✳ RICHARD B. SHER ✳

The Enlightenment & the Book

Scottish Authors & Their Publishers in
Eighteenth-Century Britain, Ireland, & America

The University of Chicago Press

Chicago & London

RICHARD B. SHER is
Distinguished Professor of History at the New Jersey Institute
of Technology. He is the author of *Church and University in the
Scottish Enlightenment: The Moderate Literati of Edinburgh.*

The University of Chicago Press, Chicago 60637
The University of Chicago Press, Ltd., London
© 2006 by The University of Chicago
All rights reserved. Published 2006
Printed in the United States of America

15 14 13 12 11 10 09 08 07 06   1 2 3 4 5

ISBN: 0-226-75252-6 (cloth)

Library of Congress Cataloging-in-Publication Data

Sher, Richard B., 1948–
      The Enlightenment and the book: Scottish authors and
   their publi███████████████████████████land, and
   America ███████████████████████████████
      p. ███████████████████████████████
      Inclu███████████████████████████
      ISBN███████████████████████████
      1. S███████████████████████████ing.
   2. English literature—Scottish authors—publishing.
   3. Publishers and publishing—Great Britain—History
   —18th century.   4. Publishers and publishing—
   Ireland—History—18th century.   5. Publishers and
   publishing—United States—History—18th century.
   6. Authors and publishers—Scotland—History—18th
   century.   7. Scottish literature—18th century—Appreciation.   8. English literature—Scottish authors—
   Appreciation.   9. Authors, Scottish—Intellectual life—
   18th century.   10. Enlightenment—Scotland.   I. Title.
   Z326.S54 2006
   070.50941109'033—dc22

                                        2006015667

The Enlightenment & the Book

FOR DORIS

Contents

List of Illustrations · ix
Abbreviations · xiii
Preface · xv
Author's Note · xxiii

Introduction	1
Toward a Book History of the Scottish Enlightenment	1
Designs and Disclaimers	25

PART I. SCOTTISH AUTHORS IN A WORLD OF BOOKS

1. Composing the Scottish Enlightenment	43
Progress through Print	43
Building a Database of Scottish Enlightenment Authors and Books	73
2. Identity and Diversity among Scottish Authors	97
The Social Contexts of Authorship	97
Unity and Representation	131
3. The Rewards of Authorship	195
Patrons, Publishers, and Places	195
Copy Money and Its Uses	209

PART II. PUBLISHING THE SCOTTISH
ENLIGHTENMENT IN LONDON AND EDINBURGH

4. Forging the London–Edinburgh Publishing Axis	265
The Framework of Collaborative Publishing	267
The Founding Publishers and Their Firms	275

5. The Heyday of Scottish Enlightenment Publishing 327
The House of Strahan and Cadell 327
Successors and Rivals 373

6. The Achievement of William Creech 401
The Career of a Bookseller 401
The Reputation of a Bookseller 428

PART III. REPRINTING THE SCOTTISH
ENLIGHTENMENT IN DUBLIN AND PHILADELPHIA

7. The Rise and Fall of Irish Reprinting 443
Publishers or Pirates? 445
In the Company of Dublin Booksellers 467

8. Making Scottish Books in America, 1770–1784 503
The Scottish Enlightenment and the American Book Trade 503
The Emergence of Scottish Enlightenment Reprinting in America 511

9. "A More Extensive Diffusion of Useful Knowledge":
Philadelphia, 1784–1800 541
Atlantic Crossings: Carey, Dobson, Young, and Campbell 541
Immigrant Booksellers and Scotch Learning 556

Conclusion 597
The Disintegration of the London–Edinburgh Publishing Axis 598
The Pattern of Scottish Enlightenment Book History 606

Appendix: Tables 611
1. Scottish Enlightenment Authors, 1746–1800 613
*2. British, Irish, and American First Editions of Scottish
Enlightenment Books, 1746–1800* 620
Index of Publishers in Table 2 690
*3. Subjects and Formats of First British Editions of Scottish
Enlightenment Books* 700
4. Popularity of British Editions of Scottish Enlightenment Books 701
5. Principal Publishers of New Scottish Enlightenment Books 702
*6. Principal Publishers of Dublin First Editions of Scottish
Enlightenment Books* 704
*7. Printing Account of Thomas Cadell, Sr., in the Strahan Archive,
1793–1798* 705

Bibliography · 709
Index · 757

Illustrations

1.1. Title page and frontispiece in Hume's *Essays and Treatises,* 1768   48–49

1.2. Hume's *Essays and Treatises* in quarto and octavo   51

1.3. *Books Printed for W. Strahan, and T. Cadell in the Strand*   57

2.1. The Cross and the Luckenbooths on the Edinburgh High Street   111

2.2. Parliament Square, Edinburgh   112

2.3. Sibbald's Circulating Library, Parliament Square, Edinburgh   113

2.4. The British Coffee House, London   130

2.5. Title page in Guthrie's *Geography,* 11th ed., 1788   134

2.6. Subscription list in the Edinburgh edition of Burns's *Poems,* 1787   137

2.7. Title page in Cullen's *Treatise of the Materia Medica,* 1789   158

2.8. Detail of line engraving (from fig. 2.16)   166

2.9. Detail of stipple engraving (from fig. 2.20)   166

2.10. David Hume engraved by Joseph Collyer the younger, 1788   170

2.11. Tobias Smollett engraved by Joseph Collyer the younger, 1790   171

2.12. William Robertson by Sir Joshua Reynolds   174

2.13. Frontispiece portrait in Robertson's *Charles V,* 2nd ed., 1772   175

2.14. Frontispiece portrait in James Macpherson's *History of Great Britain,* 2nd ed., 1776   176

2.15. Frontispiece portrait in Robert Henry's *History of Great Britain*, vol. 4, 1781 177

2.16. Frontispiece portrait in Hugh Blair's *Lectures*, 1st ed., 1783 178

2.17. Frontispiece portrait in Hugh Blair's *Lectures*, 6th ed., 1796 179

2.18. Frontispiece portrait in James Fordyce's *Poems*, 1786 180

2.19. Robert Burns by Alexander Nasmyth 182

2.20. Frontispiece portrait in the Edinburgh edition of Robert Burns's *Poems*, 1787 182

2.21. Frontispiece portrait in James Ferguson's *Select Mechanical Exercises*, 2nd ed., 1778 183

2.22. Frontispiece portrait in Benjamin Bell's *System of Surgery*, 5th ed., 1791 184

2.23. Frontispiece portrait in John Pinkerton's *History of Scotland*, 1797 185

2.24. Frontispiece portrait in Mungo Park's *Travels*, 1799 186

2.25. Frontispiece portrait in John Brown's *Elements of Medicine*, 1795 188

2.26. John Brown engraved by James Caldwall, 1790s 189

2.27. William Leechman by William Millar 192

2.28. Frontispiece portrait in William Leechman's *Sermons*, 1789 193

3.1. Contract for Alexander Adam's *Roman Antiquities*, June 1794 239

4.1. Title page in Hume's *Essays, Moral and Political*, 3rd ed., 1748 286

4.2. Kincaid & Bell's shop, Edinburgh 317

4.3. Title pages in the first three editions of Adam Ferguson's *Essay*, 1767–68 319

5.1. William Strahan by an unknown artist 328

5.2. Thomas Cadell engraved by H. Meyer 328

5.3. Page from William Strahan's printing ledgers, 1777–78 335

5.4. Title page in William Buchan's *Domestic Medicine*, 9th ed., 1786 341

5.5. Title page in *Sentimental Beauties and Moral Delineations*, 1782 358

5.6. Book advertisements in the *London Chronicle*, March 1777 364

5.7. Andrew Strahan by William Owen 377

5.8. Thomas Cadell by Sir William Beechey 377

6.1. Letter from William Strahan to William Creech, 16 July 1771 411

6.2. "Verses to the Author of the Man of Feeling," by
William Creech   421

6.3. Frontispiece portrait in William Creech's *Fugitive Pieces*,
1815   429

6.4. Archibald Constable by Andrew Geddes   437

7.1. Title page in Dublin edition of Kames's *Sketches*, 1775   477

7.2. Page from the Graisberry ledgers   480

7.3. Title page and frontispiece in William Robertson's *History
of America*, Dublin, 1777   481

8.1. Two pages from a Robert Bell advertisement, "To the
American World," 1771   520–21

8.2. Proposals for Philadelphia edition of Kames's *Sketches*,
1775   529

8.3. Robert Aitken by an unknown artist   533

8.4. Robert Aitken's logo   533

9.1. Title page in Thomas Dobson's *Encyclopaedia*, 1798   557

9.2. Advertisement for Thomas Reid's *Essays* in William
Young's *Universal Asylum*, December 1792   568

9.3. Dedication in William Young's edition of Reid's *Essays*,
1793   569

9.4. William Young by an unknown artist   571

9.5. Title page in volume 1 of Mathew Carey's edition of
Guthrie's *Geography*, 1794   580

9.6. Page from Mathew Carey's edition of Guthrie's *Geography*,
1794   581

9.7. Title page and frontispiece in Robert Campbell's edition
of Hume's *History*, 1795   583

Abbreviations

AUL = Aberdeen University Library

BL = British Library, London

BLJ = *Boswell's Life of Johnson*, ed. George Birkbeck Hill; revised by L. F. Powell, 6 vols., including the *Journal of a Tour to the Hebrides with Samuel Johnson* in vol. 5 (Oxford, 1934–64).

ECL = Edinburgh Central Library

EEC = *Edinburgh Evening Courant*

ESTC = English Short-Title Catalogue

EUL = Edinburgh University Library

HL = Houghton Library, Harvard University

HSP = Historical Society of Pennsylvania, Philadelphia

LDH = *The Letters of David Hume*, ed. J. Y. T. Greig, 2 vols. (Oxford, 1932).

NLS = National Library of Scotland, Edinburgh

NPG = National Portrait Gallery, London (www.npg.org.uk).

ODNB = *Oxford Dictionary of National Biography* (Oxford, 2004).

RSE = Royal Society of Edinburgh

RSL = Royal Society of London

SA = Strahan Archive, British Library, Add. MSS 48800–48918 (also consulted in the published microfilm edition).

WCL = William Creech Letterbooks, Blair Oliphant of Ardblair Muniments, NRAS 1915; microfilm copy, National Archives of Scotland, RH4/26/1–3

WYP = William Young Papers, William L. Clements Library, University of Michigan

Preface

My favorite definition of the word "publish" appears in Samuel Johnson's famous dictionary of 1755: "To put forth a book into the world." Granted, the word "book" is somewhat limiting, since magazines, journals, and pamphlets are also published. But this work happens to be about the publication of books, and Johnson's definition draws our attention to the prominence of that medium during the eighteenth century. It also suggests the expansive nature of book publishing, which is at once an act of production and dissemination. According to this view, the publisher—"one who puts out a book into the world," in Johnson's corresponding definition—is a kind of global broadcaster. Johnson of all people knew that every new book required an author, defined in his dictionary as "the first writer of anything" (as opposed to a translator or an editor), or "a writer in general." Yet precisely because he *was* a professional author, deeply enmeshed in the practices of London print culture, Johnson understood that the move from author/text to book was a complicated, creative, and contingent process in which the book trade, and above all publishers, had a large role to play.

This volume explores how the books of the Scottish Enlightenment were put forth into the world during the second half of the eighteenth century. Although lengthy and occasionally technical, it has been written for a general readership and therefore contains some basic information about book history and the Scottish Enlightenment, which I hope specialists in those fields will excuse. In an earlier book, *Church and University in the Scottish Enlightenment*, I located the institutional and ideological core of the Scottish Enlightenment in a circle of Moderate Party Presbyterian ministers and academics in Edinburgh. As argued there, a tolerant established church and an outstanding university, both led by the same group of distinguished clergymen of letters in Scotland's historic capital, were instrumental in creating an atmosphere highly conducive to enlightened thought and culture throughout Scotland and in promoting excellence even in areas of intellectual activity to which those "Moderate literati" did not personally make significant contributions, such as science, medicine, and law. Other factors also stimulated Scottish intellectual and cultural life in Edinburgh and other Scottish towns, including lively clubs and learned societies, progressive patronage, and a rich intellectual heritage. Yet no matter how valuable such factors may have been for encouraging the protagonists of the Scottish Enlightenment to realize their potential as teachers, preachers, lawyers, physicians, and scientific experimenters, it was chiefly when these individuals expressed themselves in print, especially books, that they gained opportunities to acquire international fame for themselves and their homeland. The Scottish Enlightenment is therefore unimaginable apart from its published books.

Throughout the research and writing of this volume, I have benefited from the assistance of many friends and fellow workers. My greatest debt is to Bill Zachs, who provided much valuable guidance as well as access to the books and manuscripts in his library. Warren McDougall and Stephen Brown were also enormously helpful. Jeff Smitten and especially Paul Wood commented usefully on drafts of the whole manuscript, and Doris Sher helped to shape the final version. Adam Budd contributed valuable criticism of parts 1 and 2, as James Raven did of chapters 4 and 5. Particular chapters or parts of chapters were also read and commented upon by David Allan, Hugh Amory, Barbara Benedict, Mark Box, Stephen Brown, James Green, Ryan Hanley, Andrew Hook, Máire Kennedy, Sarah Knott, and Fiona Stafford. Jim Green of the Library Company of Philadelphia was my principal guru for early American book culture, and I am grateful to him and Rosalind Remer for their support. Among the many people who provided materials that went into the making of this book were Bob Arner, Nigel Aston, Mike Barfoot, Tom Bonnell, Skip Brack, Philip Carter, Catherine Dille, Roger Emerson, Jane Fagg, Donald Farren, Henry Fulton, Catherine Jones, Frank Kafker, Tony Lewis, Kate Marsters, Hamish Mathison, Ian Maxted, Carol McGuirk, Martin Moonie, Mary Catherine Moran, John Morris, David Fate Norton, John Robertson, Philipp Roessner, Silvia Sebastiani, Jeff Smitten, Mark Spencer, Sandy Stewart, and Iain Whyte. Some would say that the emergence of book history as a mature historical discipline in the English-speaking world can be dated to the nearly simultaneous publication in 1979 of *The Business of Enlightenment* by Robert Darnton and *The Printing Press as an Agent of Change* by Elizabeth L. Eisenstein, and I treasure the gracious encouragement I have received from both of those eminent scholars.

It is no pleasurable task to devote a full paragraph to scholars and friends who helped to make this book possible but died before it appeared. My collaboration with Hugh Amory on the bookseller Andrew Millar was so close that neither of us knew where the contributions of one ended and the other began, but I am fairly sure I got the better of the deal. The annual Seminars on the British Book Trade, organized by the late Peter Isaac (and the still vibrant Barry McKay), provided opportunities for me to present, and later publish, my work on Millar and William Buchan, and to develop my ideas about authors and publishers in a broadly British context. I am grateful to Colin Matthew for giving me the chance to devote several years of service to the magnificent *Oxford Dictionary of National Biography*, both as an author and an associate editor, from which I obtained much valuable biographical knowledge about the authors and publishers who figure prominently in this book. Roger Robinson, the leading expert on the life and poetry of James Beattie, was enormously helpful on Beattie's relations with his publishers. Vincent Kinane alerted me to the existence of the Graisberry ledgers at Trinity College Dublin, where I discovered the means of identifying the members of the Dublin Company of Booksellers. Mary (Paul) Pollard was an inspiration to me, as she was to so many others who have worked in the field of Irish book history, and I consider my meeting with her at Marsh's Library in July 1999 one of the highlights of my Dublin research experience. I was privileged to discuss aspects of my work with Roy Porter when I visited the Wellcome Institute for the History of Medicine; I wish he were still here to debate our differences about the Enlightenment and to share his extensive learning about the eighteenth century.

Although I started working on this book in the early 1990s, serious research began when I received a much-appreciated fellowship from the John Simon Guggenheim Memorial Foundation in 1994–95. The work was significantly advanced during a second sabbatical leave in 2001–2. Between those two years of intensive research and writing, I was fortunate to receive a research grant from the Spencer Foundation in 1998–99. I am also grateful for a summer fellowship from the National Endowment for the Humanities in 1994; a summer as a visiting scholar at the University of Edinburgh in 1998, arranged by Howard Gaskill; a summer as a visiting scholar at University College Dublin in July 1999, organized by Andrew Carpenter; and a month's fellowship at the University of Edinburgh's Centre for the History of the Book in July 2000, courtesy of Bill Bell.

Many authors have obligations to libraries, archives, and the people who make them accessible to scholars, but mine are exceptionally large because of this book's heavy reliance on rare books and unpublished manuscripts. Naturally, most of my research time was spent in libraries and archives located in the four cities in which the book's principal action is set. In London, I had the good fortune to pass significant portions of three summers at the British Library, old and new, and also visited Stationers' Hall and the library of the Wellcome Institute for the History of Medicine. In Edinburgh, the incomparable National Library of Scotland was the cornerstone of my research activity, but I also benefited greatly from Edinburgh University Library, the National Archives of Scotland, the Edinburgh City Archives, the library of the Royal College of Physicians of Edinburgh, the Scottish Genealogy Society, and the wonderful Edinburgh Room at the Edinburgh Central Library. In Dublin, I made much use of the National Library of Ireland and the libraries at Trinity College Dublin and University College Dublin, and also spent productive hours at the libraries of the Royal Irish Academy, the Royal College of Physicians in Ireland, and the Royal College of Surgeons in Ireland, as well as at Marsh's Library and Dublin Public Library. In Philadelphia, I made a number of worthwhile trips to the libraries at the American Philosophical Society, the Historical Society of Pennsylvania, and the Library Company of Philadelphia.

The Thomas Fisher Rare Book Library at the University of Toronto, where in 2000 I had the pleasure of collaborating with Paul Wood and others in organizing an exhibition titled The Culture of the Book in the Scottish Enlightenment, is surely one of the best places on earth to study eighteenth-century British books and has been tremendously helpful to me. I owe huge debts to Stephen Parks, formerly of the Beinecke Library at Yale University, as well as to Gordon Turnbull, Jim Caudle, and others in the Boswell Office at Yale. At the Houghton Library at Harvard University, Leslie Morris and Rick Stattler went out of their way to help with my last-minute efforts to consult the outstanding eighteenth-century manuscript collection of Charles Hyde and Mary Hyde Eccles. Among many other libraries that I visited in preparing this book, I am happy to mention, in England, the University of Reading Library, the Bodleian Library at Oxford University, the John Rylands Library, and the Literary and Philosophical Society of Newcastle; in Scotland, Glasgow University Library, the Mitchell Library, St. Andrews University Library, and the library at the University of Aberdeen; in the United States, the Library of Congress, the Pierpont Morgan Library, and the library of the National Library of Medicine; and in Canada, the library of McGill University in Montreal. Closer to my home, countless hours were spent at the New York Public Library, the Firestone Library at Princeton University, and the Alexander Library at Rutgers University. The interlibrary loan office in the Van Houten Library at New Jersey Institute of Technology was consistently efficient in responding to my constant requests for obscure materials from faraway places.

To all the libraries that own manuscript sources and rare editions cited in this book, and their librarians, a collective thank you. In several cases, libraries that I was unable to visit provided copies of manuscript sources, the most important being the William Young Papers at the William L. Clements Library at the University of Michigan; William Young manuscripts on microfilm borrowed from the American Antiquarian Society in Worchester, Massachusetts; a family history of the Youngs at the Historical Society of Delaware; and the Thomas Cadell Papers at Duke University Library. Among privately owned collections, I thank the Blair Oliphant of Ardblair family for permission to quote from the William Creech letterbooks that I consulted by means of microfilm copies deposited at the National Archives of Scotland; Virginia Murray for permission to quote from letters in the John Murray Archive (formerly owned by John Murray Ltd., London, but now at the National Library of Scotland), copies of which were sometimes supplied to me by Bill Zachs and Warren McDougall; and Charles Maconochie Welwood for permission to quote from the correspondence of Allan Maconochie, Lord Meadowbank, using microfilm copies in the Special Collections Department at Edinburgh University Library. For permission to quote from the Boswell Papers at Yale University, I am grateful to Gordon Turnbull, the general editor, and the Editorial Committee of the Yale Editions of the Private Papers of James Boswell. I thank David Currie for allowing me to examine the manuscript roll book of Canongate Kilwinning Lodge No. 2 and to John Killen for searching the stock of eighteenth-century books owned by the Linen Hall Library in Belfast.

This book probably could not have been written without frequent on-line access to the indispensable English Short-Title Catalogue (ESTC), which was made possible by Rutgers University. I owe that affiliation, along with much else, to the Federated History Department of Rutgers–Newark and New Jersey Institute of Technology, and I am especially appreciative of the many fine students from that program who have attended the different versions of my graduate courses on the comparative Enlightenment, British intellectual and cultural history, and the social history of communication and technology. One of those students, Stephen Patnode, was particularly helpful during the early stages of research on this book. At NJIT, Joyce Davis and Erin Borry provided valuable assistance.

The book includes a number of illustrations keyed to the text, including portraits of some of the authors and publishers who are featured in its pages and scenes of bookshops, circulating libraries, and related institutions, most of which have never been published in a modern book. Among those who helped me to secure the illustrations, I must mention Verity Andrews, Iain Gordon Brown, Lois Densky-Wolff, Kevin Gumienny, Patrice Kane, Sue Killoran, Murray Lieb, Kate Marsters, Robin Myers, Antonia Reeve, Alison Rosie, Philip Weimerskirch, and above all Philip Oldfield of the Thomas Fisher Rare Book Library at the University of Toronto, which provided the largest number of them. Special thanks are due to W. F. Bauermeister of the Edinburgh Booksellers' Society for permitting me to reproduce William Borthwick Johnstone's splendid painting of James Sibbald's circulating library.

At the University of Chicago Press, the legendary Douglas Mitchell immediately grasped what I was trying to do and encouraged me to move ahead. Doug's successive associates, Robert Devens and Tim McGovern, have also made helpful contributions, and the book was further improved by the copyeditor, Kathryn Gohl. The expense associated with producing a book of this length and complexity is considerable, and I am deeply grateful to the dean of the College of Science and Liberal Arts at NJIT, Fadi Deek, for his generous support.

The Eighteenth-Century Scottish Studies Society has been at the center of my professional existence for the past two decades. If the time I have devoted to its affairs has delayed the appearance of this book by more than a few years, I have no regrets. A number of the stories in this book were originally rehearsed at ECSSS conferences, and the friendship and fellowship of its members have been a constant source of renewal. In particular, each of the society's presidents—Roger Emerson, Andrew Hook, Ned Landsman, Susan Manning, James Moore, Nicholas Phillipson, Jane

Rendall, John Robertson, Ian Simpson Ross, and M. A. Stewart—has contributed in some way to improving both this book and my life, and I am grateful to them all.

Lastly, and firstly, this book is dedicated to my wife Doris, my great love and best friend for more than thirty years.

Author's Note

ORGANIZATION

Those with a general interest in the subject of this book may wish to read the main text through without consulting the data in the back. Others—particularly students and scholars of the history of books, and of the Enlightenment and eighteenth-century thought and culture—may wish to consult the data frequently while reading the main text. Still others may wish to use this book as a reference work, focusing on the data, and reading the main text selectively.

The book has been organized to provide convenient access points to the data for readers in the last two categories, with a minimum of distractions for readers in the first category. As explained in chapter 1, the book's empirical foundation is a database containing information about 115 Scottish authors (table 1) who published 360 books (table 2) during the period 1746–1800. Throughout the main text, parenthetical references such as (no. 131) or (nos. 17 and 162) correspond to the numbers of the titles listed in table 2. These references provide a quick link to further information on books discussed in the text, but nonspecialists may choose to ignore them. Readers wishing to consult the data in table 2 may gain access by using the numbers that follow each author's name in table 1 (if the starting point is a particular author) or the numbers that follow the names of publishers in the index of publishers appended to table 2 (if the starting point is a particular publisher).

TERMINOLOGY

Although the word "publisher" was sometimes used in the eighteenth century to mean the person who arranges and finances the publication of books, the term "bookseller" was more common. This book employs both terms (and occasionally even "bookseller-publisher"), but my general preference is for "publisher" because it more clearly differentiates the function of publishing from bookselling and because it encompasses the printers William and Andrew Strahan, who were among the leading publishers of the age although they were not booksellers.

In contemporary usage, the term "copy money" (often hyphenated) referred either to the purchase price of a copyright or, more generally, to the money that authors received from publishers for their books, whether from sale of copyright or from some other arrangement. This book uses the term in the second sense.

The term "reprint" refers here to a book in which the type has been reset since the last time it was published. "Reissue" refers to a book using the unsold printed sheets from an earlier edition, usually with a new title page and sometimes with other new or revised material added.

SPELLING AND PUNCTUATION

In quotations from unpublished eighteenth-century manuscripts, standard contractions and abbreviations of the day such as "w^t." for "with," "w^h." for "which," and "Edin^r." for "Edinburgh" have normally been extended, as have ampersands that stand for "and." This practice has not been followed when quoting from published sources, however.

Ampersands have been used to link the names in formal partnerships (e.g., "Cadell & Davies") in order to avoid confusion in phrases such as "printed for Andrew Strahan and Cadell & Davies."

CURRENCY

The standard equivalencies in the British money of account were well established by the eighteenth century:

> 1 shilling (1s.) = 12 pence (12d.)
> 1 pound (£1) = 20 shillings (20s.)
> 1 guinea = 21 shillings (21s., or £1.1s.)

Nevertheless, there were differences in value between the English pound (sterling), the Scottish pound, and the Irish pound. The Scottish pound, valued at a fraction of sterling, was officially withdrawn after the parliamentary union of England and Scotland in 1707, even though it remained in use for Scottish rents, wages, and agricultural produce during the eighteenth century. Ireland continued to use an Irish pound that was worth about 8 percent less than sterling (a currency table in the 1788 edition of Guthrie's *Geography* gave the exchange at 18s.5½d. Irish to £1 sterling, which is supported by the data in McCusker, *Money and Exchange*, 31–41). In this volume, however, British and Irish book prices are given as they were advertised at the place of publication, without taking into account these differences.

British colonists in America also used the pound as a money of account, although each colony set the value of its local currency at a different rate. In colonial Philadelphia, a Pennsylvania shilling was valued at about 60 percent of a British shilling (£1 Pennsylvania currency = 12s. sterling). The dollar, equivalent to the Spanish silver coin known as a piece of eight, was worth about 22½ percent of a pound sterling during the colonial period (i.e., approximately 7s.6d. sterling and 4s.6d. Pennsylvania currency) and retained that value after the American Revolution; for example, in 1791 $4.55 was equal to £1 sterling. More detailed information may be found at the Economic History Services Web site, http://www.eh.net, and in McCusker, *How Much Is That in Real Money?*

The purchasing power of eighteenth-century British and American money can be translated into early twenty-first-century terms by using the retail price index calculators provided by Economic History Services at www.eh.net/hmit. As a very rough guide, using July 2006 as a conversion point, the purchasing power of £1 sterling during the period 1746–70 was equal to about £94 sterling or US$142 in modern terms; £1 sterling during the 1770s and 1780s was worth about £76 or $154; and £1 sterling during the 1790s was worth about £69 or $126. Thus, a standard-sized, bound octavo published in the 1770s at a price of six shillings, such as Lord Kames's *The Gentleman Farmer* or the first volume of Hugh Blair's *Sermons*, or a two-volume bound duodecimo novel such as Henry Mackenzie's *Julia de Roubigné* (also six shillings), was worth the equivalent of about £25/$46 in 2006 money; an expensive quarto edition from the same period, such as William Robertson's *History of America* or Adam Smith's *Wealth of Nations* (both priced at two guineas for two bound volumes), cost the equivalent of about £89/$162 per volume, or £178/$324 the set, in 2006 money; and a published play from the same era, such as John Home's *Alfred: A Tragedy* (priced at one and a half shillings), cost the equivalent of about £6/$11.60 in 2006 money. I am grateful to John McCusker for assistance with these calculations.

Introduction

The Problem of Enlightenment Publishing

"To a man sincerely interested in the welfare of society and of his country, it must be particularly agreeable to reflect on the rapid progress, and general diffusion of learning and civility, which, within the present age, have taken place in Great Britain." So began the preface to one of the most popular books of the late eighteenth century, *A New Geographical, Historical, and Commercial Grammar; and Present State of the Several Kingdoms of the World* by William Guthrie, Esq., first published in London in 1770. After contrasting the state of British political culture with that found in "some other kingdoms of Europe," where "illiberal prejudices" prevailed, the preface continued: "Among us, learning is no longer confined within the schools of the philosophers, or the courts of the great; but, like all the greatest advantages which heaven has bestowed on mankind, it is become as universal as it is useful." Britain was leading the way not only in the "rapid progress" of learning but also in its dissemination, for only in Britain had the "general diffusion of knowledge" advanced to the point where "the great body of the people" could share in it. This had happened, on the one hand, because "in Great Britain, the people are opulent, have great influence, and claim, of course, a proper share of attention"—which is to say, they constitute a public. On the other hand, in Britain "books have been divested of the terms of the schools, reduced from that size which suited only the purses of the rich, and the avocations of the studious, and are adapted to persons of more ordinary fortunes, whose attachment to other pursuits admitted of little leisure for those of knowledge." The diffusion of learning through popular books is exalted, even over "the works of our

Bacons, our Lockes, and our Newtons," as the means by which "the generality of our countrymen" have attained their "superior improvement" over their counterparts elsewhere.

The phenomenon described in the preface to Guthrie's *Geography* has become familiar to students of the Enlightenment and eighteenth-century British culture. "Print proved the great engine for the spread of enlightened views and values," wrote the late Roy Porter in his popular account of the Enlightenment in Britain. As part of an occurrence that Porter variously termed "the print explosion," "the print boom," and "print capitalism," "literature became a commodity circulating in all shapes and sizes" and "Britain found itself awash with print." Along with these developments on the supply side came changes in patterns of consumption, as "reading became second nature to a major swathe of the nation."[1] Similarly, John Brewer has written perceptively on the "print revolution" that occurred in eighteenth-century Britain, involving both a "remarkable transformation in British publishing" (which he sometimes calls "the publishing revolution" or "the publication revolution") and an expansion in the quantity and variety of reading, as well as in the institutions that facilitated it, such as bookshops, different kinds of libraries (e.g., subscription, circulating, church, coffeehouse), book clubs, and private collections. Like Porter and the author of the preface to Guthrie's *Geography*, Brewer views these developments as intimately connected with the growth of "modern commerce and refinement." The findings of the learned, the diffusion of knowledge, enlightened attitudes, opulence, civility, and the rise of a broad and highly commercialized public culture were all inseparable from what Brewer calls more than once "the ubiquity of books."[2]

Despite the notion of British exceptionalism that permeates the preface to Guthrie's *Geography*, many commentators who treat eighteenth-century culture within a broader geographical context have reached similar conclusions. Following the well-known thesis of Jürgen Habermas, James Van Horn Melton credits England with establishing a literary public sphere earlier than the rest of Europe, but by the time his account reaches the second half of the century, France and Germany are sharing in "the eighteenth-century print explosion."[3] Similar views have been a

1. Porter, *Enlightenment*, quoting 91, 85, 479, 76, 77 ("print explosion"), 87 and 94 ("print boom"), 95 ("print capitalism").

2. Brewer, *Pleasures of the Imagination*, chaps. 3 and 4, quoting 137, 125, 187, 191, xxvii, 190, 196.

3. Melton, *Rise of the Public*, chaps. 3 and 4, quoting 115.

fixture in social and cultural histories of the age of the Enlightenment since at least 1969, when the second volume of Peter Gay's seminal synthesis discussed the emergence of a broader reading audience, the appearance of lending libraries and coffeehouses, the development of publishing in place of aristocratic patronage, increasing financial compensation for enlightened authors, and the decline of censorship and repression as key features of the republic of letters.[4] In a general survey of Europe published in 1982, Isser Woloch asserted that "the expansion of publishing and the growth of the reading public . . . constituted the eighteenth century's pivotal cultural development."[5] More recently, Thomas Munck has argued that "an unprecedented growth in the accessibility of the printed word to those who could read" was crucially important for the expression and proliferation of the Enlightenment, and T. C. W. Blanning's explicitly Habermasian account of Old Regime culture emphasizes "a revolutionary change in the production of books" and corresponding changes in the character and sites of reading.[6] These developments have in turn been linked by Michel Foucault and others with the rise of modern institutional structures for categorizing and regulating both authors and books. In Carla Hesse's succinct summation, the modern literary system that arose in eighteenth-century Europe may be equated with "the civilization of the book," meaning "the stabilization of written culture into a canon of authorized texts, the notion of the author as creator, the book as property, and the reader as an elective public."[7]

Britain, then, was not unique in developing a ubiquitous book culture that was intimately tied to the espousal and promulgation of the Enlightenment. That was to some degree a feature of the Enlightenment everywhere. Few would deny, however, that eighteenth-century Britain was in the vanguard of the movement. As the author of the preface to Guthrie's *Geography* and other contemporaries realized, printing and publishing faced fewer constraints there than on the Continent, with significant consequences. In the absence of most forms of censorship and other restrictive regulations, such as the one that limited the number of master printers in Old Regime Paris to thirty-six, the number of printing offices and

4. Gay, *Enlightenment*, 2:57–83.

5. Woloch, *Eighteenth-Century Europe*, 189–90.

6. Munck, *Enlightenment*, chap. 4, quoting 105; Blanning, *Culture of Power*, pt. 2, "The Rise of the Public Sphere," quoting 140. See also Hesse, "Print Culture in the Enlightenment," 369–71.

7. Hesse, "Books in Time," 21.

bookshops increased dramatically in London and throughout Britain, and so did the quantity of accessible reading material, including books, periodicals, and newspapers. The Enlightenment book trade in Britain did not have to go underground or abroad, as was so often the case in France and other European countries, and the producers of learned books were not subject to the high degree of instability and uncertainty, as well as licensing requirements, that existed in seventeenth-century England.[8] In spite of disagreements over the precise nature and duration of copyright, there was widespread acceptance in eighteenth-century Britain of the principle of copyright itself, extending at least the fourteen years (or twenty-eight years, if the author were still alive) allowed by the so-called Statute of Anne, the copyright act that went into effect in 1710 and was upheld as the law of the land on appeal to the House of Lords in 1774. There arose an auxiliary species of journals, such as the *Monthly Review* and the *Critical Review*, to guide the public's selection of the best new books. Books took their place within a burgeoning culture of material consumption and commercialization, well beyond what existed elsewhere.[9]

All this is familiar enough. But the tendency to posit the existence of a print boom in eighteenth-century Britain has greatly outpaced our knowledge of what was actually taking place. We have many generalizations but little concrete understanding of the complex historical processes and interplay of human actors that connected the book trade to the Enlightenment. More than a quarter of a century has passed since Robert Darnton's pioneering publishing history of the *Encyclopédie* established book history as a vital component in Enlightenment studies.[10] Since then there have been several excellent studies of individual Enlightenment publishers and their relations with authors,[11] and book history has flourished and grown as a scholarly discipline. Despite differences among practitioners, there is universal agreement that the starting point for all approaches to the field is the conviction that books do in fact have histories which reveal a great deal about life as well as letters, and that books are therefore to be

8. Darnton, *Forbidden Best-Sellers;* Eisenstein, *Grub Street Abroad;* Birn, *Forging Rousseau;* Hesse, "Print Culture in the Enlightenment"; Johns, *Nature of the Book;* Furdell, *Publishing and Medicine.*

9. See McKendrick, Brewer, and Plumb, *Birth of a Consumer Society.*

10. Darnton, *Business of Enlightenment.*

11. Tucoo-Chala, *Charles-Joseph Panckoucke;* Selwyn, *Everyday Life in the German Book Trade;* Zachs, *First John Murray;* Birn, *Forging Rousseau;* and various studies of the Société typographique de Neuchâtel and its publications, especially by Robert Darnton.

taken seriously in every possible mode in which they appear—as homes for texts written by authors and read by readers, as physical artifacts crafted by skilled and unskilled workers using particular technologies, as commodities bought and sold in the marketplace, as instruments for the transmission of knowledge and values, as fodder for great libraries and popular amusements, as objects of government regulation and censorship, as cultural symbols, and much more.[12] Few historians of the book would deny that these modes are necessarily interrelated and therefore cannot be successfully studied in isolation from each other, or in isolation from the specific historical settings in which they occur. Yet the book history of the Enlightenment, especially the English-language Enlightenment, remains a story waiting to be told.

The second half of the eighteenth century was a particularly interesting time for author–publisher relations. It not only signified the beginning of modern notions of authorship as a commercial category but also marked a critical transitional era for publishers. During this period, substantial publishing houses emerged in Britain, but they were not yet the large, impersonal, specialized entities they would later become. Publishing was still something that members of the book trade did in addition to something else—usually bookselling (which accounts for the fact that publishers were still called "booksellers" much of the time) but in some cases printing or occasionally even bookbinding. Publishers were sometimes deeply involved with the works they produced, and authors who dealt with the leading publishing houses often had direct, substantive contact with the head of the firm. "Cadell and I are going to prepare the second edition of 'Fatal Falsehood'," wrote Hannah More to her sister in 1780. "We talked over all the affairs. He gave me some very good advice."[13] There was nothing unusual about this exchange, even though Thomas Cadell was then at the head of the largest and most prestigious publishing enterprise in Britain, if not in the world.

The success of books depended on publishers in many ways. In the process of generating new books, publishers had to make critical decisions about whether to publish, when to publish, and in what format to publish, as well as how to promote published books, how much to charge for them, and how much to pay authors for them. Of course, to say that eighteenth-century publishers had important choices to make does not mean that they were free to do whatever they pleased. Various kinds of

12. For a recent introduction with bibliography, see Bishop, "Book History."
13. Roberts, *Memoirs*, 1:103.

factors—technological, economic, institutional, legal, cultural, intellectual, ideological—operated at many levels to restrict and direct choices. But such factors did not always point toward the same conclusion, and publishers were therefore able to operate with a great deal of freedom most of the time.

The actions of publishers were not strictly determined by external forces such as the economic or technological "logic" of print, or print capitalism, favored by Alvin Kernan, or the equally rigid theory of monopoly with which William St. Clair explains book production in the period 1710–74.[14] Nor were they virtually free of technological and other material constraints, as others have suggested or implied. "Is history conditioned by print, or print by history?" Adrian Johns asks in his debate with Elizabeth Eisenstein on the status of early modern printing, answering that "the latter is the case." Perhaps the best response to Johns's question, however, is to reject its either/or premise and to opt instead for another formulation by Johns himself, "that print is conditioned by history as well as conditioning it."[15] To the extent that print can be considered apart from history at all, the relationship between print and history, like that of any technology and history, is complex and dialectical; neither one is caused or conditioned exclusively by the other. Technologies like printing do not dictate or determine the course of history, but they frequently create conditions, opportunities, and constraints that influence the construction of cultures, just as cultural factors shape the social construction of technologies.[16] Because eighteenth-century British printing was famously free of technological innovation and firmly rooted in a secure commercial system, Enlightenment publishers operated within a relatively stable environment in which the social construction of printing over the course of several centuries was taken for granted.

The publishing process was too complex to conform to any simple formula. Enlightenment book publishing cannot be reduced either to unrestrained outbursts of authorial creativity (as historians of ideas often assume) or to business endeavors involving the production and distribution of marketable commodities (as historians of books sometimes insinuate). In the second half of the eighteenth century, publication of new books was almost always a cooperative act or partnership between authors

14. St. Clair, *Reading Nation*, chap. 5; Kernan, *Printing Technology*, 76.

15. *AHR* Forum, quoting from Johns, "How to Acknowledge a Revolution," 124.

16. Smith and Marx, *Does Technology Drive History?*

and publishers. Often these partnerships were harmonious and polite, and occasionally they were intimate, but sometimes they were tense and strained, even hostile, as one might expect when the stakes involve not only money but also status and cultural authority.[17] Enlightenment book publishing, then, was a negotiated, collaborative, often contested activity that occurred within the economic, technological, legal, and intellectual contexts of the day.

The more Enlightenment book culture is viewed as the product of interaction between authors and members of the book trade, contingent to a large degree on decisions made by publishers within a given technological and social setting, the more important are questions concerning the roles of publishers and authors and their relationships with each other, as well as with that mystical, abstract entity known in the eighteenth century, and ever since, as "the public." Publishers naturally paid close attention to economic self-interest when making decisions about publishing and marketing books, but other motives frequently came into play as well. To the extent that such motives were personal, ideological, and yes, intellectual, they form a contrast with the businesslike persona that publishers frequently tried to project, especially when dealing with authors. Authors too had complicated agendas, and they therefore should not be treated as rarefied intellectuals who were unconcerned with fame, money, and other factors besides the substance of their texts. As John Brewer has remarked: "Both bookseller and author shared in the balancing act between pecuniary reward and intellectual interest that gave eighteenth-century publishing much of its energy."[18]

In their capacity as the managers of printers, stationers, and binders, publishers were largely responsible for translating authors' texts into material reality. They were therefore critically important in helping to determine not only which books would be produced but also how those books would look. Their central position between texts and books had implications that extended into the public realm. Foucault's famous concept of the "author function" has rightly drawn attention to the author's name as the primary mode of categorizing books.[19] It also seems appropriate to speak of a "publisher function," however, because in the late eighteenth

17. For an exploration of this point in a French context, see Turnovsky, "Enlightenment Literary Market," 387–410.

18. Brewer, *Pleasures of the Imagination*, 158.

19. Foucault, "What Is an Author?" 101–20.

century, like today, the names of publishers could be as important as those of authors in providing the public with a mechanism for organizing and prioritizing books.

Besides the interaction of authors and publishers, two other relevant methodological problems of Enlightenment book history concern the range of physical locations and the range of genres or subjects to be studied. In his magisterial account of the production and reception of scientific book learning in seventeenth-century England, *The Nature of the Book*, and in other writings, Adrian Johns has called for the adoption of "a local focus" as the best way to study the historical relations between "print and knowledge."[20] "In general, . . . print entailed not one but many cultures," he writes, and "these cultures of the book were themselves local in character."[21] Johns treats a time when scholarly English-language "printing and bookselling were concentrated almost exclusively in the vast social morass of London" and when communication among publishers of learned works in different places was excruciatingly slow. These circumstances may help to explain his decision to concentrate on the institutional structures and professional relationships that characterized scientific publishing in the English metropolis. But how well does such a local, metropolitan approach hold up during the late eighteenth century, when there were other centers of learned printing and publishing in Great Britain and the English-language world besides London? Has Johns given us the key to "the nature of the book" in general, or merely a rich history of the making of one genre of books in one particular time and place?

London remained the undisputed capital of the English-language book trade during the late eighteenth century, and Johns is surely correct about the contextual nature of book culture and the need for empirical investigation of local circumstances, in London as well as in every other site of publication and reception. But the development and diffusion of Enlightenment book culture cannot be explained by a local, or even a comparative, model, let alone a model that is limited to a single species of knowledge in one particular time. Robert Darnton has correctly observed that "by its very nature . . . the history of books must be international in scale."[22] From the middle of the fifteenth century, book trade practices shared many similarities throughout Europe, and printed books were "in-

---

20. Johns, "How to Acknowledge a Revolution," 117.
21. Johns, *Nature of the Book*, 30, 52.
22. Darnton, "What Is the History of Books?" 135.

ternational objects of merchandise, and therefore of reading."[23] For this reason, it can be argued that the relationship of "print and knowledge" always requires more than a local, metropolitan approach. Certainly by the mid-eighteenth century the sites of book culture were too closely interconnected, both within Britain and beyond, to be studied in isolation. This judgment applies not only to the trade in books but also to the relationships that prevailed among the makers of books: authors in France negotiated with publishers in Amsterdam, Neuchâtel, and Geneva, just as authors in Scotland dealt with publishers in London, and publishers had similarly expansive interactions with printers, booksellers, and stationers. In such circumstances, the key to understanding the relationship between print and knowledge lies not in any particular local context but rather in the dynamic interplay of authors, publishers, and other members of the book trade in a variety of locations. Enlightenment book history must be viewed through a wide geographical lens.

The foundation work in the field of book history, Lucien Febvre and Henri-Jean Martin's *The Coming of the Book* (first published in 1958 as *L'apparition du livre*), adopted a broad geographical approach, mainly European but with some attention to America too. By the late 1960s, however, the focus of most serious scholarship on eighteenth-century book history had withdrawn to a single country or region,[24] and with few exceptions it has remained so ever since. As this work goes to press, major multiauthor volumes are about to appear on the book history of the eighteenth century in each of the four geographical areas comprising the subject matter of this volume.[25] These publications represent milestones in the respective book histories of England, Scotland, Ireland, and North America, but they should also be seen as steps toward a more comprehensive, international understanding of the field.

With regard to subject matter, similarly, Enlightenment book history

23. McKitterick, *Print, Manuscript*, 5. See also Febvre and Martin, *Coming of the Book*; and Eisenstein, *Printing Press*.

24. The trend began with the publication of Furet, Bollème, and Roche's pioneering work, *Livre et société dans la France du 18e siècle*, which is discussed in Darnton, "Social History of Ideas."

25. Gillespie and Hadfield, *Irish Book in English*; Suarez and Turner, *Cambridge History of the Book in Britain*, vol. 5, which has an English emphasis; Brown and McDougall, *Edinburgh History of the Book in Scotland*, vol. 2; and Gross and Kelley, *Extensive Republic*, the sequel to Amory and Hall, *Colonial Book in the Atlantic World*. See also Fleming, Gallichan, and Lamonde, *History of the Book in Canada*, vol. 1.

must be multidisciplinary because it is necessary to consider different genres of books in order to know whether a particular form of publishing was typical or unusual, a paradigm or an aberration. Johns's contention that "piracy and plagiarism occupied readers' minds just as prominently as fixity and enlightenment" (30) may be true of scientific books in seventeenth-century London, but it is not necessarily true of books in philosophy, law, or fiction from that same time and place. Limiting his analysis to scientific books prevents Johns from establishing the universal significance of his model for book history. As far as eighteenth-century Britain is concerned, there is currently no basis for accepting his suggestion that print culture—particularly scientific print culture—was mainly perceived by contemporaries as "destabilizing and threatening to civility" rather than as a "rationalizing" force (28).

The primary genre bias in British book history is not toward science but toward English literature. The strong textual orientation of literary critics encourages a dualism of text and book that associates literature with mind and bibliography with matter. In the introduction to the January 2006 *PMLA* special issue "The History of the Book and the Idea of Literature," Leah Price traces the invisibility of books among modern literary critics to a lack of training in the analysis of material culture and "a commonsense Cartesianism [that] teaches us to filter out the look, the feel, the smell of the printed page."[26] As a result, much of what passes for book history among literary critics maintains a literary and textual emphasis. Furthermore, the genres of fiction, poetry, drama, and literary criticism tend to be privileged over other kinds of writing. Too often, the canonical writers in London who wrote books in those genres are seen as the new cultural heroes of the age of print; the professional literary author is exalted as the paradigm of modernity; and figures in the book trade are rendered worthy—or not—on the basis of their contributions to those authors and their works. This literary bias accounts for the proliferation of exaggerated claims about the place of Samuel Johnson, Robert Dodsley, and other London literary figures in eighteenth-century print culture.[27] Throw the genre net wider, to include the writing of history, political economy, philosophy, medicine, and other forms of polite literature and learning, and the situation will look very different. It may even turn out

26. Price, Introduction, 12.

27. See, for example, Solomon, *The Rise of Robert Dodsley*, 263: "Indisputably, he was the most important publisher of his period, and present histories of printing and bookselling designate his as the 'Age of Dodsley.'"

that the paradigm of the "modern" author is not independence in the sense of having no occupation other than writing for publication but rather independence in the sense of integration into appropriate professions and professional institutions.

These observations point to the need for a kind of book history that takes seriously and explores fully—in multiple genres and in local, national, and international contexts—the values, aspirations, actions, and interactions of eighteenth-century authors and publishers, and that does not seek to restrict one to the realm of the mind and the other to the realm of the purse. This book provides such a history, centered on one segment of the Enlightenment, but with methodological implications that may extend beyond it. In focusing first on authors and publishers, and then on the reprinters of their works, it shows how developments in eighteenth-century publishing served the Scottish Enlightenment, and how the Scottish Enlightenment served the domain of publishing. As this formulation implies, the relationship was symbiotic. Scottish authors of new Enlightenment texts provided British publishers with their most prestigious and potentially lucrative raw materials for books, while publishers provided Scottish authors and potential authors with opportunities for international fame, glory, and wealth.

From the Enlightenment to the Scottish Enlightenment

The January 2006 issue of the journal *American Behavioral Scientist* is devoted to the question "The End of Enlightenment?" One might think this inquiry has to do with the debate over the demise of the Enlightenment at the end of the eighteenth century, as the phrase has traditionally been used.[28] But no, in this debate, the existence of the Enlightenment itself is under review. In one contribution, Graeme Garrard discusses the history of anti-Enlightenment thought, "including the accusations that it was atheistic, morally nihilistic, and fatuously optimistic; that it perverted reason with destructive consequences; that it had a blind faith in science, which it conceived of as almost wholly benign; and that it was intolerant of difference."[29] Some of these and other accusations date back to the beginnings of "counter-Enlightenment" thought during the second half of

---

28. See, for example, Outram, *Enlightenment*, chap. 9: "The End of the Enlightenment: Conspiracy and Revolution?"

29. Garrard, "Enlightenment and Its Enemies," 671, and the articles by Robert Wokler cited by Garrard.

the eighteenth century and immediately after the French Revolution, but many have been expressed most forcefully during the past seventy-five years.[30]

The modern era of anti-Enlightenment thought began in 1931, with the publication of *The Heavenly City of the Eighteenth-Century Philosophers* by Carl Becker. The impact of that work was increased when the author's colleague at Cornell University, Preserved Smith, paraphrased Becker's thesis three years later in what was perhaps the first book to use the term "the Enlightenment" in its title. "The Enlightenment resembled a new religion," Smith wrote, "of which Reason was God, Newton's *Principia* the Bible, and Voltaire the prophet."[31] Despite a convincing rebuttal by Peter Gay, whose overly secular, antireligious interpretation of the Enlightenment was shaped largely by his antipathy to the Becker thesis, Becker's book has returned in a new edition published by Yale University Press in 2003, and it is now being hailed as "incredibly prescient" because of its anticipation of later, postmodern attacks on the Enlightenment.[32]

If Becker's essay anticipated some of the main currents of the postmodern view, so did Horkheimer and Adorno's 1947 work, translated from the German in the 1960s as *Dialectic of Enlightenment* and reissued by Stanford University Press in 2002. Here the Enlightenment's "program" is characterized as a kind of dictatorship of reason grounded in a tendency to promote "the self-oblivious instrumentation of science" and "the disenchantment of the world."[33] Building on this book and other counter-Enlightenment writings, postmodernists have continued to argue that Enlightenment thinkers were fundamentally narrow and intolerant be-

30. Garrard, *Counter-Enlightenments*; McMahon, *Enemies of the Enlightenment*; Mali and Wokler, *Isaiah Berlin's Counter-Enlightenment*.

31. Smith, *Enlightenment*, 35. Although it is commonly said that "the Enlightenment" did not come into common use in English until the appearance of the English translation of Ernst Cassirer's *Die Philosophie der Aufklärung* as *The Philosophy of the Enlightenment* in 1951, Smith's 1934 book was not only titled *The Enlightenment, 1687–1776* but contained a section, called "Character of the Enlightenment," that began with a discussion of "that vast spiritual revolution long known to the Germans as the *Aufklärung*, sometimes called by English writers the Illumination, and now coming to be known as the Enlightenment" (32).

32. McMahon, "Happiness and *The Heavenly City*," quoting 682; Wright, "Pre-Postmodernism of Carl Becker"; Gay, "Carl Becker's Heavenly City"; and Gay, *Enlightenment*, e.g., 1:18, where it is claimed that the Enlightenment's "leaders were atheists."

33. Horkheimer and Adorno, *Dialectic of Enlightenment*, quoting xvi and 3.

cause they advocated a single, universal, program founded on reason or science—what John Gray terms "the Enlightenment project of universal cultural homogenization."[34] The Enlightenment's substantial role in the creation of "modernity," which has often been cause for celebration, has been turned against the Enlightenment on the grounds that the creation of modernity entails responsibility for the ills of the modern world—from racism and sexism to colonial oppression, genocide, and nihilism. In its most extreme form, anticipated by Horkheimer and Adorno but articulated more vigorously by various postmodernists, this view holds that "the Enlightenment led straight to Auschwitz, just as it had led to the Terror" during the French Revolution.[35]

From Becker to Horkheimer and Adorno to Gray, most modern and postmodern critics of the Enlightenment have had only a superficial familiarity with it, and their writings are more often polemical attacks on an abstraction of their own creation than careful and contextual analyses of works by Enlightenment thinkers.[36] In these polemics, a single name, most commonly Voltaire or Kant, is frequently invoked to vilify a vast array of thinkers, and a movement devoted largely to the ideal of toleration is transformed into its opposite by fiat. Yet contending with these phantom critiques is taking a toll on the study of the Enlightenment, which seems to be languishing.

Faced with these external challenges, as well as with decades of internal bickering about the contours of their field, scholars of the Enlightenment have reacted in different ways. Several have tried to engage in thoughtful dialogue with postmodernist critics.[37] In the same spirit, some have ed-

---

34. Gray, *Enlightenment's Wake*, 178; Rosenau, *Post-Modernism and the Social Sciences*, 128–29; Garrard, "Enlightenment and Its Enemies," 675.

35. See David A. Hollinger's critique of this position, "Enlightenment and the Genealogy of Cultural Conflict," quoting 9.

36. See, for example, Darnton, "Case for the Enlightenment," 17: "Like Horkheimer and Adorno, Gray does not pause to consider what the French *philosophes* actually wrote. Instead, he offers a vague and unsubstantiated description of something he calls the enlightenment project and proceeds to condemn it for its failure to meet the standards set by postmodernist philosophy." Cf. Gordon, "Post-Structuralism and Post-Modernism," esp. 345 on "the Foucauldian style of writing about something that is not the Enlightenment and implicitly criticizing the Enlightenment in the process"; Williams, "Enlightenment Critique," esp. 641; and Wilson, "Postmodernism and the Enlightenment," 648–49.

37. Baker and Reill, *What's Left of Enlightenment*; Gordon, *Postmodernism and Enlightenment*.

ited Enlightenment anthologies that devote a significant portion of their space to recent critics of the Enlightenment, at the expense of authors from the Enlightenment itself or modern writers analyzing Enlightenment thought in a nonpolemical manner.[38] Others have offered substantial refutations of key aspects of the postmodernist critique, such as Sankar Muthu in his treatise on the anti-imperialist strand of Enlightenment thought in France and Germany.[39] Still others have countered with polemical defenses of the Enlightenment as a radical political movement.[40]

Another strategy, adopted by Muthu among others, has been to pluralize the Enlightenment and to qualify references accordingly. We do well to speak of "English, Arminian, Parisian" and Scottish Enlightenments, writes John Pocock, but not of "The" Enlightenment, because Enlightenment "occurred in too many forms to be comprised within a single definition and history."[41] For Dorinda Outram, similarly, the appearance in the 1970s of books on the Enlightenment in the Americas by Henry May and A. Owen Aldridge "made it impossible any longer to see the Enlightenment as a unified phenomenon." Outram and others seek to redefine the Enlightenment as "a series of interlocking, and sometimes warring problems and debates,"[42] an approach that highlights the institutional settings in which those debates occurred and emphasizes the extent to which the Enlightenment was a process rather than a common set of beliefs or values.

Finally, some commentators have attempted to reassert the unity of the Enlightenment by means of an approach that one of its supporters, Robert Darnton, has dubbed "deflation."[43] According to this view, the Enlightenment "industry" has become unwieldy because of the very multiplicity of Enlightenments that others have been so keen to create and promote: the Russian, Romanian, Brazilian, Josephinian, Pietistic, Jewish, musical, religious, radical, conservative, and Confucian Enlightenments are cited to demonstrate that "the Enlightenment is beginning to be everything and therefore nothing" (3–4). For Darnton, making "the case for

---

38. Schmidt, *What Is Enlightenment?*; Goodman and Wellman, *Enlightenment*.

39. Muthu, *Enlightenment against Empire*.

40. Bonner, *Reclaiming the Enlightenment*.

41. Pocock, *Barbarism and Religion*, 1:7–10, quoting 9–10; Hunter, *Rival Enlightenments*; Muthu, *Enlightenment against Empire*, 260–66.

42. Outram, *Enlightenment*, 2–4. Cf. Goodman and Wellman, *Enlightenment*, 3.

43. Darnton, "Case for the Enlightenment," 4.

the Enlightenment" means going back to basics by focusing on the "elitist, Voltairean, and incorrigibly Parisian" Enlightenment that consisted of
"a self-conscious group of intellectuals"—exclusively male—who set out
"to persuade, propagandize, and change the world" (5–6). Men of letters
elsewhere soon joined the fray, but they did so in emulation of the Parisian
philosophes, whose ideas and values were subsequently "diffused" among
them (7). Although John Robertson defines the problem in the same way
as Darnton and uses the same title phrase in some of his writings, his
"case for the Enlightenment" involves maintaining its broad geographical range as a European phenomenon but limiting its subject matter to a
cluster of topics involving the science of human nature, political economy,
and the historical development of human societies.[44]

If there is a common denominator in these approaches, it is that all of
them assume a defensive posture toward the Enlightenment. In contrast
with the strategies of retrenchment that are now in vogue, I contend that
the Enlightenment should be viewed as a very big movement, requiring
correspondingly broad conceptualization, geographically, intellectually,
and socially. The Enlightenment may be perceived as a grand symphony
with multiple variations. Such an approach may not yield a conception
of the Enlightenment that is as tightly demarcated as some would wish,
but the retreat to a narrowly defined Enlightenment or to a multitude
of discrete Enlightenments with no overriding unity is not likely to do
much better in this respect because there will always be uncertainties
about which thinkers and books fall within the purview of the delineated
spaces.

Although few would dispute the place of Paris as the capital of the
Enlightenment, a diffusionist model emanating from Paris is an over-
simplification of a complex process, partly because Paris did not always
dictate the terms of eighteenth-century intellectual life and partly because
men (and sometimes also women) of letters were increasingly engaged in
a complex, international exchange of ideas and information that did not
always start in one place or move in just one direction. In the same way,
restricting the content of the Enlightenment to political economy and
the science of man and society requires us to sacrifice too many rich and

44. Robertson, "Case for Enlightenment"; Robertson, "Scottish Contribution to
the Enlightenment." Robertson provides the fullest account of his position in chapter 1 of *Case for the Enlightenment*, an exemplary work of comparative intellectual
history that reached me as this book was undergoing its final revisions.

important fields of enlightened intellectual inquiry for the sake of a particular ideal of intellectual coherence.[45] Breaking up the Enlightenment into a multitude of unrelated segments exaggerates differences among geographical areas and intellectual schools at the expense of their underlying similarities. Graeme Garrard points out that the tendency to pluralize the Enlightenment "is an overreaction to the unavoidable vagueness of language and creates many problems of its own."[46] We do not discard the word "Asian" just because the boundaries of Asia are uncertain or because that word has been defined in many different ways. There will always be borderline cases, but these should not drive our understanding of concepts that prove useful for making sense of history. "Nor does the absence of complete unity among the philosophes necessarily invalidate the use of the term *the Enlightenment*," Garrard adds. "There is a common core to their views, notwithstanding differences that separate them on many points" (668).

In my view, that common core resides not in a fixed body of doctrine or a universal reform program or an institutional structure or a particular field or school of thought but rather in a set of general values to which proponents of the Enlightenment adhered. These values could be found among men of letters from the Americas in the west to Russia in the east, and from Scotland in the north to Naples in the south, despite variations within different national and regional contexts, among different schools of thought, and among particular individuals. They included improvement, or a commitment to bettering the human condition, morally and perhaps spiritually as well as materially, sometimes with a local or national focus and sometimes with an eye on mankind as a whole; humanity and cosmopolitan sensibility, or a sense of sympathy and fellow feeling toward other human beings, and opposition to torture, slavery, and other practices judged to be inhumane; sociability, or an awareness of, and a preference for, the social character of human nature and human society; toleration of those holding different beliefs about religion and other matters, and a corresponding adherence to basic liberties of worship, speech, and written communication (even if there was disagreement about just how far those and other liberties should extend); intellectualism, or dedication to cultivating the powers of the mind for understanding human nature, society, and the natural world, in accordance with Kant's famous

45. Schmidt, "What Enlightenment Was," 659.

46. Garrard, "Enlightenment and Its Enemies," 667, quoting Muthu, "Enlightenment Anti-Imperialism," 999.

motto of enlightenment, "Dare to know," and a concomitant belief in the power of learning as a means of bringing about improvement; and aestheticism, or an appreciation for the arts, including painting, music, poetry, and imaginative literature.

This list is not a closed one, and it is pitched at a high-enough level of generality to accommodate the different national, regional, and topical manifestations of the Enlightenment, as well as the differences and debates that characterized salons, academies, clubs, and lodges throughout large parts of Europe and the Americas.[47] Adhering to this general pattern of values were both secularists (including some atheists but more deists) and devout believers in moderate or rational varieties of institutionalized religion; both proponents of enlightened absolutism and those who believed that the power of rulers should be limited; both radical critics of the existing order and social and political conservatives. These core values were often promoted self-consciously by individuals and groups whose ideas and activities were sufficiently prevalent to set the tone for the age. Yet these values were not "everything and therefore nothing" because intolerance, inhumanity, injustice, ignorance, prejudice, religious enthusiasm and fanaticism, anti-intellectualism, narrow-mindedness, selfishness, immorality, sectarianism, belligerency, corruption, and insensitivity toward other human beings continued to exist, and sometimes to flourish.

Such a conception of the Enlightenment is deliberately open-ended. Like the concept of Asia, it is big enough to withstand border disputes. We may find that certain individuals and groups, even regions and nations, appear to be partly in and partly out of the Enlightenment. Commentators may explore the tensions inherent in enlightened values, perhaps even to the point of paradox.[48] Yet as long as "the Enlightenment" captures the spirit of the main trends and general tendencies of the philosophes or literati who are associated with it, the term remains useful with the definite article intact. More than that, this conception of the Enlightenment points toward a way out of the current malaise in Enlightenment studies by encouraging investigations of Enlightenment thought and practice that cross the boundaries of nations and disciplines. It provides a framework for undertaking the comparative history of variations within a larger pattern of unity.

---

47. Goodman, "Difference"; Goodman, *Republic of Letters;* Gordon, *Citizens without Sovereignty;* Jacob, *Living the Enlightenment;* Outram, *Enlightenment;* Roche, *Le siècle des lumières;* McElroy, *Scotland's Age of Improvement;* Clark, *British Clubs and Societies.*

48. Steintrager, *Cruel Delight.*

The Scottish Enlightenment was one of those variations. Although those who study it have had their share of disagreements over the nature and boundaries of their patch of the Enlightenment,[49] they have generally been spared the wrath of modern and postmodern critics. The Scottish Enlightenment's version of the "end of Enlightenment" debate has centered on a different problem, defined by two contrary trends in popular historiography. One approach, associated chiefly with a best-selling book by Arthur Herman, claims that "the Scottish Enlightenment created the basic idea of modernity," meaning nothing less than that eighteenth-century Scotland generated "the basic institutions, ideas, attitudes, and habits of mind that characterize the modern age."[50] Of course, modernity in this sense is thoroughly admirable and contains none of the reprehensible features of the modern world. "As the first modern nation and culture," Herman writes, "the Scots have by and large made the world a better place."[51] Herman is correct to draw attention to the enormous impact of Scots and the Scottish Enlightenment—far beyond what might be expected from a country of Scotland's size or previous accomplishments in the republic of letters. The Scottish influence was extensive in its global reach and intensive in the depth of its impact. Yet the Scottish Enlightenment was only one part of a much larger movement. To the extent that certain praiseworthy aspects of the modern world have been shaped by Enlightenment thinkers, we must take into account the work of Newton and Locke, Voltaire and Rousseau, Kant and Beccaria, Franklin and Jefferson, along with Hume and Smith, and countless others. We must also keep in mind that not all aspects of the Scottish contribution to the modern world were praiseworthy.[52] Overstating the case the way Herman has done may actually diminish the chances that the magnitude of the Scottish intellectual and cultural contribution will be taken seriously because such excessive boasting makes it easier to dismiss the entire phenomenon as a made-up story. That is the reaction of Ian Rankin's hard-nosed Edinburgh detective John Rebus when he encounters Herman's book at a local library: "Rebus picked a book off the shelf. It seemed to be saying

---

49. See the articles by Robertson, Sher, and Wood in Wood, *Scottish Enlightenment*.

50. Herman, *How the Scots Invented the Modern World*, quoting first the preface to the British paperback edition (*Scottish Enlightenment*, vii) and then the prologue (American ed., 9–10).

51. Herman, *How the Scots Invented the Modern World*, 361.

52. Hancock, "Scots in the Slave Trade"; and Hook, *From Goosecreek to Gandercleugh*, chap. 11, on the Scottish cultural ancestry of the Ku Klux Klan.

that the Scots had invented the modern world. He looked around to make sure they weren't in the fiction section."[53] Some scholars who are more familiar with the Scottish Enlightenment than Rebus have had a similar experience.

The other recent view, promoted by Roy Porter and Gertrude Himmelfarb, goes to the opposite extreme, by contending that the Scottish Enlightenment never existed. Not that Porter and Himmelfarb deny the importance of David Hume, Adam Smith, and other eighteenth-century Scottish thinkers, but they insist that their contributions should be considered within the framework of a larger entity called the British Enlightenment, which they view as the prime source of modernity (once again defined with reference to the features of the modern world that are deemed most admirable). They trace the concept of the Scottish Enlightenment to perspectives that are narrowly nationalistic or parochial. Porter argues that "to draw rigid distinctions between the English and Scottish enlightened traditions is anachronistic, largely because such a delineation merely reflects later nationalisms."[54] Himmelfarb justifies the eradication of the Scottish Enlightenment on the grounds of a few alleged instances of Scottish Anglicizing by Hume, Smith, and other literati (including the false claim that "many of these philosophers chose to identify themselves as North Britons rather than as Scots") and concludes that "the Scottish Enlightenment, therefore, was not as parochially or exclusively Scottish as might be thought."[55] Both Porter and Himmelfarb readily acknowledge that the Enlightenment took different forms in different national contexts,[56] and both assert the special character and significance of the British Enlightenment against the versions of the Enlightenment that prevailed in France and elsewhere. But their willingness to recognize distinctive national variations of the Enlightenment stops abruptly at the Scottish border.

Like Herman's claim that the Scottish Enlightenment was virtually everything, the counterclaim that it was, in effect, nothing cannot be substantiated. Readers of this book will see that the Scottish Enlightenment did exist as a recognizable entity, although not in a rigid or narrowly parochial sense. Here the Scottish Enlightenment is defined broadly, to

53. Rankin, *Fleshmarket*, 219.

54. Porter, *Enlightenment*, 243.

55. Himmelfarb, *Roads to Modernity*, 13.

56. Porter and Teich, *Enlightenment in National Context*, constitutes a seminal work in that tradition.

mean the Scottish manifestation of the international movement dedicated to the proliferation of polite, morally and intellectually edifying literature and learning during the eighteenth century, written by authors whose work can be identified with the general values of the Enlightenment discussed earlier. It was a cultural and intellectual phenomenon that is not reducible to any single branch, school, or mode of thought, be it history (narrative or "conjectural"), natural science, medicine, common sense philosophy (or moral philosophy generally), rhetoric and belles lettres, imaginative literature, or political economy and what are now called the social sciences.[57] In all these fields of intellectual activity, and others too, a good case can be made for regarding eighteenth-century Scottish thinkers as among the most innovative, eminent, and influential authors of their day. The books of eighteenth-century Scotland were disproportionately influential in many areas and were conspicuous in shaping modern academic disciplines and scholarly fields, from English literature, political economy, and sociology to various branches of science and medicine.[58] Equally remarkable is the fact that so much of this literature was written by individuals who associated with each other, socially and professionally, in the urban centers of Scotland, and sometimes also in London, and moved easily as authors from one enlightened genre to another. This sense of social, intellectual, and cultural integration and cohesiveness gives a distinctive character to the Scottish Enlightenment, setting it apart from the Enlightenment in England.

Almost half a century ago, Franco Venturi wrote in an essay on the European Enlightenment that "English intellectuals . . . did not constitute a party, one particular trend, but represented all the nuances of a free and diversified public opinion. Only in Scotland, where the unified action of scholars, erudites, and intellectuals sharing common ideas proved more necessary, was a movement born which had strong resemblance to the French movement." In Venturi's view, the sense of unity among Scottish men of letters, reflected in their celebrated clubs and their efforts to undo their nation's image as "a poor, abandoned, despised and

---

57. Sher, "Science and Medicine," 99–156.

58. See, for example, Broadie, *Cambridge Companion;* Crawford, *Scottish Invention of English Literature;* Court, *Institutionalizing English Literature;* Miller, *Formation of College English;* McCullough, *John Gregory;* Dean, *James Hutton;* Sakamoto and Tanaka, *Rise of Political Economy;* Hont and Ignatieff, *Wealth and Virtue;* Donovan, *Philosophical Chemistry;* Bryson, *Man and Society;* Berry, *Social Theory of the Scottish Enlightenment;* Howell, *Eighteenth-Century British Logic.*

rebellious country," was closely connected with Scotland's emergence as "one of the brightest centres of the European Enlightenment," home to "a pleiad of writers such as only Paris possessed."[59] Social conditions and intellectual accomplishments were inseparable, and it was not coincidence that Europe's two greatest national bodies of Enlightenment authors, the French philosophes and the Scottish literati, were the two national groups that displayed the highest degree of social cohesiveness and personal interaction.

In rejecting Venturi's distinction between the Scottish and English Enlightenments and Venturi's avowal of the underlying connection between the social and the intellectual spheres, Porter argues that writers in eighteenth-century Britain are best understood as "autonomous individuals," along the lines of Karl Mannheim's notion of a "free" (or free-floating) intelligentsia. They were free, that is, of primary connections with institutions and patrons, and "beholden to none but themselves, the public who bought their writings or subscribed to their lectures, and such cultural middlemen as publishers." Thus, "Mannheim's reading illuminates the British scene better than Venturi's."[60] Such an approach fits with Porter's insistence on subsuming the Scottish Enlightenment into a "British" (or, linguistically speaking, "English") Enlightenment, consisting of all authors who lived in Britain during the eighteenth century and wrote in English on enlightened themes, with little regard for their personal and institutional connections, outlooks, and identities (xviii–xix). To the extent that these factors are considered at all, they are dismissed as irrelevant because "English and Scottish thinkers were in constant dialogue" (243).

Surely this approach obscures more than it clarifies. Although Scottish and English intellectuals often interacted meaningfully during the eighteenth century, just as they interacted with men and women of letters elsewhere, there were powerful and distinct national traditions, patterns of thought, and social bonds among the Scottish literati that were often different from those that operated among their English counterparts. As we shall see, eighteenth-century Scottish men of letters were involved in a self-conscious attempt to glorify and improve the Scottish nation through the publication of learned and literary books. Even Scottish authors and publishers who resided in London were often bound by national ties and imbued with a strong sense of Scottish identity and national pride.

59. Venturi, "European Enlightenment," 22–23.
60. Porter, *Enlightenment*, 478–79.

For Venturi, the ultimate significance of the intense social interaction that prevailed among the Scottish literati lay in its authorial payoff: the creation of "a pleiad of writers such as only Paris possessed." This aspect of the Scottish achievement has not always been fully appreciated, even by scholars with a solid grasp of the social nature of enlightened knowledge and the distinctiveness of the Scottish scene. In his splendid study of chemistry as a "public" science in late eighteenth-century Britain, Jan Golinski contends that, in contrast with England's scholarly arena, "credit and reputation in the Scottish academic world rested much more on teaching performance than on success as an author." Scotland's star academic chemists, William Cullen and Joseph Black, "did not significantly exploit the potential of the printed word," whereas their English counterpart, Joseph Priestley, did.[61] Restricted to the field of chemistry, Golinski's claims may be valid. As an argument about the nature of the Enlightenment in Scotland and England, however, they are very far from the mark. Success as an author was at least as important as success in teaching for establishing the credit and reputation of Scottish professors, and Cullen himself was one of the masters at exploiting learned publishing—in his main publishing field of medicine, that is. The term "English Enlightenment" appears least problematic in regard to those topics, such as natural science and applied arts, that most interested Priestley and others in England who participated in distinct social communities of polite learning.[62] More generally, England produced large numbers of connoisseurs and dilettantes, antiquarians and virtuosi, performers and collectors; it can plausibly be argued that they gave eighteenth-century English culture its distinctive character, and that the British Museum, which opened its doors to the public in January 1759, constituted the closest thing to an institutional embodiment of enlightened learning in London.[63] As authors of Enlightenment books, however, the Scots far surpassed their southern neighbors. In short, Venturi was right.

Viewed from this standpoint, this work is about the disproportionately large Scottish component in Enlightenment book culture and the immense contribution of the book trade in cultivating it. It investigates

61. Golinski, *Science as Public Culture*, 43, 13, 71–76.

62. Gascoigne, *Joseph Banks and the English Enlightenment*; Golinski, *Science as Public Culture*; Uglow, *Lunar Men*; Levere and Turner, with Golinski and Stewart, *Discussing Chemistry and Steam*.

63. Brewer, *Pleasures of the Imagination*; Sloan with Burnett, *Enlightenment*; Anderson et al., *Enlightening the British*; Chambers, *Joseph Banks*.

how one of Europe's smallest and poorest nations became a fountainhead of Enlightenment books. This does not mean that book publishing was the sole or even the chief factor in accounting for the Scottish Enlightenment, but it was certainly a principal factor, and a neglected one too. The development and international expansion of the Scottish Enlightenment through the power and influence of books is therefore a primary theme of this study.

As we shall see, the new books of the Scottish Enlightenment resulted from interaction and collaboration between publishers in London and Edinburgh, who contracted to publish works by Scottish authors residing in various places. But the success of the Scottish Enlightenment also owed much to the propagation of Scottish books in places far from the English and Scottish capitals. To cover this subject fully, we would need to study the massive Continental dissemination of Scottish Enlightenment books, above all in France and Germany, where translations of works by Scottish authors were plentiful, often augmented by significant new introductions, prefaces, and notes by their editors and translators.[64] As a result of these developments, the Scottish Enlightenment exerted a powerful influence on European thought and culture, extending to nineteenth-century movements such as German Romanticism and French academic philosophy. These are important topics that require careful examination, but they involve different kinds of methodological issues and research skills.[65] The present study is therefore limited to the spread of Scottish Enlightenment books in the English-speaking Atlantic world during the late eighteenth century, especially as a result of reprinting in Dublin and Philadelphia. In this process of diffusion, authors eventually dropped out of the picture,

---

64. Barber, *Studies in the Booktrade*, chap. 16, treats J. J. Tourneisen of Basle, the leading Continental reprinter of books in English, whose publications included twenty-three titles by Scottish Enlightenment authors between 1787 and 1799. Recent studies of German and French translations and reprints of Scottish Enlightenment books, and their Continental impact, include Fabian, *English Book in Eighteenth-Century Germany;* Oz-Salzberger, *Translating the Enlightenment*, on Adam Ferguson; Schmidt, *"Homer des Nordens" und "Mutter der Romantik,"* on Ossian in Germany; Gaskill, *Reception of Ossian;* Gordon, *Citizens without Sovereignty*, chap. 4, on Jean-Baptiste Suard's translations in France; chapters by John Renwick and Richard B. Sher in S. J. Brown, *William Robertson;* chapters by Pierre Carboni and Deidre Dawson in Dawson and Morère, *Scotland and France;* Malherbe, "Impact on Europe"; and Rendekop, "Reid's Influence." German translations are reprinted in Klemme, *Reception of the Scottish Enlightenment in Germany* and in Schmidt's work, cited above.

65. Bassnett, *Translation Studies*.

but commercial, technological, cultural, demographical, legal, ideological, and personal factors remained in play among those who elected to reprint Scottish Enlightenment books in Ireland and America.

Once again a dynamic, comprehensive, geographically expansive approach is needed in order to explain these occurrences—an approach that encompasses all genres of polite literature and that views the Atlantic Ocean as something more than a liquid barrier separating so many local domains of print culture. Atlantic studies have become so faddish that one commentator has recently quipped: "We are all Atlanticists now—or so it would seem from the explosion of interest in the Atlantic and the Atlantic world as subjects of study among historians."[66] But Atlantic studies can mean many different things, and it has also been noted that "books and articles with 'Atlantic' in their titles rarely connect different lands bordering the Atlantic Ocean; more often they showcase one part of that oceanic geography."[67] This criticism has been applied particularly to the discipline of early American history, which currently places a premium on Atlanticization but does not consistently implement it in a manner that is both sophisticated and comprehensive, and that regards the Old World as something more than a backdrop for the New. Conversely, America often appears in recent books by historians of eighteenth-century Scotland as a site of Scottish empire-building rather than as part of an intricate process of Atlantic interaction.[68] Because it embodies immigration, diffusion, exchange, and appropriation and incorporates a broad range of historical modalities, from material to intellectual, the history of books represents one way to reconceptualize the Atlantic world and transcend the Britain–North America dichotomy.[69] In accordance with this theme, the closing chapters of this book investigate how the Scottish Enlightenment was imported and reprinted in late eighteenth-century America, especially by Scottish booksellers in Philadelphia who followed and often emulated their precursors in Dublin. The goal is both to reveal the material foundations of the "general diffusion of knowledge" exalted in the preface to Guthrie's *Geography* and to illustrate the complex, interactive manner in which American book culture was constructed.

66. Armitage, "Three Concepts of Atlantic History," 11.

67. Chaplin, "Expansion and Exceptionalism," 1439–40.

68. Devine, *Scotland's Empire*; and Michael Fry, *Scottish Empire* and *"Bold, Independent, Unconquer'd and Free."*

69. Rubin, "What Is the History of the History of Books?" 555–76, esp. 566; Amory and Hall, *Colonial Book*.

DESIGNS AND DISCLAIMERS

Copyright and Reading

Having indicated what this book is meant to be, I now add a few words about two important topics on which it has relatively little to say: literary property regulations and the reception and reading of books. Unlike many recent studies, this work does not view changes in copyright law as the central theme of eighteenth-century British book history. It is not difficult to see why the issue of literary property has attracted so much scholarly attention. Because the issue was contested in legal cases and paper wars, there exists a huge body of legal papers and published pamphlets that scholars can consult.[70] Intellectual property has continued to be a vibrant issue ever since, and it therefore possesses relevance today beyond many other eighteenth-century topics: the Statute of Anne and its affirmation by the House of Lords in February 1774 are widely recognized as the starting point for modern copyright law.

Despite all this, it can be argued that overemphasis on the issue of literary property has encouraged exaggeration and misrepresentation regarding eighteenth-century British book culture.[71] Because scholarship on this subject has often been written with what might be called an authorial bias, there has been a tendency to treat the history of copyright as the story of authors' property rights, even though those rights were not always what legislators and judges had in mind.[72] Authors were certainly affected by the Lords' decision to uphold the Statute of Anne, but the position of authors was ambiguous, and it is still not completely clear how the Lords' decision affected them. Although the bookseller-publishers who fought to establish the legal justification for perpetual copyright did what they could to recruit authors to their cause by scaring them with predictions of severe decreases in copy money if the duration of copyright were restricted by statute, their efforts met with limited success. David Hume permitted his London publishers to use his name publicly, but in private he told one of them that he did not think the elimination of per-

70. Deazley, *On the Origin of the Right to Copy*, discusses all the relevant copyright cases. Much of the pamphlet literature is discussed in Rose, *Authors and Owners.*

71. For a fuller discussion of some aspects of the argument about intellectual property presented in this section, see Sher, "Corporatism and Consensus," 32–93.

72. Deazley, "Myth of Copyright," 106–33; Ross, "Copyright and the Invention of Tradition," 1–27.

petual copyright would be likely to have "any such bad Consequences as you mention" (*LDH*, 2:288). By and large, Hume was correct. After the abolition of perpetual copyright in 1774, publishers paid authors as much or more for the rights to publish their new titles, perhaps because, among other factors, the *certainty* of copyright regulations mattered more than the *duration* of the copyright period.[73]

A single-minded focus on problems relating to copyright has led to a preoccupation with the reprinting of old books by dead authors and a failure to appreciate the more innovative, and often more cooperative, activities of the book trade in the publication of new books. It has also inflated the role of the law in relation to that of the trade. In practice, laws were not always decisive, not only because they were sometimes evaded by means of unauthorized publishing or piracy but also, and perhaps more importantly, because the men at the top of the London book trade, like their brethren elsewhere, routinely bypassed the legal regime by establishing and enforcing regulations within the trade itself. This was the principle that the elite London publishers followed after the defeat of perpetual copyright in 1774; as James Boswell observed in 1791, "honorary copyright" continued to flourish among them, regulated by "mutual compact" rather than by law (*BLJ*, 3:370). It was based in the Chapter Coffee House, where participating booksellers kept a private register of copies (now, unfortunately, lost) for the express purpose of minimizing competition and conflict.[74] In this sense, the ideology of literary property functioned as a subset of the ideology of corporate order. Moreover, sale of copyright prior to publication was only one of several publishing arrangements available to authors and publishers. For all these reasons, it seems advisable to proceed by asking not only how the law regulated literary property but also how the publication process actually worked. In this book, therefore, names such as Millar and Donaldson signify real booksellers and, beyond that, real people, rather than merely the principal parties involved in famous lawsuits about literary property.

This point leads directly to another. Exaggerating the importance of copyright law has contributed to distorting the interests, motives, and roles of publishers. The regulations governing literary property were sometimes a matter of pressing interest to the eighteenth-century British book trade, especially when the legal crisis came to a head in the early 1770s. But literary property was only one of many issues that concerned

73. Belanger, "Publishers and Writers," 21.
74. Pollard, "English Market."

the publishers of Enlightenment books, and it should be kept in perspective. By relying more heavily on personal correspondence than on copyright pamphlets, and by focusing attention on the making of new books (as well as on their reprinting), this study attempts to present the full range of issues that engaged authors and publishers as they put the Scottish Enlightenment into print.

William St. Clair's critically acclaimed book, *The Reading Nation in the Romantic Period*, marks the climax of the tendency to establish 1774 as the chief turning point in the history of eighteenth-century British books. Although St. Clair is chiefly interested in the expansion of reading during the early nineteenth century, eighteenth-century publishing and marketing practices constitute the foundation of his argument. St. Clair reasons that because readership depended on access to printed material, because access to printed material depended on price, and because price depended on intellectual property regulations grounded in the relationship of the book industry to the state (42), it follows that copyright laws were the key to the growth in reading that occurred in late eighteenth- and early nineteenth-century England. Building on this formula, St. Clair paints a dismal picture of the London publishing industry during the third quarter of the eighteenth century. In his account, the refusal of the book trade to accept limits on the duration of copyright produced an era of artificially large and expensive books catering to a small number of wealthy book buyers, "as perfect a private monopoly as economic history can show" (101). The existence of such a monopoly dictated that books would be overpriced, with little regard to production and marketing costs (28–29), and would be reprinted in smaller sizes as the high end of the market became saturated.[75] Although St. Clair acknowledges that this period saw "the publication of an impressive range of innovative texts" in a variety of fields (99) and an increase in copy money paid to some authors, he believes these developments had little to do with the general reading public. The London trade employed an imposing battery of devices to restrict access to published books, including "cartel, conspiracy, price-fixing, predatory pricing, rent seeking [i.e., "the devising of imaginative means of enhancing and maintaining the monopoly" (93)], repetitive and baseless litigation, entry barriers, market division, credit-fixing, collective refusal to deal, exclusionary joint ventures, resale price restrictions,

---

75. St. Clair calls this process "tranching down" or "moving prices in discrete stages down the demand curve" (*Reading Nation*, 32). I prefer the simpler word "downsizing."

tying, and vertical non-price constraints" (100–101). In St. Clair's analysis, the end of this unhappy age of monopoly and "the explosion of reading" that transformed England into a "reading nation" occurred as a direct result of the House of Lords' decision in 1774 to limit the duration of intellectual property, "the most decisive event in the history of reading in England since the arrival of printing 300 years before" (109). Because of that ruling, St. Clair has written elsewhere, "prices tumbled, production soared, and access widened."[76]

This book espouses a different interpretation, which suggests that Britain began to emerge as a "reading nation" long before 1774 and that the impact of the Lords' copyright decision should not be exaggerated. Contemporaries such as the author of the preface to Guthrie's *Geography* believed that the decades immediately preceding 1774 were dynamic and innovative from the standpoint of both the production and the dissemination of books, and their perceptions should not be dismissed hastily. It is true that during this period many learned books originally appeared in expensive quarto formats and were later reprinted in smaller and more affordable formats if they proved to be popular. But the ominous gloss that St. Clair places on this practice is unwarranted. Eighteenth-century publishers usually pitched their books, even scholarly books, to the general reading public, and most of the titles that were commercially successful among elite readers also appealed to a broader readership not only in Britain but also abroad. It is misleading to stress "the weight, price, and immobility" of books published before 1774 (100) because huge folios had degenerated into a novelty format by the mid-eighteenth century, if not sooner; quartos were used only for certain kinds of genres and were more readable than smaller formats (an important consideration when trying to read by candlelight or without precision eyeglasses); and octavos, which were considered affordable by much of the book-buying public, had dimensions no larger than most paperback trade books today. No matter what the format and price, new books were increasingly accessible to large numbers of readers through the various kinds of libraries that were rapidly springing up throughout Britain.[77]

If publishers were going to downsize their popular quartos within a few years anyway, what difference would it make for this practice whether they owned the copyright for fourteen years or in perpetuity? A limited

76. St. Clair, "Political Economy of Reading," 8.

77. See Robin Alston's comprehensive database, "Library History: The British Isles–to 1850," at www.r-alston.co.uk/contents.htm.

copyright, after all, is a limited monopoly, no matter how long the copyright period may be. Perhaps this is why so little changed in the way that most kinds of new books were published and marketed after the Lords' decision in 1774. In our own day, scholarly books often appear first in expensive hardcover editions for the library market and then, after a suitable time lag, in paperback editions that are priced considerably lower. But whereas price differentials between these hardbacks and paperbacks usually have little or nothing to do with the content of the editions or their production costs, in the eighteenth century a quarto first edition and an octavo second edition were very different entities (always in their paper and type, and usually in their content), and their respective prices bore some relation to differences in their costs of production.

Above all, it is necessary to apply rigorous historical methods to the study of the book trade. Why suppose that soaring book production at the end of the eighteenth century was the result of the Lords' ruling in 1774 when the same phenomenon is evident in places not affected by that decision, such as Dublin and Philadelphia? Similarly, when like formats are compared and adjustments are made for inflation, did the prices of new British books really plummet after 1774? More empirical research is needed on this issue, but it is worth noting that contemporaries such as John Nichols complained of the growing "luxury" and expense of books during the 1780s and 1790s,[78] and anyone who has compared book prices in the third and fourth quarters of the century will understand why. Furthermore, where is the evidence that during the third quarter of the eighteenth century the London book trade operated a "perfect" monopoly that was brought to an end by the Lords' ruling in 1774? The list of exclusionary business practices that St. Clair attributes to the pre-1774 London trade is drawn from a discussion of monopoly in an economics textbook rather than from an examination of the actual practices of the book trade. Whatever the state of copyright law, and however monopolistic the leading London publishers wished to be, they could never realize anything approaching a perfect monopoly during the third quarter of the eighteenth century because the textbook model of monopoly was mediated by the complexities of real life—including cheap Scottish and Irish reprints, ongoing legal disputes, competition from other publishers in London, and uncertainty about the behavior of the public. Expensive books entailed significant risk on the part of publishers, whose control over copyright—whether limited or perpetual—could not assure them

78. Quoted in Collins, *Profession of Letters*, 57, 112.

of profits at any price. All publishers who owned copyrights had to take expenses into account when setting prices, and they had to be prepared to produce smaller, cheaper editions in response to competition and demand. Moreover, after 1774 the leading London bookseller-publishers continued to assert their pretended right of perpetual copyright by enforcing, to the extent they were able to do so, the principle of "honorary copyright" within the trade. Thus, the Lords' decision in 1774 was not the critical turning point that St. Clair and others have made it out to be, and the "reading nation" was not created in that year.

St. Clair is on firmer ground when he argues that a nucleus of best-selling authors from the second half of the eighteenth century formed an "old canon" that remained popular until well into Victorian times. A high proportion of the authors whom he names in this context were Scots, such as James Beattie, Hugh Blair, William Buchan, David Hume, William Robertson, Adam Smith, and Tobias Smollett. If changes in copyright law alone cannot explain the enduring popularity of the old canon and the strong Scottish representation within it, how can we account for these developments? Although this question is too large to be answered here, it is a matter of considerable importance. Publishing and reading, production and consumption, were vital components of what Robert Darnton has described as "a communications circuit that runs from the author to the publisher . . . , the printer, the shipper, the bookseller, and the reader."[79] In order to understand the Enlightenment communication circuit, we need careful historical research into the ways in which Enlightenment books were actually received.

With regard to the Scottish Enlightenment, empirical research of this kind has just begun to appear. In a series of articles and a forthcoming book, David Allan investigates the appeal of works by Scottish Enlightenment authors such as those in St. Clair's "old canon" to late eighteenth- and early nineteenth-century English readers, using both individual reactions (found in unpublished marginalia, commonplace books, and the like) and statistical patterns (identified through the titles listed in library inventories, sale catalogues, and similar sources).[80] Allan is well aware of

79. Darnton, "What Is the History of Books?" 111. See also Adams and Barker, "New Model," which offers a process-oriented rather than a people-oriented version of the cycle of book history: publication, manufacture, distribution, reception, and survival (15).

80. See the following articles by David Allan: "Scottish Enlightenment and the Readers of Late Georgian Lancaster," 267–81; "Some Methods and Problems in the History of Reading," 91–124; "Eighteenth-Century Private Subscription Libraries,"

the difficulty of merging these two kinds of data into a coherent analysis of reading and reception that will answer James Raven's call for "an approach to the history of reading that will be various enough in its methodologies and in its objects of study to establish and explore the often conflicting, contradictory ways in which general social changes and individual experience interact."[81] Nevertheless, efforts like these are beginning to provide an empirical foundation for understanding the attraction of the Scottish Enlightenment to several generations of English readers.

The emphasis on publishing in the present volume may be justified in other ways. Under the influence of postmodernism and its offshoot, reader-response theory, recent scholarship has so thoroughly privileged reading and reception over production that some correction is necessary. "Abandoning the Author, Transforming the Text, and Re-Orienting the Reader"—this chapter title from a book by Pauline Marie Rosenau captures the postmodern turn from authors, whose intentions and concerns are minimized, to readers, who are empowered (either individually or as part of what Stanley Fish calls "interpretative communities") to create meaning out of texts.[82] The postmodern abandonment of the author has also entailed an abandonment of the publisher and the entire process of book production. What Roger Chartier has called "the dialectic between imposition and appropriation" (viii)—that is, between bookmaking and reading—has been skewed to the detriment of the former, with unfortunate results for our understanding of the history of books.

At the most basic level, publishing takes precedence over reading and reception because in the eighteenth century (unlike in our modern world of electronic communication), texts that were not widely accessible in print simply could not be read by large numbers of people. The literature on scribal or manuscript books in early modern England and America supports this point: whatever social functions such writing may

---

57–76; "A Reader Writes," 207–33; and "Opposing Enlightenment," 301–21. I am grateful to David Allan for allowing me to read a draft of his forthcoming book, provisionally titled *Making British Culture: English Readers and the Scottish Enlightenment.*

81. Allan, "Some Methods and Problems," 109: "The evidence permits us to sketch a broad picture of aggregate patterns of reading and, occasionally, to paint detailed miniatures of the responses of specific readers, but not to integrate the two." Raven is quoted from the introduction to Raven, Small, and Tadmor, *Practice and Representation of Reading*, 15.

82. Rosenau, *Post-Modernism and the Social Sciences*, 25–41; Fish, *Is There a Text in This Class?* Cf. Goldstein, "Reader-Response Theory and Criticism"; and Chartier, *Order of Books*, preface and chap. 1.

have served for certain women, elite families, colonists, and others, manuscript books were usually read only by small, select audiences, and they were far less prevalent in the eighteenth century (especially the late eighteenth century) than in the preceding two hundred years.[83] The process of making and marketing books and the nature of books themselves must be recognized as crucial factors in shaping reading and reception. I am referring not only to the size and appearance of a book, its typography, and other physical attributes that directly affect the reading process; the role of these traits in the making of meaning has already received some consideration from perceptive bibliographers and historians of books.[84] The price of a book, the number of copies printed, how it was advertised and promoted, and even the contractual arrangements between the author and the publisher, or among the copublishers, must all be taken into account, because supply-side factors such as these affected reception in various ways. As Robert Darnton has written in a slightly different context, "Our knowledge of production and distribution can compensate, to a certain extent, for the limitations of our knowledge of reception."[85]

As an illustration of the truth of Darnton's statement, let us look at the following passage from a sermon titled "On Sensibility" by the Scottish Presbyterian minister Hugh Blair:

> In modern times, the chief improvement of which we have to boast is a sense of humanity. This, notwithstanding the selfishness that still prevails, is the favourite and distinguishing virtue of the age. On general manners, and on several departments of society, it has had considerable influence. It has abated the spirit of persecution; it has even tempered the horrors of war; and man is now more ashamed, than he was in former ages, of acting as a savage to man. Hence, sensibility is become so reputable a quality, that the appearance of it is frequently assumed when the reality is wanting. Softness of manners must not be mistaken for true sensibility. Sensibility tends to produce gentleness of behaviour; and when such behavior flows from native affection, it is valuable and amiable. But the exterior manner alone may be learned in the school of the world; and often, too often, is found to cover much unfeeling hardness of heart.[86]

83. Love, *Culture and Commerce of Texts*; Fox, *Oral and Literate Culture*; Ezell, *Social Authorship*; Justice and Tinker, *Women's Writing*; Hall, *Cultures of Print*.

84. See, for example, McKenzie, *Making Meaning*; and Tanselle, *Literature and Artifacts*, 312.

85. Darnton, *Forbidden Best-Sellers*, 184.

86. Blair, *Sermons*, 3:34.

As an assertion of fundamental Enlightenment values, this passage can be read profitably without any reference to book history. The notion of modern manners, and society as a whole, being transformed by the spread of humanity or sensibility went to the heart of the Enlightenment world-view. Civilization was by definition the product of a softening of the heart stemming from this attribute, which for Blair was grounded in Christianity; without sensibility or humanity, Blair states elsewhere in the sermon, "men would become hordes of savages, perpetually harassing one another" (27). The distinction between true and false humanity is another significant part of the passage, for the Enlightenment was continually grappling with the problem of affectation, or right actions not accompanied by appropriate or authentic sentiments. Blair's aim was not only to draw attention to improvements in social and political conduct, including a lessening of "persecution" and of the brutality of warfare, but also to encourage his readers to become truly virtuous by internalizing the sentiments from which good conduct springs.

Now consider how additional information about the conditions of publication and distribution can add another dimension to the contemporary meaning of this passage. "On Sensibility" was the second sermon in the third volume of Blair's published *Sermons*. When that volume appeared in 1790, Blair was already famous for having written "the most admired sermons that ever were published" and for having "obtained the highest price that ever was given for any work of the kind," as one of his publishers put it in a pamphlet first published in the 1780s.[87] In 1807 the *Critical Review* declared the complete five-volume series "the most popular work in the English language" except for the *Spectator* (11:170). Bibliographical evidence concerning the number of printed and published editions confirms the immense scale of circulation.[88] The book crossed denominations, was translated into French, German, Dutch, and other European languages, and was widely excerpted, reprinted, pirated, and anthologized. The sermons were read aloud at family prayer and were borrowed by other clergymen. Aware of his status, Blair prefixed to the third volume a dedication to the queen, justified by "the favourable manner in which the Public has received Two Volumes."

Viewed in these terms, the quoted passage may be interpreted as a self-conscious declaration of Enlightenment principles. It came from a man who was aware of having his finger firmly on the pulse of European

87. [Creech], *Letters to Sir John Sinclair*, 12.
88. Zachs, *Hugh Blair's Letters to His Publishers*.

culture, and it was directed not to the congregation of a single church but to a vast readership throughout Europe and America. Although we will never know exactly what these words meant to each person who read or heard them during the late eighteenth century, the conditions of publication and distribution allow us to make inferences about reception that carry more weight than accounts by individual readers. Blair's preaching on humanity may seem to be an extreme case because of the special circumstances surrounding the publication and reception of the work in which it appeared. Yet the methodological principle that I have invoked it to illustrate holds true across the board: the conditions of publication and distribution can help us to recover the contemporary meaning of published books.

In these ways, I hope this study of publishing and reprinting will help to facilitate further investigations of the reading and reception of Scottish Enlightenment books by contemporaries as well as by later generations. Perhaps the postmodern formula articulated by Rosenau can be revised to represent reading as a process that commonly reflects, rather than subverts, the work of publication by authors and publishers. The new slogan might be: "Revitalizing the Author and the Publisher, Re-Situating the Text within the Book, and Re-Orienting the Reader."

Things to Come

Although this work keeps its focus on the books of the Scottish Enlightenment and the people who made them, the emphasis in part 1 on the authors of those books shifts in part 2 to their original British publishers and in part 3 to their Irish and American reprinters. Part 1 looks first at the emergence of the mature Scottish Enlightenment in the 1750s in connection with the rise of a new self-consciousness about authorship and its relationship to Scottish national identity, focusing on Francis Hutcheson's *System of Moral Philosophy*, on the preface to the first *Edinburgh Review* of 1755–56, and above all on the most neglected book by the leading figure in the movement, *Essays and Treatises on Several Subjects* by David Hume. For many Scottish authors, and for some key Scottish publishers as well, what we now call the Scottish Enlightenment was closely connected with feelings of national pride; nowhere is this more evident than in the rivalry between Scottish and English men of letters, in the enthusiastic Scottish reception to the accolades of the Italian scholar Carlo Denina, and in the lists of prominent Scottish authors that appear in contemporary works by Tobias Smollett, William Creech, and Robert Alves. The 50 Scottish authors identified by those three writers, along with 65 others whom I have added in order to broaden the representation in the same genres identified by these commentators, constitute the list of 115 authors, whose 360 major works form the empirical database of this study (tables 1 and 2). Chapter 1 analyzes the first editions of these books by examining a number of variables, including formats, subject matter, print runs, and popularity.

Chapter 2, which treats the social and cultural conditions of authorship in the Scottish Enlightenment, begins by uncovering patterns in the ages and backgrounds of authors and their social organization. There is discussion of the mainly urban context and the diverse backgrounds of these authors, who came from all over Scotland and ranged from the well-entrenched professional elite of Edinburgh to the more marginal Grub Street Scots in London. The second part of the chapter emphasizes the sense of solidarity that prevailed among Scottish authors, despite their many differences. Sometimes celebrated in the dedications to their books, this sense of unity-amid-diversity derived from extensive connections through blood and marriage, friendship, teacher–pupil relationships, schools of thought, and various kinds of professional and social ties. It was strengthened by their shared sense of Scottishness, particularly in the face of contact, and sometimes confrontation, with English attitudes, institutions, and people. The chapter concludes by considering some of the ways in which Scottish authors represented themselves to their readers and thereby proclaimed their authenticity and authority as writers. They did this chiefly by placing their names on the title pages of their books, which often were augmented by descriptive information about their academic degrees and professional positions and affiliations. Less frequently, frontispiece portraits, made from line or stipple engravings, enabled readers to associate an author's name not only with a face but also with an attitude.

Chapter 3 considers the ways in which the writing of Scottish authors was supported and compensated. It has sometimes been said that in the eighteenth century traditional aristocratic patronage of authors gave way to patronage by the bookseller-publishers or, in some versions of the story, by the public itself. The first part of the chapter suggests a different interpretation, which recognizes the continued importance of aristocratic and government patronage but contends that it operated in new ways. By enabling many authors to become self-sufficient, this new kind of patronage had the ironic effect of releasing authors from the need for further patronage. Whether it resulted from patronage, inherited income, or success in a chosen profession, the financial independence of many Scottish authors occasionally led them to adopt an aristocratic attitude toward authorship, by writing for some end other than personal profit. More commonly, however, authors wished to earn as much money as they could from their books, and their growing success at doing so created an incentive for others to take up the pen. The last part of chapter 3 relates the stories of a number of Scottish authors with respect to this theme. Every story is set within a common framework, shaped by the constraints of the possible and the customary, and yet every story is unique. Some authors got rich by selling their words to booksellers by the sheet, or by selling copyrights in advance of publication, or by selling the rights to a particular edition, or by sharing profits with booksellers, or by publishing books at their own risk (at least initially), sometimes by subscription—and some authors met failure and disappointment by means of these same arrangements. On the whole, however, we shall see that the authors of the Scottish Enlightenment took authorship to a new level of commercial success.

The second part of this book concentrates on the publishers who made it possible for Scottish authors to enjoy so much critical and financial success. Chapter 4 introduces the principal publishers of Scottish Enlightenment books in London and Edinburgh, all of whom were either Scots or English provincials by birth (or, in the next generation, their London-born sons). The second part of the chapter traces the origins of the London–Edinburgh axis in Scottish Enlightenment publishing to a generational cohort of five Scottish publishers born within six years of 1710, who helped to transform the Scottish Enlightenment into a recognizable movement in the republic of letters during the late 1740s, the 1750s, and the 1760s: Andrew Millar, William Strahan, Gavin Hamilton, John Balfour, and Alexander Kincaid. The most important of these figures, Millar, set himself up in the Strand during the late 1720s in the shop of his former master, James M'Euen, and then used a mainly Scottish network of authors, booksellers, advisers, and friends—including the emerging printing firm founded in London by William Strahan—to build a strong list of new Scottish writing. Both Millar and Strahan had to grapple with problems associated with being Scots in a foreign place. Meanwhile, the Edinburgh firms of Hamilton & Balfour and Alexander Kincaid were also beginning to publish new works of Scottish literature and learning. Beginning with Millar and Kincaid's copublication of works by David Hume in 1748, collaborative publishing projects flourished among them. Such collaboration depended in large measure on friendship and trust rooted in their early years in Edinburgh. But those bonds did not necessarily extend to their successors. Chapter 4 closes with a growing rift between the firms of Millar and Kincaid, owing not to differences between the senior partners but to disagreements on publishing policy and a personality clash between their respective junior partners, Thomas Cadell and John Bell, centered on one particular new title: *An Essay on the History of Civil Society* by Adam Ferguson.

Chapter 5 treats the heyday of Scottish Enlightenment publishing from the late 1760s to the 1790s. After the death of Andrew Millar in 1768, William Strahan joined forces with Millar's protégé and successor, Thomas Cadell, and their Edinburgh associates, especially Kincaid's last partner and successor, William Creech, to carry Scottish Enlightenment book production into its golden age. To some degree, they passed on their strategy to their progeny—Andrew Strahan and Thomas Cadell, Jr. (partnered with William Davies, as Cadell & Davies)—who continued to work together as publishers, and especially reprinters, of Scottish Enlightenment books until well into the nineteenth century. Yet maintaining the hegemony of the Strahan–Cadell publishing empire was not easy. William Strahan's surviving correspondence with Creech reveals a high level of anxiety that focused on issues such as the unsatisfactory state of the economy, the rising demands of authors, the incursions of Irish reprinters, the biases of Scottish advisers, and the uncertain condition of literary property. Attempts to forge an alliance between Balfour and Creech came to naught. Furthermore, there was competition from other British publishers, such as John Murray, Joseph Johnson, the Dilly brothers, and George Robinson in London and Charles Elliot and John Bell in Edinburgh, who also tried to secure worthy Scottish authors and to copublish their books across the London–Edinburgh axis.

Chapter 6 explores the career of Strahan and Cadell's most important Edinburgh publishing partner, William Creech. Demonized relentlessly by early nineteenth-century Scottish critics, Creech is shown to be a more complex and important figure than has often been thought. The first part of the chapter investigates his publishing career, noting his productive ties with Scottish Enlightenment authors and his close connection to Alexander Kincaid, who brought him into his household as an orphan and eventually made him his partner and successor. Equally important was his relationship with Kincaid's old friend William Strahan, who would become Creech's mentor and (with Thomas Cadell) Creech's chief London collaborator in the publication of Scottish Enlightenment books. The second part of the chapter reviews the charges leveled against Creech by Archibald Constable and his circle of early nineteenth-century critics and argues that they unfairly represent both the nature of Creech's ties with his London associates and the magnitude of his contributions as an Enlightenment publisher, and that in the process they distort the record of Constable himself.

If the London and Edinburgh publishers discussed in chapters 4–6 were responsible for producing most of the important new books of the Scottish Enlightenment, as well as for continuing to publish new editions of the titles that sold well enough to merit reprinting, this was not the whole story. Owing largely to the book trade, the Scottish Enlightenment became an international phenomenon during the second half of the eighteenth century. Part 3 explores this theme with respect to the intellectual culture of the Anglophone Atlantic world and particularly the reprinting of Scottish Enlightenment books in Dublin and Philadelphia. The focus on those cities reflects their status as the leading late eighteenth-century English-language publishing centers outside Great Britain proper. In Dublin, where no copyright laws applied, booksellers reprinted popular new literary and learned works from Britain with great speed and persistence, frequently in smaller formats and almost always at significantly lower prices. As chapter 7 demonstrates, the works of the Scottish Enlightenment were prime fodder for Irish reprinters, who succeeded in coordinating their publishing efforts under the banner of the Dublin Company of Booksellers. Dismissed as piracies by the leaders of the trade in London, Dublin reprints figured prominently in the international dissemination of the Scottish Enlightenment, and they were also significant from the standpoint of domestic Irish print culture.

Moreover, their impact extended to the other side of the Atlantic. Robert Bell, a Scottish émigré in Philadelphia who cut his entrepreneurial teeth as a Dublin reprinter, initiated aggressive reprinting and marketing of the Scottish Enlightenment in colonial America. After an introductory discussion of the American book trade and its foreign relations, chapter 8 treats Bell's exploits and antics in Philadelphia from his arrival in the late 1760s until his death in 1784. More than anyone else, it was Bell who launched the Enlightenment reprinting trade in America, and he did so in large measure with books written by authors from his homeland. Another Scottish bookseller who made his way to Philadelphia in the colonial period, Robert Aitken, joined Bell as an Enlightenment reprinter. But as a devout member of one of the most radical sects of Scottish Presbyterian dissenters, the antiburgher seceders, Aitken had to work hard at reconciling the religious and the secular in his publishing activities.

Chapter 9 examines the publishing contributions of four men who were prominent in the Philadelphia reprint trade during the last fifteen years of the eighteenth century: the Scotsmen Thomas Dobson, William Young, and Robert Campbell and the Irishman Mathew Carey. Along with several other Irish, Scots-Irish, and especially Scottish émigrés, such as Campbell's brother Samuel and Thomas Allen in New York, these men saw to it that their new nation was well supplied with American editions of Scottish Enlightenment books during the late eighteenth century, in addition to British and Irish editions that continued to be imported. Their reprinting activities, like those of Bell and Aitken, are viewed here as acts of cultural appropriation, which transformed foreign texts into native books. The prominence of the Scottish Enlightenment in the intellectual culture of late eighteenth- and early nineteenth-century America may have resulted as much from their efforts as it did from the better-known ties between American and Scottish universities.

American reprinting of Scottish Enlightenment books continued throughout the nineteenth century, underpinning the American heritage of literature and learning. As the conclusion to this volume demonstrates, however, the Scottish sources of that heritage were in a state of decline by the end of the eighteenth century, and changes in publishing conditions are among the factors that must be taken into account in order to explain that occurrence. Although the preeminent publishing house of the age remained strong and prosperous under the leadership of Thomas Cadell and his near contemporary Andrew Strahan, the partnership steadily lost ground after Cadell's retirement in 1793 and death in 1802. Cadell's son Thomas, Jr., and manager, William Davies, trading as Cadell & Davies, continued to publish their firm's star authors and best-selling titles from the heyday of the Scottish Enlightenment, but the strong personal and national bonds that had linked Scottish authors with the leading London publishers and their Edinburgh collaborators grew progressively weaker. Back in Edinburgh, William Creech was abandoned by his former publishing allies in London, and Archibald Constable replaced him as the leading Scottish publisher. The age of Sir Walter Scott and the *Edinburgh Review* had begun, but the Scottish Enlightenment was drawing to a close.

*

Enlightenment book publishing was a complex, multifaceted phenomenon. It cannot be fully understood by limiting the field of study to one species of knowledge or one physical location, or by focusing too closely on a single issue, such as copyright. John Brewer has observed that "the world of eighteenth-century publishing is best understood as an expanding maze or labyrinth."[89] The phrase refers specifically to the perceptions of literary and learned authors—and potential authors—as they attempted to guide their book manuscripts through the "hazards, pitfalls and dead ends" of the publishing process, especially in London. The same metaphor may also be applied more generally, however, to describe all aspects of eighteenth-century literary and learned publishing, including the ways that publishers and authors related to each other, to other members of the book trade, and to the purchasers and readers of their books, not merely in London but throughout Britain, Ireland, Europe, the Americas, and elsewhere. Viewed in this way, the labyrinth of eighteenth-century book culture appears no less intricate, complex, expansive, and intimidating to someone in our time than it did to authors, publishers, and readers in 1750 or 1785. Like them, we must ask ourselves how best to comprehend this maze so that we can navigate our way through it. That is the fundamental question which this book sets out to answer.

89. Brewer, *Pleasures of the Imagination*, 140.

PART I

*

SCOTTISH AUTHORS IN
A WORLD OF BOOKS

[1]

Composing the Scottish Enlightenment

The Author David Hume

"Really it is admirable how many Men of Genius this Country produces at present," wrote David Hume to his countryman Gilbert Elliot in July 1757. "Is it not strange," he continued, "that, at a time when we have lost our Princes, our Parliaments, our independent Government, even the Presence of our chief Nobility, are unhappy in our Accent and Pronunciation, speak a very corrupt Dialect of the Tongue which we make use of; is it not strange, I say, that, in these Circumstances, we shou'd really be the People most distinguish'd for Literature in Europe?" (*LDH*, 1:255). In this well-known passage, Hume articulates the central paradox of the Scottish Enlightenment: how did a poor, tiny country on the geographical fringes of Europe, which was once a sovereign kingdom but had recently lost its monarchy (in the Union of Crowns of 1603), its Parliament (in the Union of 1707 that gave rise to Great Britain), and many of its greater nobility (who now enjoyed the high life in London), and whose men of letters wrote in a language (formal English) that differed from the one most of them spoke (Scots, or more commonly a form of English heavily tinctured with Scots)—how did such a nation that was no longer a nation-state emerge as a leading force in the republic of letters? But Hume's statement is also an exaggeration. Did he really believe that in 1757 Scots were "the People most distinguish'd for Literature in Europe"? In the letter, Hume gives only two examples to support his claim: a recently published epic poem by William Wilkie, *The Epigoniad*, which never attained the Homeric stature that Hume thought it merited, and William Robertson's *History of Scotland*, which would not appear in print for another two years.

Perhaps the boast can help to resolve the paradox. Hume was not merely an observer of the phenomenon he was describing but also one of its prime movers. His words can be read as a wish, indeed as a self-fulfilling prophecy, as well as an explanation of his own behavior and that of many of his fellow men of letters. Faced with a series of national losses and disadvantages, and with the potential for political, social, and cultural union with England, the Scottish literati of Hume's circle were engaged in a self-conscious attempt to bring fame and glory to themselves and the Scottish nation by means of their intellectual accomplishments. If Hume exaggerated, he nevertheless described a process that was well under way by this time, and his boasting stirred aspirations and helped to define a program that would give it focus. Intellectual activity, and above all the production of learned and literary books, was imbued with cultural and national meaning, and Scottish national identity could be redefined in terms of it. In other areas, Hume and his fellow literati would accept their losses, but in this domain they were determined to succeed not merely as Britons but as Scots.

Books were the key to this vision because only they could generate personal and national distinction on a large scale. Such a result was not automatic, however. When published in London in 1739–40, Hume's three-volume *Treatise of Human Nature*, recognized today as a classic of philosophical literature, "fell *dead-born from the* Press," as the author wrote on his deathbed. A similar fate greeted two works that were published in London in 1740 by another Scottish philosopher, George Turnbull (1698–1748): the two-volume *Principles of Moral and Christian Philosophy* and the subscription folio *A Treatise on Ancient Painting*. Precisely because these and every other title by this author enjoyed so little commercial success, Turnbull dropped from sight until James McCosh resurrected him in 1875, noting with some exaggeration that he was probably the first person in a hundred years to read Turnbull's works.[1] Turnbull's powerful intellect may have been influential at Marischal College, Aberdeen, during the 1720s,[2] but the brevity of his Scottish teaching career and the unpopularity of his books ensured that his personal impact would be local and temporary. Unlike Turnbull, Hume learned a valuable lesson from the failure of his first book, and his subsequent publications took the form of shorter philosophical writings and a multivolume history of England that were more accessible to readers than the *Treatise* had been.

1. McCosh, *Scottish Philosophy*, 95.
2. Wood, *Aberdeen Enlightenment*, 40–49.

It is important to understand, however, that Hume's success came not only from the greater readability of his post-*Treatise* writings but also from careful management and cultivation of his career as an author. Hume frequently involved himself in every aspect of the publication process. His surviving correspondence is filled with detailed observations, requests, and demands about the format, timing, paper, quantity, printing, publishing, and marketing, as well as textual content, of his books.

The creation and evolution of Hume's *Essays and Treatises on Several Subjects* illustrates this point.[3] In 1741 Hume began publishing his essays with the Edinburgh bookseller Alexander Kincaid, who was joined in co-publication by the London bookseller Andrew Millar in 1748. Both separately and together, Kincaid and Millar issued different kinds of volumes by Hume, ranging from collections of short, less abstruse pieces on manners, literary and cultural criticism, and political economy, including *Essays, Moral and Political* (1741–42), *Three Essays, Moral and Political* (1748), and *Political Discourses* (1752), to the longer and denser reworkings of his *Treatise* that appeared as *Philosophical Essays* [later *An Enquiry*] *concerning Human Understanding* (1748) and *An Enquiry concerning the Principles of Morals* (1751). It was not immediately clear that these works fit together in a meaningful way. In spring 1753, however, they were jointly reissued by Millar in London, and Kincaid and his junior partner Alexander Donaldson in Edinburgh, in a four-volume set, under the umbrella title *Essays and Treatises on Several Subjects*. Volume 1 contained *Essays, Moral and Political*, volume 2 *Philosophical Essays concerning Human Understanding*, volume 3 *An Enquiry concerning the Principles of Morals*, and volume 4 *Political Discourses*. In effect, Hume and his publishers forged a single, affordable, comprehensive body of works out of existing volumes of his disparate writings on various subjects. They also fashioned a vehicle for propagating Hume's most skeptical philosophical essays, which benefited from being placed between the more accessible essays that framed them in volumes 1 and 4. In the autobiographical sketch that he wrote shortly before his death, "My Own Life," Hume commented that the *Enquiry concerning Human Understanding* "was at first but little more successful than the Treatise of human Nature" and that the *Enquiry concerning the Principles of Morals* "came unnoticed and unobserved into the World" (*LDH*, 1:3–4). These remarks suggest that in his mind something had to be done if these works were to avoid the *Treatise*'s unhappy fate. In fact, Hume seems to have anticipated this development as early as 13 June 1742, when

3. Sher, "Book," 43–47; and Fieser, Introduction.

he told Henry Home (later Lord Kames) that his commercially successful *Essays* "may prove like dung with marl, and bring forward the rest of my Philosophy, which is of a more durable, though of a harder and more stubborn nature" (*LDH*, 1:43).

Unfortunately, none of Hume's letters to his publishers survives from the period when *Essays and Treatises on Several Subjects* came into being. It seems likely that Hume actively participated in the process, but we cannot be sure. The next part of the story is better documented, however, and there can be no doubt of Hume's involvement. The critical passage appears in a letter that Hume sent to Millar on 4 December 1756, while he was preparing for the press another volume of essays that Millar published early in 1757 as *Four Dissertations*. In the letter, Hume recounts a meeting the previous day with Kincaid and Donaldson, in which a scheme had been hatched to publish *Essays and Treatises on Several Subjects* (augmented to include the essays in *Four Dissertations*) in a single quarto volume. Hume declares himself "extremely desirous" to have such a quarto edition. In order to achieve this end, he acts aggressively as intermediary between his Edinburgh and London copublishers, appealing to the former's preference for the smaller, duodecimo edition in order to clear out enough of the latter's stock so that a quarto edition will become economically feasible. Hume puts his scheme into the language of market sales by arguing that the anticipated success of his *History of England*, which Millar was also in the process of publishing, will stimulate sales of *Essays and Treatises* and that "the bringing these scatterd Pieces into one Volume will of itself quicken the Sale; and every new Edition has naturally that Effect" (*LDH*, 1:236).

Hume was doing more than helping his publishers to market his books more effectively. He was also repackaging himself as an author, with a view toward enhancing both his unity and his status in the eyes of readers and critics. If unity came from the process of gathering his "scatterd Pieces" within one title and volume, reordered thematically instead of chronologically, status derived from the quarto format itself. As we shall see later in this chapter, quartos were large books intended for the wealthy and the learned. The *History of England* had initially appeared in quarto; well-to-do consumers would now be able to purchase *Essays and Treatises* in a similar format, which could be bound to match the *History* on their library shelves. Furthermore, to put *Essays and Treatises* into quarto was to confer distinction not only on the author but also on the controversial ideas that the book contained. It was to give Hume's skeptical philosophy an aura of respectability that some would have wished to deny it. When James Boswell and Samuel Johnson visited Pembroke College, Oxford, in March 1776, Boswell recorded in his journal his dismay at finding in William Adams's library a copy of the "quarto edition" of *Essays and Treatises on Several Subjects*, handsomely bound in morocco leather.[4] He disapproved because he believed that an "infidel" writer should not be treated with the same marks of "politeness and respect" owed to an antagonist in a genteel scholarly dispute. Had Adams owned a duodecimo edition of *Essays and Treatises*, plainly bound, it is unlikely that Boswell would have cared so much. It was the quarto format and expensive binding that upset him because of what they signified about the status being accorded to Hume and his philosophy.

Hume, then, had good reasons for being "extremely desirous" to see his *Essays and Treatises* published in a single quarto edition, and his publishers warmly embraced his scheme. It was a substantial book of 547 large pages, closely printed and reasonably priced at fifteen shillings, with a print run of 750 copies (SA 48800, fol. 113; *EEC*, 1 Mar. 1759). Millar provided compensation that Hume deemed "generous," and the printing and correcting were done with such "great Care" by William Strahan that the author declared himself "extremely pleasd" and gave his printer a presentation copy in appreciation (*LDH*, 1:247, 251, 267). Although the printing was completed in October 1757, publication was delayed until spring 1758, presumably to avoid undercutting the sale of existing stock of *Four Dissertations* and *Essays and Treatises* in duodecimo. Clearly, the intention of the publishers was to produce a durable, flexible book and an effective working relationship with the author over the long term. Their strategy was successful. Not only were all the copies of the quarto edition sold within a few years, but for the duration of Hume's life, and for a long time afterward, Hume's essays and shorter philosophical writings continued to be published in varying formats and sizes under the title *Essays and Treatises on Several Subjects*. Editions with the joint imprint of Millar and Kincaid & Donaldson appeared in four duodecimo volumes in 1760 and in two octavo volumes in 1764 and 1767. A splendid two-volume quarto edition appeared early in 1768, larger and less cramped than the 1758 quarto, with a frontispiece portrait of the author (fig. 1.1). This was followed by a four-volume small octavo edition in 1770, two-volume octavo editions in 1772 and 1777, and so on throughout the century. Jerome Christensen

4. Boswell, *Ominous Years*, 278.

DAVID HUME
Esq.

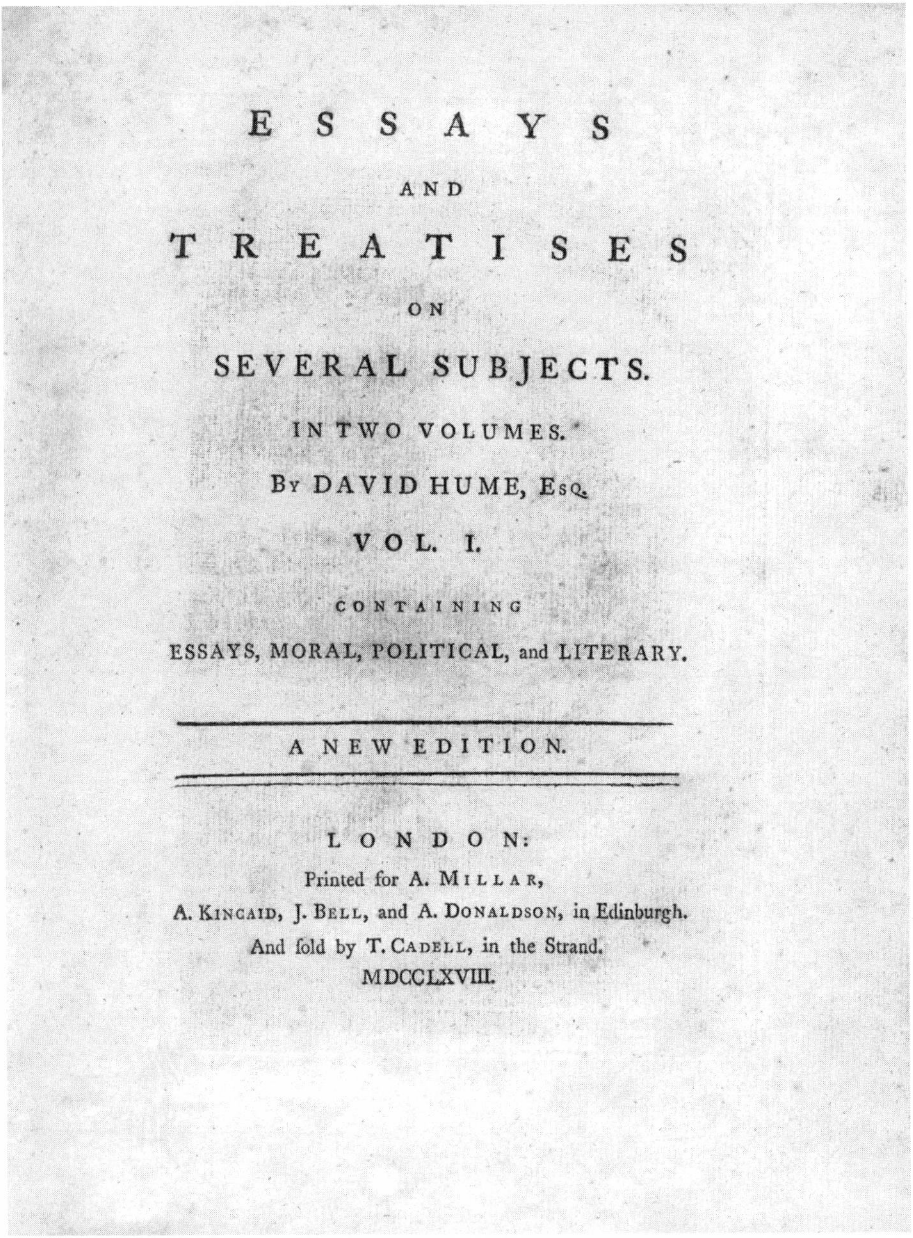

E S S A Y S

AND

T R E A T I S E S

ON

SEVERAL SUBJECTS.

IN TWO VOLUMES.

By DAVID HUME, Esq.

VOL. I.

CONTAINING

ESSAYS, MORAL, POLITICAL, and LITERARY.

A NEW EDITION.

L O N D O N:

Printed for A. MILLAR,

A. KINCAID, J. BELL, and A. DONALDSON, in Edinburgh.

And fold by T. CADELL, in the Strand.

MDCCLXVIII.

Fig. 1.1. With a frontispiece portrait engraved by Simon François Ravenet after a drawing by John Donaldson, the 1768 two-volume quarto edition of David Hume's *Essays and Treatises on Several Subjects* helped to raise Hume's stature as an author. Thomas Fisher Rare Book Library, University of Toronto.

has perceptively characterized the first two editions of *Essays and Trea-tises* as "a progressive movement of condensation,"[5] but the entire body of eighteenth-century editions of this work is more accurately described as a progressive movement of variation.

Some idea of these variations can be gleaned from figure 1.2, which shows the spines of copies of the quarto editions of 1758 and 1768 and of the octavo editions of 1764 and 1770, along with a large royal folio volume by a different author that has been included for purposes of comparison. As the image shows, because the formatting terms "folio," "quarto," "oc-tavo," and "duodecimo" referred, technically, to the number of times each sheet of paper was folded, the size of books printed in each format varied according to the size of the sheets.[6] Thus, the 1758 and 1768 quarto edi-tions of *Essays and Treatises* were not exactly the same height, and neither were the two octavo editions of 1764 and 1770. Occasionally copies of a book from the same edition were sized and priced differently because some were printed on larger paper than the rest.[7] Nevertheless, in com-mon parlance, and when not preceded by words such as "large" or "small," "crown" or "royal," the terms "folio," "quarto," "octavo," and "duodecimo" referred to books of a predictable size and shape.[8] That is why the pub-lishers of the 1764 edition of *Essays and Treatises*, which was technically a small octavo, advertised it as a duodecimo.

While *Essays and Treatises* was appearing in different formats and sizes, Hume continued to make textual revisions until his death in 1776 (the posthumous 1777 octavo contained the last of them). The *History of En-gland*, which he completed in 1761, went through a parallel process of revision and republication in various formats, and on different grades and sizes of paper, as well as a change of title from the original *History of Great Britain*. By frequently revising these two key books, Hume added to the value of the latest editions, which continually superseded all earlier ones. "It is one great advantage that results from the Art of printing, that an Author may correct his works, as long as he lives," Hume told his printer

---

5. Christensen, *Practicing Enlightenment*, 130–31.

6. Gaskell, *New Introduction to Bibliography*, 80–86.

7. For example, some copies of the individual volumes comprising the quarto first edition of Hume's *History of England* were printed on large (royal) paper, and they cost up to 50 percent more than the standard copies that were printed on standard (demy) paper. See Todd, "David Hume," 189–21.

8. The semantic complexities are discussed in Tanselle, "Concept of Format," 67–116.

Fig. 1.2. Hume's *Essays and Treatises on Several Subjects* was published in several for-mats to suit different audiences. *From right to left:* the 1770 four-volume small octavo edition that was sometimes marketed as a duodecimo, the 1764 two-volume octavo edition, the 1768 two-volume quarto edition that contained a frontispiece portrait engraved by Ravenet (fig. 1.1), and the 1758 one-volume quarto edition that first col-lected Hume's shorter pieces in a single book and gave them the respectability of the quarto format. Although quartos normally dwarfed octavos and duodecimos, large folios such as Alexander Monro's *Observations on the Structure and Functions of the Nervous System* (1783; *far left,* in a nineteenth-century binding) were sometimes twice the height of quartos. Thomas Fisher Rare Book Library, University of Toronto.

in July 1771. In another letter he went further, calling this the "Chief Advantage" of printing from the author's point of view (*LDH*, 2:247, 239; cf. 1:38).

The revision process was partly substantive, of course, but it was also rhetorical and stylistic.[9] One particularly troubling aspect of style for Scottish authors concerned idiomatic English. Hume's correspondence is filled with expressions of anxiety on this subject, and in 1752 he published a list of "Scotticisms" as an appendix to the first Edinburgh edition of his *Political Discourses*.[10] The passage in the letter to Gilbert Elliot quoted at the beginning of this chapter articulates Hume's uneasiness about speaking a language that he considered an "unhappy" and "very corrupt" dialect of English. Similarly, the letter to Millar that laid out the plan for the first quarto edition of *Essays and Treatises on Several Subjects* contains a paragraph imploring his publisher "to employ all your Interest" in an effort to secure a list of Scotticisms from David Mallet, who was then correcting the *History of England* for the press. To root out Scotticisms from his prose, Hume (formerly Home) turned to anglicized Scots like Mallet (formerly Malloch) and William Strahan (formerly Strachan; *LDH*, 1:369, 2:247, 250), who like him had changed their names to accommodate English patterns of speech.[11] But their help was not enough. "Though I make no question that your ear is well purged from all native impurities," Hume wrote to the Scotsman John Clephane in 1753, "yet trust not entirely to it, but ask any of your English friends, that frequent good company, and let me know their opinion" (*LDH*, 1:182). His fears were shared by other Scottish authors, who regarded their lack of mastery of idiomatic English as a major obstacle to be overcome before their English-language books could compete successfully in the international marketplace. "The greatest difficulty in acquiring the art of *writing* English" for Scots, wrote James Beattie, who would publish a book titled *Scoticisms* in 1787, "is to give a *vernacular* cast to the English we write. . . . In a word, *we* handle English, as a person who cannot fence handles a sword; continually afraid of hurting ourselves with it, or letting it fall, or making some awkward motion that shall betray our ignorance."[12] Hume did his best to purge Scotticisms from the books of William Robertson, Thomas Reid, and

9. Box, *Suasive Art*.

10. The subject is discussed, and the list reproduced, in Basker, "Scotticisms," 81–95.

11. On Hume's name change, see Christensen, *Practicing Enlightenment*, 57n14.

12. Beattie to Sylvester Douglas, 5 Jan. 1778, in Forbes, *Account*, 2:16–17.

others, but it was above all the attention he lavished on the style of his own works that gave younger Scottish authors the confidence to strive for mastery of English as a language of publication.

Hume capped his efforts at authorial self-construction by leaving behind two autobiographical pieces, with specific instructions for publication. The first was a "short Advertisement" that he sent to Strahan on 26 October 1775, to be prefixed to the second volume of *Essays and Treatises* as soon as possible (*LDH*, 2:301). In this advertisement, which first appeared between the title page and the table of contents in the second volume of the posthumous 1777 edition, Hume disowns his *Treatise of Human Nature* and castigates unnamed critics (identified in the letter to Strahan as Thomas Reid and "that bigoted silly Fellow, Beattie") for directing "all their batteries against that juvenile work, which the Author never acknowledged," in a manner "very contrary to all rules of candour and fairdealing." Significantly, the advertisement does not deny that Hume wrote the *Treatise*, and it does not reject its substance; it merely identifies it as a "juvenile" performance, "which the Author had projected before he left College, and which he wrote and published not long after." "The error of going to the press too early" is the only mistake that Hume admits. These, however, were autobiographical rationalizations, not philosophical arguments. The real purpose of the advertisement was to fix the boundaries of the author David Hume, not according to what he had actually written or published but according to what he himself had come to regard as the true or legitimate body of work characterizing his authorial essence.[13] The advertisement, in short, was an exercise in retrospective self-construction.

The second autobiographical work that Hume offered to the public during his final year, "My Own Life," was another attempt to shape his persona as an author for posterity. It is the story of a man with "an insurmountable Aversion to every thing but the pursuits of Philosophy and general Learning" (*LDH*, 1:1), who writes books, experiences with stoic detachment both triumphs and, more commonly, setbacks as those books are published, and concludes his life in a state of tranquility, wealth, and contentment. "My Own Life" contains little about the intellectual content of Hume's works but carefully documents each book's reception. In so doing, it draws attention to book publication as an ego event in which "the

---

13. In 1778 Hume's adversary James Beattie attempted to fix his poetic canon in precisely the same way when he made plans to issue "in one volume all the poems whereof I am willing to be considered as the author . . . renouncing all my other poems as juvenile and incorrect." Beattie, *Day-Book*, 212.

author's life . . . assumes a value larger than that of what has been written."[14] The receptions accorded to his books, and his handling of them, are portrayed as the focal point of Hume's life. The thesis of the autobiography is stated in this sentence: "Even my Love of literary Fame, my ruling Passion, never soured my humour, notwithstanding my frequent Disappointments" (*LDH*, 1:7). As one critic has observed, "a recurrent motif of disappointment," set against the backdrop of Hume's passion for literature and cheerful temperament, gives the autobiography a narrative structure as it provides Hume's life with a sense of personal identity.[15]

Nowhere is this point more evident than in Hume's treatment of the *History of England*. As usual, "My Own Life" emphasizes how poorly the different parts of this work were received by the public. The first volume, on the early Stuarts, "seemed to sink into Oblivion" when it was first published in 1754. The second volume, on the later Stuarts, had a somewhat better reception when it appeared in 1757, but two years later the third and fourth volumes, on the Tudors, set off a "Clamour . . . almost equal to that against the History of the two first Stuarts." The last two volumes, on ancient and medieval England, met with "tolerable, and but tolerable Success" when published later in 1761 (with a 1762 imprint). Yet Hume presents himself as being unfazed by these events. "My Own Life" creates the impression of an author standing above "the Misrepresentations of Faction" and "callous against the Impressions of public Folly" (*LDH*, 1:4–5). Hume portrays himself as an honest man and an impartial seeker after truth in a world permeated by partisan sentiment.

From start to finish, "My Own Life" rings half true.[16] The one major publication it never mentions, *Essays and Treatises on Several Subjects*, is the one that, along with the *History of England*, did more than any other to define Hume's authorial persona and create the circumstances that enabled him to choreograph his death as a rich, famous, contented author. For Hume to have mentioned that book would have entailed bringing into his autobiography precisely the part of himself that his sketch was meant to suppress or at least minimize to the greatest possible extent: the calculating, anxious, aggressive author, full of schemes to realize his avowed "ruling Passion," the "Love of literary Fame." It would therefore have required Hume to qualify the image of the jolly bon vivant that he often showed to his friends and of the calm, contented philosopher that he presented to

---

14. Carnochan, "Trade of Authorship," 138.

15. Sturrock, *Language of Autobiography*, 119–20.

16. Cf. Stewart, "Hume's Intellectual Development," 53–55.

the world. No one who has perused Hume's demanding, anxiety-ridden, and sometimes accusatory correspondence with his publishers is likely to accept either of those characterizations as entirely accurate.

Like the writer of "My Own Life" himself, most intellectual historians and philosophers who study Hume regard *Essays and Treatises on Several Subjects* as a bibliographical inconvenience, to be quickly dispensed with in footnotes if not entirely ignored. With one important exception,[17] *Essays and Treatises* remains practically invisible because the scholars who study Hume are focused on texts and their intellectual content, not on books and their cultural meaning. Yet without an understanding of the ways in which authors such as Hume, along with their publishers, made their books, and were in turn made by them, how well can we know Hume the man or Hume the writer?

Hume wrote "My Own Life" while his health was declining in April 1776. On 8 June he told William Strahan about it and stated his desire that "it may be prefixed to this Edition" (*LDH*, 2:322–23), meaning, apparently, the matching octavo editions of the *History of England* and *Essays and Treatises on Several Subjects* that Strahan was then preparing for the press with Hume's last revisions. Two months later Hume dictated a new codicil to his will that left "My Account of my own Life" to Strahan, with specific instructions to prefix it to the first posthumous edition of his "Works, which will probably be the one at present in the Press" (*LDH*, 2:453). He also arranged for his friend Adam Smith to write a "small addition" that would be published with it,[18] knowing full well that Smith's account would do credit to his reputation.

Strahan, however, had his own ideas about how Hume's authorial image should be managed. To the dismay of Hume's brother, John Home, who accused him of violating the express terms of Hume's will,[19] Strahan published "My Own Life" in the January 1777 issue of the *Scots Magazine* and again in March as a separate pamphlet, *The Life of David Hume, Esq. Written by Himself.* Anticipating considerable public interest, he printed 2,000 copies of the pamphlet, and another edition of 1,000 copies was

---

17. See Tom L. Beauchamp's introductions to Hume, *Enquiry concerning Human Understanding* and *Enquiry concerning the Principles of Morals*, in the Clarendon critical edition of Hume's works, in progress under the joint editorship of Tom L. Beauchamp, David Fate Norton, and M. A. Stewart.

18. John Home (Hume's brother) to Strahan, 2 Sept. 1776, in Hume, *Letters of Hume to Strahan*, 346.

19. John Home to Strahan, 25 Feb. and 13 Mar. 1777, ibid., 361–63.

soon required (SA 48815, fol. 21). Hume's autobiographical sketch was introduced with a brief preface and then the piece by Adam Smith that Hume had essentially commissioned, which took the form of a long letter addressed to Strahan. Smith's laudatory letter—which notoriously concluded with the observation that his friend approached "as nearly to the idea of a perfectly wise and virtuous man, as perhaps the nature of human frailty will permit"[20]—had the effect of confirming and objectifying Hume's reflections on his life and asserting his eminence as a man. Together, "My Own Life" and Smith's letter showed off the camaraderie that prevailed among the Scottish literati of Hume's day at the same time that they humanized and glorified an author whose writings were frequently viewed as harmful to morality and society. Two other additions to the pamphlet version further enhanced the effect: a list of available editions of Hume's two major publications and a "pretty Engraving of his Head."[21] By tampering with the codicil in these ways, Strahan deliberately modified the authorial image that Hume himself had tried to present to the world after his death.[22] Left to his own devices, the publisher would also have added a number of Hume's personal letters in order to expand the pamphlet into "a little Volume," but Smith convinced him that it would be "highly improper" for him to do so.[23] Moreover, Strahan determined, apparently contrary to Hume's codicil, to print "My Own Life" (along with Smith's letter) in the 1778 edition of the *History of England* rather than in the 1777 edition of the *Essays and Treatises*. In that form it long remained a fixture in Strahan and Cadell's editions of the *History of England*, augmented from 1782 with a frontispiece portrait of the author.

The outcome of all these developments was the author David Hume as he was known to readers during the second half of the eighteenth century and beyond. By looking at one of the catalogues issued by Hume's publishers, we can gain a sense of what this author's publications looked like to the book-buying public at a particular moment in time. A 1781 version of

20. Smith to Strahan, 9 Nov. 1776, in Smith, *Correspondence*, 217–21.

21. Strahan to John Home, 3 Mar. 1777, NLS, MS 23158, no. 44.

22. Strahan also failed to honor the codicil's instructions to publish the manuscript of Hume's controversial "Dialogues concerning Natural Religion." Hume, however, had anticipated this reaction, for the codicil stipulated that if the work "be not published within two Years and a half of my death" (*LDH*, 2:453), the manuscript would revert to Hume's nephew, who was apparently responsible for having it printed in Edinburgh in 1779.

23. Strahan to John Home, 3 Mar. 1777, NLS, MS 23158, no. 44; Strahan to Smith, 26 Nov. 1776, and Smith to Strahan, 2 Dec. 1776, in Smith, *Correspondence*, 222–24.

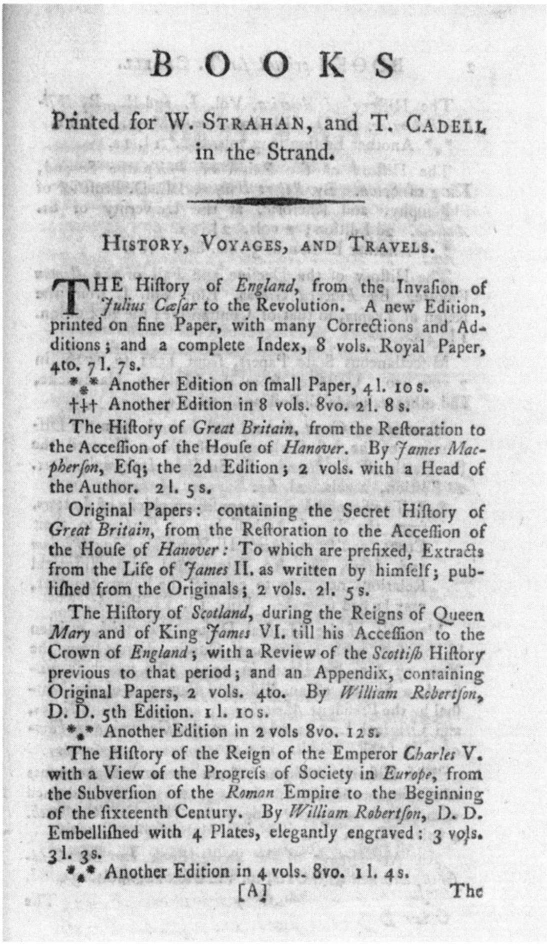

BOOKS

Printed for W. STRAHAN, and T. CADELL in the Strand.

———————

HISTORY, VOYAGES, AND TRAVELS.

THE History of *England*, from the Invasion of *Julius Cæsar* to the Revolution. A new Edition, printed on fine Paper, with many Corrections and Additions; and a complete Index, 8 vols. Royal Paper, 4to. 7 l. 7 s.

*** Another Edition on small Paper, 4 l. 10 s.
†+† Another Edition in 8 vols. 8vo. 2 l. 8 s.

The History of *Great Britain*, from the Restoration to the Accession of the House of *Hanover*. By *James Macpherson*, Esq; the 2d Edition; 2 vols. with a Head of the Author. 2 l. 5 s.

Original Papers: containing the Secret History of *Great Britain*, from the Restoration to the Accession of the House of *Hanover*: To which are prefixed, Extracts from the Life of *James* II. as written by himself; published from the Originals; 2 vols. 2l. 5 s.

The History of *Scotland*, during the Reigns of Queen *Mary* and of King *James* VI. till his Accession to the Crown of *England*; with a Review of the *Scottish* History previous to that period; and an Appendix, containing Original Papers, 2 vols. 4to. By *William Robertson*, D. D. 5th Edition. 1 l. 10 s.

*** Another Edition in 2 vols 8vo. 12 s.

The History of the Reign of the Emperor *Charles* V. with a View of the Progress of Society in *Europe*, from the Subversion of the *Roman* Empire to the Beginning of the sixteenth Century. By *William Robertson*, D. D. Embellished with 4 Plates, elegantly engraved: 3 vols. 3 l. 3 s.

*** Another Edition in 4 vols. 8vo. 1 l. 4 s.

[A] The

Fig. 1.3. From the early 1780s Strahan and Cadell advertised their publications in sixteen-page octavo catalogues like the one shown here, organized by subject category rather than by authors' names. Thomas Fisher Rare Book Library, University of Toronto.

Books Printed for W. Strahan, and T. Cadell in the Strand reveals that *Essays and Treatises on Several Subjects* was then available in three different formats: a two-volume quarto that we know to be the 1768 edition pictured in figures 1.1 and 1.2, priced at £1.16s.; a two-volume octavo, undoubtedly the 1777 edition, which cost 12s.—exactly one-third the price of the quarto; and finally, for 14s., a four-volume duodecimo "on a fine Writing Paper," which was actually the 1770 small octavo edition that is pictured in figure 1.2.[24] The *History of England*, similarly, could be purchased in an eight-volume quarto edition on large royal paper for £7.7s., or on "small Paper" for £4.10s., or in an eight-volume octavo edition for £2.8s. or six shillings per volume (fig. 1.3). Thus, in the early 1780s a "gentleman"

24. [Strahan and Cadell], *Books Printed for W. Strahan, and T. Cadell in the Strand*, 8.

could purchase Hume's philosophical and historical works in ten quarto volumes for as much as £9.3s., while those of more modest means could own the same texts in ten octavo volumes for as little as £3.2s., without recourse to pirated or used editions.

In this way, Hume's authorial persona was self-consciously constructed during the eighteenth century, in a manner that bears witness to the model that Michel Foucault defines in his seminal essay "What Is an Author?" In presenting his notion of the "author function," Foucault contends that the process of delineating authors and their works comprises a "classificatory function" in which "the author's name manifests the appearance of a certain discursive set and indicates the status of this discourse within a society and a culture." The "author" in this sense is the creation of critics and readers engaged in "author construction"; "the author is an ideological product," or "the principle of thrift in the proliferation of meaning," because the very concept structures and limits our thoughts about the nature of literary production.[25] By providing an organizing principle based on the notion of an author's authentic "works," the author function enables us to make sense of the great mass of published writing that would otherwise overwhelm us. It is therefore the key to the organization of modern Western print culture.

Useful as it is, Foucault's interpretation requires qualification in at least two respects. Whereas Foucault sees "author construction" as an activity carried out chiefly by critics and readers, most of the constructing in Hume's case was done by the author and his publishers. And whereas Foucault's notion of author construction hinges on the classification of *texts*, we have seen that in Hume's case the reconfiguring of texts *as books* was equally important. By fashioning and refashioning *Essays and Treatises on Several Subjects* and the *History of England*, and by making them available in a variety of formats and variations, priced to fit different budgets, Hume and his publishers not only stimulated sales but broadly defined Hume the author as a complex and integrated entity, with widespread accessibility and appeal. Hume's success as an author rested very largely on his skill, and that of his publishers, at self-classification and repackaging, at promoting the identification of the name "David Hume" not only with an orderly, recognizable body of discourse but also with the physical artifacts in which that body of discourse was housed.

It is therefore useful to supplement Foucault's notion of author construction with Gérard Genette's concept of "paratexts," defined as "those

25. Foucault, "What Is an Author?" quoting 107, 118–19.

liminal devices and conventions, both within the book (*peritext*) and outside it (*epitext*), that mediate the book to the reader."[26] They include the "titles and subtitles, pseudonyms, forewords, dedications, epigraphs, prefaces, intertitles, notes, epilogues, and afterwords" that constitute the "framing elements" of a work. Very often these paratextual components are formulated by authors, but they may also be devised by publishers, or authors and publishers working together, or even designated third parties (8–9). They usually take a form that is "*textual*, or at least verbal" (e.g., prefaces and afterwords among peritexts, catalogue listings and book reviews among epitexts), but they may also be "iconic" (e.g., illustrations), "material" (e.g., cover, typography, format, and other features that constitute "the publisher's peritext" proper), or "factual" (e.g., information about the life of the author) (7, 16). It is, of course, difficult to know exactly what effect paratexts may have on the public reception of authors and books, or on the public perception of authors. The example of the author David Hume, however, suggests that they were crucially important and that publishers like Strahan played a large role in shaping Hume's image through the manipulation of paratextual material, especially after Hume's death.

James Boswell was one reader who reacted strongly to the paratextual shaping of Hume's authorial persona. In the course of a critique of Hume in his *Journal of a Tour to the Hebrides with Samuel Johnson* (1785), Boswell says nothing about "My Own Life" itself but rants against Adam Smith's claim that Hume approached perfection in wisdom and virtue. He was particularly upset that the text housing Smith's sentiments was "not a confidential letter to his friend, but a letter which is published with all formality" (*BLJ*, 5:30–31). As Boswell fully understood, Smith's published letter mediated Hume's autobiography to the reader, just as the autobiography itself mediated Hume's philosophical and historical works. Layers of published paratext molded the image of the author.

Hume was not the first eighteenth-century British author to try to shape his destiny in print. Similar activities were carried out by others, most notably Alexander Pope. Early in his career, working closely with the London bookseller Bernard Lintot, Pope published translations of the *Iliad* (1715–20) and the *Odyssey* (1725–26) as well as an edition of his own *Works* (1717). All were available in a variety of formats that sold for widely different prices, and the *Works* contained a personal preface and an oversized frontispiece portrait engraved by George Vertue after a painting by

26. Genette, *Paratexts*, xviii.

Pope's friend Charles Jervas, which conveyed a carefully cultivated mixture of intelligence and sophistication, bordering on haughtiness (NPG D14071). As James McLaverty has written of the *Works:* "In this one volume Pope was able to define a canon, publish an image of himself as a man and writer, shape his relations with his reader, and guide the interpretation of individual poems through illustration and annotation."[27] Whether the prime mover behind the *Works* was Pope himself, as McLaverty believes, or Lintot, as Maynard Mack contends,[28] the effect was the same. Mack calls it "a monument to vanity," while McLaverty goes so far as to designate it as "a turning point in the history of authorship: a point at which the author's person, personality, and responsibility were becoming matters of public interest as never before."[29] The many thousands of pounds that Pope received from his translations of Homer enabled him to maintain even tighter controls over his publications and his public image, which he never stopped trying to dictate to posterity.[30]

Hume was well aware of Pope's achievement as an author. He sent the poet a presentation copy of his first major work, the *Treatise of Human Nature*, and he borrowed from him the colorful phrase "dead-born from the press" to describe its fate.[31] Perhaps after the failure of the *Treatise* he even modeled aspects of his subsequent publishing career on Pope's innovations. Nevertheless, there are significant differences between Hume and Pope as authors, and they are indicative of changing patterns in author–publisher relations between Augustan England and the era of the mature Scottish Enlightenment. The Augustan literary world was narrowly focused on London and imaginative literature, with poetry enjoying pride of place. Pope made his fortune not from his own writing but from his Homeric translations, and the subscribers to those works constituted a wealthy elite whose members functioned much like traditional patrons.[32] Although he patronized other authors, Pope had only fleeting loyalty to the booksellers who published his work; even Lintot did not escape his wrath for long. By contrast, the world of Hume and the mature Scottish Enlightenment was geographically broader and more interac-

---

27. McLaverty, *Pope, Print and Meaning*, 56; Foxon, *Pope.*

28. McLaverty, *Pope, Print and Meaning*, 48; Mack, *Alexander Pope*, 333–34.

29. Mack, *Alexander Pope*, 333; McLaverty, *Pope, Print and Meaning*, 50.

30. Nichol, *Pope's Literary Legacy*; Piper, *Image of the Poet*, chap. 2.

31. Mossner, *Life of David Hume*, 116.

32. McLaverty, "Contract," 206–25; Foxon, *Pope*, 100–101.

tive, especially between London and Edinburgh. It encompassed a much wider range of scholarly and literary fields in which authors could earn fame and wealth from their own writings. It existed within a more modern, commercial system of publishing, with less emphasis on traditional patronage and aristocratic subscription publishing and, generally speaking, more stable and supportive relations between authors and publishers. It relied on a sizable reading and purchasing public to sustain literature and make determinations about it. But it was also a good deal more national in that many of its authors, and publishers too, were acutely aware of their Scottishness and of their opportunity—even responsibility—to transform Scottish national identity through print.

What has been said of Hume and his publications also applies to many other eighteenth-century authors and their books, and to the Scottish Enlightenment as a whole. Hume and his fellow Scottish authors sought international distinction through the power of the book, both individually and collectively, and they were assisted in this effort by publishers who shared their outlook. As a number of recent studies have emphasized, early modern Scotland was not an intellectual wasteland, and the Scottish Enlightenment, like other historical phenomena, did not spring out of thin air in the middle of the eighteenth century. Nevertheless, around that time something unprecedented began to happen in Scottish intellectual life. It was characterized by a new attitude of literary and scientific cooperation and self-assertiveness among Scottish scholars and literary men, of self-consciousness about the past, present, and future place of Scotland in the republic of letters, of confidence in the nation's rising glory as a leading center of learning. It was the moment when the Scottish Enlightenment entered its mature or high phase as an intellectual movement because it was the moment when its practitioners began to think of themselves as a unified body of intellectuals, engaged in a national mission.

The Literati and the Scottish Literary Nation

The month before Hume wrote the letter quoted at the beginning of this chapter, his friend John Home, the Scottish clergyman turned playwright, also wrote a letter to Sir Gilbert Elliot, in which he alluded to "the literati who make a sort of body in this province."[33] This is the first instance known to me of Scottish men of letters referring to themselves as "the

33. Home to Elliot, 1 June [1757], NLS, MS 11009, fols. 141–42.

literati," and doing so in an almost corporate sense, much the way the term "philosophes" was sometimes used to describe their counterparts in France. The enthusiasm with which Hume and other Scottish men of letters had recently rallied to support Home during the controversy provoked by the latter's tragedy *Douglas* constitutes one example of this attitude.[34] Another is the Select Society (1754–64), an Edinburgh debating club that symbolized the self-conscious identification of the literati as an exclusive body, committed to improvement and intimately linked with the nation's social elite.[35] It spawned two other Edinburgh clubs that had broader memberships and were dedicated to technological and economic improvement on the one hand (the Edinburgh Society for the Encouragement of Arts, Sciences, Manufactures, and Agriculture in Scotland) and linguistic improvement on the other (the Society for Promoting the Reading and Speaking of the English Language in Scotland).[36] Two other examples are more relevant to the argument being made here because they appeared as printed works: Francis Hutcheson's *System of Moral Philosophy* in 1755 and the short-lived *Edinburgh Review* of 1755–56.

It is sometimes said that the Ulsterman Francis Hutcheson (1694–1746) was the "father" of the Scottish Enlightenment because he was the most important force in the development of Scottish intellectual life during the formative second quarter of the eighteenth century. Hutcheson established an international reputation with two treatises on the "moral sense" and other philosophical works that were published during the 1720s, while he was teaching in a Dublin academy.[37] After assuming the professorship of moral philosophy at Glasgow University in 1730, he concentrated on pedagogical activities, including the composition of cheap student compendia in Latin and English.[38] The Dublin treatises and the Glasgow compendia, coupled with a charismatic classroom style, secured Hutcheson's reputation within Scotland as an influential, if highly eclectic, Whig-Presbyterian moralist. But Hutcheson was never able to develop his moral philosophy lectures into the great book that he evidently wished to write. In 1741 he told a friend in Belfast that he was "adding confusedly to a confused Book all valuable Remarks in a Farrago, to refresh my Memory

34. Sher, *Church and University*, 74–92.

35. Emerson, "Social Composition," 291–329; "Select Society" in *ODNB*; Phillipson, "Culture and Society," 407–48.

36. McElroy, *Scotland's Age of Improvement*, 48–64.

37. Brown, *Francis Hutcheson in Dublin*.

38. Moore, "Two Systems," 37–59, and *ODNB*.

in my class Lectures on the several Subjects."[39] When he died in August 1746, the manuscript of that "Farrago" was still on his desk.

In 1755 Hutcheson's manuscript was published posthumously by the author's son Francis, under the title *A System of Moral Philosophy*. It was a two-volume quarto priced at one guinea, well calculated to make a statement about Hutcheson and the Scottish academic philosophy he had done so much to propagate. Inside was an impressive list of more than four hundred subscribers who had signed on to the cause, including Adam Smith, Lord Kames, William Cullen, Adam Ferguson, and many other established and emerging Scottish scholars. The book was printed at Glasgow by Hutcheson's protégés, Robert and Andrew Foulis, although the publishers appear to have been the London booksellers Andrew Millar and Thomas Longman, in whose names the copyright was registered at Stationers' Hall. Prefixed to the first volume was a copious essay on Hutcheson's life and work by the author's chief disciple, William Leechman, who was then professor of divinity at Glasgow University and soon afterward its principal. Leechman stressed Hutcheson's inspirational role as a moral teacher and preacher who labored above all to "excite a relish for virtue" (xxxi–xxxiii); to teach his students "in the warmest manner" "to rejoice above all things in the firm persuasion of the universal Providence of a Being infinitely wise and good, who loves all his works, and cannot be conceived as hating any thing he hath made" (xxxiv); "to inculcate the importance of civil and religious liberty to the happiness of mankind" (xxxv); and to base the study of mankind on an empirical method rooted in "observation and experience" (xiii). Leechman's essay was so deeply steeped in a teleological vision of its subject that it attributed Hutcheson's settlement as professor of moral philosophy at Glasgow University to "the silent and unseen hand of an all-wise Providence" (xii).[40]

Hutcheson's *System of Moral Philosophy* is a monument in print. The associations with Hutcheson's family, with the Foulis brothers, with the Scottish universities, with hundreds of eminent subscribers, with Leechman, and with the principles of Whig-Presbyterian moralizing and Newtonian science that Leechman stressed in his panegyrical preface—all packaged in two handsome quarto volumes—sent a powerful ideological message.[41] Perhaps the only thing unremarkable about these volumes is

39. Hutcheson to Thomas Drennan, 15 June 1741, Glasgow University Library, MS Gen. 1018.

40. Leechman, "Preface."

41. Sher, "Professors of Virtue," 94–99.

Hutcheson's text, which is very much the "Farrago" that the author himself had once declared it to be. There are lively and engaging passages on the various topics covered in Hutcheson's moral philosophy course, but there are also glaring inconsistencies of argument and perspective, and the style appears unpolished by the standards of elegant prose that were becoming prevalent in mid-eighteenth-century Scotland. When Dugald Stewart, who was born two years before the publication of *A System of Moral Philosophy*, wrote a biography of Hutcheson's pupil Adam Smith during the last decade of the century, he commented in the body of the work on Smith's favorable opinion of Hutcheson's "profound and eloquent" lectures but added a note revealing his own perplexity. Reading the *System* as a philosophy text, Stewart could not understand what all the fuss was about, though he correctly intimated that the real point of the *System* lay elsewhere: in the tribute it paid to the man whose moral philosophy teaching had helped to inspire "some of the most valuable productions of the eighteenth century."[42] By the word "productions," of course, Stewart meant books.

In the autumn of 1755 Hutcheson's *System* received a favorable review (despite criticism of its "careless and neglected" style) in the first number of a new periodical publication, the *Edinburgh Review*. The work of a younger generation of Edinburgh clergymen, lawyers, and others who looked on Hutcheson as a kind of mentor to the present age—including Hugh Blair (author of the review of the *System*), William Robertson, Adam Smith, and Alexander Wedderburn—the *Edinburgh Review* sets out an avowedly patriotic goal in the opening sentence of the preface: "to lay before the Public, from time to time, a view of the progressive state of learning in this country."[43] The "progress" of Scottish letters had been "very rapid and very remarkable" during the age of George Buchanan in the sixteenth century, the preface states, but during the seventeenth century a decline in public spirit, growing indifference to the state of Scottish improvement among the English, and a rise in "violence and civil dissen-

42. Stewart, "Account," 271, 333–34.

43. Preface to the *Edinburgh Review*, no. 1, i–iv, in Mizuta, *Edinburgh Reviews*. The preface is sometimes attributed to Alexander Wedderburn, a young Edinburgh lawyer who would later pursue a successful career in government, becoming lord chancellor and earning a peerage as Lord Loughborough and Earl of Rosslyn. Regardless of who penned it, however, the preface can be assumed to have reflected the collective views of all the collaborators behind the periodical.

tions" had put a halt to the nation's "hopes of attaining a distinguished rank in the literary world." "Amidst all the gloom of these times," a few individuals had "kept alive the remains of science, and preserved the flame of genius from being altogether extinguished," but only after the Revolution of 1688 and the Union of 1707 had liberty, commerce, trade, industry, the equitable administration of laws, good manners, good government, public spirit, and "a disposition to every species of improvement" been awakened to a large degree. According to this view, union with England was not in itself the critical development but rather part of a continuous process of political, economic, religious, and cultural modernization: "What the Revolution had begun, the Union rendered more compleat."

The "species of improvement" that particularly concerns the author or authors of the preface to the *Edinburgh Review* lies in the realm of intellect. As their treatment of that topic with respect to the Scottish past makes clear, their aim was not to claim that "the memory of our ancient state" should be "obliterated," as the preface puts it, but rather to demonstrate that Scotland could compete with other nations in literature and science if it was not prevented from doing so. The contrast was not only between the dismal seventeenth century and the hopeful eighteenth century but also between the dismal seventeenth century and the promising era that preceded it. The preface was based on a theory of the harmful effects of pernicious circumstances on literature and learning: "The progress of knowledge depending more upon genius and application, than upon any external circumstance; where-ever these are not repressed, they will exert themselves." Therefore, the excellent educational system "and the ready means of acquiring knowledge in this country" should make Scotland "distinguished for letters."

Why, then, had Scotland not achieved international distinction in the republic of letters after the Revolution of 1688 and the Union of 1707 had alleviated the most repressive circumstances of the seventeenth century? The preface traced the cause to "two considerable obstacles": first, "the difficulty of a proper expression in a country where there is either no standard of language, or at least one very remote," and second, the slow development of printing, because "no literary improvements can be carried far, where the means of communication are defective." But these obstacles were finally beginning to lose their force. In the first instance, Scottish writers (no doubt Hume was among those in mind) were demonstrating that with a bit of effort, "one born on the north side of the Tweed" could acquire "a correct even an elegant stile" in written English. Similarly, the preface observed—undoubtedly referring to the Foulis brothers above all—that the obstacle caused by deficient printing "has, of late, been entirely removed; and the reputation of the Scotch press is not confined to this country alone."

With the acquisition of elegant English and the development of printing, Scotland stood ready to resume the ascent to national distinction in letters that had started with Buchanan but had subsequently gone off course. At this point the preface delivers its coup de grâce: "It occurred to some Gentlemen, that, at this period, when no very material difficulties remain to be conquered; the shewing men the gradual advances of science, would be a means of inciting them to a more eager pursuit of learning, to distinguish themselves, and to do honour to their country: With this view, the present work was undertaken." This statement of intent adds a new dimension to the one articulated in the preface's opening sentence. The aim was not merely to show off "the progressive state of learning in this country" but also to stimulate intellectual activity among the inhabitants of Scotland. It was hoped that demonstration would lead to emulation, and then to national glory in the realm of literature and learning.

Thus, the purpose of the *Edinburgh Review* was nothing less than to incite a national Enlightenment. Having few significant Scottish books to review in the mid-1750s besides Hutcheson's *System*, and faced with opposition from pious Calvinists and others who had received rough treatment, the periodical realized only two numbers (published on 25 Aug. 1755 and 30 Mar. 1756) and therefore appears in retrospect to be an ill-fated venture. As a public declaration by a group of young intellectuals in mid-eighteenth-century Edinburgh, however, it may be said to embody the same spirit of Scottish national self-consciousness and to serve the same self-fulfilling prophetic function in regard to the place of Scotland in the republic of letters that one finds in Hume's boastful letter to Sir Gilbert Elliot of July 1757, as well as in inflated contemporary claims about the genius of Home's *Douglas* as national tragedy and of Wilkie's *Epigoniad* (and early in the next decade James Macpherson's *Fingal* and *Temora*) as national epic. Like Hutcheson's posthumous *System of Moral Philosophy*, the original *Edinburgh Review* represents an exercise in the construction of Scottish authorship that goes far beyond individual Scottish authors in its significance. It constitutes an attempt to fashion the collective identity of Scotland by simultaneously claiming and stimulating the production of outstanding works of literature and learning. In its narrower role as a literary journal, the *Edinburgh Review* may not have done all that much to accomplish this goal, but as a self-conscious, public statement of general

principle it defined the national aspirations of the larger intellectual enterprise that we now associate with the Scottish Enlightenment.

The attitude articulated by the Scottish literati of the mid- and late
eighteenth century has been characterized by one disparaging commentator as "smothering triumphalism."[44] It is not difficult to see why their
national pride might give rise to such a reaction, but we should be clear
about just what the literati believed that their triumph entailed. It was
not simply an expression of victory over the barbaric Scottish past in the
name of a modernizing Scottish future. One part of the Scottish past, the
age of George Buchanan, was if anything viewed as a model for emulation.
Rather, the triumph being claimed was over the repressive conditions and
"obstacles" from times past that had prevented Scotland from realizing
its full literary and scientific potential. The vision consisted not so much
in a denial of past instances of Scottish intellectual achievement as in an
assertion of what the Scottish nation could and would achieve if it were
liberated from the disadvantageous circumstances under which its men of
letters had too often labored. It entailed a realization that political, economic, cultural, linguistic, and technological conditions were finally ripe
for the appropriation of polite print culture by the literati of Scotland.

The most impressive part of the story is that Hume and the writers of
the *Edinburgh Review* accomplished exactly what they set out to do. Driven
largely by their need to overcome fears and self-doubts about their own
national identity, they led their nation to a position as an international
center of authorship and learning during the second half of the eighteenth
century. No single book or author was responsible for this phenomenon,
but by the early 1760s the general pattern was becoming apparent to English and European observers. In September 1761 a London newspaper,
the *St. James's Chronicle*, published a letter of 31 August that purported
to be from Edinburgh, reporting on the "very extraordinary" success of
public lectures given there by the Irish elocutionist Thomas Sheridan and
concluding with this sentence: "You may soon therefore expect to find
Scotland the standard of elocution and of the English tongue: And while
Britain is to be the Greece of Europe, *Scotland* is to be the Athens of Britain." The *Edinburgh Evening Courant* reprinted this item on 23 September,
acknowledging it as an extract from the *St. James's Chronicle*. The Scottish
press also printed a translation of Voltaire's review of Lord Kames's 1762
work, *Elements of Criticism*, which had dared to criticize one of Voltaire's
works under an Edinburgh imprint. "It is an admirable effect of the prog-

44. Allan, *Virtue*, 159.

ress of the human mind, that at this day we receive from Scotland rules of taste in all the arts from Epic poetry to gardening," Voltaire quipped.[45] Despite their ironic or condescending tone, such pronouncements are testimony to the growing awareness among foreigners that Scottish authors were assuming leading roles in literature and learning.

There was no hint of irony or condescension in another publication of 1762, in which the Englishman William Rider, thinking above all of David Hume, wrote: "It must be acknowledged, for the Honour of *Scotland*, that it has in the present Age produced more Men eminent for having cultivated Literature with Success, than either *Great-Britain* or *Ireland*."[46] The same point was made more forcefully the following year in a book by Professor Carlo Denina of the University of Turin on notable shifts in the republic letters, *Discorso sopra le vicende della letteratura*. "It is now an incontestable fact," Denina wrote, "that the principal authors who have adorned the British literature in these latter times, or do honour to it in the present days, have received their birth and education in Scotland."[47] To illustrate his point, Denina named Francis Hutcheson, James Thomson, David Mallet, John Home, William Wilkie, David Hume, Tobias Smollett, William Robertson, Robert Simson, Colin Maclaurin, James Ferguson, William Cullen, "etc.," making it clear that these men were representative of a larger movement of authors who might also have been cited. Hutcheson in particular was singled out for having "diffused through the whole country a happy taste for philosophical and literary researches, and planted those fertile seeds from whence so noble and such abundant fruits have sprung."

In saying that the "principal" British authors were now Scots, Denina was also commenting indirectly on the relatively poor showings made by Scottish authors of the seventeenth and early eighteenth centuries, as well as by English authors of the mid-eighteenth century. "Among the many eminent writers who flourished in G. Britain during the reign of Queen Anne," he noted, "we can scarcely reckon one who is a native of Scotland" (466). Regarding the contrast with England after that time, Denina referred to a "sensible decline in the genius and literature of England" that had gone unnoticed because many Europeans did not appreciate the distinction between English and Scottish authors.

Although literary competition with England was rarely alluded to in

---

45. Voltaire, "M. De Voltaire to the Authors of the *Literary Gazette*."

46. Rider, *Historical and Critical Account*, 13–14.

47. *Scots Magazine* 26 (1764): 465–68, quoting 466.

public pronouncements by Scots, they were sometimes less reticent in private. In 1768 Hume remarked to Robertson that literature in England was "still in a somewhat barbarous state," and barely four years later he identified several Scottish authors who might continue his *History of England*, adding: "For as to any Englishman, that Nation is so sunk in Stupidity and Barbarism and Faction that you may as well think of Lapland for an Author" (*LDH*, 2:194, 269).[48] When Edward Gibbon produced a first-rate work of history in 1776, Hume used Gibbon's achievement to denigrate English authors, writing to Adam Smith on 1 April: "I shoud never have expected such an excellent Work from the Pen of an Englishman. It is lamentable to consider how much that Nation has declined in Literature during our time." In March he had written much the same thing to Gibbon himself, and he confided to Smith his hope that the historian "did not take amiss the national Reflection" (*LDH*, 2:309–12). Other Scottish men of letters could be even more insensitive. On 10 May 1786 Hannah More wrote to her sister of a "memorable quarrel" that she and several other English men and women had with Lord Monboddo about the playwriting prowess of Shakespeare and John Home. To the consternation of More and Elizabeth Montagu, Monboddo insisted that Home's *Douglas* "was a better play than Shakespeare could have written." As the claims of "the prejudiced Scotch critic" escalated, the normally polite More grew "angry" and found it "impossible to be temperate, and difficult to be just." She added dryly, with reference to Monboddo's well-known preference for the ancients, "I suppose when, on a former occasion, he declared that no modern could turn a period finely, he meant to make an exception in favour of Scotch authors."[49]

It has been plausibly argued that Scottish literary boasting was a reaction (or overreaction) to the intensely anti-Scottish atmosphere that permeated eighteenth-century England.[50] "You cannot conceive the Jealousy that prevails against us," Tobias Smollett told John Moore early in 1758. "Nevertheless, it is better to be envied than despised."[51] But it was not long before Scots in London were both envied *and* despised. John Wilkes played upon anti-Scottish sentiment in his vicious attacks on Lord Bute,

---

48. Stoking the fire, Strahan showed this letter to an astonished James Beattie, knowing full well that doing so ensured the circulation of its contents among Beattie's many English friends. Beattie, *London Diary*, 34–35 (16 May 1773).

49. Roberts, *Memoirs of Hannah More*, 1:241.

50. Smith, "Some Eighteenth-Century Ideas," 107–24.

51. Smollett to Moore, 2 Jan. 1758, in Smollett, *Letters*, 65.

and Samuel Johnson frequently disparaged Scotland and Scottish authors such as William Robertson, leaving Boswell protesting lamely that his friend did not really mean what he said on this subject but rather "talked for victory" (*BLJ*, 2:238). Although Boswell observed that "two men more different" than Johnson and Wilkes "could perhaps not be selected out of all mankind," they were in perfect harmony at two dinner parties at the Dillys in May 1776 and May 1781. On both occasions, ridiculing the poverty and barrenness of Scotland constituted "a bond of union between them," and they "joined in extravagant sportive raillery" at Scotland's expense. At the first party, when someone said, "Poor old England is lost," Johnson asserted: "Sir, it is not so much to be lamented that Old England is lost, as that the Scotch have found it." At the second party, Wilkes spoke of "an inundation of Scotchmen, who come up [to London] and never go back again," and Johnson replied that "one Scotchman is as good as another" (*BLJ*, 3:64, 77–78, 4:101–2). It was all in good fun. Johnson "seems fond of Boswell," the Irishman Thomas Campbell wrote in his diary on 8 April 1775, "and yet he is always abusing the Scots before him, by way of joke."[52]

Yet beneath the "sportive" surface lay what John Brewer has described as "a genuine and deep-felt fear" of a Scottish conspiracy "to squeeze all worthy Englishmen from posts of power and profit and replace them by needy Scots"; in Linda Colley's words, it was "savage proof that Scots were acquiring power and influence within Great Britain to a degree previously unknown."[53] Among English men of letters, there was growing resentment about the sudden onslaught of their Scottish counterparts, which threatened to eclipse their own accomplishments and those of their national heritage. On one occasion when Boswell was not present at the Dillys, Johnson denigrated Scottish literary pretensions in relation to English ones with no trace of humor and declared himself content with Thomas Campbell's boasting about the accomplishments of medieval Irish scholars *since they are not Scotch.*[54] Whereas the Irish displayed "the impudence of a fly," Johnson told the Irishman Arthur Murphy, "the impudence of a Scotchman is the impudence of a leech, that fixes and sucks your blood."[55] "I do not *hate* the Scots," Johnson is supposed to have remarked, in an anecdote that was printed in the *London Chronicle* for

52. Campbell, *Diary*, 76.

53. Brewer, "Misfortunes," 20; Colley, *Britons*, 121.

54. Campbell, *Diary*, 74 (Campbell's emphasis).

55. Quoted in Clark, *Samuel Johnson*, 66.

29 April–2 May 1775; "Sir I do not *hate* the frogs, in the water, though I confess I do not like to have them hopping about my bedchamber."

Horace Walpole is a particularly interesting study in national bigotry because of the way his attitude shifted over time, reminding us that anti-Scottish fears among English men of letters did not constitute a momentary episode during the Bute era of the early 1760s. In *A Catalogue of the Royal and Noble Authors of England*, first published in 1758, Walpole somewhat surprisingly proclaimed Scotland "the most accomplished nation in Europe; the nation to which, if any one country is endowed with a superior partition of sense, I should be inclined to give the preference in that particular."[56] Although the precise meaning of this remark is uncertain, Walpole was making a friendly gesture to the Scots. Wilkes accordingly took him to task in various issues of the *North Briton*, such as number 2 (12 June 1762), which put Walpole's remark into the mouth of a boastful Scot celebrating the ascension of Ossian over Shakespeare on the occasion of Bute's appointment as first lord of treasury.

Before long, Walpole adopted Wilkes's anti-Scottish rhetoric. At times, his attitude took the common form of concern about aggressive or ingratiating Scots invading England and stealing its plums, such as his snide remark in 1780 about Patrick Brydone having "wriggled" himself into Lord North at a social event: "I suppose soon [he] will be an envoy, like so many other Scots."[57] But Walpole's mounting antipathy toward the Scots went deeper. Nothing written by Wilkes could surpass Walpole's extraordinary letter of 5 February 1781 to the poet William Mason, citing a reference in the *Critical Review* to "a saucy blockheadly note" in Hume's *History of England* that supposedly called "Locke, Algernon Sidney, and Bishop Hoadly, *despicable writers.*" Walpole adds, "I believe that ere long the Scotch will call the English *lousy!*" referring to the traditional English association of Scots with the "itch," "and that Goody Hunter [the Scottish medical lecturer William Hunter] will broach the assertion in an anatomic lecture." The letter continues:

> Not content with debasing and disgracing us as a nation by losing America, destroying our Empire, and making us the scorn and prey of Europe, the Scotch would annihilate our patriots, martyrs, heroes and geniuses.

56. Walpole, *Works*, 1:492.

57. Quoted in Katherine Turner's biography of Brydone in *ODNB*. The following year Brydone was appointed comptroller of the stamp office, a position worth about £600 a year.

Algernon Sidney, Lord Russel, King William, the Duke of Marlborough, Locke, are to be traduced and levelled, and with the aid of their fellow-labourer Johnson, who spits at them while he tugs at the same oar, Milton, Addison, Prior, and Gray are to make way for the dull forgeries of Ossian, and such wights as Davy and Johnny Home, Lord Kaims, Lord Monboddo, and Adam Smith!—Oh! If you have a drop of English ink in your veins, rouse and revenge your country! Do not let us be run down and brazened out of all our virtue, genius, sense, and taste by Laplanders and Bœotians, who never produced one original writer in verse or prose.[58]

In Walpole's (as in Wilkes's) bitter interpretation, the literary battle with the Scots was part of a larger war between England and Scotland over international perceptions of national greatness in a variety of fields—not merely "geniuses" but also "patriots, martyrs, heroes." It was a struggle for national glory that the Scots were winning—not on the basis of their genuine literary merit, Walpole believed, but rather as a result of what Samuel Johnson once called, in regard to the Ossian controversy, "Scotch conspiracy in national falsehood" (*BLJ*, 2:297). Like Hume, Walpole compared the opposition to "Laplanders," meaning barbarians with no literary talent. In his view, the stakes were so high that no quarter could be given: even Samuel Johnson, who "spits on" the Scots and their literary pretensions, was considered dangerous because his literary criticism had exposed weaknesses in the great English poets. Walpole closed the passage with a fiery call to arms, but it is not clear if Mason was supposed to attain revenge by composing outstanding poetry that would demonstrate the current literary greatness of England or by writing against those who had unjustly tarnished the English national image and unfairly exalted that of Scotland. Yet if Walpole was unclear about exactly what should be done to make things right, his letter leaves no doubt of his anger and frustration at the widespread perception that Scots were appropriating the cultural limelight from English authors who had traditionally, and rightfully, held it.

In this tense atmosphere, Scottish men of letters worried about whether English critics would judge their literary accomplishments fairly. When preparing for the press his loose translation from the Portuguese of Luís de Camões's sixteenth-century epic poem *The Lusiad* (1776), William Julius Mickle took a number of precautions. He had already moved to England, changed his surname from Meikle to Mickle in order to conform

58. Walpole, *Correspondence*, 29:104–5.

to English phonetics,[59] and adopted the middle name Julius, and he would see to it that Oxford and London were the only places to appear in the imprint. But a letter written sometime in 1775 to William Creech, principal publisher of the *Edinburgh Magazine and Review*, defined one more safeguard that Mickle considered necessary:

> As your magazine is much read in England, (at least I often see it in different places) when you *touch up* the Lusiad, I beg you would not maintain that the Translator is a Scotchman, for that would only set a nest of wasps, commonly called Critics, about my ears in this country. And though a book of real merit will live in spight of them, yet it is in their power to hurt the sale of a new work, and the sale, you know, is *fish* to an Author, while the Reputation is often only *a stone*. (WCL)

When an anonymous review by Thomas Blacklock appeared the following year, it commented on "the merit of the translator, whose performance, in our judgment, is an honour to British literature."[60]

BUILDING A DATABASE OF SCOTTISH ENLIGHTENMENT AUTHORS AND BOOKS

Authors, Publishers, and Books

Mickle's nervous attempt to shield his Scottish identity was one way to deal with the quandary in which Scottish authors found themselves during the second half of the eighteenth century. The opposite strategy was to celebrate their intellectual achievements in print, not only admitting their Scottishness but gloating about it. The response to Carlo Denina's book took this form. An eight-page quarto extract of the portion of Denina's work that dealt with Scotland appeared in the late spring or early summer of 1763, with the Italian and English versions in facing columns. The preface by "Scotus" (dated 16 Apr. 1763) commented that the attention and praise of learned foreigners to the achievements of Scottish authors "reflect an honour on the genius and improvement of our countrymen, and may be thought to have some effect in exciting a noble emulation, and encouraging the pursuits of literary fame." It noted that other Scottish

---

59. Mickle to Boswell, ca. 21 Sept. 1776, Boswell Papers, Yale University, C 2011; J. J. Caudle's biography in *ODNB*.

60. *Edinburgh Magazine and Review* 5 (May 1776): 208.

productions not mentioned by Denina, such as Lord Kames's *Elements of Criticism* and the Ossianic epic *Fingal*, were also attracting international attention. On 16 August the *Caledonian Mercury* printed an excerpt from the English version on its front page, "for those who love their country."[61] In early December the Foulis brothers published in Glasgow an "edizione seconda" of Denina's book in the original Italian, with a new letter from the author. The *Scots Magazine* placed Denina's comments on Scottish authors on the front page of its September 1764 issue, prefaced by remarks on the significance of a "distinguished" European professor giving "the palm at last to Scotland, in preference even to England, long deservedly esteemed the first nation in the world for learning and arts, . . . such a determination must give the highest satisfaction to every Scotsman in whose breast resides the smallest spark of love for his country" (465). The article added that Denina "might with ease have swelled his catalogue with a number of [other] names, eminent in every science" (468n). Finally, in 1771 Thomas Cadell and other London booksellers published a complete translation of Denina's book by John Murdoch.[62]

In the same year that Murdoch's translation appeared, Tobias Smollett, who had given up a medical career in Glasgow for a literary one in London, immortalized some of his countrymen in a passage in his last novel, *Humphry Clinker*, which is rarely quoted beyond its famous opening sentence:

> Edinburgh is a hot-bed of genius. I have had the good fortune to be made acquainted with many authors of the first distinction; such as the two Humes, Robertson, Smith, Wallace, Blair, Ferguson, Wilkie, etc. and I have found them all as agreeable in conversation as they are instructive and entertaining in their writings. These acquaintances I owe to the friendship of Dr Carlyle, who wants nothing but inclination to figure with the rest upon paper.[63]

In Smollett's formulation, books instruct and entertain, whereas the conversation that personal contact makes possible is merely "agreeable." Smollett excluded from the ranks of genius his good friend Alexander Carlyle because he was not well known as a published author. As Smollett knew, Carlyle had six or seven publications to his credit by this date, but they were all occasional sermons or anonymous polemical pamphlets. It

---

61. Dwyer, *"Caledonian Mercury,"* 152, quoting from the *Caledonian Mercury*.
62. Denina, *Essay*.
63. Smollett, *Humphry Clinker*, 227.

was not authorship per se that qualified an individual as a man of genius but rather authorship "of the first distinction." With the possible exception of Wallace, whose works appeared anonymously, the men whom Smollett singled out were widely known for having published major works of philosophy, history, drama, poetry, literary criticism, and social theory. Their greatness in Smollett's eyes arose from the prominent stature of their books, along with the fame they enjoyed as a result of wide readership and critical acclaim. Smollett could pull off such a shameless puff of his Scottish friends because most readers of his novel would be familiar with their names as authors.

Smollett's passage may be understood as a collective or national variation on the classificatory process of "author construction" identified by Foucault. Smollett dignifies authorship itself (or at least authorship "of the first distinction") by associating it with "genius." He then identifies the names of particular authors with a particular place—the town of Edinburgh. In so doing, he classifies the writers he names, and does so in accordance with geographical or national principles. Smollett invites the reader to categorize eight discrete individuals as a unified group of writers living together in a dynamic, urban, Scottish setting. The need for analysis, for evidence, for some kind of demonstration that these individuals are in fact men of genius is lost in the visceral imagery of known authors associating agreeably in a specific geographical context. As in Denina's work, the insertion of "etc." at the end of the list reinforces the main point: the names of these Scottish authors constitute a shorthand representation of a larger movement, associated with a place. Smollett does not use the term "Scottish Enlightenment," but he might well have done. In creating ideological meaning through the construction of authorship as a national phenomenon, he acts much like commentators in our own time who write about the Scottish literati as a collective entity.

Something similar happens in a pamphlet on the rise of Edinburgh during the latter part of the eighteenth century, *Letters containing a Comparative View of Edinburgh in the Years 1763 and 1783*, which the bookseller William Creech first published in December 1783 under the pseudonym Theophrastus and continued to revise and reprint (under different titles) at least six more times over the course of the next decade. Creech asserts that before 1763, "the Scots had made no very distinguished figure in literature as writers, particularly in the departments of History and Belles Lettres," whereas two decades later "the Scots had distinguished themselves in a remarkable manner in many departments of literature." The fact that the starting point for Creech's claim is the very year when

Denina proclaimed the remarkable ascension of Scottish literature and learning may reflect Creech's ignorance of Scottish authorship in the years before 1763, or it may indicate how dramatically the process had accelerated since that date. In any event, Creech illustrates his point with a list of "eminent authors" from all over Scotland, picked out of a larger pool of writers "too numerous to mention."[64] The latter phrase serves the same function for Creech as Smollett's (and Denina's) "etc.": it informs readers that his list of notable Scottish authors is representative of a larger intellectual movement. Creech's list of "eminent authors" grew over time from thirty-three to forty-two, as he added writers such as Alexander Adam, Joseph Black, Sir David and Sir John Dalrymple, Andrew Duncan, Sir John Sinclair, William Smellie, Dugald Stewart, and Alexander Fraser Tytler. It included one or two figures who would seem to be odd choices by the standards of his day or ours (e.g., Robert Orme), and it excluded several notable Scottish authors of the period. But these occasional irregularities do nothing to lessen the collective or national thrust of Creech's assertion. Creech uses the category of authorship for ideological purposes, in order to show that Edinburgh has become a leading center of literary and scientific genius. Merely listing the surnames of authors evokes their eminence, and the eminence of authors establishes the greatness of Scotland and its capital city.

In 1794, the Scottish language teacher Robert Alves died as he was putting to press *Sketches of a History of Literature*, one part of which was dedicated to delineating the Scots' "genius in learning." Alves focuses on his own field of literary interest, poetry, as well as the three fields of learning in which, in his estimation, Scotland was then most distinguished for "excellence": history, philosophy, and medicine. The eight historians and eight philosophers whom he cites are all on Creech's final list, with one exception: Tobias Smollett in the category of history. Alves's list of physicians is rather different from Creech's, however, and cites two new names: Robert Whytt and Charles Alston. Finally, although Alves's list of notable Scottish poets active during the second half of the eighteenth century duplicates Creech's in the selection of John Home and James Beattie, and duplicates Smollett's in the selection of Home and William Wilkie, it also adds three new figures: John Ogilvie, Thomas Blacklock, and William Richardson.

The lists of distinguished Scottish authors formulated by Smollett, Creech, and Alves are social constructions of authorship in two impor-

64. [Creech], *Letters to Sir John Sinclair*, 11–12.

tant respects—that of each individual author, whose very name came to signify a body of work in the manner indicated by Foucault, and that of the national collectivity of authors who were thought to bring credit to the Scottish nation. All three writers limited their lists to authors of books in the various genres of polite literature and learning, such as history, philosophy, science, medicine, law, political economy, rhetoric and belles lettres, travel and exploration, and poetry and novels. Although all three included a number of Presbyterian ministers, some of whom were known in part for their sermons and other religious works, every one of the clergymen whom they singled out was also the author of at least one major work of polite literature and learning.

When the names selected by Smollett, Creech, and Alves are combined, the result is a list of fifty "eminent authors," including many of the literati normally associated with the high Scottish Enlightenment that flourished during the second half of the eighteenth century. They may be regarded as one version of a contemporary canon of distinguished Scottish Enlightenment authors. In table 1 in this volume the names of these fifty authors are marked with asterisks, followed by life dates and brief summaries of their professions or means of livelihood. As we have seen, however, Smollett, Creech, and Alves each named only a representative group of individuals whom they considered the brightest lights among Scottish authors. In order to widen the representation, I have augmented table 1 with the names of sixty-five additional Scottish authors who contributed new books of polite literature and learning in the period 1746–1800. Some of these authors were probably omitted from the lists of Smollett, Creech, and Alves because their major works appeared either decades earlier (such as Francis Hutcheson and Colin Maclaurin) or else too late in the century to be considered (such as James Hutton and Joanna Baillie). Others may have been deemed too popular (such as William Buchan, James Ferguson, and James Fordyce) or too insignificant (such as Walter Anderson and James Grant). Still others may have been deemed insufficiently genteel (such as the Scots poets Robert Burns and Robert Fergusson) or insufficiently distinguished (such as the Grub Street writer Robert Heron). In adding names to table 1, I have tried to avoid biases such as these and to identify a broad cross-section of Scottish authors who wrote in a wide variety of polite literary and learned genres, including some critics of the leading literati, such as Hume's philosophical opponent James Balfour of Pilrig. In this way, this book extends the range of Scottish Enlightenment authors to include a number of figures who have not always been considered part of the movement.

Table 2 presents 360 books published in Britain during the period 1746–1800 by the 115 authors in table 1; the books are arranged chronologically by first edition. The numbers following each name in the left-hand column of table 1 correspond to the numbers of each author's works listed in table 2. Table 2 also records, in the title column, each book's original format (i.e., folio or 2°, quarto or 4°, octavo or 8°, duodecimo or 12°), number of volumes (if more than one), price (when known), subject category, and level of popularity based mainly on the number of eighteenth- and early nineteenth-century British editions. The next three columns provide publication information about the first British edition as well as about the first eighteenth-century reprint editions to appear in Ireland and America, respectively (the columns on Irish and American reprints are discussed in chapters 7–9). The assignment of each book to a single subject category is intended as a rough guide, using the same twenty subject categories that appear in William Zachs's checklist of the books published by John Murray.[65] The process is necessarily subjective: the categories are imprecise, and many books fall into more than one category. There is also some unavoidable imprecision in the designation of popularity ratings, ranging from best sellers (bs) that were frequently reprinted to poor sellers (ps) that appeared only once, but the cumulative results are useful as a way of generalizing about the dissemination of Scottish Enlightenment books.

In determining which works to include in table 2, I have excluded polemical pamphlets, individual sermons, heads of lectures (in contrast to more substantial lecture outlines), university theses, and other publications of less than about one hundred octavo pages, as well as all editions in languages other than English. However, separately published plays, and separately published poems and other shorter works of a certain stature, such as Hugh Blair's *Critical Dissertation on the Poems of Ossian*, have been included, as have the first English-language editions of translated, edited, or compiled works that have been judged to constitute significant contributions to learning in their own right (e.g., William Duncan's edition of *The Commentaries of Caesar*, Robert Simson's and John Playfair's editions of Euclid, William Julius Mickle's translation of *The Lusiad*, William Smellie's edition of Buffon's *Natural History*, the *Encyclopaedia Britannica*, John Gillies's edition of *Aristotle's Ethics and Politics*, and George Campbell's translation of the Gospels). Periodicals, the transactions of

---

65. Zachs, *First John Murray*, 254.

learned societies, and works that first appeared in parts or numbers have been included only if they were also published in book form (e.g., James Anderson's *Recreations in Agriculture,* Andrew Duncan's *Medical and Philosophical Commentaries,* Henry Mackenzie's *Mirror* and *Lounger,* the *Encyclopaedia Britannica,* and *Transactions of the Royal Society of Edinburgh*). Books consisting of multiple volumes that first appeared in different years have normally been entered only once, even though a good case can be made for regarding each volume of, say, Hugh Blair's *Sermons* or Robert Henry's *History of Great Britain* as a separate work. An exception has been made for the *History of England* and other works by David Hume, which have received preferential treatment because of their special importance.

The period 1746–1800 has been chosen because it stands out as the great age of Scottish Enlightenment book history, stretching from the end of the last major Jacobite uprising in 1745–46 to the beginning of the new century. As I have noted elsewhere, the term "Scottish Enlightenment" was coined in 1900 in William Robert Scott's biography of Francis Hutcheson, to denote "the diffusion of philosophic ideas in Scotland and the encouragement of speculative tastes amongst the men of culture of the generation following [Hutcheson's] own."[66] Although Scott's mode of expression now sounds archaic, his fundamental point about the Scottish Enlightenment involving a flowering and expansion of intellectual and cultural activity among Scottish men of letters who reached maturity in the post-Hutcheson era remains compelling after more than a century. The fact that Hutcheson died in 1746, along with another leading intellect of the second quarter of the eighteenth century, Colin Maclaurin, adds to the appeal of that year as a symbolic turning point in Scottish intellectual as well as political history. In the decades after 1746, Scotland underwent an unprecedented period of intellectual, cultural, social, and economic development, and Scotland's emergence as a major international producer of print culture was part of that broader transformation.[67] The point was recognized by Dugald Stewart, in his footnote on Hutcheson's *System of Moral Philosophy* cited earlier and in his allusion elsewhere to "the sudden burst of genius, which to a foreigner must seem to have sprung up in this country by a sort of enchantment, soon after the Rebellion of 1745."[68]

This midcentury intellectual awakening was not always sudden or

66. Scott, *Francis Hutcheson*, 265; Sher, *Church and University*, 4.

67. Sher, "Scotland Transformed."

68. Stewart, "Dissertation," 551nS.

abrupt. Both Hutcheson and Maclaurin appear in table 1 because important new books by them were published posthumously in the decade following their deaths, and a number of other men of letters who had begun publishing during the 1720s, 1730s, and 1740s, such as Hume, Kames, and Alexander Monro *primus*, ensured continuity by remaining active during subsequent decades. But the fact that the midcentury flowering of Scottish intellect had roots in the preceding period, just as it extended in some respects into the opening decades of the nineteenth century, should not be allowed to diminish the power and significance of a movement that left contemporaries, as it still leaves us, marveling at the extent to which Scotland flourished as an international center of literature and learning during the period under review.

This study rests on the belief that table 2 provides a solid foundation for understanding Scottish Enlightenment book history during the second half of the eighteenth century. The table forms the empirical cornerstone of this volume and is referred to frequently throughout these pages. However, I do not claim that the Scottish Enlightenment in its entirety can be reduced to the data contained in this table. In the first place, although I have tried to include an unusually wide range of relevant authors and books, I am aware that many have been omitted. Such omissions are inevitable because of ambiguities regarding categories like "Scottish," "Enlightenment," and "book," because all temporal boundaries are inherently artificial, and because a complete enumeration can never be attained in an interpretive exercise of this kind. Limiting the number of authors to 115 is an act of selection; the number might just as well have been 100, or 175. The crucial question, then, is not whether tables 1 and 2 are all inclusive, for they are not, but whether they are comprehensive enough to permit meaningful generalizations about the authors and books of the mature Scottish Enlightenment. I believe they are, even if a modifying word or phrase, such as Smollett's "etc." or Creech's "too numerous to mention," must always be kept in mind.

Second, table 2 does not capture the Scottish Enlightenment in its entirety because many individuals made contributions to it without ever writing a book. Some wrote pamphlets, book reviews, journal articles, or other shorter works that advanced enlightened causes. Some presented papers at learned societies, delivered academic lectures, painted pictures, composed music, designed buildings, or performed scientific experiments. Still others participated as members of clubs and societies, or as the audience that read, discussed, and absorbed the ideas contained in Enlightenment books. As Voltaire wrote in the *Encyclopédie*, "there are many *men of letters* who are not authors,"[69] let alone authors of books, and it is not my intention to exclude them from the Enlightenment solely on that account.

As discussed in the introduction to this book and elsewhere, the Scottish Enlightenment, like the Enlightenment as a whole, was a cultural and intellectual movement perpetrated by literati or philosophes who shared a common core of general values, including improvement, cosmopolitanism, humanity, sociability, toleration, and a dedication to literature and learning, even if they sometimes disagreed about just how such values should be interpreted and disseminated.[70] A book per se is not necessarily enlightened; indeed, eighteenth-century Scotland generated large numbers of pious works that did not embrace, and sometimes explicitly ridiculed or rejected, enlightened values. John Witherspoon's popular publication of 1753, *Ecclesiastical Characteristics*, which satirizes his brethren in the Church of Scotland for their pretensions to polite learning and culture, is a model of this kind of anti-Enlightenment thinking. By contrast, the books in table 2 all embodied the Enlightenment's commitment to polite literature and learning, and most of them exemplified other key values of the Enlightenment as well. Although they did not comprise the whole of the Scottish Enlightenment, therefore, these books constituted its most tangible and influential representation and were, taken collectively, the chief vehicle for the Scottish manifestation of Enlightenment print culture that forms the principal subject of this book.

Formats, Subjects, and Print Runs

In the eighteenth-century spectrum of book formats, the great majority of books were standard-sized octavos (8° or 8mo) or pocket-sized duodecimos (12° or 12mo). The quarto format (4° or 4to) was generally reserved for learned books of a certain character and standing. The size and expense of quartos gave them an elitist association with gentlemen and universities. Yet quartos were far more accessible than books in folio—an oversized, unwieldy format that was by this time usually reserved for reference or novelty works in law, medicine, and the fine arts. The extent to which Alexander Monro's folio *Observations on the Structure and Functions of the Nervous System* (no. 234 in table 2) dwarfs the other volumes in figure 1.2—even the quarto editions of Hume's *Essays and Treatises*—illus-

---

69. Voltaire, "Men of Letters," in Diderot, *Encyclopedia*, 168.
70. Sher, "Science and Medicine," 99–156.

trates this point. By the end of the century, when James Boswell talked of publishing his life of Samuel Johnson in one folio volume instead of two quarto volumes, his friend Edmond Malone quickly drove that thought from his head by asserting that he "might as well throw it into the Thames, for a folio would not now be read."[71] To be published in quarto was a mark of distinction, yet also a commercially viable option, and for this reason among others, status-minded authors campaigned vigorously for quarto format. As William Robertson wrote to one of his publishers in London, when arranging the publication details of his last work of history in 1791 (no. 299): "It is not a large work, but as I cannot descend from the dignity of a Quarto Author to the humble rank of Octavo, I propose that it should be printed in 4to form, with types similar to my other Books."[72] Similarly, octavo authors generally did not care to see their books reduced in size and price to mere duodecimos. Hugh Blair wrote to one of his publishers in regard to his popular *Sermons* that "I would not wish to have it reduced to a diminutive size . . . but to have it retain its old octavo form."[73]

Quartos were also desirable to authors, as well as publishers, because they were, potentially at least, more profitable than books in smaller formats. Although quartos were more expensive to produce—and therefore required a greater outlay of capital, and ran a greater risk of piracy in smaller and cheaper editions—prices were set higher because the target audience was wealthier and expected to pay more, and profit margins were greater. A quick perusal of book prices in table 2 shows this difference: quartos cost up to a guinea per volume, whereas thick octavos usually cost six or seven shillings per volume, and thinner octavos sometimes sold for half that amount. As we shall see more fully in chapter 3, authors could expect, and sometimes demand, hundreds or even thousands of pounds for their books in quarto, especially for works published in multiple volumes. But books published in octavo normally could not fetch such large amounts in advance of publication.

This point is illustrated by considering the copy money that Strahan and his partners were willing to pay for two books by Lord Kames in the mid-1770s. In 1774 Strahan, Cadell, and Creech published Kames's *Sketches of the History of Man* (no. 164) in two large quarto volumes, for which the

71. Boswell, *Great Biographer*, 32–33 (13 Jan. 1790). On the decline of the "luxury folio" earlier in the century, see Foxon, *Pope*, 64.

72. Robertson to Andrew Strahan, 13 Mar. 1791, EUL, La.II.241; Smitten, "Robertson's Letters," 36–54.

73. Blair to William Strahan, 10 Apr. 1778, EUL, Dc.2.76, no. 10.

author received a generous fee of £1,000. The work was expensive to produce, but at a retail price of two guineas a set, bound, the publishers had an opportunity to recoup their costs, and in 1778 they published a second, less expensive edition in four octavo volumes, followed by another octavo edition ten years later. Though not a best seller, the book performed respectably, and there is every reason to believe that the publishers made a solid profit from it. Yet when Creech passed along to Strahan Kames's request for three hundred guineas (£315) for the rights to the first edition of his next book, *The Gentleman Farmer* (no. 176), Strahan was indignant in his reply of 23 July 1776 (WCL): "300 Guineas for a simple Vol. 8vo. [i.e., octavo] on Husbandry!!! Ridiculous! What an immense Number must be sold to indemnify such a Price." He added a detailed accounting, which I have reproduced in chapter 5, to show that a single edition of 1,000 copies could not possibly yield enough profit to cover that large a payment to the author, even if every copy were sold.

In the phrase "a simple Vol. 8vo. on Husbandry," Strahan's disdain seems to be divided equally between the one-volume octavo format and the topic. There was nothing reprehensible about a subject like husbandry as such, but convention dictated that a book in that genre was suitable for no more than octavo format and, given its length, would be priced at no more than six shillings per volume (Strahan estimated an average of 3s.8d. per copy, which was presumably the wholesale price). The amount of copy money that could be paid to the author was necessarily commensurate with that circumstance. If 1,000 copies of a one-volume octavo like *The Gentleman Farmer* could be expected to produce £183.6s.8d. before expenses (as Strahan estimated it), whereas an edition of 1,000 copies of a two-volume quarto like *Sketches of the History of Man* might yield more than seven times that amount, such differences would have a significant effect on both publishers' profits and authors' incomes. "I told Strahan and Cadell, that if a Volume of a Guinea Price, was not worth £300, it was worth nothing," wrote Bishop John Douglas, when trying to negotiate more copy money for a quarto history by a fellow Scot.[74]

Bindings must also be considered. Although books were sometimes sold wholesale to the trade in quires, or loose sheets, the general public rarely encountered them in that form.[75] Rather, most books were retailed

---

74. Douglas to Alexander Carlyle, 20 Mar. 1773, EUL, Dc.4.41, no. 21, negotiating for Joseph MacCormick's *State-Papers and Letters, Addressed to William Carstares* (1774).

75. Bennett, *Trade Bookbinding.*

in hard millboard covers called boards or else fully bound in leather made from sheepskin or calfskin. Once again, formats mattered: quartos were more likely than octavos or duodecimos to be sold in boards, so that individuals with the means to do so might subsequently have them bound, lettered, and perhaps decorated to suit their tastes. Morocco, an exceptionally fine leather made from goatskin that was usually colored red (though sometimes green, blue, or black) was among the most expensive binding materials, and that fact undoubtedly contributed to Boswell's distress at discovering William Adams's quarto copy of Hume's *Essays and Treatises* in that binding. Some books, especially duodecimos and thin octavos, were sold stitched or sewed in paper wrappers, as were installments of periodicals and books that were published in parts or numbers, with a view toward binding upon completion, such as the quarto *Encyclopaedia Britannica* during the three years preceding its completion in 1771.

Thus, format, subject matter, length, price, binding, and remuneration were all inextricably linked. This does not necessarily mean that books originally published in quarto format were ultimately intended only for elite readers. If successful, they would soon be reprinted in smaller and cheaper octavo formats that could attract larger audiences. As we shall see in chapter 7, the Dublin book trade kept the pressure on British publishers by reprinting many new books in smaller formats very soon after their original publication. For this reason among others, the British publishers of new books were keen to downsize the more popular literary and scholarly titles on their lists as soon as the potential for high-end sales had been exhausted, and so were authors. Lord Kames would have been insulted if his *Sketches of the History of Man* had appeared initially in anything but quarto format, but two years after that occurrence, he was urging his Edinburgh publisher to produce a second edition in octavo as soon as possible, partly because he feared that a pirated edition might cut into their sales.[76]

Table 3 organizes the 360 works in table 2 according to their subject categories and correlates each topic with book formats. The first conclusion to be drawn from table 3 is that the books of the Scottish Enlightenment covered a very broad range of subjects, including virtually all aspects of polite literature and learning. Of course, certain kinds of books were more common than others. Two categories alone—history (including various types of historical writing and antiquarianism) and

76. Kames to William Creech, 9 Sept. 1776, Fraser-Tytler of Aldourie Papers, NRAS 1073, bundle 24.

medicine—comprise about 36 percent of the books in the database. But the breadth of the topics and genres is nevertheless striking.

When the subject categories that appear in tables 2 and 3 are correlated with the authors in the database, it becomes evident that the wide range of subjects treated in those books arose from the broadly diverse interests of individual authors rather than merely from the juxtaposition of authors with narrow specialties in different fields. Fifty-five of the 115 authors in the database, or approximately 48 percent, published books in at least two different subject categories. This number includes seven authors who published books in three different subject categories (Boswell, D. Fordyce, Gerard, Guthrie, F. Home, Thomson, and Duff), six authors with books in four different subject categories (Logan, Mackenzie, Moore, J. Ogilvie, Pinkerton, and Smollett), two authors with books in five different subject categories (Beattie and Sinclair), and one author, Kames, with books in six different subject categories.

Table 3 also indicates the formats of the first editions in table 2, arranged by subject category. Publication in the large and expensive folio format occurred in just 2 percent of the books in the database. At the other end of the scale, only thirty-eight titles, comprising nearly 11 percent of the whole database, were originally published in duodecimo format, or smaller, and almost two-thirds of them occurred in just two subject categories: fiction, because novels were usually published as inexpensive pocketbooks, and philosophy, because duodecimo was the format of choice for student texts such as Francis Hutcheson's *Short Introduction to Moral Philosophy* (no. 3), Adam Ferguson's *Institutes of Moral Philosophy* (no. 117), and John Bruce's *First Principles of Philosophy* (no. 205). By the end of the century, and especially early in the next century, even smaller formats were becoming popular, especially for cheap reprints of best sellers or multivolume series such as *Cooke's Pocket Edition of Select British Poets*, which was hawked on grounds of its cheapness, its uniformity, and its suitability for works of "Amusement" ("works of Science" being conceded to larger formats).[77] But only one book in table 2 (no. 37) made its initial appearance in a format smaller than duodecimo.

77. *Plan and Catalogue of Cooke's Uniform, Cheap, and Elegant Pocket Library* (1794), quoted in Ezell, *Social Authorship*, 137. Burns's and Ossian's *Poems*, various novels by Henry Mackenzie and John Moore, Hume's *History of England*, and Robertson's *Works* were all advertised in tiny 18mo editions in *A Catalogue of Valuable Books*, which Cadell and Davies distributed in 1816, and an even smaller 32mo edition of Hume's and Smollett's histories was also available.

Thus, almost nine out of ten Scottish Enlightenment books, rising to about 91 percent if novels are excluded, were originally published in either quarto or octavo. Of those titles, octavos outnumbered quartos by better than two to one, but the proportions do not hold equally across the different subject categories. Works of history were twice as likely to begin life as quartos than as octavos, and polite readers were sensitive to this distinction: Sir David Dalrymple, Lord Hailes, once remarked that his wife "could not bring herself to suppose that [octavo] was consistent with the dignity of History."[78] Two other categories in which quartos were not unusual were works of political economy and poetry, especially epic poetry, such as James Macpherson's two major Ossianic works, *Fingal* (no. 71) and *Temora* (no. 83), and Mickle's translation of *The Lusiad* (no. 175). At the opposite extreme, no works in table 2 of prose fiction, drama, or politics, and few in most other genres, were published in quarto. In religion, for example, sermons were usually published in octavo, or occasionally in duodecimo, but never in quarto. The only religious work in the database that originally appeared in quarto is George Campbell's *The Four Gospels*, which qualified for that format on the basis of its large size and ambitious character, as a work of scholarship intended mainly for the libraries of scholars and gentlemen.

The number of copies that were printed of each book varied according to several factors, including format, subject matter, length of the text, price, extent of the author's fame, estimates of likely sales, and the willingness of publishers to take risks. Bibliographers have also noted that, under normal circumstances, technical and economic constraints tended to limit the print runs of eighteenth-century books to a minimum of 500 and a maximum of 2,000 copies.[79] The titles in table 2 bear out this dictum. I have been able to ascertain the size of the print run of the first editions of 124 books, comprising more than a third of the database, and only 12 of them fall outside the 500–2,000 range. All but one of those 12 books were printed in runs larger than 2,000, and almost all of them ended up passing through many editions in spite of their unusually large initial print runs.[80] The print runs of the 112 books that fall within the

---

78. Hailes to Sir Adam Fergusson of Kilkerran, 3 June 1774, NLS, MS 25302, fol. 5.

79. Gaskell, *New Introduction to Bibliography*, 161.

80. Only 300 copies of the first volume of Lord Monboddo's *Antient Metaphysics* (no. 204) were printed in 1782, and the same number of the second volume two years later (SA 48815, fols. 63 and 79). The books known to have initial print runs higher

range of 500–2,000 copies can be broken down as follows: 2,000 copies, 6; 1,750 copies, 1; 1,500 copies, 11; 1,250 copies, 4; 1,000 copies, 39; 750 copies, 32; and 500 copies, 19.[81] These numbers suggest that almost three-quarters of the first editions in table 2 had print runs of 500–1,000, mostly at the higher end of the range (750 or 1,000 copies).[82] Of course, once a book was established, these numbers often rose higher. Hence William Strahan's remark to David Hume in 1771 regarding a new edition of his *History of England:* "The impression is to be 1,500 and no more, which is of all others the most proper Number."[83] The most proper number was actually the one that corresponded most closely to the potential market for a particular edition, and determining it could never be anything more than a calculated guess. Boswell, for example, took a huge gamble when he printed 1,750 copies of the quarto first edition of the *Life of Johnson,* and he had grave doubts if enough people would really pay two guineas for the set; two years after publication, however, he noted that "many more would have gone off could they have been had."[84]

---

than 2,000 are as follows: John Home's plays *Agis* in 1758 (4,500 copies) and *Siege of Aquileia* in 1760 (4,000); the third and fourth volumes of David Hume's *History of England* (on the Tudors) in 1759 (2,250); William Robertson's *History of the Reign of Charles V* (4,000), *History of America* (3,000), *Historical Disquisition concerning the Knowledge which the Ancients Had of India* (3,000), and *History of America,* bks. 9 and 10 (750 quarto and 1,500 octavo); John Moore's *A View of Society and Manners in Italy* (3,000) and *Edward* (3,000); William Buchan's *Domestic Medicine* (more than 5,000); and the *Encyclopaedia Britannica* (later said to be 3,000). This list includes several titles with popularity ratings of "n/a" because they were later incorporated into other works.

81. One book printed in a quantity of 2,098 has been counted in the 2,000-copy category; one with a print run of 800 copies has been counted in the 750-copy category; and one with a print run of 612 copies has been counted in the 500-copy category. James Beattie's *The Minstrel* has been counted as 500 based on the first book, although the print run of the first edition of the second book was 750. Alexander Dow's *History of Hindostan* has been counted as 750 based on the first volume, although the first edition of the third volume had a print run of 1,000.

82. Slightly lower estimates may be found in Zachs, *First John Murray,* 68; and in Hernlund, "William Strahan's Ledgers," 104. However, Chard, "Bookseller to Publisher," states that Joseph Johnson usually printed books in quantities of 750 copies, and Raven, "Publishing and Bookselling," 32, views 750 as the standard in the trade.

83. Strahan to Hume, 25 May 1771, NLS, MS 23157, no. 63.

84. Boswell to Andrew Erskine, 6 Mar. 1793, in Boswell, *Correspondence and Other Papers,* 399.

The Popularity of Books

The two-letter popularity rating that appears in the title column of table 2 is based primarily on the number of editions published in England and Scotland through the year 1810, or through 1820 in the case of books originally published during the 1790s. Each book has been assigned one of six rating categories: bs for best seller, defined here as a book published in at least ten distinct British editions in the designated time period; ss for strong seller, meaning a book with seven to nine British editions; gs for good seller, for a book with four to six British editions; ms for modest seller, for a book with two to three British editions; ps for poor seller, for a book that was never reprinted in Britain during the period in question; and n/a for not applicable, assigned to books that were later reprinted within other books in table 2, mainly nine works by David Hume that became best sellers as parts of *Essays and Treatises on Several Subjects* or *The History of England*, and William Robertson's posthumous history of British America (no. 341), which was immediately incorporated into his best-selling *History of America*. N/a has also been assigned to the published transactions of four scholarly societies, on the grounds that such works are not normally reprinted.

The method of counting editions to determine the popularity of books requires qualification. First, variations in the size of print runs must be considered, since a book with a large initial print run that appears to be unsuccessful on the basis of numbers of editions may actually have sold more copies than another book that moved quickly to a second edition because its initial print run was much smaller. In 1758 Andrew Millar ordered the printing of 4,500 copies of John Home's *Agis* (no. 51), the author's first play after *Douglas*, and two years later he commissioned 4,000 copies of Home's next tragedy, *The Siege of Aquileia* (no. 63). Not surprisingly, no further separate editions of either play were required, although total sales were probably the equivalent of several standard editions because of the huge size of the initial printings. In other cases, the length, format, and cost of a book must also be taken into account when determining its popularity. The *Encyclopaedia Britannica* (no. 139) originally appeared in Edinburgh between 1768 and 1771 in one hundred weekly installments, each consisting of twenty-four quarto pages; in 1771 these were bound into three large volumes (reprinted in London in 1773 and 1775), which were expanded to ten volumes in the second edition of 1778–83 and eighteen volumes in the third edition of 1788–97, all heavily illustrated and printed in increasingly large runs.[85] It would be misleading to classify it as anything less than a best seller, even though it had only three eighteenth-century editions.

It is also necessary to distinguish bona fide editions from spurious ones. Eighteenth-century publishers sometimes resorted to tactics intended to fool the public into overestimating a book's popularity, and we must be careful not to be taken in by their tricks. In one extraordinary case, William Strahan told James Beattie that he and Thomas Cadell had altered the dates on editions of William Robertson's *History of Scotland* in order to make them appear less numerous than they really were, so that David Hume's feelings would not be hurt by a comparison with his own history.[86] A more common ploy was to reissue a slow-selling book with a new title page, perhaps marked "second edition." For example, Edward Dilly reissued Thomas Blackwell's *Letters concerning Mythology* (no. 4) this way in 1757, and John Murray did so with Gilbert Stuart's *A View of Society in Europe* (no. 195) in 1783. Occasionally Murray advertised a spurious second edition so that he could lure customers into his shop and sell them a copy of the first edition.[87] Another trick that publishers sometimes used was to skip a numbered edition, so that what should have been the second edition of a particular book would appear instead as the third. Murray seems to have published a second edition and a fourth edition of William Richardson's *Essays on Shakespeare's Dramatic Characters* (no. 247), without ever publishing a third edition. Although these various ploys are sometimes difficult to discover, I have tried to locate and exclude suspicious editions and reissues whenever possible.

It has also been necessary to consider abridgments, anthologies, unauthorized editions, and other alternatives to straightforward reprints of the books in table 2. Lengthy books were sometimes abridged, often under new titles, and in one or two instances, such as James Bruce's *Travels to Discover the Source of the Nile* (no. 288; often abridged as *An Interesting Narrative, of the Travels of James Bruce, Esq.*), I have raised a book to bestseller status as a result of the great popularity of the abridgments. William Duncan's *The Elements of Logic* (no. 5) and David Fordyce's *The Elements of Moral Philosophy* (no. 7) are examples of books in table 2 that were separately published but also widely reprinted as parts of other works.

85. Kafker, "Achievement," 139–52; Yeo, *Encyclopaedic Visions*, chap. 7.
86. Beattie, *London Diary*, 35.
87. Zachs, *First John Murray*, 36.

Both are categorized as best sellers in the rating system used here (rather than as a strong seller and a modest seller, respectively) because they continued to be reprinted in Robert Dodsley's anthology, *The Preceptor,* not to mention being adapted for the articles on "logic" and "moral philosophy" in the *Encyclopaedia Britannica.* Similarly, Hugh Blair's *Critical Dissertation on the Poems of Ossian* (no. 80) never passed beyond an expanded second edition as a separate publication, but I have categorized it as a best seller on account of its inclusion in at least eleven British editions of the *Works of Ossian* or *Poems of Ossian* in the years 1765–1809. Finally, although it was uncommon for unauthorized editions of the titles in table 2 to be published in Britain in violation of statutory copyright during the period in question, some editions appeared that violated the London booksellers' conception of honorary or tacit copyright (i.e., copyright based on convention rather than statute), and these editions have been counted fully because they are legitimate indicators of a book's popularity.

The popularity ratings in table 2 reflect adjustments that have been made to correct the problems just discussed. I have taken into account extreme variations in print runs, when known, and the special circumstances associated with large works such as the *Encyclopaedia Britannica.* I have also attempted to include all varieties of real editions published in Britain, including those that were abridged, anthologized, or thought by some parties to be pirated, and to exclude all varieties of ghost (i.e., nonexistent) editions. Also excluded are foreign reprints, some of which are discussed in the last three chapters of the book.

Table 4 tabulates the results of these popularity ratings. More than a third of the 360 books in table 2 were never reprinted in Britain during the late eighteenth or early nineteenth centuries, and almost as many were reprinted no more than twice during that period. A small number of these poor and modest sellers were late bloomers that sold better in the nineteenth century than they had in the years immediately following their publication. Examples include George Campbell's *Philosophy of Rhetoric* (no. 174) and Adam Ferguson's *History of the Progress and Termination of the Roman Republic* (no. 232). Some other titles remained dormant in Britain but later emerged as popular books elsewhere, particularly in North America. William Smellie's *Philosophy of Natural History* (no. 292) is a classic instance. Originally published in Edinburgh in two volumes in 1790 and 1799, it was neglected in nineteenth-century Britain but became a standard college text in North America and was reprinted or reissued (as a one-volume abridgment) more than thirty times between 1824 and 1900, mainly in Boston but also in Dover, New Hampshire, and Halifax, Nova Scotia. Yet such cases were unusual. The great majority of the poor sellers in table 2, and most of the modest sellers too, never enjoyed widespread popularity. From a commercial point of view, most modest sellers can be assumed to have generated some profit for their publishers, especially if they reached three editions and did not entail large outlays of capital, but many of the poor sellers probably lost money. From the standpoint of authorship, few of the books in these categories brought their authors lasting fame in the republic of letters, although a few of them, such as Kames's *Sketches of the History of Man*, have proved to be exceptions over the long term.

The books in the top three categories tell a different story. Most of them, comprising about 17 percent of the entire database, were good sellers that passed through between four and six British editions during the designated time period. These titles were usually quite profitable and established the contemporary reputations of their authors to some degree, even if they often sank to a lower level over the course of time. Many of these books were reprinted overseas, as we shall see in the concluding chapters of this study, and a few of them grew increasingly popular as time passed. Among the sixty-three good sellers are such well-known works as John Millar's *Observations concerning the Distinction of Ranks in Society*, Adam Ferguson's *Essay on the History of Civil Society*, Archibald Alison's *Essays on the Nature and Principles of Taste* (another late bloomer), George Campbell's *Dissertation on Miracles*, Henry Mackenzie's *Lounger*, Dugald Stewart's *Elements of the Philosophy of the Human Mind*, and Robert Henry's *History of Great Britain*, all of which experienced some years of sustained popularity and influence after their original publication.

At the high end of the popularity scale are fifty-one strong sellers and best sellers. The first of these categories, consisting of books that appeared in seven to nine editions during the designated time period, has only five titles, or about 1 percent of the entire database. It is not clear why this category is so small. One possibility is that once a book reached seven editions, it passed a kind of popularity threshold and usually went on from there to become a best seller. Some of the books in the category of strong sellers were virtually best sellers anyway. Lord Kames's *Elements of Criticism* (no. 73), for example, went to a tenth British edition in 1824 and an eleventh in 1839 (in addition to a large number of nineteenth-century editions in America). Another strong seller, Benjamin Bell's *A System of Surgery* (no. 240), consisted of six volumes, so the fact that it had at least seven, and possibly eight, British editions between its completion in 1788 and 1801 is very impressive. The three other books in this category, Sir John Pringle's *Observations on the Diseases of the Army* (no. 20), Thomas Reid's *Inquiry into the Human Mind* (no. 88), and John Moore's *A View of Society and Manners in Italy* (no. 219), were also consistently popular late eighteenth-century titles that were still being reprinted in the early nineteenth century.

Finally, forty-six books, comprising approximately 13 percent of the 360 titles in table 2, are categorized as best sellers, and their titles appear in boldface. Thirty-two of these books were written (or in one case edited) by fifteen men who were among the fifty names cited by Smollett, Creech, and Alves as distinguished Scottish authors. The most popular of them, Smollett himself, produced seven best sellers (*Roderick Random, Peregrine Pickle, Ferdinand Count Fathom, Complete History of England, Continuation of the Complete History of England, Sir Launcelot Greaves*, and *Humphry Clinker*). William Robertson followed with four best sellers (*History of Scotland, History of Charles V, History of America*, and *Disquisition on India*), and Hugh Blair had three (*Critical Dissertation on Ossian, Sermons*, and *Lectures on Rhetoric and Belles Lettres*). Next come six authors with two best sellers each: James Beattie (*Essay on Truth* and *The Minstrel*), John Gregory (*Comparative View* and *Father's Legacy to His Daughters*), David Hume (*Essays and Treatises on Several Subjects* and the *History of England*), Henry Mackenzie (*The Man of Feeling* and *The Mirror*), James Macpherson (*Fingal* and *Temora*), and Adam Smith (*The Theory of Moral Sentiments* and the *Wealth of Nations*). Six others from this group of core authors were responsible for one best seller apiece: Alexander Adam (*Roman Antiquities*), Patrick Brydone (*Tour through Sicily and Malta*), William Cullen (*First Lines of the practice of Physic*), John Home (*Douglas*), John Moore (*View of France, Switzerland, and Germany*), and William Smellie (editor of the *Encyclopaedia Britannica*). The remaining fourteen best sellers were the work of thirteen authors who were not named by Smollett, Creech, or Alves: William Buchan (*Domestic Medicine*), James Boswell (*Life of Samuel Johnson*), James Bruce (*Travels to Discover the Source of the Nile*), Robert Burns (*Poems*), William Duncan (*Elements of Logic*), James Ferguson (*Astronomy Explained* and *Lectures on Select Subjects*), Robert Ferguson (*Poems*), David Fordyce (*Elements of Moral Philosophy*), James Fordyce (*Sermons to Young Women*), William Guthrie (*New Geographical, Historical, and Commercial Grammar*), Mungo Park (*Travels in the Interior Districts of Africa*), Robert Simson (*Elements of Euclid*), and William Smellie, M.D. (*Treatise on Midwifery*).

These best-selling titles conform to no obvious pattern. With regard to formats, ten books started their lives as duodecimos, eighteen as octavos, eighteen as quartos, and none as folios. Duodecimos, which we have seen to be relatively uncommon as a format for the first edition of Scottish Enlightenment books, had the best chance of reaching best-seller status in proportion to their total numbers: more than 25 percent of them achieved that goal, as opposed to a little over 17 percent of quartos and only 9 percent of octavos. This result can be explained by two factors: the low prices of duodecimos and the fact that so many of them were either works of imaginative literature of an entertaining nature or books that became popular texts for secondary school and university students. In the first category were five novels by Smollett and one by Mackenzie, as well as Mackenzie's periodical *The Mirror* (which featured moral fiction) and Robert Fergusson's *Poems;* in the latter category were William Duncan's *Elements of Logic* and Alexander Adam's *Roman Antiquities.* Quartos that became best sellers did so by dropping down to octavos after the first (or occasionally, second) edition or by being abridged, anthologized, or incorporated into larger works in the ways we have seen. Similarly, some octavo best sellers were downsized to cheaper duodecimos, but this practice was less common than downsizing quartos because octavos were already affordable to many book buyers, and because thick one-volume octavos, such as Buchan's *Domestic Medicine* and Guthrie's *Geography*, could not be reprinted as duodecimos without expanding them into two or more volumes. Toward the end of the century, popular books like these were sometimes available in more than one format.

The subject matter of best sellers was extraordinarily varied. Although history heads the list with 8 best sellers, this number is not very high in proportion to the enormous number of history books in the database. Fiction follows with six best sellers, and eleven different subject categories have between one and five titles on the best-seller list: philosophy (5), poetry (5), miscellaneous (5), travel (4), medicine (3), science (3), literature (2), religion (2), biography (1), drama (1) and economics (1). Medical books, which we have seen to be one of the two largest subject categories overall, were unlikely to become best sellers: just under 5 percent of the medical books in table 2 earned that distinction—the lowest percentage of any category. The best chance for a best seller lay with books whose subject matter has been designated "miscellaneous," such as William Guthrie's wide-ranging *Geography,* John Gregory's eclectic *Comparative View* (which combined elements of science, medicine, literature, fine arts, philosophy, and conduct literature), Gregory's little book of advice for young women titled *A Father's Legacy to His Daughters*, Henry Mackenzie's *The Mirror,* and the comprehensive *Encyclopaedia Britannica.*

If all this demonstrates once again the remarkable breadth and scope of the books of the Scottish Enlightenment, it also shows how difficult it was to predict what sort of books would be likely to sell well. A cheap duodecimo novel or an expensive quarto history might be in demand for decades, but works in those same formats and genres could also fall flat. Publishers believed that the best predictors of popularity were authors whose earlier books had sold well and whose names (or their associations with previous works, in the case of anonymous books that contained links to earlier ones by the same author) gave their latest books an advantage over others. "A Bookseller in a Purchase looks to the probability of the sale," John Murray told one of his authors, "and seizes hold of the manuscript of an author already well and successfully known to the Public in preference to another tho perhaps better, written by an author whose reputation is not so well established."[88] Underlying this kind of thinking was an awareness of the public's tendency to classify books by their authors as brand names, much as Foucault's concept of the "author function" would lead us to expect.

*

This chapter began with David Hume's boast about the Scots having become "the People most distinguish'd for Literature in Europe." If that statement was an exaggeration when Hume made it in 1757, it would not remain so for long. In the half-century following the last Jacobite uprising in 1745–46, Hume and his countrymen published hundreds of books in a variety of formats and in virtually all the subject categories and genres of polite literature and learning. Many had little impact, immediate or otherwise, but scores were in demand, and dozens became best sellers that not only appeared in edition after edition in Great Britain but also were frequently anthologized, excerpted, and abridged, as well as reprinted abroad.

It was a remarkable achievement, a revolution in literature, in the language of Carlo Denina. As it was taking place, English literary men like Horace Walpole and Samuel Johnson reacted with a mixture of respect, denial, condescension, anger, and outrage. Many Scots were also confused about the best course of action. Some, like William Julius Mickle, tried to hide their identity in order to protect themselves from hostile English

---

88. Murray to Gilbert Stuart, 11 Dec. 1775, quoted in Zachs, *First John Murray*, 63.

critics. Others used the medium of print to publicize as loudly as possible Scotland's new status as a center of literature and learning, broadcasting at every chance the judgment of foreign admirers such as Sheridan and Denina. Thus, the books of the Scottish Enlightenment were charged with national, political, and ideological significance.

Investigating this phenomenon requires a deeper acquaintance with the authors who wrote the books of the Scottish Enlightenment. It is necessary to give some consideration to their backgrounds and careers, their relationships among themselves as well as with patrons and publishers, their motives and rewards, and their identities as authors. These are the topics addressed in the two chapters that follow.

2

Identity and Diversity among Scottish Authors

By its very nature, writing books is usually a private activity, and often a lonely one. Yet sociability and commitment to a community and a world beyond oneself were among the core values of the Enlightenment, in Scotland at least as much as anywhere else. Different authors devised different strategies for balancing the contrary demands of the individual and the collective, the private and the social. William Robertson, for example, was able to combine personal scholarship with active participation in the cultural life of Enlightenment Edinburgh by limiting his participation in the domestic sphere: "I well remember his constant habit of quitting the drawing-room, both after dinner and again after tea, and remaining shut up in his library," recalled his nephew Henry Brougham.[1] Outside the home, sociability depended largely on access to the formal and informal institutions that comprised the public sphere. As we shall see in this chapter, the books of the Scottish Enlightenment were affected by the social interaction of their authors, and those books in turn projected images of authors as, among other things, friends, colleagues, and men of letters.

THE SOCIAL CONTEXTS OF AUTHORSHIP

Generations, Backgrounds, and Social Organization

The birth dates of the authors in table 1 span the better part of a hundred years, from Charles Alston in 1683 to Mungo Park in 1771, with the year

1. Brougham, *Lives*, 1:259.

1729 constituting the median for the 113 individuals whose birth dates are known. Those birth dates may be used to divide the authors in the table into three broad generational cohorts, which correspond roughly to "the three overlapping, closely associated generations" of European and American philosophes identified by Peter Gay.[2] Fourteen (12 percent) were born between 1680 and 1709—the contemporaries of Voltaire and Montesquieu. Several from this cohort wrote learned works that appeared during the first half of the eighteenth century, especially during the two decades preceding the 1745 uprising. Books such as Francis Hutcheson's *An Inquiry into the Original of our Ideas of Beauty and Virtue* (1725), Alexander Monro *primus*'s *The Anatomy of the Human Bones* (1726), Thomas Blackwell's *An Enquiry into the Life and Writings of Homer* (1735), and Colin Maclaurin's *Treatise on Fluxions* (1742), along with the publications by Andrew Baxter (1686/87–1750), George Cheyne (1671/72–1743), George Turnbull (1698–1748), and other Scottish authors who do not appear in table 1, mark this as a formative period in the book history of the Scottish Enlightenment, even if it lacks the explosive character of the post-'45 era. Several of the men in this cohort continued their activity as authors during the second half of the century, but only five of them—Charles Alston, Lord Kames, Alexander Monro *primus*, James Oswald, and Robert Wallace—were among the authors singled out for distinction by Smollett, Creech, and Alves.

The formative generation of Scottish Enlightenment authors born between 1680 and 1709 was followed by what might be called the prime generation, born between 1710 and 1739—the contemporaries of Diderot, d'Alembert, and Rousseau in France. Sixty-two of the individuals in table 1, comprising 55 percent of those whose birth dates are known, were born during this period, including 34 of the 50 distinguished authors named by Smollett, Creech, and Alves. Their numbers include such luminaries as William Cullen, Thomas Reid, David Hume, Lord Monboddo, Robert Whytt, Robert Henry, George Campbell, and Francis Home, born during the 1710s; William Robertson, Tobias Smollett, Adam Ferguson, Adam Smith, John Gregory, Lord Hailes, James Hutton, Joseph Black, Alexander Gerard, John Hunter, William Buchan, and John Moore, born during the 1720s; and Alexander Monro *secundus*, James Beattie, John Millar, James Macpherson, and James Anderson, born during the 1730s. The men of this generation reached their prime during the 1750s, 1760s, and 1770s, and along with a handful of figures from the previous generation,

2. Gay, *Enlightenment*, 1:17.

they were chiefly responsible for the "takeoff" of the mature Scottish Enlightenment during those years. Many of them remained active as authors during the closing decades of the eighteenth century.

Finally, the 37 authors born between 1740 and 1771, comprising 33 percent of those whose birth dates are known (but only 11 of the leading authors cited by Smollett, Creech, and Alves), constituted a younger generation of Scottish Enlightenment authors. Their numbers remained strong during the 1740s, which saw the birth of 22 of the authors in table 1, including James Boswell, William Smellie, Gilbert Stuart, Andrew Duncan, Henry Mackenzie, John Gillies, and John Playfair. More of them were troubled, and sometimes disgruntled, about their careers and their prospects in Scotland than was the case with earlier generations, and several of them ended up on Grub Street in London, as we shall see. The number of authors born during the 1750s, 1760s, and early 1770s (14, including only 3 of the 50 named by Smollett, Creech, and Alves) reveals a significant decline, with a total roughly comparable to that of the period 1680–1709. They include some important figures, however, such as James Gregory, Dugald Stewart, Sir John Sinclair, and Robert Burns among those born in the 1750s alone, as well as the only women authors in the table, Elizabeth Hamilton and Joanna Baillie. Of course, individuals born during the second half of the century are at a disadvantage for inclusion in this database, since they had less time to distinguish themselves as authors before the cutoff point for this study in 1800. Several of them published principally during the first quarter of the nineteenth century. But even when allowances are made for this chronological imbalance, it is difficult to avoid the impression of declining intellectual stature, which was a common refrain at the time. As Lord Cockburn (who was born in 1779) put it many years later, when describing his early years in the Edinburgh of Robertson, Ferguson, Black, Henry, and their contemporaries: "we knew enough of them to make us fear that no such other race of men, so tried by time, such friends of each other and of learning, all of such amiable manners and such spotless characters, could be expected soon to arise, and again ennoble Scotland."[3]

Few of the 115 authors in table 1 belonged to the titled elite. Only one, the Earl of Buchan, was noble by birth; four others (Hailes, Kames, Monboddo, and Woodhouselee) acquired the honorary title Lord in their capacity as judges of the Court of Session. Three (Sir David and Sir John Dalrymple, and Sir James Steuart) inherited baronetcies, while two others

3. Cockburn, *Memorials*, 57.

of comparable birth (Sir John Pringle and Sir John Sinclair) were created baronets on the basis of their accomplishments, and another (Sir James Mackintosh) obtained a knighthood in his capacity as a judge in Bombay. Most of the 105 individuals in table 1 whose fathers' occupations can be identified came from relatively well-off families by the standards of eighteenth-century Scotland. By far the largest number (28, comprising nearly 27 percent) were sons (or in the case of Joanna Baillie, a daughter) of the manse, having fathers who were Presbyterian ministers; another (William Guthrie) was the son of a Scottish Episcopal clergyman. Twenty (including the noble and the baronets) were the sons of landed families, though in some cases their estates were quite modest; six others were the sons of lawyers or judges, who were usually also landed, like the Boswells of Auchinleck.[4] Twelve had fathers who can be identified as farmers, ranging from moderately well off to struggling tenant farmers. Others were the children of merchants of one kind or another (13, including provosts of Edinburgh and Aberdeen), physicians and surgeons (9, including two military or foreign service surgeons), tradesmen and laborers (6, at least two of whom also did some farming), clerks, factors, and civil servants (4), architects (2), schoolmasters (2), a soldier (who was also a landed gentleman), and a professor (in addition to six other academics who have already been counted as clergymen or physicians).

Their births occurred over a remarkably wide geographical area. Thirty, or more than 27 percent of the 109 whose place of birth is known, hailed from Edinburgh and the surrounding Lothians. Thirteen were born in the greater Glasgow area (Lanarkshire, Dunbartonshire, and Renfrewshire), 9 in the Borders (Berwickshire, Roxburghshire, and Selkirkshire), 6 in the southwest (Ayrshire, Dumfriesshire, and Kirkudbrightshire), 3 in Stirlingshire, and 6 in Fife. A significant number came from the north and west. Eight were born in Angus and Perthshire, 14 in Aberdeenshire and Kincardineshire in the northeast, 6 along the Moray Firth in Morayshire, Banffshire, and Nairnshire, 8 in the Highlands and Islands proper, and 1 in the Orkneys. In fact, the number of Highlanders was even higher than this, because some individuals from Perthshire (such as Adam Ferguson) and Nairnshire (such as John Bethune) can also be considered among their number. Thus, although the Scottish Enlightenment was primarily a Lowland phenomenon, its authors came from all over Scotland. In addition, five of the figures in table 1 were born outside Scotland: two (Francis Hutcheson and Elizabeth Hamilton) to Scottish families in Ulster, and

4. Phillipson, *Scottish Whigs.*

one each in London (Alexander Monro *primus,* although the family returned to Scotland when he was a toddler), Bordeaux (Joseph Black, the son of a Scot from Belfast), and India (Robert Orme, the son of a surgeon in the East India Company).

The great majority learned to read and write English and do basic mathematics at local parish schools and at grammar or high schools, which also taught Latin. Some high-born young men such as Boswell and John Sinclair had private tutors (Sinclair's tutor was another figure from table 1, John Logan), and three attended prestigious English schools (James Bruce and Robert Orme at Harrow and Sir David Dalrymple at Eton). A few trained for commercial careers (e.g., Alexander Dow) or a trade (e.g., David Loch, who was bred a sailor, and William Russell and William Smellie, who were apprenticed in the book trade, although both attended classes at Edinburgh University while serving their apprenticeships). One (James Ferguson) was unusual in having virtually no formal education at all.

Even the two women in the database, the Belfast-born novelist and miscellaneous writer Elizabeth Hamilton and the playwright and poet Joanna Baillie, had some years of formal schooling, in Stirling and Glasgow, respectively. Although Scottish women sometimes had opportunities to attend public lectures and scientific demonstrations, they were denied access to the primary training grounds for authorship—grammar schools and universities—as well as clubs and societies. Hamilton and Baillie both made most of their contributions as authors in the early nineteenth century, when gender barriers to literary pursuits were gradually beginning to break down. In 1818 Elizabeth Benger observed, in regard to her friend Hamilton's move to Edinburgh fourteen years earlier: "A female literary character was even at that time a sort of phenomenon in Scotland. Even though most Scotchwomen read, and were not inferior to their southern neighbours in general information and good taste, very few had ventured to incur the dangerous distinction of authorship."[5]

It is significant that Benger used the word "dangerous" in this context, suggesting that Scottish women who wrote for publication were violating established conventions in a much more serious way than did women writers of late eighteenth-century England. For this reason, both Baillie and Hamilton were fortunate to have had successful, supportive brothers

---

5. Quoted from Benger, *Memoirs of Elizabeth Hamilton* (1818), in Thaddeus, "Elizabeth Hamilton's Domestic Politics," 271. Selections from some eighteenth-century Scottish women authors appear in McMillan, *Scotswoman.*

who brought them to London (in 1784 and 1788, respectively) and provided for them there, although the death of Hamilton's brother in 1792 forced her to take up residence outside the city and set the scene for her final move to Edinburgh in 1804. Women in eighteenth-century England also constituted a minority among the authors of books, but their numbers were substantial, especially in literary genres.[6] In Paris, where there were relatively few women authors, a handful of women played crucial roles in enlightened society through their work as salon managers.[7] By comparison, Scottish society remained provincial, and women not only had limited opportunities to participate in the primary institutions of Scottish intellectual life but also found it difficult to cultivate other institutions that might have served the same purpose. Alison Cockburn may have attracted some of the Edinburgh literati to her parlor,[8] but evidence of a salon life in the French or English sense is lacking until the early years of the nineteenth century. Although a number of male authors encouraged the efforts of women who dared to join their ranks, few seem to have tried.[9] The prevailing view toward female intellectual activity was

6. The literature on this topic is now too large to be cited fully here, but see Turner, *Living by the Pen*, which contains a database of 446 eighteenth-century books of prose fiction by 174 British women authors, very few of whom were Scottish; Todd, *Dictionary;* Jones, *Women and Literature;* Prescott, *Women;* Schellenberg, *Professionalization of Women Writers.*

7. Goodman, *Republic of Letters.* Robert Darnton counts only sixteen women among several hundred individuals identified as authors in mid-eighteenth-century Paris (*Great Cat Massacre,* 154). Hesse, *Other Enlightenment,* discusses the liberating effects of the French Revolution on women authors.

8. Graham, "Women of Letters," in *Scottish Men of Letters,* 311–54; and Graham, *Group of Scottish Women,* 178–98.

9. In 1772 Jean Marishall (or Jane Marshall) published in Edinburgh a comedy, *Sir Harry Gaylove,* with a prologue by Thomas Blacklock and a large subscription list that included James Beattie, James Boswell, Adam Ferguson, David Hume, Lord Kames, Henry Mackenzie, Thomas Reid, Gilbert Stuart, Alexander Fraser Tytler, and other names from table 1. Four years later, "Miss Edwards" published in Edinburgh *Miscellanies, in Prose and Verse,* with a subscription list containing the names of Beattie, Hume, Robertson, and many other leading Scottish authors. Elizabeth Hamilton contributed an essay to *The Lounger,* her first publication, and both she and Joanna Baillie were encouraged to pursue their writing by Dugald Stewart. The mathematician Mary Somerville received crucial encouragement from her uncle and father-in-law, Rev. Thomas Somerville, from the time she was a teenager in the 1790s. Neeley, *Mary Somerville,* 65.

still the cautious one articulated in John Gregory's best-selling *A Father's Legacy to His Daughters* (no. 163): "if you happen to have any learning, keep it a profound secret."[10]

Of the 113 male authors whose names appear in table 1, at least 105, or 93 percent, were educated, at least in part, at one or more of Scotland's universities. In the 97 cases in which the specific universities or colleges can be identified, two-thirds attended the University of Edinburgh exclusively or in combination with other educational institutions—more than attended the other four Scottish colleges combined.[11] Well-prepared students typically entered Scottish universities at around the age of thirteen or fourteen. They normally pursued first a basic arts course that included Latin, Greek, mathematics, logic, natural philosophy, and moral philosophy. At least 25 percent of these authors are known to have earned an M.A. (the equivalent of a formal undergraduate degree), despite the fact that doing so was increasingly unnecessary for students pursuing advanced professional training. Such students proceeded to take courses in law, medicine, or divinity, although those bound for the less prestigious levels of the legal profession (i.e., writers as opposed to advocates) and the medical profession (i.e., surgeons as opposed to physicians) commonly served an apprenticeship with a practitioner instead of (or, in some cases, before) pursuing advanced coursework and a formal thesis or examination. At least twenty-one, or almost 19 percent, enriched their education with study outside Scotland. Most of these were physicians and lawyers, about half of whom went to Leiden in the Netherlands, often supplemented by London and Paris for those in medicine, and less frequently by other European cities such as Berlin, Utrecht, and Groningen. The English universities were not a very attractive option by comparison with the Scottish ones or the Continent, although six individuals in table 1 studied for a time at Oxford and one at Cambridge. Earned doctorates did not exist other than the M.D. degree, but British universities regularly awarded the D.D. degree to clergymen and the LL.D. degree to laymen as honorary distinctions, usually in recognition of their accomplishments, combined with the right connections and the payment of a fee. At least thirty of the

10. Quoted in Marshall, *Virgins and Viragos*, 221. See Moran, "From Rudeness to Refinement."

11. At least 26 attended the University of Glasgow at some time or other, at least 21 one of the Aberdeen colleges, at least 9 St. Andrews University, and 7 a Scottish university (or more than one) that cannot be identified with certainty.

nonmedical authors in table 1 gained the right to be addressed as Dr. in this manner, and more than two dozen others earned the same right by virtue of an M.D. degree.

The authors in table 1 lend strong support to the view that the Scottish Enlightenment was dominated by professional men who were well integrated into the institutional infrastructure. More than two-thirds of them (79) were trained for a career in the clergy (33, or about 29 percent), medicine (27, or 23 percent), or law (19, or 17 percent, counting Sir James Mackintosh, who was qualified in both medicine and law, as a lawyer). A fourth major profession, education, overlapped the others. At least 42 (37 percent) of the individuals in table 1 were at one time or another professors or principals at one or more of Scotland's five institutions of higher learning: the universities of Edinburgh, Glasgow, and St. Andrews, and the two Aberdeen colleges, King's and Marischal, which would later merge to form the University of Aberdeen. Of these 42 academics, there were 14 Church of Scotland ministers, 12 physicians or surgeons, 3 advocates, and 13 who came from outside these professions. The classes they taught covered the full range of contemporary academic subjects, including moral philosophy, natural philosophy, logic, mathematics, chemistry, Latin and Greek, history, rhetoric and belles lettres, divinity, law, and the various branches of medicine. The five who rose to positions as college or university principals had considerable authority over all academic matters at their respective institutions. Add to these figures the rector of Edinburgh High School (Alexander Adam), an itinerant science lecturer (James Ferguson), an educator of young women (Elizabeth Hamilton), a law professor at the East India College at Hertford (Sir James Mackintosh), many individuals who served as private tutors or teachers, and several physicians who lectured on anatomy, midwifery, and other subjects outside the Scottish universities, and one begins to get a sense of the huge role that education played in the careers of these Scottish authors. Even when the category of educator is restricted to formal university appointments in Scotland, some 92 individuals, or 81 percent of the male database, can be categorized as belonging in some way to the four major professions of church, medicine, law, and education.[12] Nor do these totals

12. These figures, however, include a number of men who did not practice long (if at all) in the profession for which they were trained, such as James Hutton and Mungo Park in medicine, George Chalmers, John Pinkerton, Sir John Sinclair, Sir James Steuart, and Gilbert Stuart in law, and Thomas Blacklock, Robert Heron, John Home, and William Thomson in the clergy.

include other professional men in the database, such as the architect Robert Adam and civil servants and administrators such as Sir John Sinclair, Patrick Brydone, Alexander Dow, James Macpherson, and Robert Orme. Even Robert Burns, the poetic apostle of the common man, secured a minor position in the excise.

The overwhelmingly professional character of these authors helped to fix the prevailing tone of the Scottish Enlightenment: stable, scholarly, and sociable. The involvement of so many Scottish authors with the Scottish universities often gave their publications a didactic, professorial air. Several of the books in table 1 were published university lectures, such as Hugh Blair's *Lectures on Rhetoric and Belles Lettres* (no. 230), Charles Alston's *Lectures on the Materia Medica* (no. 122), John Gregory's *Lectures on the Duties and Qualifications of a Physician* (no. 129, to use the authorized title of that work), William Cullen's *Lectures on Materia Medica* (no. 145), Adam Ferguson's *Principles of Moral and Political Science* (no. 303), and George Campbell's *Lectures on Ecclesiastical History* (no. 355). Other books, such as Adam Smith's *Theory of Moral Sentiments* and *Wealth of Nations*, were drawn from classroom lectures but reshaped so as not to appear that way. James Beattie, after publishing his academic lectures on language, memory, and imagination "in the same form in which they were first composed" in his *Essays* of 1776 (no. 173), produced an "abridgement" in 1790–93 of his entire moral philosophy course, in two volumes of more than a thousand pages, under the title *Elements of Moral Science* (no. 291, quoting the advertisement prefixed to the first volume).

Some professors published book-length outlines of their lectures for the benefit of their own students, and the appeal of these works sometimes extended far beyond their classrooms. Examples include Adam Ferguson's *Institutes of Moral Philosophy* (no. 117), John Anderson's *Institutes of Physics* (no. 257), John Walker's *Institutes of Natural History* (no. 310), and Dugald Stewart's *Outlines of Moral Philosophy* (no. 320). In the preface to the first version of his *Institutes* (1777), Anderson explained that such outlines performed an important pedagogical function, providing enough guidance "to guard against the inaccuracies into which young students are apt to fall" but not enough information to prevent students from "taking notes: a custom by which their attention and ingenuity is constantly exercised; and the experiments and lectures become, as it were, their own."[13] Others published lectures delivered outside the universities, such as *Lectures on Select Subjects in Mechanics, Hydrostatics, Pneumatics, and Optics* (no. 61),

13. Anderson, preface to *Institutes of Physics* (1777).

which James Ferguson brought out in 1760 as a guide to his popular science presentations; William Hunter's posthumous *Two Introductory Lectures* (no. 243) of 1784, taken from lectures that Hunter had delivered at his anatomy school in London; and *Elements of the Philosophy of History, Part First* (no. 215), which John Logan published in 1781 to accompany and publicize a private course of lectures given in Edinburgh in an effort to secure a university chair.

The celebrated sociability that prevailed among the authors of the Scottish Enlightenment occurred in a wide range of locations, from informal sites of cultural interaction, including taverns, coffeehouses, and private homes, to formal societies. In the latter category were, first, professional organizations such as the Faculty of Advocates, the Society of Writers to the Signet, the Royal College of Physicians of Edinburgh, and the Royal College of Surgeons of Edinburgh. Among other things, these professional bodies often contributed to intellectual life by maintaining libraries that could be used by all men of letters. Of formal Scottish learned societies, the most prestigious was the Royal Society of Edinburgh, which evolved from the Philosophical Society of Edinburgh in 1783.[14] Although modeled in some respects on the most famous British organization for the study of the natural sciences, the Royal Society of London, the RSE initially differed from the RSL by encompassing all areas of polite learning. No fewer than 51 of the authors named in table 1 were fellows of either the "literary" or "physical" class of the RSE (including several nonresidential fellows), which amounts to 59 percent of the 86 men from the table who were alive when the society was founded. Sixteen of these 51 RSE fellows were also RSL fellows, and 12 others from table 1 were fellows of the RSL though not fellows of the RSE. In addition, 16 authors whose names appear in table 1 (including 4 who were not affiliated with the RSE or the RSL) were fellows of another formal learned body that emerged in Edinburgh during the last two decades of the century, the Society of Antiquaries of Scotland (established 1780; royal charter 1783). After adding 6 members of the Philosophical Society of Edinburgh who died before it became the RSE and who were not fellows of the RSL or the Society of Antiquaries, we find that 73 of the 113 male authors listed in table 1 (65 percent) belonged to at least one of these elite learned societies.

Less formal learned societies were based at the universities in Glasgow

14. See the series of articles by Roger L. Emerson on the Philosophical Society of Edinburgh. For Scottish clubs and societies generally, see McElroy, *Scotland's Age of Improvement.*

and Aberdeen: the Glasgow Literary Society (17 members from table 1) and the Aberdeen Philosophical Society or Wise Club (7 members from table 1). Despite their names, which suggest narrow specialization of subject matter, both of these clubs dealt with all fields of polite learning. There were also improving societies such as the Select Society (20 members from table 1) and its two practical offshoots—the Edinburgh Society for the Encouragement of Arts, Sciences, Manufactures, and Agriculture in Scotland, and the Society for Promoting the Reading and Speaking of the English Language in Scotland—and the Highland Society of Scotland (at least 9 members from table 1), which was also based in Edinburgh.[15]

These organizations had direct connections with the production of print culture in Scotland. Several of the learned societies published volumes of papers that had been delivered at their meetings (e.g., nos. 34, 279, and 353), and it was not uncommon for their members to present papers that would later be expanded into books of their own. Examples from table 2 include books that developed partly or wholly from Aberdeen Philosophical Society dissertations by Thomas Reid (nos. 88, 255, and 275), John Gregory (no. 90), James Beattie (nos. 123, 173, and parts of other works), George Campbell (no. 174), and James Dunbar (no. 206); from Glasgow Literary Society discourses by James Moor (no. 57), Thomas Reid (nos. 255 and 275), and John Millar (no. 271); from Edinburgh Philosophical Society or Royal Society of Edinburgh papers by Robert Whytt (nos. 21 and 110), Robert Wallace (no. 28), James Lind (no. 82), William Alexander (no. 103), Joseph Black (no. 180), James Gregory (no. 304), and James Hutton (no. 332); and from Royal Society of London discourses by William Alexander (no. 103), Robert Whytt (no. 110), Sir John Pringle (no. 236), and John Hunter (no. 265). At least three books, by Alexander Gerard (nos. 53 and 162) and Adam Dickson (no. 79), were written in response to prizes offered by the Edinburgh Society for the Encouragement of Arts, Sciences, Manufactures, and Agriculture. In February 1755 this society announced a premium for "the best printed and most correct Book," followed by five prizes for improvements in the processing of linen for making paper.[16]

Insofar as these books were revised for publication on the basis of com-

15. Emerson, "Social Composition of Enlightened Scotland"; Sher, "Commerce"; Emerson and Wood, "Science and Enlightenment"; Ulman, "Minutes of the Aberdeen Philosophical Society."

16. *Scots Magazine* (February 1755), quoted in McElroy, *Scotland's Age of Improvement*, 50–51.

ments and criticisms by members of these societies who heard oral renditions of earlier drafts or read them privately, the social aspect of Scottish club life takes on a high degree of importance for book culture.[17] The presentation of knowledge was understood to be dialectical and cumulative, partly because of the interplay of orality and print, but also because continued research brought about revisions and expansions. When James Lind published his *Two Papers on Fevers and Infection* (no. 82) in 1763, he addressed the second paper to his colleagues in the Philosophical Society of Edinburgh but added in a postscript: "Since these papers were read before the Society, and afterwards revised and enlarged, an unwearied attention to this subject, together with three years observations on fevers, in addition to those related in Paper 1st, have abundantly confirmed their contents" (114).

Freemasonry also deserves mention here, as a fraternal cosmopolitan organization that encouraged and spread enlightened principles and provided another homosocial milieu for Scottish men of letters.[18] At least twenty-four individuals from table 1 (and probably many more) were masons, no fewer than sixteen at Lodge Canongate, Kilwinning No. 2, in Edinburgh. It is significant that they included physicians, judges, professors, and gentlemen such as John and James Gregory, Alexander Monro *secundus*, John Brown, James Bruce, William Buchan, Lord Monboddo, Lord Hailes, Henry Mackenzie, John Millar, Andrew Duncan, James Boswell, Sir John Sinclair, and the noble Earl of Buchan, as well as men from humbler occupations, such as Robert Burns and the printer William Smellie, and even an occasional Presbyterian minister such as Matthew Stewart.[19] Masonic lodges also provided opportunities for authors to associate with booksellers such as Alexander Kincaid, Alexander Donaldson, and William Creech. Although it is usually difficult to connect freemasonry with the production of specific Enlightenment books, we shall see that the Edinburgh edition of Robert Burns's *Poems* fits this pattern in certain respects.[20]

17. Sher, "Science and Medicine," 131–34.

18. On the broader connections between freemasonry and the European Enlightenment, see Jacob, *Living the Enlightenment*. Although women sometimes participated in freemasonry on the Continent, they did not do so in Scotland.

19. A. Mackenzie, *History*, 237–47, as corrected against the manuscript roll book.

20. On freemasonry and Scottishness in Burns's poetry, see Andrews, *Literary Nationalism*, chap. 3.

Less formal, and more convivial, organizations included the Poker Club in Edinburgh, which was formed to agitate for a Scots militia (9 members from table 1), the Oyster Club in Edinburgh (11 members), Robert Simson's Friday Club or Anderston Club in Glasgow (at least 8 members), and the rowdy Crochallan Fencibles Club in Edinburgh to which Burns, Smellie, and Stuart belonged. If these convivial clubs did not generally have the direct connections with the books of the Scottish Enlightenment that one finds in the more formal, learned societies, there were exceptions. The Mirror Club, for example, was an Edinburgh convivial and charitable body that produced *The Mirror* (no. 217) and *The Lounger* (no. 270) under the direction of its leading member, Henry Mackenzie.[21] Even when the connections between these organizations and published books were not this straightforward, the Scottish convivial clubs fostered a sociable atmosphere that was often conducive to literature and learning.

The Oyster Club is a good example. Founded in Edinburgh by three prominent men of letters—Adam Smith, Joseph Black, and James Hutton—it added to its membership, among others, Robert Adam, Hugh Blair, William Cullen, Adam Ferguson, Henry Mackenzie, John Playfair, William Robertson, and Dugald Stewart. As Playfair wrote in his biography of Hutton, "the conversation was always free, often scientific, but never didactic or disputatious." The meetings were frequently attended by "strangers who visited Edinburgh, from any object connected with art or with science,"[22] so that the members regularly engaged in free and open exchanges of information and ideas in a convivial setting. This was precisely the ambiance of learned cosmopolitanism that, according to William Smellie, distinguished intellectual life in Edinburgh from other European cultural capitals:

> In London, Paris, and all other great cities of Europe, though they contain many literary men, the access to them is difficult; and even after that is obtained, the conversation, for some time, is shy and constrained. In Edinburgh, the access to men of parts is not only easy, but their conversation and the communication of their knowledge are at once imparted to intelligent strangers with the utmost liberality. The philosophers of Scotland have no nostrums. They tell what they know, and deliver their sentiments without disguise or reserve.[23]

21. Dwyer, *Virtuous Discourse*.
22. Playfair quoted in McElroy, *Scotland's Age of Improvement*, 169.
23. Kerr, *Memoirs*, 2:252–54.

Meetings were typically held in taverns, where claret was the beverage of choice. Drinking constituted a vital component of these convivial organizations, but food was also important. "You may rather call them the *Iterati* (Eaterati)," quipped one Edinburgh woman as a group of literati strolled past at around the dinner hour.[24]

Smellie famously quoted the observations of one English visitor to Edinburgh during the third quarter of the eighteenth century, who located the uniqueness of the city's intellectual life in the urban congestion of the Old Town. "Here stand I at what is called the *Cross of Edinburgh*," he marveled, "and can in a few minutes take fifty men of genius and learning by the hand."[25] In clarifying his subject's meaning, Smellie's biographer, Robert Kerr, explained that the "respectable inhabitants" of Edinburgh traditionally gathered at the cross in the High Street between the hours of one and three o'clock to socialize and "discuss the topics of the day." "They were further led to this habit," he added, "because all the coffee houses and booksellers shops, the usual lounges of literary idle hours, were then around the cross." Kerr employed the past tense because by the time he published this account in 1811, the physical expansion of the city had diffused the older pattern of intimate socialization: "Coffee houses and booksellers shops are now dispersed in many places; and literary men are not now to be found at the cross in change hours, as formally."

Perhaps the best way to visualize the vibrant cultural space that nourished the Edinburgh Enlightenment is to imagine a circle with St. Giles Church at its center. On one side of that church was the High Street, extending from Edinburgh Castle in the west to Holyrood Palace in the east. The Cross to which Kerr alluded was a small octagonal building in the High Street, a short distance east of St. Giles (fig. 2.1). Although the Cross itself was torn down in 1756 to facilitate urban circulation, people continued to gather on the spot where it had stood from one to three o'clock each afternoon, "for news, business, or meeting their acquaintances."[26] Adjacent to St. Giles stood the Luckenbooths (fig. 2.1), a ramshackle four-story commercial building, torn down in 1817, which jutted out into the High Street even more obtrusively than the Cross. The booksellers James M'Euen, Alexander Kincaid, and William Creech occupied in succession the prize location at the eastern end of the Luckenbooths, facing the Cross. Many other bookshops and printing offices were located directly

24. Mackenzie, *Anecdotes*, 179.

25. Kerr, *Memoirs*, 2:252.

26. Arnot, *History of Edinburgh*, 304.

Luckenbooths. Ancient Cross and Ramsay's Shop

High Street. Edinburgh

Fig. 2.1. In this engraving of the High Street by W. Forrest, the octagonal Cross that was the center of mid-eighteenth-century social life in Edinburgh is shown in the foreground, while the commercial Luckenbooths appears at the top, next to St. Giles Church. Frontispiece to volume 2 of *The Works of Allan Ramsay*, 3 vols. (London and Edinburgh: A. Fullarton & Co., 1848). Author's collection.

on and just off the High Street in the same area, and the university was just a short distance away. The south side of St. Giles bordered Parliament Square, marked by an equestrian statue of Charles II (fig. 2.2). Although the statue and square still stand, the shops and stalls that made this space a bustling commercial and cultural center are long since gone. In the late eighteenth century, book stalls lined the south side of the square, against

Fig. 2.2. This mid-nineteenth-century mixed etching and aquatint by John Le Conte and Thomas Dobbie, after a collaborative oil painting by Sir David Wilkie, Alexander Nasmyth, and others (with figures by John Kay), shows the bustle of Edinburgh's Parliament Square as it might have looked at the end of the eighteenth century. Bell & Bradfute's bookshop (formerly owned by Charles Elliot) is visible along the east side of the square, next to John's Coffeehouse. National Gallery of Scotland.

buildings that the Scottish Parliament occupied until the Union of 1707. After the Union those buildings housed the courts and members of the legal profession, including the magnificent Advocates' Library (precursor of the National Library of Scotland), where David Hume and Adam Ferguson served in succession as keepers during the 1750s and where many Scottish Enlightenment figures conducted research for their books.[27] Along the east side of Parliament Square was a particularly important

27. Cadell and Matheson, *Encouragement of Learning;* I. Brown, *Building for Books.*

Fig. 2.3. *James Sibbald's Circulating Library* (1856), by William Borthwick Johnstone. *From left to right:* Hugh Blair, Henry Mackenzie, Robert Burns, Alexander Nasmyth, David Allan, James Bruce, Lord Monboddo, his daughter Elizabeth Burnet[t], Sibbald, Adam Ferguson, and young Walter Scott. The painting hangs in the Writers' Museum, Edinburgh. Edinburgh Booksellers' Society Limited.

bookshop, occupied by Charles Elliot until his death and then, from 1791 onward, by Bell & Bradfute (far right of fig. 2.2).

The book culture of old Edinburgh is brilliantly captured in William Borthwick Johnstone's mid-nineteenth-century painting of the interior of James Sibbald's circulating library as it might have looked in late 1786 or early 1787 (fig. 2.3). The picture is supposed to represent a historic moment in Scottish literary history, when young Walter Scott (far right) cast his eyes upon Robert Burns, whose *Poems, Chiefly in the Scottish Dialect* (no. 260) was taking Edinburgh by storm. Burns is shown conversing with the two leading Scottish literary authorities of the day, Hugh Blair and Henry Mackenzie. A separate conversation occupies two artists, Alexander Nasmyth (whose famous full-length painting of Burns provided the basis for Johnstone's portrayal of the poet) and David Allan (who would soon illustrate some of Burns's poems). In the background, the proprietor of the establishment, James Sibbald, who had been the first to draw public attention to the virtues of Burns's Kilmarnock edition in a review in the October 1786 issue of his *Edinburgh Magazine*, pulls a book from the shelf for James Burnett, Lord Monboddo. Adam Ferguson reads intently through a magnifying glass, while the African explorer James Bruce, towering over the rest of the company, seems more interested in Monboddo's daughter Eliza—immortalized as "Fair B[urnett]" in the "Address to Edinburgh" that Burns was in the process of adding to the second edition of his *Poems*.

Of course, there is no evidence that these particular individuals ever congregated at Sibbald's shop in exactly this way. Yet the spirit of the painting rings true. Most of the figures in Johnstone's picture interacted extensively with Burns during his visit to Edinburgh in 1786–87, and Scott later remarked that he had a "distant view" of Burns at Sibbald's, among other "literary characters."[28] Located along the east side of Parliament Square, close to Elliot's bookshop and John's Coffeehouse, Sibbald's establishment was one of the centerpieces of late eighteenth-century Edinburgh book culture, with some twenty thousand volumes in several European languages, in addition to music and art prints.[29] Here artists and authors (and future authors) of novels, poems, and books on philosophy, history, literary criticism, sermons, travel, and other subjects engaged in reading, browsing, conversing, and socializing. These forms of interaction occurred in an intimate space, included women as well as men, and spanned the generations, from Monboddo in his seventies and Blair and Ferguson in their sixties to Burns in his twenties and Scott in his teens.

"The True Scene for a Man of Letters"

The participation of Scottish authors in formal and informal organizations and the culture of taverns, coffeehouses, professional and circulating libraries, and bookshops reflected the fundamentally urban character of the Scottish Enlightenment. "In 1751, I removed from the Countrey to the Town; the true Scene for a man of Letters," wrote David Hume in "My Own Life" (*LDH*, 1:3). Hume's migration to Edinburgh serves as a metaphor for the Scottish Enlightenment as a whole. With few exceptions, such as several clergymen residing in country parishes, Robert Burns and others who tried farming for a time, and two or three individuals whose

28. Quoted in Warren McDougall's biography of Sibbald in *ODNB*.
29. Sibbald, *New Catalogue*.

careers lay mainly outside Britain (e.g., Orme and Park), Scottish Enlightenment authors tended to reside in or very near towns—and Edinburgh was overwhelmingly the town of choice. More than half of them (at least sixty-two and very possibly more than that) lived there for a significant portion of their adult lives, including twenty professors at the university.

The centrality of Edinburgh may be gauged in many ways. The Scottish book trade was based there, and men of letters viewed it as their capital. A number of Scottish professors were drawn to Edinburgh from Glasgow or Aberdeen by academic appointments (e.g., Black, Cullen, Gregory, and Maclaurin), but Edinburgh's centrifugal pull went far beyond the lure of its university chairs. A majority of the most important clubs and societies were in Edinburgh, and only Edinburgh, among eighteenth-century Scottish towns, was large and diverse enough to sustain an urban Enlightenment that significantly transcended the local universities and their auxiliary institutions. Ambitious clergymen tried to secure parish charges there, and those who succeeded often did so in large part because of their reputations as authors. Medical men and scientists gravitated there if they could, as did advocates, writers to the signet, and judges. Landed gentlemen could and often did divide their time between their country estates and Edinburgh without the inconvenience and expense that was associated with life in London.

This combination of sociability, urbanity, proximity, professionalism, and authorship gave Edinburgh its reputation as the "Athens of the North" or the "Athens of Britain," as Thomas Sheridan called it in the early 1760s. Like Smollett's "hot-bed of genius," this phrase, or some variation of it, obtained much of its credibility from the accomplishments of the Edinburgh literati as the writers of learned and literary books. In the "greatly enlarged" third edition of his *View of the British Empire* (no. 244), published in 1785, John Knox observed: "This city is considered as the modern Athens, in politeness, science, and literature. The writings of its professors, divines, and lawyers, are every where read and admired."[30] Knox discussed Edinburgh's excellent resources and "respectable schools for both sexes; a celebrated university, in which arts, science, philosophy, and all the branches of literature, are taught on easy terms; academies; literary societies; a flourishing botanic garden; an observatory; public libraries, and all the fashionable amusements" (583). But without the presence of so many universally admired authors, these attributes would not

30. Knox, *View*, 3rd ed., 580.

have entitled Edinburgh to consideration as a city of international greatness. Polite culture and print culture were the twin bulwarks upon which the legacy of the "modern Athens" was constructed.

If Edinburgh was the capital of the Scottish Enlightenment, Glasgow and Aberdeen were also important cultural centers. Despite its small size and its location well up the northeast coast, Aberdeen was able to exert a disproportionately large influence on Scottish intellectual life through its two colleges and its academic-based philosophical society.[31] No fewer than eleven professors at King's and Marischal colleges—James Beattie, Thomas Blackwell, George Campbell, James Dunbar, William Duncan, David Fordyce, Alexander Gerard, John Gregory, Colin Maclaurin, William Ogilvie, and Thomas Reid—made names for themselves as authors of books in moral philosophy, history, religion, logic, medicine, literary criticism, mathematics, music, and other fields of learning. Although several were Presbyterian ministers, the distinguishing feature of Aberdonian culture was its Episcopalian influence, which moderated the strong Calvinist sentiments that were prevalent in some other regions of Scotland. In part for that reason, and because they lacked the ties with Dutch and other continental Calvinists that were found in larger Scottish towns, Aberdonians often had close ties with England.[32] A number migrated to London, and some, such as James Fordyce and William Guthrie, distinguished themselves as authors there. Still other Aberdonian authors who were not academics remained in Scotland, such as the poet John Ogilvie (minister of the Aberdeenshire parish of Midmar) and the agricultural improver James Anderson.

Glasgow forms a striking contrast.[33] Whereas Aberdeen was the most Episcopalian and least Calvinist of Scottish towns, Glasgow was the opposite. When Thomas Reid moved from Aberdeen to Glasgow in 1764, he was struck by the "gloomy, enthusiastical cast" of the "common people."[34] Looking westward, Glasgow had strong ties with Ireland and America and developed a particularly imposing commercial and industrial presence, based first on tobacco and later on cotton. Its university (which had its own academic club, the Glasgow Literary Society) featured a succession of

---

31. Emerson, *Professors;* Wood, *Aberdeen Enlightenment;* Ulman, *Minutes;* Conrad, *Citizenship;* Carter and Pittock, *Aberdeen.*

32. Wood, "Aberdeen and Europe," 119–42.

33. For a fuller discussion of what follows, see Sher, "Commerce," 312–59, and Hook and Sher, *Glasgow Enlightenment.*

34. Reid to Andrew Skene, 14 Nov. 1764, in Reid, *Philosophical Works,* 1:40.

prominent teachers and authors over the course of the century, including John Anderson in natural philosophy; Francis Hutcheson, Adam Smith, and Thomas Reid in moral philosophy; William Leechman in divinity; John Millar in law; James Moor in Greek; William Richardson in literary criticism; Robert Simson in mathematics; and—until their departures for Edinburgh University—Joseph Black and William Cullen in chemistry and medicine. Glasgow University emphasized a particular brand of classicism that crossed disciplinary boundaries, but it also cultivated a practical, applied species of learning. Both are evident in the university's emphasis on the arts, understood not only in the classical, aesthetic sense of that term (the fine arts) but also in the sense of practical activities and technologies (the applied or mechanical arts), which often utilized science in the service of commerce and industry. Both forms were taught at the academy founded in 1753 by the Foulis brothers, Robert and Andrew, who trained young men to paint according to aesthetic principles as well as to execute such practical arts as engraving and calico printing.[35] As the university printers and members of the Glasgow Literary Society in their own right, the brothers published a famous series of classical Latin and Greek texts edited by members of the faculty and embodying both the principles of classicism and fine craftsmanship.

Taken together, Aberdeen, Glasgow, and Edinburgh constituted a potent urban trio during the late eighteenth century. Each town embodied a distinct cultural ethos, yet they all had fine universities, societies, and other institutions that nurtured an extraordinarily rich intellectual environment. All three were crucial components of the Scottish Enlightenment. Scotland's other university town, St. Andrews, also had a part to play on a smaller scale. In all of Scotland, however, only Edinburgh had a book trade of sufficient size and diversity to sustain an ongoing program for transforming this intellectual activity into print. Authors came from all over the country and congregated in all the university towns, but as we shall see in chapter 4, within Scotland the publication of enlightened new books was heavily concentrated in the capital.

Besides Edinburgh, Glasgow, and Aberdeen, the fourth major urban center that many Scottish Enlightenment authors called home was London. At least twenty-eight individuals in table 1, or 24 percent of the total, lived in London for a year or more during their adult lives, and at least two others lived part of their lives in other areas of England—though only seven of these thirty (Hume, John Hunter, James Macpherson, Mickle,

---

35. Fairfull-Smith, *Foulis Press.*

Moore, Smollett, and Stuart) were among those whom Creech, Smollett, and Alves mentioned in their boasts about the accomplishments of Scottish authors. In his recent study of the "British Enlightenment," Roy Porter argues that London "certainly lured the literati" from Scotland, who found it less narrow and restrictive than Scottish towns. This alleged preference becomes the foundation for a broader distinction that Porter draws between "lively England and languishing Scotland."[36] Of course, London, a city of 650,000 or more people at the middle of the eighteenth century, and nearly a million by the end, is hardly comparable to towns like Edinburgh, Glasgow, and Aberdeen, which had midcentury populations of only about 50,000, 30,000, and 15,000, respectively. London was unquestionably the political, economic, and cultural center of Britain and the British Empire, as it was also the hub of the British book trade. Scots who visited London for the first time were invariably startled by its vast size, its anonymity, and its opportunities for almost every kind of amusement and activity. Vast pleasure gardens like Vauxhall and Ranelagh, the theaters at Drury Lane and Covent Garden, the shops in the Strand, the promenade on Pall Mall, the colorful coffeehouses and well-stocked bookshops, the treasures at the British Museum—there was simply nothing else like it. It is therefore to be expected that some Scottish men of letters wished to be more than visitors. Porter quotes Robert Adam and David Hume on the attractiveness of London, and England generally, and evidence of this kind could also be cited from Boswell's journals, Monboddo's letters, and many other sources.[37] "I am more and more convinced that a man used to London cannot well live out of it," wrote Sir John Pringle in a letter from Bath to another Scotsman who had adopted London as his home. "I am starving for want of good coffee."[38]

Such evidence, however, cannot sustain Porter's sweeping generalizations about London and Edinburgh, England and Scotland, the Scottish Enlightenment and the British (or English) Enlightenment. Although Porter acknowledges that Hume sometimes hurled sharp invective at "the Barbarians who inhabit the Banks of the Thames,"[39] he omits to say that

36. Porter, *Enlightenment*, 242, 246.

37. Monboddo went to London almost every spring when the Court of Session was not sitting. See Cloyd, *James Burnett Lord Monboddo*, 93, 105, 134.

38. Pringle to William Strahan, 24 May 1779, NLS, Acc. 7997.

39. *LDH*, 1:436, quoted in Porter, *Enlightenment*, 243. For a fuller discussion of Hume's view, see Livingston, "Hume," 133–47.

both the men whom he cites as examples of the Scottish literati's prefer-ence for London and England, David Hume and Robert Adam, elected to return to Edinburgh late in life. They did so not because Scotland was "languishing" but for exactly the opposite reason: for men of letters, Scotland, and especially Edinburgh, displayed a degree of intellectual vi-tality and excitement that London could not match. After Robert Adam returned to Edinburgh, he contributed to the Scottish Enlightenment by drawing up plans for rebuilding the university in 1789 and by design-ing splendid neoclassical buildings and spaces in the New Town, such as Charlotte Square.[40] A quarter of a century earlier, Hume, who had re-sided for some years in London and was becoming wealthy enough to live anywhere he pleased, put it bluntly in a letter to Hugh Blair from Paris, when pondering where to spend his remaining years: "If a man have the Misfortune in [London] . . . to attach himself to Letters, even if he suc-ceeds, I know not with whom he is to live, nor how he is to pass his time in a suitable Society. The little Company there, that is worth conversing with, are cold and unsociable or are warmd only by Faction and Cabal" (*LDH*, 1:497–98). In Paris, by contrast, "a man that distinguishes himself in Letters, meets immediately with Regard and Attention." That is why Hume experienced "great wavering and uncertainty between Paris and Edinburgh," which he considered the two most desirable cities for a man of letters, but "never allow'd London to enter into the Question" (*LDH*, 1:527). Although this assessment was harsh, it was not unique to Hume. In 1767 the Anglican clergyman William Johnson Temple wrote to James Boswell in a similar vein, contrasting the intimate, instructive, well-bred, and "honourable" literati of Edinburgh with their "ill-bred" and pedantic counterparts in England.[41] "No attachments here," Temple wrote in his diary when visiting the capital sixteen years later. "Every one indifferent to another. Neither literature nor any thing appears of consequence."[42]

Eighteenth-century London contained no universities and few institu-tions to which a reasonably learned individual like Temple might go to interact with men of letters on an equal footing. Accomplished men of sci-ence had access to the Royal Society of London; antiquaries, dilettantes, and artists had their specialized societies and academies; and anyone could visit the British Museum. But the Enlightenment as a whole was not al-

40. Sanderson, *Robert Adam;* Fraser, *Building of Old College*, chaps. 3 and 4.
41. Boswell, *Correspondence of Boswell and Temple*, 188.
42. Temple, *Diaries*, 42.

ways well served. It is true that The Club contained, in Edward Gibbon's striking phrase, "a large and luminous constellation of British stars":[43] Sir Joshua Reynolds, Samuel Johnson, Oliver Goldsmith, and Edmund Burke were among its founders, and its membership eventually included Gibbon, Thomas Percy, Sir Joseph Banks, and several other prominent men of learning, including three Scottish literati found in table 1 (Adam Smith, George Fordyce, and James Boswell). But The Club was less a learned or literary society than an exclusive supper (and subsequently dinner) club for the Reynolds circle, chatty and sometimes catty in the Johnsonian manner, and infrequently attended by most of its members.[44]

Besides Hume and Adam, a number of other figures whose names appear in table 1 returned to Scotland after making their fortunes or reputations in London or elsewhere. Having acquired wealth as a bookseller and publisher in the Strand, John Knox dedicated his later years to encouraging Scottish economic improvement, especially in the Highlands. As a member of Parliament from 1780 onward, Sir John Sinclair had to be in London during part of the year, but from the mid-1780s he made his home in Edinburgh and kept his large family there.[45] James Bruce returned to his estate at Kinnaird in Stirlingshire after his remarkable adventures in Africa. Others, such as William Duncan and John Gregory, hastened back to Scotland from London to accept academic appointments as soon as they were offered, or came back under other circumstances. Still others had opportunities to make careers in London but declined them, in some cases deliberately choosing "comfort and content" over the likelihood of "rank and wealth," as Henry Mackenzie put it, when explaining his decision to return to Edinburgh as a young man, though "urged to remain in London" by friends in the legal profession.[46] In the early 1760s William Robertson resisted Lord Bute's entreaties that he move to London to write a history of England under the earl's patronage, and later in that decade, and again in the early 1780s, William Smellie passed up the chance to manage the Strahan printing house in London.[47] In 1774 James Beattie declined two firm offers of clerical livings in the Church of England, one of them worth considerably more than his current income.[48] Pronounce-

43. Gibbon, *Memoirs*, 166.

44. *Annals of The Club*.

45. Mitchison, *Agricultural Sir John*, 62–63, 96–97.

46. Mackenzie, *Anecdotes*, 190, 186.

47. Sher, *Church and University*, 112–13; Kerr, *Memoirs*, 1:325–28.

48. Forbes, *Account*, 1:358–64.

ments expressing a preference for Scotland were common among Scottish men of letters who knew London well.[49]

A disproportionately large number of the Scottish authors who headed south for more than relatively brief periods fall into two main categories: medical men and frustrated aspirants to Scottish careers. Scottish surgeons and physicians invaded London early and enjoyed opportunities there that simply were not available to the practitioners of any other Scottish learned profession.[50] Doctors Alexander, Baillie, Fordyce, John and William Hunter, Donald Monro, Pringle, and Smellie were among those who flocked to the metropolis, often with great success. The process was exemplified by William Hunter, a younger son of a struggling Lanarkshire laird, who was trained by William Cullen and Alexander Monro in Scotland, and then by William Smellie and another Scottish doctor, James Douglas, in London. Hunter built his own anatomy lecture theater in London and announced to his students that "it is in your power not only to *chuse*, but to *have*, which rank you please in the world."[51] True to his own words, he made a fortune from a combination of his practice as a male midwife, his lectures on anatomy, and financial speculation, and then he spent it in the manner of an aristocratic connoisseur and patron, amassing a huge collection of rare books, manuscripts, paintings, specimens, coins, and other artifacts that he bequeathed at the time of his death in 1783 to the University of Glasgow for the improvement of its students and the use of the public.[52] Toward the end of the century Hunter's nephew and heir, Matthew Baillie, the son of a Church of Scotland minister, established a London medical practice that was said to be worth £10,000 a year.[53]

Others went to London chiefly because they could not make a living in Scotland, or at least could not fulfill their aspirations there. Among physicians, John Brown was disappointed in his quest for a medical chair at the University of Edinburgh and his application to the Edinburgh Philosophical Society, became embittered toward his mentor William Cullen for blocking him, and finally went to London for the last two miserable years of his life. William Buchan also ran afoul of Cullen as he tried to

49. Sher, *Church and University*, 214–15.

50. Guerrini, "Scotsman on the Make," 157–76.

51. Hunter, *Two Introductory Lectures* (London, 1784), quoted in Porter, "William Hunter," 13.

52. Brock, "Happiness of Riches," 35–54. In 1807 Hunter's gift (which included £8,000 for the construction of a museum to house his materials) spawned what is now the University of Glasgow's Hunterian Museum and Art Gallery.

53. Porter and Porter, *Patient's Progress*, 126.

obtain various chairs at the University of Edinburgh or a medical sinecure that would enable him to remain in Scotland, and he too went to
London after all his Scottish schemes failed. John Moore made several
unsuccessful attempts to enter the ranks of the medical professors at the
University of Glasgow before he accepted a generous offer to take the
Duke of Hamilton on the grand tour in 1772, after which he had sufficient
financial resources to remake himself as a London man of letters while
in his midforties.[54] Moore followed, and in some respects emulated, his
cousin Tobias Smollett, who also gave up medicine to write for a living
in London. Among lawyers found in table 1, even James Boswell, who so
loved London, would surely have stayed in Scotland if he had been offered
a judicial gown, like his father Lord Auchinleck, and his brief stint as an
English barrister during the last decade of his life turned out to be a disastrous career move.

Some Scottish authors who failed to make satisfactory careers for
themselves in Scotland became hired pens in London. Although the phenomenon of Grub Street has received much attention in English literary studies,[55] the enormous contribution of Scottish authors has hardly
been noticed. The first Grub Street writer among the figures in table 1
was William Guthrie, a schoolteacher from the northeast who seems to
have been driven from Scotland by a sex scandal, possibly compounded
by Jacobite sympathies. Arriving in London around 1730, he obtained a
pension of £200 per annum by writing zealously in the service of government and referred to himself in 1767 as "the oldest author by profession in
Britain."[56] But Guthrie also wrote and compiled a number of literary and
scholarly works that are listed in table 2, as well as a massive history of
England that has been excluded from my database only because it began
appearing two years before the starting date for this study.[57]

Smollett, born thirteen years after Guthrie, in 1721, was by far the
most successful of the Grub Street Scots. For a number of years during
the 1740s and early 1750s, he tried to establish himself as a medical practitioner in London while also producing novels and translations, but from
the age of thirty-three his career was mainly devoted to literary jobs,

54. Fulton, "John Moore," 176–89.

55. Rogers, *Grub Street*; McDowell, *Women of Grub Street*; Bloom, *Samuel Johnson*.

56. Quoted from a letter to the Earl of Buchan in Chambers and Thomson, *Biographical Dictionary*, 2:188.

57. Okie, "William Guthrie," 221–38; Forbes, *Hume's Philosophical Politics*,
253–58.

including writing novels and other kinds of books, editing periodicals
such as the *Critical Review*, compiling large compendiums and editions of
various kinds, and translating for the booksellers. Despite his success in
this role, he stated privately that he would have greatly preferred to live
among the literati in Scotland than in England, for he viewed England,
Hume-like, as a place "where Genius is lost, Learning undervalued, and
Taste altogether extinguished."[58]

The other Grub Street writers found in table 1 were younger than
Guthrie and Smollett. Perhaps the most gifted was Gilbert Stuart, whose
dissipation and impertinence made him unsuitable for the Scottish academic career that he coveted. He subsequently turned against William
Robertson, whom he blamed for his misfortune, and the Edinburgh culture that Robertson represented. "I mortally detest and abhor this place;
and everybody in it," Stuart wrote of Edinburgh in a letter to the Scottish
bookseller John Murray of 17 June 1774. "Never was there a city, where
there was so much pretension to knowledge, and so little of it. The sol-
emn fopping and the gross stupidity of the Scottish literati are perfectly
insupportable."[59] He fit in better on Grub Street in London, writing and
editing books, pamphlets, and reviews in close association with Murray.
Stuart was soon followed by Rev. John Logan, who had also tried and
failed to win an Edinburgh academic chair and had eventually been forced
to give up his parish charge at Leith as a result of sexual misconduct.[60]
Both Stuart and Logan drank too much, and they both died young, resentful and depressed.

Like Logan, William Thomson was a Church of Scotland clergyman
born in the 1740s. He made a Grub Street career for himself after it became clear that what a contemporary biographer called his "pleasurable
propensities" were not conducive to his career as a parish minister in
Perthshire.[61] After working in London "night and day . . . with unwea-
rying perseverance," "being ready to write on any subject, and for any
one who should employ his versatile talents," he retired to Kensington
near the end of his life, "in decent but not by any means affluent circumstances,"[62] and died there at the age of seventy-one. In this he was unusual, being one of the few Scottish Grub Street writers of his generation

58. Smollett to Alexander Carlyle, 1 Mar. 1754, in Smollett, *Letters*, 33.
59. Quoted in Zachs, *Without Regard for Good Manners*, 91.
60. See my entry on Logan in *ODNB*.
61. "William Thomson," 443; Scott, *Fasti*, 4:282.
62. Chambers and Thomson, *Biographical Dictionary*, 2:458.

to avoid an early death. Thomson wrote regularly for John Murray, and he assumed control of the *English Review* for a short time after Murray's death, but on at least one occasion in June 1785 he provoked Murray by going on a drunken binge that caused him to miss a deadline. The following year he was dismissed for failure to carry out his duties in accordance with Murray's wishes.[63]

Another hired pen, William Russell, was born in Selkirkshire in 1741 and apprenticed as a printer for five years with the Edinburgh firm of Martin & Wotherspoon. In the 1760s he tried his hand as a miscellaneous writer in London, also working stints as a press corrector at the London printing houses of William Strahan and Brown & Aldred. After twenty years of the Grub Street grind in the metropolis, he married and moved to a farm near Langholm in Dumfriesshire in 1787. Yet his surviving letters from the period 1787–93 to his London publisher, George Robinson, betray an almost single-minded concern over the struggle to earn enough money from his writing to sustain his family. The postscript to a letter of 20 September 1790, regarding a *History of Ancient Europe* (no. 318) that would appear three years later in two octavo volumes (though never finished), shows that Russell was living the life of a Grub Street author in the Scottish countryside:

> P.S. What staggers my perseverance, beside the apprehension of running in debt, is the necessity of looking forward to the conclusion of the History of Ancient Europe, as the first season of mental ease. If you can agree to publish it in portions, and give me three hundred pounds for the two first volumes, my industry will be reanimated, and you will be a gainer. No man can write with spirit, when he finds he is ruining himself.

Russell's last known letter to Robinson, dated 2 January 1793, capped off an angry exchange, as the desperate author tried to juggle his commitment to Robinson to continue his successful *History of Modern Europe* (no. 203) with a more lucrative offer from Cadell to continue Hume's *History of England*.[64] But the pressure to produce was enormous, and by the end of the year he was dead of a stroke at the age of fifty-two.[65]

The literary career of William Julius Mickle was a happier variation on the same theme. The son of a Scottish Presbyterian minister who gave

---

63. Zachs, *First John Murray*, 213–14.

64. Russell's letters to Robinson in the Beinecke Library, Yale University, MS Vault Shelves, Cadell & Davies.

65. Chambers and Thomson, *Biographical Dictionary*, 2:315–16.

up his parish charge to pursue a more lucrative career as a brewer in Edinburgh, Mickle worked in (and eventually owned) the family brewery for a dozen or more years before going bankrupt in 1763. At that point, while still under the age of thirty, he took leave of his Scottish creditors by taking up a literary career in London, and subsequently Oxford, where he worked as a corrector for the Clarendon Press from 1765 to 1772. His literary life in England was a constant search for patronage and place, and the alteration of his name (as discussed in chapter 1) was part of that process. In the end, sinecures and marriage into a wealthy English commercial family enabled him to write his poetry in relative affluence during the last six years of his life. He died suddenly in 1788, however, just after turning fifty-three.[66]

John Pinkerton was another member of the younger generation of Scottish Enlightenment authors who tried to make a career as an independent man of letters in London after forsaking a professional career in Edinburgh. Pinkerton was the son of a Scottish merchant who had acquired considerable wealth selling hair in Somerset and then returned to Scotland, purchasing an estate in Lanarkshire. After being educated at a grammar school and then privately in Edinburgh, Pinkerton served an apprenticeship with an Edinburgh writer of the signet. When his father died in 1780, his older brother got the family estate, but John received a modest inheritance, with "a sufficient income for a man of very moderate wishes and pleasures."[67] The following year, at the age of twenty-three, he gave up his legal career in Edinburgh for a life of letters in London, beginning with a book of his own poems (no. 221) and another that he tried to pass off as a work of old Scottish ballads.[68] There followed a long literary career so varied and peculiar that it is difficult to describe. His stable, if modest, independent income and his marriage to a sister of the bishop of Salisbury set him apart from the ordinary Grub Street writer, and his pursuit of Scottish antiquarian subjects of various kinds gave him the air

66. See J. J. Caudle's article on Mickle in *ODNB*.

67. Pinkerton to Messrs. Longman & Co., 5 Apr. 1810, in Pinkerton, *Literary Correspondence*, 2:393.

68. *Scottish Tragic Ballads* (1781). The work was reprinted in 1783 with a second volume, under the title *Select Scotish Ballads*, but the forgery was exposed in the *Gentleman's Magazine* in November 1784 and admitted by Pinkerton two years later in his two-volume *Ancient Scotish Poems*, a serious compilation that was followed in 1792 with a three-volume work, *Scottish Poems, Reprinted from Scarce Editions*. I have omitted from table 2 all Pinkerton's compilations of supposedly ancient poetry, whether spurious or authentic.

of a virtuoso scholar in the aristocratic Whig tradition of his friend and correspondent, the Earl of Buchan. Yet Pinkerton also engaged in unnamed "irregularities in his conduct" that quickly put an end to his marriage and caused him to lose social status. He wrote extensively for the periodical press (especially the *Critical Review*, which for a time he edited), published several anonymous and pseudonymous compilations that seem to have been produced for profit (such as the two-volume *Treasury of Wit* of 1786, published under the pseudonym H. Bennet, M.A.), and fought with publishers over fees in a manner that suggests a struggle to make ends meet—all more characteristic of Grub Street than of the world of Edinburgh literary lawyers he had left behind.[69] Late in life Pinkerton moved back to Edinburgh briefly and then went to live in Paris, where he died in 1826.

Besides the Edinburgh printer William Smellie, who had some of the characteristics of a Grub Street writer and was also a member of the younger generation of Scottish Enlightenment authors,[70] the only Edinburgh counterpart of Guthrie, Stuart, Logan, Thomson, Russell, Mickle, and Pinkerton in table 1 was the unfortunate Robert Heron, who supported himself as a divinity student at Edinburgh University by translating, compiling, writing, and editing for the Scottish booksellers. He was duly licensed to preach the Gospel and briefly served as an assistant minister to Hugh Blair, for whom he always maintained great respect. In time, however, Heron's extravagant lifestyle and unbalanced personality combined to undo his clerical career and put him in debtors' prison, where most of his *New General History of Scotland* (no. 330) was supposedly written.[71] In 1799 he moved to London, where, he later claimed, he published "a greater variety of light fugitive pieces than I know to have been written by any one other person," in addition to his anonymous books and

---

69. In a letter to Longman & Co. dated 5 April 1810, Pinkerton alludes to having drawn on his inheritance to publish some of his antiquarian works and remarks that "the occupations of literature do not furnish the best qualifications for conducting the pecuniary transactions of life, as I have been taught by experience." Pinkerton, *Literary Correspondence*, 2:393, 1:viii.

70. On Smellie's multifaceted career as an Edinburgh printer, editor, journalist, and author, see Brown: "William Smellie and Natural History," 191–214; "William Smellie and the Culture," 61–88; and "William Smellie and the Printer's Role," 29–43.

71. Sinton, "Robert Heron," 17–33; *ODNB*. Heron's tortured life on Edinburgh's Grub Street is chillingly depicted in his unpublished "Journal of My Conduct, begun Aug. 14, 1789," EUL, La.III.272.

articles on a wide range of subjects and at least a dozen translations of French works.[72] Nevertheless, he ended up back in prison for debt, and then in a hospital, where he died at forty-two. Sir Walter Scott recalled him harshly as "a mere sot and beast" who "starved to death."[73]

Although Heron and the other Grub Street Scots wrote or compiled a substantial number of books that appear in table 2, as well as other known publications and presumably many others that will never be identified, all were viewed after their deaths as "men of genius" whose irregular habits and eccentricities, combined with the pressures of writing too much and too fast, prevented them from living up to their considerable potential in the republic of letters.[74] In 1756 Smollett described their lot (and to some degree his own at that time) from the writer's point of view in a caustic book review, which tells of "the infinite pains and perseverance it must cost a writer" to carry out the various parts of a multivolume composition, working against tight deadlines set by mercenary booksellers "who cannot distinguish authors of merit, or if they could, have not sense and spirit to reward them according to their genius and capacity." Under these circumstances, "the miserable author must perform his daily task, in spite of cramp, colick, vapours, or vertigo; in spite of head-ach, heart-ach, and *Minerva*'s frowns; otherwise he will lose his character and livelihood, like a taylor who disappoints his customer in a birth-day suit."[75] Forty years later, in the first biography ever written of Robert Burns, Robert Heron was probably describing himself and his fellow Grub Street writers more than his subject when he wrote: "Had he but been able to give a steady preference to the society of the virtuous, the learned, and the wise, rather than to that of the gay and the dissolute, it is probable that he could not have failed to rise to an exaltation of character and of talents fitted to do high honour to human nature."[76]

The struggles of the Grub Street Scots underline the importance of professional careers for the majority of Scottish Enlightenment authors, for whom payment from publishers for writing books was normally

72. Baines, "Robert Heron," 168, quoting Heron.

73. Scott to John Murray, 6 Jan. 1814, in Scott, *Letters*, 3:396.

74. This theme runs through the biographies of Guthrie, Heron, Logan, Russell, Stuart, and Thomson, in Chambers and Thomson, *Biographical Dictionary*.

75. Quoted from the *Critical Review*, in Martz, *Later Career*, 24–25.

76. Heron, "Memoir," in Lindsay, *Burns Encyclopedia*, 173. Heron's tirade against Burns's patrons for failing to give him "any small pension, or any sinecure place of moderate emolument" (175) may be read in the same way. For a similar interpretation of other passages in Heron's life of Burns, see Baines, "Robert Heron," 167.

supplemental to their regular income, as we shall see more fully in the next chapter. When we compare the lives of these two kinds of authors, it is tempting to see an insurmountable chasm between the successful figures of the High Enlightenment and the scurrilous and resentful "low-life of literature," such as Robert Darnton claims to have discovered in eighteenth-century France.[77] Yet if the Scottish Grub Street writers in London stood far from the epicenter of the Scottish Enlightenment in more ways than one, their marginality should not be exaggerated. Even Gilbert Stuart, the most alienated of the lot, devoted most of his energy to writing works of history embodying the same scholarly standards and critical assumptions as the works of his chief antagonists among the Edinburgh literati, William Robertson and Robert Henry, and the short-lived Scottish literary magazine that Stuart cofounded and co-edited, the *Edinburgh Magazine and Review* (Nov. 1773–Aug. 1776), was intended in large measure to promote the literature of his homeland and drew upon the Scottish literati to achieve that purpose.[78] The other Grub Street Scots generally respected their better-known brethren in Scotland and often expressed gratitude for their support. The fact that Stuart, Thomson, and Russell were all awarded LL.D. degrees from Scottish universities in recognition of their literary accomplishments (Stuart from Edinburgh in 1770, Thomson from Glasgow in 1783, and Russell from St. Andrews in 1792) is another indication of their inclusion within the larger movement.

It must also be remembered that even well-established and successful Scottish authors living in mid- and late eighteenth-century London were not usually fully integrated into English society. The notion of an integrated "British" culture, so appealing to cosmopolitan Scots, was often impossible to realize. In the sometimes virulently anti-Scottish climate that existed in London during much of this period, Scottish men of letters often kept to themselves, displaying a clannishness that in turn fueled the prejudices against them. No matter what efforts they might make to assimilate, speech marked them as outsiders: during riots they were warned

77. Darnton, "High Enlightenment," in Darnton, *Literary Underground*, chap. 1. Darnton's thesis is criticized and defended in several of the articles in Mason, *Darnton Debate*.

78. Besides Smellie, who served as co-editor, at least three other figures from table 1 contributed to the *Edinburgh Magazine and Review:* James Beattie, Thomas Blacklock, and William Richardson. Although Stuart attained notoriety for his hostile reviews of works by Henry and Monboddo, most books by the Scottish literati were noticed favorably.

not to utter a word,[79] for even those who lived much of their lives in London, such as John Hunter, John Moore, and John Pinkerton, retained noticeable Scottish accents. In a coffeehouse culture that was notorious for segregation by occupation, ethnic group, or some other characteristic, Scottish identity in London was built around the aptly named British Coffee House, centrally located in Cockspur Street near Charing Cross, a short walk from the bookshops in the Strand. From at least 1714, when John Macky observed that "the *Scots* go generally to the *British*,"[80] it constituted the physical and social center of Scottish culture in London. A number of Scots resident in London belonged to clubs that met at the British Coffee House, and it was not uncommon for Scottish visitors to receive their mail there.[81] For more than twenty years during the 1750s, 1760s, and 1770s, it was run (and briefly owned) by Helen Anderson—sister of the Scottish Anglican clergyman John Douglas, later bishop of Salisbury—who performed the functions of an extremely competent *salonnière*.[82]

The British Coffee House became a convenient target for Scots baiters, such as the anonymous Wilkite author of a 1764 poem about a stupid, uncouth Scot who makes his way there and horrifies "Poor Mrs. D[ougla]s" by mistaking his own image in a mirror for an enemy and slaying it with a shout of elation, shattering the glass.[83] The poem brutally mocks the Scots in London for being clannish on the basis of both nationality and kinship, and for aggressively seeking "To tread on Englishmen, and English laws." As we saw in chapter 1, such fears were not confined to the era

79. Carlyle, *Autobiography*, 199.

80. [Macky], *Journey through England*, 108; Archibald Dalzel to Andrew Dalzel, 1 Apr. 1763, EUL, Dk.7.52.

81. On clubs, see Carlyle, *Autobiography*, 354, 362; Mackenzie, *Account*, 56. Clark, *British Clubs*, 296, alludes to a Scottish literary club that met at the British Coffee House during the 1770s; Phillips, *Mid-Georgian London*, 98, refers to "a Scottish club called 'The Beeswing'" that met there, but it is unclear if these were among the clubs mentioned by Carlyle or Mackenzie. On mail, see Lillywhite, *London Coffee Houses*, 133. Boswell's first London letter from his friend Temple, dated 5 April 1760, was addressed to him at the British Coffee House.

82. Helen Anderson is called "a woman of uncommon talents, and the most agreeable conversation," in Mackenzie, *Account*, 56–57; "a person of superior character" in Carlyle, *Autobiography*, 354–55; and "a person of great respectability" in Cumberland, *Memoirs*, 1:194. Her fame spread as far as Philadelphia, where Alexander Graydon cited Cumberland's high opinion of her in his *Memoirs*, 63.

83. *British Coffee-House.*

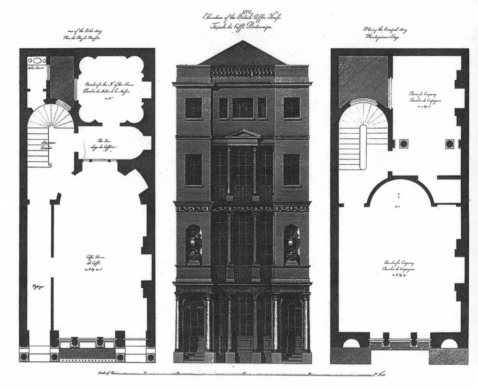

Fig. 2.4. The second volume of *The Works in Architecture of Robert and James Adam* (1779) showed off Robert Adam's 1770 redesign of the British Coffee House (demolished in 1886), which was the centerpiece of Scottish cultural and social life in late eighteenth-century London. The ground floor or "Parlor Story" (*left*) consisted of a large "Coffee Room" in the front, the bar, a room for the master of the house in the rear, and a water closet. The "Principal Story" above (*right*) had large and small rooms for "company." Private collection.

of Bute and Wilkes and extended to those in all walks of life, including men of letters. The British Coffee House was the primary physical embodiment of this perceived threat.

For this reason, the dramatic redesign of the British Coffee House in 1770 by Scotland's leading architect, Robert Adam, was infused with cultural significance, and so was the way that the redesign was publicized in print. In Rome as well as in London, Adam was always more comfortable in the company of fellow Scots—his so-called Caledonian Club.[84] At the end of the 1770s he and his younger brother James displayed their

84. Adam's term, quoted in Sanderson, *Robert Adam*, 48.

family firm's handiwork in the section on public buildings in the second volume of *The Works in Architecture of Robert and James Adam* (no. 197). As engraved by Robert Blyth, the brothers' representation of the British Coffee House supports their claim to have transfused "the beautiful spirit of antiquity" with "novelty and variety," by portraying an elegant, multi-story, neoclassical facade (fig. 2.4).[85] Inside, the parlor floor contained a small coffee bar and a large coffee room, as well as the room of the master (or mistress) of the house. On the principal floor above were two more rooms for company, one quite large, which could be used for special events such as club meetings. Both the classical redesign of the British Coffee House and the publication of the plans in the Adam brothers' handsome folio represent assertions of Scottish national pride about metropolitan cultural achievement.

UNITY AND REPRESENTATION

Modes of Bonding

The clannishness of Scottish men of letters in London was partly their way of reinforcing the familiar in response to the foreignness of England—its language, attitudes, and manners—and partly the result of other kinds of ties. Religion was one important bond. Large numbers of Scottish Enlightenment authors were Church of Scotland Presbyterians, and this circumstance, which so annoyed Samuel Johnson—who admired Hugh Blair's *Sermons* "though the dog is a Scotchman, and a Presbyterian, and every thing he should not be" (*BLJ*, 4:98)—provided a common ground of association not only among themselves and with Scottish Presbyterians in London but also with other kinds of English Dissenters. James Fordyce ministered to a congregation of Presbyterians at the Monkwell Street meetinghouse, and Thomas Somerville and other Scots routinely heard him preach there when they were in London. William Leechman and some other Scottish ministers established strong ties with Dissenters in England. At the same time, the fact that the British Coffee House was presided over by the sister of a Scot who had taken Anglican orders and would rise to become a prominent bishop reminds us that a minority of the Scottish literati were Anglicans or Episcopalians, especially from Aberdeen and the northeast. The cosmopolitan spirit of the Scottish lite-

85. Adam and Adam, *Works in Architecture*, 46; Phillips, *Mid-Georgian London*, 98.

rati enabled all varieties of polite Scottish Christians to associate among themselves without the narrow parochialism that Johnson represented.

For the literati, whether in England or Scotland, family connections were important bonding agents. The 115 individuals in table 1 include five sets of fathers and sons: the Gregorys, the Monros, the Stewarts, the Tytlers, and the Wallaces, and in the case of the Monros there are two sons on the list (Alexander *secundus* and Donald). The table also contains three additional sets of siblings besides the Monros: the Baillies, the Fordyces (David and James), and the Hunters. Other kinds of kinship ties are represented there as well. The mother of the Fordyce brothers was the sister of Thomas Blackwell, and George Fordyce was their nephew. A sister of the Hunter brothers, Dorothea, was the mother of Joanna and Matthew Baillie, who was William Hunter's sole heir; Joanna was particularly close with her other uncle, John Hunter, and his wife Anne Home (a poet in her own right). Sir James Steuart was the uncle of the Earl of Buchan, being the brother of the earl's mother. Thomas Reid was a cousin of the Gregorys, and John Gregory's daughter Dorothea (sister of James Gregory) married Archibald Alison; the Alisons' daughter would in turn marry Alexander Gerard's grandson. Adam Dickson was the uncle and tutor of Thomas Somerville (who was the uncle and father-in-law of the mathematician Mary Somerville). William Cullen was the first cousin of John Millar's mother, and his daughter Robina married Millar's son John. William Robertson was the first cousin of Robert Adam. There were family connections between James Beattie and John Bethune, Boswell and James Bruce, Hugh Blair and Robert Watson, Sir James Mackintosh and Alexander Fraser Tytler, William Buchan and Sir John Pringle, Henry Mackenzie and Lord Monboddo, Sir David Dalrymple (Lord Hailes) and Sir John Dalrymple, John Moore and Tobias Smollett, and the two William Smellies. One sister of James Balfour of Pilrig, Bridget, married William Leechman, while another, Louisa, married Robert Whytt, and a third married the Edinburgh natural philosopher James Russell, the first cousin of Joseph Black. Adam Ferguson's mother was the great aunt of the wife of George Campbell and the aunt of Joseph Black, whose niece Ferguson married. By his marriage to a daughter of John Simson, the controversial Glasgow divinity professor, John Moore was connected with the mathematician Robert Simson, who was his wife's first cousin. Colin Maclaurin's niece was the mother of Agnes Craig M'Lehose—Robert Burns's lover "Clarinda."

Other bonds were forged through teacher–student and mentor–protégé relationships of various kinds, as well as through close friendships. It would be tedious to mention all the individuals in table 1 who studied with others in the list at the Scottish universities or looked to them for patronage or were influenced by their ideas, but a few special connections may be mentioned. Among the formative generation of Scottish Enlightenment authors, Francis Hutcheson, Colin Maclaurin, Lord Kames, and Alexander Monro *primus* stand out as major influences on those who followed them. Hutcheson was closely connected with Robert Simson and had a strong influence on a number of students who would later join the ranks of the Glasgow University faculty, including James Moor (with whom he translated an edition of Marcus Aurelius's *Meditations* that was published in 1742), Adam Smith (who later referred to him as "the never-to-be-forgotten Hutcheson"), and William Leechman (his principal protégé). Maclaurin was revered by an entire generation of Edinburgh University students who were educated in the years before the 1745 uprising. Unlike Hutcheson and Maclaurin, Kames did not hold an academic chair, but he was active in encouraging learning and in helping to determine academic appointments. Sir John Dalrymple, Thomas Reid, John Millar, John Walker, Alexander Fraser Tytler, and William Smellie were among the many literati of later generations who were grateful for his support. Among medical men, both in Edinburgh and in London, the internal networks of patronage and support were particularly extensive, and Alexander Monro *primus* was a mentor for several of those who came after him.

Close ties among the Scottish literati often led to support for publication projects and sometimes to direct collaboration. William Cullen contributed an essay on the cold produced by evaporating fluids to Joseph Black's 1777 *Experiments* (no. 180). In 1752 James Fordyce placed a sermon in his brother David's posthumous *Theodorus* (no. 18), which he edited for the press. Robert Heron was hired by Sir John Sinclair to oversee the compilation of the great *Statistical Account of Scotland* (no. 301). In the early 1750s Tobias Smollett edited the first two volumes of William Smellie's *Treatise on the Theory and Practice of Midwifery* (no. 22). James Ferguson added an introductory section on "astronomical geography" to the second edition (1771) of William Guthrie's *Geography* (no. 130) and was named on the title page from the third edition (also 1771) onward (fig. 2.5).[86] According to the *ODNB*, at the time of his premature death in 1760, William Duncan was writing a continuation of Thomas Blackwell's *Memoirs of the Court of Augustus* (no. 29).

Much effort went into editing, revising, and reprinting each other's

86. Millburn, *Bibliography*, 81.

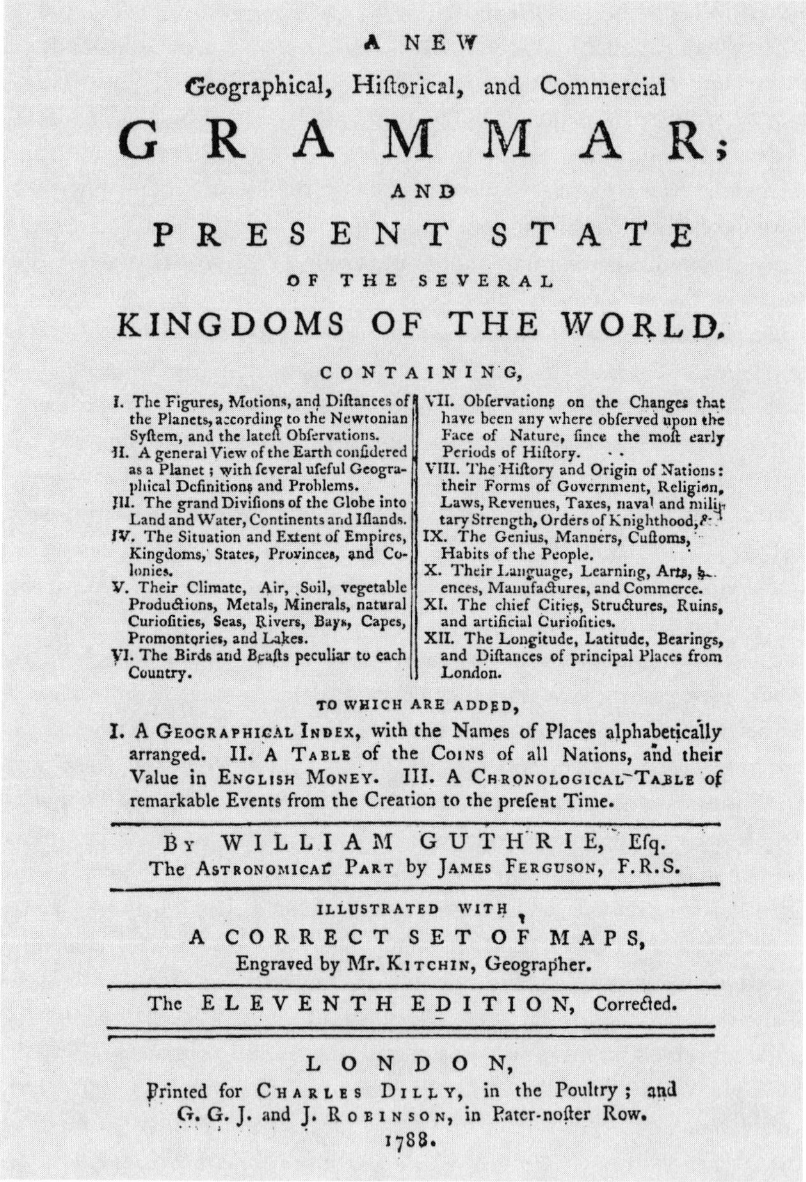

A NEW

Geographical, Hiftorical, and Commercial

GRAMMAR;

AND

PRESENT STATE

OF THE SEVERAL

KINGDOMS OF THE WORLD.

CONTAINING,

I. The Figures, Motions, and Diftances of the Planets, according to the Newtonian Syftem, and the lateft Obfervations.

II. A general View of the Earth confidered as a Planet ; with feveral ufeful Geographical Definitions and Problems.

III. The grand Divifions of the Globe into Land and Water, Continents and Iflands.

IV. The Situation and Extent of Empires, Kingdoms, States, Provinces, and Colonies.

V. Their Climate, Air, Soil, vegetable Productions, Metals, Minerals, natural Curiofities, Seas, Rivers, Bays, Capes, Promontories, and Lakes.

VI. The Birds and Beafts peculiar to each Country.

VII. Obfervations on the Changes that have been any where obferved upon the Face of Nature, fince the moft early Periods of Hiftory.

VIII. The Hiftory and Origin of Nations: their Forms of Government, Religion, Laws, Revenues, Taxes, naval and military Strength, Orders of Knighthood, &c.

IX. The Genius, Manners, Cuftoms, Habits of the People.

X. Their Language, Learning, Arts, Sciences, Manufactures, and Commerce.

XI. The chief Cities, Structures, Ruins, and artificial Curiofities.

XII. The Longitude, Latitude, Bearings, and Diftances of principal Places from London.

TO WHICH ARE ADDED,

I. A GEOGRAPHICAL INDEX, with the Names of Places alphabetically arranged. II. A TABLE of the COINS of all Nations, and their Value in ENGLISH MONEY. III. A CHRONOLOGICAL TABLE of remarkable Events from the Creation to the prefent Time.

By WILLIAM GUTHRIE, Efq.

The ASTRONOMICAL PART by JAMES FERGUSON, F.R.S.

ILLUSTRATED WITH

A CORRECT SET OF MAPS,

Engraved by Mr. KITCHIN, Geographer.

The ELEVENTH EDITION, Corrected.

LONDON,

Printed for CHARLES DILLY, in the Poultry ; and G. G. J. and J. ROBINSON, in Pater-nofter Row.

1788.

Fig. 2.5. William Guthrie's *Geography* (1770) was among the most popular books of the age, although the principal compiler was not Guthrie but the original publisher, John Knox. By the time of the eleventh edition of 1788, Knox had relinquished the publication rights to Charles Dilly and the Robinsons. Author's collection.

books. When it became clear that William Thomson was not going to succeed as a parish minister in Scotland, Hugh Blair and William Robertson arranged for him to edit and complete Robert Watson's posthumous *History of Philip III* (no. 239), which launched Thomson's literary career in London. In the same way, Matthew Baillie completed William Hunter's work on anatomy (no. 326); Malcolm Laing edited and completed the last volume of Robert Henry's *History of Great Britain* (no. 144); and James Macpherson had a hand in revising and editing John Macpherson's posthumous *Critical Dissertations on the Ancient Caledonians* (no. 108). William Robertson helped to edit his cousin Robert Adam's *Ruins of the Palace of the Emperor Diocletian at Spalatro* (no. 85) and ghostwrote the introduction, receiving ten cases of claret for his trouble. Joseph Black and James Hutton edited the papers of their late friend Adam Smith as *Essays on Philosophical Subjects* (no. 336). Hugh Blair performed the same service for John Logan, resulting in the posthumous publication of Logan's *Sermons* (no. 290).[87] William Smellie helped to edit the books he printed, including William Buchan's *Domestic Medicine* (no. 115) and other titles in table 2.[88] As editor of the first edition of the *Encyclopaedia Britannica*, Smellie drew heavily on the published works of other Scottish literary men, such as David Fordyce (whose *Elements of Moral Philosophy*, no. 7, was adapted for the article "Moral Philosophy"), the obstetrician William Smellie (whose *Treatise on Midwifery*, no. 22, was used for the article "Midwifery"), William Duncan (whose *Elements of Logic*, no. 5, was employed for the article "Logic"), Sir James Steuart (whose *Principles of Political Oeconomy*, no. 101, was drawn on for the articles "Commerce" and "Money"), and James Ferguson (whose *Astronomy Explained*, no. 39, formed the gist of the article "Astronomy," and whose *Lectures on Select Subjects*, no. 61, was the basis of several other articles).[89] In 1816 Sir James Mackintosh reprinted the

87. Blair to Mackenzie, 6 Mar. 1790, in Mackenzie, *Literature and Literati*, 166.

88. Brown, "William Smellie and the Printer's Role," 31.

89. Millburn, *Wheelwright*, 222. Smellie named many of his sources in a "List of Authors" prefixed to the first volume of the work (though he wrongly attributed "Moral Philosophy" to Duncan rather than Fordyce). Other Scottish authors from whose works he borrowed were Charles Alston, James Balfour, George Campbell, William Cullen, Adam Dickson, Francis Home, David Hume, Lord Kames, Colin Maclaurin, Alexander Monro, Robert Simson, Sir James Steuart, and Robert Whytt. The tradition of lifting passages from Scottish authors continued, and in the mid-1780s John Murray sued the publishers over passages in the second edition of the *Encyclopaedia Britannica* that were taken from two books by Gilbert Stuart that Murray had published, as discussed in Zachs, *First John Murray*, 189–91.

only two published issues of the original *Edinburgh Review* from the mid-1750s, noting in a new preface that the appearance there of the earliest publications of Adam Smith and William Robertson went far toward justifying the act.[90]

Older, established writers reached out to help deserving younger ones. In a letter to Robert Burns, Hugh Blair wrote: "I know no way in which literary persons who are advanced in years can do more service to the world than in forming the efforts of rising Genius, or bringing forth unknown merit from obscurity."[91] He was referring specifically to his role in advancing Burns's career and in encouraging James Macpherson to "translate" and publish the poems of Ossian—two important examples of collective literary patronage by Scottish men of letters.[92] In both cases, subscriptions were undertaken to advance the work of these needy authors. Figure 2.6, showing two sample pages from the subscription list that appeared in the Edinburgh edition of Burns's *Poems*, includes five figures from table 1 (the Earl of Buchan, Thomas Blacklock, Joseph Black, Benjamin Bell, and Blair) as well as Lord Monboddo's daughter, Elizabeth (or Eliza) Burnett. Blair also patronized the African traveler James Bruce and younger Church of Scotland clergymen, including John Logan and William Thomson.[93] William Robertson advised younger historians such as Thomas Somerville about how to break into print on favorable terms. At the same time, Robertson and Blair continued throughout their lives the practice of reading and critiquing every manuscript the other man wrote before it was published, and in Aberdeen George Campbell performed a similar service for his friend James Beattie.[94] Beattie returned the favor by negotiating aggressively with the booksellers on Campbell's behalf. Henry Mackenzie also expended much effort encouraging publications by fellow Scottish men of letters. The promotion of each other's book manuscripts by the Scottish literati was so prevalent that it sometimes damaged their credibility, as we shall see in a later chapter.

90. Mackintosh, *Miscellaneous Works*, 2:466–75.

91. Blair to Burns, 4 May 1787, NLS, MS 3408, fols. 3–4.

92. Seventeen names from table 1 appear in the subscription list of the Edinburgh edition of Burns's *Poems, Chiefly in the Scottish Dialect*. On the role of the Scottish literati in promoting Macpherson's Ossianic poetry, see Sher, *Church and University*, chap. 6.

93. E.g., Blair to Cadell, 20 Feb. 1794, BL, Add. MSS 28098, fols. 18–19.

94. Beattie to Creech, 28 Oct. 1789, AUL, 30/1/290: "Dr. Campbell, without whose *imprimatur* I never publish any thing."

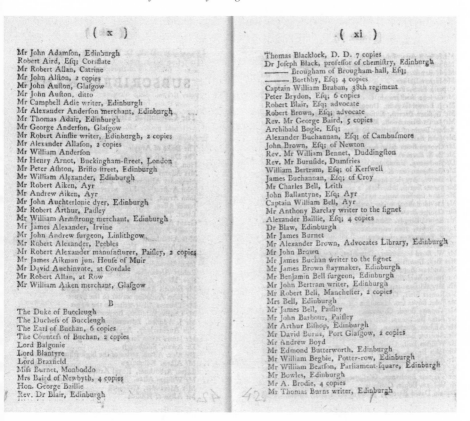

(x)

Mr John Adamfon, Edinburgh
Robert Aird, Efq; Corsflate
Mr Robert Allan, Catrine
Mr John Alfton, 2 copies
Mr John Auſton, Glaſgow
Mr John Auſton, ditto
Mr Campbell Adie writer, Edinburgh
Mr Alexander Anderfon merchant, Edinburgh
Mr Thomas Adair, Edinburgh
Mr George Anderſon, Glaſgow
Mr Robert Ainflie writer, Edinburgh, 2 copies
Mr Alexander Allaſon, 2 copies
Mr William Anderfon
Mr Henry Arnot, Buckingham-ſtreet, London
Mr Peter Athton, Briſto ſtreet, Edinburgh
Mr William Alexander, Edinburgh
Mr Robert Aiken, Ayr
Mr Andrew Aiken, Ayr
Mr John Auchterlonie dyer, Edinburgh
Mr Robert Arthur, Paiſley
Mr William Armſtrong merchant, Edinburgh
Mr James Alexander, Irvine
Mr John Andrew furgeon, Linlithgow
Mr Robert Alexander, Peebles
Mr Robert Alexander manufacturer, Paiſley, 2 copies
Mr James Aikman jun. Houſe of Muir
Mr David Auchinvote, at Cordale
Mr Robert Allan, at Row
Mr William Aiken merchant, Glaſgow

B

The Duke of Buccleugh
The Ducheſs of Buccleugh
The Earl of Buchan, 6 copies
The Counteſs of Buchan, 2 copies
Lord Balgonie
Lord Blantyre
Lord Braxfield
Miſs Burnet, Monboddo
Mrs Baird of Newbyth, 4 copies
Hon. George Baillie
Rev. Dr Blair, Edinburgh

(xi)

Thomas Blacklock, D. D. 7 copies
Dr Joſeph Black, profeſſor of chemiſtry, Edinburgh
———— Brougham of Brougham-hall, Efq;
———— Borthby, Efq; 4 copies
Captain William Braban, 38th regiment
Peter Brydon, Efq; 6 copies
Robert Blair, Efq; advocate
Robert Brown, Efq; advocate
Rev. Mr George Baird, 5 copies
Archibald Bogle, Efq;
Alexander Buchannan, Efq; of Cambuſmore
John Brown, Efq; of Newton
Rev. Mr William Bennet, Duddingſton
Rev. Mr Burnfide, Dumfries
William Bertram, Efq; of Kerfwell
James Buchannan, Efq; of Croy
Mr Charles Bell, Leith
John Ballantyne, Efq; Ayr
Captain William Bell, Ayr
Mr Anthony Barclay writer to the fignet
Alexander Baillie, Efq; 4 copies
Dr Blaw, Edinburgh
Mr James Burnet
Mr Alexander Brown, Advocates Library, Edinburgh
Mr John Brown
Mr James Buchan writer to the fignet
Mr James Brown flaymaker, Edinburgh
Mr Benjamin Bell furgeon, Edinburgh
Mr John Bertram writer, Edinburgh
Mr Robert Bell, Mancheſter, 2 copies
Mrs Bell, Edinburgh
Mr James Bell, Paiſley
Mr John Barbour, Paiſley
Mr Arthur Biſhop, Edinburgh
Mr David Burns, Port Glaſgow, 2 copies
Mr Andrew Boyd
Mr Edmond Butterworth, Edinburgh
Mr William Begbie, Potter-row, Edinburgh
Mr William Beatfon, Parliament-ſquare, Edinburgh
Mr Bowles, Edinburgh
Mr A. Brodie, 4 copies
Mr Thomas Burns writer, Edinburgh

Fig. 2.6. The second, or Edinburgh, edition of Robert Burns's *Poems, Chiefly in the Scottish Dialect* (1787) contained a subscription list with the names of about 1,500 individuals who paid five shillings per copy. On these two sample pages can be found five of the authors listed in table 1 of the present volume as well as one wife (the Countess of Buchan), one daughter Elizabeth Burnet[t]), and one leading patron (Adam Smith's benefactor, the Duke of Buccleuch [or Buccleugh] and his wife, the duchess). Thomas Fisher Rare Book Library, University of Toronto.

Once their books were published, the literati often helped each other by writing favorable reviews. Reviewing did not always live up to the high standards of impartiality that the leading journals and newspapers claimed for themselves, and authors sometimes had doubts about the nature of their involvement. When asked by his publisher how the poor initial sales of his *Philosophy of Rhetoric* (no. 174) might be improved, George Campbell observed that favorable reviews "may be of some use. . . . But I should be sorry to think there were occasion for attempting to corrupt the integrity of a judge."[95] Others had no such qualms. When James Beattie asked Thomas Blacklock to insert a favorable account of his forthcoming *Essay on the Nature and Immutability of Truth* (no. 123) in the Edinburgh press, he added: "Puffing is so constantly used on these occasions that the omission of it would seem to bespeak either total unconcern about public approbation or that the production is altogether unsupported or friendless."[96] Hugh Blair sent a complimentary copy of the third volume of his *Sermons* to Archibald Alison in 1790 with a cover letter that read: "You was so obliging as to say that after looking over them, it might be in your power to give some account of them, which you could send to some of your friends in London to be inserted in some of the Periodical Publications."[97] When Charles Dilly was about to publish John Pinkerton's *History of Scotland* (no. 345) in 1797, he reminded the author that, "from the conversation which passed between you and Dr. [John] Gillies in my counting-house," Gillies was likely to review it in the *Monthly*, while the *Critical Review* "will be ready to receive what may be given from yourself or a friend" because Pinkerton had formerly been connected with that periodical.[98]

If the library of Adam Smith was typical, many of the Scottish literati acquired copies of each other's books either by purchase or presentation. Of 287 titles listed in table 2 that had been published by the time of Smith's death in 1790 (excluding Smith's own works), at least 84 (29 percent) appear to have been in his library in one edition or another, including two or more different titles by Kames, Hume, Hutcheson, Mackenzie, Reid, Robertson, James Ferguson, Adam Ferguson, Robert Wallace, John Bruce, and several other authors. This number does not take into account multiple editions of the same book (e.g., Smith owned three different editions of Hume's *Essays and Treatises on Several Subjects*, in three different formats) or the fact that several titles represented in table 2 as single books actually consisted of separately published volumes that may have been acquired through several discreet purchases or presentations (e.g., Smith owned volumes 1–3 of Robert Henry's *History of Great Britain*, published in 1771, 1774, and 1777, respectively). It is also likely that many other titles from table 2 were in Smith's library besides the ones that have

95. Campbell to William Strahan, 8 Jun. 1776, HL, MS Hyde 76, 5.2.90.2.

96. Quoted in Forbes, *Beattie and His Friends*, 46.

97. Blair to Alison, 16 Apr. [1790], Beinecke Library, Yale University, Osborn MSS 1376.

98. Dilly to Pinkerton, 26 Jan. 1797, in Pinkerton, *Correspondence*, 1:437–39.

been traced. As to how books by Scottish authors came to be in Smith's possession, it is unfortunate that in Smith's day presentation copies were often sent directly from publishers and therefore lack telltale inscriptions. Nevertheless, Hiroshi Mizuta has ascertained that several of the books in Smith's library were sent to him as gifts, especially by younger authors such as John Bruce, George Chalmers, Henry Mackenzie, William Thompson, and George Wallace.[99]

Younger writers also showed their respect and gratitude by memorializing their elders in print. As we saw in the last chapter, William Leechman glorified the career of Francis Hutcheson in the biographical preface to Hutcheson's posthumous *System of Moral Philosophy* of 1755 (no. 36). Matthew Stewart concluded the preface to his *Tracts, Physical and Mathematical* (no. 69) with a tribute to Robert Simson, "whose reputation is already great in the learned world, and must continue to increase, as long as true geometry is understood, or valued." In the 1790s James Anderson placed admiring accounts of Adam Smith, William Cullen, and Sir James Steuart in his periodical *The Bee* (the last of them written by Steuart's nephew, Lord Buchan), as well as a poem "On the Death of William Cullen, M.D." by Mungo Park.[100] Dugald Stewart presented to the Royal Society of Edinburgh lives of Smith (read January and March 1793), Robertson (read March 1796), and Reid (read at various meetings in 1802), which were subsequently published in a variety of formats and became the standard biographical accounts of all three men. John Playfair did the same for Matthew Stewart and James Hutton, and he also popularized Hutton's geological findings in his influential *Illustrations of the Huttonian Theory of the Earth* (1802).[101] In 1781 Andrew Duncan added a brief account of the life of Alexander Monro *primus* to the second edition of his *Medical Cases* (no. 190) and also published it separately. In 1812 Henry Mackenzie read to the Royal Society of Edinburgh a life of John Home that was in some respects an account of Home's entire coterie of Edinburgh literati; it was published a decade later, both separately and in the first volume of a new edition of Home's *Works*.[102] Mackenzie had already idealized the life of

99. Mizuta, *Adam Smith's Library*, xix.

100. Erskine, *Anonymous and Fugitive Essays*, 264–83; Duffill, "Notes on a Collection of Letters by Mungo Park," 41.

101. Playfair's lives of Stewart and Hutton were read to the Royal Society of Edinburgh in April 1786 and January 1803, respectively, and published in the first (1788) and fifth (1805) volumes of its *Transactions*.

102. Mackenzie, *Account*.

Hume in a fictional piece in *The Mirror*, "The Story of La Roche," and had composed a life of Thomas Blacklock for an edition of Blacklock's poems in 1793.[103] In 1800 William Smellie's son Alexander published a posthumous volume containing biographies of John Gregory, Kames, Hume, and Smith that his father had written some forty years earlier (no. 360), but that book was only part of a much larger, unfinished biographical project that would have included the lives of at least fifteen more subjects in table 1 if Smellie had lived to complete it.[104] Boswell seriously intended to write a life of Kames, who was an influential father figure to him,[105] and he toyed fleetingly with the idea of writing a life of Hume. In 1807 Alexander Fraser Tytler, Lord Woodhouselee, produced a long biography of Kames that, like Mackenzie's biography of Home, broadened its subject to include "every species of improvement, whether of an intellectual or a political nature, that took place in Scotland during [Kames's] age."[106] Archibald Alison, in turn, published a biographical account of Woodhouselee in the *Transactions of the Royal Society of Edinburgh* for 1818. Sir John Sinclair filled the first of two carefully manicured volumes of his correspondence and reminiscences with tributes to "the celebrated Dr. Blair," Adam Smith ("truly a great man"), William Robertson ("a truly great mind"), Joseph Black ("not only a distinguished philosopher, but a worthy man"), John Playfair ("among the greatest ornaments of the University of Edinburgh"), Dugald Stewart ("one of the most eminent persons of his time"), and several other eighteenth-century Scottish authors.[107]

Author-sons generally did what they could to promote the reputations of their author-fathers. George Wallace published a brief biographical obituary of his father Robert in the *Scots Magazine* in 1771. Alexander Monro *secundus* arranged for the posthumous publication of his father's works in quarto in 1781, with a biographical introduction by Donald

103. Mackenzie to Cadell, 30 Apr. 1793, in Mackenzie, *Literature and Literati*, 181–82; Spencer, *Hume and Eighteenth-Century America*, 202–4.

104. Kerr, *Memoirs*, 2:417–22. Smellie's list names Arnot, Alston, Blair, Beattie, Black, Blacklock, Monboddo, Campbell, Cullen, Hailes, Adam Ferguson, Hutton, Monro *primus*, Robertson, and Wilkie, as well as six others who do not appear in table 1.

105. Ross, *Lord Kames*, esp. chap. 13; Sher, "Something That Put Me in Mind of My Father," 64–86.

106. Tytler, *Memoirs of Kames*, v.

107. Sinclair, *Correspondence*, 1:238, 387, 433, 435–36. Sinclair also praised his former tutor John Logan, as well as John Gillies, James Bruce, the Earl of Buchan, Lord Hailes, John Pinkerton, John Home, William Cullen, and James Gregory.

Monro (no. 218). Seven years later James Gregory arranged for the publication of a posthumous quarto edition of his father's *Works*, with a biography by Alexander Fraser Tytler. Among those found in table 1 who were near contemporaries, John Moore was the biographer of Smollett, Adam Ferguson of Black, and Robert Heron of Burns, while James Fordyce praised his brother David in a brief biographical advertisement prefixed to the latter's *Theodorus* (no. 18).[108] We have seen that Adam Smith commemorated Hume in the laudatory letter that was published along with Hume's brief autobiography in most posthumous editions of the *History of England*.

The dedications contained in some of the books listed in table 2 provide additional evidence of the camaraderie that existed among Scottish Enlightenment authors. Many of the books in the table have no dedications. A small number, usually quarto works of history and other subjects that were thought to possess sufficient dignity, bear dedications to the king, such as William Robertson's *History of Charles V* (no. 119), John Gillies's *History of Ancient Greece* (no. 263), James Bruce's *Travels to Discover the Source of the Nile* (no. 288), Thomas Robertson's *History of Mary Queen of Scots* (no. 317), Thomas Somerville's *History of Great Britain during the Reign of Queen Anne* (no. 346), and (unusually, because it was an octavo) Lord Kames's *Elements of Criticism* (no. 73). A much larger number of works were dedicated to other kinds of patrons, especially noblemen—a practice that reminds us of the continued importance of aristocratic patronage.

Still other books in table 2 were dedicated to fellow authors among the Scottish literati, and these public expressions of gratitude and affection deserve special mention here. John Dalrymple dedicated *An Essay towards a General History of Feudal Property* (no. 43) to Kames, "as the following thoughts were directed by your lordship." Robert Heron dedicated his *New General History of Scotland* (no. 330) to Sir John Sinclair, in a manner that stressed the theme of national improvement through arts and letters (he also dedicated his 1789 edition of James Thomson's *The Seasons* to Hugh Blair). The second edition of James Anderson's *Essays Relating to Agriculture and Rural Affairs* (no. 172), which appeared in 1777, carried a dedication in the same spirit to William Cullen, with whom the author had studied; the first edition lacked a formal dedication but contained an advertisement that identified "the late ingenious Dr John Gregory" as

108. Moore, "Life of Smollett"; Ferguson, "Minutes" (read to the Royal Society of Edinburgh in Aug. 1801); Heron, "Memoir," in Lindsay, *Burns Encyclopedia*, 166–82.

the inspiration behind the book's enlightened objective: "to turn the attention of mankind to the pursuit of what was solid and useful in arts and sciences." Among medical books, Alexander Hamilton's *Outlines of the Theory and Practice of Midwifery* (no. 242) was dedicated to Cullen and Benjamin Bell's *System of Surgery* (no. 240) to Alexander Monro *secundus.* The second edition of William Buchan's *Domestic Medicine* (no. 115), John Gregory's *Lectures on the Duties and Qualifications of a Physician* (no. 129), and Lord Kames's *Gentleman Farmer* (no. 176) were all dedicated to the president of the Royal Society of London, Sir John Pringle. Andrew Duncan, writing in the name of "A Society in Edinburgh" on 12 January 1773, dedicated the first volume of his *Medical and Philosophical Commentaries* to the principal of the University of Edinburgh, William Robertson, as an expression of "sincere thanks" for his efforts on behalf of the university's "celebrated School of Medicine." Archibald Alison dedicated the second edition of his *Essays on Taste* (no. 287) to his companion from his student days at the University of Glasgow, Dugald Stewart.

Four of these "internal" dedications in the books of the Scottish literati stand out because they express fundamental Enlightenment ideals about the proper relationships among men of letters. The dedication in David Hume's *Four Dissertations* of 1757 (no. 45) to John Home, "Author of *Douglas,* a Tragedy"—the only dedication that Hume ever wrote—was both a gesture to a personal friend and an endorsement of politeness and cosmopolitanism. Home and his associates in the Moderate party of the Church of Scotland were then under attack from stricter members of the Kirk over the propriety of clergymen writing and attending stage plays. Without mentioning this controversy directly, Hume's dedication sought to negate it by reference to an idealized classical world in which "men of letters," guided by the principle of "liberty of thought," maintained "a mutual friendship and regard" in the face of differences of opinion. For these enlightened ancients, "Science was often the subject of disputation, never of animosity." Although Hume found it necessary to suppress the dedication after its initial appearance, under pressure from friends who feared that it would do more harm than good, it circulated widely in the press, and it is significant that he defended his actions privately in a strongly worded letter to a close friend in Scotland: "I am sure I never executed any thing, which was either more elegant in the Composition, or more generous in the Intention" (*LDH,* 1:242).[109] The dedication may have been

---

109. See Mossner, *Life of David Hume,* chap. 26; Lonsdale, "Thomas Gray," 57–70.

deemed inexpedient, but it accurately reflected the enlightened beliefs of Hume and his friends.

Later in the century, the lengthy tribute to Dugald Stewart and James Gregory—"My Dear Friends"—that appears in Thomas Reid's *Essays on the Intellectual Powers of Man* (no. 255) espouses similar principles, but the scene has moved from the ancient world to the modern Athens and its environs (see fig. 9.3). Signed "Glasgow College, June 1, 1785," when the author was nearly seventy-five years old, Reid's dedication paints an idealized picture of eighteenth-century Scotland as a place where men of letters debate ideas in a calm and pleasurable manner, sometimes disagreeing but generally using the give-and-take of philosophical discourse to clarify and sharpen their principles in an atmosphere of "friendship" and mutual respect. That Reid's book was dedicated to two fellow philosophers was unusual; even more unusual was the fact that those philosophers were both forty-three years younger than the author. Reid notes their enormous age differences in the first sentence of the dedication and also mentions that one of them (Stewart) had been his pupil. He then proceeds to invoke the name of an inspirational Scottish man of letters much older than he, the late Henry Home, Lord Kames, who had lived long enough to engage in philosophical exchanges with Stewart and Gregory, and who was distinguished for "his zeal to encourage and promote every thing that tended to the improvement of his country, in laws, literature, commerce, manufactures, and agriculture." "On some points we differed in opinion," Reid observes in regard to Kames's patronage of his philosophical investigations, "and debated them keenly, both in conversation and by many letters, without any abatement of his affection, or of his zeal for the work's being carried on and published." Without the encouragement of men like Kames, Stewart, and Gregory, Reid might never have published this book, because "without social intercourse, even a favourite speculation languishes."[110] Thus, a reader of this dedication would see that Reid considered his book to be the product of a continuous period of intellectual discourse and social interaction, which encompassed several generations of Scottish men of letters and permeated the Scottish universities.[111]

110. Letters to James Gregory, such as those of 7 April and 8 June 1783, reveal the great debt that Reid felt toward Gregory for reading and critiquing his book manuscript and seeing it through the press, as well as for providing moral support, and it is clear that he felt similarly indebted to Stewart. Reid, *Correspondence*, 162–63.

111. Stewart's and Gregory's academic titles at Edinburgh are recorded after their names, and Reid alludes indirectly to his lectures at Marischal College, Aberdeen,

Seven years later, Dugald Stewart and James Gregory dedicated their books to Reid. Stewart's *Elements of the Philosophy of the Human Mind* (no. 309) contained a brief statement "in Testimony of the Respect and Affection of the Author." Although Gregory's *Philosophical and Literary Essays* (no. 304) also bore a 1792 imprint, the author signed his dedication "January 1, 1790." It is an eight-page open letter to an aging mentor, composed in much the same spirit as the dedications by Hume and Reid. Differences "on certain points of philosophy" are acknowledged but transcended by the "pleasure and instruction" derived from Reid's writings and "the high sense that I have of the merit of your philosophy." Reid is placed among "those authors who have contributed by their labours, either to make men wiser, or to make them better"—or both. The last word of the dedication—"Farewell"—stands by itself, beckoning the reader to consider the ebb and flow of philosophical generations. Reid would die in 1796, but Gregory and Stewart would live on into the 1820s.

The same spirit of corporate identity and cosmopolitanism among authors that characterizes these dedications by Hume, Reid, Stewart, and Gregory appears in the body of the texts of many works in table 2. When they published books that chronicled their travels in Scotland, Scottish authors typically puffed their fellow literati in the major towns. Mention has already been made of John Knox's complimentary references to Edinburgh authors in his *View of the British Empire*, which bore similarities to Smollett's remarks in *Humphry Clinker*. Boswell's *Journal of a Tour to the Hebrides, with Samuel Johnson* (1785; no. 250) ranged more widely. Visiting Edinburgh in August 1773, Boswell and Johnson socialized with William Robertson, Adam Ferguson, William Cullen, Thomas Blacklock, Lord Hailes, and James Gregory. In St. Andrews they were entertained chiefly by Robert Watson, "a well-informed man of very amiable manners." In Aberdeen they met George Campbell, Alexander Gerard, and James Dunbar among the professors in the two Aberdonian colleges. In Glasgow in October, after their Highland excursion, they conversed with Thomas Reid, John Anderson, and William Leechman. Back in Edinburgh at the conclusion of the journey the following month, they spent time with Robertson and Hugh Blair (whom Johnson declared "good men,

---

and the University of Glasgow. Reid enclosed the "Epistle" that would become the dedication with a letter to Gregory of 2 May 1785, leaving it up to Gregory and Stewart to determine "whether your [Gregory's] Name should go first on account of your Doctor's degree or Mr Stewarts on account of his Seniority as a Professor" (Reid, *Correspondence*, 173).

and wise men"), as well as with Hailes, Blacklock, Sir John Dalrymple, and William Tytler and his son, Alexander Fraser Tytler. There is talk throughout the book of David Hume, James Beattie, Adam Smith, Lord Kames, and of course James Macpherson and his controversial Ossianic poetry. Whatever disagreements Johnson may have had with the Scottish literati over particular issues, and however much he may have questioned their merit as authors when sparring with Boswell, the overall impression is one of provincial cosmopolitanism and politeness. In this way, Boswell's *Tour* publicized and often praised the authors of the Scottish Enlightenment and placed many of them in their appropriate geographical contexts in Scotland's university towns.

Scottish Grub Street writers in London followed the lead of Knox and Boswell. In 1788 William Thomson, writing as "An English Gentleman," published an account of an excursion to Scotland three years earlier (no. 277), which he reprinted in 1791 in an expanded version under the pseudonym Thomas Newte, Esq., of Devon. The following year the Earl of Buchan cited "Captain Newte's admirable Tour in Scotland" in the introduction to his *Essays on the Lives and Writings of Fletcher of Saltoun and the Poet Thomson* (no. 302). The authorial ruse represents an attempt to use a gentrified English identity to legitimize what was essentially Scottish Grub Street boasting and boosting. Passing through Oxford and Cambridge on his northward route, "Newte" declares them "venerable monuments of ancient times." In Glasgow, by contrast, he finds "professors here, of all the sciences, many of whom, as Simson, Hutcheson, Smith, Muir [Moor], Millar, and Reid, are celebrated in the republic of letters." There is a long passage praising the writings of the improver David Loch and an extensive discussion of the University of Edinburgh, which includes this sentence: "The names of Smith, Robertson, Black, Fergusson, Cullen, Monro, Gregory, and other *Edinburgenses*, distinguished by their writings, are well known." Two other professors, Dugald Steward [*sic*] and John Playfair, are also singled out as men likely to make a name for themselves as authors before long. When discussing Aberdeen, Thomson mentions no names but notes the "liberal and active spirit that prevails" there, due mainly to the influence of the two colleges.[112] Robert Heron's *Observations Made in a Journey through the Western Counties of Scotland* (1793; no. 314) is another example of a tour of Scotland by a Grub Street Scot who incorporates into the narrative a long, laudatory discussion of

112. [Thomson], Thomas Newte, *Prospects and Observations*, 2–3, 61–67, 188–89, 200, 366–67.

the academic literati of Edinburgh, including Blair, Robertson, Ferguson, Stewart, Playfair, and the medical professors. In doing so, Heron retells the by-now familiar story of how "the scientific and literary fame of the [Edinburgh] professors spread into England and over the continent of Europe" as a result of their publications (2:480).

Philosophical works often carried a similar message. John Bethune's anonymous *Essays and Dissertations on Various Subjects* (1770; no. 125) praises Adam Ferguson and Adam Smith, "one of the most rational and acute philosophers of this philosophical age" (2:348). In a footnote in one of the essays, Bethune playfully comments on the refutation of David Hume's skeptical arguments on the nature of the self by the Aberdonians Beattie, Gerard, Campbell, and Reid. It has been rightly noted that the Aberdonians' relationship with Hume "is better characterized as a dialogue than as a simple refutation,"[113] and the point holds true for many other Scottish Enlightenment authors. Opposition to Humean skepticism was a common theme in a number of the philosophical works found in table 2 besides those written by the Aberdonians mentioned by Bethune, including all the books by James Balfour (nos. 23, 104, and 222), James Oswald's *An Appeal to Common Sense in Behalf of Religion* (no. 97), Lord Monboddo's *Antient Metaphysics* (no. 204), John Ogilvie's *Inquiry into the Causes of the Infidelity and Scepticism of the Times* (no. 235), William Russell's *History of Modern Europe* (no. 203), and William Julius Mickle's anonymous *Voltaire in the Shades* (no. 131), in which a character named Sceptic (H———e) joins in a debate with Voltaire, Rousseau, Socrates, and others. Although the subject provoked strong feelings, most of these works were distinguished by an enlightened attitude that lived up to the cosmopolitan ideal of disagreement without animosity. Bethune, for example, follows his statement about the demise of Hume's skeptical philosophy with a comment about the pleasing nature of Hume's "genius and character" (1:131), and Russell's strictures on Hume's infidelity are accompanied by praise of "this great man."[114] When harsher language was used, as in Beattie's *Essay on Truth* (no. 123), there was controversy and concern about whether the bounds of politeness had been overstepped.[115]

---

113. Suderman, *Orthodoxy and Enlightenment,* 28.

114. [Russell], *History of Modern Europe,* 5:514.

115. In the preface to the first volume of *Antient Metaphysics* (1779), for example, Monboddo ostensibly defends Beattie against the complaints of Hume and "his friends" about the abusive nature of Beattie's "style," but he emphasizes that his own

As the opposition to Hume's skepticism illustrates, we should not conclude that all these connections, all this bonding among the Scottish literati, gave rise to universal agreement among them on all important issues. Peter Gay's statement that "unity did not mean unanimity" still holds true, and so does his comparison of the philosophes of the Enlightenment to a squabbling family.[116] The Hunter brothers' savage attacks on other physicians, such as Alexander Monro *secundus*, in William's *Medical Commentaries* (no. 76), demonstrate that relations with fellow Scots who were not kin could sometimes be strained; the bad blood that developed between the brothers themselves after 1780 shows that even kinship did not always ensure close and supportive relationships. There were intellectual debates, ideological disputes, and personal rivalries among the literati. Political differences existed between a conservative Whig majority and a more radical Whig minority, along with some Tories and Jacobites.[117]

The crucial point, however, is that differences and disagreements were overshadowed by the larger setting in which they occurred: an environment of mutual support and common cause on behalf of economic and moral improvement, polite learning and literature, cosmopolitanism, and other enlightened values. Within such a setting, even rivalries and differences could stimulate rather than inhibit enlightened book culture. The Scottish Enlightenment was firmly grounded in personal relationships among its leading practitioners. It functioned as a constellation of overlapping urban communities of scholars and literary figures who were joined through a multiplicity of common ties of nationality, kinship, religion, occupation, education, patronage, friendship, and outlook. Scottishness, far from being a tangential component of this identity package, let alone an anachronistic construction imposed on eighteenth-century intellectuals by nationalist scholars from a later period, constituted one of the fundamental elements that united the authors whose names appear in table 1, including those who resided in London.

---

answer to Hume is "strictly philosophical" and avoids "that illiberal abuse, which no zeal, even in the best cause, can justify" (vi).

116. Gay, *Enlightenment*, 1:6.

117. Among the left-leaning literati, whose ideology has never been properly examined, were Alexander Adam, James Anderson, John Anderson, Robert Burns, the Earl of Buchan, Francis Hutcheson, Malcolm Laing, Sir James Mackintosh, John Millar, John Moore, William Ogilvie, John Pinkerton, John Playfair, Thomas Reid, William Smellie, and Gilbert Stuart.

Naming the Author

Although the public identity of authors hinges mainly on the outcome of their decision either to conceal or to reveal themselves in their books, this polarity can be broken down into a number of practices that fill the space between total concealment at one extreme and full disclosure of an author's name, sometimes supported by additional biographical information, at the other. The author column in table 2 reveals some of these nuances. I have placed square brackets around an author's name to signify "true anonymity" whenever the author's name is not to be found on the title page, in the front matter, or in the body of the text of at least the first three editions of a book. I use angle brackets if these conditions apply but a pseudonym has been employed. Combining all the titles with square and angle brackets, we can say that 58 of the 360 books in table 2 (16 percent) were published under conditions of true anonymity.

This number is actually not as high as it may at first seem, however, because the identity of the author of an anonymous book was often an open secret, or no secret at all, as a result of information available outside the book. Although Hume told Hutcheson of his determination "to keep my Name a Secret for some time" after publishing the first two volumes of his *Treatise of Human Nature* in January 1739, by mid-March 1740 he admitted he had "fail'd in that point" (*LDH*, 1:38). If Hume's identity was leaked through word of mouth, that was not the only way such news could spread. One of the works written against Hume's philosophy, *An Appeal to Common Sense in Behalf of Religion* (no. 97), was also published anonymously, but a newspaper advertisement announcing its appearance identified the author as James Oswald, D.D., minister of the Gospel at Methven (*EEC*, 24 Nov. 1766). Henry Mackenzie's identity as the author of *The Man of Feeling* (no. 135), *The Man of the World* (no. 155), and *Julia de Roubigné* (no. 183) was forced into the open in 1777, in response to a claim that all three novels had been written by a deceased English clergyman.[118] In 1769 David Garrick orchestrated a scheme to hide the fact that John Home was the author of *The Fatal Discovery* (no. 118) for fear that English prejudice would hurt the reception given to a play by a Scotsman who was closely attached to the hated Lord Bute, but the ruse could not be maintained for long, and the true author was soon discovered.[119] In this case,

---

118. Mackenzie, *Letters to Elizabeth Rose*, 205n6.
119. Carlyle, *Autobiography*, 534–35.

like that of Henry Home's controversial *Essays on the Principles of Morality and Natural Religion* (no. 14), anonymity was grounded in subterfuge of the sort that Voltaire and other French *philosophes* employed frequently in order to elude censorship and legal prosecution when they wished to publish works that would be deemed improper by the authorities. Scottish Enlightenment authors rarely had to contend with such legal constraints, however, and only occasionally did they feel the need to conceal themselves as authors for fear of giving offense. The most likely reasons for them to publish their works anonymously were modesty and anxiety in the face of public exposure and criticism, at least until they discovered how their books would be received.[120]

Anonymous publication correlates to some extent with age, status, and genre. Some older writers, such as Francis Hutcheson and Robert Wallace, always published anonymously. Grub Street writers such as William Thomson were also more likely to conceal their authorship, whereas established members of the liberal professions did so much less frequently. But the highest correlation is with subject matter and genre. If we exclude multiauthor works such as the *Encyclopaedia Britannica* and the papers published by learned societies, almost half the cases of true anonymity found in table 2 occur in fictional prose works of novels and tales (18) or plays (10). Or, to look at the matter another way, 86 percent of the works of fiction (18 of 21) and 83 percent of the works of drama (10 of 12) in table 2 were published anonymously,[121] whereas in all other genres combined, true anonymity occurred less than 10 percent of the time, and in some fields it was virtually unknown.

These figures are of particular interest in light of Foucault's claim that the seventeenth century saw a major reversal in the way that literary and scientific works achieved credibility. Before that time, Foucault argues, literature could stand on its own when produced anonymously, while science required the authority of a great name in order to gain acceptance; after the reversal, however, "the author function faded away" from scientific works, which now obtained their credibility by appearing to embody "redemonstrable truth" in and of itself, whereas "literary discourses came to be accepted only when endowed with the author function," and literary

120. On this point and several others discussed below, see Griffin, introduction to *Faces of Anonymity.*

121. These figures are consistent with those given for late eighteenth-century British and Irish novels in Raven, "Anonymous Novel," 141–66.

anonymity became intolerable except when it appeared in "the guise of an enigma."[122] The evidence in table 2 runs counter to Foucault's claims, since literary works tended toward anonymity while scientific and medical works were the least likely to be published in that manner. Indeed, true anonymity can be found in only two of ninety-one works of science, mathematics, and medicine in table 2.

Yet nothing that has been said negates Foucault's larger point about the importance of the author function in literary publications.[123] Among British novelists, it was standard practice since at least the 1740s for a body of fiction to be linked together not under a proper name but under the titles of earlier novels by the same author. Thus, in 1762 the title page of Tobias Smollett's *Sir Launcelot Greaves* (no. 78) contained the phrase "By the Author of Roderick Random." The title page of Henry Mackenzie's 1777 novel, *Julia de Roubigné*, affirms that this book was written by the author of two novels from earlier that decade, *The Man of Feeling* (no. 135) and *The Man of the World* (no. 155). The title page of John Moore's 1800 novel, *Mordaunt* (no. 359), links the author to two earlier novels, *Zeluco* (no. 284) and *Edward* (no. 340), without mentioning either the author's name or other nonfiction works he had written. The title page of William Guthrie's anonymous novel of 1759, *The Mother* (no. 54), states that the book is by the author of *The Friends* (no. 32), which had also appeared anonymously five years earlier, and the title page of William Thomson's *Mammuth* (1789; no. 286) informs readers that it is written by the Man in the Moon—an allusion that would carry them back to Thomson's 1783 work with that title (no. 237). Newspaper advertisements of anonymous books by established authors performed the same function (see fig. 5.6). In such cases, the author function is clearly in play as a means of encouraging the reading public to make sense of a number of fictional books by categorizing them under a single author, even though that author's name is never stated.

Foucault's point about the attraction of literary anonymity when it appears in "the guise of an enigma" is well illustrated by Henry Mackenzie's periodical-turned-book, *The Mirror* (no. 217). Mackenzie devoted the entire second number of 30 January 1779 to this question. Comparing anonymity to the power of "invisibility" conferred by magical caps and rings in children's fairy tales, the unnamed author visits the shop of the paper's publisher, William Creech, in order to hear what people are saying about

122. Foucault, "What Is an Author?" 109–10. Cf. Chartier, *Order of Books*, 31–32.
123. Cf. Griffin, introduction to *Faces of Anonymity*, esp. 4 and 9–10.

his identity. The trap has been set by deliberately placing several copies of the first issue on the table, in addition to the subscription paper hanging near the front door. The customers are overheard to speculate in turn that the author is a clergyman, a professor, a player, a lawyer, a judge, a nobleman, a gentleman or baron of the exchequer, or a commissioner of customs. One believes that the paper will be used to advance the Humean system of skepticism, another that it will promote Methodism, a third that its purpose is to pursue a political agenda. Someone says it is to be "very satirical," someone else that it will be "very stupid." And so on. After hearing all this, the author finds himself "for some time in doubt, whether I should not put an end to these questions at once, by openly publishing my name and intentions to the world." "A certain bashfulness" finally leads him to decide against shedding his cloak of invisibility, however, and he contents himself with restating the point of the project from the first number: "I mean to shew the world what it is, and will sometimes endeavour to point out what it should be." The work's title is explicitly associated with this aim of reflecting reality. Yet most of the second number uses the mirror concept in a different, implicit sense, to suggest the illusory images of a conjuring trick: now you think you see the author, and now you don't. The deception is enhanced by situating the action in Creech's shop, a "real" and identifiable setting.

Moving along the spectrum from concealed to revealed identity, I have placed curly brackets around names of authors in table 2 to signify what I call "mitigated anonymity" and "temporary anonymity." In cases of mitigated anonymity, the name of the author does not appear on the title page but can be ascertained from other information in the book, usually the front matter. For example, Henry Home, Lord Kames, never put his name on the title page of a first edition, but readers usually knew his identity because he signed his name to the preface or introduction (nos. 62, 176, 182, and 214) or to the dedication (no. 73). In other forms of mitigated anonymity, readers had to work a little harder to discover the name of the author, though it was available to them if they wished to pursue the matter. The title page of Hume's *Philosophical Essays concerning Human Understanding* (no. 8), published in April 1748, does not identify the author, but it states that the book is "by the author of the *Essays Moral and Political*"—a work reprinted in a new edition later that same year (fig. 4.1), with Hume's name on the title page. Although John Gregory's name does not appear on the title page of *Observations on the Duties and Offices of a Physician* (no. 129), references in the text to the author's "learned and ingenious colleagues" in the medical faculty at the University of Edinburgh, "particularly Dr. Cullen and Dr. Monro" (165–66), leave no doubt about who wrote the book. Another example is the attribution of *Essays and Observations, Physical and Literary* (no. 34) to "A Society in Edinburgh," which any informed reader would know to be the Edinburgh Philosophical Society.

Curly brackets around an author's name in table 2 have also been used to designate "temporary anonymity," which is defined here as occurring whenever authors fully concealed their identities in the first edition but revealed it by the third edition. This was done in roughly a score of books in the database. William Wilkie's epic poem *The Epigoniad*, a work that failed to live up to the high expectations of its supporters when originally published anonymously in Edinburgh in 1757, was recast two years later with additional material and published in London rather than Edinburgh, with the author's name on the title page. Hugh Blair published his *Critical Dissertation on the Poems of Ossian* anonymously in 1763, although his authorship was common knowledge in literary circles. In 1765 Blair produced a greatly expanded second edition of the work, with his name on the title page. A third example of temporary anonymity involves James Beattie's poem *The Minstrel*. After the great success of the anonymous book 1 in 1771, the author put his name on the title page of the third edition in 1772 and kept it there in all subsequent editions of book 1, book 2 (first published in 1774), and the complete poem in two books. According to Margaret Forbes, Beattie left his name off at first because he "did not wish to append his name to an unfinished production,"[124] but it is also possible that he was merely being cautious at first and added his name to the third edition after it became clear that his poem was going to be successful. James Fordyce's *Sermons to Young Women* (no. 93), John Moore's *A View of Society and Manners in France, Switzerland, and Germany* (no. 201), and Elizabeth Hamilton's *Memoirs of Modern Philosophers* (no. 357) are other examples of works that were originally published anonymously but added the author's name to the title page after the success of the first edition.

In the same way, Thomas Reid encouraged William Ogilvie to add his name to the title page of his *Essay on the Right of Property in Land* (no. 220), remarking that an acquaintance of his "cannot see a reason (neither can I) why it should go about like a foundling without its father's name."[125] Reid's terminology is of interest because it removes anonymity from its traditional association with selfless nobility—the opposite of vanity—and

124. Forbes, *Beattie and His Friends*, 57.
125. Reid to Ogilvie, 7 Apr. 1789, in Reid, *Correspondence*, 204.

links it instead with the pejorative imagery of paternal desertion and illegitimacy. Perhaps Ogilvie would have complied with Reid's suggestion if there had been a demand for another edition of his book. This circumstance reminds us that many of the poor- and modest-selling books that were published anonymously might have become instances of temporary anonymity if the opportunity for another edition had presented itself to their authors.

Altogether, thirty-eight titles in table 2, almost 11 percent of the total number of entries, fall under the combined categories of mitigated and temporary anonymity. In a small number of these books, both mitigated and temporary anonymity came into play. Henry Home, later Lord Kames, published *Essays upon Several Subjects concerning British Antiquities* (no. 2) anonymously in Edinburgh in 1747 but then signed the introduction to the second edition that was published in London two years later. In 1779 he signed the preface to the third edition of his *Essays on the Principles of Morality and Natural Religion* (no. 14), although his identity as the author had never been in doubt.[126] William Russell published the first part of *The History of Modern Europe* (no. 203) in 1779 anonymously, but the second part appeared in 1784 with a signed dedication to the Duke of Bedford. When Alexander Fraser Tytler was preparing to publish the third edition (1813) of his anonymous *Essay on the Principles of Translation* (no. 300), he told his publisher that "I have put my name to the dedication, because, as I was well known to be the author of the work, it would have had a look of affectation to present it again in an anonymous form."[127]

The complexities of anonymity are well illustrated by the literary career of William Richardson. When Richardson wrote to William Creech on 7 September 1773 about the possibility of publishing his first book, *A Philosophical Analysis and Illustration of Some of Shakespeare's Remarkable Characters* (1774; no. 166), along with another manuscript of fictional tales, he was nervous about the prospect of identifying himself as an author. "I cannot prevail with myself to put my name to them till I see what success they will have," he states. "Let me therefore beg of you not to be known as the author" (WCL). His way of phrasing his concern supports the hypothesis that temporary anonymity was often a way for authors to use a first edition in order to test the waters: a cold reception shielded an author from exposure, but if the book drew critical acclaim and sold well enough to call forth further editions, the author could confidently add his name

126. Ross, *Lord Kames*, chaps. 6 and 8.
127. Constable, *Archibald Constable*, 2:203.

to the title page. In this instance, however, the author changed his mind several months later, when he wrote to Creech on 12 December that "I am determined to put my name to the work, not on the title page nor in the advertisements, but at the end of a short dedication to Lord Cathcart" (WCL). This he did, but when a third edition of the book appeared in 1784, Richardson's name appeared on the title page.

Richardson's correspondence with Creech about the second work he was planning to publish in the mid-1770s reveals a different motive for withholding one's identity as author, a motive more suited to true anonymity than to its mitigated or temporary forms. Writing on 23 November 1773 of poems that he had first given to the London publisher John Murray, who had passed them along to Creech, Richardson states: "Let me beg of you not to show them to any one. I would not be answerable to the good people of Glasgow for writing a tragedy" (WCL). Richardson's fear of putting his name to a stage play, at a time when the theater was considered immoral by many pious Presbyterians in Scotland, especially in Glasgow, is another illustration of how concern about giving offense could sometimes affect the way that authors identified themselves. Richardson solved this problem by excluding the play from *Poems, Chiefly Rural* that he published in 1774 (no. 167). Even so, he kept his name off the title page of that work, though his anonymity was once again compromised by his signing another dedication to Cathcart, and he put his name on the title page of the second edition that appeared later in the same year. When he finally published his tragedy, *The Indians*, in 1790 (no. 289), the work appeared anonymously. Richardson's *Anecdotes of the Russian Empire* of 1784 (no. 246) also appeared without his name on the title page, though with a signed dedication to Cathcart. Thus, despite his modesty, which caused him to leave his name off the title pages of the first editions of most of his books, Richardson rarely tried to conceal his identity as an author.

Most Scottish Enlightenment authors made no attempt whatsoever at concealment. Approximately three-quarters of the books in table 2 reveal the author's name on the title page of the first edition, and the figure rises to well over 80 percent when works of fiction and drama are excluded. Add the fact that the concealment of authorship in formally anonymous works was not often rigorously maintained for all the reasons that have been discussed and it soon becomes clear that anonymity was a practice of little consequence except in certain types of literary writing: novels, some plays, and some literary periodicals. Overwhelmingly, the authors of the Scottish Enlightenment wrote to be known by their readers. This finding runs counter to current scholarship on author identification, which maintains that before the twentieth century anonymous publication was "at least as much a norm as signed authorship."[128] But it lends support to the notion, grounded in Foucault's concept of the "author function," that the book culture of the mature Scottish Enlightenment was characterized by author recognition and a number of attributes that flow from it, including author construction, author categorization, author accountability, and author criticism.

The power of the author function could lead to some strange twists. *A New Geographical, Historical, and Commercial Grammar* (no. 130)—the most popular of all eighteenth-century geography books and one of the biggest best sellers of the age in any genre—always identified the author on its title page as "William Guthrie, Esq." (fig. 2.5). It is unlikely, however, that much of the book was actually written by Guthrie, who had died on 9 March 1770, about six months before publication. Rather, attention must be focused on the publisher, John Knox, a Scottish bookseller with a shop in the Strand who is the only person listed in table 2 as both an author and a publisher. The first edition of Knox's *A View of the British Empire* (no. 244) identified the author on the title page as "The Original Editor of Guthrie's Geographical Grammar." Knox elaborated in a footnote in the preface to the fourth edition of the *View*, which appeared in 1789:

> Perceiving that the books of geography were extremely defective respecting Scotland, I formed a design of publishing a more accurate and complete work on geography, history, etc. an undertaking which required more time and patience than I was aware of. After labouring upon it, more than a twelvemonth, with intense application, I applied to Mr. William Guthrie for assistance in such parts of the work as I should point out, as well as for the use of his name in the title-page.

Knox, then, claimed to have used Guthrie as a hired hand in the service of a project that was essentially his own and to have placed Guthrie's name on the title page to capitalize on that writer's fame. An anonymous periodical writer went further, asserting that "a geographical grammar has been printed under [Guthrie's] name; but it is generally understood,

---

128. Griffin, introduction to *Faces of Anonymity*, 6, 15. Griffin's claim may be accurate for the totality of late eighteenth-century print culture, because certain forms of printed works, such as pamphlets and ephemera, and certain genres, such as fiction, were so heavily anonymous. But unless Scottish authors were atypical, a completely different pattern prevailed in regard to nonfiction books.

that he had no share in its composition."[129] This does not mean that Knox was the principal "author" of the book any more than Guthrie was. He may have written much of it, but he identified himself as the "editor," meaning presumably one who commissioned, organized, compiled, and adapted materials and perhaps even lifted text from other published books.[130] As Robert Mayhew has argued, the issue of attribution is particularly problematic in regard to eighteenth-century geography books, "a genre where textual usurpation and the breach of copy were the norm."[131] All that can be said with certainty is that Knox understood the advantages of placing Guthrie's name on the title page and keeping it there, and so did others. In part 3 of this study, we shall see how, toward the end of the century, Irish and American booksellers appropriated this work for purposes of their own, tampering aggressively with its contents but never daring to replace or supplement Guthrie as the named author.

There is more to the matter of author identification than naming the author. Although one would not know it from ESTC, most of the title pages of works in table 2 contain additional biographical information after the author's name. These identification tags can be extremely revealing. Even the relatively innocuous "Esq." that follows the names of authors such as Robert Adam, David Hume, William Guthrie, James Macpherson, James Balfour, and James Boswell tells us that these authors wished to be identified as gentlemen. Authors with earned M.A.'s from Scottish universities sometimes placed their degrees after their names (e.g., "By W. Duff, A.M." in no. 126), but the M.D., D.D., and LL.D. degrees were more prestigious and were usually recorded by authors who possessed them. Besides degrees, authors sometimes identified their occupations in a straightforward way, such as "By George Wallace, Esq., Advocate" (no. 238) or "By William Alexander, Surgeon in Edinburgh" (no. 103). Authors who held academic or other important institutional positions usually listed them fully, along with their academic degrees. Clergyman typically identified themselves as ministers of particular parishes. Authors who were fellows of the Royal Society of London or the Royal

129. "Critical Remarks," 91.

130. An advertisement for a rival geography book, *A New and Complete System of Universal Geography* by John Payne [Robert Heron?], charged that some of the text in Guthrie's *Geographical Grammar* was lifted from an earlier German geography text, Anton Friedrich Büsching's *Neue Erdbeschreibung*, which had been translated into English by Patrick Murdoch and published in London by Andrew Millar in 1762 as *A New System of Geography*.

131. Mayhew, *Enlightenment Geography*, 40.

Society of Edinburgh commonly recorded that information, written out or abbreviated as F.R.S. and F.R.S.E., and membership in other learned societies was increasingly noted as well, as were certain kinds of prestigious sinecures and positions.

These bits of biographical information were not mutually exclusive; rather, they accumulated as authors obtained new degrees, positions, and honors. The title page of *The History of Great Britain during the Reign of Queen Anne* (no. 346) identifies the author as "Thomas Somerville, D.D. F.R.S.E. One of His Majesty's Chaplains in Ordinary, and Minister at Jedburgh." It thus managed to include an honorary doctorate of divinity, a fellowship in a learned society, an ecclesiastical sinecure, and a position as a parish minister in the Church of Scotland. In the first volume of *A System of Surgery* (no. 240), published in 1783, Benjamin Bell is identified on the title page as "Member of the Royal College of Surgeons of Edinburgh, and one of the Surgeons to the Royal Infirmary of that City." By the time the second volume appeared the following year, Bell added "and Fellow of the Royal Society of Edinburgh." When his next book was published in 1793 (no. 312), he supplemented all this with a reference to his membership in the Royal College of Surgeons of Ireland. Robert Whytt's *Observations on the Dropsy* (no. 110) identifies the author as "M.D. Late Physician to his Majesty, President of the Royal College of Physicians, Professor of Medicine in the University of Edinburgh, and F.R.S." In Andrew Duncan's *Medical Cases* (no. 190), the author's name is followed by "M.D. Fellow of the Royal College of Physicians, Lecturer in Medicine, and Physician to the Public Dispensary of Edinburgh, Member of the Royal Societies of Medicine in Paris, Copenhagen, Edinburgh, etc." This form of author embellishment peaked in 1789 when the title page of *A Treatise of the Materia Medica* (no. 281) named William Cullen as the author and then identified him in eighty-four words that listed his M.D. degree, his professorship at the University of Edinburgh, his sinecure as first physician to his majesty for Scotland, and his fellowships or memberships in ten learned societies in Britain, Europe, and America (fig. 2.7).[132]

The presence on title pages of additional information about authors is significant for four reasons. First, it shows how authors thought about themselves, or more precisely, how they wanted to be perceived. The fact

132. James Anderson's *Recreations* (no. 351) was a close second, with "LL.D., FRS and FSA. E." (the Society of Antiquaries of Scotland, apparently), the full names of ten learned societies in England, France, Russia, Germany, and America, and the words "and author of several performances."

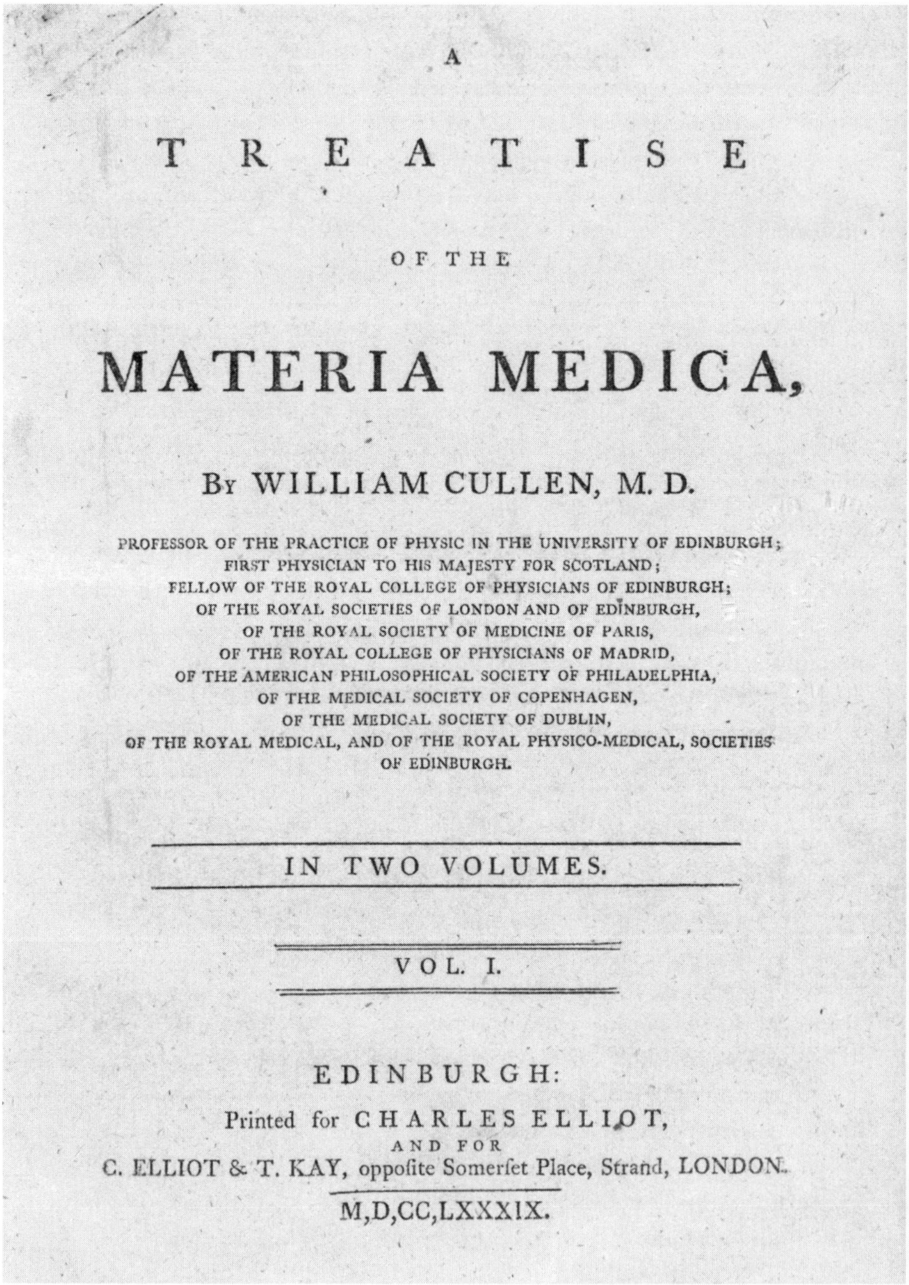

A

TREATISE

OF THE

MATERIA MEDICA,

By WILLIAM CULLEN, M. D.

PROFESSOR OF THE PRACTICE OF PHYSIC IN THE UNIVERSITY OF EDINBURGH;
FIRST PHYSICIAN TO HIS MAJESTY FOR SCOTLAND;
FELLOW OF THE ROYAL COLLEGE OF PHYSICIANS OF EDINBURGH;
OF THE ROYAL SOCIETIES OF LONDON AND OF EDINBURGH,
OF THE ROYAL SOCIETY OF MEDICINE OF PARIS,
OF THE ROYAL COLLEGE OF PHYSICIANS OF MADRID,
OF THE AMERICAN PHILOSOPHICAL SOCIETY OF PHILADELPHIA,
OF THE MEDICAL SOCIETY OF COPENHAGEN,
OF THE MEDICAL SOCIETY OF DUBLIN,
OF THE ROYAL MEDICAL, AND OF THE ROYAL PHYSICO-MEDICAL, SOCIETIES
OF EDINBURGH.

IN TWO VOLUMES.

VOL. I.

EDINBURGH:

Printed for CHARLES ELLIOT,
AND FOR
C. ELLIOT & T. KAY, oppofite Somerfet Place, Strand, LONDON.

M,D,CC,LXXXIX.

Fig. 2.7. The title pages of Scottish Enlightenment books often identified authors by their degrees, titles, and positions, but William Cullen's *Treatise of the Materia Medica* (1789) took this practice to its farthest extreme. Thomas Fisher Rare Book Library, University of Toronto.

that Cullen elected to list so many honors, for example, says something about his character, which one commentator has described as "ambitious and self-confident, intelligent and interested in a broad range of subjects, generous yet shrewd."[133] There is evidence of other authors pondering the wording of their identifications on title pages. The first edition of Adam Ferguson's *History of the Progress and Termination of the Roman Republic* (no. 232), published in 1783, identifies the author simply as "Adam Ferguson, LL.D. Professor of Moral Philosophy in the University of Edinburgh." In the second edition of 1799, however, Ferguson added his fellowship in the Royal Society of Edinburgh ("F.R.S.E.") and his membership in four Continental academies, but privately he expressed concern about whether he had "done right in Spelling my forreign honours at full length."[134] William Robertson had many international honors and distinctions, but he omitted them when he referred to himself on the title pages of his books as "William Robertson, D.D., Principal of the University of Edinburgh, and Historiographer to His Majesty for Scotland." As he was about to publish his last book on 9 May 1791, however, Robertson asked one of his publishers, Andrew Strahan, if he thought he should place after that description the words "Member of the Imperial Academy of Sciences of St Petersburgh, and of the Royal Academy of History at Madrid," adding uncertainly, "I think it better to omit them" (SA 48901, fols. 44–45). Strahan agreed, and Robertson's *Historical Disquisition* (no. 299) identified him on the title page in the usual way.

Besides telling us something about how authors wished to project their self-images and the anxiety they sometimes felt about it, this mode of representation reinforces Foucault's thesis about the importance of the author function. Indeed, the reasoning that Andrew Strahan employs in his reply to Robertson's query may be read as powerful supporting evidence for that concept. "We think with you," Strahan writes, on behalf of Cadell and himself, "it is better to omit in the Title Page and Advertisements your additional Titles, as the more important ones would be less noticed by increasing the Number, and *we wish to preserve the Appearance of the same Dr. Robertson with whom the Public are so well acquainted.*"[135] More important than the proliferation of titles and honors were the coherence

133. Donovan, *Philosophical Chemistry*, 5.

134. Ferguson to Sir John Macpherson, 15 July 1799, in Ferguson, *Correspondence*, 2:456.

135. Strahan to Robertson, 17 May 1791, NLS, MS 3944, fols. 42–43 (emphasis added).

and authenticity of the public's image of the author as an individual whose works were joined together to form a unified and immediately recognizable whole. As publishers, Strahan and Cadell were sensitive to the fact that the reading public used the name of the author to organize the vast amount of books in print, and they were therefore reluctant to alter the way in which a known entity such as Robertson was identified. Like Foucault, they understood that author identification and author commodification had become inseparably linked.

Third, placing titles, offices, occupations, degrees, and honors on the title page gave authors author-*ity*. The fact that the fullest embellishment of authors' identities often occurred in medical books like Bell's and Cullen's illustrates this point. In dealing with sickness and health, life and death, surgeons and physicians had the most at stake, and in the eighteenth century they were constantly in danger of being considered quacks and charlatans.[136] Showing readers that an author was a person of prominence and credibility, not merely in his native city and country but elsewhere too, was among other things an attempt to convince them that the author wrote with the authority of the international medical and scientific community. The same principle applied in other fields of scholarship. It is significant that three of the four "forreign honours" that Adam Ferguson added to the second edition of his Roman history were memberships in academies and learned societies in the country where his book was set (the Royal Academy in Florence, the Etruscan Society of Antiquaries in Cortona, and the Arcadia in Rome). In a pamphlet on trade, commerce, and manufacture of 1775, David Loch is identified on the title page simply as "Merchant in Edinburgh," but his greatly expanded *Essays on the Trade, Commerce, Manufactures, and Fisheries of Scotland* (1778–79; no. 196) gained authority from the designation "Merchant, and General Inspector of the Fisheries in Scotland." Sometimes authors even showed off their degrees and titles when writing about seemingly unrelated subjects. The fact that Smollett was a qualified medical practitioner may not have improved his ability to write English history, but he nevertheless appeared on the title pages of his published histories as "Tobias Smollett, M.D." Conversely, it may well be that some Grub Street writers concealed their identities as authors in their nonfiction works more frequently than did other kinds of authors because many of them lacked authoritative titles and distinctions.

136. Porter and Porter, *Patient's Progress*, esp. 23–24 and chap. 6.

Finally, this mode of identification is significant because it demonstrates the extent to which Scottish Enlightenment authors perceived themselves, and in turn would be perceived by their readers, as being associated with their native land and its institutions. The connection with the Scottish universities is particularly important. When readers encountered a book by Robertson, Reid, Stewart, Cullen, Black, Gerard, Campbell, Ferguson, Blair, or the many other authors who were professors or principals in the Scottish universities, they immediately knew they were reading a work by a Scottish academic author because of the designations that followed the author's name on the title page, and their evaluation of the book colored their perceptions not only of the author but also of the institutions and the nation with which the author was affiliated. In February 1766 David Hume pointed out to Hugh Blair that if the manuscript of Adam Ferguson's *Essay on the History of Civil Society* were allowed to go into print in its current and (he believed) flawed state, "any Failure of Success . . . , besides the Mortification attending it, operates backwards, and discredits his Class" (*LDH*, 2:12); in defending the manuscript, Blair broadened the point still further when he conceded that "much depends on the Success of this work, for Ferguson's reputation, and Class, and indeed for our College in general."[137] The international reputation of an eighteenth-century university, much like the reputation of a university today, was built chiefly on the reception given to the publications of its faculty, and the immediate identification of an author as a member of that faculty was a vital part of this process.

This point applies to other Scottish learned institutions besides universities. By identifying themselves on the title page as fellows or members of such institutions as the Royal College of Physicians of Edinburgh (as did Charles Alston, William Buchan, Andrew Duncan, Francis Home, James Lind, Alexander Monro *primus* and *secundus*, Robert Whytt, and other physicians), the Royal College of Surgeons of Edinburgh (Benjamin Bell and Alexander Hamilton), or the Royal Society of Edinburgh (Bell, Somerville, Thomas Robertson, John Bruce, Playfair, Logan, and others), or as the minister of a particular Scottish parish (Somerville, Dickson, Blair, John Macpherson, Thomas Robertson, and other clergymen), authors informed readers of their nationality and contributed to the perception that Scotland—and Edinburgh in particular—was indeed a "hot-bed of genius." Even the identifying institutions that appear in anonymous

---

137. Blair to Hume, 24 Feb. 1766, NLS, MS 23153, no. 56.

works such as the *Encyclopaedia Britannica* ("By a Society of Gentlemen in Scotland") and Andrew Duncan's *Medical and Philosophical Commentaries* (some volumes "by a Society in Edinburgh," some "by a Society of Physicians in Edinburgh") left no doubt that these works emanated from Scotland and were to be associated collectively with the men of letters there.

As a final example, consider the ways in which Adam Smith's name was modified in the title pages of the various lifetime editions of the *Theory of Moral Sentiments* (no. 59) and the *Wealth of Nations* (no. 177).[138] In the first and second editions of the *Theory of Moral Sentiments* (1759 and 1761), Smith's name is followed by the phrase "Professor of Moral Philosophy in the University of Glasgow." When preparing the third edition, Smith sent William Strahan explicit instructions to "call me simply Adam Smith without any addition either before or behind."[139] Nevertheless, in the third edition of 1767, the fourth of 1774, and the fifth of 1781, Smith's name was followed by the designation "L.L.D."—the honorary doctorate of laws that Smith had received from the University of Glasgow in October 1762.[140] Meanwhile, the title page of the first edition of the *Wealth of Nations* (1776) identified the author as "LL.D. and F.R.S. Formerly Professor of Moral Philosophy in the University of Glasgow," and in the fourth edition of 1784 this description was expanded further to include Smith's positions as a fellow of the new Royal Society of Edinburgh and "One of the Commissioners of his Majesty's Customs in Scotland." This very full form of identification was added to the title page of the sixth edition of the *Theory of Moral Sentiments*, published just before Smith's death in 1790, and it also traveled overseas, to appear on the title pages of the Irish and American editions of the *Wealth of Nations*. Thus, in spite of the misgivings that Smith once expressed, his name came to be associated by readers with his honorary degree, his fellowships in Britain's two most prestigious learned societies, his present and former professional positions, and his homeland. In this way, the representation of the name Adam Smith on the title pages of his books projected an image of the author as a coherent, authentic, and recognizable individual who was the creator of a distinctive body of writing, backed by the authority of an impressive—and identifiably Scottish—array of degrees, titles, and offices.

138. See Sher, "Early Editions," 13–26.

139. Smith to Strahan, [winter 1766–67], in Smith, *Correspondence*, 122.

140. Ross, *Life of Adam Smith*, 151.

Picturing the Author

Roger Chartier has observed that the pictorial representation of authors in their books has a long history, going back to miniatures in late medieval manuscripts. Whether the image of the author is realistic or symbolic, "the function of the author's portrait is to reinforce the notion that the writing is the expression of an individuality that gives authenticity to the work."[141] The author is shown to exist in flesh and blood, as a unique human being whose face, and perhaps body, can be linked to a particular book or a group of books in the same way that they are associated with an author's name. But Chartier's emphasis on authenticity is only part of the story. An authorial portrait may also signify authority of one kind or another, depending on the genre of the book in which it appears and the overall effect that is intended. In this regard, what matters is not only the representation of the subject but also the setting in which the portrait occurs, the way the subject is dressed, and the nature and placement of various objects and accessories that are pictured on the page.

One particularly important accessory in eighteenth-century authorial portraits was the male wig. Wigs signified authority in a manner that was linked both to gender and to class. Men of learning frequently projected the aura of refined dignity associated with gentlemen's wigs, augmented by appropriate attire and other relevant accessories. But such a representation was not considered equally desirable for every author and every genre, in every era. If wigs represented polite, male authority, they also embodied what Marcia Pointon has called "prosthetic ambiguity" on account of their associations with effeminacy and artifice.[142] While enhancing the authority of learned authors, wigs could also challenge their authenticity as men. Thus, when threatened by a riotous London mob in 1746, Smollett, Carlyle, and their friends "were glad to go into a narrow entry to put our wigs in our pockets, and to take our swords from our belts and walk with them in our hands,"[143] replacing one ambiguous accessory with another whose meaning was unmistakable. Increasingly toward the end of the century, authors began to appear in frontispieces with their own hair, sometimes powdered to look like a wig (in accordance with

141. Chartier, *Order of Books*, 52.

142. Pointon, *Hanging the Head*, 128. Cf. Festa, "Personal Effects"; Rauser, "Hair"; Carter, *Men and the Emergence of Polite Society*, chap. 4.

143. Carlyle, *Autobiography*, 199.

the tendency of new technologies to copy those they are challenging) but sometimes without any embellishment. Although it is tempting to see this development as a straightforward movement from the affected to the natural, such an interpretation would be naïve. All frontispiece portraits of authors were calculated to create a certain visual effect that would enhance the author's image; all were carefully staged.

Changes in the technology of artistic reproduction have altered our visual perceptions of eighteenth-century authors. Today, not only is there widespread public access to painted portraits of authors, many of which hang in museums devoted entirely to portraiture, but original paintings of eighteenth-century authors are also routinely reproduced in biographies and other books, as well as on the Internet. In the eighteenth century, however, few people had access to original portraits, and it was almost always by means of prints engraved from them, whether published in books or sold separately, that the public could see visual images of authors.[144] As a result, some representations of authors that are widely known in our time but never were the basis for prints in theirs, such as Allan Ramsay's first portrait of David Hume (1754), were probably seen by relatively few contemporaries, whereas other likenesses, which are not so well known today, were familiar to the late eighteenth-century reading public, such as portraits of Hume based on a contemporary drawing by John Donaldson that cannot now be traced. Even when the same images form the foundation of eighteenth- and twenty-first-century ideas of what an author looked like, our perceptions may differ because we are accustomed to seeing reproductions of oil paintings rather than prints modeled on those paintings. All modes of reproducing art introduce deviations from the original, but the process of printmaking necessitated a considerable degree of variation because it relied on the skill of artists working in one medium to translate the vision of artists operating in different media. A dramatic example concerns Rousseau, who originally spoke highly of the portrait that David Hume arranged for Allan Ramsay to paint of him but later, after apparently viewing the similar but much less flattering engraving that Ramsay's assistant David Martin made from it, came to believe that Hume had conspired to make him appear ugly.[145] Ultimately,

144. Clayton, *English Print*. The discussion that follows is confined to frontispiece portraits in books, but prints of authors' portraits that never appeared in books were sometimes sold separately or published in magazines.

145. Smart, *Allan Ramsay, Painter*, 204–7.

it was the engraver, at least as much as the painter, who defined the visual images of authors in the minds of the eighteenth-century public.

Adding an author's likeness to a book was labor-intensive, time-consuming, and expensive, and the outcome was never certain. Although various methods were used to create prints during the late eighteenth century, the most common techniques for reproducing images in books—and the only kinds used in the portraits discussed in this chapter—were line and stipple engraving, especially the former.[146] Both required high levels of skill and involved several stages that preceded printing and publication. First came the painting or drawing of a portrait, for which the author would normally sit over a period of time, and which usually would be acknowledged on the lower left side of the finished print (e.g., "Painted by D. Martin" or "S.Jos.ᵃ Reynolds Eq. pinx."). Next, a draftsman would make a drawing of the desired size. In line engraving (fig. 2.8), this image would be traced or burnished onto a thin layer of wax set above a polished piece of copper and then carefully incised into the copper with a graver or burin. Removal of the wax would leave an engraved copperplate that could be touched up, inked, wiped clean (leaving the ink only where incisions had been made), and printed onto paper using a special copper-plate rolling press. Stipple (fig. 2.9) involved the same initial steps, but the impressions in copper consisted mainly of multiple dots made with a blunt tool rather than lines made by a pointed graver. This technique had the advantage of rendering light and dark tones more effectively than line engraving and could be enriched by the use of etching and short engraved lines or flicks made with a graver. Since both line and stipple engravers usually identified themselves on the lower right side of a print (e.g., "Engraved by J. Caldwall" or "J. K. Sherwin sculp."), most frontispiece portraits could immediately be associated with three distinct individuals whose identities were known to informed readers: the subject (whose name often appeared prominently on the page), the artist who painted or drew the original portrait, and the engraver.

The process of adding frontispiece portraits was fraught with difficulties for the authors and makers of books. The chief obstacle was expense. The softness of copper, which made it so desirable during the engraving

146. See Gaskell, *New Introduction to Bibliography*, 158–59; Griffiths, *Prints and Printmaking*; Hind, *History of Engraving*; Gascoigne, *How to Identify Prints*; and Clayton, *English Print*, 13–14. Information on particular portraits has sometimes been taken from Ormond and Rogers, *Dictionary*, vol. 2.

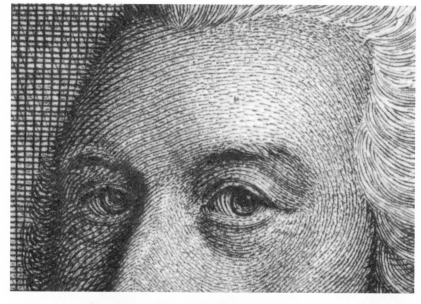

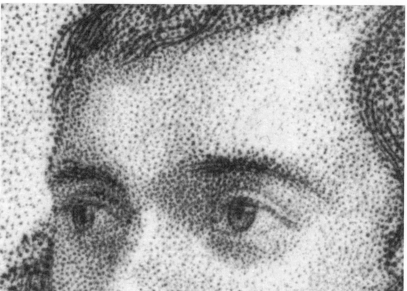

Figs. 2.8 and 2.9. Virtually all frontispiece portraits in Scottish Enlightenment books used the technology of either line engraving or stipple. Fig. 2.8 (top) shows a detail from James Caldwall's line engraving of Hugh Blair (see fig. 2.16), while fig. 2.9 (bottom) shows a detail from John Beugo's 1787 stipple portrait of Robert Burns (fig. 2.20). Caldwall engraving: Special Collections, Fordham University Library; Beugo engraving: Thomas Fisher Rare Book Library, University of Toronto.

process, was costly in the long run because copperplates wore down quickly with use and then had to be touched up or replaced—unlike durable steel plates, which became technologically feasible in the nineteenth century. More problematic in the short run was the high cost of obtaining both an original portrait and a print made from it. In the late 1760s Allan Ramsay charged twenty guineas (£21) to paint a bust-length portrait (the standard format for use in frontispieces), and in 1777 Sir Joshua Reynolds raised his price for the same service to thirty-five guineas (£36.15s.).[147] A decade later James Caldwall charged £30 for a frontispiece line engraving of William Leechman. Not only was Caldwall's price roughly comparable to the cost of sitting for a bust-length portrait by the most famous and expensive portrait painters of the age but it also represented almost 40 percent of the cost of printing 1,250 copies of the two-volume book in which the frontispiece appeared (no. 283), including the type, many days of labor by compositors and pressmen, extra charges for corrections, and all other production expenses except paper (SA 48815, fol. 126, where the total printing charge is reported as £76.8s.). The high price of engraving was dictated by supply and demand, since line and stipple engravers who were willing and able to make accurate portrait prints were always in short supply. For the same reason, the most sought-after engravers worked at their own pace, and publication of books with frontispiece portraits was sometimes delayed for months while they finished their work.

Frontispiece portraits of authors were therefore relatively uncommon during the age of the Scottish Enlightenment. When they occurred in books by living authors, they were usually not in the first volume of the first edition but rather were added after a book had achieved some critical and commercial success, presumably because this made it easier to justify the addition of an authorial portrait as a response to public interest. As far as I have been able to ascertain, the earliest instance among the books listed in table 2 occurred in 1763, when the first volume of a "new" (i.e., second) edition of Tobias Smollett's *Continuation of the Complete History of England* (no. 67) contained a frontispiece head-and-shoulders portrait of the author engraved by François Aliamet after a painting by Sir Joshua Reynolds. A few years later David Hume received the same honor. It was not Hume himself, but his publisher, Andrew Millar, who had insisted on a frontispiece portrait. "I am much, much better pleasd to have the Edition come out without it," Hume told Millar in October 1766;

---

147. Smart, *Allan Ramsay, Painter*, App. B; Weindorf, *Sir Joshua Reynolds*, 96. Of course, half-length and full-length portraits by these painters cost much more.

"I am indeed averse to the prefixing a Print of the Author, as savouring of Vanity" (*LDH*, 2:97–98). Vanity or not, Hume had reluctantly agreed that his friend Allan Ramsay, who had just painted his portrait for the second time, dressed in a magnificent scarlet and gold coat, would select a suitable engraver, but Ramsay told him that none could be found in Scotland "that is capable of doing a head tolerably" (*LDH*, 2:97).[148] When the matter surfaced again a year later, Millar wanted Hume to sit for James Ferguson, who had made his living painting miniature portraits before achieving success as a science lecturer and author. Hume, however, recommended an existing portrait drawn by John Donaldson, "in every body's Opinion, as well as my own . . . the likest that has been done for me, as well as the best Likeness" (*LDH*, 2:169).

Two engravings were accordingly made from the Donaldson drawing at this time. The 1767 octavo reissue of the *History of England* used one by the Irishman Patrick Halpen or Halpin, showing Hume turned to his left. The 1768 quarto edition of *Essays and Treatises* used a different engraving by Simon François Ravenet, showing Hume turned to his right (fig. 1.1). As we saw in the last chapter, this was an important edition of *Essays and Treatises*, which marked a critical moment in the repackaging of Hume as an eminent philosophical author. The addition of a newly commissioned frontispiece portrait was a significant component in that process. Looking portly and distinguished in a white powdered wig, Hume is set within an oval frame, which rests against a masonry wall on whose ledge the words "DAVID HUME ESQ" have been inscribed. Between those words and the portrait itself are two partially concealed quill pens and two bound volumes. One of the volumes lies open, with the words "History and" displayed on one page and "Philosophy" on the other. This arrangement not only conveys a sense of intellectual permanence but also presents the author as a versatile man of letters who was the master of two distinct scholarly genres.

Although subsequent editions of *Essays and Treatises* did not contain Hume's likeness, a frontispiece portrait after the Donaldson drawing graced most late eighteenth-century editions of Hume's *History of England*. From 1782 onward, such frontispiece portraits, together with Hume's autobiographical sketch "My Own Life" and the laudatory letter that Adam Smith had written shortly after Hume's death, created a powerful paratextual effect. Readers encountered Hume as a unique individual, and the tex-

148. However, in 1767 a mezzotint was made from Ramsay's portrait by David Martin. See Smart, *Allan Ramsay: Complete Catalogue*, 139.

tual description and self-description of the author were reinforced by visual imagery. As sales increased, the principal publisher of Hume's *History of England*, Millar's successor Thomas Cadell, sought a way to extend the coverage beyond Hume's ending point in 1688. After several false starts, he obtained his goal in 1785 by joining forces with Richard Baldwin to publish a *History of England* by Tobias Smollett that could be marketed, through a slight of hand, as a "continuation" of Hume.[149] Smollett's *History* was deliberately printed in the same typeface and format as Hume's *History*, "so that any gentleman, possessed of the latter, may take up his History at the Revolution, where Hume breaks off, and find a regular connexion in this complete History given by Smollet."[150] In 1788, presumably to commemorate the centenary of the Glorious Revolution, the well-worn John Donaldson drawing of Hume was reengraved by Joseph Collyer the younger in a more elaborate setting that shows an armed Britannia looking on with approval as a muse inscribes Hume's name beneath his portrait (fig. 2.10). This plate was used for the frontispiece in the first volume of a new octavo edition of Hume's *History*, bearing the imprint 1789, which also included prints of historical figures and events. In the following year a new octavo edition of Smollett's *History* appeared with similar illustrations, including a new frontispiece portrait of the author engraved by Collyer to match the one of Hume (fig. 2.11). Collyer closely copied the oval portrait by Aliamet that had originally appeared in the 1763 "new" edition of Smollett's original *Continuation* of his own *Complete History of England*, but he set the portrait above a mythological scene that featured Clio, the muse of history, with a quarto volume in one hand and a quill pen in the other. This double-barreled *History of England* was extremely popular, particularly in the form of a thirteen-volume, illustrated octavo set (eight volumes by Hume, five volumes by Smollett), and it is significant that most contemporary reprints by competitors in London, Scotland, and even America found it advisable to include frontispiece portraits of the authors as well as plates of historical figures and events.

149. Smollett had actually been a friendly competitor of Hume. His *Continuation of the Complete History of England*, originally published by Baldwin between 1760 and 1765, was meant to continue to 1765 not Hume's work but his own *Complete History of England* (no. 49), which stopped in 1748. Cadell and Baldwin combined the last part of the *Complete History* (covering the period 1688–1748) with the first four volumes of the *Continuation* (covering the period 1748–60), added some revisions and a new title, and marketed the work under Smollett's name. See, for some aspects of this story, Knapp, "Publication," 295–308.

150. Advertisement prefixed to the first volume of Smollett, *History of England*.

In describing "English" intellectual life during the reign of George II, Smollett's *History of England* paid tribute to "the ingenious, penetrating, and comprehensive Hume, whom we rank among the first writers of the age, both as an historian and philosopher."[151] It also praised a younger

---

151. Smollett, *History of England*, 5:299. When originally published in Smollett's *Continuation*, this section had immediately been excerpted in the Scottish press (e.g., *EEC*, 17 Oct. 1761).

Figs. 2.10 and 2.11. After Thomas Cadell and his partners found a way to extend
David Hume's *History of England* by combining it with portions of two books on the
subject by Tobias Smollett, portraits of Hume (by John Donaldson) and of Smollett
(by Sir Joshua Reynolds) were engraved by Joseph Collyer the younger to serve as
matching frontispieces in new editions. Hume's print dates from 1788 but is shown
here from the frontispiece in the 1790–91 edition of his *History* (left), covering the
period up to the Revolution of 1688; Smollett's dates from 1790 and is pictured here
from the frontispiece in the 1791 edition of his *History of England*, covering the period
from the Revolution to 1760 (above). Thomas Fisher Rare Book Library, University
of Toronto.

Scottish historian who had published only one book at the time Smollett wrote his account, "the learned and elegant Robertson." William Robertson's second book, *The History of the Reign of Charles V,* had no illustrations when it first appeared in three quarto volumes in 1769, but after the success of the first edition, a decision was made to add four engravings to the second, octavo edition of 1772, including a frontispiece portrait of the author. In the interim between the editions, a portrait of Robertson was painted by Sir Joshua Reynolds in London (fig. 2.12), and in late summer 1771 he pressed his London publishers, Strahan and Cadell, to have it "copied properly for an engraving" and then elegantly engraved.[152] In doing so, they saw to it that the size would be suitable for both the octavo second edition and the quarto first edition, which seems to have risen in price from two and a half to three guineas after the plates were added.[153] Engraved by John Hall, the frontispiece portrait of Robertson, in his clerical gown and wig, bolstered the stature of *Charles V* as a book that entitled its author to the largest amount of money ever paid for a copyright of a new work (fig. 2.13). It also placed Robertson in a grander setting and softened his facial features, removing both the writing accessories and the suggestion of craftiness that make Reynolds's original representation so memorable.

Hume and Robertson set the standard for other Scottish historians, and a frontispiece portrait in an expensive quarto edition was sometimes part of the process of emulation. Two quarto histories from the 1770s bearing the title *The History of Great Britain* illustrate this point. The chronological coverage of one of them, by James Macpherson (no. 170), overlapped with the last part of Hume's *History of England* but then continued that work from the Revolution of 1688 to the accession of George I in 1714. Although Macpherson's *History* did not include a frontispiece portrait in the first edition, published by Strahan and Cadell in 1775, the second edition of 1776, like the second edition of Robertson's *Charles V,* contained a frontispiece portrait engraved from an oil painting by Sir Joshua Reynolds (NPG 983). When Reynolds painted this portrait in 1772, he was obviously thinking of his subject as the translator of Ossian. Macpherson is shown in a poetic pose, dreamy eyed and with what appears to be his own hair rather than a wig, holding a manuscript that suggests

152. Robertson to Strahan, 7 Aug. 1771 (quoted), and Robertson to Cadell, 6 Sept. 1771, Bodleian Library, Oxford, MS 25435, fols. 307–8, 312–13.

153. Sher, *"Charles V,"* 177.

an Ossianic poem more than a historical document.[154] Whether intention-
ally or not, John Keyse Sherwin's line engraving altered Macpherson's
expression slightly, achieving an effect that is a little less wistful,
though it still appears better suited for a work of poetry than of history
(fig. 2.14).

The other *History of Great Britain* in table 2, by Robert Henry (no. 144),
was printed by Strahan for the author, in self-conscious emulation of Robertson's quarto histories. A frontispiece portrait of Henry completed the
effect, but it made its appearance not in the first volume in 1771 but in the
fourth volume ten years later.[155] Engraved by the London artist James
Caldwall (or Caldwell) from a painting by David Martin, it showed Henry,
like Robertson, in the clerical collar and powdered wig that constituted
the standard accessories for Scottish Presbyterian clergymen of letters
(fig. 2.15). One way in which Henry deviated from Robertson was by having the engraving made to fit the full size of a quarto page. This was fine
at the time, but when Strahan and Cadell published a second edition in
1788, the portrait had to be cut down awkwardly in order to fit into the
smaller octavo format.

Historians were not the only Edinburgh clergymen of letters whose
portraits found their way into print. In 1783 Hugh Blair, who was well
known for his genial vanity, became the first living author whose name
appears in table 1 to place a frontispiece portrait in the first edition of
one of his own books. A hint of his intention occurred in a postscript to
a letter to William Strahan of 5 May 1780, in which Blair remarked: "A
Picture which is reckoned tolerably good is done for me here by [Da-
vid] Martin, who is painting away in this place at a great rate and with
considerable reputation. I mention this to you in case you think it might
be of any advantage to your book [i.e., Blair's *Sermons*] to take an engraving from it."[156] Strahan was receptive to the idea and suggested
that the picture be engraved in Edinburgh, but Blair's reply of 5 August

154. Cf. George Romney's very different portrait of Macpherson in a powdered
wig, painted in 1779–80 (NPG 5804).

155. *EEC*, 3 Mar. 1781. Similarly, a frontispiece portrait of Catharine Macaulay
was published in the third volume of her *History of England*, four years after the work
began to appear.

156. Blair to Strahan, 5 May 1780, in Zachs, *Hugh Blair's Letters to His Publishers*.
References to other letters from Blair in the following discussion are drawn from
this source.

Figs. 2.12 and 2.13. Between the quarto first edition of William Robertson's *History of the Reign of Charles V* in 1769 and the first London octavo edition three years later, Robertson had his portrait painted in London by Sir Joshua Reynolds (above). A line engraving by John Hall, after Reynolds's portrait (right), appeared in the first volume of the second edition and was also added to unsold copies of the first edition. Reynolds portrait: Scottish National Portrait Gallery; Hall engraving: Special Collections, Fordham University Library.

WILLIAM ROBERTSON D.D.

Painted by Sʳ Josʰ Reynolds   Engraved by Jnº St

JAMES MACPHERSON ESQ^R

Fig. 2.14. John Keyse Sherwin's line engraving of a dreamy-eyed James Macpherson, after an even dreamier oil painting by Sir Joshua Reynolds (1772), became the frontispiece in the first volume of the second edition of Macpherson's *History of Great Britain* (1776). Special Collections, Lake Forest College Library.

recommended a different plan, as well as a possible new place for the engraved portrait to appear:

> There is no good hand here to whom the engraving of my picture can be committed. Mr Creech therefore proposed that it should be sent up to you. Accordingly by the first ships it will come up in a box directed to your care. I know you will not fail to employ the best engraver you have for doing it to advantage: for a paultry engraving is a very ugly thing and deforms a book. I have no direction to give about it, but only to desire that you will give orders to have it done in as large a form as an octavo volume will admit; so that it might serve also to be prefixed to a quarto volume; as I have in view the publication of my Lectures in 4to, in a year or two hence.

Blair's plan was agreed to but took time to implement. In a letter to Strahan of 12 November 1781, the author fretted about why the engraver, James Caldwall, was taking so long, since the painting had been in his possession for a year. As it turned out, no frontispiece portrait of Blair was

Fig. 2.15. This line-engraved portrait of Robert Henry by James Caldwall, after David Martin's oil painting, was used as the frontispiece in the fourth volume of Henry's self-published *History of Great Britain*, which appeared in 1781. Thomas Fisher Rare Book Library, University of Toronto.

put in the *Sermons*, but one did appear in his *Lectures on Rhetoric and Belles Lettres* (no. 230). In the quarto edition of 1783, Blair is pictured in wig and clerical attire, with his right hand across his heart (fig. 2.16), as in Martin's original oil painting, which it closely replicates. When the octavo second edition came out in 1785, however, a new engraving by Caldwall was used; the setting was unchanged, but the portrait achieved a more natural effect by removing Blair's hand from his heart. This pose was reproduced in

Painted by D. Martin
Engraved by J. Caldwall

HUGH BLAIR D.D.

subsequent authorized editions of the *Lectures*, although the quality of the workmanship deteriorated noticeably. By the sixth edition of 1796, the sitter looks nothing at all like Blair as he appears in contemporary portraits by Martin and Sir Henry Raeburn, even though the engraving was still being credited to Caldwall (fig. 2.17). The commercial success of Blair's *Lectures* must have placed a heavy burden on the publishers to commission fresh portraits as one plate after another wore out.

Figs. 2.16 and 2.17. The first edition of Hugh Blair's *Lectures on Rhetoric and Belles Lettres* (1783), in quarto, featured as the frontispiece in volume 1 a fine line-engraved portrait by James Caldwall (left), after an oil painting by David Martin, showing Blair's right hand on his heart. In all later, octavo editions the pose was changed, as in the sixth edition of 1796 (above), which displayed an inferior engraving that was still being attributed to Caldwall. Thomas Fisher Rare Book Library, University of Toronto.

Fig. 2.18. The full profile frontispiece portrait in James Fordyce's *Poems* (1786), a stipple engraving by Thomas Trotter after John Flaxman, was meant to evoke an ancient Roman rather than a modern Presbyterian minister. Thomas Fisher Rare Book Library, University of Toronto.

As noted earlier, portraits of poets were not subject to the same formal constraints as portraits of scholarly authors. This is clear from the first (and only) edition of *Poems* by the Presbyterian minister James Fordyce (no. 262), which uses as its frontispiece a portrait engraved by Thomas Trotter from a likeness by John Flaxman (fig. 2.18). Fordyce appears in the toga of an ancient Roman, viewed in profile in order to accentuate his prominent "Roman" nose. Full profile was rarely employed in eighteenth-century portraiture, partly, it is sometimes said, because contemporary dentistry could not disguise the unflattering lower jaws of many of the toothless middle-aged men and women who typically sat for portraits, but also because gentlemen's wigs threatened to overwhelm the faces they covered.[157] Fordyce did not have to worry about the latter problem because he is bald in this print—a mode of presentation that was akin to nakedness for gentlemen in other contexts,[158] but that apparently was acceptable in a stylized Roman portrait prefixed to a volume of verse.

The image of Robert Burns in the second (Edinburgh) edition of *Poems*,

157. Pointon, *Hanging the Head*, 131.

158. See Boswell, *Great Biographer*, 11, on Boswell's crisis when he lost his wig while traveling in northern England in 1789.

Chiefly in the Scottish Dialect (no. 260) represents another poetic alternative to the dignified, somber frontispiece portraits of scholarly authors. When Burns came to Edinburgh late in 1786 to arrange this publication, the first edition, published by subscription earlier in the year in Kilmarnock, Ayrshire, had already begun to cause a stir. Early in 1787 the nominal publisher of the Edinburgh edition, William Creech, allegedly used the local freemasonry network to arrange for Alexander Nasmyth to paint Burns's picture and then for John Beugo to make a stipple engraving from the unfinished Nasmyth portrait, for use as the frontispiece of the new edition.[159] After six sittings, Nasmyth rendered Burns as a pretty boy whose head, flanked by trees, mountains, and an expansive sky, is turned to his right to show off his long, dark hair (fig. 2.19). It would appear that Beugo was not entirely pleased with Nasmyth's work, for he took the unusual step of having Burns sit for his engraving in February 1787. "I am getting my Phiz done by an eminent Engraver," Burns wrote to a friend during this process, "and if it can be ready in time, I will appear in my book looking, like other fools, to my title page."[160] The engraving *was* ready in time, though it would show Burns looking away from his title page rather than toward it. Beugo's portrait retains the pose and background of Nasmyth's painting but depicts Burns somewhat fuller faced and hardier—ruggedly handsome rather than elegantly romantic (fig. 2.20). This image, which has been called "the best, most reliable, and most factual account of what Burns looked like,"[161] was widely associated with Burns in his own time, although Nasmyth's softer and more refined portrait is much better known today. As a result of the Edinburgh edition, furthermore, it became standard practice to include a frontispiece portrait in contemporary editions of Burns's *Poems.* That is why eight years later Burns could joke that "my phiz is *sae kenspeckle*" (i.e., my face is so famil-iar) that even a joiner's apprentice recognized the poet as soon as he laid eyes upon a portrait.[162] The illusion of naturalness in these frontispiece portraits supported the author's peasant persona, deliberately masking a

159. Burns was hailed as "Caledonia's Bard" at a joint meeting of the Edinburgh masons, and both Nasmyth and Beugo, along with Burns's patron the Earl of Glen-cairn and William Creech, were members of Canongate Kilwinning Lodge No. 2, which embraced Burns upon his arrival in Edinburgh. Neither artist charged Burns for his work. See Burns to [John Ballantine], 14 Jan. 1787, in Burns, *Letters*, 1:82–84, 96; Lindsay, *Burns Encyclopedia*, 26, 137, 269.

160. Burns to [John Ballantine], [24 Feb. 1787], in Burns, *Letters*, 1:96.

161. Skinner, *Burns*, 8.

162. Burns to George Thomson, [May 1795], in Burns, *Letters*, 2:355–56.

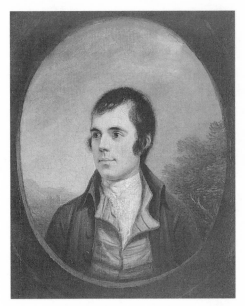 

Figs. 2.19 and 2.20. Although Alexander Nasmyth's unfinished portrait of Robert Burns (left) is by far the best-known likeness of the poet today, contemporaries were much more familiar with John Beugo's hardier-looking (and probably more accurate) stipple engraving after Nasmyth (right), which first appeared as the frontispiece in the Edinburgh edition of Burns's *Poems* (1787). Nasmyth portrait: Scottish National Portrait Gallery; Beugo engraving: Thomas Fisher Rare Book Library, University of Toronto.

self-consciously creative poet who was actually quite well versed in English and Scottish literature.[163]

James Ferguson's *Select Mechanical Exercises* (no. 153) is yet another book that acquired a frontispiece portrait in its second edition, in this case posthumously. Ferguson prefixed to the first edition a brief autobiographical account of his extraordinary journey from unschooled son of a laborer in the north of Scotland to respected member of the Royal Society of London. When the book was reprinted in 1778, two years after the author's death, the publishers, Strahan and Cadell, added a frontispiece portrait engraved by Thomas Cook. This image of Ferguson, based on an original portrait by John Townshend,[164] shows a practical man with an intelligent, wizened face who is dressed as a gentleman wearing a pow-

163. McGuirk, *Robert Burns*.

164. Townshend's portrait appears in Millburn, *Wheelwright*, 247.

Fig. 2.21. The second, posthumous edition of James Ferguson's *Select Mechanical Exercises* (1778) featured a frontispiece line engraving of the author by Thomas Cook (after John Townshend), to which a variety of scientific artifacts were added. Historical Society of Pennsylvania.

dered wig. But whereas the only external prop in the Townshend portrait was a small part of a globe on which the subject rests his hand, the frontispiece portrait placed Ferguson's likeness amid an array of scientific and learned artifacts, including a substantial portion of a globe, a telescope, a thermometer, two bound books, and a scroll (fig. 2.21). If the portrait itself, along with the autobiography, established Ferguson's authenticity as a unique individual, the surrounding objects served to augment his authority as a man of science and letters.

The choice of accessories and visual associations was not always obvious. Sir Henry Raeburn's painting of the Edinburgh surgeon Benjamin Bell, engraved by W. & J. Walker for the frontispiece in the first volume of the fifth edition of Bell's strong-selling *A System of Surgery* (1791), situated Bell not among surgical tools and instruments but rather in his study (fig. 2.22). Well dressed and bewigged, the author sits in a plush chair,

Fig. 2.22. W. & J. Walker's line engraving of the Edinburgh surgeon Benjamin Bell, after an oil painting by Sir Henry Raeburn, was used as the frontispiece in the first volume of the fifth edition of Bell's *System of Surgery* (1791). It portrayed Bell as an author in his study rather than a surgeon in practice. Special Collections, University of Medicine and Dentistry of New Jersey Libraries.

with books, quill pen, and ink visible on his writing table. By appearing in this manner, Bell deliberately chose to define his image as a man of letters rather than as a surgeon working at his craft. He may have done so partly in order to emphasize his credentials as an author and a gentleman,[165] but his decision may also have been influenced by the fact that the social and intellectual status of surgeons was traditionally suspect, especially in relation to physicians.

John Pinkerton also appeared in his study in a stipple portrait by William Nelson Gardiner, after a painting by Silvester Harding, which was used as the frontispiece in the first volume of the first edition of Pinkerton's 1797 quarto work, *The History of Scotland from the Accession of the House of Stuart to That of Mary* (no. 345; fig. 2.23). Pinkerton's dress and pose, with hands clasped atop a book, are carefully mannered. The setting defines the message: the author is framed by quills and ink to his right,

---

165. Jordanova, *Defining Features*, 120, 160–61, makes a similar point regarding Sir Joshua Reynolds's and Allan Ramsay's portraits of the surgeons John and William Hunter.

Fig. 2.23. This line-engraved portrait by William Nelson Gardiner, after a painting by Silvester Harding, appeared as the frontispiece in the first volume of John Pinkerton's *History of Scotland* (1797) and showed off the author's spectacles as a scholarly accessory. Thomas Fisher Rare Book Library, University of Toronto.

writing paper to the front, and learned books to his left, which ascend from weighty folios at the bottom to quartos and octavos. But the crucial prop, replacing the wig as the defining facial ornament, is the set of spectacles through which the author peers intently at the viewer. Armed with these learned accoutrements, Pinkerton claims authority as a historian while at the same time appealing to the reader to recognize his authenticity as a genuine man of letters.

An authorial portrait also graces the frontispiece of the first edition of Mungo Park's 1799 best seller, *Travels in the Interior Districts of Africa* (no. 350). Because this book dealt mainly with unknown lands and cultures, its credibility was intimately connected with Park's own. Less than a decade earlier, James Bruce's *Travels to Discover the Source of the Nile* (no. 288) had failed the credibility test, chiefly because Bruce offended contemporary standards of taste with his exotic tales of eating lions and pieces of flesh from living cattle, performing blood-letting on naked women in an Abyssinian harem, and impressing the Abyssinian royal court with martial feats. Even though scholars now believe that most of these stories were true, the author appeared to contemporaries as boastful

Fig. 2.24. Mungo Park's *Travels in the Interior Districts of Africa* (1799) gained credibility from this dashing frontispiece portrait engraved by T. Dickinson after an original by Henry Edridge. Special Collections Library, Pennsylvania State University Libraries.

and inauthentic. The book sold well, especially in its abridged form, but not necessarily because it was considered a reliable account. Kate Ferguson Marsters has discussed various ways in which Park overcame the credibility problem that plagued Bruce, including adopting the persona of an ordinary man, withholding (or relating as hearsay) information that might have seemed exaggerated or sensationalized to contemporary British readers, and keeping to the pattern announced in his preface, that his was "a plain, unvarnished tale; without pretentions of any kind, except that it claims to enlarge, in some degree, the circle of African geography."[166] The credibility of Park's *Travels* was increased by the author's credentials as a surgeon, by the sponsorship of the London-based African Association, and by the inclusion of an appendix by Major James Rennell. But it also helped that Park's book, unlike Bruce's, contained an effective frontispiece portrait of the author (fig. 2.24). Engraved by T. Dickinson from a likeness by Henry Edridge, the frontispiece shows Park as a dashingly handsome, intelligent-looking man in his twenties, with his

166. Marsters, introduction to Park, *Travels*, esp. 18–20, and Park's preface, quoting 45.

own hair (or possibly a natural-looking wig) and locked in a penetrating gaze that marks him as a keen observer of the world. A comparison with a watercolor miniature (NPG 1104) that is based on the same original demonstrates the variability of artistic translation into other media: Dickinson's rendition appears more intense and less sentimental, and therefore much better suited to the main purpose to which it was put. Its effectiveness can also be measured from a comparison with Thomas Rowlandson's 1805 caricature of Park as a bald, arrogant man (NPG 4924). Also used to illustrate the glowing front-page review of *Travels* in the *European Magazine, and London Review* for June 1799, Dickinson's engraving helped to establish Park's persona as a credible, even heroic figure whose stories of distant adventures could be believed.

Still another kind of frontispiece portrait appeared in posthumous editions that were specially edited to fix or alter the public's perception of a recently deceased author. Dr. John Brown, founder of the Brunonian medical system, enjoyed some notoriety with his *Elements of Medicine*, which appeared first in Latin in 1780 and then six years later in his own English translation, published by Joseph Johnson (no. 273). Like James Ferguson, Brown had risen from poverty to attain an international reputation, but unlike Ferguson he remained mired in controversy and misfortune as a result of his ineffective social and political skills, his uncompromising and often disagreeable personality (exacerbated by his apparent addictions to drugs and alcohol), and his unrelenting challenge to the medical theories of his powerful mentor, William Cullen. In 1795, seven years after Brown died in poverty in London, Joseph Johnson published for the benefit of the author's family a posthumous new edition of the *Elements of Medicine*. In a dedication "To the Ingenious, the Candid, and Humane," the editor, Thomas Beddoes, presented Brown's story as an object lesson in "Unfortunate Genius."[167] Though brilliant, the story went, Brown had been unable to profit from his intelligence. In an "Account of the Origin and Object of this Edition," Beddoes observed that Brown had even failed to provide an adequate English translation of his own Latin text, making it necessary for the editor to "refit" the style (1:ix). The addition of a frontispiece portrait, engraved by William Blake from a miniature painting by John Donaldson, buttressed Beddoes's interpretation (fig. 2.25). Although dressed as a gentleman, Brown appears strangely out of place amid such finery, as if distracted or perhaps depressed. There is a hint of clownishness in his expression, reinforcing Beddoes's description of him in the

167. Brown, *Elements of Medicine*, 1795.

Figs. 2.25 and 2.26. William Blake's line-engraved portrait of Dr. John Brown
(above), after an original miniature by John Donaldson, was ideally suited to serve as
the frontispiece in the posthumous 1795 London edition of Brown's *Elements of Medicine* because it captured the clownish yet sad character of the author that the edition
sought to convey. By contrast, a portrait that James Caldwall engraved from the same
source at about the same time presented Brown in a more positive light, as a "creative" rather than an "unfortunate" "Genius" (right). Blake engraving: Thomas Fisher
Rare Book Library, University of Toronto; Caldwall engraving: KBooks, Ltd.

long biographical preface as "a comic figure . . . not inferior to Sancho
Panza" (1:lxix). He tries to smile, but his eyes betray a deep sadness—or
is it fear?—that is not present in another posthumous print engraved four
years later from the same source by James Caldwall (fig. 2.26). Whereas
Blake pictured the pathetic or "unfortunate" genius that Beddoes was describing, Caldwall portrayed Brown as a "creative Genius," as the caption to his print put it; the impression of vulnerability, clownishness, and
misfortune was replaced by one of smug complacency. Since Donaldson's

JOHN BROWN, M.D.

Engraved by J. Caldwall from the Miniature painted by M. Donaldson.

Hail! creative Genius, by whose sense divine
Sprung forth a glorious System, ever form'd to shine
Envy and Prejudice in vain oppos'd thy might,
And Æsculapius self acknowledg'd all thy right.

miniature cannot now be traced,[168] it is impossible to know which of these interpretations is truer to the original representation on which they were both based.

Like the 1795 edition of Brown's *Elements of Medicine*, the *Sermons* of William Leechman (no. 283) may be considered an example of posthumous author construction by means of paratextual materials, both verbal and iconographic. In this case, the book's editor, Rev. James Wodrow, who was Leechman's disciple and relation by marriage, was engaged in unabashed hagiography.[169] The book begins with Wodrow's long, admiring portrayal of Leechman as a Presbyterian clergyman of perfect piety, complemented by the frontispiece portrait of the author looking suitably austere in a wig and clerical attire. From Wodrow's surviving correspondence with his friend Samuel Kenrick, we learn that the editor had some difficulty arranging to have William Millar's painting of Leechman shipped to him in London by Mrs. Leechman in order to serve as the source of an engraving (fig. 2.27). Only after prickly negotiations involving an intermediary did the principal publishers, Strahan and Cadell, agree to pay half the £30 engraving fee. Besides the expense, the print—engraved once again by James Caldwall (fig. 2.28)—took longer than expected and caused the entire publication to be delayed for a season. Worst of all, when it was finally finished, Wodrow expressed displeasure because he thought "it wants the sweet and pleasant look that I think the picture had. The countenance is too grave or thoughtful."[170] Whether or not one agrees with Wodrow's complaint, the very fact that he voiced it confirms the precariousness of putting likenesses of authors in books: after so much time and expense, one was ultimately at the mercy of the engravers, whose images of authors could deviate considerably from the models on which they were based and the purposes they were meant to achieve.

When all eighteenth-century British editions are taken into account, at least 24 of the 115 authors in table 1 (21 percent) were pictured in at least one frontispiece portrait during the eighteenth century.[171] But liv-

168. Essick, *William Blake's Commercial Book Illustrations*, 66.

169. Another example of a posthumous celebratory edition is the *Works of the Late John Gregory, M.D.*, which contained a flattering frontispiece stipple portrait of the author as a younger man, engraved by John Beugo.

170. Wodrow to Kenrick, 5 Aug. 1789, in *Wodrow–Kenrick Correspondence*, no. 149.

171. In addition to those already discussed, frontispiece portraits of the author appear in the following editions: the 1798 Edinburgh edition of John Home, *Douglas*

ing authors were portrayed in the first (or only) volume of a first edition in just 5 of the 360 books in table 2 (Blair's *Lectures,* Fordyce's *Poems,* Pinkerton's *History of Scotland,* Park's *Travels,* and Gilbert Stuart's *History of the Establishment of the Reformation in Scotland*), or about 1 percent of the database. The main reason for the rarity of such images was undoubtedly the large amount of time and money required to have portraits painted or drawn and then engraved for insertion in books, though reluctance to appear too forward or vain may also have been a factor in some cases. When frontispiece portraits were employed, they usually served to authenticate the identities of individual authors and to represent them as authorities in their fields. The specific means of accomplishing these ends varied widely according to the nature of the author and the particular book in question. A work of history, philosophy, science, or medicine might gain support from a portrait of an author looking suitably somber and scholarly, surrounded by appropriate accessories and artifacts, including such items as wigs, clerical or fashionable attire, scientific instruments, spectacles, books, and writing implements. However, certain kinds of authors, such as poets and explorers, were better served by a youthful, handsome appearance, plain clothes, the subject's own hair arranged in a casual and unaffected manner, and in Burns's case at least, what passed for a rustic background. Depending on the specific individual and context, an author might be portrayed as a troubled genius or a pious clergyman, an ancient Roman or a polite gentleman. Every visual representation was intended to project an authorial image of one kind or another, encouraging readers to associate an author's name not merely with a face but also with an attitude toward literature and learning. Just as Edgar Wind contended in the 1930s that every portrait by a Reynolds or a Ramsay captured a "social situation" along with the countenance of the sitter, in that sense constituting "an argument in paint,"[172] so were frontispiece portraits en-

---

(no. 44); volume 10 of William Guthrie, *General History of Scotland* (1767–68; no. 102); the 18mo, 1799 edition of Robert Fergusson, *Poems* (no. 158); the first volume of the second edition of Lord Monboddo, *Of the Origin and Progress of Language* (1774; no. 160); the second edition of Andrew Duncan, *Medical Cases,* in 1778 (no. 190); the only edition of Gilbert Stuart, *History of the Establishment of the Reformation in Scotland* (1780; no. 210); the first volume of the second edition of Sir John Sinclair, *History of the Public Revenue of the British Empire* (1790; no. 256); the second (1787) and third (1792–93) editions of John Gillies, *History of Ancient Greece* (no. 263); and William Julius Mickle's posthumous *Poems, and a Tragedy* (1794, no. 329).

172. Wind, *Hume and the Heroic Portrait,* 3.

Figs. 2.27 and 2.28. When preparing for publication the posthumous *Sermons* (1789) of his mentor and relation by marriage, William Leechman, James Wodrow insisted on adding a frontispiece portrait engraved from an original oil painting of Leechman by William Millar (above). But the resulting line engraving by James Caldwall (right) delayed publication and disappointed Wodrow because of its gravity. Millar painting: Hunterian Art Gallery, University of Glasgow; Caldwall engraving: Harris Manchester College Library, Oxford University.

graved and printed arguments on behalf of particular ways of seeing the authors of books.

*

What was true of Scottish Enlightenment books was also true of Scottish Enlightenment authors: they were extraordinarily diverse, yet they embodied patterns and connections that demonstrate their unity and cohesiveness. We have seen that the authors of the Scottish Enlightenment came from virtually every part of Scotland, including a surprisingly large

WILLIAM LEECHMAN, D.D.
late Principal of the College of Glasgow.

Engraved by J. Caldwell from a Picture painted by W. Miller.

number from the Highlands. Their backgrounds varied widely, ranging from the offspring of day laborers and poor farmers to descendants of the landed elite, and by the end of the century women had begun to appear among them. In the main, however, they were male, born into the middle and upper (but rarely noble) echelons of society, and educated at Scottish universities, largely for the liberal professions. They gravitated to urban centers of culture, particularly Edinburgh, but also Glasgow, Aberdeen, and the British metropolis, London. Whether living in Scotland or England, they frequently displayed patterns of attachment and mutual support rooted in religion, blood and marriage, and academic and social relationships. Their Scottish connections gave them a strong sense of collective identity, which sometimes appeared clannish and sectarian to outsiders, especially in London.

These modes of bonding affected the production and reception of books in various ways. Scottish authors regularly collaborated on publications, patronized each other's works in public and behind the scenes, and referred to each other in print—sometimes critically, but usually in a manner that was friendly and collegial, even when they disagreed on substantive issues. The title pages of their books usually bore their real names, followed by biographical information that tended to strengthen the public perception of their association with Scottish institutions and with each other. Occasionally, they were pictured in frontispiece portraits, with appropriate props and expressions for achieving a desired effect.

Thus, in Britain and abroad, the reading public viewed Scottish authors through a national lens. As individuals, they were generally known by name and were associated with a personal body of published works. But most of them were also known by place, through biographical accounts, book reviews, newspaper articles and advertisements, travel literature, and information on title pages, which frequently proclaimed their affiliations with Scottish universities, learned societies, and other institutions. This union of text and paratext was crucial for their personal reputations as authors, as it was for the reputation of their country. At the same time that they gained credibility as authentic individuals who were recognized as authorities in their respective fields of intellectual endeavor, they established their collective identity as Scottish authors and marked their nation as a wellspring of literary and learned books.

3

The Rewards of Authorship

PATRONS, PUBLISHERS, AND PLACES

Publishers as Patrons

In a famous passage in the *Life of Samuel Johnson*, James Boswell expresses sorrow that Johnson received only £1,575 for his monumental *Dictionary of the English Language*, from which he had to pay his staff of editorial assistants and support himself for almost a decade. "I am sorry too," Johnson replies. "But it was very well. The booksellers are generous liberal-minded men." Boswell then elaborates upon Johnson's ideas about booksellers: "He, upon all occasions, did ample justice to their character in this respect. He considered them as the patrons of literature; and, indeed, although they have eventually been considerable gainers by his Dictionary, it is to them that we owe its having been undertaken and carried through at the risk of great expence, for they were not absolutely sure of being indemnified" (*BLJ*, 1:304–5). In an age when patronage often defined power, Boswell's attribution to Johnson of the view that booksellers were "the patrons of literature" was significant. It was an assertion that publishers constituted the driving force behind serious writing—an assertion borne out in this particular case by the evidence of Johnson's own career as a writer who regularly responded to commissions from booksellers.

This passage occurs at the end of a long section on the making of the *Dictionary*, and it must be understood within that context. Early in the section Boswell reproduces Johnson's caustic letter to Lord Chesterfield of 7 February 1755, in which Johnson spurns the earl's pretense of patronage on the eve of publication by pointing out that when he was struggling to complete his work and badly in need of support, his supposed patron never provided "one act of assistance, one word of encouragement, or one smile of favour. Such treatment I did not expect, for I never had a Patron before" (*BLJ*, 1:261–62). Some pages later Boswell prints a letter from Johnson to Charles Burney of 8 April 1755, directing those who wish to purchase copies of the newly published *Dictionary* to "Mr. Dodsley, because it was by his recommendation that I was employed in the work" (*BLJ*, 1:286). From there Boswell moves directly to a discussion of Andrew Millar and William Strahan, Scottish publishers "with whom Johnson chiefly contracted for his literary labours" (*BLJ*, 1:287). The passage concludes with Johnson's praise of Millar for having "raised the price of literature," an honor that Boswell also extends to Strahan and to Charles-Joseph Panckoucke in Paris (*BLJ*, 1:288).

Thus, when readers arrive at the "patrons of literature" passage several pages later, they already understand the sharp contrast between the superficial or false patronage of the nobility and the real patronage of the booksellers. The paragraph immediately preceding that passage revives the contrast and sets the stage for what follows: "No royal or noble patron extended a munificent hand to give independence to the man who had conferred stability on the language of his country" (*BLJ*, 1:304). "We may feel indignant that there should have been such unworthy neglect," Boswell adds. But then he provides a positive gloss by contending that this neglect enabled Johnson to overcome the "natural indolence" of his constitution and to compose his "valuable productions." When readers encounter Boswell's lament about how little Johnson was paid for his labors, they are well prepared for Johnson's moderate response. Compared to Lord Chesterfield, his ostensible patron, Dodsley, Millar, and Strahan were the new heroes of literature.

Taken as a whole, Boswell's discussion of Johnson's *Dictionary* implies a general progression in the eighteenth century from aristocratic patronage to patronage by booksellers or, to be more precise, publishers. This idea is now commonplace. Arnold Hauser developed it at length in his *Social History of Art and Literature* (1951), and a decade later Jürgen Habermas drew on Hauser's work when he observed that "serious reading by an interested public . . . arose only in the first decades of the eighteenth century, after the publisher replaced the patron as the author's commissioner and organized the commercial distribution of literary works."[1] For Habermas and others, these developments marked the transition from an aristocratic to a "bourgeois" or modern, commercial mode of organization of the book

1. Hauser, *Social History of Art*, 2:548; Habermas, *Structural Transformation*, 38.

trade and, in some respects, of society itself. In Alvin Kernan's similar formulation, a new literary order emerged, featuring print technology, a broader reading audience, a book trade regulated by market economics, and authors who, like Johnson, wrote chiefly for money.[2] Kernan represents the liberation of authors as being so complete that they seem not to have exchanged one kind of patron for another but rather to have escaped from the bondage of patronage entirely and to have become fully professional men of letters, dependent only on the taste of the public. In fact, this is more or less the way Johnson himself put the matter in a conversation on 19 August 1773 that is recorded in Boswell's *Journal of a Tour to the Hebrides with Samuel Johnson* (1785), in which patronage of literature by "the great" is contrasted not so much with literary patronage by booksellers as with the judgment of "the multitude" (*BLJ*, 5:59). A dozen years earlier, Oliver Goldsmith had made the same point, at least in regard to English poets, who "no longer depend on the great for subsistence; they have now no other patrons but the public."[3] In such formulations, however, publishers and booksellers continue to play a crucial behind-the-scenes role as "cultural middlemen," in Roy Porter's phrase, occupying the space between authors and their publics.[4]

How much truth is contained in these observations? Certainly the professionalization of authorship and the commercialization of literature increased dramatically during the eighteenth century. Nevertheless, the details and dynamics of the process are not well understood, and it often seems that a formula about traditional patrons being replaced by booksellers or publishers—or the public whom they represent—is being continually repeated with little hard evidence to support it or analysis to explain it. In what ways were publishers "the patrons of literature" and (what is not always the same thing) of authors? And does it follow from the answer to this question that traditional patrons were superseded by publishers?

Perhaps the most obvious sense in which publishers became the patrons of literature relates to the copy money that authors hoped to receive from their books; this subject is discussed more fully in the last section of this chapter. Boswell himself emphasized a rather different, entrepreneurial notion of patronage by publishers when he observed, in the course of explaining the meaning of Johnson's phrase "the patrons of literature,"

2. Kernan, *Printing Technology*.
3. Quoted in Kent, *Goldsmith*, 8.
4. Porter, *Enlightenment*, 479.

that booksellers sometimes took long-term financial risks in order to produce books from which they might realize no profit, or even lose money. The entrepreneurial mission of publishers included commissioning major works like Johnson's *Dictionary*, which could not otherwise have been undertaken. Writing of "our booksellers" in the *Gentleman's Magazine* three years before the appearance of Boswell's *Life of Johnson*, John Pinkerton made the same point by contrasting the role of the London booksellers with those on the Continent:

> Without their assistance, where should we have been in other respects? To their enterprise we are indebted for Biographias, Systems of Geography, Encyclopedias, Dictionaries. In France and Italy such works were projected, and carried into execution, by the Literati, supported by the patronage of kings and nobles; and the booksellers knew nothing of the matter till the manuscripts were put into their hands. Here, on the contrary, the booksellers projected the works, and engaged the authors. They are, in fact, the sole patrons of literature in this country.[5]

Although Pinkerton's views were expressed in the context of his own attempt to stir up interest in a large publishing project devoted to the cultivation of Britain's "National History," they articulate one of the genuine sources of authors' admiration for the great London publishers during the late eighteenth century.

A third way in which publishers functioned as patrons of literature concerns a range of services they performed for authors and literary men. Much hospitality was offered in their shops and homes. According to Boswell, in the early 1760s Alexander Donaldson entertained in Edinburgh "like a prince."[6] During the latter part of the century, William Creech's Edinburgh bookshop, and the room above it, constituted a well-known literary gathering place, where fraternizing among the Scottish literati regularly occurred. In London, Boswell first met Johnson in May 1763 in the back room of Thomas Davies's London bookshop, where the discussion was suitably literary. The printer William Strahan had no bookshop, but the services he performed for men of letters were extensive, including serving as Johnson's banker and assisting young literary men from Scotland. The fact that James Fordyce used Strahan's daughter Rachel as the

---

5. *Gentleman's Magazine* 58 (1788): 126.

6. Boswell's journal for 27 October 1762, quoted in Boswell, *General Correspondence*, 22n.

model for one of the characters in his *Sermons to Young Women* (no. 93) is probably a reflection of Strahan's hospitality, for Strahan remarked that Fordyce had become "intimately acquainted" with her before her premature death in November 1765.[7]

Elaborate dinners and parties at the private homes of booksellers were a common feature of London literary life. Describing a visit to London in 1791, Thomas Somerville wrote that the "entertainments" of Andrew Strahan and his publishing partner, Thomas Cadell, "were the most elegant and splendid I had ever seen before."[8] A contemporary account of the London bookseller George Robinson stated that "his generosity to his authors was well known, and his house became a general rendezvous for the literary men of the day, who were heartily welcome whenever they chose to turn up, provided always that they did not come late for dinner."[9] The Longmans entertained in similar fashion, and so did the Dilly brothers, whose establishment in the Poultry was characterized by one American visitor as "a kind of Coffee house for authors."[10] Joseph Johnson combined all these functions by holding weekly dinners for authors in an upstairs room, serving, in the words of a modern commentator, as their "banker, postal clerk and packager, literary agent and editor, social chairman, and psychiatrist" and sometimes providing their room and board as well.[11] Andrew Millar sponsored science lectures by one of his authors, James Ferguson, at Bath and other fashionable spas that the bookseller frequented late in life; Millar's successor, Cadell, was named an executor in Ferguson's will, and William Strahan was one of the six pallbearers at Ferguson's funeral on 23 November 1776.[12] In short, wealthy publishers now took responsibility for providing authors with the social support system that was formerly supplied by aristocratic patrons.

7. Strahan to David Hall, [ca. 1767], in Pomfret, "Some Further Letters," 462; Cochrane, *Dr. Johnson's Printer*, 110–11.

8. Somerville, *My Own Life*, 247.

9. Quoted in Curwen, *History of Booksellers*, 70.

10. Benjamin Rush, quoted in Butterfield, "American Interests," 290. Cf. Richard Cumberland's account of the hospitality bestowed on literary men by Charles Dilly, who "kept a table ever open to the patrons and pursuers of literature, which was so administered as to draw the best circles together, and to put them most completely at their ease," in Cumberland, *Memoirs*, 2:113. On the Longmans, see Rees, *Riminiscences*, 52.

11. Chard, "Bookseller to Publisher," 141.

12. Millburn, *Wheelwright*, 93, 250, 253; Andrew Millar to Thomas Cadell, 22 Dec. 1766, Boston Public Library, Ch.H.1.43.

Consider the relationship of James Boswell with his London publishers, Edward and Charles Dilly, as recorded in Boswell's journal.[13] In August 1767 the Dilly brothers paid one hundred guineas for the copyright to the *Account of Corsica* (no. 105), Boswell's first major work. More significant than the copy money was the personal attention that accompanied it. From the time of their initial meeting in London on 23 March 1768, a month after publication, the brothers spoiled Boswell shamelessly: fine food, beer and port, grand parties, and friendly, almost deferential treatment were lavished upon him. In September 1769 he was invited to stay at their house, where he was tended to with great care by the housekeeper and the "most obsequious" footman; even his linen was "washed and dressed by a city laundress" (17 Sept. 1769). On his next trip to London in 1772, he once again went first to his publishers, who gave him "a hearty welcome" and his own room in their house, for use "whenever I was late in the City end of the town" (19 Mar. 1772). From then on he regularly went first to the Dillys' house upon coming to London (2 Apr. 1773). In his journal, Boswell makes it clear that the generous hospitality he received from the Dilly brothers was rooted in "the great connection between author and bookseller" (23 Mar. 1768). "I liked to see the effects of being an author," reads his entry for 1 September 1769. "Upon the strength of that, here were two booksellers who thought they could not do enough for me." Charles Dilly, the surviving brother, loaned Boswell money on more than one occasion, as his grateful author acknowledged in his "Ode to Mr. Charles Dilly."[14] In the end, Dilly would be rewarded for all those years of hospitality and support with the right to put his name on the title page of Boswell's *Journal of a Tour to the Hebrides* in 1785 and *Life of Johnson* in 1791. Yet it was not merely to obtain these uncertain prizes that he and his brother had so warmly opened their home and their hearts to Boswell. Indeed, Dilly would graciously decline Boswell's offer to share the profits from the *Tour*,[15] would shield both that book and the *Life of Johnson* from the stigma of self-publication by issuing them under his own imprint ("Printed by Henry Baldwin, for Charles Dilly"), and would even offer advice about the publishing terms for the *Life* that went against his own monetary interests, as we shall see.

Still another sense in which publishers served as literary patrons con-

13. See the journal references under the dates cited below in Boswell, *Boswell in Search of a Wife* and *Boswell for the Defence*.

14. *Gentleman's Magazine* 61 (1791): 367.

15. Brady, *Later Years*, 272.

cerns the bridge they provided to "the public." There were three broad categories of the public in the book world of eighteenth-century Britain. First, the public meant readers, or what we might call the reading public. Second, the public meant consumers, in the sense of buyers of books or the market for books. Third, the public meant public opinion, or the general consensus of book readers and book buyers about the meaning, value, and quality of books. Precisely because these three categories were often indistinguishable, authors and booksellers generally used "the public" as a deliberately vague catchall term, often to connote all these meanings at once.

Three examples involving Scottish authors demonstrate the complexity of the topic. In the *Life of Johnson,* Boswell records that in conversation on 29 April 1778 William Robertson stated: "An authour should sell his first work for what the booksellers will give, till it shall appear whether he is an authour of merit, or, which is the same thing as to purchase-money, an authour who pleases the publick" (*BLJ,* 3:334). In this sentence, the public's aesthetic and economic functions are difficult to separate; pleasing the public is equated both with literary merit and with book sales and profits, which in turn produce or justify proportionate amounts of "purchase-money" paid to authors. It is also noteworthy that Robertson assigns a primary role to the bookseller-as-publisher, whose judgment of the anticipated public response takes precedence over that of the author himself. The patronage of the publisher is affirmed.

In a letter written a decade earlier, David Hume commented to the Abbé Morellet on the unprecedented amount of copy money that had just been given to Robertson himself for his second book, *The History of the Reign of Charles V:* "M. Suard would tell you what noble encouragement is given to literature in England, without the intervention of the great, by means of the booksellers alone, that is, by the public" (*LDH,* 2:203) Hume's remark once again suggests the shift from aristocratic patronage to patronage by the book trade. The focus is not on Robertson personally but on the general significance of Robertson's financial arrangement, which gives literature "noble encouragement"—a phrase that highlights the perceived shift of true nobility and literary patronage from the aristocracy to the booksellers. The most interesting aspect of Hume's statement, however, occurs at the end, when bookseller-publishers are equated with the public itself. Although Hume's precise meaning is far from clear, he seems to be saying that booksellers, in their dual capacity as the publishers and vendors of literature, have their fingers so firmly on the pulse of the public that they represent its interests and desires.

A third perspective on the relationship between authors, publishers, and the public occurs in an extraordinary article titled "On the History of Authors by Profession," published in installments in four early numbers of James Anderson's magazine *The Bee*—two shortly before and two just after the publication of Boswell's *Life of Johnson* in mid-May 1791. This piece argues that authors have always been supported "either by *becoming objects of the munificence of individuals*, or by *ministering to the pleasure of the public*. The first is the state of *patronage:* The second is that to which has been annexed the vulgar obloguy of *authorship*."[16] This fundamental tension between private patronage and public support has operated from ancient times to the present, but the emergence of printing introduced a new intermediary between the author and the public: the bookseller, whose rise to dominance over authors is described in highly unfavorable terms:

> The art of printing, by enlarging the sphere of the commerce of books, gave utility and importance to its conductors; they speedily became to authors, what the monied capitalist is to the manufacturer. In simple times, the manufacturer and the author distribute their own produce: But, in the progress of society, by a sort of *division of labour*, separate professions arise for this distribution, the merchant and the bookseller. Placed in circumstances more favourable to the growth of wealth, than the original producer, they soon obtain over him the superiority conferred by the command of capital, and, instead of agents, become the employers and masters. It is this circumstance that renders the state of *authorship* less eligible among us than it was in the ancient world. A *medium* is now interposed between the author and the public. The profits of literature are abridged, while its professors are subjected to a new dependence. (3:88–89)

Up to this point, the article can be read as an elaborate historical defense of authors against rapacious booksellers. But immediately after the passage just quoted, the article takes an unexpected twist by arguing that the interests of authors and the public

> are, in fact, opposite: for it is the object of the author to enhance the value of his produce, and that of the public, to procure it as easily as they can. The art of printing, and the profession of bookseller, facilitate the dispersion of literary produce. In the same proportion, they perhaps *lower the market* of

16. "On the History of Authors," 3:13.

knowledge, and perhaps, in some degree, diminish the importance of authors, as they diffuse information more widely among men. (3:89)

With the introduction of a distinction between learning and the diffusion of knowledge, or between authors on the one hand and publishers, booksellers, and the public on the other, the writer of this article asserts that the interests of literature cannot be identified absolutely with the interests of those who write it. Boswell's Johnson, let us remember, spoke of booksellers as the patrons of *literature*, not necessarily of *authors*. To individual authors, these two interests may have appeared to be inextricably bound together, and very often they were. As we shall see later in this chapter, it was not uncommon for authors to regard booksellers or publishers with suspicion, on the assumption that they were always liable to exploit authors, or at least capable of doing so under certain circumstances. Yet perceptive critics, such as Robertson, Hume, and the writer in *The Bee*, realized that this was not always so and that publishers sometimes represented the interests of the public more thoroughly and judiciously than did authors, whose perspective was sometimes skewed by their self-interest.

Traditional Patronage Transformed

If eighteenth-century publishers were sometimes the patrons of literature and of authors, this does not mean that traditional patronage by aristocratic and cultural elites no longer had a role to play in the world of commercial print culture. Roger Chartier has observed that from the Renaissance onward "the traditional system of patronage, far from being dismantled by the diffusion of the printed book, adapted to the new technique for the reproduction of texts and to the market logic that it set up."[17] Similarly, Dustin Griffin points out that the "myth of liberation" of authors from aristocratic patrons is no more accurate a representation of the literary world in the eighteenth century than are contrary myths that stress the growth of corruption and victimization.[18] Writing about English poets, Griffin argues that aristocratic patronage persisted during the eighteenth century in ways that have not always been fully appreciated and that the age is best characterized as "a mixed system of patron-

17. Chartier, *Order of Books*, 48.
18. Griffin, "Fictions," 181–94.

age and market."[19] This phrase applies equally well to the authors of the Scottish Enlightenment.

The fact that so many Scottish Enlightenment authors enjoyed professional positions with regular, secure, and often substantial incomes, as well as pensions and sinecures from the government or from other established institutions, has a bearing on their status as authors. Obviously, authors whose main income was derived from their employment as professors, physicians, lawyers, and clergymen, or who were independently well-off, did not depend wholly on the patronage of the book trade. If we carry the analysis back one step by asking how so many Scottish Enlightenment authors attained the professional positions that enabled them to assert their independence, it becomes clear that patrons continued to perform an important function in the process of publication during the late eighteenth century, even if their role was often different from what it had been in earlier centuries. Although aristocratic patrons were less likely to retain authors in their households or to fund their scholarship and publications directly, another kind of patronage became more prominent. This mode involved bestowing academic positions, church livings, and other offices that enabled authors to write in comfort, and sometimes in affluence. Virtually all Scottish professors, judges, parish ministers, and holders of pensions and sinecures owed their appointments to powerful patrons, who used influence effectively on their behalf. Usually these appointments came with no external restrictions. Barring a scandal, total incapacity, unauthorized absenteeism over a period of years, or voluntary retirement, professors in Scottish universities served for life, and so did judges and parish ministers.

A great deal hinged, therefore, on the ability of people in positions of power to recognize worthy scholarly and literary accomplishments, or promise of same, as well as on their willingness to dispense patronage in accordance with their best judgment. The book culture of the Scottish Enlightenment was deeply indebted to a number of patrons who made outstanding appointments to deserving men of letters, but the third Duke of Argyll and his nephew the third Earl of Bute are particularly noteworthy.[20] The patronage appointments that Argyll made or influenced during

19. Griffin, *Literary Patronage*, 291. See also Korshin, "Types of Eighteenth-Century Literary Patronage," 453–73.

20. The fullest account will appear in Emerson, *University Patronage*. At least eighteen authors from table 1 were among the dozens of Scots who owed their academic, judicial, or other appointments to Argyll, as listed in Emerson, "Catologus Li-

the two decades preceding his death in 1761, and those that Bute made or influenced in the several years that followed, when nearly all desirable positions in Scotland (and in Bute's case, England also) were theirs to bestow, not only gave full-time livings or positions with supplemental incomes to many of the authors listed in table 1 but also established a standard for encouraging and rewarding merit among authors. Although relatively few men of letters could realistically hope to obtain the extraordinarily large amounts of copy money that went to a small number of best-selling quarto authors, many more could aspire to indirect rewards of this kind.

The transformation in the nature of aristocratic literary patronage is illustrated by the career of John Home. After his tragedy *Douglas* took Britain by storm in 1756–57, provoking the animosity of orthodox Calvinists, who regarded theater as inherently sinful, Home was obliged to resign his position as a parish minister in the Church of Scotland. He then went to live with the Earl of Bute in London as a private secretary or personal assistant. Bute's ally at the time, William Pitt, had already been instrumental in convincing David Garrick to produce *Douglas* at Covent Garden, but Bute himself became the chief patron of Home's theatrical career, which was so closely tied to the earl that Home's second play to be produced and published, *Agis*, was widely seen as a vehicle for Bute's party at Leicester House.[21] All this was patronage in the grand old style of lords and literary men. But it was no longer acceptable to the Scottish literati, who campaigned vigorously for Home to be given an independent living. "Every man of Worth shoud have a firm bottom on which he may stand however narrow it is," wrote Adam Ferguson to Gilbert Elliot, a Scottish politician in Bute's circle, in 1760. "I therefore wish most earnestly that every other act of Friendship for Home was thought of no avail till he is fixed in some moderate reasonable or even little provisions sure for his Life."[22] Ferguson was a clergyman's son from Perthshire who had just obtained his own "firm bottom" the previous year, when his political patrons (including Bute and Ilay's agent Lord Milton, in whose families he had served as a tutor) had prevailed on the town council of Edinburgh to appoint him to a university chair in a field (natural philosophy) in which

---

brorum," 38n3. This list does not include ecclesiastical chaplaincies and certain other positions. See also Emerson, "Scientific Interests," 21–56; Emerson, "Lord Bute," 147–79; Andrew, *Patrons of Enlightenment*, chap. 6.

21. Sher, "Favourite of the Favourite," 83–98.

22. Ferguson to Gilbert Elliot, 6 Nov. 1760, in Ferguson, *Correspondence*, 1:42.

he had virtually no expertise. Now he was lecturing politicians about the proper way to dispense patronage. Moreover, Ferguson appealed in part on national grounds, by stating that doing the right thing for his friend was "of more consequence than half the Public measures you will pursue this Twelve months for more than that proportion of them will result finally in getting more Victuals for John Bull, for which I do not care one single farthing." In the end, the literati got their way: Home received a government pension of £300 a year and then, just before Bute left office, an additional sinecure worth the same amount, and anti-Bute, anti-Scottish pundits gained a new target for their barbs and taunts about Scottish favoritism. Perhaps the clearest indication of the triumph of the new attitude toward literary patronage is the fact that Bute received little credit for his actions from Home's friends and was seen instead as having delayed too long what he should have done much earlier.[23]

The career of William Richardson provides another illuminating case study. Like Ferguson, he was the son of a Presbyterian minister in Perthshire and was himself bound for a career in the clergy. When an opportunity arose to serve as tutor to the sons of Lord Cathcart, however, Richardson withdrew from divinity school at Glasgow and took his young charges to Eton for two years. In 1768, following Cathcart's appointment as ambassador to Russia, he accompanied the family to St. Petersburg, where he served for four years both as family tutor and as Cathcart's secretary. Shortly after the entourage returned to Scotland, Cathcart used his influence as lord rector of Glasgow University to secure the appointment of Richardson to the chair of humanity (Latin), which he occupied with distinction from autumn 1773 until his death in 1814. Richardson wasted no time making the transition from retainer to gentleman: on 25 November 1773 he told the London bookseller John Murray that his writings were merely for amusement rather than for profit, and he took no fee for his *Philosophical Analysis and Illustration of Some of Shakespeare's Remarkable Characters* (no. 166), a profitable title.[24] At the same time, he remained close with Cathcart, frequently residing at his estate and taking care to acknowledge his debt in the dedications to his books.

Traveling tutors like Richardson could use their time abroad to gather materials for books that would contribute to their careers in Britain. *Anecdotes of the Russian Empire* (no. 246) was the product of Richardson's period in Cathcart's household in St. Petersburg. Similarly, John Gillies

23. Mackenzie, *Account*, 1:51; Carlyle, *Autobiography*, 378.
24. Zachs, *First John Murray*, 75.

accompanied the sons of the Earl of Hopetoun on two Continental tutoring tours, which yielded not only a fixed, lifetime annuity for the tutor but also a biography of Frederick the Great of Prussia (no. 282). When Richardson and Gillies became tutors, they had no other means of employment. As Scottish men of letters attained independent careers of their own, however, aristocratic patrons seeking the most experienced and well-regarded tutors for their sons had to offer long-term support in order to convince the men they wanted to give up the positions they already had, either temporarily or permanently. The problem became particularly serious when the object was to find someone to accompany one's son on the grand tour. Adam Ferguson, Adam Smith, and John Moore were all lured away from professional positions in Edinburgh or Glasgow for this purpose, and in each case the aristocratic employer paid the tutor £200–300 a year for life in exchange for a year or two of Continental service.[25] Such lifetime annuities allowed these men of letters to spend more time on their writing than they might otherwise have been able to do, without requiring continued service to their patrons.

Government patronage must also be taken into account. In fact, the line between aristocratic and government patronage was often invisible in eighteenth-century Britain. Increasingly, men of letters obtained pensions, ecclesiastical offices, regius chairs and other academic professorships, civil service positions, and various kinds of sinecures from the government. A growing number were receiving such places less as a reward for political pamphleteering and other services on behalf of government policies and officials, which had long been an avenue to preference, than as a reward for having made significant contributions to literature and learning. The distinction was sharply drawn in 1763, when Samuel Johnson, who prided himself on his independence, accepted a £300-a-year government pension that was offered by the Bute administration on a recommendation by Alexander Wedderburn, solely in consideration of Johnson's accomplishments as an author and lexicographer. On this oc-

---

25. Moore's employment for the Duke of Hamilton, briefly noted in the last chapter, brought him a £300 annuity for life. Smith got the same amount for accompanying the Duke of Buccleuch on the grand tour in the 1760s—enough for him to resign his chair of moral philosophy at the University of Glasgow. Ferguson took an unauthorized leave from his position at the University of Edinburgh in order to accompany the fifth Earl of Chesterfield to Europe in the 1770s, and after some difficulties he managed to reclaim his chair and secure a lifetime annuity of £200 from the earl's family. See Ross, *Life*, chap. 13, 231, and 253–54; Fagg, "Biographical Introduction," 1:xliv–xlvi.

casion, Bute made a point of emphasizing that the pension "is not offered to you for having dipped your pen in faction, nor with a design that you ever should"; "it is not given you for any thing you are to do, but for what you have done."[26]

Such pronouncements cannot be taken at face value, however, because patronage often created subtle pressures and allegiances rather than straightforward obligations. As Griffin has noted, "the system of patronage was *always* political."[27] "The Truth is, Dr Johnson's Heart and Soul is with the Government," Strahan informed a government official in 1771, when explaining Johnson's willingness to write a pamphlet defending the government in a dispute with the magistrates of London, "and he will be extremely happy if his Pen can be made instrumental to its support in any way that shall be deemed seasonable, proper, and efficacious."[28] The difference between factional service and independent literary achievement is far from clear in regard to some of the Scottish men of letters whom Bute was using his authority to advance at this time, and who continued to serve him loyally, such as John Home and James Macpherson. Bute viewed government patronage for William Robertson, including his positions as principal of the University of Edinburgh and historiographer royal for Scotland, in conjunction with a scholarly commission to write a modern history of England.[29] But the model of government preferment articulated by Bute on the occasion of Johnson's appointment ultimately prevailed as the ideal. As the century wore on, authors increasingly came to expect government preferment of one kind or another as a reward for literary labors past, with less expectation of specific future services, whether political or literary. Many of the authors in table 1 received government preferment of this kind.

Thus, instead of the view that traditional forms of patronage were replaced by patronage from publishers, or simply withered away in the face of modern market forces, it is more accurate to say they were transformed into a new phenomenon, which generally supported authors indirectly rather than directly, and which had as one of its consequences the elevation of many men of letters to a state of social respectability and financial independence. In Scotland, as in France and elsewhere in Europe, for ev-

26. Quoted in Bate, *Samuel Johnson*, 356.

27. Griffin, *Literary Patronage*, 10, 67–69.

28. Strahan to John Robinson, 1 May 1771, with a letter from Strahan to Johnson, HL, MS Hyde 77, 4.300.

29. Sher, *Church and University*, chap. 3.

ery author who made a decent living solely from publications, there were many who regarded whatever they earned from their writing as supplementary income.[30] What it supplemented was usually a salary that derived in one way or another from patronage, even though it was patronage of a quite different sort from the traditional model of retainers serving at the whim of their lord and master or hack writers hiring their pens to one faction or another. In this new form, patronage served to establish professional autonomy, and professional autonomy enabled the majority of Scottish Enlightenment authors to deal with the book trade on terms of strength rather than weakness, according to their own individual motives and objectives.

COPY MONEY AND ITS USES

Authors write books for a combination of reasons that are seldom fully articulated. A love of learning, a desire for fame and glory, aspirations for a position or a promotion, a wish to spread a particular set of values or advance a school of thought, an intention to be useful to society, personal rivalries with other authors, and yes, cold cash—who can say how much weight to place on each of these and other factors? It is likely that most eighteenth-century authors undertook book projects largely because they believed they had something meaningful to say, and it is not my intention to minimize these intellectual motives. But in the context of the growing commercialization of literature that was occurring in Britain, it is also necessary to consider the role of material factors. The remainder of this chapter discusses the varied ways in which the authors of the Scottish Enlightenment approached this issue.

Aristocratic Variations

At one extreme, a number of authors had little or no interest in profiting from their books. Some aspired to the aristocratic ideal of the gentleman-author, whose writing career does not require patronage or profits of any sort because he is already a man of independent means. Although only a small minority of Scottish Enlightenment authors were born into these circumstances, many in effect grew into them by virtue of their professional positions and careers. Once financially independent, they were in a position to adopt the stance of a gentleman-author if they wished.

30. Chartier, "Man of Letters," 151–52.

Behavior of this kind was most common among landed gentlemen whose books were written solely for scholars and who were not likely to make a profit anyway. James Hutton, for example, printed his *Dissertations on Different Subjects in Natural Philosophy* (no. 306) at his own expense, though it was a huge quarto volume. He then offered the printed sheets to Strahan and Cadell, who published the book in London. In making the arrangements on Hutton's behalf, Henry Mackenzie told Cadell: "I may frankly say, that money is not his Object so much as the Book being well respectably announced to the world."[31] This way of putting the matter demonstrates once again the public importance of the publisher as a mode of classifying and ordering books—the "publisher function." Readers would not know the details of Hutton's publication arrangements, but they would immediately see that Hutton's book was appearing with the imprimatur of Britain's most prestigious publishing partnership.

Lord Monboddo's *Antient Metaphysics* (no. 204) also fits this category. In the preface to the first volume (1779), Monboddo expresses disdain for ordinary and "fashionable" readers. Appealing exclusively to a learned audience, he deliberately scorns the commercial ethos of polite publishing: "Nor do I believe there is a bookseller in Great Britain, who upon the credit of the title-page, would offer me a shilling for my copy, if I had a mind to sell it."[32] In keeping with this elitist posture, Monboddo financed the publication himself, and the print run was a mere three hundred copies (SA 48815, fol. 63). "I am very sensible that you do not profit much by the sale of my Books, as they are not of common use," he wrote to his primary publisher, Thomas Cadell, in 1784, when the third volume of *Antient Metaphysics* appeared; "but what profit you make is sure and without any risk; and therefore I expect that you will give the proper attention to what concerns them, and at least answer the Letters that I write to you."[33] The haughty tone of this letter, while partly reflecting the author's personality, was meant to remind Cadell of the social gap that separated a gentleman-author from a mere bookseller-publisher. A somewhat similar attitude marked the pronouncements of the Earl of Buchan, who contrasted "writing . . . for a bookseller," which is to say, for profit, with

31. Mackenzie to Cadell, 2 Aug. 1792, NLS, Acc. 9546.

32. Quoted in Moran, "From Rudeness to Refinement," 108. Remarkably, four years later Monboddo tried to sell the copyrights to *Antient Metaphysics* and *Of the Origin and Progress of Language* (no. 160) to Strahan and Cadell. See his letter to Cadell of 30 June 1783, HL, MS Hyde 69, item 27.

33. Monboddo to Cadell, 30 July 1784, NLS, Acc. 11313, no. 3.

the loftier activity of voluntarily, and patriotically, contributing papers to volumes of scholarly proceedings or transactions that would display and encourage national learning.[34] When Buchan wrote books, like the biographies of John Napier (no. 191) and Fletcher of Saltoun and James Thomson (no. 302), his avowed purpose was "to rescue from oblivion the memory of every man who has been usefull to Scotland."[35] Of course, being a wealthy nobleman made it easier to pursue this idealistic goal without any concern for material rewards.

In another variation on the gentleman-author ideal, authors sometimes attempted to obtain as much copy money as possible from their publishers, but not for themselves. The most formidable instance of an undertaking of this kind was Sir John Sinclair's twenty-one-volume *Statistical Account of Scotland* (no. 301), which was intended to raise money for the Society for the Benefit of the Sons of the Clergy. As we shall see in chapter 6, it never obtained this objective, but the sincerity of Sinclair's motives was never in doubt. A more successful instance of a charitable publication was *The Mirror* (no. 217), the literary periodical that Henry Mackenzie and his friends first published in 1779–80. When it became clear that there was a large audience for this work in book form, William Creech offered £100 for the copyright but was rebuffed by Mackenzie because he was acting as "a Trustee for charitable uses; and in that Capacity must make as good a Bargain as I can."[36] Creech apparently replied that he was willing to accept any arrangement agreed to by Strahan and Cadell. Mackenzie accordingly set out for London, and on 17 May he reported the results of his negotiations to Creech: "I found them a little hard with me and I was (for the first time) a Stickler in the Bargain, because I was bargaining not for myself but for the poor. At last we settled Matters at £180 in Hand, and if there was a 4th Edition, (that is, one after that now printing) that they would give me the additional £20 then" (115). As a result of Mackenzie's tenacity as a negotiator, the Mirror Club was able to make a donation of £100 to the Orphan Hospital in Edinburgh as well as to purchase a large supply of claret for the club itself. Other donations to charitable causes may also have been made with the remaining copy money. Mackenzie did even better when negotiating the book rights for a sequel, *The Lounger* (no. 270), which brought him £300, presumably also for charitable purposes (SA 48814A, fol. 14).

34. Quoted and discussed in Sher, "Science and Medicine," 133.
35. Earl of Buchan to Robert Chalmers, 6 Sept. 1791, HL, MS Hyde 76, 2.3.177.5.
36. Mackenzie to Creech, 11 Apr. 1781, in Mackenzie, *Literature and Literati*, 108.

Some years later, Creech, in partnership with Cadell & Davies, agreed to purchase the copyright to the first volume of the Highland Society's *Prize Essays and Transactions* (no. 353), which Mackenzie had edited, for the amount of money it had cost the society to print 750 copies of the work. The arrangement negotiated with Mackenzie also extended to future volumes, with Creech agreeing in mid-1799 "to give the society such a sum of money as shall be deemed reasonable by yourself" (212). Andrew Duncan's *Medical Cases, Selected from the Records of the Public Dispensary at Edinburgh* (no. 190) was also a work of a charitable nature, published to promote Duncan's pet project.

Still another version of this charitable ideal occurred when an author's estate negotiated a publication arrangement that would provide income for the author's family or heir. In the same letter in which he informed Cadell that Hutton was not especially interested in profiting financially from his book, Mackenzie remarked that he was taking a more aggressive stance in the negotiations for Adam Smith's posthumous *Essays on Philosophical Subjects*, because Smith's nephew and heir needed the money.[37] He succeeded in getting £300 in copy money for the first (and as it turned out, only) edition, with a stipulation calling for £200 more in the event of a second edition. Another posthumous work, *An Account of Sir Isaac Newton's Philosophical Discoveries* (no. 10) by Colin Maclaurin, was published by subscription to raise money for the author's children.

Profiting from Books

The great majority of Scottish Enlightenment authors did not express disdain for profits or write books for charity. Rather, they tried to make the most advantageous bargains they could with the publishers of their books. But what sort of bargains, and with which publishers or booksellers? Who could be trusted? What "hazards, pitfalls and dead ends" were waiting to snare an unsuspecting author,[38] and how could they be avoided?

In an effort to discover answers to these questions, a young Aberdonian in London, Sylvester Douglas, the future Lord Glenbervie, appealed to James Beattie in 1775 for advice about how to deal with booksellers. In his reply, Beattie remarks that "my experience . . . (small as it is) has taught me, that few of them wish to see an Author grow rich under their

---

37. Mackenzie to Cadell, 2 Aug. 1792, NLS, Acc. 9546.
38. Brewer, *Pleasures of the Imagination*, 140.

influence, and that the case of a young author bargaining with them about his first performance is by no means to be envied." William Strahan ranks highest among them, says Beattie, being "at once a judge of merit, and a liberal Encourager of it"; Edward Dilly is another possibility, but "he is very slow in making a bargain; as he is determined entirely by the opinion of some people about him, who must read the manuscript and deliberate upon it, before he can be brought to speak a word about terms."[39]

Similar suspicions were voiced by Henry Mackenzie in a letter of 19 April 1770, as he was about to publish his first book, *The Man of Feeling* (no. 135): "I have hitherto felt only the Pleasure of Composition; I begin now to experience the Troubles of an Author: Booksellers, and Managers of Play-houses, are of all Men of Business the least to be depended on."[40] Three years later, after his book had succeeded beyond expectation, Mackenzie would write to the same correspondent of "my worthy Friend and Bookseller Mr Strahan," and he continued to refer to Strahan in this manner throughout his life.[41] But there is no indication of a general change in his attitude toward the book trade. Like Beattie, Mackenzie might consider Strahan to be the best of the lot, but booksellers as a whole were to be regarded with suspicion because they stood on the other side of the divide separating authors from their books.

Authors usually expressed these suspicions among themselves, not wishing to alienate those responsible for putting their words into print. When authors conversed or corresponded with publishers directly, or wrote about them publicly, they often adopted a respectful, sometimes deferential, tone. James Fordyce began his volume of *Poems* (no. 262) with "To Mr. Cadell, Bookseller: An Ode," in which Cadell defends himself against the charges of a disgruntled author:

> "Hold, Friend; I did not write the book
> "Nor at it had I time to look."

The publisher is likened to a midwife whose "part" is not

> To form the child, but help it forth,
> And with due care direct the birth:
>   A necessary art!
> That art is yours; and, honest still,
> Whate'er you promise you fulfill.

39. Beattie to Douglas, 14 Aug. 1775, in Beattie, *Correspondence*, 2:308–9.
40. Mackenzie, *Letters to Elizabeth Rose*, 41.
41. Ibid., 138; Mackenzie, *Anecdotes*, 181.

Should Fordyce's book "prove dead-born" (as indeed it did), the fault would lie not with the publisher but with the author. Underlying such pronouncements was the ideal of the bookseller-publisher as the consummate professional, whose judgment should not be disputed.

By contrast, when Beattie's letter to Sylvester Douglas enters into details, it retains the skeptical tone of author-to-author communications:

> I would not advise you to make a conditional bargain, stipulating for a price proportioned to the sale of the Book. You cannot imagine what a monstrous list of expences and deductions a Bookseller draws forth in array against an author, when they come to settle their accounts upon an agreement of that sort. . . . I think it would be better if you could finish the matter at once, and sell your manuscript finally for a sum of money.

The preference Beattie expresses for selling the copyright to a bookseller for a fixed fee in advance of publication was widespread among eighteenth-century authors. The main alternatives seemed to them to rely too much on the integrity of the booksellers, who might easily cheat the author out of profits or, if books were printed "for the author," fail to promote publications in which they had no financial stake.

It is certainly true that the highest-paid Scottish author of the age, William Robertson, sold his copyrights in advance of publication for handsome sums. After receiving £600 for his two-volume *History of Scotland* (no. 58) in 1759, Robertson was paid more than £1,000 per quarto volume for his next three histories: £4,000 (including £500 for the second edition) for his three-volume *History of the Reign of Charles V* (no. 119), £2,667 for his two-volume *History of America* (no. 185), and £1,111 for his one-volume *Historical Disquisition concerning the Knowledge which the Ancients Had of India* (no. 299).[42] All this was the equivalent of more than £700,000 or well over $1 million in early twenty-first-century money. Yet the matter is not as simple as Beattie made it seem. Many other authors did better with "conditional" publishing arrangements than they would have done if they had sold their copyrights in advance. These matters are so complex, and the contingencies so plentiful, that it is advisable to examine a number of individual cases, arranged according to major categories of contractual arrangements. We shall see that no two instances were exactly alike. Publishers could be strikingly devious but also remarkably generous in their dealings with authors, and the terms of publication varied enormously from book to book, and sometimes from volume to volume and edition

---

42. Sher, *"Charles V,"* 164–95; and Sher, "Boswell," 205–15, esp. n. 20.

to edition. In short, there were many ways for authors to make and lose money in the business of Scottish Enlightenment books.

Payment by the Sheet or by the Job

Authors who wrote on commission from publishers, such as Grub Street hacks, were commonly paid by the printed sheet. As we saw in the last chapter, this species of author–publisher relations sometimes resulted in a difficult, even desperate form of existence for writers who struggled to meet tight deadlines. Yet some Grub Street authors could make a respectable living by selling their words to the booksellers. Robert Heron claimed earnings of more than £300 a year as a Grub Street writer after moving to London in 1799, although he had to work sixteen-hour days and could not sustain this rate of production for very long.

A half-century earlier, William Duncan and Tobias Smollett each negotiated profitable piece-rate agreements with publishers. Duncan, a skilled Latinist, contracted with Robert Dodsley in October 1744 to produce a translation of Julius Caesar's account of the Gallic wars, with English and Latin on facing pages and scholarly notes.[43] The contract specified that the work would use "the same type and letter" as a 1743 octavo edition of Horace's satires that presumably had also been translated and edited by Duncan. For Caesar, Duncan would be paid a guinea and a half per printed sheet for the first edition, which would be limited to 1,000 copies; if a second edition were called for, he would receive an additional half guinea per sheet. Dodsley would own the copyright, and Duncan had to agree not to publish anything similar with anyone else. When the work finally appeared in 1753, it was a large illustrated folio (no. 24) to which Duncan prefixed a learned discourse on the Roman art of war. From this edition, and the two-volume octavo edition that followed two years later, Duncan must have realized several hundred pounds.

Tobias Smollett earned a good deal more than that from *A Complete History of England* (no. 49). The bankruptcy records of one of that book's publishers, James Rivington, reveal that in 1757–58 Smollett was paid a generous three guineas per sheet for the first edition, which came to a total of 999 guineas, or £1,048.19s., for the 333 sheets that made up four quarto volumes.[44] When the book sold well, the publishers called

43. BL, Egerton MSS 738, fol. 9.

44. Hernlund, "Three Bankruptcies," 86. In 1753 Rivington, Robert Dodsley, and William Strahan contracted to pay Smollett a guinea and a half per sheet to compile

upon the author for another £500 worth of "alterations and additions" that were both textual and paratextual, including a number of boastful puffs intended to boost sales of the second and third editions.[45] The total earnings of £1,549 that Smollett realized from this work in the space of three years were exceptional, and they brought him a newfound sense of financial independence.[46]

Sometimes publishers commissioned men of letters to work by the job rather than by the sheet. Johnson's *Dictionary* and *Lives of the Poets* (consisting of biographical prefaces that Johnson famously offered to write for only two hundred guineas, when the London booksellers approached him with a commission in 1777) are the best-known eighteenth-century instances, but there were many others, such as the *Encyclopaedia Britannica* (no. 139). When the printer Colin Macfarquhar and the engraver Andrew Bell conceived the plan of the *Britannica*, they shrewdly secured the services of the multitalented printer and writer William Smellie to compose fifteen scientific articles and "likewise to prepare the whole work for the press, etc. etc.," for a total fee of just £200. Although Smellie used to say that he created this work with a pair of scissors, because he compiled so much of it from other publications, it was by any reckoning an enormous undertaking for which his payment turned out to be thoroughly inadequate. Unfortunately for Smellie, he then turned down the publishers' offer of a one-third share of the work to continue as editor of the second edition. The *Britannica* succeeded, and Bell and Macfarquhar became wealthy (their net profits from the third edition alone were said to be £42,000), while Smellie continued to struggle to support his large family.[47]

Self-Publication

Even if some men of letters managed to make a decent living from selling their writings or their editorial services by the sheet or by the job, they

---

A Compendium of Authentic and Entertaining Voyages. HL, MS Hyde 10, item 646. Cf. Feather, "John Nourse and His Authors," 206.

45. Hernlund, "Three Bankruptcies," 86; and Brack, "Tobias Smollett," 267–88.

46. Knapp, *Tobias Smollett,* 192. Knapp relied on Robert Anderson's assertion that Smollett earned £2,000 from his *Complete History* and the five-volume *Continuation* (no. 67), but this estimate is probably too low, considering the amount that he received for the *Complete History* alone.

47. Kerr, *Memoirs,* 1:361–63; Kafker, "Achievement," 139–52.

had little or no control over these publications. Control could be obtained, however, by publishing their books themselves, usually by paying a book-seller a commission to take charge of production and marketing. Several Scottish authors elected this option successfully. Mungo Park obtained a thousand guineas (£1,050) from the first edition of his popular *Travels in the Interior Districts of Africa* (no. 350), which appeared in spring 1799 with the designation "Printed for the Author." By the beginning of January 1800, Park told his wife that his profits from three editions had reached "about two thousand pounds," with more to come.[48] In 1756 the self-educated science lecturer James Ferguson published in London his first major book, *Astronomy Explained upon Sir Isaac Newton's Principles* (no. 39), in a one-volume subscription quarto, featuring engravings made from the author's own drawings. An unabashed exercise in the popular diffusion of difficult scientific concepts, *Astronomy Explained* was an immediate suc-cess. The following year the author published an expanded second edi-tion, also in quarto and also marked "Printed for, and sold by the Author." Although it was unusual for an author to market his own book, Ferguson could do it because at this time he was keeping a shop in the Strand, where he sold globes of his own manufacture.

Although Ferguson must have earned hundreds of pounds from the first two editions of *Astronomy Explained*, self-publishing was an uncer-tain and time-consuming activity. Unless one was prepared to manage every aspect of the process, as John Hunter did with his *Treatise on the Venereal Disease* (no. 264) and *Observations on Certain Parts of the Animal Oeconomy* (no. 265), it was often wise to sell the rights to a successful self-published work to professionals in the book trade.[49] In 1757 Ferguson gave up his manufacturing business, and therefore his shop at the sign of the globe, and the following year he sold the copyright of *Astronomy Explained* for £300 to his former neighbor in the Strand, Andrew Millar, who published the third edition in 1764 under his own imprint. Millar, and subsequently his successor Cadell, in partnership with Strahan, be-came the publishers of all of Ferguson's major books, and the author prof-ited enough from copy money and lecturing to have accumulated £6,000 in savings at the time of his death.[50]

---

48. Hallett, *Records*, 165n1, citing correspondence from the bookseller George Nicol to Sir Joseph Banks; Mungo Park to Allison Park, 10 Jan. 1800, in Lupton, *Mungo Park*, 123, 110.

49. Sher, "Science and Medicine," 143–46.

50. Millburn, *Wheelwright*, 85–93, 253.

Robert Henry's *History of Great Britain* (no. 144) was another success-ful book that was originally printed for the author.[51] It was a huge un-dertaking, in which Henry set out to treat a fixed sequence of topics in a series of chronologically ordered volumes, from the ancient Romans to the present. After reading the manuscript of the first volume in 1770, Hume provided William Strahan with a mixed review: the scholarship was admirable, but the scope of the enterprise made it unlikely that Henry would be able to complete it (*LDH*, 2:230–31, 234)—a correct assessment, as it turned out, because the first five volumes of Henry's *History* got only as far as 1485, and the posthumous sixth volume, partially composed by Malcolm Laing, went to 1547. We do not know how much money Henry was requesting for the copyright, but it must have been a large amount, and it was in this context that William Robertson made his previously quoted statement about the impropriety of authors refusing to take what the booksellers offered for their first books. Yet, as Hume recognized, Robertson's £4,000 advance contract for *Charles V* colored everything that came after it: "I wish that Dr Robertson's Success may not have ren-derd the Author too sanguine in his pecuniary Expectations," he told Strahan (*LDH*, 2:230–31, 234).

Rather than back down, Henry decided to publish the book himself. Doing so was not only financially risky but also an enormous drain on the author's time and energy. Strahan printed 1,000 copies of the first volume in London in 1771, and Cadell served as the sales agent for all five volumes that appeared in the author's lifetime. From the second volume (1774) onward, Henry personally oversaw the printing in Edinburgh, ar-ranged to have copies shipped to London, wrote the London newspaper advertisements and provided detailed instructions on when and where to publish them, pressed Cadell for annual accounts of sales, and announced in the Edinburgh newspapers that the book could be purchased at the home of the author in Potter-row Street—unusual behavior for an Edin-burgh clergyman.[52] He worried privately that Cadell and his associates did not put enough effort into marketing the book in England because "it is not their property."[53] Nevertheless, the quarto edition sold well enough

51. See Sher, "Book," 20–40; and my article on Robert Henry in *ODNB*.

52. Henry to Cadell, 1 Oct. 1776, HL, Autograph File C; 11 Jan. 1777, NLS, MS 948, no. 3; and 30 Jan. 1777, EUL, La.II.219, no. 23; *EEC*, 1 Jan. 1774.

53. Henry to R. Harrison, 17 Jan. 1783, privately owned. The London bookseller James Lackington believed that his brethren resented authors who tried to publish

for Henry to realize a profit of £1,600 by 1786, when he released 140 unsold quarto sets to Andrew Strahan and Thomas Cadell for £455 (at £3.5s. per five-volume set). As part of the same agreement, Strahan and Cadell paid him £1,000 for the copyrights to the first five volumes, which they wished to publish in a more affordable octavo edition.[54] This brought Henry's total profit from these volumes to the sizeable sum of £3,055. Yet in a letter written to Thomas Percy on 2 May 1787, Henry remarked that this amount, augmented by a government pension of £100 per annum that he considered part of his book earnings, "is all I have made by these volumes" (*BLJ*, 3:526)—as if his income from the *History of Great Britain* was not all it should have been.[55] There can be no better demonstration of the rising expectations of Scottish authors regarding copy money.

William Buchan's *Domestic Medicine* (no. 115), one of the biggest sellers of the age, was also initially published by the author.[56] Thanks to an aggressive subscription campaign and much advertising in Scottish newspapers, more than 5,000 copies were sold a short time after the book's appearance in 1769, apparently without even tapping into the large English market. It is not known how much profit Buchan earned from the first edition. Since the book was a thick octavo priced at just five shillings (20 percent of which went to subscription agents), his profit margin could not have been anything like what Henry got from his multivolume quarto history with a retail price of a guinea per volume. But Buchan could partially compensate for this deficiency with high-volume sales.

A coalition of four publishers—Strahan and Cadell in London, Creech and Balfour in Edinburgh—grasped the commercial potential of Buchan's

---

their own books and that they often sabotaged such works (Collins, *Profession of Letters*, 109).

54. Letters exchanged between Henry and Cadell, between 22 March and 8 April 1786, in SA 48901, fols. 27–30, and two contract letters from Henry to Cadell dated 15 November 1786, NLS, Acc. 11693. The Strahan ledgers reveal that Henry's widow was paid four hundred guineas (£420) when the posthumous sixth volume appeared in 1793 (SA 48814A, fol. 13).

55. Similarly, when the fourth volume appeared, Henry told Strahan on 21 April 1781 that so far he had received "a decent, though not an adequate recompense for my labour, having made rather better than £300 of each of my former volumes besides 200 copies of each volume still on hand of which I may still make something" (HL, MS Hyde 10, item 316).

56. For additional details on what follows, see Sher, "William Buchan's *Domestic Medicine*," 45–64.

book and purchased the rights to it for £500 in October 1770. Yet even that agreement was in part conditional, because it apparently stipulated that the author would receive additional compensation in money (£50) or in kind (100 copies of the book) for each new edition he prepared for the press. These terms, along with seemingly insatiable demand by the public, led the publishers to print very large editions, rising from a print run of 3,500 for the second edition of 1772 to 6,000 copies for the eighth edition of 1784 (SA 48801, fol. 65, and 48815, fol. 43). Even so, new editions were required every two or three years. Strahan and Cadell also paid Buchan an additional fee of £300 to renew the copyright in 1803. All told, Buchan earned a total of perhaps £1,500 from *Domestic Medicine* during his lifetime.[57]

The high degree of anxiety that authors sometimes experienced over the terms of publication is illustrated by the drama surrounding another self-published best seller, James Boswell's *Life of Samuel Johnson* (no. 295). In the years leading up to the publication of this work, Boswell's anxiety about the book's critical reception was compounded by financial anxiety, and the terms of publication became the focus of his concerns. One option was to publish the book himself under the imprint of his friend Charles Dilly, who would receive a commission of 7.5 percent. In this arrangement—which had worked well enough for the *Journal of a Tour to the Hebrides* (no. 250)[58]—Boswell would continue to own the copyright and would receive all the profits, but he would also be responsible for all production and marketing expenses and would risk losing money if the book sold poorly. The second option—selling the copyright to a publisher for a flat fee—entered Boswell's consciousness in April 1790, a little more than a year before publication, when the author was informed by his trusted editor, Edmund Malone, that an unnamed bookseller was willing to pay £1,000 for the property.

Over the next eleven months, Boswell passed through three distinct stages as he tried to determine the best course of action. In the first period, stretching from April to November 1790, he was increasingly con-

57. This sum would be considerably higher if we accept the assertion of William West, who claimed to know Buchan "extremely well," that Buchan received for every revised or corrected addition not £50 (as Buchan's surviving correspondence suggests) but £100. See [West], "Letters," 71.

58. Brady, *Later Years*, 271–72, 296. The first edition of 1,500 copies of the *Tour* sold out almost immediately in the autumn of 1785, and two more editions appeared within a year. But then sales dropped off abruptly, and no more editions were published.

fident about the prospects of self-publication. The very fact that he had turned down *"A Cool thousand"* on the advice of Malone and the book-seller John Nichols fueled hopes that his "Magnum Opus . . . will be the most entertaining Book that ever appeared," as he playfully remarked to a friend.[59] During this period Boswell saw his book swell "unavoidably" from one to two quarto volumes, to be priced at two guineas the set, and he made the bold decision to print 1,750 copies. In a letter of 11 October, he boasted that "I would not now accept of £1500 for the property," which Malone told him he could get but should turn down.[60] A few days later, still riding high, he borrowed money to purchase at an inflated price the estate of Knockroon, adjoining his own estate, Auchinleck, in Ayrshire.

Then the bubble burst. Early in November Boswell had to assign the rents from his Ayrshire estate and "the copyright and profits" from his forthcoming book as security for a £1,000 bond from Dilly and his printer Henry Baldwin to help cover the high cost of production.[61] Plagued by mounting financial pressures and problems completing the book, he grew depressed and lapsed into a state of "timidity" and indecision, as he informed Malone on 29 January 1791, "quite at a loss what to do" and wondering seriously if he should accept the offer to sell the copyright for (as he now put it in his journal) "1000 guineas."[62] At a particularly bleak moment in late February, after it was learned that the book had been depreciated because someone with access to the manuscript had spoken against it, Dilly himself advised him to sell the copyright for £1,000 to George Robinson (by this time revealed to be the interested bookseller), even though he would lose his commission if Boswell did so.[63] A few days later Boswell told Malone that he was "in a distressing perplexity how to decide as to the property of my Book" and was willing to accept "even of £500" for it.[64] His confusion was exacerbated by his feelings of loyalty to Dilly, "with whom my name had been so long connected" as an author.[65]

After hitting this low point, Boswell reached an equilibrium between

59. Boswell to Bennet Langton, 9 Apr. 1790, and Boswell to Sir William Forbes, 2 July 1790, in Boswell, *Correspondence and Other Papers*, 244, 256; Boswell to Robert Boswell, 28 Sept. 1790, quoted in Boswell, *Great Biographer*, 110.

60. Quoted in Boswell, *Correspondence and Other Papers*, 264.

61. Boswell Papers, Yale University, A 59, item 1.

62. Boswell, *Correspondence and Other Papers*, 295.

63. Boswell, *Great Biographer*, 126.

64. Boswell to Malone, 25 Feb. 1791, in Boswell, *Correspondence and Other Papers*, 298.

65. Boswell, *Great Biographer*, 126.

his initial phase of euphoric optimism and his subsequent period of dire pessimism and depression. On 5 March 1791 Malone explained that if the copyright was worth £1,000 to Robinson when he believed it would be a one-volume quarto, it could not conceivably be worth less than £1,200 to him now that the book was twice as big. Four days later Boswell reported that Dilly and Baldwin had each agreed to lend him an additional £200 against the value of the *Life*; together with a £600 loan in Scotland, this would provide the money for a payment that would enable him to keep Knockroon. With financial pressures relaxing, Boswell gained clarity: "I am quite resolved now to keep the property of my *Magnum* Opus," he told Malone, "and I flatter myself I shall not repent it."[66] Writing in his journal on 18 March, he added that, after considering an approach to Robinson, "I resolved to take the fair chance of the public."[67] Although this decision seems to have been grounded at least partly in his fear of humiliation if he should contact Robinson directly and be rebuffed, the important thing was that a choice had been made. In the two months that remained until publication, Boswell never again expressed doubts about whether to publish the book himself or sell the copyright to a bookseller.

When the *Life of Johnson* finally appeared on 16 May 1791, its rapid sales vindicated Boswell's decision. Almost half the copies were sold in the first two weeks, and by late September the relieved author told a friend that "the profits will exceed the offer which I refused."[68] At a "hearty breakfast" with Dilly and Baldwin on 24 November 1792, when the entire edition was gone, Boswell learned that he was entitled to a profit of £1,555.18s.2d., an amount he considered "very flattering to me as an author." When additional deductions were made for the considerable amounts that Boswell owed his printer and bookseller, among others, the author was left with only £608.[69] But most of those debts would have been called in anyway, and Boswell would have come away with much less if he had accepted Robinson's offer. Moreover, because he had not yet sold the copyright, Boswell could also lay sole claim to the substantial profits—said to be as high as £950—from the second edition that appeared

66. Malone to Boswell, 5 Mar. 1791, and Boswell to Malone, 9 Mar. 1791, in Boswell, *Correspondence and Other Papers*, 301–2.

67. Boswell, *Great Biographer*, 136.

68. Boswell to Forbes, 27 Sept. 1791, in Boswell, *Correspondence and Other Papers*, 345.

69. Boswell, *Great Biographer*, 200–201.

in three octavo volumes in 1793.[70] And after his death, his four youngest
children, to whom he had willed the copyright, were able to profit from
the four-volume octavo third edition of 1799, which proved to be the last
of the Dilly editions, and *then* to sell the copyright to Cadell & Davies for
£300. In this case, self-publication proved to be vastly preferable to prior
sale of the copyright for Boswell and his heirs, but it was also a good deal
harder on the author's nerves.

How did Dilly and Baldwin determine that Boswell's profit from the
first edition of the *Life of Johnson* was £1,555.18s.2d.? The Boswell papers
at Yale University contain a little-known set of documents that answers
this question and reveals a great deal about the financial workings of self-
publication in the late eighteenth century.[71] The first step was to establish
the total income from the sale of the edition. Although 1,750 copies had
been printed, 52 were charged to the author for his private use, mostly as
presentation copies, and 9 more were sent to Stationers' Hall to register
the book there. The income from the remaining 1,689 copies was figured
at a flat rate of 32s. each, which was presumably the wholesale price for
a handsomely bound copy (exactly two-thirds of the retail price, in this
case), for a total income of £2,702.8s. Dilly used this figure to calculate
his 7.5 percent commission—£202.13s.6d. This was Dilly's publishing
profit, as opposed to the profit of 16s. that he (or any other bookseller)
might have earned every time he sold a bound set at the retail price of
£2.8s. A separate account listed £943.16s.4d. in additional expenses, including £552.15s. for 502½ reams of paper, £286.2s.6d. paid to Baldwin
for the printing, £47.5s. paid to James Heath for engraving the frontispiece portrait of Johnson, £14.7s. for newspaper advertisements in London and Edinburgh, and numerous other itemized charges for everything
from putting boards on forty-nine presentation copies (£4.18s.) to paying
the fees for entering the book in the register at Stationers' Hall (6d., and
6d. more for registering each of two pamphlets containing excerpted material). Here was the dreaded "monstrous list of expences and deductions
a Bookseller draws forth in array against an Author" that Beattie warned
of in his letter to Sylvester Douglas about the dangers of "conditional"
bargains—and there was no kind of bargain more conditional than self-
publication. But Boswell trusted Dilly and Baldwin, and the total expenses of £1,146.9s.10d. (all the charges plus Dilly's commission), when

70. Brady, *Later Years*, 577.
71. Boswell Papers, Yale University, A 59, items 4 and 5.

subtracted from the income of £2,702.8s., left a balance that kept his spirits high: £1,555.18s.2d. We can appreciate the full extent of Boswell's risk, however, by observing that if the first edition of the *Life of Johnson* had sold, say, 600 copies at the time of the "hearty breakfast" when this accounting was done, the author would still have been deep in the red. Self-publication on a grand scale was not for the faint of heart.

Of course, most self-published books were not productions on the grand scale of Boswell's *Life of Johnson* or Henry's *History of Great Britain*. Thomas Blacklock started his career as a poet with a slim pamphlet of *Poems on Several Occasions*, "Printed for the Author" in Glasgow in 1746. Eight years later he produced a more substantial volume with that title in Edinburgh (no. 31), with an imprint that identified Hamilton, Balfour, and Neill as the printers but did not indicate for whom the book was printed. A letter from David Hume establishes that this edition was self-published, and in a most unusual manner: since publication in what Hume calls "the common way" (meaning an arrangement with a publisher) would have resulted in "the greatest part of the profit" going to "the booksellers," Hume—along with other friends who wished to patronize a Scottish poet trying to overcome the dual disabilities of poverty and blindness—had arranged to "take copies from him and distribute [i.e., sell] them among their acquaintances" (*LDH*, 1:184). In this way, Blacklock earned "about one hundred guineas" from the three-shilling 1754 Edinburgh edition (1:203). Equally important, that edition spurred interest in Blacklock in England, where in 1756 a much more lucrative quarto "second edition" (with a biographical introduction by Joseph Spence of Oxford University) would be "Printed for the Author" by the Dodsley brothers and financed by subscription.[72]

Subscription

The previously mentioned article on the history of "authors by profession" in *The Bee* characterized the reign of Queen Anne in early eighteenth-century England as "the age of *subscription*," driven by "an aristocracy of *patrons*" whose numbers were "small enough to be pervaded by individual solicitation or influence." In this view, subscription publishing was

---

72. We do not know the total amount of money that Blacklock received for this edition, but in a letter to Robert Dodsley of 13 March 1756, the author mentions a final payment of £232 and thanks Dodsley and Spence for having placed him in "Independent Circumstances." HL, MS Hyde 10, item 52.

a "remnant of patronage" in its original form, and it broke down during the course of the eighteenth century under the pressure of a growing public that "left men of letters to be patronized only by those who derived profit from the distribution of their works"—which is to say, the book trade.[73] This view of subscription publishing as "a way-station on the road from personal patronage to commercial authorship," in the words of one modern commentator,[74] is familiar today, but in fact it applies only to one particular kind of subscription publishing, which may be described as traditional or elitist. Such books were normally published in quarto or even folio, often at inflated prices, and they nearly always contained lists of subscribers, which were headed by prominent members of the aristocracy. The purpose of these books was typically to patronize a worthy (and often needy) author, who received the profits from the subscription as well as a conspicuous display of support in the form of the subscription list itself. The 1756 second edition of Blacklock's *Poems* is a good example of such display, because it was available in both standard quarto and "large paper" issues, and an asterisk was placed next to the name of every subscriber who had signed up for the latter. Readers could therefore see at a glance that the Archbishop of Canterbury and the Duke of Newcastle had each subscribed for two copies of the large-paper variant, whereas many lesser lights had each subscribed for one copy of the standard issue. Although I have not located any subscription proposals for this edition, it would be surprising if subscribers paid much less than a guinea for a book of poems in quarto that was just a little larger than the 1754 three-shilling octavo edition.

Only five first editions in table 2 fit this traditional, elitist pattern of subscription publication. Two were the posthumous productions honoring Francis Hutcheson and Colin Maclaurin (nos. 10 and 36). The others were Robert Adam's *Ruins of the Palace of the Emperor Diocletian at Spalatro in Dalmatia* (no. 85), the quarto edition of James Beattie's *Essays* (no. 173), and William Julius Mickle's translation of Luís de Camões's epic poem about the Portuguese exploration of India, *The Lusiad* (no. 175). Adam's *Spalatro* was a magnificently illustrated folio volume funded by wealthy subscribers who paid three guineas apiece for the privilege of having their names listed among the patrons. Even at that high price, the book probably lost money, for in addition to the high cost of printing 500 copies of the text and the engravings and 1,000 copies of the subscription propos-

73. "On the History of Authors," 3:53.
74. Lockwood, "Subscription-Hunters," 132.

als, as well as advertising the work in the newspapers, Adam had to pay an army of draftsmen, artists (most notably Charles-Louis Clérisseau), engravers, designers, advisers, and agents. The production costs must have been enormous, and Strahan had to wait three years for payment.[75] But immediate financial gains were not the only way that a publication could be profitable to its author. As Iain Gordon Brown has shown, *Spalatro* constituted "a public-relations exercise designed to impress potential clients," and the subscription list functioned as a self-constituting elite of "patrons and would-be connoisseurs" of fashion and taste.[76] Everything about the book—the folio format, the dedication to the king, the recruitment of key members of the nobility among the subscribers, the minimizing of Clérisseau's contribution to create the impression that Adam himself had executed most of the drawings, and even the occasional alteration of the historical record in order to improve upon the taste of the ancients—was calculated to achieve those ends. It was an aristocratic showpiece, intended to enhance the reputation of the architect-author at a critical time in his career.

Mickle and Beattie obtained more tangible rewards. Mickle is said to have earned almost £1,000 from the *Lusiad* subscription (*ODNB*), but I have been unable to obtain any details about the publishing arrangements. More is known about the subscription edition of Beattie's *Essays*, the most profitable of that author's publications. It was a thick one-volume quarto, which contained the sixth edition of the *Essay on Truth* and three previously unpublished essays—on poetry and music, laughter and humorous writing, and the usefulness of classical education. Conceived by the English bluestocking Elizabeth Montagu for the express purpose of generating income for the author,[77] this edition can also be viewed as a public endorsement of Beattie's opinions, which defended Britain from Humean skepticism and from challenges to the classics-based system of education. For one guinea per volume in boards, 476 individuals subscribed for 732 copies, from which the author said he received approximately four hundred guineas after expenses were deducted. The publishing arrangements for this book were peculiar. In exchange for the profits from the quarto subscription edition, Beattie gave the copyright to the three new essays to Creech and the Dilly brothers, who already owned the copyright

75. Harlan, "William Strahan," 155–56.

76. Brown, *Monumental Reputation*, 46.

77. Beattie, *London Diary*, 33; Robinson, introduction to Beattie, *Essays*, xxii–xxvi.

to the *Essay on Truth*.[78] The new essays also appeared without the *Essay on Truth* in a moderately priced octavo edition, which sold in bookshops for seven shillings bound. Beattie deliberately limited the quarto edition to 800 copies. He was able to restrict the number of subscribers because the subscription proposals circulated privately among a select group of (mainly English) admirers and were never seen by the general public.[79] Yet when the book was finally published in February 1777, the announcement that subscribers could pick up their copies was published in the newspapers for all to see.[80]

Beattie's actions may seem paradoxical in one respect. Why would an author deliberately restrict the size of the print run of an edition published for his benefit? Beattie addressed this question in a letter to Mrs. Montagu of 7 December 1776. One reason was concern for Creech and the Dilly brothers, for he "thought it unfair to print more than were absolutely necessary, lest I should hurt the sale of the octavo edition, which is the only thing (including the copyright of the three additional Essays) which they have to indemnify themselves for granting me this indulgence." But there was another reason: from the beginning, Beattie "was determined to give no ground even to the adversary to charge me with avarice."[81] Friends had urged him to terminate the project in its early stages for this very reason.[82] As Cheryl Turner has commented in regard to women authors like Frances Burney, whose 1796 novel *Camilla* was a profitable subscription venture, "subscription was tainted with commercialism, involving an undignified touting of work or reputation for profit."[83] Beattie and Burney relied on networks of friends and admirers—mostly women from the upper echelons of English society—to handle the business details of the subscription process, enabling the authors themselves to remain aloof. But this tactic alone was not enough to remove the taint of rapaciousness associated with this kind of subscription publishing, especially for established authors like these. Just as Beattie limited his profit to an amount that he hoped would be considered moderate and dignified, Burney rationalized her decision to adopt such an "unpleasant and unpalatable" mode

78. Beattie to Edward Dilly, 5 Apr. 1776, HL, MS Hyde 77, 4.314.2.

79. Forbes, *Beattie and His Friends*, 95–96.

80. *London Chronicle*, 4–6 Feb. 1777. The announcement was repeated two months later (3–5 Apr. 1777) with a note stating that "a few Copies were printed more than subscribed for" and could be purchased for a guinea in boards.

81. Quoted in Forbes, *Beattie and His Friends*, 129.

82. William Mason to Beattie, 19 Dec. 1773, AUL, MS 30/2/166.

83. Turner, *Living by the Pen*, 111.

of publishing by declaring that the anticipated profits were for the sake of her young son.[84]

Another way of dealing with this problem was to disguise it. Whereas subscription lists appear in a total of seven first editions in table 2, constituting about 2 percent of the whole database,[85] subscription was a factor in other books in table 2 that do not contain subscription lists or, often, any other evidence of subscription publication. James Ferguson's *Astronomy Explained* and William Buchan's *Domestic Medicine* are important examples that have already been mentioned. These were straightforward commercial undertakings by their authors, without any display of conspicuous patronage by elite subscribers, and with prices set lower rather than higher than the industry standard. In the case of Buchan's book, at least, the process of selling subscriptions was commercialized by providing subscription sellers with a 20 percent commission. Subscribers to such editions would be attracted by the opportunity to obtain desirable new books at low prices rather than to demonstrate support for particular authors or to see their own names in print. For aspiring authors who had not yet published a book, this mode of publishing represented a relatively inconspicuous way to maintain control over production and maximize profit while avoiding the elitist trappings of the older form of subscription. It was very different from the model of subscription that the anonymous writer in *The Bee* had in mind, and it has been neglected in modern treatments of subscription publishing, which usually confine themselves to books with subscription lists.

The distinction I have drawn between traditional and commercial subscription publishing is not a hard-and-fast one, and many variations and combinations involving subscription were possible. William Smellie

84. Burney to Mrs. Waddington, 19 June 1795, in Burney, *Journals and Letters,* 3:124–25. *Camilla* contained "a star-studded subscription list" with 1,060 names, including many who ordered multiple copies (Thaddeus, *Frances Burney,* 132–33). Subscribers paid a guinea apiece in advance of publication, yielding more than £1,000 before expenses and many hundreds after. A few months after publication, Burney told her friend Mrs. Waddington that "guarding" the copyright "was our motive to the subscription," but she sold the copyright anyway for £1,000 in order to be free of the problems associated with managing the work (Burney, *Journals and Letters,* 3:227; see also Salih, "Camilla in the Marketplace," 122–26).

85. Besides the five just discussed, they include David Loch's patriotic guide to national improvement, *Essays on the Trade, Commerce, Manufactures, and Fisheries of Scotland* (no. 196), and William Julius Mickle's posthumous *Poems, and a Tragedy* (no. 329).

initially intended to publish the first volume of his *Philosophy of Natural History* (no. 292) by subscription but ended up selling the copyright to Charles Elliot for one thousand guineas (£1,050) in advance of publication, apparently using the considerable number of subscriptions he had already secured as collateral for the copy money.[86] In some instances, such as Adam Dickson's posthumous *Husbandry of the Ancients* (no. 274) and the first two volumes of Thomas Blackwell's *Memoirs of the Court of Augustus* (no. 29), subscription proposals have survived, but publication did not necessarily take place on those terms.[87] Conversely, no subscription proposals are known to have survived for John Bethune's *Essays and Dissertations on Various Subjects* (no. 125) or William Duff's *Sermons on Several Occasions* (no. 261), but external evidence establishes that both books were in fact published by subscription. In Duff's case, an entry in James Beattie's daybook for 2 April 1788 states: "Paid my subscription to Mr. W. Duff's sermons," and a debit of one pound is displayed. In Bethune's case, one of Beattie's unpublished letters from 1770 reveals that Bethune received 500 copies "for the use of his subscribers" and that the remaining 500 copies from the impression were retained for retail sale by the copublishers in Edinburgh and London, using various imprints, in order to cover "the expence of the publication" and the publishers' profit.[88] Still other books, such as William Guthrie's *English Peerage* (no. 81) and *History of Scotland* (no. 102) and William Russell's *History of America* (194), belong to a special category of subscription publications called part or number books, which were usually produced in inexpensive weekly or biweekly installments.[89] In the late 1750s the unfinished third edition of

86. Kerr, *Memoirs*, 2:263.

87. The first volume of Blackwell's book was printed for the author by Hamilton, Balfour, & Neill in April 1753 without a subscription list. Four months later a group of five London booksellers that included Andrew Millar and Robert Dodsley contracted to pay the author £500 for the copyright to volumes 1 and 2, although Blackwell had to provide the plates. It was stipulated that the publishers would receive the subscription proceeds for the second volume, which appeared in March 1756 (bearing a 1755 imprint) without either a subscription list or any indication that the property was now owned by London booksellers. McDougall, "Catalogue of Hamilton, Balfour and Neill Publications," 198; HL, MS Hyde 10, item 53.

88. Beattie, *Day-Book*, 160; Beattie to James Dun, 14 Aug. 1770, quoted in my entry on Bethune in *ODNB*.

89. Wiles, "Relish for Reading," 98–100. For example, before being published in book form, Russell's *History of America* appeared in sixty quarto installments beginning on 3 January 1778.

Smollett's *Complete History of England* (no. 49) carried this technique to the point of mass marketing, with print runs of 11,000–13,000 copies for each of thirty-six numbers to appear before the bankruptcy of the publishers halted the project.[90] The *Encyclopaedia Britannica* (no. 139) subsequently made profitable use of this technique, which was nearly always instigated and controlled by publishers rather than by authors.

Robert Burns stands out as the eighteenth-century Scottish author whose literary career was most clearly and completely made by subscription publishing.[91] At first, subscription provided a means for Burns to break into print on the strength of a local reputation based on manuscript circulation and oral recitation—"known in the neighbourhood as a maker of rhymes," as he described his pre-book status in an important autobiographical letter to John Moore of 2 August 1787. Proposals dated 14 April 1786 announced that an octavo edition of "Scotch Poems" by Burns would be sold for three shillings per copy, stitched.[92] John Wilson of Kilmarnock, Ayrshire, began printing the edition of just over 600 copies in mid-July, and *Poems, Chiefly in the Scottish Dialect* (no. 260) was published at the end of that month. The book contained no subscription list, but the author thanked his subscribers in the preface and told John Moore, in the letter just mentioned, that "about three hundred and fifty" copies were ordered through advance subscriptions. However, Wilson's records reveal that more than 400 copies were ordered by seven individuals alone: Robert Aiken (145), Robert Muir (72), Burns's brother Gilbert (70), James Smith (41), Gavin Hamilton (40), Logan of Laight (20), and David McWhinnie (20).[93] The Kilmarnock Burns, then, was what might be called a distribution subscription edition on the model of the Edinburgh Blacklock: friends and well-wishers bought up large quantities for local sale by word of mouth. This variety of subscription could work only if a book were priced very low, so that the distributors could afford to purchase many copies for resale to people of modest means.

Although the proposals stated that "the Author has not the most distant *mercenary* view in Publishing," Burns actually intended to raise money for his planned emigration to Jamaica. His autobiographical let-

---

90. Hernlund, "Three Bankruptcies," 87.

91. Unless otherwise noted, the discussion that follows is based on Burns, *Letters*, under date.

92. A facsimile of the proposals is printed in Ross, *Story of the Kilmarnock Burns*, 16.

93. Ibid., 64.

ter to Moore stated that he received "near twenty pounds" after expenses from the Kilmarnock edition, but he probably earned more than twice that amount.[94] At this critical juncture, when Burns had both the ways and means to leave Scotland forever, he was shown a complimentary letter that Thomas Blacklock wrote to Rev. George Lawrie of Loudon on 4 September 1786. There Blacklock announced that "the whole impression is already exhausted" and suggested that an expanded second edition might have "a more universal circulation than any thing of the kind which has been published within my memory."[95] Burns's autobiographical letter to Moore stated that Blacklock's letter "overthrew all my schemes" of emigration "by rousing my poetic ambition."[96] His first thought was to produce a second edition of 1,000 copies at Kilmarnock, but as he told Aiken in a letter around 8 October, that idea was negated by Wilson's insistence "t'other day" that the author would have to advance the £27 for the cost of paper. Then the October number of James Sibbald's *Edinburgh Magazine* (published 3 Nov.) carried an anonymous review, sometimes attributed to Robert Anderson, that proclaimed Burns "a striking example of native genius bursting through the obscurity of poverty and the obstructions of laborious life."[97] In late November the poet set out for Edinburgh with growing confidence that a second edition could be published there.

In Edinburgh, Burns was soon befriended by the fourteenth Earl of Glencairn, who rallied the support of his aristocratic club, the Caledonian Hunt.[98] Glencairn also introduced Burns to his childhood friend, the bookseller William Creech, who agreed to publish a subscription edition for the benefit of the author. As Burns was feted by the Edinburgh literati, subscription proposals appeared by mid-December 1786. The Ayrshire farmer was about to make the transition from a regional to a national—and international—poet. His experience replicated that of Blacklock: just

94. The supposition that Burns earned substantially more than £20 from the Kilmarnock edition is based on the differential of roughly £54 between Wilson's bill of £35.17s for paper and print and the £90 that 600 copies should have generated at the minimum price of three shillings apiece. See Ross, *Story of the Kilmarnock Burns*, 60; Lindsay, *Burns Encyclopedia*, 378.

95. Blacklock's letter is reproduced in Snyder, *Life of Robert Burns*, 153–54.

96. The letter to Moore also streamlined the story by creating the false impression that Blacklock's letter immediately fixed Burns's determination to publish the second edition in Edinburgh.

97. The review is reprinted, along with others, in Ross, *Story of the Kilmarnock Burns*, quoting 26.

98. On this connection, see Mathison, "Gude Black Prent," 70–87.

as the cheap Edinburgh distribution edition of Blacklock's poems had prepared the way for a much more expensive and conspicuous London edition, so did the Kilmarnock Burns prepare the way for a slightly more expensive and much more conspicuous Edinburgh edition. Both men were perceived as novelties—one on account of his blindness, the other on account of his rusticity—and this circumstance added to their appeal within an expanding geographical base of subscribers.

The 1787 Edinburgh edition of Burns's *Poems* was a hybrid of publication modes. Burns made two different kinds of agreements prior to publication: the subscription agreement for the Edinburgh edition itself and an agreement to sell the copyright. According to the first, Burns was to receive all profits from this edition but also had to pay all expenses, in the standard manner of self-published books. When the work appeared during the third week of April, the imprint accordingly read "Printed for the author, and sold by William Creech." Since the printed subscription list included some 1,500 names, pledged to receive 2,876 copies at five shillings apiece, Burns knew that hundreds of pounds would be coming to him. Creech himself had subscribed for 500 copies at the regular subscription price, to be resold in his shop at the higher retail price of six shillings each.[99] This difference of a shilling per copy was "Creech's profit" from the edition, Burns noted in a letter to Alexander Pattison of 17 May 1787, and it could have amounted to no more than £25. Creech managed the subscription out of his shop (no small task for a project on this scale), procured the paper, took charge of the printing of 3,000 copies by his partner William Smellie and subsequently of the binding of the printed sheets, handled the advertising and publicity, and arranged, as we saw in chapter 2, for Burns to have his portrait painted and engraved for reproduction as the frontispiece.

In addition to the subscription arrangement, on 17 April 1787, just four days before publication, Creech met with Burns at the home of Henry Mackenzie and signed a memorandum of agreement to purchase the copyright for one hundred guineas. Creech wanted Cadell (presumably with Andrew Strahan) to take half the copyright, and there is evidence that his plan succeeded: not only did Strahan reprint 1,500 copies of the

---

99. Although it was not unusual for booksellers to sell extra copies of a subscription book at a higher retail price, Michael F. Suarez has found evidence of the opposite pattern among poetry books in England; further research is needed to account for such radical differences in trade practice. Cf. Suarez, "Production," 217–51, esp. 220, 224.

Edinburgh edition in July 1787 (SA 48815, fol. 115), for a London edition in which Strahan, Cadell, and Creech were named in the imprint as copublishers, but on 8 May 1787 the copyright was registered to Creech and Cadell at Stationers' Hall in London. On 23 April, however, Creech, not yet having heard from Cadell, acted independently in Edinburgh to guarantee the copyright agreement.[100]

After publication, relations between author and publisher steadily deteriorated. Burns was desperate for his money, whereas Creech was in no hurry to finalize the settlement. It was not uncommon for conditional publishing agreements to be settled only after an edition was completely gone (we have seen that the settlement for Boswell's *Life of Johnson* occurred a year and a half after publication), and Creech was always slow to part with money anyway. But in this case the settlement seems to have been delayed by special circumstances. Soon after the Edinburgh edition appeared, Creech went to London for an extended visit that was, as we shall see in chapter 5, crucial for his career as a Scottish Enlightenment publisher. While he was away, there were some misunderstandings about collecting payments for subscription copies from country agents, and Smellie apparently mismanaged the partnership's finances.[101] When he returned to Edinburgh, Creech gave Burns an IOU for the copyright fee of one hundred guineas, dated 23 October 1787, but he did not actually pay him this amount until 30 May 1788, following a period of several months in which Burns was in a panic over false rumors of Creech's impending bankruptcy. Creech did not finally settle accounts on the subscription profits from the Edinburgh edition until February 1789, although Burns had been receiving money from him sporadically well before then.

When Burns was trying to get his money, he wrote a letter to Agnes M'Lehose (his lover "Clarinda") on 19 March 1788 that dubbed his publisher "that arch-rascal Creech." He told John Moore on 4 January 1789 that "I cannot boast of Mr. Creech's ingenuous fair-dealing to me" and on 20 January sent Dugald Stewart a poetical sketch of his bookseller that began, "A little upright, pert, tart, tripping wight, / And still his precious self his chief delight." Yet on 20 February he informed Jean Armour that "I have settled matters greatly to my satisfaction with Mr. Creech," though he still believed Creech had not provided everything "I should have." A week later even that grievance was resolved by a final payment

100. Chambers, *Life and Works*, 2:92; *Records of the Worshipful Company of Stationers*, reel 7.

101. Parks, "Justice," 453–64; Brown, "William Creech," 75–80.

of £18.5s.,[102] and Burns wrote to Moore again on 23 March, retracting his former criticisms of Creech and admitting that "at last, he has been amicable and fair with me." Two days later he wrote to Mrs. Dunlop in a similar frame of mind, reporting that "I clear about 440 or 450 £." This was a significant amount of copy money for the second edition of a relatively inexpensive first book of poetry, and there is reason to suspect that it was not the full amount that Burns obtained from this work. Creech told Robert Heron that Burns received almost £1,100 in all, from which the expenses of publication were deducted, and if this figure is correct, or nearly so, the assertion in the anonymous biographical sketch of Burns in the *Supplement* to the third edition of the *Encyclopaedia Britannica* (first published in 1799), that Burns received "a clear profit of at least 700 pounds," is plausible.[103] Although 2,876 subscription copies at five shillings apiece works out to just £719, before expenses, Burns's letter to Pattison of 17 May 1787 told of additional subscribers whose names may have been left off the "very incorrect" printed list. But most of the additional money to which Creech referred probably came from sales of the London edition that appeared later in 1787 with the Edinburgh subscription list prefixed to it.

As the Edinburgh edition of Burns's *Poems* illustrates, subscription provided eighteenth-century authors with a flexible mode of publishing that could be combined with other publishing alternatives, such as self-publication and outright sale of copyright. It allowed prominent patrons like "the Noblemen and Gentlemen of the Caledonian Hunt," to whom the volume was formally dedicated, to take an active part in the publication process, but the moderate subscription price of five shillings also opened the door to hundreds of ordinary men and women to become patrons of a worthy and needy young poet. In this sense, the Edinburgh edition of Burns was among the eighteenth-century subscription publications that "democratized literary patronage," in Paul Korshin's phrase.[104] This work is also of interest because Burns's changing attitudes toward Creech during the course of publication embodied the full range of emotions that

102. Donaldson, "Burns's Final Settlement," 38–41.

103. Mackey, *Biography*, 297, argues that Creech's figure was probably correct, and Lindsay, *Burns Encyclopedia*, 123, appears to say the same when he estimates that Burns netted £855 from the first Edinburgh edition, including the sale of the copyright.

104. Korshin, "Types of Eighteenth-Century Literary Patronage," 464; Griffin, *Literary Patronage*, 267.

authors might experience in their dealings with publishers: from close personal friendship and admiration early in the process, to intense hostility when Burns believed he was being cheated, to a calmer and more dispassionate attitude after financial matters were finally resolved to the author's satisfaction.

Above all, Burns's early forays into print confirm that subscription publishing was varied and complex in late eighteenth-century Britain and that the options for authors were therefore much greater than is usually thought. As we have seen, this point can be fully grasped only by going beyond books that contain subscription lists, using external evidence to locate editions that might not otherwise appear to be subscription publications. Yet even when this is done, and when all the first editions in table 2 in which subscription played some role are added together (seven with subscription lists and eleven without), the total number constitutes just 5 percent of the entire database. And publication of a second edition by subscription, in the manner of Blacklock and Burns, was even more unusual. Thus, despite its importance for Burns and several others, subscription was not a numerically significant factor in the publication of Scottish Enlightenment books in Britain, and the bold claims that have sometimes been made about the prevalence of this mode of publication during the age of the Enlightenment are not borne out by the collective experience of Scottish authors.[105]

Profit Sharing

It was chiefly profit sharing that James Beattie had in mind when he advised Sylvester Douglas to avoid conditional bargains with booksellers. In arrangements of this kind, the publisher paid for all or part of the expenses of production and promotion and then shared profits with the author for a single edition. For authors, profit-sharing arrangements had three main advantages over self-publication, including self-publication by subscription: such arrangements eliminated or significantly decreased

105. Cf. Korshin, "Types of Eighteenth-Century Literary Patronage," 463: "the subscription method touched nearly all eighteenth-century authors of ambitious works"; and Melton, "Rise of the Public," 128: "the most successful British writers of the [Enlightenment] period published their work through subscription at one time or another." My findings are more in tune with Lockwood, "Subscription-Hunters," 121–22, where it is argued that the two thousand to three thousand books published by subscription in eighteenth-century Britain "never made more than a fraction of the total published: perhaps five per cent of all new books each year."

risk and the anxiety that went with it, removed responsibility for personally managing production and marketing, and abolished from the imprint the odious phrase "Printed for the Author," or words to that effect. Thus, when a book was published with a profit-sharing arrangement, the author both retained the copyright and avoided the stigma of self-publication.

Adam Smith's *Wealth of Nations* (no. 177) was an unlikely best seller that emerged from a profit-sharing publication arrangement.[106] Like Boswell's *Life of Johnson*, the first edition was a big book of two quarto volumes, expensive at £1.16s. in boards or £2.2s. bound. Circumstantial evidence indicates that Strahan and Cadell published it on the basis of shared costs and shared profits. The publishers and their mentor, Andrew Millar, had been disappointed by a similar undertaking a decade earlier, when they purchased the copyright to Sir James Steuart's *Inquiry into the Principles of Political Oeconomy* (no. 101) for £500 in advance of publication. In Smith's case, the results were very different. The first edition of the *Wealth of Nations* sold extremely well, and eight months after publication the author was paid £300, which was probably a partial payment on profits from the first edition. The second edition of 1778, again in two volumes quarto, also seems to have been published on the basis of shared profits between Smith and his publishers, but with the latter covering all costs. Smith prepared major revisions for the third edition of 1784, which was the first to appear in a more affordable three-volume octavo format, and he presumably made a tidy profit when the entire print run of 1,000 copies was sold in less than two years. Before the fourth edition could be published in 1786, Smith accepted an offer from Cadell and Andrew Strahan to pay him £200 in advance instead of sharing profits. Finally, the publishers, realizing that the market for this book was continuing to increase, purchased the copyright outright for £300 in 1788 (retroactive to the date of original publication in March 1776), and when Smith was dying in April 1790 they paid him the same amount in order to renew the copyright for another fourteen years. Thus, we know that Smith received at least £1,100 for the *Wealth of Nations*, and this amount does not include whatever he received for the second and third editions on a profit-sharing basis or additional income that he may have received from the first edition. I estimate that the total amount of copy money paid to the author in the fourteen years from publication until his death was between £1,500 and £1,800. The book was a much bigger commercial

106. For a fuller account, see Sher, "New Light," 3–29.

success, both for its publishers and for its author, than one might surmise from recent revisionist scholarship on its contemporary reception.[107]

Roman Antiquities (no. 293) by Alexander Adam, rector of Edinburgh High School, was another best seller that was initially published on a profit-sharing basis. In 1791, shortly after Strahan, Cadell, and Creech had published the first edition as a duodecimo with a modest print run of 750 copies, Adam wrote to Cadell to seek continued support for his plan, which the bookseller had approved "above two years ago." Now that the book had been published and introduced into several of the leading public schools in England, Adam had no intention of letting the matter rest. "I am sensible it is yet an imperfect work," he asserts, "but no exertion on my part shall be wanting to complete it; for I must inform you it is only part of a great plan I have formed. My object is, to make it literally a *key* to illustrate all the classics." His intention was to embellish the existing text and eventually to add illustrations and new sections on ancient mythology and Greek antiquities, as well as to compose "a Summary of ancient and modern geography and history."

Then Adam addresses the delicate issue of compensation:

> Money is no object with me in comparison of the desire I have to be useful. But if a price is to be affixed to my work, I wish it to be respectable. The sum I mentioned to Mr. Creech I am sensible is too much for the work in its present form; but not for what I hope to make it. . . . My great wish is that the work be useful. The labour I have undergone is such [that] it would not be overpaid, although I received the sum I mentioned. I meant only part of it to be paid at present, and the rest to depend on the success of the book, under whatever limitations you think proper. But if you chuse rather to fix a less sum at present, and to allow so much on every subsequent edition for the improvements and alterations, according to the number of the copies, I have no objection.[108]

Notice how this passage weaves and bobs through the subject of copy money. "Usefulness" is twice said to be Adam's primary concern, compared to which "money is no object." And yet he has proposed a high fig-

107. Teichgraeber, "Less Abused," 337–66; Teichgraeber, "Adam Smith," 85–104; Rashid, *Myth*, 135–81.

108. Adam to Cadell, 3 July 1791, Beinecke Library, Yale University, Osborn MSS, no. 55.

ure to Creech for his work. He is willing to be flexible and patient about how the payments are apportioned as the revisions develop, but he will not surrender his claim to be well paid. Although we do not know how much money Adam received for the first edition of *Roman Antiquities*, or what figure he had proposed to Creech for his planned revisions, we can be sure he had not yet sold the copyright by the time of this letter, and that is what gives him leverage in negotiating for later editions.

Adam's ambition was well rewarded. The "considerably enlarged" second edition of 1792 was upgraded to an octavo, with separate printings in Edinburgh and London, the latter with a print run of 2,000 copies (SA 48817, fol. 18). Adam continued to revise and expand the book in accordance with the scheme he had set out in his letter to Cadell, and on 30 June 1794 Strahan, Cadell, and Creech made an outright purchase of the copyright for £600, with a stipulation that Adam would receive up to fifty "well and handsomely bound" copies of every revised octavo edition (see fig. 3.1).[109] The book continued to sell exceedingly well, both in Britain and America, where it became a set text at Harvard and other universities.[110] By the time of the sixth edition of 1807, if not sooner, the size of the print run had increased to 4,000 copies.[111] Furthermore, Adam's *Summary of Geography and History* (no. 321) was published separately in 1794, apparently earning its author an additional sum of £800 for the copyright (SA 48814A, fol. 44).

George Campbell's *The Four Gospels* (no. 280), which appeared in 1789, teaches a very different lesson about conditional publishing. Two years earlier, when Campbell was preparing his text for the press, his friend James Beattie had informed William Creech that "Dr. Campbell's Great Work" was "without doubt the greatest and most useful work in theology that Scotland ever produced" and therefore deserved a substantial amount of copy money.[112] Cadell and Strahan did not agree, however, and they appear to have published it on the basis of profit sharing.[113] Unable to get adequate sales information from the publishers, the anxious author

109. Contract for Roman Antiquities, University of Reading Library, Longman Archive, MS 1393, 26/8; SA 48814A, fol. 29, records the payment of Andrew Strahan's third of the copy money (£200) to the author in July 1794.

110. McKean, *Questions*.

111. The impression account of the sixth edition appears in *Archives of the House of Longman*, reel 37, H6, fol. 67.

112. Beattie to Creech, 7 May 1787, WCL; and Beattie to Creech, 24 May 1787, in Beattie, *Correspondence*, 4:19–20.

113. Suderman, *Orthodoxy and Enlightenment*, 48.

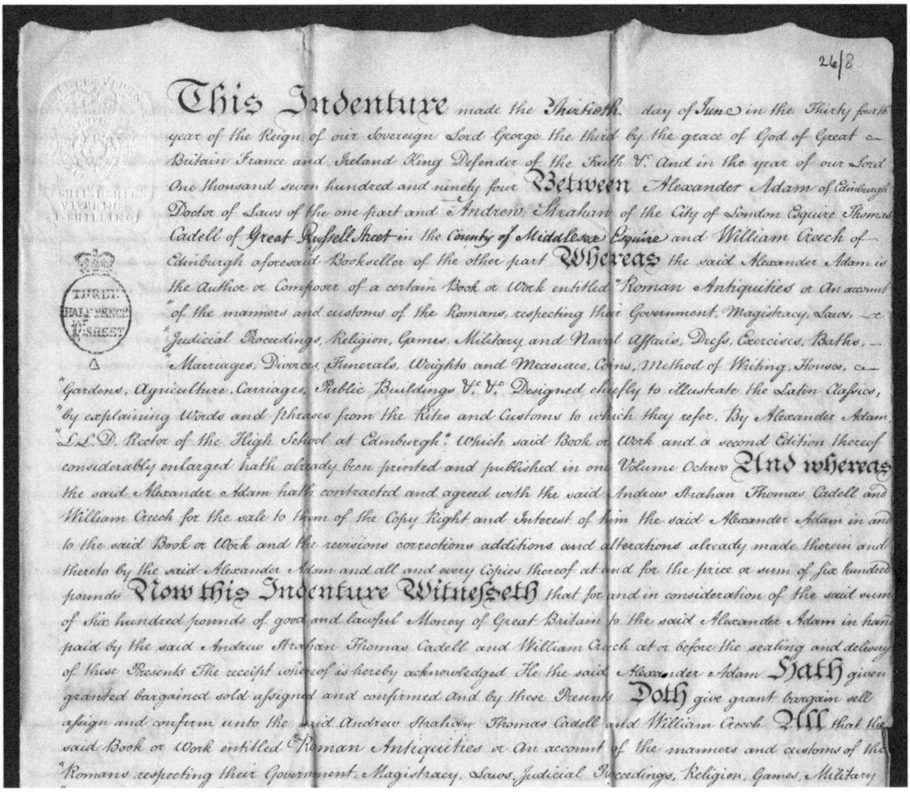
26/8

THREE HALF PENCE SHEET

This Indenture made the Thirtieth day of June in the Thirty fourth year of the Reign of our Sovereign Lord George the third by the grace of God of Great Britain France and Ireland King Defender of the Faith &c. And in the year of our Lord One thousand seven hundred and ninety four Between Alexander Adam of Edinburgh Doctor of Laws of the one part and Andrew Strahan of the City of London Esquire Thomas Cadell of Great Russell Street in the County of Middlesex Esquire and William Creech of Edinburgh aforesaid Bookseller of the other part Whereas the said Alexander Adam is the Author or Composer of a certain Book or Work entitled "Roman Antiquities or An account "of the manners and customs of the Romans, respecting their Government, Magistracy, Laws, "Judicial Proceedings, Religion, Games, Military and Naval Affairs, Dress, Exercises, Baths, "Marriages, Divorces, Funerals, Weights and Measures, Coins, Method of Writing, Houses, "Gardens, Agriculture, Carriages, Public Buildings &c. &c. Designed chiefly to illustrate the Latin Classics, "by explaining Words and Phrases from the Rites and Customs to which they refer. By Alexander Adam "LL.D. Rector of the High School at Edinburgh." Which said Book or Work and a second Edition thereof considerably enlarged hath already been printed and published in one Volume Octavo And whereas the said Alexander Adam hath contracted and agreed with the said Andrew Strahan Thomas Cadell and William Creech for the sale to them of the Copy Right and Interest of him the said Alexander Adam in and to the said Book or Work and the revisions corrections additions and alterations already made therein and thereto by the said Alexander Adam and all and every Copies thereof at and for the price or sum of six hundred pounds Now this Indenture Witnesseth that for and in consideration of the said sum of Six hundred pounds of good and lawful Money of Great Britain to the said Alexander Adam in hand paid by the said Andrew Strahan Thomas Cadell and William Creech at or before the sealing and delivery of these Presents The receipt whereof is hereby acknowledged He the said Alexander Adam Hath given granted bargained sold assigned and confirmed and by these Presents Doth give grant bargain sell assign and confirm unto the said Andrew Strahan Thomas Cadell and William Creech All that the said Book or Work entitled "Roman Antiquities or An account of the manners and customs of the "Romans respecting their Government, Magistracy, Laws, Judicial Proceedings, Religion, Games, Military

Fig. 3.1. In June 1794, after his *Roman Antiquities* (1791) had appeared in two successful editions in duodecimo and octavo, Alexander Adam signed a contract (the first part of which is shown here) to sell the copyright to Andrew Strahan, Thomas Cadell, and William Creech for £600, plus up to fifty bound copies of every revised octavo edition. Longman Archives, University of Reading Library.

turned to John Douglas, the Scottish Anglican bishop and intermediary between authors and booksellers, who had been present when Beattie and Campbell had negotiated the terms of publication in Cadell's "backshop" in the Strand. In a letter of 11 March 1790 Campbell expressed concern that the price of the book—two guineas for two large quarto volumes in boards—"is too high for a theological work. I suspected it from the beginning, but considered the booksellers as having a better title to decide, in a question of that kind." He hoped for a second edition of three octavo volumes at a guinea a set "or cheaper." Four months later Campbell gratefully acknowledged receipt of a favorable notice in the June number of the *Monthly Review*, and his hopes were once again raised for a more affordable second edition. By September, however, Campbell saw the disappointing conclusion of the *Monthly*'s review, and Strahan and Cadell made it clear to him that a second edition was unlikely, because 400 copies out of an impression of 750 remained unsold. Frustrated and incredulous, Campbell tells Douglas that Cadell has charged him at the wholesale rate for about a dozen presentation copies that were supposed to be free, treatment that gives "some notion of the man." In this foul mood, Campbell begins to see authorship itself as a precarious activity: "When I think of the vexations one is exposed to, from booksellers, reviewers, etc., and the misrepresentations which are often given of their works to the public, I am almost surprized that a man should form a resolution to publish any thing."[114]

Sale of the Rights to Single Editions

Another way for authors to retain their copyrights and at the same time escape the uncertainty of conditional publishing that Campbell found so discouraging was to sell the rights to a particular edition for a fixed sum, in advance of publication. We have already encountered this arrangement in regard to Lord Kames's *Gentleman Farmer* and the fourth edition of Adam Smith's *Wealth of Nations*. Other examples include Robert Watson's *History of Philip II* (no. 186; £800 for the first edition) and John Gillies's edition of Aristotle (no. 343; £400 for the first edition), both of which brought their authors much additional income when subsequent editions were published.

David Hume used the sale of single-edition rights to great advantage. As a young man he secured fifty guineas from the London bookseller John Noon for the first two volumes of his first book, *A Treatise of Human Nature* (1739). He soon realized he had made "a hasty Bargain" (*LDH*, 1:38) because the contract stipulated that he could not publish a second edition unless he bought back from Noon all unsold copies of the first edition at the wholesale price. Later he employed the principle of single-edition rights more effectively. Hume stated in his deathbed autobiography that "the Copy Money, given me by the Booksellers, much exceeded any thing formerly known in England: I was become not only independent, but opulent" (*LDH*, 1:5). Most of this copy money came from

114. Campbell to Douglas, 11 Mar., 22 July, and 22 Sept. 1790, BL, Egerton MSS 2186, fols. 5–6, 10–11, 12–15.

his most popular work, the *History of England*. Hume received £400 from Hamilton, Balfour, and Neill for the rights to the first edition of the first volume on the early Stuarts (no. 33) and apparently £700 from Andrew Millar for the rights to the first edition of the second volume on the later Stuarts (no. 46). By selling the rights only to the first edition of the first Stuart volume, Hume was able to switch publishers for the second volume. Equally important, since he still owned the copyright and had never agreed to a safety clause such as the one in his contract with Noon for the *Treatise*, he could then offer Millar "the full Property" of both Stuart volumes for an additional sum of eight hundred guineas (£840) without having to reimburse Hamilton, Balfour, and Neill for any unsold copies of the first edition of volume 1. For the next segment of the *History*, the volume he was writing on the Tudors (no. 56), Hume asked Millar for the same amount of money he had received for the second Stuart volume. When the Tudor history expanded into a two-volume work, however, he probably received considerably more than that for it. Finally, in 1759 Hume sold Millar the copyright to his projected two volumes on the period from the ancient Romans to the Tudors (no. 74) for £1,400, noting in a letter to Adam Smith that this was the first time he had ever made a "previous Agreement . . . with a Bookseller"—meaning the sale of copyright in advance of composition (*LDH*, 1:193, 244, 266, 314). All told, Hume's income from the *History of England* was certainly more than £4,000, and very possibly more than £5,000, as William Creech asserted in 1783.[115]

William Cullen sold the rights to the first edition of the first volume of his *First Lines of the Practice of Physic* (1777; no. 187) to John Murray for £100. The book was roughly the same size and format as Kames's *Gentleman Farmer*, had the same size print run (1,000 copies), and sold for the same price (six shillings), so it should come as no surprise, in light of Strahan's calculations for Kames's book (mentioned in chapter 1, and presented in more detail in chapter 5), that Murray considered the terms for *First Lines* so hard that he could not make any profit from it, even though all the copies were sold.[116] We do not know how much money Cullen received for the second and third volumes in 1779 and 1783, or for later editions of the first and second volumes, but Charles Elliot agreed to pay him £1,200 for the copyright to the full set when the fourth and final volume was added in 1784. Four years later Elliot told the author that he still had

---

115. [Creech], *Letters to Sir John Sinclair*, 12.
116. Zachs, *First John Murray*, 191–95, 275.

not recouped his expenses, even though the book had reached a fifth edition by then.[117] *First Lines* always appeared in octavo, and the retail price of seven shillings per volume for the full set was simply not high enough to offset both production costs and the large fee paid to the author. Cullen was uncompromising as a negotiator and maintained complete control at every stage, and he set off a huge furor when he blocked separate sales of the fourth volume, leaving Murray unable to sell his remaining copies of earlier volumes and the purchasers of those volumes unable to complete their sets.

An interesting variation on the single-edition arrangement occurred when authors produced editions at their own expense and then sold all the printed copies to a bookseller, whose name appeared in the imprint as the publisher. Earlier in this chapter we saw that James Hutton used this approach with his *Dissertations on Different Subjects in Natural Philosophy* (no. 306). So did James Bruce, whose *Travels to Discover the Source of the Nile* (no. 288) constitutes a particularly enterprising adventure in bookmaking by an author. Control over printing was a key factor in both instances, but whereas Hutton used this technique to maximize the prestige of his book, without concern for profit, Bruce had other ideas. After composing his long, fascinating, albeit disorganized, account of his African adventures during the late 1760s and early 1770s, Bruce had the work printed at his own expense in Edinburgh. With five large quarto volumes on royal paper, as well as maps and engravings, it was a tremendously expensive undertaking. But Bruce was a man of means and determination, and he understood that by proceeding in this manner he could maintain control not only over production but also, to some extent, over domestic reprints and foreign sales. The London bookseller George Robinson was willing to pay him £4,000 for 1,500 printed copies of the book if it retailed for four guineas the set (£4.4s.), or £5,000 for 1,500 copies retailing for five guineas (£5.5s.).[118] In the end, Robinson paid Bruce the prodigious sum of £6,666 for 2,000 printed sets that retailed for five guineas each.[119] In spring 1790 the work appeared in bookshops with an imprint that identified the publishers as G. G. J. & J. Robinson but gave no hint of the author's role in the production process. Bruce apparently made

117. Elliot to Cullen, 3 Apr. 1789, cited in McDougall, "Charles Elliot's Medical Publications," 222.

118. Robinson to Bruce, 25 Feb. 1789, NLS, Acc. 4490; the originals of the letters in this collection are in the James Bruce Archive, Yale Center for British Art.

119. Warren McDougall's article on Sibbald in *ODNB*.

separate agreements for foreign sales with Charles-Joseph Panckoucke in Paris and Philip Erasmus Reich in Leipzig, and in March 1794 Cadell & Davies were willing to pay him £2,500 for another British edition of 2,000 copies, supplied by the author.[120] But a month later Bruce suffered an incapacitating fall that led to his death in the same year, bringing an abrupt end to his negotiating. Although he made a great deal of money from the first edition of his book, the process of putting it together took a huge toll, and his production costs must have been so high that his net profit was probably less than William Robertson received for the copyright to *Charles V*.[121] Yet if Bruce had lived longer, he might well have earned more money from his *Travels* than any other eighteenth-century author received for a single book.

Like self-publishing and profit sharing, sales of single editions allowed authors to retain possession of copyrights. It is evident from the registration records of the Stationers' Company in London that many Scottish authors took this matter seriously.[122] Since nine copies had to be deposited at Stationers' Hall at the time of registration, the value of the deposited books could be substantial, especially for multivolume quartos like the *Wealth of Nations* and the *Life of Johnson*. But registration was considered a meaningful assertion of copyright ownership, and necessary in order for a book to be fully covered by the provisions of the Statute of Anne. Almost 40 percent of the 360 titles in table 2 were entered at Stationers' Hall at least once, and nearly one-third of the first-edition registrations (at least forty-three titles, or 12 percent of the entire database) were registered in the name of the author or editor, not the publisher. This includes most of the works discussed in the last three sections: the first volume of Hume's *History of England* (registered on 11 Nov. 1754), Buchan's *Domestic Medicine* (17 July 1769), the first two volumes of Henry's *History of Great Britain* (29 Mar. 1771 and 26 Jan. 1774), Kames's *Gentleman Farmer* (18 Jan. 1776), Smith's *Wealth of Nations* (7 Mar. 1776), Watson's *History of Philip II* (12 Dec. 1776), vols. 2–4 of Cullen's *First Lines* (10 June 1784), Adam's *Roman Antiquities* (15 Mar. 1791), and Boswell's *Life of Johnson* (11 May 1791). After these books had proved themselves, publishers who had purchased

---

120. Thomas Cadell, Jr., to Bruce, 24 Mar. 1794, NLS, Acc. 4490.

121. Peter Elmsley to Bruce, 2 Nov. 1789, NLS, Acc. 4490, suggests that Bruce might have netted £3,500 from his agreement with Robinson. Some of the difficulties that Bruce encountered in producing the book are discussed in McDougall's *ODNB* article on Sibbald.

122. *Records of the Worshipful Company of Stationers*, reels 6–9.

the copyrights sometimes reregistered them in their own names.[123] Until then, however, the books were the property of their authors to do with as they pleased.

Sale of Copyright before Publication

If copyright registrations at Stationers' Hall show that many Scottish authors were savvy about their rights, it is also true that few of them wished to become too deeply involved in the business of publishing. Even Hume, who knew how to profit from his books as well as any author, grew weary of dealing with his publishers on an edition-by-edition basis. "It is chiefly in order to avoid the Trouble and Perplexity of such Schemes that I desire at once to part with all the Property," he told Strahan, when explaining his offer to sell the copyright to the first two published volumes of his *History of England* to Millar in 1757 (*LDH*, 1:244). As we have seen repeatedly, authors of popular books who sold their copyrights *after* publication often increased their returns by maximizing their leverage. But authors did not know beforehand whether their books were going to be popular, and this circumstance, along with suspicion of booksellers and the "Trouble and Perplexity" associated with continually negotiating terms, made it attractive to many authors to surrender all rights to their books in advance of publication in exchange for a fixed amount of compensation.

John Moore's experiences during the 1780s demonstrate that even advance sales of copyrights sometimes contained gray areas or contingent elements that kept authors on their guard. When Moore sold the copyright to his *View of Society and Manners in France, Switzerland, and Germany* (no. 201) to Strahan and Cadell, the written contract stipulated that he would receive £100 for the first edition of 1,000 copies and £50 for every subsequent edition of that size. But Moore believed there was also a verbal understanding that the payment for each new edition would be increased if sales warranted it, and when the book went to a third edition in the year of its initial publication, 1780, the publishers silently doubled the grateful author's fee.[124] At the end of the 1780s, however, Moore fumed over the manner in which Cadell had tricked him (as he thought) into

---

123. For example, the second edition of *Domestic Medicine* was registered on 7 November 1772 to William Strahan (one-third share), Cadell (one-third), Balfour (one-sixth), and Kincaid (one-sixth), and the second edition of *Roman Antiquities* was registered to Andrew Strahan, Thomas Cadell, and William Creech on 24 May 1792.

124. Moore to William Strahan, 1 Feb. 1780, HL, MS Hyde 10, item 483.

relinquishing the copyright to his novel *Zeluco* (no. 284) in advance of publication for less than its true value, and he demanded additional compensation despite the terms of the contract:

> You must be sensible Gentlemen that you have been far greater gainers by my works than I have been. Since I decline the trouble of printing them on my own account I am willing that this should continue to be the case. But in the instance of Zeluco I do think, and I am sure all the world must think the disproportion by far too great. And as it is now evident that Mr Cadell's arguments by which he prevailed on me to fall at once from what I thought the fair value, to terms so very far under it, were ill founded, I have no doubt of your acting on this occasion in such a manner as will give me no reason to regret my own conduct in this business.[125]

Andrew Strahan's ledgers reveal that Moore received a first payment of £250 for *Zeluco* in July 1789, as well as a second £250 payment in December (SA 48814A, fol. 8). The first payment was probably the amount of the copyright purchase, while the second may have been a response to Moore's protest. In addition, the success of *Zeluco* and the dissatisfaction that the author expressed about his compensation for it may have influenced Andrew Strahan and Cadell & Davies to grant Moore the handsome sum of £800 for the copyright to his next novel, *Edward* (no. 340), which had an initial print run of 3,000 copies (SA 48814A, fols. 17, 40).

Hugh Blair always sold the copyrights to his books in advance of publication, but the sale itself was not always the end of the story. Late in 1776, after Blair sold the copyright to the first volume of his *Sermons* (no. 188) to Alexander Kincaid for £100, his friend William Robertson apparently persuaded Strahan and Cadell to purchase shares in the book, sight unseen. Strahan, who had initially wanted no part of this project,[126] remained unimpressed after he read some of the printed sheets that were sent to him by Creech (who assumed control after Kincaid's death in January 1777), but Samuel Johnson reassured him by enthusiastically praising one sermon that he read at Strahan's request (*BLJ*, 3:97).[127] When a small

125. Moore to Andrew Strahan and Thomas Cadell, 10 July 1789, ibid., no. 484. Note that in the second sentence of this passage, Moore treats self-publication as a mode of publishing that is both potentially more lucrative and more troublesome for authors.

126. Strahan to Cadell, 19 Sept. 1776, HL, MS Hyde 77, 7.116.

127. Boswell's account of this incident exaggerates the role of Johnson, who read this sermon in print—not manuscript—and did not help to bring about the publication of the book, as Boswell claimed.

print run of perhaps 500 copies appeared in Edinburgh in a one-volume octavo edition in February 1777, expectations were not high. But the book quickly became a runaway best seller.

Although Blair had certainly not published his *Sermons* with the intention of making large amounts of money, financial matters could not be ignored as he prepared subsequent volumes for the press over the course of the next two decades. The fee that Creech, Strahan, and Cadell were willing to pay for the copyright to the second volume in 1780 rose to £500 after Charles Dilly offered the author £300, using Boswell as his intermediary.[128] Blair received £600 for each of the next two volumes (published in 1790 and 1794), and the posthumously published fifth volume of 1801 fetched the same sum for Blair's estate.

Blair was well aware that these amounts, while unprecedented for volumes of sermons, were small sums relative to the wealth that this book was generating. After informing a relation of his that his publishers had agreed "without the least hesitation" to pay him £600 for the copyright to the third volume, he added, "and well they might; considering what profit they made of 15 Editions of the two former ones."[129] But Blair also knew that he could expect his publishers to supplement the copy money specified in the contract by sending him cash presents from time to time, in appreciation of their profits from reprints of the published volumes. So far it has been possible to trace three £50 gifts in association with volume 1, two gifts of that amount for volume 2, and a present of one hundred guineas (£105) for volume 4.[130] Thus, Blair and his estate received no less than £2,765 for the five volumes of his sermons, and the actual total was probably higher because we do not have a complete record of the cash gifts he obtained from his publishers. Such gifts represented another way in which apparently straightforward legal agreements between authors and their publishers were sometimes complicated in practice.

Strahan, Cadell, and Creech also contracted in advance of publication to pay Blair £1,500 for the copyright to his *Lectures on Rhetoric and*

128. Boswell, *Laird of Auchinleck*, 31. In the *Life of Johnson* (*BLJ*, 3:98), Boswell correctly recalled being one of the "subscribing witnesses" of this contract, which survives in the British Library (SA 48901, fol. 20), but he apparently confused the amount Blair actually received with the amount offered by Dilly. In a letter to Cadell of 6 January 1790 (HSP, Dreer, English Clergy, vol. 1), Blair himself recalled receiving only £400 for volume 2.

129. Blair to Robert Blair, 14 Apr. 1790, NLS, MS 588, no. 1374.

130. Schmitz, *Hugh Blair*, 83; SA 48814A, fol. 34; Blair to Thomas Cadell, Jr., 14 Apr. 1795, in Zachs, *Hugh Blair's Letters to His Publishers*.

Belles Lettres (no. 230), which appeared in two quarto volumes in 1783 and became yet another profitable best seller. Like Robertson, Blair already had a respectable base salary of several hundred pounds per annum from his academic and ecclesiastical positions, and in 1780 the government granted him an annual pension of £200 on account of his *Sermons*. He became one of the first ministers in the Church of Scotland to maintain his own carriage, bought a handsome home in Edinburgh's Argyll Square and a fine library for it, acquired a second home in nearby Leith, and left behind approximately £4,000 in bonds.[131] The supplemental income from his publications had made him rich. No wonder, then, that late in life Blair told one of his own publishers that he had counseled another author, James Bruce, to put his faith in the booksellers when preparing his book for the press: "My advice to him was to enter into transaction with a creditable Bookseller and after stipulating the price that was to be paid himself, to leave all inferiour articles to the Bookseller, who has as much interest in them as he had; which I told him was the Method I had always followed."[132]

If Blair's five volumes of published sermons are noteworthy on account of their astonishing popularity, James Wodrow's posthumous edition of William Leechman's *Sermons* (no. 283) stands out for a different reason: the letters that Wodrow sent to his friend Samuel Kenrick while he was trying to arrange the terms of publication constitute a remarkably informative account of negotiations over the prepublication sale of copyright.[133] In September 1788 Wodrow traveled to London with some of Leechman's sermons and a long biographical sketch of their author, as well as a letter of introduction to Thomas Cadell from Leechman's successor as principal of Glasgow University, Archibald Davidson, who was the kinsman of Andrew Millar.[134] When he learned that Cadell was not in London, Wodrow met with another bookseller, Joseph Johnson, through the intervention of Johnson's Scottish friend, Thomas Christie (letter of 16 Sept. 1788). On 27 September Wodrow described his first meeting with Johnson: "He offered me two Alternatives Either to take the whole risk of the Impression of 1000 copies on himself and divide the profits or 2d to give me 200 copies. The last is the best offer tho' I cannot specify the reasons." The second

131. See my account of Blair in *ODNB;* and Amory, "Hugh Blair," 159–64.

132. Blair to Cadell, 20 Feb. 1794, BL, Add. MSS 28098, fols. 18–19.

133. In the following discussion, Wodrow's letters are cited from *Wodrow–Kenrick Correspondence.*

134. Oliver, *History,* 2:265.

option was presumably considered more desirable because it guaranteed Wodrow some income from the sale of his copies, whereas the profit-sharing plan would only begin to yield income if the publisher's break-even point were passed. Johnson sweetened the offer by agreeing to pay for a frontispiece portrait that was to be engraved in London from an original painting sent up from Glasgow, as discussed in the last chapter.

Rather than agree hastily to the offer from Johnson, which was lower than he had hoped for, Wodrow told him of his intention to meet with Cadell. He was impressed that Johnson replied "very politely and frankly that my application to him or any other Bookseller so far from giving him any offense was what he rather wished. It was what I ought to do, and what my friends woud expect. If their offers were better than his, it was well. If not, he would abide by his." Having just returned from the Continent, Cadell was now taking the waters at Tunbridge Wells in Kent, where another intermediary sent him a letter about Wodrow's manuscript, along with Davidson's letter of introduction. On 15 October 1788 Wodrow told Kenrick that Cadell had written that he considered it "an honour to be concerned in the Publication." Since Cadell would not be returning to London until the end of October, however, Wodrow was invited either to meet with him then or else "settle the business with Mr. Strahan." Unfortunately, Andrew Strahan was also out of town, but upon return-ing he met with Wodrow in early October and was "polite and obliging." Wodrow's letter to Kenrick gives this account of the negotiations:

> I asked at our first meeting 100£ and 100 copies for the property of the two vols. and continued on this footing for two subsequent visits. He de-clined making the bargain on these terms as he was to see Mr. Cadell in a few days. But by his Mr Str[ahan's] calculations (which were the same with Mr. John[so]n's) he brought me to abate a little in my offers and then woud have struck the barg[ai]n on these lower terms which I on my part de-clined; telling him at the same time that I woud not flinch from my lowest offer but expected something better from his and Mr. C's honour and gen-erosity when they should meet and consult about it. I parted with him on Saturday [11 October] on this footing, and he left the town on Sunday. In the mean time however he had without my knowledge communicated my first offer to Mr. Cad[el]l by Letters. In consequence of which I received a Letter from Mr. Cad[el]l on Monday offering me what I had first asked viz £100 and 100 copies which I immediately by another Letter accepted.

After more than a month of hard bargaining in London, Wodrow had finally settled the publication arrangements for his edition of Leechman's

Sermons, and done so on his own terms. Although the £100 and one hundred books that he received as compensation may not seem impressive, it was a relatively large amount for a posthumous new book of sermons by an author who was only moderately well known outside Scotland. Indeed, it turned out to be more than the copyright was probably worth, since a second edition was never required. As the pastor of the Ayrshire parish of Stevenston, Wodrow was not affluent; his entire living (including the "glebe," or plot of land assigned to the minister) was worth only about £96 a year, mainly in the form of victual,[135] and it is likely that he had never held £100 cash in his hands. Yet the author's enjoyment of this financial triumph was short-lived. Having forgotten to secure the frontispiece portrait, Wodrow reported to Kenrick from Scotland on Christmas Day 1788 that "Messrs Cadell and Strahan on their return to London declined any part of the Expense of the engraving which they said woud cost £30." Although another intermediary eventually prevailed on them to divide this charge evenly with Wodrow, the editor was resentful. "I impute this to Mr. Strahan," he told Kenrick, "who knows that he coud have concluded the bargain on lower terms with me had it been left entirely to him, and has taken hold of this circumstance left a little loose in my Letters to bring down what he thought too high a price." To this Kenrick replied, in his letter of 16 January 1789: "So Mr Strahan has plaid you a bookseller's trick after all."

Disappointment came to authors in many forms, but all the worst cases were rooted in the growing gap between expectation and reality. If William Robertson could sell his quarto histories to publishers for large sums in advance of publication, others wondered if they could do the same. "All the Solan geese of Orkney can hardly furnish quills for the historical hands that are now said to be at work in Scotland," quipped James Beattie in 1771, when discussing the large profits that "the great quarto historians" were earning from their books. "In short, history is the word." In the same spirit, Beattie explained why his *Essay on Truth* had not earned him nearly as much as Sir John Dalrymple had received for his "affected" and "uninteresting" *Memoirs of Great Britain and Ireland:* "We little octavo philosophers must not pretend to vye with the great quarto historians."[136] Scottish Presbyterian ministers in particular were smitten by the quarto history bug. "The men of letters of Scotland seem to be seized with a rage

---

135. Sinclair, *Statistical Account,* 6:610.

136. Beattie to James Williamson, 13 Apr. 1771, in Beattie, *Correspondence,* 2:136.

for this species of writing," wrote Gilbert Stuart in a review of the third volume of a *History of France* by Rev. Walter Anderson (no. 121), "and . . . the deserved celebrity procured in it by an eminent divine has engaged, perhaps, too many of his order in attempts to imitate his example."[137] Boswell struck a similar chord in an unsigned newspaper article of May 1777, in which he observed that "several of our Scots clergy, who are so fond of imitating the Doctor in every particular, thought that they might also like him acquire some of the rewards due to literary merit." For this reason, the public was "pestered with historical compositions by Scots clergymen" who lacked Robertson's ability to find a way through "the intricate and mazy paths of History."[138]

The troubled literary career of Thomas Somerville exemplifies this trend and its possible consequences. A Presbyterian clergyman with a modest income as minister of Jedburgh, Somerville openly acknowledged in his autobiography that "pecuniary embarrassments . . . first suggested to me the idea of becoming an author."[139] Not surprisingly, in light of this confession, he decided to write a book in that most lucrative of genres, history. Somerville related how William Robertson raised his expectations for the manuscript of his history of British politics in the age of William III (no. 308)—in a manner very different, incidentally, from what one would expect Robertson to have said on the basis of his remark about the obligation of unproven authors to accept whatever the booksellers offered them. "He asked me what sum I expected from the booksellers," Somerville recalled, "and, upon my mentioning £300, he said it was too moderate, that I ought to make my stand at £500, and that he could almost assure me of obtaining that sum from Messrs. Strahan and Cadell, to whom he would recommend the publication, in a joint letter with Dr. Blair, who coincided with his opinion of its merit" (244).

Somerville then went to London, sent a copy of the introduction to his book to Andrew Strahan and Thomas Cadell, and was invited to meet with them and to provide the finished portions of the manuscript for evaluation. His account continues:

> After my manuscript had passed through the ordeal of critical inquisition under the eyes of their advisers, I concluded my bargain with Messrs. Stra-

---

137. *Edinburgh Magazine and Review* 3 (Dec. 1774): 43.

138. Quoted in Sher, "Boswell," 205–6.

139. Somerville, *My Own Life*, 287, 205.

han and Cadell pleasantly, and in a few words. They said that £500, the sum specified, was too large for the work of an unknown author, and more than Dr. Robertson had received for his first publication, but that they would consent to my demand on the following conditions, viz.—£300 to be paid on the publication of the first edition, to consist of 700 copies; and £200 on the publication of the second edition. (245)

Whether owing to faulty recollection by the author, miscommunication, or some other factor, the print run of Somerville's book turned out to be 1,000 copies (SA 48817, fol. 17), and it never went to a second edition. Indeed, when the author inquired about that possibility in 1798, his publishers told him bluntly that "so far from our having at present any Intention to reprint it, we can safely assure you that we have not sold a Dozen Copies within the same number of Months last past, and nearly half of the Impression is still on hand."[140]

In his autobiography, Somerville attributed the poor showing of his first book to "the coincidence of its publication with the horrors of the French Revolution" (256). Nevertheless, he set out to continue his history into the regime of Queen Anne, stopping, significantly, when he had "reached the number of pages to which booksellers wish to confine a quarto volume" (291). In August 1795 Andrew Strahan and Thomas Cadell, Jr., "made me the offer of £300 for the copyright, which was so much beneath my expectation that I abruptly declined any farther conversation on the business" (291). When the book was ready for the press two years later, however, "the alarming state of public affairs" as a result of the ongoing war with France "had in the meantime depreciated all literary property" (293), and Strahan and Cadell & Davies published *The History of Great Britain during the Reign of Queen Anne* (no. 346) in 1798 "on terms which proved less advantageous than those they had originally offered" (293). Somerville used this diplomatic language to describe his disappointment in his autobiography, written fifteen years after the event. But correspondence at the time shows him to have been in a state of despair, as the two hundred copies of the book that he ended up receiving as compensation (possibly in addition to £150 in cash) turned out to be more difficult to sell for a profit than he had hoped. At times he came close to accusing his publishers of cheating him by failing to market the book properly, provoking an indignant reply from Cadell & Davies and a sheepish apology from

---

140. Cadell & Davies to Somerville, 12 Oct. 1798, EUL, Dc.4.102.

the author.[141] Although Somerville did receive some indirect rewards for his scholarly and (especially) political writings, in the form of a chaplaincy worth £50 a year in 1793, raised to a government pension of £100 a year in 1800, the main theme of his relations with his publishers is frustration over his failure to achieve anything remotely approaching the pecuniary success of his role model, William Robertson. At the same time, the fact that Somerville was compensated wholly or partially with copies of his second book, as Wodrow had been before him, reminds us that even authors who sold their copyrights in advance of publication were not always completely removed from the realm of conditional publishing.

For ambitious authors of quarto histories, Adam Ferguson's *History of the Progress and Termination of the Roman Republic* (no. 232) constituted a memorable cautionary tale. Offered £1,000 for the copyright by Strahan, Cadell, and Creech in July 1776, as the soaring sales of the first volume of Edward Gibbon's *Decline and Fall of the Roman Empire* were demonstrating that ancient Rome was a surprisingly marketable historical topic,[142] Ferguson held out for twice that amount. Eventually he got it, thanks to the expansion of the work from two to three quarto volumes and unrelenting pressure from the author's Scottish friends.[143] But the contract contained a crucial safety or saving clause, requiring the author or his heirs to buy back all the copies that were unsold eighteen months after publication, at the wholesale price of £2 per set.[144] With a print run of 1,500 copies, Ferguson had taken a huge gamble by signing such a contract, and he would soon regret it. When his book was finally published in March 1783, sales were sluggish. The author's friends put the blame on

141. See Somerville to Cadell & Davies, 3 Feb. and 18 Feb. 1799; and Cadell & Davies to Somerville, 13 Feb. 1799, all at Duke University Library, Thomas Cadell Papers.

142. Strahan to Creech, 23 July 1776, WCL. At this time the first volume of Gibbon's work was in its third edition, with more than 2,500 quarto copies in circulation at a guinea apiece in boards.

143. Strahan to Creech, 14 May 1782, WCL: "I don't know how it was, we were so pressed by his Friends that we could not well avoid agreeing to it." For evidence of the pressure being exerted by the author's friends, see Blair to [Strahan], 17 Dec. 1781, NLS, MS 2257, fols. 9–10; and Alexander Carlyle to John Douglas, 14 Mar. 1781, asking for Douglas's help in negotiating with the booksellers on Ferguson's behalf and noting that Adam Smith, Joseph Black, and James Edgar had all read and approved Ferguson's manuscript. BL, Egerton MSS 2185, fols. 103–4.

144. The memorandum that forms the foundation of the contract, dated 28 February 1782, is printed in Ferguson, *Correspondence*, 2:576.

everything from personal resentment by jealous critics to the fact that the author had not "followed Mr. Gibbon's Plan of making the Narrative only a Vehicle for attacking the Religion of his Country."[145] In 1784 Ferguson had to buy back all the unsold copies at considerable expense, requiring a loan from William Pulteney that was repaid three years later with income from sales of the books. After several years of trying to manage the sale of the surplus copies himself, Ferguson sold the remainder to the London bookseller John Stockdale for a lump sum in 1790, with the stipulation that a new edition could not be published for five more years.[146]

Even if Ferguson recovered some of his losses this way, it must have been a humiliating experience. Stockdale announced in the *Edinburgh Evening Courant* for 8 August 1791 that he had purchased "the few remaining copies" of the work from the author, and he tried to stimulate interest by stating that "this book takes up the Roman History from the earliest period, and closes where Mr. Gibbon's work commences, so that the two works form a Complete history of the Roman Empire." Ferguson's only consolation was that he regained the copyright to his Roman history when the safety clause was activated by Strahan and Cadell, enabling him to arrange for the Robinsons in London and Bell & Bradfute in Edinburgh to copublish a revised edition in five octavo volumes in 1799. Ironically, the book became extremely popular during the first half of the nineteenth century. But the author had paid a high price for demanding so much money for the copyright in advance of publication. There were evidently no hard feelings between the author and the original publishers, however, because Andrew Strahan, Cadell, and Creech purchased the copyright to Ferguson's next book, *Principles of Moral and Political Science* (no. 303), for £800 in advance of publication, as we shall see in chapter 5.

The copyrights to many other titles in table 2 were sold to publishers in advance of publication for respectable sums, including Patrick Brydone's popular tour of Sicily and Malta (no. 150) for £500 in 1773; Lord Kames's two-volume quarto, *Sketches of the History of Man* (no. 164), for £1,000 in 1774 (although this arrangement had complications);[147] William Cullen's two-volume quarto, *Treatise of the Materia Medica* (no. 281), for £1,500 in 1789; and Dugald Stewart's single quarto volume, *Elements of the Human Mind* (no. 309), for £500 in 1792. In certain circumstances, even novels,

145. John Douglas to Alexander Carlyle, 2 Nov. 1783, EUL, Dc.4.41, no. 24; Carlyle, *Autobiography*, 298.

146. Fagg, "Biographical Introduction," lxvi–lxvii.

147. Ross, *Lord Kames*, 337, 347.

which traditionally made their authors relatively little money, were also becoming valuable properties, as we saw in regard to John Moore's *Zeluco* and *Edward*.

Of course, some authors sold their copyrights in advance of publication for smaller amounts of money. Among novelists, Henry Mackenzie was paid fifty guineas (£52.10s.) for his best-selling *The Man of Feeling* (no. 135), and even after the great success of that work he got only twice as much for each of his next two novels, *The Man of the World* (no. 155) and *Julia Roubigné* (no. 183). Alexander Gerard received £50 for the copyright to his *Essay on Genius* (no. 162). James Mackintosh obtained just £30 from George Robinson for the copyright to his answer to Edmund Burke on the French Revolution, *Vindiciae Gallicae* (no. 298), although after the book sold well Robinson is believed to have shared some of the profits with the author.[148]

Even the copyrights to quarto histories, which made so many Scottish authors rich, were sometimes sold in advance of publication for relatively modest amounts, such as Adam Ferguson's *Essay on the History of Civil Society* (no. 99) for £200; John Millar's *Observations concerning the Distinction of Ranks* (no. 137) for 100 guineas (£105); Sir David Dalrymple, Lord Hailes's *Annals of Scotland* (no. 178) for 130 guineas (£136.10s.); and various histories by Gilbert Stuart, which generally brought the author between £60 and £100. In 1766 John (later Sir John) Macpherson made the London publisher Thomas Becket a final offer of £100 for the copyright to his late father's *Critical Dissertations on the Ancient Caledonians* (no. 108), explaining that although the offer was "not high" and was twenty pounds less than an unnamed "Scotch Bookseller" was willing to pay, "the reputation of the Book weighs more with me than its little profits." But Becket rejected even that amount, and we do not know on what terms he and his partners (de Hondt in London and John Balfour in Edinburgh) finally copublished this work two years later.[149]

In accordance with his advice to Sylvester Douglas, James Beattie usually sold the copyrights to his books in advance of publication: *Dissertations, Moral and Critical* (no. 229) for £200, *Evidences of the Christian Religion* (no. 258) for sixty guineas (£63), and *Elements of Moral Science* (no. 291) for two hundred guineas (£210). Beattie's first and best-selling

148. O'Leary, *Sir James Mackintosh*, 25–26.

149. John Macpherson to Thomas Becket, [early Dec. 1766], BL, Add. MSS 40166, fols. 104–6. A copy of Becket's reply of 13 December 1766 is scribbled on the address page of this letter.

prose work, *An Essay on the Nature and Immutability of Truth* (no. 123), is a more interesting case. The author initially received fifty guineas (£52.10s.), which he believed came from the publishers, Kincaid & Bell of Edinburgh. In fact, Beattie's friends and agents, Sir William Forbes and Robert Arbuthnot, had secretly funded the publication, including the copy money paid to the author, because they were sure that Beattie "would never agree" to publish the work at his own expense, as Kincaid & Bell wished to do.[150] The controversial *Essay on Truth* immediately became a surprise best seller among elements of the public looking for quick answers to Hume's skepticism, and it was frequently reprinted during the 1770s. After the success of the first edition, Beattie sold the copyright to Kincaid & Bell for one hundred guineas. He seems to have received another fifty guineas from Creech and the Dilly brothers (who had purchased half the copyright from Kincaid) around the time of the fourth edition of 1773, bringing the total amount of his earnings from this work to about two hundred guineas[151]—in addition to the four hundred guineas or so that he got from the quarto subscription edition of his *Essays*, as discussed earlier. All told, Beattie earned more than £1,200 over the course of his career from his various works of poetry, criticism, and philosophy. This was a respectable amount of money for a professor earning about £140 a year, though certainly not at the high end as book earnings go. Together with his academic income and a royal pension of a little under £200 per annum that he received in 1773 as a reward for his writings, it was enough "to render him independent," in the judgment of one contemporary who knew him well.[152]

*

The evidence presented in this section demonstrates a wide variation in the kinds of arrangements that Scottish authors made with their publishers, as well as in the amounts of copy money they received from their publications. Authors could be hired by publishers to write or edit books by the sheet or the job, could hire booksellers or printers to produce their books on a commission basis, could organize a subscription, could share profits with their publishers (sometimes also sharing expenses), could sell

150. Forbes, *Account*, 1:147.

151. Beattie to Creech, 13 Apr. 1773, WCL; and Robinson, introduction to Beattie, *Essay on Truth*.

152. Forbes, *Account*, 1:268; Forbes, *Beattie and His Friends*, 97n1.

the rights to a particular edition of a work to a publisher for a fixed sum, or could sell their copyrights before publication (usually for cash, but sometimes for copies of the book, or some combination of cash and copies), with fixed fees for later editions and voluntary publishers' "presents" among the possibilities for additional income. The publication history of a single book sometimes involved several of these publication arrangements, overlapping or in sequence. Although certain variables, such as format and genre, operated as constraints, there was still a great deal of room for negotiation—and therefore for contingency, conflict, and cooperation—in the arrangement and implementation of the terms of publication.

The complexity and variety of publishing arrangements were a source of endless fascination to contemporaries. One day in June 1781 Boswell and Johnson passed their time on the road conversing about "the uncertainty of profit with which authours and booksellers engage in the publication of literary works" (*BLJ*, 4:121). Uncertainty about authors' profits arose not only because no one could ever be sure how well books were going to sell but also because so much depended on the terms of publication. If Thomas Somerville was resentful that he could not sell the copyrights to his histories for £500, William Buchan must have rued the day that he parted with the copyright to his phenomenally popular *Domestic Medicine* for that very amount. As a result, Buchan was bitter for the rest of his life about earning just £50 for every revised edition of his book while his publishers got rich from it.

It is sometimes tempting to regard authors as essentially profit driven, the way some book historians have portrayed booksellers and publishers. Although few were as blunt as Thomas Somerville about the pecuniary motives for writing and publishing books, there were others who admitted that money was an important incentive. "I am far from wishing to surfeit the public," wrote Rev. Alexander Gerard to William Strahan, after Strahan had apparently turned down his plan for a book of sermons. "At the same time, you will not wonder that, with a scotch stipend and six children, I should be willing to lay hold of a favourable opportunity, if it should happen to cast up."[153] Of course, such opportunities did not normally just "happen to cast up." A prospective author seeking financial rewards had to be prepared to venture into the marketplace with a manuscript or at least an idea for one, and then to make an offer, withstand rejection, and negotiate the most favorable terms. Gerard tried again with

153. Gerard to Strahan, 20 Dec. 1774, HL, MS Hyde 76, 5.2.92.3. Gerard had offered the work to Strahan in a letter of 21 July 1774, HSP, Gratz, case 11, box 7.

Charles Dilly, and this time he succeeded, although we do not know the details of the publication arrangement or the extent to which Gerard's *Sermons* (no. 211) augmented his "scotch stipend."

"No man but a blockhead ever wrote, except for money" and "nothing excites a man to write but necessity" are statements that have been attributed to Samuel Johnson.[154] Yet Johnson himself wrote many things for which he was not paid and sometimes sold his services for much less than they were worth. By contrast, David Hume drove a hard bargain with his publishers, especially for his *History of England*, but he evidently did not believe that money could provide an adequate incentive for authors to write books of quality. "If your commendations of Henry's *History* are well founded," William Strahan wrote to him, after Robert Henry refused to sell his book to the London publishers on their terms, "is not his work an exception to your own general rule, that no good book was ever wrote for money?"[155] Hume's "general rule" implies a sharp distinction between higher and lower forms of authorship, based not on the amount of copy money that authors received but on their reasons for writing books. It was acceptable to him for authors to become wealthy from their publications, and even to boast about it, as he would do in his own autobiography, yet "good" books would not be produced by authors who took up their pens chiefly with that end in view. Others registered similar views, such as the anonymous writer in *The Bee* who noted that Smollett "often wrote merely for wages; and on such occasions, nothing above mediocrity can with reason be demanded."[156] But the Irish author Philip Skelton contended that the poverty and barrenness of Scotland constituted the chief cause for the literary achievements of "the Scotch professors," because "hunger is a most powerful spur to genius."[157] In general, however, we would do well to set aside all categorical pronouncements and to recognize that financial gain was one among several reasons for Scottish Enlightenment authors to write their books and that the true motives of authors (to the extent they can be known) cannot be neatly correlated with the quality of their works or their success in the marketplace.

Whatever their motives for writing books, Scottish authors as a whole did extremely well for themselves in the material realm. Forty-seven of the 93 titles in table 2 about which I have been able to discover at least partial

154. Quoted in Bate, *Samuel Johnson*, 526–27.
155. Strahan to Hume, 9 Apr. 1774, in Hume, *Letters of Hume to Strahan*, 285.
156. "Critical Remarks," 91.
157. Burdy, *Life of Skelton*, 18.

information concerning copy money netted their authors at least £450, including known income from all volumes and editions published during the authors' lifetimes (but not including income from pensions, promotions, and places that were often bestowed as rewards for these publications, or income from performances of plays).[158] In at least 27 instances, involving 22 different authors, the copy money was £1,000 or more. These results are probably on the low side for the sample of 93 titles, because it is not always possible to learn about every gift and additional payment that authors received. On the other hand, the figures might look a little less impressive if more data could be found about copy money from minor books in the database, books published only in Edinburgh, and books published during the late 1740s, 1750s, and early 1760s, when payments were lower than later in the century.

Such qualifications, however, should not be allowed to blunt the impact of these findings. During the second half of the eighteenth century, the financial rewards available to Scottish authors increased far beyond anyone's earlier experience or expectation, and authors entered a new era of potential status and wealth. A number of them grew rich, while many others became comfortably well off. Even some relatively low figures were respectable sums in their day: the £50 that Thomas Reid received for his *Inquiry into the Human Mind* in 1764, for example, had purchasing power equivalent to more than £4,500 sterling or roughly $8,000 in the early twenty-first century. The conventional wisdom on these matters among eighteenth-century book historians who have generalized on the basis of English novelists—that with a few exceptions "authors were paid paltry sums" for their books—does not seem to apply. Neither does the standard view that the abolition of perpetual copyright by the House of Lords in February 1774 fundamentally "transformed" the book trades and the status of authors,[159] for the explosion in the amounts of copy money paid to authors occurred earlier and does not seem to have been affected by the Lords' decision. The authors of the Scottish Enlightenment were in the vanguard of this movement, and the consequences of the new order they helped to inaugurate were considerable. Educated Scots acquired an incentive to associate with and emulate the most successful authors among their countrymen, thus ensuring that the revival of Scottish let-

---

158. Two posthumous publications have also been included: William Leechman's *Sermons* (no. 283) and Adam Smith's *Essays on Philosophical Subjects* (no. 336).

159. Raven, "Book Trades," quoting 16; Raven, "Publishing and Bookselling," 34–35; and Feather, *Publishing, Piracy, and Politics*, 94.

ters, which had begun during the second quarter of the eighteenth century and had taken off at midcentury under the leadership of David Hume, would continue for some time. Some English authors were similarly affected. When contemplating a literary career as a young man, Edward Gibbon later wrote in his autobiography, the historical prose of William Robertson "inflamed me to the ambitious hope, that I might one day tread in his footsteps," just as reading the volumes of Hume's *History of England* on the Stuarts filled him "with a mixed sensation of delight and despair."[160] Gibbon succeeded in his quest to emulate Robertson and Hume and in the process earned as much fame from his publications as either of them—and even more money.[161]

Yet Gibbon was exceptional in more ways than one. Although some other English writers shared in the high profits of authorship during the second half of the eighteenth century, the number who did so appears to have been considerably smaller than among the Scots, especially when demographic differences are taken into account and attention is paid to the full range of enlightened genres (rather than just to poetry, novels, and plays).[162] "You cannot imagine how much it has astonished all the London authors," William Robertson commented to a friend, after reporting the

160. Gibbon, *Memoirs*, 99. Elsewhere in his memoirs Gibbon refers to himself as Robertson's "disciple" (158). The importance of Robertson, Hume, and other Scottish Enlightenment thinkers in establishing one of the primary historiographical contexts from which Gibbon emerged is explored in Pocock, *Barbarism and Religion*, vol. 2, pts. 2 and 3, and vol. 3, chap. 16.

161. I calculate that Cadell and the Strahans paid Gibbon £9,077 for *The History of the Decline and Fall of the Roman Empire*, published in six quarto volumes between 1776 and 1788. This amount surpassed the sum of £8,578 that Robertson received for his four major histories in eight quarto volumes (including a gift of two hundred guineas for revising his first three works late in life, as indicated in a letter from Cadell and Andrew Strahan to Robertson, 17 Apr. 1788, NLS, MS 3943, fol. 237). Like Strahan and Cadell's other great publication of 1776, Adam Smith's *Wealth of Nations*, Gibbon's work began as a conditional publication, but after the great success of the first volume, the publishers purchased the copyright retroactively and bought the copyrights to volumes 2–6 in advance of their publication. See Barker, *Form and Meaning*, 248–59; also see the receipt for £750.16s. for the first two editions of the first volume, HL, Autograph File.

162. In the absence of recent, comprehensive scholarship on the amounts of copy money that eighteenth-century English authors received for their books, especially outside the realm of creative literature, one must still rely on two pioneering but badly dated and largely undocumented studies by A. S. Collins: *Authorship in the Days of Johnson* and *Profession of Letters*.

sale of the copyright to his *History of Scotland* to Andrew Millar for "more than was ever given for any book except David Hume's."[163] Ten years later, when word spread that Robertson's next book would be sold for thousands of pounds more than the *History of Scotland*, the London literary world was once again incredulous.[164] Faced with this growing imbalance, as well as with the fact that so many of the publishers and patrons involved in the process were Scotsmen themselves, English authors often reacted either by glorifying Scottish authors and trying to imitate their success, in the manner of Gibbon, or else by attributing their success to national conspiracy and deception rather than to merit. Whatever their nationality, authors who tried and failed to partake of the new wealth that fell to the lot of Hume, Robertson, and Gibbon were more likely to feel frustrated and embittered by their experience as a result of the heightened expectations that were engendered by these acclaimed authors. Moreover, as we shall see more fully in chapter 5, the publishers who were largely responsible for bringing about the transformation in the profitability of Scottish authorship had doubts of their own and sometimes wondered if they had created a new species of ravenous monster that could not be controlled.

*

For Scots in the second half of the eighteenth century, the material rewards of learned and literary authorship were expanding simultaneously on several fronts. With regard to aristocratic and government patronage, many Scottish authors could look forward to obtaining professional positions, sinecures, and pensions that would give them greater financial autonomy. In this sense, enlightened patronage helped to free authors from the need for further patronage. At the same time, the leading publishers of books in Edinburgh and especially London began to assume much of the responsibility for providing authors with personal services, including hospitality and social support, which were formerly associated with traditional patrons. They also took on the role of sponsoring large, risky book projects, such as multivolume dictionaries and encyclopedias, and of mediating the relationship between authors and the public in a variety of ways.

163. Robertson to John Jardine, 20 Apr. 1758, in Brougham, *Lives*, 1:278–79 (misdated by Brougham).

164. Sher, *"Charles V,"* 166.

Scottish authors could also look forward to receiving higher amounts of income from their books than had ever been known. May each of your lines be paid like Robertson's, Voltaire wrote to a fellow French author (La Harpe) early in 1770, as news of these new developments spread through Europe. Another French observer commented that a bookseller in Paris would consider himself "very generous" if he had given an author an eighth of the amount that Robertson received for his history *Charles V*.[165] When authors like Robertson sold their copyrights for large amounts of money in advance of publication, many contemporaries surmised that the publishers who purchased those copyrights were the new patrons of authors. In other instances, when authors published their books on a contingency basis, "to take the fair chance of the public," as Boswell put it, it seemed that even the publisher was unnecessary and that the "public" had become the true patron of authors deemed worthy of its support. Each of these formulations contains a portion of the truth, but it is necessary to take into account the entire range of existing options—emanating from aristocratic patrons, from government, from publishers, and from the "public"—in order to understand the sense of almost boundless potential for worldly success that characterized the booming book culture of the Scottish Enlightenment.

165. Quoted in Lough, *Writer and Public*, 200.

PART II

*

PUBLISHING THE
SCOTTISH ENLIGHTENMENT IN
LONDON AND EDINBURGH

[4]

Forging the London–Edinburgh
Publishing Axis

Readers and consumers of books, in the eighteenth century as well as today, are often cognizant of where and by whom a book has been published, and this information may affect not only whether they buy or read it, but also how they categorize it in their own minds. Publishers' catalogues and printed advertisements (and today also Web sites) add to this effect by providing a link between books and their makers. The name of the publisher, like that of the author, may take on the role of a brand name, influencing perceptions of the "product" and patterns of consumption in profound ways. As Michael Suarez has asked rhetorically, by way of example: "Is a book published by Gypsy Lane Press likely to be accorded the same reception as a work produced and marketed by Viking Penguin?"[1]

In examining the relationship of this "publisher function" to the "author function," we must take into account the effect of time on our perceptions of the printed word. As time passes, publishers often drop out of the consciousness of readers, leaving authors alone as the sole standard for ordering texts. Consider how the makers of Scottish Enlightenment books were represented in the *Dictionary of National Biography*, the classic record of Victorian perceptions of personal merit and distinction in British history. The *DNB* contains entries for every one of the 115 Scottish authors in table 1, but only sixteen of the many individuals who produced the books in table 2 have separate entries in the *DNB*, and some of them were included for reasons other than their contributions to publishing

1. Suarez, "Business of Literature," 131.

(e.g., John Knox appears as a "philanthropist"). In London, the first John Murray, Andrew Strahan, and Thomas Cadell, Jr., are briefly mentioned within biographies of their sons or fathers, and George Robinson appears in a token entry of just over one hundred words. The disparity is particularly marked with regard to authors and publishers resident in Scotland. Only two of the latter—William Creech (who was also an author in his own right) and Robert Foulis (who was mainly esteemed for his editions of the classics and for his academy of arts)—have their own entries in the *DNB*. Important figures such as Gavin Hamilton, John Balfour, Alexander Kincaid, Alexander Donaldson, Charles Elliot, and John Bell are excluded.

Although the recently updated edition of the *DNB*, the *Oxford Dictionary of National Biography*, has greatly increased the representation of eighteenth-century booksellers and publishers, the authorial bias to which I am referring is not limited to the Victorians. I suspect that relatively few current specialists in the various disciplines of eighteenth-century thought would be able to identify in more than a cursory way the people responsible for making and selling many of the eighteenth-century books that they study. Why should they? Outside of bibliographers and book historians, and perhaps biographers explaining how their individual subjects came to publish their works, scholars classifying books from the past generally do so by reference to their authors alone, with little or no attention paid to publication information. When eighteenth-century texts are republished in modern editions—the main way they are encountered by modern readers—the details of contemporary publication are usually stripped away or at most mentioned in passing. Even among bibliographers and book historians who specialize in the eighteenth-century book trade, relatively little work has been done to connect publishers and the conditions of publication with authors and their books.

One of the primary tasks of this book is to reestablish that connection. To do so, it is necessary to alter the way that the book trade and its cultural role are perceived. So long as we persist in viewing publishers apart from the books they produce, except in the narrowest sense of businessmen appropriating what has come to be known as "intellectual property" for personal gain, we will have little chance of success. This chapter and the two that follow it treat the publishers of the Scottish Enlightenment with the same degree of consideration that the previous three chapters accorded to authors. Like authors, publishers had their alliances and rivalries and struggled to define their identities in an age marked by growing commercialization and Anglo-Scottish tensions. And like authors, they gravitated to the English and Scottish metropolises, London and Edinburgh, which became the twin bulwarks of Scottish Enlightenment publishing.

THE FRAMEWORK OF COLLABORATIVE PUBLISHING

At first glance, the column near the middle of table 2 that indicates the places and publishers of British first editions appears muddled and confusing. Unlike the author column, which usually contains just one name per book, the publisher column consists of a complicated array of places and names, arranged in what may initially appear to be bewildering combinations and sequences. The imprints reveal that some books were published by a single firm in a single place but that far more were published by two or more firms in the same town or—as indicated in the table by a solidus or slash (/)—in more than one town. In addition to the standard phrase for identifying publishers, "printed for"—which is so commonly found in these imprints that its presence is assumed unless otherwise noted—some of these books identify only the selling agents ("sold by") or the printers ("printed by" rather than "printed for"). When the words "printed for" do not appear, printers may have served as publishers, or authors may have footed the expense of publication; in some instances, the presence of the phrase "printed for the author" (represented in the table simply as "author") leaves no doubt that the author took most if not all the risk, although the precise nature of the arrangements between authors and the printing or bookselling firms with which they contracted cannot always be ascertained from the imprint alone. Finally, the names of publishing firms identified in imprints changed as individual booksellers retired, died, and formed new combinations and partnerships with their colleagues.

To make sense of all this, we must focus on essentials. First, looking at the locations where printing and publication occurred,[2] we find that the production of new Scottish Enlightenment books was highly concentrated geographically. Only two books in table 2 bear the imprint of an English town other than London: Elizabeth Hamilton's *Memoirs of Modern Philosophers* (no. 357), which has a Bath imprint although it was printed for a London firm, and William Julius Mickle's translation of *The Lusiad* (no. 175), which Mickle published by subscription with an Oxford imprint,

---

2. As a rule, the primary location shown in the imprint is the site of printing. The sites of printing and publishing were usually the same, but not always, as discussed later in the chapter.

but with a number of prominent London booksellers as its principal selling agents. The Kilmarnock edition of Robert Burns's *Poems, Chiefly in the Scottish Dialect* (no. 260) is the sole title in table 2 bearing an imprint from a Scottish town with fewer than 10,000 inhabitants, but the subsequent fame of that book, and of its author, was generated by the Edinburgh and London reprints that appeared the next year. One might expect the larger Scottish towns of Perth, Aberdeen, and especially Glasgow to have been important centers for publishing the new books of the Scottish Enlightenment. Yet the evidence in table 2 does not support this hypothesis. Despite the extraordinarily high level of academic and scholarly activity in Aberdeen, that town's contribution to book publishing was negligible during the eighteenth century.[3] The only item in the database with an Aberdeen imprint is a duodecimo set of sermons printed in 1786 for its author, Rev. William Duff, by an unidentified firm (no. 261). In Perth, Robert Morison and his son ran a productive printing and publishing firm, but it was mainly involved with reprinting. Aside from one title by Robert Heron published with an Edinburgh imprint (no. 339), the Morisons' only new publications in the database were the Earl of Buchan's biography of John Napier (no. 191) and two other works by Robert Heron (nos. 314 and 330). All three books showed London copublishers on their title pages.

Glasgow's story is more complicated. During the second half of the eighteenth century, Glasgow ranked sixth in English-language imprints, behind London, Dublin, Edinburgh, Philadelphia, and Boston.[4] Moreover, Glasgow was the home of the famous Foulis brothers, Robert and Andrew, who had put the Scottish printing industry on the map with their fine editions of the Latin and Greek classics during the 1740s and 1750s, and who continued to reprint the ancient classics in their original languages and in English translations, as well as modern English classics by the likes of Milton, Dryden, Addison, Pope, and Gray, until their deaths in the mid-1770s. The Foulis brothers' press may be considered the publishing arm of the Glasgow Enlightenment.[5] It was created in the image of Francis Hutcheson, who was the spiritual and probably also the financial force behind the brothers' book business. As the official printers of Glasgow University, the Foulis brothers printed textbooks (in Latin and English) and course outlines for Glasgow professors such as Hutcheson

3. Carnie, "Scholar-Printers," 298–308, esp. 305.

4. Sher, "Corporatism and Consensus," 34.

5. Sher, "Commerce," 312–59, esp. 325–34; Sher and Hook, "Introduction." See also Brown, "Robert and Andrew Foulis," 135–42.

in moral philosophy (no. 3), James Moor in Greek, John Millar in law, John Anderson in natural philosophy, and William Wight in ecclesiastical history, as well as handsome Latin and English editions of Euclid by the mathematics professor Robert Simson (no. 42), a volume of essays that Moor read to the university's literary society (no. 57), and a book of poems by the Humanity (Latin) professor William Richardson (no. 166).[6] The Foulis brothers were occasionally called on to print other titles found in table 2, such as Hutcheson's *System of Moral Philosophy* (no. 36) and James Boswell's *Account of Corsica* (no. 105).

Yet when Scottish men of letters, including Glasgow professors such as Millar, Richardson, and Adam Smith, wished to publish substantial books of their own composition, they scarcely ever approached the Foulis brothers. Whether this was because Glasgow lacked the resources for promoting major literary and scientific works, or because the Foulis brothers were more interested in their reprinting business, their academic job printing, and eventually their arts academy, the firm played a relatively minor role in publishing the new books of the Scottish Enlightenment. Other Glasgow booksellers and printers contributed still less. The only other titles in table 2 bearing a Glasgow imprint are *Disquisitions concerning the Antiquities of the Christian Church* (no. 231) by Sir David Dalrymple, Lord Hailes, which was printed by Robert Foulis's son Andrew, and the expanded fourth edition of John Anderson's *Institutes of Physics* (no. 257), a course outline partially issued by the Foulis brothers but first printed as a complete book by Chapman and Duncan, probably for the author. Eighteenth-century Glasgow was also home to Robert Urie, who published English-language editions of works by Voltaire, Rousseau, and many classical authors, and it nurtured a thriving trade in the publishing and reprinting of evangelical sermons and other religious books, notably bearing the imprint of the antiburgher seceder John Bryce.[7] But Urie and Bryce had nothing to do with the first editions listed in table 2. Glasgow was a force in Enlightenment reprinting, and like Aberdeen, it vied with Edinburgh in academic and club life and sustained many literati who became Enlightenment authors. But neither Glasgow nor Aberdeen had much to do with publishing the new literary, philosophical, and scientific books of the Scottish Enlightenment.

A total of 15 books in table 2, representing just 4 percent of the whole,

6. For further details, see Gaskell, *Bibliography of the Foulis Press.*

7. M'Lean, "Robert Urie," 88–108; R. A. Gillespie's entries on Urie and Bryce in *ODNB.*

bear an imprint from any of the places just mentioned—8 from Glasgow, 3 from Perth, and 1 each from Aberdeen, Bath, Kilmarnock, and Oxford. The remaining 345 titles, representing 96 percent of the database, show the place of imprint as either London (218 titles, comprising 61 percent of the entire database) or Edinburgh (127 titles, or 35 percent of the database). These numbers establish a fundamental fact about the geography of Scottish Enlightenment printing and publishing: as far as new books are concerned, only London and Edinburgh mattered much.

The publishing connections between those two cities were significant. Roughly a quarter of the London titles in table 2 can be linked with Edinburgh through the presence in the imprint of at least one Edinburgh copublisher or selling agent. About two-thirds of the Edinburgh titles can be linked to London in the same manner. In many of these cases, the participating booksellers would agree among themselves about how many shares each of them would take in a book and where it would be printed, and the publication expenses, including paper, printing, and any copy money paid to authors, would be divided up among them according to their respective shares. Upon publication, a participating publisher in the secondary city might be shipped the number of copies of the book that corresponded to his shares in the copyright, for sale in his bookshop at retail prices and wholesale to the local or regional trade. Advertising was often handled locally by the copublishers in each town. Another kind of collaborative arrangement gave the secondary publisher the rights to a specified number of copies at a low price, without actually owning a share of the work or dividing production costs.[8] Sometimes publishers in Edinburgh and London added to their imprints the names of booksellers in the other city as selling agents, or as a courtesy, or in exchange for the same favor done for them. In other cases, a book with an Edinburgh imprint would show the name of a London bookseller as the publisher without any counterpart from Edinburgh; such works were either printed in Edinburgh for a London bookseller (e.g., nos. 26 and 238) or else printed in Edinburgh for the author and then sold to the London publisher as printed books (e.g., nos. 288 and 328).

Thus, the title pages reveal that collaborative publishing between members of the book trade in London and Edinburgh was widespread and took many forms. It also performed several functions. At the most ba-

8. This was the policy followed by Charles Elliot, as McDougall explains in "Charles Elliot and the London Booksellers," 81–96.

sic level, collaboration served to distribute the capital outlay and the risk of publishing new books among two or more firms, as well as to establish order within the trade. There was nothing new about such practices within London, where older publishing "congers" formed the foundation of the book trade's corporate system of copyright.[9] But a large, intercity copublication network was not only new but extraordinary, in light of the well-known efforts of London publishers to protect their titles from reprinters elsewhere. In economic terms, it made good sense. Whereas copublishing new books within one's own city would be likely to cut into a bookseller's local trade, intercity collaboration had the opposite effect. London functioned as the distribution center for books in England,[10] much as Edinburgh did for Scotland. Some overlap might occur regarding sales to parts of northern England and America, but the arrangement generally worked smoothly as a means of dividing bookselling labor. London–Edinburgh collaborative publishing also diffused tensions about Scottish reprinting practices that the leading London publishers considered piracy, both before and after the House of Lords' landmark decision on copyright in 1774. It also provided opportunities to take advantage of optimal conditions for printing and the supply of paper, and sometimes catered to the needs of authors who wanted their books printed locally so that corrections and revisions could be made more easily.

Furthermore, improvements in communication and transportation were making London–Edinburgh collaborative publishing increasingly feasible. For large shipments, the Leith packet that sailed between London and Edinburgh's port on the Firth of Forth was reliable, cheap, and relatively quick, even in winter. The land route witnessed a dramatic change during the second half of the eighteenth century. As William Creech boasted in his pamphlet on Edinburgh, the number of London–Edinburgh stage coaches increased from one a month in 1763, taking two weeks to complete the journey, to fifteen a week two decades later, taking two and a half to four days.[11] As a result of these developments, private letters, contracts, proof sheets, and books themselves moved ever more quickly from one city to the other.

Of the many publishers in London and Edinburgh, twelve firms were principally responsible for making the London–Edinburgh axis so im-

---

9. Mumby, *Publishing and Bookselling*, 140–41; Feather, *History*, chap. 6.

10. Feather, *Provincial Book Trade*.

11. [Creech], *Letters to Sir John Sinclair*, 10–11.

portant for the publication of new Scottish Enlightenment books. Of the 360 first editions given in table 2, 291 or 81 percent were published, printed, or sold by one or more of these twelve major firms, whose representatives appear in boldface in the British publisher column in table 2. In most of these cases, at least one of those firms was the book's principal publisher. Dozens of other names are displayed in the column that identifies the British publishers of these books, but few of them are present in more than two or three imprints, and several appear only as printers or sellers of books printed "for the author."

Table 5 lists the twelve principal publishing firms of Scottish Enlightenment books and their primary operatives, as well as the number of first-edition imprints from table 2 in which their names appear and the chronological range of those appearances. Five of these firms—the Dodsley brothers, the Dilly brothers, Joseph Johnson, and the partnership of Thomas Becket and the Dutchman Peter Abraham de Hondt in London, as well as Charles Elliot in Edinburgh—were each involved in publishing between nine and sixteen titles found in the database and sometimes in serving as the selling agents of several more. Each of the other seven firms appears in the imprints of at least thirty books in table 2. The largest by far was the firm founded in London by Andrew Millar, continued by Thomas Cadell after Millar's death, and subsequently run by Cadell's son Thomas, Jr., and William Davies, trading as Cadell & Davies; this firm is listed in 140 imprints in table 2 as a publisher and 14 more as a selling agent. Its closest competition comes from the Edinburgh firm founded by Alexander Kincaid and continued by William Creech, which appears in 89 imprints as publisher and 8 as selling agent, the majority during Creech's tenure. Next, with 56 imprint entries, is the London printing firm founded by William Strahan and continued by his son Andrew—the only nonbooksellers among the dozen leading publishers. This firm's contribution was actually much greater than the table indicates, both because the Strahans were sometimes silent publishing partners and because they printed many of the books in table 2 even if they did not publish them. The Edinburgh bookseller John Bell, on his own or in partnership with John Bradfute, trading as Bell & Bradfute, can be found in the imprints of 22 books as a publisher and 2 more as a selling agent, in addition to almost the same number of titles that he was involved with publishing or selling during his years as Kincaid's junior partner. The London bookseller George Robinson, on his own and with various partners, appears in 37 imprints as a publisher and 4 more as a selling agent. The imprints of 32 books name as publisher or printer,[12] and 3 more as seller, the Edinburgh firm that began publishing as Hamilton & Balfour, added the printer Patrick Neill, and subsequently published under the name of its surviving principal partner, John Balfour, and later his son Elphingston (or Elphinston). Finally, the London firm of John Murray appears in 29 imprints as a publisher and 4 as a selling agent.

Although the figures in table 5 are based entirely on information contained in the imprints, there were many instances in which collaboration occurred behind the scenes, in ways that one could not suspect from the imprint alone. Some of these instances are indicated by square brackets around the names of publishers in table 2. For example, private correspondence and newspaper advertisements establish that William Creech was either the copublisher or the distributor of works by John Millar (no. 137), Adam Smith (no. 177), Thomas Robertson (no. 248), and James Boswell (no. 250), although his name does not appear in the imprints of any of them. William Strahan was a silent partner in the publication of at least five titles in table 2, but probably many more, and the firm of Bell & Bradfute was a silent partner in a book by John Moore (no. 315).[13] Even if every instance of silent publishing of the books in table 2 could be identified, they would not reveal the full extent of publishing cooperation between the main London and Edinburgh publishers because table 2 records only the first editions of works published in Britain. When a book originally published by a minor firm or "for the author" showed promise of unusually strong sales, its publishing rights would often be acquired by one or more of the twelve principal firms. Smollett's *Continuation of the Complete History of England* (no. 67) and most of Smollett's novels, William Smellie's *Treatise of Midwifery* (no. 22), James Ferguson's *Astronomy Explained* (no. 39), William Buchan's *Domestic Medicine* (no. 115), William Guthrie's *Geography* (no. 130), and Robert Burns's *Poems* (no. 260) are all books that achieved best-seller status after being acquired and repeatedly reprinted by one or more of the twelve major Scottish Enlightenment publishers. Buchan's *Domestic Medicine* and Mackenzie's *Lounger*

---

12. Since it is sometimes difficult to know when the imprint words "printed by" are to be taken literally with Hamilton & Balfour, I have excluded from their totals only those imprints that unambiguously identify one of Balfour's specialist printing firms (nos. 115 and 151).

13. Charles Dilly to John Bell, 28 Oct. 1785, NLS, Acc. 10662, folder 10; Sher, "New Light," 26n2; advertisements in *EEC*.

(no. 270) are examples of books that were initially published in Edinburgh but from the second edition onward were regularly copublished by prominent booksellers in London and Edinburgh. In short, both London–Edinburgh collaborative publishing and publishing by the twelve principal firms in table 5 were even more extensive than one might surmise from the imprints of first editions alone.

All twelve of the leading firms shown in table 5 participated to some degree in the culture of collaborative London–Edinburgh publishing, and table 2 is filled with the resulting combinations: books printed for Cadell and Elliot, for Murray and Elliot, for Robinson and Elliot, for Murray and Bell, for Creech and the Dilly brothers, for Robinson and Bell, and so on. However, the London–Edinburgh publishing axis, and Scottish Enlightenment publishing generally, was dominated by one powerful publishing syndicate. At its core was an alliance between the Scottish founders of two London businesses that each became the largest of its kind: the bookselling firm established by Andrew Millar and the printing firm started by William Strahan. From the late 1740s onward, this London syndicate collaborated extensively with the Edinburgh firm founded by Alexander Kincaid and continued by William Creech. They also allied themselves at times with the Edinburgh firm that began publishing as Hamilton & Balfour, especially after Balfour took over the business.

Considering the atmosphere of tension and distrust that characterized mid-eighteenth-century relations between publishers in London and Edinburgh over the problem of copyright, how did a different, indeed opposite, tradition of collaborative publishing emerge in regard to the publication of new books by Scottish authors? Previously mentioned factors concerning the economics of publishing and improved communication and transportation suggest that conditions were ripe for collaboration among publishers in these two cities, but propitious conditions alone cannot explain this development. Why, then, did it happen?

The remainder of this chapter seeks to answer this question by examining the careers of the five founding fathers of the London–Edinburgh publishing axis: Gavin Hamilton (1704–1767), Andrew Millar (1705–1768), Alexander Kincaid (1710–1777), John Balfour (1715–1795), and William Strahan (1715–1785). Born within six years of 1710, they constituted the seminal generation of Scottish Enlightenment publishers, corresponding in age to authors like William Cullen, David Hume, and Thomas Reid. In addition to comprising a generational cluster, they were all born in Scotland, even though two of them founded firms in London. This temporal and spatial juxtaposition was crucial. All of them knew each other from their childhood or youth, and friendships they established in that period of their lives sometimes blunted the effects of individual and regional competition and smoothed the way for collaboration. Like many of the Scottish authors whose work they published, they bonded personally and professionally among themselves, with productive results. By the late 1750s, when Hume was boasting about the rise of Scotland in the republic of letters, the London–Edinburgh publishing axis was firmly in place as a means of propagating Scottish Enlightenment book culture.

THE FOUNDING PUBLISHERS AND THEIR FIRMS

Scotland in the Strand: A. Millar's Tale

By almost any measure, the story of Scottish Enlightenment publishing begins with Andrew Millar, the greatest bookseller and publisher of the mid-eighteenth century. Yet Millar's career has not been well understood. Contemporaries in London who knew nothing of his early years beyond the fact that he came from Scotland believed he was, in John Nichols's words, "literally the artificer of his own fortune," and modern commentators have usually taken these words at face value.[14] Building on research that the late Hugh Amory and I engaged in independently at first, and subsequently in collaboration, I pursue a very different line of thought. Millar's career as a London bookseller and publisher can only be explained by understanding his Scottish background, which shaped his future in more ways than one.[15]

Andrew Millar was the son and grandson of Presbyterian clergymen from western Scotland, the stronghold of evangelical Calvinism. His father Robert (1672–1752) was educated at the University of Glasgow and began his ecclesiastical career in the aftermath of the Revolution Settlement of 1690, which restored Presbyterianism as the established church of Scotland.[16] On 16 October 1705 Andrew was born in Port Glasgow, where his father was then the minister. Four years later Robert Millar moved to the Abbey Kirk, Paisley, where he would remain until his death.

Robert Millar was an ecclesiastical historian of some standing. In 1723 he published his greatest work, *The History of the Propagation of Christianity,*

---

14. Hart, *Minor Lives,* 270; Hall, "Andrew Millar," 184–90.

15. For a fuller account, see Sher, with Amory, "From Scotland to the Strand," 51–70. See also Hugh Amory's biography of Millar in *ODNB.*

16. See my account of Robert Millar in *ODNB.*

and Overthrow of Paganism, now considered one of the classics of Scottish global evangelism.[17] It is a book of enormous learning, piety, and evangelical conviction, published in Edinburgh with a fifteen-page subscription list that contains the names of many Scottish Presbyterian clergymen and professors, including young Francis Hutcheson (then a "Preacher in Dublin") and the Edinburgh professor of divinity William Hamilton. Robert Millar recognized the historical importance of printing, first among the Chinese, and then in Europe, where it "made books and learning have a more easy passage over the world. It is much cheaper and easier to buy a printed book, than to transcribe a manuscript out of a library." Millar believed that printing was intimately connected with "the reviving of arts and sciences, knowledge and learning" since the fifteenth century, which had been ordered by "Divine Providence" as a means of crushing "infidelity and heathenish idolatry."[18] In a second book of 1730, also published by subscription but in folio rather than octavo, Millar traced the spread of Christianity in the ancient Jewish world and appended a "Discourse to Promote the Conversion of the Jews to Christianity."[19]

The Millar family was thick with Church of Scotland clergymen. Andrew's oldest brother, John, served as minister of nearby Old Kilpatrick in Dunbartonshire from 1728 until his premature death in 1738, and a younger brother, Henry, was minister of Neilston, a parish five miles south of Paisley, from 1737 until his death in 1771. His sisters married into the local clergy: Anna Millar married Peter Scott, who was assistant minister, and subsequently sole minister, of the Laigh Kirk, Paisley, from 1740 until his death in 1753, while Elizabeth Millar wed James Hamilton, who was briefly the colleague of Robert Millar as the second minister of the Abbey Kirk, Paisley, from 1751 to 1753, and then served as his successor until his own death in 1782. Thus, the Millars and their kin were well entrenched in the manses of Renfrewshire, to the west of Glasgow, and particularly that shire's largest town, Paisley.

Paisley was one of the central sites of Scottish industrialization in the late eighteenth century. It featured pious handloom weavers and other tradesmen laboring in cottages and small workshops, along with workers in rural and semirural factories driven by waterpower. We can see many of their names in a subscription list appended to the eight-volume duodecimo

---

17. Davies, "Robert Millar," 143–56; Foster, "Scottish Contributor," 138–45; De Jong, *As the Waters,* 113–14.

18. Millar, *History of the Propagation of Christianity,* 2:227–28, 207.

19. Millar, *History of the Church.*

edition of *The Whole Works of the Reverend Robert Millar, A.M.*, which appeared in Paisley in 1789; more than a thousand names appear, most of them identified by their occupations as artisans and tradesmen, including more than 350 weavers from Glasgow, Renfrewshire, and Ayrshire. Andrew Millar continued to have close ties with his Renfrewshire relations after he attained wealth and fame in London. He published editions of his father's books in Edinburgh and London, and in 1767 he erected a handsome monument in Paisley in honor of his mother and father, whom the Latin inscription called "an exemplary, wise, indefatigable, blameless pastor."[20] He and his wife sometimes made visits to Paisley, and his will left substantial amounts of money to his Renfrewshire relations. His brother Henry appears to have inherited his estate after the bookseller's widow remarried an even wealthier Scotsman, and the money was used to finance the construction of an inkle (linen tape) mill at Neilston.[21] Three other brothers went overseas to seek their fortunes: Robert as a surgeon and botanist whom Andrew once tried unsuccessfully to promote for a Glasgow University professorship,[22] Archibald as a naval captain, and William as a physician in Antigua, who returned to acquire the Walkinshaw estate near Paisley and was named an executor in Andrew's will.

Andrew Millar came from a family in which professional careers were

20. In 1731 Andrew Millar published the third edition of his father's *History of the Propagation of Christianity*, with a full-page advertisement (headed "Just Published, Printed for A. Millar") for Robert Millar's second major work, *The History of the Church under the Old Testament* (1730), although Andrew's name does not appear in the imprint of the latter work. The inscription to Millar's monument to his parents appears in Crawfurd and Semple, *History*, 304.

21. Andrew Millar's will, dated 20 February 1768 (Oliver, *History*, 2:265), left £200 to his brother Henry, £50 a year during the life of his widow to Henry's son Alex, £200 each to his sisters Anna and Elizabeth, and an additional £300 to Elizabeth's husband James Hamilton, as well as other legacies to some Scottish cousins. In the history of Neilston in the *New Statistical Account of Scotland*, Rev. Henry Millar, "a man of great spirit and enterprise," is credited with starting the parish's move toward industrialization by projecting and establishing with some partners an important new factory to make inkle with the "fine fortune" he inherited from his brother, "the celebrated bookseller in the Strand, London" (7:335). Since Andrew Millar's will left the profits from his estate to his wife "unless she shall marry again" (all three of their children having died in infancy or childhood), it would appear that Henry Millar inherited his brother's "fine fortune" when Jane Millar married Sir Archibald Grant of Monymusk in May 1770.

22. Andrew Millar to Sir Hans Sloane, n.d., BL, Sloane MSS 4059.

the norm, and it would be surprising if he had not attended a grammar (or Latin) school as a boy. Knowledge of Latin and the liberal arts was an advantage for booksellers, as was the possession of a cultivated literary taste. There is no firm evidence about his formal education, although the fact that he later issued Latin catalogues and commemorated his parents with a Latin inscription certainly suggests that he had some knowledge of that language. Almost without exception, however, contemporary anecdotal literature portrayed him as a man with little expertise in the world of learning, who relied on the judgment of others because he lacked the ability to discern literary merit himself. Even if this assessment is exaggerated, as seems likely, there is little doubt that Millar had a first-rate business mind, which he used to compensate for deficiencies in his education and learning. He was barely twenty-two when he set himself up as a London bookseller and publisher. In light of his youth and his background as an outsider to London and its institutions—including the Stationers' Company, with which he acquired an affiliation a full ten years after establishing his business in London—one may well wonder how he managed to do it.

The key to this mystery lies in Millar's relationship with his master, James M'Euen or McEuen. M'Euen was the leading figure in the Edinburgh book trade during the 1710s and 1720s. He cofounded and printed Scotland's first successful newspaper, the *Edinburgh Evening Courant*, in 1718; published an important collection of local poetry in 1720, the *Edinburgh Miscellany*, which included the earliest published poems by James Thomson and David Mallet; auctioned fine libraries and learned books, for which he often issued catalogues; and published many books under his own imprint, especially sermons and polemical works by Presbyterian divines such as John Willison of Dundee. M'Euen's ties with Church of Scotland ministers included a friendship with the prominent church historian Robert Wodrow of Eastwood in Renfrewshire, who called Robert Millar "my worthy and learned neighbour, and dear brother" when praising his first book in a letter to Cotton Mather in America.[23] Ecclesiastical connections of this kind probably helped to bring about the apprenticeship agreement that was made by Millar and M'Euen in 1720, bonding Millar's second son Andrew, then fourteen or fifteen years old, for a fee of £40.[24] As we have seen, Robert Millar appreciated the power of the

23. Wodrow to Mather, 29 July 1724, in Wodrow, *Correspondence*, 3:154.
24. Maxted, *British Book Trades*, no. 1015.

printed word to spread knowledge and religious truth, and M'Euen was apparently the model of a learned and devout bookseller.

Successful in his trade, M'Euen undertook unprecedented expansion. By 1722 some of his imprints, such as the second edition of Willison's *Treatise concerning the Sanctifying the Lord's Day*, referred to "his shops in London, Edinburgh and Glasgow." Catalogues that he issued in the spring of 1723 and the following winter show that M'Euen was then auctioning learned books in Latin and English, sometimes "Collected Out of Private Libraries Both in Scotland and England." The address of his London bookshop was given on these catalogues as "Buchanan's [or Buchannan's] Head opposite to St. Clements Church Door in the Strand." It was a bold move for a Scottish bookseller to open a shop in the Strand in the early 1720s, using a likeness of the head of the sixteenth-century Scottish patriot and Presbyterian humanist George Buchanan on the shop sign. At some point during his apprenticeship, Andrew Millar went to work at the Strand shop. He was certainly there toward the end of his apprenticeship in 1727, when he appeared in court for his master in a piracy case, and it is likely that he began working in London some years before then.

In January 1728 Millar took over M'Euen's London shop. Although the details of the transition are not known, it seems to have been a smooth succession from master to former apprentice. Millar not only retained Buchanan's head as the sign of the shop but also acquired M'Euen's stock, as shown by a comparison of newspaper advertisements in the *Daily Journal* for November 1727 (under M'Euen's name) and January 1728 (under Millar's name). This stock was largely Scottish, including the second edition of Robert Millar's *History of the Propagation of Christianity* (which had been published in London in 1726 by "J. Mac-Euen in the Strand" and others), Robert Wodrow's *History of the Sufferings of the Church of Scotland, from the Restauration to the Revolution* (1721–22), James Anderson's *Collections Relating to the History of Mary Queen of Scotland* (1727–28), and *The Tea-Table Miscellany* by "the famous Allan Ramsay," with whom M'Euen was closely connected. Millar also emulated M'Euen by selling off learned libraries in London, although he did so by marking discount prices in the front of the books rather than auctioning them. In May 1728 Millar issued the seventy-two page *Librorum, In Omnibus ferè Facultatibus & Linguis, Catalogus: Being the Libraries of an Eminent Physician, and of a Gentleman of the Inner-Temple, Both Lately Deceased*, and the following spring he printed a similar catalogue that was twice as long: *Catalogus Librorum Praestantissimorum in omnibus ferè Artibus & Scientiis: or, a Catalogue of the Libraries of the Learned and Judicious James Anderson, Esq; Famous Antiquary, and Late Post-Master-General of Scotland.*

The aspirations of Andrew Millar, however, were not limited to selling books, new or secondhand, and he immediately began to carve out his own niche as a London publisher. Many of Millar's early publications were essentially offshoots of M'Euen's early stock, such as the fifth edition of Ramsay's *Tea-Table Miscellany*, which Millar published in 1729; the "second edition" (also 1729) of James Anderson's *Collections Relating to the History of Mary Queen of Scotland*, which was in fact a reissue, with a new title page, of the first edition acquired from M'Euen; and the third edition of his father's *History of the Propagation of Christianity*, which he published under his own imprint in 1731. A high proportion of his other publications were by Scottish authors or about Scottish subjects. Ties with the Church of Scotland remained strong, particularly with regard to his contemporaries, Revs. Robert Wallace and William Wishart, who were disciples of William Hamilton of Edinburgh University and closely connected with Millar's chief printer, William Strahan.[25] During the 1730s and early 1740s Millar also began to appear as the publisher, or more commonly as the London selling agent, of philosophical works by Scottish authors, including Andrew Baxter, David Hume, and George Turnbull, and in 1735 he published the first play by David Mallet, *Eurydice*. By September 1742 Millar was doing well enough as a publisher and a bookseller to move the sign of "Buchanan's Head" to a more prestigious location elsewhere in the Strand, where the firm would remain until well into the nineteenth century.[26] He also began to publish important new work by English authors, such as Henry Fielding and Samuel Johnson. But the foundation of his identity as a publisher was thoroughly Scottish, deeply grounded in authors and books with links to his father and his master.

Among these Scottish authors, one stands out as the cornerstone of Millar's entire publishing business. It is probable that Millar first made the acquaintance of the poet James Thomson in Edinburgh during the early 1720s, when Millar was the apprentice of M'Euen (who had first put Thomson's poetry into print) and Thomson (who was five years Millar's senior) was a divinity student under William Hamilton, overlapping with

25. Sefton, "Early Development of Moderatism."

26. The building, opposite Catherine Street, is pictured in Phillips, *Mid-Georgian London*, 170. The common story that Millar's new shop was the one formerly owned by Jacob Tonson is false, for Phillips discovered that since 1714 the site had been occupied by a mercier and a hosier.

William Wishart, Robert Wallace, and George Turnbull.[27] The first title ever registered by Millar at Stationers' Hall was Thomson's *Spring* (registered 23 Jan. 1728; published 5 June 1728), originally printed for the author but subsequently bought and reissued by the bookseller.[28] On 11 March 1729 Millar registered Thomson's play, *The Tragedy of Sophonisba*, which went through numerous impressions when it appeared in print the following year and was perhaps the first big seller for both men. He paid a relatively large sum for these titles—a total of £137.10s. for the rights to both of them—and from this time forward he purchased every copyright by Thomson that he could, including several already owned by another Scottish bookseller in London, John Millan (formerly McMillan).[29] In years to come Millar would register at least fifteen of Thomson's titles at Stationers' Hall and would have his name in the imprints of nearly one hundred of Thomson's publications, including twenty-five editions of *The Seasons*, one of the century's most popular and most litigated books of poetry, and more than a dozen editions of the *Works*.

Both the poet and the publisher were sons of the Scottish manse, and they remained lifelong friends, with nearby villas at Kew Green. A few months before he died in 1748, Thomson made reference in one of his letters to "Good-natured obliging Millar."[30] Millar's devotion continued long after Thomson's death. In 1762 Millar published a fine quarto edition of Thomson's *Works* in two volumes, with an impressive list of subscribers headed by the young King George III (who contributed £100) and including his chief minister, the Earl of Bute, as well as an admiring biography of the author by Patrick Murdoch that drew attention to the bookseller's generous tribute to "his favourite author and a much-loved friend."[31] Millar used the income from this edition to pay for an elaborate classical monument to Thomson in Westminster Abbey, designed by Robert Adam. Tobias Smollett publicly commended Millar for having "sacrificed his interest, by giving up the advantages of his copy, for the

27. Scott, *James Thomson*, 245–47.

28. Sambrook, "A Just Balance," 137–53.

29. The contract for *Spring* and *Sophonisba*, dated 16 January 1729–30, is printed in Thomson, *Letters and Documents*, 69–70, along with other contracts and correspondence. There are summaries of Millar's relations with Thomson and other major literary figures in Hall, "Andrew Millar," 184–90. For details on Thomson's publishing career, see Sambrook, *James Thomson*, and the introduction to Sambrook's edition of *The Seasons*.

30. Thomson, *Letters and Documents*, 197–98.

31. Thomson, *Works*, 1:xx.

advancement of such a generous design."[32] At the same time, building the monument was an act of Scottish patriotism, because it literally thrust a Scot into the pantheon of English poets commemorated in Westminster Abbey—in the space between Shakespeare and Nicholas Rowe.[33] The subscription list was accordingly filled with prominent Scotsmen and included three Scottish bookselling firms: Hamilton & Balfour (two sets), Kincaid & Bell (six sets), and Alexander Donaldson.

The Millar–Thomson relationship shows Millar at his best. It established his reputation as a publisher who was not only generous but also genuinely concerned about his authors, a publisher who could make money, lots of it, without exploiting those responsible for his wealth. It was this view of Millar that Samuel Johnson immortalized when he called him "the Maecenas of the age," who "raised the price of literature" (*BLJ*, 1:288, 287n3). One way he did so was by outbidding other booksellers for titles he wanted, such as William Robertson's *History of Scotland* (no. 58), which he secured in 1758 with an offer of £600 after Gavin Hamilton had offered Robertson £500. Another tactic was to give authors monetary bonuses if their books sold well: Fielding supposedly obtained a £100 gift for *Tom Jones* in 1749, in addition to the impressive sum of £600 that he had already contracted to receive.[34] That kind of generosity got the attention of authors (we know about it from a letter of Horace Walpole) and strengthened Millar's image as the London publisher of choice. Samuel Kenrick heard about this policy of gift giving directly from Millar, his friend and relation: "He told me himself that he had lost by many more publications than he had gained, and when his gains exceeded expectation, he was ready to allow the authors or their heirs to partake of them."[35] There is also a story of Millar giving an additional £100 to Mrs. Sheridan for a comedy that sold poorly, evidently out of sympathy for the author, who was told that the demand for her play was "uncommonly great" (*BLJ*, 1:287n3). Even in death Millar cultivated his image as the grateful friend of authors by willing £200 to David Hume, £250 to

32. Smollett, *Continuation*, 4:129n.

33. For a different interpretation of the patriotic significance of the monument, see Connell, "Death and the Author," 573–76.

34. Dobson, "Fielding and Andrew Millar," 184.

35. Kenrick to James Wodrow, 16 Aug. 1808, *Wodrow–Kenrick Correspondence*, no. 265. Kenrick's and Millar's mothers were cousins, and Kenrick spent his student holidays at the home of Millar's parents in Paisley. Kenrick, *Chronicles of a Nonconformist Family*, 33–34.

another of his best-selling authors, Richard Burn, £250 to Patrick Murdoch, and £200 to each of Fielding's needy sons.[36]

Millar's ability to raise the price of literature relied on professionalizing the process by which manuscripts were selected for publication. John Nichols observed that Millar "had little pretensions to Learning; but had a thorough knowledge of mankind; and a nice discrimination in selecting his literary counsellors."[37] Boswell wrote that "Millar, though himself no great judge of literature," had amassed "a very large fortune" by having "good sense enough to have for his friends very able men to give him their opinion and advice in the purchase of copy-right" (*BLJ*, 1:287). According to Kenrick, "my old friend . . . never read a book in his life; but he paid others well to read them for him, and was directed by their judgment."[38] Advice of this kind enabled Millar to make specific recommendations to authors before publication, such as suggesting to Sir James Steuart that a section on money and coinage be cut from his forthcoming *Inquiry into the Principles of Political Oeconomy* (no. 101).[39]

Who were these "literary counsellors," or "triers," as the booksellers called those who judged manuscripts for publication at their request?[40] Millar favored his Scottish authors and friends, such as Hume, Mallet, Sir John Pringle, William Rose, John Blair, John Douglas, and Patrick Murdoch.[41] Sir Andrew Mitchell, William Rouet, George Scott, and Dr. John Armstrong may also have been used in this manner. Millar entertained his Scottish triers and sometimes involved them in his publishing affairs. Writing to Mitchell on the Continent on 4 May 1764, for example, he tells of dining with Armstrong, John Forbes (son of Duncan Forbes), and "Dr Pringle, on which I depend more."[42] A particularly revealing letter, sent to William Robertson when his *History of Scotland* was published in 1759, demonstrates that decisions about publication matters were some-

36. See Millar's will, in Oliver, *History*, 2:265.

37. Hart, *Minor Lives*, 271–72.

38. Kenrick to James Wodrow, 8 May 1780, *Wodrow–Kenrick Correspondence*, no. 68.

39. Andrew Millar to Sir James Steuart, 15 Apr. 1766, University of Reading Library, MS 1393/26/2 (a).

40. Burdy, *Life of Skelton*, 92.

41. Nichols singles out Rose and also names, interestingly, William Strahan (Hart, *Minor Lives*, 272). There are many examples in the correspondence of Millar, such as his mentioning Pringle's opinion of a manuscript under consideration for publication in a letter to Cadell of 5 February 1767 (BL, Stowe MSS 755, fol. 79).

42. BL, Add. MSS 6858, fols. 31–32.

times made by a confederation of Scottish friends who met at Millar's home over a few bottles of claret or port:

> Your friend Mr Hume called last night[;] he, Rouet, G. Scott, Murdoch, Douglas, and Mallet spent the evening with me, when your health and success to your book was remembered and we agreed not to publish Hume[']s history of the Tudors] till the 20th of March which is giving you full 2 Months of Time you desire, which he most cordially agreed to, and it is my Interest more than yours to prevent their interfering.[43]

Millar also had some good English friends and literary counselors, such as Thomas Birch, Hans Sloane, and the bookseller Thomas Longman, who was appointed an executor in Millar's will. But the social and cultural world Millar inhabited in London was chiefly composed of men who have been fairly described as Anglo-Scots.[44]

Thomson and Millar were part of the first substantial wave of professional Scots to settle in London and achieve distinction there after the Union of 1707. They and some of the other members of their circle were role models for later generations of Scottish publishers and men of letters. Yet Millar's accomplishment had the effect of diminishing the appeal of the particular path to literary fame and glory followed by expatriate authors such as Thomson. Once a patriotic Scottish publisher like Millar was entrenched in London, eager to support Scottish authors with generous payments for manuscripts, those authors themselves did not have to leave Scotland; rather, they could stay at home and reap the rewards of London publication and distribution, all the while advancing themselves within the institutional framework of their chosen professions. Millar could be relied on to work out matters satisfactorily, partly because, as the bookseller put it in his letter to Robertson, it was in his personal or financial "interest" to do so, but also because he was known to have the best interests of his native land at heart. Alexander Carlyle's description of Millar as "the generous patron of Scotch authors" neatly captures this view, which combines Johnson's emphasis on booksellers as the new patrons of literature—and Millar as a particularly generous patron of that kind—with an appreciation for Millar's partiality for his countrymen.[45]

43. Millar to Robertson, 27 Jan. 1759, NLS, MS 3942, fols. 11–12.

44. See Scott, *James Thomson*, chap. 8, for an excellent discussion of the Thomson–Millar circle of Scots in London.

45. Carlyle, *Autobiography*, 456. "Millar's preferential treatment of Scottish literary figures" is noted in Abbattista, "Business of Paternoster Row," 5–50, esp. 30–31.

Similarly, David Hume spoke for many Scottish authors when he wrote to William Strahan from Edinburgh on 12 June 1758, after hearing that Millar was seriously ill: "I know few who would make a greater Loss to this Country, especially to the young Men of Letters in it" (*LDH*, 1:281). Many years later Samuel Kenrick recollected that "for personal kindnesses and services to his young countrymen, I knew of no man to whom they were under greater obligations."[46] The existence of the Scottish Enlightenment owed much to this development, for as we saw in chapter 2, during the second half of the eighteenth century repatriation in London was not usually a desirable option for professional men with successful careers in Scotland.

Beginning around the middle of the century, Millar began collaborating with Scottish partners in the publication of important new work by Scottish authors. The transitional year was 1748, when Millar and Alexander Kincaid copublished David Hume's *Three Essays, Moral and Political* (no. 9) and the "third" edition of Hume's *Essays, Moral and Political* (fig. 4.1), incorporating the three new essays from the former volume. In the same year both men also took part (along with Hamilton & Balfour at Edinburgh and three other booksellers in London, Glasgow, and Dublin) in the publication of Colin Maclaurin's posthumous *Account of Sir Isaac Newton's Philosophical Discoveries* (no. 10), edited by Millar's chief literary associate, Patrick Murdoch. In 1753 came *Essays and Treatises on Several Subjects*, in four duodecimo volumes (no. 25)—a neglected milestone in Hume's career, as I argued in chapter 1, but also significant as a seminal collaboration between Millar in London and Kincaid & Donaldson in Edinburgh. It seems likely that Millar's ties with Kincaid were rooted in a shared association with their master James M'Euen, for Kincaid had taken over M'Euen's shop in Edinburgh, as Millar had succeeded to his shop in London.

Toward the end of the 1750s this trend evolved into a significant publishing pattern, especially in association with Kincaid and his second junior partner, John Bell. In 1757 Millar copublished with Kincaid & Donaldson James Lind's *Essay on the Health of Seamen* (no. 47). The following year Kames's *Historical Law-Tracts* (no. 50) appeared with the imprint "Edinburgh: printed for A. Millar, London; and A. Kincaid, and J. Bell, Edinburgh, 1758." Then came Alexander Gerard's *An Essay on Taste* (no. 53), Francis Home's *Medical Facts and Experiments* (no. 55), and Adam Smith's *Theory of Moral Sentiments* (no. 59), all copublished in 1759, with a

46. Kenrick to Wodrow, 16 Aug. 1808, *Wodrow–Kenrick Correspondence*, no. 265.

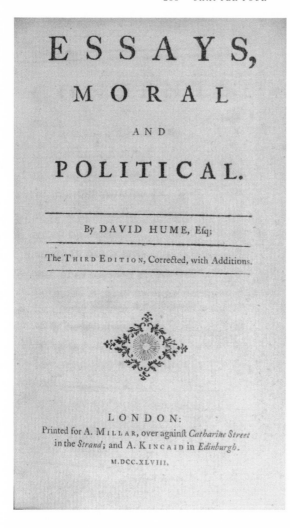

ESSAYS,

MORAL

AND

POLITICAL.

By DAVID HUME, Efq;

The THIRD EDITION, Corrected, with Additions.

LONDON:

Printed for A. MILLAR, over againſt *Catharine Street*
in the *Strand*; and A. KINCAID in *Edinburgh*.

M.DCC.XLVIII.

Fig. 4.1. The copublication in 1748 of David Hume's *Three Essays, Moral and Political* and a new edition of Hume's *Essays, Moral and Political* by Andrew Millar and Alexander Kincaid—both of whom had been apprentices of James M'Euen of Edinburgh—marked the beginning of large-scale collaboration between London and Edinburgh booksellers in publishing the new books of the Scottish Enlightenment. Thomas Fisher Rare Book Library, University of Toronto.

London imprint. The same publishers produced Lord Kames's folio *Principles of Equity* in 1760 (no. 62), Matthew Stewart's *Tracts, Physical and Mathematical* in 1761 (no. 69, also with Nourse in London and Sands in Edinburgh), Kames's *Elements of Criticism* (no. 73) and George Campbell's *Dissertation on Miracles* (no. 72, sold by Millar and others) in 1762, the supplement to Matthew Stewart's *Tracts* in 1763 (no. 69), Thomas Reid's *An Inquiry into the Human Mind* in 1764 (no. 88), and Alexander Gerard's *Dissertations on the Genius of Christianity* in 1766 (no. 94). After Millar began to cultivate Thomas Cadell as his junior partner and successor, Millar & Cadell combined with Kincaid & Bell to copublish Adam Ferguson's *Essay on the History of Civil Society* in 1767 (no. 99). It was a remarkable run, during which the book history of the Scottish Enlightenment may be said to have entered its mature phase. For the first time, booksellers in London and Edinburgh were collaborating on a regular basis in the production of important new work by a growing number of Scottish authors whose books covered a wide variety of genres and whose birth dates spanned more than three decades—from Kames, born in 1696, to Gerard, born in 1728.

At the same time, Millar continued to publish books by Scottish authors under the imprint of his own firm alone, including, among others, Hume's *Philosophical Essays concerning Human Understanding* (no. 8), all the volumes of Hume's *History of England* from the second onward (nos. 46, 56, and 74), Robertson's *History of Scotland* (no. 58), two books by his old friend Robert Wallace (nos. 52 and 70), several plays by John Home (nos. 44, 51, and 63, the first of which was also published separately by Hamilton & Balfour), James Ferguson's *Lectures on Select Subjects* (no. 61), John Dalrymple's *Essay towards a General History of Feudal Property* (no. 43), and Sir James Steuart's *Inquiry into the Principles of Political Oeconomy* (no. 101, with Cadell and, silently, Strahan).

During the two decades preceding his death in 1768, Millar had a hand in more than forty titles in the database and was by far the most prolific and influential publisher of Scottish Enlightenment books. We can only speculate about the full impact of his publishing policies on the Scottish Enlightenment, for it will never be known how many Scots he inspired to become authors, or how many manuscripts that might otherwise have ended up as obscure or provincial publications became popular and profitable tomes as a result of his involvement. Furthermore, the publishing policies that Millar began lived on after his death, when his successor Thomas Cadell and his principal printer William Strahan, along with their associates in Edinburgh, continued his legacy.

Yet for all his greatness as a publisher, Andrew Millar had other, less commendable attributes. A member of his circle of Anglo-Scots described him as "a good-natured fellow, and not an unpleasant companion, but he was a little contracted by his business; had the dross of a bookseller about him."[47] He cut a ludicrous figure at Harrogate, where he came into fashionable company each morning, with his extravagant "city-wife" (Jane Johnston, daughter of a London printmaker, whom Millar had married in 1729), wearing an "old well-worn suit of clothes" and looking so "ridicu-

47. Dr. William Robertson, the physician, in *The Bee* (1791), quoted in Scott, *James Thomson*, 247.

lous" that other guests called him "Peter Pamphlet."[48] He was commonly said to be uncouth and unlettered, even "illiterate," according to one who knew him well,[49] although this judgment is certainly too severe.

If it were no more than dressing shabbily and not being a man of high culture, Millar might have come off as merely odd, or perhaps endearingly eccentric. But there was more. He was sometimes ruthless in his dealings with other booksellers, printers, and even, on occasion, the same authors whom he patronized. Samuel Johnson said privately that "A. Millar, who got £60,000 by his trade, [was] so habitually drunk that Strahan for twenty years did not know it."[50] Perhaps due to the effects of alcohol, Millar had a reputation for sometimes being overly aggressive and even dishonorable in his business dealings. In a satirical survey of the London booksellers written in 1766 by one of their number, Henry Dell, he is mocked for his Scottishness—still a distinguishing characteristic after some four decades in London—and his "meanness":

> A *Scotchman* next, the muse presents to view;
> True to his int'rest, and to meanness too:
> For no bright deed the muse can him prefer;
> Like *Druger*'s dog he's always snarling *er*.[51]

Examples of his bad form are plentiful. Sir Walter Scott told the story of Millar's protecting the huge investment he had made in Fielding's *Amelia* (1751), for which the author had received as much as £1,000, by generating an unwarranted competition among the other London booksellers.[52] Precisely because he rewarded his best authors so generously, and sometimes paid large amounts for a copyright before knowing if a book would sell, Millar was adamant about protecting his property, and he led the parade of lawsuits that London publishers brought against Scottish booksellers for reprinting titles they claimed to own by right of common law, even though the statutory copyright had expired. In particular, Millar was not prepared to let booksellers in Scotland get away with reprinting James Thomson's profitable poetry; ironically, it was his zeal to protect his claim

48. Carlyle, *Autobiography*, 456.

49. Kenrick to James Wodrow, 16 Aug. 1808, *Wodrow–Kenrick Correspondence*, no. 265.

50. Boswell, *Laird of Auchinleck*, 99. The anecdote appears differently in the *Life of Johnson*, where Millar is identified only as "a bookseller" and Strahan as "his most intimate friend" (*BLJ*, 3:389).

51. Belanger, "Directory," 10.

52. Dobson, "Fielding and Andrew Millar," 186.

to unrestricted ownership of *The Seasons* that ultimately resulted in the House of Lords quashing the principle of perpetual copyright in 1774 on Donaldson's appeal. He was eager to sue Alexander Kincaid and others for allegedly violating his copyrights at the same time that he was carrying on a thriving business with Kincaid in joint publications of new work by Scottish authors.

Some authors also had reason to complain. Thomas Hollis claimed (though the bookseller denied it) that Millar agreed to terms for publishing two different editions he had edited—one of Locke's *Letters on Toleration* and the other of Milton's prose works—and broke his word on both occasions. Hollis was so furious about Millar's alleged treachery that he is said to have thrown into the fire Millar's letter of 14 May 1767 denying his claims about the nature of the agreement for the Milton edition.[53] Boswell relates a famous anecdote about the messenger who carried to Millar the last sheets of Johnson's monumental *Dictionary* relaying Millar's response to Johnson: "thank GOD I have done with him"; but attention is usually placed on Johnson's witty retort ("I am glad . . . that he thanks GOD for anything") rather than on the inappropriate and ungracious nature of Millar's remark. Even the memorial edition of Thomson's *Works* that Millar published to raise money for the poet's monument is open to a more cynical interpretation: in praising Thomson, Millar also contributed to his own reputation as Thomson's nurturing bookseller-patron.

Many questionable incidents occurred in Millar's relationship with David Hume. Millar would help to make Hume rich and famous, and when things were going well the philosopher was proud to be numbered among his publisher's friends (*LDH*, 1:466). But things did not always go well. Millar promised to burn two controversial essays that Hume wished to suppress but actually allowed some copies to get into circulation.[54] In January 1757 he apparently showed David Garrick a letter from Hume that criticized the touchy theater manager for rejecting John Home's tragedy of *Douglas*, leading Garrick to commission John Hawkesworth to write an anonymous pamphlet against Hume.[55] The following May Hume angrily accused Millar of showing his personal letters to John Brown, who used them in a published attack (*LDH*, 1:249–50). Five months later Hume wrote a confidential letter to Strahan, asking advice about an unscrupulous attempt by Millar to renege on a prior offer for his next book

53. Blackburne, *Memoirs of Thomas Hollis*, 1:232, 365–67.

54. Mossner, *Life of David Hume*, 328–31.

55. Lonsdale, "Thomas Gray," 63.

"and extort it from me at a somewhat lower Price, which is so ungenteel a Method of Proceeding that I cannot allow myself to believe it, and it woud much discourage me from dealing with him" (*LDH*, 1:269–70). On 23 May 1764 Hume scolded Millar from Paris for publishing a new edition of part of his *History* "without consulting me" (*LDH*, 1:443). In 1768 he caught Strahan in a lie about the number of copies that had been printed of the first octavo edition of his *History of England* in 1763. Strahan, in admitting his complicity, insisted that he had been "only the Mouth of another Person, who was afterwards sorry he had occasion to conceal the Number of the Impression from you."[56] That other person was Andrew Millar, who had overestimated the market by printing 5,000 copies in April 1763 (SA 48800, fol. 141) and then, in an attempt to conceal the fact that so many copies had been printed and remained unsold (*LDH*, 2:360), reissued them in 1767 as if they constituted a new edition.[57] Two years after the bookseller's death, Hume was still carping about "the Rapaciousness of Mr Millar" because of this incident (*LDH*, 2:228).

Thus, Millar epitomized two opposite types: the avaricious bookseller who acts only from narrow self-interest, and the generous bookseller who is well loved by his authors. Both aspects of Millar's personality are conveyed in two adjacent articles in *The Bee* for June 1791. In the first article, a writer identified as "Authenticus" draws a sharp distinction between two different aspects of books: their power to generate profit and their "intrinsic value, by which I mean the power of informing the understanding, directing the judgement, or improving the heart of the reader."[58] Determining the "intrinsic value" of books is the rightful task of legislators, moralists, and divines, argues Authenticus, but not of booksellers:

> The proper business of the bookseller is *to make money in his vocation;* all other concerns are, to him, matters of little importance; and the art of *book-making,* as fostered by these Maecenases, must, of course, consist in dressing up high-seasoned dishes, calculated to provoke the appetite of their customers, without troubling their heads about the effects that these may afterwards have upon their constitutions. If it brings money into their pockets, that is all *their* concern.—And do they not, in this respect, act upon the same principle with men in almost every other vocation? (128)

56. Strahan to Hume, 27 July 1768, NLS, MS 23157, no. 59.

57. SA 48800, fol. 141; *LDH*, 2:360; Van Holthoon, "Hume," 133–52.

58. Authenticus, "Anecdotes of Mr. Andrew Millar," 128.

This piece appeared around the same time as Boswell's *Life of Johnson*, in which Johnson refers to Millar as "the Maecenas of the age" (*BLJ*, 1:288), but Authenticus invokes the comparison facetiously. As the last sentence makes clear, his aim is not only to show that booksellers act exclusively from self-interested motives but also to establish that in doing so they are no different from the rest of us. Millar is the model for booksellers, and booksellers, in turn, are the models for mankind.

To substantiate his cynical interpretation of booksellers' motives, Authenticus recounts an amusing anecdote about Millar's early years in the trade. When Millar first set up his business in the Strand, Authenticus writes, he had "but a scanty stock," and his first ten or twelve publications were "good books in philosophy, history and morality, that tended to enlarge the understanding, and improve the heart" but did not sell well. When his "stock of cash was nearly exhausted," a more worldly friend advised him to publish a translation of a popular, "b[*awd*]y" work on the notorious case of Catherine Cadière and Father Girard, a French scandal concerning a Jesuit priest accused of raping a girl in his care.[59] "The scruples of Mr. Andrew began to subside," says Authenticus, and he published the book after paying £20 to have it translated. His wife, however, "expressed her disapprobation of the undertaking, in very unequivocal terms" (129). Absorbing her abuse in silence ("for Mr. Andrew was a man of a meek and patient disposition"), Millar earned seven hundred guineas (£735) from three editions published in the space of a month. One evening after dinner he spread the guineas on the table, to the astonishment of his wife, who declared, upon learning the source of the money, "praised be God for such a lucky discovery; could we find twenty such books, our fortune might be made" (130).

Should Authenticus's story be taken literally, or is it merely a moral (or immoral) tale? We cannot be certain. Millar seems to have been involved in publishing some of the many pamphlets on the Father Girard scandal in 1732,[60] and Hume referred to the "Extravagance" and "tenacious Avarice" of his wife Jane (*LDH*, 1:311, 2:226). On the other hand, we have seen that Millar himself was not a one-dimensional figure, interested only in maximizing his profits. To illustrate this point, the editor of *The Bee*, James Anderson, appended to the Girard anecdote a brief note, followed by an article of his own. Anderson does not take issue with the verac-

59. Maza, *Private Lives*, 38.
60. Sher, with Amory, "From Scotland to the Strand," 64–65.

ity of the story related by Authenticus, but he does challenge the latter's cynical interpretation of Millar the bookseller, and of mankind in general. Authenticus's anecdote had been introduced with a critical remark about Anderson's idealism as a moralist: "I have a strong suspicion, Mr. Editor, that you have not been initiated into the mysteries of the bookseller's business" (127–28). Anderson responds by pledging to continue his moralizing ways and to cease publishing when the audience for such an approach no longer exists. He also offers a very different anecdote to show that Millar "never altogether abandoned those antiquated principles, which many of his profession would now laugh at as unfashionable and ridiculous;—yet honest Andrew Millar, with all these follies, made more money in the end, than any of his profession I have yet heard of."[61]

Anderson's anecdote concerns Richard Burn (1709–1785), author of *The Justice of the Peace, and Parish Officer*, which Millar originally published in 1755 in two octavo volumes. According to Anderson, when Burn brought his manuscript to London, another publisher offered him £20 for it. He then tried Millar, who showed him every mark of courtesy, including dining with the author each day that he had the manuscript in his care. Millar, "who did not depend upon his own judgment in cases of this sort" (132), sent the manuscript to his usual adviser on legal subjects, who told him it would be a bargain at £200 because it was well written and was likely to have a large sale. The next day Millar offered Burn the full £200, and they drank a bottle of "good port" to celebrate the arrangement. The book turned out to be one of his most profitable titles, and "Mr. Millar, with a spirit of candour and liberality, that does not always belong to men of his profession, frankly sent a hundred guineas to the author for every edition of the book that was printed in his lifetime; and there were many: in so much, that by the sale of this book alone, he cleared no less than eleven thousand pounds" (132–33). Although there is no way to confirm the accuracy of Anderson's account, we know that Millar published ten editions of Burn's book during his lifetime, including one in quarto (1764) and two in folio (1756 and 1758). It continued to be profitable for his successor, Thomas Cadell, whose carriage was said to be kept in motion by "the four wheels" of his best-selling "four B's": Blackstone, Blair, Buchan, and Burn.[62]

According to Anderson, Millar not only paid Burn one hundred guineas for every edition (even though he had no legal obligation to do so) but

61. A[nderson], "Second Anecdote," 131–33, quoting 131.
62. [West], "Letters to My Son," 310.

also bought him a pipe or large cask of the best port in London every year and arranged for this practice to continue in later generations. (We have also seen, though Anderson does not mention it, that Millar left Burn £250 in his will.) For Anderson, the moral of the story is that honesty and generosity, rather than greed, constituted the chief source of Millar's wealth:

> It was because of Mr. Millar's candid manner in this and other instances of a similar kind, that he was enabled to acquire that immense fortune of which he was possessed; for during his life, every man who had a good book either to print on his own account, or to dispose of, went directly to Mr. Millar with it. They seldom higgled on terms, because they knew he would not hesitate to give an additional allowance if the sale should be such as to enable him to do it. Thus, his profits were for the most part very sure. In this way, he experienced the fate of many other men, *That honesty, though it may not seem to be the most direct road to wealth, is in the end the best policy.*
>
> Let those who have sense and spirit to do it, profit by his example. (133)

The exchange of Millar anecdotes in the pages of *The Bee* was less about Millar himself than about the character of publishing and, beyond that, the nature of formal relationships in a commercial world. Both Authenticus and James Anderson consider large profits to be a legitimate end of publishing; the point in dispute is how a publisher achieves that end. For Authenticus, the process is essentially sordid, because human beings are fundamentally selfish creatures. For Anderson, a patriotic improver by vocation, honesty and generosity are the key traits, and morality and prosperity go hand in hand.[63] If Millar had merely "raised the price of literature" by paying more than any other bookseller for manuscripts, he would not have seemed so praiseworthy to a moralist like Anderson. It was the fact that he gave authors substantial gifts, over and above what he agreed to pay them by contract, that separated Millar from other publishers of his day and made him a symbol of the man of business who is both ethical and successful.

The international significance of this aspect of Millar's reputation is shown by a letter that the Philadelphia physician Benjamin Rush sent to James Madison in 1790—a year *before* Authenticus and Anderson crossed

---

63. Cf. the preface to Anderson's *Observations on the Means of Exciting a Spirit of National Industry* (no. 179).

paths in *The Bee* and Johnson complimented Millar in Boswell's *Life*. In justifying the proper course of action for the U.S. Congress to take on a particular matter, Rush commented that Andrew Millar had made so much money from William Robertson's *History of Scotland* that "he sent him every year as long as he lived afterwards a pipe of madeira wine. This was natural justice."[64] Whether or not the story is true, it demonstrates once again how Millar's generosity toward authors grew over the course of several decades into an ideal of ethical conduct in commercial transactions, embodying a kind of justice that was "natural" because it went beyond the letter of the law to do what was morally right.

Was Andrew Millar a greedy, drunken hypocrite driven strictly by hunger for profit, or was he a generous benefactor who frequently forsook his private interest for the sake of doing the right thing and assisting worthy authors, particularly those from Scotland? There is a great deal riding on the answer to this question, because it goes to the issue of the prime motive for putting the Scottish Enlightenment into print. It will not do to deny the existence of either of these aspects of Millar's personality and career, in the face of so much evidence to the contrary. Nor is it helpful to divide each publisher into a businessman who seeks monetary gain and a private citizen who may have other, loftier motives, as Robert Darnton has suggested.[65] Rather, it is necessary to recognize publishers, like authors, as complex individuals, whose actions cannot be easily compartmentalized or reduced to a single motivating factor. Millar undoubtedly published for profit, and he ended his life a very wealthy man, with a splendid home in Pall Mall that Robert Adam designed for him. But he also wished to be seen as a patron of literature and learning, and of authors, especially those who hailed from his native country. From such complexities were the books of the Scottish Enlightenment made.

From Strachan to Strahan: Alienation and Identity

Like Andrew Millar, William Strahan—or Strachan, as he was known in Scotland—emigrated to London while in his early twenties and made his fortune there. Born in Edinburgh on 24 March 1715, he enjoyed a moderately privileged upbringing, for his father was a graduate of the University of Edinburgh who had practiced law before becoming a customs clerk, and William was educated at a grammar (or Latin) school, probably

---

64. Rush to Madison, 27 Feb. 1790, in Rush, *Letters*, 1:538–39.

65. Darnton, "Two Paths," 282.

the prestigious High School of Edinburgh.[66] He was well connected, being a relation of the influential Wishart family that produced two principals of the University of Edinburgh in this period, William Wishart I and II, as well as the latter's brother George, dubbed "the Addison of Scottish preachers."[67] Although he is almost certainly the William Strachan who appears in the matriculation roll of Adam Watt's Humanity (Latin) class in 1729–30, along with John Balfour and Gavin Hamilton,[68] Strahan never got an opportunity to complete his education at the university. Around this time, if not sooner, he was apprenticed to an Edinburgh printing firm. This event defined his self-image for life, since he always minimized the advantages he had enjoyed in Scotland and portrayed himself as a completely self-made man. "When People, like you and I, who were born to little or nothing, follow their Business with the time spent of Industry in the early Part of their Lives," he wrote to William Creech on 21–22 February 1777, "it generally, unless some very unforeseen Calamities interpose, brings them into a respectable and independent Situation, which richly rewards them for the many anxious and careful Hours necessarily spent in Pursuit" (WCL). He once remarked that if he had £100 a year as a young man in Edinburgh, he would never have moved to London.[69] His obituary in *The Lounger* observed that some people were inclined to censure Strahan for boasting about his humble origins, considering it "as a kind of ostentation in which he was weak enough to indulge."[70]

It is usually thought that Strahan was apprenticed to John Mosman and William Brown. However, the only evidence to support this claim is a letter of 17 January 1743 that Strahan wrote to James Read in Pennsylvania, stating that David Hall (whose name appears in Edinburgh guild records as an apprentice of Mosman and Brown from 1729) was "my Fellow-prentice."[71] Since Hall was born one year before Strahan, in 1714, they would indeed have been Edinburgh apprentices at the same time, but the letter does not actually say that they were apprentices in the same firm. In September 1756 Strahan told Hall, now comfortably settled in

---

66. That Strahan attended a grammar school is stated in the anonymous obituary published in *The Lounger* on 20 August 1785, reproduced in Hart, *Minor Lives*, 279. Cochrane, *Dr. Johnson's Printer*, 2, identifies this school as the Edinburgh High School.

67. Ramsay, *Scotland and Scotsmen*, 1:229–30, 247–49, quoting 249.

68. McDougall, "Gavin Hamilton, John Balfour and Patrick Neill," 3, 10.

69. Boswell, *Ominous Years*, 100.

70. Hart, *Minor Lives*, 279.

71. Quoted in Cochrane, *Dr. Johnson's Printer*, 2, 60.

Philadelphia, that most of their old acquaintances in Scotland "are dwindled away to nothing," and he proceeded to list ten men who apparently once comprised, with Strahan and Hall, a tight-knit "Sett of Printers." The only two among them whose masters can now be identified were Walter Pearson (apprentice of James Watson from 1721) and Peter Mathie (apprentice of John Moncur from 1722). Strahan might have called this group of ten young printers "fellow-prentices," but their apprenticeships were not necessarily served with Mosman and Brown.[72]

It is more likely that Strahan, like Kincaid and Millar, was apprenticed to James M'Euen. A footnote in Robert Fleming's anonymous life of William Creech, published in 1815, asserts that Creech's master, Kincaid, had succeeded "James Macewen . . . a bookseller of considerable note, who had also an establishment in London. Mr William Strahan, Mr Andrew Millar, (both of whom early settled in London,) and Mr Kincaid were his apprentices, a circumstance which no doubt laid the foundation of the intimate connection between these eminent men."[73] Circumstantial evidence supports the feasibility of Fleming's claim. Mosman, Brown, and M'Euen were in business together in 1718, and it is entirely possible that Mosman and Brown's apprentices remained closely associated with M'Euen's in subsequent years. Because M'Euen was both a printer and a bookseller, members of both professions could have served apprenticeships with him. Andrew Millar was more than eight years older than Strahan, but the two men were closely associated in London, and a shared connection with M'Euen would help to explain the genesis of their relationship even if their periods of apprenticeship did not actually coincide.

Strahan was only five years younger than Kincaid, about whom he reminisced affectionately to Creech on 30 January 1777, a few days after Kincaid's death: "Mr. Kincaid was the *oldest Friend* I had in the World; for we were acquainted *half a Century;* the best part of the time, and till I left Scotland, intimate Friends; and since that Period, maintained, as you know, a pretty constant Correspondence, considering the Distance of our abodes" (WCL). This statement is consistent with Fleming's contention that their intimacy grew out of their apprenticeships with M'Euen. As in Millar's case, the M'Euen connection also helps to explain how Strahan initially got started in London, perhaps during the latter part of his apprenticeship. Another link was George Strahan of Cornhill, a possible relation who served a London apprenticeship (as George Strachin) from

72. Strahan to Hall, 11 Sept. 1756, American Philosophical Society.

73. [Fleming], "Account," xvi–xvii, note.

1692 to 1702. George Strahan was one of the sellers of M'Euen's London catalogues and copublished the second edition of Robert Millar's *History of the Propagation of Christianity* with M'Euen, and his name appears in the Strahan Archive as William's first printing account.

Whatever the precise nature of William Strahan's path to London, there can be no doubt that Andrew Millar was the key to his success there. Strahan struck out on his own as a London printer in 1738, after serving as a compositor in the firm of William Bowyer from May 1736 to February 1738,[74] and perhaps briefly as the partner of Thomas Hart. Millar first used Strahan for printing a publication in April 1739 and by early 1740 was employing him to print several of his Scottish books, including 750 copies of George Turnbull's *Principles of Moral Philosophy* in the winter and 2,000 copies of Allan Ramsay's *Tea-Table Miscellany* in the spring (SA 48800, fol. 3). By then he was using Strahan regularly for large undertakings and important titles, such as Fielding's *Joseph Andrews* and *Miscellanies* in 1743, the *Universal History* in 1747, and Hume's *Essays, Moral and Political* and Maclaurin's *Account of Sir Isaac Newton's Philosophical Discoveries* in 1748. It has been calculated that, in the period from 1751 until Millar's retirement, Strahan's account with Millar generated about £9,000 worth of printing.[75] Once their relationship was well established, Strahan was called on to print most of the major works by Scottish authors that Millar published or copublished in London during the 1750s and 1760s. Occasionally Millar would place one of his Scottish books with another London printer, as when he had William Bowyer print Alexander Gerard's *Essay on Taste* (no. 53) in April 1759,[76] and other London booksellers would sometimes hire Strahan to print Scottish books for them, as Becket & de Hondt did with James Macpherson's Ossianic epics (nos. 71 and 83). By and large, however, Strahan was, for the better part of thirty years, "the fawning humble servant of A. Millar," in the words of Samuel Kenrick, referring to the period around 1760.[77]

Strahan steadily built his career as a book printer in London, and his family grew along with his business. Although Presbyterian himself, he married in July 1738 Margaret Elphingston, the daughter of an Edin-

74. Maslen, "William Strahan," 250–51.

75. Harlan, "William Strahan," 144.

76. Maslen and Lancaster, *Bowyer Ledgers*, 325.

77. Samuel Kenrick to James Wodrow, 8 May 1780, *Wodrow–Kenrick Correspondence*, no. 68. Kenrick was contrasting Strahan's stature in 1780 with the scene he had witnessed in London "20 years ago."

burgh Episcopalian minister, and from 1740 the birth of their five surviving children, coupled with the growth of the firm, created pressures
for more space. In 1748 Strahan moved from Wine Office Court, where
he had been based throughout the 1740s, to larger quarters at 10 Little
New Street, which he expanded within a few years into a seventeen-room
home along with business premises that he privately called "beyond Dispute the largest and best Printing-house in Britain."[78] The motives for
the move and the subsequent expansion were largely technological and
economic: as his business prospered, Strahan needed more space to accommodate more presses, as he told Hall, with whom he built up a profitable transatlantic trade.[79] When the renovations were complete, he had
nine presses in operation (eleven by 1753), although his letters to Hall
from the early 1750s express some concern about his ability to keep them
all going. Whether or not one interprets this development in the manner of Alvin Kernan, as a technological impetus to greater production of
printed material, it is certainly a matter of some importance for our story.
During the early and mid-1750s, at the very time that the Scottish Enlightenment was beginning to emerge as a large-scale publishing project,
Strahan was building the technological infrastructure that enabled him
to print the many texts that Millar and other publishers sent his way. At
the same time, he was increasingly able to assume a role as a printer, and
partial proprietor, of newspapers and periodicals, which would become
valuable tools in promoting the authors whose works he printed. His expanded printing facilities also put him in a position to buy into the lucrative patents in law printing (1762) and state printing (as king's printer,
1767, taking effect in 1770); these patents, in turn, generated greater profits and increased the need for more presses, which numbered more than
two dozen in all parts of the business by 1770 and continued to increase
after that time.[80] The culmination of this process of technological expan-

78. Strahan to David Hall, 1 Nov. 1753, quoted in Cochrane, *Dr. Johnson's Printer*,
102. For a description of the rooms in his private home and their contents at the time
of his death, see SA 48901, fols. 282–83.

79. Harlan, "William Strahan's American Book Trade," 235–44; Cochrane,
Dr. Johnson's Printer, chap. 6.

80. Hernlund, "William Strahan," table 1, p. 42, shows a breakdown in 1770 of
twelve presses in his private business, nine presses doing the work of king's printer,
and four presses devoted to patent law printing—a grand total of twenty-five presses,
not counting four additional proof presses distributed through the three branches of
the business.

sion and capital accumulation was Strahan's career as a major publisher of Enlightenment books in association with Thomas Cadell, as discussed in the next chapter.

Strahan's sense of personal and national identity held considerable significance for his life in the book trade. Strahan's change of his surname suggests the fundamental tension in the identity of Scots who attempted to remake themselves in London during the eighteenth century. By omitting the letter *c* from the name Strachan, he was removing a guttural sound that had no English equivalent and that threatened to conjure up barbarous associations in London. In some respects, Strahan's entire career can be viewed as a successful exercise in anglicization. Once he brought his wife to London in 1738, he did not set foot in Scotland again for eleven years, and for the rest of his life he purported to view it as an outsider. His early hero as a printer was the Londoner Samuel Richardson, at least until a suspicion of unethical behavior turned Richardson violently against him in 1758.[81] Strahan worked his way up in the Stationers' Company, becoming free of it by redemption on 3 October 1738, a liveryman in 1742, and master of the company in 1774, and he bequeathed to it £1,000 from his fortune. His family penetrated a very different English institution when his son George took orders in the Church of England, and Strahan himself, like Millar before him, was buried in an Anglican church despite his Presbyterianism.[82] He also followed the example of Millar by becoming active among London publishers in their struggle against booksellers and printers in Scotland who reprinted works that the Londoners considered their perpetual property, and after the House of Lords struck down that concept in 1774, he played a leading role in scheming to keep perpetual copyright alive in practice if not in law.[83] Strahan was deeply concerned about eliminating Scotticisms and worked hard to purify his English prose, eventually becoming a recognized arbiter of English style and vocabulary among his countrymen, including even the fastidious David Hume (*LDH*, 2:259). As we shall see, he sometimes castigated Scottish authors for their clannish ways. He eventually entered

81. Sale, *Samuel Richardson*, 84, quotes a letter from Richardson of June 1758 on "a false and perfidious Scotchman," believed to be Strahan, who had endeared himself to him while secretly attempting to undermine his business. See also Eaves and Kimpel, *Samuel Richardson*, 504

82. Cochrane, *Dr. Johnson's Printer*, 154–55.

83. Sher, "Corporatism and Consensus," 32–93.

Parliament as a member for Malmesbury (1774–80) and Wootton Bassett (1780–84) in Wiltshire, fervently supporting Lord North during the American war.[84]

While remaking himself as a kind of Englishman, Strahan could not escape the lure of his native land. He remained preoccupied with his Scottishness even as he tried to transcend it. In 1749, during his first trip back to Scotland after settling in London, he opened his soul in a series of letters to his beloved mentor Samuel Richardson.[85] The admission that "I am now almost become a stranger to this country" (24 Aug.; 1:139–42) motivates him to experience the ancient and "curious" aspects of Scotland, which he sets out to do, beginning with a visit to Holyrood Palace in Edinburgh, and continuing for more than twenty years. His experience is complicated by the realization that, in addition to the trauma of rediscovering his homeland from the outside, he must accept that Scotland itself had undergone extensive changes during his absence, causing him to reflect on "the mutability of human affairs" (17 Aug.; 1:137). At Glasgow he is particularly impressed, like most eighteenth-century travelers, by the town's alteration "for the better, in trade, since I was last there" (2 Sept.; 1:143); the same is true at nearby Paisley, where he finds the economy has made advances even since Andrew Millar visited the previous year. By the end of the summer, Strahan seems almost awestruck by all the things he has seen ("What an amazing variety in one little island" [21 Sept.; 1:154]) and then waxes sentimental about his "parting with dear friends, some of whom I am sure I shall see no more" (1 Oct.; 1:156). "Had I a tolerable pen," he continues, "I could tell you how exquisitely pleasing the sight of my native country has been to me; and how easily, how naturally, how cordially, I have renewed old friendships. . . . I could paint to you the analogy between an excursion of this kind, and the journey of life itself" (1:156–57).

Strahan subsequently made at least seven more excursions to Scotland. Although he left no accounts comparable to those in his correspondence with Richardson in 1749, he wrote occasional letters documenting his

84. Namier's account in Namier and Brooke, *House of Commons*, 3:489–91; Cochrane, *Dr. Johnson's Printer*, chaps. 12 and 13.

85. In the following paragraph, Strahan's letters to Richardson from the summer and early autumn of 1749 are cited parenthetically from Richardson, *Correspondence*. Strahan's father had died sometime before 1742, and in the first of these letters Strahan tells Richardson: "I love you as my father" (17 Aug.; 1:138). Cf. Eaves and Kimpel, *Samuel Richardson*, 160–61

ongoing sense of estrangement amid hospitality and friendship. At the time of his second Scottish jaunt in 1751, for example, he wrote to David Hall: "All your Friends that I know of are dead except some of the Geds and Freebairns; so that this wou'd be a Strange place to you as indeed it is to me; tho' I know a good many People in it."[86] Strange place or no, Scotland was very much on Strahan's mind, and in 1756 he allowed himself to dream of traveling there with his old friend: "Shall we never travel to Scotland together, and view the many Changes that have happened in Auld Reekie since you left it? Lord, how it would strike you, were you just now at the Cross! Take my Word for it, such a Jaunt would give you more Joy than you can easily conceive. I am sure there would not be two happier Souls in the Country."[87] In 1780 Strahan published an anonymous letter in *The Mirror* (1 Apr. 1780) that is devoted mostly to the theme of mutability and estrangement. Returning to Scotland after settling in London, he writes, "I found myself, in almost every sense of the word, an utter stranger." He is upset by many of the changes he has encountered in the city of his youth and speculates, in the same spirit as in his letters to Richardson more than three decades earlier, that such changes may incur our displeasure because they remind us of our own impermanence. He is delighted by some new developments, such as the "spirit of industry" that he detects in the recent growth of Scottish manufacturing, and in regard to at least one issue—the need for replacing the "plain, mean, unadorned building" housing the University of Edinburgh—he makes a passionate appeal for action. But the prevailing tone of his *Mirror* article is melancholy over Scotland's changing face—a sentiment deeply rooted in Strahan's sense of personal loss, or abandonment, of his native land.

Strahan also kept travel diaries that outlined his activities and meetings during his Scottish jaunts of 1751, 1759, 1766, 1768, 1773, and 1777.[88] They reveal his constant quest to experience the most interesting and unusual features in his homeland, and they demonstrate his continuing concern with Scottish social questions such as health care, poverty, agricultural improvement, and economic change. "The whole Country wears a quite new Face," he observes in his diary at the end of his 1768 visit, in reference to agriculture, manufacturing, and architecture, "and affords a striking Proof, to those who remember it half a Century ago, how very

---

86. Strahan to Hall, 27 July 1751, in Pomfret, "Some Further Letters," 461.

87. Strahan to Hall, 11 Sept. 1756, quoted (but misdated) in Cochrane, *Dr. Johnson's Printer*, 88. Hall would die in America without ever returning to Britain.

88. American Philosophical Society, B/St 83, cited under date.

transitory every thing is in this Life, and how very quickly the Fashion of this World passeth away." The Scottish jaunts gave Strahan a chance to escape from the pressures of business in the metropolis and to see relations, renew acquaintances with old friends, and discuss publishing projects with booksellers and authors. Most of the individuals he visited in Scotland fall into one or more of these three categories.

With regard to family, Strahan records visits to his mother and his in-laws, the Elphingstons or Elphinstons, as well as frequent encounters with William and George Wishart. The Wishart connection illustrates how closely linked the categories of kin, friend, and author, as well as pastor, could sometimes be, for Strahan always considered William and George Wishart to be friends as well as relations,[89] and two of the ways he showed his respect were to hear them preach in Edinburgh and to print or publish their sermons. Andrew Millar had begun publishing sermons by the Wisharts almost at the outset of his publishing career; when Strahan set up shop in London he printed their works for Millar more than once, and perhaps for himself on at least one other occasion.[90] George Wishart continued to be one of his closest friends, and when he died, in the same year as Strahan himself, Strahan willed £50 to each of Wishart's sons.[91]

The Wisharts were not Strahan's only link with the Scots Presbyterian clergy. On his Scottish jaunts Strahan regularly visited Paisley, "where Mr. Millar's father is minister, a venerable old man."[92] He continued to visit the Millar family after the death of Robert Millar in 1752 and also made a point of visiting Andrew's brothers Henry, the minister of Neilston, and William of Walkinshaw.[93] Strahan had a close bond with Robert Wallace,

89. E.g., Strahan to Hume, 14 May 1769, NLS, MS 23157, no. 60.

90. ESTC lists one sermon by George Wishart that Strahan printed for Millar in 1746, and two works by William Wishart (one a volume of sermons) that were printed by Strahan and sold by Millar in London and by Hamilton & Balfour in Edinburgh. Another sermon by George Wishart that appeared in 1746 was printed by Strahan without any indication of a bookseller's involvement.

91. Public Record Office, Probate 11, no. 1132. Strahan's travel journals record frequent meetings with Wishart in Edinburgh. In November 1782 Hugh Blair wrote to Strahan in London: "Your old friend Geo. Wishart, now in his 81st or 82d year, is surprisingly well; and still preaches away." In Zachs, *Hugh Blair's Letters to His Publishers.*

92. Strahan to Richardson, 2 Sept. 1749, Richardson, *Correspondence*, 1:144. Cf. Strahan Journals, American Philosophical Society, 6 Aug. 1751.

93. Strahan Journals, American Philosophical Society, 24 Aug. 1759, 28 Aug. 1768, 18 and 27 Aug. 1773, and 13 Aug. 1777.

another clergyman whom Millar published, and Strahan printed, and once again the relationship was personal as well as professional. Strahan socialized with Wallace on his Scottish jaunts (e.g., 30 Aug. 1759) and later negotiated with him about publishing one of his works. After discussing publication details in a letter of 7 March 1768, Strahan switches to a personal mode, remarking that "I propose paying you a Visit next Summer" when in Scotland.[94] He proceeds to pay his compliments to Mrs. Wallace and their son George, another author with whom Strahan would continue to have a close personal and professional relationship, despite some differences.[95] The following summer Strahan did in fact visit Scotland, when his journal records seeing Robert Wallace several times (on 5, 6, 25, and 27 Aug. 1768). As already noted, Wallace and the Wishart brothers were connected as moderate Presbyterians and as friends and disciples of the Edinburgh divinity professor William Hamilton, who was the father of Strahan's friend, the Edinburgh bookseller Gavin Hamilton; in a letter to Hume of 1775, Strahan recalls how Hamilton, "in my early Days, gave so much Satisfaction" in the divinity chair.[96]

Strahan was very supportive of younger Scots with literary aspirations, especially Presbyterian ministers. Like Andrew Millar, he patronized the historian William Robertson, and would be among the copublishers of Robertson's major works. He was also Robertson's friend, entertaining him in London and meeting with him frequently on his Scottish jaunts. Strahan's patronage of Scottish authors in London was as well known as Andrew Millar's: "at his table in London every Scotsman found an easy introduction," wrote the anonymous author of Strahan's obituary in *The Lounger*.[97] When Rev. John Logan was in London in 1781, trying to publish a volume of poems (no. 216), he found Strahan receptive and wrote home that "Mr Strahan is not only obliging but partial to his Countrymen. I find that he will not be adverse to publish the poems you have seen."[98]

Another Scottish clergyman of letters, Thomas Somerville, gained entrée to Strahan through George Wishart on a visit to London in 1769. He frequently dined at Strahan's house and was flattered to receive an

---

94. Strahan to Wallace, 7 Mar. 1768, EUL, II.96/1, fol. 13.

95. See esp. George Wallace to Strahan, 25 Sept. 1772, HL, MS Hyde 10, item 730, and 6 June 1780, MS Hyde 76, 2.1.53.2.

96. Strahan to Hume, 30 Oct. 1775, NLS, MS 23157, no. 66.

97. Hart, *Minor Lives*, 279.

98. Logan to Alexander Carlyle, 2 Apr. 1781, EUL, La.II.419/3.

invitation to a literary party that included Hume, Sir John Pringle, and Benjamin Franklin. As a young minister from the small parish of Minto, in the Scottish Borders, Somerville was counseled by his new friend to pursue a literary career in London: "In a private conversation I had one day with Mr. Strahan, after regretting the scanty provision of the Scottish clergy, he warmly recommended to me to think of some scheme of literary employment in London, assuring me of his patronage in such friendly terms as impressed me with a full persuasion of the sincerity of his kind attentions, and of the probability of their leading to flattering success."[99] Instead of heeding this advice, Somerville chose to emulate Robertson by pursuing a scholarly vocation while maintaining his character as a parish minister, eventually turning to Strahan's son Andrew and his partners to publish two quarto histories (nos. 308 and 346), as we have seen. Among the young Scottish laymen benefiting from Strahan's hospitality in London were James Beattie in 1773 and James Boswell, who was encouraged by Strahan at a breakfast discussion in 1775 to pursue a career in English law. Boswell was well pleased with his host's "wealthy plumpness and good animal spirits" when he visited him in 1779, although on another occasion he agreed with Garrick's assessment of Strahan as *an obtuse man.*"[100]

When Strahan visited Scotland, he often met with his authors, especially those who lived in the vicinity of Edinburgh. Among those mentioned in his travel journals are David Hume, Henry Mackenzie, John Gregory, Lord Kames, Adam Ferguson, William Cullen, and (in Glasgow and Edinburgh) Adam Smith. Strahan's diaries do not usually provide much information about the nature of these meetings, but they can sometimes be supplemented by other sources. On 6 August 1773, for example, Henry Mackenzie told a correspondent that "my worthy Friend and Bookseller Mr Strahan was in Town . . . and took up some part of my little Leisure during his Stay."[101] While visiting Edinburgh, Strahan also met frequently with his closest contemporary associates in the book trade, Alexander Kincaid and John Balfour (though never at the same time). Once again, the details of what went on are not known, but we can safely speculate that the time was passed in a mixture of business and pleasure, as copublication deals were negotiated in an atmosphere of trust grounded in a lifetime of personal and professional association. The rest of Strahan's

---

99. Somerville, *My Own Life*, 142–43.

100. Cochrane, *Dr. Johnson's Printer*, 143–44, 149, 152.

101. Mackenzie, *Letters to Elizabeth Rose*, 138.

time in Scotland was filled up with visits, churchgoing, excursions, and travel to tourist sites that continually increased his range of Scottish acquaintances and experiences.

The attraction of Scotland was strong, but that of his adopted city was stronger. In 1777 Strahan told Thomas Cadell that "no Man leaves London for any length of Time, without repenting it, or at least wishing himself back again"; to him, London was "in every Respect the most desirable [place], perhaps, on the Face of the Earth."[102] Whether in London or Edinburgh, Strahan was always aware of Scotland's uneasy relationship with John Bull. His attitude fluctuated according to circumstances. Sometimes he was proud, even boastful, of his achievements as a successful Scot in London, as in his assertion to Hall about Millar and he being the first Scots to penetrate the inner circle of the Stationers' Company by being made members of its Court of Assistants.[103] When trying to persuade David Hume to come to London in the midst of the Wilkes and Liberty hysteria of 1769–70, he was moderately conciliatory, hoping his friend would "become reconciled to Mr Bull, who is, at bottom, I hope, a very honest and sensible Fellow; tho', at times, he is troubled with violent Fits, and those of considerable Duration too, nearly bordering upon down right madness."[104] At other times he shared Hume's feelings of resentment toward the English. In 1772 he remarked to Hume that promoting both Andrew Stuart and Adam Ferguson in the same issue of the *London Chronicle* would be difficult because "John Bull would not fail commenting upon two Scotchmen being praised at once in a paper printed by a *Scotchman*."[105] There were also occasions when he adopted the role of John Bull himself, criticizing his Scottish friends for unfairly favoring their countrymen.

William Strahan's conflicting attitudes toward his native and adopted lands reveal the fundamental anxiety and self-consciousness of transplanted Scots in eighteenth-century England who were struggling to find themselves amid the process—sometimes painful, frequently rewarding—that contemporaries called "completing the Union." By reinforcing Scottish connections and by providing opportunities to promote Scotland's genius and glory, patriotic publishing was in part an attempt by

---

102. Strahan to Cadell, 25 July 1777, quoted in Cochrane, *Dr. Johnson's Printer*, 139.

103. Strahan to Hall, 23 Mar. 1764, American Philosophical Society.

104. Strahan to Hume, 13 Jan. 1770, NLS, MS 23157, no. 6.

105. Strahan to Hume, 27 Feb. 1772, in Hume, *Letters of Hume to Strahan*, 244. For Hume's critical view of England, see Livingston, "Hume," 133–47.

Strahan, as also by Millar, to resolve his complex feelings about national and personal identity. Scottish authors and the Scottish Enlightenment were the beneficiaries of these tensions.

Hamilton & Balfour, Kincaid, and Edinburgh Publishing

Until around the middle of the eighteenth century, Edinburgh lacked a critical mass of booksellers with whom their London counterparts could collaborate in the production of new learned and literary books. Printing had existed in Edinburgh since 1507, and what Alastair F. Mann has called a distinctive "Scottish tradition in book culture" emerged over the next two centuries, emphasizing a form of limited "copyright" based on government patents granted to publishers for fixed periods. During the first quarter of the eighteenth century, Edinburgh supported 20–40 printers and 30–55 booksellers, bookbinders, and stationers and became, in Mann's words, "the epicentre for book trading in the northern British Isles."[106] One learned printer of the early eighteenth century, the Jacobite controversialist Thomas Ruddiman, would produce a number of scholarly books, mainly in Latin, and his exploits would be recounted by George Chalmers in one of the titles that appears in table 2 (no. 323).[107] We have also seen that James M'Euen was active during this period in scholarly printing, auctioneering, and publishing.

Nevertheless, the Edinburgh book trade remained small during the opening decades of the eighteenth century. In chapter 1 we saw that the preface to the original *Edinburgh Review* asserted in the mid-1750s that the standing of Scotland in the republic of letters had been greatly retarded by the poor condition of its printing industry but that this state of affairs had recently been remedied. By 1781 the Edinburgh printer William Smellie complained to Strahan that competition among practitioners of their trade had reached crisis proportions because the number of Edinburgh printing houses had increased from "not above half a dozen" when Strahan emigrated to London in the late 1730s to "near thirty."[108] Moreover, the growth of the Edinburgh book trade extended to all aspects of the industry, including the publishing of new books by Scottish authors. As in London, many individuals participated in this process, but we

106. Mann, *Scottish Book Trade*, 227, 234, and 220, graph 10. For the late seventeenth century, see also Emerson, "Scottish Cultural Change," 121–44.

107. For a modern assessment, see Duncan, *Thomas Ruddiman*.

108. Smellie to Strahan, [1781], in Kerr, *Memoirs*, 1:330.

are concerned here with the two seminal mid-eighteenth-century firms: Hamilton & Balfour, and Alexander Kincaid and his early partners.

Thanks chiefly to the research of Warren McDougall, a great deal is now known about Hamilton & Balfour.[109] John Balfour joined the firm of Gavin Hamilton as a clerk around 1733 and became a partner in 1739, the date of their first joint imprint. During the period with which we are concerned, the firm added a printing partner and became known from 1750 onward as Hamilton, Balfour, & Neill, though not all subsequent imprints included Patrick Neill's name. A dispute having to do with the addition of a second printing partner, John Reid, and another involving an unsuccessful newspaper venture, the *Edinburgh Chronicle*, led to dissolution of the firm in 1762.[110] Gavin Hamilton died less than five years later, on New Year's Day 1767. But John Balfour continued as a force in Edinburgh bookselling until well into the 1780s, even though he became steadily less adventurous as a publisher of new books.[111] From 1766 to 1782 he was in partnership with the learned printer William Smellie (who appears in tables 1 and 2 as an author in his own right) and was joined for part of that period by another printer, William Auld.[112] Later Balfour was associated with his sons, Elphingston and John, in John Balfour & Co. (*EEC*, 5 July 1777) and John Balfour & Sons (*EEC*, 27 Nov. 1784).

Hamilton & Balfour strengthened their position as an Edinburgh publisher by means of several expansive maneuvers. First, there were the printing partnerships mentioned above, especially with Patrick Neill. Bookselling–printing partnerships were particularly advantageous in Edinburgh, where the division of labor between these two essential branches of the trade was not as sharply defined as in London.[113] In addition to a print shop that Neill managed separately, Hamilton & Balfour built a paper mill at nearby Colinton. With their own paper manufactur-

109. McDougall, "Gavin Hamilton, John Balfour and Patrick Neill." Convenient summaries are provided in McDougall, "Gavin Hamilton," 1–19, and in McDougall's separate entries on Hamilton, Balfour, and Neill in *ODNB*.

110. McDougall, "Hamilton, Balfour, and Neill's *Edinburgh Chronicle*," 24–28.

111. Smellie to Strahan, [1781], in Kerr, *Memoirs*, 1:331: "My partner [Balfour] has for some years printed little or nothing; and it is not likely that he will again become an adventurous publisher."

112. The dates of the Balfour–Smellie partnership derive from Kerr, *Memoirs*, 1:319, 2:170–71, and the same source also gives the years 1766–71 as the period of the three-way partnership with the printer William Auld (1:319, 325).

113. Smellie complained to Strahan that every notable Edinburgh bookseller except Balfour and Creech was also a printer (ibid., 1:331–32).

ing and printing facilities, they were able to produce hundreds of publications in a little more than a decade, including many Scottish Enlightenment titles.[114] On the distribution side, the firm maintained a bookshop in the High Street, where the literati could congregate. It also operated a warehouse and a large auction room and marketed books aggressively outside Edinburgh, including extensive sales through a mostly Scottish network in America.[115] By combining printing, paper manufacturing, publishing, warehousing, bookselling, auctioneering, and marketing, the firm operated according to the modern principle of vertical integration, or the coordinated control of all the key components in the production and distribution process. This experiment in integration ended upon the dissolution of the firm, after which Hamilton got the paper mill, Balfour the bookselling business, and Balfour and Neill the print shop. In 1770, however, Balfour purchased the paper mill from Hamilton's heirs, and his son John soon rebuilt it.[116] In subsequent years the Balfours continued Hamilton & Balfour's old practice by using the firm's paper and print shop to produce publications that appeared wholly or partly under their name, were stored in their warehouse, and were sold in two Edinburgh bookshops that they owned by 1774 (*EEC*, 12 Nov. 1774).

Hamilton & Balfour's move to a basic form of vertical integration was connected with another distinguishing feature of their firm: a strong sense of Scottish national sentiment and self-sufficiency. The *Edinburgh Review* of 1755–56, with its preface boasting of Scotland's rise to literary greatness, was among their productions; so were John Home's tragedy, *Douglas* (no. 44); William Wilkie's *The Epigoniad* (no. 48), which was supposed to be the first modern epic by a Scot; and James Macpherson's *Fragments of Ancient Poetry* (no. 64), which started the Ossian craze. Even before these works appeared, the firm had attempted an ambitious adventure in Scottish national publishing: the publication in 1754 of the first volume of *The History of England* (no. 33; then titled *The History of Great Britain*) by David Hume, "our scots author," as Gavin Hamilton tellingly referred to him in a letter to his old friend and London agent, William Strahan. Addressed "My dear Willie," the letter described in detail the financial aspects of this "very bold," some said "rash," undertaking. Hume received £400 for the firm's right to print 2,000 copies of the first quarto

---

114. McDougall, "Catalogue," 187–232.

115. McDougall, "Scottish Books," 35–38.

116. [Hamilton], *Short Memoir of Gavin Hamilton*, 7–8.

volume.[117] An undertaking on that scale required strong London sales, but Hamilton was unable to secure them on his own, even though he set up a temporary shop in London expressly for that purpose.[118] In a letter to Strahan of 3 May 1755, Hume himself traced Hamilton's failure partly to English readers' antipathy to the book's controversial views on politics and religion and partly to a "Conspiracy of the Booksellers" in London, who supposedly wished to teach the Edinburgh book trade a lesson about the folly of pursuing a policy of independent publishing (*LDH*, 1:222).[119] Most modern commentators have focused on the alleged conspiracy and suggested that Andrew Millar—who purchased the unsold copies from Hamilton and later benefited from the book's profitability—was behind it.[120] McDougall argues, however, that the book's controversial nature was the main issue and that far from undermining the London sale, Millar was an ally in the struggle against what he would later term "prejudice."[121] Nevertheless, the affair sent a clear message to Scottish authors and booksellers about the need for collaboration between London and Edinburgh publishers.

The firm of Hamilton & Balfour also illustrates the intimate, familial nature of eighteenth-century Edinburgh society and the close personal relationships that existed between the Scottish Enlightenment and the Scottish book trade. As first cousins and brothers-in-law (Hamilton was married to Balfour's sister Helen), the two men were doubly intertwined with each other, and it was these personal and kinship ties that originally led them into a business partnership despite some significant personality

---

117. Hamilton to Strahan, 29 Jan. 1754, in Hume, *Letters of Hume to Strahan*, 3. Hamilton was anticipating three volumes in all, for which Hume was to receive a total of £1,200.

118. More than twenty letters that Hamilton sent home from London during the last three months of 1754 are in the Thomson of Banchory Papers, THO1, in New College Library, Edinburgh.

119. On 22 March Hume had written in another letter, probably also to Strahan: "The London Booksellers, who are jealous of the Edinburgh Press, are glad to see us fail in any Undertaking, and help to keep us down." In Klemme, "Ein unveröffentlichter Brief von David Hume an William Strahan," 661.

120. Mossner and Ransom, "Hume and the 'Conspiracy of the Booksellers,'" 162–82. One contemporary account, Pratt, *Supplement*, charged Millar with loaning copies of Hume's book instead of selling them, so that he could take over Hamilton & Balfour's interest in the *History* "for a trifle."

121. McDougall, "Copyright Litigation," 27–28.

differences, which sometimes led to clashes.[122] Both were well educated and cosmopolitan: in 1754 Hamilton wrote home of attending Latin plays put on at the Westminster School in London; Balfour dealt easily with French booksellers such as Charles-Joseph Panckoucke, with whom he was in "constant correspondence."[123] Their families were as deeply imbedded as any in the powerful network of Presbyterian academic and landed society that formed the principal seedbed of the Scottish Enlightenment. Gavin Hamilton's father William, professor of divinity and briefly principal of the University of Edinburgh, inspired a generation of liberal-minded divines, including three of the authors in table 1: William Leechman, James Oswald, and Robert Wallace. Two of Gavin's brothers were clergymen, and one of them, Robert, followed in their father's footsteps as professor of divinity at the University of Edinburgh. Gavin's sister Jean married William Cleghorn, who would best David Hume for the Edinburgh moral philosophy chair in 1745, thanks largely to the Hamilton interest.[124]

One of the authors listed in table 1, the philosopher James Balfour, was John Balfour's eldest brother, and therefore heir to the family estate at Pilrig; he published his first book in 1753 with Hamilton, Balfour, & Neill (no. 23), his second in 1768 with John Balfour alone (no. 104), and his third in 1782 with John & Elphingston Balfour and Thomas Cadell (no. 222). Elphingston Balfour (who was apparently named after the family of William Strahan's wife) married Margaret Bruce, the niece of William Robertson, whose histories of Charles V and America were copublished by John Balfour (nos. 119 and 185) and whose last major historical work (no. 299) was copublished by Elphingston himself, at Robertson's personal request.[125] As we saw in chapter 2, two sisters of James and John Balfour married other authors whose names appear in table 1: William Leechman and Robert Whytt, whose medical works appeared under the imprint of Hamilton, Balfour, & Neill (nos. 17, 21, and 38).

Family connections were reinforced by political ties. During the 1730s and 1740s Gavin Hamilton was regularly elected to the Edinburgh Town Council as a senior magistrate, or bailie, and in that capacity he exerted

122. See, for example, Hamilton's letter to Strahan of 16 August 1762 on Balfour's discourteous treatment toward him in the period leading up to the dissolution of their firm (NLS, Acc. 10832).

123. Hamilton to his son John, 9 Dec. 1754, and to his son Robert, 9 Jan. 1755, New College Library, Edinburgh, Thomson of Banchory Papers, THO1, fols. 22–23, 26–27; Balfour to Richard Gough, 23 Dec. 1774, NLS, Adv. MSS 29.5.7(1), fol. 180.

124. Nobbs, "Political Ideas," 575–86.

125. Robertson to Andrew Strahan, 13 Mar. 1790, EUL, La.II.241.

some authority over the university, which was under the jurisdiction of the town council. John Balfour also served on the town council as a merchant councilor in 1754. Such political influence must have helped to secure the appointments of Hamilton & Balfour as printers to the city of Edinburgh as well as printers to the university. McDougall has shown that Gavin Hamilton was also an active civic improver who served as treasurer of the Royal Infirmary, director of the Society in Scotland for Propagating Christian Knowledge, a cosponsor of the dancing assembly, and a manager of the Edinburgh Society for the Encouragement of Arts, Sciences, Manufactures and Agriculture. What emerges is a picture of two men with a strong sense of public spirit, deeply committed to the betterment of Edinburgh, Scotland, and the world.

The second seminal eighteenth-century publishing firm in Edinburgh was founded by another civic-minded bookseller, Alexander Kincaid.[126] Like Gavin Hamilton, Kincaid served as a bailie or magistrate on the Edinburgh Town Council, elected six different times between 1738 and 1751 (and again in 1772, though he declined to serve). His political career was undoubtedly helped by his "zealous" Hanoverian sentiments during and after the 1745 Jacobite uprising, which gave him access to the third Duke of Argyll.[127] He was a member of Masonic Lodge Canongate Kilwinning No. 2 from 5 December 1769, and from 3 November 1775 he belonged to the Society of Captains of the Trained Bands. In 1776 he was elected lord provost. By that time, and apparently for a good while before, he enjoyed all the trappings of wealth, including a "large and convenient house in the Cowgate," with a coach house and stables for six horses (*EEC*, 14 Jan. 1778).[128] When he died suddenly in office on 21 January 1777, he was accorded a funeral with one of the grandest processionals in the modern history of Edinburgh (*EEC*, 29 Jan. 1777). According to his intimate friend William Strahan, his character was marked by a meek and gentle temper and an inability to act deceitfully. He gave extensively, but secretly, to charity and died "revered, beloved, and honoured by all who knew him."[129]

Kincaid's career as a bookseller began in March 1734, when he completed his apprenticeship with James M'Euen. Like Millar, he seems to have acquired from his master his publishing skills as well as certain con-

126. See my entry on Kincaid in *ODNB*.

127. Mackenzie, *Anecdotes*, 180–81.

128. Gilhooley, *Directory of Edinburgh*, places Kincaid in President's Close off the Cowgate, which is presumably where his "large and convenient house" was located.

129. *London Chronicle*, 25–28 Jan. 1777; *EEC*, 22 Jan. 1777.

nections with Scottish men of letters. M'Euen, for example, appears as the
selling agent in the imprint of the first book published by Henry Home
(later Lord Kames) in 1732, *Essays upon Several Subjects in Law,* and fifteen
years later Kincaid was the sole publisher of Home's next book, *Essays
upon Several Subjects concerning British Antiquities* (no. 2). Perhaps Kincaid's
greatest debt to M'Euen was the famous bookshop in the Luckenbooths
that he took over from him.[130] Although the site is most closely associated with Allan Ramsay, who operated Scotland's first circulating library
in the same building from the mid-1720s, and with Kincaid's successor,
William Creech, it must have been useful to Kincaid as well. Besides the
bookshop, Kincaid also operated a printing office in Pearson's Close, just
across High Street from the Luckenbooths, and like M'Euen he was active
as an auctioneer of fine books.

By 1735 Kincaid was copublishing (with Robert Fleming) and printing
the successful newspaper that M'Euen had cofounded, the *Edinburgh Evening Courant.* In July 1741 he published David Hume's first volume of *Essays, Moral and Political,* followed in 1742 by a second volume. Eight years
later Kincaid took a decisive step by obtaining the office of His Majesty's
Printer and Stationer for Scotland, whose patent took effect, for Kincaid
and his heirs, for forty-one years beginning 6 July 1757. That gave him
the lucrative monopoly on the printing of Scottish bibles, just as William Strahan would later acquire the monopoly on bible printing in England.[131] Kincaid's upward ascent continued with his marriage in 1759 to
Caroline Kerr (or Ker), a cultured woman of noble descent who possessed,
according to an obituary by Strahan himself, "in an eminent degree, every
amiable virtue."[132] Her library was impressive enough to receive separate
billing in the sale catalogue that circulated in Edinburgh in the winter of
1778 (*EEC,* 28 Feb. and 6 Mar. 1778).

Besides his marriage, Alexander Kincaid engaged in a second union in
1751, with a junior partner named Alexander Donaldson (1727–1794).[133]
The son of a well-to-do textile manufacturer from whom he is said to have
inherited £10,000, Donaldson entered the book business in style. He be-

130. Grant, *Cassell's Old and New Edinburgh,* 155. Grant's dates may be off, but the
rest of his story appears to be accurate. In the early 1740s the address of Kincaid's
shop was usually given as "the east side of the Luckenbooths."

131. Kincaid's commission is reproduced in Lee, *Memorial,* App. 32. For his Bible
publishing, see Darlow and Moule, *Historical Catalogue.*

132. *London Chronicle,* 18–20 Aug. 1774.

133. See the entry on Donaldson by J. J. Caudle and Richard B. Sher in *ODNB.*

came an Edinburgh burgess by right of his father in 1750, apparently in lieu of an apprenticeship in the trade, and it is likely that his marriage to a merchant's daughter the following year brought him a substantial dowry.[134] All indications are that he bought his way into the partnership with Kincaid, whose business almost immediately began to change. Whereas during the 1740s Kincaid published no new learned books besides Hume's and Home's *Essays*, the Kincaid–Donaldson partnership was more ambitious. Two new Scottish books were published by Kincaid & Donaldson in the firm's first year: Francis Home's *Essay on the Contents and Virtues of Dunse-Spaw* (no. 13) and Henry Home's controversial *Essays on the Principles of Morality and Natural Religion* (no. 14). The next year the firm was the sole publisher of Hume's *Political Discourses* (no. 19). James Lind's *Treatise of the Scurvy* (no. 26) was another of Kincaid & Donaldson's 1753 productions, indicative of the niche the firm was carving out for itself in the area of practical medical works. But it was yet another 1753 venture, an eight-volume duodecimo edition of the *Works of Shakespear*, that seems to have set Donaldson on his true career path, as a reprinter of English classics.

As McDougall has demonstrated, a 1751 decision by the Scottish Court of Session gave Scottish booksellers reason to believe that they had defeated the London booksellers' claims of perpetual copyright and established the right to reprint any title no longer protected by the Statute of Anne.[135] In fact this impression was premature: the London booksellers would continue to contest the issue for another quarter of a century, first with a 1759 campaign of intimidation against English booksellers selling Scottish reprints, and then with a barrage of lawsuits against Scottish reprinters (particularly Alexander Donaldson), until the House of Lords finally settled the issue in 1774.[136] During the early 1750s, however, Scottish booksellers felt confident enough to produce multivolume reprints of London editions, including some of the English classics. A self-consciously patriotic Scottish edition of the *Spectator* in eight volumes set the stage in 1745.[137] It was followed by a number of Scottish reprint editions of Swift (1752 and 1756), Shakespeare (1753), Milton (1755), and oth-

---

134. Plomer et al., *Dictionaries*, 299.

135. McDougall, "Copyright Litigation," 8–9.

136. Walters, "Booksellers in 1759 and 1774," 287–311; Deazley, *On the Origin of the Right to Copy*; Feather, *Publishing, Piracy and Politics*; Rose, *Authors and Owners*; Saunders, *Authorship and Copyright*, 21–59.

137. Sher, "Commerce," 314.

ers, and Hamilton & Balfour, Kincaid & Donaldson, or both were usually among the publishers.

In 1758 the Scottish book publishing industry stood at a crossroads, and Kincaid and Donaldson reflected the two alternate directions. One path, represented by Kincaid, led to the new books of the Scottish Enlightenment. The other, taken by Donaldson, pointed toward continuing the pattern of intensive reprinting of English books no longer protected by copyright according to the Statute of Anne. After the breakup of the partnership with Kincaid in 1758, for reasons that have never been determined but may well have had to do with their different philosophies of publishing, Donaldson opened his own bookshop in Edinburgh and cultivated young literary men who congregated there, such as James Boswell and his friend Andrew Erskine. He also opened an Edinburgh print shop at Castlehill, eventually operated by his son James. Although Donaldson continued to publish new material from time to time, such as a two-volume *Collection of Original Poems* by "Scotch Gentlemen" (1760–62) that included Boswell, Thomas Blacklock, and John Home among the contributors, his involvement with the new books of the Scottish Enlightenment was essentially over as soon as he left Kincaid.

Donaldson concentrated on reprinting, especially literary reprinting, which he found he could do more cheaply than the London booksellers could or would. The works of Milton and Swift, which he had reprinted while still partners with Kincaid, remained central to his business, but they were augmented by the writings of Dryden, Defoe, Pope, James Thomson, Edward Young, John Locke, and other, mostly English, writers. Donaldson's problem was marketing: how could he find enough buyers to justify the kind of high-volume, low-margin publishing that he wished to pursue? The answer was to set up a bookshop in the Strand in London with his brother John for the express purpose of underselling the London trade. This was the "shop for cheap books" that Boswell mentions in his *London Journal* in May 1763.[138] Donaldson must have known that his actions would be seen as a call to arms by the London booksellers, whose literary and geographical territory was being invaded; for the next eleven years they harassed him mercilessly in the courts for reprinting titles whose copyrights they claimed to possess among themselves in perpetuity. But Donaldson fought them off and eventually beat them in the House of Lords, in the process becoming a Scottish national hero for having

138. Boswell, *London Journal*, 257.

liberated the Scottish publishing industry from the stigma of piracy that the London booksellers had attempted to place upon it (*ODNB*).

Donaldson, or his lawyers and friends, sometimes stated or implied that his motives had been largely ideological all along: he wanted to break the monopoly of the London booksellers and lower the price of books for the good of the public and of Scotland. This is how the Scottish MP George Dempster portrayed him in debate with Samuel Johnson on 20 July 1763, causing Johnson to exclaim that Donaldson was then "no better than Robin Hood" (*BLJ*, 1:438–39). Although such idealistic motives may not tell the whole story, neither should we assume that they are merely a rationalization for the actions of a greedy bookseller. Can we be so certain, after all, that a bookseller who was already quite wealthy in Edinburgh would be motivated to subject himself to a torrent of abuse merely in order to make more money? In January 1764 Donaldson founded a successful newspaper, the *Edinburgh Advertiser*, which also appears to be the result of complex motives. Its name suggested the source of revenue it was meant to attract, and it served additionally as another vehicle for marketing the cheap reprints that Donaldson's print shop was churning out. On the other hand, in an editorial message to "the Public" at the beginning of the first issue, Donaldson spewed patriotic rhetoric about the newspaper's preference for "home productions" over "foreign" (i.e., English) ones and vowed that the editors were "the servants of the Public" in all things. Rather than view Donaldson either as a one-dimensional profit seeker who cleverly employed the rhetoric of public service and national sentiment as a front, or as a patriot and altruist who hardly cared about making money, it is probably best to view him as a man whose complex motives were both economic and ideological.

Whatever his motives, Donaldson made a fortune in the reprint trade. Thomas Somerville later recalled that in 1769 Donaldson entrusted him with a chest of eight to ten thousand guineas meant for the Bank of Scotland, which left the poor clergyman "haunted with dreams of robbery and assassination" as he made his way north from London on the stagecoach.[139] In 1786 Donaldson purchased Broughton Hall near Edinburgh, where he lived after retiring from the book trade around 1789. His son James inherited that house as part of an estate valued at £100,000. For Alexander Donaldson, a career in reprinting had paid off.

In the standard, London-centric accounts of eighteenth-century publishing, reprinting of English books is viewed as the soul of the Scot-

---

139. Somerville, *My Own Life*, 162–65.

tish book trade, and Donaldson is sometimes portrayed as "the leader of the Edinburgh industry."[140] But Donaldson never occupied that position, and reprinting was not the only option open to Scottish booksellers. Indeed, the Scottish Enlightenment would have been much diminished, if not unrecognizable, if Donaldson's emphasis on reprinting of English classics had been shared by all his colleagues in the Edinburgh trade. When the partners in Kincaid & Donaldson went their separate ways in 1758, Kincaid took John Bell (1735–1806) as his new partner.[141] Bell had been apprenticed to Kincaid & Donaldson since 1754, and he was only twenty-two years old when he got the opportunity to share the management of one of Edinburgh's two largest and most prestigious bookselling firms. His influence was felt immediately. During the thirteen years of the partnership, the firm occasionally produced editions of English classics, but it also assumed a much more active role as a publisher of new books by Scottish authors, often in collaboration with London firms such as Edward & Charles Dilly and especially Andrew Millar and his partner and successor, Thomas Cadell. In his career as a publisher between 1741 and 1758, first alone and then with Donaldson, Kincaid had published a total of ten new titles listed in table 2, nearly all of them by three authors who shared a single surname: David Hume, Henry Home (after 1751 Lord Kames), and Francis Home. The partnership with John Bell began at the very moment when younger authors were beginning to add significantly to the output of new works emanating from Scotland, and the firm of Kincaid & Bell was perfectly positioned to copublish many of them with Millar while continuing to issue new books and reprints by their established authors. At the same time, the firm seems to have associated itself with the politics of the Moderate Party in the Church of Scotland, which was struggling to promote its vision of enlightened culture in opposition to the pious and less tolerant views of their opponents in the Popular or orthodox party. An image of Kincaid & Bell's bookshop that appears in a political print from around December 1762, satirizing the Moderates' high-handed ways in one such skirmish, suggests that the shop served as a meeting place for Moderate Party conspirators (fig. 4.2).[142]

Mention has already been made of Kincaid & Bell's extraordinary record of copublications with Millar from 1758 to 1767. Some sense of the impact of this publishing pattern on Scottish authors can be gleaned from

140. St. Clair, *Reading Nation*, 107; Feather, *History*, 77–83.

141. For biographical details, see my entry on Bell in *ODNB*.

142. On the dispute in question, see Sher, "Moderates, Managers," 179–209.

Fig. 4.2. The Edinburgh partnership of Alexander Kincaid and John Bell from 1758 to 1771 played a crucial role in the development of Scottish Enlightenment publishing, often in collaboration with the London firm of Andrew Millar. Here their bookshop at the east end of the Luckenbooths in the High Street is pictured in a political cartoon that probably dates from December 1762. The figures seem to have been blackened at a later date. Edinburgh Room, Edinburgh Central Library, Edinburgh City Libraries.

a 1769 letter of James Beattie concerning the publication arrangements for his *Essay on Truth* (no. 123). After explaining that he would prefer to have the book printed in Edinburgh, mainly so "that I might myself revise the sheets as they came from the press," he adds:

> only I could wish a London Bookseller engaged in the publication, because otherwise it would be impossible to make it circulate in England. It is very common in the publication of Scotch books for English and Scotch booksellers to have a joint concern. Smith's Theory of Moral Sentiments is printed for Kincaid and Bell at Edinburgh and Miller at London: the same is the case with Gerards Dissertations on Christianity, Reid's Inquiry into the human mind, and Campbell on miracles. I could wish the property of my book to be divided in the same manner.[143]

143. Beattie to Robert Arbuthnot, 8 Aug. 1769, in Beattie, *Correspondence*, 2:89.

Beattie saw the trend and wanted to be part of it, and we can assume that other Scottish authors felt the same way.

Although all the books that Beattie named were copublished by Kincaid & Bell in Edinburgh and Andrew Millar in London, the London copublishers of his *Essay on Truth* turned out to be the Dilly brothers. The death of Millar in 1768 may have been one reason for Beattie's decision to employ the Dillys on this occasion, instead of Millar's fledgling successor, Thomas Cadell. It is also possible that Cadell did not want to copublish this book because it gave such rough treatment to one of his principal authors, David Hume. But the factor jeopardizing collaboration that I wish to emphasize most is the growing tension between key personalities in the firms of Millar and Kincaid, dating back to the time when Millar was still alive. In a letter to Cadell dated 5 February 1767, Millar accused Bell of supplying London booksellers with copies of their copublished titles that were printed in Edinburgh, in violation of bookselling conventions associated with joint publications. "It is realy as bad as robbery for Bell to supply the [London] market with every book before I can," he wrote, "particularly the Principles of equity [no. 62], which should be more saleable at Edinburgh."[144] By this time, these two firms were being run mainly by their respective junior partners, Bell and Cadell,[145] and the possibility of collaboration hinged on the relationship between them. As we shall now see, a London–Edinburgh publishing syndicate could not rest comfortably on such shaky foundations.

Bell, Cadell, and the Crisis over Ferguson's
Essay on the History of Civil Society

The ill feeling between John Bell and Thomas Cadell is revealed in Bell's surviving letterbooks from the period 1764–71.[146] The two junior part-

144. BL, Stowe MSS 755, fol. 79.

145. Cadell's management of Millar's firm is discussed in chapter 5. On Kincaid's declining involvement in the book trade, the following sentence in a letter that Charles Dilly sent to Beattie on 21 August 1771 (AUL, MS 30/2/58) was probably accurate several years before it was written: "Mr Kincaid, of Edinburgh, is a worthy and an honourable gentleman; he is past the time for an active part in business—it lay'd with his partner—Mr Bell to manage affairs in regard to Printing and vending articles for the shop."

146. John Bell Letterbooks, Bodleian Library, Oxford, MS Eng. Letters, C20–21. Parenthetical page citations in the following discussion refer to the letters in this collection.

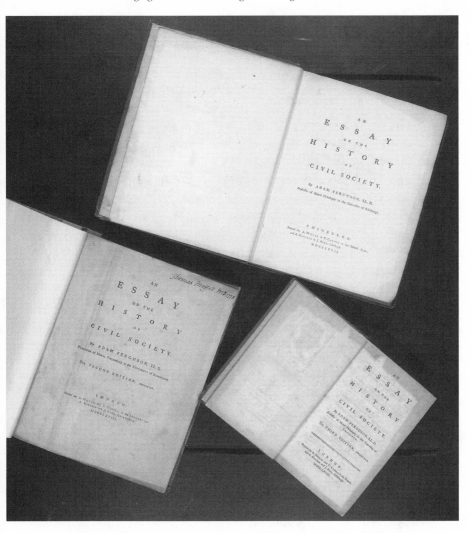

Fig. 4.3. Conflict over the formats and timing of the second and third editions of Adam Ferguson's *Essay on the History of Civil Society* drove a wedge between the houses of Millar and Kincaid, enabling William Creech to replace John Bell as Kincaid's junior partner. Thomas Fisher Rare Book Library, University of Toronto.

ners fell out particularly over Adam Ferguson's *Essay on the History of Civil Society* (fig. 4.3), which their firms originally copublished in late February 1767 in a quarto volume printed in Edinburgh. A detailed consideration of this dispute, seen primarily from Bell's point of view, conveys some sense of the way in which differences in personalities, relationships, and local circumstances could affect copublication along the London–Edinburgh axis.

Market conditions were a crucial part of the problem. The quarto edition of Ferguson's *Essay* that appeared in 1767 cost 12s. wholesale (though it was sometimes discounted for as little as 10s.6d.) and 15s. retail, whereas the octavo third edition of 1768 cost 3s.9d. wholesale and 6s. retail (8 Apr. 1769, C20, fols. 124–25). Thus, the profit margin for the quarto edition was considerably higher for the copublishers as well as for the retail booksellers. In London, where quartos considerably more expensive than this one could sometimes be sold in large quantities, there was a strong economic incentive to push quarto sales to their limit, and brisk initial sales of the first edition of Ferguson's *Essay* convinced Cadell that a second quarto edition was needed. In Edinburgh, however, Kincaid & Bell anticipated having large numbers of the first edition on hand by the winter of 1767–68, and they therefore wanted to publish the second edition in a more affordable octavo rather than in quarto (early March 1767, C20, fol. 29).[147] Sometime later, in the spring or summer of 1767, Bell wrote that "since Mr Millar and you are of opinion that a Quarto Edition may be proper, we shall submitt," but he asked that the new edition be delayed until they could dispose of their stock of 120 copies of the first edition. Presumably he meant by this only two or three months. He also proposed that he and Kincaid print 1,000 copies of the third edition in octavo and receive assurances that they would not get caught with a surplus of quarto copies, which were thought to be too expensive for the Scottish market (no date, fols. 46–47).

Cadell chose not to reply, causing Bell to write again in mid-August, invoking Ferguson's own preference for the Edinburgh booksellers' plan to print 1,000 copies of an octavo edition in Edinburgh, "which the author wishes much as this small Edition will sell amongst his [moral philosophy] Class" (15 Aug. 1767, C20, fol. 55). By late September Bell was threatening to sell his firm's half share in Ferguson's *Essay* to an unnamed London bookseller, who was probably William Johnston (30 Sept. 1767, C20, fol. 66). Cadell seems to have talked him out of this ploy, but with the

147. There is evidence that Bell had been trying to lower the price of the first edition of Ferguson's *Essay* from the outset, for Millar tells Cadell in a letter of 5 February 1767 (BL, Stowe MSS 755, fol. 79) that he "must write to Kincaid. The [retail] price of Ferguson must be 15 [shillings]" because the publishers' real costs would rise to eight shillings or more when advertising and freight were included.

academic term beginning in Edinburgh, Bell reported in early November that Ferguson was "Extremely anxious about the 8vo Edition of his Book being Done here just now to Supply his Class" (3 Nov. 1767, C20, fol. 67). In delaying the second (quarto) edition that he insisted on publishing, Cadell was in turn delaying the third (octavo) edition that was important to the author and the Edinburgh copublisher.

The second edition of Ferguson's *Essay* was finally printed by Strahan in December 1767 (SA 48800, fol. 158), and it appeared in London early in 1768. Judging from the way that Bell acknowledged its appearance in a letter of 13 February to William Johnston—"I see Mr Caddel has published Mr Fergusons Book" (C20, fols. 71–72)—it would seem he had not been informed of the publication by his London copublisher. By the summer of 1768 Bell was so angry at Cadell for blocking publication of an authorized octavo edition of Ferguson's *Essay* that he resorted to desperate measures: "Wish you could inform us . . . if Fergusons C[ivil]: Society be near Done as we want the 8vo Edition much. Mr Balfour having Imported the 8vo from Ireland and be so good as write, what you would chuse to have done in this, as I wish the prosecution against him to begin Instantly. . . . would you chuse to supply us in Dr Robertsons new History" (11 July 1768, C20, fol. 97). Bell's charge that his Edinburgh rival John Balfour was illegally importing the octavo edition of Ferguson's *Essay* that Boulter Grierson had reprinted in Dublin in 1767, though perfectly plausible, remains unsubstantiated, but the very fact that Bell was making it reveals a great deal about his lack of prudence and his agitated state of mind. As the copublisher of Ferguson's *Essay*, Bell should have enjoyed an advantage in the sale of an octavo edition of that book. Instead, he was forced to watch helplessly as his London partners, oblivious to the special needs of the Scottish market, deprived him and the author of an octavo edition and put him at the mercy of pirates in regard to it. The first edition of the *Essay* had been printed at Edinburgh, but after its appearance and early success, London began to call all the shots, including dealing with the author in regard to corrections and revisions.[148] Adding to Bell's frustration was the fact that Millar & Cadell and their printing partner Strahan were negotiating with Strahan's old friend John Balfour to copublish William

148. As early as his undated letter to Cadell that was apparently written in late spring or early summer 1767, Bell made reference to Ferguson having just received from Cadell a letter "desireing that his Essay may be sent to you [Cadell] with what corrections he has made" (C20, fols. 46–47).

Robertson's *History of the Reign of Charles V*—an undertaking on a scale so vast that it dwarfed all Kincaid & Bell's copublications with London. Bell would have been angrier still if he had known (or perhaps he did) that in March 1768 Strahan had already printed 1,000 copies of the octavo third edition of Ferguson's *Essay* (SA 48801, fol. 27), which were presumably sitting in a London warehouse while Cadell sold off more copies of the second quarto edition.

When the octavo third edition of Ferguson's *Essay* was finally published late in 1768, the controversy escalated rather than subsided. Bell was outraged at Cadell for, among other things, dumping unsold copies of the quarto second edition on him after the octavo was published (30 Dec. 1768, C20, fols. 118–19). Bickering over the accounting for this book continued for years. In August 1769 the disagreement caused Bell to decline payment on a draft that Cadell had authorized another bookseller, William Chapman, to draw on Kincaid & Bell (C20, fols. 151–52). On 24 May 1770, responding to a letter that Cadell sent directly to Kincaid twelve days earlier, Bell reminded Cadell that he could have sold his share of the *Essay* to another London bookseller but had not done so at Cadell's request, only to be cheated, in his estimation, when Cadell sent him an accounting. "It is needless to say, how I *have been* used" (fols. 33–35), he commented.

The bad feelings over Ferguson's *Essay* spilled over into other collaborative projects. Cadell believed that when Kincaid visited London in the spring of 1769 the two men had agreed to copublish the second edition of Gilbert Stuart's *English Constitution* (no. 109). On 7 August, however, Bell wrote:

> I would not wish to be concerned in Mr Stewarts English Constitution as I mentioned to Mr Kincaid, on his arrival here. You may conclude we are no partner here as Mr Kincaid did not agree to take any concern and if the author uses us well he will take care that no new Edition be published untill the first is sold, his bargin with you I do not know. (C20, fols. 151–52)

This forceful statement provoked a sharp reply from Cadell, sent directly to Kincaid:

> I have received a Letter from Mr Bell, in which he tells me you decline having any Concern in Stewarts Book on the English Constitution, and he

Absolutely Declares, he will have nothing to do with it. You know when you was here, I told you I had Purchased the Copy of him, and you agreed to have one half share in consequence of which, I Refused Mr Dillys being a Proprietor, and others who Applied to me for that Purpose. (15 Aug. 1769, C20, fols. 152–53)

Having gone over Bell's head, Cadell had the satisfaction of seeing his rival humiliated: the second edition of Stuart's book appeared in January 1770 with the imprint "London: printed for T. Cadell, Successor to Mr Millar; and A. Kincaid and J. Bell, Edinburgh."[149] For his part, Bell scolded Cadell in August 1770 for not dealing fairly with new London editions of Reid's *Inquiry* (no. 88) and Hume's *Essays and Treatises on Several Subjects* (no. 25), which Cadell had published without so much as informing him: "these little things always create jeallouses and Mistrust which ever ought to be avoided" (17 Aug. 1770, C21, fols. 44–45).[150]

Ferguson's *Essay*, however, remained the focal point of hostilities. In September 1770 Bell tried to soothe an angry William Johnston, to whom he had sold, through Cadell, fifty copies of the second edition of that work, by stating that "we had not the Least Idea Mr Cadell was to publish the 8° almost immediately upon the 4° being advertised" (C21, fols. 51–52). Cadell had acted without the consent or approbation of Kincaid & Bell "and much contrary to our Interest," he noted, since "we have about a 100 4°s on hand. From this conduct and worse than I have leisure to tell you now arose a Dispute betwixt us which is not seteled to this hour." Left with a surplus of quarto editions that he could not sell once the more affordable third edition appeared in octavo, Bell was filled with resentment over the highhanded way he thought he had been treated by Cadell. A quarter of a century later he was still advertising new copies of the quarto second edition of Ferguson's *Essay* for the original price of fifteen shillings, although several octavo editions had come and gone over the course of that

149. It was reissued in 1771 with a new title page that replaced Bell's name with that of Kincaid's next partner, Creech. Zachs, *Without Regard to Good Manners*, 216.

150. Since both books had originally been joint publications of Millar & Cadell and Kincaid & Bell (or Donaldson), Cadell was honor-bound to include their names in the imprints of later editions (which he did) as well as to consult with them about plans for new editions (which he evidently did not do). Bell seems to have learned about the 1768 quarto edition of Hume's *Essays* when the author happened to mention it two years later (7 Aug. 1770, C21, fols. 43–44).

period.[151] As late as 1815, William Creech had eleven copies of the second edition in stock.[152]

While the dispute over Ferguson's *Essay* was at its height, Bell blurted out another source of his resentment. "Why can't you order sometimes a few of our Books or any Books printed in this Country," he asks Cadell in a letter of 13 February 1768, listing titles by Lord Kames, James Oswald, and Adam Dickson among the books he has in mind. "Do give us an order of some kind or other and oblidge" (C20, fols. 72–73). There is evidence in the letterbook that Cadell did buy some of Kincaid & Bell's Scottish publications; the first volume of Oswald's *Appeal to Common Sense*, for example, was ordered in successive quantities of 50, 27, 20, and 12 copies between October 1766 and February 1768, according to an accounting statement that Bell prepared in 1769 (C20, fols. 127–28). In general, however, the books by Scottish authors that were most marketable in London were the ones that Cadell or other London booksellers snatched up for publication or copublication in the first place. When a Scottish book performed better than expected, or seemed to hold promise for London sales, Cadell could always become a partner in a later volume, as he did with the second volume of Oswald's *Appeal* in 1772, or in a later edition, as he did with the third edition of Kames's *Introduction to the Art of Thinking* (no. 68) in 1775 and a "new" edition of Adam Dickson's *Treatise of Agriculture* (no. 79) in 1770.

What emerges from a perusal of John Bell's letterbooks from the last years of his partnership with Kincaid is a picture of an aggressive young Scottish bookseller who did not like being at the mercy of his London associates. He was outspoken, and sometimes appeared rude, imprudent, and openly antagonistic in his dealings with a London firm much bigger than his. By this time Bell was in his early thirties, with nearly a decade of experience as a partner, much of it spent running his firm. He may well have resented having to defer to Cadell, who was seven years his junior and had been a mere apprentice during the first seven years of Bell's partnership with Kincaid, when so many major works by Kames, Smith, Reid, and other Scottish authors had appeared. It happened that Cadell's coming of age occurred just after the publication of Ferguson's *Essay*: the second edition of that work was the first substantial book to be charged to Cadell rather than to Millar in the Strahan printing ledgers. Whatever

151. See *A Catalogue of Books for the Year M,DCC,XCIV*, the Bell & Bradfute catalogue published in December 1793.

152. *Catalogue of Books and Copyrights*, 19.

the causes for it, there is no doubt that Bell was seething about his treatment at the hands of Cadell.

Although different market conditions in London and Edinburgh created tensions between the publishers in those towns, personality conflicts exacerbated the situation. One of the London booksellers with whom Bell sometimes collaborated, John Murray, privately called him "difficult to deal with" owing to "the peculiar turn of his mind."[153] Yet others found him good-natured and worthy, and Archibald Constable, who was a close friend of Bell's nephew and partner, John Bradfute, called Bell "the most thorough gentleman of the profession in Edinburgh at this period . . . a man of most excellent talents, kind and benevolent in his intercourse with his brethren, of rather a humorous and facetious turn of mind, particularly when associated of an evening with a few friends."[154] The son of a Church of Scotland minister who was intended for the ministry himself, Bell apparently had a grammar school and university education, and he was sociable, civic-minded, and popular with his fellow booksellers in Edinburgh. As soon as his apprenticeship ended in 1758, he became a member of Masonic Lodge Canongate Kilwinning No. 2, and he was elected the first praeses of the reconstituted Edinburgh Booksellers' Society in December 1792. From the mid-1780s, Bell forged his own version of a successful London–Edinburgh publishing alliance with the firm of George Robinson, as discussed in the next chapter.

The problem was not an inherent deficiency in Bell's personality or background but bad chemistry, or a rivalry, between Bell and Cadell. The crisis over the first three editions of Adam Ferguson's *Essay on the History of Civil Society* demonstrates the delicacy of collaborative publishing endeavors between booksellers in London and Edinburgh. The tradition of intercity copublishing of major new books by Scottish authors had been forged by a generational cohort of Scottish bookmen, and it rested on foundations of friendship and trust that were strong enough to survive copyright suits and other kinds of disagreements between them. But the junior partners of the founding fathers did not necessarily have the same personal connections with their counterparts, and collaborative publish-

153. John Murray to Gilbert Stuart, 4 Oct. 1777, quoted in Zachs, *Without Regard to Good Manners*, 96. Later, Murray squabbled with Bell over finances, remarking in a letter to Stuart of 5 September 1778 that "this Gentleman insists upon acting diametrically opposite to the rules laid down by the trade here" (John Murray Archive, NLS).

154. Constable, *Archibald Constable*, 1:536.

ing ties could easily disintegrate without them. Had Bell and Cadell succeeded their respective senior partners in Edinburgh and London, that is almost certainly what would have happened. As we shall see in the next two chapters, Kincaid was succeeded not by Bell but by a different junior partner, William Creech, who had the blessing of Kincaid's old friend in London, Strahan, as well as Cadell. Far from disintegrating, the London–Edinburgh copublishing connection between the firms of Millar-Cadell and Strahan in London and their affiliates in Edinburgh grew closer and more productive in the decades following Millar's death. Together with formidable but lesser rivals who also pursued similar versions of a collaborative publishing strategy, the publishing syndicate headed by Cadell and Strahan would carry Scottish Enlightenment book production to its highest level of achievement.

[5]

The Heyday of Scottish Enlightenment Publishing

THE HOUSE OF STRAHAN AND CADELL

Visions of Empire

On 15 March 1785 Thomas Cadell told a parliamentary committee investigating illegal importation of books from Ireland that "in the House of Strahan and Cadell above £39,000 have been paid, in 18 Years, to Authors for Copy Right."[1] Coming less than four months before Strahan's death on 9 July, this statement represents one important measure (but only one, for we have seen that publishers did not always purchase copyrights) of the scale of operations of the publishing partnership between William Strahan (fig. 5.1) and Thomas Cadell (fig. 5.2). It was a spectacular accomplishment, especially when one considers that the books in question included so many major works by the leading writers of the age. Although several of their most distinguished authors were English, such as Edward Gibbon, Samuel Johnson, and Sir William Blackstone, a disproportionate number of them were Scots. The House of Strahan and Cadell was the preeminent publisher of the Scottish Enlightenment.

Strictly speaking, it wasn't a "house" at all, because no legal partnership is known to have existed between the bookselling business that Thomas Cadell took over from Andrew Millar and the printing firm founded by Strahan. The bond between them was a shared sense of mutual benefit, cooperation, and trust that fostered dozens of individual book publishing arrangements. A sensible division of labor lay at its core: Strahan did the printing and Cadell did the bookselling.[2] Yet the relationship quickly

1. Lambert, *Sessional Papers*, 52:359.

2. Harlan, "William Strahan," 168, calculates that Cadell expended about £15,000 on printing by Strahan between 1771 and 1785.

Figs. 5.1 and 5.2. The publishing partnership of the printer William Strahan (left, artist unknown) and the bookseller Thomas Cadell (right, engraved by Henry Meyer, after a drawing by W. Evans from a picture by Sir William Beechey that appears as fig. 5.8) dominated London publishing from the late 1760s until Strahan's death in 1785. Strahan: British Library, Add. MSS 38730, fol. 180v; Cadell: Providence Public Library.

developed into something much greater: a deep family friendship and an effective publishing partnership of equals, using the address of Cadell's bookshop in the Strand as the site of publication. "You may place every Confidence in him, as well as in me," Strahan wrote to Hume on 14 May 1769, when striving to build up confidence in Cadell among Scottish authors, "for he is very much your humble Servant."[3] "You rightly consider writing to Mr Cadell or to me as the same, when you write about Business," Strahan told Adam Smith in June 1776.[4] On 6 December of that year he made a similar remark in a letter to William Creech: "In matters of Business we have one Mind and one Interest, so that the Sentiments of one are those of both."[5] For his part, Cadell added a postscript to Strahan's letter to Creech of 4 October 1779 about various collaborative publishing

3. Strahan to Hume, 14 May 1769, NLS, MS 23157, no. 60.

4. Strahan to Smith, 10 June 1776, in Smith, *Correspondence*, 199.

5. All letters from William and Andrew Strahan to William Creech in this chapter are cited from WCL.

projects with Scottish authors, commenting that he "cannot add or alter one word" in Strahan's account because Strahan "writes on this, as on all occasions, exactly to my sentiments." In short, long before Cadell's parliamentary testimony in 1785, it was standard practice to consider their publishing business as a single, unified enterprise.

Thirty-two titles in table 2 contain the joint imprint of Strahan and Cadell in the first edition, and that number is only the beginning of the story of their joint contributions. Aside from a number of new books that Strahan merely printed for Cadell, as he had formerly printed books for Andrew Millar, the two men copublished some later editions of popular titles that were initially produced by others, such as William Buchan's *Domestic Medicine* (no. 115), as well as several first editions that did not reveal their collaboration on the title page. The first edition of Henry Mackenzie's *Man of Feeling* (no. 135), for example, shows only Cadell's name as the publisher, even though Strahan owned half the copyright (his name was added to the imprint of the second edition). Similarly, although Cadell's name alone appeared in the imprints of David Hume's historical and philosophical works, it is clear from Hume's correspondence that Strahan was a silent copublisher of those titles, which were included in their joint catalogues, *Books Printed for W. Strahan, and T. Cadell in the Strand.*

In 1776 Strahan returned the favor by giving Cadell half ownership of the copyright of Hume's autobiography, "My Own Life." *"Tho' a present"* from the author, he wrote to Cadell on this occasion, "I think myself bound in Honour to you, agreable to the sense and spirit of our Agreement, which I hope neither of us will ever think of departing from."[6] In Strahan's view, the "Agreement" with Cadell was worth preserving because it constituted a means of dominating the publication of new books of quality over the long term. It would be a profitable union, Strahan assured his friend, but their profits would be kept within proper bounds:

Indeed I see clearly we have the Ball at our Feet, and as all the rest of the Trade can but little interfere with us, we shall both have enough to satisfy our utmost Desires for Accumulation, unless they should become boundless and insatiable, which I hope in God will never be the case with either of us; for tho' it is a most agreeable Time to be adding to our Fortunes every year *something*, it is by no means necessary to our Happiness, that that *something*, should be a very large sum.

6. Strahan to Cadell, 19 Sept. 1776, HL, MS Hyde 77, 7.116.1.

The agreement, then, reflected a vision of just and moderate acquisition through enlightened publication, grounded in principles of honor and collaboration.

Both Strahan and Cadell emerged from under the shadow of Andrew Millar during the second half of the 1760s. Cadell entered the book trade at age fifteen as Millar's apprentice, bound by his father on 7 March 1758 for a fee of £105.[7] Born on 27 October 1742,[8] he was the same age as Strahan's own children, who were born between 1740 and 1750, and Strahan seems to have played a paternal role in the relationship. Of Cadell's real father and mother, William and Mary, almost nothing is known beyond the fact that they resided in Wine Street, Bristol, where Thomas was born. His father's brother, also called Thomas, was a prominent bookseller in Wine Street, known for his Whig-Presbyterian sympathies,[9] and it was most likely through his influence that young Thomas gained his connection with the London trade. Although the family probably emigrated to Bristol from Scotland, Cadell, like Strahan's children, was English by birth. Yet his Scottishness can be detected in various ways besides his surname, including his telltale use of the Scottish spelling "Strachan" when referring to his publishing partner in some of his letters to Scottish authors.[10] Horace Walpole considered him part of the dreaded cabal of Scottish publishers who showed favoritism toward their countrymen. "Our Scotch Alduses and Elzevirs keep down every publication they do not partake," he wrote bitterly of Strahan and Cadell.[11]

Cadell must have been exceptionally competent, for upon completing his apprenticeship on 2 April 1765, he obtained a partnership with his master.[12] It was Cadell's good fortune that Millar wished to spend more time away from London, especially at the spas of Bath and Tunbridge

7. McKenzie, *Stationers' Company Apprentices*, 235 (no. 5461).

8. "Cadell (Thomas)," 8:13. Unless otherwise noted, biographical information about Cadell is drawn from this source, Catherine Dille's biography in *ODNB*, and John Nichols's obituary in the *Gentleman's Magazine* 71 (Dec. 1802): 1173–1222, as reprinted in Hart, *Minor Lives*, 265–70.

9. [West], "Letters to My Son," 251; British Book Trade Index.

10. For example, Cadell to Hugh Blair, 3 Nov. 1793, NLS, MS 948, no. 9.

11. Walpole to William Mason, 15 May 1773, in Walpole, *Correspondence*, 28 (1955): 86.

12. A fragment of a letter to Millar from William Cadell in Bristol, dated 25 April 1765, expresses the joy of Cadell's parents on this occasion and the hope that "my sons future conduct will be such as not to Disgrace your Patronage" (Beinecke Library, Yale University, Osborn MSS 33, box 1, folder 16).

Wells, where among other things he sponsored popular science lectures by one of the Scottish authors whose works he published, James Ferguson.[13] Since Millar had no surviving sons or other relations to take over his business, nor any other employee with a claim to succeed him, Cadell had no competition. He was fortunate, however, to have the support of Millar's assistant, the Dubliner Robin Lawless, whose importance can be measured by the fact that Cadell would later commission Lawless's portrait to hang in the drawing room of his home in Bloomsbury Place.

Millar's semiretirement began by the summer of 1766: on 28 August of that year he told his friend Andrew Mitchell that since midsummer he had put matters in the hands of "Mr. Cadell one every way deserving." Millar would visit his shop in the Strand just once or twice a week "to see and be seen," and "not one minuet [*sic*] have I regretted it nor one hour has lain heavy on my hands." He was then living at his house in Kew Green but planning to go to Bath from November through the end of January, when Cadell would again be left in charge of the business. Thus, from the age of twenty-three, Cadell was already running the largest bookselling and publishing operation in Britain on a day-to-day basis for sizable periods of time. Soon the phrase "Printed for A. Millar and T. Cadell" began to appear in some new titles that Millar was publishing or copublishing with other booksellers, such as Adam Ferguson's *Essay on the History of Civil Society* in 1767 (no. 99). Millar retired during the course of that year, and his business passed to his protégé, who was also named in his will as one of the executors of his estate. One contemporary noted that Cadell was "greatly dependent" on Millar as late as 1767, and there is evidence that Millar continued to play a role in publishing after his retirement.[14] When Millar died on 8 June 1768, however, Thomas Cadell found himself in sole command of the firm at the age of twenty-five.

Strahan was then in his early fifties and eager to assume a major role as a publisher. For all the printing work he had thrown Strahan's way over the years, Millar had never encouraged his printer's forays into publishing. When Millar did allow Strahan to purchase a share in a new publication, no one would know it from the title page. In 1758 the two men

13. See, for example, Millar to Andrew Mitchell, 28 Aug. 1766, BL, Add. MSS 6858, fols. 33–34; Millar to Cadell, from Bath, 22 Dec. 1766, Boston Public Library, Ch.H.1.43; and Millar to Cadell, 7 Feb. 1767, BL, Stowe MSS 755, fol. 79.

14. Blackburne, *Memoirs of Thomas Hollis*, 366. The contract for Robertson's *Charles V* was originally offered in Millar's name in 1768. See Sher, "*Charles V*," 167.

had joined forces to publish Robert Wallace's *Characteristics of the Present Political State of Great Britain* (no. 52),[15] for example, but the imprint reads "Printed for A. Millar in the Strand." In spite of Millar's lack of encouragement, Strahan had used his friendship with Smollett and other authors whose works he had printed, as well as debts owed to him by booksellers such as John Knapton, as a means of purchasing shares of many copyrights.[16] Yet he was usually a silent owner on these occasions (e.g., nos. 22 and 27), and he was not a major player in Scottish Enlightenment publishing as long as Millar was active. A turning point of sorts was reached when Millar invited Strahan and Cadell to take one-quarter shares (as against Millar's own one-half share) in Sir James Steuart's *Principles of Political Oeconomy* (1767; no. 101).[17] This was the last major book that Millar registered at Stationers' Hall and the first major book that he permitted Strahan to copublish, although as usual Strahan's role was not detectable in the imprint.

For several years after taking control of Millar's firm, Cadell identified himself in imprints as Millar's successor. At first he continued his master's tradition of disguising Strahan's role as a publisher, as in the first two volumes of Walter Anderson's *History of France*, published in February 1769 with the imprint "Printed for T. Cadell, (Successor to Mr. Millar) in the Strand" (no. 121), even though Strahan owned the other half of the copyright. However, with the publication of William Robertson's *History of Charles V* a few weeks later, Strahan's name appeared not only *with* Cadell's, as one of the publishers of the book, but *before* Cadell's, presumably in acknowledgment of Strahan's seniority. The copublishing "Agreement" between Strahan and Cadell probably dates from this time. From then until Strahan's death in 1785, the imprint "Printed for W. Strahan; and T. Cadell, in the Strand" became a common sight, normally with each man owning an equal share of the copyright or the publishing profits.

Cadell enjoyed success in every aspect of his life and career. On 1 April 1769, at the age of twenty-six, he married the daughter of Thomas Jones, an Anglican clergyman. His marriage not only demonstrated confidence in his ability to sustain a career in the trade but also marked a step toward

15. Strahan to Hume, 9 Apr. 1774, in Hume, *Letters of Hume to Strahan*, 283: "*Characteristics of Great Britain* Mr. Millar and I bought for £30." Cf. Harlan, "William Strahan," 69, 106.

16. Brack, "William Strahan," 185–86.

17. Contract in University of Reading Library, MS 1393/26/2(d); Stationers' Hall register, 16 Apr. 1767.

his integration into the London establishment. Cadell's only daughter would marry Charles Lucas Eldridge, chaplain to George III. Especially after his retirement in 1793, Cadell assumed a number of civic and professional responsibilities in London, including serving as a governor of the Foundling Hospital in 1795 and becoming master of the Stationers' Company in 1799. In 1798 he was elected alderman of Walbrook ward, and two years later was elected sheriff of London and Middlesex. It was rumored that he was in line to become lord mayor of London at the time of his death from an asthma attack on 27 December 1802.

Cadell's good fortune was not guaranteed from the outset. Scarcely two months after his marriage, on 13 June 1769, Cadell had an opportunity to demonstrate the extent of his entrepreneurial vision when many of Andrew Millar's shares in copyrights were auctioned to the trade at the Queen's Arms Tavern. Strahan and Cadell bought heavily, becoming in the process the sole or principal owners of the copyrights of some of the Scottish titles that Millar had published or copublished over the past decade, such as Smith's *Theory of Moral Sentiments*, Kames's *Elements of Criticism*, Reid's *Inquiry into the Human Mind*, and several works by James Ferguson.[18] These titles supplemented other Millar copyrights that do not appear in the Millar auction catalogue, either because they were sold separately or because Millar had turned them over to Cadell before his death, sometimes allowing Strahan to purchase a minority interest.[19] All told, Strahan and Cadell each purchased almost 36 percent of what came to be known as the "Millar Stock."[20] At about the same time, the pair began publishing new books by several of Millar's old Scottish authors as well as by a number of English writers.

In a letter to David Hall of 15 June 1771, Strahan boasts of being a copyright owner or shareholder of "above 200" books.[21] He explains how his transformation from printer to publisher had astonished his fellow printers in London, "who never dreamt of going out of the old beaten Track," and "taught them to emancipate themselves from the Slavery in which the Booksellers held them" (118). Instead of just getting by, as he

18. *Catalogue of the Copies and Shares, of the late Mr Andrew Millar.* Harlan, "William Strahan," 105, notes that Strahan alone spent £379.1s.10d. at the sale to purchase shares of forty-two titles.

19. Harlan, "William Strahan," 106.

20. Lutes, "Andrew Strahan," 19, 88.

21. Strahan to Cadell, 15 June 1771, in "Correspondence between William Strahan and David Hall," 12:117.

might have done if he had confined himself to "mere *printing for Book-sellers,*" he had gone his own way, with great success, and he proudly tells Hall that no printer had "ever before extended [his business] so far as I have done" (117). Other London printers had owned property in books before Strahan, however. William Bowyer the younger, who had employed Strahan as a compositor during his early days in London, owned shares in more than 160 books over the course of his long career.[22] Strahan himself had begun purchasing shares in copyrights early in his career, so the process had been going on for a long time. Moreover, as late as his boastful letter to Hall, he was still giving serious consideration to "selling all my property in Copies, and confining my whole Attention to printing" (117). Despite these qualifications, in 1771 Strahan really was marking a new path for an eighteenth-century British printer. Its uniqueness consisted not in owning copyrights as such but in publishing the most important new literary and learned works of the age.

Andrew Millar had prepared the foundations. The special encouragement shown toward Scottish authors; the emphasis on works of polite learning, often published originally in expensive quarto editions that appealed to the most prominent segment of the book-buying public; the practice of paying authors more than any other firm for publication rights, thereby acquiring first choice of the most desirable new books; the willingness to make cash presents to authors whose books sold better than expected; the tradition of cooperative publication with booksellers in Edinburgh; the pattern of registering many major new books at Stationers' Hall in London in order to provide them with statutory protection under the copyright act of 1710; the determination to regard ownership of copyright shares as perpetual property and to take a hard line against perceived copyright violations emanating from Scotland, Ireland, or anywhere else—all were adopted from Millar. What distinguished the House of Strahan and Cadell was the scale of operations: more printing presses, more publications, more money paid to authors, more profits, more fame and glory. These developments were in turn made possible by personal and institutional factors that greatly expanded Millar's operation.

A page from one of Strahan's surviving ledgers, showing all the printing that was charged to Cadell's account from November 1777 through April 1778, provides some idea of the enterprise (fig. 5.3). In the space of

22. Maslen, "William Strahan," 250–51; Maslen, "Slaves or Freemen?" 145–55; Maslen and Lancaster, *Bowyer Ledgers,* xxxviii.

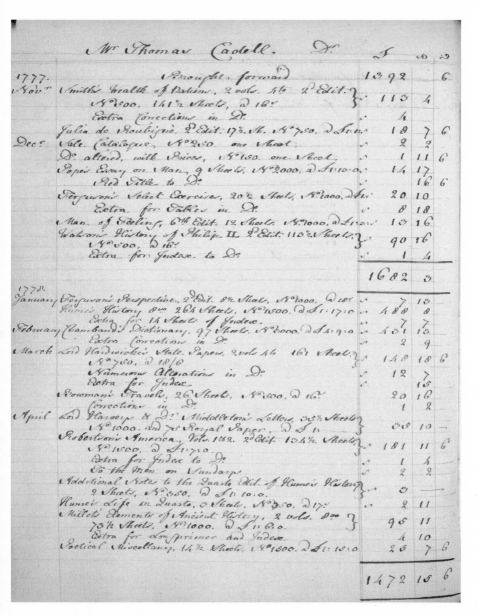

Mr Thomas Cadell.   Dr   £   s   d

1777.   (Brought forward)   1392   6
Novr Smith's Wealth of Nations, 2 vols. 4to 2d Edit.
        No 500, 141½ Sheets, a 16s   }   113 4
        Extra Corrections in Do   4
      Julia de Roubigné, 2d Edit. 17½ Sh. No 750, a   18 7 6
Decr Sale Catalogue, No 250, one Sheet.   2 2
      Do altered, with Prices, No 150, one Sheet.   1 11 6
      Pope's Essay on Man, 9 Sheets, No 2000, a   14 17
      Red Title to Do   16 6
      Ferguson's Select Exercises, 20½ Sheets, No 1000.   20 10
        Extra for Tables in Do   8 18
      Man of Feeling, 6th Edit. 12 Sheets, No 1000,   13 16
      Watson's History of Philip II 2d Edit. 113½ Sheets,
        No 500, a 16s   }   90 16
        Extra for Index to Do   1 4
                                                        1682 3

1778.
January Ferguson's Perspective, 2d Edit. 8¾ Sheets, No 1000, a   7 13
      Hume's History 8vo 264 Sheets, No 1500, a £1:17:0   488 8
        Extra for 14 Sheets of Index   7 7
February Chambaud's Dictionary, 97 Sheets, No 2000, a £4:9:0 431 13
        Extra Corrections in Do   2 9
March Lord Hardwicke's State Papers, 2 vols 4to 16¾ Sheets,
        No 750, a 18/6   }   148 18 6
        Numerous Alterations in Do   12 7
        Extra for Index   15
      Bowman's Travels, 26 Sheets, No 500, a 16s   20 16
        Corrections in Do   1 2
April Lord Harcourt & Do Middleton's Letters, 35½ Sheets
        No 1000. and on Royal Paper, a   }   88 10 —
      Robertson's America, Vols 1 & 2. 2d Edit. 134½ Sheets,
        No 1000, a £1:7:0   }   181 11 6
        Extra for Index to Do   1 4
        To the Men on Sundays   2 2
      Additional Notes to the Quarto Edit. of Hume's History,
        2 Sheets, No 250, a £1:10:0   }   3 —
      Hume's Life in Quarto, 3 Sheets, No 250, a 17s   2 11
      Millot's Elements of Ancient History, 2 vols. 8vo
        73½ Sheets, No 1000, a £1:6:0   }   95 11
        Extra for Longprimer and Index   4 10
      Poetical Miscellany, 14½ Sheets, No 1500, a £1:15:0 25 7 6
                                                        1472 15 6

Fig. 5.3. The Strahan printing ledgers are a goldmine of information about eighteenth-century book production. This image shows the books that Strahan charged to Cadell's account from November 1777 through April 1778, including various editions of Scottish Enlightenment books that were copublished by Strahan and Cadell. British Library, Add. MSS 48816, fol. 21v.

just five months, Strahan printed for the publishing partnership 500 copies of the second edition of Adam Smith's *Wealth of Nations* (no. 177), 750 copies of the second edition of Henry Mackenzie's *Julia de Roubigné* (no. 183), 1,000 copies of the first edition of James Ferguson's *Select Mechanical Exercises* (no. 153), 1,000 copies of the sixth edition of Mackenzie's *Man of Feeling* (no. 135), 500 copies of the second edition of Robert Watson's *History of Philip II* (no. 186), 1,000 copies of the second edition of James Ferguson's *Art of Drawing in Perspective* (no. 168), 1,500 copies of an eight-volume octavo edition of David Hume's *History of England* (no. 75), and 1,500 copies of the second edition of William Robertson's *History of America* (no. 185). We can see that Strahan was also printing other books for the partnership during this period, from a cheap reprint of Alexander Pope's *Essay on Man* (1777) to a two-volume quarto edition of Louis Chambaud's French-English dictionary (1778; copublished by Peter Elmsley). But literary and learned works by Scottish authors constituted the core of their publishing program. At the end of each year, Strahan would total the printing bill and the account would be settled. The amounts were not trivial: £1,682.3s. in 1777, and £1,472.15s.6d. in just the first third of 1778. However, the published books were bringing in revenues that far exceeded these printing costs, and large profits were generated.

Besides the basic agreement between Strahan and Cadell themselves, the publishing partnership was sustained through the cultivation of closer ties with the book trade in Edinburgh. In this respect, Cadell seems to have thrown his net somewhat wider than Strahan, particularly in his greater willingness to collaborate with one of the rising stars of Edinburgh publishing, Charles Elliot. But the key to the London–Edinburgh axis lay with Strahan's old friends in the Scottish capital. We have already seen that on his periodic excursions to Scotland Strahan spent much of his time in the company of Alexander Kincaid and John Balfour, near contemporaries who operated the leading Scottish bookselling and publishing firms for much of the third quarter of the eighteenth century. On 26 June 1768 Strahan made his most important summer jaunt to Scotland. Millar had died less than three weeks earlier, leaving behind both uncertainty and opportunity regarding the publication of new works by Scottish authors. In Scotland Strahan met frequently with both Kincaid and Balfour. A typical entry was the one Strahan made in his journal on 1 August: "Dined at home. Called on Mr Kincaid, Dr. Robertson, Marchioness of Lothian, etc. Supt at Mr Balfour."

Strahan was then preparing to copublish William Robertson's *History of Charles V* with Balfour, and we know that some of his meetings with both Balfour and Robertson were meant to finalize the details of that ambitious project. It is also likely that on this visit Strahan met Balfour's son John, who would serve an apprenticeship with him in London from 1771 to 1778 and then return to Scotland to manage Balfour's paper mill near Edinburgh. As we have seen, Strahan and Balfour had been friends since their childhood days in Edinburgh. Just as Strahan visited Balfour on his periodic jaunts to Edinburgh, Balfour sometimes traveled to London for the express purpose of seeing his friend.[23] The two men held similar, conservative views on British foreign policy and American affairs.[24] Balfour's deference to his old friend was such that he confided in Strahan about the prospect of building a gunpowder mill in Scotland in 1780, adding that Strahan's advice on the matter would "go a great way" toward determining his decision.[25] Still another link between them was the Edinburgh printer-scholar William Smellie, who was Balfour's partner during the 1760s and a great favorite of Strahan's. For all these reasons, the association with Balfour would form one of the Edinburgh pillars supporting the Strahan–Cadell publishing edifice.

The other pillar of the Edinburgh connection was the bookselling firm headed by Alexander Kincaid, whose long friendship with Strahan was noted in the last chapter. More significant than any particular copublication project they may have discussed during the summer of 1768 was the attempt by Strahan to map out a comprehensive strategy for publishing new work by Scottish authors. In a letter of 19 September, two weeks after his return to London, Strahan explained to Creech (who had been out of town when Strahan visited during the summer) that he had made a "very bold Push" to influence Kincaid in regard to Creech's career. The arguments he had made in person were subsequently reinforced in a letter to Kincaid that he quoted to Creech, including this revealing passage: "I wanted to concert such measures with you (at this Juncture on Mr Millar's Demise) that you, Mr Cadell and I might secure any Author's of our Country, whether resident here or with you, that were worth notice; which I am certain might very easily be done." There follows a passage—

23. Strahan to Hall, 24 Aug. 1770, in "Correspondence between William Strahan and David Hall," 11:352.

24. For example, Balfour's support for the war against the American "rebels" is evident in his letters to James Ross of 21 May 1777 and 10 March 1778, in the Gordon Castle Muniments, National Archives of Scotland, GD44/43/173. For Strahan's views on this subject, see Cochrane, *Dr. Johnson's Printer*, chap. 13.

25. Balfour to Strahan, 10 July 1780, Pierpont Morgan Library, Misc. English.

quoted at greater length in chapter 6, where Creech's career is considered more fully—in which Strahan tries to convince Kincaid "to hasten your Separation from Mr Bell" and replace him with Creech.

Thus, Strahan made it clear to Kincaid that his exertions on behalf of Creech were driven by his wish to establish a reliable London–Edinburgh syndicate that would corner the market on publishing what we now call the Scottish Enlightenment in the post-Millar era. He knew that Kincaid was no longer an aggressive force in publishing and that his junior partner John Bell did not get along well with Cadell. He therefore wanted Kincaid to select a younger partner who would be Strahan and Cadell's principal associate in Edinburgh. Strahan was well aware that meddling in the business affairs of his old friend, and corresponding with Creech behind Kincaid's back, was hardly behavior of which to be proud, but he was hopeful that Kincaid would not take offense. "I securely trust in my long and intimate Friendship with him," Strahan confided to Creech in his letter of 19 September, "that he will not be angry at my Interfering in a matter which a Person not so good naturedly-disposed as he is, might be apt to be." As Strahan continued to pressure Kincaid on this matter over the next three years, he relied on Creech for inside information about what was happening in the world of Edinburgh publishing. "Let me have any news that may be stirring with you," he wrote on 22 December 1768, "especially among the trade."

Once Creech was finally installed as Kincaid's partner and successor in 1771, Strahan laid out his publishing strategy. "I shall be very well pleased to be concerned in any thing along with you and Mr Cadell," he tells Creech on 4 January 1772: "I mean any thing of Consequence, for small Shares of small Books are hardly worth the Trouble of keeping an Account of them, especially as I have a great many different Acc[oun]ts to adjust and keep already. But in a Work of any Bulk or Consideration I have no Objection to being joined with you and Mr Cadell, as we understand one another perfectly well." The first two Scottish manuscripts that fell under this instruction were the first volume of Lord Monboddo's *Of the Origin and Progress of Language* (no. 160) and Lord Kames's *Sketches of the History of Man* (no. 164), both of which were sent to Strahan for evaluation late in 1773. On 13 November Strahan regretfully declined to copublish Monboddo's manuscript on the grounds that "it will not be a popular Book" (Cadell would, however, play a role in its publication), but in a letter of 17 January 1774 he praised Kames's work ("every Page I have yet dipp'd into contains some what [i.e., thing] amusing or instructive, or both") and declared that "Mr Cadell and I . . . thankfully accept your

Offer, and will do what in us lies to usher it into the Public, with every Advantage we can give it, and push the Sale here to the utmost."

As Monboddo's work demonstrates, Strahan did not mean it literally when he told Creech that he and Cadell would be happy to collaborate on *any* substantial new book. Unlike Millar, Strahan seems to have personally read, or at least "dipp'd into," all manuscript submissions, and he had great confidence in his own judgment. His correspondence with Creech is filled with rejections of manuscripts offered for copublication, some of which were subsequently published or copublished by other booksellers, such as John Murray, Charles Elliot, and Creech himself. Nor did Strahan abide in every instance by his policy of declining to collaborate on "small Books." Not long after Strahan, Cadell, and Creech began to copublish Scottish authors, Strahan told Creech in a letter of 17 January 1774 that young James Gregory had offered him a little manuscript by his father, the late Dr. John Gregory of the University of Edinburgh, "only 50 Pages in Writing," which the three men would copublish that spring under the title *A Father's Legacy to His Daughters* (no. 163). The low retail price of this little book (just two shillings) must have held down the profits on each edition, but it was immediately hugely successful as a guide to female social behavior and moral values and therefore profitable for its publishers, in spite of competition from many unauthorized editions. Although Strahan, Cadell, and Creech published the early editions of *A Father's Legacy* on a conditional basis, Strahan subsequently pushed Creech to secure the copyright and was delighted when he did so on favorable terms late in the summer.[26]

The most impressive collaborative accomplishments of Strahan, Cadell, and Creech were the large number of major books by Scottish authors that they copublished during the 1770s and early 1780s. Besides the second volume of Sir John Dalrymple's *Memoirs of Great Britain and Ireland* (1773; no. 143), which was the last major new title to include Kincaid's name in its imprint along with Creech's, the trio copublished in succession Alexander Gerard's *Essay on Genius* (no. 162)—along with Gregory's *Father's Legacy* and Kames's *Sketches of the History of Man*—in 1774; George Campbell's *Philosophy of Rhetoric* (no. 174) in 1776, Robert Watson's *History of Philip II* (no. 186), Henry Mackenzie's *Julia de Roubigné* (no. 183), and the first volume of Hugh Blair's *Sermons* (no. 188) in 1777; most of Smellie's multivolume translation of Buffon's *Natural History* (no. 212) in 1780; the book version of *The Mirror* (no. 217) in 1781; and

---

26. Moran, "From Rudeness to Refinement," 122–26; and chap. 3 in this volume.

Adam Ferguson's *Progress and Termination of the Roman Republic* (no. 232), Hugh Blair's *Lectures on Rhetoric and Belles Lettres* (no. 230), and James Beattie's *Dissertations, Moral and Critical* (no. 229) in 1783. In reality, the extent of their collaboration was even greater, because all their names did not always appear in the imprints of works they copublished. For example, in 1776 Adam Smith's *Wealth of Nations* (no. 177) was advertised in the Edinburgh newspapers by Creech as if he were its publisher, even though the imprint contains only the names of Strahan and Cadell; other evidence seems to corroborate Creech's involvement.[27] Other books by Scottish authors were published by Strahan and Cadell alone, by Creech and Cadell without Strahan, or, in the case of William Robertson's histories, by Strahan and Cadell along with Balfour. Taken as a whole, the London–Edinburgh publishing syndicate led by Strahan and Cadell stood at the head of the profession.

Holding the syndicate together was not always easy. As we shall see in chapter 6, Strahan lectured and disciplined Creech whenever he believed the younger man was not behaving properly. He never relaxed his control, and even his good wishes were peppered with instructional proverbs, as in the closing to his letter of 10 November 1773: "I hope all goes well with you, and that you grow in favour with all Mankind. Punctuality, Regularity, and Precision are the very Life of Business. And none of these, I hope will be wanting with you." Early in the relationship, Creech complained to Strahan about Cadell's lack of punctuality in his correspondence, to which Strahan replied on 18 March 1774 that "this must be purely accidental" because Cadell "possesses, in truth, the true Spirit of Business, as you will every Day be more and more convinced of." It would not be surprising if Strahan then lectured Cadell (who was, it must be remembered, only two and a half years older than Creech) on the importance of punctuality in *his* correspondence, for the problem does not seem to have arisen again.

The final component in Strahan's imperial vision proved more difficult to attain. Strahan wished to see his two Edinburgh copublishers, John Balfour and (after Kincaid's retirement) William Creech, collaborating with each other—and ultimately with Strahan and Cadell—in what he called, in a letter to Creech of 21–22 February 1774, a "Coalition between you in regard to the Purchase of Copies." The plan started on a high note in 1772, when Strahan, Cadell, Balfour, and Kincaid & Creech joined forces to copublish the revised second edition of William Buchan's *Domestic Medicine*, originally printed for the author in 1769 by Balfour's firm

27. Sher, "New Light," 26n2.

Domeſtic Medicine:

O R, A

T R E A T I S E

ON THE

PREVENTION AND CURE

O F

D I S E A S E S

B Y

REGIMEN and SIMPLE MEDICINES.

W I T H

An APPENDIX, containing a DISPENSATORY
for the Uſe of Private Practitioners.

By W I L L I A M B U C H A N, M.D.
Fellow of the Royal College of Phyſicians, Edinburgh.

THE NINTH EDITION:

To which is now added,
An ADDITIONAL CHAPTER on COLD BATHING,
and Drinking the MINERAL WATERS.

L O N D O N:
Printed for A. Strahan; T. Cadell in the Strand;
and J. Balfour, and W. Creech, at Edinburgh.
M DCC LXXXVI.

Fig. 5.4. William Buchan originally published his popular medical advice book, *Domestic Medicine*, by subscription in 1769, but from the second edition in 1772 it was copublished by Strahan and Cadell in London and Balfour and Creech in Edinburgh—an unwieldy partnership that could not be sustained. The ninth edition of 1786 was the first to contain a chapter on the medicinal effects of mineral waters. Thomas Fisher Rare Book Library, University of Toronto.

(then including the printers Smellie and Auld). As we have seen, Buchan's book subsequently became one of the century's biggest best sellers, and the firms of Strahan, Cadell, Balfour, and Creech continued to appear in the imprint throughout its glory years (fig. 5.4). Although Strahan continually campaigned for a regular publishing partnership that would build on the success of the Buchan collaboration, he never could achieve his goal. Writing to Creech on 10 November 1773, for example, he asks if Balfour is to be concerned in the publication of Kames's *Sketches of the History of Man*, adding,

> I think he should, and that you should cultivate a close Friendship and Intimacy with him, as he is really a Man who understands Business in gener-

all, and in particular Bookselling, extremely well. . . . As for the Coalition, I am, and so is Mr Cadell, willing to enter into any Engagement in regard to it that you shall propose. I mean, only with you and Mr Balfour, for we will be concerned with no other. And I am sure between us there can never be any misunderstanding, else I am vastly mistaken.

But vastly mistaken Strahan was, because Creech and Balfour had difficulty agreeing about anything.

At first Strahan remained optimistic. Although Creech convinced him that he should be the sole Edinburgh copublisher of Kames's book, apparently in order to establish his reputation as a young bookseller, Creech also agreed to some kind of arrangement with Balfour. The latter prospect caused Strahan to proclaim, in a letter of 17 January 1774: "You two firmly united in Sentiment and Interest will form a Phalanx which nothing will be able to withstand in Scotland." Both reported to Strahan on the results of a "conference" they held in Edinburgh the following month, to which he responded on 21–22 February with a letter to both men, to be opened

> in the Presence of one another. It contains my Sentiments of the Outlines of a Written Agreement, which I wish you to enter into, if you approve of it, leaving the undertakings now in hand to be settled according to your now separate Pleasures, without Impeachment of one another. I imagine you will very soon feel the good Effects of a thorough Confidence and Agreement so sensibly, that it will be henceforth unnecessary for me ever more to mention the Subject.

The same letter, however, referred to "past Grievances on either Side, whether real or imaginary," and these evidently proved difficult to overcome. In a letter to Creech of 18 March 1774, Strahan was still campaigning aggressively for an agreement based on three principles, which he listed in numbered sequence:

1. That a Coalition between Mr Balfour and you will be mutually beneficial
2. That to make it useful and lasting, it ought to be in writing. And
3. To make it cordial, the very first Article ought to be That all past Offences, real or imaginary, be burried in everlasting Oblivion.

Once again Strahan offered to broker such a coalition with "some very plain and simple Rules, that, if followed, would forever prevent any future misunderstanding between you."

When the Creech–Balfour union floundered, Strahan pushed for a new variation in a letter to Creech of 12 July 1774: Creech was to join Balfour as a partner in the printing business of "the able industrious and sensible [William] Smellie," after which "a compleat Coalition with Mr Balfour will quickly follow." On 25 August Strahan told Creech of his hope that "you are now a Partner in the Printing-house with Smellie, whom I much esteem; and that Mr Balfour and you will strongly coalesce and draw together, which will do well for both. There is nobody to interfere or indeed can interfere with you, if you two agree." Negotiations dragged on, however. Balfour countered Creech's offer of £150 for a one-third interest in Smellie's concern with a demand for £200, prompting Strahan to advise, in a letter to Creech of 27 December 1774, that they split the difference for the greater good. Further details on the Smellie affair are lacking, but it appears that the scheme finally collapsed in 1775. Other aspects of the coalition scheme fared no better. On 29 January 1776 Strahan admitted to Creech that Balfour's recent conduct has been "unaccountably mean, but exactly of a piece with all the rest of his Conduct." Soon both Balfour and Creech were complaining to Strahan of incivilities by the other, and in his letters to Creech of 4 and 23 July 1776 Strahan agreed that Balfour had acted deplorably in attempting to secure copies of Buchan's *Domestic Medicine* from Creech for just 2s.6d., when Creech was getting at least 4s.8d. for them from other Edinburgh booksellers. They had another falling out over an Edinburgh edition of Justamond's translation of Raynal's history of the West Indies, causing Charles Elliot to write to Cadell of "a good deal of altercation between Mr Balfour and Mr Creech."[28] All talk of a printing partnership with Smellie or a full-scale publishing "coalition" now ceased, and the most Strahan could muster was a wish, in his letter of 4 July, that Creech and Balfour "will yet come to a better Understanding" with each other for their mutual interest. They did not, and in 1781 their rivalry would culminate in a fierce contest between Creech and Balfour's son Elphingston for the position of bookseller to the Society of Antiquaries of Scotland, which Creech obtained.

Why was Strahan so concerned about forging a coalition between his two Edinburgh associates during the early and mid-1770s? Two answers

28. Quoted in McDougall, "Charles Elliot and the London Booksellers," 94.

appear in the following passage from one of Strahan's letters to Creech, dated 9 April 1774:

> I still sincerely wish a firm and lasting Coalition between you and Mr Balfour may take place; because I am not clearer that I exist than I am that it will be for your mutual Advantage. . . . The Coalition would be of great use in future Purchases, and prevent Authors from raising their Demands to the enormous Heighth they have done of late: But indeed the precarious Terms upon which we now hold Literary Property of every kind, will effectually ease That End, both here and with you. You might, besides, be of particular Service to Mr Balfour in the Printing and Paper-selling, if he printed and sold Paper as cheap as others, as I doubt not he would do. In short, you ought to have but one mind, and live like Brothers, and then you must carry all before you.

Taking the second of these reasons first, we see that Strahan was anticipating a mutually advantageous collaboration if Creech could take advantage of the Balfour printing partnership with Smellie as well as the Balfour paper mill at Colinton. Such an arrangement would also have been advantageous for Strahan and Cadell whenever a joint production was printed in Scotland. Even though the Creech–Balfour coalition failed, there were occasions when Strahan and Cadell benefited from the vertical integration of the Balfour family firm—a legacy from the days of Hamilton & Balfour. Strahan anticipated that a strong coalition between Balfour and Creech would provide additional opportunities for cheap and efficient joint publications through the savings in printing and paper that the Balfour–Smellie connection could provide.

The other reason cited by Strahan—to "prevent Authors from raising their Demands to the enormous Heighth they have done of late"—opens up a large, important topic that was discussed in chapter 3 from the point of view of authors. Publishers naturally saw matters differently. Along with their Edinburgh partners, Strahan and Cadell had continued Millar's policy of paying large amounts to their premier authors. At times they recognized the status value of their practice and even boasted publicly about it, as Cadell did when he testified before Parliament in 1785 about the large amount of copy money his house had paid to authors since Millar's death. In his *Letters containing a Comparative View of Edinburgh in the Years 1763 and 1783*, Creech asserts, with considerable exaggeration, that in 1763 "literary property, or authors acquiring money by their writings, was hardly known in Scotland." Twenty years later, however, "the value of literary property was carried higher by the Scots than ever was known among any people."[29] Creech's pamphlet was explicitly endorsed by Strahan, who remarked in a letter of 26 January 1784: "Every Word of it I know to be true."

William Strahan's private correspondence with Creech also reveals another side of the story. To these publishers, the copy money paid to authors seemed to be getting out of hand, and Strahan hoped that a four-way coalition with Cadell, Creech, and Balfour would lower authors' demands by reducing competition among the leading publishers in London and Edinburgh. Strahan and his colleagues were constantly grumbling among themselves about the outrageous demands of Scottish authors. Creech must have done so in his letters to Strahan of 15 and 18 July 1776, for in his reply of 23 July Strahan writes: "You paint the extravagent Demands of Modern Authors in very lively, as well as in just Colours. They are indeed beyond all Credibility." The immediate context of these words was a request by Lord Kames for three hundred guineas for the right to publish the first edition of his *Gentleman Farmer* (no. 176), a thick, illustrated octavo of more than four hundred printed pages. Strahan laid out a full, speculative accounting in order to demonstrate to Creech that the publishers would stand to lose more than £240 if they paid Kames the full amount he was requesting, even if they sold the entire print run of 1,000 copies at the estimated wholesale price of 3s.8d. Here are his calculations:

Printing 30 Sheets, No. 1,000 @ £1:1:0	£31:10:0
Paper 60 Reams @ 16 Shillings	48:0:0
Engraving 6 Cutts, suppose	6:6:0
Paper and printing off Do., suppose	10:10:0
Advertising and Incidentals, suppose	13:14:0
[Total Expenses]	110:0:0
1,000 Books @ 3s.8d.1s	183:6:8
Subtract Charges	110:0:0
Remains [Profit]	73:6:8

Strahan refused to have anything further to do with Kames, whom he called "quite a Jew in his dealings" in a letter to Creech of 12 March 1779.

Kames was not the only Scottish author whose demands for copy money were upsetting Strahan. After Creech reported that Adam Fer-

29. [Creech], *Letters to Sir John Sinclair*, 11–12.

guson had reacted badly to a recent offer for his Roman history (no. 232), Strahan exclaimed in his letter of 23 July 1776: "Dr Ferguson to treat the offer of £1,000 with Disdain! a Sum which till very lately, a Scots Professor, or indeed any Professor, never possessed. I do assure you Mr Cadell and I both, who have suffered greatly by our Profession to Authours, are determined to be more cautious in all our future Bargains." He was also annoyed that Robert Watson had requested £2,000 for his *History of Philip II* (no. 186): "Ten or twenty years ago I told him, he would have been glad of as many hundreds." Having raised expectations by paying Robertson so much for *Charles V,* perhaps Strahan should not have been so surprised to find that other Scottish men of letters were trying their best to emulate Robertson's performance. Although Strahan and his associates were obtaining great wealth and status from their Scottish publishing, and were personally responsible (and publicly proud of it) for significantly increasing the level of copy money paid to authors, they were not always comfortable in the new world they had created.

Strahan sometimes regarded Scottish authors as a cabal bent on driving up the price of book manuscripts. He particularly resented established authors for raising the expectations of younger ones, who had not yet proved themselves with their pens. "I have at length agreed, but after much difficulty, with Captain Bryden," Strahan wrote to David Hume on 25 January 1773, in reference to Patrick Brydone's *A Tour through Sicily and Malta* (no. 150). He proceeded to scold Hume for having "raised his expectations so very high, and so much beyond the real worth of the book . . . that he could not be satisfied with the very utmost the size and nature of the book would admit of. You spoil all young authors, by leading them to expect prices only due to veterans in literature and men of established reputation."[30] Brydone's *Tour* became a best seller,[31] and we do not find Strahan complaining about it again in his extant correspondence.

Strahan's belief that the Scottish literati were engaged in a high-handed conspiracy to raise the value of copy money was not without foundation. Besides the fact that Scottish authors tended to band together to support each other's projects in the various ways discussed in chapters 2 and 3, authors sometimes entertained unrealistic expectations about copy money because they did not understand the book business and adopted a condescending attitude toward those who did. This was certainly true of Lord Monboddo, who pontificated about the proper price of his book in London

30. In Burton, *Letters of Eminent Persons,* 99.

31. On the grounds for its appeal, see Turner, *British Travel Writers,* 115–21.

and Edinburgh on the basis of his fantasies about how much profit was justified for a bookseller in each of those places.[32] In 1800 Creech would tell Cadell & Davies that in order for a particular book they were copublishing to yield a reasonable profit, the price would have to be raised to six shillings in boards, even though the author was insisting it could not go above five. "Authors must be drove out of [the] Idea that we make such great sums of every impression of their Works," he added.[33]

Similar feelings surfaced in negotiations about the manuscript of Robert Wallace's "Treatise on Taste." In April 1774 Wallace's son George, backed by David Hume, requested £500 from Strahan and Cadell (*LDH*, 2:289–90). Unfortunately for Wallace, Strahan and Cadell were still edgy from an embarrassing incident of the previous year, when they had paid John Hawkesworth £6,000 to edit a three-volume work of voyages by Captain Cook and others that Hawkesworth actually had done little to improve.[34] If the Hawkesworth episode "does not cure Authors of their delirium" about copy money, Strahan told Hume in the context of discussing Wallace's request, "I am sure [it] will have the proper effect upon booksellers."[35] Even though he had not read a word of Robert Wallace's manuscript and had been a close friend of the late author, Strahan reacted almost as sharply as he would later to Kames's demands for *The Gentleman Farmer:* such fees were simply too high for works of uncertain popularity, especially coming from an author who had "never in his lifetime produced anything that was so received by the public, as could in any manner justify such a price as £500."[36] He believed it would be necessary to sell 2,000 bound copies at a guinea each to justify such a transaction, and he simply did not believe that was going to happen. As usual, he placed the blame on the high fees that were being requested, and paid, for new books. "The prices demanded, and indeed given of late for copies, hath had a most strange effect upon our present Authors," he observed, "as every one is abundantly apt to compare his own merit with his contemporaries, of which he cannot be supposed to be an impartial judge." In the end, Strahan consented to print Robert Wallace's book at the publishers' ex-

32. Monboddo to Cadell, 22 Sept. 1780, HL, MS Hyde 69, item 26.

33. Creech to Cadell & Davies, 12 Nov. 1800 (copy), ECL, William Creech Letterbook, Green Box 120, 33–36.

34. Hawkesworth, *Account of the Voyages for Making Discoveries in the Southern Hemisphere;* Cochrane, *Dr. Johnson's Printer,* 140.

35. Strahan to Hume, 9 Apr. 1774, in Hume, *Letters of Hume to Strahan,* 283.

36. None of the three titles by Robert Wallace in table 2 ever reached a second edition during the eighteenth century.

pense, sharing the profits with the author's son. But George Wallace may have considered this offer demeaning, and he elected to leave "A Treatise on Taste" unpublished. It remains so to this day.[37]

The profit-sharing proposal that Strahan made to Wallace was among the most popular of several tactics used by publishers to counter the growing demands of authors. When negotiating with John Bell in January 1781 about the possibility of copublishing Lord Kames's *Loose Hints upon Education* (no. 214), Charles Dilly took issue with Bell's plan to purchase the copyright for the undisclosed amount that Kames had requested, because "'tis wrong for a bookseller to yield to demand of authors in paying an Extravagant price for copy right. The surest way is to reward an author according to the real sale of his works. I have seen and felt too much in purchasing new copies."[38] Dilly favored limiting the publisher's risk to paper and print and sharing profits with authors, just as Strahan had offered to do for Wallace's "Treatise on Taste." But as we saw in chapter 3, authors were often suspicious of that mode of publishing, and this was certainly true of Kames. After Dilly refused to collaborate on Kames's terms, Bell purchased the copyright of *Loose Hints* from the author and recruited John Murray as the London copublisher.[39]

Another tactic was to purchase a copyright with strings attached. In chapter 3 we saw how Strahan, Cadell, and Creech resorted to the use of a safety or saving clause that enabled them to purchase the copyright to Adam Ferguson's *Roman Republic* (no. 232) for £2,000 without the slightest risk to themselves. A less severe version of this procedure was to pay authors or their estates less than they requested for the copyright of a book, with a proviso for an additional payment if the book should reach a second edition. A saving clause of this kind was used with Kames's *Sketches of the History of Mankind* (no. 164), and Hume recommended a similar arrangement for Wallace's "Treatise on Taste."[40] In chapter 3, we saw that on at least two occasions during the 1790s Andrew Strahan and the Cadells saved hundreds of pounds by making a £300 plus £200 arrangement of this kind for books by Thomas Somerville (no. 308) and Adam Smith (no. 336) that never required a second edition. Charles Dilly did much the same thing in 1796, when he offered John Pinkerton £400 for

---

37. A critical edition of the text is appended to Smith, "Literary Career."

38. Dilly to Bell, 27 Jan. 1781, NLS, Dep. 317, box 1.

39. Zachs, *First John Murray,* 296.

40. Hume to Strahan, 2 Apr. 1774, in *LDH,* 2:290; Strahan to Hume, 9 Apr. 1774, in Hume, *Letters of Hume to Strahan,* 284.

the copyright of his *History of Scotland* (no. 345), plus an additional £200 if all one thousand copies of the first edition sold off within two years and the author made revisions and corrections for a second edition.[41]

Sometimes this kind of arrangement was modified to allow for an additional fee, in money or in copies of the book, to be paid for every later edition that the author revised. Strahan and Cadell and their Edinburgh partners adopted this strategy with Alexander Adam's *Roman Antiquities* and William Buchan's *Domestic Medicine.* This option appealed to publishers because it encouraged authors to make substantive revisions, which constituted one of the main ways that statutory copyright could be extended beyond the twenty-eight-year limit established by law. In addition, exceptionally popular books like Buchan's could be reprinted in very large print runs of several thousand copies per edition, thus reducing the impact of the fees that authors received for later editions. Buchan can also be used to illustrate another, particularly shrewd publishers' ploy. In 1781 Strahan and Cadell agreed to pay him £500 for a new book he was supposedly writing, with the projected title *Preventive Medicine,* and they gave him £100 as an advance, "purely to prevent him from disposing of it to any other of the Trade," Strahan told Creech in a letter of 23 August 1781, "as in that Case he might have been tempted to insert in it the most valuable Part of *our* Volume [i.e., *Domestic Medicine*], and by that means have injured the Sale of it very naturally."[42] The new contract was simply a means of keeping Buchan in the Strahan–Cadell stable.

Still another variation was to pay a fixed amount for the rights to the first edition only, leaving one's options open about what might happen later. As we saw in chapter 3, savvy authors like Hume and Cullen used this tactic to their own advantage, but it also appealed to publishers under certain circumstances. A case in point concerns Strahan's response to Robert Watson's previously mentioned request for £2,000 for his *History of Philip II.* "I would not give half of what he asks, or agree upon any other Terms than for an Impression of 1,000, upon which though little will be got, little can be lost, if this Book has any Sale at all," Strahan told Creech in his letter of 23 July 1776. Together with Creech and Balfour in Edinburgh, therefore, Strahan and Cadell paid Watson £800 for the first edition of 1,000 quarto copies that appeared early in 1777. In this instance, the book was successful, and the publishers then negotiated a new con-

41. Dilly to Pinkerton, 11 Jan. 1796, in Pinkerton, *Literary Correspondence,* 1:395–96.

42. See Sher, "William Buchan's *Domestic Medicine,*" 45–64.

tract that gave the author £400 for a second quarto edition of 500 copies, published in 1778, and £100 for a third edition in octavo, published in 1779.[43] Although the publishers did not own the copyright and therefore had to pay the author's estate an additional fee for the fourth edition in 1785, they saved money by not giving in to the author's initial demands. Above all, this arrangement protected them against catastrophic loss in the event that the book turned out to be a commercial failure.

Besides the matter of rising pecuniary demands, publishers like Strahan had differences with their Scottish authors over questions of status, professional authority, and national identity. During the negotiations over copy money for Adam Ferguson's *Roman Republic* in the early 1780s, Strahan told an acquaintance that he resented being treated by Ferguson as a mere "mechanick."[44] The word choice is significant: almost ten years earlier Samuel Johnson had censured Alexander Gerard at a dinner party in Aberdeen for saying that Strahan was "very intimate with [William] Warburton," because according to Johnson "the intimacy is as one of the professors here may have with one of the carpenters who is repairing the college" (*BLJ*, 5:92). Besides being personally hurt by such condescension, Strahan expected authors to respect his reputation for fair dealing and to defer to his professional judgment about publishing.

This expectation sometimes became a point of contention due to the constant stream of books by Scottish authors that the literati believed Strahan and his associates should publish on their say-so. Whenever a book published on the recommendation of his Scottish authors failed, Strahan did not let them forget it. In a letter of 9 September 1774, he told Creech of his decision to reject John Gillies's edition of the orations of Lysias and Isocrates (no. 192) on the basis of his own reading of the manuscript, despite the positive opinion of the Scottish literati: "Mr. Hume and Dr. Robertson and Dr. Blair too, [Gillies] tells me, approve of them, which I doubt not is true; but there is no Dependence to be placed on what they say of the Works of young Authors. They are either by accident or design, inclined to be favourable in their Reports, which I have suffered by more than once; witness Anderson's History of France and Carstairs's Papers, etc." As Strahan and Cadell's first major Scottish publication after Millar's death, the first two volumes of Rev. Walter Anderson's *History of France* (1769; no. 121) had been a costly mistake for its publishers at a vulnerable time in their careers, and five years later Strahan was still

43. Watson to Strahan, 8 Apr. 1777, SA 48901, fol. 8.
44. John Fletcher Campbell's diary for 10 Apr. 1782, NLS, MS 17753, fol. 209.

angry at William Robertson and his circle for promoting it to them.[45] Strahan's reference to "Carstairs's Papers" is an allusion to *State-Papers and Letters, Addressed to William Carstares* (1774), which Strahan and Cadell had recently copublished with John Balfour in a quarto volume; no other edition ever appeared. The work was edited by William Robertson's close associate, the Moderate minister Joseph MacCormick, whose sketch of Carstares's life can be viewed as Moderate Party propaganda, and Robertson himself had organized the campaign to sell the manuscript to a London publisher for £300 after an Edinburgh publisher offered the author £200.[46]

Strahan reached his highpoint of irritation over the publication of Hugh Blair's *Sermons* (no. 188). Writing to Cadell in September 1776, he contends that the partners should not take part in publishing Blair's sermons, "however well Dr. Robertson speaks of them," not only because he expects little from the English sale but also because "by taking shares in these little Things (not at all worth our while) they will think themselves entitled to a concern in large works, where we do not want them."[47] Three months later Strahan expressed himself more forcefully in a remarkable letter to Robertson himself, in which he rebukes his correspondent for displaying, on this occasion and others, "the most unbounded Partiality to your Friends."[48] The issue in this instance was not money, since the £100 fee that Blair received for the copyright, divided among three copublishers, was insignificant. Rather, the issue was the relative authority of authors and publishers, and beyond that, Strahan's fears about Scottish authors leading him down a path of national prejudice as he was trying to refashion his identity in London. In regard to Blair's work, however, it was Strahan's critical judgment that was blinded by prejudice, for he had become so consumed with the notion that Robertson was inclined to mislead him into publishing inferior books by Scottish Presbyterian ministers that he could not (until reassured by Samuel Johnson) appreciate the critical or commercial potential of what would prove to be one of the most popular books of its age. Yet even after what he called, in a letter to Creech of 18 November 1777, the "unexpected Success" of Blair's *Sermons*,

45. The printing alone had cost them approximately £120 for 750 quarto copies, and the author had received 250 guineas in copy money. SA 48801, fol. 40.

46. Sher and Murdoch, "Patronage and Party," 212–13; Alexander Carlyle to John Douglas, 11 Mar. 1773, BL, Egerton MSS 2185, fols. 90–91.

47. Strahan to Cadell, 19 Sept. 1776, HL, MS Hyde 77, 7.116.1.

48. Strahan to Robertson, 6 Dec. 1776, NLS, MS 3942, fols. 299–300.

Strahan continued to put more faith in his own assessment of manuscripts than in any judgment he might receive from Robertson or Blair. In two letters written to Creech in the autumn of 1779, for example, Strahan rejected a manuscript by Rev. John Smith (published the next year by Charles Elliot as *Galic Antiquities*) because he was convinced that "the Public Curiosity" on the subject of Gaelic poetry "is at an End" (15 Oct.), "whatever may be Dr. Blair's opinion" (19 Nov.). Nor did he heed Blair's advice to pay £400 for Robert Watson's posthumous *History of Philip III* (no. 239),[49] which was subsequently brought out by rival publishers.

The problems that publishers faced were not limited to relations with their authors. Strahan's letters to Creech are filled with complaints about a variety of other factors that were thought to be creating a hostile climate for publishing projects. Sometimes the problem was nothing more than a bad investment. In a letter of 20 May 1776, Strahan responded to Creech's inquiry about the price of Buchan's projected new book by observing that "Mr Cadell and I have of late suffered so much by buying Gold too dear, that we shall in future, be very cautious how we give large Sums for any Work whatever, the Merit of which is not well known, and the Subject popular." There were frequent laments about the general state of the economy. On 11 December 1780 Strahan asserted, in connection with the particularly difficult negotiations over Ferguson's history of the Roman republic: "I am more and more confirmed in my Opinion, that it is both foolish and dangerous to give large Sums for new Works of any kind, in these untoward Times, when almost every Circumstance in the literary Way is against us." Tight money, bankruptcies, and similar problems were commonly cited.

Unfavorable economic conditions were compounded by "the precarious Terms upon which we now hold Literary Property of every kind," as Strahan put it in his letter to Creech of 9 April 1774. Strahan feared that the ruling against the principle of perpetual copyright by the House of Lords in February 1774 would make publishing disastrously competitive and drive down the value of copyrights that the London booksellers regularly purchased and resold among themselves. Consequently, publishers would be more reluctant to take risks with expensive publications, and authors would receive less money for their works. "In the present precarious State of Literary Property," he wrote to Creech on 18 October 1781, "it would be downright Madness to venture a large Sum of Money on any Book." Yet Strahan's logic was contradicted by his own experience: the

49. Blair to Strahan, 10 Sept. 1782, HL, MS Hyde 77, 5.404.2.

copy money paid to authors continued to rise after 1774, notwithstanding the complaints, predictions, and schemes of publishers.

Although powerless in regard to general economic conditions, the Strahan syndicate was not always so in other respects. After spearheading the propaganda effort on behalf of perpetual copyright that came to an end in February 1774, as well as the equally unsuccessful attempt to pass new legislation that would have eased the plight of the London copyright-holders, Strahan and Cadell played a leading part in developing and sustaining the system of honorary or tacit copyright that operated during the second half of the eighteenth century.[50] This arrangement kept up the value of literary property by means of an informal understanding among the booksellers themselves rather than a legal decision or legislative act. A "general Association" was devised for this purpose,[51] although Strahan was so confident of the support of all but "a very few inconsiderable Individuals," as he put it to Creech in a letter of 25 August 1774, that the plans do not seem to have been implemented. While not ruling out the possibility of another try at parliamentary legislation, Strahan told Creech on 27 December that "our best Protection is in our own Power; I mean to underprint [i.e., undersell and undercut] every Person instantly that invades our Books."

In more than one letter to Creech, Strahan emphasized that he and Cadell were motivated to defend perpetual copyright not from personal interest but from "a Desire of saving the Trade in general from universal Destruction" (18 Mar. 1774; cf. 1 Jan. 1773 and 9 Apr. 1774). Their intention was to maintain order and stability in the face of the disorder and confusion that they believed would arise if every bookseller and printer were free to publish any work not protected by statutory copyright. Most of their own literary property was invested in relatively new books, protected by statutory copyright, but some of their "brethren" in the trade "have their whole Property vested in Copies not protected by Q. Anne's Statute," and it was chiefly for their sake that Strahan and Cadell were engaged. Whether one accepts this principled argument or regards it as a mere rationalization for economic self-interest, there is no doubt that Strahan and Cadell were determined to defend their copyrights even after

50. Pollard, "English Market," 27–29 (Pollard uses the term "*de facto* copyright" to describe this practice); Sher, "Corporatism and Consensus," 32–93. For a different view based on the analysis of a single work, see Amory, "*De Facto* Copyright?"

51. Plan for an Association of the Booksellers for the Preservation of their Trade, ca. 1774, in Hodgson and Blagden, *Notebook*, 219–21.

they were no longer protected by law. In March 1792 Cadell expressed his commitment to this policy in a letter to the Edinburgh booksellers Bell & Bradfute, in connection with recent Edinburgh reprints of two works no longer protected by statutory copyright, Hume's *History of England* and Macpherson's *Poems of Ossian* (containing *Fingal* and *Temora*): "I trust the time will arrive when the Booksellers in Scotland as well as England will see it [in] their mutual Interest not to invade each others property *whether protected by the Statute or not*—on my part I engage to trade upon such terms as will allow them encouragement not to print my Books, and I will also oppose to the utmost of my power every invasion."[52]

Protecting honorary copyright meant devising strategies to stop booksellers and printers from violating the rules of publishing and reprinting set down by Strahan, Cadell, and their associates. Within London, alleged pirates were initially excluded or shunned, but in the long run cooption proved a better strategy. At the end of the century, a group of dissidents, including Thomas Hood of Vernor & Hood (who were among the worst offenders of honorary copyright) and the famous seller of "cheap" books, James Lackington, formed themselves into an independent body known as the Associated Booksellers.[53] Yet Thomas Vernor was buying shares in London trade books from 1787, and Lackington was doing so from 1796 despite his carefully cultivated reputation as a renegade.[54] When shares of many of Strahan and Cadell's great properties from the Scottish Enlightenment were made available to "a Select Number" of the London trade in December 1805, Vernor & Hood and George Lackington (successor to his uncle James) each purchased shares of Gregory's *A Father's Legacy to His Daughters*, which had been out of copyright for seventeen years. Vernor & Hood bought shares of other "honorary" copyrights at this sale, such as Hume's *History of England*, Ferguson's *Astronomy Explained*, and Macpherson's *Poems of Ossian*, and both firms also bought shares of titles that were protected by statutory copyright only in their later, revised editions, such as Buchan's *Domestic Medicine* (Lackington) and Robertson's *History of Scotland* and *History of Charles V* (Vernor).[55]

52. Cadell to John Bell or John Bradfute, 23 Mar. 1792, NLS, Dep. 317, box 2, folder 1 (emphasis added).

53. Mumby, *Publishing and Bookselling*, 204–5.

54. Lutes, "Andrew Strahan," 147; Lackington, *Confessions* and *Memoirs*.

55. *A Catalogue of Copies, and Books in Quires, which will be sold to a Select Number of Booksellers of London and Westminster at the London Coffee-House Ludgate Hill on Thursday, December 19, 1805*, in SA 48901, fols. 284–87; for a list of Vernor & Hood's purchases, see also BL, Add. MSS 38730, fol. 35.

Policing the Edinburgh trade was a greater challenge. Strahan complained to Creech in a letter of 1 January 1773 that the book trade was being destroyed by the unscrupulous behavior of "about ten Printers with you, that print every Thing, and who are now beginning to print upon one another." Following Strahan's lead, Creech responded by attempting to establish a booksellers' society in Edinburgh from 1776 onward.[56] In a letter of 20 May 1776 Strahan praised him for proposing to the new society that the Edinburgh booksellers act aggressively to ban the trafficking in books protected by the Statute of Anne as well as indiscriminate reprinting by Edinburgh printers of books whose statutory copyrights had expired.

Creech's proposals were never enforced, however. The Edinburgh booksellers lacked the legal authority to control the Edinburgh printers, and attempts to do so through the authority of the trade were hampered by the fact that London booksellers sometimes commissioned Edinburgh printers directly. "Many of the London Booksellers have been here this summer," Creech casually told Cadell in August 1785,[57] and it was understood that he did not mean they had come merely on holiday. The presence of London publishers looking for new titles and cheap printing of old ones made it more difficult for the Edinburgh trade to police itself. Furthermore, the leading Edinburgh booksellers themselves, including Creech and Balfour, were not always prepared to abide by the conventions of honorary copyright, even if infringements on statutory copyright were relatively rare among them. There is considerable irony in the fact that the only time Creech and Balfour ever joined forces in a major publishing project of their own was to copublish an inexpensive, forty-four-volume edition of *The British Poets* (1773–76), which infuriated Strahan even *after* 1774 because it represented a gross violation of honorary copyright.[58] John Murray undoubtedly had the Balfour-Creech edition of the British poets in mind when he told Creech on 8 April 1774: "you appear to be as great a pirate as the worst [the London booksellers] complain of."[59]

Strahan was even more distressed about the problem of Irish reprinting, because it typically involved new titles, covered by statutory rather

56. Sher, "Corporatism and Consensus."

57. Creech to Cadell, 15 Aug. 1785, HL, MS Hyde 69, item 12.

58. Writing to Creech on 1 Jan. 1773, Strahan remarked: "I have had a good deal of Altercation with Mr Balfour on the Subject of the proposed Edition of the English Poets."

59. Quoted in Zachs, *First John Murray*, 59.

than honorary copyright. On 17 October 1780, during the course of the negotiations on Adam Ferguson's Roman history, Strahan warned Creech that "above all" the publishers must take into account, in addition to "the Situation of the Times, very unfavourable to Works of Genius in general," the fact that Irish reprinters would immediately publish, "in an inferior [i.e., smaller] Size, and at a low Price, every new Book the Instant it is published here, which they are by a late Act of Parliament permitted to export to America." The following year (4 Oct. 1781) he added that cheap Irish reprints of books like Ferguson's were not only enabling the Irish to "run away with the whole American Trade, but even import them, with Impunity, into all the Western Coast of Britain." These charges are addressed from the standpoint of the Irish book trade in chapter 7.

In all cases in which statutory copyright was violated, Strahan tried to follow an uncompromising policy that was relayed to Creech in a letter of 25 August 1774: "when they meddle with Books still protected by Q. Anne's Statute . . . we must prosecute Offenders, when we can come at them." To "come at them" was not easy, but by registering titles at Stationers' Hall, practicing vigilance, and privately rewarding customs inspectors who reported violations, Strahan, Cadell, and Creech managed to prosecute some Scottish importers of illegal Irish reprints, such as the notorious William Anderson of Stirling.[60] Although reputable Scottish booksellers seem to have steered clear of the illegal Irish trade most of the time, there were significant exceptions. Charles Elliot, one of the leading figures in the Edinburgh trade and a pillar of corporate order in the Edinburgh Booksellers' Society, regularly collaborated in secret with Anderson and also dealt directly with Irish booksellers, and we have seen that John Balfour himself was once accused of importing the Dublin octavo edition of Adam Ferguson's *Essay on the History of Civil Society* at a time when that book was available in Britain only in an expensive quarto edition.

Thus, Strahan's letters to Creech from the 1770s and early 1780s depicted the publishing trade as a profession under siege. Economic conditions always seemed to be bad for books. Authors were increasingly demanding vast amounts for their works and promoting each other's efforts in unreasonable ways. Printers in Edinburgh were destroying the trade by indiscriminately reprinting books no longer protected by statutory copyright, and Edinburgh booksellers were unable or unwilling to control them, or even to place restrictions on themselves. Irish reprinters and

60. McDougall, "Smugglers," 151–83.

their Scottish associates were exacerbating the crisis, especially in regard to new books, by illegally exporting into Britain cheap Dublin editions of legally protected titles. The book trade was a battlefield, and respectable publishers were surrounded by enemies. Early in 1780 Strahan received a letter from his old friend John Balfour that summed up the prevailing attitude within their circle: "Bookselling is at so low a pass, that I have sometimes . . . had thoughts of giving it up. It is a laborious business at present without any profit, and it is only the hope of its emending, that makes me continue."[61] Several years later Creech complained to Cadell about still another problem: "[John] Murray's scandalous abridgements" of the syndicates' books. "If such things are allowed," he continued, "what is literary property? There is no book almost but what may be abridged, and how can booksellers afford to give money to authors!"[62] Strahan, Cadell, and Creech's stable of best-selling authors made them vulnerable to this practice, and Murray was not the only culprit (fig. 5.5).

Amid these complaints, which reflect a mixture of harsh reality and self-serving exaggeration, Strahan and his friends insisted on the need to fight back by aggressively negotiating, underselling, prosecuting, publicizing, posturing, and organizing. It was thought necessary for the London booksellers to band together by enforcing honorary copyright among themselves and by keeping a printing ledger in the Chapter Coffee House; the Edinburgh booksellers were encouraged to follow a similar plan.[63] Within Strahan's own publishing syndicate, every effort was made to maintain cooperation and discipline across the London–Edinburgh axis, ideally with Creech and Balfour in federation with each other as well as with their London partners, Strahan and Cadell. When disagreements between Creech and Balfour made this ideal unworkable, Strahan settled for the next best thing: a firm coalition with Cadell and the young and ambitious Creech, along with a separate, secondary coalition with Balfour.

For all his bickering and complaining, Strahan generally succeeded in implementing the plan he envisioned. One measure of its success was the remarkable output of important new books by Scottish authors that the Strahan–Cadell syndicate published. "There will be no Books of Reputation now . . . printed in London but through your hands and Mr Cadel's," Hume assured Strahan in April 1776, shortly after the appearance of

61. Balfour to Strahan, 10 July 1780, Pierpont Morgan Library, Misc. English.

62. Creech to Cadell, 9 Nov. 1784, ibid.

63. See the passage from Strahan's letter to Creech of 20 May 1776 that is quoted in Sher, "Corporatism and Consensus," 42.

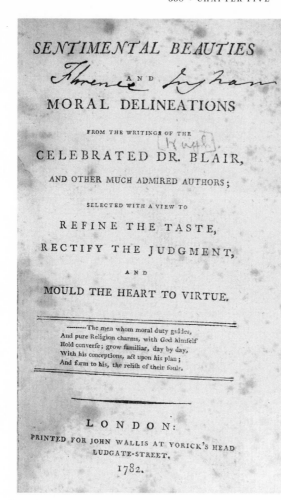

Fig. 5.5. Cheap abridgments and miscellanies like the one shown here tried the patience of their original publishers, but it is doubtful that they seriously weakened the market for authorized titles within Great Britain. Thomas Fisher Rare Book Library, University of Toronto.

Smith's *Wealth of Nations* and the first volume of Gibbon's *Decline and Fall* (*LDH*, 2:518). Hume exaggerated, but not by much. Another measure of success was the enormous wealth that these books generated for their publishers. "The most profitable trade now in Edinburgh appears to be that of a Bookseller," wrote Edward Topham in 1776, apparently with Creech and Balfour chiefly in mind.[64] Balfour, Creech, Elliot, and Bell were each worth many thousands of pounds. And if the Edinburgh publishers of the Scottish Enlightenment grew rich, their London associates became still richer. George Robinson's book stock alone was auctioned

64. [Topham], *Letters from Edinburgh*, 179.

after his death in June 1801 for £54,000.[65] Strahan left behind assets valued at more than £100,000, and Cadell was worth over £150,000 at the time of his death.[66] Yet profits were not everything. Alarmed by the £1,500 that Strahan and Cadell had contracted to pay for Hugh Blair's *Lectures on Rhetoric and Belles Lettres* (no. 230), Creech received a reassuring reply from Strahan, dated 13 June 1782, explaining that more was involved in dealing with authors than simply making as much money as possible: "We endeavour to make the best Bargains we can; and if we have been upon some Occasions rather too easy and too liberal we hope we have got some Reputation by it, which may be of some Use to us in future." Despite his reservations, Creech must have accepted this argument, since he copublished Blair's book.

Kames's *Gentleman Farmer* constitutes a different kind of example. Although, as we have seen, Strahan wanted nothing to do with this book on account of its author's excessive demands for copy money, he was aware that Creech was in a more delicate position because Kames was a powerful judge on the Scottish Court of Session, a literary patriarch in Edinburgh, and one of Creech's regular customers, as well as a friend and patron.[67] When Strahan recommended not publishing the book in his letter to Creech of 23 July 1776, he added: "if you have not some good Reasons (other I mean than any thing you can possibly get by such an Impression) to the contrary." He even commented that if Creech thought he must publish the book, he was welcome to affix "Mr. Cadell's name, or mine" to the imprint in order to improve the sale, "and I will answer for Mr Cadell he will endeavour to sell as many of them as he can, the very same as if it were his own Property." In this passage, Strahan explicitly acknowledges, approvingly, that booksellers sometimes published for reasons other than financial gain. In the case at hand, Creech took advantage of Strahan's offer to use Cadell's name in the imprint, for *The Gentleman Farmer* appeared in February 1777 under the joint imprint (dated 1776) of Creech and Cadell.

There never was a sharp break between the various motives that drove

65. Stockdale, *'Tis Treason*, 374.

66. See Raven, "Book Trades," 28–29. In a letter to Hannah More of 23 March 1793, Walpole said Cadell's shop was grossing £15,000 a year until the early 1790s. *Correspondence* 31 (1961): 386–87.

67. Benedict, "Service to the Public," 123–25; Fraser-Tytler of Aldourie Papers, NRAS 1073, bundle 24.

the Scottish publishing mission of the Millar–Strahan–Cadell syndicate. The profit motive was basic, of course, for publishers could not stay in business without making money, and the attainment of wealth was an alluring goal. But it would be wrong to jump from this undeniable premise to the conclusion that Robert Darnton has applied to both booksellers and publishers in eighteenth-century France, that "all seemed to live by the supreme principle of the book trade: make money. It was the profit motive, 'the great driving force of everything,' that kept them fairly neutral in the role of cultural broker."[68] On the contrary, the great Scottish Enlightenment publishers were far from neutral in their role as cultural brokers, and we must take into account their desire for personal fame, prestige, and status; their feelings of Scottish national pride; their personal concern for some of the authors they published, often as genuine friends; and their sense of commitment as purveyors of significant ideas and doers of good works.

The evidence to support this position is plentiful. Commenting to Hume on the daily growth of his business activities in 1771, Strahan placed his actions within a broader context of social welfare when he observed that "there is a Pleasure, and that no inconsiderable one, in being of use to others, in ones Progress through Life."[69] His publishing partner Thomas Cadell once remarked, in regard to an unidentified publishing project which he considered "truly magnificent," that he was "more desirous of the honour of being concerned in the publication of this grand Work than with any view of present profit."[70] If authors were sometimes demonized by publishers for their excessive demands and ignorance of the book business, they were often lionized as well. After completing the publication arrangements for Edward Gibbon's *Decline and Fall of the Roman Empire* in 1787, in a manner that he considered almost without precedent "in the Annals of Authors and Booksellers," Cadell added: "As for myself I had rather risk my fortune with a few such Authors as Mr Gibbon, Dr Robertson, D Hume, etc than be the publisher of a hundred insipid publications."[71] "There is no Man upon the Face of the Earth, whom I more highly respect and esteem, and whom I more wish to oblige, than yourself," Strahan told the ever-skeptical Hume in the month following

68. Darnton, "Sounding the Literary Market," 491.

69. Strahan to Hume, 1 Mar. 1771, NLS, MS 23157, no. 62.

70. Cadell to ?, 6 Apr. 1769, Pierpont Morgan Library, folio extra-illustrated edition of Boswell's *Life of Johnson*, 3:10.

71. Cadell to Gibbon, 9 May 1787, BL, Add. MSS 34886, fols. 151–52.

Andrew Millar's death, when he was anxious about keeping this author in the stable of Scottish writers he was starting to construct with Cadell. After learning of Hume's death, Strahan wrote to Cadell: "We have really lost in him a very good Friend."[72] These were not the utterances of people who considered profit the sole determining factor of their professional lives, or were reluctant to play the parts of committed cultural brokers. Rather than try to claim either this idealistic tone or the cynical tone that surfaces in some of Strahan's letters to Creech as the "true" voice of these publishers, we must regard both voices as equally legitimate characteristics of the men who led the Scottish Enlightenment publishing project.

The Tools of Publicity:
Advertisements, Excerpts, Reviews, and Catalogues

However we assess the motives of these publishers, and whatever friction sometimes existed with their authors, or among themselves, once they decided to produce a new book, the focus was on cooperative efforts to raise the work as high as possible, both critically and commercially. Broadly speaking, if a book was being produced in London, it was Strahan's job to see to it that it was reasonably well printed. In this capacity, Strahan's reputation as a Scotsman who had mastered idiomatic English was a source of reassurance to his Scottish authors, who felt they could rely on his assistance without embarrassment. "I have endeavoured to avoid Scotticisms as much as possible," wrote William Richardson, as Strahan was preparing to print his *Anecdotes of the Russian Empire* (no. 246), "but should be much obliged to anyone who would point out or alter any that may have escaped me."[73] Cadell's primary role was to ensure widespread distribution through wholesaling as well as retailing. Either man might take the lead in negotiating terms and discussing publication plans with authors, and both made contributions to the three major marketing techniques used to increase sales of their new books: advertisements and excerpts in newspapers and periodicals, book reviews, and catalogues of their published works.

When the Strahan–Cadell syndicate published a major new book, their newspaper advertisements usually appeared in both London and Edinburgh—often in more than one newspaper in each town—as well as, in some cases, newspapers elsewhere. They typically began advertising sev-

---

72. Strahan to Cadell, 7 Sept. 1776, HL, MS Hyde 69, item 42.
73. Richardson to Strahan, 1 Oct. 1782, HL, MS Hyde 10, item 582.

eral weeks before the publication date, in an effort to raise expectations by indicating when the book was scheduled to appear. The campaign would reach a climax with a "This Day is Published . . . " advertisement that would often continue to run beyond the actual publication date. For example, the *Edinburgh Evening Courant* first carried an advertisement for Hugh Blair's *Sermons* (no. 188) on Wednesday, 15 January 1777, introduced with the words "In the Press, and speedily will be published, by William Creech." Exactly three weeks later it carried another advertisement that gave the publication date as "Saturday morning." On the Saturday in question, 8 February, the paper contained a "This Day is Published" advertisement that indicated the size of the book (a one-volume octavo) but not the price. Finally, an advertisement on Saturday, 15 February, contained another "This Day is Published" announcement, with the addition of details about the price of the book both in boards (5s.3d.) and bound in calf and lettered (6s.).

Since advertisements like these were costly, especially when they ran repeatedly, in different newspapers and in different cities, launching a new title could be expensive.[74] As we saw earlier, in his anticipated accounting of Kames's *Gentleman Farmer*, Strahan figured £13.14s. for "advertising and incidentals," as against just £31.10s. for printing 1,000 copies of that large book. Even though printing and advertising together did not equal the enormous expense of paper (figured at £48 in this case), the cost of advertising still appears quite substantial for a book that would retail for only six shillings bound. Strahan was calculating advertising and incidental costs that were about 17 percent of the cost of paper and print. For the first edition of Smollett's *Humphry Clinker* (no. 140), William Johnston and Benjamin Collins spent about 10 percent of the cost of paper and print on advertising.[75] John Murray's advertising costs ranged from 15 percent to as much as 30 percent of the cost of production for books published during this period.[76] Of course, as a percentage of production costs, the advertising budgets for expensive books were often much lower than this:

74. Tierney, "Advertisements," 159, gives the following rates for a two-inch advertisement in an eighteenth-century London newspaper: two shillings until 1759 (one to the paper, one in duty); three shillings (one to the paper, two in duty) from 1759, when the duty was doubled; three and a half shillings (one to the paper, two and a half in duty) from 1780, when the duty was increased again.

75. Plant, *English Book Trade*, 235–36: the cost of paper and print totaled £155.15s.6d., while £15.10s. was spent on advertising.

76. Zachs, *First John Murray*, 86.

the sum of £14.7s. that Boswell was charged for advertising his *Life of Johnson*, for example, was less than 2 percent of his total cost for paper and print.[77] Nevertheless, £14 or £15 was a significant expense.

One way that Strahan helped the syndicate was by becoming one of the principal owners (with Robert Dodsley) of the *London Chronicle*, which he printed from the time of its first appearance on 1 January 1757.[78] That newspaper, which is said to have surpassed all its rivals in circulation and to have been "something of a literary clearing-house of the time,"[79] was a prime vehicle for book advertisements, and Scottish Enlightenment books were heavily represented. Part of a page from the 22–25 March 1777 issue is a case in point (fig. 5.6). It includes a John Murray advertisement for the latest number of Andrew Duncan's *Medical and Philosophical Commentaries*, pitched to medical professors and students along with Duncan's *Elements of Therapeutics* and a pamphlet by William Cullen; a Strahan–Cadell advertisement for Henry Mackenzie's anonymous novel *Julia de Roubigné* (with reference to two earlier novels "by the same Author"); a Cadell–Creech advertisement for Kames's *Gentleman Farmer* (with reference to three other titles by Kames); and a Strahan–Cadell advertisement for the second edition of James Macpherson's *History of Great Britain* (with reference to another of Macpherson's historical publications)—all in addition to advertisements for a number of other Scottish books and pamphlets that are not included in table 2. Note the detailed information that these advertisements contained about the number of volumes, formats, prices, states of binding (e.g., sewed, boards, or neatly bound), illustrations, dates of publications, and names and addresses of publishers of the works in question.

Equally important, the *London Chronicle* sometimes printed excerpts from the latest books, including, of course, new works published by Andrew Millar and the Strahan–Cadell syndicate. Excerpts from Hume's *History of England* graced its pages from the outset,[80] defining a pattern to be followed in the years ahead. For example, on 23 February 1779 Strahan and Cadell published John Moore's *A View of Society and Manners in France, Switzerland, and Germany* (no. 201) in an edition of 1,000 copies, and on

77. See the discussion of the publication of the *Life of Johnson* in chap. 3.

78. At some point Strahan also acquired an interest in another London newspaper that carried book advertisements, the *Public Advertiser*.

79. Chard, "Bookseller to Publisher," 146.

80. Solomon, *Rise of Robert Dodsley*, 178–81.

SONG. Mr. Moody.
And now, Sir, I'll tell you, you've done what
  you ought,
A blessing will surely 'light down on your head,
  You've made a heart easy,
  Instead of being crazy,
The thought won't displease you, not after you'r
  dead.

To have but one glimpse of this sweet little
  jewel,
I'd walk all the way from the north to the south,
  When she hears of her fate,
  How her breast will elate,
The poor creature's heart will jump out of her
  mouth.

SALE of LEAD MINES.
To be peremptorily SOLD *to the best Bidder*,
At the House of Mr. Proctor, the Spread Eagle, in
Settle in the County of York, on Saturday the
5th Day of April 1777,

A THIRD SHARE in the Lead Mines called
  Coldstone's Lead Mines, situate on Grenow-
hill, near Pately-bridge, in the county of York;
held by Lease from John White, Esq; for a term of
years, Six of which are yet unexpired.

Also A FOURTH SHARE in the valuable Lead
Mine called Golegrove-head Lead Mine, situate on
Gressington-moor, near Shipton, in the co-nty of
York.

For further Particulars apply to Mess. Birtbeck of
Settle, or Mr. John Summers of Gressington.

This Day was published, Price 1s.

THEODOSIUS to CONSTANTIA.
  A POETICAL EPISTLE.
Printed for J. Walter, at Homer's Head, Charing-
cross.

This Day was published,

T. LOWNDES's CATALOGUE for 1777.
  Containing the Library of a Merchant.
To which are added some Modern Books; which
in general are in good condition, and now selling,
for ready money, at the prices printed in the Cata-
logue,
  By T. LOWNDES, Bookseller,
At his Sale Rooms behind his house in Fleet-street.
  Catalogues may be had at Mr. Davis's, Piccadilly;
Mr. Walter's, Charing-cross; Mr. Brown's, corner
of Essex-street; Mr. Sewell's, opposite the Royal
Exchange; and at the Place of Sale.

This Day was published,
In one Vol. Quarto, Price 12s. 6d. in Boards, printed
for John Donaldson, the Corner of Arundel-street
in the Strand,

THE History of the Province of MORAY,
  extending from the Mouth of the River Spey
to the Borders of Lochaber in length; and from the
Moray-Frith to the Grampian Hills in breadth: and
including a part of the Shire of Banff to the East;
the whole Shire of Moray and Nairn; and the greatest
part of the Shire of Inverness; all which was an-
ciently called the Province of Moray, before there
was a division into counties.
  By the Reverend Mr. LACHLAN SHAW,
    Minister of the Gospel at Elgin.
N. B. John Donaldson has no concern in any other
shop.

To the Faculty and Students in Medicine.
On *Tuesday, April* 1, *will be published*,
    Price 1s. 6d.
    NUMBER XIV. Of

MEDICAL and PHILOSOPHICAL
    COMMENTARIES.
  By a Society of Physicians in Edinburgh.
London: Printed for J. Murray, No. 32, Fleet-
street.   Where may be had,
  Any of the preceding Numbers, 1s. 6d. each.
As also,
  1. Dr. Cullen's Letter to Lord Cathcart on the
Recovery of Drowned Persons, price 1s. 6d.
  2. Dr. Duncan's Elements of Therapeutics; or,
First Principles of the Practice of Physic, 3 vols. 5s.
sewed.
  3. Dr. Young's Treatise on Opium, 8vo. 3s. in
Boards.
  4. Dr. Mead's whole Works, 8vo, 6s. bound.

THE CREDITORS of Ensign ROBERT
  MUNRO, late of his Majesty's first (or
Royal Scotch) regiment, are desired to send in an
account of their demands to Mr. George Gun Munro,
the Administrator, No. 67, Basinghall-street, in
order to their being paid, and the residue of his
estate divided among the heirs.

In a few Days will be published,
In Two Volumes, Price 5s. sewed,

JULIA DE ROUBIGNE: A TALE. In a
  SERIES of LETTERS.
Published by the Author of the Man of Feeling.
Printed for W. Strahan; and T. Cadell in the
Strand.
  Of whom may be had by the same Author,
  1. The Man of Feeling, a new Edition, 3s.
  2. Man of the World, 2 vols. 2d Edition, 6s.

This Day was published, Price 2s. sewed,
Illustrated with Plates,

A PRACTICAL TREATISE on
  CHIMNIES: Containing full Directions for
preventing or removing Smoke in Houses.
Printed for T. Cadell in the Strand; and C. Elliot
at Edinburgh.
  Of whom may be had,
  Miscellaneous Observations on planting and train-
ing Timber Trees, Price 3 s. sewed.

This Day was published. Price 2s. 6d. sewed,
  The Second Volume of

THE SCOTCH PREACHER; or,
  A Collection of Sermons by some of the most
eminent Clergymen of the Church of SCOTLAND.
Printed for T. Cadell in the Strand; and J. Dick-
son at Edinburgh.
  Of whom may be had,
The First Volume, Price 2s. 6d. sewed, or the
Two Volumes, uniformly bound, for 6s.

This Day was published, Price 5s. in Boards,
  Illustrated with Plates,

THE GENTLEMAN FARMER: Being
  an Attempt to improve Agriculture, by sub-
jecting it to the Test of Rational Principles.
By the Author of the Elements of Criticism, &c.
Printed for T. Cadell in the Strand; and
W. Creech at Edinburgh.
  Of whom may be had, by the same Author,
  1. The Elements of Criticism, in 2 vols. the 5th
Edition, Price 12s.
  2. Sketches of the History of Man, 2 vols. 4to,
Price 2l. 2s.
  3. The Principles of Equity, folio, Price 16s.

This Day was published, Price 6s. in Boards,
Elegantly printed in Octavo, illustrated with Plates,
  The Third Edition, corrected, of

THE LIFE of WILLIAM of WYKEHAM,
  BISHOP of WINCHESTER, collected from
records, registers, manuscripts, and other authentic
evidences.
  By ROBERT LOWTH, D.D.
    Now Lord Bishop of Oxford.
Printed for J. Dodsley, Pall-mall; and T. Cadell
in the Strand.
  Of whom may be had,
Two new Editions of A Short Introduction to
English Grammar, with Critical Notes, for 3 s. on a
fine paper, the other for schools at 1 s. 6d.

This Day was published,
Elegantly printed in Two Volumes, Quarto, Price
    2l. 2s. in Boards,
The Second Edition, illustrated with a Head of the
    Author, of

THE HISTORY of GREAT BRITAIN,
  from the RESTORATION to the ACCESSION
of the HOUSE of HANOVER.
  By JAMES MACPHERSON, Esq.
Printed for W. Strahan; and T. Cadell, in the
Strand.
  Of whom may be had,
  Original Papers, containing the Secret History of
Great Britain, from the Restoration to the Accession
of the House of Hanover: To which are prefixed,
Extracts from the Life of James II. as written by
himself, 2 vols. 4to, 2l. 2s. in Boards.

6 and 14 March the *London Chronicle* carried front-page, first-column excerpts from that work on Frederick II and Voltaire, continued on inside pages of the numbers for 22 March, 3 April, and 8 April. By the summer a second edition of 1,000 copies of Moore's book was called for, and it was well on its way to becoming a best seller.[81] Similarly, the *Chronicle* printed excerpts from *The Mirror* and *The Lounger* when those works appeared and devoted the entire front page of its 30 June–2 July 1785 issue to paper no. 17 from the latter, prefaced with a paragraph that begins: "It is somewhat remarkable, that the metropolis of Scotland should, within the space of a few years, produce two periodical papers. The *Mirror*, of which we formerly presented our readers with several extracts, and this present one, the *Lounger*; while London, with all its advantages in point of size, manners, fashion, and extravagance, has produced none of any note since the Connoisseur." Considering that Strahan was a copublisher of *The Mirror* and *The Lounger*, this brand of journalism was blatantly self-serving. It was in effect free advertising, at a time when newspaper publishers were feeling increased pressure to use more space for advertisements that generated income.[82] But Strahan was promoting the literary accomplishments of his native city and country at the same time that he was advertising his own wares.

The syndicate was similarly well positioned for securing reviews of its new works in the major review journals of the age, the *Critical Review* and especially the *Monthly Review*. The *Critical* was founded in March 1756 by the Scottish printer Archibald Hamilton, who had formerly managed Strahan's printing business, and Tobias Smollett, another Scot whose career owed more to Strahan than has usually been thought.[83] Since Smollett appealed to his "Scotch friends" in the William Robertson circle to

81. Fulton, "Eighteenth-Century Best Seller," 428–33.

82. Tierney, "Advertisements," 153–64.

83. Knapp, "Smollett's Works as Printed by William Strahan," 282–91; Harlan, "William Strahan," 62–70. On Smollett and the *Critical*, see Basker, *Tobias Smollett*; on Hamilton, see Barbara Laing Fitzpatrick's biography in *ODNB*.

Fig. 5.6. These two columns from Strahan's *London Chronicle* for 22–25 March 1777 contain a variety of advertisements for Scottish Enlightenment books. Note how the advertisements for anonymous works, such as Henry Mackenzie's *Julia de Roubigné* (*top right*) and Lord Kames's *The Gentleman Farmer* (*middle right*) were linked with previous publications by the same authors. Houghton Library, Harvard University.

provide reviews of new Scottish books, publications by Scottish authors had a distinct advantage as long as Smollett was associated with that journal.[84] Relations were cooler with Hamilton, who had left Strahan's shop on somewhat disagreeable terms, but the journal's Scottish ties remained strong. From 1774 the *Critical* was published by George Robinson, who was becoming heavily involved in Scottish Enlightenment publishing. The *Monthly Review* was more directly tied to Strahan, who printed it from its beginnings in 1749 and then used the debt owed him by its editor and publisher, Ralph Griffiths, to purchase a one-quarter share of the ownership in 1761.[85] Although Griffiths and Smollett came to dislike each other, Strahan seems to have played a mediating role between them and stayed on good terms with both men.[86]

Thus, the leading British book review journals were closely intertwined with the system of publishing that was dominated by a handful of powerful figures in the book trade, and Scottish printers, booksellers, and men of letters occupied a leading position in both. Similar patterns can be detected in several other review journals, such as the *English Review* (owned by John Murray) and the *Edinburgh Magazine and Review* (jointly owned by Murray and Creech).[87] As one might expect, influence was frequently exerted. John Murray's correspondence with his friend Gilbert Stuart shows him scrambling to fix favorable reviews of Stuart's works and unfavorable ones of books by Stuart's avowed enemies, Robert Henry and William Robertson. But debunking Robertson was made difficult, Murray told Stuart, by the influence exerted in the opposite direction by Robertson's powerful publishers, Strahan and Cadell.[88] To his credit, Strahan appears not to have abused his journalistic influence as much as

84. Robertson's review of Lord Kames's *Historical Law-Tracts* in the *Critical Review* for April 1759 was the result of what Robertson called, in a letter to Smollett of 15 March 1759, "a permission which you granted your Scotch friends" to provide reviews of new Scottish books. The letter, the review, and my discussion of this matter appear in Robertson, *Works*, 12:xxv–xxviii, 95–114.

85. Harlan, "William Strahan," 86, 292.

86. See Strahan's letters to Griffiths, Bodleian Library, Oxford, MS. Add. c.89, fols. 341–46; and Smollett to Strahan, 20 July 1759, in Smollett, *Letters*, 80–81. Donoghue, "Colonizing Readers," 54–74, reads the tension between these periodicals as indicative of ideological differences between the informative *Monthly* and the more discriminating *Critical.*

87. Zachs, *Without Regard to Good Manners*, chap. 3; and Zachs, *First John Murray*, chap. 11.

88. Murray to Stuart, 11 Mar. 1779, quoted in Zachs, *First John Murray*, 167.

he probably could have done. When Creech complained in 1781 about the tone of the *Monthly*'s review of *The Mirror*, Strahan's reply of 23 August stressed his impotence in such matters: "The account of the *Mirror* in the Monthly Review is, as you observe, rather cold; but, upon the whole, it is pretty tolerable. However, had it been much worse, I could not have remedied it, unless by speaking to Mr. G[riffiths] in a friendly way, to persuade him to soften it, which I did. I have not other Cognizance over that Work. Mr. G. has the sole and uncontrouled Management of it."[89] Even in attempting to demonstrate his distance from the reviewing practices of the *Monthly*, however, Strahan revealed that a friendly word to the editor could be used (and in this case, *had* been used) to "soften" a harsh notice. The fact that Strahan was not officially in control of the *Monthly* did not prevent him from using subtle forms of influence that served to promote his books and those of his associates.

The rise to prominence of the classicist and historian John Gillies illustrates this point. As noted earlier, Strahan had rejected Gillies's first book, *The Orations of Lysias and Isocrates* (no. 192), which was published instead by Murray in 1778. Strahan printed the book, however, and Gillies soon ingratiated himself with Strahan and Cadell by taking on various literary tasks, including reviewing books in the *Monthly Review*. The success of John Moore's *A View of Society and Manners in France, Switzerland, and Germany* probably owed something to the appearance in the June 1779 number of the *Monthly* of the first and most enthusiastic review of that book—written by Gillies.[90] Gillies functioned as an antidote to the dreaded Gilbert Stuart, who might well have ruined a book like Moore's if he had the opportunity and the inclination. Just as Stuart performed miscellaneous services for John Murray, so we find Cadell steering the Earl of Hardwicke from William Thomson to "a Dr Gillies . . . an exceptional man," when Hardwicke needed an editor to prepare a second volume of state papers that Strahan and Cadell intended to publish.[91] Gillies's reward, if it is fair to call it that, came in 1786, when his next book was elegantly published by Strahan and Cadell in two quarto volumes as *The History of Ancient Greece* (no. 263). The book was a huge success and led

89. Strahan's remarks support the interpretation offered in Roper, *Reviewing before the Edinburgh*, 31, although Roper does not mention Strahan in his discussion of the *Monthly*.

90. Fulton, "Eighteenth-Century Best Seller," 431–32.

91. Cadell to Hardwicke, 10 Dec. 1784, BL, Add. MSS 35621, fols. 119–20. The work in question never appeared.

to Gillies's appointment as historiographer royal for Scotland upon the death of William Robertson in 1793.

The schoolmaster and literary critic William Rose was another Scot in the London area who was intimately connected with Strahan and Cadell and active in puffing his countrymen's books in the *Monthly*, which he had cofounded with Griffiths, his brother-in-law.[92] More than thirty books listed in table 2 were reviewed in the *Monthly* by Rose, and sometimes the arrangement bordered on impropriety, even by eighteenth-century standards. Consider Rose's reviews of books by Hugh Blair.[93] When the first volume of Blair's *Sermons* was in the press, Rose read the book in advance, presumably at Strahan's request, and sent Strahan a glowing account. Strahan in turn forwarded Rose's letter to William Robertson, who showed it to the author, and on 20 January 1777 Blair replied gratefully to Rose via Strahan, secure in the knowledge that Rose would be writing a complimentary notice in the *Monthly Review* (see *Monthly*, 56:278). Three years later, when Blair's second volume was in the press, the author enclosed a letter to Rose with one to Strahan (dated 15 Feb. 1780), to whom he remarked: "I have beg'd him to take the charge of giving an account of it in the Monthly Review; which he did in a very friendly and favourable manner on the former occasion." After some concern about the feasibility of this scheme, Blair wrote on 5 May to thank Strahan for sending him an advance copy of Rose's laudatory review (*Monthly*, 62:293). In letters to Strahan dated 10 March and 15 April 1783, Blair went through an almost identical scenario regarding his *Lectures on Rhetoric and Belles Lettres*, which was once again reviewed very favorably (and at great length) by Rose in response to a specific request from the author (*Monthly*, 68:489, 69:186, and 70:173).

A fourth major marketing device used by Strahan and Cadell was to issue printed catalogues of books published by the syndicate. Thomas Cadell began issuing lists of his new publications almost as soon as he took over Andrew Millar's business, but he seems to have used the device sparingly and on a small scale.[94] In 1774 he placed a two-page advertisement

92. Nangle, *Monthly Review*, 37. In a letter to Gibbon of 5 December 1786 (BL, Add. MSS 34886, fols. 149–50), Cadell notes that the recently deceased Rose had named him as the executor of his estate.

93. The letters cited in this paragraph appear in Zachs, *Hugh Blair's Letters to His Publishers*.

94. The earliest version I have discovered, [Cadell], *Books Printed for and Sold by T. Cadell, opposite Catherine-Street in the Strand*, contains only twelve entries (including two books from table 2: James Fordyce's *Sermons to Young Women* and James Fer-

for sixteen "Books printed for T. Cadell in the Strand" in the back of the fourth edition of Adam Smith's *Theory of Moral Sentiments*. Significantly, it began with a list of six books in the expensive quarto category, all by Scottish authors: Robertson's *History of Scotland* and *Charles V*, Hume's *History of England* and *Essays and Treatises on Several Subjects*, Dalrymple's *Memoirs of England and Ireland*, and Ferguson's *Essay on the History of Civil Society*. An identically titled list in the back of the second edition of Macpherson's *History of Great Britain* (1776) was limited to fourteen pricey quartos. Another list of twenty-five "Books printed for, and sold by T. Cadell" appeared in a publication of 1779, but by that time more substantial lists of new publications were appearing regularly under the title *Books Printed for W. Strahan, and T. Cadell in the Strand*. At least four different versions of publication lists so titled have survived from the late 1770s and early 1780s, some printed in more than one format and all containing more than one hundred titles. They were printed in large quantities, especially in octavo, and were apparently given away gratis as well as bound in the back of Strahan and Cadell's books. For example, in August 1780 Strahan charged to Cadell's account a total of £6.3s. (not including the cost of 6,000 sheets of paper) for an updated "List of Books" that was printed in the following formats: 1,000 in duodecimo (twenty-four pages), 1,000 in quarto (eight pages), and 4,000 in octavo (sixteen pages); a year later another impression of 5,500 was printed in the three formats for £5.9s., plus paper (SA 48816, fols. 61–62). These one-sheet publication catalogues testify to the status of the Strahan–Cadell syndicate as a major publishing empire, unrivaled within the English-speaking world by this time. Although the costs associated with printing, distributing, and updating these catalogues were not insignificant, Strahan and Cadell evidently considered them a worthwhile way to advertise their books and promote their position at the head of the trade.

The fundamental problem they faced in regard to their publication catalogues was structural: how best to organize and present their books. Many printed eighteenth-century book catalogues were designed for auctions or mail-order sales. Often they followed the order in which books were shelved in private libraries that were being put up for auction or for sale in bookshops; that is, books were listed by size, beginning with large, expensive folios and quartos and moving down to smaller, cheaper octavos and duodecimos. This is how Cadell arranged his publication list

---

guson's *Tables and Tracts*) and may date from 1767. In 1768 Cadell also began printing catalogues under the title *A Select Catalogue of the Most Approved English Books*.

in his 1774 advertisement, for example. Sometimes the entries were numbered continuously, and there is evidence of buyers requesting particular titles from larger catalogues by number. Books were rarely listed in strict alphabetical order by title or author until the end of the century, but organization by topic was not unknown. In their joint publication catalogues that began appearing in the late 1770s, Strahan and Cadell mixed titles in different formats according to a topical arrangement, using seven basic categories that remained constant throughout the last two decades of the century, both in name and sequence: (1) History, Voyages, and Travels; (2) Divinity; (3) Miscellanies, Books of Entertainment, Poetry, etc.; (4) Law; (5) Physic; (6) Philosophy [i.e., science], Mathematics, Mechanics, etc.; and (7) Agriculture, Botany, Gardening, etc.

Within each section, the books were loosely organized by subtopic, with the names of authors placed in light italics after the titles. The effect of this mode of organization was to deemphasize individual authors, whose names are sometimes difficult to pick out and whose works often appear in different sections, or in different areas within particular sections. Thus, Hume's *History of England* (which, oddly enough, was always listed anonymously) is in the History section, whereas Hume's *Essays and Treatises on Several Subjects* appears under Miscellanies. Adam Smith's *Wealth of Nations* is listed with works on political economy within the Miscellanies section, while his *Theory of Moral Sentiments* is found later in the same section among works of philosophy. In playing down the prominence and unity of individual authors, these catalogues drew attention to the role of publishers as the producers of works in most major areas of polite knowledge. They presented the publisher both as a brand name and as the primary mode of classifying books, with topical categories and the names of authors appearing as subdivisions. In this sense, the Strahan–Cadell publication catalogues exemplify the publisher function.

Although the majority of the books in Strahan and Cadell's publication catalogues are not by Scottish authors, the lists have a strong Scottish emphasis. It is evident on the opening page (see fig. 1.3), where all the titles are by Scottish authors—David Hume, James Macpherson (two titles, one without his name), and William Robertson (two titles); the pattern continues on the second page with a third title by Robertson and one by Robert Watson, until a work by an English author finally appears in the form of Edward Gibbon's *Decline and Fall of the Roman Empire*. Not only are the first seven books in the list by Scots but they are all available in expensive quarto editions as well as, in most cases, less expensive octavo editions. Later in this section, there appear Sir John Dalrymple's

Memoirs of Great Britain and Ireland, Lord Kames's *Sketches of the History of Man*, William Smellie's nine-volume edition of Buffon's *Natural History*, and three travel books by Patrick Brydone and John Moore. The Divinity category includes Hugh Blair's popular *Sermons*, then in two volumes and an eighth edition, James Fordyce's *Sermons to Young Women* and *Addresses to Young Men*, and the *Sermons* of John Farquhar.

The section titled "Miscellanies, Books of Entertainment, Poetry, etc." begins with Bolingbroke and Bacon and then shifts into a Scottish mode: six of the next eleven places are occupied by Adam Smith's *Wealth of Nations*, Sir James Steuart's *Inquiry into the Principles of Political Oeconomy*, Hume's *Essays and Treatises on Several Subjects* (available in three different formats), Adam Ferguson's *Essay on the History of Civil Society*, James Dunbar's *Essays on the History of Mankind*, and Smith's *Theory of Moral Sentiments*. With the exception of James Thomson from earlier in the century, none of the poetry in the publication list is Scottish, but toward the end of this section one finds John Gregory's *A Father's Legacy to His Daughters*, *The Mirror*, and three novels by Henry Mackenzie (*The Man of Feeling*, *The Man of the World*, and *Julia de Roubigné*) along with one by Tobias Smollett (*Adventures of Peregrine Pickle*). In the Physic or medicine category, the first entry is always William Buchan's *Domestic Medicine*, described more fully than any other title, and there are also works listed by John Gregory, William Fordyce, William Hunter, and William Smellie. The section titled "Philosophy, Mathematics, Mechanics, etc." is almost completely given over to six titles by a single Scottish author, James Ferguson.

Newspaper advertisements and excerpts from books, book reviews, and publication catalogues are all examples of what Gérard Genette calls "epitexts," or paratextual materials that are situated outside a book but serve, in a sense, as its extension.[95] Advertisements, excerpts, and catalogues were normally fashioned by publishers and booksellers, and book reviews were often arranged and influenced by them. Together with other epitexts, such as favorable articles and portraits planted in magazines,[96] these materials enabled publishers not only to publicize their books but also to mediate the public's response to them. To a large degree, epitexts were dependent on the willingness of publishers to spend money on ad-

95. Genette, *Paratexts*.

96. For example, it is likely that the reverential puff of William Robertson in the *London Magazine* in April 1772, which coincided with the publication of the second, octavo edition of Robertson's *History of Charles V* (no. 119), was planted by Strahan and Cadell.

vertisements and catalogues, but publishers who could influence or control a variety of print media such as newspapers and magazines, as well as printing presses themselves, had an enormous advantage over those who could not. In all these ways, the House of Strahan and Cadell was at the top of its profession.

*

When Thomas Cadell testified before Parliament in March 1785, the House of Strahan and Cadell was indisputably preeminent. Its two component firms constituted the leading printing and bookselling establishments in London, and perhaps the world. Their heads had achieved great status and wealth: one had become a member of Parliament and a master of the Stationers' Company, while the other would become a master of the company in the next decade and was on his way to becoming a man of consequence in the civic and political life of London. The house's list of authors and published books was unrivaled. It had solid copublishing connections with the Edinburgh firms run by Balfour and especially Creech. The syndicate was connected with a major English newspaper, the *London Chronicle*, and a prominent literary journal, the *Monthly Review*. And it had developed the publishers' catalogue as a device for marketing not only its publications but also itself. Of course, there was much to complain about: greedy and clannish authors, unfavorable legal decisions on literary property, tight money, bad investments, Irish piracies, unauthorized abridgments. But these were relatively minor considerations compared to the enormous success of the publishing syndicate.

Within a matter of months of Cadell's testimony, however, the Strahan–Cadell publishing partnership would suffer a devastating blow. When William Strahan died on 9 July 1785, the future of the publishing empire he had built with Thomas Cadell on foundations laid by Andrew Millar was suddenly in doubt. Like Millar before and Cadell afterward, Strahan's passing set off choruses of mourning for a man who seemed to embody the principle of merit combined with industry. "Lament with me such worth should be withdrawn, / And all who knew his worth must weep for STRAHAN!" wrote one wit.[97] Could the House of Strahan and Cadell withstand the passing of its elder statesman and retain its preeminence as publishers of the Scottish Enlightenment?

97. From verses by J. Noorthouck, quoted in Timperley, *Encyclopaedia*, 2:756.

SUCCESSORS AND RIVALS

Sons of the Empire

In the immediate aftermath of William Strahan's death, the endurance of the Strahan–Cadell syndicate depended chiefly on the viability of the succession on the Strahan side of the partnership. Strahan had three sons who survived infancy, born between 1740 and 1750. As his printing business prospered, he made plans for his sons to enter different branches of the book trade, "so that they will all have a Connection with one another, and yet not interfere."[98] The eldest, William or Billy (1740–81), was to be a printer, and to that end apprenticed with his father from 1754 to 1761, becoming in the process the manager of the main Strahan print shop (also called the "private" branch, to distinguish it from the law branch and the king's branch, which Strahan held by patent) after Archibald Hamilton left the firm. To launch the bookselling career of his second son, George (1744–1824), Strahan trained him himself from 1758 to 1761 and then sent him to Thomas Durham, with whom he was partner in a bookselling firm in the Strand; indeed, Strahan had originally brought Durham to London from Scotland, perhaps with this purpose in mind. As Strahan explained the plan to his friend David Hall on 15 July 1761, George was to assume his own share in the Durham partnership as soon as his apprenticeship was complete. His third and youngest son, Andrew (1750–1831), was slated to be a stationer. The boys were extremely close. As late as 1768, a friend who visited Strahan's house while Strahan himself was in Scotland called them "the bold Triumverate," who displayed the most "unaffected appearance of cordial affection" he had ever seen.[99]

Had Strahan's scheme succeeded, his firm might have become a vertically integrated family business, with a different son heading its printing, bookselling, and stationery concerns. But the scheme was never implemented. George was the first to bolt, quitting his apprenticeship as a bookseller in 1763 in order to attend Oxford University and take orders as an Anglican clergyman. In 1772 Strahan dutifully procured for him the vicarage of St. Mary's, Islington, where George remained until his death in 1824. Young William stayed in his appointed trade, but not in the way Strahan intended. A partner in the firm from 1767, he shared

---

98. Strahan to Hall, 15 July 1761, quoted in Cochrane, *Dr. Johnson's Printer*, 99.

99. Owen Ruffhead to William Strahan, 21 July 1768, HL, MS Hyde 77, 8.196.2.

the imprint with his father as coprinter of William Robertson's *History of Charles V* in March 1769 ("Printed by W. and W. Strahan"). He also served the Strahan–Cadell publishing network by supervising apprentices who were the sons of important connections, including Andrew Wilson (son of the type-founder and Glasgow University professor Alexander Wilson) in 1762 and Andrew Becket (son of the Strand bookseller Thomas Becket) in 1765—not to mention his own brother Andrew in 1763.[100] But in October 1769 William, Jr., decided to go into business for himself, launched with £2,000 from his father.[101] After an undistinguished career as an independent printer, he died prematurely in April 1781.

That left only Andrew, "a very decent little Rogue," as his father had described him when he was only six,[102] to succeed William Strahan. He was named after his godfather, Andrew Millar, whose will left him £100.[103] Andrew Strahan spent some time at a boarding school and then, contrary to the original plan, was apprenticed as a printer to his older brother William at the age of thirteen on 4 October 1763, the year of George's departure. He completed his apprenticeship on 6 November 1770 and was soon managing the private print shop, as William, Jr., had done before him. In January 1777 he again followed in the footsteps of William, Jr., by becoming a partner in the firm. There followed some years of hard work behind the scenes, as Andrew administered the firm's day-to-day operations while his father attracted national attention as a member of Parliament and a prominent leader of the trade. Cadell and Creech had emerged from the shadows of their respective senior partners, Millar and Kincaid, during the late 1760s and early 1770s, long before their thirtieth birthdays. Although Andrew Strahan was only eight years younger than Cadell and just five years younger than Creech, he did not assume a leading position in the book trade until after his father's death in July 1785, when he was thirty-five years old. In the meantime, the elder Strahan did all he could to cement the connection between his primary publishing partner and his heir. On 25 July 1777, for example, he wrote to Cadell from Scarborough: "I hope you dine with Andrew at least three or four times a Week, and help to support his Spirits during our Absence."[104] Andrew and Cadell were

100. McKenzie, *Stationers' Company Apprentices*, 341.

101. Strahan to Hall, 7 Oct. 1769, in Pomfret, "Some Further Letters," 474.

102. Strahan to Hall, 11 Sept. 1756, quoted in Cochrane, *Dr. Johnson's Printer*, 95.

103. Millar's will in Oliver, *History*, 2:265.

104. Strahan to Hall, 11 Sept. 1756, quoted in Cochrane, *Dr. Johnson's Printer*, 95, 139.

named joint executors in Strahan's will. Cadell received a gift of £500, while Andrew inherited much of his father's printing and publishing assets, and would purchase some of his father's other copyrights from the estate in August 1786.[105] Although the personal estate of William Strahan, including the family house and "farm" in the country, was willed to his wife Margaret, her death within weeks of her husband's left Andrew in possession of the family fortune as well as the family firm.

On 12 July 1785 Andrew Strahan sent a remarkable letter to William Creech in Edinburgh in order to explain how the death of his father three days earlier would affect the publication of new books by Scottish authors.

> Some years ago my Father and Mr Cadell entered into an Agreement that the Copies [i.e., copyrights] in which they were jointly concerned should not be subject to Division at their Deaths, but should devolve to such of their Sons as might be bred up to the Business. This Branch of course falls to my Lot; which is particularly satisfactory to me, as (independent of any Connection in Business) I regard Mr Cadell as one of my most steady and intimate Friends. I have thought it necessary therefore to write to Drs Robertson, Blair, etc. informing them of this Circumstance, and soliciting the Continuance of their Friendship, and Interest with their Friends; assuring them that they would find this Branch of my Father's Business pursued with the same Spirit and Attention as ever. I flatter myself you will think I have done right, lest it should be imagined that the Business was to be given up; and if it shall occur to you that any further measures should be adopted, I will thank you to give me a Hint.
>
> Whenever you come to this Quarter, I shall be happy to see you, and I hope you will find the House what it was wont to be, as far as may be considering our Loss.

There would be no sale of William Strahan's copyrights, the way there had been of Andrew Millar's in 1769. Nor would the publishing business be given up. Rather, "the House" would remain much as it had been, physically as well as personally and professionally. The letter's reference to the closeness of Andrew's friendship with Cadell, "independent of any Connection in Business," may be read as a reminder that the core of the Strahan–Cadell publishing empire was the relationship between those two London families, based on deep personal ties that included, yet transcended, the

---

105. Lutes, "Andrew Strahan," 241.

quest for profit. Above all, the sentence in which Andrew tells of writing to William Robertson and Hugh Blair, among others, seeking their support and that of "their Friends," served to demonstrate the determination of Andrew Strahan and Thomas Cadell to hold together their stable of Scottish authors, just as they meant to hold together the alliance with their most important ally in the Edinburgh book trade, William Creech.

That is more or less how things turned out. In October 1786 Creech wrote to James Beattie about the arrangements for publishing his *Evidences of the Christian Religion* (no. 258): "Young Mr. Strahan, Mr. Cadell and I continue the same co-partners as to Scots literary property that we did when old Mr. Strahan lived. In consequence of this Mr. Strahan got 1/3 of your Evidences and Mr. Cadell 1/3," in addition to Creech's own third.[106] The following spring and summer Creech visited Andrew Strahan and Cadell in London. As we saw in chapter 3, in the context of Robert Burns's dealings with his bookseller over the Edinburgh edition of his *Poems*, his absence on this occasion caused difficulties for his Edinburgh business, which floundered under the management of his partner, William Smellie. But a visit to London was necessary for Creech to maintain his connections and secure the publishing partnership with "Young Mr. Strahan" and Cadell. For his part, Andrew Strahan traveled north from time to time, as his father had before him. We know that he did so in 1796, for example, because at the end of that year Hugh Blair wrote: "It was a great Satisfaction to me that your Jaunt here proved so agreable to you and that you express so much pleasure in the Remembrance of it."[107] Another letter places Strahan and Blair at a dinner at Creech's two years later.[108] In this way, the publishing partnership was sustained, both within London and along the London–Edinburgh axis. It was good news for Scottish authors who had been affiliated with Millar, Strahan, and Cadell over the years.

Frances Burney described Andrew Strahan in 1798 as someone with "all the appearance of a very worthy, sensible, unpretending man, well-bred and good natured."[109] There is a suggestion of these traits in his por-

106. Creech to Beattie, 6 Oct. 1786, AUL, MS 30/2/523.

107. Blair to Andrew Strahan, 26 Dec. 1796, Pierpont Morgan Library, extra-illustrated folio edition of Boswell's *Life of Johnson*, 3:86.

108. Writing to Andrew Strahan in the third person on 13 September [1798], Blair states that "he hopes to have the pleasure of meeting Mr Strahan at Mr Creech's this day at dinner." Quoted in Zachs, *Hugh Blair's Letters to His Publishers.*

109. Cited in the life of Andrew Strahan that appears in Thorne, *House of Commons*, 5:301–2, quoting 302.

Figs. 5.7 and 5.8. Andrew Strahan (left, by William Owen) and Thomas Cadell (right, by Sir William Beechey, 1798) were near contemporaries whose close friendship and publishing partnership were carefully cultivated by Andrew's father, William. These impressively framed portraits hang in the Stock Room (Strahan) and Court Room (Cadell) of Stationers' Hall, London. Cadell is pictured in his midfifties, when he was serving as a London alderman, five years after his retirement from the book trade. The date of Strahan's portrait is unknown, but it appears to be from late in life, perhaps near the time of his death in 1831 at the age of eighty-one and almost certainly well after his retirement from the trade in 1819. Master and Wardens of the Worshipful Company of Stationers.

trait by William Owen, apparently painted when he was well on in years (fig. 5.7). It hangs in the Stock Room of Stationers' Hall in London, as the portrait of his partner Thomas Cadell by Sir William Beechey hangs in the Court Room in a similarly elegant frame (fig. 5.8). In the only existing full-length study of his business practices, Richard Lutes shows that Andrew Strahan "did all the things his father had done, but on a larger scale."[110] In 1788 he expanded the printing capacity of the private branch of his business from eleven to fifteen presses, with fifty-four composition frames, and in 1800 he built a new two-story printing office that soon accommodated eight additional presses and twenty more composition

110. Lutes, "Andrew Strahan," 21. The pages cited parenthetically in this paragraph and the next refer to this helpful work.

frames (29–30). He and his partners kept up with new developments in printing technology by replacing their wooden presses with iron ones by the time of his retirement in 1819 (30–31). The size of the payroll soared, from £2,940 at the time of his father's death in 1785 to roughly twice that amount in 1800 and nearly £10,000 in 1818 (35). Profits apparently continued to rise as well. From 1796 to 1820 Andrew, like his father before him, served as a member of Parliament for various English boroughs, supporting the government on most occasions. In 1802 he became a governor of the Foundling Hospital.[111] A lifelong bachelor, with no family to support, he grew fantastically wealthy and was worth over a million pounds at the time of his death in 1831.[112]

Collaboration with the Cadells never faltered. Lutes has calculated that the Cadells did more printing with Andrew Strahan in his first decade running the family firm than Thomas Cadell had done in the two decades preceding the death of William Strahan: £18,780 in the period 1767–86, £20,584 in the period 1787–96. When Cadell retired in 1793, he left his firm in the hands of his well-respected manager, William Davies (d. 1820), along with his son, Thomas, Jr. (1773–1836), trading as Cadell & Davies. Despite serious shortcomings, the new partnership remained a major player in the British book trade for decades to come. In 1794 Andrew Strahan joined them to build a large new warehouse (89), replacing Cadell's warehouse in the Strand where, according to one frequent customer from the years 1785–88, "many hundred waggon loads of unbound books were deposited."[113]

Andrew Strahan's name appears in the imprints of some two dozen titles in table 2, all dating from the period 1786–98, and all published jointly with Thomas Cadell or, from 1796 onward, with Cadell & Davies. Nine were copublished in Edinburgh by Creech (occasionally joined by Bell or Balfour), and another was copublished by Balfour alone. Creech's name also appears along with Cadell & Davies alone in the imprints of four other titles from table 2, and Bell and Balfour each had one individual collaboration with Cadell & Davies as well. The list of the writers they published continued to include many of the stars of the Scottish Enlightenment, as well as Gibbon, Blackstone, and other prominent English authors. For these reasons, it is sometimes difficult to perceive a significant

111. Nichols and Wray, *History*, 391.

112. Obituary in the *Gentleman's Magazine* for 1831, quoted in Thorne, *House of Commons*, 5:302.

113. [West], "Letters to My Son" 252.

break in the publishing output and status of the Strahan–Cadell syndicate in the years immediately following William Strahan's death.

One of the ways that Andrew Strahan and Thomas Cadell, and later Cadell & Davies, cultivated this impression was by resuming the practice of issuing substantial catalogues of their publications. No such catalogues are to be found for several years during the mid-1780s. Toward the end of that decade, however, there appeared *The Following Valuable Books Are Printed for A. Strahan and T. Cadell, in the Strand. 1788,* and similarly titled catalogues are known to exist for 1790, 1791, 1792, and 1793, often bound in the back of books published by Strahan and Cadell. These catalogues differ from the ones that William Strahan and Thomas Cadell produced in the late 1770s and early 1780s only by being dated and by including a number of newer titles and editions, as these came to be published. Like their predecessors, they were printed on one sheet of paper in different formats; copies of the 1788 catalogue have survived in duodecimo, octavo, and quarto. After Cadell's retirement in 1793, this series of publication lists seems to have halted for a short time, but in 1796 it reappeared, once again unchanged in its organization, under the title *The Following Valuable Books Are Printed for T. Cadell, Jun. and W. Davies (Successors to Mr. Cadell) in the Strand, 1796,* and from that date onward Cadell & Davies produced various lists and catalogues, which never again included the name of Andrew Strahan in the title even though he was usually a partner in copyright ownership.

As we shall see in the concluding chapter of this book, the sons ultimately could not live up to the high standards of their fathers as publishers of new books. Yet the decline of the publishing syndicate was gradual, masked for some time by continuity in reprinting large quantities of the most popular titles from the golden age of William Strahan and Thomas Cadell, as well as some new ones by authors from that era. Buoyed by an ongoing association with William Creech in Edinburgh, the House of Strahan and Cadell remained a major force in the publication of new works of literature and learning for some time after beginning its downward trajectory during the 1790s.

Challenging the House of Strahan and Cadell

Even at its peak, the Strahan–Cadell syndicate had no monopoly over the publication of Scottish Enlightenment books. It was not a monolithic entity, and its component firms often collaborated with other publishers. Cadell, without the Strahans, sometimes copublished books with members of the Edinburgh trade from outside the syndicate, just as Creech some-times collaborated with members of the London trade other than Strahan and Cadell. These instances arose when Strahan, Cadell, or Creech de-clined to participate in a publication that had initially been offered to all of them by another member of the syndicate, or else when the initiative for a publication came from outside their ranks. Thus, the situation was fluid rather than rigid.

Furthermore, many new Scottish books were published by promi-nent booksellers operating independently from the men involved with the Strahan–Cadell syndicate. At the time of William Strahan's death in July 1785, Charles Dilly (the surviving member of a partnership with his brother Edward), Joseph Johnson, John Murray, and George Robinson were all active in London, as were Charles Elliot and John Bell in Edin-burgh. These booksellers appear in table 5 as substantial publishers of Scottish Enlightenment books, and most of them engaged extensively in collaborative publishing. This section looks at their achievements as Scot-tish Enlightenment publishers, as well as some of the factors that pre-vented them from presenting a more serious challenge to the preeminence of the Strahan–Cadell syndicate.

From a metropolitan point of view, the principal publishers were all outsiders. This is true not only of the Scots but also of the Englishmen among them. None came from London or its environs, and their religious and political views placed them outside the establishment. For example, Edward (1732–1779) and Charles (1739–1807) Dilly, bachelor brothers based in the Poultry district of London, were Dissenters with strong American connections.[114] As we saw in chapter 3, they had a special rela-tionship with James Boswell, whose biographer has identified him as "the Dillys' prime author."[115] But the Dillys also copublished, with Edinburgh booksellers, three books by James Beattie, including his best-selling *Essay on Truth* (no. 123) and *The Minstrel* (no. 141). Otherwise, there were few major works among their Scottish Enlightenment titles. This may be be-cause, for all their hospitality toward authors, the Dillys generally did not pay them very much for copyrights, and some of their prime publications were in fact printed for the author under the Dilly imprint, such as Bos-well's *Life of Samuel Johnson*.

Joseph Johnson (1738–1809) of St. Paul's Churchyard was even more

114. Butterfield, "American Interests," 283–332; J. J. Caudle's biographies of the Dilly brothers in *ODNB*.

115. Pottle, *Earlier Years*, 541n.

closely linked to radicalism and Nonconformity (specifically Unitarianism) than were the Dilly brothers, and late in the century he was imprisoned for six months for publishing a controversial pamphlet.[116] Best known for his connections with English authors such as Joseph Priestley, Erasmus Darwin, William Cowper, and Mary Wollstonecraft, and the Anglo-Irish novelist Maria Edgeworth, Johnson was a formidable figure in British publishing. With regard to new publications by Scottish authors, he specialized in science and medicine. Of fifteen titles in table 2 of which Johnson was the principal publisher, only two that were published at the very end of the century, William Thomson's *Enquiry into the Elementary Principles of Beauty* (no. 347) and George Campbell's *Lectures on Ecclesiastical History* (no. 355), did not belong to those genres. Most of the rest of Johnson's Scottish publications were penned by Scottish physicians resident in London, such as George Fordyce (whose *Elements of the Practice of Physic*, no. 113, and *Elements of Agriculture and Vegetation*, no. 134, were among Johnson's most popular scientific publications), John Hunter, William Hunter, and Matthew Baillie. According to the obituary by John Aiken in the *Gentleman's Magazine* for December 1809, Johnson "was not remarkable for the encouragement he held out to Authors," but he voluntarily gave authors a share of the profits "when the success of a work surpassed his expectations."[117] Perhaps because he harbored suspicions about Scottish booksellers, whom he privately accused of pleading ignorance about publishing improprieties "when it is their interest" to do so,[118] Johnson did not copublish books with them as readily as the other leading London booksellers were inclined to do. Yet even he did so occasionally, such as his collaboration in the publication of two new medical books by Alexander Monro *secundus* (nos. 234 and 344).

John Murray (1737–1793), whose name appears in more imprints in table 2 than do the Dillys and Johnson combined, entered the London book trade as an outsider in more ways than one. The son of an Edinburgh legal writer (equivalent to an English solicitor), he left the University of Edinburgh after only one year and went to sea.[119] After a brief

---

116. Tyson, *Joseph Johnson;* Andrews, *Unitarian Radicalism.*

117. The obituary is reprinted in Hart, *Minor Lives*, 282–84, quoting 283.

118. Johnson to Mr. Fauche, June 1796 (copy), Joseph Johnson Letterbook, 1795–1810, New York Public Library, Carl H. Pforzheimer Collection.

119. Unless otherwise noted, biographical details on Murray are drawn from Zachs, *First John Murray*, which presents the fullest picture yet of an eighteenth-century British bookseller as a man of business.

career as a naval lieutenant during and after the Seven Years' War, he retired on half pay in 1768 and purchased the Fleet Street bookshop and stock of William Sandby for £1,000. Upon beginning his new career as a London bookseller, he shortened his name from McMurray to Murray. This alteration was indicative of his willingness to remake himself as a bookseller in the metropolis at the age of thirty-one, although it may also have been a response to the strong anti-Scottish feeling that existed in London during the decade of Ossian and Lord Bute. Murray remained closely connected with Scotland. He is said to have made frequent visits to Edinburgh, and he sent his son and successor to Edinburgh High School for a year.[120] He also cultivated close ties with a select group of Scottish authors and with members of the book trade in Scotland.

Because he had not been bred to the London book trade, Murray was excluded from the sales at which the leading London booksellers bought and sold copyright shares among themselves. He was so adamant in his opposition to those who excluded him that during the literary property crisis of 1774 he testified against the elite London booksellers in the House of Commons. In this sense, he identified more with his publishing colleagues in Edinburgh than with those in London. In March 1774 Murray expressed indignation toward Creech and Balfour for failing to stand up to the principal London booksellers on the copyright issue, declaring them "contemptible men" because they "stand aloof and will not join in a public opposition to them."[121] Believing the Lords' decision on copyright in February to be "a *magna charta* . . . to the Scotch booksellers," he charged Creech with hypocrisy for supporting schemes that would "reinstate [the London booksellers] in their usurpation" while at the same time benefiting from the decision by reprinting relevant titles himself.[122] Meanwhile, to Edinburgh booksellers who felt the way he did, such as John Bell, he sent assurances of "my zealous co-operation with Mr A. Donaldson."[123] When the hysteria of 1774 died down, and he was accepted into the fold, Murray appeared to conduct himself like any other prominent London bookseller, buying and selling copyright shares and making bargains at the Chapter Coffee House. Yet he always remained somewhat enigmatic and independent, if not downright belligerent, and

120. Smiles, *Publisher and His Friends*, 1:21, 27.

121. Murray to Gilbert Stuart, 21 Mar. 1774. Murray letters cited in this section are copies located in his letterbooks in the John Murray Archive, NLS.

122. Murray to Creech, 8 Apr. 1774.

123. Murray to Bell, 5 Apr. 1774.

for these reasons he was never fully trusted by some of the leading citizens of the London trade. William Strahan wrote to Creech on 18 March 1779, for example, that Murray remained "a Man with whom we wish to have no Concern in any Shape."

Murray normally copublished his new books by Scottish authors with Edinburgh booksellers, particularly Bell, Creech, and Elliot. Of the thirty-three books in table 2 with his name in the imprint as publisher or selling agent, only eight contain his name alone. The fee of one hundred guineas that John Millar received for the first of those works, *Observations on the Distinction of Ranks* (no. 137), was a great deal of copy money for Murray to lay out by himself, and his correspondence shows him scrambling to recoup it. He persuaded a Dublin bookseller, Thomas Ewing, to purchase the Irish rights for fifteen guineas, and he was compelled to set the price of the British edition higher than he would have liked, even though the text turned out to be shorter than anticipated.[124] When the relatively high retail price and dumping by other London booksellers led to slower than expected sales in Scotland, Murray had reason to wonder if he had over-extended himself: "I am sorry that the price of Millar is complained of," he wrote to Kincaid & Creech, who handled the book in Edinburgh; "such is the consequence of buying a copy too dear."[125] As it turned out, Millar's book had some life left in it despite the problems of the quarto first edition, and Murray reaped the rewards of reprinting a "greatly enlarged" octavo second edition in 1773 and a further enlarged (and retitled) octavo third edition in 1779 (which he reissued in 1781). He also maintained the loyalty of Millar when it came time to publish his next book, *An Historical View of the English Government* (no. 271).

Nevertheless, Murray was, as Zachs has shown, a cautious business-man who generally avoided taking large risks as a publisher because of a "lack of capital and fear of failure."[126] When bargaining with Sir David Dalrymple, Lord Hailes, for the rights to his *Annals of Scotland* (no. 178), which he seems to have wanted to publish more for the status than the anticipated profit, he based his case on the degree to which he could provide quality service, not large amounts of copy money.[127] The copy money he

124. Zachs, *First John Murray*, 70, 112. See also Murray's letters to Thomas Ewing of 22 March and 22 April 1774.

125. Murray to Kincaid & Creech, 1 July 1771.

126. Zachs, *First John Murray*, 29.

127. See Murray's correspondence of autumn 1775 with Gilbert Stuart on the publication of the *Annals*.

paid to authors rarely exceeded one hundred guineas, and copublication with Edinburgh booksellers often helped to defray his expenses. Several of the books he copublished were medical works by Scottish physicians or surgeons such as Andrew Duncan (no. 190, with Elliot), William Cullen (no. 187, with Creech), Francis Home (no. 207, with Creech), and Benjamin Bell (no. 312, with Watson and Mudie; and no. 322, with Bell & Bradfute and the Robinsons). Murray was also attracted to history, and he copublished works in this genre by John Gillies (no. 192, with John Bell), Hugo Arnot (no. 199, with Creech), John Millar (no. 271, with A. Strahan and Cadell), and above all his friend Gilbert Stuart (no. 195, with John Bell; no. 202, with Creech; no. 210, with Bell; and no. 226, with Bell).

Since Murray could not or would not compete aggressively in the amount of copy money he offered, potential authors frequently came to him only after their manuscripts had been turned away by his larger and more adventurous rivals. Thomas Cadell seems to have had first refusal of Millar's *Observations on the Distinction of Ranks*, for example.[128] In a letter to Creech of 9 September 1774, William Strahan emphatically rejected "Mr. Ogilvie's Poem"—presumably *Rona*, which Murray published in 1777 (no. 184)—declaring that "poetry, unless excellent, is good for nothing, and seldom sells to pay Paper and Print." In the same letter, Strahan turned down John Gillies's *Orations of Lysias and Isocrates* (no. 192) with greater delicacy, after having patiently critiqued the manuscript to the young author, whom he considered a friend; when he wrote again on 29 October, he was plainly relieved to learn that Murray had purchased the copyright for £100. In other instances, Murray published minor authors like William Thomson, or minor books by major authors, such as Lord Kames's *Loose Hints upon Education* (no. 214). More than 80 percent of the titles in table 2 that Murray published or copublished sold poorly or modestly. Only one, Cullen's *First Lines of the Practice of Physic* (no. 187), was a best seller, and Murray managed to lose that book, along with a valuable title by Duncan, before the final volumes appeared.[129]

Murray's principal Scottish author was Gilbert Stuart, whose career reveals large gaps between both publishers and authors at different levels of success. Blaming William Robertson for blocking his appointment to an Edinburgh University chair in 1777, Stuart tried to compete by composing handsome quarto histories that took issue with Robertson's argu-

128. Murray to John Moore (who was handling Millar's negotiations), 7 Sept. 1770.

129. Zachs, *First John Murray*, 179–80, 191–95.

ments and sometimes harshly attacked Robertson himself.[130] From the four histories that he published between 1777 and 1782 with Murray and his Edinburgh copublishers, Bell and Creech, Stuart literally did not earn as much in hundreds as Robertson received in thousands from Strahan, Cadell, and Balfour for the histories of Charles V and America. And what is true of payments is equally so of sales: Murray typically sold several hundred copies of each edition of Stuart's histories, whereas his counterparts printed and sold several thousand copies of Robertson's histories at a clip.

Murray sometimes attributed this disparity to the malicious activities of his rivals, whom he privately accused of manipulating reviews of Stuart in the press, refusing to stock and sell Stuart's works in Cadell's shop, and generally using their "interest" to turn public opinion against them.[131] "It is impossible to select men fonder of their interest or more diligent to preserve it than the proprietors in question," Murray told Stuart on 11 March 1779. Writing to Creech on 24 May 1776, he was somewhat more charitable, though no less envious: "Publications in general are a lottery and most of the prizes . . . fall to the share of our friend Cadell." Whether the real reason was malicious behavior, luck, or some other factor, Murray correctly assessed the sizeable chasm that separated him from his more successful competitors. The death of William Strahan does not seem to have had any effect on Murray's pattern of publishing, although it is possible that his offering young Andrew Strahan and Thomas Cadell quarter shares of the copyright of John Millar's *Historical View of the English Government* in 1786, and then placing their names ahead of his own in the imprint,[132] was calculated as a peace offering to a publishing partnership with which Murray had enjoyed little connection as long as the elder Strahan lived.

Murray died in 1793 in possession of stock in trade worth almost £9,000, in addition to other assets.[133] He was succeeded by his son, John Murray II (1778–1843), who would become the leading literary publisher of the early nineteenth century as a result of his associations with writers

130. Zachs, *Without Regard to Good Manners*, esp. chaps. 4 and 5.

131. See Murray's letters to Stuart of 30 May 1778, insinuating that an initially favorable review of Stuart's *View of Society in Europe* in the *Monthly Review* by John Gillies had been tampered with by the editor, Ralph Griffiths; 11 March 1779, on the mobilization of the Strahan–Cadell "interest" against Stuart; and 23 April 1779, on Cadell refusing to sell Stuart's *Observations concerning Public Law*.

132. Zachs, *First John Murray*, 78.

133. Ibid., 242.

such as Lord Byron, Walter Scott, and Jane Austen. In 1807 young Murray married Anne Elliot, whose father, Charles Elliot (1748–1790), had been a major Edinburgh publisher with whom the first John Murray had frequently collaborated. As a result of this union, Elliot's papers ended up in the Murray Archive.

From his analysis of Charles Elliot's unpublished correspondence and imprints, Warren McDougall has found that Elliot had an independent, entrepreneurial spirit that was unprecedented in the Edinburgh trade.[134] Archibald Constable, writing more than thirty years after Elliot's death, would dub him "the most distinguished among the booksellers of Edinburgh" in his day and "the first bookseller who gave money for literary property in Scotland to any great amount."[135] Through his family ties with the Elliots of Minto,[136] in the Borders region where he was born, Elliot had powerful and wealthy patrons who were well connected with the Scottish literati. He learned the book business in Kirkcaldy, Fife, and in Edinburgh, but he was barely twenty-three when he acquired the premises and stock of a recently deceased Edinburgh bookseller, William Sands, in May 1771—the very same month in which his chief Edinburgh rival, William Creech, became a partner in the firm of Alexander Kincaid. In the two decades following his emergence as an independent Edinburgh bookseller, Elliot was aggressive in purchasing copyrights, especially in the field of medicine, and he used copublishing with London booksellers such as Murray, Robinson, and Cadell as a device for assuring widespread circulation of his books without actually surrendering any copyright shares.[137] In at least three instances—Cullen's *First Lines of the Practice of Physic* (no. 187) and *A Treatise of the Materia Medica* (no. 281), and the first volume of William Smellie's *Philosophy of Natural History* (no. 292)—Elliot paid authors one thousand guineas or more for the copyrights to multivolume scientific or medical works, something that few other eighteenth-century booksellers ever contemplated doing on their own.

In May 1776 Elliot renovated his premises in Parliament Square, and the next year he boasted to John Murray that he had "as good a shop as any in Fleet Street."[138] But Elliot was not content to be among the

134. See especially McDougall, "Charles Elliot's Medical Publications," 215–54; and McDougall, "Charles Elliot and the London Booksellers," 81–96.

135. Constable's memoir, in Constable, *Archibald Constable*, 533.

136. Smiles, *Publisher and His Friends*, 1:18.

137. McDougall, "Charles Elliot and the London Booksellers," 86.

138. Ibid., quoting 95.

premier booksellers in Edinburgh. In 1787 he established a shop in the Strand in London, run by his sister's husband, Thomas Kay, and bearing as its sign the head of his best-known author, William Cullen. This was the first London incursion by a major Edinburgh bookseller since Alexander Donaldson's "shop for cheap books" in the early 1760s. But whereas Donaldson used his London shop chiefly as an outlet for distributing his cheap reprints, mainly of the "English" classics, Elliot wanted an outlet for his new Scottish medical books, which the London booksellers were said to be conspiring against. The imprint of his two-volume quarto edition of Cullen's *Treatise of the Materia Medica*, "Edinburgh: Printed for Charles Elliot, and for C. Elliot & T. Kay, London, 1789," was clearly intended as a future model, which cut the established London booksellers out of the publication. Elliot also joined forces with Newcastle booksellers in the sale of books and medical tonics, dabbled in Irish and Scottish piracies, issued large book catalogues, and made huge investments in America, chiefly through Thomas Dobson, a former apprentice whom he set up in business in Philadelphia.[139]

In spite of his unbounded energy and ambition, it can be argued that Elliot was largely responsible for his own undoing. Both his London shop and his American adventures demonstrated poor business judgment. Kay proved to be an incompetent manager, and Dobson was able to delay repayment for many years because Elliot had never formalized or specified the terms of their arrangement.[140] Although his estate would ultimately be worth more than £30,000, Elliot was having cash-flow problems when he was crippled by a stroke in September 1789; he died four months later, at just forty-one years of age. As a result of a combination of bad business decisions and bad health, his contribution as a Scottish Enlightenment publisher was limited to a relatively brief period, and it was heavily concentrated in medicine and science.

The most serious challenge to the Strahan–Cadell publishing syndicate began around the middle of the 1780s, when George Robinson expanded his bookselling business in London into a large family concern and joined into an informal partnership with John Bell of Edinburgh (1735–1806).

---

139. McDougall, "Charles Elliot's Book Adventure," 197–212; McDougall, "Charles Elliot and the London Booksellers," esp. 82–83, 95; Isaac, "Charles Elliot and the English Provincial Book Trade," 97–116; and Isaac, "Charles Elliot and Spilsbury's Antiscorbutic Drops," 157–74.

140. McDougall, "Charles Elliot's Book Adventure"; and chap. 9 of the present volume.

After Kincaid replaced him with Creech in 1771, Bell had set up his own shop at Addison's Head. He made a specialty of law books and continued to be a major force in Scottish Enlightenment reprinting, keeping nearly everything written by Lord Kames in print, for example. But it was some time before Bell got back into the business of publishing new work by Scottish authors: as an independent publisher, his name does not appear in the imprints of any of the first editions in table 2 until 1778. From then on, however, he began to collaborate more frequently with London booksellers such as John Murray, especially in the publication of new works by Gilbert Stuart (nos. 195, 210, and 226).[141] It was also in 1778 that Bell moved his bookshop to a new location in Parliament Square. As his business expanded, Bell made a partner of his nephew and former apprentice John Bradfute (d. 1763), trading as Bell & Bradfute from November 1788. Following the death of Charles Elliot in 1790, the firm purchased his handsome shop on the east side of Parliament Square from Elliot's estate (see fig. 2.2). Bell & Bradfute issued large catalogues from which buyers ordered by number,[142] and when Bell died in 1806 he bequeathed his partner one-half the firm's stock in trade valued at £4,155.

Bell's upward surge coincided with his association with George Robinson in London, with whom he did a booming business that is documented in the many surviving business papers of Bell himself and Bell & Bradfute. An admiring contemporary bookseller, William West, recalled that Robinson was popularly known in the trade as the "king of booksellers, George Robinson the *first*," partly on account of his "noble appearance and manners," partly to distinguish him from his rather less imposing son, George II, and partly because he ran "perhaps . . . the most extensive publishing and wholesale book establishment in Europe."[143] According to West, "Mr. Robinson's conviviality . . . would fill a volume" (133). He was "a six-bottle man" (85) with a talent for storytelling and conversation and "a great share of wit and vivacity" (156), who "might appropriately be considered the pride of Paternoster Row, from his hospitality and liberality to

141. In the case of one of these titles, Stuart's *History of the Reformation in Scotland* (no. 210), Murray placed Bell's name on the title page without his knowledge, "to make some return for your favours" (Murray to Bell, 1780, NLS, Dep. 317, box 1, folder 1). In another instance, Stuart's *View of Society in Europe* (no. 195), Bell placed Murray's name on the title page in exchange for Murray's placing his name on the title page of John Gillies's *Orations of Lysias and Isocrates* (no. 192). See Zachs, *Without Regard for Good Manners*, 205n4.

142. Several of them are conveniently bound in NLS, NG.1615.d.15 (1–5).

143. [West], "Letters to My Son," 132.

authors, artists, printers, booksellers and even to the most distant of his English, Irish, and Scotch correspondents" (132). West referred repeatedly to Robinson's "conviviality and connections with his Irish and Scotch friends" (133) and implied that until late in life Robinson frequently traveled to Ireland and Scotland (156), where he was warmly received. West did not identify Robinson's Scottish friends (though we can be certain that one of them was John Bell), but the sampling of Dublin friends whom he named—John Archer, Patrick Byrne, John Exshaw the younger, John Jones, William Jones, James Moore, Peter Moore, John Rice, and Luke White (85, 133)—included several of the most aggressive reprinters of Scottish Enlightenment books in late eighteenth-century Ireland, both Protestant and Roman Catholic. Like his intimate friend and near neighbor Joseph Johnson, Robinson was a Dissenter, a fact that may also have contributed to the ease of his associations with some of his counterparts from outside England.

Robinson was born in December 1736 in the village of Dalston, near Carlisle, in the far northwest of England.[144] Lacking much formal education but possessing a mind that West called "shrewd, penetrating, and enriched by various experiences" (156), he went to London in the mid-1750s. Nothing is known of his training before that time, but in light of his religion, his connections with Glasgow and the Scottish trade, and his rapid integration into the London trade after arriving there at about eighteen years old, it is quite possible that he served an apprenticeship in Scotland. In London he worked for John Rivington, and then William Johnston, before entering into a partnership in 1764 with John Roberts at Addison's Head, 25 Paternoster Row. This was a central location in the heart of the "narrow, crowded, confined" book trade district, where Robinson remained for the rest of his life.[145] Robinson & Roberts appear in the imprints of three titles in table 2 that date from this period: William Guthrie's ten-volume *General History of Scotland* (no. 102), which they sold for the author; Tobias Smollett's eight-volume *Present State of All Nations* (no. 112), which they copublished with three other London booksellers, including William Johnston; and Smollett's anonymous *History and Adventures of an Atom* (no. 120), which they published independently. Even before he became involved with these publications, however, Robinson was suffi-

144. For biographical information about Robinson, see G. E. Bentley's account in *ODNB*, supplemented by West and other contemporary sources, as noted.

145. Raven, "Location, Size, and Succession," 100–101; and Raven, "Memorializing a London Bookscape," quoting 199.

ciently known and respected in Scotland to be granted the freedom of the city of Glasgow by the magistrates on 7 July 1766 (*EEC*, 9 July 1766), and one wonders what services he had performed to merit that honor.

After the death of Roberts in 1776, Robinson carried on the firm on his own at Addison's Head. He continued to involve himself with new Scottish books from time to time, particularly quarto and multivolume works that required large capital outlays. In 1781 we find him collaborating with Charles Elliot on *The Works of Alexander Monro*, a large quarto volume (no. 218). Two years later he copublished with two other London booksellers Robert Watson's posthumous *History of Philip III* (no. 239), another quarto, this one complicated by the fact that William Thomson had to be hired to write the last two books of the unfinished manuscript that Watson had left behind. Also in 1783, Robinson joined Charles Elliot in the publication of Benjamin Bell's *A System of Surgery* (no. 240), which took five years and six volumes to complete. The third volume (1785) contained an advertisement for twenty-seven medical books "Printed for and sold by C. Elliot, Edinburgh; and G. Robinson, London."

If George Robinson's Scottish publishing achievements were promising during his first two decades in business, they became considerably more so during the last fifteen years of the century. The mid-1780s marked the emergence of Robinson as a premier publisher of the Scottish Enlightenment. From a business point of view, the formation in 1784 of a strong partnership with his younger brother John (1753–1813) and his son George (d. 1811) was crucial. For the remainder of the century the imprint of G. G. J. & J. Robinson (or some variation, such as G. G. & J. Robinson) would appear in scores of volumes, including more than two dozen titles found in table 2. In one those publications from 1796, the third volume of James Anderson's *Essays Relating to Agriculture and Rural Affairs* (no. 172), the imprint identifies the firm simply as "the Robinsons," so well known had they become by then. Around the same time that George Robinson was reorganizing his firm along family lines, the death of William Strahan in July 1785 appeared to create opportunities in Scottish publishing. In that year the Robinsons published or copublished (with Elliot or Bell) no fewer than four new Scottish Enlightenment titles (nos. 249, 252, 253, and 255). During this period Robinson visited Edinburgh personally on at least one occasion, when he spent time with John Bell and, presumably, Charles Elliot and other Edinburgh booksellers.[146]

The growing collaboration between Bell and Robinson as Scottish En-

---

146. Robinson to Bell, 4 Oct. 1785, NLS, Acc. 10662, folder 10.

lightenment publishers was made viable by the combination of Robinson's large scale of operations and vast supply of capital in London and Bell's long experience as an Edinburgh publisher and bookseller who was well connected with many Scottish authors. The key book in the development of the partnership was Thomas Reid's *Essays on the Intellectual Powers*. In 1764 Bell had been among the copublishers of Reid's first book, *An Inquiry into the Human Mind* (no. 88), when he was the junior partner of Alexander Kincaid, and in that capacity he had supervised the printing by Patrick Neill.[147] Though a modest octavo, the *Inquiry* was eventually a strong seller, and it is widely considered the prime text in the emergence of the Scottish common sense school of philosophy with which Reid has often been associated. In the twenty years since the publication of the *Inquiry*, Reid had been developing his philosophical ideas in his moral philosophy lectures at the University of Glasgow and in his discourses in the Glasgow Literary Society, and he had other discourses on hand from his earlier years in the Aberdeen Philosophical Society. By 1784 he had accumulated enough papers to fill a large volume, and after so long a hiatus he obviously wanted the book to appear to best advantage. Who should publish it?

Strahan and Cadell may have seemed the obvious choice to publish Reid's new book on account of their prominence. In addition, as the successor to Andrew Millar, Thomas Cadell had been involved in the publication of the third edition of Reid's *Inquiry* in 1769, and he would be involved in the publication of the fourth edition of 1785. But John Bell was also a copublisher of those editions, and Reid seems to have had no personal attachment to Cadell. Situated in Glasgow, Reid was not in a position to negotiate easily with any London or Edinburgh publisher. He therefore turned over the negotiations for his book to William Rose, who was empowered to bargain on his behalf in London. Reid reported the arrangement in a letter to James Gregory of 14 March 1784: "Dr Rose at Chiswick—who, you know, has all along had a principal concern in *The Monthly Review*—has made me a very kind offer, that, if I please to send the MSS. to him, he will both give me his remarks, and treat with a bookseller about the sale of it."[148] An old acquaintance of Reid from his days in Aberdeen, Rose had been a student at Marischal College when Reid began teaching at King's College. Reid's manuscript was carried to Rose by his son Samuel, who was then attending Reid's current university at Glasgow. In addition, William Rose had favorably noticed Reid's

147. NLS, Dep. 196, fols. 17–18.
148. Reid, *Correspondence*, 167.

Inquiry in the *Monthly Review* for May 1764, giving rise to a 1775 article in the *London Review* which asserted that this notice had been planted unscrupulously by "a *friend* and *countryman* of the Author's."[149] Under the circumstances, one might have expected Rose's involvement to increase the odds that Reid's book would be published by Strahan and Cadell, with whom, as we have seen, Rose was closely connected through personal friendship and a long association with the *Monthly Review*.

How, then, did George Robinson and John Bell secure this prestigious title? On 13 August 1784 Bell wrote to Robinson to inform him that Rose was in charge of the negotiations and that quick action was necessary. Upon reading Bell's letter eight days later, Robinson replied that he had been away but would go to see Rose the next day "and will treat with him for the Manuscripts you mention and write to you concerning it in a few days."[150] Two weeks later Robinson wrote again:

> London Septr. 6 1784
>
> Sir
>
> Dr Rose of Chiswick who has the disposal of Dr Reids *Manuscripts* writes to him this night with Mr Cadells answer vizt. that he will give two hundred pounds down, print 1,000 Copies in Quarto and on reprinting the Book give one Hundred more. I have commissioned Mr Rose to write to Dr Reid that with you I will give the full Sum of three Hundred pounds. Now least there should be any farther correspondence on the subject I wish you to write to Dr Reid as soon as you recieve this and get his final answer, if the Dr asks time to write once more to London to try Cadell farther I decline any concern in it. No doubt the Dr will give time for payment of the Money which is generally twelve Months from the date of the Publication for which a note of hand is given, however do as well as you can and I will take two thirds.
>
> I am Sir   Y[our] H[umble] Servt.
>   Geo. Robinson
>
> Please to give me a line when you have Dr Reids answer.

Bell accordingly wrote directly to the author on 11 September, as we know from Reid's reply of 12 September. There Reid explained that he had given

149. The anecdote appears, along with Rose's review, in Fieser, *Scottish Common Sense Philosophy*, 3:1–39.

150. Robinson to Bell, 21 Aug. 1784, NLS, Acc. 10662, folder 9 (1784). Bell's letter to Robinson is now apparently lost but is referred to in Robinson's reply.

Rose the exclusive power to conclude a bargain but intimated that he was willing to include Bell in any agreement that met his minimum price of £300.[151] Meanwhile, Rose wrote to Reid on 9 September to say (in Reid's words) that an unnamed "respectable Bookseller of London" (meaning Robinson) had visited him and stated "that he would willingly take an equal Share with Mr Bell, and give 300£ for the Copy," whereas Cadell was unwilling to do so. At this point, Rose relinquished the negotiations to the author, who told Bell that he was "very willing" to conclude the arrangement for £300, provided that he also received a dozen presentation copies at no charge and, if necessary, "a few more" beyond that at the wholesale price.[152] It was presumably on these terms that the negotiations were concluded.

The economics of this business seem clear enough: Robinson and Bell got Reid's book because they offered the author £300 clear, whereas Cadell would do no better than £200, plus a promise of another £100 in the event of a second edition. But as significant as the outcome was the way the process unfolded and the meaning it held for Scottish Enlightenment publishing. Robinson was more aggressive than Cadell in seeking out William Rose and in manipulating the negotiations to his advantage. His ability to act quickly and decisively was critical, and so was his skill at using London–Edinburgh copublication as a means of raising capital for securing the copyright: Robinson would pay the author £200 and Bell the remaining, and apparently decisive, £100.[153] As an agent, Rose acted in the best interest of his "client" by not allowing his friendship with Strahan and Cadell to sway his decision. For his part, Reid hid behind his agent in his letter to Bell of 12 September 1784, in an apparent effort to raise the stakes still higher, much the way Robinson anticipated. But a clever strategy and a firm stance assured Robinson's triumph.

Printed in Edinburgh and published jointly by John Bell, Parliament Square, and G. G. J. & J. Robinson, London, in the third week of July 1785, Reid's *Essays on the Intellectual Powers of Man* was a massive one-volume quarto of 766 pages that could be purchased for £1.5s. in boards or £1.8s.

151. Reid, *Correspondence*, 170–71.

152. Reid to Bell, 26 Sept. 1784, in Reid, *Correspondence*, 171. The contents of Rose's lost letter of 9 September are given by Reid in this letter.

153. Robinson apparently told Rose that he would take "an equal Share with Mr Bell" (Reid to Bell, 26 Sept. 1784, in Reid, *Correspondence*, 171), but as we know from Robinson's letter to Bell of 6 September, reproduced above, Robinson actually took a two-thirds share.

bound. Since an authorized second edition never appeared in Reid's lifetime, the author seems to have made the right choice of publishers from
the standpoint of copy money (assuming, of course, that publication with
Strahan and Cadell would not have stimulated higher sales and multiple
editions). The fact that three years later the same London–Edinburgh
team copublished a second large volume of Reid's essays, the 493-page
quarto *Essays on the Active Powers of Man* (no. 275), suggests that the author and the publishers were both pleased with the arrangement.[154] As
always, motives having to do with prestige and status must be taken into
account along with those involving pecuniary gain, and on this score
Robinson and Bell seem to have done rather well in their first foray into
Scottish philosophical publishing. Personal rivalry may also have been
a factor, and perhaps ideology, as discussed later. The death of William
Strahan less than two weeks before the publication of Reid's *Intellectual
Powers* may also have encouraged the partners in their ambitious new
enterprise.

It seems clear that the publishing partnership of Robinson and Bell
was conceived as a long-term challenge to Strahan and Cadell, rather
than merely a way of making a quick profit off one or two new books.
When Reid's *Active Powers* got off to a slow start in 1788, Robinson looked
hopefully for steady progress over the long haul. "The Sale mends and no
doubt in time it will sell very well," he reassured his partner.[155] Bell's re-
organization later in the year as Bell & Bradfute strengthened this Edinburgh–London publishing partnership, which soon contracted to publish
another new philosophical quarto by a Scottish author, *Essays on the Nature and Principles of Taste* (no. 287) by Archibald Alison. In a letter to Bell
of 14 May 1789, Robinson discussed the publication of Alison's book in
terms that suggest a pattern of continuity with the two volumes of Reid's
essays: high-prestige quarto editions that were printed relatively cheaply
in Edinburgh, underwritten mainly by Robinson, and designed to turn a
small profit over an extended period of time, with modest print runs in
order to reduce risk: "I think 750 copies of Mr Alisons Book should be
printed in Quarto in the manner of Dr Reids Works, these will yield some
profit, and without running too great a risk determine the character
of it[;] if you are of the same opinion you will please to proceed with

154. For his part, Reid told James Gregory on 31 December 1784, seven months
before the *Essays on the Intellectual Powers* appeared, that Bell would have "the first
offer" of the *Essays on the Active Powers*.

155. Robinson to Bell, 10 May 1788, NLS, Dep. 317, box 1, folder 2.

the printing immediately[;] you have a third share with [us]."[156] Seven months later, when Bell had completed production in Edinburgh, Robinson assumed primary responsibility for marketing Alison's book, which he did in a manner that once again emphasized continuity with their two volumes of Reid's *Essays:* "We have given you Credit for the amount of the paper and printing of our 2/3ds of Alisons Book which we have fixed to sell for 16/ [sixteen shillings] in boards and will publish it on the first of next Month. You will see we advertise Reid['s] two Quarto's with it."[157] Alison received £200, plus £50 for a second edition.[158] But Alison's book also sold slowly at first, and a second edition did not appear until 1811, under the imprint of Bell & Bradfute and Archibald Constable.

The informal publishing partnership of George Robinson and John Bell continued to operate during the 1790s. The titles in table 2 that they copublished included two popular volumes of posthumous sermons by John Logan, which appeared in 1790–91 (no. 290); Thomas Robertson's quarto history of Mary Queen of Scots in 1793 (no. 317); the third volume of James Anderson's *Essays Relating to Agriculture and Rural Affairs* in 1796 (no. 172); and mathematical and medical works by Benjamin Bell in 1794 (no. 322; with John Murray), John Playfair in 1795 (no. 334), and Alexander Monro *secundus* in 1797 (no. 344; with Joseph Johnson). In addition, during the 1790s Robinson's firm was the sole publisher of several books in table 2, including works by James Bruce (no. 288), James Mackintosh (no. 298), John Moore (nos. 315, 333, and 359), and Elizabeth Hamilton (nos. 338 and 357).[159]

Yet considering their potential for ascendancy in this field and the elimination of competition from Elliot, Robinson and Bell did not do as

156. Robinson to Bell, 14 May 1789, ibid., box 2, folder 1.

157. Robinson to Bell, 16 Jan. 1790, NLS, Acc. 10662, folder 11. The Robinsons' two-thirds share of the printing charge for Alison's book is given as £80.10.10 in Bell & Bradfute's ledger under 31 December 1789 (NLS, Dep. 193, ledger 1, fol. 146; and Bell & Bradfute Ledgers, City Chambers, Edinburgh, SL 138/1). On 1 February Bell & Bradfute ran a similar advertisement in the *Edinburgh Evening Courant*, announcing the publication of Alison's quarto for sixteen shillings and noting the availability of Reid's *Intellectual Powers* and *Active Powers*.

158. Sir William Forbes to James Beattie, 3 June 1789, NLS, Acc. 4796, box 98.

159. In some of these cases, Bell & Bradfute may have been silent copublishers. For example, the first volume of John Moore's *Journal during a Residence in France* (no. 315) names only the Robinsons in its imprint but is advertised in the Edinburgh press as "published by" Bell & Bradfute (*EEC*, 23 May 1793).

well for themselves in the late 1780s and 1790s as they might have initially hoped. After Reid and Alison, few of the Scottish titles they subsequently produced were important texts by major authors. During the 1790s, William Robertson, Adam Ferguson, Dugald Stewart, James Gregory, James Hutton, and Thomas Somerville all had their new quartos published by Andrew Strahan and Thomas Cadell, or the latter's successor, Cadell & Davies. Meanwhile, Robinson and Bell often could compete only with relatively minor books such as *The History of Mary Queen of Scots* by Thomas Robertson, a clergyman who shared the same surname, occupation, topic, and expensive publishing format as William Robertson but had little success in his attempt to replace his rival's carefully balanced treatment of Mary with an approach that set out to glorify her. Robinson's only best seller in table 2, James Bruce's *Travels to Discover the Source of the Nile* (no. 288), was a work that Strahan and Cadell had apparently rejected and that the author sold to Robinson as a finished product, to be marketed under his name. And it became a best seller in abridged editions published by others.

There would seem to be three principal reasons for Robinson and Bell's failure to take command of Scottish Enlightenment publishing during the late 1780s and 1790s. First, as we have already seen, the publishing partnership of Strahan and Cadell showed surprising resiliency under Andrew Strahan and, to a lesser extent, Cadell & Davies. Second, the French wars of the 1790s depressed the value of literary property and reduced the demand for new books. "The present times are against Authors and Booksellers; books being little read," wrote the author of one of Robinson and Bell's slow-selling books in 1793.[160] This situation affected all publishers, of course, but the Strahans and Cadells had a large number of Scottish authors who remained loyal to them, whereas Robinson and Bell had to discover fresh talent at an inopportune time. Third, Robinson's political radicalism, apparently shared by Bell, placed an added financial and psychological strain on their publishing partnership and probably impaired their willingness and ability to attract leading Scottish authors (other than radicals) to their presses during the 1790s.

The ideology of Robinson and Bell must be pieced together bit by bit. Bell was certainly public-spirited, and his position in the early 1780s as a manager of the Edinburgh Public Dispensary, founded under the patronage of the radical Whig Henry Erskine to provide medical and pharma-

---

160. Thomas Robertson to Bell & Bradfute, 26 Feb. [1793], EUL, La.II.419, no. 21.

ceutical relief to the poor, may reveal something about his views (*EEC*, 29 Jan. 1783). Perhaps it is coincidence that in the years preceding the French Revolution Bell and Robinson copublished two works by Reid, whose political sentiments were among the most liberal of any major Scottish Enlightenment author. It was certainly not by chance, however, that in April 1791 Robinson published James Mackintosh's popular answer to Edmund Burke's *Reflections on the French Revolution*, titled *Vindiciae Gallicae: Defence of the French Revolution and Its English Admirers* (no. 298). He subsequently was the publisher, copublisher, or selling agent of various radical books, the most famous of which, William Godwin's *An Enquiry Concerning Political Justice* (1793), would probably not have been completed if he had not supported Godwin while he was writing it.[161] In November 1793 Robinson and his London firm were convicted of wholesaling to the trade Thomas Paine's *Rights of Man* and fined a significant amount.[162] For his part, Bell seems to have been responsible for providing the Scottish, and later American, radical James Thomson Callender with his copy of Paine, for on 5 March 1792 Callender stated in a postscript to a letter to Bell: "I have bid the servant ask for Paine's book, which should come this day."[163]

When Bell tried unsuccessfully to interest his partner in copublishing a new edition of a book on insurance by the son of Professor John Millar of Glasgow, who was well known for his radical political views, Robinson penned this reply on 24 July 1794: "Altho' I should prefer dealing with a Democrat to an Aristocrat yet I decline taking any share in his Book. I have no doubt of his abilities, but from the very nature of the Book it must have a slow sale and these are not times to add to a heap already much too large. Business is very dull here, and not a guinea to be had for Books."[164] Later in the same letter, Robinson expressed regret that he and Bell could not visit Ireland together, as Bell had apparently suggested, and revealed the heavy toll the political crisis was taking on him: "I should like very well to call upon you and take you in my hand to Ireland, but I really

161. Bentley, "Copyright Documents," 67–110, contains details of the agreement as well as Godwin's testimony about Robinson's continued patronage since the early 1780s. Cf. Philp, *Godwin's Political Justice*, 74–75.

162. [West], "Letters to My Son," 133.

163. NLS, Dep. 317, box 2, folder 1.

164. Ibid.. The book in question was *Elements of the Law relating to Insurances* by John Millar, Jr., which Bell and the Robinsons had copublished in 1787. Cf. Robinson's letter to Bell of 21 November 1797, declining an offer from John Balfour on account of "these times of a flourishing War" (box 3, folder 1796–99).

have neither Strength nor Spirits to undertake the Journey. I might add that it is impossible for me to be so long from home in these Critical times." The reference to Ireland is significant in light of Robinson's close connections with one of the founding members of the United Irishmen, the Dublin bookseller John Chambers.[165] Robinson published two books on revolutionary France by the sympathetic Scottish author John Moore—*A Journal during a Residence in France* in 1793 (no. 315) and *A View of the Causes and Progress of the French Revolution* in 1795 (no. 333)—and Bell advertised them under his own name in the Edinburgh newspapers. Robinson promoted the latter title to Bell on 6 May 1795 and ten days later sent a bill for fifty copies, adding: "We hope you will want many more of Dr Moore's Book."[166] Yet when Moore negotiated the sale of a large new novel that would appear in the following year, *Edward* (no. 340), the right to publish went not to Robinson or Bell but to the leaders of the firms that had regularly published Moore's popular fiction—Andrew Strahan and Cadell & Davies—who were prepared to pay him the substantial sum of £800 for the copyright.

*

As we saw in the last chapter, the Scottish Enlightenment experienced its "take-off" around the middle of the eighteenth century, when its five founding booksellers—Millar, Strahan, Hamilton, Balfour, and Kincaid—began to publish and promote new work by Scottish authors, using London and Edinburgh as their bases of operation. In this chapter we have seen that Scottish Enlightenment publishing grew into an even larger enterprise after Millar's death in 1768. Founded in that year as an extension of Millar's firm, the House of Strahan and Cadell became a publishing empire that took full advantage of the London–Edinburgh publishing axis, especially after Creech replaced Bell as Kincaid's junior partner in 1771. At around the same time, other booksellers began to follow the lead of the founders by publishing new books of literature and learning by Scottish authors, often demonstrating collaboration between London and Edinburgh. The dates when some of their names first appear in the imprints of first editions in table 2 are revealing: the Dilly brothers

165. Pollard, *Dictionary*, 100, quoting an Irish informer's report from 1797 on Chambers's visit to London, allegedly for "private political business. When in London he will be often at Robinsons, Booksellers."

166. NLS, Dep. 317, folder 1795.

and George Robinson, 1767; Joseph Johnson, 1768; and John Murray and Charles Elliot, 1771. John Bell also went into business for himself in 1771 and was an active reprinter of Scottish Enlightenment books from that time onward, even though he did not start publishing new work again until later in the decade.

This second wave of Scottish Enlightenment publishers was once again mainly Scottish, whether located in Edinburgh or London. However, it also included a number of English booksellers who settled in London, though they came from the provinces and were generally as much outsiders to the English establishment as their Scottish colleagues were. It is quite possible that the Dissenters George Robinson, who was born and raised not far from the Scottish border, Joseph Johnson, and the Dilly brothers were drawn to Scottish authors by religious, political, and social ties. Thus, when James Wodrow was planning to publish sermons by William Leechman, he went first to Joseph Johnson in London because of Johnson's associations with Dissenters who were sympathetic to Leechman's brand of moderate Presbyterianism. And when John Moore considered a publisher for his liberal works on revolutionary France, he naturally turned to George Robinson. By contrast, the established London houses of Rivington and Longman were scarcely ever approached by Scottish authors and rarely published their works.

The second wave of publishers broadened the base of Scottish Enlightenment publishing, with two main effects. First, there was increased competition for the most desirable authors and manuscripts, and the copy money paid to the most profitable authors kept rising. Despite their preeminence, Strahan and Cadell were occasionally outbid, especially by Elliot and Robinson (with Bell), and they were increasingly aware that in order to maintain their place at the top of the profession, they had to pay authors more than they might have wished. The Lords' final judgment on the literary property issue in 1774, establishing limited copyright once and for all, had no appreciable effect on this trend, in spite of Strahan's belief that it would. That is because copy money was affected less by the duration of copyright than by other factors, including competition among publishers, the stability of laws and policies, and, ultimately, the public's willingness to consume books in large quantities. The principal publishers moaned incessantly about their plight, but they all became rich, and so, as we saw in chapter 3, did most of their best-selling authors.

Second, an outlet was created for publication of books that could not command great amounts of copy money. It was all very well if aspiring authors could sell their manuscripts to Strahan and Cadell, or perhaps

Elliot, for many hundreds or even thousands of pounds. But if no publisher was willing to pay large amounts for their manuscripts, they could still go to John Murray, the Dilly brothers, Joseph Johnson, or John Bell. Although they would not receive as much money, they would have their books published by reputable booksellers in appropriate formats, and there was always the chance of their books becoming strong sellers or best sellers that would receive critical acclaim and perhaps generate additional material rewards in one form or another. In this way, the second wave of Scottish Enlightenment publishing that began in the late 1760s provided incentives for authors to write books in emulation of Hume and Robertson, and new ways were found to satisfy the demands of an international reading public that looked to Scotland for much of its intellectual sustenance.

6

The Achievement of William Creech

Although the London–Edinburgh publishing axis was dominated by the London firms of Millar–Cadell, the Strahans, and the Robinsons, their counterparts in Edinburgh were also significant. This chapter examines the publishing career and reputation of the most prominent bookseller in late eighteenth-century Edinburgh, William Creech (1745–1815), whose name appears in the imprint of more than sixty first editions listed in table 2. It shows how Creech emerged as the protégé not only of Kincaid in Edinburgh but also of Strahan and Cadell in London and how he balanced feelings of loyalty and deference toward his London partners with a strong commitment to publishing Enlightenment books. These findings are then contrasted with the unsympathetic portrayal of Creech's career by commentators associated with a younger rival in the Edinburgh book trade, Archibald Constable, whose views have shaped perceptions of Creech's reputation since the early nineteenth century.

THE CAREER OF A BOOKSELLER

William Creech was the offspring of a marriage between a Scottish Presbyterian minister of the same name and an English woman known as Mary Buley or Bulley, who had come to Scotland as a young girl in the late 1720s and subsequently had been employed in the household of the fifth Lord Cranstoun at Crailing House in Roxburghshire. She probably met William Creech, Sr., during the 1730s, when he was also working at Crailing House as tutor to George Cranstoun, a brother of the woman whom Mary Buley served. Crailing being a seat of the third Marquess of Lothian, whose sister Jean was Lord Cranstoun's wife, both William Creech and Mary Buley received the patronage of that noble family. Thanks to the Lothian interest, in 1739 Creech became the minister of Newbattle, a small parish adjacent to Dalkeith, a few miles southeast of Edinburgh. The following year William and Mary married, and in the span of five years they had four children, three of whom survived infancy. The future bookseller was the youngest, born early in May 1745. His father died just three months later, and his two older sisters died of smallpox in 1749. Writing to an English relation around 1750 in an effort to claim a ring that she believed was intended for her by her grandmother, of the surname Quarme, Mary Creech described her plight and that of her young son, noting that in the event of her death, "I leave a poor orphan in a strange countrey."[1] It was Mary Creech's good fortune, however, that the third Marquess of Lothian and his first wife, Margaret Nicholson, "have acted like parents to me and my fatherless Children and still dos." As a result, young William Creech received a privileged upbringing despite the lack of a father.

Creech was educated at the most prestigious Scottish grammar school of the day, Dalkeith Academy, and then at the University of Edinburgh. Beyond a solid foundation in the classics and other marks of elite education, this combination brought the right social connections and lifelong patterns of bonding that cut across social classes. According to his contemporary biographer, Robert Fleming, who was the executor of his estate, Creech and other men who had been educated at Dalkeith Academy during the days of its famous teacher, James Barclay, subsequently "assembled at social parties, under the name of 'Barclay's Scholars,' to talk over their youthful exploits." Creech was actively involved in these gatherings until he died in 1815, some forty years after Barclay's death, and so were more than a score of others who moved "in a respectable rank of life, and some of them of great opulence and consequence," such as the politicians Alexander Wedderburn, Lord Loughborough, and Henry Dundas, Viscount Melville.[2] Some of the highborn students at the academy—in-

1. Mary Creech to Dr. Cousin, [1750], ECL, Y2325C91[G44823]. In this letter Mary also mentions her sister Judith, "who is still in a state of servitude" in Scotland.

2. [Fleming], "Account," xii, note. Creech's lifelong political association with Dundas is noted by Fleming (xx). On Barclay, see Hutchison, "Eighteenth-Century Insight," 233–41.

cluding Lord Kilmaurs, the future fourteenth Earl of Glencairn—lived in Creech's household, at the Dalkeith boardinghouse that Mary Creech operated after her husband's death.

The matriculation records at Edinburgh University place Creech in Hugh Blair's rhetoric and belles lettres class in 1762–63 and James Russell's natural philosophy class in 1763–64. He was also a central figure in an intimate coterie of young men who shared a love of Rousseau and things sentimental, at least four of whom would later become Edinburgh professors: Alexander Tytler (later Lord Woodhouselee), Allan Maconochie (later Lord Meadowbank), John Bruce, and James Gregory.[3] He was, along with Maconochie, Bruce, and three others, one of the founding members of the famous student debating club, the Speculative Society (established November 1764), where he presented discourses on "The Advantages of Society in General, and of Literary Institutions in Particular," "The Immortality of the Soul," "The Attributes and the Providence of God," "The Instability of Conduct," and "The Principles of Belief."[4] Creech, then, was primed for success in the polite Presbyterian world of late eighteenth-century Edinburgh. His credentials were further strengthened by his character as an upstanding citizen with a strong sense of piety and civic commitment, evidenced later by his service as an elder in the High Kirk at St. Giles Church, a cofounder of the Edinburgh Chamber of Commerce in 1786, secretary of the Society for the Benefit of the Sons of the Clergy, commandant of the Edinburgh Trained Bands, a member of the town council (1779), a magistrate (1788, 1789, and 1791), and in 1811 lord provost.

Had Creech completed the Edinburgh course in medicine for which he was intended, he might have unambiguously entered the professional elite to which so many of the leading figures of the Scottish Enlightenment belonged. Instead, he took a different course by becoming an apprentice to the bookseller Alexander Kincaid and his junior partner, John Bell. He owed this opportunity to the patronage of the same noble family that had brought him this far in the world, for Kincaid's wife, Caroline Kerr,

3. See the letters of Creech, Gregory, and Tytler to Maconochie in the Meadowbank Papers, EUL, Mic. M 1070, especially Creech's letters of 10 January 1772 and [March 1772]. On 27 January 1773 Creech tells James Beattie that he is "an enthusiastic admirer of Rousseau" (AUL, MS 30/2/100). However, he later changed his mind, and in a newspaper article of 1786, reprinted in his *Edinburgh Fugitive Pieces*, 151, he described Rousseau as a "paradoxical, whimsical, ingenious, eloquent, weak, and dangerous author."

4. *History of the Speculative Society*, 70.

was the granddaughter of the first Marquess of Lothian by his son, Lord Charles Kerr, and the first cousin of the third marquess. The connection was further strengthened in October 1760, when Mrs. Kincaid's older sister, Jean Janet, became the third marquess's second wife.[5] When his mother died in 1764, just a month after his nineteenth birthday, Creech was taken into the Kincaid household and became more like an adopted son than an apprentice. The Kincaids hoped he would be a role model for their biological son, Alexander, whose behavior never lived up to their expectations. Eight years later, when Creech took young Alexander along with him on a trip to London, Mrs. Kincaid would write to Creech of her wish that he and her son would "live and love like brothers."[6]

Yet Creech faced an uncertain future. On the one hand, he was an exceedingly well-educated and well-connected "lad o parts," with eminent patrons and encouraging prospects. On the other hand, he was a teenage orphan apprentice, living in the household of a bookseller who already had both an heir apparent and a competent junior partner in the person of John Bell. The ambiguity of Creech's personal situation was never fully resolved, even when he attained success later in life. Although he would live a genteel life of letters much like that of the elite professionals whom he served—selected by the Earl of Buchan as a charter member of the Society of Antiquaries of Scotland and elected a fellow of the Literary Class of the Royal Society of Edinburgh in its early days (26 Jan. 1784)— he could never forget that as a man of business he *was* in the service of others. Barbara Benedict has suggested that Creech's situation was not unique in this regard: it was the plight of the cultured eighteenth-century bookseller, who stood at once among and apart from the readers and consumers of books because his relationship to print culture was largely mediated through commerce.[7] But Creech carried this dichotomy to the farthest extreme and was sometimes resented by booksellers and men of letters alike for blurring the distinction between them.

In July 1766, at the age of twenty-one, Creech set off for London "for improvement in his profession," as Fleming put it.[8] He would end up visiting Holland and France as well as London and would not return to Scot-

5. Paul, *Scots Peerage*, 5:480.

6. "Replies for Mr Creech to the Answers for Mr Kincaid's Trustees," 52, ECL, William Creech Papers.

7. Benedict, "Service to the Public," 119–46.

8. [Fleming], "Account," xv.

land until January 1768. His diary from this expedition is revealing.[9] Like the more detailed London journal kept by James Boswell in 1762–63, it reveals the sense of awe and alienation that marked a young Scot's first visit to London in the 1760s. Estrangement is evident from the moment his ship docks near a public house along the Thames on 1 August 1766: when one of his party "who spoke broad Scotch" asked questions of the landlord and his maid, "they star'd at him as if he had been a foreigner and laugh'd at his way of speaking" (11). There was worse treatment at their ship's next stop near Flamstead Observatory: "at our very landing at the wharf we were insulted by some fellows in an ale house because we were Scotch" (19). Like Boswell before him, Creech immediately begins the process of cultural adaptation to protect himself from such abuse. "I avoided staring or any marks of surprise as much as possible," he writes, "to avoid being thought a stranger" (19).

Everything surprises him during his first week in London. He is shocked by the "impudence" of the common people. He is startled by the anonymity of the public houses, where perfect strangers smoke their pipes, drink their pints, and talk politics (21–22), and by the impersonal efficiency of the eating houses, such as the Crown and Rose in Beau Lane:

> There you see all different meats you can think of—roast, boil'd, baked, etc. etc. having made choice, we tell the waiter to bring us such a thing. We then went upstairs into a prodigious long room—there were above 50 people all at dinner—the room is all divided into a kind of boxes so [Creech draws a diagram]—into one of these we step'd—and had our plate of meat and pint of porter brought in a very little. (29)

He is impressed by the convenience of the coffeehouses, to which "any single gentleman may go in breakfast dine or supper at a very reasonable rate" (27–28). He is "confounded" by the sale of fruit, cakes, and milk on a Sunday (22). He is amazed by the lack of reserve among women, who are free to take hold of the arm of any gentleman "without the imputation of forwardness—nay it is fashionable" (24).[10] He is much taken by the cosmopolitan nature of the Royal Exchange that had been so well described

9. Journal of William Creech 1766–67, NLS, MS 56. The references in the following discussion are drawn from the bound typescript edition in the Edinburgh Room of the ECL, YZ325C91 [B3085].

10. Cf. Creech to Maconochie, 9 Sept. 1766, Meadowbank Papers, EUL.

in Voltaire's *Letters concerning the English Nation* (1733), where each ethnic group did business on its own walk. He is appalled by the hustle and bustle of the city, observing that "one must not here stand to look at any thing upon the street—the people croud so fast you'll be knocked over if not very attentive" (31).

These reactions are similar to those of other Scottish travelers and remind us of the sizable cultural gap that existed between London and Edinburgh some six decades after the Union.[11] Yet Creech soon becomes acclimated to the ways of London. His journal tells of frequent visits to the popular debates at the Robin Hood Club, to the pleasure gardens at Vauxhall and Ranelaugh, and to the theater to see Garrick act. There is even an entry that reminds one of Boswell in its matter-of-fact approach to urban prostitution: "Charing Cross—Whores—home at 11." Boarding with his late mother's relation, Mrs. Strachey, on Downing Street in Westminster, Creech is presumably spared the rent of £3.10s. a month, plus a shilling per meal, that Boswell had to pay his landlady.[12] Additional support may have come to Creech from another relation of his mother, a Mr. Quarme, who is occasionally mentioned.

What was Creech doing in London in 1766–67? This question became an issue in the Kincaid household while he was away, when a young member of the family who is referred to in letters as Miss Peggy tried to convince young Alex Kincaid that Creech paid "small Attention" to the firm's business. On that occasion, Creech was ably defended by the family tutor, Alexander Adam, who reported all the details to a worried Creech and acted as intermediary in his defense with Alexander Kincaid and his wife.[13] The issue surfaced again following the death of Alexander Kincaid in 1777, when his executors scoured his account books from the 1760s and found numerous payments to Creech in London, which they tried to collect on the assumption that they were unpaid loans. Creech defended himself by contending that he had made his trip to London on one day's notice at Kincaid's request, that he had paid his own way while there, and

11. Cf. Boswell, *London Journal*; and Adam Ferguson's letter, 11 Sept. 1745, in Ferguson, *Correspondence*, 1:3. Ferguson, who visited London in 1745 at about the same age that Creech would be in 1766, wrote with astonishment that "every fellow reads the publick papers and talks his mind concerning them with all the vehemence imaginable. . . . You or I may go to an Eating House a Beer or any house, set at what Board join what company you will, and talk familiarly with people who neither know you nor one another, and whom perhaps you never will have another sight of."

12. Boswell, *London Journal*, 50.

13. Adam's letters to Creech, 7 (quoted) and 20 Feb. and 4 Apr. 1767, WCL.

that "from the day he reached London to the day he left it, he was wholly engaged in Mr Kincaids business, and was only anxious how he could be of service to him."[14]

The diary confirms that in London Creech spent a portion of his time (though not every day) working for Kincaid & Bell, for there are entries that say he "received letters from Mr Kincaid with Commissions," "came to town employ'd for Mr Kincaid till 4," "did business for Mr Bell," "went about Mr Kincaid's business all the forenoon," and so on. Other sources support these entries. In a letter from London of 13 November 1766, Creech wrote to a friend in Edinburgh: "I have had so much business to do for Mr Kincaid and the Company that I have wasted above 3 quires of paper in answering letters within these few weeks."[15] More vivid details appear in copies of several letters that John Bell sent to Creech in London in 1767.[16] On 27 March, for example, Bell listed Scottish books that Creech was to try to exchange for English ones and discussed negotiations for a possible reprint of Nathan Bailey's *Dictionary* despite the copyright claims of the leading London booksellers. On 12 June Creech was told to obtain twelve copies of William Robertson's *History of Scotland* and to ask Andrew Millar if he wanted to copublish a new edition of Kames's *Elements of Criticism* (such an edition appeared in 1769). On 22 June Bell laid out a plan for Creech to visit booksellers in The Hague, Rotterdam, Amsterdam, and Paris, where he was to purchase a list of specific foreign-language books and to arrange book exchanges for any foreign titles likely to sell in Edinburgh. "You may happen to want the Money that we are indebted to you," Bell adds; "you may draw for it, from London or any Place you may happen to be in."

Establishing that Creech was employed as an agent for Kincaid & Bell in London and on the Continent, however, does not answer the larger question that must have confused Kincaid's executors. Why did Kincaid entrust such duties to an inexperienced lad of twenty-one, who had been an employee in the firm for just two years, as a kind of apprentice? Creech's legal defense against the accusations of Kincaid's executors contains a re-

14. "Replies for Mr Creech," 21, 29. This defense also states that "Mr Creech was daily laying out money for Mr Kincaid in London and transacting business for him to a great extent altho' he is not credited for one Shilling of these advances after May 1767 about two months before he set out for the Continent" (17).

15. Creech to Maconochie, Meadowbank Papers, EUL.

16. John Bell Letterbooks, Bodleian Library, Oxford, MS Eng. Letters c. 20, fols. 31–32, 41, and 44–46.

markable answer: "Before [Creech] left Edinburgh Mr Kincaid who was then in Company with Mr Bell had formed a Scheme of dropping his [Bell's] share in that Co[pan]y in Mr Creeches favours and had sent him to London and the Continent on purpose to improve his knowledge of that very business which he intended him to follow."[17] If this recollection was correct, Creech went to London knowing that he was being groomed as Kincaid's successor, much the way Andrew Millar was training Thomas Cadell to take over his bookselling firm in London. The presence of John Bell, however, added a complication that Millar and Cadell never had to face, and it would cause difficulties for the implementation of the plan.

The best way for Creech to learn the book business in London, especially the publication end of it, was to associate with Cadell and his publishing partner, Kincaid's old friend William Strahan. This he certainly did, as we know from entries in his diary that refer to both men (e.g., "with Cadell till near 2—dined with Mr Strahan"). Even so, the diary does not convey the full extent to which Creech became attached to Cadell and especially Strahan while he was in London. Robert Fleming commented on the closeness of these relationships,[18] and from later correspondence it is clear that Creech became Strahan's protégé during that time. As we have seen, Strahan and Cadell were about to expand Millar's business into a publishing empire centered on their ties to Scottish authors, as well as to the Edinburgh firms of Kincaid and Balfour. The problem from Strahan and Cadell's point of view was that they did not consider John Bell the right person to be their chief confederate in Edinburgh. Creech's visit to London happened to coincide with the escalation of hostilities between Cadell and Bell, especially over publication strategies regarding Adam Ferguson's *Essay on the History of Civil Society*, as discussed at the end of chapter 4. Creech's career as a bookseller probably owed much to that coincidence.

When Creech returned to Edinburgh in January 1768, his position was once again uncertain. He resumed his studies at the university, where, according to the matriculation records, he attended Blair's rhetoric class for the second time and Adam Ferguson's moral philosophy class. Such training was valuable both in preparing Creech for his future role as a bookseller of letters, who could associate on equal terms with authors and critically evaluate their manuscripts, and in connecting him with some of Edinburgh's leading academic minds, whose works he would later publish.

17. "Replies for Mr Creech," 20–21.
18. [Fleming], "Account," xxxii.

Whatever promises Kincaid may have made privately before Creech traveled to London, nothing was said or done publicly about his future status in the firm after his return. But Creech now had a powerful London ally who was willing to use his influence to advance his young friend's career in Edinburgh. As we saw in chapter 5, in the summer of 1768 Strahan visited Edinburgh and made what he later called, in a letter to Creech of 19 September, a "very bold Push" to convince Kincaid to oust Bell in favor of Creech. Kincaid then "promised me, that he would instantly get rid of B[ell]," Strahan states. Quoting from another letter he had written to Kincaid four days earlier, Strahan shows how he had tried to "press" his old friend

> by every argument I could think of to hasten your Separation from Mr Bell, and to associate with you some decent practicable young Fellow, upon whose Industry, Honesty, Sobriety, and obliging Disposition, you could surely depend, as it is impossible for you to attend to that Branch of Business [i.e., copublishing Scottish authors] yourself. Such a Person, to all appearance, Mr Creech is; but of this you must necessarily be a more capable Judge than I can be.[19]

Kincaid's reply of 25 October carried assurances of his "determined Resolution" to follow this plan, Strahan tells Creech in a letter of 22 December. "But still, it seems, nothing is yet done." Faced with Kincaid's reluctance "to do what he really intends to do," Strahan presents his frustrated friend with a series of options, including the one he had followed as a young Edinburgh printer who set off to "push his own way" in London:

> I am really at a loss how to advise you. To him I can say no more than I have said already. In short, I see nothing for you to do, but to come up [to London] with him in the Spring, if he keeps his Resolution; and if not, by all means, come up by yourself. You had better put yourself apprentice to a Cobler here, than remain where you are in a State of the most disgusting Inactivity and Suspense. If you think you could settle in Edinburgh by yourself with any tolerable Prospect of Success, you may then settle a Correspondence here. If not, even resolve at once to remain here, without looking back, and push your own way, as many Scotsmen have done before you. I see nothing else for it. Your remaining longer in the unsettled, dis-

19. Strahan to Creech, 19 Sept. 1768, WCL. All subsequent references to Strahan's letters to Creech in this chapter are cited from this source.

sipated, idle Way you are in at present, will be altogether inexcusable, for if you cannot bring Things to a fixed Settlement before next Spring, I do not think you have the least Reason to imagine you ever will.

"I have no doubt, after all," Strahan adds, "that when you begin the World (what a Pity tis you are yet to *begin*) you will distinguish yourself by your Industry, Alacrity, and Readiness to oblige, and will be adding to the number of your Friends every Day."

Creech followed Strahan's advice by joining Kincaid on a visit to London in April 1769. Still nothing happened. The following year Creech accompanied his childhood companion Lord Kilmaurs on the grand tour, visiting some of the same European sites as in 1767, as well as others.[20] When he returned to Scotland in January 1771, he found to his dismay that Kincaid was still not prepared to act. A letter Creech sent to "Allie" Maconochie on 1 February describes his dilemma: he was unwilling to abandon Kincaid, yet he could not afford to lose any more time. Then "an offer from London" brought matters "to a crisis," and Kincaid finally agreed that a "total separation" from Bell would take place on Whitsunday in May. Creech was to "come in for the one half, and have the promise of the whole in two years, so that if I keep my health I am hopeful I shall do tolerably." The effect was to end Creech's period of uncertainty and raise his self-confidence. "The die is cast and Fate hath fixed my situation to Edinburgh," he exclaimed; "I am quite another creature[;] my mind is freed from suspense, and now I can enjoy myself and my friends."[21]

On 27 February 1771 the *Edinburgh Evening Courant* printed the announcement that Creech had been anticipating for several years: the partnership between Kincaid and Bell would be dissolved on Whitsunday, when Kincaid "assumes another partner, and carries on business in the old shop." The unnamed new partner was of course Creech, and the old shop was the one that Kincaid operated in the Luckenbooths. On 16 July William Strahan, who had presumably orchestrated the London job offer that forced Kincaid's hand, wrote to Creech "purely to give you Joy upon the happy Commencement of your Connexion with my old and ever-honoured Friend, which I hope and indeed have no doubt will be daily productive of mutual Satisfaction. . . . United, I expect to hear you carry all before you" (fig. 6.1). Strahan had every reason to be pleased. He

20. "Fragmentary Notes of a Tour Made by William Creech 1 Aug. 1770 to Holland, Belgium, France, Switzerland, and Germany," ECL, Y2325C91 [G44823].

21. Creech to Maconochie, 1 Feb. 1771, Meadowbank Papers, EUL.

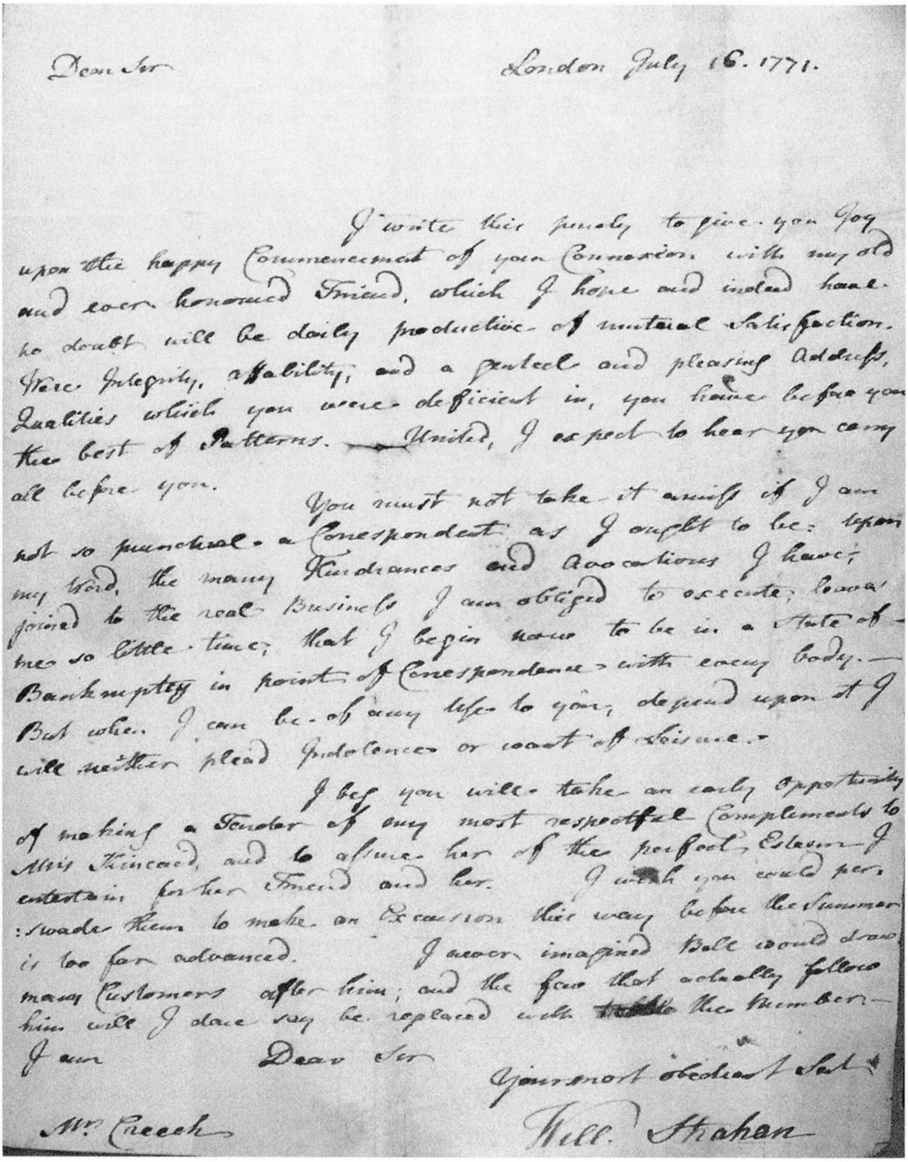

Fig. 6.1. After William Strahan engineered the replacement of John Bell by William Creech as the junior partner of his friend Alexander Kincaid, Strahan sent Creech this letter of congratulations, dated 16 July 1771. It begins: "I write this purely to give you Joy upon the happy Commencement of your Connexion with my old and ever-honoured Friend, which I hope and indeed have no doubt will be daily productive of mutual Satisfaction. . . . United, I expect to hear you carry all before you." William Creech Letterbooks, Blair Oliphant of Ardblair Muniments.

had landed his man in a key Edinburgh bookselling firm and so assured himself that the book publishing empire that he and Cadell were building would have a firm Scottish connection long after Kincaid's retirement from the trade. Two years later Kincaid officially ended the partnership, signing over to Creech stock in books worth £1,779.13s.11d., which with interest and Kincaid's share of a particular copyright brought the total amount of his loan to £2,008.13s.3d.[22] Creech was heavily in debt but in business for himself. By summer 1773 he was advertising occasional publications with his name alone in the imprint, and for several months he identified himself in newspaper advertisements as "William Creech (successor to Mr Kincaid)." In the space of less than two and a half years, Creech had gone from uncertainty about his career to a partnership with Kincaid and finally to a position as Kincaid's sole successor in the well-situated Luckenbooths shop. Creech remained close to Kincaid, and when the latter died suddenly in January 1777, less than a year after the death of Creech's fiancé (a Miss Kerr, who was probably a relation of Kincaid's wife), he confided to James Beattie that the event "has rendered me perfectly incapable of attending to business. . . . I cannot express to you how much this melancholy event has shocked me."[23]

When Creech replaced John Bell in 1771, Kincaid was past his prime as a bookseller and only occasionally involved himself in publishing matters. The business was essentially left in Creech's care. It quickly became clear that Bell did not pose a serious threat. "I never imagined Bell would draw many Customers after him," Strahan wrote to Creech on 16 July 1771, "and the few that actually follow him will I dare say be replaced with the Number." This judgment was certainly true of authors, largely because Kincaid and Creech retained the crucial publishing connection with Strahan and Cadell after Bell left the firm. The relationship was cemented when Creech visited London again in the spring of 1772 with Alexander Kincaid, Jr. "Mr Creech will stay some time in London," John Balfour wrote to a correspondent at this time. "You will hear of him at Mr. Strachan's Printer Mr. Cadell's etc."[24]

22. National Archives of Scotland, Register of Deeds, vol. 311 Dur, fols. 1592–98. The deed is dated 17 July 1773 but took effect the preceding May.

23. Creech to Beattie, 22 Jan. 1777, AUL, MS 30/2/282.

24. Balfour to George Paton, 18 Apr. 1772, NLS, Adv. MSS 29.5.7(1), fols. 47–48; Alexander Fraser Tytler's letter of 8 May 1772, WCL, addressed "to the care of Mr Cadell Bookseller London."

In partnership with Kincaid and on his own, Creech collaborated with Strahan and Cadell, or less frequently Cadell alone, in the publication of more than forty first editions listed in table 2, in addition to a number of popular titles that the partners acquired after the first edition, such as Buchan's *Domestic Medicine* and Burns's *Poems*. Even these impressive figures do not tell the whole story, since there were several books, such as Adam Smith's *Wealth of Nations,* that Creech effectively copublished in Edinburgh even though his name is not found in the imprint with those of Strahan and Cadell.[25] As far as the Scottish Enlightenment is concerned, the collaboration among the firms of Strahan, Cadell, and Creech was the most important London–Edinburgh publishing partnership of the late eighteenth century.

Creech's relationship with his London partners was complex. London was a much larger market for books than Edinburgh, especially for expensive quartos. Creech was also at a disadvantage because he often made smaller investments and therefore owned smaller amounts of the properties they copublished, typically a one-third share as against their combined total of two-thirds. For these reasons, Creech understood, and accepted, that his role was subordinate. Furthermore, he never forgot that Strahan and Cadell had been instrumental in teaching him the book business and in setting him up in the Kincaid partnership. More than his partners, they were his mentors.

Strahan in particular was considerably Creech's senior and a father figure in the life of the orphan bookseller. Although Strahan's letters to Creech are friendly and sometimes intimate, they occasionally contain strong criticism. A letter that Creech sent Strahan on 25 March 1776 must have been too lighthearted for Strahan's taste, for in his reply of 11 April Strahan harangues about the need to avoid "the Appearance of trifling Conduct" and "seeming Levity of Behavior," and to make his point he returns the offending epistle so that Creech might ponder the error of his ways. Two years later Strahan threatens to apply stricter discipline. Surprised and annoyed that Creech has drawn on his account at an inappropriate time, Strahan announces in a letter of 19 November 1778 that he has decided to postpone accepting his friend's bills until the matter is resolved to his satisfaction. He again returns Creech's letter with his own, this time with instructions that it be altered to conform to his reading of the accounts. Strahan then turns down two manuscripts that Creech

25. Sher, "New Light," 26n2.

had recently offered for joint publication—an unnamed medical work by Francis Home (presumably no. 207) and a multivolume translation of Buffon (no. 212)—and uses Buffon's work as a pretense for a lecture about the danger of publishers overextending themselves:

> Nothing hurts a Man in Business, especially a young Trader, more than getting out of Depth, by engaging in too many Schemes at once, which naturally occasions a Pressure for Money that embarrases him, and prevents him from following his Business with Credit and Satisfaction. This Propensity *to do a great deal*, is a Rock I have known many worthy and otherwise intelligent Men split upon.

Toward the end of the letter, Strahan continues the lesson with a firm reminder about who is in charge:

> When you write next, be particular in answering the several Parts of Mr Cadell's Letter, as it appears to me you do not duly consider how matters really stand between you, nor how much more we are concerned in than you are. This has, you will see, . . . been the case from the first, till the present time.

Having given Creech a sufficient fright, Strahan concludes by changing his mind and accepting his bills after all, "Lest it should be any Injury to your Credit, either here or at home." Strahan's letter of 11 April 1776 also concludes by making it clear that his rebuke is meant in a spirit of fatherly advice: "This plain and friendly Admonition I hope you will take as it is meant, as a Mark of my Esteem, and of my Confidence in your good Sense that you will make a proper use of it."

As a rule, Creech tried to avoid acting in a manner that might have struck his London partners as arrogant, the way John Bell did during the ongoing dispute with Cadell over Ferguson's *Essay on the History of Civil Society*. When the struggle over copyright came to a head in 1774, Creech was caught in an awkward position: he felt obligated to support Strahan and Cadell's position in favor of perpetual copyright, at least in private letters to Strahan, but doing so gave him the appearance of a traitor among other members of the trade in Scotland—a situation that Strahan exacerbated by quoting from one of Creech's personal letters in the House of Commons. From the perspective of John Bell, who was a leader of the Edinburgh opposition to the London booksellers during the copyright struggle, Creech's behavior was reprehensible. It was in this context that another opponent of perpetual copyright, John Murray, characterized "C——ch the dancing Master bookseller" as a "non-entity." In the same letter, Murray observed that in supporting perpetual copyright, Creech was acting against his own financial interest.[26]

Creech's loyalty was sometimes tested by his partners. Many years later, when Thomas Cadell, Jr. (of Cadell & Davies) contacted him about regularizing their arrangements, Creech recollected with some resentment (and almost certainly much exaggeration) how unfairly Thomas, Sr., had managed their joint publications from London. Instead of giving Creech the number of copies that corresponded to his share of the copyright and then allowing him to manage the wholesale distribution of the book to other Scottish booksellers, "your father chose to have the command of the market." This meant that Creech usually ordered and purchased his copies of their joint publications from London in the same way that every other Scottish bookseller did, only at a lower price, and sometimes he was completely neglected:

> Many editions were printed and sold, of which I got no notice and of many of them I never saw a Book. No doubt editions can be produced more rapidly in London than here, and London is the great mart for the sale of Books. No share of mine that I recollect of, ever was delivered but scanty supplies furnished as my sale demanded and for many years that sale cramped by every one of the Trade in Scotland being supplied by your house at sale prices while the trifling number of my shares were stated to me at subscription price. In this practice there was manifest absurdity and injustice. I do not say intentional, but from inattention and mistake.[27]

According to Creech, the only collaborative publication printed in London in which he received his fair share of books from every edition was William Buchan's *Domestic Medicine*, which was managed by Strahan rather than Cadell, even though "when I printed or reprinted any of our mutual property, I always sent to London the complete shares."

Even when he believed he was being slighted, Creech never wavered in his allegiance to Strahan and Cadell. Yet there were definite limits to his subordination to his London mentors. In chapter 5 we saw that Creech could never bring himself to join forces with his archrival in Edinburgh, John Balfour, in spite of Strahan's insistence that he do so. The order in which publishers' names appear in imprints is another revealing topic. Although Creech usually put the names of Strahan and Cadell before his

---

26. Murray to Gilbert Stuart, 21 Mar. 1774 (copy), John Murray Archive, NLS.

27. Creech to Cadell, Jr., 3 July 1807 (copy), ECL, William Creech Letterbook, Green Box 120, fols. 118–20.

own when he oversaw the printing of a joint edition, he had inherited that practice from his master Kincaid, who put the names of Andrew Millar or Strahan and Cadell ahead of his own in eight first editions found in table 2 that bear an Edinburgh imprint. Other Edinburgh booksellers commonly did this also, sometimes as an act of courtesy, sometimes because the London copublisher had seniority or owned a larger share of the copyright.[28] Creech copublished more than a dozen first editions listed in table 2 with London booksellers other than Strahan and Cadell, particularly John Murray, and he did not normally give them priority in the imprint.[29] Indeed, he did not always do so in copublications with Strahan and Cadell. He put his own name before theirs, for example, when he printed the first edition of Kames's *Sketches of the History of Man* in 1774 (no. 164), the first edition of the first volume of Blair's *Sermons* in 1777 (no. 188), the first book edition of *The Mirror* in 1781 (no. 217), and the title page of James Beattie's *Scoticisms* in 1787 (no. 267, with Cadell only).

The publishing history of Hugh Blair's *Sermons* bears closer examination. The first edition of the first volume was printed in Edinburgh in 1777, as the imprint indicates. According to ESTC, however, the dozens of editions of the various volumes of Blair's *Sermons* that subsequently appeared in late eighteenth-century Britain all had London imprints. Yet this fact should not lead us to assume that they were all printed in London. The third volume, for example, was initially printed in Edinburgh with a London imprint.[30] Similarly, in a letter to Cadell of 25 October 1793, when the fourth volume was about to go to press, Blair writes: "Mr Creech is decidedly of opinion that the book should be printed here, as all the other volumes of my Sermons have been; and indeed I incline to this my self, in order to save the troublesome transmission of so many sheets to and fro, from London; and to have the press at hand is always some advantage." In his reply of 3 November, Cadell "cheerfully" acquiesces with this re-

28. Examples include nos. 66, 91, 179, 222, 249, and 287.

29. John Murray expressed displeasure that Creech's name appeared ahead of his in a joint publication printed in Edinburgh in 1774 (no. 166), since Murray was "his senior in business" (Murray to William Smellie [copy], 9 Apr. 1774, John Murray Archive, NLS); some copies had a London imprint with Murray's name first. In January 1777 Creech offended Edward Dilly by printing Beattie's *Essays* (no. 173) in Edinburgh rather than London, with his own name alone in the imprint of the copies of the quarto edition that were intended for subscribers (Creech to Beattie, 16 Jan. 1777, AUL, MS 30/2/281).

30. Hugh Blair to Robert Blair, 14 Apr. 1790, NLS, MS 588, no. 1374.

quest.[31] Blair would later write that the printing was taking longer than expected due to a scarcity of paper and "the very large Edition they are printing"; other sources identify the initial print runs of both volumes 3 and 4 at 6,000 copies, although this number was meant to cover the first two editions of each volume.[32] No sign of the fourth volume appears in the Strahan Archive until September 1794, when Andrew Strahan printed 3,000 copies of the third edition (SA 48817, fol. 19). Thus, although the Strahan Archive establishes that dozens of editions of Blair's *Sermons* were in fact printed in London, often in very large print runs (SA 48815, 48816, 48817, and 48818), some were also printed in Edinburgh, bearing a "false" London imprint. This evidence suggests that Creech supervised the printing in Edinburgh of many more books than one would conclude from the imprints alone. It also demonstrates that Creech sometimes assumed the dominant role, normally attributed to the London booksellers, of overseeing the first edition of new volumes in close association with their authors.

Creech's greatest asset as a publisher was his skill at attracting Scottish men of letters and nurturing their growth as authors. James Beattie is one good example. When Creech replaced Bell in the Kincaid partnership, Beattie was unhappy with Kincaid for allegedly not selling *The Minstrel* (no. 141) aggressively enough, shortchanging him in regard to its profits, and not responding quickly enough to inquiries from the London copublishers about a second edition.[33] Creech took over the Beattie account and developed it into one of the century's warmest author–publisher relationships.[34] He copublished the first editions of all Beattie's later works, sometimes with the Dillys (nos. 141, book 2, and 173), some-

31. NLS, MS 948, nos. 8 and 9. Blair was clearly referring only to first editions; even so, he exaggerated, because Zachs, *Hugh Blair's Letters to His Publishers*, establishes that the first edition of the second volume of the *Sermons* was printed by Strahan in London.

32. Zachs, *Hugh Blair's Letters to His Publishers*, items 1790.S.3.1 and 1794.S.4.1. See also Blair to Cadell, 20 Feb. 1794, BL, Add. MSS 28098, fols. 18–19; Creech to Cadell, 18 Apr. 1794, NLS, Acc. 8205; Blair to Cadell, 26 Apr. 1794, Pierpont Morgan Library, Misc. English.

33. Beattie to Sir William Forbes, 6 May 1771, NLS, Acc. 4796, box 94; Beattie to Robert Arbuthnot, 18 May 1771, in Beattie, *Correspondence*, 2:140–42.

34. See Beattie's fifty-one letters to Creech, spanning the period May 1771 to April 1793, WCL, and additional letters from Beattie to Creech and from Creech to Beattie, December 1772 to April 1794, AUL.

times with Strahan and Cadell (nos. 229 and 258) or Cadell alone (nos. 267 and 291). He took particular pains to make certain that the quarto edition of Beattie's *Essays* would be "as elegant and correct a Book as ever was printed in this country,"[35] though he did not stand to gain from it; indeed, he insisted on subscribing for one hundred copies at the full price (one guinea), rather than at the trade price (fourteen shillings) that Beattie recommended. In 1778 Beattie turned over the copyright of his poems to Dilly and Creech in gratitude for "some favours I have received from them, particularly their refusing to take money for the trouble of distributing the subscription Copies of my Quarto [volume of *Essays*]."[36] Three years later, after Dilly offended him by refusing to pay £200 for the copyright of his *Dissertations*, Beattie turned to Creech and his London partners, "as I was certain you would have no objection to the price."[37] Beattie confided in Creech and considered him an ally, and he never spoke ill of him.

Publication arrangements for the first volume of Beattie's *Elements of Moral Science* (no. 291) demonstrate how Creech and Beattie resolved their differences. Creech favored a quarto format, whereas Beattie preferred a cheaper duodecimo for student use. They compromised on an octavo. When Beattie fretted about the timing of this publication, Creech made sure that two dozen prepublication copies of the first volume were available for the author's college class in late February or early March 1790. Creech generated some confusion when he told Beattie to "name your terms" for the copyright, although in practice he would not go above one hundred guineas (£105) per volume after "much argument" with Beattie's agents.[38] As we have seen, Beattie could be extremely sensitive about such matters, but in this case he did not hold it against his publisher, perhaps because he understood that his own insistence that the book not be published in quarto had adversely affected the amount of copy money he could receive. He had no reason to doubt Creech's pronouncement in his letter of 27 April 1789: "I feel a pride in being your publisher for I love the man and I love his works. Be assured you deal with no mercenary vendor of

35. Creech to Beattie, 7 June 1776, AUL, MS 30/2/255.

36. Beattie, *Day-Book*, 212–13.

37. Beattie to Creech, 28 June 1781, HL, MS Hyde 77, 7.150.

38. Creech to Beattie, 27 Apr. 1789, AUL, MS 30/2/596; Sir William Forbes to Beattie, 3 June 1789, NLS, Acc. 4796, box 98. See Robinson, introduction to Beattie, *Elements of Moral Science*, 1:xxxi.

literature." Creech understood the language of sentimental poetry, and he was so moved by *The Minstrel* that in 1784 he addressed a poem to Beattie about it, which was included in his published miscellany of 1791.[39] The lasting friendship and emotional bond between Beattie and Creech went far beyond their pecuniary relations.

Beattie was only one of several authors with whom Creech built a personal relationship that transcended the issue of payments to authors. For all his anger with Creech about money matters, Robert Burns valued his friendship.[40] Alexander Fraser Tytler was an intimate college friend with whom Creech was so close that, upon leaving Scotland on one of his youthful excursions to England and the Continent, he printed a ten-page poem celebrating their friendship, "An Epistle to a Friend on Leaving Scotland. W.C.—to A.T." Not surprisingly, Tytler turned to Creech to publish his writings after he became professor of civil history at the University of Edinburgh in 1780 (nos. 228 and 300). He would go on to publish his best-known works with Creech in the early nineteenth century: *Elements of General History, Ancient and Modern* (1801) and, after being raised to the bench as Lord Woodhouselee in 1802, *Memoirs of the Life and Writings of the Hon. Henry Home of Kames* (1807). John Bruce was an old friend from their student days at Dalkeith Academy and Edinburgh University, where he was one of the other founding members of the Speculative Society. Creech published Bruce's *First Principles of Philosophy* (no. 205) in 1780 and six years later copublished with Strahan and Cadell his *Elements of the Science of Ethics* (no. 259).

We have seen that Alexander Adam, who would become rector of the Edinburgh High School in 1768 through the patronage of Alexander Kincaid, supported Creech when they were both members of Kincaid's household in the mid-1760s. Most of Adam's letters from that period in Creech's letterbooks are intimately addressed ("My Dear Willie" or "Dear Willie"), and a remark in one of them, dated 3 September 1766, establishes that Creech was sending Adam portions of his London diary to read: "Your journal however gave me great Entertainment" (WCL). Later their friendship would form the basis of a professional relationship: Creech would be involved in the publication of all Adam's works in association with his London partners (nos. 293, 321, and 354) and would

39. "Stanzas Addressed to Dr Beattie, Author of The Minstrel," in Creech, *Edinburgh Fugitive Pieces*, 221–22.

40. Carrick, *William Creech*.

include Adam among the eminent Scottish authors cited in his published *Letters* on Edinburgh.

Creech was in partnership with William Smellie when the latter undertook a multivolume translation of Buffon's *Natural History* (no. 212), and he published that extremely ambitious production in spite of Strahan's chastisement on grounds of overextension, as discussed earlier. "With Lord Kames," his biographer observed, "Mr Creech was in habits of particular intimacy,"[41] and he copublished the first edition of two of Kames's works: *Sketches of the History of Man* (no. 164) with Strahan and Cadell, and *The Gentleman Farmer* (no. 176) over Strahan's objections. Another of his authors, Dugald Stewart, referred to Creech as "my old friend."[42] Creech was on excellent terms with Henry Mackenzie, whose sentimental fiction he greatly admired. A poem that appeared in Creech's *Edinburgh Fugitive Pieces* celebrates Mackenzie's ability "To teach the tear of sympathy to flow" in the cause of virtue and refinement (fig. 6.2).[43]

Gilbert Stuart, no easy person to get on with, was yet another Edinburgh man of letters who appreciated Creech's skills as a publisher. Stuart and the London bookseller John Murray collaborated with Creech on the *Edinburgh Magazine and Review* during the mid-1770s. When Murray was looking for a copublisher for Lord Hailes's *Annals of Scotland* (no. 178) around that time, Stuart strongly recommended "our common friend Creech as the most proper publisher in this country." He explained that Creech benefited from "being acquainted with all the first people here. And, in the other natural advantages of trade I need not mention his superiority over the book sellers of Edinburgh."[44] Although in the end Creech did not agree to Murray's terms for this particular publication,[45] the fact that Stuart viewed him as the leading Edinburgh publisher so early in his career shows how well connected and competent he was thought to be. John Bell and several other booksellers were more senior, but they did not possess Creech's widespread connections and extensive ties with both men of letters and the portion of the reading public who possessed, in Stuart's words, "money and taste." Masonic lodges and the

41. [Fleming], "Account," xvii. See also Benedict, "Service to the Public," 122–25.

42. Stewart to Archibald Constable, 28 Dec. 1809, NLS, MS 675, fols. 79–80.

43. Creech, *Edinburgh Fugitive Pieces*, 223.

44. Stuart to Murray, Nov. [1775], John Murray Archive, NLS.

45. Stuart to Murray, 3 Dec. 1775, ibid.

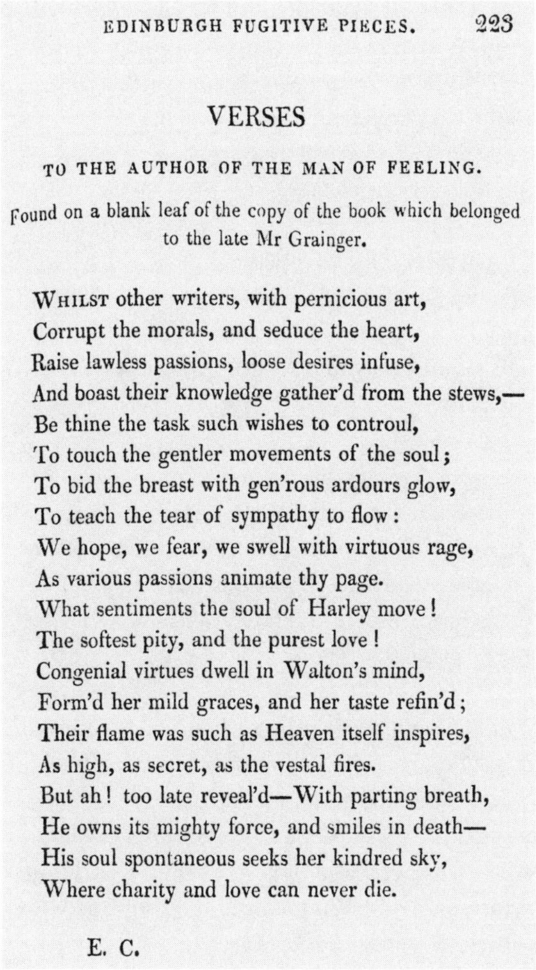

EDINBURGH FUGITIVE PIECES.   223

VERSES

TO THE AUTHOR OF THE MAN OF FEELING.

Found on a blank leaf of the copy of the book which belonged
to the late Mr Grainger.

WHILST other writers, with pernicious art,
Corrupt the morals, and seduce the heart,
Raise lawless passions, loose desires infuse,
And boast their knowledge gather'd from the stews,—
Be thine the task such wishes to controul,
To touch the gentler movements of the soul;
To bid the breast with gen'rous ardours glow,
To teach the tear of sympathy to flow :
We hope, we fear, we swell with virtuous rage,
As various passions animate thy page.
What sentiments the soul of Harley move !
The softest pity, and the purest love !
Congenial virtues dwell in Walton's mind,
Form'd her mild graces, and her taste refin'd ;
Their flame was such as Heaven itself inspires,
As high, as secret, as the vestal fires.
But ah ! too late reveal'd—With parting breath,
He owns its mighty force, and smiles in death—
His soul spontaneous seeks her kindred sky,
Where charity and love can never die.

E. C.

Fig. 6.2. William Creech was a great admirer of Henry Mackenzie, several of whose works he published. Creech's *Edinburgh Fugitive Pieces* (1791) contains this poem, which contrasts the praiseworthy sentimental moralizing of "the Man of Feeling" with the base appeals to sentiment by authors who corrupt and seduce their readers. Copy of the 1815 edition, from the author's collection.

Edinburgh Musical Society were two of the Edinburgh cultural institutions where Creech associated with such people.[46]

Creech cultivated his authors with great care. His breakfast room, located above his shop, in the rooms where Allan Ramsay once operated his famous circulating library, was known as "Creech's levee" in honor of the gatherings that were held there each morning. Burns celebrated these levees in a stanza from a poem he wrote for Creech, featuring James Gregory, Alexander Fraser Tytler, Henry Mackenzie, Dugald Stewart,

46. Macleod, "Freemasonry and Music," 123–52.

and Hugh Blair's protégé, William Greenfield, all of whom suddenly had to meet elsewhere on account of Creech's unfortunate absence:

> Now worthy Gregory's latin face,
> Tytler's and Greenfield's modest grace;
> M'Kenzie, Stewart, such a brace
>   As Rome ne'er saw;
> They a' maun meet some ither place,
>   Willie's awa'.[47]

The bookshop itself was also an intellectual meeting place, as Creech's contemporary biographer explains:

> Many of his literary friends were particularly attached to him; indeed, for a long course of years his shop, during a part of the day, was the resort of most of the clergy of the city, of the professors of the University, and other public men and eminent authors; and his dwelling-house was equally frequented in the morning hours by many of the same characters, who met to discuss with him their literary prospects.[48]

"I sat some time in the room behind Creech's shop," James Boswell wrote in his journal on 12 January 1786, "and had an impression of Edinburgh being a very good place."[49] In his memoirs, Henry Cockburn recalled how as a boy he attended a handwriting school on the High Street, not far from Creech's shop, and "always tried to get a seat next a window, that I might see the men I heard so much talked of moving into and out of this bower of the muses, or loitering about its entrance."[50]

The best test of the degree of independence that Creech displayed in his relations with his London mentors concerns titles that Strahan and Cadell chose not to copublish. After receiving Strahan's previously cited letter of 19 November 1778, which not only declined to participate in the publication of a work by Francis Home and a translation of Buffon

47. Quoted in Thompson, *Scottish Man of Feeling*, 228.

48. [Fleming], "Account," xx. According to Robert Chambers, *Traditions of Edinburgh*, the levee in the breakfast room lasted until noon each day; soon afterward Creech went down to the shop, "where the same company lasted till four" (quoted in Brown, "William Creech," 76).

49. Boswell, *English Experiment*, 27.

50. Cockburn, *Memorials*, 170.

but lambasted Creech for planning such ambitious publishing projects, Creech simply ignored Strahan's advice. In the first instance, he copublished Francis Home's *Clinical Experiments, Histories and Dissections* with John Murray early in 1780 (no. 207)—printing it in Edinburgh with his own name first in the imprint. The decision to publish Smellie's translation of Buffon's *Natural History* was a good deal more complicated, because of its large size and many engravings. But Creech persevered, even issuing a twenty-page prospectus in order to attract subscribers, with Creech's own name conspicuously displayed on the title page, while those of the translator and engraver are not even shown. Eventually he succeeded in getting Strahan and Cadell to join him as copublishers in spite of Strahan's initial misgivings.

Whenever Creech defied the advice of Strahan and Cadell, there are indications that he was concerned with more than profits. His front-page newspaper advertisement for Home's *Clinical Experiments* reproduced the book's entire preface, which argues that a society's institutions for the relief of the sick constitute "the most certain tests of polished and humane manners" (*EEC*, 3 Jan. 1780). The prospectus for Smellie's Buffon asserted that the work's facts, reasonings, and inferences about the natural world "every where lead to reflections which are momentous and interesting. They expand the mind, and banish prejudices. They create an elevation of thought, and cherish an ardor of inquiry."[51] Like Smellie, Creech viewed science as a force for enlightenment, and he acted aggressively to publish scientific works that he valued, with or without the collaboration of his London partners.

The same commitment to enlightened publishing is evident from a consideration of Hugo Arnot's *History of Edinburgh* (no. 199). Creech had a passion for the subject, and he would have been particularly interested in the chapter that discussed the development of printing and periodical publishing in Edinburgh and the growth of freedom of the press, as well as an appendix on the elaborate funeral procession for his master, Alexander Kincaid, who had died in office as lord provost in 1777. At one point Creech approached Strahan and Cadell to serve as London copublishers, but in his reply of 18 March 1779, on behalf of Cadell and himself, Strahan declined to take part in the publication in spite of his admiration for the work, mainly because he doubted that it would have much of a market in

---

51. [Smellie], *In the Press, and to be Published by William Creech*, 7–8. The prospectus is dated 23 June 1779.

London. Creech and Arnot went ahead anyway, collaborating with a reluctant John Murray to produce an overly large print run of 1,000 copies of an expensive quarto edition. Many copies went unsold, and in 1782 it was necessary to lower the price in boards from £1.5s. to one guinea.[52] But Creech did not give up. In 1788 he secured the Robinsons as London sales agents for a posthumous second edition, which was actually a reissue of the slow-selling first edition with Creech's own *Letters containing a Comparative View of Edinburgh in the Years 1763 and 1783* appended, as well as new illustrations and several revised sections inserted as replacements.

Observations on the Structure and Functions of the Nervous System by Alexander Monro *secundus* (no. 234) also demonstrates Creech's entrepreneurial spirit on behalf of enlightened projects (see fig. 1.2). When the book was being printed, Creech ran a large newspaper advertisement that declared it to be, "without exception, the most splendid [work] that has ever been produced from the Scottish press" (*EEC*, 8 Jan. 1783). Adopting the persona of "The Editor" writing to "the Public," Creech proclaims the book "so interesting to philosophy and science" that he has prepared a separate prospectus, available gratis at his shop. The book's merit as a work of science is matched by its grandeur as a material artifact: "The tables are accurate and elegant representations of nature, and they are accompanied with full explanations. The drawings and engravings were executed under the immediate inspection of the author. With regard to the mode of publication, the work will be splendidly printed on a new great printer type, and a fine royal paper made on purpose (in colour and substance like the French plate paper), in one large volume in folio." Creech states that the copies of this work will be distributed in proportion to the dates of the orders, so that individuals who are "zealous in promoting the cause of literature and science" may be assured of receiving copies with "the first impressions" from the plates. The fact that the book was dedicated to Scotland's powerful lord advocate, Henry Dundas, is also mentioned in the advertisement, placing its political stature on a par with its form and content. Of course, a royal folio of this caliber would be costly, although Creech's advertisement gave the price optimistically as "only Two Guineas in Boards." Even at that high price, it was not likely to be profitable, and a second edition was out of the question.

Finally, attention must be paid to the most ambitious of all Creech's publishing projects, *The Statistical Account of Scotland* (no. 301), which appeared in twenty-one thick octavo volumes over the better part of a de-

---

52. Arnot to Creech, 6 May 1782, WCL; Zachs, *First John Murray*, 68, 71.

cade, from 1791 to 1799. It was by any reckoning an extraordinary undertaking, compiled parish by parish from accounts submitted by more than nine hundred ministers in response to Sir John Sinclair's comprehensive questionnaire and twenty circular letters. The *Statistical Account* has been cited as an example of national information-gathering that had no equal during the eighteenth century and for some time afterward. Sinclair himself constantly publicized the vast scale and enlightened purpose of his achievement, as when he stated, in the advertisement prefixed to the second volume in 1792, that "there is no work, now extant, which throws such light upon the actual state of human society, or furnishes so many useful hints, of the most likely means of promoting its happiness and improvement." One modern commentator has gone so far as to claim the work as the defining text of the Scottish Enlightenment.[53] But the euphoric secondary literature on the *Statistical Account* gives almost all credit to the compiler, Sinclair, and the clergymen who submitted accounts of their parishes; its publishing history, in some respects its most remarkable feature, has received little attention.[54] As a member of Parliament, Sinclair paid nothing to send mail through the post, and his wealth enabled him to support a staff, which apparently did most of the editorial and clerical work.[55] All other production expenses fell to the publisher, who had no sources of capital available to him besides the proceeds from sales.

As the son of a Presbyterian minister, Creech became secretary of the newly formed Society for the Benefit of the Sons of the Clergy and agreed to publish Sinclair's series on its behalf. Besides charity for the society, he was motivated by a spirit of Scottish patriotic improvement, and the section on Edinburgh contained his often-printed *Letters containing a Comparative View of Edinburgh in the Years 1763 and 1783*, expanded and retitled *Letters Addressed to Sir John Sinclair, Bart.* Initially, Creech may not have grasped the full extent of what he was volunteering to do, but he persevered, and it is probably safe to say that without his dedication and sacrifice, the *Statistical Account* would never have been completed. We know something about his contribution because of his correspondence with Sinclair, who was pressing him to settle accounts and determine how much money the publication had raised for the Sons of the Clergy a decade after the last volume appeared in print. Sinclair was more

---

53. Withrington, "What Was Distinctive?" 9–19.

54. But see Grant, "Note on Publicity," 1:xlvii–lxxiii.

55. Mitchison, *Agricultural Sir John*, 122. Volume 2 was the only one edited by Sinclair himself.

than a little suspicious of the publisher's accounting procedures when he heard that there were as yet no profits, causing Creech to explain himself in letters to Sinclair dated 2 November 1807 and 27 October 1809.[56] "There are a multitude of expenses attending the publication that you have not taken into consideration," Creech states in the first of these letters. Among them he mentions "a separate warehouse . . . hired for this extensive and voluminous publication" and "still solely appropriated for the purpose." Two years later Creech itemized other factors, including the following: too many copies had been printed, at Sinclair's insistence and over Creech's objections; sales had initially been strong but had tailed off after the tenth volume, leaving "an accumulating mass of unsold Books to above 12,000"; "the Publication was burthened with printing and paper etc. etc. of numerous separate Parishes—Views—Addresses—Circular Letters—and corrections and alterations when at Press, beyond any publication that ever was known," though Sinclair "never advanced a shilling for paper and print of so great an undertaking"; "Numerous copies of the work beyond any example were given away in presents [584 sets, to be exact]—diminishing by their circulation the sale of the Book"; and postage and announcements had subjected the publisher to "great expense and trouble." Anyone familiar with the *Statistical Account* knows what Creech is talking about. What must it have cost, for example, to prepare a lengthy specimen, translate it into French, print it, and then transmit it "to every person of power, political influence, or literary merit, on the continent of Europe," as was done in 1792, according to the "Advertisement to the 3d and 4th Volumes"? Even if some of the expenses associated with such activities were covered by Sinclair himself, or by the government, in the case of postage, much if not most of the burden fell on Creech. Moreover, since the individual volumes were so large, yet cost as little as six shillings in boards, the profit margin must have been very thin, even without so many additional expenses.

According to Creech, if the remaining volumes could be sold, a profit might still be made for the Sons of the Clergy. "Had it not been with a view to aid that benevolent purpose," he adds, "I never would have undertaken so arduous and laborious a task, which entirely interrupted my business, and occupied my Clerks and warehousemen for years. . . . the

56. Copies of both letters, along with an angry one from Sinclair of 20 October 1809, are in Creech's Letterbook, ECL, and the two from Creech are published in Grant, "Note on Publicity," lxii–lxvi, from which the following citations are taken.

advance of money upon this work cramped my other views and operations of business." Creech objects that he told the society "what was likely to happen" after the publication of the tenth volume in March 1794, so that they "cannot be disappointed." Sinclair, however, was more than disappointed—he was furious, a circumstance that Creech attributes to the universal plight of authorship: "Every author is extremely sanguine respecting the success of his work, till experience checks it." In the end, the *Statistical Account* brought the Sons of the Clergy little or no income and probably cost Creech a great deal of money. Seven years after his death, in March 1822, the society issued a memorandum assigning blame to "the carelessness and inattention of the Publisher as well as . . . other causes over which they had no control." Sinclair went further, charging that "gross mismanagement on the part of the Publisher" had deprived the society of the "handsome sum" intended for it.[57]

All this scapegoating disguised the real problem, which was not mismanagement by the publisher but overextension and unrealistic expectations by the compiler, who donated profits that were not likely ever to materialize. As Creech apparently understood better than Sinclair, the success of the *Statistical Account* was to be measured not by financial profits but by the service it did as a source of enlightenment about the nature of late eighteenth-century Scottish society. In addition, because it was produced entirely in Edinburgh, it provided jobs for Scottish printers and other laboring men of the book trade, from clerks to warehousemen, far exceeding any other Scottish publication of the century.

The common denominator in the books that Creech published in defiance of Strahan is that they all sought to advance the cause of the Enlightenment. The program of agricultural improvement heralded in Kames's *Gentleman Farmer;* the association of medical institutions with civilization that Francis Home announces in his *Clinical Experiments;* the claims about Buffon's *Natural History* enlarging the mind, rooting out prejudice, and encouraging a spirit of inquiry; the determination to chronicle the growth of Scotland's capital in Arnot's *History of Edinburgh;* the placing of the bookmaker's art in the service of zeal for "the cause of literature and science" in Monro's book on the nervous system; the commitment to national improvement on the basis of comprehensive, empirical fact-finding that underlies Sinclair's *Statistical Account*—all showed Creech to be a publisher who was willing to take substantial financial risks for

57. Quoted in Grant, "Note on Publicity," lxvii–lxx.

the sake of scientific learning and enlightened principles, whether or not there was a likelihood of profit, and whether or not he had the support of his principal London partners.

THE REPUTATION OF A BOOKSELLER

Soon after William Creech died on 14 January 1815, he was eulogized by Robert Fleming in a biographical sketch prefixed to a new edition of Creech's *Edinburgh Fugitive Pieces*. It was published by John Fairbairn, "successor to Mr Creech," along with Cadell & Davies, John Murray, and a number of other London booksellers. The book included a frontispiece portrait of Creech (fig. 6.3), engraved by W. & D. Lizars from an early nineteenth-century painting by Sir Henry Raeburn, one of two Raeburn likenesses of Creech from this period.[58] The pose, showing its subject seated, with the index finger of his right hand marking his place in a book, is that of a book reader, not a book vendor: a man of letters rather than a man of business. It deliberately copies the well-known pose of his mentor, William Strahan, as painted decades earlier by Sir Joshua Reynolds (NPG 4202); even the style of the wig is remarkably similar. Fleming's text emphasized Creech's accomplishments as a publisher, noting that "for above forty years . . . Mr Creech had a concern in most of the principal literary productions which appeared in Scotland, and was intimately acquainted with all the eminent authors who, during that period, conferred such luster on our country."[59]

This view of Creech as a great Enlightenment publisher in Scotland did not go uncontested. In a bitter autobiographical memoir that was composed in 1821 and later published posthumously by his son, the Edinburgh publisher Archibald Constable provided a harsh depiction of Creech and his age.[60] Although "an accomplished gentleman and most agreeable companion" who "told a story remarkably well,"[61] Creech was "narrow-minded and contracted in his views," Constable charged, and unwilling to avail himself of "the advantages which his education and position afforded him in his relations with the literary men of Scotland." That is why when John

---

58. The other Raeburn portrait, in the Scottish National Portrait Gallery, is reproduced in Dwyer and Sher, *Sociability and Society in Eighteenth-Century Scotland*.

59. Creech, *Edinburgh Fugitive Pieces*, xvii.

60. Constable, "Edinburgh Booksellers of the Period," in Constable, *Archibald Constable*, 1:533–40.

61. Cf. Black, *Memoirs*, 24: "He was the best story-teller I ever heard."

Fig. 6.3. This portrait
of William Creech
at about sixty years
of age, engraved by
W. & D. Lizars from
one of two original oil
paintings by Sir Henry
Raeburn, was used
as the frontispiece in
the posthumous 1815
edition of Creech's *Ed-
inburgh Fugitive Pieces.*
Thomas Fisher Rare
Book Library, Univer-
sity of Toronto.

Bell left Kincaid and set himself up independently, "much of the literary connexion and respectability of Mr. Kincaid's trade accompanied him." To illustrate Creech's shortcomings, Constable cited Hugh Blair's *Sermons,* which he castigated Creech for never printing in Edinburgh "as he ought to have done, and which would have brought much money and credit to the profession here." In Constable's view, Creech was too subservient to his London masters, as evidenced by his printing title pages with "the names of the London booksellers before his own." Constable believed that Charles Elliot was a far more eminent figure in Scottish publishing than Creech and that both Elliot and John Bell were more likable and polite. His conclusion about Creech as a publisher was dismissive: "His publications were neither very important nor voluminous." Moreover, Constable broadened this judgment into a general critique of Scottish publishing during the last quarter of the eighteenth century, when in his estimation "there were few original books published in Edinburgh, and intercourse with London was consequently neither extensive nor important." In an-other part of his autobiographical fragment, he commented that, in light of the "highly respectable" number of literary men in Edinburgh during the second half of the eighteenth century, publishers of that time missed "an opportunity of publishing a much greater number of new books than are to be met with in the annals of the period."[62]

Some of Constable's charges had already been aired publicly during Creech's lifetime. In 1806 Constable published *Picture of Edinburgh*, by the printer John Stark. After paying tribute to "Hume, Smith, Robertson, and Kames," along with John Gregory and William Cullen, who "were the first in Edinburgh who led the way to that excellence in literature that is almost without a parallel," the book laments the absence in eighteenth-century Edinburgh of great bookseller-patrons, such as "the Lintots, the Dodsleys, the Millars, the Strahans, and the Cadells of the sister King-dom," without whom many great authors who "do honour to Britain" might not have arisen.[63] Without identifying any particular booksellers in Scotland, Stark then charges that "the former booksellers in this city were unable . . . to encourage genius, by the purchase of copy-rights, and consequently most of the great works produced in Scotland for the last half century, were sold and published in London." As a result, "many authors, whose modesty, diffidence, or want of interest, prevented the publication of their works in this circuitous manner, were thus lost to themselves, and to their country" (261). Just as Creech's name was meant to flash through the minds of readers of the preceding passage, so is Constable's easily discernible in the one that follows:

> That obstacle, however, has now in part been happily surmounted; and of late there have appeared some booksellers in Edinburgh, whose names will be recorded to posterity as the best benefactors of science and learn-ing in their country. One house, in particular, besides the many valuable original works which they occasionally print, publish no less than four of the most popular and approved periodical journals in Britain. It is trusted, that the example which has been given so nobly, will inspire others of equal abilities and fortune, in this manner to patronise genius; to draw, by the encouragement of her votaries, 'fair science from her coy abode;' and thus not only secure to themselves great emolument, but leave an envied lustre to their names which time shall not be able to destroy. (261–62)

When a new edition of *Picture of Edinburgh* appeared in 1819, Creech had been dead for four years and was now considered fair game. Before

---

62. "Autobiographic Fragment" in Constable, *Archibald Constable*, 1:32–33.
63. Stark, *Picture of Edinburgh* (1806), 259–60.

the launching of the *Edinburgh Review* in 1802, writes Stark, "most of the great literary works of Scotland were sold to publishers in London. The late Mr William Creech, the greatest Edinburgh bookseller of his time, held merely small shares in those works to which his name is attached; and the printing, to the inconvenience of the authors, and the discouragement of the Edinburgh press, was chiefly executed in London." Since 1802, however, "the house of Messrs. Archibald Constable and Co. have not only secured to Edinburgh all the works of native talent, but have drawn to this city works from every quarter of the island."[64] In another section of the 1819 edition, dealing specifically with the history of printing in Edinburgh, a discussion of the classical printing of the Foulis brothers of Glasgow is followed immediately by an equally laudatory passage about how "the appearance of Mr Walter Scott as an author, and the establishment of the Edinburgh Review, and the enterprise of the House with which that celebrated publication originated, have procured for Edinburgh, not only the printing of works of native genius, but transferred to this city the printing and publication of books from every quarter of the empire" (221). The 1806 edition supported claims about the growth of Edinburgh as a printing center with statistics: 6 printing houses in 1763, 21 in 1790, 30 in 1800, and 40 in 1805, operating more than 120 presses (242). In the 1819 edition the number of Edinburgh printing houses was said to be 47 as of 1819, operating nearly 150 presses (222), and in the third edition of 1823 the number of printing houses was given as 44 as of 1822, operating the same number of presses (197).

Also in 1819, J. G. Lockhart outdid both Stark and Constable himself in his hostility to Creech and the Edinburgh book trade of the late eighteenth century. Lockhart's popular *Peter's Letters to His Kinfolk* contrasts the age of Creech and the age of Constable at length, to the great advantage of the latter. According to Lockhart, the Edinburgh booksellers of the late eighteenth century "were all petty retailers, inhabiting snug shops, and making a little money in the most tedious and uniform way imaginable"; they were so timid and dull, and so subservient to the London booksellers (who sometimes included their names in title pages merely as a "courtesy"), that "there was no such thing in Edinburgh as the great trade of Publishing."[65] The embodiment of this short-sighted eighteenth-

---

64. Stark, *Picture of Edinburgh* (1819), 233. Perhaps because the blatantly self-serving nature of the project was so transparent, Constable dropped his connection with this popular title from the 1819 edition onward.

65. Lockhart, *Peter's Letters*, 2:157–58.

century Scottish attitude toward publishing was William Creech, "then the Prince of the Edinburgh Trade" (158). Lockhart's Creech is a pathetically paradoxical figure, inordinately fond of money yet unwilling to pursue it persistently for several reasons. One was that "he had been trained in all the timid prejudices of the old Edinburgh school of booksellers." In addition, as a prominent magistrate who had been well educated and done the grand tour, who dabbled in literature himself, and who put on the airs of a great man, he evidently "thought it beneath his dignity to be a mere ordinary money-making bookseller" (159–60). "He never had the sense to perceive, that his true game lay in making high sweep-stakes," Lockhart observes, and as a result he settled for preeminence in Edinburgh rather than risk competition with "the great booksellers of the metropolis." "Had he possessed either the shrewdness or the spirit of some of his successors," Lockhart adds, thinking mainly of Constable, "there is no question he might have set on foot a fine race of rivalry among the literary men about him" (159)—a race that would have yielded him huge profits. The climax of Lockhart's story is the sudden and simultaneous emergence in Edinburgh of a "new tribe of authors" (the Edinburgh Reviewers and Sir Walter Scott) and a "new race of booksellers" (led by Constable, "by far the greatest publisher Scotland ever has produced") who turned the tables on the booksellers of London by making Edinburgh into "a great mart of literature" (156) and the new center of British publishing (162–67). As a result of this revolution, "in one moment, Mr Creech was supplanted in his authority" (163).

Creech's personality and lifestyle made him an easy target for these attacks. That he could be somewhat priggish and more than a little parsimonious is beyond doubt. His staunch Calvinism may have caused him to appear narrow-minded to some, and his vanity could be grating. To Maria Riddell he was "a great rogue as well as an intolerable pedant," who "should be avoided like plague or pestilence."[66] He was self-righteous about infringements on his copyrights and dictatorial in persecuting those who violated the rules of the Edinburgh Booksellers' Society that he founded and tried his best to control.[67] A bachelor all his life, by the early nineteenth century Creech had a fashionable house on George Street in the New Town as well as a cottage and grounds at Trinity, from which he was in the habit of riding into Edinburgh each day on horseback with

66. Riddell to James Currie, 6 Dec. 1797, *Burns Chronicle* (1921): 43.
67. Sher, "Corporatism and Consensus," 32–93.

his manservant, in what one commentator called "the old style of a gentle-man in the Scottish metropolis."[68] Once at the shop, he would pass each morning and much of the afternoon entertaining literary men and others, leaving business transactions in the care of clerks.[69] As a result, he had a reputation for sometimes neglecting his business affairs. Worse, Robert Burns wrote in his commonplace book of Creech's "extreme vanity" and questioned his integrity in dealing with authors. William Smellie, Creech's printing partner during the 1780s, was equally severe in charging that Creech cheated him out of money, just as Sir John Sinclair came to believe that Creech squandered the profits from the *Statistical Account of Scotland*. John Pinkerton told the Earl of Buchan that "the booksellers have a mean opinion of Creech" and asked "if your lordship would recommend some other bookseller in Edinburgh, who does not, like Creech, set up for a genius and a gentleman."[70]

Recent research suggests that in these transactions Creech was not always the villain he has been made out to be. As we have seen, Sinclair seems to have used his publisher as a scapegoat for an enterprise that had little chance of commercial success. And chapter 3 showed that Burns's anger was largely due to the poet's misunderstanding of the bookselling business and to confusion surrounding subscriptions. Moreover, it is now believed that Smellie's financial mismanagement contributed significantly to Creech's difficulties with both Burns and Smellie himself.[71] With regard to his character, Creech had his strengths as well as weaknesses. As secretary of the Edinburgh Chamber of Commerce, he was a party to the first Scottish petition to Parliament against the slave trade in February 1788 (*EEC*, 1 Mar. 1788), and he joined an Edinburgh society dedicated to that cause. The Earl of Buchan applauded him as "a man of taste and spirit and at the heart of the literary profession in Scotland," and Burns asserted that "his social demeanour and powers, particularly at his own table, are the most engaging I have ever met with."[72] The same former

68. Anderson, *History of Edinburgh*, 325; Minute Book of the Trustees of William Creech, 17, ECL, William Creech Papers.

69. This account by a former employee, in Chambers, *Life and Works*, 2:266, may be a more accurate description of Creech near the end of his bookselling career than during his prime.

70. Pinkerton to Buchan, 2 Feb. 1788, in Pinkerton, *Literary Correspondence*, 1: 177.

71. Brown, "William Creech," 75–80.

72. Buchan to Creech, 4 Sept. 1791, quoted in Mathison, "Gude Black Prent," 73.

employee who testified to his neglect of his bookselling duties called him "a very good-natured man."[73] As for his stinginess, when encouraging a new edition of Rev. John Erskine's sermons, Creech spoke loftily of the need for spreading Erskine's thoughts on "the most momentous concerns of human nature" and openly declared his intention to take no money himself.[74]

The core of the charges leveled by Constable, Stark, and Lockhart, however, was not that Creech lacked integrity or business acumen or good manners or a good nature but that he failed as a publisher because his flawed entrepreneurial vision, his inability to provide adequate encouragement to Scottish authors, and his subservience to London booksellers prevented him from building Edinburgh into the great publishing center that it later became. Writing in 1840, Henry Cockburn spared Creech the personal invective but adopted essentially the same line on Edinburgh publishing when he stated that Constable had rescued Edinburgh from "the old timid and grudging system" and transformed it into a "literary mart, famous with strangers, and the pride of its own citizens."[75] The same interpretation lives on today, in assertions that Creech was "ultimately parochial" in his approach to publishing, whereas Constable was "truly international."[76]

It should now be clear that these charges cannot stand up to scrutiny. Before proceeding further, however, it will be helpful to reflect on the context and credibility of Creech's nineteenth-century accusers. Archibald Constable was born in 1774, did not come to Edinburgh to begin his career in bookselling until he was apprenticed to Peter Hill at the age of fourteen, and did not go into business for himself until 1795, when he was twenty-one years old.[77] He therefore could scarcely have been acquainted with Charles Elliot (who was immobilized by a stroke in September 1789 and died the following January) and could not have had much firsthand knowledge of William Creech or the Edinburgh book trade generally during the great age of Scottish Enlightenment publishing. The Creech he knew had his best years as a publisher behind him and was heavily

73. Chambers, *Life and Works*, 2:266.

74. Creech to Erskine, 24 Jan. 1801, NLS, MS 682, fols. 44–46.

75. Cockburn, *Memorials*, 168–69.

76. Brown, "William Creech," 75.

77. Information on Constable's life is drawn from the autobiographical fragment that concludes the first chapter of Constable, *Archibald Constable*, 5–33; and David Hewitt's entry on Constable in *ODNB*.

involved in town politics; the Edinburgh book trade he knew was the one stumbling through the difficult days of the late 1790s, when times were hard as a result of incessant war with France. Constable seems to have obtained his information about the previous era from John Bell, the uncle and partner of his good friend John Bradfute, who was hardly an impartial source. He may also have been influenced by the second John Murray, the copublisher of the first edition of Stark's *Picture of Edinburgh*, who had married Charles Elliot's daughter. And if Constable, along with Stark and Cockburn, had little firsthand knowledge of publishing in the age preceding their own, Lockhart, who was born in 1794, had none at all. He apparently obtained most of his information from Sir Walter Scott (Constable's senior by just three years), who would become his father-in-law the year after *Peter's Letters* appeared. In a letter to the printer James Ballantyne, Scott laid out the plan that Lockhart was to follow in *Peter's Letters:* "Creech, with his peculiar habits of conducting business in the mode of the old school should be contrasted with Constable at the head of the new. . . . Nothing offensive should be said. Creech's penurious and short-sighted mode of doing business might partly emanate from his personal habits but it was chiefly the narrow views of his time."[78] As an author in his own right, Lockhart was partial to publishers who paid their authors handsomely; the incident that best illustrated Constable's greatness in his eyes was his offering Scott one thousand guineas for a single, unwritten poem, *Marmion.*[79]

Constable's excesses and grandiose claims about his accomplishments as a publisher reflect a deep sense of insecurity. His autobiographical account was designed to justify a career that was the opposite of Creech's in most respects. Whereas Creech had all the advantages of a privileged education, extensive connections with eminent booksellers who greased his path to the top, and much experience in London and on the Continent, Constable attended a humble parish school in Carnbee, Fife, until the age of fourteen and then, after his apprenticeship, worked his way up in the trade on his own by selling "scarce old books" on Scottish topics. His professional training outside Edinburgh was confined to a single month in London in January 1795, when he met Thomas Cadell, Jr., Thomas Longman, and the Robinsons.

The two men could hardly have been more different in appearance. As painted by Andrew Geddes in 1813, when he was not yet forty years

78. Scott to Ballantyne, 9 Apr. 1819, in Scott, *Letters*, 6:89.

79. Lockhart, *Memoirs*, 1:463.

old (fig. 6.4), Constable lacks the air of gentility, refinement, and self-assurance that Creech possessed when Raeburn painted him just a few years earlier, around the age of sixty. The setting for the Geddes portrait is deliberately plain, and the usual literary props do little to alter the sense of commonness that is conveyed by Constable's inelegant pose, ungainly figure, and poorly tailored clothing. Their attitudes toward business were equally different. Creech built his publishing business carefully—based in large part on loyal relations with Scottish authors and lifelong relationships with his London connections—and died worth more than £20,000.[80] Constable followed a very different course. Although he made a fast, vast fortune from the *Edinburgh Review* (founded in 1802) and the poetry and novels of Sir Walter Scott, his publishing career was marked by instability, overextension, grandstanding, and an inability to maintain viable relations with London partners.[81] In January 1826 his empire came tumbling down in the largest British book trade bankruptcy up to that time, and he died the following year.

The earlier accounts by Constable, Stark, Scott, and Lockhart may be read as expressions of hubris that were subsequently contradicted by the course of events. A decade after the bankruptcy, Lockhart, in his life of Scott, further perpetuated the story of Constable's heroic career while also revealing that Constable and his partners had brought about their own downfall. In the latest biography of Constable, however, Lockhart's financial criticism is challenged on the grounds that "the accusations of financial incompetence against [Constable & Co. and James Ballantyne & Co.] are incompatible with the fact that Constable as publisher and Ballantyne as printer had conducted two extraordinarily successful businesses for twenty-five years" and that they fail to take into account the severe financial crisis during the winter of 1825–26.[82] But success in good times is no guarantee that a poorly managed firm will continue to thrive during a crisis. Constable went under because he became vulnerable as a result of a series of bad business decisions regarding expenditures and alliances, and his illusions of grandeur may well have affected his judgment. There is considerable irony in Scott's telling Constable in 1825, in connection with a mass-marketing scheme, that the bookseller would become

---

80. "Inventory of the Personal Estate belonging to the deceased William Creech Esq. at his death 14 Jan'y 1815," ECL, William Creech Papers, item 1, no. 62.

81. Millgate, "Archibald Constable," 110–23.

82. David Hewitt's entry on Constable in *ODNB*.

Fig. 6.4. Archibald Constable in his late thirties, painted by Andrew Geddes (1813). Scottish National Portrait Gallery.

known as "the grand Napoleon of the realms of *print*."[83] His bankruptcy was his Waterloo.

It is questionable if the myth of Constable as a revolutionary publisher was ever justified. Aside from the *Edinburgh Review* and Scott, Constable pursued a publishing program that was generally unadventurous, and he relied heavily on works and authors from the late eighteenth century. "We seldom undertake the risk of a first production," he told one aspiring author in 1816, preferring instead to manage the sale after the author covered the expenses of "Printing, Paper and advertising."[84] Among the 185 titles in the *Catalogue of Books Printed for Archibald Constable & Co. Edinburgh* that appeared in 1814—the year of Scott's *Waverley*—one finds of course the *Edinburgh Review* and Scott's popular works of poetry (not to mention Stark's *Picture of Edinburgh*), but the catalogue is dominated by such familiar names as Archibald Alison, James Bruce, George Chalmers, James Grant, Henry Mackenzie, John Playfair, Sir John Sinclair, Dugald Stewart (both his philosophical writings and his lives of Adam Smith, William Robertson, and Thomas Reid), Alexander Fraser Tytler, Robert Wallace, the *Scots Magazine*, the *Encyclopaedia Britannica*, the *Transactions of the Royal Society of Edinburgh*, the *Prize Essays and Transactions of the Highland Society of Scotland*, and Sir William Forbes's *Account of the Life and Writings of James Beattie*. This is hardly the stuff that one would expect from the leader of Lockhart's "new race of booksellers."

Similarly, Constable and his supporters exaggerated the extent to which he was personally responsible for building up Edinburgh as a printing center—and in the process greatly shortchanged Creech's contribution. When accounting for the rosy condition of Edinburgh printing in 1805, the first edition of Stark's *Picture of Edinburgh* commented that "a great part of it is done on account of the booksellers of London, and other places; and considerable quantities of books are printed for exportation to Ireland and America" (242). Regarding the first of these points, James Anderson stated in 1792 that it was "at the desire of the [London] booksellers" that "half the books printed in Edinburgh and the country towns in England bear to be printed in *London*."[85] Allowing for exaggeration, Anderson's statement suggests that the pattern identified by Stark in the next decade had deep roots in the period before Stark or Constable were

83. Ibid., as quoted from Lockhart's biography of Scott.

84. Constable to James Graham, 1 July 1816, NLS, MS 789, p. 605.

85. Anderson to John Pinkerton, 12 Feb. 1792, in Pinkerton, *Literary Correspondence*, 1:295.

in business for themselves. Stark's statement also identifies two overseas markets that were providing new sources of opportunities for the Edinburgh printing trade: Ireland, where union with Britain at the turn of the century had decimated the once-proud Dublin reprinting industry, and America, where the demand for books continued to grow. Constable was not responsible for either of those developments. Moreover, Stark's own statistics on the growth of Edinburgh printing firms, as previously cited, demonstrate an unprecedented rate of expansion from 1790 to 1805, when the number of printing houses doubled, but very modest growth over the course of the next seventeen years, during Constable's period of ascendancy.

In the process of constructing a heroic identity for themselves, Constable and his friends went out of their way to debunk what had come before them. Although they never denied that Creech attracted men of letters to his shop and levees, these activities were somehow turned against him. Some, such as Cockburn, attributed Creech's achievement to "the position of his shop in the very tideway of all our business."[86] The location at the east end of the Luckenbooths certainly was advantageous, and the fact that the building was torn down almost immediately after Creech's death prevented any comparisons with later booksellers.[87] But no one ever accused Creech's predecessors in the Luckenbooths—M'Euen and Kincaid—of having an unfair advantage because of the location of their shops. And how much can this location have mattered when so many other booksellers with shops in the immediate vicinity never achieved the same level of social and cultural importance as Creech?

In *Peter's Letters*, Lockhart provided a more sinister explanation when he suggested that Creech developed his shop into a literary lounge in order to compensate for his reluctance to contend with the London booksellers as a serious publisher: "Not thinking, therefore, of entering into competition with the great booksellers of the metropolis, in regard to the stimulating of literary ardour by the weight of his purse, his ambition was to surpass all his own brethren in Edinburgh, in the attractions of his shop—which, if the account I hear be true, he must certainly have succeeded in rendering a very delightful lounge."[88] Lockhart grossly un-

---

86. Cockburn, *Memorials*, 169.

87. In 1797 Creech sold his shop to the town for £670, with the right to remain a tenant for life. Town Council Minutes, Edinburgh City Chambers, 8 Mar. 1797, 127:100.

88. Lockhart, *Peter's Letters*, 160.

derestimated the extent to which Creech participated in large, expensive publishing ventures, both on his own and in association with his London partners. In addition, he failed to see that massive payments to authors of the sort that Constable paid to Scott were not the only way for publishers to stimulate "literary ardour." Creech used his levees and his shop generally as a means of cultivating relationships with authors and potential authors—as a publishing catalyst rather than as an alternative to publishing. He attracted men of letters through the force of his lively personality—well suited for literary conversation and storytelling, at which he excelled—and through his stature as a well-educated, well-read man of letters in his own right, well versed in science and medicine as well as philosophy and literature. Exploiting his excellent location to the fullest possible extent was a personal achievement based on his ability to develop and maintain relations with Scottish men of letters, many of whose works he published.

Creech's defects as a bookseller and a man did not include failing to encourage vigorously the production of new works of literature and learning by Scottish authors, or failing to generate much printing of such works in Edinburgh, or slavishly following his London mentors no matter where their advice might lead. Constable and his followers never understood that Creech viewed his relations with the London trade in terms of cooperation, not conquest, and that many of his publishing projects were motivated largely by enlightened causes and civic concerns. At critical moments, he stood up to London and went his own way. The publication of the *Statistical Account of Scotland* alone discredits those who criticized him for lacking independent vision and enterprise as a publisher and who blamed him for failing to provide work for Edinburgh printers. Creech collaborated effectively with his more powerful London associates, the House of Strahan and Cadell, in order to publish much of the best new work of the Scottish Enlightenment. In his prime, he was an Enlightenment publishing entrepreneur of the first order, and it is difficult to dispute his boast in a letter of 28 September 1803: "I believe I have published more Books and paid more money to Authors than any man of my profession in Scotland during my time."[89]

89. Creech to Gilbert Hutchison, 28 Sept. 1803, quoted in Brown, "William Creech," 75.

PART III

﹡

REPRINTING THE
SCOTTISH ENLIGHTENMENT IN
DUBLIN AND PHILADELPHIA

7

The Rise and Fall of Irish Reprinting

During the second half of the eighteenth century, Dublin prided itself on being the second city of the British Empire. With regard to publishing, there is considerable merit in this claim. A rough count drawn from ESTC reveals that during this period Dublin was surpassed only by London in the production of English-language printed material.[1] Its only competition was Edinburgh, which it barely nosed out, each town printing approximately 14,000 items between 1751 and 1800. During the 1780s (to take a sample decade) Dublin and Edinburgh had about 2,800 and 2,100 imprints, respectively. If their combined total of approximately 5,000 items was small compared to the more than 25,000 imprints that were generated in London during the same years, it nevertheless exceeded the number of English-language imprints that appeared during the 1780s in all the other localities of Britain, Ireland, and America put together. In a study of Enlightenment publishing, such unrefined statistics must be used with care, since the raw numbers include everything from broadsides, squibs, and printed legal documents to multivolume quarto editions of major works. Nonetheless, the figures indicate the undeniable impor-

---

1. See the table in Sher, "Corporatism and Consensus," 34, as updated from a search of ESTC in January 2006. Although the results for British and Irish towns have not changed significantly since the table was compiled in 1997, the numbers of imprints in North American towns have been adjusted downward in ESTC since then.

tance of Edinburgh and Dublin as publishing centers in the age of the Enlightenment.

There was a great difference, however, in the way the Enlightenment was served by the book trades in these two towns. In Edinburgh, as we have seen, a number of booksellers published new works by Scottish men of letters, either on their own or in association with publishing partners in London. This activity often entailed negotiating directly with authors and paying them copy money, as well as collaborating with other British booksellers in the production of new books. A considerable amount of reprinting also went on in Edinburgh, including some that violated statutory copyright or (more commonly) the principle of "honorary" copyright that the established London booksellers tried to uphold as trade custom. Thus, Edinburgh contained a full-service publishing industry in the eighteenth century, in which initiative and enterprise took many different forms and in which relationships among the authors and publishers of polite literature were varied and complex.

In Dublin, by contrast, the business of Enlightenment publishing was focused more narrowly on the reprinting of British editions, with no concern for the British copyright provisions established by the statute of Queen Anne. As a result of this circumstance, eighteenth-century Irish publishing has often been neglected by scholars, if not simply dismissed as mere piracy. Fortunately, recent work by Mary Pollard, Máire Kennedy, Richard Cargill Cole, and others, along with the publication in 1998 of *Printing and Bookselling in Dublin*, James W. Phillips's notable 1952 doctoral thesis, has rejuvenated the field. It now seems clear that publishing in eighteenth-century Dublin is a rich and complex topic that deserves more careful consideration than it has previously received.

In focusing on the Dublin trade in Scottish Enlightenment books, this chapter recounts and then critically assesses the views on Dublin reprinting held by some of the leading British publishers of the Scottish Enlightenment. It then looks more closely at the individuals who were chiefly responsible for reprinting Scottish Enlightenment books in Dublin and examines some of their most ambitious efforts to equal, and occasionally outdo, their counterparts in London and Edinburgh. Finally, it considers the reasons for the decline of the Dublin book trade at the turn of the nineteenth century and the significance of late eighteenth-century Dublin reprinting for the international dissemination of the Scottish Enlightenment.

PUBLISHERS OR PIRATES?

On 15 March 1785 four London booksellers testified before a parliamentary committee appointed to consider reforming the trade with Ireland: Thomas Cadell, Sr., Cadell's leading competitor George Robinson, Cadell's close friend Thomas Longman, and the law publisher Edward Brook. Although the published account of their testimony does not report the names of the particular witnesses who were speaking at any given time, an identifying phrase at one point in the testimony ("Mr. Cadell added . . .") and internal evidence regarding another answer (the assertion about the accomplishments of "the House of Strahan and Cadell" that is mentioned at the beginning of chapter 5) suggest that Cadell, whose name appears first among them, was the booksellers' chief spokesman.

Cadell and his colleagues presented four main reasons for what they took to be Ireland's unfair advantage in book publishing. First, because Ireland had no copyright laws, the booksellers there could reprint new British books, as well as new British editions of old books, with "all the Benefit of the Expence we have been put to" in paying authors. Second, "the Price of Paper of every Sort is much cheaper there than here" because the Irish trade paid a lower duty on paper. Third, booksellers in Ireland could bind books more cheaply because they paid a much cheaper duty on leather. Fourth, the wages of journeymen printers "are much lower there than here."[2]

According to Cadell and his associates, these advantages had two primary consequences. First, the British export trade to Ireland had been rendered inconsiderable "except in such heavy Works as they cannot print there," such as dictionaries and multivolume books, which were commonly sent to Ireland in the form of unbound sheets. "Mr. Cadell added" that the Irish booksellers reprint British books "soon after they are printed here, and often get the Sheets as they come from the Press"—implying by the latter phrase that they received the printed sheets surreptitiously from unscrupulous British printers or their employees. Second, the London booksellers asserted that there was "no Doubt" of "a great clandestine Importation of Books from Ireland into this Country," including books protected by copyright according to the statute of Queen Anne. Although they did not use the word "piracy" in their testimony, the implication was clear. In their final statement, they conceded that the Irish advantages in duties on paper and leather did not constitute a serious grievance for the

2. Lambert, *Sessional Papers*, 52:358–59.

British trade. Rather, "the Protection of our Copy Right is the great Point to be attended to."

On 5 March 1785, Cadell wrote a strongly worded letter on this topic to the leading parliamentary authority on Irish trade, Charles Jenkinson, later first Earl of Liverpool. The letter contained some of the same arguments that would appear in Cadell's testimony before Parliament ten days later, as well as a straightforward assertion that Cadell was representing "the Booksellers and Printers of Great Britain."[3] This sweeping claim enhances the significance of Cadell's parliamentary testimony. It also gives added importance to the following speculation in Cadell's letter about the disastrous consequences of allowing Irish books to compete freely in Britain: "No Bookseller will in future venture to give a Sum of money for the property of a Book if he cannot be protected in the exclusive Sale, at least in this Country, for the Term given by the Act of Queen Anne. The very great encouragement given to Literary productions has most certainly produced a number of Capital Publications viz Robertson, Hume, Gibbon, Blackstone, Lyttleton, Blair, Johnson, Sterne, etc etc which do honour to this Country." Of course, the London booksellers had made similar assertions a decade earlier, when proclaiming the harmful effects that would result from the abolition of perpetual copyright. But I know of no statement in the debate over perpetual copyright that exalts the role of the publisher quite so forcefully as this passage. In contending that great books or "Capital Publications" by well-known authors were "most certainly produced" by generous payments for copyrights, Cadell was putting forward the British booksellers' theory of literary production. It held that British bookseller-publishers like himself were not merely participants in the system of book production, responding to market forces or to the creative works that authors placed before them. They stood behind the entire process, as the first cause of great literature and learning. And the greater the importance of the British publishers in the creation of great books, the more the significance of the Dublin reprinters was diminished.

One problem with assessing the opinions that Cadell expressed privately and publicly in March 1785 is that they were intended to serve a specific political purpose, namely, blocking a bill that would have opened up the British market to Irish books and supporting, at least implicitly, the opposite plan of extending British statutory copyright law to Ireland. Another kind of ulterior motive occasionally turns up in the communica-

3. Cadell to Jenkinson, 5 Mar. 1785, BL Add. MSS 38218, fols. 296–97.

tions of British publishers with their authors. For example, in 1777 John Murray told one of his Scottish medical authors, who had inquired about the Irish sale of his book: "At Dublin the Booksellers reprint every new book without regarding literary property, so that there is no chance of disposing of your edition in that Kingdom."[4] As it happened, this particular book, Alexander Hamilton's *Elements of the Practice of Midwifery* (no. 169), was never reprinted in Ireland. Murray may have been discouraged from selling the book there by one circumstance or another, but the reason in this case could not have been the one he gave his author. We are left to believe, therefore, that the specter of Dublin reprinting sometimes provided a convenient scapegoat for late eighteenth-century British publishers who wished to pacify their anxious authors.

Yet it would be wrong to conclude that the London publishers were being disingenuous when they articulated their misgivings about the Irish trade to politicians and authors. Extant letters from William Strahan to his Edinburgh associate William Creech during the late 1770s and early 1780s demonstrate the sincerity and intensity of their concerns. "The importations from Ireland, I am afraid it is not in our Power to prevent," Strahan writes on 19 November 1778. In his view, Irish reprinting and "the laying open Literary Property in Britain [i.e., the abolition of perpetual copyright], are two incurable Evils, which are likely to render Bookselling one of the most unprofitable and precarious, and of course the most disreputable of all Trades."[5] As noted in chapter 5, on 17 October 1780 Strahan cited the Irish threat in connection with Strahan and Cadell's reluctance to meet Adam Ferguson's asking price for a new book on ancient Rome, remarking, in language not unlike that found in Murray's letter to Alexander Hamilton, that the Dublin booksellers "immediately" reprint "in an inferior Size, and at a low Price, every new Book the Instant it is published here." Unlike Murray, however, Strahan was thinking not of book sales in Ireland, which he seems to have conceded as a lost cause, but of sales in America and the West Indies, where he believed that British publishers were being "totally deprived of the Sale of new Works" as a result of recent legislation that legalized Irish exports there.[6]

A year later, in a letter dated 4 October 1781, Strahan voices a similar

4. Murray to Alexander Hamilton, 25 Oct. 1777, quoted in Zachs, *First John Murray*, 113.

5. All references to letters from Strahan to Creech cited in this chapter are from WCL.

6. On this legislation, see Pollard, *Dublin's Trade in Books*, 135–39.

complaint, adding, with regard to cheap Dublin reprints, that the Irish booksellers "not only run away with the whole American Trade, but even import them, with Impunity, into all the Western Coast of Britain." In subsequent letters (18 Oct. and 20 Nov. 1781), he is cheered by Creech's reports of a prosecution of Scottish booksellers who had received Irish reprints of books protected by statutory copyright. By singling out one of the largest and most persistent of the Scottish smugglers, William Anderson of Stirling, Strahan hopes that "we may be able to put a Check to this illicit Trade, which tears up our Property by the very Roots." In more pessimistic moments, however, Strahan acknowledges that British publishers and booksellers could do little to prevent the importation of illegal Irish books.

So much for the views of the leading British booksellers, expressed both privately and publicly. How accurately did they portray the Irish trade in Scottish Enlightenment books? The column of Irish first editions in table 2 provides some answers. Shown are the first Irish editions of all titles in the database that were reprinted in Dublin during the second half of the eighteenth century, along with information on the date, publisher(s), format, number of volumes, and price, all of which can be used to compare the Irish editions with the first British (original) editions. Although it is likely that the proportion of Scottish Enlightenment titles reprinted in Ireland was considerably higher than that of British publications generally, the Dublin book trade did not reprint the majority of Scottish Enlightenment books, let alone all of them. In fact, 38 percent of the original British titles listed in table 2 (136 of 360) generated Irish editions during the eighteenth century (including a few abridgements and reissues). So Murray and Strahan's assertions that British books were always reprinted in Ireland during this period cannot be taken literally.

Nevertheless, the number of Dublin reprints in table 2 is significant. Virtually all new books with strong sales potential generated at least one Irish reprint, and several were reprinted more than once. Although Murray and Strahan exaggerated, their opinion was grounded in reality. The Dublin booksellers reprinted the Scottish Enlightenment extensively, and any commercially successful Scottish Enlightenment title was almost certain to be reproduced by them.

It is worth emphasizing, to avoid any misunderstanding, that Scottish Enlightenment books constituted a small percentage of the total number of books reprinted in late eighteenth-century Dublin, just as they made up only a small fraction of the total number of books published in eighteenth-century Britain. Within the realm of learned and literary books, however, they occupied an important place. The foundation of Scottish Enlightenment reprinting in Dublin lay in the success of Scottish Enlightenment books within Britain, which helped to determine which titles were selected for reprinting elsewhere. But the substantial presence of Scots and Scottish culture in Ireland may also have been a factor. A number of the booksellers who reprinted Scottish Enlightenment titles in Dublin are known to have been Scottish immigrants, such as Robert Main and Thomas Stewart, or sons of Scottish immigrants, such as Boulter Grierson, or Ulster Scots, such as John Magee and John Smith; many more about whom less is known had Scottish surnames, such as Beatty, Burnet, Ewing, Gunne, Hay, M'Allister, M'Kenzie, Moncrieffe, Spotswood, Walker, Watson, Williamson, and Wilson. Although we do not yet know if ethnic ties encouraged Scottish Enlightenment reprinting in Ireland, it is certainly possible that they did.

In northern Ireland, the prevalence of Scottish culture was unmistakable, and at least one contemporary reported in 1774 that the people "read more in the north than in the south" and have far more bookshops.[7] A Dubliner visiting Belfast around this time noted that "the men in general are well read," though "the common people speak broad Scotch, and the better sort differ vastly from us, both in accent and language."[8] When the learned of Belfast began to build libraries, they naturally turned to Scottish authors. On 5 November 1791 the members of the Linen Hall Library in Belfast directed their secretary to purchase William Robertson's *History of Scotland* and Lord Kames's *Essays* and *Sketches of the History of Man*, as well as "the most approved History of Ireland"; two months later (2 Jan. 1792) they added, among other titles, Buffon's *Natural History* (undoubtedly referring to William Smellie's translation), Robertson's *Historical Disquisition on India*, and the *Encyclopaedia Britannica*. In 1792 they added John Gillies's *History of Ancient Greece* (3 Mar.); the transactions of the Edinburgh Philosophical Society (10 Mar.); David Hume's *History of England*, with Tobias Smollett's *Continuation* (14 Apr.); and Boswell's *Life of Johnson*, the *Transactions of the Royal Society of Edinburgh*, and Alexander Monro's *The Structure and Physiology of Fishes* (22 Sept.).[9] Some of these titles existed only in their original British editions, but most had recently been reprinted in Dublin, and it was presumably to the Dublin booksellers that the members turned for some of these purchases.

7. Quoted in Adams, *Printed Word*, 26.
8. Quoted in McClelland, "Amyas Griffith," 13.
9. Anderson, *History of the Belfast Library*.

The library's records confirm that they did so when they bought the 1791 Dublin edition of James Bruce's *Travels to Discover the Source of the Nile*, which is discussed later in this chapter.

Belfast had presses of its own, of course, but the Scottish literature they printed was mainly popular and religious. With the exception of three editions of Robert Burns's *Poems, Chiefly in the Scottish Dialect* (1787, 1789, and 1793) and reprints of John Home's plays *Douglas* (1757) and *Alonzo* (1773)—all published by the Ulster Presbyterian James Magee—the book trade in Belfast and the rest of Ulster did not reprint any of the titles in table 2.[10] On the other hand, when Dublin booksellers published reprints of Scottish books by subscription, they often attracted subscribers from the north. The subscription list in James Williams's 1772 edition of Hume's *History of England*, about which more is said later in the chapter, contains the names of two Belfast booksellers, John Hay and James Magee, in addition to at least one gentleman and two merchants from Belfast. The Belfast bookseller Hugh Warren subscribed for twelve copies of John Archer's 1791 Dublin reprint of William Julius Mickle's translation of *The Lusiad* (no. 175). It therefore seems likely that the Dublin reprinters of Scottish Enlightenment titles counted on support in the north of Ireland, and this circumstance may have encouraged them to give preference to some books by Scottish authors.

Let us look more closely at the Scottish Enlightenment titles selected for reprinting in Dublin. No significant pattern can be identified regarding genres, except that lighter forms of entertaining literature, such as popular novels and travel books, were particularly popular with the Dublin trade. In general, good books with potential for strong sales got reprinted, no matter what their subject matter. Scanning the Dublin reprints recorded in table 2, one encounters most of the best-known books by Scottish authors of the second half of the eighteenth century: David Hume's philosophical and historical works; Adam Smith's *Theory of Moral Sentiments* and *Wealth of Nations*; key works by Adam Ferguson, Hugh Blair, Thomas Reid, Lord Kames, and John Millar; the histories of William Robertson; the novels of Tobias Smollett and Henry Mackenzie; *The Life of Samuel Johnson* and other books by James Boswell; the *Encyclopaedia Britannica*; Robert Burns's *Poems*; James Macpherson's Ossianic poetry;

---

10. Anderson, *Catalogue of Early Belfast Printed Books*. A list of eighteenth-century Ulster publications is appended to Adams, *Printed Word*, 175–81. In addition, in 1766 an edition of Smollett's *Travels through France and Italy* and an edition of Fordyce's *Sermons to Young Women* were printed in Dublin for Belfast booksellers.

John Home's tragedies; most of the medical books by William Cullen. Of the 136 Scottish Enlightenment books that were reprinted in Dublin during the second half of the eighteenth century, 98, or 72 percent, were written by the core canon of fifty authors whose names are marked by asterisks in tables 1 and 2 because they were singled out for distinction by Smollett, Creech, and Alves.

There were several ways in which Dublin booksellers could determine which British books to reprint. One of the most important was to consult the leading London book review journals, the *Critical Review* and the *Monthly Review*, which were occasionally referred to in newspaper advertisements for Dublin editions. Two examples from among many involve William Wilson, who included praise from the *Critical Review* of January 1777 in his advertisement for the Dublin reprint of Robert Watson's *History of Philip II* (no. 186) in the *Hibernian Journal* (24–26 Feb.), and William Hallhead, who put an extract from the *Monthly Review*'s notice of the first volume of Hugh Blair's *Sermons* in his advertisement in *Magee's Weekly Packet* (2 Aug. 1777). Besides reviews, Dublin booksellers naturally kept themselves informed about books that were selling well in Britain. In the advertisement for his edition of Blair's *Sermons* (no. 188), Hallhead observed: "Two Editions of this valuable Work were sold off in London in the Space of Three Weeks." When Wilson was trying to attract attention to a new Dublin edition of John Moore's *View of Society and Manners in France, Switzerland, and Germany*, his advertisement in the *Dublin Evening Post* for 22 July 1780 observed that three large editions of the book had recently appeared in London. Of course, such information was intended to induce the Irish public into buying the book, but it may also have encouraged Dublin booksellers like Hallhead and Wilson to proceed with their reprint editions in the first place.

The Dublin booksellers tried to obtain copies of new books from Britain as soon as possible because convention dictated that whoever first announced an intention to reprint a book (or in a different version, whoever was first to begin to print a book) was considered the copyright owner by the Dublin trade. For this reason, regular and rapid communications with Britain were crucial. In late September 1766 William Colles announced his establishment as a Dublin bookseller with an advertisement stating that he had "fixed a regular Correspondence in London."[11] Seven years later James Williams advertised that "a parcel leaves London for him every ten Days, containing all the new Books, Plays, Pamphlets, etc. pub-

11. Quoted in Phillips, *Printing and Bookselling*, 115

lished in Britain."[12] In 1784, when struggling to obtain supremacy over Luke White as Dublin's leading publisher of (mainly Scottish) medical books, William Gilbert informed "his Friends in the Medical Faculty, and the Public in general, that he has established a regular Correspondence in Edinburgh and London, from whence he will be constantly supplied with every new Work of merit in the physical line."[13] Others traveled to London from time to time and socialized with some of the London booksellers both there and in Dublin.[14] In some cases the Dublin booksellers may have received the unbound sheets of British books "as they come from the Press," as Cadell testified before Parliament, but it is impossible, on the basis of current evidence, to know whether this happened "often," as Cadell claimed.

Nor can we know whether Dublin booksellers who were supplied with the printed sheets of British books were more often the beneficiaries of above-board arrangements among booksellers, of surreptitious dealings with workers in London or Edinburgh print shops, or of other circumstances.[15] Warren McDougall has demonstrated direct connections between the Edinburgh bookseller Charles Elliot and various booksellers in Dublin,[16] but we do not yet know if Elliot ever arranged to sell his new publications to Dublin for authorized reprinting there. Collaboration between booksellers can be inferred in the case of John Ogilvie's *Philosophical and Critical Observations on the Nature, Character, and Various Species of Composition* (no. 165), which first appeared in London in 1774 under the imprint of George Robinson and five years later was reissued in Dublin by William Hallhead with a new title page. In this instance (and there must have been others), Dublin publishing was generated by the commercial failure, rather than success, of the original British edition.

There is also some evidence of Dublin booksellers paying British

12. *Freeman's Journal*, 11–16 Nov. 1773.

13. *Dublin Evening Post*, 3 June 1784.

14. Colles mentions having just returned from London in his advertisement. [West], "Letters to My Son," 85, 133, refers to Luke White, John Archer, Patrick Byrne, John Exshaw, John Jones, William Jones, John Rice, James Moore, and other Irish booksellers socializing warmly with George Robinson, both in Dublin and at Robinson's premises in London, and John Chambers is known to have visited Robinson as well.

15. For an illustration of the complexities of a famous case, see Sale, "Sir Charles Grandison," 80–86.

16. McDougall, "Smugglers," 166–72. See also Tierney, "Dublin–London Publishing Relations," 133–39.

publishers for the opportunity to reprint—rather than merely reissue—their books. Robert Main paid fifteen guineas to William Johnston and William Strahan for the rights to Smollett's 1753 novel *The Adventures of Ferdinand Count Fatham* (no. 27), which he reprinted in Dublin in the same year in a densely printed edition that sold for slightly less than the London original.[17] In another case involving a work by Smollett, George Faulkner claimed in 1758 to have paid the unscrupulous James Rivington the substantial sum of forty guineas (£42) for the printed sheets of his popular edition of the *Complete History of England* (no. 49), only to lose his investment when Rivington reneged on the agreement. Another example involves the London bookseller John Murray, who personally traveled to Ireland and maintained close ties with Dublin booksellers such as Thomas Ewing. Ewing paid Murray fifteen guineas for a prepublication copy of the London quarto edition of John Millar's *Observations on the Distinction of Ranks* (no. 137), for the explicit purpose of producing a quick reprint in Dublin.[18] Murray then informed Millar about the existence of the Irish reprint without revealing his own complicity and even asked him to discourage its sale in Glasgow! "Authorized" Irish reprinting of this kind was not the norm, but we now know that it sometimes did occur.

Once a British book was in hand, whether bound or in loose sheets, it could be carefully examined and read by the Dublin booksellers themselves or by experts whom they consulted for that purpose. Lawrence Flin's Dublin reprint of Robert Wallace's *Characteristics of the Present State of Great Britain* (no. 52) prints the letter of one such evaluator, dated 30 March 1758 and signed R.C., as an advertisement for the book itself. The letter praises the book for its firm adherence to the principles of the Revolution of 1688 and declares it "adviseable to reprint the Book here," adding that "it is impossible so good a Work can lye upon your Hands." Despite the enthusiasm of this reader, it is unlikely that Wallace's book enjoyed much of an Irish sale, judging from the fact that it attracted little notice and was never again reprinted.

This outcome was not uncommon, but sometimes publishers were more fortunate. Almost one out of four of the 136 titles that generated Irish reprints were reprinted in Dublin on at least three separate occa-

---

17. For this episode and the one that follows, see Phillips, *Printing and Bookselling*, 113–15; Pollard, *Dictionary*, 394; and Pollard, *Dublin's Trade in Books*, 97–100.

18. Zachs, *First John Murray*, chap. 7, esp. 112. Murray later included Ewing in the imprint of several volumes of Andrew Duncan's *Medical and Philosophical Commentaries* (1773, 1775–76, 1776–77), but those were not Dublin reprints.

sions before 1801. These books, which are marked by an asterisk in the column of Irish editions in table 2, may be considered the Scottish Enlightenment best sellers in late eighteenth-century Dublin.[19] By far the most popular of them, with a total of twelve Dublin editions, was Buchan's *Domestic Medicine* (no. 115). It was followed by Smollett's *Roderick Random* (no. 12) with nine Dublin editions, and then by two European travel books with eight editions each: Patrick Brydone's *A Tour through Sicily and Malta* (no. 150) and John Moore's *A View of Society and Manners in France, Switzerland, and Germany* (no. 201). Then came Robertson's *History of Charles V* (no. 119) and Smollett's *Peregrine Pickle* (no. 16) and *Humphry Clinker* (no. 140), with seven each. Of course, books published toward the end of the century had less time to be reprinted three or more times during the designated period, and perhaps for that reason none of the Dublin editions that are marked as best sellers in table 2 was initially published in Britain after 1789.

With few exceptions, these Dublin best sellers were written by men who were among the fifty notable Scottish authors cited by Smollett, Creech, and Alves. Indeed, more than half of the 31 Dublin best sellers were written or edited by just five authors: Hugh Blair (2 titles), Henry Mackenzie (5), John Moore (3), William Robertson (3), and Tobias Smollett (5). Anonymous books were at a disadvantage unless they were novels by writers like Smollett and Mackenzie, whose works were widely known even though their names were not on their title pages. Robert Wallace had published his *Characteristics* anonymously in London, and the previously quoted Irish evaluator could only say that "the Author, whoever he be, is a Friend to Mankind." Conversely, many Scottish authors acquired international reputations that helped both booksellers and the reading public in Ireland to make decisions about which books to reprint, purchase, and read.

The Irish press contributed to this process in various ways. The book-

19. In counting numbers of reprints for this purpose, we must be careful to exclude instances when an apparently new Dublin edition was actually the previous Dublin edition, reissued with a new title page. Examples include the 1790 (J. Jones) edition of John Millar's *Historical View of the English Government* (no. 271) and the 1796 (Gilbert) edition of Benjamin Bell's *Treatise on Gonorrhoea Virulenta* (no. 312). In two instances, Macpherson's *Fingal* (two 1763 Dublin editions with same pagination) and Cullen's *Lectures on the Materia Medica* (two 1781 editions with the same pagination), I have been unable to determine if the editions in question were reissues of this kind.

sellers' advertisements that regularly appeared in the Dublin newspapers sometimes editorialized about the authors and books they were promoting. Occasionally they personalized books and authors by linking them with a particular segment of the population or group of readers. William Wilson's advertisement for Gilbert Stuart's *View of Society in Europe* (no. 195) in the *Dublin Evening Post* for 22 October 1778 contains a paragraph intended to show the relevance of Stuart's book for Irish political circumstances in the age of the American Revolution and the patriotic Irish Volunteer movement. It begins: "This ingenious Author, hath not only plainly delineated the Progress of Society, but ably defended the Rights of its Individuals, against the Encroachments of assuming Tyranny." In the previous year, an advertisement in the *Hibernian Journal* for the Dublin reprint of Henry Mackenzie's new novel *Julia de Roubigné* (no. 183) identified its intended audience in its heading: "To the Ladies: A NEW NOVEL. By the admired author of the Man of Feeling; the Man of the World; etc." (2–4 June 1777). Although Mackenzie was not identified by name, in keeping with standard convention among many novelists of the period (as discussed in chapter 2), the naming of his earlier sentimental novels in the advertisement had the effect of connecting the author with a fixed body of work and alerting female readers to the likelihood that this new novel would affect them in a familiar and desirable way.

Dublin periodicals frequently contained biographical stories about Scottish authors. When James Boswell visited Ireland in the spring of 1769 to promote the Corsican cause and his book on that subject, the Dublin press covered his every move.[20] The *Hibernian Magazine* published biographical pieces and anecdotes about William Robertson (June 1772), Tobias Smollett (June 1775), David Hume (April and July 1777; 1778 appendix; July 1779; June 1788), Francis Hutcheson (1778 appendix; November 1788), James Beattie (February 1782), Gilbert Stuart (December 1786), James Boswell (December 1785), Robert Burns (1796), Lord Kames (February 1796), James Macpherson (April 1796), and Adam Smith (March and April 1797). The occasion for such items could be a recent death (e.g., Hume, Stuart, Burns, and Macpherson), or a new book, edition, or biography, such as Boswell's *Journal of a Tour to the Hebrides with Samuel Johnson* in 1785. There were also occasional critical pieces, such as a "Comparison of Hume and Robertson, as Historians," which appeared in the *Hibernian Magazine* for June 1799. An article in the April 1781 issue of *Exshaw's*

20. Cole, *Irish Booksellers*, 94–99.

Magazine took issue with Samuel Johnson's negative judgment of modern historical writing by naming "Hume, Robertson, and Gibbon" as modern authors of outstanding historical works.[21]

A steady stream of book reviews and excerpts from new publications, sometimes containing editorial content, also helped to transform the leading authors of the Scottish Enlightenment into household names in late eighteenth-century Ireland. The *Hibernian Magazine* introduced a selection from *Domestic Medicine* with a favorable allusion to its author, "the able and ingenious Dr. Buchan" (December 1772). A July 1771 advertisement in the *Dublin Mercury* for the first Irish reprint of Smollett's *Humphry Clinker* informed readers about the "justly established" reputation of the author, complimented his special skills as a novelist, and praised this particular work, and especially "that part of it that describes the Scotch Nation, . . . at once calculated to entertain the most gay and to give the serious a very useful fund of information."[22] A brief notice of the second part of William Russell's *History of Modern Europe* (recently reprinted by John Exshaw) in the July 1784 number of *Town and Country Magazine, or, Irish Miscellany* identified the author as "a gentleman well known to the literary world, and whose merit, by this publication, is still more firmly established."

Some newspapers also printed biographical articles and excerpts, along with other articles showing interest in the progress and institutional framework of Scottish literature and learning. Immediately after Adam Smith's death in July 1790, the *Dublin Chronicle* published a story about his being kidnapped by gypsies as a child (29 July 1790); this was followed by "Anecdotes of the Late Adam Smith" (14 Aug. 1790) and an extract from the *Wealth of Nations* (19 Aug. 1790). The next month the *Chronicle* ran a human-interest story on "Burns, the Scottish Poet" (7 Sept. 1790). The paper followed the construction of the new Edinburgh University buildings with careful attention (5 and 28 Oct. 1790, 8 Oct. 1791). The 3 November 1791 issue included "Scots Literary News," containing the latest gossip about what the Scottish literati were writing, with numbered paragraphs on publications rumored to be coming from the "Royal Society of Antiquaries in Scotland," the Royal Society of Edinburgh, James Hutton, William Cullen, Lord Monboddo, Dugald Stewart, and James Beattie. Although most of the material in these Irish newspapers and

21. Ibid., 141.

22. Quoted by Cole, ibid., 78. The Dublin edition was probably a publication of the Company of Booksellers.

magazines was probably lifted from the London and Edinburgh press, which regularly printed accounts of the Scottish literati's latest writing projects,[23] the point being made here relates not to the authors or the sources of these pieces but to the tendency of the Irish periodical press to print them, apparently with a view toward humanizing and popularizing Scottish authors.

Cadell testified that Dublin editions appeared "soon" after the British originals, and Strahan wrote privately that Dublin reprinting occurred "immediately." The evidence in table 2 lends strong support to their statements. The imprint year in the title page of the first Dublin edition of books that generated Irish reprints is usually identical to that of the original British edition; in one case, John Home's tragedy *Alfred* (no. 193), the Dublin imprint year actually precedes the London one, presumably because the play (first produced in January 1778) was published at the end of the year and postdated in London but not in Dublin. Judging from the imprints, more than three-quarters of the Dublin reprints in table 2, and nearly all the books I have designated as Dublin best sellers, appeared within one year after the first British edition, and more than 90 percent appeared within four years of the British original. Clearly, the Dublin reprint trade was geared for speed,[24] and this circumstance raised the level of anxiety experienced by the publishers of new books in Britain.

On the relatively rare occasions when Dublin reprints of Scottish Enlightenment books did not occur until four or more years after the British original, there was usually a special reason for delay. The Dublin edition of Francis Home's *Experiments on Bleaching* (no. 41) appeared fifteen years after the British edition, and the publisher, Thomas Ewing, made a point of remarking in his publication catalogue that his edition contained three additional essays "not to be found in any English or Scotch Edition of that Book."[25] David Hume's *Essays and Treatises on Several Subjects* (no. 25) was not reprinted in Dublin until the late 1770s, at a time when controversy in the aftermath of Hume's death probably encouraged the publisher, James Williams, to produce his two-volume octavo edition. The first Dublin reprint of Adam Smith's *Theory of Moral Sentiments* (no. 59) occurred eighteen years after the appearance of the original edition in London, as a result of the popularity of Smith's next book, the *Wealth of Nations* (no. 177).

23. See, for example, "Scottish Literary News" in the *Edinburgh Advertiser*, 23–26 Nov. 1773; and the *London Chronicle*, 30 Nov–2 Dec. 1790.

24. Phillips, *Printing and Bookselling*, 274–75.

25. [Ewing], *Select Catalogue of Books*, 31.

On this occasion the publishers of the Dublin edition placed a conspicuous advertisement in the *Hibernian Journal* (21–23 Apr. 1777) that addressed the publicity for the *Theory of Moral Sentiments* to "the Admirers of the *Writings* of Dr. SMITH, the celebrated Author of 'An Enquiry into the Nature and Causes of the WEALTH OF NATIONS.'"[26]

Although Scottish authors generally had little to do with Dublin reprints of their books, there are some intriguing hints to the contrary. As he was putting out the first volume of his *History of England* in the autumn of 1754, Hume remarked to a Scottish friend: "We shall also make a Dublin Edition; and it were a Pity to put the Irish farther wrong than they are already" (*LDH*, 1:210). It is not known whether Hume was referring to the Dublin reprint published by John Smith in 1754 (no. 33), whether he was using the word "we" to encompass his Edinburgh publishers, Hamilton & Balfour, or whether he meant to put fresh corrections and revisions in the Dublin edition, as he was then preparing to do for a French translation. In August 1785 Boswell sent Thomas Barnard, bishop of Killaloe, the printed sheets of his *Journal of a Tour to the Hebrides* as they came from the press in London, apparently intending him to arrange publication in Ireland. But Barnard seems to have misunderstood his friend's wishes.[27] In November, however, Boswell successfully arranged for Barnard to soften an anecdote about Alexander Fraser Tytler by replacing a cancel page in remaining copies of the Dublin edition published by Luke White and others.[28] Besides Barnard, Boswell relied on the Irish antiquary Joseph Cooper Walker, who functioned as an intermediary between some British authors and the Dublin book trade at this time.[29] Irish authors were

26. Sher, "Early Editions of Adam Smith's Books," 25–26.

27. Boswell to Barnard, 24 Aug. 1785: "pray do not let it get into the hands of any printer or publisher *till you have the whole*" (my emphasis); Barnard replied on 15 October as if Boswell had not written the last five words. Boswell, *Correspondence with Certain Members of The Club*, 211, 216.

28. Boswell to Barnard, 8 Nov. 1785, ibid., 221; Joseph Cooper Walker to Boswell, 31 Dec. 1785, ibid., 221n2; and Boswell Papers, Yale University, C 3055.

29. On 26 July 1785 Walker advised Boswell to "make a bargain with the Dublin booksellers" in order to prevent them from keeping all the profits from the Irish edition, and he repeated the advice on 20 August. Yet judging from the matter-of-fact way in which Walker reported the publication (on 12 November) of the Dublin edition in a letter to Boswell of 13 November, it does not appear that Boswell followed his advice (Boswell, *Correspondence and Other Papers*, 93–95, 100). On 20 December Boswell told Walker that if "the Irish booksellers should have occasion to reprint my book, it will be obliging if you will suggest that the reprint should be made from my second

sometimes capable of exerting direct influence on Dublin reprinters, even to the point, in one extraordinary case involving the professor of medicine at Trinity College Dublin, David MacBride, of postponing a Dublin reprint edition in conformity with the author's wishes.[30] I have not, however, been able to discover any firm evidence of Scottish Enlightenment authors being directly and decisively involved with the reprinting of their works in Ireland.

Strahan believed that the Dublin booksellers reprinted British books "in an inferior Size, and at a low Price." By and large, he was right. More than three-quarters of the Irish reprints represented in table 2 were printed in Dublin in a smaller (and therefore cheaper) format than the British original. In the great majority of these cases, the size of the format was reduced by one (i.e., from quarto to octavo, or from octavo to duodecimo) without affecting the number of volumes, so that, for example, an expensive two-volume British quarto became a less costly two-volume Irish octavo, or a one-volume octavo became a one-volume duodecimo. In several cases, reducing the format resulted in the Irish reprint having more volumes, examples being Adam Smith's *Wealth of Nations* (no. 177) and Hugh Blair's *Lectures on Rhetoric and Belles Lettres* (no. 230), which went from two-volume quartos in London to three-volume octavos in Dublin (Smith's book was also published in two octavo volumes). Less frequently, the Irish reprinters managed to squeeze the original text into a smaller format and *fewer* volumes. In a handful of instances, Dublin reprint editions were two format sizes smaller than the original, sometimes even in the same number of volumes. Thus, James Macpherson's Ossianic

---

and more perfect edition" (quoted in Cole, *Irish Booksellers*, 101–2). But this advice was moot because a second edition was never published in Dublin.

See also Charlotte Smith to Thomas Cadell, 28 Sept. 1790, in Taylor, "The Evils I was born to bear," 312–18: "Mr [Joseph Cooper] Walker says, that by sending a copy of any new Work to Dublin before it is printed here [i.e., in London], A Bookseller there will give me a Sum of money for it, which mode he wishes me to adopt."

30. In 1772 MacBride had his *Methodical Introduction to the Theory and Practice of Physic* published in quarto by Strahan and Cadell in London, in collaboration with Kincaid & Creech and Balfour in Edinburgh, and certain Dublin booksellers promptly advertised their intention of reprinting it. When MacBride asked them not to do so, however, they consented "out of deference to him." See the "Advertisement from the Publisher" that is prefixed to the two-volume "enlarged and corrected" (and retitled) octavo edition that William Watson finally published in Dublin in 1777 with the author's approval. On Edmund Burke's authorizing London and Dublin editions of one of his works, see Cole, *Irish Booksellers*, 183.

epics *Fingal* and *Temora* (nos. 71 and 83), which first appeared in Britain as quartos, printed in large type with generous spacing, were each immediately reprinted in Dublin as cheap duodecimos. When *Fingal* was noticed in the *Dublin Magazine* in January 1762, the mere presentation of the publishing facts at the head of the review drew readers' attention to the large price differential between the London and Dublin editions: "*Fingal* London 4to 12s.; reprinted in Dublin 12mo 2s.8d.½" (49–50).

Even when Dublin reprinters maintained the same format as the British original, they could save pages, and therefore money, by putting more words on the page. In a half-dozen instances shown in table 2, the Dublin trade used the same format as the British edition being reprinted but reduced the number of volumes. The second edition of Robert Henry's *History of Great Britain* (no. 144) is one example. When Patrick Byrne and John Jones reprinted this book in 1789 (with an additional volume added in 1794 to complete the set, under the imprint of Byrne and James Moore), they retained the octavo format of the second London edition (1788–95) but halved the number of volumes by putting more words on the page and making their volumes much thicker, and they omitted the portrait of the author that served as the frontispiece of the London edition. In this way, they reduced the number of volumes from twelve to six and the retail price by up to a third (from £3.10s. to about £2.6s., bound) while retaining the same textual content and format. In other cases, Dublin editions saved significant amounts of paper by reprinting books in the same format and with the same number of volumes as the British original, but with fewer pages. For example, the Dublin octavo reprint of Adam Smith's *Theory of Moral Sentiments* (no. 59) was 52 pages, or 11 percent, shorter than the latest London octavo, while the Dublin octavo reprint of John Gillies's *View of the Reign of Frederick II* (no. 282) reduced the 500-page British octavo by more than 80 pages, or 17 percent.

The process of lowering the cost of books by reducing formats or decreasing the number of pages was closely related to the speed of reprinting. Dublin booksellers knew that the publication of a new book in Britain normally restricted its publisher's actions until most copies of the first edition were sold. At that point, the British publisher might let the book die or else reprint it, either in the same format as the first edition or in a smaller format. Reprinting in a smaller, octavo format was the standard option with marketable titles originally published in quarto, whereas books originally published in octavo were more likely to continue in the octavo format in later British editions. Particularly in the case of expensive British quartos, therefore, Dublin booksellers had to move quickly in order to capitalize on the enormous price disparity between a British quarto and an Irish octavo. Once an authorized British octavo edition appeared in print, the Irish advantage would be greatly reduced. And in the absence of a substantial price advantage, other factors, including the perception of reliability, authenticity, status, and (depending on the date and the market) legality, were likely to have an adverse effect on the sales of Dublin editions relative to British ones. Thus, when Luke White priced his 1787, five-volume Dublin reprint of Smollett's continuation of Hume's *History of England* (no. 49) at £1.12s.6d., or 7s.6d. higher than the "original" (that is, the posthumously revised and retitled) edition that Cadell and Baldwin had published in London in 1785, in the same number of volumes and the same octavo format, he learned that the usual inclination of Irish library-owners to buy Irish books whenever possible did not apply in this case.[31] Only a Dublin edition purporting to be superior in quality to an otherwise comparable London edition could possibly compete at an equal or slightly higher price.

"Production costs were certainly lower in Dublin," Mary Pollard observed in her important study of 1989, *Dublin's Trade in Books*, "but without the sort of printing archive that exists for the London trade it is impossible to discover by how much they fell below London costs, and indeed, what they actually were."[32] Fortunately, the ledgers of the Dublin printer Daniel Graisberry that are now housed at Trinity College Dublin provide the sort of evidence that Pollard wished to have.[33] In covering the period 1777–85, one of Graisberry's extant ledgers records many books printed for the prominent Dublin bookseller James Williams and his sometime partner Richard Moncrieffe. Williams frequently reprinted the same books that were being printed in London by William Strahan, whose printing ledgers have also survived. Strahan and Graisberry used the same system of costing, which was standard in the eighteenth century: for each printing job, a unit charge was determined on the basis of the number of copies printed and the format and type(s) used, and the unit charge was then multiplied by the number of sheets of paper required for each copy of the book in order to arrive at the total printing charge.[34] Since unit charges had to be high enough to cover the price of labor and other local costs, such as type, they can be used to obtain a rough com-

---

31. Cole, *Irish Booksellers*, 131–32.

32. Pollard, *Dublin's Trade in Books*, 110.

33. Kinane and Benson, "Graisberry Ledgers," 139–50.

34. Hernlund, "William Strahan's Ledgers," 89–111.

parison of the overall expense of printing (exclusive of the cost of paper) in London and Dublin.

In September 1777 Strahan printed 1,000 copies of a two-volume octavo edition of Hume's *Essays and Treatises on Several Subjects* (no. 25), using pica type with long primer notes. He needed 69½ sheets of paper for each copy and set a unit price of £1.10s., for a total printing charge of £104.5s (SA 48815, fol. 21). Graisberry reprinted the work in two octavo volumes for James Williams in March 1779. He used an almost identical amount of paper (71½ sheets) for the main body of the work, also printed in pica type with long primer notes. Graisberry's unit charge was six shillings less than Strahan's—£1.4s. instead of £1.10s.—and his base printing charge was therefore only £85.16s. instead of £104.5s. Graisberry did add some extra charges for altering margins and for printing an additional 6½ sheets of paper in large pica, bringing his total printing charge to £91.13s. But the edition he was printing for Williams was 500 copies larger than the one printed by Strahan, and the unit charge normally rose several shillings under those circumstances. Thus, Graisberry was able to print 1,500 copies that closely resembled the British original in length, format, and typeface for twelve guineas less than Strahan could print 1,000 copies of the same work.

Hume's *Essays and Treatises* provides some indication of the economic advantage enjoyed by Dublin booksellers when they engaged in "copycat" reprints. Such cases prove that labor and other printing costs were lower in Dublin than in London, but they do not reveal a cost differential that was great enough to result in huge differences in retail prices. In fact, Williams charged more for his edition of *Essays and Treatises* than Strahan and Cadell charged for the London edition (thirteen shillings as opposed to twelve). But dramatic disparities in printing costs occurred when an expensive British quarto edition was reprinted in Dublin in octavo format. An example from the Strahan and Graisberry ledgers is Adam Ferguson's *Progress and Termination of the Roman Republic* (no. 232). It was originally printed by Strahan in February 1783 in three quarto volumes, requiring 202 sheets of paper per set; for a print run of 1,500 copies, the unit price was £1.7s., and the total printing cost was therefore £272.14s., which rose to £304.19s. when charges for "Extraordinary Corrections" were added (SA 48815, fol. 78). The book was published in London and Edinburgh in March 1783 at a retail price of £2.12s.6d. in boards. The Dubliners wasted little time. Graisberry's ledgers reveal that on 7 June 1783 the printing of 1,000 copies of the second volume of Ferguson's work was charged to the account of Richard Moncrieffe, who was apparently representing the group of thirteen Dublin booksellers (all members of the Company of Booksellers, as discussed more fully later in the chapter) whose three-volume octavo edition also bore a 1783 imprint.[35] Graisberry charged £42.7s. for the job, based on 38½ sheets of paper printed with pica typeface and side and bottom notes, at a unit price of just £1.2s. If the two other volumes were printed at the same rate (perhaps simultaneously by other Dublin printers, in order to speed production), then printing this octavo edition of 1,000 copies cost its Irish publishing partners about 42 percent as much as the British publishers had to pay for printing a quarto edition of 1,500 copies—£128 as against £305. That difference concerns only printing charges. The difference in the cost of paper would also have been significant, since the Dublin octavo edition used cheaper paper and approximately 40 percent less of it (i.e., fewer than 120 sheets, as against 202 sheets, per three-volume set). Not surprisingly, the Dublin three-volume octavo retailed for close to 60 percent less than the London three-volume quarto: £1.2s.9d. instead of £2.12s.6d.

A comparison of retail prices for British and Irish books listed in table 2 confirms that these kinds of price differentials were not uncommon when the Dublin reprinters downsized a London quarto, even when the process required an additional volume. Adam Smith's *Wealth of Nations* (no. 177) retailed for £1.16s. in boards or £2.2s. bound as a two-volume London quarto, but less than half as much as a three-volume Dublin octavo priced at 19s.6d bound. The original two-volume quarto edition of Hugh Blair's *Lectures on Rhetoric and Belles Lettres* (no. 230) sold in Britain for £2.12s.6d. in boards, but the Dublin three-volume octavo was once again only 19s.6d. bound, a reduction of more than 65 percent. Thomas Reid's *Essays on the Intellectual Powers of Man* (no. 255) retailed in Britain for £1.8s. bound as a single large quarto volume; the Dublin reprint of 1786 was a two-volume octavo set that sold for less than half that amount (13s. bound). Adam Ferguson's *Essay on the History of Civil Society* (no. 99) was reprinted in Dublin as a bound octavo that cost 5s.5d., as against 15s. bound for the London quarto—a savings of more than 60 percent.

Once these Dublin octavos appeared, the domestic Irish market for the British quarto editions of these books must have contracted. Octavo editions of British quartos also gave the Dublin booksellers a huge advantage in the American trade, especially after the conclusion of the American Revolutionary War. But were Irish reprints like these also exported

35. The other publishers were Price, Whitestone, Colles, Jenkin, Walker, Exshaw, Beatty, White, Burton, Byrne, Cash, and Sleater, Jr.

to Britain with "Impunity," as Strahan related to Creech in 1781? Was there in fact "a great clandestine Importation of Books from Ireland into this Country," as Cadell and his associates testified before Parliament?

For many years, few questioned such pronouncements. In *Dublin's Trade in Books*, however, Pollard argued that the charges were not supported by the existing evidence, including the evidence of book seizures by the British authorities.[36] Pollard was correct on the basis of available sources, but her challenge had the effect of stimulating scholarship that has produced a considerable amount of evidence in support of the British booksellers' claims. In an earlier chapter, we saw that the Edinburgh bookseller John Bell angrily informed Thomas Cadell in London that John Balfour was selling an Irish reprint of Adam Ferguson's *Essay on the History of Civil Society*—meaning the octavo edition that Boulter Grierson published in Dublin in 1767. Although Bell's charge cannot be substantiated, it is certainly feasible, now that we have seen the extent of the price differential between the London quarto and the Dublin octavo editions of this book. Warren McDougall has discovered evidence of Irish imports being intercepted by Scottish authorities, both at sea and on land. For example, in August 1776 Scottish customs officials stopped a ship from Dublin carrying fourteen sets of a three-volume octavo edition of Smith's *Wealth of Nations* in unbound sheets, along with twenty-one unbound sets of an octavo edition of the first volume of Gibbon's *Decline and Fall of the Roman Empire*. And in 1786 books from the Dublin bookseller Luke White were seized at Greenock, near Glasgow, including his octavo reprint of Reid's *Essays on the Intellectual Powers*.[37]

These are all examples of Irish octavos being smuggled into Scotland at a time when the only British editions of the books in question were expensive quartos. It was the extreme vulnerability of the British publishers during such periods that accounts for their concern, sometimes bordering on panic, about Irish smuggling when a quarto was the only edition in print. In June 1777, the month after they copublished Robertson's *History of America* (no. 185) in quarto, Balfour, Strahan, and Cadell prevailed on the Board of Customs Commissioners in Scotland to circulate an order to the nine western Scottish ports, informing them of the publishers' apprehensions "that a pirated edition of the said book will soon be smuggled

36. Pollard, *Dublin's Trade in Books*, 74–87.

37. McDougall, "Smugglers," 161 (Smith and Gibbon), 170 (Reid). Cf. Feather, "Country Trade in Books," 170, which identifies Preston as "a favourite port of entry for Irish books" in England.

from Ireland contrary to law" and requesting their vigilance.[38] Two weeks later Robert Watson informed Strahan that an Irish edition of his *History of Philip II* (no. 186) "has found its way both into England and the west of Scotland."[39] Watson wondered if advertising the forthcoming second edition of his book, with "corrections and additions," would be helpful "in checking the sale" of the Irish work; the second British edition would not appear until the end of the year, however, and it would be another quarto because strong sales of the first edition had not yet exhausted that lucrative market. Until the appearance of the three-volume, eighteen-shilling British octavo edition in the latter part of 1778, the Dublin two-volume octavo edition, which was sold in Britain for "12 or 14" shillings according to Watson, had a huge price advantage over the London quarto, which cost at least three times more.

Once British publishers produced their own moderately priced octavo editions, as they did in all the cases just mentioned except for Reid's *Essays*, the price difference between Dublin and London octavos was usually no longer high enough to justify the risk of illegal importation. Smuggling of Irish editions continued, however, under two sorts of circumstances. First, local, temporary demand sometimes came into play, as in the following example. In spring 1783 Charles Elliot ordered copies of a Dublin edition of William Cullen's *Lectures on Materia Medica* (no. 145). Although the Irish edition was smaller and cheaper than the British one, its main appeal in this case was simply that it was available, whereas the British edition was either out of print or out of stock at a time when Edinburgh medical students were about to require it as a class text.[40] Second, high-volume sales of popular books could sometimes compensate for high profit margins and create an incentive for smuggling. Thus, in July 1784 more than 400 Irish copies of the first two volumes of Hugh Blair's *Sermons* (no. 188), mostly half bound, were seized at Greenock, bearing a false London imprint (165). Earlier in the 1780s authorities caught Robert Morison & Son of Perth with Irish octavo editions of William Robertson's histories of Scotland, Charles V, and America, even though by this time authorized, moderately priced octavo editions of all those titles were widely available in Britain. In the course of defending Morison & Son in court, James Boswell remarked on "the open manner in which Irish books are bought and sold in this Country" (177).

38. Quoted in McDougall, "Smugglers," 157; Pollard, *Dublin's Trade in Books*, 77.

39. Watson to Strahan, 3 July 1777, HL, MS Hyde 77, 6.91.

40. McDougall, "Smugglers," 168.

McDougall has produced evidence of other Irish editions of Scottish Enlightenment titles being smuggled into Britain, including John Moore's *View of Society and Manners in France, Switzerland, and Germany* and David Hume's *History of England.* Regardless of format, nearly all the illegal imports were reprints of best sellers. Since seizures of smuggled Irish books seem to have been haphazard rather than systematic, it is probably safe to assume that the known instances represent a small proportion of the illicit trade in Dublin reprints of books by Scottish authors. Despite some convictions, and the occasional payment of reward money to diligent customs officials by concerned British publishers, Strahan was probably correct when he acknowledged to Creech that ultimately little could be done to stop illegal imports from Ireland. There were too many ships, ports, loopholes, and tricks, and too few customs inspectors (who were too poorly motivated and too badly paid), to make much of an impact. Once pirated books with false London imprints got into general circulation, they were extremely difficult to detect.[41] But some books with straightforward Dublin imprints also seem to have circulated in Scotland, and probably also in parts of England.

Even when smugglers were caught red-handed, prosecution was difficult and costly, with relatively light penalties, and exposure of a Scottish bookseller as an importer and seller of illegal Irish books carried only a slight stigma. McDougall quotes the Edinburgh bookseller Charles Elliot telling his Dublin counterpart Luke White in 1786, in regard to the importation of illegal Irish books: "It is, do you know, a kind of affront to have such detected." He also observes that Elliot seemed relatively calm about a seizure of illegal Irish books intended for him, apparently accepting it as little more than a temporary inconvenience that was to be expected from time to time.[42] According to the Scottish Book Trade Index, Elliot's collaborator in the book-smuggling business, William Anderson, served six terms as lord provost of Stirling.

If all this demonstrates that the Dublin booksellers did export their

41. When testifying before Parliament in March 1774, the London bookseller William Johnston, the original publisher of Smollett's *Humphry Clinker* (1771), described a pirated edition of that work with his name on it, "so that the original and copy could not be distinguished one from the other" (*EEC,* 23 Mar. 1774). This particular piracy had been printed in Edinburgh, and Johnston successfully prosecuted those behind it (see McDougall, "Smugglers," 173), but it is likely that other, undetectable facsimile editions of best sellers were sometimes produced in Ireland and smuggled into Britain.

42. McDougall, "Smugglers," 170–71.

Scottish Enlightenment reprints to Britain and that Pollard may have erred in asserting that smuggling of Irish reprints into Britain "did not exist on a very large scale,"[43] the argument should not be overstated. Existing evidence does not refute Pollard's chief point: "piracy" apparently accounted for a relatively small proportion of the activity of the Dublin reprinting industry during the second half of the eighteenth century. The focus of that trade was usually on the home market, and later also on exports to the Americas. Recent research on the large Irish audience for French books indirectly supports the former point, for if Ireland could sustain a sizable domestic trade in French Enlightenment books, including some works imported in their original language and others printed in Ireland,[44] they could surely sustain a domestic trade in English-language books as well. The many Dublin newspapers carrying booksellers' advertisements for Scottish Enlightenment books and the many stories about Scottish authors in Dublin newspapers and periodicals, as well as excerpts from and reviews of their works, suggest a thriving domestic market for the Scottish Enlightenment in Ireland. As for the Irish connection with America, Cole has discussed it in considerable detail, if only in regard to a handful of authors, and has shown that it involved not only the movement of books printed in Ireland but also the movement of Irish booksellers, who flocked to Philadelphia and other American towns in large numbers, especially after the Irish paper duty of 1795, the failure of the 1798 Irish political uprising, and the turn-of-the-century union with Britain broke the will of many radical Irish booksellers and facilitated the extension of British copyright law to Ireland (as of 2 July 1801), signaling the end of the great age of Irish reprinting.[45]

IN THE COMPANY OF DUBLIN BOOKSELLERS

The booksellers who reprinted the Scottish Enlightenment in Dublin during the second half of the eighteenth century are difficult to penetrate. Unlike their brethren in London and Edinburgh, they have left us few business records and scarcely any private correspondence, and it is difficult to identify a small number of firms that constituted the core of the Dublin trade. Almost half of the dozens of individuals who participated

43. Pollard, *Dublin's Trade in Books*, 87.

44. Kennedy, *French Books;* Kennedy, "Readership in French," 3–20; Kennedy and Sheridan, "Trade in French Books," 173–96.

45. Cole, *Irish Booksellers*, esp. chaps. 3 and 8.

in the publication of the Dublin first editions that appear in table 2 are named in only one or two imprints. The Dublin book trade tended to band together in large groups as copublishers of the books they reprinted, sometimes more than forty strong. Collaborative publishing on this scale reduced risk, though it also reduced the potential for profit, especially when reprinting small, cheap books. John Home's play *The Siege of Aquileia* (no. 63), which probably sold for the standard Irish price of just 6½d. per play, was reprinted in 1760 by a group of eight Dublin booksellers, none of whom could have earned much from it, even if the edition were unusually large and every copy sold. It is easy to see how these practices would have created the impression among elite British publishers like Thomas Cadell that the Dublin trade was cheap, quick, mercenary, and despicable.

Suppose, however, that we look at the matter differently. Table 6 shows the publishing output of the twenty-five Dublin firms whose names appear in at least ten different first-edition Dublin reprints of Scottish Enlightenment books, along with their addresses in the randomly chosen year 1786 (the publishers in these firms appear in boldface in table 2). These were relatively stable and substantial firms by Dublin standards. As the table shows, they tended to congregate in shopping streets near Trinity College: Grafton Street (2), College Green (3), Great George's Street (1), and above all Dame Street (10), or else just across the Liffey from the northern end of Dame Street, in and around Capel Street (4), including the north ends of Great Strand (1) and Abbey (1) streets.[46] The only bookseller in the table who does not fit this geographical pattern is Patrick Wogan, located well up the river on Old Bridge. Two others, James Hoey, Jr., and William Jones, were not in business in 1786, but Jane Hoey was then still trading at her husband's shop at 19 Parliament Street, near Dame Street, and Jones would commence bookselling in 1789 at 86 Dame Street, after buying out Luke White. Furthermore, of the first ten booksellers listed in table 6, six were located on Dame Street in 1786, and the other four on either College Green or Grafton Street.

All this points to a well-established, geographically focused trade. To stroll from Trinity College down College Green and its extension, Dame Street, must have been a book lover's delight in the second half of the eighteenth century. Bookshops were everywhere. Stocks numbered in the thousands and consisted of books that were both imported from Britain

46. Unless otherwise noted, addresses and other biographical details about the Dublin booksellers discussed in this section are drawn from Pollard, *Dictionary*.

and the Continent and, more and more commonly, printed in Dublin itself. Binders, printers, and later engravers were also part of the picture,
even though the division of labor among different occupations within the
book trade was not always as much in evidence here as elsewhere. Mention has already been made of local newspapers with book advertisements
and magazines with coverage of the republic of letters; it may now be
added that these periodicals were usually owned and edited by leading
booksellers, such as the Exshaws, who published *Exshaw's Magazine* from
1741 to 1794; James Potts and, in particular, Thomas Walker, who were
responsible for the *Hibernian Magazine* from 1771 to 1812; the Faulkners,
who produced the *Dublin Journal* for decades; James Hoey, Jr., who ran the
Dublin Mercury during the late 1760s and 1770s; and William Sleater, Jr.,
and subsequently Patrick Byrne, who owned the *Dublin Chronicle* in the
1780s and early 1790s. A supporting relationship existed between such
periodicals and the books that were reprinted by their operators: newspapers and magazines were needed to advertise, review, and promote the
reprints that the Dublin booksellers published.[47] There were also increasingly comprehensive sale catalogues, book auctions both for the trade and
for the public, and circulating libraries and literary lounges for reading
without necessarily buying.[48]

In short, Dublin was a thriving center of print culture, operating on a
scale that dwarfed all English-speaking cities except London. Once this
point is fully understood, physically as well as conceptually, it becomes
even more difficult to accept the traditional stereotype of the Dublin trade
as fundamentally piratical, even if its members sometimes shipped protected books to Britain. But the same realization also throws into relief
the great paradox, or Achilles Heel, of Dublin book culture, to which we
shall return: the town had an abundant supply of bookmakers and booksellers, and evidently no shortage of book buyers and book readers, but
it lacked a substantial body of native book-writers; instead it relied on
Britain (including Irish writers who had emigrated there), and especially
Scotland, for its most prestigious and popular Enlightenment authors and
texts.

Like London, but unlike Edinburgh, the Dublin book trade was organized into a guild, albeit an unusually diverse and frequently ineffective one called the Guild of St. Luke the Evangelist, which included

47. Cole, *Irish Booksellers*, 9–10, 197–98.
48. Phillips, *Printing and Bookselling*, esp. chap. 3.

painters and cutlers as well as "stationers"—the general term that encompassed many different occupations within the English and Irish book trades. Dublin booksellers came from varied backgrounds, ranging from Northern Irish to Scottish to English and Huguenot, but during the late eighteenth century a high percentage seem to have been native Dubliners, whatever their ancestry. Although the great majority were Protestants, Roman Catholics were allowed membership in the guild as quarter brothers, and in 1793 several of them became full brothers according to the guild (though their status was not accepted by the city government). Catholic booksellers mixed imperceptibly with Protestant members of the trade in the publishing of polite and scholarly literature, and it is significant that the person whose name appears in more Dublin first editions of Scottish Enlightenment titles than any other, Patrick Byrne, came from their ranks, as did at least three other Dublin booksellers who were active enough to be represented in table 6: James Hoey, Jr., James Moore, and Patrick Wogan.[49]

It has sometimes been observed that the Dublin book trade supported few partnerships and that the ones that did occur were invariably short-lived. Yet the Dublin trade had an unusually strong tradition of survival among individual firms across generations. Often such continuity was achieved by means of succession from father to son, as in the examples of Peter and William Wilson, John Exshaw, Sr. and Jr., William Sleater, Sr. and Jr., William Watson, Sr. and Jr., and William and Henry Whitestone. In several instances when sons were unavailable, widows attempted to continue their husbands' businesses. Sometimes they did not last long. Anne Colles tried to sustain her husband William's business at 17 Dame Street after his death in May 1790 and continued his four-volume edition of Hugh Blair's *Sermons* (1790), putting her own name in the imprint of some volumes instead of his; within just a year and a half, however, another, unrelated bookseller, George Folingsby, announced that he had assumed ownership of the Colles house and shop.

In a number of other instances, Dublin firms sustained themselves through complicated lines of succession in which the widows of deceased booksellers played crucial roles. One such firm, identified in table 6 as Chamberlaine–Rice, was founded by 1757 by the bookseller Dillon Cham-

49. On Catholic bookselling in Dublin, see Wall, *Sign of Doctor Hay's Head*, chaps. 1 (on Wogan) and 3 (on the Hoeys). Byrne's career in Dublin and America is discussed in Cole, *Irish Booksellers*, 182–90.

berlaine, whose name appears in the imprints of fifteen Dublin reprints in table 2, spanning the years 1765–77. When Chamberlaine died in 1780, he was succeeded at his shop at 5 College Green by his widow Hannah, whose name appears in the imprints of two more titles listed in table 2, published in 1781 and 1789. Hannah Chamberlaine allied herself with the bookseller John Rice, a specialist in music publishing who had married her daughter Maria. In 1790 Rice returned to Dublin from America, where he had been working in the trade with his brothers, to join Hannah in a short-lived partnership, Chamberlaine & Rice, whose name appears in the imprints of two more titles in table 2 under that year. Finally, upon Hannah's death later in 1790, Rice took over the well-situated Chamberlaine shop on College Green and, trading under his own name, copublished during the years 1791–1800 twelve more books that are listed in table 2—making a total of thirty-one Dublin first editions of Scottish Enlightenment titles that the firm copublished over a period of thirty-five years, the second-highest total on the list. After the extension of British copyright law to Ireland in 1801, Rice returned to America, where he set up shop in Baltimore and died in 1805.

The firm identified in table 6 as Leathley–Hallhead–M'Kenzie is another good example of this distinctive Dublin pattern of continuity. The Dame Street bookseller and bookbinder Joseph Leathley (or Leathly) was an important figure in the Dublin trade from about 1719 until his death in 1757, when he was succeeded by his widow Ann. During the eighteen years that she owned the business, Ann Leathley was involved in four Dublin reprints of Scottish Enlightenment books listed in table 2: Smollett's *Travels* and *Humphry Clinker* (nos. 96 and 140), Macpherson's *Temora* (no. 83), and Fordyce's *Sermons to Young Women* (no. 93). After her death in 1775, she was succeeded by her nephew, William Hallhead, who had probably been her foreman for some time before that. Hallhead was actively engaged as a publisher of Enlightenment reprints during the late 1770s and early 1780s, including eight titles by Scottish authors and, in May 1781, a costly edition of Gibbon's *Decline and Fall of the Roman Empire* in six octavo volumes. When Hallhead died seven months later, apparently leaving the business at 63 Dame Street bankrupt, his widow Sarah managed to keep the firm afloat, and her name appears in the imprint of the first Dublin edition of Robert Watson's *History of Philip III* (no. 239). Then, in 1783, Sarah Hallhead married another Dublin bookseller (and bookbinder), William M'Kenzie (or McKenzie), who had apprenticed with William Gilbert and supposedly had published a 1782 Dublin edition of

Adam Smith's *Wealth of Nations*.[50] McKenzie ran the firm until his death in 1817 and was involved in the publication of twelve Dublin first editions of Scottish Enlightenment titles during the period 1783–1800. Thus, the firm of Leathley–Hallhead–M'Kenzie not only survived but thrived, and it ranks sixth among the bookselling firms shown in table 6.

The fourth name in table 6, Luke White, is well known because of his extensive Continental and British connections and the enormous wealth that he accumulated, largely from lottery sales.[51] But until his retirement from bookselling in 1789, White was also an active reprinter of Enlightenment books; his name appears in twenty-eight of the Dublin imprints in table 2. Although White's establishment at 86 Dame Street did not survive as a family firm, continuity of a sort was achieved when the building and stock were purchased by William Jones, who put his name on the title pages of sixteen first-edition Dublin reprints of Scottish Enlightenment books from 1789 to 1800. In another sense, Jones was a disciple not of White but of his master, James Williams, who ranks third in the table with twenty-eight imprints, including one publication that was the product of a brief partnership with Richard Moncrieffe. Williams spent more than twenty years in Skinner Row before assuming a more fashionable Dame Street address in 1784. All in all, he was the most aggressive, ambitious, and enterprising Dublin reprinter of Enlightenment books, with a strong affinity for the works of the Scottish literati, and he trained as apprentices not only Jones but also two others whose names appear in table 6: John Beatty and John Cash. After Williams died suddenly in 1787, his widow Dorothea tried to succeed him as a bookseller and lottery seller, in partnership with his former apprentice William Jones, but the partnership and the Williams firm both ended in 1789.

Like the collaborative publishing practices that developed among booksellers in London and Edinburgh, those that arose among Dublin firms such as the ones in table 6 represented a means not only of pooling economic resources but also of minimizing potentially destructive disturbances within the trade. In particular, collaborative publishing was a way to maintain order by avoiding overly competitive practices that could result in conflict and bankruptcy. The Dublin book price war of May 1767 marks a critical moment in this process. It occurred after four rising fig-

---

50. It was advertised by M'Kenzie in the *Dublin Evening Post* for 15 October 1782 (as cited in Pollard, *Dictionary*, 386), but no copies of M'Kenzie's edition have been traced.

51. Gough, "Book Imports," 35–48.

ures in the Dublin trade—Dillon Chamberlaine, James Potts, James Williams, and Robert Bell—began to sell cheap editions of popular British books, such as *Tom Jones* and *The Vicar of Wakefield*. Unfortunately for them, the books in question were already spoken for by more established Dublin booksellers, who considered themselves the rightful owners of the titles according to Dublin trade conventions, even though they had never paid a single shilling for the copyrights. James Fordyce's *Sermons to Young Women*, the only Scottish Enlightenment title among the books in dispute, had been reprinted in Dublin as the "fourth edition" in 1766 (the year of its original London publication by Andrew Millar and others) by Ann Leathley (as Leathly), James Hoey, Sr. and Jr., John Exshaw, Sr., Henry Saunders, and William Watson. Leathley, Exshaw, and Watson joined with a number of other established Dublin booksellers, including George Faulkner, W. & W. Smith, Peter Wilson, and Thomas Ewing, to challenge the dissidents' editions in a newspaper advertisement in the *Dublin Gazette* for 12–16 May 1767. Ironically, their rhetoric replicated that of the London booksellers who might have accused *them* of piracy: "The Proprietors of the undermentioned Books, being materially injured in their Properties, by the Publication of several Piratical Editions of them, have (in order to discountenance such unfair Practices, tending to destroy the printing Business of this Kingdom) resolved to offer them to the Publick, upon the following very disadvantageous Terms to themselves." There followed a list of price cuts intended to undersell the rival editions of their upstart competitors. The price of Fordyce's *Sermons to Young Women*, in two volumes duodecimo (sewed in one volume), was dropped from 3s.3d. to an absurdly low 1s.4d., at a time when the London edition of the same work cost 6s. or 7s. in two octavo volumes.

When they attempted to undercut their rivals for the sake of order in the trade, the leaders of the Dublin book trade took a bold step by giving themselves a name: the Company of Booksellers. Their advertisement in the *Dublin Gazette* cited the Company's imprint exactly as it appeared in a new publication of 1767, *The Death of Abel:* "Printed for the Company of Booksellers, and sold by Mrs. A. Leathley, Messrs. W and W. Smith, G. Faulkner, P. Wilson, J. Exshaw, H. Bradley, W. Watson, S. Watson, and T. Ewing." The response by Chamberlaine, Potts, Williams, and Bell in the next issue of the *Dublin Mercury* (16–19 May) began with a facetious reference to "some persons who chuse to distinguish themselves by the title of 'The Company of Booksellers.'" The implication was that no such body actually existed and that the dispute was simply between two groups of Dublin booksellers, neither of which was entitled to claim corporate status. Lurking beneath this aspect of the confrontation was the fact that all four of the chief renegades were at this time either, like Chamberlaine and Bell, mere quarter brothers in the guild (the same marginal status that was accorded to Roman Catholics and hawkers) or else, like Potts and Williams, not members of the guild at all. The establishment figures, by contrast, included guild grandees such as Exshaw, Faulkner, William Smith, and Wilson. In spite of this disadvantage, the rebels pressed their challenge by matching the new, unprofitably low prices that the Company of Booksellers was now charging for three of its titles, including Fordyce's book, and almost matching the Company's price for a fourth title, *Tom Jones*. If this were not enough, they ended their advertisement with a reckless sentence charging that it was not them but some booksellers in the Company (which they call "the junto") who were attempting to suppress Irish printing "by importation and contracting for books printed in London with their names," which would then be sold under value in Ireland.

This was a war the dissidents could not win. Although much remains unclear about this affair,[52] we know that three of the renegades made their piece with the Company of Booksellers and became respected members of the Dublin trade. The fourth member of their party, Robert Bell, suffered a different fate. On 2 December 1767 Bell's bound stock was auctioned at a sheriff's sale, and he departed abruptly (leaving behind his Irish wife), to enter upon an important career in Philadelphia that is explored in the next chapter. Bell's bankruptcy and departure from Dublin within a few months of the May price war may have been hastened by overexpansion, but a strained relationship with other members of the Dublin book trade also played a role. It has been suggested that Bell's problems can be traced to "antagonism among the Dublin booksellers" because Bell and another Scottish bookseller in Dublin, Robert Main, were selling books printed in Scotland.[53] As discussed in chapter 8, Bell started his Dublin career that way around 1759–60, but there are no grounds for supposing that Bell and his associates were still selling books made in Scotland when they provoked the Company of Booksellers in May 1767. However, there is circumstantial evidence that Bell's group of dissidents was selling at least two books made by Scots residing elsewhere. The edition of *The Vicar*

52. Particularly baffling is the fact that James Williams is named as a copublisher of some of the editions published by the Company, such as the 1766 and 1767 editions of *The Vicar of Wakefield*.

53. Phillips, *Printing and Bookselling*, 124–25.

of Wakefield that Bell's faction put up for sale was undoubtedly the one bearing the imprint "Dublin: Printed in the Year 1767" (ESTC W39851), and their edition of Fordyce's *Sermons to Young Women* was probably the one marked simply "Printed in M,DCC,LXVII" (ESTC W24605). Bibliographical research has determined that both of these editions were in fact printed in Boston by the Scotsmen John Mein and John Fleeming.[54] I suspect that John Fleeming of Boston was the former John Fleming of Dublin, who had joined forces with Bell in 1764 to reissue the handsome folio volumes of Walter Harris's editions of works on Irish history and antiquities by Sir James Ware (originally published 1739–46) and then disappeared from Ireland in 1765.[55] Whether or not this hypothesis is correct, the existing evidence raises the fascinating possibility that the Company of Booksellers in Dublin was founded in part to combat the threat of an Atlantic network of Scots selling books printed outside Ireland.

Bell also earned the animosity of the leaders of the Dublin book trade because of his outspoken justification of aggressive, competitive publishing practices. They could not have taken it lightly when Bell reprinted in Dublin the attack on perpetual copyright and monopoly that the Scottish bookseller Alexander Donaldson had directed against the London booksellers. Prefixed to Bell's edition of this pamphlet is an "Advertisement, in Ireland," which forcefully extends Donaldson's argument to Dublin:

> The following Thoughts on Literary Property are reprinted here, because some booksellers in the city of Dublin assert they are injured in their property: this pretended injury is nothing more than that other booksellers claim the right they have to print as many books as they judge proper, when they can save above fifty per cent, by causing them to be printed for themselves, without applying to those Dictators; and on account of this pretended injury they have contrary to common sense, equity, even law, and the natural rights of mankind, entered into a combination to distress or destroy all the other booksellers that will not submit to be the slaves of their USURPED AUTHORITATIVE DETERMINATIONS concerning the printing and selling of BOOKS, which they endeavour to monopolize, not only in the city of Dublin but in the whole kingdom, to the prejudice and injury of all the people of Ireland.

54. Alden, "John Mein, Publisher." Mein & Fleeming also published from the same impression an edition of *Sermons to Young Women* with the imprint "Boston: Printed by Mein and Fleeming," for sale in America (see table 5, no. 93).

55. Pollard, *Dictionary*, 215–16.

With its rhetoric of dictators, slavery, monopoly, and even "the natural rights of mankind," this advertisement marked Bell as the ringleader of the rebels. In the equally vigorous editorial comments that were appended to this edition, Bell asserted that a Dublin bookseller had no more right to claim ownership of British literary property than would a baker to claim a monopoly on bread and to presume to say of a fellow baker that "His loaves were *pirated*."[56] In America, Bell would continue both to preach this philosophy and to live by it. In Dublin, it may well have proved his undoing.

Bell notwithstanding, the Company of Booksellers (also called the United Company of Booksellers) flourished. By the mid-1770s Dublin books began to appear under the Company's imprint, and nearly two hundred titles were published in that fashion before the organization petered out during the 1790s. Among them were at least fifteen editions of Scottish Enlightenment titles, including Patrick Brydone's *Tour* in 1775 and 1780, John Home's *Alfred* in 1777 and *Douglas* in 1787, David Hume's *History of England* (eight volumes, octavo) in 1775, Lord Kames's *Sketches* in 1775 (fig. 7.1), Henry Mackenzie's *Julia de Roubigné* in 1777 and *Prince of Tunis* in 1779, Thomas Reid's *Inquiry* in 1779, four novels by Tobias Smollett in 1775, and another edition of Smollett's *Humphry Clinker* in 1790.

Writing in the early 1950s, James Phillips argued that the imprint of the Company of Booksellers was "a mask," designed to protect Dublin publishers from the wrath of English copy owners, or else to enhance the "economy and appearance" of the title page. It was definitely not "indicative of the existence of a semi-official body apart from the Guild of St Luke the Evangelist."[57] But Phillips's arguments do not stand up to scrutiny in the light of recently discovered evidence. Although far less is known about the Company than we could wish, there is now no doubt that it was a real organization, which employed for a time in the 1770s its own London agent (John Murray, then Robert Baldwin, then John Wallis), maintained its own secretary (William Colles, who had sided with Bell's faction in 1767), registered Dublin publications that sometimes bore the phrase (obviously copied from the Stationers' Company in London) "Entered with the Company of Booksellers," held an anniversary dinner every August, required its members in 1778 to purchase a new suit made in Ireland as a demonstration of support for native manufacture, appointed a committee in 1791 to negotiate changes in the price of bookbinding with

56. [Donaldson], *Some Thoughts*, 1, 16.
57. Phillips, *Printing and Bookselling*, 32–35.

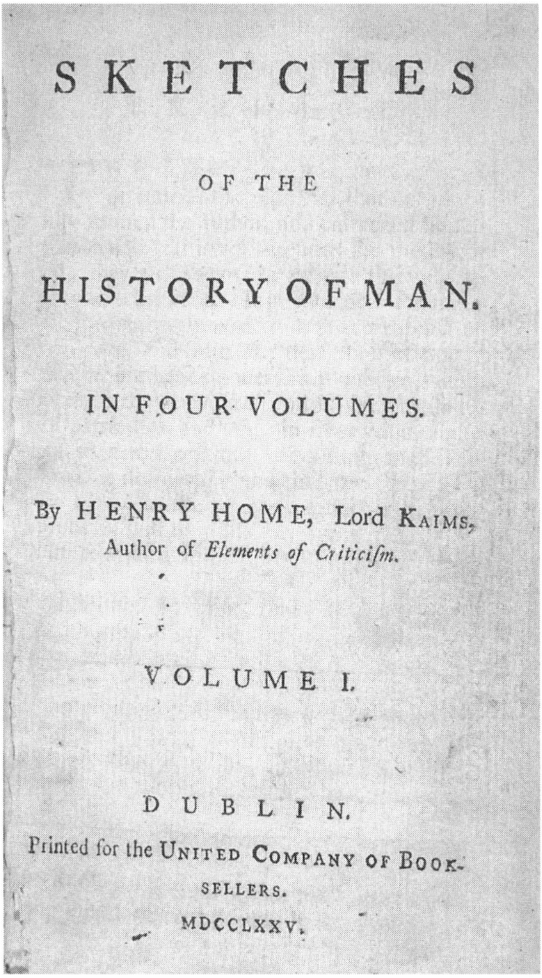

S K E T C H E S

OF THE

HISTORY OF MAN.

IN FOUR VOLUMES.

By HENRY HOME, Lord KAIMS,
Author of *Elements of Criticism.*

VOLUME I.

DUBLIN.
Printed for the UNITED COMPANY OF BOOK-
SELLERS.
MDCCLXXV.

Fig. 7.1. The Company (or United Company) of Booksellers dominated Dublin publishing during the second half of the eighteenth century, and new Scottish Enlightenment books were among its prime fodder for reprinting. The company's imprints frequently listed all the participating publishers, sometimes running to several dozen, but in other cases, such as this 1775 reprint of Kames's *Sketches of the History of Man*, the company itself appeared as the publisher. Special Collections, Lake Forest College Library.

the Company of Bookbinders, and met in 1792 to take a stand on the high price of paper.[58]

A 1793 magazine article on literary property noted that "the invasion of copy right"—which is to say, copyright as it was understood in Ireland, as a convention among booksellers rather than a legal entity—"is in some measure prevented in Dublin, by the institution which is called the United Company of Booksellers."[59] It seems clear that protecting liter-

58. Pollard, *Dictionary*, 114; Pollard, *Dublin's Trade in Books*, 168–69; Zachs, "John Murray and the Dublin Book Trade," 26–33.

59. Quoted in Pollard, *Dublin's Trade in Books*, 169.

ary property in this manner, which had nothing to do with copyright in Britain, was the Company's primary purpose. In this sense, the Company of Booksellers was more like the Edinburgh Booksellers' Society than the Dublin and London stationers' guilds, which were too diffuse to address the specific concerns of publishers. If the Company of Booksellers in Dublin was more successful at accomplishing this goal than its counterpart in Edinburgh, it was chiefly because the Company recognized the importance of cooperation among its members, for whom the best defense against invasions of literary property lay in a successful offense based on collaborative publishing.

The 1793 article goes on to say that the effectiveness of the Company of Booksellers was limited because it was "a mere voluntary association of individuals . . . not extending beyond the metropolis, and not comprising even all the printers and booksellers in Dublin." This problem affected almost all eighteenth-century occupational organizations; nearly two-thirds of the Dublin book trade, after all, may not even have belonged to the Guild of St. Luke.[60] Furthermore, by the time this article appeared in print, the Company was in serious decline, judging from the scarcity of imprints bearing its name after the early 1790s. In the era of its heyday during the 1770s and 1780s, however, the Company could claim virtually all the most prominent Dublin publishers among its members. We know this because the printer Daniel Graisberry recorded in his ledgers two jobs that he printed for the Company of Booksellers: the notes for 2,000 copies of an octavo edition of William Robertson's *History of America* in October 1777 (no. 185; fig. 7.2) and the notes for volume 1 of a duodecimo edition of John Moore's *View of Society and Manners in Italy* (no. 219) in February 1781. Although there is some uncertainty about which of two 1777 octavo editions of Robertson's *History of America* was referred to by Graisberry, in reality it hardly matters, because the imprints of these two editions are so similar that we can safely conclude that both were printed for the company. One edition, in two volumes, contains 43 names in the imprint, while the other, in three volumes, contains 46 (fig. 7.3), in addition to a poorly executed frontispiece portrait that bears little resemblance to Reynolds's original (see fig. 2.12) or even to the first engraving made from it in Britain (see fig. 2.13). In the case of Moore's book, the edition that Graisberry partially printed for the Company is undoubtedly the first of two Dublin editions that appears in table 2, with 22 booksellers shown in the imprint. None of these books bears the imprint "Company of Book-

60. Pollard, *Dictionary*, ix.

sellers" on its title page, even though that is to whom the account was charged by the printer. Instead of employing a corporate name to represent a large number of publishers, as they sometimes did (e.g., nos. 156, 183, and 193; see fig. 7.1), the publishers of these editions did just the opposite: they used "Company of Booksellers" as shorthand in their private dealings with a printer while listing all their names in the imprints of the books themselves, using a conspicuous trapezoidal design.

Except for three names that appear only in the three-volume edition—Samuel Price, Peter Hoey, and William Kidd—the 43 and 46 names in the imprints of the two 1777 Dublin octavo editions of Robertson's *History of America* are identical. The 22 names in the 1781 edition of Moore's *View of Society and Manners in Italy* all appear in the two 1777 octavo editions of Robertson's *History of America* except those of Robert Burton and Patrick Byrne, both of whom had begun publishing only in 1778. Thus, these three books together provide a total of 48 Dublin booksellers or firms that can be confidently identified as members of the Company of Booksellers during the period 1777–81. Since members of the Company were not obliged to collaborate on every publication that the Company sponsored, the actual membership must have been higher than this. Although membership may have been voluntary, very few publishers of consequence could afford to remain outside the fold. Of the 25 firms listed in table 6, the names of 21 (including the former dissidents Chamberlaine, Potts, and Williams) appear in at least one of the imprints of the Robertson and Moore editions that were printed for the Company. The remaining four booksellers in the table—John Cash, John Jones, William Jones, and James Moore—were not yet in the publishing business in 1781; the inclusion of their names in later Dublin imprints containing groups of Company booksellers would seem to indicate that they too joined as soon as they were able to do so.

It is no coincidence that the greatest period of Irish reprinting, from the late 1760s to the early or mid-1790s, was also the prime era of the Company of Booksellers. With dozens of booksellers voluntarily organized into a unified body, the Dublin reprinters achieved a degree of harmony and collaboration among themselves that publishers in London, Edinburgh, and Philadelphia could not equal, and they did it entirely on their own, without the support of laws, government interference, or even formal guild regulations. The results were dramatic. Recall that Cadell and his associates testified before Parliament in 1785 that "heavy Works" were the only ones that British booksellers could export profitably to Ireland, because the Irish booksellers could not reproduce them. The remark was in keeping with the London booksellers' condescending view of the

1777		Mr. Jas. Williams to Printing House		Dr	
		Amount of Sundries brought over			
Sep.	13	Catalogue 1 Sheet, Pica Folio, 100 No. (Thos. Armitage)	1	0	6
	19	Job for Mr. Richardson Folio Page 1500		6	9
	27	Job Lottery Tickets Left 250	1		6
		Gordon's Tacitus Vols. 1, 2 & 3, S. Pica 12s. 500 No. 42 Sheets d 19/6			
		Do. Vols 4 & 5 Bottom Notes, 31 Sheets d 1:1:0 /a	} 73	15	9
		Titles to 4th & 5th Vols of Do. 5 4			
		Book & Print Scheme 2000		6	0
		Tickets for Do. 2 Qrs.		8	10½
Oct. 4		2000 Lottery Schemes for Mr. L. White		14	3
		150 Resolutions of Lottery Office Keepers, Folio Page		4	6
		14 Qrs. of Shilling Chances		2	3
	6	Les Incas Pica & L. P. Notes, 25 Sheets No. 500 d 18/0	22	10	0
	11	500 Job Hay to be Sold	1		10½
		32 Qrs. of Shilling Tickets		4	6
	25	Annual Register L. P. 8vo. 6 Sheets 750 d 1:6:3	7	17	6
		Catalogue 2 Sheets 8vo. S. P. 500 No. d 19/6 (J. Vallance)	1	19	0
		French & Italian Catalogue 1 Sheet 750 No. L. White	1	3	6
		Hist. of America Pica 8vo. J. & B. Notes 12 Sheets, 2000 No.	} 17	8	0
		d 1:9:0 Company of Booksellers			
		Tickets for Song & Memorandum Book 3 Qrs.		8	3
Nov. 1		500 Hand Bills (J. Vallance)	1		10½
		250 Copy Job for Nordh...l Dictionary			

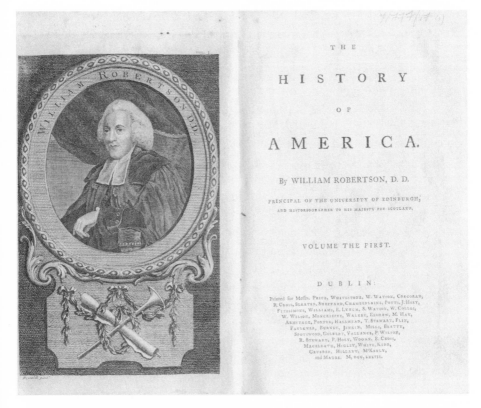

Figs. 7.2 and 7.3. This entry of 25 October 1777 from the ledgers of the Dublin printer Daniel Graisberry (left) shows expenses for printing part of an octavo edition of William Robertson's *History of America* that was charged to the Company of Booksellers. The entry establishes that the individuals named in the imprint of the two 1777 Dublin octavo editions of Robertson's book were among the members of the company. Fig. 7.3 shows the title page of one of those editions, containing forty-six names arranged in a trapezoidal shape, as well as the company's feeble attempt to reproduce John Hall's frontispiece portrait of Robertson after Reynolds (figs. 2.12 and 2.13). Graisberry ledger: Board of Trinity College Dublin; Robertson volume: Harris Manchester College Library, Oxford University.

Dublin trade, but the data on Scottish Enlightenment reprinting under consideration here show it to be a gross exaggeration. By pooling their resources through the Company, the Dublin booksellers soon found that most large, prestigious, and multivolume works were now within their grasp. Apparently emboldened by this realization, and in a few cases (notably Luke White and James Williams) further empowered by the large profits yielded by sales of lottery tickets and patent medicines, several of them also became more aggressive and ambitious in their individual reprinting activities. No longer content merely to churn out cheap copies, they began to turn their attention from crude imitation to a higher form of emulation.

The critical year was 1769, when William Strahan, Thomas Cadell, and John Balfour published in London and Edinburgh their handsome and expensive three-volume quarto edition of William Robertson's *History of Charles V* (no. 119). The response of the Dublin booksellers was extraordinary.[61] Within two years, the Company of Booksellers and others produced five different Dublin editions in a variety of formats, including two highly condensed, two-volume octavo editions that appeared in 1771. The process began in 1769 with page-for-page reprints of the British original in both quarto and octavo format. Although these editions were still cheaper than the British quarto, they were expensive works by the standards of the Dublin reprint trade. Equally important, they retained the trappings of finery associated with books suited for gentlemen's libraries. The publishers of the Dublin quarto—William Watson, Thomas Ewing, and Samuel Watson—advertised in *Freeman's Journal* of 11–14 March 1769 that the public was invited to examine a specimen of their handiwork on display in one of their bookshops, and the *Public Gazetteer* for 21–25 March announced that the page-for-page octavo edition, which was almost certainly a Company of Booksellers production, came "bound in Calf and lettered." Similarly, when the quarto edition of Robertson's two-volume *History of America* appeared in London in 1777, a large group of Dublin booksellers reprinted it in a two-volume quarto of their own, followed by the elegant three-volume octavo and the two-volume octavo that have already been discussed as collaborative products of the Company of Booksellers. This was clearly not the gutter industry that Strahan and Cadell made it out to be when they spoke or wrote about Dublin reprinting.

It was also in 1769 that James Williams, one of the twenty-one copublishers of the Dublin page-for-page octavo edition of *Charles V*, brought out the first complete Irish edition of David Hume's *History of England* (no. 75) in eight octavo volumes. Williams reprinted the work in the same format in 1772, as we shall see, and again in 1780, and it was supplemented by his reprints of *The Life of David Hume, Esq. Written by Himself* in 1777 and Hume's *Essays and Treatises* in 1779. In 1780 Williams even printed

61. Sher, "*Charles V*," 179–80.

a title page and front matter (containing the *Life of David Hume*) for an edition of *The Works of David Hume, Esq.*—the only one ever attempted anywhere in the eighteenth century—evidently intended to introduce his editions of Hume's *History* and *Essays and Treatises*. We have seen that another eight-volume octavo edition of Hume's *History of England* appeared in 1775 with the imprint of the United Company of Booksellers, and in 1788 Luke White produced yet another, which he marketed together with his 1787 five-volume edition of Smollett's continuation as a uniform, thirteen-volume *History of England*.[62]

One of the ways that Williams obtained the capital for undertaking such large ventures on his own was by organizing subscriptions. At the beginning of November 1770 Williams and Richard Moncrieffe published subscription proposals in *Freeman's Journal* for a new edition of Sir James Steuart's *Inquiry into the Principles of Political Oeconomy* (no. 101). The subscription price was 16s.3d. bound for a three-volume octavo edition, less than one-third the price of £2.12s.6d. in boards that they quoted for the London quarto. They tried to stir up enthusiasm among potential subscribers by appealing to individuals "inclined to encourage and promote the useful Arts" and by referring to "the great Demand . . . for the London Edition of this valuable Work," even though the London edition of Steuart's book actually did not sell particularly well.[63] Another of their ploys was to assert in the beginning of November that they had printed "very few" copies above the number subscribed for, implying that those wishing to obtain a copy at the subscription price (or possibly at any price) needed to act quickly. Yet when publication was announced in *Freeman's Journal* on 8–10 November, the book was offered to the general public at the subscription price.

The list printed in some copies of Steuart's *Inquiry* names 252 subscribers, who ordered 405 two-volume sets. Most were Irish gentlemen and merchants, but large numbers of sets were taken by other Dublin booksellers, such as Thomas Ewing (50 sets), Charles Ingham (25), William Smith (14), Samuel Watson (14), Peter and William Wilson (12), John Milliken (10), Elizabeth Lynch (6), James Potts (6), Henry Saunders (6), James Vallance (3), Dillon Chamberlaine (2), and William Sleater (2).

---

62. Cole, *Irish Booksellers*, 132. Phillips, *Printing and Bookselling*, 101–2, records that in June 1776 Saunders, Chamberlaine, and Potts advertised a limited-time sale of an eight-volume octavo edition of Hume's *History of England* for just 14s.1d., but it is not clear whose edition they were selling.

63. Sher, "New Light," 22–23.

Quite a few of the subscribers were British officers stationed in America and colonists in South Carolina, including the Scottish bookseller Robert Wells of Charleston, who took six sets. This pattern suggests that support for ambitious reprints of this kind was widespread among members of the Dublin book trade and that it also extended to the Americas some years before the Irish booksellers were legally permitted to export their publications there.

In the issue of *Finn's Leinster Journal* for 18–22 January 1772, Williams issued subscription proposals for his new edition of Hume's *History of England*, promising to print subscribers' names in the book "not only as Encouragers of this Work, but of the Arts and Manufactures of Ireland." The list that appears in some extant copies of that edition includes 117 names. The subscribers were mainly gentlemen and merchants in Ireland, along with seventeen members of the book trade and a smattering of others, including a few individuals in America. The relatively small size of the list compared to the one in Steuart's *Inquiry* may have been due in part to the higher price of the eight-volume Hume edition, but it probably owed more to the fact that the book's London publishers were already producing a comparably priced, eight-volume octavo edition of Hume's *History* at this time, whereas Steuart's *Inquiry* was then available only in an expensive London quarto edition. The two-guinea subscription price for Williams's edition of Hume's *History* was six shillings less than the retail price being charged by Strahan and Cadell for bound copies of the London edition in the same number of volumes and the same format, and Williams's sets were bound and lettered more handsomely. The regular retail price for the Williams edition, £2.5.6d. (as advertised in the *Public Register: or, Freeman's Journal* for 27–30 Mar. 1773) was still 2s.6d. less than the price charged by Strahan and Cadell.

All this activity by James Williams and his colleagues in the Company of Booksellers was plainly meant to compete directly with Strahan and Cadell, the publishers or copublishers of the original editions of these books. But Williams was not content merely to undersell the great London publishers of the Scottish Enlightenment. He also wanted to outdo them in the quality of his editions. The subscription proposals for his 1772 edition of Hume's *History of England* noted that it would be printed "Page for Page with the London Quarto Edition, on a new Type cast on Purpose, and the same fine Paper as the Specimen," and "neatly bound in Calf, and double-lettered." Corrections that appeared on an errata page in the London quarto edition were to be incorporated into the body of the work, and "no Expense will be spared, in order to render it worthy of the

Encouragement of the Public: Two Correctors will be employed to read every Sheet; and a head of the Author, finely engraved, will be prefixed to the first Volume." Williams's edition would therefore be distinguished by its "superior Elegance" and would also be "considerably larger than those of any Edition in Octavo, published either in Great Britain or Ireland, although offered to the Public so much under the Price of the cheapest." The "finely engraved" head of Hume turned out to be by Patrick Halpen or Halpin, who had produced the first frontispiece portrait of Hume after Donaldson in the 1767 London octavo reissue of Hume's *History* and was, according to the *ODNB*, "the only native line engraver in Dublin" until the mid-1780s. Williams had either managed to secure the original plate from London or else prevailed on Halpen to engrave another portrait of comparable quality for his Dublin edition.

In July 1778 Williams began an advertisement in the *Dublin Evening Post* with these controversial words: "James Williams at No. 21, Skinner-Row, has, at a very great Expence, printed Editions of the following Works, and many others, as far superior to the London Editions, as the London Editions of Books formerly were to Irish Editions." The conclusion of the advertisement pressed the point by inviting "Ladies and Gentlemen [who] have indifferent English, or other Editions, of some of the above Works" to "have them exchanged on a reasonable Valuation," and the public was invited to examine Williams's editions at his shop. The list of superior reprint editions included a new edition of Robertson's *History of Scotland* (to which Williams added engravings of Mary Queen of Scots and Lord Darnly that he said cost him £20), his latest edition of Hume's *History of England*, and an edition of Cullen's *First Lines of the Practice of Physic* (no. 187). Also on the list is a notable work by an Irish author living in London, *An History of the Earth, and Animated Nature* by Oliver Goldsmith, which Williams had published a year earlier in a subscription edition of eight octavo volumes, with plates.[64] In a two-page "Advertisement, by the Printer of the Irish Edition of Goldsmith's History of the Earth, to the Public" that is prefixed to some copies of this work, Williams boasts of having equaled the original edition (published in London in 1774 by John Nourse) in textual accuracy while surpassing it in typography and quality of paper; along with other books he published, including Hume's *History of England*, it is said to be "superior to the London editions."

The front matter in Goldsmith's *History of the Earth* presented Williams's three aims. First, he was attempting to demonstrate that the Irish

---

64. Cole, *Irish Booksellers*, 133.

trade could turn out quality books, in an effort "to remove," as he puts in it the book's dedication to Edmund Sexton Pery, the Speaker of the Irish House of Commons, "the reproaches which Ireland has laboured under for bad printing." The inclusion of so many Irish booksellers in the subscription list, many of them ordering multiple copies, is indicative of the degree to which the Irish trade had come to view Williams, the former renegade, as their spokesman on this issue.[65] Second, Williams expressed a genuine interest in advancing the cause of enlightenment in Ireland by making learned books like Goldsmith's available for widespread consumption there. His "principal desire," the advertisement states, is to put "a work of merit, beautifully printed, into every one's hands," and the bookseller is delighted "that thro' me, my Countrymen will be gratified with this charming repast." Finally, Williams openly acknowledged the extent to which his actions were driven by his personal aspirations, not only for wealth but also for glory. "I confess," he writes, "that my ambition glows with the probable expectation of soon finding my name inrolled with those of *Tonson, Millar,* and *Foulis;* who, at the same time that they have enriched themselves, and contributed to propagate science, have done honour to their respective countries." Thus, the Goldsmith advertisement and dedication reveal the intentions of an ambitious Dublin bookseller driven to produce excellent reprint editions from a mixture of patriotic, cultural, and personal motives. The desire for profits was certainly part of that mixture, but it was by no means the whole, and perhaps not even the major, part.

James Williams set the tone for late eighteenth-century Dublin publishers who wished to emulate the practices of their better-known counterparts in England and Scotland. Of several attempts to equal or surpass his achievement, one of the most important was John Chambers's remarkable edition of Guthrie's *Geography.*[66] Chambers had begun his career printing for Williams and had been among the subscribers to Williams's edition of Goldsmith's *History of the Earth.* According to the subscription proposals, his edition of Guthrie would start to appear at the end of May

65. William Hallhead ordered twenty sets; Laurence Flin II, Caleb Jenkin, Elizabeth Lynch, Richard Moncrieffe, William Wilson, Thomas Walker, and William Whitestone each ordered a dozen; and William Colles, George Burnet, Arthur Grubere (Grueber), John Chambers, Peter Hoey, William Spotswood, William Sleater I, William Watson, Peter Wilson, Luke White, and Patrick Wogan were among those who each took between one and twelve copies.

66. Pollard, "John Chambers," 4–5; and Pollard, *Dublin's Trade in Books,* 207–8.

1788 in weekly numbers of four sheets (thirty-two pages) and could be purchased by paying either a shilling for each of the thirty-two numbers or the subscription price of a guinea and a half for the complete volume (published in mid-May 1789), one-third payable as a deposit at the time of subscription.[67] Inscribed by permission of the new Royal Irish Academy, the book attracted 806 subscribers. Chambers asserted in the advertisement prefixed to the book that the project had been "undertaken not more with a view to profit, than to prove, that this country has spirit, when encouraged, not only to undertake literary publications on an English scale of liberality, but even to attempt improvement thereon."[68] It was in this improving spirit that he changed the main title of the book from *A New System of Modern Geography* to *An Improved System of Modern Geography*, with the words "Chambers's Edition" placed conspicuously at the top of the title page.[69]

On 16 December 1788 the *Dublin Chronicle* ran an advertisement for Chambers's quarto edition of Guthrie's *Geography* along with one for the octavo edition of John Exshaw, Jr., which sold for 9s.9d., less than one-third the price of Chambers's volume. Exshaw had a claim on the Irish "copyright" of the book because his father, John, Sr., had joined with Boulter Grierson and James Williams to reprint a cheap (6s.) Dublin edition in 1771, and in 1780 John, Jr., himself had copublished another Dublin edition with James Williams, with a print run (according to the Graisberry ledgers) of 2,000 copies. There is some evidence that Exshaw's relatively cheap editions were exported generously to America, for the preface to the first volume of Mathew Carey's American edition of Guthrie's *Geography* of 1794 remarked that Irish editions "have frequently supplied the American market." On 20 December 1788 Chambers responded with an

67. Subscription proposals published separately (Chambers, *Proposals*) and in the *Dublin Chronicle*, 22 May 1788. The retail price of £1.14s.1½d. was a few shillings higher than the subscription price (*Dublin Chronicle*, 27–29 Oct. 1789).

68. Guthrie, *Improved System of Modern Geography*, v.

69. *A New System of Modern Geography* was the title of the London quarto edition that first appeared in 1780 under the imprint of Charles Dilly and George Robinson, whose firms had purchased the copyright from John Knox in the late 1770s. The octavo title, *A New Geographical, Historical, and Commercial Grammar; and Present State of the Several Kingdoms of the World*, was used (without the word "New") as the subtitle of the quarto, although Chambers changed the phrase "the Several Kingdoms of the World" to read "All the Empires, Kingdoms, States, and Republics in the Known World." In 1788 Dilly and the Robinsons published the fourth London edition of the quarto and the eleventh edition of the octavo.

advertisement in the *Dublin Chronicle* that blasted his rival's "cheap Geography . . . printed in the School-Book stile in OCTAVO with a few small old Plates (according to the surveys of the last century) furbished up for the purpose, and the work itself (however obviously imperfect in other respects) does not contain the recent occurrences of the world." By contrast, his edition was executed "in the manner of the LONDON QUARTO, and on superior paper and type; the plates more numerous, engraved in a finer style, and of a medium and demy size," and the text updated. So Chambers had to stave off a challenge from "below," within Dublin itself, at the same time that he mounted his own challenge to the best work of the London trade. Regarding the latter offensive, he must have taken some satisfaction when the *Dublin Chronicle* for 27–29 October 1789 pronounced "the Dublin Edition of Guthrie's Geographical Grammar . . . much superior to any published in London."

The main improvements intended by Chambers were of two kinds. First, in the tradition of James Williams, he was trying to outdo the London trade in all aspects of book production and to break its hold on the publication of high-quality books. As he put it in his advertisement of 16 December 1788, he intended to inflict "a new wound to English Monopoly." In this same spirit, in February 1796 he would advertise a four-volume octavo edition of Smollett's translation of *Don Quixote* as "the most elegant Typographical Performance ever attempted and executed in Ireland."[70] Second, Chambers aspired to surpass the London trade in the quality of the text itself. Although updating the accounts of each nation was part of that effort, his chief contribution to textual improvement involved providing a new and greatly expanded account of Ireland. In an effort to keep pace, Exshaw asserted that the article on Ireland in *his* 1789 edition was also "almost entirely new wrote," but Chambers impatiently dismissed his rival's claim,[71] with considerable justification. Although Exshaw added some new material on Trinity College and other subjects, his revisions were not nearly so significant as he claimed, and the article on Ireland in his 1789 edition was expanded only slightly, from twenty-three to twenty-eight octavo pages.

In order to understand the significance of Chambers's accomplishment, it is necessary to look more closely at Guthrie's *Geography* and Ireland's place in it. Robert Mayhew has shown that from the time of its original

70. Quoted in Cole, *Irish Booksellers*, 79.

71. *Dublin Chronicle*, 16 and 20 Dec. 1788; and Guthrie, *New Geographical, Historical, and Commercial Grammar*, 10th ed. (Dublin, 1789), advertisement.

publication in 1770, Guthrie's *Geography* was permeated with the patriotic, Whig-Presbyterian improving ethos of the Scottish Enlightenment, including the stadial or stage theory of social development.[72] Readers encountered this perspective as soon as they opened the book.[73] The preface, almost certainly written by John Knox, was already cited at the beginning of the introduction to this book to illustrate an attitude affirming "the rapid progress, and general diffusion of learning and civility, which, within the present age, have taken place in Great Britain" (5)—and only there. "To promote and advance this improvement," the preface adds, "is the principal design of our present undertaking" (5–6). By studying the nations of the world, comprehensively and historically, we can discover "a natural and striking picture of human manners, under the various stages of barbarity and refinement" (7). Of course, Great Britain stands at the top of this ladder of refinement, followed at some distance by the rest of Europe; as the dominant power in Britain, and therefore in the world, England receives more coverage in the book than the whole of continental Europe. Asia is deemed less interesting because of its uniformity, bred of tradition and tyranny, and Africa is considered "so immersed in rudeness and barbarity" that to dwell upon it "would be disgusting to every lover of mankind" (9). Thus, the preface prepares readers for an ideologically structured global survey, and it is likely that this feature helped to distinguish this book from its less successful competitors.

The account of Ireland in the London octavo editions of Guthrie's *Geography* is short—23 pages, as against 50 for Scotland, and 213 for England—and generally unexceptionable. Dublin, "which may be classed among the second order of cities in Europe," is praised for its "elegance and magnificence" and its "spirit of national improvement," but derided for lacking a single decent inn (428). The university is described in some detail, and Swift, Steele, Berkeley, and Goldsmith are among the writers cited as proof of Irish distinction in the republic of letters (425). When the work treats the Roman Catholic majority, however, the substance and tone are very different:

> With respect to the present descendants of the old Irish, or, as they are termed by the Protestants, the *mere Irish*, they are generally represented

72. See Mayhew, *Enlightenment Geography*, 168–80; and Mayhew, "William Guthrie's *Geographical Grammar*," 19–34.

73. All parenthetical citations in the following discussion are drawn from the eleventh octavo edition of Guthrie, *New Geographical, Historical, and Commercial Grammar* (London, 1788).

as an ignorant, uncivilized, and blundering sort of people. Impatient of abuse and injury, they are implacable and violent in all their affections; but quick of apprehension, courteous to strangers, and patient of hardships. Though in these respects there is, perhaps, little difference between them and the more uninformed part of their neighbours, yet their barbarisms are more easy to be accounted for from accidental than natural causes. By far the greatest number of them are Papists, and it is the interests of their priests, who govern them with an absolute sway, to keep them in the most profound ignorance. (422)

The account continues in this manner, describing their extreme poverty, their "offensive" Sunday gatherings, their superstitions (422), and their "popery, and that too of the most absurd, illiberal kind" (423). The primitive level of society among the "mere Irish"—a term laden with strong connotations of English contempt[74]—is placed in its international and historical context in this memorable sentence: "The common Irish, in their manner of living, seem to resemble the ancient Britons, as described by Roman authors, or the present Indian inhabitants of America" (422). In short, the "common Irish" were no better than common savages or barbarians.

The text of Guthrie's *Geography* often underwent modifications as new London editions appeared, and after the American war several new paragraphs were added that spoke approvingly of the patriotic Volunteers and of recent legislation that liberalized Irish trade restrictions. This liberal stance is not surprising, considering that the rights to Guthrie's *Geography* had been purchased by the London booksellers Charles Dilly and (later) George Robinson, English Dissenters with liberal outlooks, who maintained close ties with the Dublin trade. Their editions expressed skepticism about Ireland's future but remained thoroughly British in outlook, as they pondered how to raise Ireland to the exalted level of England and Scotland and facilitate Ireland's integration into greater Britain. Significantly, Dilly and Robinson's 1788 edition retained the notorious passages that relegated the "mere Irish" to a primitive rung on the social evolutionary ladder.

In the early Dublin reprint editions, these derogatory passages were not only retained but sometimes embellished. For example, Exshaw and Williams's 1780 Dublin edition inserted this sentence immediately after the lengthy passage quoted above: "Hence that settled aversion to En-

74. Leerssen, *Mere Irish*.

glishmen, and even to their own countrymen of a different persuasion; and to this also, more than local situation, may be attributed those acts of savage cruelty so frequent in that country, as well as the irregularities attending all their public meetings, which generally end in bloodshed."[75] Although Exshaw's 1789 and 1794 editions carefully excised the most offensive references to the Irish majority, they were replaced with others that were merely more subtle in their expression of British-Protestant superiority. Noting the severity of the penal laws against Roman Catholics in Ireland, these editions observed that "the people at large . . . had not such opportunities of cultivating their rational qualities as could be wished, and consequently could not be expected to be remarkably industrious and civilized."[76] If only "they had but an equal chance with their neighbours, of being instructed in the real principles of Christianity, and been enured and encouraged to industry and labour," they would be both happier and more supportive of government. Fortunately, "Protestantism is making a very rapid progress in the towns and communities" (423). Thus, Exshaw's revised edition continued to equate the values and religion of British Protestantism with civilization itself, in keeping with the original improving spirit of Guthrie's *Geography*.

John Chambers implemented a complete break with this tradition. He was a political radical and a zealous supporter of Irish liberty, who would be a founding member of the United Irishmen in 1791. A Protestant, he had taken a Catholic wife in December 1780 and was a firm believer in Catholic rights. In Chambers's edition of Guthrie's *Geography*, Ireland was covered in no fewer than 127 quarto pages, compared with 165 for England, 34 for Scotland (plus 6 more on the Scottish isles), and 28 for France. But it was not just the number of pages that mattered. The article on Ireland in Chambers's edition provided a detailed account of recent Irish history that culminated in a specially commissioned section on the Volunteers by the Edinburgh-educated Ulster physician William Drennan.[77] Drennan presented the Volunteers as a prodigious force for civil and national liberty. Writing in a civic humanist vein, he contended that

75. Guthrie, *New Geographical, Historical, and Commercial Grammar* (Dublin, 1780), 354.

76. Guthrie, *New Geographical, Historical, and Commercial Grammar* (Dublin, 1794), 422.

77. On Drennan and his connections with Chambers, see Agnew, *Drennan–McTier Letters*, esp. 1:331–32 ("a grand edition of Guthrie's *Geography*"), 385 ("that worthy man"), 483 ("my friend Chambers"). For Drennan's Scottish ties, see McBride, "William Drennan," 49–61.

"the Volunteers of Ireland promoted, perhaps created, national liberty" by uniting "the characters of citizen and soldier" and renouncing "the insidious and arbitrary claims of Britain" to legislative authority over Ireland.[78] He looked forward to "the coming of a time, which will give all Irishmen a country to boast of, liberties to enjoy, not merely of sufferance; and a God to worship as they think best" (497). With regard to political liberty, nothing less than "extending the elective franchise to Roman Catholics" would do: "To build a liberal system of freedom" upon the "general principles" of this idea "was an ambition worthy the friends of liberty and reform" (507).

In this way, Chambers used a conspicuous Dublin reprint edition of Guthrie's *Geography* as a vehicle for reshaping Irish national identity, and the enlightened values with which this book had always been associated were extended to a nation (or part of a nation) to which they had previously been denied. This feature of Chambers's project suggests another aspect of his contest with John Exshaw over rival reprint editions of Guthrie. Like Chambers, Exshaw was deeply engaged in politics, but on the opposite side. An alderman since 1782, closely connected with the police, Exshaw became, while still in his thirties, the youngest man ever to be elected lord mayor of Dublin in May 1789, just one week before the publication of Chambers's edition of Guthrie, and served another term in 1800.[79] In October 1789 Exshaw took office as lord mayor while Chambers took office as warden of the Guild of St. Luke, rising to master in 1793. A primary point of tension between the guild and the town government concerned the rights of Catholics, who were granted full guild membership for the first time during Chambers's term as master but were continually blocked by the rigidly anti-Catholic Corporation of Dublin.[80] The presentations of Irish Catholics in Exshaw's and Chambers's competing editions of Guthrie's *Geography* were reflections of these fundamental political differences as well as instruments for influencing public opinion about them. In this contest, Chambers was at a severe disadvantage because his quarto edition had a smaller print run and was much more expensive than the octavos published by his Dublin rival. Even worse from the standpoint of Chambers's intentions, neither Chambers's nor Exshaw's revisions of the article on Ireland had any apparent impact in Britain, and the most

78. Guthrie, *Improved System of Modern Geography* (Dublin, 1789), 497–98.

79. Pollard, *Dictionary*, 192–93. In 1790 he stood for Parliament as a government man but was defeated.

80. Pollard, "John Chambers," 9–10.

derogatory passages on the uncivilized character of the "mere Irish" continued to be reproduced in every London edition, at least through the twenty-first edition of 1808 (the latest I have examined).

No sooner had Chambers produced his landmark edition of Guthrie's *Geography* than another Dublin bookseller, James Moore, began an even more ambitious campaign to publish a new and improved edition of the *Encyclopaedia Britannica* (no. 139), which he advertised in the *Dublin Chronicle* for 26 June 1790 as "an undertaking the most expensive and spirited ever attempted in Ireland." In the conditions of subscription, Moore promised that "the Work will be printed in a superb style, suitable to the spirit and taste of the Irish Nation: the paper will be a superfine and the types occasionally renewed, before they contract a worn appearance." It would consist of between twelve and fifteen quarto volumes, each costing one guinea in boards, and the last volume would be accompanied by "an elegant Frontispiece, the Dedication and Preface, together with a complete list of the Subscribers." There would be "near four hundred Copperplates, newly engraved with neatness and accuracy."

With the exception of the number of volumes, which finally rose to eighteen in accordance with the number of volumes in the third edition that he was reprinting as it appeared in Edinburgh between 1788 and 1797, Moore kept every one of these promises. When he finished the work eight years later, he proudly announced on the title page of volume 1 that it was "Illustrated With Near Four Hundred Copperplates," including the grand frontispiece showing men of learning studying and teaching the various arts and sciences in a classical setting. The first volume also contained two pages of subscribers' names, headed by the Earl of Westmoreland, the lord lieutenant general and general governor of Ireland. There were 333 subscribers in all, demonstrating strong support from the upper echelon of Irish society. Many Dublin booksellers were represented, including John Archer (2 sets), George Folingsby (16), Grueber & M'Allister (25), John Jones (12), William Jones (10), John Milliken (3), and Peter Moore (16), in addition to William Magee (40) and Hugh Warren (6) of Belfast, and an occasional bookseller elsewhere in Ireland.

As framed by Moore, the Dublin *Britannica* was a patriotic and heroic undertaking in the name of enlightened learning. When announcing the publication of the first volume in the *Dublin Chronicle* on 26 June 1790, Moore stated: "The Publisher presumes to recommend this Work, as the completest and most Compendious System of Universal Information ever presented to the Public, or that these Kingdoms can boast of." The final version of volume 1 contained an authorized dedication to the king (dated

1797) that characterized the publisher's motivation as an "ardent desire of extending the line of his profession, and diffusing knowledge amongst his Countrymen." What Moore never mentioned was that the "Universal Information" in the third edition of the *Britannica* had a strong Scottish bias. The entry on Scotland was more than twice as long as the one on England, for example, and the article on Edinburgh (replete with a complete list of the faculty of the University of Edinburgh as of 1790) was only a little shorter than the article on Ireland itself. The editor of the third edition, George Gleig, was a Scottish Episcopal bishop, and his preface cited a number of Scottish writers who had contributed new articles, including Thomas Blacklock, David Doig, Andrew Duncan, Robert Heron, and John Robison.

The most important way that the third edition of the *Britannica* promoted the Scottish Enlightenment was by adding additional biographies of deceased historical figures. Eighteenth-century Scottish authors received a disproportionately high level of representation. The entries included James Ferguson, David Fordyce, John Gregory, Robert Henry, Henry Home (Lord Kames), David Hume, William Hunter, Francis Hutcheson, Colin Maclaurin, William Julius Mickle, Alexander Monro *primus*, Robert Simson, Adam Smith, Tobias Smollett, Matthew Stewart, Gilbert Stuart, Robert Watson, and Robert Whytt. The *Supplement* to the third edition that appeared in Edinburgh between 1799 and 1801, which Moore reprinted in Dublin in two volumes in the latter year, added lives of Thomas Blacklock, James Boswell, John Brown, James Bruce, Robert Burns, George Campbell, William Cullen, David Dalrymple (Lord Hailes), James Fordyce, Alexander Gerard, John Hunter, James Macpherson, Thomas Reid, Sir James Steuart (under Stewart), William Tytler, and William Wilkie, most of whom had died during the 1790s. These biographical sketches, often quite lengthy, promoted and contextualized the eighteenth-century Scottish achievement in the republic of letters. They also bestowed celebrity status on many of the figures they treated: Bruce was introduced as "the celebrated Abyssinian traveler," Hume as "a late celebrated philosopher and historian," Kames as "an eminent Scottish lawyer, and author of many celebrated works on various subjects," Robertson as "one of the most celebrated historians of his age."

Much of Moore's boasting concerned the national significance of his accomplishment as a publisher. The dedication expressed the hope that the work "will in some degree prove, that however inferior Ireland may be in wealth and commerce to Great Britain, Irishmen are not deficient in enterprize and industry, and that they need only encouragement to become as eminent in trade (for which Nature qualifies their country) as they have ever been renowned for valour and steady loyalty." In a brief "Preface from the Publisher of the Irish Edition" that was also added to the first volume at the end of the project, Moore reiterated that this work was "the most expensive ever attempted in Ireland, engaging nearly 20,000l. [£20,000] and that in a country where in times the most prosperous the Art of Printing and the Trade of Bookselling has many disadvantages, but much more at a period of peculiar distress" such as the nation had recently endured. Asserting that his edition had disproved the common opinion "that works of this magnitude will fail in Ireland," he further declared it "superior" to the original *Encyclopaedia Britannica* both in the "manner of its execution" and its "matter," the result of his having "in many instances consulted men of the first talents and information, and agreeable to their opinion, made many corrections and additions." Moore's edition thus represents another significant example of the Dublin book trade not only disseminating, but also attempting to improve upon, the book learning of the Scottish Enlightenment. Furthermore, it seeks to appropriate the work for Ireland, as if what mattered most was not the effort that had gone into editing, writing, and illustrating the third edition of the *Britannica* in Edinburgh but the act of revising and reprinting it in Dublin.

There was more national boasting on 17 February 1791, when John Rice advertised in the *Dublin Chronicle* a six-volume octavo edition of James Bruce's *Travels to Discover the Source of the Nile* (no. 288), with approximately fifty engravings. In general, engravings posed a serious problem for Dublin reprinters, and the appearance of Irish editions of works requiring them, such as the *Encyclopaedia Britannica* and Bruce's *Travels,* signifies the emergence of a more sophisticated publishing industry, containing aspects of the book arts besides printing itself. Rice announced that his edition of Bruce had cost him "upwards of ONE THOUSAND GUINEAS" to produce, and would sell for the imposing price of £2.5s.6d. in boards. It was, he proclaimed, "an honourable proof of the excellence which the Arts of Printing and Engraving have attained in Ireland." Yet another ambitious Scottish Enlightenment reprint in this period was Patrick Byrne and John Jones's previously mentioned edition of Robert Henry's *History of Great Britain,* published in five thick octavo volumes in 1789, to which the posthumous sixth volume was added in 1794 under the joint imprint of Byrne and James Moore.

A final example of Irish publishing ambitions concerns a Scottish Enlightenment work that does not actually appear among the Dublin reprints in table 2. Mention was made in the last chapter of William Smellie's nine-volume translation of Buffon's *Natural History* (no. 212), published in 1780–85 by William Creech, in association with Strahan and Cadell. It was an extremely expensive project, not only because of the enormous size of the text but also because of the large number of plates—about three hundred of them—engraved by Andrew Bell, who had also done the engravings for (and copublished) the original *Encyclopaedia Britannica*, which Smellie had edited. Writing to Strahan and Cadell on 22 November 1783, in an effort to increase the amount of their copy money from £800 to £1,000, Smellie and Bell commented that "the Irish would print the book if the expence of the plates did not deter them. The plates, indeed, secure the property, and make the sale of the book unrivalled, and therefore the more valuable."[81] The same letter claimed that a Dublin bookseller (probably Luke White) had recently offered to buy five hundred impressions of the plates, "but Mr Creech declined entering into any terms with him."

Immediately after the appearance of the final volume of Smellie's edition of Buffon in 1785, Luke White launched a subscription campaign to reprint Smellie's octavo edition in Ireland on fine paper, using new type and new plates "engraved by the best Artists."[82] At the high price of three guineas per set (though several shillings cheaper than the original Edinburgh–London edition), the subscription was apparently slow to take hold, but the Dublin booksellers persisted. In autumn 1790 White's former clerk, Arthur Grueber, took over the subscription campaign, pledging in an appeal in the *Dublin Chronicle* (12 and 14 Oct.) that "the plates, paper, and press work shall do credit to his country." The following June the subscription proposals began to appear in the newspapers under the name of Grueber's former partner, Randal M'Allister. Yet despite the costs associated with continually running large newspaper advertisements for more than six years, the Dublin reprint of Smellie's edition of Buffon's *Natural History* was never published. We do not know exactly what went wrong, but perhaps the project was brought down by the appearance in London of a severely abridged, one-volume octavo translation of Buffon's work in 1791. In October this one-volume edition was reprinted in Dublin by a group of thirteen booksellers, including Grueber, Moore, Rice, and John

81. Smellie and Bell to Strahan and Cadell, 22 Nov. 1783, EUL, La.II.584.

82. Subscription proposals, with conditions, dated September 1785. I have used the copy of this item that is appended to White's book catalogue in the back of University College Dublin's copy of Woodfall, *Impartial Sketch*.

Jones; in all likelihood, it was a Company of Booksellers publication.[83]
According to Jones's advertisement in the *Dublin Chronicle* for 22 Octo-
ber, it sold for just 8s.8d. neatly bound or 7s.7d. in boards—a fraction of
the cost of the projected reprint of Smellie's more comprehensive edition.
Although M'Allister continued to advertise the proposals for the longer
Buffon reprint at least through the end of 1791, the Dublin booksellers
were never able to reproduce this particular product of the French and
Scottish Enlightenments.

∗

Despite the failure to publish an Irish edition of Buffon, the Dublin reprint trade of the late eighteenth century requires no apologies. If the
data on Scottish Enlightenment titles presented here are representative of
Irish reprinting in general, then most of what the leading British publishers had to say about the Dublin trade was at best half true. Although the
Dublin booksellers benefited from the absence of a copyright law, as they
did from the lack of any obligation to make payments to authors and editors, and the capability to print and publish less expensive editions than
their counterparts in London usually could, it does not follow that their
books were meant mainly, or even largely, for illegal export into Britain,
as Cadell and his associates implied when they raised the specter of "a
great clandestine Importation of Books from Ireland into this Country."
Although piracy of this kind was one component in the Irish reprint trade
and was probably more prevalent than Pollard has suggested, the focus
of that trade was on the home market, along with the American market that was opened up to Irish booksellers during the American war for
independence.

As we have seen, the Dublin booksellers reprinted vast quantities of
books by Scottish authors, but they did not reprint all British books indiscriminately, as British booksellers sometimes said; they were selective,
and generally chose the best books (in both a critical and commercial
sense) in the various genres of polite literature. Though they normally
reprinted books very soon after their original appearance, evidence does
not exist to substantiate the London booksellers' testimony—with its
insinuation of prepublication complicity by London printers—that Irish

83. *Buffon's Natural History, Abridged* (Dublin, 1791). The booksellers named in
the imprint were Wogan, Byrne, Grueber, M'Kenzie, J. Moore, J. Jones, Halpen,
W. Jones, R. White, Rice, Draper, P. Moore, and A. Porter.

booksellers "often" got the sheets of British books "as they come from the Press." The Dublin reprinters frequently published books in smaller formats, and at lower prices, than the original British editions they were reproducing. Yet they also printed books in the same formats as the British originals, and particularly during the last three decades of the century they made a number of ambitious attempts, mostly successful, to reprint exactly the kind of multivolume, expensive works that Cadell and other London booksellers claimed they could not reproduce. Moreover, in several of these cases their goal was not merely to equal, but to surpass, the British original in regard to the quality of their work. In these instances, individual initiative was evident, but it operated against the backdrop of a publishing industry that was predominantly cooperative and surprisingly orderly, owing not to law or even to guild organization but to conventions devised by the Dublin publishers themselves, acting as the Company of Booksellers.

Three factors were chiefly responsible for bringing about the collapse of the Dublin book trade in the closing years of the eighteenth century and opening years of the nineteenth. First, the turbulent 1790s took a huge economic and political toll on Ireland, and the book trade was particularly hard hit. Bankruptcies became increasingly common among Irish publishers whose names appear in table 2, such as George Draper, Arthur Grueber, and Randal M'Allister in 1793, Thomas Walker in 1794, and William Jones in 1796. The radical society known as the United Irishmen was attractive to a number of Dublin publishers, among them Patrick Byrne, John Chambers, William Gilbert, Randal M'Allister, and James Moore.[84] They were invariably disappointed, as political and religious oppression worsened, and the uprising of 1798 failed dismally. Byrne, who probably owned the biggest bookselling firm in Dublin by that time, was imprisoned after the uprising and finally emigrated to Philadelphia in 1800. Chambers confided to Mathew Carey in 1794 that the situation in Ireland was bleak and likely to remain so "however long I may continue to speak of this Country";[85] he too was imprisoned after the uprising and made his way to New York in 1805. Gilbert did a three-month stint at Newgate in 1797 for breach of privilege in his newspaper, the *Dublin Evening Post*, and M'Allister was imprisoned for the same crime in 1793 and went bankrupt soon after. Moore, like Byrne a politically radical Roman Catholic, managed to make it through the 1790s but not by much; he put

84. McDowell, "Personnel," 12–53.

85. Chambers to Carey, 26 Mar. 1794, HSP, Lea and Febiger Papers.

his stock up for auction in 1802 and died the following year. Following the death of James Williams in 1787 and the retirement from bookselling of Luke White in 1789, these bankruptcies, imprisonments, retirements, and departures for America deprived the Dublin book trade of many of its shining lights, and the decline and apparent demise of the Company of Booksellers during the 1790s only made matters worse. The fact that American booksellers were now producing more reprints of their own did not help matters either.

Second, the Dublin reprint trade was adversely affected by two legislative actions: the large increase in the paper duty in 1795 and the extension of British copyright law to Ireland as a result of the union in 1801. Both of these changes fulfilled the wishes of London booksellers like Cadell, who believed they were necessary in order to prevent publishers in Ireland from having an unfair advantage over their counterparts in Britain. In Ireland the matter was viewed differently, of course, and the imposition of British copyright law was seen as the straw that broke the back not only of the native reprinting industry but also of Irish print culture in general. Writing in 1818, Dublin's contemporary historians lamented that "great numbers who formerly were in the habits of reading are by this act interdicted from doing so, as the books which once, by their comparative cheapness, were within their means of purchasing, cannot be procured."[86] At the opposite end of the book-buying spectrum, the Union sparked an exodus to London of many prominent Protestant families, weakening the domestic market for Enlightenment books.[87]

Yet were these factors really enough to bring the Dublin publishing industry to its knees? As difficult as the 1790s were for Dublin booksellers, statistics culled from ESTC indicate that the number of Dublin imprints continued to grow at a prodigious rate during that decade, just as they did elsewhere. Indeed, the 1790s witnessed by far the largest growth rate for Dublin imprints of any decade during the second half of the eighteenth century. Furthermore, as hard as the introduction of British copyright law must have been for a trade that had never known it before, it cannot, in and of itself, account for what subsequently occurred. After all, Edinburgh in the age of Archibald Constable enjoyed a thriving culture of print and publication (even if, as I have suggested in chapter 6, it did not reach the mythic proportions attributed to it by its loyal boosters), and it did so in spite of British statutory copyright law, the enforcement of

---

86. Warburton, Whitlaw, and Walsh, *History,* 2:1158.
87. Kennedy, "Domestic and International Trade," 101–2.

"honorary" copyright among the more reputable booksellers, the growth of American reprinting and cheap reprinting in London, and other potentially threatening developments. Why didn't Dublin do the same?

Writing in the *Dublin Journal* when a change in the Irish commercial laws was being contemplated in April 1785, just a few weeks after Cadell and his colleagues gave parliamentary testimony on this matter, Thomas Todd Faulkner—the nephew of one of Ireland's greatest booksellers, George Faulkner—argued that just as Scottish writers like Tobias Smollett had gone to London because the prices paid to authors were higher there, so would Irish writers do the same if the Irish trade had to compete with the London booksellers on equal terms. Building on sources like this one, Richard Cole has formulated a modern version of the "poor Ireland" argument: "Ireland was small, poor, and ignorant, and there were not enough Irish writers to keep many printers and booksellers in business or the resources to publish original works from manuscript."[88]

This approach, however, oversimplifies a complicated story. We have seen that Dublin was a thriving center of print culture during the late eighteenth century, with some wealthy individual publishers and a tradition of collaborative reprinting that could generate wealth through numbers. Dublin far surpassed Edinburgh in numbers of inhabitants, bookshops, and imprints, and its access to the American market was growing. Yet Dublin never hosted a broad-based Irish Enlightenment, the way that Edinburgh became a center for authors of the Scottish Enlightenment. Long before the extension of British copyright law to Ireland in 1801, Oliver Goldsmith, Edmund Burke, Hugh Kelly, Edmond Malone, Arthur Murphy, the Sheridans, and other prominent Irish authors were in the habit of publishing their writings in London, and most of them lived there, too. In 1842 one Irish writer pointed out that "until within the last ten or twelve years an Irish author never thought of publishing in his own country, and the consequence was that our literary men followed the example of our great landlords; they became absentees, and drained the country of its intellectual wealth precisely as the others exhausted it of its rents."[89] Allowing for exaggeration and partial exceptions, such as the tradition of Irish antiquarian writing that has been expertly analyzed by Clare O'Halloran,[90] the statement may provide an accurate description

88. Cole, *Irish Booksellers*, 195–96.

89. William Carleton, quoted in Benson, "Printers and Booksellers," 47.

90. O'Halloran, *Golden Ages*, shows that the discourse of the Irish antiquarians frequently intersected with that of the Enlightenment—and particularly with that of

of the situation in late eighteenth-century Ireland. But its logic is faulty. As the example of Scotland proves, the undeniable attraction of London as a publishing center did not necessarily entail a mass migration of local authors and the depletion of local book culture. Much depended on the relationships of the local book trade with the London trade on the one hand and with authors on the other.

This brings us to the third reason for the demise of the Dublin book trade, which I referred to previously as the trade's Achilles' heel. The fundamental flaw in Irish publishing was not that it was piratical but that it was so largely parasitical. If we go back to the 1720s, when the Dublin bookseller George Faulkner was the friend, editor, and publisher of Jonathan Swift and collaborated with prominent London booksellers and printers,[91] we can get some idea how differently things might have turned out. In subsequent decades, the Dublin book trade grew in every way except one: it did not cultivate viable publishing relationships with prominent Irish authors, either by competing with London publishers for the right to publish new literary and scholarly works or by collaborating with London publishers in that process, the way that some Edinburgh booksellers did. As a result, the Dublin trade remained almost completely dependent on reprinting and could not withstand the series of blows it received at the end of the eighteenth century, culminating in the extension of British copyright law to Ireland.

The rapid decline of the Irish book trade in the early nineteenth century

---

the Scottish Enlightenment. Nevertheless, their writings were too narrowly focused on the ancient and medieval Irish past to generate much interest outside their homeland. Even within Ireland, several of them, such as Charles O'Conor and Edward Ledwich, felt isolated in the countryside, and they lacked institutional support in Dublin until the foundation of the Royal Irish Academy in 1785 (4). Most of their major works were published in Dublin rather than London, and the few that initially had London imprints were sometimes published for the author (e.g., Sylvester O'Halloran, *General History of Ireland*) or reissued from a Dublin original with a new title page (e.g., John Murray's 1772 edition of O'Halloran's *Introduction to the Study of the History and Antiquities of Ireland*, which appeared in the same year as Thomas Ewing's Dublin edition). When Richard Moncrieffe paid Thomas Leland £300 for the copyright to *The History of Ireland from the Invasion of Henry II* (published separately in Dublin and London in three quarto volumes in 1773), Leland was touted as the first Irish author to sell the copyright to a literary work to the Dublin trade. But the publisher lost money on the transaction (Pollard, *Dictionary*, 413), and the experiment did not did not set off a trend.

91. Ward, *Prince of Dublin Printers;* Pollard, *Dictionary*, 198–206.

seemed to confirm the views of London booksellers like Thomas Cadell, who portrayed it as a quick and dirty business, incapable of carrying out large-scale publishing projects and fundamentally shady in its practices, with regard both to the reception of the texts to be reprinted and the uses to which the reprinted books were eventually put. From the standpoint of the book history of the Scottish Enlightenment, however, the situation looks rather different. The Dublin reprint trade of the second half of the eighteenth century served a critical function by making the books of the Scottish Enlightenment available to a much wider readership because they cost less yet maintained reasonably high (sometimes extremely high) publishing standards. Had the London booksellers not felt the sting of competition from across the Irish Sea during the late eighteenth century, they might have priced their books higher and been slower to bring out cheaper octavo editions of major quarto works. It is unlikely that their editions of Scottish Enlightenment books would have penetrated the Irish market to anything like the degree that those of the Dublin booksellers did. And what happened in Ireland had enormous ramifications elsewhere, especially in the Americas, where Dublin-trained booksellers and Dublin-printed books would play a leading part in the dissemination of literature and learning, much of it Scottish.

When the Scottish Enlightenment is viewed from this broadly Atlantic perspective, the significance of the Irish reprint trade becomes clear. Dublin was the hinge on which the Atlantic dissemination of Enlightenment books turned. Whether they were making cheap editions or attempting to surpass the British originals they were copying, and whether their products were ultimately bound for readers in Ireland, the Americas, Britain, or the Continent, the Dublin reprinters were above all else appropriators of culture. To the extent that the culture they appropriated was that of enlightened Scotland, their actions contributed almost as much as those of the Strahans, the Cadells, and other major publishers of new books in London and Edinburgh to the creation and diffusion of the Scottish Enlightenment as an Atlantic cultural phenomenon. The Scottish Enlightenment was crossing the Atlantic, and Irish booksellers were among its principal agents.

8

Making Scottish Books in
America, 1770–1784

THE SCOTTISH ENLIGHTENMENT AND
THE AMERICAN BOOK TRADE

In their influential 1976 article, "The Enlightened Reader in America," David Lundberg and Henry F. May charted the reading habits of late eighteenth-century Americans by searching the holdings of nearly three hundred libraries. Among their findings was the existence of "a sharp growth in the popularity of the Scots" during the years 1777–90 and the continued or increased popularity of Scottish authors from 1790 until the closing date of their study in 1813.[1] Lundberg and May based these conclusions on works by seven prominent Scottish authors: James Beattie, Hugh Blair, Adam Ferguson, David Hume, Lord Kames, Thomas Reid, and Adam Smith. They categorized most of the books by these men under the heading "Scottish Common Sense," placing the works of Hume and (strangely) Ferguson under the designation "skepticism and materialism."

As Mark G. Spencer has shown in regard to Hume, Lundberg and May seriously underestimated the colonial influence of some of the authors whose works they attempted to analyze.[2] Moreover, the full impact of Scottish books in America involved a much larger number of authors than the seven in the Lundberg-May sample, transcended Lundberg and May's narrow and often misleading categories, and was evident before 1777.[3] The influence of the Scottish Enlightenment on the American founding

---

1. Lundberg and May, "Enlightened Reader," 262–71, quoting 269.

2. Spencer, *Hume and Eighteenth-Century America*, 12–16.

3. Sher, "Introduction: Scottish-American Cultural Studies," 1–27, esp. 10–11.

fathers has now been placed on firm ground, and recent studies by Roger Emerson, Nina Reid-Maroney, and others, along with classic works by Andrew Hook on Scottish-American cultural and literary interactions and by Douglas Sloan on the role of Scots and Scotland in the making of American higher education, have informed us of the richness and complexity of Scottish intellectual influences both well before and long after the American Revolution.[4] Yet little scholarship has appeared on the material foundations of the transmission of Scottish thought and culture to America.

Thomas Jefferson's famous letter to Robert Skipwith of 3 August 1771, recommending 148 titles for the establishment of a gentleman's library in America, constitutes one interesting piece of evidence about the awareness of Scottish Enlightenment books in the colonial period. The list contains, in one form or another, 28 of the 122 books in table 2 that had been published by 1769, as well as works by two other Scottish authors, David Mallet and James Thomson, who are not represented in the table.[5] Among the titles from table 2 that Jefferson recommended were works of history by David Hume and William Robertson, fiction by Tobias Smollett, drama by John Home, poetry by John Ogilvie and Ossian, philosophy by Hume, Adam Smith, Thomas Reid, and Lord Kames, jurisprudence by Lord Kames, literary criticism by Kames and Hugh Blair, political economy by Sir James Steuart, and science by Francis Home. It has been plausibly argued that Kames is the central figure in the Skipwith list.[6] In advising Skipwith about how to obtain the books on his list, Jefferson referred him to the London bookseller Thomas Waller. He did so because in 1771 no

4. Emerson, "Scottish Literati and America," 183–220; Reid-Maroney, *Philadelphia's Enlightenment;* Hook, *Scotland and America;* Sloan, *Scottish Enlightenment and the American College Ideal.* On Scots and the American founding fathers, see Spencer, *Hume and Eighteenth-Century America,* chaps. 4–8; Fleischacker, "Adam Smith's Reception," 869–96, and "Impact on America," 316–37; and, on the previously neglected influence of Lord Kames, Jayne, *Jefferson's Declaration of Independence,* esp. chap. 4. For older studies, see the comprehensive footnotes and bibliography in Spencer's book and my bibliographical essay cited in the preceding note.

5. Jefferson, *Papers,* 1:76; Wilson, "Thomas Jefferson's Library," 56–72. By the phrase "in one form or another," I mean that three of the works Jefferson cites—Ossian's *Poems* with Blair's *Dissertation,* Hume's *Essays and Treatises,* and John Home's *Plays* (i.e., *The Dramatic Works of John Home,* 1760)—contain works that also appear separately in table 2.

6. Wilson, "Thomas Jefferson's Library," 66–68; Berman, *Thomas Jefferson,* 22–31.

bookseller in America would have stocked all the books on Jefferson's list, and a Virginia planter like Skipwith could save both time and money by importing them directly from a London bookseller.

By the end of the century, some things had changed, and some had not. Although a small number of Americans with narrowly defined specialties continued to import their books directly from booksellers in London,[7] the ordinary American reader of enlightened literature now had other options. In 1796 Elihu Hubbard Smith wrote to his sister Abigail in New York, recommending a suitable program of modern reading for her to pursue:

> It will be best to direct your principal attention to such writings as will assist you in forming just notions in morality and criticism. In the former, read [Dugald] Stewart's "Philosophy of the Mind," and [William] Godwin's "Political Justice"—you will get them both of Mr. Allen—as also [Adam] Smith "Theory of Moral Sentiments"; in the latter, read [Lord] Kames's "Elements of Criticism" — and [Hugh] Blair's Lectures. I mention these books, because I know that you *can* obtain them; and because they are, perhaps, as good as any you can procure.[8]

In purpose and content, Smith's recommendations were not so different from Jefferson's. Both men demonstrated an appreciation for the moral and critical thought of what we now call the Scottish Enlightenment. They even cited three of the same authors—Adam Smith, Lord Kames, and Hugh Blair—and two of the same titles by them. There is a considerable difference, however, in the way that the recommended books were to be procured. Abigail Smith could obtain her books immediately, simply by visiting the New York City bookshop of Thomas Allen; indeed, her brother says he selected these particular titles for her on account of their accessibility as well as their excellence.

Smith's confidence in the availability of these books probably rested on knowledge that most of them had recently been reprinted, or were then being reprinted, in America. British editions of these books would also have been available in bookshops like Allen's. To historians of ideas, it may not matter whether a particular book arrived on a ship from Britain or Ireland or was reprinted in America, so long as Americans had the opportunity to purchase and read the text and absorb its ideas. Lundberg

7. See, for example, Ewan, "One Professor's Chief Joy," 312.

8. Smith, *Diary*, 141 (19 Mar. 1796).

and May do not distinguish the provenance of the books they are charting in American libraries, and they describe the general field to which
they believe their study has contributed as "the spread of the European
Enlightenment in America."[9] From one perspective, this makes sense, for
during this period Americans unquestionably looked to Europe for most
of the books they read.

Yet the matter was more complex than a simple case of European diffusion and American reception. American reprints can be regarded as acts
of appropriation, with enormous significance for understanding American
culture. Through the process of reprinting, the fledgling American book
trade laid claim to certain works from among the vast corpus of European
books. Such books may have been written and originally published in
Europe, but they were also made in America.

The development of the American reprint trade during the last three
decades of the eighteenth century was encouraged by three main factors:
financial incentive, convenience, and a patriotic ideology of material and
intellectual improvement. Some contemporaries claimed that it was more
costly to reprint books in America than to import them from Edinburgh,
Dublin, and London,[10] where prices were kept down by relatively cheap,
specialized labor, sophisticated distribution networks, and the widespread
availability of paper, type, and presses. But importing heavy items like
books across the Atlantic Ocean was expensive (especially bound books,
which were preferred because of the high cost of bookbinding in America),
and the additional costs of shipping and handling, duty, and insurance
were passed along to American consumers as a surcharge. These circumstances created a sufficiently powerful financial incentive for American
booksellers to try their hand at reprinting books that would be cheaper
for consumers yet profitable for their publishers. A second reason for reprinting derived from the slow, uncertain nature of transatlantic importing. If a desired book or edition were not available in America, it could
take months to order it from abroad, and shipments were sometimes lost
along the way, damaged, or delayed for long periods. Third, importation
was a constant reminder to Americans of their dependence on Europeans,
not only for the content of most of the books they read but also for the
books themselves, considered as material artifacts. Homegrown products
began to seem increasingly patriotic, especially as tensions with Britain

9. Lundberg and May, "Enlightened Reader," 264.

10. A statement to this effect appeared in the Philadelphia *Evening Star* as late as
30 October 1810, as quoted in Green, "From Printer to Publisher," 42n2.

mounted after 1763. In advertisements for their own publications, therefore, late eighteenth-century American booksellers frequently drew attention to the lower cost, immediate or imminent availability, and native manufacture of the editions they were producing, and they often stressed as well the importance of their undertakings for the betterment of their countrymen.

Importing books involved a certain amount of selectivity and risk, but reprinting was a good deal more selective and considerably riskier. Importers were sure to sell books that were designated for specific buyers, or that were likely to sell under any circumstances, such as bibles. They could also hedge their bets by ordering a wide range of titles, and they could exchange books with other American booksellers, sell books at auction, and sometimes return books to their distributors. If all else failed, they could delay making payments for a long time after receiving a shipment of books from across the sea—or never pay at all.[11] To publish a book, however, entailed gambling that demand for a particular edition was sufficient to make the undertaking worthwhile. It meant putting up capital for paper, type, ink, and other materials, and for the printing itself, advertising, and incidentals, without knowing in advance how well a book was going to sell. The level of uncertainty was considerably higher for unproven new books, scholarly books, and above all very large books. Organizing a subscription was one popular way to lessen the risk and uncertainty associated with publications of this kind.[12] But subscription campaigns entailed additional expenses of their own, because it was necessary to print and publicize the proposals, and hopeful publishers sometimes found it advisable to print a free specimen of the proposed book in order to stir up additional interest. Moreover, subscription publications did not yield full returns until the final product was delivered and paid for, and not all subscribers honored their commitments. Too many subscription projects could flood the potential market. Thus, publishing books, especially large, scholarly books, was risky business in eighteenth-century America.

The far right-hand column of table 2 provides publication information about the Scottish Enlightenment books that were reprinted in late eighteenth-century America. A comparison of that column with the one

---

11. There are several known instances of nonpayment, beginning with the episode depicted in Nolan, *Printer Strahan's Book Account*. Other cases are discussed later in this chapter and in chapter 9.

12. Farren, "Subscription."

adjacent to it reveals similarities as well as differences in the patterns of Irish and American reprinting. Perhaps the most obvious difference concerns the scale of reprinting. Of the 360 British first editions in table 2, a total of 80 (22 percent) were reprinted in some form in eighteenth-century America, as against 136 (38 percent) in eighteenth-century Dublin. This difference is not surprising since Dublin reprinting started earlier and was a larger, better-organized, and more centralized industry. Nevertheless, the fact that more than one out of every five Scottish Enlightenment books was reprinted in America during the second half of the eighteenth century, despite large numbers of imports, signifies a flourishing American reprint trade.

The pace of reprinting changed toward the end of the century, when the American book trade was growing rapidly. As a result, Scottish books from the last two decades of the century stood a much better chance of being reprinted quickly in America than were titles originally published during the 1750s and 1760s; indeed, by 1789 it was possible (though still unusual) for a book like William Cullen's *Treatise of the Materia Medica* (no. 281) to be reprinted in America in the same year that it was originally published in Edinburgh and reprinted in Dublin. American reprinters of the late 1780s and 1790s were also engaged in an attempt to catch up with older titles while they continued to reprint new material. This period often saw the appearance of the first American editions of works that had been in print in Britain, and often Ireland too, for several decades. Mathew Carey published the first American editions of William Duncan's *Elements of Logic* and William Guthrie's *Geography* twenty-four and forty-four years, respectively, after their original dates of publication. Thomas Dobson published the first American edition of Adam Smith's *Wealth of Nations* thirteen years after the first London edition. Robert Campbell brought out the first American edition of Hume's *History of England* more than thirty years after the first complete edition appeared in London. This pattern continued in the early nineteenth century, when Irish reprinting of Scottish Enlightenment books died out.

This time lag in American reprinting had certain advantages. American booksellers enjoyed the luxury of waiting to see which British books maintained their popularity, and they were able to avoid some of the mistakes made by the Dublin booksellers, who sometimes rushed into print their own editions of books that ended up being poor sellers. Approximately two-thirds of the Scottish Enlightenment books that were reprinted in eighteenth-century America had already been reprinted in Dublin, and the percentage was even higher for books I have designated as Dublin best sellers. The stream of Irish booksellers emigrating to America toward the end of the century made for an ongoing Atlantic dialogue that must have affected the selection of books for reprinting.[13]

We have seen that Irish reprinters typically used smaller formats and a denser printed page to produce cheaper editions of the British originals they were reprinting. American reprinters often followed the same practices, and sometimes they went further. The *Wealth of Nations* was originally published in London in two volumes quarto in 1776, downsized to a three-volume octavo in Dublin in the same year, and then reprinted as a three-volume duodecimo in Philadelphia in 1789. But this was unusual. A more common practice was for American publishers to save money through the use of close printing and volume reduction rather than duodecimo formats. For example, Henry Mackenzie's *Julia de Roubigné* (no. 183), originally published in London in 1777 as a two-volume duodecimo, and reprinted in Dublin in the same year and in the same format, was first reprinted in America as a one-volume octavo. John Moore's best-selling Continental travel books (nos. 201 and 219) both started off in Britain as two-volume octavos, were reduced to two-volume duodecimos in Dublin, and then appeared in America as one-volume octavos (gathered from separately published numbers). Sometimes close printing enabled American publishers to save money by reducing the number of pages rather than the number of volumes or the format. Cullen's *Treatise of the Materia Medica* (no. 281), for example, was published almost simultaneously in Dublin and Philadelphia as a two-volume octavo. Both editions undersold the expensive two-volume Edinburgh quarto, but the Philadelphia edition had significantly more words on the page and was therefore more than one hundred pages shorter than the Dublin edition.

Geographical differences between America and Ireland were also significant. We have already seen that the vast distance separating America from Europe created difficulties as well as opportunities for the American book trade. Geographical diversity must be taken into account along with distance. Whereas Irish reprinting was heavily concentrated in the capital city, Dublin, American reprinting was divided among Boston, New York, and Philadelphia. As time passed, the locus of reprinting activity shifted, and Philadelphia emerged as the cultural capital of the new republic. Although it was significantly outpaced by Boston in the production of books and other separately printed items during the 1740s and 1750s, Philadelphia steadily increased its share of American printed matter during the

13. Cole, *Irish Booksellers*, esp. chaps. 3, 8, and 9.

third quarter of the century, and during the 1770s it surpassed Boston for the first time in total number of imprints. Remarkably, more than three-quarters of the first American editions of books listed in table 2 were produced in Philadelphia. Boston and New York City together accounted for about 20 percent, and Providence, Albany, Mount Pleasant (New York), and Hartford had one first edition apiece. Other evidence from ESTC confirms the ascent of late eighteenth-century Philadelphia as an international printing and publishing center. In the 1750s Dublin had almost nine times as many imprints as Philadelphia (2,410 versus 275), and in the 1760s Dublin's advantage was still more than five imprints to one (2,400 versus 440). But Philadelphia gained ground dramatically during the 1770s and 1780s. By the end of the century, Philadelphia, with just over 3,000 imprints from 1791 through 1800, joined Dublin (4,400 imprints) and Edinburgh (3,230 imprints) in the second tier of English-language publishing cities behind London (35,910 imprints), almost doubling the combined output for the decade of Boston (1,228 imprints) and New York (452 imprints).[14]

The environments for reprinting also differed substantially. Despite occasional disputes, the Dublin trade was relatively orderly, and it became more so when the Company of Booksellers established procedures for collective reprinting, sometimes placing dozens of names in a single imprint. By contrast, the book trade in America was more individualistic and competitive, and it relied more on publishing by subscription than on group publishing on a large scale. As in Dublin, Edinburgh, and London, the leading booksellers in late eighteenth-century Philadelphia tried their best to control the industry by means of corporate organization, but their attempts came relatively late and did not succeed.[15] Instead, publishing collaborations tended to be sporadic and temporary.

Under these circumstances, who in America was prepared to reprint literary and learned books, and with what degree of success? The focus of this chapter and the next is on six prominent Philadelphia booksellers who were the key figures in the development of the Enlightenment reprint trade in America. These bookseller-publishers emigrated to America from Scotland and Ireland in two generational waves. In the first wave, which is discussed in the second part of this chapter, two booksellers who were born in Scotland in the early 1730s, Robert Bell and Robert Ait-

14. See chap. 7, n. 1.

15. Remer, *Printers and Men of Capital*, 55–65; Sher, "Corporatism and Consensus," 32–93.

ken, established the practice of Enlightenment reprinting in America in the period from 1770 to the mid-1780s. Bell was especially important in this respect, and it is not too much to say that he revolutionized American publishing, using the Scottish Enlightenment as his primary source. The second wave, discussed in the next chapter, occurred during the mid-1780s and 1790s, when four booksellers who were born in the 1750s and 1760s greatly expanded the scale of Scottish Enlightenment reprinting in America. Three of them—Thomas Dobson, William Young, and Robert Campbell—were Scots, while the fourth, Mathew Carey, was a Dubliner.

The names of Aitken, Bell, Campbell, Carey, Dobson, and Young appear in boldface in table 2 to highlight their prominence. Of course, many other booksellers also appear in the table as the publishers of first American editions of Scottish Enlightenment books, in Philadelphia and elsewhere. In 1766 John Mein, an immigrant from Edinburgh, reprinted in Boston John Ogilvie's *Providence: An Allegorical Poem* (no. 87) as a thin quarto. As mentioned in chapter 7, the next year Mein and his new Scottish partner, John Fleming or Fleming, produced a two-volume duodecimo edition of James Fordyce's *Sermons to Young Women* (no. 93). But Mein and Fleming soon dropped out of the picture,[16] and no other Scottish Enlightenment titles were reprinted in America until Robert Bell brought out his edition of William Robertson's *History of Charles V* in 1770–71. After that event, nothing would be the same in what Bell called "the American World of Books."

THE EMERGENCE OF SCOTTISH ENLIGHTENMENT REPRINTING IN AMERICA

The Odyssey of Robert Bell

The career of Robert Bell illustrates the complex nature of book production in America, Ireland, and Britain, as well as the beginnings of Philadelphia's challenge to Dublin as the leading city of the Scottish Enlightenment reprint trade. Bell was born and trained in Glasgow, worked as a journeyman in Berwick-upon-Tweed on the border of Scotland and

---

16. Thomas, *History of Printing*, 149–52; Alden, "John Mein: Scourge," 571–99, and "John Mein, Publisher," 199–214; Franklin, *Boston Printers*, 365–69. According to Thomas (150), Mein and Fleeming sometimes printed books in Boston with false London imprints, but I have been unable to identify any Scottish Enlightenment titles of this kind.

England, operated his own bookshop in Dublin, and passed the mature phase of his life in Philadelphia. Along the way he was a bookbinder, a bookseller, an auctioneer, a printer, and a publisher. As a result of this extraordinary geographical and occupational diversity, his range of experiences in the late eighteenth-century Atlantic book trade was unique. In Philadelphia, he was personally responsible for introducing a dynamic approach to reprinting and marketing, and particularly for applying this method to the works of the Enlightenment. For all these reasons, much can be learned by examining Bell's life in the trade.

Little is known about Bell's background. Isaiah Thomas and William M'Culloch, who were active in the American book trade in the late eighteenth and early nineteenth centuries, both asserted that he was born in Glasgow.[17] According to an obituary in the *Pennsylvania Journal* for 6 October 1784, his death the previous month occurred while he was in his fifty-third year. Although there appears to be no entry in the Old Parish Register of Scotland that conforms precisely with these chronological and geographical claims, the closest match is a Robert Bell who was baptized in Glasgow on 28 June 1730, the son of Malcome Bell and Marion Kello. That Robert Bell would have been fifty-four years old in September 1784. Thomas and M'Culloch agree that Bell served an apprenticeship in bookbinding in Glasgow and then worked for some years as a journeyman in Berwick-upon-Tweed, and M'Culloch fills in further details that lend credence to this story. Bell allegedly worked in Berwick for Samuel Taylor, a known figure in the Berwick book trade, and was the co-worker there of William Woodhouse, who would later turn up in Philadelphia as a bookbinder-bookseller and a close associate of Bell's. By working in a small-town firm like Taylor's, Bell would have been exposed to many more facets of the book trade than if he worked as a bookbinder in a larger town, with a more highly developed division of labor.[18] According to M'Culloch, as an apprentice Bell was "so very religious, and had the men and boys of the office so often convened for prayers, that his de-

17. Thomas, *History of Printing*, 394–96; McCulloch, "William McCulloch's Additions," 176.

18. A document dated 17 January 1774, which Bell printed and circulated in opposition to a proposed ban on auctioneering in Philadelphia, mentions "Robert Taylor's, at the Town of *Berwick* upon *Tweed*, on the Borders of *England* and *Scotland*, into both which Kingdoms, he penetrates annually, and sells thousands of BOOKS BY AUCTION" (Bell, *Memorandum*). Since Robert Taylor was the relation of Samuel Taylor, it seems probable that Bell also learned the art of auctioneering from the Taylors during his days as a journeyman in Berwick.

votional exercise[s] were downright intrusions."[19] This statement makes sense in light of the religious climate of Glasgow in the early 1740s, when evangelical revivals centered at nearby Cambuslang rocked the region.[20] Later in life, Bell would lose his religious convictions and would say that "he had religion enough in his youth to last him all his life time."[21]

By 1759, while still not yet twenty, Bell was in Dublin, copublishing a Gaelic book with the Irish bookseller Lawrence Flin. It has been plausibly suggested that Flin and Bell intended their book for export to Scotland.[22] This interpretation is consistent with the fact that in the following year Bell issued in Dublin an edition of James Thomson's *The Seasons* that had been printed in Glasgow. At this early stage, then, Bell may have been operating in Dublin as a Scottish book agent. If so, he did not remain one for long. By October 1760 Bell was a quarter brother in the Guild of St. Luke the Evangelist, and the following month he advertised his first known Dublin book auction. On 28 February 1761 he married a woman called Ann James, and there is every indication that he was beginning to settle in as a member of the Dublin trade. By 1763 he had a shop at the corner of Stephen and Aungier streets with a stock of "several Thousand Volumes," which he listed in *Bell's Sale Catalogue of Books for 1763 and 1764*. Although no copy of the full catalogue is known to exist, Bell put selections of titles from it in the back of two of his reprints of works by Scottish authors, James Burgh's *The Art of Speaking* (1763) and John Bell's *Travels from St. Petersburg* (1764). In 1767 Bell published another Dublin edition of James Thomson's *The Seasons*. Yet there is no indication that any of these works were printed in Scotland, and the rest of his imprints and the existing fragments of his book catalogues are not particularly Scottish.

Bell probably could not afford to be overly discriminating about his publications at this stage in his career because he was operating at the margins of the Dublin trade. Most of his stock was secondhand, sold at "the lowest Price (for ready Money) being mark'd to each Book,"[23] and the opportunity to reprint the choicest new British books generally eluded

19. McCulloch, "William McCulloch's Additions," 97.

20. Fawcett, *Cambuslang Revival*.

21. McCulloch, "William McCulloch's Additions," 97.

22. See the entry on Bell in Pollard, *Dictionary*, 29, from which some other biographical details have been drawn.

23. *Bell's Sale Catalogue of Books for 1763 and 1764*, as quoted in Bell's advertisement in the back of the second volume of his edition of John Bell, *Travels from St. Petersburg*.

him. In 1767 Bell took a huge gamble by moving his stock of more than five thousand bound books to a large "Theatre" in Capel Street, which he renovated at "a very considerable Expence."[24] At the same time, he took a different kind of risk by joining with several other young booksellers to challenge the established procedures of the Dublin trade, as discussed in the last chapter.

Although these initiatives failed, and Bell went bankrupt before the end of 1767, his years in Dublin had not been wasted. Dublin turned out to be his true apprenticeship for the experience that lay ahead—in Philadelphia. His timing could not have been better. Until the arrival of Benjamin Franklin and Samuel Keimer in the 1720s, Philadelphia had only one print shop, run by William and Andrew Bradford.[25] Subsequent growth in printing did not generate much book production, however, let alone the publication of Enlightenment books. Franklin, for example, printed few substantial tomes.[26]

In the mid-1740s William Strahan arranged for his old Edinburgh friend and fellow London printer, David Hall, to become Franklin's printing partner. From the time he arrived in Philadelphia in 1745 until his death in 1772, Hall received from Strahan a steady supply of bound books for wholesale distribution in America and for retail sale in his bookshop.[27] The arrangement worked well because of the personal relationship of trust between Strahan and Hall, and because Strahan, as a copyright owner himself, was able to deal with the London booksellers on the most favorable terms.[28] Any thoughts Hall might have had of trying his hand at reprinting instead of importing British books were checked by the fact that his contract required him to share half the profits of all his printing work with his retired partner, Franklin, whereas in bookselling he was on his own.[29] Hall occasionally dealt with British exporters other than

24. *Catalogue of Books, which Will Begin to Be Sold by Auction.* It is unfortunate that the only known copy of this informative bankruptcy catalogue (in the National Library of Ireland) is incomplete.

25. For an overview of the development of the Philadelphia trade, see Green, "English Books," 248–98.

26. Green, "Benjamin Franklin," 98–114; Miller, *Benjamin Franklin's Philadelphia Printing.*

27. Harlan, "David Hall's Bookshop," 2–23; Cochrane, *Dr. Johnson's Printer,* chap. 6.

28. Strahan to Hall, 11 July 1758, in Cochrane, *Dr. Johnson's Printer,* 83; Botein, "Anglo-American Book Trade," 70.

29. Green, "English Books," 278.

Strahan, including Hamilton & Balfour and Kincaid in Edinburgh, and he even imported some books illegally from Dublin.[30] Several other American booksellers also imported books in sizable quantities, and by the end of the 1760s Britain was exporting more books to its American colonies than to Europe.[31] Scottish Atlantic networking played a disproportionately large role in this process, even among booksellers in America who were not Scottish, such as James Rivington of New York.[32] Although the import trade in books died down during the American Revolution, the full legalization of Irish imports to America after 1780 further enriched the opportunities for importing books from abroad, and the end of hostilities with Britain set off a golden age of international, competitive book importing that is revealed by the titles of published catalogues and advertisements such as *Hugh Gaine's Catalogue of Books, Lately Imported from England, Ireland, and Scotland* (New York, 1792) and *Mathew Carey, No. 158, Market-Street, Philadelphia, Has Imported from London, Dublin, and Glasgow, an Extensive Assortment of Books* (Philadelphia, 1792).

A broadside advertisement issued by David Hall around 1768 provides some idea of the availability of Scottish books at the time that Robert Bell arrived in Philadelphia. Bearing the heading *Imported in the Last Vessels from England, and to be Sold by David Hall, at the New Printing-Office, in Market-street, Philadelphia*, Hall's list includes the *History of England* and *Essays* (presumably *Essays and Treatises on Several Subjects*) by David Hume, along with Sir James Steuart's *Inquiry into the Principles of Political Economy*, William Robertson's *History of Scotland*, Adam Smith's *Theory of Moral Sentiments*, Lord Kames's *Elements of Criticism*, and two books by Robert Wallace. This was a representative assortment, and if a desired book was not available, a copy could be ordered specially from Britain, either through an American bookseller like Hall or Rivington or directly from a British bookseller, as Jefferson advised Skipwith to do. In this way, Americans were able to keep up with the latest literary and learned publications from abroad. But, as we have seen, the process of importing books had serious disadvantages that opened the door to American reprinting.

When he arrived in Philadelphia at the end of 1767 or beginning of

30. McDougall, "Scottish Books for America," 21–46; David Hall Letterbook, Salem County Historical Society, Salem, New Jersey.

31. Raven, "Export of Books," 21–49, citing 21; Raven, "Importation of Books," 183–98; Barber, *Studies in the Booktrade*, 223–64.

32. Raven, "Commodification and Value," 78; Raven, *London Booksellers and American Customers*, 103.

1768, Bell was in his late thirties, filled with boundless energy, and ready to put to use the wide range of skills he had acquired in Dublin. His auctions up and down the East Coast were so lively that people attended them for their entertainment value; M'Culloch proclaimed them "as good as a play."[33] Bell's showmanship was inseparable from his salesmanship. The early auctions, in the spring of 1768, were accompanied by printed catalogues showing the full retail price of each book. The rules stipulated that the bidding would begin at half the retail price and that no sale could be made without at least three bidders. In addition, anyone purchasing six shillings' worth of books "shall receive, *gratis*, a Paper Cutter and Folder worth One Shilling."[34] The stock at these auctions consisted entirely of new books, which Bell presumably acquired at low prices from other booksellers who could not sell them.

On Third Street, next to St. Paul's Church, Bell opened a bookshop that attracted all varieties of men of letters and served as an intellectual center. By the end of his career, in 1784, a comical poem titled "The Philadelphiad," apparently written by Jon McLewes, drew attention to this aspect of his shop: "Here authors meet who ne'er a sprig have got, / The poet, player, doctor, wit and sot." One occasional visitor to the shop, Peter Stephen Du Ponceau, called Bell "a shrewd sensible man" and added that "we have had few of his profession who could be compared to him."[35] He recalled the advice Bell had given him about how to write, which became the young man's guiding principle: "Think a great deal before you write, and when you have well matured your subject, then take up your pen, and write as long as you have something new or interesting to say, and when you have nothing more to say, stop."

Other aspects of his behavior were less respectable. Although Bell's Irish wife followed him to Philadelphia in 1774, she did not stay long. Two years later, Bell and his American mistress had a daughter, Margaret Green, and he seems to have lived the rest of his life with them and his son, who had come to Philadelphia with his mother and remained there until his father's death. As if this behavior were not scandalous enough, Bell openly thumbed his nose at established religion by working (and making his men work) on Sundays and "ridiculing the clergy" at his book

33. McCulloch, "William McCulloch's Additions," 232.

34. Bell, *Catalogue of Books, to be Sold by Auction* [Mar. 1768]; and Bell, *Catalogue of Books, to be Sold by Auction* [early May? 1768].

35. Du Ponceau, "Autobiography," 461.

auctions. M'Culloch labeled him "profane," but his irreverence often took the form of "buffoonery," which he displayed "without limit."[36]

The content of his printed catalogues reveals that Bell was much more active as an importer of books than some commentators have thought and sold both used and new books.[37] Five years after his arrival in Philadelphia, for example, he issued *Robert Bell's Sale Catalogue of a Collection of New and Old Books, in all the Arts and Sciences, and in various Languages, Also, a large Quantity of entertaining Novels; with the lowest Price printed in each Book; Now Selling, at the Book-Store of William Woodhouse* (dated 15 July 1773), which contains 947 titles in all formats, almost all of them imported from Britain or Ireland. Other catalogues were more specialized, such as *New and Old, Medical, Surgical, and Chemical Works, Lately Imported, and Now Selling at Bell's Book-Store, under St. Paul's Church in Third-Street, Philadelphia* (1784), which contained 352 titles in medicine and the sciences. As his stock grew and his operations expanded to include a printing press, Bell acquired an additional site on the other side of St. Paul's Church. He started a circulating library and put a bookplate in its volumes that identified his shop as a place "where Sentimentalists, whether Ladies or Gentlemen, May Become Readers" by agreeing to one of several subscription plans.[38]

Like David Hall, then, Bell would be worthy of recognition for his achievements in the dissemination of enlightened literature and learning in America even if he had never published a single book. To take the medical and scientific works of the Scottish Enlightenment as an example, his specialist catalogue of 1784, cited earlier, contains numerous titles by William Alexander, Benjamin Bell, William Buchan, William Cullen, Andrew Duncan, Francis Home, James Lind, Alexander Monro *primus*, Donald Monro, William Smellie (on midwifery), and Robert Whytt, as well as the Philosophical Society of Edinburgh's *Essays and Observations, Physical and Literary*, the Edinburgh Pharmacopoeia and Dispensatory, and many other works of this kind, few of which had been reprinted in

---

36. McCulloch, "William McCulloch's Additions," 176, 219, 228, 232. The practice of working on Sundays was not uncommon in the Philadelphia book trade, to the horror of pious Scots. See Remer, "Scottish Printer," 3–25.

37. Most of Bell's known catalogues are listed in Winans, *Descriptive Checklist*.

38. Green, "English Books," reproduces the bookplate on 290 and discusses Bell's idiosyncratic use of the term "sentimentalists" on 288. See also Knott, "Culture of Sensibility," 32–56.

America. In a characteristically idiosyncratic phrase in one of his adver-
tisements, Bell remarked that his bookstore provided "a variety of NEW
WORKS OF ENTERTAINMENT; With every curiosity that is *come-at-able* in the
American world of Books."[39]

Bell made his greatest contribution to the American Enlightenment as
a publisher. He began modestly in 1768 with light fare, including Samuel
Johnson's *Rasselas* and Oliver Goldsmith's poem *The Traveller*, both of
which bore the curious imprint "America: Printed for every Purchaser"
and made no reference to Bell himself.[40] On the title page of editions of
Laurence Sterne's *Sentimental Journey* and Marmontel's *History of Belisarius* that appeared in 1770, the place of publication remains America (or
North-America, in one instance), but the publisher is identified as "R. Bell,
Bookseller and Auctioneer." These early Philadelphia publications were
cheap duodecimos, and they betrayed no connection to Scottish authors.
It would seem that Bell was simply adapting the style of reprinting he had
practiced in Ireland, involving inexpensive editions of popular works of
imaginative literature..

All that changed in 1770, when Bell undertook a three-volume octavo reprint of William Robertson's *History of Charles V* (no. 119). Isaiah
Thomas remarked that this book and another that Bell reprinted soon afterward, William Blackstone's *Commentaries on the Laws of England*, "may
be considered as the first fruits of a spirit of enterprise in book printing
in that city."[41] More generally, Bell's edition of *Charles V* has been called
the first major work of history, geography, or biography ever to be printed
in its entirely in America.[42] The book was published by subscription in
Philadelphia (though the imprint once again reads America) between
November 1770 and April 1771. To attract subscribers throughout the
American colonies, Bell noted in advertisements that his edition, which
sold for three dollars in boards or four dollars bound, was one-fifth the
price of the British edition (of course, he did not mention that the British
edition was a luxurious quarto rather than a workmanlike octavo). He

39. Advertisement appended to the first number of Bell's edition of John Moore,
A View of Society and Manners in Italy (no. 219), 117. Bell used the phrase "American
World of Books" on other occasions, such as in his advertisements in the *Pennsylvania
Gazette* for 30 October 1782 and 19 March 1783.

40. Metzdorf, "First American 'Rasselas,'" 374–76.

41. Thomas, *History of Printing*, 395.

42. Wolf, *Book Culture*, 79.

gave seven copies for the price of six and after publication promoted the book by reprinting a laudatory sketch of Robertson's life from the *London Magazine*.[43]

In addition to price, Bell played up the issue of American patriotism. He preached the gospel of mental enrichment through enlightened reading, asserting that the diffusion of learned books would make Americans wise and good. Underlying this belief was a philosophy of national improvement through print. In a 1773 pamphlet, Bell proclaimed printing to be "the noblest and most beneficial [art] that ever was invented among the sons of men," and he spoke of "learning as the glory of a nation, and of printing as an art that gains reputation to a people among whom it flourishes."[44] He summed up his views in four lines of verse by George Fisher at the end of the "Address to the Subscribers" in the third volume of his edition of *Charles V*, dated 4 April 1771:

> Since to the Pen and Press we mortals owe,
> All we believe, and almost all we know,
> Go on ye great preservers of these arts,
> Which raise our thoughts and cultivate our parts.

Another aspect of Bell's patriotic philosophy of reprinting was, in his terms, "material" rather than "formal," meaning that it related to "the benefits which arise to the publick" from printed works that "consume a considerable quantity of our paper manufacture, employ our artisans in printing, and find business for great numbers of indigent persons."[45] Importing books from Britain sent thousands of pounds "across the great Atlantic ocean," whereas native publications circulated that money within "the American World" (fig. 8.1). It was this kind of material or economic patriotism that Bell had in mind when he audaciously supplemented Robertson's original dedication to the king in the *History of Charles V* with a separate dedication from "The Editor" to the Pennsylvania patriot John Dickinson and all the subscribers to the American edition, who "contributed their names as encouragers of American manufactures, thus practically demonstrating true patriotism, a real affection for the welfare of their country." At a time when a policy of non-importation was the order

43. *Character of the Celebrated Dr Robertson.*
44. [Bell], *Observations.*
45. Ibid.

TO THE AMERICAN WORLD.

THE inhabitants of this continent have now an eafy and advantageous opportunity of effectually eftablifhing literary manufactures
in the Britifh colonies, at moderate prices calculated for this meridian,
the eftablifhment of which will abfolutely and eventually produce mental
improvement, and commercial expanfion, with the additional recommendation of poffitively faving thoufands of pounds to and among the
inhabitants of the Britifh empire in America.—Thus—The importation of
one thoufand fets of Blackftone's Commentaries, manufactured in Europe, at
ten pounds per fet, is fending very near ten thoufand pounds acrofs the great
Atlantic ocean. Whereas—One thoufand fets manufactured in America,
and fold at the fmall price of three pounds per fet, is an actual faving of fe-
ven thoufand pounds to the purchafers, and the identical three thoufand
pounds which is laid out for our own manufactures is ftill retained in the
country, being diftributed among manufacturers and traders, whofe refidence
upon the continent of courfe caufeth the money to circulate from neighbour
to neighbour, and by this circulation in America there is a great probability
of its revolving to the very hands from which it originally migrated.—

American Gentlemen or Ladies who, at this juncture, retain any degrees
of that antient and noble, but now almoft extinguifhed, affection denominated
patriotifm, and are now pleafed to exemplify it by extending with celerity
and alacrity their aufpicious patronage through the cheap mode of repofing
their names and refidences *(no money expected till the delivery of an equivalent)*
with any Bookfeller or Printer on the continent, as intentional purchafers of
any of the literary works now in contemplation to be reprinted by fubfcripti-
on in America——will render an effential fervice to the community, by encouraging native manufactures——and therefore deferve to be had in grateful
remembrance——by their country——by pofterity——and by their much obliged, humble fervant, the Publifher——

ROBERT BELL.

SUBSCRIPTIONS for Hume, Blackftone, and Fergufon, are re-
ceived by faid Bell, at the late Union Library, in Third-ftreet, Philadelphia;
and by the Bookfellers and Printers in America.

Printed SPECIMENS, with Conditions annexed, for reprinting the
above Books by Subfcription, may be feen at all the great Towns in America.

of the day among American colonists wishing to send a message to Westminster, Bell's dedication tapped into a growing determination to build a
strong and self-reliant American economy.

A further aspect of Bell's notion of patriotic publishing involved his
commitment to the liberty of the press and his resentment toward any
nation or body that attempted to limit it. Most of the "Address to the Subscribers" in his edition of *Charles V* is devoted to this subject, using Ireland

ROBERT BELL, BOOKSELLER,

[At the late UNION LIBRARY, *in Philadelphia,]*

BEING encouraged by feveral Gentlemen of Eminence in the different Provinces, to undertake the Re-publication of the following *literary* Works in America, doth, by this Conveyance, *Give Notice,* he hath now ready to be feen, *at the Bookfellers Shops in the* capital *Towns on the* American *Continent,* printed PROPOSALS, with Specimens and Conditions annexed, for

RE-PRINTING BY SUBSCRIPION,

[No Money expected except on the Delivery of each Volume]

HUME'S ELEGANT HISTORY of ENGLAND, in EIGHT VOLUMES Octavo, at *One Dollar* each Volume, which is only *Eight Dollars* for the whole Set, *although the* Quarto *Edition is* SOLD at *Thirty Dollars.*

ALSO,

FERGUSON'S *celebrated* Effay *on the* Hiftory *of* CIVIL SOCIETY, in ONE VOLUME, Octavo, at *One Dollar, although the* Britifh *Edition is* SOLD at *Four Dollars.*

ADVERTISEMENT.

ANY perfon poffeffed of the moft minute doubt, concerning the legality of literary publications in America, may be fully fatisfied of their rectitude, by looking into the Editor's addrefs to the numerous fubfcribers to the American edition of Robertfon's Hiftory of Charles the Fifth, prefixed to the third volume of that work, where the practice of all the people in the kingdom of Ireland, and the fplendid authority of that magnificent Oracle of Knowledge, the learned judge Blackftone, concerning the internal legiflation of colonies, are produced as fufficient fupport for Americans to perfevere in re-printing any, or every work of excellence, without the fmalleft infraction of the Britifh embargo upon literature.-----And if an exiftence breathes who wifheth to enjoy a fmaller fhare of liberty than the good people of Ireland,-----may not Americans, with great propriety wifh he would confign himfelf to a certain fpot of Earth, defcribed by fome Englifh travellers as,-----

"*A land! where one may pray with curs'd intent,*
"*Oh! may they never fuffer banifhment.*

Fig. 8.1. Robert Bell became an aggressive reprinter of Scottish Enlightenment books soon after he emigrated to Philadelphia from Dublin in the late 1760s. Reproduced here are two pages from an advertisement addressed "To the American World," which was prefixed to the first volume of Bell's 1771 reprint of Sir William Blackstone's *Commentaries on the Laws of England.* Here Bell presents a version of his philosophy of reprinting, defends the legal right to reprint copyrighted British books in America, and hawks proposals for subscription editions of Hume's *History of England* and Ferguson's *Essay on the History of Civil Society*—neither of which ever appeared. John Carter Brown Library at Brown University.

as a model for America to follow. Although they live in "a dependent and subordinate kingdom," Bell writes, "the depressed, I had almost said, the opp[*ré*]ss[*é*]d people of Ireland" have reprinted "every valuable Work produced in Great-Britain, without rendering the smallest pecuniary regard either to Authors or to Booksellers." Citing Blackstone, he argues that just as British copyright law does not extend to Ireland, neither does it extend to America. But the rhetorical thrust of Bell's case lies not in the fine points of legal interpretation but in the act of "depressed" nations asserting their natural right to improve themselves through printing and learning. Thus, Bell contends that "the Representatives of the people of Ireland will never give up this high-born privilege of freely disseminating knowledge, because the nation, when compared with the former inhabitants have been by this means, not only Humanified, but almost Angelified: For 'tis a Godlike attribute to know." As for the state of affairs in America, he can barely contain the hostility he feels for "the British embargo upon literature":

> Is it not enough that their embargo prevents Americans from shipping their manufactures of this kind into Britain — Would it not be incompatible with all freedom, if an American's mind must be entirely starved and enslaved in the barren regions of fruitless vacuity, because he doth not wallow in immense riches equal to some British Lords, the origin of whose progenitors are lost in the chaos of antiquity?
>
> The Editor hopeth, that the facts above exhibited are sufficient support for Americans, to persevere in reprinting whatsoever books merit their approbation, without leave or license from the Bibliopolists or Monopolists of Great-Britain.

Bell subsequently publicized his views in a relentless advertising campaign to justify the legitimacy of American reprinting.

All these strategies had their desired effect. The third volume of Bell's edition of *Charles V* contains the names of more than five hundred subscribers, from almost all walks of life and from a broad geographic span of colonies along the eastern seaboard, who committed themselves to a total of 1,019 three-volume sets.[46] With revenues of several thousand dollars, *Charles V* must have been extremely profitable for its American publisher. Bell and other booksellers then began to contemplate the possibility of saturating the American colonies with native editions of im-

---

46. A fuller account of these subscribers appears in Sher, "*Charles V*," 184–92.

portant new British works. Bell succeeded again with his four-volume, eight-dollar, royal octavo edition of Blackstone's *Commentaries* (1771–72), which attracted a relatively narrow but dedicated core of subscribers from the legal profession. Yet Bell soon learned the limits of his plan to bring the Enlightenment to America by subscription: his proposals for editions of David Hume's *History of England* in eight octavo volumes and Adam Ferguson's *Essay on the History of Civil Society* in one octavo volume, which he advertised widely (e.g., fig. 8.1), failed to attract enough subscribers to warrant publication.[47]

In spite of their unsuccessful outcomes, these attempts to stimulate American interest in works by Hume and Ferguson merit closer inspection. The subscription proposals that Bell issued in April 1771 for his projected edition of Hume's *History* incorporate variations on the sales techniques that Bell had used so successfully to generate interest in Robertson's *Charles V.* Bell appeals to cultural patriotism in an effort to associate his edition of Hume's *History* with "elevation and enriching of THE LAND WE LIVE IN." Once again, the patriotic appeal contains both a material and an intellectual component. Economically, it rests on the desirability of "the extension of useful Manufactures in an Infant-Country," or the promotion of "NATIVE FABRICATIONS." Intellectually, Bell is hinting here, as he did more fully elsewhere, that American editions of the best British and European works of history, philosophy, and literature constitute an important development in the education of the American colonies, enhancing the lives of Americans in significant ways. Bell's edition of Hume will consist of "instructive Volumes" and will advance what the bookseller calls "the progress of literary entertainment"; it will "durably support the honour of that glorious vehicle of KNOWLEDGE AND LIBERTY." Bell's model for the colonies is London, "where FOOD FOR THE MIND is almost as merchantable as BREAD FOR THE FAMILY." Taken together, the economic and intellectual aspects of the argument are said to be a matter of "PUBLIC SPIRIT," and it is specifically to those who possess this quality that the proposals are addressed.[48]

Another argument in the Hume proposals concerns quality of workmanship. The paper used in the proposed edition of the *History of England*

47. In 1771 another Philadelphia bookseller, James Humphreys, tried to interest the American public in a two-volume octavo reprint of William Robertson's first book, *The History of Scotland*, to be sold, like *Charles V,* for one dollar per volume, but his subscription was also abandoned. See Wolf, *Book Culture*, 113.

48. Bell, *Proposals, Addressed to Those Who Possess a Public Spirit.*

will be "fine" in its "colour and consistence"; "the goodness of the type, and the neatness of the artist's manual-exercise at the PRINTING PRESS" will be evident. It is not only to be an American edition but "a handsome American Edition," not only an example of American craftsmanship but of "the excellence of NATIVE FABRICATIONS," not only a work of learning but "an elegant sett of instructive Volumes." Once the edition is complete, it will be "either neatly and uniformly bound in sheep and lettered" or "beautifully finished in calf binding." Thus, public-spirited consumers will not have to sacrifice quality when they subscribe to Bell's edition.

Bell also emphasizes the good value and accessibility of his proposed edition of Hume's *History*. As in the advertisements for *Charles V,* he contrasts the "moderate" price of his proposed edition (one dollar per volume, or eight dollars the set) with the high cost of the London quarto edition, which he computes in local currency at no less than thirty dollars per set. The proposals encourage subscriptions by noting that payment is expected only upon delivery of each volume, and they attempt to assure readers of the legitimacy of publishing the edition "periodically" by noting that this method is common among "some of the most excellent literary works" published in London. One volume will appear every month for eight months, and the project will be capitalized as it goes along. This mode of publication will enable "the Editor" (as Bell again calls himself) "to proceed in large works with certainty" and to provide "a desirable opportunity, for persons in the middle walk of life, to purchase and to read at an easy and convenient rate." With the addition of binding for two dollars per set in sheep or three dollars in calf, Bell presents the American reading public with a complete publication package, designed to compete favorably with London editions in cost as well as quality.

In one of the advertisements for his proposed editions of Blackstone, Hume, and Ferguson, Bell states that the public can examine free "Specimens" of these works at bookstores "in the capital Towns on the American Continent." As well as providing additional evidence of the extent of Bell's commitment to Enlightenment reprinting, surviving examples of these specimens or prospectuses contain clues about Bell's perception of the works he planned to publish. Bell's 1771 prospectus for Adam Ferguson's *Essay on the History of Civil Society,* misleadingly headed *Now in the Printing-Press, and Speedily Will Be Published by Subscription,* excerpts the first ten paragraphs from part 4, section 3, of Ferguson's book, dealing with "the Manners of Polished and Commercial Nations." Here Ferguson reflects on the generally positive effects of the "Advancement of Civil and Commercial Arts" in the modern world, and particularly on the advantages associated with the growth of variety and diversity in commercial society. In one revealing passage, he discusses a subject dear to Bell's heart: the growing sophistication of learning as "matters that have little reference to the active pursuit of mankind, are made subjects of inquiry, and the exercise of sentiment and reason itself becomes a profession." In this new world, "the works of fancy, like the subjects of natural history, are distinguished into classes and species; the rules of every particular kind are distinctly collected; and the library is stored, like the warehouse, with the finished manufacture of different arts, who, with the aids of the grammarian and the critic, aspire, each in his particular way, to instruct the head, or to move the heart." At the end of the prospectus, Bell adds an awkwardly phrased note of his own, inviting "Gentlemen who wish Prosperity to the Increase of the Means for the Enlargement of the human Understanding in America" to come forward as subscribers. The note is signed not by the anonymous "Editor," as he often called himself, but by the "Publisher, ROBERT BELL."

In 1773 Bell printed another advertisement for Ferguson's book, addressed *To the Sons of Science in America*. "This is a living Author of much Estimation," Bell writes, "whose elegant Performance will greatly delight, by giving an Opportunity of being intimately acquainted with the *Sentiments of the Man*, whom Sir John Dalrymple, (Author of the celebrated Memoirs of Great-Britain and Ireland) is pleased to stile, 'one of the greatest of *Modern Philosophers*.'" Bell's language conveys his genuine enthusiasm about the contents of Ferguson's book, as a reader rather than merely as a merchant. The reference to Dalrymple, and to Ferguson as "a living Author of much Estimation," suggests that Bell was also well aware of the vitality of intellectual activity in Edinburgh, where men like Robertson, Hume, Ferguson, and Dalrymple were producing important new works in an atmosphere of mutual admiration. As in several of his other advertisements and proposals, Bell associates books not only with intellectual enrichment but also with pleasure. Ferguson's *Essay* "will greatly delight" readers, and potential subscribers are invited to partake of "this sentimental banquet." Subscription to a project for reprinting a work of philosophical history is portrayed as a passionate, sensuous experience, like the enjoyment of a good meal. These emotional appeals are supplemented with the usual assurances about high-quality workmanship and the opportunity for a bargain.

In spite of all this publicity, no American edition of Ferguson's *Essay* would appear until the early nineteenth century. Why did both of Bell's ambitious schemes to reprint editions of Hume and Ferguson fail? It is possible that Bell was just testing the waters with his simultaneous proposals for editions of Blackstone, Hume, and Ferguson, never intending to publish all of them. The fact that he mentioned all three projects in some of his advertisements from this period might be cited to support this interpretation.[49] Yet the money and effort that Bell spent on promotion, especially by printing free specimens, would seem to argue against it. Perhaps after the great success of his edition of *Charles V*, Bell simply miscalculated what the American market could bear in the early 1770s. Even if he published them "periodically" (as he put it in the proposals), the eight projected volumes of Hume's *History of England*, in particular, were probably more than colonial America could handle.

Another factor must also be taken into account. The books that Bell wanted to reprint by Hume and Ferguson, unlike those by Robertson and Blackstone, were already being imported from Britain in octavo format. We have seen that a relatively inexpensive British octavo edition of Ferguson's *Essay* was available from the time of the third edition of 1768. Three eight-volume octavo editions of Hume's *History of England* had been published in London by 1771, and the book was widely available in America.[50] These British octavos were nicely printed, contained their authors' latest corrections and revisions, and bore the imprints of prestigious British publishers. The retail price in Britain for Hume's *History* in eight octavo volumes was only £2.8s., or less than eleven dollars in Pennsylvania money. The London octavo edition of Ferguson's *Essay* cost only six shillings, or about $1.33, and the claims that Bell sometimes made for his one-dollar edition (also priced on occasion at ten Pennsylvania shillings, bound) being one-fourth the price of the British edition apply only to a comparison with the London quartos. Even with allowances for surcharges to cover the cost of shipping and insurance, the British octavos would still have been available in the American colonies for only a little more than the prices Bell was planning to charge.

After scrapping his projected editions of Hume and Ferguson, Bell did not stop trying to reprint Scottish Enlightenment books in America. In November 1774 he issued proposals for a subscription edition of William Cullen's *Lectures on the Materia Medica*, followed the next year by proposals for editions of John Gregory's *Lectures on the Duties and Qualifications of a Physician* (March 1775) and Lord Kames's *Sketches of the History of*

49. For example, *Pennsylvania Chronicle*, 22–29 Apr. 1771 and 23 Oct.–4 Nov. 1771; and *Boston-Gazette, and Country Journal*, 2 Sept. 1771.

50. Spencer, *Hume and Eighteenth-Century America*, 25–27.

Man (May 1775).[51] The first two of these works were intended mainly for medical students at the new Philadelphia Medical School, which was closely modeled on the medical school at Edinburgh.[52] Thanks largely to the enthusiasm of Edinburgh-educated Benjamin Rush, Cullen in particular was revered, despite some doubts about the skepticism implicit in his method. Bell played up Cullen's stature in his advertisements, which targeted an audience of "American physicians who wish to arrive at the top of their profession" by studying "the great Professor Cullen's Lectures on the Materia Medica, containing the very cream of physic."[53] This reverential attitude accounts in part for Bell's success in producing his subscription edition of Cullen's *Lectures* in 1775 (no. 145).[54] But equally important is the fact that Cullen's *Lectures on the Materia Medica* had been published only in quarto format in Britain and retailed there for eighteen shillings. This situation provided Bell with some room to maneuver, and he was able to publish his Philadelphia edition in a thick octavo volume of 512 pages, with an imprint that read "America: Printed for the Subscribers, by Robert Bell."[55] By comparison, Gregory lacked the devoted following that Rush helped to generate for Cullen in Philadelphia, and since Gregory's book was already available in a modest five-shilling British octavo edition, it did not offer the same opportunities for price-cutting. Consequently, no American edition of Gregory's work ever appeared.

Another 1775 subscription publication by Bell, in collaboration with his former Berwick associate, William Woodhouse, was a three-volume edition of *Political Disquisitions* by the Scottish-born London radical James Burgh. The subscribers whose names were listed in the third volume included George Washington, Thomas Jefferson, John Dickinson,

51. Farren, "Subscription," 125–36, esp. 133n87.

52. Brunton, "Transfer of Medical Education," 242–74, esp. 249.

53. Advertisement quoted in Reid-Maroney, *Philadelphia's Enlightenment*, 106.

54. Admiration for Cullen is even more evident in the Philadelphia edition of the first two volumes of Cullen's *First Lines of the Practice of Physic* (no. 187), which includes a subscription list with seventy-nine names, thirty-nine of whom were local medical students, as well as a note by the editor, Benjamin Rush, declaring that Cullen "has produced a revolution in medicine." Although *First Lines* was published by Steiner and Cist of Philadelphia, Robert Bell, "Printer and Bookseller," subscribed for a dozen copies.

55. Another selling point was that Bell claimed to have made improvements because Cullen's "Emendanda" that appeared at the end of the London edition of 1772 were "carefully inserted at each proper place, throughout the body of the Work in this American Edition" (viii).

John Hancock, James Wilson, and Benjamin Rush. Rush would arrange for Bell to publish Thomas Paine's *Common Sense* the following year because he knew that this "intelligent Scotch bookseller and printer" was "as high-toned as Mr. Paine upon the subject of American independence."[56] But Bell subsequently had a bitter public feud with Paine about the profits from *Common Sense*,[57] and he occasionally published pamphlets on the other side of the controversy. Among them was James Macpherson's *The Rights of Great Britain Asserted against the Claims of America* (1776), to which Bell appended, however, strong words on the necessity for freedom of the press. Bell also lost face with some American patriots because he remained in Philadelphia during the British occupation of the city in 1777–78 and appeared to cultivate the favor of British officers.[58]

The first volume of Bell and Woodhouse's edition of Burgh's *Political Disquisitions* contains proposals for an edition of *Sketches of the History of Man* by Lord Kames (fig. 8.2). Originally published anonymously in Edinburgh in 1774 in two large quarto volumes, Kames's book had been reprinted in Dublin in 1774–75 by Bell's sometime collaborator from the 1760s, James Williams, in a four-volume duodecimo edition that placed the author's name on the title page. Bell's octavo edition, to be undertaken with Woodhouse (who later withdrew) and Robert Aitken, was projected to be four volumes in two, neatly bound and lettered, at a price (twenty-four Pennsylvania shillings) that was said to be less than one-third as much as the British quarto. A two-page specimen of Kames's *Sketches* appears at the end of the second volume of *Political Disquisitions*, with a sample title page showing the place of publication as "America" and listing Bell's name alone in the imprint. The content of the specimen (drawn from book 2, sketch 3) was obviously chosen with care: it discusses "the deplorable effects of despotism" and concludes with praise for republics because they tend to inspire patriotism. In order to achieve the desired effect, Bell silently altered Kames's text by juxtaposing two separate passages.

Unlike all Bell's previous subscription projects, which either appeared in their entirety or else never appeared at all, Bell and Aitken's edition of

---

56. Rush to James Cheetham, 17 July 1809, in Rush, *Letters*, 2:1008. When recounting this incident in his *Autobiography*, Rush called Bell "a Scotch bookseller of a singular character, but a thoughtless and fearless Whig, and an open friend to independence" (114).

57. Gimbel, *Thomas Paine*.

58. McCulloch, "William McCulloch's Additions," 176; Mishoff, "Business in Philadelphia," 171.

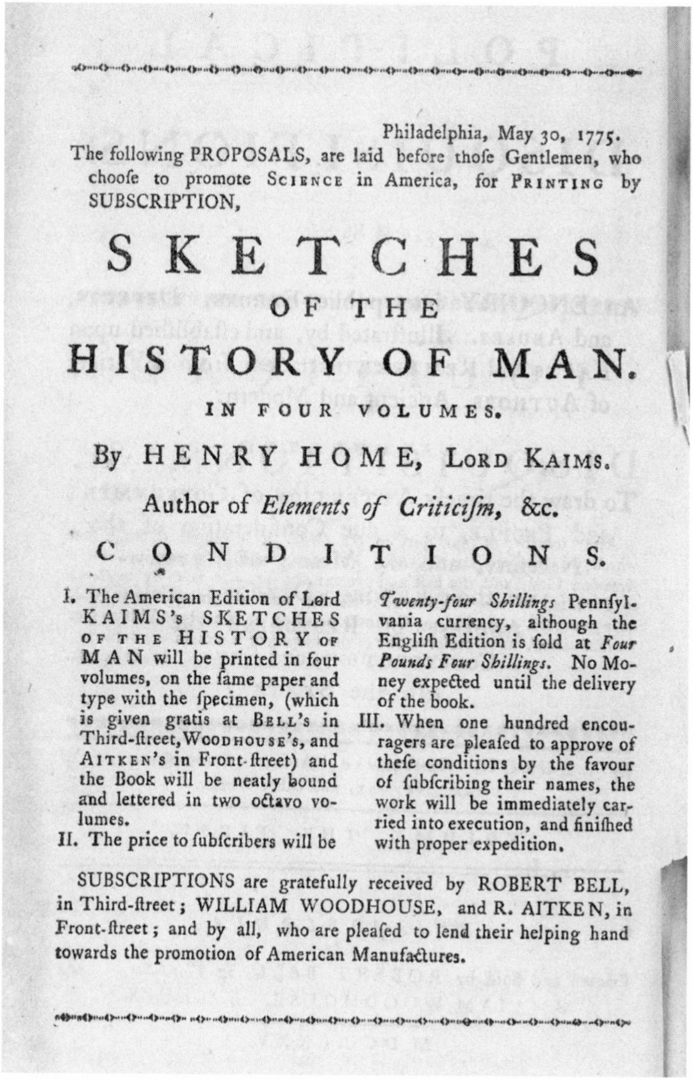

Philadelphia, May 30, 1775.

The following PROPOSALS, are laid before thofe Gentlemen, who choofe to promote SCIENCE in America, for PRINTING by SUBSCRIPTION,

S K E T C H E S

OF THE

HISTORY OF MAN.

IN FOUR VOLUMES.

By HENRY HOME, LORD KAIMS.

Author of *Elements of Criticifm*, &c.

C O N D I T I O N S.

I. The American Edition of Lord KAIMS's SKETCHES OF THE HISTORY OF MAN will be printed in four volumes, on the fame paper and type with the fpecimen, (which is given gratis at BELL's in Third-ftreet, WOODHOUSE's, and AITKEN's in Front-ftreet) and the Book will be neatly bound and lettered in two octavo volumes.

II. The price to fubfcribers will be *Twenty-four Shillings* Pennfyl-vania currency, although the Englifh Edition is fold at *Four Pounds Four Shillings.* No Money expected until the delivery of the book.

III. When one hundred encou-ragers are pleafed to approve of thefe conditions by the favour of fubfcribing their names, the work will be immediately car-ried into execution, and finifhed with proper expedition.

SUBSCRIPTIONS are gratefully received by ROBERT BELL, in Third-ftreet; WILLIAM WOODHOUSE, and R. AITKEN, in Front-ftreet; and by all, who are pleafed to lend their helping hand towards the promotion of American Manufactures.

Fig. 8.2. Prefixed to the first volume of Robert Bell and William Woodhouse's Phila-delphia reprint of James Burgh's *Political Disquisitions* (1775) were these proposals for a four-volume edition of Lord Kames's *Sketches of the History of Man*, to which Robert Aitken was also a party. In 1776 Bell and Aitken published only one volume of Kames's book. John Carter Brown Library at Brown University.

Kames's *Sketches* was published in the late summer or autumn of 1776 in a severely abridged form, and it lacked a subscription list. Titled *Six Sketches on the History of Man*, the book contained only six of the eight segments from book 1 ("The Progress of Men as Individuals")—those on the development of languages, food and population, property, commerce, arts, and "the female sex"—in addition to an appendix on animals. The rest of Kames's work never appeared, including the sketch on government in book 2 from which the printed specimen on despotism and patriotism had been taken. *Six Sketches* corresponded to the first volume in James Williams's four-volume Dublin edition of Kames's work, including the identification on the title page of the previously anonymous author as "Henry Home, Lord Kaims." Although we do not know exactly why Bell and Aitken's edition was stopped after one volume, it seems likely that the escalation of hostilities between Great Britain and its American colonies forced the Philadelphia partners to terminate the original project after the printing had begun and to cut their losses by publishing the first volume as if it were a complete work.

The general reduction in Bell's wartime publishing program provides circumstantial support for this interpretation. With rare exceptions, such as octavo editions of Beccaria's *Essay on Crimes and Punishments* and *Miscellanies by M. de Voltaire* (consisting of three philosophical tales), which appeared in 1778, Bell limited his Enlightenment publications during the early years of the war to smaller works. The fare was generally lighter, too. In 1777 he published the first American edition of James Thomson's *The Seasons* as well as John Home's tragedy *Alonzo* under a title of his own devising, *Alonzo and Ormisinda* (no. 154). Chesterfield's *Principles of Politeness* and La Rochefoucauld's *Maxims and Moral Reflections* followed in 1778, along with the irreverent *Songs, Comic, Satyrical, and Sentimental* by George Alexander Stevens, who is said to have been Bell's partner for a time in Dublin. In the same year, Bell published an edition of David Hume's autobiography, titled *The Life of David Hume, Esq; the Philosopher and Historian, Written by Himself. To which Are Added, The Travels of a Philosopher, containing Observations on the Manners and Arts of Various Nations, in Africa and Asia*. Even with the addition of an English translation of an account by Pierre Le Poivre of his African and Asian travels in the service of the French government, Hume's little autobiographical sketch and Adam Smith's accompanying letter came to no more than a sixty-two-page octavo volume. If this was a far cry from the eight-volume *History of England*, it was nevertheless the first work of Hume's to be separately published in North America. Bell found it necessary to identify

Hume in the title as "the Philosopher and Historian," perhaps because he was uncertain about the extent of the American public's familiarity with the author. Sales were evidently slow, for later in 1778 Bell reissued his editions of Hume–Le Poivre, Chesterfield, La Rochefoucauld, and three other published pamphlets in a single bound volume called *Miscellanies for Sentimentalists*. Soon afterward, the reprinting industry in Philadelphia collapsed completely, not only because the cultural and political climate was ill suited to it but also because American booksellers could not obtain new British works to reproduce. According to ESTC, Bell's name appeared in no more imprints until 1782, except one brief pamphlet of 1779 on the military exploits of Ethan Allen.

At the end of the war, Bell returned to his old ways as a reprinter of Scottish authors, but without resorting to subscription campaigns. In 1782 he reprinted Henry Mackenzie's novel *The Man of Feeling* (no. 135) as a one-dollar octavo. Later that year he published the first volume of Mackenzie's *The Man of the World* (no. 155) for half a dollar; two more volumes followed early in 1783 at the same price. Next he reprinted John Moore's *A View of Society and Manners in France, Switzerland, and Germany* (no. 201) in three parts or numbers, which were subsequently bound together to make a one-volume book that cost three dollars, and he used the same device to publish Moore's sequel, *A View of Society and Manners in Italy* (no. 219). In 1784 he brought out the first American edition of James Beattie's *The Minstrel* (no. 141) and collaborated with three other booksellers on an edition (though not the first to be printed in America) of William Buchan's *Domestic Medicine* (no. 115). Bell also reprinted literary works by English and European authors, such as an edition of Goethe's *The Sorrows and Sympathetic Attachments of Werter* in 1784, as well as some publications by American authors. But Scottish books remained central to his publishing program. Much of his postwar energy also went into fighting the restrictions on book auctions that had been imposed by the authorities with the support of several prominent Philadelphia booksellers. While traveling to Charleston, South Carolina, with books to auction, Bell died in Richmond, Virginia, on 23 September 1784, and was buried in a churchyard there.

Piety and Enlightenment: The Two Worlds of Robert Aitken

Innovative as he was, Robert Bell did not transform American publishing single-handedly. His achievement depended both on the growing size and sophistication of the book trade in Philadelphia and throughout British

America during the 1770s and early 1780s and on the growing size and sophistication of the American audience for learned and literary books.

Of several booksellers who began to follow Bell's example by undertaking large reprinting projects of their own during the late colonial and revolutionary war period, the most important was Bell's countryman and contemporary, Robert Aitken (1735–1802; fig. 8.3). Aitken hailed from Dalkeith, near Edinburgh, where he had served a bookbinding apprenticeship. By 1759, if not sooner, he was operating as a bookseller, bookbinder, and proprietor of a circulating library in Paisley. The fact that he worked at the sign of Buchanan's Head suggests not only a commitment to Scottish patriotism, Whig political principles, and learned Presbyterianism but also a respectful awareness of the London bookshop maintained by one of Paisley's most successful native sons, Andrew Millar. Aitken belonged to the radical denomination of Presbyterian seceders from the Church of Scotland known as the antiburghers, about which more is said in the next chapter. He also had close relations with the Church of Scotland minister in Paisley, John Witherspoon, whose emigration to America in 1768, when he became president of the College of New Jersey (Princeton), may have influenced Aitken's own move to Philadelphia the following year.[59] On that occasion, Aitken went to America not as an emigrant but as a sojourner, bringing books and other goods to be sold during a brief stay.[60] Two years later, however, he returned for good, bringing his wife, Janet Skeoch, and their two young children. He also brought a large stock of books, and in June 1771 he opened a shop on Front Street, where he sold and bound books and eventually performed "all kinds of printing-work."[61] According to William M'Culloch, Aitken's was "the largest and most valuable bookstore at that time in Philadelphia."[62] Significantly, the logo on his shipping forms contained the outline of an ocean-going vessel (fig. 8.4), reminding his customers of the Atlantic trade that supplied him with most of the books that he sold and reprinted.

In Paisley, Aitken catered exclusively to the evangelical Presbyterians who dominated the local readership. Between 1759 and 1769 his name appeared in the imprints of seven publications, all religious works of this kind. Four of them were brief, collaborative endeavors, chiefly with

59. Spawn and Spawn, "Aitken Shop," 431.

60. On Scottish sojourning, see Karras, *Sojourners in the Sun*.

61. [Aitken], *R. Aitken, Printer, Book-Binder, and Bookseller*.

62. McCulloch, "William McCulloch's Additions," 105. Later he moved his shop to Market Street.

Figs. 8.3 and 8.4. The Scottish publishing career of the antiburgher seceder Robert Aitken (fig. 8.3, artist and date unknown) was limited to religious works, but in Philadelphia he fared better as a bookseller and reprinter of a wider range of books, including several Scottish Enlightenment texts. Aitken's logo (fig. 8.4) drew attention to the Atlantic connection by showing a ship on the ocean. Aitken: Historical Society of Pennsylvania; logo: Marian S. Carson Collection, Library of Congress.

another antiburgher seceder, John Bryce, Glasgow's foremost evangelical publisher. The other three were lengthy works printed in Glasgow exclusively for Aitken, the last and longest being a 600-page reprint of Rev. William Wilson's *A Defence of the Reformation-Principles of the Church of Scotland*, which provided justifications for the secession. When Aitken went to Philadelphia, he stayed true to his religious principles, becoming an elder in the antiburghers' Scots Church and often printing or publishing religious, especially Presbyterian, works. But his American experience also paralleled that of Witherspoon, who constantly struggled to balance his religious beliefs with his intellectual and political concerns. Sometimes the religious and the secular made a snug fit, as in Witherspoon's celebrated sermon in support of the American Revolution, *The Dominion of Providence over the Passions of Men*, which was "Printed and Sold by R. Aitken" in the spring of 1776. There, the rhetoric of the traditional Scottish Presbyterian jeremiad was effectively harnessed in support of a secular issue: American independence.[63] Frequently, however, the two paths diverged, as Aitken's reprinting career reveals.

The first attempt by Aitken to reprint a Scottish book in America occurred within months of his return to Philadelphia. In the supplement to the first number of the *Pennsylvania Packet* (28 Oct. 1771), he advertised a subscription for the first American edition of William Buchan's *Domestic Medicine* (no. 115), to be published like the original as a thick one-volume octavo. Aitken had probably brought a copy of the original Edinburgh edition of Buchan's book with him from Scotland to use as his copy text. His advertisement claimed that this work would be "peculiarly useful in this new and growing country," where many large families live far from "approved physicians." The book was to cost one dollar by subscription but a bit more (eight Pennsylvania shillings) when sold in shops. Four variations of the first edition have survived, three dated 1772 and one undated, and in two of them William Cadogan's "Dissertation on the Gout" (first published in London by James Dodsley in 1771) is appended to Buchan's text.

The first American edition of *Domestic Medicine* was a huge success. In the second American edition of 1774, Aitken reprinted the substantially revised text of the second British edition that the Strahan–Cadell syndicate had published in London in 1772. Perhaps because he did not wish to confuse the public, however, he retained the longer subtitle of the original Edinburgh edition that began with the words *or, the Family Physician*. His

---

63. Sher, "Witherspoon's *Dominion of Providence*," 46–64.

waste book in the Library Company of Philadelphia (on deposit in HSP) records extensive wholesale distribution of this edition throughout the colonies, especially to other Scots, such as William Aikman of Annapolis, Maryland (thirty-six copies in spring 1774) and Samuel Loudon of New York (one hundred copies in July 1774). A less welcoming reception was accorded Aitken's other major reprint of 1772, a 300-page duodecimo edition of *Sermons on Practical Subjects* by Witherspoon's evangelical ally in the Popular Party of the Church of Scotland, Robert Walker. Eighteen years later, Aitken and his son would reissue the surviving stock of Walker's book with a new title page.

Although he remained religious, and would gain respect for printing the first American edition of the New Testament in 1777 and the first complete American Bible five years later,[64] Aitken was learning the difference between the book cultures of Paisley and Philadelphia. The potential American readership for sectarian works on Scottish Presbyterianism was small and divided, and Aitken lost thousands of pounds on his edition of the Bible when English and Scottish imports became available after the war. On the other hand, the American audience for reprints of new works of literature and learning by Scottish authors was growing. Aitken's next major American reprint was accordingly another secular title listed in table 2, William Russell's translation and expanded edition of Antoine Léonard Thomas's *Essay on the Character, Manners, and Genius of Women in Different Ages* (no. 157). Although the London edition had been published in two octavo volumes in 1773, Aitken condensed the work into a one-volume duodecimo that appeared in Philadelphia in 1774 and was also advertised separately by Loudon in New York.[65] Around this time, Aitken's move toward reprinting new literary and instructional books by Scottish authors formed the basis for an association with Robert Bell. In 1775 he subscribed to Bell's edition of James Burgh's *Political Disquisitions* and published his own edition of Burgh's *The Art of Speaking* (which Bell himself had once reprinted in Dublin), and the following year he and Bell copublished their edition of Kames's *Six Sketches*.

Meanwhile, in late November 1774 Aitken issued proposals for a new periodical, *The Pennsylvania Magazine; or, American Monthly Museum*, which would begin appearing in January 1775. Thanks in part to Tom Paine, who contributed as an author and an editor, and Witherspoon, who also wrote some of the articles, it is said to have had 1,500 subscribers

64. Gutjahr, *American Bible*, 20–23; Gaines, "Continental Congress," 274–81.
65. [Aitken], *This Day Is Published, at Samuel Loudon's Book Store.*

by the beginning of March.[66] A prominent component was "Select Passages from the Newest British Publications," designed to keep American colonials up to date on "the best and latest" British books. The first two numbers, for January and February 1775, featured excerpts from Lord Kames's *Sketches of the History of Man* (no. 164; 33–34, 77–80) and Patrick Brydone's *A Tour through Sicily and Malta* (no. 150; 35–37, 80–84).[67] Brydone's book is called "very ingenious" (35), while Kames and his book are praised in three different places (33, 34, 77). When introducing the third and longest excerpt from Kames, on the origins of society, the magazine states: "We find almost every page of this celebrated work so abounding with curious investigations, that we are at a loss where to select a part, that shall most readily convey the plan, design, and abilities of the Author, which appears to us, to be that of tracing Man from the most simple state, he can be supposed to have existed in, to the present; and of comparing his natural inclinations, and policies, with the animal creation" (77). This appreciation of a key element of the intellectual program of the Scottish Enlightenment is significant, especially in light of the attempt that Aitken and Bell would soon make to reprint Kames's book in Philadelphia. The "List of New Books" that followed the excerpts in the February 1775 issue was dominated by Robert Bell's recent publications (84), including Robertson's *History of Charles V* (no. 119) and Cullen's *Lectures on the Materia Medica* (no. 145). In the descriptions of these titles, as in the description of the British edition of William Richardson's *Philosophical Analysis and Illustration of Some of Shakespeare's Remarkable Characters* (no. 166) that appears in the same list, the authors are always identified by their Scottish academic positions.

The March 1775 issue of the *Pennsylvania Magazine* continued the earlier pattern. The section titled "Select Passages from the Newest British Publications" (127–32) contained an excerpt from Sir John Dalrymple's *Memoirs of Great Britain and Ireland* (no. 143), and the "List of New Books" section announced the second volume of Robert Henry's *History of Great Britain* (no. 144), the second volume of Lord Monboddo's anonymous *Origin and Progress of Language* (no. 160), and William Richardson's anonymous *Poems, Chiefly Rural* (167), all credited to Scottish publishers. The May and June issues featured excerpts from Samuel Johnson's *Journey to*

---

66. Richardson, *History of Early American Magazines*, 174–96.

67. Pages from volume 1 (1775) and volume 2 (1776) of the *Pennsylvania Magazine* are cited parenthetically in the text.

the Western Islands of Scotland (221–22, 274–75), including its most controversial attacks on Ossian and the integrity of the Scots. The editor
criticizes the work for its "pompous" style and "illiberal attacks on the
kirk of Scotland" (275) and observes that most Scots, and particularly
Highlanders, would be likely to find the work offensive (222).

The strong initial emphasis on Scottish literary culture in the *Pennsylvania Magazine* was not subsequently maintained. From July 1775 the "List
of New Books" section became sporadic, and when it did appear, as in the
issue for December 1775, the emphasis was increasingly placed on military works and pamphlets on the American crisis (574). The "Publisher's
Preface" to the second volume in January 1776 asserted that "the struggle
for *American Liberty*" would now take precedence over intellectual activity: "Till this important point is settled, the pen of the poet and the books
of the learned must be in a great measure neglected." At the same time,
the January 1776 issue silently dropped the word "British" from the "Select Passages" section, which featured a new American publication with
which Aitken was affiliated, *A Concise Natural History of East and West-
Florida* by Bernard Romans. Although the March 1776 issue included an
excerpt from Walter Anderson's *History of France* (no. 121; 141–43), and
the June 1776 issue contained a long excerpt on the growth of human understanding and personal freedom from David Hume's *History of England,
under the House of Tudor* (no. 56; 274–77), originally published seventeen
years earlier, the *Pennsylvania Magazine* did less and less to promote the
book culture of the Scottish Enlightenment, and it ceased publication entirely after the next issue, a casualty of the American Revolution. The
first number of January 1775 had reprinted the epitaph of Tobias Smollett
(30), and the last issue of July 1776 fittingly reprinted Smollett's "Ode to
Independence" (325–328), noting that it "breathes a spirit of liberty that
would not have disgraced a citizen of Sparta, or of Rome" (325).

When British troops occupied Philadelphia in 1777–78, Aitken was
jailed. This was apparently not, as Isaiah Thomas assumed, because of
his support for the American cause, but rather because Aitken had failed
to provide adequate compensation to Robert and Thomas Duncan of
Glasgow for books and stationery they had given him to sell in America on
commission.[68] Among those who mattered in Philadelphia society, however, Aitken was an upstanding citizen, quite unlike the maverick Robert
Bell. Besides his position as a church elder, Aitken served as an overseer

---

68. McCulloch, "William McCulloch's Additions," 96.

of the city's poor and became a member (along with Witherspoon) of the St. Andrew's Society, which had been founded in 1749 by twenty-five Scots (including the bookseller David Hall), who rigorously restricted membership to Scotsmen and their sons.[69] Aitken was also called on to print part of the catalogue of the Library Company of Philadelphia in 1775, to be the official printer to the Continental Congress during the Revolutionary War, and to do binding and printing for the American Philosophical Society. In the last of these capacities, he printed in 1787 a little book by Witherspoon's son-in-law, Samuel Stanhope Smith, *An Essay on the Causes of the Variety of Complexion and Figure in the Human Species*, which challenged Kames's *Sketches of the History of Man* on the origins of mankind and had the unusual distinction for an American learned book of being reprinted in Edinburgh in 1788 and in London in 1789.[70]

As the war was ending, Aitken tried to reestablish himself as a publisher, but his financially disastrous edition of the Bible appears to have sapped much of his money and entrepreneurial energy. He tended to play it safe by reprinting tried-and-true advice books such as Chesterfield's *Principles of Politeness* and Gregory's *A Father's Legacy to His Daughters*, both in 1781. In the winter of 1784, however, Aitken made one last attempt at reprinting on a grand scale, when he produced the first American edition of Hugh Blair's *Lectures on Rhetoric and Belles Lettres*. Blair's book had been published in London in the summer of 1783 by Strahan, Cadell, and Creech in two large quarto volumes that retailed for two guineas per bound set, leaving it vulnerable to reprinting elsewhere in a less expensive format. Later in 1783, fourteen booksellers in Dublin followed established Irish practice by banding together to produce an octavo edition in three volumes, anticipating the three-volume London octavo that the original publishers put out in 1785. Aitken took a different approach. Instead of reducing the format and increasing the number of volumes, he maintained the quarto format while lowering the number of volumes from two to one. In condensing 1,046 pages of quarto text into just 454 quarto pages, Aitken could not avoid using a smaller typeface and tighter spacing than Strahan. But if his edition looked cramped on the inside, it was cheap enough for him to ship two hundred unbound sets to Robert Dun-

---

69. [Beath], *Historical Catalogue of the St. Andrew's Society*; Spawn and Spawn, *Aitken Shop*, 432.

70. Noll, *Princeton and the Republic*, 115–24; Wood, introduction to Smith, *Essay on the Causes of the Variety of Complexion and Figure*, v–xxi.

can and John Bryce in Glasgow, as well as two dozen sets in boards.[71] In addition, the allure of a quarto edition to an accomplished binder like Aitken lay partly in its potential for external beauty: the Free Library of Philadelphia's copy of Aitken's edition of Blair's *Lectures*, splendidly bound by Aitken in gilt red morocco, has been recognized as one of the most beautiful books ever made in eighteenth-century America.[72]

The 1784 edition of Blair's *Lectures* marked the culmination of the publishing career of Robert Aitken and his greatest contribution to the American appropriation of the Scottish Enlightenment. After 1784, Aitken continued in business but never again undertook a major publishing initiative. By the end of that year his shop was eclipsed by a new one opened by Jackson and Dunn, which Benjamin Rush called "the largest book store that has ever been set up in Philadelphia."[73] The next year Aitken had difficulty executing a binding order for David Ramsay's new book, *The History of the Revolution of South-Carolina*, explaining that "my finances are so low on Account of My Losses in trade that I find Cr[editors] ready for it before I am possess'd of my income."[74] When he hired Aitken to print his next book, *The History of the American Revolution* (1789), reasoning that "because he was a Scotchman [he] must be a linguist and grammarian," Ramsay was disappointed by the outcome and judged him incompetent "either from old age forgetfulness or something else." "Aitkens work offends against every principle of good printing," Ramsay told Ashbel Green. "The printing the spelling the ink the form of the lines are in many cases execrable."[75] Poor investments and bad loans marred Aitken's later years, and he died deep in debt on 15 July 1802, leaving his daughter Jane to try to rescue his failing business.[76] Long before then, the leadership in American publishing had shifted to a younger generation of immigrant Philadelphia booksellers, who built on the accomplishments of

71. Aitken's Waste Book, Library Company of Philadelphia (on deposit at HSP), 12 May 1784. Aitken's edition was printed at least two months earlier, for the waste book records a copy sold to a customer on 11 March.

72. Spawn, "Extra-Gilt Bindings of Robert Aitken," 415–17.

73. Rush to William Creech, 22 Dec. 1784, WCL.

74. Aitken to Ramsay, 26 Dec. 1785, in Brunhouse, *David Ramsay*, 95.

75. Ramsay to Ashbel Green, 4 Oct. 1791, ibid., 130. Ramsay and Aitken also fought over shipping, payments, and the book's price of three dollars in boards, which Aitken considered ruinously high. See Aitken to John Eliot, 3 May 1790, ibid., 126n1; and Brunhouse's evenhanded assessment, ibid., 223.

76. Hudak, *Early American Women Printers and Publishers*, 547–75.

Bell and Aitken while carrying Enlightenment reprinting in America to a higher level.

*

In the space of fifteen years, Robert Bell and Robert Aitken brought about a radical alteration in American book culture. Bell in particular showed that Dublin-style reprinting could be conducted on a reasonably large scale in colonial America, using progressive marketing techniques. He established American reprinting as a patriotic activity in both an economic and a cultural sense, and he defined the role of the publisher as a cultural hero who enriches the lives of his customers emotionally as well as intellectually. The evangelical fervor of Bell's youth was transferred from Christianity to the culture of books, and his mission in America was to convert as many people as possible to the gospel of enlightened literature and learning.

Scottish Enlightenment books lay at the heart of Bell's program for national improvement through print. The works he attempted to reprint, and usually did reprint, spanned many genres, including history, philosophy, medicine, travel literature, novels, drama, and poetry. In most cases, they were best sellers in Britain that had been reprinted in Ireland, but Bell also reprinted some Scottish books that were not big sellers, and he did not shy away from making changes in titles and texts, or from adding new materials adapted to the American scene, when he believed they would constitute improvements. By insisting that these books be not merely *read* in America but *made* there as well, Bell transformed them into what James Green has called "declarations of independence from the London book trade."[77] They were artifacts of the American, as well as of the Scottish, Enlightenment.

77. Green, "English Books," 287.

9

"A More Extensive Diffusion of Useful Knowledge"

Philadelphia, 1784–1800

ATLANTIC CROSSINGS:

CAREY, DOBSON, YOUNG, AND CAMPBELL

The year 1784—the year of Robert Bell's death, Robert Aitken's edition of Hugh Blair's *Lectures*, and the opening of Jackson and Dunn's large bookstore—was also the year in which Mathew Carey (1760–1839), Thomas Dobson (1750–1823), and William Young (1755–1829) arrived in Philadelphia. With the war over, the United States of America appeared to be a land of boundless prosperity for many Europeans, particularly in areas of the economy that had been cut off from European supply during the war, such as books. As Benjamin Rush explained to William Cullen in a letter of 16 September 1783, scarcely any books had been received from Britain during the war, and "we are eight years behind you in everything."[1] The possibilities for both importing and reprinting books had never been so promising. In addition to economic opportunity, the new nation's atmosphere of religious toleration and its potential for denominational growth were attractive to members of pious religious sects, such as Young (an antiburgher seceder in Scotland), and of oppressed religious minorities, such as Carey (a Roman Catholic in Ireland). In some cases, notably that of Carey, America's relatively open political atmosphere was equally important. All these factors helped to create the influx of Scottish and Irish bookmen who dominated the American book trade in the late eighteenth century. The phenomenon was especially evident in Philadelphia, the cultural and political capital of the new republic and a center of ethnic and religious diversity. Carey, Dobson, Young, and Robert Campbell (1769–

---

1. Rush, *Letters*, 1:310.

1800) emigrated for different reasons and encountered different kinds of obstacles, but all found ways to overcome them. By the early 1790s they were among the most prominent figures in their profession.

Carey emigrated to Philadelphia in desperation.[2] He was born in Dublin in 1760, the son of a prosperous baker. After suffering a childhood injury that left him lame for life, he developed a "voracious" reading habit by subscribing to a circulating library without his parents' knowledge (3). At fifteen he was apprenticed to the Dublin bookseller and printer Thomas McDonnel (formerly McDaniel), whose shop was then located on Meath Street. Although the autobiographical sketch that Carey penned late in life has no kind words for his master, it is possible that he acquired his outspoken commitment to Roman Catholic activism and radical politics from this source.[3] Patrick Wogan, who gave printing work to McDonnel until the two men quarreled violently, may also have influenced Carey more than one might think from his characterization in the autobiography as "a ruffian bookseller" (3). Wogan was a fervent Catholic rights activist who dared to use a likeness of the outspoken eighteenth-century Scottish Catholic bishop George Hay as the sign of his shop on Bridge Street.[4]

Equally important, at the time that Carey apprenticed with McDonnel, Wogan was beginning to become a significant force in Irish reprinting, and his name would later appear in thirteen Dublin first-edition reprints of Scottish Enlightenment books (see table 6). McDonnel's shop may also have been printing literary and learned texts for other Dublin booksellers during this period. At the very least, Carey would have learned about this kind of Irish reprinting from William Spotswood, an experienced Catholic printer and bookseller whose name appears in the imprints of three multivolume Dublin reprints of Scottish works of history and political economy during the late 1770s (nos. 172, 186, and 203). Spotswood emigrated to Philadelphia in the same year as Carey, and the two Dubliners would collaborate closely during their early years in America.[5] It seems likely, then, that Carey absorbed more information about Enlightenment

2. Unless otherwise noted, information on Carey's life is drawn from his *Autobiography*. Quotations from this source are cited parenthetically in the text.

3. On McDonnel's radical politics, until he became a government spy, see Pollard, *Dictionary*, 383. Among other things, McDonnel printed from 1788 the *Hibernian Journal*, an opposition newspaper. See Curtin, *United Irishmen*, 212.

4. Wall, *Sign of Doctor Hay's Head*.

5. On Spotswood, see Pollard, *Dictionary*, 545–46; and Cole, *Irish Booksellers*, 51, 177–82.

reprinting from the Dublin trade than he later revealed, or perhaps than he himself realized.

In the autumn of 1781, Carey wrote a polemical pamphlet titled "The Urgent Necessity of an Immediate Repeal of the Whole Penal Code against the Roman Catholics."[6] A contemporary advertisement, bound with other promotional materials in Carey's personal copy of the printed portion of this pamphlet in the Library Company of Philadelphia, identifies the publisher as A. Johnson and the selling agent as Patrick Wogan.[7] Another advertisement, penned by Carey himself and partially reproduced in his autobiography, called on Irish Catholics to emulate the Americans by shaking off "an unjust *English yoke*" (4–5). The phrase is significant because it indicates that for Carey, in Ireland as later in America, the religious struggle for Catholic rights and the political struggle for Irish freedom from English dominance were closely connected.

Although Carey's pamphlet was never fully printed or properly published, the "obnoxious advertisement" created an uproar (5). To avoid possible prosecution, Carey was rushed off to France, where he worked for several months in the printing office of Benjamin Franklin at Passey and that of Didot the younger in Paris. Returning to Dublin early in 1783, after things had quieted down, he was able to buy out the remainder of his apprenticeship from McDonnel. He became the editor of a newspaper, *Freeman's Journal*, and then, with financial backing from his father, and in partnership with his younger brother Thomas, started a new, zealously patriotic paper, the *Volunteer's Journal*. In late winter and early spring 1784 it harangued against "OUR BLASTING CONNECTION WITH BRITAIN" and suggested that the speaker of the Irish House of Commons be tarred and feathered, if not hanged, for treason.[8] Carey was arrested, interrogated, imprisoned briefly in Newgate, and released on a technicality while charges were pending. He then published in his newspaper an indignant account of the abuses he suffered during the early days of his imprisonment, which was soon reprinted in a Dublin magazine, along with a print of Carey defiantly holding the *Volunteer's Journal*, in a piece

6. In his autobiography, Carey misdated this incident, and the *Miscellaneous Essays* that he published in 1830 printed an advertisement for this pamphlet, dated 9 December 1779 (452). However, Pollard, *Dictionary*, 86, establishes the correct dating based on contemporary newspaper accounts.

7. A. Johnson's address is given as "No. 67, High-Street (nearly opposite Michael's Church)," but no such bookseller appears in Pollard, *Dictionary*.

8. Quoted in Wilson, *United Irishmen, United States*, 18.

titled "Memoirs of Mr. Mathew Carey."[9] Soon afterward, disguised as a woman, he narrowly escaped prosecution by sailing to Philadelphia on the *America*, arriving on 1 November. According to his account, he selected a ship bound for Philadelphia rather than New York or Baltimore because he knew that the press there had reported on "the oppression I had undergone" (9), thus increasing his chances of a sympathetic reception.

He was right. With just a few pounds to his name, Carey was soon summoned by the Marquis de Lafayette, who had read the accounts of his persecution in Ireland. In an extraordinary gesture of solidarity, Lafayette gave him an unsolicited gift of $400 so that he could start a newspaper. Carey never forgot that this "most extraordinary and unlooked-for circumstance . . . changed my purpose, gave a new direction to my views, and, in some degree, coloured the course of my future life" (10).[10] Of course, Lafayette's generosity toward a man he scarcely knew must be understood politically: the gift was an investment in the vision of American liberty to which the marquis was personally committed.

Carey moved as quickly as he could to put his newfound capital to work. Purchasing printing equipment proved difficult because of its scarcity in America, and in December 1784 he was forced to spend one-third of Lafayette's gift on an old, dilapidated press that had belonged, ironically, to "a Scotch bookseller and printer, of the name of Bell" who "had recently died" (11).[11] Before the end of January 1785, Carey, Spotswood, and another Irish-Catholic bookseller who had emigrated to Philadelphia in 1784, Christopher Talbot, were publishing a short-lived newspaper, the *Pennsylvania Evening Herald*. The following year Carey, Spotswood, and Talbot joined three other partners to launch one of the most important early American periodicals, the *Columbian Magazine*. The first issue contained four pieces by Carey himself, including "The American Dream," which articulated his utopian vision of America in the year 1850, when schoolteachers would be paid respectable salaries and slavery would no longer exist. Carey soon broke with the *Columbian* and in January 1787 started a new magazine of his own, the *American Museum*, which had an influential six-year run, through the end of 1792. During this period he

9. *Town and Country Magazine, or Irish Miscellany,* June and July 1784. The print is reproduced on the cover of Green, *Mathew Carey.*

10. Among other things, Carey concluded the second volume of his edition of Guthrie's *Geography* with a tribute to Lafayette.

11. Silver, "Costs," 85–122.

married and gradually began his career as a publisher of books, first on Front Street and then, as he prospered, on Market Street.[12]

In his autobiography, Carey draws attention to his role in the early 1790s in founding the Hibernian Society "for the relief of emigrants from Ireland" (29). Other Irish booksellers joined, and it served to reinforce Irish cultural identity in Philadelphia in a manner that paralleled the role played by the St. Andrew's Society for Scottish immigrants. Carey does not mention his involvement with another, more controversial organization that was founded in Philadelphia in 1797, the American Society of United Irishmen. Although Carey always denied any involvement with this revolutionary body and played down his radicalism by emphasizing his opposition to a scurrilous attack on George Washington by some of its principal proponents, the current consensus is that Carey (along with his brother James) was not only a member but one of the organization's leaders.[13] Carey had emigrated seven years before the Society of United Irishmen had been established in his homeland, but his master, his brother William, and most of his like-minded friends were early members, and there is little doubt where Carey's own sympathies lay. For our purposes, the most important connection was with the radical Dublin bookseller and printer John Chambers, whom we encountered in chapter 7 as the publisher of an ambitious reprint edition of William Guthrie's *Geography*. Carey later identified Chambers as the printer of the Catholic-rights pamphlet that had first brought him to the attention of the authorities in Ireland.[14]

In contrast with Carey's frantic dash to America, Thomas Dobson's emigration was carefully planned.[15] Born in Galashiels in May 1750, Dobson became a clerk in the Edinburgh shop of another bookseller from the Scottish Borders, Charles Elliot. After seven years of employment, during which he married and had a child, Dobson was still earning just £26 a year. Then, at the age of thirty-four, he got his big break when Elliot decided to send him to Philadelphia to sell his books. In the autumn

12. The chronological development of Carey's publishing is presented in Clarkin, *Mathew Carey*. For Carey's career as an author, see Axelrod, "Mathew Carey," 89–96.

13. Wilson, *United Irishmen, United States*, 11, 43–44, citing Carter, "Political Activities of Mathew Carey."

14. Carey, *Miscellaneous Essays*, 452n.

15. Unless otherwise noted, the following account is drawn from McDougall, "Charles Elliot's Book Adventure," 197–212.

of 1784 Dobson sailed on the *Ann* from Glasgow's main Atlantic port, Greenock, with nearly £2,000 worth of Elliot's books and other goods on board. More books would follow. The following April, Elliot arranged cabin passage for Dobson's wife on the *Alexander*, which had among its other cabin passengers Rev. Charles Nisbet of Montrose (en route to the founding presidency of Dickinson College in Carlisle, Pennsylvania) and Dobson's mother and her companion, a devout Edinburgh bookbinder by the name of Samuel Campbell. In steerage were a maidservant meant for employment in the Dobson household and Samuel Campbell's nineteen-year-old son Samuel, Jr., who had with him a modest shipment of books sent by his former master, the Edinburgh bookseller John Bell, for sale in New York.

Trusting Dobson completely, Elliot foolishly made no formal contract and even instructed Dobson to pretend he was the owner of the books in his possession, to avoid offending their countryman William Jackson (of Jackson and Dunn) and other customers in America who dealt directly with Elliot. Elliot's understanding was that Dobson would take 25 percent of every purchase for himself and send the rest of the money back to him in Edinburgh. Dobson, however, used Elliot's stock and the secrecy surrounding it to set himself up as an independent Philadelphia bookseller and publisher. After initially opening a shop on Front Street in February 1785, he moved in the spring to a better location on Second Street, and finally, in January 1788, to an impressive new home and shop, also on Second Street, which was said to be the only fine stone building in eighteenth-century Philadelphia.[16] Elliot's last years were made miserable by Dobson's failure to reduce a debt that stood at £3,691 when Elliot died in January 1790. Only the threat of legal action by Elliot's heirs finally induced Dobson to pay off the debt (which totaled £6,457 in all) between 1801 and 1805. By that time Dobson had become a formidable American bookseller and publisher.

William Young's route to Philadelphia followed a very different path. Young was born in May 1755 in the Kilmarnock region of Ayrshire, not far from Glasgow. His father, a semiliterate farmer, had four children with William's mother, Agnes Wallace, who died in childbirth when William was four years old, and then six more children with her younger sister Elizabeth. According to an unpublished biography by a descendant, William attended grammar school until the age of fourteen, when his father, citing his son's love of books, apprenticed him to the master printer John

16. Arner, "Thomas Dobson's American Edition," 206–7.

M'Culloch.[17] When his apprenticeship ended, Young decided to pursue a calling in the clergy of the strict sect of seceders known as antiburghers, to which his family and M'Culloch belonged. But even the antiburghers valued secular education enough to require all boys to attend university before entering the ministry. In 1776, therefore, Young matriculated under Professor William Richardson at the University of Glasgow, just a few miles from his home.[18] At the age of twenty-one, he was seven or eight years older than most of his classmates and was able to support himself in part by working in the book trade, particularly for Robert Aitken's former collaborator, John Bryce (ca. 1717–1786), Glasgow's leading evangelical publisher and an elder in the antiburgher church.[19]

Besides studying under Richardson, who was the professor of humanity (Latin), Young would have studied Greek with George Young, logic with George Jardine, natural philosophy with John Anderson, and most importantly, moral philosophy with Thomas Reid—as fine a constellation of teachers as any university could boast of during the late eighteenth century.[20] A recommendation letter from Anderson calls him "a worthy Young Man, and an assiduous Student" on the basis of his performance as a "gown student" in Anderson's class during the 1779–80 session.[21] At the shop of his master, John M'Culloch, Young met a devout young woman, Agnes McLaws (1754–1793), who was M'Culloch's niece and sister-in-law.[22] They married, and in 1780 Agnes gave birth to the couple's first child. According to an account that Young wrote after her death, the marriage was an extraordinarily happy one, in which the couple "never dis-

17. Bassler, "Story of William Young." Identified in the typescript as Young's great-great-great-granddaughter, Bassler had access to a number of contemporary documents that I have been unable to trace.

18. Addison, *Matriculation Albums*, 115.

19. Years later Young received a letter from John Newall, who recalled his own time as "apprentice to John Bryce, when you was going about the shop." Newall to Young, 14 July 1793, WYP, box 2, no. 56.

20. See Sher, "Commerce," 312–59, esp. 345–46; and Hook and Sher, *Glasgow Enlightenment*.

21. Letter of John Anderson, 28 June 1780, WYP, box 1, no. 11. On Anderson, see Muir, *John Anderson*; and Wood, "Jolly Jack Phosphorous," 111–32.

22. Bassler, "Story of William Young," 3. Agnes McLaws's mother, Elizabeth M'Culloch, the second wife of Agnes's father John McLaws, was John M'Culloch's sister. In addition, John and Elizabeth's brother Michael married Agnes's stepsister, who was the daughter of the first wife of Agnes's father. Such inbreeding was not uncommon among the close-knit community of antiburghers in the west of Scotland.

agreed about any one article of our faith; our minds were like two sticks each having fire, and closely united, burst forth into a flame."[23] Faced with the economic pressures of a growing family, Young had begun teaching in Glasgow, which enabled him to become economically self-sufficient for the first time.[24] He seems to have taught all subjects to boys preparing for university, and there is evidence that he did it well.[25]

In 1781 Young was one of thirteen students entering the antiburgher divinity class taught by Rev. William Moncrieff, Jr., of Alloa, near Stirling.[26] After completing two or three years of training, he dropped out of divinity school and took a full-time position in a print shop, probably Bryce's. He had suffered no lapse in faith and would remain a devoutly religious seceder throughout his life. His change of direction occurred in response to a letter from John M'Culloch, who was apparently either the son or nephew of the man of the same name with whom Young had apprenticed and therefore the first cousin of Young's wife Agnes. Born a year before Young, in 1754, M'Culloch had served his printing apprenticeship with Bryce and emigrated to America in 1774, just in time to fight for the American cause during the Revolutionary War.[27] Now he extended an invitation to Young to join him in the new nation:

23. Young, "Yellow Fever in Philadelphia," 622. The account continues: "We had no secrets, our minds and money were one common stock, to which either might go with the greatest freedom."

24. On 22 May 1784 his father John wrote to him: "I simpathised with you when you . . . went first to Glasgow, when your grandfather refused to help you, and assisted you as far as my ability would allow me both with money and cloths for a number of years, until that you took up a school and shifted for yourself." WYP, box 1, no. 32.

25. Many years later, a Glasgow schoolteacher by the name of John Eadie recalled that he had studied with Young for five and a half years "till I entered the University which I did immediately after you went with your family to America." "The instructions I recieved from you in English writing and Latin," Eadie added, "were the means of my making a respectable appearance at College and by my education I have still lived." John Eadie to William Young, 25 Sept. 1828, HSP. Since William Young does not appear to have taught school for as long as five and a half years, it is possible that Eadie failed to distinguish him from his brother John, who took over the school when William was a divinity student.

26. All information on the antiburgher divinity students and professors is drawn from the "List of Students of Theology" in Mackenvie, *Annals and Statistics*, 654–64.

27. McCulloch, "William McCulloch's Additions," 104. William McCulloch or M'Culloch was John's son.

Why don't you come over to Philadelphia. America has won its independence, and has to stand on its own feet. It needs many things, among them good and intelligent printers. We need you here. No books came through from England during the war, and there is a great scarcity of them. Why don't you collect as many as you can, bring them over, and open a book store. Later you could branch out into printing and publishing, when you have some profits from the book store. You will be getting here at the beginning of a great new country, and I will do all I can to help you. Opportunity awaits you here and now. Do write and tell me you are coming.[28]

After receiving this letter, Young overcame his wife's reluctance to leave Scotland and began planning to emigrate. His full-time job in a Glasgow print shop was meant to raise money for the voyage as well as for the purchase of books to sell in America.

The Youngs booked passage on the *Friendship*, which left Greenock in late March 1784, bound for Philadelphia by way of Belfast. Even though Young had informed some relatives and friends of his intention to emigrate someday, his family was shocked by the abruptness of his departure.[29] Traveling in the relative luxury of cabin class rather than steerage, the Youngs paid eight guineas each for their passage, and another guinea for their young son, with additional charges of 15d. per cubic foot for the seven containers of books and other merchandise in their possession. They brought along their own food, including dried and cured meats, dried fruits and vegetables, biscuits, oatmeal for porridge, laying hens, and a cow for milk. Accompanying them was Peter Stewart, a Scottish printer who had been recommended by young M'Culloch. After a strenuous voyage of more than two months at sea, they arrived in Philadelphia on 27 June 1784.

Young benefited from an institutional support network established by Scots who had preceded him to America. Two years after arriving in his new home, he became a member of the St. Andrew's Society of Philadelphia, and in 1789 he and Robert Aitken (who had been a member since 1774) were both enshrined in that organization's "Honorary Roll."[30] Like

28. Quoted in Bassler, "Story of William Young," 4. Bassler does not date this letter, which I have been unable to trace.

29. John Young to William Young, 22 May 1784, WYP, box 1, no. 32; John McLaws to William and Agnes Young, 24 June 1784, WYP, box 1, no. 27.

30. [Beath], *Historical Catalogue of the St. Andrew's Society*, 1:101–2, 372–73. At the end of his life, Young served as vice president of the society from 1823 to 1828.

many other seceder immigrants from Scotland and northern Ireland, Young and his family also joined the antiburgher or Associate Presbyterian Church in Philadelphia. The earliest extant letters to him in America are addressed to Mr. William Young, Student of Divinity, in the care of Revd. Mr. Marshall Philadelphia,[31] and at least one letter in April 1785 was addressed to the care of Robert Aitken. Marshall was the charismatic and sometimes cantankerous pastor of the antiburgher church on Spruce Street, popularly known as the Scots Church or the Scots Presbyterian Church. He was a member of the St. Andrew's Society who retained a thick Fifeshire accent throughout his life.[32] Like Aitken and M'Culloch (who would later write Marshall's biography),[33] Young would remain closely connected with Marshall until the latter's death in 1802. Marshall was the intimate friend of Benjamin Rush, whose autobiography describes him as "a profound divine, an eminent Christian and systematic preacher, and a most instructing and entertaining companion."[34] Since Rush acknowledged Marshall's importance in building up his medical practice by sending him "nearly every family in his congregation" (80–81), it is probable that Marshall was responsible for establishing Young's intellectual and professional relationship with Rush.

Although Marshall, M'Culloch, and virtually all other Scottish seceders were strong supporters of the American Revolution, the subordination of their church to a foreign body—the antiburgher or Associate Synod (renamed the General Associate Synod in 1788) in Edinburgh—put them at a disadvantage during the war years. This issue opened the door to ecclesiastical division, and in 1782 most of the antiburgher ministers and congregations in America opted for a union with the rival branch of seceders (the burghers) and the Reformed Presbyterian Church in America (the Covenanters) to form a new, independent American religious body called the Associate Reformed Church, headed by the Associate Reformed Synod. Marshall and another minister, however, refused to go along with the union. Remaining loyal to the antiburgher synod in Scotland, they continued to call themselves the Associate Presbytery. As a result,

31. Examples include letters from William's brother John, 29 May 1784, and from Frederic McFarlan, Aug. 1784, WYP, box 1, nos. 33, 35.

32. Scouller, *Manual of the United Presbyterian Church*, 487.

33. [M'Culloch], *Memoirs of the Late Rev. William Marshall*. The attribution of this pamphlet to M'Culloch derives from notes in the margin of William Young's copy of M'Culloch's history of the United States, as reported by Young's granddaughter Agnes Young McAllister, WYP, box 8, folder 11.

34. Rush, *Autobiography*, 312.

Marshall and his followers were literally locked out of their own church building by its unionist elders. When Young arrived in Philadelphia in 1784, Marshall's antiburgher remnant in Philadelphia was worshipping in the college hall. It was a small and generally poor congregation, "Scotch with a considerable sprinkling of Irish," and its ethnic heritage remained central to its doctrine and theology.[35] Following in the footsteps of both Aitken and M'Culloch, Young became an elder in Marshall's congregation just a year or two after his arrival in America. A few years later he took charge of the building program that enabled Marshall and his flock to occupy new quarters in the Associate Presbytery Church on Walnut Street in 1790.

In accordance with M'Culloch's original suggestion, Young initially concentrated his efforts on selling books imported from Britain. In addition to the books he had brought with him, he used his brother-in-law William McLaws in London (who dealt at least once with John Murray in Fleet Street) and other purchasing agents to buy more, and as time passed he increasingly bought books directly from suppliers in London, Dublin, and Glasgow.[36] On the Philadelphia side, he was assisted by his fellow antiburgher printers, M'Culloch and Aitken, as well as Thomas Dobson, who became a close friend.[37] At the same time, Young was actively engaged, through his brother-in-law John McLaws in Greenock and his business agent Robert Galloway in Glasgow, in transatlantic trading of commodities such as indigo, tar, turpentine, barley, and cheese. He was generally successful, and as early as September 1784 he and William Marshall engaged in a substantial land purchase.[38] By the beginning of

35. Letter of John McAllister, Jr. (William Young's son-in-law), 28 Feb. 1853, in Sprague, *Annals of the American Pulpit*, vol. 9, "Associate Presbytery," 15. On the ties between ethnicity and religion in the Associate and Associate Reformed churches in America (reunited in 1858 as the United Presbyterian Church), centering on allegiance to the Scottish covenanting tradition, see Fisk, *Scottish High Church Tradition*.

36. E.g., William McLaws to Young, 5 July 1786 and 5 Jan. 1787, WYP, box 2, nos. 5 and 9; and Young's correspondence with William Gilbert of Dublin and others in HSP and in Young's letterbook, 1790–91, WYP, box 8, folder 32.

37. John McAllister, Jr., to Charles A. Poulson, 24 Oct. 1855, HSP, Dreer Autograph Collection, partially quoted in Arner, *Dobson's Encyclopaedia*, 22n6. In a portion of this letter that Arner does not cite, McAllister states, in regard to the books that Dobson brought over from Scotland, "some of these he put into Mr. Young's hands for sale."

38. Daniel Mcfarland to Young and Marshall, 20 Sept. 1784, WYP, box 1, no. 36.

1785 a former divinity classmate wrote to him: "Tell me in your next if it is true that you have £300 pr annum. If this is the case, we would better all leave Scotland, where we think ourselves well if we have £30."[39]

The second stage in M'Culloch's plan was for Young to expand his business into printing and publishing. In the spring of 1785 Young paid £17.8s.6d. for printing materials and a printing press made by John Wilson and Co. of Glasgow, purchased through an antiburgher friend in Scotland.[40] John Bryce added type made by the Glasgow type-founding firm of Alexander Wilson, which at £70.14s.11d. was far more expensive than the press and accessories, and he sent all these materials to John McLaws in Greenock, for shipment to America on the *Alexander* in May.[41] Because of his connections, Young got high-quality Scottish printing equipment at a low cost, and he was able to charge the total value of these goods (£88.3s.5d., in addition to the cost of shipping and insurance) against his account with his brother-in-law in Greenock, to be paid off with commodities shipped back from America.[42]

During his first months in Philadelphia, Young seems to have bought and sold books and other goods without a shop of his own. A joint newspaper advertisement with Robert Aitken in the *Freeman's Journal* for 5 January 1785, however, places him on Third Street "above the Golden

39. Alexander Balfour to Young, 7 Jan. and 14 Feb. 1785, WYP, box 1, no. 41. Balfour thought Young was making his money from teaching, not realizing that he had left that career behind in Scotland. In the same letter, Balfour wrote: "You enjoy Liberty (the dearest of outward blessings) while we groan under Taxes, disagreeable and many of them absurd. You live unmolested and enjoy the comforts of life cheaper than we do here. Our taxes are multiplied every Session of Parliament." He went on to list taxes on horses (now extended to clergymen), candles, windows, marriages, burials, and births.

40. Patrick Main to Young, 3 Apr. 1785, WYP, box 1, no. 47. Patrick Main and his wife Molly were close friends of Young from the antiburgher community in Glasgow, and in the first part of this letter they warned William not to let his newfound prosperity in America cause him to "neglect religion."

41. Bryce to Young, 18 Apr. 1785, WYP, box 1, no. 53. A letter from John McLaws dated 21 May 1785 informs Young that the types and press have been insured and shipped.

42. John McLaws to William and Agnes Young, 22 Apr. and 19 Sept. 1785, WYP, box 1, nos. 55 and 60. In his letter of 3 Apr. 1785 (WYP, box 1, no. 47), Patrick Main assured Young that "you have these [the press and printing accessories] at the same prices that I sell it to my merchant hear at 4 months credit"—which is to say, wholesale.

Swan," and that spring (14 April and 2 May) he announced the opening of his new "Book and Stationery Store" on Chestnut Street, with catalogues of books in all the major genres of polite learning and religion. This was probably 7 Chestnut Street, below Third Street, as he identified it in a joint newspaper advertisement with Thomas Dobson in the 10 August 1785 issue of the *Pennsylvania Journal.*[43] Young had been collaborating with Dobson since the late spring, while preparations were being made for a formal partnership with Peter Stewart and John M'Culloch. Trading from September as Young, Stewart, & M'Culloch, the new partnership was launched with a reprint of one of the classic evangelical sermons of eighteenth-century Scotland by Colin Maclaurin's brother John, *Glorying in the Cross of Christ.* "I am persuaded you will do well," wrote John Bryce when he heard of the plans for the triple partnership in April, "as you are connected with two very discreet clever lads. John M'Culloch, is as good a lad as you could have engaged with."[44] In 1786 the partnership moved to Young's new property at the corner of Chestnut and Second streets, where Young would make his home and continue in business, alone or with various partners, until he sold out to William Woodward in 1801 in order to concentrate his attention on his paper-making activities in Rockland, Delaware.

It is remarkable how quickly Young and Dobson moved up the ranks as booksellers, printers, and publishers. In March 1787 Benjamin Rush informed his old friend William Creech in Edinburgh that "Mr Dobson, and a Mr Young, from Glasgow have succeeded, and will probably make fortunes in the course of a long life. But I am afraid there is not room eno' for another in their way."[45] Four years later Rush called Dobson's bookstore "the most public place of resort for literary people in our city."[46] Young's success is all the more impressive because, as far as I can tell, no benefactor like Charles Elliot or Lafayette provided him with substantial stock or capital, although he did receive considerable assistance from a network of enterprising Scottish friends and family on both sides of the Atlantic. In the summer of 1790 Young's stock-in-trade was worth £1,500 sterling, and he proceeded to buy out his partners because, as he wrote to his brother-in-law in Scotland, "my business has been much

---

43. Some of these advertisements have been preserved among Young's papers, WYP, box 1, no. 66, and box 8, no. 11.

44. Bryce to Young, 18 Apr. 1785, WYP, box 1, no. 53.

45. Rush to Creech, 30 Mar. 1787, WCL.

46. Rush to Jeremy Belknap, 6 June 1791, in Rush, *Letters,* 1:583; see also 1:573.

superior to that of the whole company."[47] With three printing presses and a large inventory of types,[48] his shop was probably as capable of undertaking extensive periodical and reprinting projects as any in America. And reprinting, as Rush told Creech in March 1787, was now "the most profitable method of dealing in books in our country."

The fourth major figure in late eighteenth-century Philadelphia publishing, Robert Campbell, was another Scotsman, born in Edinburgh in April 1769. We have already encountered his father, Samuel Campbell, Sr. (1736–1813), and his older brother, Samuel Campbell, Jr. (1765–1829), on the same passage to America that carried Thomas Dobson's wife in the spring of 1785. Robert, who turned sixteen that spring, was apparently still in Scotland, perhaps following in the footsteps of his brother in the shop of John Bell. His emigration to Philadelphia had occurred by 1789, however, for in that year his name appeared in the imprint of an American edition of William Cullen's *Treatise of the Materia Medica* (no. 281). Two years later Campbell issued a large catalogue of books and stationery for sale in a shop on Second Street,[49] near where William Young was based. Although it contains some American editions (including twenty-three "Books printed for Robert Campbell"), the catalogue is overwhelmingly British and heavily Scottish, and its exceptional size and range suggest that Campbell, like his brother Samuel and Thomas Dobson, was supplied with a large stock by an Edinburgh bookseller. Later in the decade Campbell received some books from William Creech, who had difficulty collecting payment and complained bitterly to his American agent that "the trouble and delay in getting business settled in America really sickens mercantile people in Britain with regard to answering orders."[50]

Campbell's rise was meteoric. By February 1795, when he was just twenty-five years old, he boasted that his shop had "the largest and most

47. Young to John McLaws, 29 Aug. 1791, in Young's letterbook, 1790–91, WYP, box 8, folder 32, no. 14.

48. "Inventory of Printing Materials" [1792?], WYP, box 8, folder 21. Young continued to order type from the Wilson foundry in Glasgow, as in his letter to Alexander Wilson of 22 November 1791, in Young's letterbook, 1790–91, WYP, box 8, folder 32, no. 28.

49. [Campbell], *Robert Campbell's Sale Catalogue of Books*.

50. Creech to W. H. Tod, 28 Dec. 1798 (copy), ECL, William Creech Letterbook, Green Box 120. Other letters in this collection show that Campbell finally paid his £166 debt, but Creech had a more difficult time recovering a smaller debt from Samuel Campbell, Sr., who had taken up farming in Elizabethtown, New Jersey.

general assortment of books ever offered for sale in this city."[51] Later that year he moved his shop to larger quarters at 40 Second Street.[52] Campbell's brother Samuel had already established himself as a leading bookseller and publisher in New York as part of a publishing partnership that included yet another Scottish immigrant bookseller, Thomas Allen, whom we encountered briefly in the last chapter.[53] By subsequently placing Robert in Philadelphia, the Campbells were able to engage in intercity collaboration more effectively than most members of the book trade. As Rosalind Remer has argued, this factor—along with his fondness for underselling the competition—probably accounts for the refusal of Robert Campbell to join the Philadelphia Company of Printers and Booksellers that Young, Dobson, Carey, and others established in 1791 as a means of reducing competition and increasing cooperation among members of the Philadelphia trade.[54] Like James Lackington in London, to whom he was compared by Carey's agent, Mason Locke Weems, Campbell was "made" by "Cheapness."[55]

There was another side to Campbell's bookselling career, however, and it involved reprinting enlightened books that were often Scottish and frequently not cheap. In this capacity, Campbell appears not as a renegade who was alienated from other leading figures of the Philadelphia book trade but rather as one of their number. As in Dublin, books from the Scottish Enlightenment never constituted more than a small proportion of the works that were reprinted in late eighteenth-century Philadelphia. But they nevertheless were produced in significant numbers, and they included a majority of the most important and largest reprint editions, which involved the greatest risk and expense on the part of their projectors and had a disproportionately large influence on American intellectual life.

51. *Philadelphia Gazetteer and Universal Daily Advertiser,* 12 Feb. 1795.

52. See Campbell's catalogue of 1 January 1796, cited in Winans, *Descriptive Checklist,* 140.

53. Allen is identified as a "Scotchman" in a letter from David Ramsay to Benjamin Rush, 29 Dec. 1785, in Brunhouse, *David Ramsay,* 95.

54. Remer, *Printers and Men of Capital,* 57–59. In 1793 Young was president of this organization, Dobson its treasurer, and Carey a member of its executive committee. The reasons for the failure of the organization are stated in Carey's 1796 broadside, *Sir, Having, on Mature Deliberation, Resolved to Withdraw from the Company of Booksellers,* reproduced in Clarkin, *Mathew Carey,* 43.

55. Quoted in Remer, *Printers and Men of Capital,* 173n58.

IMMIGRANT BOOKSELLERS AND SCOTCH LEARNING

Thomas Dobson and the *Encyclopaedia Britannica*

The tradition of Scottish Enlightenment reprinting that Robert Bell introduced to America in 1770 was not immediately evident after the American Revolution. The four subjects of this chapter reprinted no Scottish Enlightenment books until 1787, when Dobson produced two works by James Beattie (nos. 92 and 258). In 1788 one of William Young's partners, Peter Stewart, copublished the first American edition of the poems of Robert Burns (no. 260). In the same year, William Spotswood produced a Philadelphia edition of *A Philosophical Analysis and Illustration of Some of Shakespeare's Remarkable Characters* (no. 166), by Young's former Latin instructor at the University of Glasgow, William Richardson, and another bookseller in the same city, Joseph Crukshank, reprinted Francis Hutcheson's *Short Introduction to Moral Philosophy* (no. 3). A Boston edition of William Cullen's *Institutions of Medicine* also appeared in 1788 (no. 146). Yet there was nothing about these publications to suggest that books by Scottish authors occupied a special place in late eighteenth-century American reprinting or that Campbell, Carey, Dobson, and Young would ever match the earlier accomplishments of Robert Bell and Robert Aitken as appropriators of the Scottish Enlightenment in America.

All that changed dramatically in 1789. On the last day of March, Thomas Dobson published proposals for an American reprint of the third edition of the *Encyclopaedia Britannica* (no. 139), then being published in Edinburgh,[56] and the first volume began appearing in weekly numbers at the beginning of January 1790. Dobson would have been familiar with the second edition of the *Britannica* (1778–84), since Charles Elliot copublished and sold it during the years when Dobson worked for him.[57] But there was a great difference between selling a large, illustrated encyclopedia as a clerk in someone else's Edinburgh bookshop and undertaking the reprint of such a work in Philadelphia. Moreover, with its eighteen volumes, the third edition, which appeared in Edinburgh between 1788 and 1797 and in Philadelphia between 1790 and 1798 (fig. 9.1), would turn out to be much larger than the second—more than twice the size, counting

---

56. Dobson's proposals are discussed in Arner, *Dobson's Encyclopaedia*, 30–31. In this section, parenthetical citations refer to this book. See also Arner, "Thomas Dobson's American Edition," 208–9.

57. McDougall, "Charles Elliot's Book Adventure," 198.

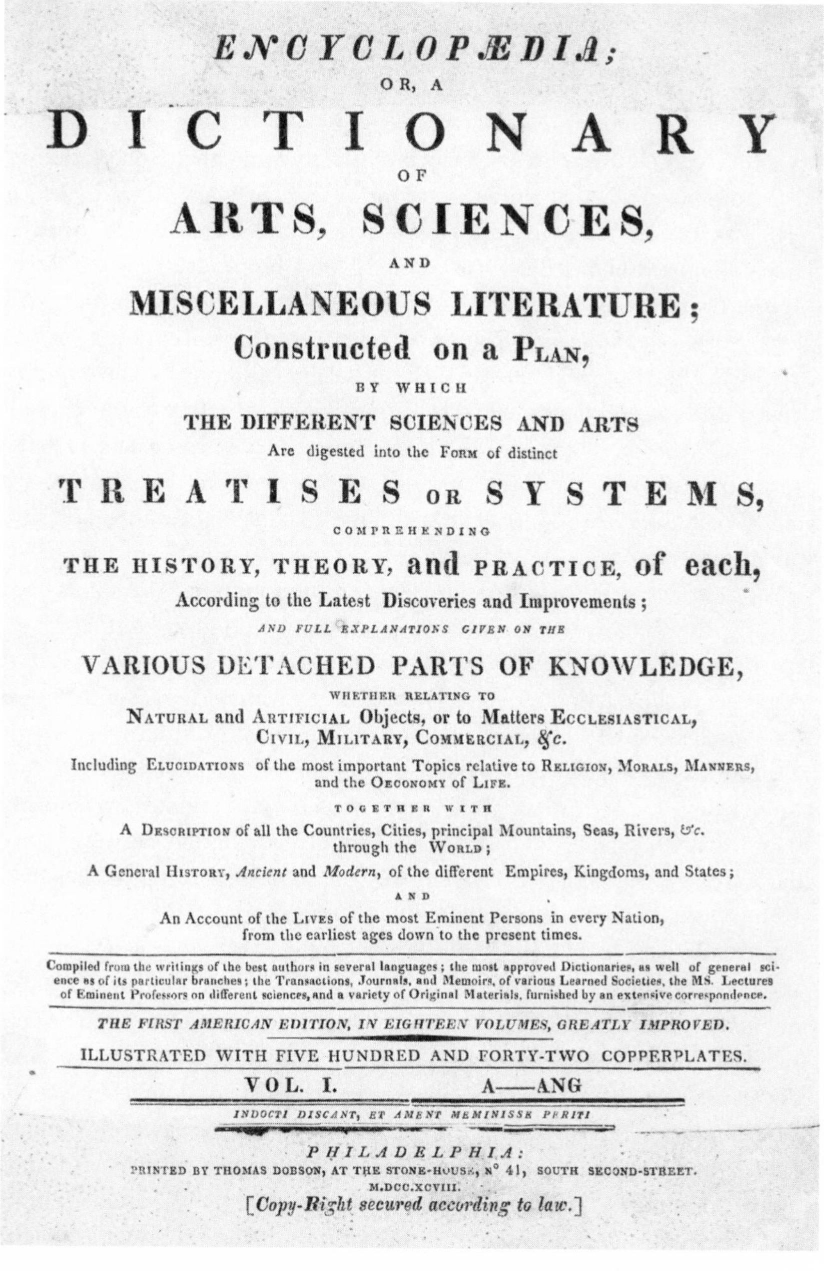

ENCYCLOPÆDIA;

OR, A

DICTIONARY

OF

ARTS, SCIENCES,

AND

MISCELLANEOUS LITERATURE;

Constructed on a PLAN,

BY WHICH

THE DIFFERENT SCIENCES AND ARTS

Are digested into the FORM of distinct

TREATISES OR SYSTEMS,

COMPREHENDING

THE HISTORY, THEORY, and PRACTICE, of each,

According to the Latest Discoveries and Improvements;

AND FULL EXPLANATIONS GIVEN ON THE

VARIOUS DETACHED PARTS OF KNOWLEDGE,

WHETHER RELATING TO

NATURAL and ARTIFICIAL Objects, or to Matters ECCLESIASTICAL,
CIVIL, MILITARY, COMMERCIAL, &c.

Including ELUCIDATIONS of the most important Topics relative to RELIGION, MORALS, MANNERS,
and the OECONOMY of LIFE.

TOGETHER WITH

A DESCRIPTION of all the Countries, Cities, principal Mountains, Seas, Rivers, &c.
through the WORLD;

A General HISTORY, Ancient and Modern, of the different Empires, Kingdoms, and States;

AND

An Account of the LIVES of the most Eminent Persons in every Nation,
from the earliest ages down to the present times.

Compiled from the writings of the best authors in several languages; the most approved Dictionaries, as well of general science as of its particular branches; the Transactions, Journals, and Memoirs, of various Learned Societies, the MS. Lectures
of Eminent Professors on different sciences, and a variety of Original Materials, furnished by an extensive correspondence.

THE FIRST AMERICAN EDITION, IN EIGHTEEN VOLUMES, GREATLY IMPROVED.

ILLUSTRATED WITH FIVE HUNDRED AND FORTY-TWO COPPERPLATES.

VOL. I.   A——ANG

INDOCTI DISCANT, ET AMENT MEMINISSE PERITI

PHILADELPHIA:
PRINTED BY THOMAS DOBSON, AT THE STONE-HOUSE, N° 41, SOUTH SECOND-STREET.
M.DCC.XCVIII.
[Copy-Right secured according to law.]

Fig. 9.1. The Scottish emigrant Thomas Dobson raised American reprinting to a new
level with his eighteen-volume, heavily illustrated reprint of the third edition of the
Encyclopaedia Britannica, which he altered and retitled to suit his own designs. Shown
here is the title page of the first volume, dated 1798. John Carter Brown Library at
Brown University.

the *Supplement*, which Dobson reprinted in three volumes between 1800 and 1803. The number of copperplate engravings alone—estimated in Dobson's initial proposal at "nearly four hundred" but ending up at almost six hundred, including those in the *Supplement*—was staggering. So was the required quantity of paper, which has been estimated at 7,200 reams for the 2,000 copies that were printed (108).

It was a remarkably ambitious endeavor, paralleling the edition that James Moore would soon begin printing in Dublin (see chap. 7). Like Moore, Dobson did not intend his edition as a cheap imitation; the proposals stressed that he would use superfine paper and new types, specially cast for the purpose by Baine & Co. of Philadelphia. Dobson's subscription drive was directed at "all the lovers of science and literature in the United States of America" (30, quoting Dobson), very much in the tradition of enlightened, patriotic publishing that Robert Bell had introduced to America before the Revolution. It is unfortunate that the full subscription list was never printed in the work itself and does not appear to have survived. There were at least 246 subscribers at the time that Dobson began printing the first edition in December 1789, but the final number must have been much higher. Dobson's announcement on 8 April 1790 that demand had required him to double the size of the print run—from 1,000 to 2,000 copies—suggests that the number of subscribers ultimately reached 1,500 or more, including George Washington, Thomas Jefferson, Benjamin Franklin, and other prominent citizens (48).[58] Robert Arner has shown that Dobson built a subscription and distribution network centered around the many booksellers whose names appeared in the imprint (27–44). Dobson himself, William Young, and Robert Campbell were the first three names listed in Philadelphia, while Samuel Campbell and Thomas Allen headed the New York contingent. Other subscription agents were identified in Boston and Worcester, Massachusetts (Isaiah Thomas); Wilmington, Delaware; Baltimore and Annapolis, Maryland; Fredericksburg, Norfolk, and Richmond, Virginia; Wilmington, North Carolina; and Charleston, South Carolina. It stands to reason that some of these booksellers would have subscribed for multiple editions with the standard quantity discount, for resale to nonsubscribing customers at a higher price. To accommodate the subscribers' financial situations and

---

58. See also Arner, "Thomas Dobson's American Edition," 213, 216–19. The estimate of at least 1,500 subscribers is mine, based on materials presented by Arner. But Arner also shows that not all subscribers paid their bill, with serious consequences for Dobson.

generate income on a rolling basis, Dobson made the work available in three different forms: forty-page weekly numbers, half volumes, and full volumes. By charging five Pennsylvania dollars per volume in boards, Dobson barely matched the one guinea price of the Edinburgh edition. However, the surcharge that Americans had to pay for books imported from Britain enabled him to beat the Philadelphia selling price of the Edinburgh edition by 15 percent (32).

Dobson originally intended to reprint the Edinburgh text without significant alterations. For the most part, that is what he did, although certain articles of local or national interest, such as "America" and "Philadelphia," were rewritten for the American edition. The principal writer whom Dobson employed for this purpose was Jedidiah Morse, whose best-selling *American Geography* (1789) was used in the Edinburgh edition.[59] A pious clergyman with an almost messianic faith in the United States as a land of liberty, Morse added little to the geographic representation of America but altered the historical representation considerably.[60] Dobson's *Encyclopaedia* also drew on local publications for the article on Philadelphia, including Mathew Carey's popular account of the yellow fever epidemic of 1793. In spite of these uniquely American articles, however, the overall effect of Dobson's *Encyclopaedia* was to publicize Scotland as well as America. As noted in chapter 7, the third edition of the *Britannica* devoted a great deal of text to Scotland, and the American edition reproduced all of it. Similarly, Dobson included all of the dozens of biographies of Scottish Enlightenment authors that appeared in the third edition of the *Britannica* and the first edition of its *Supplement*,[61] and he added no new ones of American figures. The presence in Dobson's *Encyclopaedia* of so many biographies of Scottish authors supported and encouraged the reprints of their works that were appearing in America in such substantial numbers during this period.

Regarding the technology of book production, Dobson intended to make a significant patriotic statement by employing only American crafts-

59. Ibid., 224–49.

60. Short, *Representing the Republic*, 104.

61. In *Dobson's Encyclopaedia*, 168, and "Thomas Dobson's American Edition," 245–46, Arner speculates about why Dobson deleted from his edition the biographies of Hugh Blair and James Burnett, Lord Monboddo. However, the biographies of Blair and Monboddo first appeared in the second edition of the *Supplement*, published in Edinburgh in 1803, two years after the first Edinburgh edition of the *Supplement* that Dobson used as his copy text.

men and by using only American paper, type, engravings, and other materials. Again, he was generally successful, although some adjustments
were necessary on account of a fire in September 1793 and other unforeseen hazards. But it must be remembered that American-made products
were actually often fashioned by foreign-born immigrants, and once again
Scots played a disproportionately large role in the process. For example,
the Baine type-founding firm, which established the industry in America
and supplied most of the type used in the early volumes of Dobson's *Encyclopaedia*, was headed by two Scots—John Baine and his grandson of the
same name—whom William Young had lured to Philadelphia in 1787.[62]
Similarly, of more than eighteen "American" engravers whose work Arner
has identified in Dobson's *Encyclopaedia* and the *Supplement*, the most productive and important were Scottish born: Robert Scot, Samuel Allardice,
John Vallance, and Alexander Lawson (chap. 6 and App. B). Thus, Dobson's American edition of the *Britannica* was a Scottish, or chiefly Scottish, work not only because it originated in Scotland and was reprinted
by a Scottish immigrant but also because Scottish immigrants dominated
the local distribution network and the craft technology.

For Dobson, the *Encyclopaedia* was not an isolated episode in Scottish
Enlightenment reprinting. Before the first number had even appeared,
Dobson had produced a three-volume edition of Adam Smith's *Wealth of
Nations*. By printing his edition in duodecimo rather than octavo, he was
able to advertise the work in the *Pennsylvania Mercury* on 13 January 1790
as selling "at not more than *one half the price* for which the London [oc-
tavo] Edition can be imported and sold," even though it was "printed on
a superfine paper and good type, handsomely bound and lettered" (12).
The duodecimo format should not mislead us, however. As expanded by
Smith in the third edition of 1784, the *Wealth of Nations* was a very large
book, and the appearance of an American edition was a significant development in American publishing. The fact that Dobson found it necessary
to reprint the work again in 1796 indicates that the 1789 edition sold well.
It also lends credibility to Arner's conjecture that Dobson's other reprints
supported the American edition of the *Encyclopaedia Britannica* by generating capital, associating Dobson's name with major publications, and
demonstrating the existence of an American market for learned works
(12). In 1790 Dobson continued to draw upon Scottish learning by publishing the first American editions of John Brown's *Elements of Medicine*
(no. 273), Alexander Hamilton's *Outlines of the Theory and Practice of Mid-*

62. Silver, *Typefounding in America*, 1–10, citing William McCulloch.

wifery (no. 242), and George Campbell's *Dissertation on Miracles* (no. 72), as well as Benjamin Rush's *An Eulogium in Honour of the Late Dr. William Cullen.*

The *Encyclopaedia*, however, remained Dobson's greatest achievement. A year after its completion, Joseph Johnson wrote from London:

> Before this time no doubt you have completed the expensive work you undertook of reprinting the Scots Encyclopedia, which has certainly answer'd your purpose. What I have seen of it does you credit, but it wants to be curtaild and improv'd very much indeed. You make such rapid strides in printing that in no long time it should seem you will want nothing from a London bookseller but his authors which may be exported in a single copy for half a crown or a guinea! What a glorious business it would be could *we* obtain copyrights on the same easy terms![63]

Besides showing Johnson's respect for Dobson's accomplishment in regard to the *Britannica* itself, this passage reveals the growing awareness that large-scale reprinting was steadily liberating American booksellers from dependency on the London book trade. It also contains a gentle reminder that Americans enjoyed a considerable advantage because they did not have to pay copy money to British authors. Since the American copyright law of 1790 was silent on the issue of international rights, and the Irish reprinting trade was about to be subsumed under British copyright law, American booksellers could, and did, continue to expand their reprinting operations with impunity.

William Young and Common Sense Philosophy

While Dobson was beginning work on his *Encyclopaedia*, other American booksellers were pursuing extensive Scottish publication projects of their own. In 1789 Samuel Campbell reprinted *The Lounger* in two small volumes (no. 270) and joined with his New York partners, Robert Hodge and Thomas Allen, as well as his twenty-year-old brother Robert and Joseph Crukshank of Philadelphia, to publish William Cullen's two-volume *Treatise of the Materia Medica* (no. 281). The next year Samuel Campbell and his New York partners published an edition of John Moore's *Zeluco* (no. 284), as well as the first volume of Hugh Blair's *Sermons* (no. 188), which listed Robert Campbell in the imprint as the Philadelphia selling

---

63. Johnson to Dobson, 17 July 1799 (copy), Joseph Johnson Letterbook, 1795–1810, New York Public Library, Pforzheimer Collection.

agent. The first two volumes of Blair's *Sermons* appeared together in 1791, jointly published by Mathew Carey (then partnered, briefly, with James H. Stewart)[64] and William Spotswood. In the same year young Robert Campbell released his first major solo production, a 500-page octavo edition of the first volume of William Smellie's *Philosophy of Natural History* (no. 292).

In 1792 William Young entered the fray. For several years Young had been reprinting a small number of English classics, such as Milton's *Paradise Lost* (1787, with Joseph James) and *Paradise Regained* (1790), as well as popular works of education, reference, and advice.[65] His contribution to the dissemination of the Scottish Enlightenment in America began early in 1790, when he purchased the *Columbian Magazine* from William Spotswood.[66] The change of ownership was marked by a change of title, to the *Universal Asylum, and Columbian Magazine,* as well as a statement, possibly fictitious, that the work was published by a "Society of Gentlemen." All indications are that from the time the *Universal Asylum* came into existence in March 1790, William Young had full control of all aspects of the magazine, from printing to editing.[67]

The initial issue of Young's *Universal Asylum* contained the first of three installments from Adam Smith's *Theory of Moral Sentiments*, extracts from Hugh Blair's *Critical Dissertation on the Poems of Ossian* (including the section in which Ossian is compared favorably with Homer), and an "original" translation of an Ossianic poem, with the promise, which was kept, of another "original" Ossianic translation in the next issue.[68] The three installments from the *Theory of Moral Sentiments* reproduced the chapter

64. Carey to John Chambers, 9 Sept. 1791, HSP, Lea and Febiger Papers.

65. Examples include Thomas Rudiman, *The Rudiments of the Latin Tongue* (1786); Hannah More, *Essays on Various Subjects, Principally Designed for Young Ladies* (1786); and Thomas Sheridan, *A Complete Dictionary of the English Language* (1789).

66. Young may have been printing the *Columbian* before he purchased it, for Spotswood told Jeremy Belknap on 9 October 1788 that "Young is a journeyman printer who has been a considerable time in my employment" (Belknap, *Belknap Papers*, 420). But Spotswood's remark, if it did not refer to a different printer named Young, distorted the nature of the relationship, and at least one modern commentator has erroneously asserted on the basis of this letter that Young had been Spotswood's apprentice (Cole, *Irish Booksellers*, 182).

67. Free, *Columbian Magazine*, 25.

68. Renewed interest in Ossian was probably generated by the appearance in Philadelphia in 1790 of the first American edition of *The Poems of Ossian*, under the imprint of Thomas Lang (no. 64).

"Of the Beauty which the Appearance of Utility Bestows upon All the Productions of Art, and of the Extensive Influence of this Species of Beauty" (pt. 4, chap. 1), which includes the book's only mention of the well-known Smithian term "invisible hand." However, the magazine silently removed one sentence, which pays tribute to "an ingenious and agreeable philosopher, who joins the greatest depth of thought to the greatest elegance of expression, and possesses the singular and happy talent of treating the abstrusest subjects not only with the most perfect perspicuity, but with the most lively eloquence."[69] That philosopher was Smith's close friend David Hume, and the exclusion of this complimentary sentence, coupled with later developments, suggests the nature of Young's perspective on Scottish thought.

Until the *Universal Asylum* ceased publication at the end of 1792, the magazine promoted many Scottish authors and books. There were excerpts from James Beattie's moral philosophy and Benjamin Bell's *System of Surgery*, for example, and a front-page review of Benjamin Rush's *Eulogium in Honour of the Late Dr. William Cullen*, followed by strictures on Cullen's Scottish rival, Dr. John Brown. Rush was a frequent contributor to the *Universal Asylum*, and his influence is apparent. Through him, enlightened Scottish thought and Christianity were blended in ways that Young apparently found attractive.[70]

The prominence of Rush in the pages of the *Universal Asylum* may also be seen as emblematic of Young's keen interest in promoting the fledgling American Enlightenment. The June 1790 number introduced a new column titled "Impartial Review of Late American Publications," which was said to be the first of its kind in the New World (though we saw in chapter 8 that Robert Aitken's *Pennsylvania Magazine* was moving in that direction just before the Revolution). The column opened with a review of David Ramsay's *History of the American Revolution*, "Printed and Sold by R. Aitken and Son" in two volumes in 1789. More significant than the review itself was the general introduction to the new book review section, probably written by Young himself, or at the very least produced under his authority. It began by glorying in the "rising greatness of these United States" with regard to "manufactures, and the useful arts," and proceeded to speculate on the additional greatness that might be expected

69. Smith, *Theory of Moral Sentiments*, 179.

70. Reid-Maroney, *Philadelphia's Enlightenment*, contains an insightful discussion of the outlook of Rush's circle, focusing on the notion of a "redemptive Enlightenment" in relation to science and medicine.

if "science," by means of "a more extensive diffusion of useful knowledge," could attain the same degree of perfection in America that "agriculture, commerce, and manufactures" had already begun to demonstrate (372).

By the diffusion of useful knowledge, Young did not mean merely the importation of European learning. Rather, he meant the dawning of an indigenous American Enlightenment. "We begin at length to realize that independence, which, for some years after the termination of the late arduous conflict with Britain, existed only in name," he writes. "To import the clothes we wore, and the books we read, we were badly calculated for the enjoyment of freedom and independence." A transformation in the print trades was necessary if Americans were to become something more than "servile copyists of foreign manners, fashions, and vices" (372). In the tradition of the Scottish Enlightenment, Young argued that this transformation had occurred in a series of four increasingly complex and sophisticated stages, from importing books, to reprinting minor books, to reprinting important books, and finally to publishing new work by native authors:

> To effect this has been a work of time. In literature, for instance, though our booksellers were numerous, we had but few printers; nor had our authors sufficient inducements to publish their works at home—they were obliged to seek encouragement in a foreign country. The reform, in this case, has been gradual; our printers first ventured to republish school-books, and such other low-priced publications, as were most in demand; they next advanced to books of higher repute, and some of the best works in the English language have, of late years, been reprinted in America. It was not, however, till very lately that we could boast of *original* publications, of any considerable note. A beginning, in this way, has at length been made, and we trust every American citizen will be ready to encourage the works of genius, in his own country. (372–73)

In hindsight, Young's vision was unrealistic. New books by American authors, especially books embodying the scope and enlightened content of a work like Ramsay's,[71] were still infrequent in 1790. However much Young may have wished for a new age of learned books that were American in the double sense of composition and production, that goal could not be realized at this time. As an ambitious printer and bookseller, he himself was still deeply enmeshed in his third stage, involving the reprinting of major British and European works, particularly from the Scottish En-

71. On Ramsay as an Enlightenment historian, see O'Brien, *Narratives of Enlightenment*, chap. 7.

lightenment. The first such book that he undertook was an octavo edition of William Robertson's *Historical Disquisition* (no. 299), which had appeared in London in early June 1791. The *Universal Asylum* carried a full-page advertisement to announce the subscription proposals for an American edition for just ten shillings, said to be 60 percent less than the American price of the London quarto. A lengthy excerpt titled "Robertson's Account of the Distinction of Ranks, Separation of Professions, and Political Constitutions of India" constituted the lead article in the October 1791 issue (219–25), and briefer excerpts appeared in the November and December numbers. Publication was announced in the January 1792 issue, with the retail price set at 11s.3d. or $1.50 in boards (later raised to $1.75). Young's edition was a substantial work of 420 pages, with no subscription list. There is some irony in the fact that this book by Robertson, the celebrated leader of the Scottish kirk's "prevailing party," which the seceders associated with the degeneration of the Godly tradition of Scottish Calvinism, was introduced into America by a bookseller who was firmly committed to the seceder cause in its narrowest form.

In 1792–93 Young made his greatest contribution to the diffusion of the Scottish Enlightenment in America when he reprinted three major works of Scottish philosophy. The first hint of an interest in this topic occurred in the April 1791 issue of the *Universal Asylum*, which featured a front-page essay by Benjamin Rush titled "Thoughts on Common Sense." An introduction by "A Constant Reader" explained that the essay had been read before the American Philosophical Society on 18 February but subsequently was withdrawn from the society's papers because of its metaphysical subject matter. The point of the essay was to take issue with Thomas Reid's interpretation of common sense in the *Essays on the Intellectual Powers of Man* by arguing that it should be defined as the view of the majority in any given time and place rather than (as Rush took Reid to mean) a faculty for reasoning in its most basic form. Nevertheless, Rush used Reid as his starting point, and he not only quoted Reid extensively but devoted an entire paragraph to his "great diffidence" at objecting "to any thing that comes from a gentleman from whose writings I have derived so much entertainment and instruction, and who has done so much towards removing the rubbish that has for many ages obscured the science of metaphysics" (211–15).

One year later, the *Universal Asylum* for May 1792 announced that Thomas Reid's *Essays on the Intellectual Powers of Man* and *Essays on the Active Powers of Man* (nos. 255 and 275) would be combined into a single, integrated edition and was in press in two large octavo volumes, to be priced at $4, as opposed to $6 for the Dublin edition and $12 for the separate London editions. Young was evidently following the example of the Dublin reprinters Patrick Byrne and John Milliken, who had published an integrated edition of Reid's *Essays* in three octavo volumes in 1790. Even with a surcharge on imported books, Young did not actually improve on the Dubliners' price per volume ($2), but by decreasing the number of volumes from three to two, he reduced the overall cost of the book by a third.

The sheer scale of this work is impressive. Young's edition of Reid consists of some 1,200 octavo pages, and unlike virtually all other large scholarly books reprinted in America at this time, it was not published by subscription. A full-page advertisement in the December 1792 issue of the *Universal Asylum* (fig. 9.2) declared the book "Just Published," although the imprint reads 1793; thus, it took more than six months to complete the production from the time Young announced that it was in press. The advertisement, like the title page of the book itself, prominently displays the author's position as "Professor of Moral Philosophy in the University of Glasgow." It contains a long paragraph on the author and the book, "a work, whose importance is universally acknowledged." Reid is praised for playing the same role in moral philosophy that Newton and the scientific popularizer James Ferguson have played in natural philosophy: by liberating their fields from the tyranny and confusion of the past, they made it possible for philosophy to become "not only an useful, but a pleasant exercise, and a more safe introduction to the most important studies." In crediting Reid with having "divested moral science, from that veil under which for so many ages it has been concealed, by ambiguous words, and the jargon of the schools," the advertisement echoed Rush's reference to "removing the rubbish" in his essay of April 1791. From all this, it seems clear that Young did not publish Reid's *Essays* merely or mainly as a way to make money. Rather, a number of other factors were at work, including, I suspect, respect for a former teacher, a personal love of philosophy and learning, Scottish national pride, the influence and example of Rush, and a belief, which would become increasingly common among American intellectuals and theologians, that Scottish common sense philosophy provided a bulwark against Humean skepticism and an ideal foundation for educating the new nation in the liberal arts and Christian values.[72] In addition, the attraction of common sense philosophy at this time may also

72. See Meyer, *Instructed Conscience;* Ahlstrom, "Scottish Philosophy and American Theology," 257–72; and other works cited in Sher, "Introduction: Scottish-American Cultural Studies," 1–27.

have been linked to the growth of French atheism, as the French Revolution entered its most radical phase.

Young almost immediately undertook the reprinting of another large work of Scottish common sense philosophy, Dugald Stewart's *Elements of the Philosophy of the Human Mind* (no. 309). This book had just been published in a 1792 London quarto edition that retailed for £1.5s. By bringing out a 500-page octavo edition in Philadelphia in 1793, Young was in a position to undercut the British price substantially. Even so, it was an enormous risk, undertaken without the safety net of a subscription or (since the *Universal Asylum* ceased publication with the December 1792 number) the advantages that came from having a popular magazine in which to advertise one's latest publications. The continuity between the Reid and Stewart volumes is unmistakable. As we saw in chapter 2, Reid's *Essays on the Intellectual Powers* began with a long and exceedingly liberal-minded dedication to Dugald Stewart and James Gregory, and Young placed this dedication at the front of his integrated edition of Reid's *Essays* (fig. 9.3). Stewart's *Elements* began with a dedication to Reid, and in the back of that book Young placed an advertisement for his publications that gave pride of place to his edition of Reid's *Essays*.

All told, Young printed and published 1,700 octavo pages of common sense philosophy by Reid and Stewart in 1793. It was a colossal achievement that set the stage for the celebrated conquest of American higher education by common sense philosophy. Although we do not know how many copies of each book were printed, it appears that all the copies were sold within a year or two.[73] In his popular account of the Scottish Enlightenment and its influence, Arthur Herman uses the colorful phrase "remote control" to describe the mechanism by which Dugald Stewart's philosophical teachings became the "standard guides" for generations of Americans.[74] He means that, unlike the emigrant John Witherspoon, Stewart did not personally go to America, although his philosophy did. In reality, however, it was mainly flesh-and-blood booksellers who brought the ideas of Dugald Stewart and other Scots to North America, and they did it by choosing to import, reprint, and promote certain books rather than others. In this case, William Young was instrumental in transforming Scottish common sense philosophy into a commodity that was not only purchased and used, but literally remade, in America.

---

73. Neither book appears in *A Catalogue of Books, Published by the Different Members of the Philadelphia Company of Printers and Booksellers*.

74. Herman, *How the Scots Invented the Modern World*, 330.

JUST PUBLISHED,

By WILLIAM YOUNG, Bookſeller, No. 52, *Second-ſtreet,*
the Corner of Cheſnut-ſtreet,

In two large 8vo. vols. neatly bound, price 4 dollars,

E S S A Y S

ON THE

INTELLECTUAL AND ACTIVE

POWERS OF MAN.

By THOMAS REID, D.D. F.R.S. Edinburgh,

PROFESSOR OF MORAL PHILOSOPHY

IN THE UNIVERSITY OF GLASGOW.

IT would be improper for the publiſher to mention any thing, re-
ſpecting the literary talents of an author, ſo generally known and
eſteemed. Nor does it appear neceſſary to requeſt attention, to pe-
ruſe a work, whoſe importance is univerſally acknowledged. Thoſe
who have read the ancient ſyſtems, and theſe volumes, will readily
perceive, that the knowledge of philoſophy, advances from a ſtate of
infancy, towards maturity; nor will it appear too much, when it is ſaid,
that Dr. REID has diveſted moral ſcience, from that veil under which
for ſo many ages it has been concealed, by ambiguous words and the
jargon of the ſchools. Thus he has acted that friendly part to
moral ſcience, which the ingenious Newton and Ferguſon did to natural philoſophy; their united and ſkilful efforts, render philoſophy, not only an uſeful, but a pleaſant exerciſe, and a more ſafe introduction to the moſt important ſtudies.——It is impracticable to inſert
the lengthy reviews of this work, and to give a part, would be un-
friendly to the author and reviewers.

POCKET BIBLE.

Juſt Publiſhed by WILLIAM YOUNG, *Bookſeller,*

THE FIRST AMERICAN EDITION of the *BIBLE* 18mo. either with or without Pſalms, bound in one or two vols. to ſuit
the buyer.

The generous encouragement of the public to former publications,
gave the publiſher the greateſt ſatisfaction; at the ſame time, he believes the preſent edition will claim a preference *to any imported* at the
ſame rate.—*Price per dozen without pſalms,* 75ſ, *Ditto with pſalms,* 78ſ.
Five per cent diſcount for caſh.

In the history of Philadelphia, 1793 is remembered not for William
Young's reprint editions of key works by Reid and Stewart but rather
as the year of the first yellow fever epidemic.[75] As that deadly disease
swept the city, Young's whole family became ill. Young himself report-
edly had the disease twice "and was worse the second time than the first,"

75. Powell, *Bring Out Your Dead.*

TO

Mr. DUGALD STEWART,

LATELY

PROFESSOR OF MATHEMATICS

NOW

PROFESSOR OF MORAL PHILOSOPHY,

AND

Dr. JAMES GREGORY,

PROFESSOR OF THE THEORY OF PHYSIC,

In the Univerſity of Edinburgh.

MY DEAR FRIENDS,

I KNOW not to whom I can addreſs theſe Eſſays with more propriety than to You; not only on account of a friendſhip begun in early life on your part, though in old age on mine, and in one of you I may ſay hereditary; nor yet on account of that correſpondence in our literary purſuits and amuſements, which has always given me ſo great pleaſure; but becauſe, if theſe Eſſays have any merit, you have a conſiderable ſhare in it, having not only encouraged me to hope that they may be uſeful, but favoured me with your obſervations on every part of them, both before they were ſent to the Preſs and while they were under it.

I have

Figs. 9.2 and 9.3. The December 1792 issue of the *Universal Asylum, and Columbian Magazine* (left) announced the publication of William Young's integrated Philadelphia edition of Thomas Reid's two volumes of *Essays* (1793). By prominently reproducing Reid's lengthy dedication to Dugald Stewart and James Gregory from the *Essays on the Intellectual Powers of Man* (above), Young's edition not only promoted Scottish common sense philosophy in America but also popularized the ideal of Scotland as a land of intellectual camaraderie and toleration. *Universal Asylum, and Columbian Magazine:* APS online; dedication: Washington and Lee University.

according to the account published by Mathew Carey, who, along with John M'Culloch, took an active role in organizing the city's response to the crisis.[76] Young was so sick that his friend Charles Nisbet told him in December that he "believed that you were no more."[77] Although he recovered, publicly crediting his good fortune to the purging powders of his physician, Benjamin Rush, his wife Agnes died on 22 September 1793 and was buried in the yard of the Walnut Street Church that her husband had helped to build two years earlier.[78] Young was devastated by his loss. As late as February 1795, he was still receiving consolation from Rush, who wrote that "gods favours are not withdrawn when he visits with the rod and shows us how frail we are."[79] Although it is difficult to know with certainty how the death of his wife affected his career, Young never again showed the same interest in reprinting and promoting Enlightenment books. He soon began shifting his interests to his paper mill in Rockland, Delaware, and in 1802 he remarried and moved his family to a handsome new house there, which still stands. A portrait from around this time shows him as a fashionably dressed businessman, holding a document rather than a book (fig. 9.4).

Young's religious faith never wavered. In 1804 he wrote to his successor at the corner of Chestnut and Second streets, William Woodward, who had recently published the first volume of the first American edition of Thomas Scott's annotated Bible: "nothing gave me more satisfaction than to realize all my expectations that [Chestnut and Second] should [be] the Emporium of Calvinistic publications in the United States," through which "thousands I hope shall be shown the way of salvation so as to become the happy subject[s] of the grace of god."[80] Like his predecessor and colleague Robert Aitken, Young seems to have experienced no conflict between an all-consuming faith in Presbyterianism of the Scot-

76. Mathew Carey, *Short Account of the Malignant Fever which Prevailed in Philadelphia in the Year 1793*, in Carey, *Miscellaneous Essays*, 75. When another epidemic struck the city later in the decade, Young himself organized private support for the poor. See Harrison, *Philadelphia Merchant*, 146–47.

77. Nisbet to Young, 12 Dec. 1793, HSP.

78. *Federal Gazette*, 23 Oct. 1793, cited in Rush, *Letters*, 2:724n2. Agnes Young's passing is lovingly recounted in Young, "Yellow Fever in Philadelphia in 1793." A bloodletting by Rush supposedly brought her relief near the end, but in a letter to his wife of 22 September 1793, Rush blamed the death on "bark and laudanum" (Rush, *Letters*, 2:675).

79. Rush to Young, HSP, Rush Papers, 20 Rush, fol. 133.

80. Young to William Woodward, 29 Sept. 1804, WYP, box 3, no. 70.

Fig. 9.4. William Young appears to be about fifty years old in this early nineteenth-century portrait by an unknown artist, who shows Young looking more like the affluent Delaware industrialist he then was than the aggressive Philadelphia bookseller and publisher he once had been. Historical Society of Pennsylvania.

tish seceder variety, with its strong commitment to national covenanting, and a wish not merely to tolerate but actively to promote the polite learning associated with Scottish historians, philosophers, and physicians such as Robertson, Reid, Stewart, Smith, and Cullen.

Mathew Carey and Guthrie's *Geography*

Shortly before the yellow fever epidemic visited Philadelphia in the summer of 1793, William Young joined Thomas Dobson, Mathew Carey, William Spotswood, and two other Philadelphia bookselling firms to reprint one of the many editions of William Buchan's *Domestic Medicine* (no. 115) that appeared in late eighteenth-century America. Ever since Robert Aitken published the first American edition in 1772, Buchan's book had remained a sure seller, the bible of medical homecare on both sides of the English-speaking Atlantic, and much of continental Europe too. Yet at nearly eight hundred octavo pages, it represented a sizable investment, and collaborative publishing was one way to ease the burden. The two other firms participating in this enterprise were led by the Philadelphia-born Quaker Joseph Crukshank and by Henry and Patrick Rice—immigrants from Ireland and brothers of the prominent Dublin bookseller John Rice, whose reprinting was discussed in chapter 7.[81] Although Spotswood appears to have resettled in Boston when Philadelphia succumbed to yellow fever, these booksellers formed the nucleus of a loose-knit publishing alliance that would produce at least eight reprint editions between 1792 and 1796, including Edmund Burke's *Reflections on the Revolution in France*, Pope's translation of the *Iliad*, several schoolbooks, and Helen Maria Williams's controversial *Letters containing a Sketch of the Politics of France*. But the 1793 edition of *Domestic Medicine* was the group's most ambitious undertaking.

Although William Buchan had been living for some time in London, American reprints of *Domestic Medicine* like this one still identified him on the title page as "William Buchan, M.D. / Fellow of the Royal College of Physicians, Edinburgh." We have seen that such authorial identifications were common in books published in London and Edinburgh, and they were almost never omitted or abridged in Dublin and American reprints. Particularly in the field of medicine, they established the authority of the author through association with respected institutions in a country and city famed for learning. For American reprinters, readers, and consumers, they served a branding function, conferring a certain status on Scottish books. They also help us to answer an important question raised by Andrew Hook, about whether eighteenth-century Americans understood that certain books were the products of a distinctively Scottish intellectual movement rather than merely being part of an amorphous body of "English, or European" work.[82] How could they have failed to notice?

In all probability, the 1793 edition of *Domestic Medicine*, along with the other collaborative editions alluded to, constituted the publishing output of the Philadelphia Company of Printers and Booksellers that was founded on 4 July 1791.[83] If so, *Domestic Medicine* was probably the "one

81. On 25 February 1795 the London bookseller George Robinson told his Edinburgh publishing partners, Bell & Bradfute, that his firm had been making large book shipments to the Rice brothers in Philadelphia "on their promise that we sh[ould] receive a large Sum before this time from their Bro[the]r John of Dublin, which however is not come and we are begin[nin]g to wish our Books were yet in our warehouse." NLS, Dep. 317, box 3, folder 1795.

82. Hook, *Scotland and America*, 116–17.

83. *Constitution, Proceedings, etc. of the Philadelphia Company of Printers & Booksellers*. Although the printed minutes refer to only two publications by the company, Carey's broadside cited in the next note demonstrates that there were more.

valuable book" referred to by Mathew Carey in a broadside of 1796, when he resigned from that organization in part because of the poor selection of titles that the company had chosen for reprinting.[84] At this time Carey was seriously overextended, and deeply in debt, as a result of heavy importing and an overly aggressive publishing program.[85] In his *Autobiography*, he explained: "Had I limited my printing and publication within proper bounds, instead of having my substance eaten up by interest and brokerage, I might have paid for paper and printing in cash, and had handsome discounts, particularly on the former. But, by my folly, I was, to use a homely, but very significant phrase, 'burning the candle at both ends'" (43). He then discussed, as the prime examples of his folly, two publication projects that James Green has called "an almost unprecedented publishing risk" for their day:[86] a two-volume quarto edition of William Guthrie's *Geography* (1794–95; no. 130), with an accompanying atlas, and a heavily illustrated, four-volume octavo edition of Oliver Goldsmith's *An History of the Earth, and Animated Nature* (1795).

Carey's edition of Guthrie's *Geography* is worthy of detailed consideration. In the autumn of 1788, John Chambers wrote to Carey about the quarto edition of Guthrie he was printing in Dublin. "I rejoice in your undertaking Guthrie," Carey replied in a letter addressed to "My Dear Friend," "and am happy you will do our much-abused island justice. This is a most acceptable service to every Irishman who feels for the honour of his country."[87] The following year Carey acknowledged receiving a copy of Chambers's edition, noting that "the animated and glowing character you have drawn of Ireland and Irishmen, must endear the work and its editor to every patriotic Irishman."[88] Chambers had hopes of reprinting his edition in Dublin for an American audience. But Carey had other ideas, and by the summer of 1792 he had informed his friend of his own intention to reprint the book in Philadelphia and had

84. See Carey, *Sir, Having, on Mature Deliberation, Resolved to Withdraw from the Company of Booksellers.* Even in the case of the "one valuable book" that the Company reprinted, Carey complained that the print run had been too small to generate much of a profit.

85. Green, "From Printer to Publisher," 26–44. The extent of Carey's book importing during this period is revealed in Kinane, "'Literary Food' for the American Market," 315–32, which states that Carey imported more than £2,000 worth of books from Byrne alone during the period 1793–95.

86. Green, "From Printer to Publisher," 27.

87. Carey to Chambers, 15 Nov. 1788 (copy), HSP, Lea and Febiger Papers.

88. Carey to Chambers, 9 Nov. 1789 (copy), ibid.

inquired about the possibility of securing impressions of the plates from Chambers.[89]

Carey decided to go all out. Like Chambers, he reprinted the expensive quarto version of the work, titled *A New System of Modern Geography*, using a subscription campaign and publication in weekly numbers to ease the financial strain. Carey also spread out his expenses over a longer period by producing his edition in two large volumes, published separately, the first in the winter of 1794 (fig. 9.5) and the second in the spring of 1795. Not content to limit his press run to the 1,250 copies ordered by subscription, he optimistically printed twice that number.[90] If all the copies had been sold at the subscription price of $12 a set in boards, the edition would have grossed the impressive sum of $30,000.[91] But publication expenses cut deeply into Carey's profits. By miscalculating the number of weekly issues that would be necessary to complete the work, Carey ended up providing his weekly subscribers with numbers 49–56 gratis. Chambers apparently did not come through with the plates, and Carey spent $5,000 on the engraving of maps alone, in addition to $1,000 for payments to editors and thousands more for paper.[92] The distractions and expenses of running a print shop with eight employees were such that Carey sold his printing establishment in the period between volumes one and two, so that he could concentrate on publishing.[93] Moreover, Guthrie's *Geography* represented less than half of Carey's output in the mid-1790s.[94] Shortly after publishing the first volume, Carey told Chambers that his business had nearly gone under but was now almost out of danger. As proof of his current "prosperous train," he listed a number of his works in the press, mostly by Scottish authors.[95]

89. Chambers to Carey, 12 Apr. and 1 Sept. 1792, ibid.

90. Among the 1,200 subscribing individuals and institutions were George Washington, Edmund Randolph, James Wilson, Richard Stockton, Benjamin Rush, and Rev. William Marshall. Thomas Dobson subscribed for a dozen copies, and Carey's old friend William Spotswood, now in Boston, took seven.

91. Carey to John Barclay, 28 Oct. 1795 (copy), HSP, Lea and Febiger Papers.

92. Guthrie, *New System of Modern Geography* (Philadelphia, 1794–95), vol. 2, preface. Subsequent page references to volume 1 of Carey's edition are cited parenthetically in the text.

93. Green, "From Printer to Publisher," 30.

94. Carey to John Barclay, 28 Oct. 1795 (copy), HSP, Lea and Febiger Papers.

95. Carey to Chambers, 19 June 1794 (copy), ibid.. Besides Guthrie, Carey's list included two other American reprints that appear in table 2—James Beattie's *Elements of Moral Science* (no. 291) and Tobias Smollett's *Roderick Random* (no. 12), both in two

Earlier we saw that John Knox had begun putting together the first edition of Guthrie's *Geography* in the late 1760s in response to the "extremely defective" geographical accounts of Scotland that were then available and that John Chambers had been motivated to produce his Dublin edition in order to present Ireland in a better light. In the same way, Carey was inspired principally by the prospect of mitigating the book's British (or English) bias in volume 1 and providing better coverage of the United States of America in volume 2. In the curious "Preface of the American Editor" in volume 1, Carey mercilessly critiqued the book he was reprinting in order to promote his own revisions. He charged that Thomas Salmon's once-popular geography, "though in many points a much better book," had gone out of favor because "the principal booksellers of London" had conspired to promote Guthrie at all costs (3). This was highly unlikely,[96] but Carey was closer to the mark when he noted that Guthrie's *Geography* "was exactly calculated to flatter the grossest prejudices of the English nation, at the expense of every other part of the human species" (3). He bristled at the fact that the article on England occupied one-fifth of the book. As an example of Guthrie's "English" bias, Carey quoted and mocked a remark in the article on England about "an Englishman of education and reading" being "the most accomplished gentleman in the world" (8), even though that statement was actually meant to introduce and soften a paragraph quite critical of English attitudes toward learning. Clearly, Carey's hatred of English domination, grounded in his personal experiences in Ireland, colored his perceptions.

Carey believed that the article on Ireland in Chambers's edition was too long for his American readership, just as the coverage of Ireland in British editions of Guthrie's *Geography* was too short. Striving for "a middle course" between "these two rival publications" (4), he devoted 56 quarto pages to Ireland in volume 1. The article on Scotland was also enlarged, but at 50 pages (plus 5 pages for the islands) it remained a little shorter than that on Ireland. The article on England was reduced by more than a third, to 129 pages; even so Carey lamented in the preface that it was "still

volumes duodecimo—as well as a French translation of John Moore's *Journal during a Residence in France* (no. 315) in two octavo volumes.

96. When John Knox brought out Guthrie's *Geography* in 1770, Salmon's *New Geographical and Historical Grammar* had just appeared in an eleventh edition, published by a coalition of seventeen London booksellers. If anything, the leading London booksellers had a vested interest in resisting Knox's challenge and maintaining Salmon as the standard work.

disproportionably large" (9). The article on France was moved from its traditional place in volume 1 to the end of volume 2, to allow for the latest news on the French Revolution, but still it occupied only 57 pages. The article on the United States, however, was expanded from 39 to 357 pages, thanks largely to new text by Jedidiah Morse, and it occupied more than half of the second volume. It was here that Carey saw an opportunity to make his biggest contribution. Before printing volume 2, Carey wrote to the book's London publisher, George Robinson, with a scheme to print an octavo overrun of the account of America, along with the state maps. "I feel pretty confident, that 2,000 copies might be sold in England," he wrote, "provided any bookseller of eminence undertook the business, so as to prevent its being pirated by any of the trade." Promising good paper, a reasonable price, and "a proper commission," Carey enclosed a specimen of paper and print from his quarto edition.[97] But Robinson apparently was not interested, and Carey never printed a separate octavo edition of the article on America, although he did publish the American maps separately in 1795 as *Carey's American Atlas* and in 1796 as *Carey's American Pocket Atlas*.[98]

Like Chambers, Carey wished to do much more than alter the amount of space allotted to various "nations"—a term that, significantly, replaced the traditional word "kingdoms" in his version of the book's title. Particularly in the article on Ireland, he aimed to counter the Anglocentric tone of the London editions with text that was more critical of English hegemony. In the preface to volume 1, he observed that sixteen pages had been added to the historical account of Ireland, "which the London editor would not, and the Irish editor durst not, have written. Enjoying the inestimable advantage of living in a free country, where truth may be announced without dread or hesitation, we have spoken of nations, of statesmen, and of kings, with a frankness, to which, even in the best days of the British press, its authors hardly could aspire" (4). One hears Carey's voice in the strident, Anglophobic strains of the article on Ireland. David Hume is sharply criticized for distorting Irish history in his *History of England* (365, 391–94), much as he would be in the defense of Irish history that Carey later wrote.[99] The article makes frequent references to "the despotism of England" (404), the "chains of tyranny" under British rule (410), and the "oppression and despair" of Irish Catholics subjected

97. Carey to Robinson, 15 May [1794] (copy), HSP, Lea and Febiger Papers.

98. Short, *Representing the Republic*, 100–102.

99. Carey, *Vindicaiae Hibernicae*.

to "ecclesiastical rapine" (409). The Irish House of Commons is said to be "constituted on the same absurd and corrupt principles as that of England" (407), and its system of elections is dismissed as a "farce" (411). Language used to discuss the Volunteers and the idea of extending the franchise to Catholics is lifted straight from Chambers's Dublin edition: "To build a liberal system of freedom on its genuine principles, was a design worthy of the friends of liberty and reform" (408). The United Irishmen are praised for grasping this principle, in opposition to "English and domestic despotism" (411). The article concludes with a strongly worded denunciation of "universal bankruptcy" in Ireland as a result of a war with France "in which the Irish have no interest, and in which they have been involved without their consent, as has occurred so often before, by their fatal subjection to England, a subjection which has, for a period of five hundred years, operated as the most dreadful scourge to an island as well calculated to promote the happiness of its inhabitants, as perhaps any equal extent of country under the canopy of heaven" (411).

The articles on England and Scotland received similar treatment, almost certainly from the pen of the radical Scottish immigrant James Thomson Callender, whom Carey hired to help revise the text.[100] Although Callender's duplicity and laziness drove Carey to despair,[101] personal feelings did not interfere with his sympathy for Callender's political outlook. In 1796 Carey would reissue Callender's strongest statement of his Anglophobic position, *The Political Progress of Britain*, at the beginning of a miscellaneous volume titled *Select Pamphlets*. The first part of Callender's book had appeared in Edinburgh in 1792, and Callender's emigration to Philadelphia in the following year, like Carey's nine years earlier, was undertaken to elude the authorities, who were preparing to arrest

100. Both articles mixed text from the latest London edition (1792) with new material. A footnote indicates that the last six pages of the article on Scotland (213–19) were composed by "the American editor" (213n.). The prose immediately turns radical and nationalist, referring to "the indignity of a foreign yoke" enslaving Scotland. The two authors who are cited as authorities, James Macpherson and James Anderson, have been identified among Callender's favorites in Durey, *"With the Hammer of Truth,"* 30. The article on England cites another of Callender's prime sources, Sir John Sinclair, and is filled with comparisons between England and Scotland, usually to the detriment of the former.

101. In a letter of 25 April [1794], Carey told Callender that "[you have] occasioned me more inconvenience than any other man has ever done before you." His grievances were stated more fully in a letter of 28 May that referred to his displeasure over "the Scotch business." HSP, Lea and Febiger Papers.

and prosecute him for his published writings.[102] Unmistakable echoes of Callender's experiences can be found in Carey's edition. In the conclusion to the article on England, reference is made to "some hundreds of prosecutions" against "authors, printers, booksellers, presidents of reforming societies, and others" who responded positively to Thomas Paine's *Rights of Man* and the French Revolution, and these and other attempts by the government "to alarm the people," in Edinburgh as well as in London, are called a "farce" (347).[103] The concluding paragraph in the article on Scotland is more plainly autobiographical:

> Some recent attempts have been made in Scotland to excite in the people a spirit for reformation. Political topics have been treated with much boldness and ingenuity in a variety of newspapers and pamphlets; and on the other hand, numerous prosecutions have been commenced against the authors, printers, and booksellers. Mr Sheridan lately observed, in a speech in the house of Commons, that the people of Scotland had about as much influence in the government of Britain, as the miners of Siberia had in the government of Russia. The parallel is perfectly just; but what is to be the sequel of the present discontents, time only can determine. (218–19)

In this way, Carey's edition of Guthrie's *Geography* transformed John Knox's improving, Whiggish ethos into something altogether more radical and controversial.

In the preface to volume 1, Carey observed, correctly, that "the work of Guthrie has the appearance of being written at various times, and by different hands" (10). He also asserted, in reference to certain unnamed works that apparently borrowed heavily from Guthrie's *Geography*, that "the alterations and additions in the present [edition], are so numerous, that it better deserves the title of an original work, than some mutilated transcripts of Guthrie, which, under a different name, have been introduced to the world" (10). Considering the effort and expense that Carey put into his edition, this boast is understandable, but it is misleading in two respects. First, the statement disguises how much of the text from the

102. On Callender's life and political writings, in Scotland as well as America, see Durey, *"With the Hammer of Truth."*

103. Elsewhere in the article, we read that "the crown is at present making rapid strides towards an utter extinction of the liberty of the press, and the advantages of a trial by jury, in all cases where the interest of government is particularly concerned" (264).

1792 London edition remained intact, or very nearly so, in Carey's edition. Second, Carey's assertion assumes the existence of an original, authentic text by the author William Guthrie. As we have seen, however, no such text ever existed. From the first edition in 1770, the use of Guthrie's name as the author had been a fabrication, or at least a gross exaggeration, and the alterations that John Knox and subsequent publishers made in later editions simply continued a process that Knox had begun before the book ever appeared. By making "improvements" of his own, yet preserving the branding phrase "by William Guthrie, Esq." on the title page, Carey continued this tradition and gave it an American twist. Foucault's concept of the author function has seldom been demonstrated so powerfully.

Of the many services that were performed by Carey's edition of Guthrie's *Geography*, one of the most important for our purposes was its role in disseminating throughout America a well-defined image of eighteenth-century Scottish intellectual achievement. To a certain extent, this image had always been a feature of Guthrie's book. The article on Scotland in London editions noted that the University of Edinburgh "is supplied with excellent professors in the several branches of learning; and its schools for every part of the medical art are reckoned equal to any in Europe," and it singled out for praise the work of some of the forerunners of the Scottish Enlightenment, such as the physicians Alexander Monro *primus*, William Smellie, and Robert Whytt, the mathematicians Colin Maclaurin and Robert Simson, and above all the guru of Whig-Presbyterian moral philosophy, Francis Hutcheson, whose work "deserves to be read by all who would know their duty, or who would wish to practice it."[104] Unlike England, there was no doubt about the status of Scotland as a learned nation.[105]

Carey's edition went much further. The article on England cites Adam Smith's *Wealth of Nations* on the superiority of Scottish to English universities (244). A page in the article on Scotland finds much to praise about eighteenth-century Scottish intellectual life (fig. 9.6). The

104. Guthrie, *New System of Modern Geography* (London, 1792), 165, 167.

105. The article on England in London and Dublin editions of Guthrie's *Geography* contained this sentence, or one like it: "Learning and genius often meet not with suitable regard even from the first-rate Englishmen; and it is not unusual for them to throw aside the best productions of literature, if they are unacquainted with the author" (ibid., 201). However, several pages later the laudatory section on English learning and learned men began with the sentence "England may be looked upon as another word for the seat of learning and the Muses" (209). Carey's edition did nothing to alleviate this ambiguity.

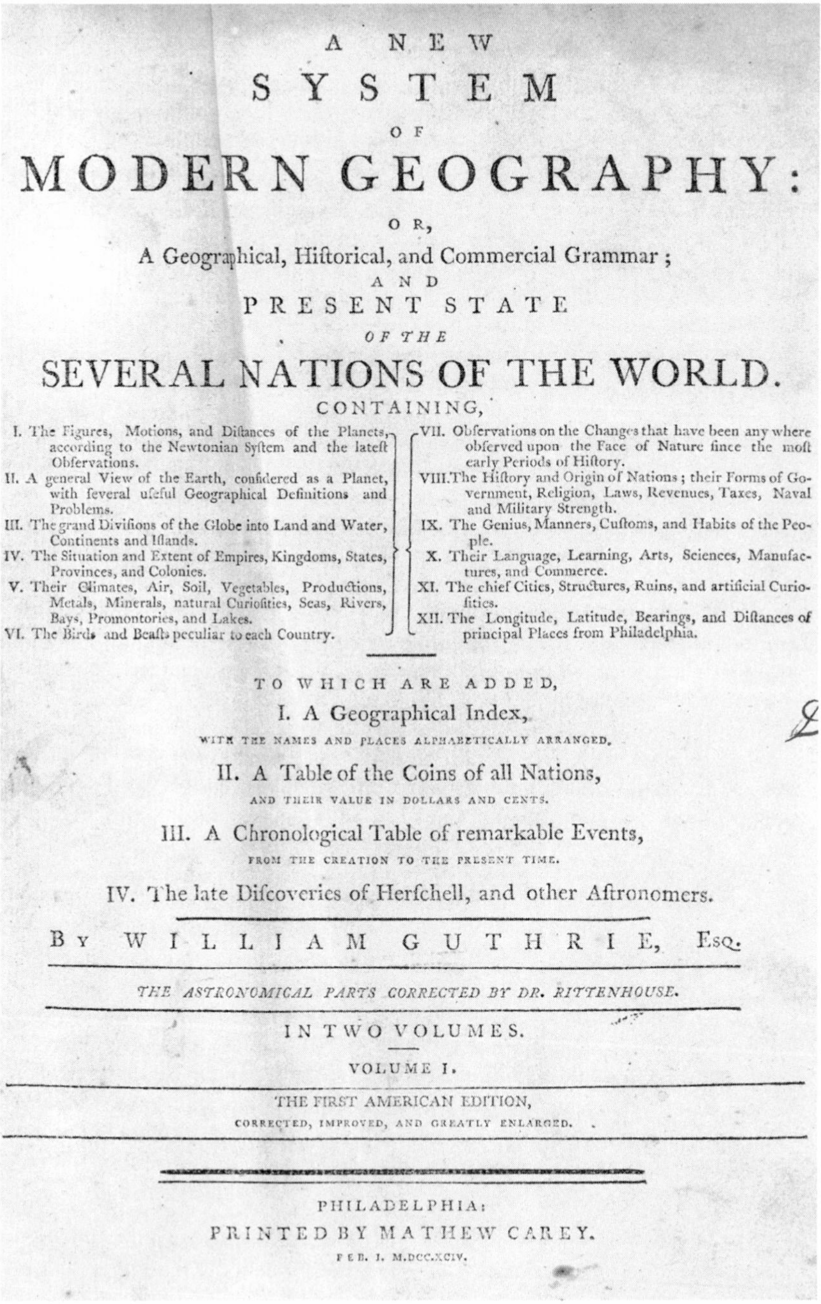

A N E W

S Y S T E M

O F

MODERN GEOGRAPHY:

O R,

A Geographical, Historical, and Commercial Grammar ;

A N D

PRESENT STATE

OF THE

SEVERAL NATIONS OF THE WORLD.

CONTAINING,

I. The Figures, Motions, and Distances of the Planets, according to the Newtonian System and the latest Observations.

II. A general View of the Earth, considered as a Planet, with several useful Geographical Definitions and Problems.

III. The grand Divisions of the Globe into Land and Water, Continents and Islands.

IV. The Situation and Extent of Empires, Kingdoms, States, Provinces, and Colonies.

V. Their Climates, Air, Soil, Vegetables, Productions, Metals, Minerals, natural Curiosities, Seas, Rivers, Bays, Promontories, and Lakes.

VI. The Birds and Beasts peculiar to each Country.

VII. Observations on the Changes that have been any where observed upon the Face of Nature since the most early Periods of History.

VIII. The History and Origin of Nations ; their Forms of Government, Religion, Laws, Revenues, Taxes, Naval and Military Strength.

IX. The Genius, Manners, Customs, and Habits of the People.

X. Their Language, Learning, Arts, Sciences, Manufactures, and Commerce.

XI. The chief Cities, Structures, Ruins, and artificial Curiosities.

XII. The Longitude, Latitude, Bearings, and Distances of principal Places from Philadelphia.

TO WHICH ARE ADDED,

I. A Geographical Index,

WITH THE NAMES AND PLACES ALPHABETICALLY ARRANGED.

II. A Table of the Coins of all Nations,

AND THEIR VALUE IN DOLLARS AND CENTS.

III. A Chronological Table of remarkable Events,

FROM THE CREATION TO THE PRESENT TIME.

IV. The late Discoveries of Herschell, and other Astronomers.

BY W I L L I A M G U T H R I E, ESQ.

THE ASTRONOMICAL PARTS CORRECTED BY DR. RITTENHOUSE.

IN TWO VOLUMES.

VOLUME I.

THE FIRST AMERICAN EDITION,

CORRECTED, IMPROVED, AND GREATLY ENLARGED.

PHILADELPHIA:

PRINTED BY MATHEW CAREY.

FEB. 1. M.DCC.XCIV.

Fig. 9.5. Mathew Carey's ambitious quarto edition of Guthrie's *Geography* (1794–95) was undertaken largely to alter perceptions of Ireland and especially America. The title page of the first volume, pictured here, announced that it was "Corrected, Improved, and Greatly Enlarged." Washington and Lee University.

is the more remarkable, not only as the fubject is little fufceptible of ornament, but as he wrote in an ancient language. Of all writers on aftronomy, Gregory is allowed to be one of the moft perfect and elegant. Maclaurin, the companion and the friend of fir Ifaac Newton, was endowed with all that precifion and force of mind, which rendered him peculiarly fitted for bringing down the ideas of that great man to the level of ordinary apprehenfions, and for diffufing that light through the world, which Newton had confined within the fphere of the learned. His treatife on fluxions is regarded, by the beft judges in Europe, as the cleareft account of the moft refined and fubtile fpeculations on which the human mind ever exerted itfelf with fuccefs. While Maclaurin purfued this new career, a geometrician no lefs famous, diftinguifhed himfelf in the almoft deferted track of antiquity. This was the late dr. Simfon, well known for his illuftration of the ancient geometry. His Elements of Euclid, and his conic fections, are fufficient to eftablifh the fcientific reputation of his native country. This, however, does not reft on the character of mathematicians and aftronomers. The fine arts have been called fifters, to denote their affinity. There is the fame connexion between the fciences, particularly thofe which depend on obfervation. Mathematics and phyfics, properly fo called, were in Scotland accompanied by the other branches of ftudy to which they are allied. In medicine, particularly, the names of Pitcairn, Arbuthnot, Monro, Whytt, Cullen, Brown, &c. hold a diftinguifhed place. In political economy, or the grand art of promoting the happinefs of mankind, by a wife adminiftration of government, Scotland can boaft of fome highly and juftly celebrated writers, Smith, Anderfon, and Steuart, whofe works fhould be the ftatefman's and legiflator's conftant ftudy, and who merit the warmeft thanks from fociety, for the pains they have taken to advance its deareft interefts.

Nor have the Scots been unfuccefsful in cultivating the belles lettres. Foreigners, who inhabit warmer climates, and conceive the northern nations incapable of tendernefs and feeling, are aftonifhed at the poetic genius and delicate fenfibility of Thomfon. But of all literary purfuits, that of rendering mankind more virtuous and happy, which is the proper object of what is called *morals*, ought to be regarded with peculiar honour and refpect. The philofophy of dr. Hutchefon, not to mention other works more fubtile and elegant, but lefs convincing and lefs inftructive, deferves to be read by all who would know their duty, or who would wifh to practife it. Among thofe modern philofophers whofe writings have done honour to North Britain, we readily diftinguifh dr. James Beattie of Aberdeen, dr. Thomas Reid of Glafgow, and mr. Dugald Stewart, profeffor of moral philofophy in the univerfity of Edinburgh. The abilities and various works of dr. Beattie and dr. Reid are long fince known to the literary world. Upon a fubject of a nature fo abftracted as metaphyfics, it requires peculiar felicity of genius to become extremely interefting; yet the elements of the philofophy of the human mind by mr. Stewart, is one of the moft pleafing and inftructive works, which we remember to have perufed. It would be endlefs to mention all the individuals who have diftinguifhed themfelves in the various branches of literature; particularly as thofe who are alive (fome of them in high efteem for hiftorical compofition) difpute the palm of merit with the dead, and cover their country with laurels. However, it would be improper to pafs over the names of Hume and Robertfon, which ftand eminently confpicuous, and will not fhrink from a comparifon with thofe of the moft celebrated hiftorians of ancient or modern times.

UNIVERSITIES.] The univerfities of Scotland are four, viz. St. Andrew's,*

---

* St. Andrew's has a chancellor, two principals, and eleven profeffors in

Greek,	Logic,	Mathematics,	Divinity,
Humanity,	Moral philofophy,	Civil hiftory,	Medicine.
Hebrew,	Natural philofophy,	Church hiftory,	

Fig. 9.6. The article on Scotland in volume 1 of Carey's American edition of Guthrie's *Geography* (1794) was probably written by the Scottish radical James Thomson Callender. The page pictured here contains a new, celebratory discussion of the achievements of eighteenth-century Scottish authors. Washington and Lee University.

discussion of Scottish moralists goes beyond Hutcheson to applaud James Beattie of Aberdeen, Thomas Reid of Glasgow, and especially Dugald Stewart of Edinburgh, whose *Elements of the Philosophy of the Human Mind* is called "one of the most pleasing and instructive works, which we remember to have perused" (192). The same section compares David Hume and William Robertson with "the most celebrated historians of ancient or modern times" (192) and appends the names of William Cullen and John Brown to the list of distinguished Scottish medical men. Then comes a new sentence about another discipline in which "Scotland can boast of some highly and justly celebrated writers": political economy. The works of three such writers—Adam Smith, James Anderson, and Sir James Steuart—"should be the statesman's and legislator's constant study," and these men are said to "merit the warmest thanks from society, for the pains they have taken to advance its dearest interests" (192). The full array of distinguished Scottish authors is declared "endless" (192). Several of them—including Tobias Smollett, James Ferguson, Sir John Pringle, Lord Kames, William Hunter, Gilbert Stuart, and George Campbell— make their first appearance in the list of "Men of Learning and Genius" that had been a fixture of Guthrie's *Geography* since the early 1770s. Still others, such as James Bruce and Sir John Sinclair, are named as authorities in other parts of the book. All told, Carey's edition cited favorably at least 25 of the 115 Scottish authors who appear in table 1. In doing so, it contributed to spreading the gospel of enlightened Scottish literature and learning among its thousands of American readers.

Robert Campbell and the *History of England*

As Mathew Carey was producing his massive edition of Guthrie's *Geography*, Robert Campbell, the youngest member of our quartet of booksellers in late eighteenth-century Philadelphia, was preparing to publish his magnum opus: David Hume's *History of England to the Revolution of 1688* (no. 75) in six octavo volumes (1795–96; fig. 9.7), followed by a six-volume continuation of Hume's history by Tobias Smollett (no. 49) and others (1796–98). In the last chapter we saw that Robert Bell had issued subscription proposals for an American edition of Hume's history in the early 1770s but apparently failed to generate enough interest, and the work never appeared. By the 1790s, however, circumstances had changed markedly on both sides of the Atlantic. By the end of the century Hume's book had become a huge best seller for the Strahan–Cadell publishing syndicate, and it had come to be linked with an equally popular *History*

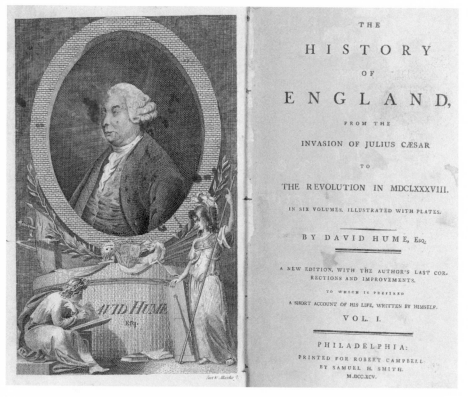

THE

HISTORY

OF

ENGLAND,

FROM THE

INVASION OF JULIUS CÆSAR

TO

THE REVOLUTION IN MDCLXXXVIII.

IN SIX VOLUMES. ILLUSTRATED WITH PLATES.

BY DAVID HUME, ESQ.

A NEW EDITION, WITH THE AUTHOR'S LAST COR-
RECTIONS AND IMPROVEMENTS.

TO WHICH IS PREFIXED

A SHORT ACCOUNT OF HIS LIFE, WRITTEN BY HIMSELF.

VOL. I.

PHILADELPHIA:

PRINTED FOR ROBERT CAMPBELL
BY SAMUEL H. SMITH.
M.DCC.XCV.

Fig. 9.7. In 1795–96 Robert Campbell accomplished what Robert Bell had failed to do more than twenty years earlier: publish by subscription a Philadelphia edition of David Hume's *History of England*. Pictured here are the title page of the first volume and the undistinguished frontispiece portrait of Hume by the Scottish emigrant engravers Robert Scot and Samuel Allardice. Washington and Lee University.

of England by Tobias Smollett that was marketed as a "continuation" of Hume. These developments had serious implications for Campbell and the American market.

The enormous success of the Strahan–Cadell editions of Hume's *History of England* generated competition, which grew more intense when Smollett's volumes were packaged with the work. In Dublin, as we saw in chapter 7, James Williams, among others, produced octavo editions of Hume's *History* during the late 1760s and 1770s, and in 1787–88 Luke White reprinted the whole of Hume's *History* and Smollett's continuation in an integrated thirteen-volume Dublin edition. Strahan and Cadell feared that Irish reprints like these would be exported illegally to Britain (which they sometimes were) and that they would capture the entire

American market. By the early 1790s they had reprint troubles closer to home. The copyright on the 1778 edition of Hume's *History of England*—with its significant paratextual front matter—expired after fourteen years, in 1792. Copyright claims for Smollett's continuation of Hume were tenuous, since the original text dated from the late 1750s and early 1760s. Although Cadell fervently believed that the code of honor within the British book trade precluded others from reprinting works that he considered his property, regardless of the legal status of their copyrights, a number of renegade British booksellers did not agree. In London, for example, John Parsons reprinted Hume's *History of England* in 1793 and Smollett's continuation of it in 1794 as an integrated "pocket" (i.e., small duodecimo) edition in sixteen volumes. Charles Cooke went one better in his thirteen-volume small octavo edition of 1793 (also billed as a "pocket edition"), which not only included both Hume's *History* and Smollett's continuation of it but also "a farther continuation, from George II. to the present time" by T. A. Lloyd. Both these editions contained plates of the author and of English rulers, and in 1793 Robert Bowyer of the "Historic Gallery" began publishing, by subscription and in numbers, a "Most Splendid National" folio edition with a continuation by George Gregory, in which the engravings received primary attention.[106] In Scotland, meanwhile, teams of booksellers headed by George Mudie of Edinburgh published in quick succession an eight-volume octavo edition, "By T. Smollett, *M.D.* and Others," from the Revolution of 1688 to 1783 (1791), and then a matching eight-volume reprint of the first posthumous edition of Hume's *History* (1792), covering the earlier period.[107] Even though Hume's *History* was no longer under copyright in a legal sense, Mudie's edition provoked Cadell to issue strong words about his determination to protect his literary property at all costs.[108]

Considering all this, it is remarkable that an American bookseller would have contemplated reprinting the Hume-Smollett *History of England* in the mid-1790s. Britain and Ireland were swarming with illustrated editions in all shapes, sizes, and price ranges, some of which were

106. Roman, "Pictures for Private Purses."

107. Mudie was joined in the Smollett reprint by A[lexander Guthrie] and J[ohn] & J[ames] Fairbairn of Edinburgh. The Hume imprint named, in addition, J[ohn] Elder, J[ames] Hunter, T[homas] Brown, J[ohn] Guthrie, [Alexander] Lawrie and [James] Symington, J[ames] Watson & Co., and C[ornelius] Elliot of Edinburgh, W[illiam] Cole of Leith, and W[illiam] Anderson of Stirling.

108. Cadell to Bell or Bradfute, 23 March 1792, NLS, Dep. 317, box 2, folder 1, as discussed in Sher, "Corporatism and Consensus," 38–42.

available for purchase in America.[109] By entering this competition, Campbell was clearly trying to make his mark as a publisher. Although no copy of the subscription proposals for his edition of Hume's *History of England* has yet surfaced, the proposals for Smollett's continuation, which appear at the end of the Hume edition with the date 1 June 1796, assert that "this work will be printed on a fine paper, and new type, (in the same elegant style as the American edition of Hume's History of England), in six octavo volumes, each of which shall be embellished with an elegant engraving executed by one of the best American artists."[110] Reducing the number of octavo volumes for Hume's *History* from eight to six was one way to save money; another was to limit the number of plates to six instead of the thirty-one (including the frontispiece of Hume) that typically appeared in Cadell's octavo editions at this time.

On the other hand, the very fact that Campbell illustrated his edition at all shows that cheapness was not his primary goal. Five of the six plates in Campbell's edition of Hume's *History*, including the one of Hume himself (fig. 9.7), were engraved by the Scottish immigrants Robert Scot and Samuel Allardice, who were principally engaged in work for Dobson's *Encyclopaedia* (the sixth was by Joseph H. Seymour). In Campbell's edition of Smollett's continuation, three engravings were done by Allerdice alone, one by Seymour, and one by still another Scottish immigrant whom Dobson would use heavily, Alexander Lawson. Although the quality of their work does not compare with that of the London engravers of Cadell's editions of the Hume-Smollett *History of England*, Campbell was doing the best he could under the circumstances. In Robert Bell's day, after all, no community of engravers even existed in Philadelphia.

Campbell's edition of Hume's *History of England* printed the names of 326 subscribers in the final volume, but 40 of them ordered multiple sets, raising the total number of subscribed sets to 612.[111] Over 40 per-

109. See, for example, [Allen], *Thomas Allen's Sale Catalogue of Books* (1792), 19, which advertised the standard eight-volume octavo edition of Hume's *History* and, immediately following it, Smollett's "continuation of Hume's *History of England*" in five volumes octavo. These were probably Cadell's editions, which dominated the market.

110. A reference to the proposals at the end of a review of the first volume of Hume's *History of England* in the *American Monthly Review* 3 (1795): 29–43, establishes that reprinting Smollett's continuation of Hume was part of Campbell's original plan.

111. Spencer, *Hume and Eighteenth-Century America*, 259–69 and App. B. The following account is based on Spencer's analysis.

cent of the subscribers came from the greater Philadelphia area, including Thomas Dobson and John M'Culloch. Robert Campbell was never keen on limiting his publishing associations to the Philadelphia trade, and his prospects for networking are suggested by the appearance on the list of his brother Samuel Campbell, Thomas Allen, and James Rivington of New York, William Spotswood (now of Boston), and the partnership of Isaiah Thomas and Loring Andrews in New England. As Mark Spencer has argued, the subscribers do not make up an elite group, but they do constitute a solid cross-section of "an improving or middling sort" (269). Perhaps the most surprising feature of Spencer's thorough analysis of the subscription list is the inclusion of at least seventy names, comprising 22 percent of the total, from the Scottish and Scots-Irish enclaves of western Pennsylvania, Ohio, and surrounding regions. This finding suggests that Campbell was engaged in innovative ethnic, and possibly also religious, networking.

Campbell charged the subscribers to Hume's *History of England* $1.67 per volume in boards and probably a little under $2 bound. It would have been reasonable for him to have printed additional copies of each volume, in order to have a small surplus of stock for retail sale at a higher price. He did have copies on hand after publication and advertised them for $13.50 per set, or $2.25 per volume, bound. Campbell employed different Philadelphia printers for different volumes, a common practice that kept down prices and sped up production. Fortunately, the records of the printer of volume 1, Samuel Harrison Smith, have survived, and they reveal that the print run was no less than 2,000 copies. The labor charges for this volume were $282.45 for composition and $207 for presswork, for a total of $489.45.[112] If we extrapolate for the full edition on the basis of this figure, taking into account the number of pages in each of the six volumes and assuming that Campbell's costs for paper were no more than his costs for the labor of printing (they were probably much higher), Campbell could not have paid less than $5,000 for paper and print. His total expenses, including binding and advertising, would have been much higher than that. Of course, he stood to take in more than $5,000 from his subscribers alone, if they all honored their subscription pledges, leaving the income from retail sales as profit. If the edition sold out, Campbell stood to make a great deal of money, but it took an enterprising spirit to extend the print run so far beyond the subscription list.

The fact that Campbell immediately proceeded to a new subscription

---

112. Kropf, "Accounts of Samuel Harrison Smith," 20–21.

for Smollett's continuation of Hume's *History* suggests that the risks he took on this occasion did not go unrewarded. Once again Campbell lowered the number of volumes, this time from the five (or sometimes six) volumes in which Smollett normally appeared in British octavo editions to four volumes; however, two additional volumes took the *History* from Smollett's ending point in 1760 to 1783. Campbell also increased the price thirteen cents per volume more than his Hume edition, to $1.80 in boards or $2 bound, "to be raised to non-subscribers." The subscription list for his edition of Smollett is slightly larger than the one for Hume (410 subscribers for a total of 636 copies) but very similar to it, indicating that most subscribers were happy with the product they were receiving and considered Smollett's work to be a valuable extension of Hume's. Campbell placed a frontispiece portrait of Smollett in volume 1, followed by a short life of the author.

One of the most interesting aspects of Campbell's sequel to Hume's *History* concerns the parts of the work that were not written by Smollett. In his subscription proposals, Campbell announced the project as "Smollett's Continuation to Hume's History of England, from the Revolution in 1688, to the Death of George II, and from that Period to the End of the American War, *by a Society of Gentlemen in Edinburgh*" (emphasis added). We have seen that during the early 1790s several British reprinters advertised editions that extended Smollett's account from the death of George II in 1760 to a more recent date, but only one of them—the 1791 edition published by George Mudie and his associates—had an Edinburgh connection. Campbell used the text in volumes 7 and 8 of Mudie's Edinburgh edition as the basis for volumes 5 and 6 of his own edition, and his title pages identified the author of those volumes as "A Society of Gentlemen."

Campbell's adaptation of the Edinburgh edition is not difficult to explain. Campbell came from Edinburgh and was something of a renegade within the Philadelphia book trade, just as Mudie was among the booksellers of Edinburgh.[113] More significantly, the Edinburgh edition's account of the history of "England" from 1760 to 1783 centered on the American crisis, ending with the American victory in the war for independence. Campbell altered the iconography by replacing a frontispiece portrait of the Prince of Wales with one of Benjamin Franklin, engraved by the Scottish-American artist Samuel Allardice. In general, however, the work by the Society of Gentlemen required no editing. Although

---

113. On Mudie, see Sher, "Corporatism and Consensus."

the perspective was British, the antiwar parliamentary opposition was distinctly privileged over government. For example, several pages were devoted to the "violent opposition" in Parliament to the government's attempt in 1769 to revive a law from the reign of Henry VIII that would have tried Americans suspected of treason in England. They included the following passage:

> The endeavour of the ministry had constantly been to represent the colonists as in a state of actual rebellion, or very little less; but this was far from being the case. The people were indeed exasperated, by a continued series of ministerial blunders, to discover their impatience by several rash and very irregular acts; but they had no intention of throwing off the authority of the mother country. It was at all times dangerous to meddle with popular prejudices; but, instead of yielding any thing to those of the colonists, every method had been taken to inflame them to the utmost. . . . It was no wonder that the Americans, now finding themselves deceived and disappointed in their expectations, should run into some extravagancies. But whatever might be their crimes, nothing could be more unjust than the method now in agitation for punishing them.[114]

The first volume of the supplemental material (Mudie's volume 7 and Campbell's volume 5) ended with Americans setting "no bounds" to their joy at the surrender of Cornwallis in October 1781; the conclusion to the second volume (Mudie's volume 8 and Campbell's volume 6) alluded to the happy state of the nation when the "the most dangerous and unfortunate war in which Great Britain had ever been engaged" was formally terminated two years later. Thus, the history of England evolved into the history of the British Empire, and the growth of America and its independence from Britain were presented as the culmination of almost two thousand years of "English" history.[115]

The twelve-volume *History of England* that Robert Campbell published in Philadelphia between 1795 and 1798 was composed mainly of elements that first appeared in London and Edinburgh. Yet the complete work—consisting of a particular version of the texts, printed in a manner that

114. Smollett and others, *History of England, from the Revolution to the End of the American War,* 7:165.

115. Accordingly, in 1798 Campbell published separately some copies of volumes 5 and 6 of his edition of the *History of England* by Smollett and others, under the title *The History of the British Empire,* by a Society of Gentlemen.

was different from every British edition in format and number of volumes, and containing unique engravings and other paratextual components, such as American subscription lists—was different from anything else in existence. It was a great publishing achievement, finished in the same year that Dobson published the eighteenth, and last, volume of his *Encyclopaedia*. It was also Robert Campbell's swan song as a publisher. On 14 August 1800, at the age of thirty-one, Campbell succumbed to the disease that had been tormenting Philadelphia throughout the decade, yellow fever, and three months later his death was reported in his native city.[116]

*

Taken together, Dobson's reprint of the third edition of the *Encyclopaedia Britannica*, Young's editions of three philosophical works by Thomas Reid and Dugald Stewart, Carey's edition of the quarto version of Guthrie's *Geography*, and Campbell's integrated edition of the *History of England* by David Hume, Tobias Smollett, and others reveal a pattern. They were all large, ambitious publishing projects that appeared during the years 1790–98, when Philadelphia was establishing itself as one of the leading publishing cities in the English-speaking world. Excepting Young's editions of Reid and Stewart, which were published without external support, these projects were multivolume subscription publications, with locally engraved plates and print runs of 2,000 copies or more. All of these works required huge capital investments, which almost ruined at least one of their publishers (Carey) and probably stretched the others to their limits. At the same time, these booksellers were publishing American editions of other large books by best-selling Scottish authors such as Cullen, Robertson, Beattie, Smith, and Blair.

In January 1797 the publishing contributions of "Scots and Irish booksellers" were recognized in the *American Annual Register, or, Historical Memoirs of the United States, for the Year 1796*. Amid calls by some prominent citizens for restrictions against immigrants, the writer, believed to be James Thomson Callender, points out that in Philadelphia, as also in New York and Baltimore, "with three or four exceptions, the whole trade centers among foreigners" (133). "If emigrants had never done any other service to America," he adds, "the importation and reprinting of so many good books should entitle them to respectful notice on the floor of Con-

116. *Scots Magazine* 62 (Nov. 1800): 779.

gress. To them Philadelphia has been largely indebted for its superior progress in printing." Contrasting present-day Philadelphia, which has "about thirty offices exclusively for printing of books," with a time, "but lately past, when four booksellers held a consultation about the printing of Dilworth's Spelling book," Callender singles out for praise "a Scotchman" who republished "the Encyclopedia . . . with valuable editions" and "an Irishman" who reprinted Guthrie's *Geography* with extensive alterations and corrections "at an expence of a thousand dollars" (133–34). But the greatest share of credit for the transformation of the Philadelphia book trade is given to a third immigrant:

> The first regular office for book printing in the city was established by Mr. William Young, a native of Scotland. This took place only twelve years ago, and the plan was regarded as chimerical. Before that time the trade was almost entirely, if not altogether, carried on as it is now in Lancaster, Alexandria, and other places, by printers of newspapers and almanacks. Mr. Young hath since done ten times more in the way of printing books than any person had attempted before him. (133)

It was largely through such efforts that the Enlightenment took root in the United States, not merely as a European import but (ironically, in light of the anti-immigration movement to which Callender was responding) as a homegrown product. Reviewing the first volume of Robert Campbell's edition of Hume's *History of England* in 1795, the *American Monthly Review* proclaimed "the art of Printing" to be among the manufactures in which the citizens of the United States had made "rapid progress" and established a claim "to the most Successful rivalship with European industry." In political publications and newspapers, the printed word was being propagated to "enlighten the public mind" and to excite

> a disposition in the mind to read and think for itself. This thirst for information has produced a demand for most of the works of established merit, and has invigorated the enterprize of our printers and booksellers; who have already republished a great many European performances of merit. Among these the subject of this article may be reckoned. For accuracy and depth of reasoning, for neatness, and frequently elegance, or diction, HUME is deservedly celebrated.[117]

117. Quoted in Spencer, *Hume and Eighteenth-Century America*, 208–9. The complete review is reproduced in Spencer, *Hume's Reception in Early America*.

The anonymous reviewer then reproduced an excerpt not from the text of Hume's *History* itself but from the paratextual front matter that had first appeared in the London edition of 1778: Hume's "My Own Life" and Adam Smith's letter to William Strahan on Hume's character and last days, both in their entirety. Like the dedication to Dugald Stewart and James Gregory in William Young's edition of Reid's *Essays*, the revised account of Scottish learning in Carey's edition of Guthrie's *Geography*, and the biographies of various Scottish men of letters in Dobson's *Encyclopaedia*, such writing, both textual and paratextual, invoked a vibrant institutional and social context in which Scottish authors wrote their books and engaged in creative intellectual exchanges in Scotland and London.

The importance of the link between the manufacture of learned books and the enlightenment of the United States was emphasized in another publication of 1795. Eight years earlier, William Young and John M'Culloch had published M'Culloch's *Introduction to the History of America*. Now M'Culloch reprinted the work with a new title and new material, including a chapter on the development of American thought and culture. After postulating that "knowledge is necessary for the preservation of liberty," M'Culloch discussed the colleges, learned societies, libraries, and other institutions that were sustaining knowledge, and therefore liberty, in America. Then he drew attention to the role of printing and publishing in this process: "Learning has been much advanced by the increase of the art of printing; and the multiplying of books and newspapers. Printing presses are erected in every state, and in every considerable town, as far west as Pittsburgh, and the falls of the Ohio. Books in different languages, and on a great variety of subjects, are daily publishing, whereby science is advanced, and the acquisition of it rendered easy to the citizens."[118] Coming from an author who was also a printer and occasionally a publisher, these words may not have been entirely free from self-interest. Yet there is no reason to doubt M'Culloch's sincerity. Like the British publishers whose productions they reprinted, immigrant booksellers in late eighteenth-century America did not usually see a conflict between publishing for profit and for enlightenment. "I would not circulate a bad book merely for the sake of money," Thomas Dobson once told a correspondent,

---

118. M'Culloch, *Concise History of the United States*, 189, 195. The popularity of this edition of the *Concise History* is indicated by M'Culloch's boast in the preface to the next edition, dated 1 March 1797, that the 1795 edition had "met with approbation from individuals and was introduced into seminaries in various parts of the States" and sold out within a year.

even though he was obliged to "consider even a good one as an article of trade."[119]

Nor did these men perceive a conflict between enlightenment and religion. Although nothing is known about the faith of Campbell, the other booksellers treated in this chapter can be placed within distinct religious traditions. Dobson was a believer in universal salvation who not only published books by the English Unitarian Joseph Priestley, and others with similar views, but also wrote and published religious books of his own.[120] Carey published the first Roman Catholic Bible in America in 1790. Young, a strict Calvinist of the covenanting variety, also published a Bible in that year, and he (like M'Culloch and Aitken) devoted much of his time during the late 1780s and 1790s to printing books and pamphlets on behalf of the Associate Presbyterian cause led by his doctrinally rigid pastor, William Marshall. Despite such personal differences, and the fact that they were often in competition with each other as booksellers operating in the same city, they generally associated with each other on friendly terms and often collaborated closely. This point is demonstrated most clearly by their involvement in the Philadelphia Company of Printers and Booksellers during the years 1791–96, but it is also established by other, more personal acts of kindness and good will. When Dobson's printing office burned down in September 1793, it was Carey who saved his business (and his *Encyclopaedia*, then almost halfway done) by providing type that he "had just imported for his own use."[121] Similarly, in the early 1790s, William Young recruited Carey as a subscriber to the fund for rebuilding Marshall's Associate Presbyterian Church on Walnut Street,[122] and Marshall (whose religious beliefs were fervently anti-Catholic) returned the favor by subscribing to Carey's edition of Guthrie's *Geography*. The families of Young and Dobson were "on such intimate terms" that the booksellers' wives cared for each other's sons.[123]

The Enlightenment provided the common ground that made such conciliation possible in America. In a 1772 advertisement for a subscription

119. Dobson to Charles Thomson, 10 Aug. [1814], quoted in Arner, *Dobson's Encyclopaedia*, 207.

120. Arner, *Dobson's Encyclopaedia*, 14–18.

121. Dobson's advertisement in the *Gazette of the United States*, 18 Sept. 1793, reprinted in Arner, *Dobson's Encyclopaedia*, 58.

122. "Memoir of W. Young by his Grandson W. Y. John McAllister, Sept 1885," 119, HSP (microfilm copy in the possession of the American Antiquarian Society).

123. John McAllister, Jr., to Charles A. Poulson, 24 Oct. 1855, quoted in Arner, *Dobson's Encyclopaedia*, 22n6.

publication of *An Interesting Appendix to Sir William Blackstone's Commentaries on the Laws of England,* Robert Bell had appealed to "the Lovers of Religious Freedom—the right of private judgment—Universal and Impartial Liberty in Matters of Conscience."[124] Bell's interpretation of the English juristic tradition was highly selective, reflecting the enlightened ideals of Bell himself, which would also be the ideals of his most prominent successors in the Philadelphia trade. Late eighteenth-century Philadelphia was peopled by English Anglicans and Quakers, German Lutherans, French and Irish Catholics, Huguenots, Old Side and New Side Presbyterians, and others. Bell's own religious views had run the gamut from evangelical enthusiasm to apparent unbelief. With no established church, Americans learned to coexist in an atmosphere of toleration, jealously guarding the liberties that Bell articulated. In Philadelphia, neither intense political hostilities nor the yellow fever epidemics of the 1790s could dispel this fundamental Enlightenment belief.

The Enlightenment also provided common ground in another sense to which I have already alluded. No matter what their religious or political beliefs, Americans of this era shared the Enlightenment's faith in the critical importance of polite literature and learning in all its variations. What William Young called "a more extensive diffusion of useful knowledge" was a common goal, infused with patriotic purpose, and the appropriation of books by leading Scottish authors from the second half of the eighteenth century was crucial for its implementation. By building on the tradition of large-scale, learned reprinting that Bell and Aitken brought to Philadelphia in the early 1770s, Dobson, Carey, Young, and Campbell defined Scottish Enlightenment books as the vessels of "useful knowledge" in almost every field of American learning.

This trend did not stop after 1800. The first two decades of the nineteenth century saw the publication of the first American editions of numerous Scottish Enlightenment titles from the second half of the eighteenth century,[125] as well as new editions of other works that had already

124. R. Bell, *To the Encouragers of Literature.*

125. They include John Logan, *Sermons* (Boston, 1804); Adam Ferguson, *Roman Republic* (Philadelphia, 1805); James Ferguson, *Easy Introduction* (i.e., *Young Gentleman and Lady's Astronomy*) (Philadelphia, 1805); James Ferguson, *Astronomy Explained* (Philadelphia, 1806); James Ferguson, *Lectures on Select Subjects* (Philadelphia, 1806); John Playfair, *Elements of Geometry* (Philadelphia, 1806); Robert Simson, edition of Euclid (Philadelphia, 1806); Alexander Adam, *Roman Antiquities* (Philadelphia, 1807); James Boswell, *Life of Johnson* (Boston, 1807); George Campbell, *Lectures on Ecclesiastical History* (Philadelphia, 1807); Adam Ferguson, *Essay on the History of Civil Society*

appeared in America. Since a number of Scottish Enlightenment books were becoming set texts in American schools and colleges during this period, Henry F. May and other scholars of American intellectual history have tended to identify it as the prime era of Scottish intellectual influence. In his popular work on the subject, May associates the Scottish Enlightenment chiefly with the last, "didactic," phase of the Enlightenment in America, from 1800 to 1815, when common sense philosophy was "assimilated" in American institutions.[126]

We are now in a position to see that both the substance and chronology of May's argument must be modified. The institutionalization of Scottish Enlightenment book culture in early nineteenth-century America was the culmination of a movement that had been building momentum from at least as early as 1770. It certainly included works of common sense philosophy, but it also encompassed other aspects of moral philosophy as well as history, literary criticism, science, medicine, religion, political economy, geography, travel literature, moral fiction, and the full range of topics covered in the *Encyclopaedia Britannica*. Some of the booksellers who were chiefly responsible for this development had personal contacts with Scottish authors before emigrating—either while attending their lectures (Young) or working in bookshops (Dobson). More importantly, all of them had firsthand knowledge of British publishing or Irish reprinting, and the prominent role that books by Scottish authors had come to play in those processes. Armed with this Old World experience and filled

---

(Boston, 1809); James Beattie, *Essay on Truth* (Philadelphia, 1809); Sir James Pringle, *Observations on Diseases of the Army* (Philadelphia, 1810); William Robertson, *History of Scotland* (Philadelphia, 1811); Archibald Alison, *Essay on Taste* (Boston, 1812); John Gillies, *History of Ancient Greece* (New York, 1814); George Fordyce, *Five Dissertations on Fever* (Boston, 1815); George Campbell, *Philosophy of Rhetoric* (Boston and Philadelphia, 1818); Lord Kames, *Art of Thinking* (New York, 1818); Robert Watson, *History of Philip II and Philip III* (New York, 1818). To these may be added William Smellie, *Philosophy of Natural History* (Dover, NH, 1808), the first volume of which had appeared in Philadelphia in 1791. Several of these titles, including those by Adam, Alison, Campbell, Adam Ferguson, Playfair, Robertson, Simson, and Smellie, passed through many American editions, sometimes in abridged form.

126. May, *Enlightenment in America*, in particular pt. 4, "The Didactic Enlightenment, 1800–1815," esp. 358. At one point, May shows an awareness of American reprinting and institutionalizing of Scottish Enlightenment authors during the 1790s (346), but his observations are confined to common sense philosophy, and they do not sit well with the chronological framework established elsewhere in his book.

with a mixture of personal ambition and faith in the power of print to effect national progress, they remade a significant number of the literary and learned books of the Scottish Enlightenment as recognizably American artifacts and in the process helped to transform their adopted city, Philadelphia, into an international publishing center.

Conclusion

Books were the basic building blocks of the Enlightenment, an edifice erected one block at a time. In reconstructing the book history of the Scottish Enlightenment, therefore, we have been engaged in a study of the architecture of book culture. We have followed a trail from David Hume's boastful pronouncement in the 1750s about Scotland being "the People most distinguish'd for Literature in Europe" to a time less than fifty years later when that boast had considerably more merit than most contemporaries might have thought possible when it was first uttered. To a very large extent, what made it so was the production of new learned and literary books by Scottish authors and their publishers in London and Edinburgh, along with the subsequent reprinting of those books, especially in Dublin and Philadelphia.

But built environments do not last forever. If the argument of this book is correct, it stands to reason that the Scottish Enlightenment would have difficulty outlasting the publishing patterns that sustained it during its golden age. Those patterns did not deteriorate overnight, and their deterioration did not constitute the sole reason for the waning of the Scottish Enlightenment. Among other things, a broader cultural crisis has been identified, caused partly by the political corruption of literature and partly by the very success of the Enlightenment print project itself. Increasingly, the boundless optimism about the expansion of book knowledge voiced by the author of the preface to Guthrie's *Geography* in 1770 had to compete with an awareness of what Paul Keen has called "the disruptive possibility of an endlessly accelerating, self-regenerating inflation of print which threatened to exceed any strategy for its assimilation."[1] Yet this perception of "literary overproduction" (117) coexisted with a transformation in the relations between Scottish authors and their publishers that was in many ways symptomatic of a decline, or a process of ossification, rather than an expansion of publishing possibilities. This development must be accounted for in order to understand what happened to the house that the Scottish literati and their publishers designed and built.

THE DISINTEGRATION OF THE LONDON–EDINBURGH PUBLISHING AXIS

As we have seen, the overwhelming majority of Scottish Enlightenment books were initially published by a small number of individuals and firms in London and Edinburgh. Springing from the founding generation of Andrew Millar, William Strahan, Gavin Hamilton, John Balfour, and Alexander Kincaid, the late eighteenth-century Scottish publishing network eventually included a dozen associates, successors, and rivals of these men. Most of them were Scottish Presbyterians or their London-born sons; nearly all the rest were Dissenters from the English provinces. They were linked extensively by birth (father and son, uncle and nephew, brothers), marriage, religion, apprenticeships, discipleships, and partnerships, both formal and informal. As ambitious entrepreneurs and businessmen, they were sometimes competitors, but they were also collaborators, whose relationships were marked by mutual cooperation and trust as well as personal friendships with Scottish authors, respect for polite literature and learning, and often feelings of Scottish national pride. The London–Edinburgh publishing axis was a product of their relationships and a crucial component in Scottish Enlightenment book culture.

At the summit of this relatively small network of Scottish Enlightenment publishers stood the London-based publishing empire of Millar–Strahan–Cadell. The key to its success lay in a complex system of personal relations and institutional management. By deciding what to publish; by producing new books by their Scottish authors, followed by reprint editions, in appropriate formats; by raising to unprecedented heights the amounts of copy money paid to authors through a variety of publishing arrangements; by nurturing their authors with personal attention and hospitality; by publishing collaboratively with each other and with a limited number of trusted associates in Edinburgh in order to attract authors,

1. Keen, *Crisis of Literature*, 107.

reduce costs, limit risk, and facilitate distribution; by manipulating and sometimes controlling media outlets for advertising and book reviews; by producing sales catalogues that drew attention to themselves as well as to their wares; and by establishing enduring traditions of Scottish publishing that linked London and Edinburgh, bookselling and printing—Millar, Strahan, and Cadell established themselves as the prime movers behind the Scottish Enlightenment and got rich in the process.

How did the House of Strahan and Cadell fare as a publisher of Scottish books at the end of the period we have been considering? As we have seen, little ground was lost when Andrew Millar and William Strahan died in 1768 and 1785, respectively, because others—Thomas Cadell in the first instance and Andrew Strahan in the second—were both qualified and motivated to fill their shoes as Enlightenment publishers. But conditions changed as Andrew Strahan and Cadell aged. Cadell retired in his early fifties, and a few years later Andrew Strahan apparently lost interest in publishing new books. Because Cadell's only son, Thomas, Jr., was not prepared to manage a prominent bookselling and publishing firm, Cadell arranged for his manager, Thomas Davies, to become the new managing partner. Under these circumstances, the publishing partnership of Strahan and Cadell was hard-pressed to maintain its past level of greatness.

The decline of the House of Strahan and Cadell as Scottish Enlightenment publishers is evident from the Strahan printing ledgers in the 1790s. Well after the retirement of Thomas Cadell, Sr., in 1793, the ledgers continued to record the printing of his books separately from those of his successors, Cadell & Davies. Table 7 lists all the books (with their edition numbers, when provided, and their print runs) that were charged to the account of Thomas Cadell, Sr., in the six-year period from the beginning of 1793 through the end of 1798. The table shows the extent to which Cadell & Davies and Andrew Strahan were in the business of reprinting the Scottish Enlightenment at the end of the eighteenth century. Along with two English authors—Edward Gibbon and the legal writer Richard Burn—John Gregory, David Hume, Henry Mackenzie, John Moore, William Robertson, Adam Smith, and above all Hugh Blair and William Buchan remained their principal authors. For the most part, other Scottish authors from table 1 fill up the remainder of the list: Alexander Adam, James Beattie, Adam Ferguson, James Ferguson, John Gillies, Robert Henry, Robert Watson, and James Macpherson's Ossian. No new publications appear in this account, except for separately published later volumes of books that had begun appearing in the 1770s, such as the fourth volume of Blair's *Sermons*, the posthumous sixth volume of Henry's

History of Great Britain, and the posthumous ninth and tenth books of Robertson's *History of America.* Thus, the 1790s account of Thomas Cadell, Sr., in the Strahan Archive represents an era frozen in time. It was comprised mainly of large print runs of popular books in a wide range of learned and literary genres, initially published some years earlier, mainly by Scottish authors.

A separate account for Cadell & Davies did not begin to appear in the Strahan ledgers until 1796, and from the outset it was dramatically different from that of Cadell, Sr. The list of new books published by Cadell & Davies was not particularly Scottish, and the new Scottish titles it did contain were usually by authors who had long been affiliated with Strahan and Cadell, such as Moore, Gillies, Smith, Mackenzie, and Somerville. There were fewer best sellers, and there were more expensive quartos that sold poorly, such as Adam Smith's *Essays on Philosophical Subjects* and Thomas Somerville's *History of Queen Anne.*

In fairness to Cadell & Davies, the 1790s was a decade ill suited to the publication of expensive new scholarly books because of incessant war with France, and we cannot be sure that Thomas Cadell, Sr., would have done much better if he had continued in business. A case in point concerns Adam Ferguson's *Principles of Moral and Political Science* (no. 303), copublished by Andrew Strahan, Thomas Cadell, and William Creech in 1792, just before the senior Cadell's retirement. The copyright was purchased from the author in advance of publication for £800. Andrew Strahan's ledgers reveal that £142.10s. was spent on printing and £254 on paper. One thousand copies were printed in two quarto volumes, and the book retailed for £1.16s. per set in boards. There was still some room for profit if sales were strong, and with no more copy money to pay, later editions could have been lucrative. But a second edition was never called for, and by 1821 a total of only £783.17s.3d. had come in from sales of the book (SA 48814A, fol. 33).[2] Thus, the publishers lost £412.12s.9d., in addition to whatever money they spent on advertising and other incidentals, and Cadell's share of the loss was passed along to Cadell & Davies.

Calculations obtained from the Strahan ledgers by Richard Lutes tell the same story in a different way. Of the £20,584 worth of printing for the Cadells recorded in the Strahan Archive in the decade 1787–96, a

---

2. At the time of Creech's death, twenty-three years after publication, Cadell & Davies had 307 copies in stock and Creech had 136. Constable, *Archibald Constable,* 1:41; *Catalogue of Books and Copyrights,* 19.

total of £19,155 (93 percent) was done for Cadell, Sr., rather than Cadell & Davies. Of £31,999 worth of business in the decade 1797–1806, no less than 50 percent was charged to the account of the senior Cadell (who died in 1802) rather than to Cadell & Davies. Indeed, as late as the period 1807–16, the senior Cadell's books accounted for more than 37 percent of the printing business that Strahan charged to the Cadells.[3] Thus, the House of Strahan and Cadell continued to live off the publishing capital of the High Scottish Enlightenment until well into the nineteenth century.

There are other signs that the house was weakening, especially as a Scottish publishing syndicate. Although Andrew Strahan continued to build up his family printing firm, in association with partners such as his foreman William Preston (1740–1818), he paid less and less attention to publishing. As Lutes has observed, Andrew's greatness lay in investing (94–95). His name was left off the Strahan–Cadell publication catalogues, which appeared from 1796 under the imprint of Cadell & Davies alone. The same shift is noticeable in book imprints from around this time. In December 1798 Malcolm Laing, who had edited the posthumous sixth volume of Robert Henry's *History of Great Britain* for Strahan and Cadell, approached Andrew Strahan with an offer to publish (jointly with Cadell & Davies) his continuation of William Robertson's *History of Scotland* (no. 358).[4] Even though the offer had been made to Strahan, who printed 1,000 copies of the book in June 1800 (SA 48817, fol. 114), the imprint shows Cadell & Davies as the sole London publisher. Similarly, the Strahans and Cadells had always appeared as copublishers of Adam Smith's *Wealth of Nations*, but the title page of the tenth edition of 1802, like that of the ninth edition of Smith's *Theory of Moral Sentiments* in the previous year, stated that the book had been printed by Strahan for Cadell & Davies.

More fundamental changes were occurring on the Cadell side of the syndicate. In the opinion of Archibald Constable and other contemporaries, by the mid-1790s Cadell & Davies had slipped behind the Robinsons to become the second firm in London.[5] This judgment was probably based on several factors besides publishing, including the Robinsons' domination of the wholesale trade, but it probably would not have been made while Cadell, Sr., was in charge. Thomas Cadell, Jr.'s grandson, Ar-

---

3. Lutes, "Andrew Strahan," 92.
4. Laing to Strahan, 19 and 24 Dec. 1798, EUL, La.II.81–83.
5. Besterman, *Publishing Firm of Cadell & Davies*, xiii.

thur H. Beavan, said that by the time the elder Cadell died in 1802, the family firm "had fallen into a state of comparative decrepitude."[6] Although Beavan may have exaggerated, by 1811 the firm was in serious trouble, and it would have gone bankrupt during the years 1811–14 if Andrew Strahan had not saved it with a £20,000 bond. In the midst of this crisis, William Davies suffered an incapacitating stroke in November 1813 and never returned to work; he died seven years later.[7] According to one contemporary account, Davies had become "too adventurous and liberal in his literary purchases," and this policy brought the firm huge debts. It was only after Davies's stroke that the younger Cadell took charge of the firm. He "prudently relinquished" Davies's policy of overextension "but continued to publish, in conjunction with his Edinburgh friends, on a more limited scale."[8]

By this time the firm's Edinburgh friends had changed: soon after Davies's retirement, Blackwood became Cadell's closest Edinburgh ally. But the London–Edinburgh axis of the Strahan–Cadell publishing syndicate had begun to disintegrate long before then. Born in 1773, Thomas Cadell, Jr., was only about twenty years old at the time of his father's retirement. He had little experience in the trade or intimacy with the authors and booksellers of the Scottish Enlightenment, and regarding the latter point it is not clear that his older and more experienced partner, William Davies, was much different. In a hesitant letter of 1796 to one of their father's old Scottish authors, James Fordyce, they described themselves as "young Beginners, with many Engagements on our Hands, . . . at present not very rich."[9]

Cadell and Davies knew that they needed an Edinburgh connection, of course, but mainly as a marketing convenience. The long-standing publishing partnership with William Creech apparently meant nothing to them. Surviving correspondence with Archibald Constable indicates how effectively Constable and his friends undercut Creech, whose unspoken name looms large in the following letter from Davies, dated 31 May 1805:

> Your Correspondence with our Paternoster-row Friends [i.e., the Long-mans, with whom Constable had been allied since the late 1790s] . . . has

6. Ibid., x, quoting Beavan.
7. Lutes, "Andrew Strahan," 85–86, 93.
8. William West, quoted in Besterman, *Publishing Firm of Cadell & Davies*, xi.
9. NLS MS 2618, fol. 67.

satisfied me that they consider both you and themselves at Liberty to form Connections with other Houses both in London and in Edinburgh, and the Circumstance of its becoming known that the Firms of Constable & Co and Cadell and Davies have every Disposition to act together, will be very satisfactory to many of our most respectable literary Friends who, driven by Circumstances to seek new Publishers at Edinburgh, will yet be anxious to see their Works flow into the old Channel in London.[10]

Aware that Constable was the rising star in Scottish publishing and that Creech's sun was setting, Cadell and Davies were willing to sacrifice their firm's traditional ties with Creech in order to prevent their "most respectable" Scottish authors from leaving their orbit.

When they wanted an Edinburgh copublisher for Laing's *History of Scotland* (1800), Cadell & Davies turned not to Creech but to the younger partnership of Alexander Manners and Robert Miller. A few years later, when Creech was arranging the publication of Alexander Fraser Tytler's *Memoirs of the Life and Writings of the Honourable Henry Home of Kames,* he insisted that Cadell & Davies be the sole London copublishers, even though Robert Miller "solicited hard" for John Murray.[11] Yet Cadell & Davies continued to cultivate Manners & Miller as their Edinburgh partners, and Creech grew increasingly bitter. "With regard to the future management of our mutual property printed or reprinted at London or Edinburgh," he wrote to Thomas Cadell, Jr., on 3 July 1807,

a material circumstance has recently taken place which must be explained and clearly understood otherwise plans cannot fail to be adopted hurtful to both Houses. Your House has lately publicly announced by printed Catalogues that Manners & Miller are your agents for Scotland, and every one of the Books in which I have a concern are there offered in small quantities at inferior prices. . . . This plan of your House forms a new aera in our connection. Your new publications are sent to Manners & Miller, and by them subscribed [i.e., wholesaled] to the Trade. The Books advertised and my name excluded, after a mutual intercourse of six and thirty years!

10. Besterman, *Publishing Firm of Cadell & Davies*, 31.

11. Archibald Constable to John Murray, 28 Nov. 1806, in Constable, *Archibald Constable*, 1:355–56.

Creech was devastated. "What would your father or old Mr. Strahan have thought of such a situation?" he wondered. "Many excellent properties I have given to your House, but never received any, and this is my reward! I cannot help feeling hurt on this occasion."[12]

What Creech experienced as an affront was interpreted by his Edinburgh critics as evidence of subservience to his London masters. Either way, it signified the end of an era. A mercenary relationship had replaced one grounded in decades of close personal relationships and loyalty. Meanwhile, Creech himself was declining as a publisher, and so were others from the golden age of the Enlightenment. The deaths (often preceded by retirement or reduced activity) of Charles Elliot in 1790, John Murray in 1793, John Balfour in 1795, George Robinson in 1801, Thomas Cadell, Sr., in 1802, John Bell of Bell & Bradfute in 1806, Charles Dilly in 1807 (retired 1800), Joseph Johnson in 1809, Thomas Becket in 1813, and Creech in 1815 gradually put an end to more than two generations of London and Edinburgh booksellers whose publishing, copublishing, and reprinting activities had helped to mold the Scottish Enlightenment. When Andrew Strahan became less active as a publisher and Cadell & Davies weakened their ties with Creech and softened the long-standing commitment of their firm to publishing the latest works of Scottish literature and learning, the London–Edinburgh publishing axis was no longer functioning in the same way it had been since the days of Andrew Millar and Alexander Kincaid in the late 1740s.

After Creech died in January 1815, Archibald Constable joined with Manners & Miller and John Fairbairn to purchase his stock and copyrights, which they then auctioned to the Edinburgh trade. But Constable himself retained the most valuable copyrights (and "honorary" copyrights) of books by Scottish authors that Creech had published jointly with Strahan and Cadell, including strong sellers and best sellers by Alexander Adam, Hugh Blair, Robert Burns, William Buchan, David Hume, Lord Kames, and Henry Mackenzie. In the same letter of 16 September 1815 that informed Cadell & Davies of this fact, Constable announced his intention to "resume the Management of such of them as were originally in Mr Creech's hands, in particular [Alexander Fraser] Tytlers Elements [of General History, first published by Creech in 1801], Adams Roman Antiquities [no. 293] and Geography [no. 321]."[13] Three days later Cadell

12. Creech Letterbook, ECL, Green Box 120.

13. Besterman, *Publishing Firm of Cadell & Davies*, 1:39–41.

& Davies replied that they were "very well pleased that shares in these works have fallen into such good hands," but

> We are sorry however to observe that, amongst your earliest acts, is the expression of a desire to dispossess us of the management of many of the works in question which we have so long had in our care. When you duly reflect on the very large share which we hold, in proportion to those which you are now becoming possessed of, we are persuaded you will presently relinquish the idea, and dispose yourselves to suggest to us, from time to time, such measures for their several improvement as you may think worth recommending. (40)

To this Constable shot back a sharp reply on 22 September, observing that "although [Creech] may have permitted you to adopt the management of late Editions, that circumstance surely does not as we apprehend entitle you to retain it now" (42). Constable backed off in a letter of 20 October, affirming his desire "of doing nothing to interfere with your rights" in regard to "reprinting any of the Litrary property in which we are mutually interested" (43). But the damage was done. Just as he had allowed his crucial connection with Longman to deteriorate some years earlier, Constable was never able to sustain a firm relationship with Cadell & Davies or any other major London publishing house, and this circumstance eventually contributed to his undoing.[14]

The contentiousness that Constable displayed in his dealings with London was only part of the problem. His independence was supposed by his supporters to herald a new age of brilliance not only in Edinburgh publishing but also in Scottish intellectual life. As we saw in chapter 6, the first edition of John Stark's *Picture of Edinburgh*, which Constable published in 1806, praised Hume, Smith, Robertson, Kames, Gregory, and Cullen for leading the way to that "excellence in literature that is almost without a parallel." It can now be added that the work of Malcolm Laing, Dugald Stewart, John Playfair, and Walter Scott caused Stark to proclaim that the movement was probably in its "infancy": Scottish literature, in the broadest sense, would continue to improve as a result of the entrepreneurial spirit embodied by Constable and his kind.[15]

Things did not quite work out that way. Scott was unique, and Playfair, Stewart, and Laing merely continued the work they had been doing before Constable's rise to prominence. The aging literati of the Scottish

14. Millgate, "Archibald Constable," 110–23.
15. Stark, *Picture of Edinburgh*, 259–60.

Enlightenment were unable to reproduce themselves.[16] Although Scotland remained an important intellectual center in certain fields, such as periodical literature, fiction, medicine, and common sense philosophy, its authors, taken collectively, never again occupied a place in the forefront of European and Atlantic intellectual life. Far from being in its "infancy," the age of unparalleled greatness was nearing its end—a point that Stark silently conceded by removing the passage on authors from later editions of his book.

With Constable & Co., as with Cadell & Davies, it is difficult to avoid the view that these firms were continuing to live largely on capital borrowed from the Scottish Enlightenment. That is why so much importance was attached to the issue of managing the reprints of their jointly owned titles. As far as new titles were concerned, most of their major collaborative publishing projects during the first two decades of the nineteenth century were books by older authors from the age of the Scottish Enlightenment, such as George Chalmers's *Caledonia* (1807–24), John Playfair's *Outlines of Natural Philosophy* (1812 and later editions), and the second and third volumes of Dugald Stewart's *Elements of the Philosophy of the Human Mind* (no. 309) in 1814 and 1827. Although Constable characterized Creech's publications as "neither very important nor voluminous,"[17] he tried to buy his way into the Scottish Enlightenment by purchasing the copyrights to those very books. He succeeded to a point, but since he never learned the art of cultivating and nurturing Scottish authors in a wide range of fields, as Creech did so well, his contributions were limited to a relatively small sphere. Throughout the first quarter of the nineteenth century, the book culture of the Scottish Enlightenment continued to be important, both in Britain and elsewhere, but it began to take on the characteristics of a set of classics from a bygone age—continually reprinted but seldom replenished or revitalized. Increasingly, it acquired the characteristics of what William St. Clair has called the "old canon."[18]

THE PATTERN OF SCOTTISH
ENLIGHTENMENT BOOK HISTORY

It is a truism among historians of books, though often a surprise to historians of ideas, that "authors do not write books: they write texts that

16. Sher, *Church and University*, 298–323.
17. Constable, *Archibald Constable*, 1:535.
18. St. Clair, *Reading Nation*, chap. 7.

become written objects."[19] Much of the action in this book has occurred within what Roger Chartier has called "the space between text and object"—the space, as I define it, between the realms of authors who write texts and of publishers who are chiefly responsible for making those texts into books and marketing them as commodities. Although this space "has too often been forgotten," Chartier adds, it is "precisely the space in which meaning is constructed" (10).

From an investigation of this space, we have seen that the book culture of the Scottish Enlightenment was remarkably collaborative. Scottish authors worked with publishers to transform their texts into books on a wide range of subjects, reflecting the intellectual fecundity of the Scottish literati. They also cooperated with each other, and with some sympathetic Scottish publishers, to bolster the identity and reputation of Scotland as a land of learning. Publishers in London and Edinburgh joined forces to disperse the costs, increase the status, and enhance the marketability of their books. In their dealings with each other and with authors, the decisive factors were often personal connections and friendships, values and ideals, and relationships built on trust.

Yet all these collaborative patterns existed within a competitive, commercial framework in which authors and publishers exhibited personal and professional rivalries, entertained mutual suspicions, and vied among themselves for critical acclaim and pecuniary gain. Scottish Enlightenment publishers attained affluence and influence, and a substantial number of their leading authors became rich and famous. At the same time, authors commiserated with each other about the stinginess of the publishers who were providing them with unprecedented amounts of copy money, and those publishers waxed indignant about the insatiable demands of the very authors whose works were making them rich. High stakes bred high anxiety. It may not be too much to say that the Scots transformed the "business of Enlightenment" into the "big business of Enlightenment."

The result of this complex mixture of cooperation and competition was a vibrant book culture, capable of stimulating and producing handsome quarto, more affordable octavo, and relatively cheap duodecimo editions of important new works in the various genres of polite literature and learning. Intellect and integrity coexisted with intrigue and avarice, generosity and trust with selfishness and vanity. The sum of the individual, diverse stories of authors, publishers, and books was a creative tension that sustained the intellectual culture of the Scottish Enlightenment. This book

19. Chartier, *Order of Books*, 9–10, citing Roger E. Stoddard.

has been written in the conviction that the publishing history of the Scottish Enlightenment can best be illuminated by relating those stories and by bringing their protagonists to life in the context of the historical conditions of the late eighteenth century. In this sense, the brand of book history practiced here is first and foremost human history constructed on a material foundation.

This point holds true even when the focus shifts from publishing first editions of Scottish Enlightenment books in London and Edinburgh to reprinting them in Dublin and Philadelphia—when it shifts, that is, from the space between texts and the original or authorized objects made from them to the space between those objects and new renditions of them constructed abroad. Despite the fact that the Dublin booksellers who reprinted the Scottish Enlightenment in vast quantities left relatively few clues about their personal and professional lives, their imprints, combined with newspaper advertisements, prefatory remarks, and other sources, are enough to sketch their impressive, largely collaborative, efforts to spread the book learning of the Scottish Enlightenment to Ireland and beyond. More is known of the Scottish and Irish immigrant bookmen who took the lead in disseminating the Scottish Enlightenment in America by reprinting many of its major titles, especially in Philadelphia. Their achievements demonstrate the dynamic, expansive character of the Scottish Enlightenment as it became a mainstay of Atlantic culture.

In 1770 the preface to William Guthrie's *Geography* that is quoted at the beginning of this book used the phrase "general diffusion of knowledge" to refer to the unprecedented spread of information and enlightened values throughout British society: more good books, in popular formats and at lower prices, were reaching and influencing an increasingly large proportion of the population. Twenty years later, when William Young's *Universal Asylum, and Columbian Magazine* made a similar reference to "a more extensive diffusion of useful knowledge" in America, the notion of diffusion was still grounded in the spread of knowledge through books, but it had broader geographical connotations, signifying an outward as well as a downward transmission of polite literature and learning. It also implied an active or interactive, rather than passive, response to Scottish Enlightenment books. For enlightened immigrant booksellers like Young, reprinting such books was a mode of patriotic appropriation, enabling them to put the cultural capital of Scotland into the service of the American Enlightenment.

The Enlightenment publishing revolution encompassed both the production of large numbers of important new works in a variety of formats and the widespread reprinting of those works, often in foreign places and in smaller formats. Without those developments, the brilliance of the Scottish literati would have been at best local and fleeting, rather than extensive and enduring. Only printed books, produced and marketed within a commercial network such as the one that emerged in eighteenth-century Britain, could have given Scottish men of letters access to the vast international audience that they acquired. It is not that print contained this transformative capacity inherently, as an essential property or an internal logic that could not be denied. But print was a necessary component in the creation and development of the Scottish Enlightenment.

If the Scottish Enlightenment as we know it is inconceivable without the publishing revolution, the reverse is also true. Whether one looks at contemporary transformations in publishing from the standpoint of authors, publishers, or the material products of their joint labors, Scots were among the leaders of the movement. In genres as varied as history and travel writing, science and medicine, literary criticism and philosophy, sermons and conduct literature, poetry and novels, biography and political economy, geography and encyclopedias, Scottish authors were collectively in the forefront in popularity, critical acclaim, and income from copy money. Most of them achieved what they did not as free-floating professional authors but as members of the liberal professions who were well integrated into the social and cultural institutions of their age. They saw no contradiction between cultivating minds and advancing careers, and they embraced the core values of the Enlightenment as an international movement as they forged a collective, national identity that was distinctively Scottish. Their success as authors owed much to their intellect and initiative, but it could not have happened without the collaboration and commitment of several generations of publishers in London and Edinburgh, Dublin and Philadelphia, who helped to create and disseminate the works of Scottish authors for reasons that frequently transcended the profit motive. This unique merger of intellectual, ideological, and commercial enterprise shaped the literary and learned publishing of the Scottish Enlightenment. At the center of the "expanding maze or labyrinth" of late eighteenth-century book culture stood a distinguished body of Scottish authors and publishers, whose accomplishments had a profound effect on the Enlightenment and the book trade not only in Scotland but throughout Britain and beyond.

Appendix: Tables

Table 1. *Scottish Enlightenment Authors, 1746–1800*

No.	Names/Life Dates/Index to Table 2	Career Summary
1.	Alexander Adam* (1741–1809) 293, 321, 354	Rector of Edinburgh High School
2.	Robert Adam (1728–1792) 85, 197	Architect in England and Scotland; OC, RSE, RSL, SAS
3.	William Alexander (1742?–1783) 103, 133, 198	Edinburgh surgeon, then physician; in London from 1768; PSE, RSE
4.	Archibald Alison (1757–1839) 287	Episcopal clergyman from Edinburgh; RSE, RSL
5.	Charles Alston* (1683–1760) 30, 122	Edinburgh physician and EU professor of medicine and botany; PSE
6.	James Anderson (1739–1808) 172, 179, 249, 351	Economic and agricultural improver in Aberdeenshire; in Edinburgh from 1783; editor of *The Bee*; HSS, PSE, RSE, SAS
7.	John Anderson (1726–1796) 257	GU professor of natural philosophy; GLS, PSE?, RSE, RSL, SS
8.	Walter Anderson (1723–1800) 35, 121, 294	CS minister at Chirnside, Berwickshire
9.	Hugo Arnot (born Pollock) (1749–1786) 199	Edinburgh advocate
10.	Joanna Baillie (1762–1851) 349	Playwright and poet; in Lanarkshire, then London
11.	Matthew Baillie (1761–1823) 311, (326), 352	Physician and anatomy teacher in London; RSE, RSL
12.	James Balfour of Pilrig (1705–1795) 23, 104, 222	Landowner and lawyer; EU professor of moral philosophy, then of public law
13.	James Beattie* (1735–1803) 60, 92, 123, 141, 173, 229, 258, 267, 291	MC professor of moral philosophy and logic; APS, RSE
14.	Benjamin Bell (1749–1806) 189, 240, 312, 322	Edinburgh surgeon; PSE, RSE
15.	John Bethune (1725–1774) 124, 125	CS minister at Rosskeen, Ross and Cromarty; RSL
16.	Joseph Black* (1728–1799) 180 (336)	Physician; GU, then EU professor of chemistry/medicine; GLS, OC, PSE, RSE
17.	Thomas Blacklock* (1721–1791) 31	Blind CS minister/poet; lodged and tutored Edinburgh students
18.	Thomas Blackwell (1701–1757) 4, 29	MC professor of Greek and principal
19.	Hugh Blair* (1718–1800) 80, 188, 230, (290)	Edinburgh CS minister and EU professor of rhetoric and belles lettres; OC, RSE, SS
20.	James Boswell (1740–1795) 105, 250, 295	Edinburgh advocate; practiced law in London from 1786; SS
21.	John Brown (1735–1788) 268, 273	Physician, medical tutor, and lecturer in Edinburgh, and briefly in London; SAS

(*continued*)

Table 1 (*continued*)

No.	Names/Life Dates/Index to Table 2	Career Summary
22.	James Bruce (1730–1794) 288	African explorer; RSL
23.	John Bruce (1745–1826) 205, 259, 313	EU professor of logic, later MP; RSE, RSL
24.	Patrick Brydone* (1736–1818) 150	Traveling tutor, then comptroller of stamp office; PSE, RSE, RSL, SAS
25.	William Buchan (1729–1805) 115, 337	Physician in Yorkshire and Edinburgh, then London from 1778
26.	James Burnett, Lord Monboddo* (1714–1799) 160, 204	Edinburgh advocate and judge; SAS, SS
27.	Robert Burns (1759–1796) 260	Ayrshire farmer, later exciseman
28.	George Campbell* (1719–1796) 72, 174, 280, 355	Aberdeen CS minister; MC principal and professor of divinity; APS, RSE
29.	George Chalmers (1742–1825) 223, 241, 323	Scottish-trained loyalist lawyer in Baltimore; in London from 1775 as man of letters and civil servant; RSL
30.	William Cullen* (1710–1790) 145, 146, (180), 187, 281, 356	Physician; GU, then EU professor of chemistry/medicine; GLS, OC, PSE, RSE, RSL, SS
31.	Sir David Dalrymple, Lord Hailes* (1726–1792) 151, 178, 231	Edinburgh advocate and judge; SAS, SS
32.	Sir John Dalrymple* (1726–1810) 43, 143	Edinburgh advocate and baron of exchequer; GLS, PSE, RSE, SAS, SS
33.	Adam Dickson (1721–1776) 79, 274	CS minister at Dunse, Berwickshire, then at Whittinghame, East Lothian
34.	Alexander Dow (1735/36–1779) 114, 116, 161	Lieutenant colonel in the East India Company
35.	William Duff (1732–1815) 98, 126, 152, 261	CS minister at Glenbucket, Peterculter, and then Foveran, Aberdeenshire
36.	James Dunbar (1742–1798) 206	KC regent; APS, RSE
37.	Andrew Duncan* (1744–1828) 127, 147, 159, 190	Surgeon; EU professor of medicine; PSE, RSE, SAS
38.	William Duncan (1717–1760) 5, 24	Miscellaneous writer in London; then MC natural philosophy professor
39.	David Stewart [or Steuart] Erskine, eleventh Earl of Buchan (1742–1829) 191, 302	Antiquary in Edinburgh; from 1787 at Dryburgh in Berwickshire; GLS, PSE, RSL, SAS
40.	Adam Ferguson* (1723–1816) 99, 117, 232, 303	CS military chaplain; EU professor of natural, then moral, philosophy; GLS, HSS, OC, PSE, RSE, SS
41.	James Ferguson (1710–1776) 39, 61, 100, 106, 128, (130), 153, 168	Banffshire laborer, then portrait painter, then itinerant natural philosophy writer/lecturer, based in London; RSL

Table 1 (*continued*)

No.	Names/Life Dates/Index to Table 2	Career Summary
42.	Robert Fergusson (1750–1774) 158	Edinburgh copy clerk and poet
43.	David Fordyce (1711–1751) 6, 7, 18	MC professor of moral philosophy
44.	George Fordyce (1736–1802) 113, 134, 296, 324, 331, 348	Physician, scientific/medical lecturer in London; PSE?, RSL
45.	James Fordyce (1720–1796) (18), 93, 181, 251, 262	CS minister in Brechin, Angus, then Alloa, Clackmannanshire; from 1760 dissenting minister in London
46.	Alexander Gerard* (1728–1795) 53, 94, 162, 211	CS minister, Aberdeen; MC professor of moral philosophy, then divinity; then KC divinity professor; APS, RSE
47.	John Gillies* (1747–1836) 192, 263, 282, 343	Traveling tutor, then independent author in London; RSE, RSL
48.	James Grant (1743–1835) 252	Edinburgh advocate; HSS
49.	James Gregory* (1753–1821) 304	Physician and EU professor of medicine; PSE, RSE
50.	John Gregory* (1724–1773) 90, 129, 148, 163	Physician and professor of medicine in KC, then EU; APS, PSE, RSL
51.	William Guthrie (1708–1770) 32, 54, 81, 89, 102, 130	Political and literary writer in London from ca. 1730
52.	Alexander Hamilton (1739–1802) 169, 213, 242, 305	EU professor of midwifery; RSE
53.	Elizabeth Hamilton (1756?–1816) 338, 357	Novelist and educational philosopher, living in Scotland and England
54.	Robert Henry* (1718–1790) 144	Clergyman in Carlisle and Berwick-on-Tweed, then CS minister, Edinburgh; RSE, SAS
55.	Robert Heron (1764–1807) 297, (301), 314, 330, 339	Independent author and journalist, in and out of debtors' prison
56.	Francis Home* (1719–1813) 13, 40, 41, 55, 207	Military surgeon, then Edinburgh physician and EU professor of medicine; PSE, RSE, SS
57.	Henry Home, Lord Kames* (1696–1782) 2, 14, 50, 62, 68, 73, 164, 176, 182, 214	Edinburgh advocate and judge; PSE, SS
58.	John Home* (1722–1808) 44, 51, 63, 118, 154, 193	E. Lothian CS minister, secretary to Earl of Bute, and playwright; RSE, SS
59.	David Hume* (born Home) (1711–1776) 8, 9, 15, 19, 25, 33, 45, 46, 56, 74, 75, 200	Edinburgh philosopher and historian; GLS, PSE, SS
60.	John Hunter* (1728–1793) (76), 142, 264, 265, 325	Surgeon and medical lecturer in London; RSL
61.	William Hunter (1718–1783) 76, 243, 326	Surgeon and anatomy lecturer in London; RSL
62.	Francis Hutcheson (1694–1746) 3, 36	Master of Dublin academy, then GU professor of moral philosophy

(*continued*)

Table 1 (*continued*)

No.	Names/Life Dates/Index to Table 2	Career Summary
63.	James Hutton (1726–1797) 306, 327, 328, 332, (336)	Agricultural improver and geologist, in Edinburgh from 1768; OC, PSE, RSE
64.	John Knox (1720–1790) 130, 244, 269	London bookseller, then traveler and economic improver in Scotland; HSS
65.	Malcolm Laing (1762–1818) (144), 358	Edinburgh advocate
66.	William Leechman (1706–1785) (36), 283	CS minister at Beith, then GU divinity professor, then principal; GLS
67.	James Lind (1716–1794) 26, 47, 82, 107	Navy surgeon; then physician in Edinburgh; from 1758 physician to the Naval Hospital at Haslar, specializing in tropical diseases; PSE, RSE, RSL
68.	David Loch (d. 1780) 196	Merchant, shipbuilder, inspector general of Scottish woolen industry, then of Scottish fisheries
69.	John Logan (1748–1788) 215, 216, 233, 290	CS minister at S. Leith, near Edinburgh; London writer after 1785; RSE, SAS
70.	William Lothian (1740–1783) 208	CS minister at Canongate Church, near Edinburgh; RSE
71.	Henry Mackenzie* (1745–1831) 135, 155, 156, 183, 217, 270, 353	Edinburgh writer (solicitor); HSS, OC, RSE
72.	Sir James Mackintosh (1765–1832) 298	Physician, then London lawyer; RSE, RSL
73.	Colin Maclaurin (1698–1746) 10, 11	Mathematics professor at MC, then EU; PSE
74.	James Macpherson* (1736–1796) 64, 71, 83, 136, 170	Tutor, then London political agent
75.	John Macpherson (1710–1765) 108	CS minister at Sleat, Isle of Skye
76.	William Julius Mickle* (born Meikle) (1734/35–1788) 131, 175, 329	Edinburgh brewery owner, then press corrector at Oxford University Press
77.	John Millar* (1735–1801) 137, 271	Glasgow advocate and GU professor of law; GLS
78.	Alexander Monro I* (1697–1767) (34), 218	Edinburgh physician and EU professor of medicine; PSE, RSL, SS
79.	Alexander Monro II* (1733–1817) (34), (218), 234, 253, 344	Edinburgh physician and EU professor of medicine; HSS, PSE, RSE
80.	Donald Monro (1727–1802) 37, 86, 132, 209, (218), 278	Physician in London; PSE, RSE, RSL
81.	James Moor (1712–1779) 57	GU professor of Greek; GLS
82.	John Moore* (1729–1802) 201, 219, 266, 284, 315, 333, 340, 359	Glasgow physician, then traveling tutor and London author; RSE

Table 1 (*continued*)

No.	Names/Life Dates/Index to Table 2	Career Summary
83.	John Ogilvie* (1732–1813) 77, 87, 95, 165, 184, 235, 316	CS minister at Midmar, Aberdeenshire; RSE
84.	William Ogilvie (1736–1819) 220	KC professor of humanity; APS, GLS, RSE, SAS
85.	Robert Orme* (1728–1801) 84, 224	East India Company civil servant and historian in India to 1758, then London
86.	James Oswald* (1703–1793) 97	CS minister at Dunnet, Caithness, then at Methven, Perthshire
87.	Mungo Park (1771–1806) 350	Surgeon at sea and in Peebles; African explorer
88.	John Pinkerton (1758–1826) 221, 245, 254, 272, 285, 345	Edinburgh writer (solicitor), then author in London and Edinburgh
89.	John Playfair (1748–1819) 279, 334	CS minister at Liff and Benvie, Angus; traveling tutor; EU professor of mathematics, then natural philosophy; OC, PSE, RSE, RSL
90.	Sir John Pringle (1707–1782) 20, 236	Edinburgh physician and EU moral philosophy professor; then physician general of army and London physician; PSE, RSL
91.	Thomas Reid* (1710–1796) 88, 255, 275	CS minister; KC regent, then GU professor of moral philosophy; APS, GLS, RSE
92.	William Richardson* (1743–1814) 166, 167, 246, 247, 289	Tutor, then GU professor of humanity; GLS, RSE
93.	Thomas Robertson (d. 1799) 248, 317	CS minister at Dalmeny, near Edinburgh; RSE
94.	William Robertson* (1721–1793) 58, 119, 185, 299, 341	Edinburgh CS minister and EU principal; OC, PSE, RSE, SAS, SS
95.	William Russell (1741–1793) 138, 149, 157, 194, 203, 318	Printer in Edinburgh, then press corrector for Strahan in London; miscellaneous writer in London from 1770; Dumfriesshire from 1787
96.	Robert Simson (1687–1768) 42, 171	GU mathematics professor with specialty in geometry; GLS
97.	Sir John Sinclair* (1754–1835) 225, 256, 301, 319, 335	Agricultural improver, MP, commissioner of excise; HSS, RSE, RSL
98.	William Smellie, M.D. (1697–1763) 22	Surgeon in Lanark, then physician and teacher of midwifery in London
99.	William Smellie* (1740–1795) (115), 139, 212, 292, 360	Edinburgh printer, editor, and journalist; PSE, RSE, SAS

(*continued*)

Table 1 (*continued*)

No.	Names/Life Dates/Index to Table 2	Career Summary
100.	Adam Smith* (1723–1790) 59, 177, 336	GU professor of moral philosophy; then tutor and customs commissioner; GLS, OC, PSE, RSE, RSL, SS
101.	Tobias Smollett* (1721–1771) 12, 16, 27, 49, 67, 78, 96, 112, 120, 140	Physician in Glasgow, navy, London, Bath; then London novelist and writer
102.	Thomas Somerville (1741–1830) 308, 346	CS minister at Minto, Roxburghshire, then Jedburgh; RSE
103.	Sir James Steuart [Steuart Denham from 1773] (1712–1780) 101	Edinburgh advocate; Jacobite exile after 1745; returned to estate 1763
104.	Dugald Stewart* (1753–1828) 309, 320	EU professor of moral philosophy; GLS, OC, PSE, RSE, RSL
105.	Matthew Stewart* (1717–1785) 1, 69	CS minister at Roseneath; then EU professor of mathematics; PSE, RSE, RSL
106.	Gilbert Stuart* (1742–1786) 109, 195, 202, 210, 226	Edinburgh writer (solicitor), then author and journalist, in London from 1783; SAS
107.	William Thomson (1746–1817) 227, 237, 239, 276, 277, 286, 342, 347	CS minister, then miscellaneous writer in London from 1778
108.	Alexander Fraser Tytler (born Alexander Tytler), Lord Woodhouselee* (1747–1813) 228, 300	Edinburgh advocate, EU professor of universal history, then judge; HSS, PSE, RSE, SAS
109.	William Tytler* (1711–1792) 65	Edinburgh writer (solicitor); RSE, SS
110.	John Walker (1731–1803) 310	CS minister at Moffat, then Colinton, and EU regius professor of natural history; GLS, HSS, PSE, RSE, SS
111.	George Wallace (1727–1805) 66, 238	Edinburgh advocate and commissary; RSE
112.	Robert Wallace* (1697–1771) 28, 52, 70	CS minister at Moffat and then at Edinburgh; PSE, SS
113.	Robert Watson* (1730?–1781) 186, 239	CS minister, SAU professor of logic and college principal
114.	Robert Whytt* (1714–1766) 17, 21, 38, 91, 110	Edinburgh physician and EU professor of medicine; PSE, RSL, SS
115.	William Wilkie* (1721–1772) 48, 111	Farmer, CS minister at Ratho, Midlothian, then SAU professor of natural philosophy; PSE?, SS

Sources: The fifty names marked with asterisks are identified as notable Scottish authors in one or more of the following contemporary works: Smollett, *Humphry Clinker* (letter from Matthew Bramble to Dr. Lewis, 8 Aug.); [Creech], *Letters Addressed to Sir John Sinclair*, 12–13; and Alves, *Sketches of a History of Literature*, 153–84. The other names have been added by the author in accordance with the fields of publication specified by Smollett, Creech, and Alves.

Notes: The numbers following the life dates of each author are keyed to the list of books in table 2. Institutions: CS = Church of Scotland; EU = Edinburgh University; GU = Glasgow University; KC = King's College, Aberdeen; MC = Marischal College, Aberdeen; SAU = St. Andrews University. Clubs and societies (final entries in Career Summary): APS = Aberdeen Philosophical Society; GLS = Glasgow Literary Society; HSS = Highland Society of Scotland; OC = Oyster Club; PSE = Philosophical Society of Edinburgh; RSE = Royal Society of Edinburgh; RSL = Royal Society of London; SAS = Society of Antiquaries of Scotland; SS = Select Society.

Table 2. *British, Irish, and American First Editions of Scottish Enlightenment Books, 1746–1800*

	Imprint Date	Author	First British Edition: Title/(Format/Volumes)/ Price/Topic/Popularity Rating
1.	1746	Matthew Stewart*	*Some General Theorems of Considerable Use in the Higher Parts of Mathematics* (8°) 3s. sewed SCI ps
2.	1747	{Henry Home, Lord Kames}*	*Essays upon Several Subjects concerning British Antiquities* (8°) 3s. HIST gs
3.	1747	Francis Hutcheson	*A Short Introduction to Moral Philosophy, in Three Books; Containing the Elements of Ethicks and the Law of Nature** (8°) (trans. of Latin 1745 2nd ed.) PHIL gs
4.	1748	{Thomas Blackwell}	*Letters concerning Mythology* (8°) 6s. LIT ps
5.	1748	William Duncan	**The Elements of Logic** (12°) (also published in Dodsley's *The Preceptor,* 1748 [8°2v]) PHIL bs
6.	[1745–] 1748	[David Fordyce]	*Dialogues concerning Education* (8°2v) 12s. EDU gs
7.	1748	{David Fordyce}	**The Elements of Moral Philosophy** (originally published anonymously in Dodsley's *The Preceptor,* 1748 [8°2v], then as a separate duodecimo volume in 1754) PHIL bs
8.	1748	{David Hume}*	*Philosophical Essays concerning Human Understanding* (12°) 3s. PHIL n/a
9.	1748	David Hume*	*Three Essays, Moral and Political* (8°) 1s. sewed PHIL n/a
10.	1748	Colin Maclaurin	*An Account of Sir Isaac Newton's Philosophical Discoveries** (4°) SCI ms
11.	1748	Colin Maclaurin	*A Treatise of Algebra** (8°) 6s. SCI gs
12.	1748	[Tobias Smollett]*	**The Adventures of Roderick Random** (12°2v) FICT bs
13.	1751	Francis Home*	*An Essay on the Contents and Virtues of Dunse-Spaw* (8°) 3s.6d. MED ps
14.	1751	{Henry Home, Lord Kames}*	*Essays on the Principles of Morality and Natural Religion* (8°) 5s. PHIL ms
15.	1751	David Hume*	*An Enquiry concerning Morals* (12°) 3s. PHIL n/a
16.	1751	[Tobias Smollett]*	**The Adventures of Peregrine Pickle** (12°4v) 12s. FICT bs

Table 2 (*continued*)

Place and Publisher(s) of the First British Edition	First Irish Edition (Dublin): Date/Publisher/ (Format/Volumes)/Price (if known)	First American Edition: Date/Place (Philadelphia unless otherwise noted)/ Publisher/(Format/ Volumes)
1. E: sold by Sands/J. & P. Knapton		
2. E: **Kincaid**		
3. Glasgow: printed and sold by R. Foulis	1787: **McKenzie** (12°)	1788: Crukshank (12°)
4. L: no printer, seller, or publisher named		
5. L: **R. Dodsley**	*1749: G. Faulkner (in *The Preceptor*, 12°2v)	1792: **Carey** (12°)
6. L: no printer, seller, or publisher named; vol. 1 (1745), vol. 2 (1748)		
7. L: **R. Dodsley** (published separately* in 1754 by **R. & J. Dodsley,** 12°, 3s.)	*1749: G. Faulkner (in *The Preceptor*, 12°2v)	
8. L: **Millar**	See no. 25 below.	
9. L: **Millar/Kincaid**	See no. 25 below.	
10. L: for the author's children; sold by **Millar,** Nourse/**Hamilton & Balfour, Kincaid**/Barry in Glasgow/J. Smith in Dublin		
11. L: **Millar,** Nourse		
12. L: Osborn	*1749: R. James (12°2v)	1794: **Carey** (12°2v)
13. E: **Kincaid & Donaldson**		
14. E: **Kincaid & Donaldson**		
15. L: **Millar**	See no. 25 below.	
16. L: author; sold by D. Wilson	*1751: Main (12°3v)	

(continued)

Table 2 (*continued*)

	Imprint Date	Author	First British Edition: Title/(Format/Volumes)/ Price/Topic/Popularity Rating
17.	1751	Robert Whytt*	*An Essay on the Vital and Other Involuntary Motions of Animals* (8°) 5s. SCI ms
18.	1752	David Fordyce (ed. James Fordyce)	*Theodorus: A Dialogue concerning the Art of Preaching** (12°) 3s. REL gs
19.	1752	David Hume*	*Political Discourses* (8°) 3s. PHIL n/a
20.	1752	Sir John Pringle	*Observations on the Diseases of the Army, in Camp and Garrison* (8°) 6s. MED ss
21.	1752	Robert Whytt*	*An Essay on the Virtues of Lime-Water* (12°) 2s.–2s.6d. MED ms
22.	1752–64	William Smellie (M.D.)	**A Treatise on the Theory and Practice of Midwifery** (8°3v) 18s. (plus £2.5s. for plates in sheets) MED bs
23.	1753	[James Balfour]	*A Delineation of the Nature and Obligation of Morality* (12°) 2s.6d. PHIL ms
24.	1753	Julius Caesar (ed. and trans. William Duncan)	*The Commentaries of Cæsar, Translated into English. To which is Prefixed A Discourse concerning the Roman Art of War* (2°) MIL ms
25.	1753	David Hume*	**Essays and Treatises on Several Subjects** (12°4v) 12s. PHIL bs
26.	1753	James Lind	*A Treatise of the Scurvy. In Three Parts. Containing an Inquiry into the Nature, Causes, and Cure, of that Disease* (8°) 6s. MED ms
27.	1753	[Tobias Smollett]*	**The Adventures of Ferdinand Count Fathom** (12°2v) 6s. FICT bs
28.	1753	{Robert Wallace}*	*A Dissertation on the Numbers of Mankind in Antient and Modern Times* (8°) 4s.6d. POL ms
29.	1753–63	Thomas Blackwell	*Memoirs of the Court of Augustus* (4°3v) £3.3s.; some large-paper copies, £3.15s. (v3* completed from Blackwell's papers by John Mills) HIST ms
30.	1754	Charles Alston*	*A Dissertation on Botany* (8°) 1s.–1s.6d. (trans. of 1753 Latin original) SCI ps
31.	1754	Thomas Blacklock*	*Poems on Several Occasions* (8°) 3s. brds. POET gs

Table 2 (*continued*)

Place and Publisher(s) of the First British Edition	First Irish Edition (Dublin): Date/Publisher/ (Format/Volumes)/Price (if known)	First American Edition: Date/Place (Philadelphia unless otherwise noted)/ Publisher/(Format/ Volumes)
17. E: **Hamilton, Balfour, & Neill**		
18. L: **R. Dodsley**	1752: G. & A. Ewing (12°)	
19. E: **Kincaid & Donaldson**	See no. 25 below.	
20. L: **Millar,** D. Wilson, T. Payne I		
21. E: **Hamilton, Balfour, & Neill**	1762: R. Watts, S. Watson (12°) 2s.8½d.	
22. Vol. 1—L: D. Wilson; vols. 2, 3—L: Wilson & Durham [**Strahan**]		
23. E: **Hamilton, Balfour, & Neill**		
24. L: J. & R. Tonson, Draper, and **R. Dodsley**		
25. Vol. 1—L: **Millar/Kincaid & Donaldson;** vols. 2, 3—L: **Millar;** vol. 4—E: **Kincaid & Donaldson** (also L: **Millar/ Kincaid & Donaldson,** 1754)	1779: J. Williams (8°2v) 13s.	
26. E: **Millar** (also E: **Kincaid & Donaldson**)		
27. L: Johnston [**Strahan**]	1753: Main (12°2v) 5s.5d.	
28. E: **Hamilton & Balfour**		
29. Vols. 1, 2 (1753–55)—E: [author]; printed by **Hamilton, Balfour, & Neill** [Hitch, Longman, **Millar, R. Dodsley,** Rivington]; vol. 3 (1763)—L: **Millar**		
30. L: Dod		
31. E: [author]; printed by **Hamilton, Balfour, & Neill**		

(*continued*)

Table 2 (continued)

	Imprint Date	Author	First British Edition: Title/(Format/Volumes)/ Price/Topic/Popularity Rating
32.	1754	[William Guthrie]	*The Friends: A Sentimental History, describing Love as a Virtue, as well as a Passion* (12°2v) 6s. FICT ps
33.	1754	David Hume*	*The History of Great Britain, Vol. I. Containing the Reigns of James I and Charles I* (4°) 14s. brds.; some large-paper copies, £1.1s. HIST n/a
34.	1754–71	A Society in Edinburgh (Edinburgh Philosophical Society) [ed. Alexander Monro I* and II* et al.]	*Essays and Observations, Physical and Literary. Read before a Society in Edinburgh.* (8°3v) 6s.–7s.6d. per vol. SCI n/a
35.	1755	[Walter Anderson]	*The History of Croesus King of Lydia* (12°) 2s.6d. HIST ps
36.	1755	Francis Hutcheson (with a biographical preface by William Leechman)	*A System of Moral Philosophy, in Three Books* (4°2v) £1.1s.–£1.5s. PHIL ps
37.	1755	Donald Monro	*An Essay on the Dropsy, and Its Different Species* (24°) 4s. MED ms
38.	1755	Robert Whytt*	*Physiological Essays* (12°) 2s.6d.–3s. MED ms
39.	1756	James Ferguson	**Astronomy Explained upon Sir Isaac Newton's Principles, and Made Easy to Those Who Have Not Studied Mathematics** (4°) 15s. sewed (subscription price) SCI bs
40.	1756	Francis Home*	*The Principles of Agriculture and Vegetation* (8°) 3s. AGR gs
41.	1756	Francis Home*	*Experiments on Bleaching* (8°) 4s. SCI ps
42.	1756	Euclid/Robert Simson	**The Elements of Euclid, viz. the First Six Books, Together with the Eleventh and Twelfth** (4°) 12s.6d. sewed SCI bs
43.	1757	[Sir] John Dalrymple*	*An Essay towards a General History of Feudal Property in Great Britain* (8°) 5s. HIST gs

Table 2 (*continued*)

Place and Publisher(s) of the First British Edition	First Irish Edition (Dublin): Date/Publisher/ (Format/Volumes)/Price (if known)	First American Edition: Date/Place (Philadelphia unless otherwise noted)/ Publisher/(Format/ Volumes)
32. L: Waller		
33. E: **Hamilton, Balfour, & Neill**	1755: J. Smith (8°2v)	See no. 75 below.
34. Vols. 1 (1754) and 2 (1756)—E: **Hamilton & Balfour** (for the Edinburgh Philosophical Society); vol. 3 (1771)—E: **Balfour**		
35. E: printed by [and for] **Hamilton, Balfour, & Neill**		
36. Glasgow: printed and sold by R. & A. Foulis/sold by **Millar, Longman**		
37. L: Wilson & Durham		
38. E: **Hamilton, Balfour, & Neill**		
39. E: author		
40. E: **Kincaid & Donaldson** [also issued under the imprint of **Hamilton & Balfour,** 1757, although the copyright was registered to Wilson & Durham of London]	1759: G. & A. Ewing (8°) 2s.2d.	
41. E: **Kincaid & Donaldson**	1771: T. Ewing (12°) [expanded] 3s.3d.	
42. Glasgow: printed by R. & A. Foulis		
43. L: **Millar**	1759: Cotter (8°) 4s.10½d.	

(*continued*)

Table 2 (*continued*)

Imprint Date	Author	First British Edition: Title/(Format/Volumes)/ Price/Topic/Popularity Rating
44. 1757	{John Home}*	***Douglas: A Tragedy*** (8°) 1s.6d. DRAM bs
45. 1757	David Hume*	*Four Dissertations* (12°) 3s. PHIL n/a
46. 1757	David Hume*	*The History of Great Britain. Vol. II. Containing the Commonwealth, and the Reigns of Charles II. and James II* (4°) 13s.–14s.; some large-paper copies, £2.2s. brds. HIST n/a
47. 1757	James Lind	*An Essay, on the Most Effectual Means, of Preserving the Health of Seamen, in the Royal Navy* (12°) MED ms
48. 1757	{William Wilkie}*	*The Epigoniad: A Poem in Nine Books* (8°) 4s. POET ms
49. 1757–58	Tobias Smollett*	***A Complete History of England Deduced, from the Descent of Julius Cæsar, to the Treaty of Aix la Chapelle, 1748*** (4°4v) £3.3s. HIST bs

Table 2 (*continued*)

Place and Publisher(s) of the First British Edition	First Irish Edition (Dublin): Date/Publisher/ (Format/Volumes)/Price (if known)	First American Edition: Date/Place (Philadelphia unless otherwise noted)/ Publisher/(Format/ Volumes)
44. E: **Hamilton & Balfour,** Gray & Peter (also L: **Millar**)	*1757: G. Faulkner, J. Hoey I, **P. Wilson, Exshaw I,** A. James, M. Williamson, **Sleater I** (12°) [6½d.] (note: two different eds., one attributed to "the Rev. Mr. Hume" and the other to "the Rev. John Home," with additional materials added)	1790: Story (12°)
45. L: **Millar**	See no. 25 above.	
46. L: **Millar**	1757: J. Smith (8°2v)	See no. 75 below.
47. L: **Millar/Kincaid & Donaldson**		
48. E: **Hamilton, Balfour, & Neill**		
49. L: Rivington & Fletcher	1787: **L. White** (8°5v) £1.12s.6d. (the latter part of the *Complete History of England*, combined with vols. 1–4 of Smollett's *Continuation of the Complete History of England* of 1760–61 [no. 67 below]; a reprint of Cadell and Baldwin's posthumously revised 1785 London ed. titled *The History of England: From the Revolution to the Death of George the Second*)	1796–98; **R. Campbell** (8°6v) (a variation on the 1785 London ed. of Smollett's *History of England* cited in the previous entry, following the 1791 Edinburgh reprint [Mudie ed.] and titled *The History of England, from the Revolution to the End of the American War, and Peace of Versailles in 1783*; vols. 1–4 by Smollett, and vols. 5 and 6 by "A Society of Gentlemen")

(*continued*)

Table 2 (*continued*)

	Imprint Date	Author	First British Edition: Title/(Format/Volumes)/ Price/Topic/Popularity Rating
50.	1758	⌈Henry Home, Lord Kames⌉*	*Historical Law-Tracts* (8°2v) 9s. LAW gs
51.	1758	{John Home}*	*Agis: A Tragedy* (8°) 1s.6d. DRAM ms
52.	1758	⌈Robert Wallace⌉*	*Characteristics of the Present Political State of Great Britain* (8°) 3s.–4s. POL ms
53.	1759	Alexander Gerard*	*An Essay on Taste* (8°) 3s.–4s. ARTS ms
54.	1759	⌈William Guthrie⌉	*The Mother: or, The Happy Distress. A Novel* (12°2v) 5s.6d.–6s. FICT ps
55.	1759	Francis Home*	*Medical Facts and Experiments* (8°) 4s.–5s. MED ps
56.	1759	David Hume*	*The History of England, under the House of Tudor* (4°2v) £1.1s. brds. HIST n/a
57.	1759	{James Moor}	*Essays; Read to a Literary Society; at their Weekly Meetings, within the College of Glasgow* (8°) ARTS ps
58.	1759	William Robertson*	**The History of Scotland** (4°2v) £1.1s. brds.–£1.10s. HIST bs
59.	1759	Adam Smith*	**The Theory of Moral Sentiments** (8°) 6s. PHIL bs
60.	1760	James Beattie*	*Original Poems and Translations* (8°) 3s.6d. POET ps
61.	1760	James Ferguson	**Lectures on Select Subjects in Mechanics, Hydrostatics, Pneumatics, and Optics** (8°) 7s.6d. SCI bs
62.	1760	{Henry Home, Lord Kames}*	*The Principles of Equity* (2°) 17s. LAW gs
63.	1760	{John Home}*	*The Siege of Aquileia: A Tragedy* (8°) 1s.6d. DRAM ps

Table 2 (*continued*)

Place and Publisher(s) of the First British Edition	First Irish Edition (Dublin): Date/Publisher/ (Format/Volumes)/Price (if known)	First American Edition: Date/Place (Philadelphia unless otherwise noted)/ Publisher/(Format/ Volumes)
50. E: **Millar/Kincaid & Bell**		
51. L: **Millar**	1758: G. & A. Ewing, J. Hoey I, **P. Wilson, Exshaw I,** A. James, W. Williamson, R. Watts, Flin I, **Sleater I,** B. Gunne, J. Rudd, **W. Watson,** R. Smith (12°) [6½d.]	
52. L: **Millar** [**Strahan**]	1758: Flin I (12°)	
53. L: **Millar/Kincaid & Bell**		
54. L: author; printed and sold by Baldwin		
55. L: **Millar/Kincaid & Bell**		
56. L: **Millar**	1759: Cotter (8°3v)	See no. 75 below.
57. Glasgow: printed by R. & A. Foulis		
58. L: **Millar**	*1759: G. & A. Ewing (8°2v) 10s.10d.	
59. L: **Millar/Kincaid & Bell**	1777: **Beatty,** Jackson, "6th ed." (8°) 5s.5d.	
60. L: sold by **Millar**		
61. L: **Millar**		
62. E: **Millar/Kincaid & Bell**		
63. L: **Millar**	1760: 1. G. & A. Ewing (12°); and 2. W. Smith I, A. James, M. Williamson, R. Watts, Bradley, **Potts,** W. Smith II, S. Smith (12°) [6½d.]	

(*continued*)

Table 2 (*continued*)

	Imprint Date	Author	First British Edition: Title/(Format/Volumes)/ Price/Topic/Popularity Rating
64.	1760	[James Macpherson]* [ostensible trans.]	*Fragments of Ancient Poetry, Collected in the Highlands of Scotland, and Translated from the Galic or Erse Language* (8°) 1s. POET ms
65.	1760	[William Tytler]*	*An Historical and Critical Enquiry into the Evidence produced by the Earls of Murray and Morton, against Mary Queen of Scots* (8°) (later eds. published as *An Inquiry, Historical and Critical, into the Evidence against Mary Queen of Scots*) HIST gs
66.	1760	George Wallace	*A System of the Principles of the Law of Scotland,* "Vol. I" (no more published) (2°) £1.5s. brds. LAW ps
67.	1760–65	Tobias Smollett*	**Continuation of the Complete History of England** (8°5v) 1.1s.–£1.10s. HIST bs
68.	1761	[Henry Home, Lord Kames]*	*Introduction to the Art of Thinking* (12°) 2s.6d.–3s. EDU gs
69.	1761	Matthew Stewart*	*Tracts, Physical and Mathematical* (8°) 7s.6d. SCI ps [1763 supplement: *The Distance of the Sun from the Earth Determined, by the Theory of Gravity*]
70.	1761	[Robert Wallace]*	*Various Prospects of Mankind, Nature, and Providence* (8°) 5s. POL ps
71.	1762	James Macpherson* [ostensible trans.]	**Fingal, An Ancient Epic Poem** (4°) 10s. 6d.–12s.6d. POET bs
72.	1762	George Campbell*	*A Dissertation on Miracles* (8°) 4s. REL gs
73.	1762	{Henry Home, Lord Kames}*	*Elements of Criticism* (8°3v) 15s. LIT ss

Table 2 (*continued*)

Place and Publisher(s) of the First British Edition	First Irish Edition (Dublin): Date/Publisher/ (Format/Volumes)/Price (if known)	First American Edition: Date/Place (Philadelphia unless otherwise noted)/ Publisher/(Format/ Volumes)
64. E: **Hamilton & Balfour**	1760: Cotter (12°)	1790: Lang (8°) *The Poems of Ossian, the Son of Fingal* (8°2v, first published under this title in London, 1773) (includes *Fragments of Ancient Poetry, Fingal, Temora,* and Hugh Blair's *Critical Dissertation*)
65. E: printed and sold by Gordon/ sold by Owen, Longman, Scott, Davie, & Law, Johnstone, **Becket,** D. Wilson		
66. E: **Millar,** Wilson & Durham/ **Hamilton & Balfour**		
67. L: Baldwin	1787: **L. White** (8°5v) £1.12s.6d. (see no. 49 above)	1796–98: **R. Campbell** (8°6v) (see no. 49 above)
68. E: **Kincaid & Bell**		
69. E: **Millar,** Nourse/Sands, **Kincaid & Bell**		
70. L: **Millar**		
71. L: **Becket & de Hondt**	*1762: Fitzsimons (12°) 2s.8½d.	See no. 64 above.
72. E: **Kincaid & Bell**/sold by **Millar, R. & J. Dodsley,** Johnston, Baldwin, J. Richardson		1790: **Dobson** (12°)
73. E: **Millar/Kincaid & Bell**	1762: Cotter (12°2v) 6s.6d.	1796: Boston— J. White, Thomas & Andrews, Spotswood, D. West, Blake, Larkin, J. West (12°2v)

(*continued*)

Table 2 (*continued*)

	Imprint Date	Author	First British Edition: Title/(Format/Volumes)/ Price/Topic/Popularity Rating
74.	1762	David Hume*	*The History of England, from the Invasion of Julius Cæsar to the Accession of Henry VII* (4°2v) £1.10s. brds. HIST n/a
75.	1762	David Hume*	**The History of England, from the Invasion of Julius Cæsar to the Revolution of 1688** (4°6v) £4.10s. HIST bs
76.	1762	William Hunter (with two papers by John Hunter*)	*Medical Commentaries. Part I* (no more published) (4°) 6s. sewed MED ms
77.	1762	John Ogilvie*	*Poems on Several Subjects* (4°) POET ms
78.	1762	[Tobias Smollett]*	**The Adventures of Sir Launcelot Greaves** (12°2v) 5s. sewed FICT bs
79.	1762–69	{Adam Dickson}	*A Treatise of Agriculture* (8°2v) 2nd ed., 13s. AGR gs
80.	1763	{Hugh Blair}*	**A Critical Dissertation on the Poems of Ossian** (4°) 2s.6d. LIT bs
81.	1763	William Guthrie	*A Complete History of the English Peerage; from the Best Authorities* (4°2v) £1.10s. per vol. sewed HIST ps
82.	1763	James Lind	*Two Papers on Fevers and Infection. Which Were Read before the Philosophical and Medical Society, in Edinburgh* (8°) MED ps
83.	1763	James Macpherson* [ostensible trans.]	**Temora, An Ancient Epic Poem** (4°) 10s.6d. POET bs
84.	1763–78	[Robert Orme]*	*A History of the Military Transactions of the British Nation in Indostan from the Year 1745* (4°2v) vol. 1: £1.1s. MIL ms
85.	1764	Robert Adam	*Ruins of the Palace of the Emperor Diocletian at Spalatro in Dalmatia* (2°) £3–£3.3s. (subscription price) —£4.4s. ARTS ps
86.	1764	Donald Monro	*An Account of the Diseases which Were Most Frequent in the British Military Hospitals in Germany, from January 1761 to the Return of the Troops to England in March 1763* (8°) 5s. MED ps
87.	1764	John Ogilvie*	*Providence: An Allegorical Poem* (4°) 8s. sewed POET ps

Table 2 (*continued*)

Place and Publisher(s) of the First British Edition	First Irish Edition (Dublin): Date/Publisher/ (Format/Volumes)/Price (if known)	First American Edition: Date/Place (Philadelphia unless otherwise noted)/ Publisher/(Format/ Volumes)
74. L: **Millar**	1762: G. & A. Ewing (8°4v) £2.12s.	See no. 75 below.
75. L: **Millar**	*1769: **Williams** (8°8v)	1795–96: **R. Campbell** (8°6v)
76. L: sold by **Millar**		
77. L: Keith	1769: S. Watson (8°2v)	
78. L: Coote	*1762: **J. Hoey II** (12°) 2s.8½d.	
79. Vol. 1 (1762)—E: author and **A. Donaldson**/sold by **Millar, R. & J. Dodsley**, J. Richardson; vol. 2 (1769)—E: **Kincaid & Bell**	1766 (vol. 1 only): Cotter (8°) 4s.4d.	
80. L: **Becket & de Hondt**	1765: **P. Wilson**, "3rd ed." (12°) 1s.1d.	1790: Lang (8°) See no. 64 above.
81. L: Newbery, Crowder & Co. and Coote, Gretton, Davies, Johnston, Kearsly, Osborne		
82. L: D. Wilson		
83. L: **Becket & de Hondt**	1763: **Leathly, P. Wilson** (12°) 3s.3d.	See no. 64 above.
84. L: Nourse		
85. [L]: author [printed by **Strahan**]		
86. L: **Millar**, D. Wilson, Durham; and T. Payne I		
87. L: Burnet		1766: Boston— Mein (8°)

(continued)

Table 2 (*continued*)

	Imprint Date	Author	First British Edition: Title/(Format/Volumes)/ Price/Topic/Popularity Rating
88.	1764	Thomas Reid*	*An Inquiry into the Human Mind, on the Principles of Common Sense* (8°) 5s.–7s. PHIL ss
89.	1764–67	William Guthrie et al.	*A General History of the World, from the Creation to the Present Time* (8°12v) £3.12s. HIST ps
90.	1765	[John Gregory]*	**A Comparative View of the State and Faculties of Man. With those of the Animal World** (8°) 3s.–4s. MISC bs
91.	1765	Robert Whytt*	*Observations on the Nature, Causes, and Cure of Those Disorders which Have Been Commonly Called Nervous Hypochondriac, or Hysteric* (8°) 6s. MED gs
92.	1766	James Beattie*	*Poems on Several Subjects* (8°) 3s. POET ps
93.	1766	{James Fordyce}	**Sermons to Young Women** (8°2v) 6s.–7s. REL bs
94.	1766	Alexander Gerard*	*Dissertations on Subjects relating to the Genius and Evidence of Christianity* (8°) 6s. REL ps
95.	1766	John Ogilvie*	*Sermons on Several Subjects* (8°) 3s. REL ps
96.	1766	Tobias Smollett*	*Travels through France and Italy* (8°2v) 10s. TRAV ms

Table 2 (*continued*)

	Place and Publisher(s) of the First British Edition	First Irish Edition (Dublin): Date/Publisher/ (Format/Volumes)/Price (if known)	First American Edition: Date/Place (Philadelphia unless otherwise noted)/ Publisher/(Format/ Volumes)
88.	E: **Millar/Kincaid & Bell**	1764: A. Ewing (12°) 3s.3d.	
89.	L: Newbery, Baldwin, Crowder, Coote, Withy, Wilkie, J. Wilson & J. Fell, Nicoll, Collins, Raikes; vols. 1–8 (1764), vols. 9, 10 (1765), vol. 11 (1766), vol. 12 (1767)		
90.	L: **J. Dodsley**	1768: **Sleater I, D. Chamberlaine, Potts, Williams, W. Colles** (12°) 2s.8½d.	
91.	E: **Becket & du [*sic*] Hondt/ Balfour**		
92.	L: Johnston		1787: **Dobson** (8°) (this is actually a reprint of Beattie's *Poems on Several Occasions*, first published in Edinburgh in 1776, but it incorporates key odes, elegies, and poems from *Poems on Several Subjects*, as well as *The Minstrel*)
93.	L: **Millar & Cadell, J. Dodsley,** J. Payne	*1766, "4th ed.": 1. Sheppard (12°2); and 2. **Leathly,** J. Hoey I, **Exshaw I,** Saunders, **W. Watson, J. Hoey II** (12°2v) 4s.4d.	1767: Boston— Mein & Fleeming (12°2v)
94.	E: **Millar/Kincaid & Bell**		
95.	E: **Balfour**		
96.	L: Baldwin	*1766: J. Hoey I, **Leathly, P. Wilson,**	

(*continued*)

Table 2 *(continued)*

Imprint Date	Author	First British Edition: Title/(Format/Volumes)/ Price/Topic/Popularity Rating
97.	1766–72	{James Oswald}*	*An Appeal to Common Sense in Behalf of Religion* (8°2v) 10s. PHIL ps
98.	1767	{William Duff}	*An Essay on Original Genius; and Its Various Modes of Exertion in Philosophy and the Fine Arts, Particularly in Poetry* (8°) 5s. LIT ms
99.	1767	Adam Ferguson*	*An Essay on the History of Civil Society* (4°) 14s.–15s.; 8° ed., 1768, 6s. HIST gs
100.	1767	James Ferguson	*Tables and Tracts, relative to several Arts and Sciences* (8°) 5s. SCI ms
101.	1767	Sir James Steuart	*An Inquiry into the Principles of Political Oeconomy: Being an Essay on the Science of Domestic Policy in Free Nations* (4°2v) £2.2s. brds. (later up to £2.10s. bound) ECON ps
102.	1767–68	William Guthrie	*A General History of Scotland* (8°10v) £3 HIST ps
103.	1768	William Alexander	*Experimental Essays* (8°) 5s. MED ms
104.	1768	James Balfour	*Philosophical Essays* (8°) PHIL ps
105.	1768	James Boswell	*An Account of Corsica, the Journal of a Tour to that Island; and Memoirs of Pascal Paoli* (8°) 6s. POL gs
106.	1768	James Ferguson	*Young Gentleman and Lady's Astronomy* (8°) 5s. (later retitled *An Easy Introduction to Astronomy*, except in Ireland) SCI gs
107.	1768	James Lind	*An Essay on Diseases Incidental to Europeans in Hot Climates* (8°) 6s. MED gs
108.	1768	John Macpherson	*Critical Dissertations on the Origins, Antiquities, Language, Government, Manners, and Religion of the Ancient Caledonians, Their Posterity the Picts, and the British and Irish Scots* * (4°) 10s.6d. brds. HIST ps
109.	1768	{Gilbert Stuart}*	*An Historical Dissertation concerning the Antiquity of the English Constitution* (8°) 5s. brds. HIST ms

Table 2 (*continued*)

Place and Publisher(s) of the First British Edition	First Irish Edition (Dublin): Date/Publisher/ (Format/Volumes)/Price (if known)	First American Edition: Date/Place (Philadelphia unless otherwise noted)/ Publisher/(Format/ Volumes)
	Exshaw I, E. Watts, D. Chamberlain[e], Murphy, Sleater I, Saunders, J. Hoey II, Potts, S. Watson, Williams (12°2v) 5s.5d.	
97. Vol. 1—E: Kincaid & Bell; vol. 2—E: Kincaid & Creech/Cadell		
98. L: E. & C. Dilly		
99. E: Millar & Cadell/Kincaid & Bell	1767: B. Grierson (8°) 5s.5d.	
100. L: Millar & Cadell		
101. L: Millar & Cadell [Strahan]	1770: Williams & Moncrieffe (8°3v) 16s.3d.	
102. L: author; sold by Robinson & Roberts		
103. L: E. & C. Dilly		
104. E: Balfour		
105. Glasgow: E. & C. Dilly	*1768: Exshaw I, Saunders, Sleater I, D. Chamberlaine, Potts, Williams, "3rd ed." (12°) 2s.8½d.	
106. L: Millar & Cadell	*1768: B. Grierson (8°) 5s.5d.	
107. L: Becket & de Hondt		
108. L: Becket & de Hondt/Balfour	1768: B. Grierson (8°) 3s.3d.	
109. E: Kincaid & Bell/Sandby, J. Dodsley, E. Dilly, Cadell		

(*continued*)

Table 2 *(continued)*

	Imprint Date	Author	First British Edition: Title/(Format/Volumes)/ Price/Topic/Popularity Rating
110.	1768	Robert Whytt*	*Observations on the Dropsy in the Brain . . . To which Are Added His Other Treatises Never Hitherto Published by Themselves* (8°) MED ps
111.	1768	William Wilkie*	*Fables* (8°) 4s. FICT ps
112.	1768–69	Tobias Smollett*	*The Present State of All Nations* (8°8v) £2.8s. POL ps
113.	1768–70	George Fordyce	*Elements of the Practice of Physic* (8°v2) MED gs
114.	1768–72	Alexander Dow [and Muhammad Ferishta]	*The History of Hindostan* (4°3v) (vols. 1, 2 mainly a trans. of Ferishta's *History*) HIST ms
115.	1769	William Buchan (ed. William Smellie*)	*Domestic Medicine; or, The Family Physician: Being an Attempt to Render the Medical Art More Generally Useful, by Shewing People What Is in Their Own Power Both with Respect to the Prevention and Cure of Diseases. Chiefly Calculated to Recommend a Proper Attention to Regimen and Simple Medicines* (8°) 5s. sewed MED bs [from the 2nd ed. of 1772, published in London, the full subtitle reads: *or, a Treatise on the Prevention and Cure of Diseases by Regimen and Simple Medicines*]
116.	1769	Alexander Dow	*Zingis. A Tragedy* (8°) DRAM ms
117.	1769	Adam Ferguson*	*Institutes of Moral Philosophy* (12°) 2s.6d. brds.–3s. PHIL ms
118.	1769	[John Home]*	*The Fatal Discovery: A Tragedy* (8°) 1s.6d. DRAM ms

Table 2 (*continued*)

Place and Publisher(s) of the First British Edition	First Irish Edition (Dublin): Date/Publisher/ (Format/Volumes)/Price (if known)	First American Edition: Date/Place (Philadelphia unless otherwise noted)/ Publisher/(Format/ Volumes)
110. E: **Balfour**		
111. L: **E. & C. Dilly/ Kincaid & Bell**		
112. L: Baldwin, Johnston, Crowder, **Robinson & Roberts**		
113. Vol. 1—L: **Johnson** & Payne; vol. 2—L: **Johnson**		
114. L: **Becket & de Hondt**	1792: **L. White** (8°3v)	
115. E: [author]; printed by **Balfour,** Auld, & Smellie	*1773: Saunders, **Sleater I, Potts, D. Chamberlaine, Moncrieffe** (8°) 7s.7d. in 1786	1772: **Aitken** (8°)
116. L: **Becket & de Hondt**	1769: W. & W. Smith, G. Faulkner, B. Grierson, Powell, Saunders, **Sleater I, D. Chamberlaine, Potts, Williams, W. Colles, Moncrieffe,** J. Porter (12°)	
117. E: **Kincaid & Bell**		
118. L: **Becket & de Hondt**	[1769]: W. & W. Smith, G. Faulkner, **P. & W. Wilson,** Saunders, **Potts, Sleater I, D. Chamberlaine, J. Hoey II, Williams,** J. [i.e., C.] Ingham, J. Porter (12°) [6½d.]	

(*continued*)

Table 2 (*continued*)

	Imprint Date	Author	First British Edition: Title/(Format/Volumes)/ Price/Topic/Popularity Rating
119.	1769	William Robertson*	**The History of the Reign of the Emperor Charles V** (4°3v) £2.12s.6d. brds. or (from 1772) £3.3s. bound, with plates HIST bs
120.	1769	[Tobias Smollett]*	*The History and Adventures of an Atom* (12°2v) 6s. FICT gs
121.	1769–82	Walter Anderson	*The History of France* (4°5v) £1.1s. per vol. HIST ps
122.	1770	Charles Alston*	*Lectures on the Materia Medica* * (4°2v) MED ps
123.	1770	James Beattie*	**An Essay on the Nature and Immutability of Truth; In Opposition to Sophistry and Scepticism** (8°) 6s. PHIL bs
124.	1770	[John Bethune]	*A Short View of the Human Faculties and Passions* (12°) (marked 2nd ed., but no copy of the 1st ed. has been traced) PHIL ps
125.	1770	[John Bethune]	*Essays and Dissertations on Various Subjects, Relating to Human Life and Happiness* (12°2v) PHIL ps
126.	1770	William Duff	*Critical Observations on the Writings of the Most Celebrated Original Geniuses in Poetry* (8°) LIT ps
127.	1770	Andrew Duncan*	*Elements of Therapeutics* (8°2v) 5s.–6s. MED ms
128.	1770	James Ferguson	*An Introduction to Electricity* (8°) 4s. SCI ms

Table 2 (*continued*)

	Place and Publisher(s) of the First British Edition	First Irish Edition (Dublin): Date/Publisher/ (Format/Volumes)/Price (if known)	First American Edition: Date/Place (Philadelphia unless otherwise noted)/ Publisher/(Format/ Volumes)
119.	L: **Strahan & Cadell/Balfour**	*1769: **W. Watson, T. Ewing;** and S. Watson (4°3v) £1.5s. brds.	1770–71: America [i.e., Philadelphia]— [**Bell**] (8°3v)
120.	L: **Robinson & Roberts**	1769: **P. & W. Wilson, Exshaw I,** Powell, Saunders, Bradley, **Sleater I,** B. Grierson, **D. Chamberlaine,** Potts, **J. Hoey II, Williams,** C. Ingham (12°2v) 2s.8½d.	
121.	Vols. 1, 2 (1769)—L: **Cadell [Strahan];** [vol. 3] (1775)— [L]: author; sold by **C. Dilly,** Robson, **Becket & de Hondt,** Wilson & Nichol [Nicol]/**Balfour,** and the booksellers of Edinburgh; vols. 4, 5 (1782)— L: author; sold by Robson, **Becket** & Nichol/**J. & E. Balfour, Creech**		
122.	L: **E. & C. Dilly/ Kincaid & Bell**		
123.	E: **Kincaid & Bell**/sold by **E. & C. Dilly**	1773: T. Ewing, "3rd ed." (12°) 3s.3d.	
124.	E: A. Neill; sold by **Kincaid & Bell/E. & C. Dilly**		
125.	E: **Kincaid & Bell/ E. & C. Dilly** [various imprints, some marked 1771]		
126.	L: **Becket & de Hondt**		
127.	E: Drummond		
128.	L: **Strahan & Cadell**		

(*continued*)

Table 2 (*continued*)

	Imprint Date	Author	First British Edition: Title/(Format/Volumes)/ Price/Topic/Popularity Rating
129.	1770	{John Gregory}*	*Observations on the Duties and Offices of a Physician; and on the Method of Prosecuting Enquiries in Philosophy* (8°) 3s. sewed (2nd ed. of 1772 published under Gregory's name as *Lectures on the Duties and Qualifications of a Physician;* 5s.) MED ms
130.	1770	<William Guthrie> (i.e., John Knox?) (astronomical part by James Ferguson from 2nd ed. onward)	**A New Geographical, Historical, and Commercial Grammar and Present State of the Several Kingdoms of the World** (8°) 6s. MISC bs
131.	1770	[William Julius Mickle]*	*Voltaire in the Shades; or, Dialogues on the Deistical Controversy* (8°) 2s.6d. sewed PHIL ps
132.	1770	Donald Monro	*A Treatise on Mineral Waters* (8°2v) 12s. MED ps
133.	1771	William Alexander	*An Experimental Enquiry concerning the Causes which Have Generally Been Said to Produce Putrid Diseases* (8°) 4s.6d. MED ps
134.	1771	George Fordyce	*Elements of Agriculture and Vegetation* (8°) AGR gs
135.	1771	[Henry Mackenzie]*	**The Man of Feeling** (12°) 3s. FICT bs
136.	1771	James Macpherson*	*An Introduction to the History of Great Britain and Ireland* (4°) 18s. HIST ms
137.	1771	John Millar*	*Observations concerning the Distinction of Ranks in Society* (4°) 9s. brds. HIST ms
138.	1771	[William Russell]	*Sentimental Tales* (12°2v) FICT ps
139.	1771	A Society of Gentlemen in Scotland [William Smellie,* ed.]	**The Encyclopaedia Britannica** (originally issued in 100 parts, 1768–71) (4°3v) £1.1s. per vol. (also £2.10s. and £3.7s. per set, depending on the paper) MISC bs

Table 2 (*continued*)

Place and Publisher(s) of the First British Edition	First Irish Edition (Dublin): Date/Publisher/ (Format/Volumes)/Price (if known)	First American Edition: Date/Place (Philadelphia unless otherwise noted)/ Publisher/(Format/ Volumes)
129. L: **Strahan & Cadell**		
130. L: Knox	*1771: 1. "2nd ed.": **Exshaw I,** B. Grierson, **Williams** (8°); and 2. "2nd ed.": Saunders and **Potts** (8°) 6s.	1794–95: **Carey** (4°2v), titled *A New System of Modern Geography: or, A Geographical, Historical, and Commercial Grammar; and Present State of the Several Nations of the World*
131. L: Pearch, T. & J. Merril in Cambridge/Prince in Oxford		
132. L: sold by Wilson & Nicol, Durham		
133. L: **Becket & de Hondt, Cadell**		
134. L: **Johnson**		
135. L: **Cadell [Strahan]**	*1771: **Sleater I, D. Chamberlaine, J. Hoey II, Williams, Potts, and Moncrieffe** (12°) 4s.4d. or 2s.8½d. [another imprint adds **Walker**]	1782: **Bell** (8°, abridged) (first complete American ed.); 1791: Taylor (12°)
136. L: **Becket & de Hondt**	1771: **Williams** (12°, abridged) 3s.3d.	
137. L: **Murray [/Kincaid & Creech]**	1771: T. Ewing (8°) 5s.5d.	
138. L: sold by Wilkie		
139. E: Bell & Macfarquhar	1790–98: **J. Moore** (4°18v + two-vol. *Supplement,* 1801) (reprint	1790–98: (under the title *Encyclopaedia*) **Dobson** (4°18v + 3v

(*continued*)

Table 2 (*continued*)

Imprint Date	Author	First British Edition: Title/(Format/Volumes)/ Price/Topic/Popularity Rating
140. 1771	[Tobias Smollett]*	***The Expedition of Humphry Clinker*** (12°3v) 9s. FICT bs
141. 1771–74	{James Beattie}*	***The Minstrel; or, The Progress of Genius A Poem*** (4°) 1s.6d. per vol. POET bs
142. 1771–78	John Hunter*	*The Natural History of Human Teeth* (4°) £1.1s. (16s. for pt. 1 alone) MED ps
143. 1771–88	Sir John Dalrymple*	*Memoirs of Great Britain and Ireland* (4°3v) vols. 1–2: £2.6s.; vol. 3: £1.2s. brds. HIST ms
144. 1771–93	Robert Henry* (2 bks. in vol. 6 by Malcolm Laing)	*The History of Great Britain, from the First Invasion of It by the Romans under Julius Caesar* (4°6v) £1.1s. per vol. brds., but £1.5s. for vol. 6* HIST gs
145. 1772	William Cullen*	*Lectures on the Materia Medica* (4°) 18s. MED ms
146. 1772	{William Cullen}*	*Institutions of Medicine Pt. I* (no more published) (12°) 3s.–5s. MED ms
147. 1772	Andrew Duncan*	*Observations on the Operation and Use of Mercury in the Venereal Disease* (8°) 3s. MED ps

Table 2 (*continued*)

Place and Publisher(s) of the First British Edition	First Irish Edition (Dublin): Date/Publisher/ (Format/Volumes)/Price (if known)	First American Edition: Date/Place (Philadelphia unless otherwise noted)/ Publisher/(Format/ Volumes)
	of the 3rd Edinburgh ed.) £1.1s. per vol.	*Supplement,* 1800–1803) (reprint, with revisions, of the 3rd Edinburgh ed.)
140. L: Johnston/Collins in Salisbury	*1771: **Leathley, Exshaw I,** Saunders, **Sleater I, D. Chamberlaine, Potts, J. Hoey II,** Mitchell, **Williams, W. Colles, Walker,** Husband, **Moncrieffe, W. Wilson,** D. Hay (12°2v) 5s.5d.	
141. Bk. 1 (1771)—L: **E. & C. Dilly/ Kincaid & Bell;** bk. 2 (1774)— L: **E. & C. Dilly/Creech**	1771 (bk. 1): C. Ingham (8°) 6½d.; 1775 (bks. 1, 2): **Williams** (8°)	1784: **Bell** (8°)
142. L: **Johnson**		
143. Vol. 1 (1771)—E: **Strahan and Cadell/Kincaid & Bell, Balfour;** vol. 2 (1773)–**Creech** replaces Bell; vol. 3 (1788)—E: **Bell, Creech /A. Strahan and Cadell**	1771 (vol. 1): B. Grierson (8°) ; 1788 (vol. 2): G. Grierson (8°)	
144. Vol. 1 (1771)—L: author/sold **by Cadell;** vols. 2, 3 (1774, 1777)— E: ditto; vol. 4 (1781)—E: ditto + Longman; vol. 5 (1785)— E: ditto + "all the booksellers in Edinburgh"; vol. 6 (1793)—L: **A. Strahan and Cadell**	1789–94: **Byrne, J. Jones** (8°6v) £1.17.11 for first five vols. as of 1791	
145. L: Lowndes	*1773: T. Ewing (8°) 6s.6d.	1775: **Bell** (4°)
146. E: no publisher named		1788: Boston— Norman (4°)
147. E: **Kincaid & Creech/Cadell; Murray**		

(*continued*)

Table 2 (*continued*)

	Imprint Date	Author	First British Edition: Title/(Format/Volumes)/ Price/Topic/Popularity Rating
148.	1772	John Gregory*	*Elements of the Practice of Physic* (8°) 3s. MED ms
149.	1772	William Russell	*Fables Moral and Sentimental. In Familiar Verse* (8°) POET ps
150.	1773	Patrick Brydone*	**A Tour through Sicily and Malta. In a Series of Letters to William Beckford** (8°2v) 12s. TRAV bs
151.	1773	Sir David Dalrymple, Lord Hailes*	*Remarks on the History of Scotland* (8°) HIST ps
152.	1773	[William Duff]	*The History of Rhedi, the Hermit of Mount Ararati. An Oriental Tale* (12°) 3s. FICT ps
153.	1773	James Ferguson	*Select Mechanical Exercises* (8°) 5s. SCI ms
154.	1773	[John Home]*	*Alonzo: A Tragedy* (8°) 1s.6d. DRAM ms
155.	1773	[Henry Mackenzie]*	*The Man of the World* (12°2v) 6s. FICT gs
156.	1773	[Henry Mackenzie]*	*The Prince of Tunis: A Tragedy* (8°) DRAM ms
157.	1773	M. [Antoine Léonard] Thomas (trans. and enlarged by William Russell)	*Essay on the Character, Manners, and Genius of Women in Different Ages* (8°2v) HIST ps
158.	1773–79	Robert Fergusson	**Poems** (from 1779 *Poems on Various Subjects**) (12°) 2s.6d.–3s. POET bs
159.	1773–86	A Society in Edinburgh [Andrew Duncan]*	*Medical and Philosophical Commentaries* (8°10v) MED gs
160.	1773–92	[James Burnett, Lord Monboddo]*	*Of the Origin and Progress of Language* (8°6v) 5s.–7s.6d. brds. per vol. LANG ps

Table 2 (*continued*)

Place and Publisher(s) of the First British Edition	First Irish Edition (Dublin): Date/Publisher/ (Format/Volumes)/Price (if known)	First American Edition: Date/Place (Philadelphia unless otherwise noted)/ Publisher/(Format/ Volumes)
148. E: **Balfour**		
149. L: Flexney, Richardson, & Urquhart		
150. L: **Strahan and Cadell**	*1773: **Potts, Moncrieffe** (8°) 5s.5d.	1792: Boston—Boyle, [D. West], and Larkin, Jr. (12°2v)
151. E: [author?]; printed by **Balfour** & Smellie		
152. L: **Cadell**	1781: Jackson (12°) 2s.2d.	
153. L: **Strahan and Cadell**		
154. L: **Becket**	1773: **W. Wilson** (12°) [6½d.]	1777: **Bell** (8°) (retitled *Alonzo and Ormisinda*)
155. L: **Strahan and Cadell**	*1773: **Sleater I, Potts, Williams, D. Chamberlaine,** Husband, **Walker, Moncrieffe, Jenkin** (12°2v)	1782–83: **Bell** (8°3v)
156. E: **Kincaid & Creech**	1779: Company of Booksellers (12°)	
157. L: **G. Robinson**		1774: **Aitken** (12°)
158. E: printed by W. & T. Ruddiman		See no. 260 below.
159. Vol. 1—L: **Murray/Kincaid & Creech,** Drummond/T. Ewing in Dublin (publishers vary in later vols.)		1793–97: **Dobson** (8°11v) (some "By a Society of Physicians in Edinburgh," but most "Collected and Published by Andrew Duncan")
160. Vol. 1 (1773)—E: **Kincaid & Creech/Cadell;** vols. 2, 3 (1774, 1776)—E: **Balfour/ Cadell;** vols. 4, 5 (1787, 1789)—E: **Bell/ Cadell;** vol. 6 (1792)—E: **Bell & Bradfute/Cadell**		

(*continued*)

Table 2 (*continued*)

	Imprint Date	Author	First British Edition: Title/(Format/Volumes)/ Price/Topic/Popularity Rating
161.	1774	{Alexander Dow}	*Sethona. A Tragedy* (8°) DRAM ms
162.	1774	Alexander Gerard*	*An Essay on Genius* (8°) 6s. LIT ps
163.	1774	John Gregory*	***A Father's Legacy to His Daughters**** (8° and 12°) 2s. sewed MISC bs
164.	1774	⌈Henry Home, Lord Kames⌉*	*Sketches of the History of Man* (4°2v) £2.2s. HIST ms
165.	1774	John Ogilvie*	*Philosophical and Critical Observations on the Nature, Character, and Various Species of Composition* (8°2v) 12s. LIT ps
166.	1774	{William Richardson}*	*A Philosophical Analysis and Illustration of Some of Shakespeare's Remarkable Characters* (8°) 3s. LIT gs
167.	1774	{William Richardson}*	*Poems, Chiefly Rural* (8°) 3s. POET gs
168.	1775	James Ferguson	*The Art of Drawing in Perspective* (8°) 4s.–4s.6d. ARTS gs
169.	1775	Alexander Hamilton	*Elements of the Practice of Midwifery* (8°) MED ps
170.	1775	James Macpherson*	*The History of Great Britain, from the Restoration, to the Accession of the House of Hannover* (4°2v) £2.5s. HIST ms
171.	1775	Robert Simson	*Elements of the Conic Sections,* bks. 1–3 (8°) 4s.6d. (trans. of 1735 Latin original) SCI ms

Table 2 (*continued*)

Place and Publisher(s) of the First British Edition	First Irish Edition (Dublin): Date/Publisher/ (Format/Volumes)/Price (if known)	First American Edition: Date/Place (Philadelphia unless otherwise noted)/ Publisher/(Format/ Volumes)
161.	L: **Becket & de Hondt**	1774: **Exshaw I, Sleater I, Potts, D. Chamberlaine, Williams, W. Wilson, J. Hoey II,** Husband, **W. Colles, Walker, Jenkin, Moncrieffe,** M. Hay (12°)	1774: Sparhawk (12°)
162.	L: **Strahan and Cadell/Creech**		
163.	L: **Strahan and Cadell/Creech**	*1774: 1. T. Ewing, **Jenkin** (8°); and 2. J. Colles, "6th ed." (12°) 1s.1d.	1775: Dunlap (8°); also 1775: Aikman (8°); also 1775: New York—Loudon (8°)
164.	E: **Creech/Strahan and Cadell**	*1774–75: **Williams** (12°4v) 10s.10d.	1776: **Bell** and **Aitken** (8°, abridged and retitled *Six Sketches on the History of Man*)
165.	L: **G. Robinson**	1779: **W. Hallhead** (8°2v) 10s.10d. (the London ed. with a canceled title page)	
166.	E: **Creech/Murray** (also L: **Murray/Creech**)		1788: Spotswood (12°)
167.	Glasgow: printed by R. & A. Foulis		
168.	L: **Strahan and Cadell**	1778: **Williams** (8°) 4s.4d.	
169.	L: **Murray**		
170.	L: **Strahan and Cadell**	1775: **Exshaw I, D. Chamberlain, Potts, Sleater I, Williams, W. Wilson, Walker, Moncrieffe, Jenkin,** Mills (8°2v)	
171.	E: **Elliot**/sold by **Cadell, Murray**		

(*continued*)

Table 2 (*continued*)

	Imprint Date	Author	First British Edition: Title/(Format/Volumes)/ Price/Topic/Popularity Rating
172.	1775–96	{James Anderson}	*Essays Relating to Agriculture and Rural Affairs* (8°3v) 6s.–8s. brds. per vol. AGR gs
173.	1776	James Beattie*	*Essays* (4° and 8° eds., the latter omitting the *Essay on Truth*); 4° ed.: £1.1s. brds.; 8° ed.: 7s. MISC gs
174.	1776	George Campbell*	*The Philosophy of Rhetoric* (8°2v) 10s.6d. brds. LIT ms
175.	1776	Luís de Camões (trans. William Julius Mickle,* with additional materials by him)	*The Lusiad; or, the Discovery of India. An Epic Poem* (4°) £1.1s. brds. POET gs
176.	1776	{Henry Home, Lord Kames}*	*The Gentleman Farmer. Being an Attempt to Improve Agriculture, by Subjecting It to the Test of Rational Principles* (8°) 6s. AGR gs
177.	1776	Adam Smith*	**An Inquiry into the Nature and Causes of the Wealth of Nations** (4°2v) £2.2s. ECON bs
178.	1776–79	Sir David Dalrymple, Lord Hailes*	*Annals of Scotland* (4°2v) 15s.–£1.7s.6d. HIST ms
179.	1777	James Anderson	*Observations on the Means of Exciting a Spirit of National Industry; Chiefly Intended to Promote the Agriculture, Commerce, Manufactures, and Fisheries, of Scotland* (4°) £1.1s. ECON ps

Table 2 (continued)

Place and Publisher(s) of the First British Edition	First Irish Edition (Dublin): Date/Publisher/ (Format/Volumes)/Price (if known)	First American Edition: Date/Place (Philadelphia unless otherwise noted)/ Publisher/(Format/ Volumes)
172. Vol. 1 (1775)—E: **Cadell/ Creech;** vol. 2 (1777)—E: **Creech/Cadell;** vol. 3 (1796)— E: **Bell & Bradfute/"the Robinsons"**	1779 (vols. 1, 2 only): **W. Hallhead,** Lynch, Flin II, **Jenkin, Williams, L. White,** Spotswood (8°2v); 10s.10d.	
173. E: **Creech/E. & C. Dilly** (some copies of the 4° ed. contain only Creech's name)	1778: **Jenkin** (8°2v) 13s.	
174. L: **Strahan and Cadell/Creech**		
175. Oxford: sold in London by **Cadell,** [**E. & C.**] **Dilly,** Bew, Flexney, Evans, Richardson & Urquhart, Goodsman	1791: Archer (8°2v) 13s. brds.	
176. E: **Creech/Cadell**	1779: **Williams** (8°) 5s.5d.	
177. L: **Strahan and Cadell** [**/Creech**]	*1776: **W. Whitestone, D. Chamberlaine, W. Watson, Potts,** S. Watson, **J. Hoey II, Williams, W. Colles, W. Wilson,** Armitage, **Walker, Moncrieffe, Jenkin, Gilbert,** R. Cross, Mills, **W. Hallhead,** T. Faulkner, Hillary, J. Colles (8°3v) 19s.6d.	1789: **Dobson** (12°3v) (also 1796)
178. L: **Murray**		
179. E: **Cadell/Elliot**	1779: Price, **W. & H. Whitestone, Williams, W. Colles, W. Wilson, Jenkin, Walker,** Flin II, **L. White, Exshaw II, Beatty,** James Parker (8°2v) 10s.10d.	

(continued)

Table 2 (*continued*)

	Imprint Date	Author	First British Edition: Title/(Format/Volumes)/ Price/Topic/Popularity Rating
180.	1777	Joseph Black* (with an essay by William Cullen*)	*Experiments upon Magnesia Alba, Quick-Lime, and Other Alcaline Substances* (8°) 2s.6d. SCI ms
181.	1777	James Fordyce	*Addresses to Young Men* (8°2v) 8s. MISC ms
182.	1777	{Henry Home, Lord Kames}*	*Elucidations respecting the Common and Statute Law of Scotland* (8°) LAW ms
183.	1777	[Henry Mackenzie]*	*Julia de Roubigné* (12°2v) 6s. FICT gs
184.	1777	John Ogilvie*	*Rona: A Poem* (4°) 12s.6d. brds. POET ps
185.	1777	William Robertson*	**The History of America** (4°2v) £2.2s.18s. HIST bs
186.	1777	Robert Watson*	*The History of the Reign of Philip the Second King of Spain* (4°2v) £2.2s. HIST gs

Table 2 *(continued)*

Place and Publisher(s) of the First British Edition	First Irish Edition (Dublin): Date/Publisher/ (Format/Volumes)/Price (if known)	First American Edition: Date/Place (Philadelphia unless otherwise noted)/ Publisher/(Format/ Volumes)
180. E: **Creech/Murray;** Wallis & Stonehouse		
181. L: **Cadell**	1777: **Exshaw II** (12°2v) 6s.6d.	1782: Boston—Green (12°)
182. E: **Creech**/sold by **Cadell**		
183. L: **Strahan and Cadell/Creech** (also L: **Strahan and Cadell** alone)	*1777: Company of Booksellers (12°2v) 2s.8½d.	1782: Cist (8°2v)
184. L: **Murray**		
185. L: **Strahan and Cadell/Balfour**	*1777: Price, **W. Whitestone, W. Watson,** R. Cross, Corcoran, **Sleater I, D. Chamberlaine, Potts, J. Hoey II, Williams,** Lynch, M. Hay, S. Watson, T. Stewart, **W. Colles, W. Wilson, Moncrieffe,** Armitage, **W. Hallhead, Walker, Exshaw II,** Flin II, **Burnet,** T. Faulkner, **Jenkin, Beatty, Gilbert,** Vallance, **Wogan,** E. Cross, Mills, **Grueber,** R. Stewart, **L. White,** M'Kenly, Magee (4°2v) (also in 1777: 8°3v ed. published by 46 individuals, 16s.3d.; and 8°2v ed. published by 43 individuals, 13s.)	1798: New York— S. Campbell (8°2v)
186. L: **Strahan and Cadell/Balfour, Creech**	1777: Price, **W. Watson, W. Whitestone, Sleater I, D. Chamberlaine,** R. Cross, **J. Hoey II, Williams,**	

(continued)

Table 2 (*continued*)

Imprint Date	Author	First British Edition: Title/(Format/Volumes)/ Price/Topic/Popularity Rating
187. 1777–84	William Cullen*	***First Lines of the Practice of Physic*** (8°4v) £1.8 MED bs
188. 1777[–1801]	Hugh Blair*	***Sermons*** (8°5v) 6s. per vol.; full set (including v5*) £1.11s. REL bs
189. 1778	Benjamin Bell	*A Treatise on the Theory and Management of Ulcers* (8°) 7s. MED gs
190. 1778	Andrew Duncan*	*Medical Cases, Selected from the Records of the Public Dispensary at Edinburgh* (8°) 5s. MED gs
191. 1778	David Stewart [Erskine], Earl of Buchan, and Walter Minto	*An Account of the Life, Writings, and Inventions of John Napier, of Merchiston* (4°) BIOG ps
192. 1778	Lysias and Isocrates (trans. and ed. John Gillies*)	*The Orations of Lysias and Isocrates, Translated from the Greek: with Some Account of their Lives; and a Discourse on the History, Manners, and Character of the Greeks* (4°) 18s. brds.; £1.1s. HIST ps

Table 2 (*continued*)

Place and Publisher(s) of the First British Edition	First Irish Edition (*Dublin*): Date/Publisher/ (Format/Volumes)/Price (if known)	First American Edition: Date/Place (*Philadelphia unless otherwise noted*)/ Publisher/(Format/ Volumes)
	W. Colles, Potts, W. Wilson, Mon- crieffe, Armitage, Flin II, Jackson, Walker, [J.] Porter, Gilbert, Jenkin, P. Hoey, Burnett, E. Cross, W. Hallhead, Spotswood, Exshaw II, L. White, J. Colles, Higly, Hillary, Beatty (8°2v) 13s.	
187. E: **Murray/Creech** (later vols. **Elliot/Cadell**)	1777–84: vol.1, Armit- age (8°); vols. 2–4, **Wil- liams** (8°) £1.8s.	1781–85: Steiner & Cist (8°3v)
188. Vol. 1 (1777)—E: **Creech/ Strahan and Cadell;** vol. 2 (1780)—L: **Strahan and Cadell/ Creech;** vol. 3 (1790) and vol. 4 (1794)—L [i.e., E]: **A. Strahan and Cadell/Creech;** (vol. 5 pub- lished posthumously in 1801—L: **A. Strahan and Cadell/Creech**)	*1777–94 (vols. 1–4; 8°): vol. 1 (1777): **W. Hallhead;** four-vol. set (1790): **W. Colles** (vols. 1, 4) and **A. Col- les** (vols. 1–3), 6s.6d. per vol. [£1.6s. for four vols.]	1790 (vol. 1): New York—Hodge, Al- len, & S. Campbell; sold by **R. Campbell,** P (8°); 1791 (vols. 1, 2): Spotswood, and **Carey,** Stewart & Co. (12°); 1795 (vol. 3): Boston—Spotswood (12°); 1794 (vol. 4): **R. Campbell** (12°)
189. E: **Elliot**/sold by **Cadell**		1791: Boston— Thomas & Andrews (8°) (also 1797)
190. E: **Elliot/Murray**		
191. Perth: R. Morison & Son; sold by **Murray/Creech**		
192. L: **Murray/Bell**		

(*continued*)

Table 2 *(continued)*

	Imprint Date	Author	First British Edition: Title/(Format/Volumes)/ Price/Topic/Popularity Rating
193.	1778	[John Home]*	*Alfred: A Tragedy* (8°) 1s.6d. DRAM ms
194.	1778	William Russell	*The History of America, from Its Discovery by Columbus to the Conclusion of the Late War* (4°2v) HIST ps
195.	1778	Gilbert Stuart*	*A View of Society in Europe* (4°) 18s. brds. HIST ms
196.	1778–79	David Loch	*Essays on the Trade, Commerce, Manufactures, and Fisheries of Scotland* (12°3v) ECON ps
197.	1778–79 [vol. 3, 1822]	Robert and James Adam	*The Works in Architecture of Robert and James Adam* (2°2v) (originally issues in five parts, 1773–78) £10.15s. unbnd. ARTS ps
198.	1779	William Alexander	*The History of Women, from the Earliest Antiquity, to the Present Time* (4°2v) £1.10s. brds. HIST gs
199.	1779	Hugo Arnot	*The History of Edinburgh* (4°) £1.5s. brds. HIST ms
200.	1779	David Hume*	*Dialogues concerning Natural Religion* * (8°) 4s. sewed PHIL ms
201.	1779	{John Moore}*	**A View of Society and Manners in France, Switzerland, and Germany** (8°2v) 12s. TRAV bs
202.	1779	Gilbert Stuart*	*Observations concerning Public Law, and the Constitutional History of Scotland* (8°) 6s. LAW ms
203.	1779–84	{William Russell}	*The History of Modern Europe* (8°4v) HIST gs

Table 2 (*continued*)

Place and Publisher(s) of the First British Edition	First Irish Edition (Dublin): Date/Publisher/ (Format/Volumes)/Price (if known)	First American Edition: Date/Place (Philadelphia unless otherwise noted)/ Publisher/(Format/ Volumes)
193. L: **Becket**	1777 [1778?]: Company of Booksellers (12°) 6½d.	
194. L: Fielding & Walker		
195. E: **Bell/Murray**	1778: **W. Whitestone, W. Colles, J. Hoey II, W. Wilson, Williams, Walker, Jenkin,** Flin II, **Burnet, L. White, Beatty, Exshaw II** (8°) 5s.5d.	
196. E: author		
197. L: authors; sold by Elmsly and "the other Booksellers in Town and Country"		
198. L: **Strahan and Cadell**	1779: Price, R. Cross, **Potts,** Flin II, **W. Wilson, Walker, Jenkin, Exshaw II, Beatty, L. White** (8°2v) 13s.	1796: Dobelbower (8°2v) (first issued in parts, 1795)
199. E: **Creech/Murray**		
200. [E?]: no printer, seller, or publisher named	1782: **Exshaw II** (8°) 5s.5d.	
201. L: **Strahan and Cadell**	*1780: 1. **Byrne** (12°2v); and 2. **W. Wilson** (12°2v) 6s.6d.	1783: **Bell** (8°) (first issued in three parts)
202. E: **Creech/Murray**		
203. L: pt. 1 [vols. 1, 2] (1779), pt. 2 [vols. 3, 4] (1784): **G. Robinson,** Robson, Walter, Sewell	1779 (pt. 1): Price, **W. Whitestone,** R. Cross, Lynch, **Walker, Jenkin,** E. Cross, Higly, **Moncrieffe,** Spotswood,	1800[–1801]: Birch & Small (8°5v)

(*continued*)

Table 2 (*continued*)

Imprint Date	Author	First British Edition: Title/(Format/Volumes)/ Price/Topic/Popularity Rating
204. 1779–99	[James Burnett, Lord Monboddo]*	*Antient Metaphysics* (4°6v) 15s.–£1.1s. per vol. PHIL ps
205. 1780	John Bruce	*First Principles of Philosophy* (12°) 6s. PHIL ms
206. 1780	James Dunbar	*Essays on the History of Mankind in Rude and Cultivated Ages* (8°) 6s. HIST ms
207. 1780	Francis Home*	*Clinical Experiments, Histories and Dissections* (8°) 7s. MED ms
208. 1780	William Lothian	*The History of the United Provinces of the Netherlands* (4°) 16s. HIST ps
209. 1780	Donald Monro	*Observations on the Means of Preserving the Health of Soldiers; and of Conducting Military Hospitals* (8°2v) 10s. MED ps (first book ed., though marked as 2nd ed.)
210. 1780	Gilbert Stuart*	*The History of the Establishment of the Reformation in Scotland* (4°) 10s.6d. HIST ps
211. 1780–82	Alexander Gerard*	*Sermons* (8°2v) 12s. REL ms
212. 1780–85	Buffon (ed. and trans. William Smellie*)	*Natural History, General and Particular* (8°9v) £4.1s. SCI ms
213. 1781	Alexander Hamilton	*A Treatise of Midwifery, Comprehending the Management of Female Complaints, and the Treatment of Children in Early Infancy* (8°) 6s. brds. MED ms
214. 1781	{Henry Home, Lord Kames}*	*Loose Hints upon Education, Chiefly concerning the Culture of the Heart* (8°) 5s. EDU ms

Table 2 (*continued*)

	Place and Publisher(s) of the First British Edition	First Irish Edition (Dublin): Date/Publisher/ (Format/Volumes)/Price (if known)	First American Edition: Date/Place (Philadelphia unless otherwise noted)/ Publisher/(Format/ Volumes)
		W. Hallhead, Exshaw II, Beatty, L. White, Byrne (8°2v); 1784 (pt. 2): Exshaw II (8°2v);	
204.	Vol. 1 (1779)—E: **Cadell/Balfour;** vols. 2, 3 (1782, 1784)— L: ditto; vol. 4 (1795)—E: **Bell & Bradfute/Cadell;** vols. 5, 6 (1797, 1799)—E: **Bell & Bradfute/Cadell & Davies**		
205.	E: **Creech**/sold by **Cadell**		
206.	L: **Strahan and Cadell/Balfour**	1782: **W. Colles, Gilbert** (12°) 3s.3d.	
207.	E: **Creech/Murray**		
208.	L: **J. Dodsley,** Longman/Dickson	1780: **W. & H. Whitestone, Walker, Jenkin,** E. Cross, **L. White, Beatty** (8°) 6s.6d.	
209.	L: **Murray, G. Robinson**		
210.	L: **Murray/Bell**		
211.	L: **C. Dilly**		
212.	E: **Creech;** vol. 9: add **Strahan and Cadell** (also L: **Strahan and Cadell/Creech**)		
213.	L: **Murray**/Dickson, **Creech** (also E: Dickson, **Creech, Elliot**)		
214.	E: **Bell/Murray**	1782: Price, **W. & H. Whitestone, Walker, Beatty,** Burton, **Byrne** (12°) 2s.8½d.	

(*continued*)

Table 2 (*continued*)

	Imprint Date	Author	First British Edition: Title/(Format/Volumes)/ Price/Topic/Popularity Rating
215.	1781	John Logan	*Elements of the Philosophy of History, Part First* (no more published) (12°) 2s. HIST ps
216.	1781	John Logan	*Poems* (8°) 2s.6d. sewed POET gs
217.	1781	[Henry Mackenzie* et al.]	**The Mirror** (originally published as a periodical, 1779–80) (12°3v) 9s. MISC bs
218.	1781	Alexander Monro I* (ed. Alexander Monro II*; biography by Donald Monro)	*The Works of Alexander Monro* (4°) £1.8s. MED ps
219.	1781	John Moore*	*A View of Society and Manners in Italy* (8°2v) 14s. TRAV ss
220.	1781	[William Ogilvie]	*An Essay on the Right of Property in Land* (8°) ECON ps
221.	1781	{John Pinkerton}	*Rimes* (8°) 3s.6d. brds. POET ms
222.	1782	James Balfour	*Philosophical Dissertations* (8°) 2s.6d. sewed PHIL ps
223.	1782	George Chalmers	*An Estimate of the Comparative Strength of Britain during the Present and Four Preceding Reigns, and of the Losses of Her Trade from Every War since the Revolution* (4°) ECON gs
224.	1782	[Robert Orme]*	*Historical Fragments of the Mogul Empire* (8°) 5s. HIST ps
225.	1782	[Sir] John Sinclair*	*Observations on the Scottish Dialect* (8°) 5s. LANG ps

Table 2 (*continued*)

Place and Publisher(s) of the First British Edition	First Irish Edition (Dublin): Date/Publisher/ (Format/Volumes)/Price (if known)	First American Edition: Date/Place (Philadelphia unless otherwise noted)/ Publisher/(Format/ Volumes)
215. E: **Creech, Elliot**		
216. L: **Cadell**		
217. E: **Creech/Strahan and Cadell**	*1782: **Walker, Beatty,** Burton, **Byrne,** Webb, **Cash** (12°2v) 6s.6d.	1792: Boston—Gould or Blake (12°2v)
218. E: **Elliot/G. Robinson** (also **Elliot** alone)		
219. L: **Strahan and Cadell**	1781: 1. Price, **W. Watson, W. & H. Whitestone, H. Chamberlaine, Williams, W. Colles, W. Wilson, Moncrieffe, Walker,** Flin II, **Jenkin, Burnet, W. Hallhead, Exshaw II, Gilbert,** Vallance, R. Cross, E. Cross, Burton, **L. White,** John Parker, **Byrne** (12°3v); and 2. **W. Wilson** (12°3v) 9s.9d.	1783: **Bell** (8°) (first issued in three parts)
220. L: Walter		
221. L: **C. Dilly**		
222. E: **Cadell/J. & E. Balfour**		
223. L: **C. Dilly,** Bowen		
224. L: Nourse		
225. L: **Strahan and Cadell/Creech**		

(*continued*)

Table 2 (*continued*)

	Imprint Date	Author	First British Edition: Title/(Format/Volumes)/ Price/Topic/Popularity Rating
226.	1782	Gilbert Stuart*	*The History of Scotland, from the Establishment of the Reformation, till the Death of Queen Mary* (4°2v) £1.5s. HIST ms
227.	1782	[William Thomson, ed. or author] (attributed to "William Mackintosh")	*Travels in Europe, Asia, and Africa; Describing Characters, Customs, Manners, Laws, and Productions of Nature and Art* (8°2v) TRAV ps
228.	1782	Alexander [Fraser] Tytler, later Lord Woodhouselee*	*Plan and Outlines of a Course of Lectures on Universal History, Ancient and Modern, Delivered in the University of Edinburgh* (8°) 6s. HIST ps
229.	1783	James Beattie*	*Dissertations, Moral and Critical* (4°) £1.1s. MISC ps
230.	1783	Hugh Blair*	**Lectures on Rhetoric and Belles Lettres** (4°2v) £2.2s. LIT bs
231.	1783	[Sir David Dalrymple, Lord Hailes]*	*Disquisitions concerning the Antiquities of the Christian Church* (8°) REL ps
232.	1783	Adam Ferguson*	*The History of the Progress and Termination of the Roman Republic* (4°3v) £3.3s. HIST ms
233.	1783	[John Logan]	*Runnamede: A Tragedy* (8°) 1s.6d. DRAM ps
234.	1783	Alexander Monro II*	*Observations on the Structure and Functions of the Nervous System* (2°) £2.2s. brds. MED ps

Table 2 (*continued*)

Place and Publisher(s) of the First British Edition	First Irish Edition (Dublin): Date/Publisher/ (Format/Volumes)/Price (if known)	First American Edition: Date/Place (Philadelphia unless otherwise noted)/ Publisher/(Format/ Volumes)
226.	L: **Murray/Bell** (also L: **Murray** alone)	1782: **Gilbert, Walker, Beatty,** Burton, **Exshaw II, Byrne, Cash** (8°2v) 13s.	
227.	L: **Murray**		
228.	E: **Creech**/sold by **Cadell,** Longman		
229.	L: **Strahan and Cadell/ Creech**	1783: **Exshaw II, Walker, Beatty, L. White, Byrne, Cash, M'Kenzie** (8°2v) 13s.	
230.	L: **Strahan and Cadell/Creech**	*1783: **W. Whitestone, W. Colles, Burnet, Moncrieffe, Gilbert, Walker, Exshaw II, L. White, Beatty,** Burton, **Byrne,** John Parker, **Cash, M'Kenzie** (8°3v) 19s.6d.	1784: **Aitken** (4°)
231.	Glasgow: printed by A. Foulis II		
232.	L: **Strahan and Cadell/Creech**	1783: Price, **W. Whitestone, W. Colles, Moncrieffe, Jenkin, Walker, Exshaw II, Beatty, L. White,** Burton, **Byrne, Cash, Sleater II** (8°3v) £1.2s.9d.	
233.	L: **Cadell/Creech**		
234.	E: **Creech/Johnson** (second title page shows **Cadell,** Elmsley, **Murray,** and Longman instead of Johnson)		

(*continued*)

Table 2 (*continued*)

	Imprint Date	Author	First British Edition: Title/(Format/Volumes)/ Price/Topic/Popularity Rating
235.	1783	John Ogilvie*	*An Inquiry into the Causes of the Infidelity and Scepticism of the Times* (8°2v) 6s. PHIL ps
236.	1783	Sir John Pringle	*Six Discourses, Delivered by Sir John Pringle, Bart. When President of the Royal Society* (8°) 6s. SCI ps
237.	1783	[William Thomson]	*The Man in the Moon; or, Travels into the Lunar Regions, by the Man of the People* (8°2v) 5s.–6s. FICT ps
238.	1783	George Wallace	*Thoughts on the Origin of Feudal Tenures, and the Descent of Ancient Peerages, in Scotland* (4°) 12s. brds. HIST ps
239.	1783	Robert Watson* (2 of 6 bks. are by William Thomson)	*The History of the Reign of Philip the Third, King of Spain** (4°) HIST ms
240.	1783–88	Benjamin Bell	*A System of Surgery* (8°6v) £2.2s. MED ss
241.	1784	George Chalmers	*Opinions on Interesting Subjects of Public Law and Commercial Policy* (8°) ECON ms
242.	1784	Alexander Hamilton	*Outlines of the Theory and Practice of Midwifery* (8°) 6s. MED gs
243.	1784	William Hunter	*Two Introductory Lectures, Delivered by Dr. William Hunter, to His Last Course of Anatomical Lectures** (4°) MED ps
244.	1784	John Knox	*A View of the British Empire, more especially Scotland, with Some Proposals for the Improvement of that Country, the Extension of Its Fisheries, and the Relief of the People* (4°) 3s. sewed,

Table 2 (*continued*)

Place and Publisher(s) of the First British Edition	First Irish Edition (Dublin): Date/Publisher/ (Format/Volumes)/Price (if known)	First American Edition: Date/Place (Philadelphia unless otherwise noted)/ Publisher/(Format/ Volumes)
235. L: Richardson & Urquhart/Gordon, **Creech,** Dickson		
236. L: **Strahan and Cadell**		
237. L: **Murray**		
238. E: **Strahan and Cadell**		
239. L: **G. Robinson,** Robson, Sewell	1783: Price, **W. Whitestone, W. Watson, Moncrieffe, W. Colles, Jenkin, Walker, Exshaw II, Beatty, Burnet, W. Wilson,** R. Cross, Mills, [**J.**] Porter, Burton, **L. White, Byrne,** Higly, N. Cross, **Cash,** Doyle, **Sleater II,** Lynch, **S. Hallhead** (8°) 6s.6d.	
240. E: **Elliot/G. Robinson**		1791: **Dobson** (8°, abridged) (unabridged 1791: Boston— Thomas, vols. 1–4, 8°)
241. L: Debrett		
242. E: **Elliot/G. Robinson**		1790: **Dobson** (12°)
243. [L]: **Johnson**		
244. L: Walter, Sewell/Gordon		

(*continued*)

Table 2 (*continued*)

	Imprint Date	Author	First British Edition: Title/(Format/Volumes)/ Price/Topic/Popularity Rating
			rising to 10–12s. for the "greatly enlarged" 3rd ed. (8°2v), 1785 ECON gs
245.	1784	{John Pinkerton}	*An Essay on Medals* (8°) 4s. sewed MISC ms
246.	1784	{William Richardson}*	*Anecdotes of the Russian Empire* (8°) 6s. TRAV ps
247.	1784	William Richardson*	*Essays on Shakespeare's Dramatic Characters of Richard the Third, King Lear, and Timon of Athens* (8°) 2s.6d. brds.–3s. LIT gs
248.	1784	Thomas Robertson	*An Inquiry into the Fine Arts* ("Volume the First," but no more published) (4°) 18s. brds. ARTS ps
249.	1785	James Anderson	*An Account of the Present State of the Hebrides and Western Coasts of Scotland* (8°) 8s. ECON ps
250.	1785	James Boswell	*The Journal of a Tour to the Hebrides, with Samuel Johnson, LL.D.* (8°) 7s. TRAV gs
251.	1785	James Fordyce	*Addresses to the Deity* (8°) 2s.6d. sewed–3s. REL ms
252.	1785	James Grant	*Essays on the Origin of Society, Language, Property, Government, Jurisdiction, Contracts, and Marriage* (4°) 6s.–7s.6d. brds. HIST ps
253.	1785	Alexander Monro II*	*The Structure and Physiology of Fishes Explained, and Compared with Those of Man, and Other Animals* (2°) £2.2s. brds. SCI ps
254.	1785	<Robert Heron> (i.e., John Pinkerton)	*Letters of Literature* (8°) 6s. brds. LIT ps
255.	1785	Thomas Reid*	*Essays on the Intellectual Powers of Man* (4°) £1.8s. PHIL ms
256.	1785–90 [vol. 3, 1804]	[Sir] John Sinclair*	*The History of the Public Revenue of the British Empire* (4°2v) £1.18s. ECON ms
257.	1786	John Anderson	*Institutes of Physics* (8°) "Fourth Edition" (vols. 1 and 3 published in 1777) SCI ps
258.	1786	James Beattie*	*Evidences of the Christian Religion* (8°2v) 5s. sewed REL gs

Table 2 (*continued*)

Place and Publisher(s) of the First British Edition	First Irish Edition (Dublin): Date/Publisher/ (Format/Volumes)/Price (if known)	First American Edition: Date/Place (Philadelphia unless otherwise noted)/ Publisher/(Format/ Volumes)
245. L: **J. Dodsley**		
246. L: **Strahan and Cadell**		
247. L: **Murray**		
248. L: **Strahan and Cadell** [**/Creech**]		
249. E : **G. G. J. Robinson/Elliot**	1786: **L. White, Byrne, M'Kenzie,** Marchbank, **J. Jones, J. Moore** (8°)	
250. L: **C. Dilly**[**/Creech**] [author]	1785: **L. White, Byrne, Cash** (8°) 6s.6d.	
251. L: **Cadell**	1785: **L. White, Byrne, Cash** (12°) 2s.8½d.	
252. L: **G. G. J. & J. Robinson/Elliot**		
253. E: **Elliot/G. G. J. & J. Robinson** (also E: **Elliot** alone)		
254. L: **G. G. J. & J. Robinson**		
255. E: **Bell/G. G. J. & J. Robinson**	1786: **L. White** (8°2v) 13s.	1793: **Young** (8°2v) (as *Essays on the Intellectual and Active Powers;* see no. 275)
256. L: **Cadell**	1785: **Byrne** (8°) 6s.6d.	
257. Glasgow: [author?]; printed by Chapman & Duncan		
258. E: **A. Strahan and Cadell/Creech**	1786: **Moncrieffe, W. Colles,** [**W.**] **Wilson, L. White, Byrne, Cash,** W. Porter,	1787: **Dobson** (8°)

(*continued*)

Table 2 (*continued*)

Imprint Date	Author	First British Edition: Title/(Format/Volumes)/ Price/Topic/Popularity Rating
259. 1786	John Bruce	*Elements of the Science of Ethics* (8°) 6s. PHIL ps
260. 1786	Robert Burns	**Poems, Chiefly in the Scottish Dialect** (8°) 3s. sewed (subscription price); POET bs
261. 1786	William Duff	*Sermons on Several Occasions* (12°2v) REL ps
262. 1786	James Fordyce	*Poems* (8°) 3s.6d. POET ps
263. 1786	John Gillies*	*The History of Ancient Greece, Its Colonies, and Conquests* (4°2v) £2.10s. HIST gs
264. 1786	John Hunter*	*A Treatise on the Venereal Disease* (4°) £1.1s. brds. MED ms
265. 1786	John Hunter*	*Observations on Certain Parts of the Animal Oeconomy* (4°) 16s. brds. SCI ms
266. 1786	John Moore*	*Medical Sketches* (8°) 7s. MED ps
267. 1787	James Beattie*	*Scoticisms, Arranged in Alphabetical Order, Designed to Correct Improprieties of Speech and Writing* (8°) LANG ps
268. 1787	[John Brown]	*Observations on the Principles of the Old System of Physic, Exhibiting a Compend of the New Doctrine* (8°) MED ps
269. 1787	John Knox	*A Tour through the Highlands of Scotland, and the Hebridean Isles, in 1786* (8°) 7s. brds.–8s. TRAV ps

Table 2 (*continued*)

Place and Publisher(s) of the First British Edition	First Irish Edition (Dublin): Date/Publisher/ (Format/Volumes)/Price (if known)	First American Edition: Date/Place (Philadelphia unless otherwise noted)/ Publisher/(Format/ Volumes)
	McKenzie, J. Moore, J. Jones (12°) 3s.3d.	
259. L: A. Strahan and Cadell/Creech		
260. Kilmarnock: [author]; printed by J. Wilson	1787: Gilbert (12°) 3s.3d.	1788: Stewart & Hyde (8°) (also 1788: New York—printed by J. & A. M'Lean, 8°; *To which Are Added, Scots Poems, Selected from the Works of Robert Fergusson*)
261. Aberdeen: author		
262. L: Cadell		
263. L: A. Strahan and Cadell	1786: Burnet, W. Colles, Moncrieffe, Exshaw II, L. White, Byrne, Cash, Marchbank, M'Kenzie, J. Moore, J. Jones (8°3v) £1.2s.9d.	
264. L: author; sold at No. 13, Castle-street, Leicester-Square		1787: Cist (8°, abridged) (unabridged 1791: Hall, 8°)
265. L: author; sold at No. 13, Castle-street, Leicester-Square		
266. L: A. Strahan and Cadell		1794: Providence, RI—Carter & Wilkinson (8°)
267. E: Creech/Cadell (printed in Aberdeen)		
268. E: author; printed by the Apollo Press		
269. L: Walter, Faulder, W. Richardson/Gordon and Elliot/Dunlop & Wilson in Glasgow		

(*continued*)

Table 2 (*continued*)

	Imprint Date	Author	First British Edition: Title/(Format/Volumes)/ Price/Topic/Popularity Rating
270.	1787?	[Henry Mackenzie* et al.]	*The Lounger. A Periodical Paper, Published at Edinburgh in the Years 1785 and 1786* (2°) 10s.6d. MISC gs
271.	1787	John Millar*	*An Historical View of the English Government, from the Settlement of the Saxons in Britain to the Accession of the House of Stewart* (4°) £1.1s. HIST ms
272.	1787	John Pinkerton	*A Dissertation on the Origin and Progress of the Scythians or Goths* (8°) 3s.6d. brds. HIST ps
273.	1788	John Brown	*The Elements of Medicine* (8°2v) (trans. of 1784 Latin original) MED ms
274.	1788	Adam Dickson	*The Husbandry of the Ancients* (8°2v) 12s. brds. (subscription price) −14s. AGR ps
275.	1788	Thomas Reid*	*Essays on the Active Powers of Man* (4°) £1.1s. PHIL ms
276.	1788	[William Thomson]	*Memoirs of the Late War in Asia* (8°2v) MIL ms
277.	1788	[William Thomson]	*A Tour in England and Scotland, in 1785* (8°) TRAV ms
278.	1788–90	Donald Monro	*A Treatise on Medical and Pharmaceutical Chymistry, and the Materia Medica* (8°4v) £1.7s. MED ps
279.	1788 [–present]	Royal Society of Edinburgh (ed. John Playfair et al.)	*Transactions of the Royal Society of Edinburgh* (4°) £1.5s. brds. per vol. SCI n/a
280.	1789	George Campbell*	*The Four Gospels, Translated from the Greek. With Preliminary Dissertations, and Notes Critical and Explanatory* (4°2v) £2.2 brds.–£2.10s. REL ps

Table 2 *(continued)*

	Place and Publisher(s) of the First British Edition	First Irish Edition *(Dublin): Date/Publisher/ (Format/Volumes)/Price (if known)*	First American Edition: Date/Place *(Philadelphia unless otherwise noted)/ Publisher/(Format/ Volumes)*
270.	E: **Creech** (from 2nd ed. add **Strahan and Cadell**)	1787: **W. Colles, Burnet, Moncrieffe, Gilbert, Exshaw II,** Burton, **L. White, Byrne, H. Whitestone,** W. Porter, Heery, **M'Kenzie, J. Moore,** Dornin (12°3v) 9s.9d.	1789: New York—S. Campbell (17cm. 2v) "sixth ed." (i.e., reprint of the 4th London/Edinburgh ed. of 1788)
271.	L: **A. Strahan and Cadell, Murray**	1789: **Grueber & M'Allister** (8°) 7s.7d.	
272.	L: Nicol		
273.	L: **Johnson**		1790: **Dobson** (8°)
274.	E: Dickson, **Creech/ G. Robinson, Cadell**		
275.	E: **Bell/G. G. J. & J. Robinson**	1790: **Byrne,** Milliken (8°) 6s.6d.	1793: **Young** (see no. 255 above)
276.	L: author; sold by **Murray**		
277.	L: **G. G. J. & J. Robinson**		
278.	Vols. 1–3 (1788)—L: **Cadell;** vol. 4 (1790)—L: **Cadell** as *Appendix or Supplement*		
279.	Vol. 1 (1788)—L: **Cadell;** vol. 2 (1790)—E: **Cadell**/Dickson; vol. 3 (1794)—E: **Cadell**/Dickson, **E. Balfour;** vol. 4 (1798)—E: **Cadell & Davies**/Dickson, **E. Balfour**		
280.	L: **A. Strahan and Cadell**		1796: **Dobson** (4°)

(continued)

Table 2 (continued)

	Imprint Date	Author	First British Edition: Title/(Format/Volumes)/ Price/Topic/Popularity Rating
281.	1789	William Cullen*	*A Treatise of the Materia Medica* (4°2v) £2.2s. brds. MED ps
282.	1789	John Gillies*	*A View of the Reign of Frederick II of Prussia* (8°) 7s. HIST ps
283.	1789	William Leechman	*Sermons, by William Leechman, D. . . . To Which Is Prefixed Some Account of the Author's Life, and of His Lectures, by James Wodrow** (8°2v) 12s.–14s. REL ps
284.	1789	[John Moore]*	*Zeluco. Various Views of Human Nature, Taken from Life and Manners, Foreign and Domestic* (8°2v) 14s. FICT gs
285.	1789	John Pinkerton	*An Enquiry into the History of Scotland Preceding the Reign of Malcom III. or the Year 1056* (8°2v) 12s.–14s. HIST ms
286.	1789	[William Thomson]	*Mammuth; or, Human Nature Displayed on a Grand Scale: in a Tour with the Tinkers, into the Inland Parts of Africa* (12°2v) 6s. FICT ps
287.	1790	Archibald Alison	*Essays on the Nature and Principles of Taste* (4°) 16s. brds. ARTS gs
288.	1790	James Bruce	**Travels to Discover the Source of the Nile, in the Years 1768, 1769, 1770, 1771, 1772, and 1773** (4°5v) £5.5s. TRAV bs

Table 2 (*continued*)

Place and Publisher(s) of the First British Edition	First Irish Edition (Dublin): Date/Publisher/ (Format/Volumes)/Price (if known)	First American Edition: Date/Place (Philadelphia unless otherwise noted)/ Publisher/(Format/ Volumes)
281. E: **Elliot/Elliot & Kay**	1789: **L. White** (8°2v) 15s.2d.	1789: Crukshank, **R. Campbell;** New York—Hodge, S. Campbell, & Allen (8°2v)
282. L: **A. Strahan and Cadell**	1789: **H. Chamberlaine, Byrne, J. Moore, J. Jones, Grueber & McAllister, W. Jones** (8°) 6s.6d.	
283. L: **A. Strahan and Cadell/ E. Balfour, Creech**		
284. L: **A. Strahan and Cadell**	*1789: 1. **Grueber & M'Allister** (12°2v); and 2. **L. White, Byrne, Grueber, W. Jones** (8°2v) 6s.6d.	1790: New York— Hodge, Allen, & S. Campbell (12°2v)
285. L: Nicol/**Bell**		
286. L: **Murray** (also L: G. & T. Wilkie)		
287. E: **G. G. J. & G. Robinson/ Bell & Bradfute**	1790: **Byrne, J. Moore, Grueber & M'Allister, W. Jones,** R. White (8°) 5s.5d.	
288. E: **G. G. J. & J. Robinson** [**/sold by Creech**]	1790–91: **Wogan, L. White, Byrne,** W. Porter, **Sleater I, J. Jones, J. Moore,** Dornin, Lewis, **W. Jones,** Draper, Milliken, R. White (8°6v) £2.5s.6d.	1790: New York— Berry & Rogers (12°); reprint of Samuel Shaw's one-vol. London abridgment: *An Interesting Narrative of the Travels of James Bruce, Esq., into Abyssinia, to Discover the Source of the Nile*

(*continued*)

Table 2 (*continued*)

	Imprint Date	Author	First British Edition: Title/(Format/Volumes)/ Price/Topic/Popularity Rating
289.	1790	[William Richardson]*	*The Indians, a Tragedy* (8°) DRAM ps
290.	1790–91	John Logan (ed. Hugh Blair*)	*Sermons** (8°2v) 12s. brds. REL gs
291.	1790–93	James Beattie*	*Elements of Moral Science* (8°2v) 15s. PHIL ms
292.	1790–99	William Smellie*	*The Philosophy of Natural History* (4°2v); vol. 1, £1.1s. brds.–£1.4s.; vol. 2*, £1.1s. brds. SCI ps
293.	1791	Alexander Adam*	**Roman Antiquities; or, An Account of the Manners and Customs of the Romans** (12°) 5s. HIST bs
294.	1791	Walter Anderson	*The Philosophy of Ancient Greece Investigated, in Its Origin and Progress, to the Areas of its Greatest Celebrity, in the Ionian, Italic, and Athenian Schools* (4°) £1.8s. PHIL ps
295.	1791	James Boswell	**The Life of Samuel Johnson, LL.D.** (4°2v) £2.8s. BIOG bs

Table 2 (*continued*)

Place and Publisher(s) of the First British Edition	First Irish Edition (Dublin): Date/Publisher/ (Format/Volumes)/Price (if known)	First American Edition: Date/Place (Philadelphia unless otherwise noted)/ Publisher/(Format/ Volumes)
289.	L: **C. Dilly**	1791: **Wogan, Byrne, J. Jones, McKenzie,** Corbet, **Grueber, W. Jones, Rice** (12°) [6½d.]	
290.	E: **Bell & Bradfute/ G. G. J. & J. Robinson**		
291.	E: **Cadell/Creech**	1790, vol. 1 only: **Chamberlaine & Rice, Wogan, Byrne, M'Kenzie, J. Moore, Gru[e]ber & M'Allister, W. Jones,** R. White, Milliken (8°) 6s.6d.	1792–94: **Carey** (12°2v)
292.	Vol. 1—E: heirs of Charles Elliot/Elliot & Kay, **Cadell, G. G. J. & J. Robinsons** [*sic*]; vol. 2—E: **Bell & Bradfute,** Dickson, **Creech, E. Balfour,** Hill, Lawrie, Manners & Miller, Jack, A. Smellie/**G. G. & J. Robinson, Cadell & Davies,** Kay	1790, vol. 1 only: **Chamberlaine & Rice, W. Wilson, Wogan, L. White, Byrne, McKenzie, J. Moore, Grueber & McAllister, W. Jones,** R. White, Milliken (8°) 13s.	1791: **R. Campbell** (8°) (vol. 1 only; first American ed. of two-vol. set: Dover, NH, 1808)
293.	E: **A. Strahan and Cadell/Creech**		
294.	E: [author?]; printed by Smellie/sold by **C. Dilly, G. G. J. & J. Robinson, Johnson, Murray,** T. Payne II, Nicol, Debrett, Clarke		
295.	L: **C. Dilly** [author]	1792: R. Cross, **W. Wilson, Byrne, Grueber, J. Moore, J. Jones, M'Kenzie, W. Jones,** M'Allister, R. White, **Rice,** Draper (8°3v) £1.2s.9d.	

(*continued*)

Table 2 (*continued*)

	Imprint Date	Author	First British Edition: Title/(Format/Volumes)/ Price/Topic/Popularity Rating
296.	1791	George Fordyce	*A Treatise on the Digestion of Food* (8°) 3s.6d. brds. MED ms
297.	1791	{Robert Heron}	*Scotland Delineated, or a Geographical Description of Every Shire in Scotland* (8°) 6s. TRAV ms
298.	1791	⌜Sir⌝ James Mackintosh	*Vindiciae Gallicae: Defence of the French Revolution and its English Admirers against the Accusations of the Right Hon. Edmund Burke* (8°) 5s. sewed POL gs
299.	1791	William Robertson*	**An Historical Disquisition concerning the Knowledge which the Ancients Had of India** (4°) 18s. HIST bs
300.	1791	{Alexander Fraser Tytler, later Lord Woodhouselee}*	*Essay on the Principles of Translation* (8°) 4s. brds.–5s. brds. LIT ms
301.	1791–99	Sir John Sinclair* (superintended by Robert Heron)	*The Statistical Account of Scotland* (8°21v) 6s. per vol. brds.–9s. MISC ms
302.	1792	D⌜avid⌝ S⌜tewart Erskine⌝, Earl of Buchan	*Essays on the Lives and Writings of Fletcher of Saltoun and the Poet Thomson: Biographical, Critical, and Political* (8°) BIOG ps
303.	1792	Adam Ferguson*	*Principles of Moral and Political Science: Being Chiefly a Retrospect of Lectures Delivered in the College of Edinburgh* (4°2v) £2.2s. PHIL ps
304.	1792	James Gregory*	*Philosophical and Literary Essays* (8°2v) 12s. brds. PHIL ps
305.	1792	Alexander Hamilton	*A Treatise on the Management of Female Complaints, and of Children in Early Infancy* (8°) 6s. brds. MED ms

Table 2 (*continued*)

Place and Publisher(s) of the First British Edition	First Irish Edition (Dublin): Date/Publisher/ (Format/Volumes)/Price (if known)	First American Edition: Date/Place (Philadelphia unless otherwise noted)/ Publisher/(Format/ Volumes)
296. L: **Johnson**		
297. E: J. Neill; sold by **Bell & Bradfute, Creech/G. G. J. & J. Robinson**		
298. L: **G. G. J. & J. Robinson**	1791: R. Cross, **Burnet, Wogan, Byrne, J. Moore, Grueber, W. Jones,** R. White, **Rice,** M'Allister (8°)	1792: **Young** (8°)
299. L: **A. Strahan and Cadell/ E. Balfour**	1791: **Burnet, L. White, Wogan, Byrne, Grueber,** W. Porter, **J. Moore, J. Jones,** Dornin, **W. Jones,** R. White, **Rice,** M'Allister, A. Porter, P. Moore (8°) 7s.7d.	1792: **Young** (8°)
300. L: **Cadell/Creech**		
301. E: printed and sold by **Creech** (also sold by J. Donaldson, Guthrie/**Cadell,** Stockdale, Debrett, Sewel/Dunlop & Wilson in Glasgow/Angus & Son in Aberdeen)		
302. L: Debrett		
303. E: **A. Strahan and Cadell/Creech**		
304. E: sold by **Cadell/Creech**		
305. E: Hill/**Murray**		1792: New York—S. Campbell (12°)

(*continued*)

Table 2 (*continued*)

	Imprint Date	Author	First British Edition: Title/(Format/Volumes)/ Price/Topic/Popularity Rating
306.	1792	James Hutton	*Dissertations on Different Subjects in Natural Philosophy* (4°) £1.5s. SCI ps
307.	1792 [–present]	Society of the Anti-quaries of Scotland	*Transactions of the Society of the Antiquaries of Scotland . . . Volume I* (4°) £1.1s. brds. HIST n/a
308.	1792	Thomas Somerville	*The History of Political Transactions and of Parties, from the Restoration to the Death of King William* (4°) £1.5s. brds. HIST ps
309.	1792	Dugald Stewart*	*Elements of the Philosophy of the Human Mind* (4°) £1.5s. PHIL gs
310.	1792	John Walker	*Institutes of Natural History* (8°) 2s.6d. SCI ps
311.	1793	Matthew Baillie	*The Morbid Anatomy of Some of the Most Important Parts of the Human Body* (8°) MED gs
312.	1793	Benjamin Bell	*A Treatise on Gonorrhoea Virulenta and Lues Venerea* (8°2v) 14s. MED ms
313.	1793	[John Bruce]	*Historical View of Plans, for the Government of British India, and Regulation of Trade to the East Indies* (4°) £1.1s. ECON ps
314.	1793	Robert Heron	*Observations Made in a Journey through the Western Counties of Scotland* (8°2v) 12s. brds. TRAV ms
315.	1793	John Moore*	*A Journal during a Residence in France, from the Beginning of August, to the Middle of December, 1792* (8°2v); vol. 1, 7s. brds.–8s. brds.; vol. 2, 9s.6d. POL ms
316.	1793	John Ogilvie*	*The Theology of Plato, compared with the Principles of Oriental and Grecian Philosophers* (8°) 4s.6d.–5s. PHIL ps
317.	1793	Thomas Robertson	*The History of Mary Queen of Scots* (4°) 15s.–18s. HIST ms
318.	1793	William Russell	*The History of Ancient Europe, with a View of the Revolutions in Asia and Africa* (8°2v) 12s. brds. HIST ps

Table 2 (*continued*)

Place and Publisher(s) of the First British Edition	First Irish Edition (*Dublin*): *Date/Publisher/* (*Format/Volumes*)/*Price* (*if known*)	First American Edition: *Date/Place* (*Philadelphia unless otherwise noted*)/ *Publisher/*(*Format/* *Volumes*)
306. E: **A. Strahan and Cadell**		
307. E: **Creech/Cadell**		
308. L: **A. Strahan and Cadell**	1793: **Byrne, W. Jones, Rice** (8°)	
309. E: **A. Strahan and Cadell/ Creech** (vol. 2, 1814; vol. 3, 1827)		1793: **Young** (8°)
310. E: printed by Stewart, Ruthven, & Co.		
311. L: **Johnson** (also L: **Johnson**, and Nicol)		1795: Albany, NY— Spencer (8°)
312. E: Watson, Mudie/**Murray**	1793: **W. Jones** (8°2v)	1795: **R. Campbell** (8°2v)
313. L: Sewell, Debrett (also issued with no place of publication or publisher in the imprint)		
314. Perth: R. Morison & Son/**Bell & Bradfute**/Vernor & Hood		
315. L: **G. G. J. & J. Robinson** [**/Bell & Bradfute**]	1793: 1. **J. Moore** (12°2v); and 2. **Byrne,** Dugdale, **W. Jones, J. Jones,** Colbert, **Rice** (12°2v) 2s.8½d.	1793–94: Baltimore— H. & P. Rice, and J. Rice & Co. (12°2v)
316. L: Deighton		
317. E: **Bell & Bradfute/ G. G. J. & J. Robinson**		
318. L: **G. G. J. & J. Robinson**		

(*continued*)

Table 2 (*continued*)

	Imprint Date	Author	First British Edition: Title/(Format/Volumes)/ Price/Topic/Popularity Rating
319.	1793	Sir John Sinclair*	*Specimens of Statistical Reports; Exhibiting the Progress of Political Society, from the Pastoral State, to that of Luxury and Refinement* (8°) ECON ps
320.	1793	{Dugald Stewart}*	*Outlines of Moral Philosophy* (8°) 5s.–6s. PHIL gs
321.	1794	Alexander Adam*	*A Summary of Geography and History, Both Ancient and Modern* (8°) 9s. HIST gs
322.	1794	Benjamin Bell	*A Treatise on the Hydrocele, or Sarcocele, of Cancer, and Other Diseases of the Testes* (8°) 4s. brds. MED ps
323.	1794	George Chalmers	*The Life of Thomas Ruddiman* (8°) 7s. brds. BIOG ps
324.	1794	George Fordyce	*A Dissertation on Simple Fever* (8°) MED ms
325.	1794	John Hunter*	*A Treatise on the Blood** (4°) £1.16s. MED ms
326.	1794	William Hunter (ed. Matthew Baillie)	*An Anatomical Description of the Human Gravid Uterus, and Its Contents* (4°) (meant to accompany Hunter's elephant folio [1°] pictorial vol. of 1774, *Anatomia uteri humani gravidi tabulis illustrata*) MED ps
327.	1794	James Hutton	*An Investigation of the Principles of Knowledge, and of the Progress of Reason, from Sense to Science and Philosophy* (4°3v) £3.15s. brds. PHIL ps
328.	1794	James Hutton	*A Dissertation upon the Philosophy of Light, Heat, and Fire* (8°) 6s. brds. SCI ps
329.	1794	William Julius Mickle*	*Poems, and a Tragedy** (4°) 15s. POET gs
330.	1794–99	Robert Heron	*A New General History of Scotland* (8°5v) £2.2s. (advertised as 6 vols.) HIST ps
331.	1795	George Fordyce	*A Second Dissertation on Fever* (8°) MED ms
332.	1795	James Hutton	*Theory of the Earth, with Proofs and Illustrations* (8°2v) 14s. brds. SCI ps
333.	1795	John Moore*	*A View of the Causes and Progress of the French Revolution* (8°2v) 16s. POL ms

Table 2 (*continued*)

Place and Publisher(s) of the First British Edition	First Irish Edition (Dublin): Date/Publisher/ (Format/Volumes)/Price (if known)	First American Edition: Date/Place (Philadelphia unless otherwise noted)/ Publisher/(Format/ Volumes)
319. L: **Cadell,** Debrett, Sewell		
320. E: **Creech/Cadell**		
321. E: **A. Strahan and Cadell/Bell & Bradfute, Creech;** also E: **Cadell & A. Strahan**		
322. E: **Bell & Bradfute/ G. G. J. & J. Robinson, Murray**		
323. L: Stockdale/Laing		
324. L: **Johnston** (i.e., **Johnson**)		
325. L: Nicol		1796: Bradford (8°2v)
326. L: Nicol		
327. E: **A. Strahan and Cadell**		
328. E: **Cadell & Davies**		
329. L: Egerton; W. Richardson/ Fletcher & Hanwell in Oxford (also issued without Hanwell)		
330. Perth: R. Morison & Son/ Vernor & Hood		
331. L: **Johnson**		
332. E: **Cadell & Davies/Creech**		
333. L: **G. G. J. & J. Robinson**	1795: **J. Jones,** Halpin, Butler, P. Moore,	

(*continued*)

Table 2 (*continued*)

Imprint Date	Author	First British Edition: Title/(Format/Volumes)/ Price/Topic/Popularity Rating
334. 1795	Euclid/John Playfair	[Euclid's] *Elements of Geometry* (8°) 6s.(with Playfair's "Elements of Plane and Spherical Trigonometry") 6s. brds. SCI gs
335. 1795	Sir John Sinclair*	*General View of the Agriculture of the Northern Counties and Islands of Scotland; . . . with Observations on the Means of Their Improvement* (4°) AGR ps
336. 1795	Adam Smith* (ed. Joseph Black* and James Hutton)	*Essays on Philosophical Subjects** (4°) 15s. brds. PHIL ps
337. 1796	William Buchan	*Observations concerning the Prevention and Cure of the Venereal Disease* (8°) 3s.6d. sewed MED ms
338. 1796	Eliza[beth] Hamilton	*Translation of the Letters of a Hindoo Rajah; . . . To which is prefixed a Preliminary Dissertation on the History, Religion, and Manners, of the Hindoos* (8°2v) 12s. FICT gs
339. 1796	Robert Heron	*A Philosophical View of Universal History* (8°) HIST ps
340. 1796	[John Moore]*	*Edward. Various Views of Human Nature, Taken from Life and Manners, Chiefly in England* (8°2v) 18s. FICT ms
341. 1796	William Robertson*	*The History of America. Books IX and X. Containing the History of Virginia, to the Year 1688, and the History of New England, to the Year 1652** (4° and 8°) HIST n/a
342. 1796	[William Thomson]	*Letters from Scandinavia, on the Past and Present State of the Northern Nations of Europe* (8°2v) POL ps

Table 2 (*continued*)

Place and Publisher(s) of the First British Edition	First Irish Edition (Dublin): Date/Publisher/ (Format/Volumes)/Price (if known)	First American Edition: Date/Place (Philadelphia unless otherwise noted)/ Publisher/(Format/ Volumes)
	Byrne, Wogan, W. Jones, Rice, J. Moore (12°2v)	
334. E: **Bell & Bradfute/G. G. & J. Robinson**		
335. L: printed by Macrae		
336. L: **Cadell & Davies/Creech**	1795: **Wogan, Byrne, J. Moore,** Colbert, **Rice, W. Jones,** [W.] Porter, Folingsby (8°)	
337. L: author; sold by Chapman/ Mudie & Sons (also issued with Chapman and Mudie as sole publishers)	1796: **Wogan,** Milliken, **Sleater II, Rice,** P. Moore (8°)	
338. L: **G. G. & J. Robinson**	1797: Colbert (12°2v)	
339. E: R. Morison & Son		
340. L: **A. Strahan, and Cadell & Davies**	1797: **Wogan, Byrne, J. Moore, Rice, W. Watson & Son,** Dugdale, P. Moore, Milliken, Colbert, W. Porter, Fitzpatrick, Kelly, Folingsby (12°2v)	1798: Mount Pleasant, NY—Judah (12°2v)
341. L: **A. Strahan, and Cadell & Davies**		1799: Humphreys (8°)
342. L: **G. G. & J. Robinson**		

(*continued*)

Table 2 (*continued*)

	Imprint Date	Author	First British Edition: Title/(Format/Volumes)/ Price/Topic/Popularity Rating
343.	1797	John Gillies*	*Aristotle's Ethics and Politics, Comprising His Practical Philosophy, Translated from the Greek. Illustrated by Introductions and Notes; the Critical History of His Life, and a New Analysis of His Speculative Work* (4°2v) £2.2s. brds. PHIL ms
344.	1797	Alexander Monro II*	*Three Treatises. On the Brain, the Eye and the Ear* (4°) £2.5s. brds. MED ps
345.	1797	John Pinkerton	*The History of Scotland from the Accession of the House of Stuart to That of Mary* (4°2v) £2.10s. HIST ps
346.	1798	Thomas Somerville	*The History of Great Britain during the Reign of Queen Anne* (4°) £1.5s. brds. HIST ps
347.	1798	William Thomson	*An Enquiry into the Elementary Principles of Beauty, in the Works of Nature and Art* (4°) ARTS ps
348.	1798–99	George Fordyce	*A Third Dissertation on Fever. Part I* (pt. 2 published in 1799) (8°) MED ms
349.	1798[–1812]	[Joanna Baillie]	*A Series of Plays: In Which It Is Attempted to Delineate the Stronger Passions of the Mind. Each Passion Being the Subject of a Tragedy and a Comedy* (8°3v) DRAM gs
350.	1799	Mungo Park	**Travels in the Interior Districts of Africa: Performed under the Direction and Patronage of the African Association, in the Years 1795, 1796, and 1797** (4°) £1.11s.6d. TRAV bs
351.	1799[–1802]	James Anderson, ed.	*Recreations in Agriculture, Natural-History, Arts, and Miscellaneous Literature* (8°6v) AGR ps
352.	1799[–1803]	Matthew Baillie	*A Series of Engravings, Accompanied with Explanations, which Are Intended to Illustrate the Morbid Anatomy of Some of the Most Important Parts of the Human Body* (4°) MED ms
353.	1799[–1824]	Henry Mackenzie*	*Prize Essays and Transactions of the Highland Society of Scotland* (8°) ECON n/a

Table 2 (*continued*)

Place and Publisher(s) of the First British Edition	*First Irish Edition (Dublin): Date/Publisher/ (Format/Volumes)/Price (if known)*	*First American Edition: Date/Place (Philadelphia unless otherwise noted)/ Publisher/(Format/ Volumes)*
343. L: **A. Strahan, Cadell & Davies**		
344. E: **Bell & Bradfute/ G. G. & J. Robinson; Johnson**		
345. L: **C. Dilly**		
346. L: **A. Strahan, Cadell & Davies**		
347. L: **Johnson**		
348. L: **Johnson**		
349. L: **Cadell & Davies;** vol. 2 (1802), vol. 3 (1812)		
350. L: author; sold by G. & W. Nicol		1800: Humphreys (8°)
351. L: sold by Wallis, R. H. Evans		
352. L: **Johnson,** Nicol & Nicol		
353. Vol. 1 (1799)—E: **Cadell & Davies/Creech** (five more vols. published in the nineteenth century)		

(*continued*)

Table 2 (*continued*)

	Imprint Date	Author	First British Edition: Title/(Format/Volumes)/ Price/Topic/Popularity Rating
354.	1800	Alexander Adam*	*Classical Biography* (8°) 8s. BIOG gs
355.	1800	George Campbell*	*Lectures on Ecclesiastical History* (8°2v) REL ms
356.	1800	William Cullen*	*Nosology: or, A Systematic Arrangement of Diseases, by Classes, Orders, Genera, and Species* (8°) (trans. of 1769 Latin original) MED gs
357.	1800	{Elizabeth Hamilton}	*Memoirs of Modern Philosophers* (8°3v) 18s. FICT gs
358.	1800	Malcolm Laing	*The History of Scotland, from the Union of the Crowns on the Accession of James VI . . . to the Union of the Kingdoms in the Reign of Queen Anne* (8°2v) 18s. HIST ms
359.	1800	[John Moore]*	*Mordaunt. Sketches of Life, Character, and Manners in Various Countries* (8°3v) FICT ps
360.	1800	William Smellie*	*Literary and Characteristical Lives of John Gregory, Lord Kames, David Hume, and Adam Smith* (8°) 8s. BIOG ps

Table 2 (*continued*)

Place and Publisher(s) of the First British Edition	First Irish Edition (Dublin): Date/Publisher/ (Format/Volumes)/Price (if known)	First American Edition: Date/Place (Philadelphia unless otherwise noted)/ Publisher/(Format/ Volumes)
354. E: **Creech/Cadell & Davies**		
355. L: **Johnson**/Brown in Aberdeen		
356. E: **Creech**/sold by **Robinsons,** Kay, Cox		1792: Hartford, CT— Thomas (8°, abridged trans. of the fourth ed. [1785] of Cullen's *Synopsis Nosologiae Methodicae,* originally published in Edinburgh in 1769, titled *Synopsis and Nosology*); unabridged 1793: Hall; *A Synopsis of Methodical Nosology* (8°)
357. Bath: **G. G. & J. Robinson**	1800: **Wogan, Burnett, Gilbert & Hodges,** Brown, **Rice,** [W.] Porter, Dornin, Folingsby, Fitzpatrick (12°2v)	
358. L: **Cadell & Davies**/Manners & Miller		
359. L: **G. G. & J. Robinson**	1800: **W. Watson & Son, Burnet, Wogan, Byrne,** Colbert, W. Porter, **M'Kenzie,** Dugdale, **W. Jones, Rice,** Fitzpatrick, Kelly, Folingsby, Stockdale, Mercier & Co., P. Moore, J. Parry (12°3v)	
360. E: printed and sold by A. Smellie, **Bell & Bradfute,** Dickson, **Creech, E. Balfour,** Hill, Simpson, Laing, Lawrie, Manners & Miller, J. Ogle, Guthrie, Constable, Jack, Gray/**G. G. & J. Robinson, Cadell & Davies,** Kay, R. Ogle		

Sources: Bibliographical information has been drawn from on-line searches of ESTC from 1997 through January 2006, and from examinations of copies of books, facsimile reprints, and microform copies in the Eighteenth Century microfilm series. Data on book prices have been obtained from booksellers' advertisements; book reviews in periodicals; *A New and Correct Catalogue of All the English Books which Have Been Printed from the Year 1700, to the Present Time, with Their Prices* (London, 1767); [William Bent], *The London Catalogue of Books* (London, 1791); and other sources.

Notes:

Imprint Date column: Date(s) indicate the imprint year(s) as given on the title page of first editions. The actual years of publication may vary from the imprint years, since books published in December, and sometimes November, commonly bore the imprint of the following year, and books published in January or February occasionally bore the imprint of the preceding year. Square brackets ([ ]) indicate the portion of a book that was published before or after the period 1746–1800.

Author column: Names followed by an asterisk (*) are the authors identified by Smollett, Creech, and Alves, as listed in table 1. Square brackets ([ ]) around an author's name indicate that the work was published anonymously (true anonymity); curly brackets ({ }) around an author's name indicate that the author's name is discernable from the book (e.g., from a signed preface or dedication, or from a reference to another book that contains the author's name, or from the text itself), although the name does not appear on the title page (mitigated anonymity), or they indicate that the author's name was added to a second or third edition of a work that was originally published without it (temporary anonymity); angle brackets (< >) around an author's name indicate that the work was written under a pseudonym. M.D. differentiates the William Smellie who wrote on midwifery in London from the William Smellie who was a printer in Edinburgh.

First British Edition column: An asterisk (*) indicates a posthumous publication. Formats are recorded as follows: 2° = folio; 4° = quarto; 8° = octavo; 12° = duodecimo. The number of volumes appears as a numeral immediately following the format abbreviation, followed by a "v," and includes the first editions of additional volumes published later in the eighteenth century. Prices (when known) signify bound books unless otherwise noted. When books were sold mainly in loose sheets (quires), or sewed, or in boards (brds.), that information has been recorded. Price disparities (which may represent typographical errors, regional variations, or actual price changes, among other possibilities) are separated by a dash (e.g., 4s.–5s.).

A topic has been assigned to each book from among the twenty subject categories in Zachs, *First John Murray,* 254. These are as follows: AGR = agriculture; ARTS = arts; BIOG = biography; DRAM = drama; ECON = economics; EDUC = education; FICT = fiction; HIST = history; LANG = language; LAW = law; LIT = literary criticism (including rhetoric); MED = medicine; MIL = military; MISC = miscellaneous; PHIL = philosophy; POET = poetry; POL = politics; REL = religion; SCI = science (including mathematics): and TRAV = travel and topography.

A popularity rating has been assigned to each book on the basis of the number of editions (including abridgments, works appearing in anthologies or collections, and pirated editions) published in Britain through 1810 (or through 1820 for books originally published after 1790), as recorded in table 4: bs = bestseller (10 or more editions); ss = strong seller (7–9 editions); gs = good seller (4–6 editions); ms = modest seller (2–3 editions); ps = poor seller (never reprinted);

and n/a = not applicable (applied to books that were incorporated into other books in the list, or to works not normally reprinted, such as society proceedings or transactions). These ratings have sometimes been adjusted to account for print runs and special circumstances related to large, multivolume works. Boldface type indicates a British bestseller.

British Publishers column: The primary city of printing and (usually) publication, as shown in the imprint of the first edition, appears first, abbreviated as L = London and E = Edinburgh. A city in square brackets ([ ]) indicates the assumed place of printing/publication. The names of publishers (or in some cases, the selling agents, set off in the imprint and in the table by the phrase "sold by") follow the primary city of printing/publication, the words "printed for" being assumed; boldface type indicates the principal publishers identified in table 5. Ampersands (&) signify publishing partnerships. Slashes (/) separate copublishers or selling agents operating in different cities (London or Edinburgh should be assumed unless otherwise noted). An author appears as the publisher when an imprint states that a work has been printed "for the author." Square brackets ([ ]) around the name of a publisher or a selling agent indicate information drawn from a source other than the imprint, such as publishers' records, correspondence, or a contemporary book review. Only the surnames of publishers and selling agents are given except when first-name initials are required for clarity. The names Balfour, Cadell, and Strahan signify John Balfour, Sr., Thomas Cadell, Sr., and William Strahan unless otherwise noted. The names of printers, set off in the imprint and the table by the phrase "printed by," are included only in the absence of adequate information about publishers other than authors.

First Irish Edition column: An asterisk (*) denotes a Dublin bestseller. Boldface type indicates the principal Scottish Enlightenment publishers and publishing firms identified in table 6.

First American Edition column: All imprints are Philadelphia unless otherwise noted. The names of the six primary publishers in chapters 8 and 9 appear in boldface type.

Index of Publishers in Table 2

Numbers correspond to the books listed in table 2. Square brackets around book numbers indicate books whose publishing involvement is known from a source other than the imprint or books that were reprinted as parts of other books. Boldface type indicates featured publishers.

ENGLAND

Cambridge

Merril, T. & J.: Thomas Merrill and John Merrill (no. 131)

London

Baldwin: Robert Baldwin (nos. 54, 67, 72, 89, 96, 112)

Becket: Thomas Becket or Beckett (nos. 65, 154, 193) (see also Becket & de Hondt)

Becket & de Hondt: Thomas Becket or Beckett and Peter Abraham de Hondt (nos. 71, 80, 83, 91, 107, 108, 114, 116, 118, 121, 126, 133, 136, 161) (see also Becket)

Becket & Nichol: not traced (no. 121)

Bew: John Bew (no. 175)

Bowen: Joseph Bowen (no. 223)

Burnet: George Burnet or Burnett (no. 87)

Cadell: Thomas Cadell, Sr. (nos. 97, 109, 121, 133, 135, 144, 147, 152, 160, 171, 172, 175, 176, 179, 181, 182, 187, 189, 204, 205, 216, 222, 228, 233, [234], 251, 256, 262, 267, 274, 278, 279, 291, 292, 300, 301, 304, 307, 319, 320) (see also Millar & Cadell; Strahan & Cadell; Strahan, A., & Cadell)

Cadell & Davies: Thomas Cadell, Jr., and William Davies (nos. 204, 279, 292, 328, 332, 336, 349, 353, 354, 358, 360) (see also Strahan, A., and Cadell & Davies)

Chapman: Thomas Chapman (no. 337)

Clarke: William Clarke (no. 294)

Collins: Benjamin Collins (no. 89)

Coote: John Coote (nos. 78, 81, 89)

Cox: Thomas Cox (no. 356)

Crowder: Stanley Crowder/Crowder and Co. (nos. 81, 89, 112)

Davie & Law: not traced (no. 65)

Davies: Thomas Davies (no. 81)

Debrett: John Debrett (nos. 241, 294, 301, 302, 313, 319)

Deighton: John Deighton (no. 316)

Dilly, C.: Charles Dilly (nos. 121, 211, 221, 223, 250, 289, 294, 295, 345) (see also Dilly, E. & C.)

Dilly, E.: Edward Dilly (no. 109) (see also Dilly, E. & C.)

Dilly, E. & C.: Edward and Charles Dilly (nos. 98, 103, 105, 111, 122, 123, 124, 125, 141, 173, 175) (see also Dilly, C.)

Dod: Benjamin Dod (no. 30)

Dodsley, J.: James Dodsley (nos. 90, 93, 109, 208, 245) (see also Dodsley, R. & J.)

Dodsley, R.: Robert Dodsley (nos. 5, 7, 18, 24, [29]) (see also Dodsley, R. and J.)

Dodsley, R. & J.: Robert and James Dodsley (nos. 72, 79) (see also Dodsley, J., and Dodsley, R.)

Draper: Somerset Draper (no. 24)

Durham: Thomas Durham (nos. 86, 132) (see also Wilson & Durham)

Egerton: Thomas Egerton (nos. 234, 329)

Elliot & Kay: **Charles Elliot** and Thomas Kay (nos. 281, 292) (see also Kay; Edinburgh: Elliot)

Elmsley: Peter Elmsley (no. 197)

Evans: Robert Harding Evans (no. 351)

Evans: not traced (no. 175)

Faulder: Robert Faulder (no. 269)

Fielding & Walker: John Fielding and John Walker (no. 194)

Flexney: William Flexney (nos. 149, 175)

Goodsman: David Goodsman (no. 175)

Gretton: John Gretton (no. 81)

Hitch: Charles Hitch [no. 29]

Johnson: Joseph Johnson (nos. 113, 134, 142, 234, 243, 273, 294, 296, 311, 324, 331, 344, 347, 348, 352, 355) (see also Johnson & Payne)

Johnson & Payne: Joseph Johnson and John Payne (no. 113) (see Johnson; Payne, J.)

Johnston: William Johnston (nos. 27, 65, 72, 81, 92, 112, 140)

Johnstone: see Johnston

Kay: Thomas Kay (nos. 292, 356, 360) (see also Elliot & Kay)

Kearsly: George Kearsly (no. 81)

Keith: George Keith (no. 77)

Knapton, J. & P.: John Knapton and Paul Knapton (no. 1)

Knox: John Knox (no. 130) (see also table 1)

Longman: Thomas Longman (nos. [29], 36, 65, 144, 208, 228, 234)

Lowndes: Thomas Lowndes (no. 145)

Macrae (printer): Colin Macrae (no. 335)

Millar: Andrew Millar (nos. 8, 9, 10, 11, 15, 20, 25, 26, 29, 36, 43, 44, 45, 46, 47, 50, 51, 52, 53, 55, 56, 58, 59, 60, 61, 62, 63, 66, 69, 70, 72, 73, 74, 75, 76, 79, 86, 88, 94, 99, 100, 101, 106) (see also Millar & Cadell)

Millar & Cadell: Andrew Millar and Thomas Cadell, Sr. (nos. 93, 99, 100, 101, 106) (see also Cadell; Millar)

Murray: John Murray (nos. 137, 147, 159, 166, 169, 171, 178, 180, 184, 187, 190, 191, 192, 195, 199, 202, 207, 209, 210, 213, 214, 226, 227, 234, 237, 247, 271, 276, 286, 294, 305, 312, 322)

Newbery: John Newbery (nos. 81, 89)

Nicol: George Nicol (nos. 272, 285, 294, 311, 325, 326) (see also Nicol, G. & W.; Nicol & Nicol; Wilson & Nichol/Nicol)

Nicol, G. & W.: George Nicol and William Nicol (no. 350) (see also Nicol; Nicol & Nicol)

Nicol & Nicol: (no. 352) (see also Nicol; Nicol, G. & W.)

Nicoll: William Nicoll (no. 89)

Nourse: John Nourse (nos. 10, 11, 69, 84, 224)

Ogle, R.: Robert Ogle (no. 360)

Osborn[e]: John Osborn[e] (nos. 12, 81)

Owen: William Owen (no. 65)

Payne: John Payne (no. 93) (see also Johnson & Payne)

Payne I, T.: Thomas Payne I (nos. 20, 86)

Payne II, T.: Thomas Payne II (no. 294)

Pearch: George Pearch (no. 131)

Raikes: Robert Raikes (no. 89)

Richardson, J.: Joseph Richardson (nos. 72, 79)

Richardson, W.: William Richardson (nos. 269, 329) (see Richardson & Urquhart)

Richardson & Urquhart: William Richardson and Leonard Urquhart (nos. 149, 175, 235) (see Richardson, W.)

Rivington: John Ribington [no. 29]

Rivington & Fletcher: James Rivington and James Fletcher (no. 49)

Robinson, G.: George Robinson (nos. 157, 165, 203, 209, 218, 239, 240, 242, 274) (see also Robinson, G. G. J. & J.; Robinson & Roberts; Robinsons)

Robinson, G. G. & J. (nos. 315, 333, 334, 338, 342, 344, 356, 357, 359, 360) (see Robinson, G.; Robinson, G. G. J. & J.)

Robinson, G. G. J.: see Robinson, G. G. J. & J.

Robinson, G. G. J. & J. (and variations): George Robinson, George Robinson, John Robinson, and James Robinson
(nos. 172, 249, 252, 253, 254, 255, 275, 277, 287, 288, 290, 292, 294, 297, 298, 315, 317, 318, 322, 333, 334, 338, 342, 344, 357, 359) (see also Robinson, G.; Robinson, G. G. & J.)

Robinson & Roberts: George Robinson and John Roberts (nos. 102, 112, 120) (see also Robinson, G.; Robinson, G. G. & J.; Robinson, G. G. J. & J.)

Robinsons: see Robinson, G. G. J. & J.

Robson: James Robson (nos. 121, 203, 239)

Sandby: William Sandby (no. 109)

Scott: John Scott (no. 65)

Sewell [Sewel]: John Sewell (nos. 203, 239, 244, 301, 313, 319)

Stockdale: John Stockdale (nos. 301, 323)

Strahan: William Strahan as silent partner (nos. [22], [27], [52], [101], [121], [135], [200]) (see also Strahan anad Cadell)

Strahan and Cadell: William Strahan and Thomas Cadell, Sr. (nos. 119, 128, 129, 143, 150, 153, 155, 162, 163, 164, 168, 170, 174, 177, 183, 185, 186, 188, 198, 201, 206, 212, 217, 219, 225, 229, 230, 232, 236, 238, 246, 248) (see also Cadell; Strahan; Strahan, A., and Cadell)

Strahan, A., and Cadell: Andrew Strahan and Thomas Cadell, Sr. (nos. 143, 144, 188, 258, 259, 263, 266, 271, 280, 282, 283, 284, 293, 299, 303, 306, 308, 309, 321, 327) (see also Cadell; Strahan and Cadell; Strahan, A., and Cadell & Davies)

Strahan, A., and Cadell & Davies (nos. 340, 341, 343, 346) (see also Cadell & Davies; Strahan, A., and Cadell)

Tonson, J. & R.: Jacob Tonson and Richard Tonson (no. 24)

Vernor & Hood: Thomas Vernor and Thomas Hood (nos. 314, 330)

Waller: Thomas Waller (no. 32)

Wallis: James Wallis (no. 351)

Wallis & Stonehouse: John Wallis and ? Stonehouse (no. 180)

Walter: John Walter (nos. 203, 220, 244, 269)

Wilkie: John Wilkie (nos. 89, 138)

Wilkie, G. & T.: George Wilkie and Thomas Wilkie (no. 286)

Wilson, D.: David Wilson (nos. 16, 20, 22, 65, 82, 86) (see also Wilson & Durham; Wilson & Nichol/Nicol)

Wilson & Durham: David Wilson and Thomas Durham (nos. 22, 37, [40], 66) (see also Durham; Wilson; Wilson & Nichol/Nicol)

Wilson & Fell: Jacob Wilson and Isaac Fell (no. 89)

Wilson & Nichol/Nicol: David Wilson and George Nicol (nos. 121, 132) (see also Nicol; Nicol,
    G. & W.; Nicol & Nicol; Wilson; Wilson & Durham)
Withy: Robert Withy (no. 89)

Oxford

Fletcher & Hanwell: James Fletcher and William Hanwell (no. 329)
Prince: Daniel Prince (no. 131)

Salisbury

Collins: Benjamin Collins (no. 140)

SCOTLAND

Aberdeen

Angus & Son: ? (no. 301)
Brown: Alexander Brown (no. 355)

Edinburgh

Apollo Press (printers): John Martin ? (no. 268)
Balfour: John Balfour (nos. 34, 91, 95, 104, 108, 110, 119, 121, 143, 148, 160, 185, 186, 204,
    206) (see also Balfour, J. & E.; Hamilton & Balfour; Hamilton, Balfour, & Neill; Balfour, E.;
    Balfour, Auld & Smellie)
Balfour, J. & E.: James Balfour and Elphinston (or Elphingstone) Balfour
    (nos. 121, 222)
Balfour, E.: Elphinston (or Elphingstone) Balfour (nos. 279, 283, 292, 299, 360) (see also
    Balfour, J. & E.)
Balfour, Auld, & Smellie (printers): John Balfour, William Auld, and William Smellie
    (no. 115)
Balfour & Smellie (printers): John Balfour and William Smellie (no. 151)
Bell: John Bell (nos. 143, 160, 192, 195, 210, 214, 226, 255, 275, 285) (see also Kincaid & Bell;
    Bell & Bradfute)
Bell & Bradfute: John Bell and John Bradfute (nos. 160, 172, 204, 287, 290, 292, 297, 314,
    [315], 317, 321, 322, 334, 344, 360) (see also Bell)
Bell & Macfarquhar: Andrew Bell and Colin Macfarquhar (no. 139)
Constable: Archibald Constable (no. 360)
Creech: William Creech (nos. 121, 141, 143, 162, 163, 164, 166, 172, 173, 174, 176, [177],
    180, 182, 183, 186, 187, 188, 191, 199, 202, 205, 207, 212, 213, 215, 217, 225, 228, 229, 230,
    232, 233, 234, 235, [248], [250], 258, 259, 267, 270, 274, 283, [288], 291, 292, 293, 297,
    300, 301, 303, 304, 307, 309, 320, 321, 332, 336, 353, 354, 356, 360) (see also Kincaid &
    Creech)
Dickson: James Dickson (nos. 208, 213, 235, 274, 279, 292, 360)
Donaldson, A.: Alexander Donaldson (no. 79) (see also Kincaid & Donaldson)
Donaldson, J.: James Donaldson (no. 301)
Drummond: William Drummond (nos. 127, 159)

Elliot: Charles Elliot (nos. 171, 179, 187, 189, 190, 213, 215, 218, 240, 242, 249, 252, 253, 269, 281) (see also London: Elliot & Kay)

Gordon: William Gordon (nos. 65, 235, 244)

Gordon & Elliot: not traced (no. 269)

Gray: George Gray (no. 360)

Gray & Peter: William Gray and Walter Peter (no. 44)

Guthrie: Alexander Guthrie (nos. 301, 360)

Hamilton, Balfour, [& Neill]: Gavin Hamilton, John Balfour, [and Patrick Neill] (10, 17, 21, 23, 28, [29], 31, 33, 34, 35, 38, 40, 44, 48, 64, 66) (see also Balfour, J.)

Hill: Peter Hill (nos. 292, 305, 360)

Jack: Robert Jack (nos. 292, 360)

Kincaid: Alexander Kincaid (nos. 2, 9, 10) (see also Kincaid & Bell; Kincaid & Creech; Kincaid & Donaldson)

Kincaid & Bell: Alexander Kincaid and John Bell (nos. 50, 53, 55, 59, 62, 68, 69, 72, 73, 79, 88, 94, 97, 99, 109, 111, 117, 122, 123, 124, 125, 141, 143) (see also Kincaid; Kincaid & Creech; Kincaid & Donaldson; Bell)

Kincaid & Creech: Alexander Kincaid and William Creech (nos. 97, [137], 147, 156, 159, 160) (see also Kincaid; Kincaid & Bell; Kincaid & Donaldson; Creech)

Kincaid & Donaldson: Alexander Kincaid and Alexander Donaldson (nos. 13, 14, 19, 25, 26, 40, 41, 47) (see also Kincaid & Bell; Kincaid & Creech)

Laing: William Laing (nos. 323, 360)

Lawrie: Alexander Laurie (nos. 292, 360)

Manners & Miller: Alexander Manners and Robert Miller (nos. 292, 358, 360)

Mudie: George Mudie (no. 312) (see also Mudie & Son[s])

Mudie & Son(s): George Mudie, William Mudie, and ? Mudie (no. 337) (see also Mudie)

Neill, A.: Adam Neill (no. 124)

Neill, J.: James Neil (no. 297)

Ogle, J.: John Ogle (no. 360)

Ruddiman, W. & T. (printers): William Ruddiman and Thomas Ruddiman (no. 158)

Sands: William Sands (nos. 1, 69)

Simpson: James Simpson (no. 360)

Smellie, A.: Alexander Smellie (nos. 292, 360)

Stewart, Ruthven & Co. (printers): Charles Stewart and James Ruthven (no. 310)

Watson: James Watson (no. 312)

Glasgow

Barry: John Barry (no. 10)

Chapman & Duncan (printers): Robert Chapman and Alexander Duncan (no. 257)

Dunlop & Wilson: [individual names not traced] (nos. 269, 301)

Foulis, A. (printer): Andrew Foulis II (no. 231)

Foulis, R.: Robert Foulis (no. 3) (see also R. & A. Foulis)

Foulis, R. & A.: Robert Foulis and Andrew Foulis (nos. 36, 42, 57, 167) (see also R. Foulis)

Kilmarnock

Wilson (printer): John Wilson (no. 260)

Perth

R. Morison & Son: Robert Morison and James Morison (nos. 191, 314, 330, 339)

Dublin

Archer: John Archer (no. 175)
Armitage: Thomas Armitage (nos. 177, 185, 186, 187)
Beatty: John Beatty (nos. 59, 179, 185, 186, 195, 198, 203, 208, 214, 217, 226, 229, 230, 232, 239)
Bradley: Hulton Bradley (nos. 63, 120)
Brown: Charles Brown (no. 357)
Burnet: George Burnet (nos. 185, 186, 195, 219, 230, 239, 263, 270, 298, 299, 357, 359)
Burnett: see Burnet
Burton: Robert Burton (nos. 214, 217, 219, 226, 230, 232, 239, 270)
Butler: Richard Martin Butler (no. 333)
Byrne: Patrick Byrne (nos. 144, 201, 203, 214, 217, 219, 226, 229, 230, 232, 239, 249, 250, 251, 256, 258, 263, 270, 275, 282, 284, 287, 288, 289, 291, 292, 295, 298, 299, 308, 315, 333, 336, 340, 359)
Cash: John Cash (nos. 217, 226, 229, 230, 232, 239, 250, 251, 258, 263)
Chamberlain: see Chamberlaine
Chamberlaine, D.: Dillon Chamberlaine (nos. 90, 96, 105, 115, 116, 118, 120, 135, 140, 155, 161, 170, 177, 185, 186, 219)
Chamberlaine, H.: Hannah Chamberlaine (no. 282) (see also Chamberlaine & Rice)
Chamberlaine & Rice: Hannah Chamberlaine and John Rice (nos. 291, 292) (see also Chamberlaine, H.; Rice)
Colbert: Harriet Colbert (nos. 315, 336, 338, 340, 359)
Colles, A.: Ann Colles (no. 188)
Colles, J.: John Colles (nos. 163, 177, 186)
Colles, W.: William Colles (nos. 90, 116, 140, 161, 177, 179, 185, 186, 188, 195, 206, 219, 230, 232, 239, 258, 263, 270)
Company of Booksellers (nos. 156, 183, 193)
Corcoran: Bartholomew Corcoran I (no. 185)
Cotter: Sarah Cotter (nos. 43, 56, 64, 73, 79)
Cross, E.: Edward Cross (nos. 185, 186, 203, 208, 219)
Cross, N.: Nicholas Cross (no. 239)
Cross, R.: Richard Cross (nos. 177, 185, 186, 198, 203, 219, 239, 295, 298)
Dornin: Bernard Dornin (nos. 270, 288, 299, 357)
Doyle: Matthew Doyle (no. 239)
Draper: George Draper (nos. 288, 295)
Dugdale: Bennett Dugdale (nos. 315, 340, 359)
Ewing, A.: Alexander Ewing (no. 88) (see also Ewing, G. & A.)
Ewing, T.: Thomas Ewing (nos. 41, 119, 123, 137, 145, 159, 163)
Ewing, G. & A.: George Ewing and Alexander Ewing (nos. 18, 40, 51, 58, 63, 74) (see also Ewing, A.)
Exshaw I: John Exshaw I (nos. 44, 51, 93, 96, 105, 120, 130, 140, 161, 170)

Exshaw II: John Exshaw II (nos. 179, 181, 185, 186, 195, 198, 200, 203, 219, 226, 229, 230, 232, 239, 263, 270)

Faulkner, G.: George Faulkner I (nos. 5, 7, 44, 116, 118)

Faulkner, T.: Thomas Todd Faulkner (nos. 177, 185)

Fitzpatrick: Hugh Fitzpatrick (nos. 340, 357, 359)

Fitzsimons: Richard Fitzsimons (no. 71)

Flin I: Lawrence Flin I (nos. 51, 52)

Flin II: Lawrence Flin II (nos. 172, 179, 185, 186, 195, 198, 219)

Folingsby: George Folingsby (nos. 336, 340, 357, 359)

Gilbert: William Gilbert (nos. 177, 185, 186, 206, 219, 226, 230, 260, 270) (see also Gilbert & Hodges)

Gilbert & Hodges: William Gilbert and Robert Hodges (no. 357) (see also Gilbert)

Grierson, B.: (Hugh) Boulter Grierson (nos. 99, 106, 108, 116, 120, 130, 143)

Grierson, G.: George Grierson II (no. 143)

Grueber: Arthur Grueber (nos. 185, 284, 289, 295, 298, 299) (see also Grueber & M'Allister)

Grueber & M'Allister: Arthur Grueber and Randal M'Allister (nos. 271, 282, 284, 287, 291, 292) (see also Grueber; M'Allister)

Gunne: Benjamin Gunne (no. 51)

Hallhead, W.: William Hallhead (nos. 165, 172, 177, 185, 186, 188, 203, 219)

Hallhead, S.: Sarah Hallhead (no. 239)

Halpin: John Halpen (no. 333)

Hay, D.: David Hay (no. 140)

Hay, M.: Mary Hay (formerly Grierson) (nos. 161, 185)

Heery: Thomas Heery (no. 270)

Higly: Patrick Higly (nos. 186, 203, 239)

Hillary: John Hillary (nos. 177, 186)

Hoey I, J.: James Hoey I (nos. 44, 51, 93, 96)

Hoey II, J.: James Hoey II (nos. 78, 93, 96, 118, 120, 135, 140, 161, 177, 185, 186, 195)

Hoey, P.: Peter Hoey (no. 186)

Husband: John Abbot Husband (nos. 140, 155, 161)

Ingham, C.: Charles Ingham (nos. 118, 120, 141)

Ingham, J.: see Ingham, C.

Jackson: Christopher Jackson (nos. 59, 152, 186)

James, A.: Alice James (nos. 44, 51, 63)

James, R.: Richard James (no. 12)

Jenkin: Caleb Jenkin (nos. 155, 161, 163, 170, 172, 173, 177, 179, 185, 186, 195, 198, 203, 208, 219, 232, 239)

Jones, J.: John Jones I (nos. 144, 249, 258, 263, 282, 288, 289, 295, 299, 315, 333)

Jones, W.: William Jones I (nos. 282, 284, 287, 288, 289, 291, 292, 295, 298, 299, 308, 312, 315, 333, 336, 359)

Kelly: Nicholas Kelly (nos. 340, 359)

Leathly: Ann Leathley/Leathly (nos. 83, 93, 96, 140)

Lewis: Christopher Lewis (no. 288)

Lynch: Elizabeth Lynch (see Watts, E.)

Magee: John Magee I (no. 185)

Main: Robert Main (nos. 16, 27)

Marchbank: Robert Marchbank (nos. 249, 263)

M'Allister: Randal M'Allister (nos. 295, 298, 299) (see also Grueber & M'Allister)

M'Kenly: Henry M'Kenly (no. 185)

M'Kenzie/McKenzie: William M'Kenzie or McKenzie (3, 229, 230, 249, 258, 263, 270, 289, 291, 292, 295, 359)

Mercier & Co.: Richard Edward Mercier (and John Dumoulin) (no. 359)

Milliken: John Milliken (nos. 275, 288, 291, 292, 337, 340)

Mills: Michael Mills (nos. 170, 177, 185, 239)

Mitchell: John Mitchell (no. 140)

Moncrieffe: Richard Moncrieffe (nos. 115, 116, 135, 140, 150, 155, 161, 170, 177, 185, 186, 203, 219, 230, 232, 239, 258, 263, 270)

Moore, J.: James Moore (nos. 139, 249, 258, 263, 270, 282, 287, 288, 291, 292, 295, 298, 299, 315, 333, 336, 340)

Moore, P.: Peter Moore (nos. 299, 333, 337, 340, 359)

Murphy: John Murphy (no. 96)

Parker, James: James Parker (no. 179)

Parker, John: John Parker I (nos. 219, 230)

Parry: John Parry II (no. 359)

Porter, A.: Alexander Porter (no. 299)

Porter, J.: James Porter (nos. 116, 118, 186, 239)

Porter, W.: William Porter (nos. 258, 270, 288, 299, 336, 340, 357, 359)

Potts: James Potts I (nos. 63, 90, 96, 105, 115, 116, 118, 120, 130, 135, 140, 150, 155, 161, 170, 177, 185, 186, 198)

Powell: Samuel Powell I (nos. 116, 120)

Price: Samuel Price (nos. 179, 185, 186, 198, 203, 214, 219, 232, 239)

Rice: John Rice (289, 295, 298, 299, 308, 315, 333, 336, 337, 340, 357, 359) (see also Chamberlaine & Rice)

Rudd: James Rudd (no. 51)

Saunders: Henry Saunders (nos. 93, 96, 105, 115, 116, 118, 120, 130, 140)

Sheppard: Josiah Sheppard/Shepherd (no. 93)

Sleater I: William Sleater I (nos. 44, 51, 90, 96, 105, 115, 116, 118, 120, 135, 140, 155, 161, 170, 185, 186, 288)

Sleater II: William Sleater II (nos. 232, 239, 337)

Smith, J.: John Smith I (nos. 10, 33, 46)

Smith, R.: Richard Smith I (no. 51)

Smith, S.: Samuel Smith I (no. 63)

Smith I, W.: William Smith II (no. 63) (see also W. & W. Smith)

Smith II, W.: William Smith IV (no. 63) (see also W. & W. Smith)

Smith, W. & W.: William Smith II and William Smith IV (nos. 116, 118) (see also W. Smith I and W. Smith II)

Spotswood: William Spotswood (nos. 172, 186, 203) (see also Philadelphia: Spotswood)

Stewart, R.: not traced (no. 185)

Stewart, T.: Thomas Stewart (no. 185)

Stockdale: John Stockdale (no. 359)

Vallance: James Vallance (nos. 185, 219)

Walker: Thomas Walker (nos. 135, 140, 155, 161, 170, 177, 179, 185, 186, 195, 198, 203, 208, 214, 217, 219, 226, 229, 230, 232, 239)

Watson, S.: Samuel Watson (nos. 21, 77, 96, 119, 177, 185)

Watson, W.: William Watson (nos. 51, 93, 119, 177, 185, 186, 219, 239)

Watson, W. & Son: William Watson I and William Watson II (nos. 340, 359)

Watts, E.: Elizabeth Watts (later Lynch) (nos. 96, 172, 185, 203, 239)

Watts, R.: Richard Watts (nos. 21, 51, 63)

Webb: Thomas Webb (no. 217)

White, L.: Luke White (nos. 49, 67, 114, 172, 179, 185, 186, 195, 198, 203, 208, 219, 229, 230, 232, 239, 249, 250, 251, 255, 258, 263, 270, 281, 284, 288, 292, 299)

White, R.: Richard White (nos. 287, 288, 291, 292, 295, 298, 299)

Whitestone, H.: Henry Whitestone (no. 270) (see also W. & H. Whitestone)

Whitestone, W.: William Whitestone (nos. 177, 185, 186, 195, 203, 230, 232, 239)

Whitestone, W. & H.: William Whitestone and Henry Whitestone (nos. 179, 208, 214, 219)

Williams: James Williams (nos. [8], [9], [15], [19], 25, [45], 75, 90, 96, 105, 116, 118, 120, 130, 135, 136, 140, 141, 155, 161, 164, 168, 170, 172, 176, 177, 179, 185, 186, 187, 195, 219) (see also Williams & Moncrieffe)

Williams & Moncrieffe: James Williams and Richard Moncrieffe (no. 101) (see also Moncrieffe; Williams)

Williamson, M.: Matthew Williamson (nos. 44, 63)

Williamson, W.: William Williamson (no. 51)

Wilson, P.: Peter Wilson I (nos. 16, 44, 51, 80, 83, 96)

Wilson, P. & W.: Peter Wilson I and William Wilson (nos. 118, 120)

Wilson, W.: William Wilson (nos. 140, 154, 161, 170, 177, 179, 185, 186, 195, 198, 201, 219, 239, 258, 292, 295)

Wogan: Patrick Wogan (nos. 185, 288, 289, 291, 292, 298, 299, 333, 336, 337, 340, 357, 359)

AMERICA/UNITED STATES

Albany

Spencer: Thomas Spencer (no. 311)

Baltimore

Rice, J.: James Rice (no. 315) (see also Dublin: Rice)

Boston

Blake: William Pynson Blake (nos. 73, 217?)

Boyle: John Boyle (no. 150)

Green: William Green (no. 181)

Guild: Benjamin Guild (no. 217?)

Larkin: Ebenezer Larkin (no. 73)

Larkin II: Ebenezer Larkin, Jr. (no. 150)

Mein: John Mein (no. 87) (see also Mein & Fleming)

Mein & Fleming: John Mein and John Fleming or Fleming (no. 93)

Norman: John Norman (no. 146)

Spotswood: William Spotswood (nos. 73, 188) (see also Philadelphia: Spotswood; and Dublin: Spotswood)

Thomas: Isaiah Thomas (no. 240) (see also Thomas & Andrews; Hartford: Thomas)

Thomas & Andrews: Isaiah Thomas and ? Andrews (nos. 73, 189) (see also Thomas, I.)

West, D.: David West (nos. 73, [150])

West, J.: J.? West (no. 73)

White: J.? White (no. 73)

Hartford, CT

Thomas: Isaiah Thomas (no. 356) (see also Boston: Thomas)

Mount Pleasant, NY

• Judah: Nap[h]tali Judah (no. 340)

New York City

Berry & Rogers: ? (no. 288)
Campbell: Samuel Campbell (nos. 185, 270, 305) (see also Hodge, S. Campbell, & Allen)
Hodge, S. Campbell, & Allen: Robert Hodge, Samuel Campbell, and Thomas Allen (and variants) (nos. 188, 281, 284) (see also Campbell)
Loudon: Samuel Loudon (no. 163)
M'Lean, J. & A.: ? M'Lean and ? M'Lean (no. 260)

Philadelphia

Aikman: William Aikman (no. 163)
Aitken: Robert Aitken (nos. 115, 157, 164, 230)
Bell: Robert Bell (nos. 119, 135, 141, 145, 154, 155, 164, 201, 219)
Birch & Small: William Young Birch and Abraham Small (no. 203)
Bradford: Thomas Bradford (no. 325)
Campbell: Robert Campbell (nos. 49, 67, 75, 188, 281, 292, 312)
Carey: Mathew Carey (nos. 5, 12, 130, 291) (see also Carey, Stewart & Co.)
Carey, Stewart & Co.: **Mathew Carey** and Peter Stewart (no. 188) (see also Carey)
Cist: Charles Cist (nos. 183, 264) (see also Steiner & Cist)
Crukshank: Joseph Crukshank (nos. 3, 281)
Dobelbower: J. H. Dobelbower (no. 198)
Dobson: Thomas Dobson (nos. 72, 92, 139, 159, 177, 240, 242, 258, 273, 280)
Dunlap: John Dunlap (no. 163)
Hall: Parry Hall (nos. 264, 356)
Humphreys: James Humphreys (nos. 341, 350)
Lang: Thomas Lang (nos. 64, [71], 80, [83])
Rice, H. & P.: Henry Rice and Patrick Rice (no. 315)
Sparhawk: John Sparhawk (no. 161)
Spotswood: William Spotswood (nos. 166, 188) (see also Boston: Spotswood; and Dublin: Spotswood)
Steiner & Cist: ? Steiner and Charles Cist (no. 187) (see also Cist)
Stewart & Hyde: Peter Stewart and George Hyde (nos. 158, 260)
Story: Enoch Story (no. 44)
Taylor: H.? Taylor (no. 135)
Young: William Young (nos. 255, 275, 298, 299, 309)

Providence, RI

Carter & Wilkinson: ? Carter and ? Wilkinson (no. 266)

Sources: ESTC and imprints of works cited; Maxted, *London Book Trades;* British Book Trade Index; Scottish Book Trade Index; Plomer, H. R., et al., *Dictionaries;* Pollard, *Dictionary.*

Table 3. *Subjects and Formats of First British Editions of Scottish Enlightenment Books*

Genre	No. of Titles	2°	4°	8°	12°
History	68	0	44	21	3
Medicine	61	1	12	43	5
Philosophy	39	0	10	19	10
Science (incl. mathematics)	29	1	7	21	0
Fiction	21	0	0	7	14
Poetry	20	0	8	11	1
Religion	15	0	1	12	2
Travel/topography	13	0	2	11	0
Economics	13	0	7	5	1
Literary criticism/rhetoric	13	0	2	11	0
Drama	12	0	0	12	0
Miscellaneous	11	1	3	6	1
Politics	9	0	0	9	0
Agriculture	8	0	1	7	0
Arts	8	2	3	3	0
Biography	6	0	2	4	0
Law	5	2	0	3	0
Education	3	0	0	2	1
Military	3	1	1	1	0
Language	3	0	0	3	0
Total	360	8	103	211	38
Percentage (%)		2	29	59	11

Notes: 2° = folio; 4° = quarto; 8° = octavo; 12° = duodecimo. Nos. 163, 173, and 341 have been counted in the larger of the two formats in which they originally appeared. One book published in 24° format has been counted in the 12° column.

Table 4. *Popularity of British Editions of Scottish Enlightenment Books*

Category	Number of Books	% of Whole
Best sellers (10 or more editions)	46	13
Strong sellers (7–9 editions)	5	1
Good sellers (4–6 editions)	62	17
Modest sellers (2–3 editions)	100	28
Poor sellers (1 edition only)	133	37
Not applicable	14	4
Total	360	100

Note: Editions have been counted through the year 1810 for books in table 2 published between 1746 and 1790, and through the year 1820 for books publishing during the 1790s. Abridgments, works reprinted in anthologies and collections, and pirated British editions have been included, but "ghost" editions and editions known to have been printed outside Great Britain have been excluded. In a few unusual cases, such as Smollett's *Complete History of England* and the *Encyclopaedia Britannica*, popularity levels have been adjusted to take account of exceptionally large print runs and other special circumstances.

Table 5. *Principal Publishers of New Scottish Enlightenment Books*

	"Printed For"	"Sold By"
London		
Robert & James Dodsley, 1748–84		
Robert Dodsley, 1748–52	4	0
Robert & James Dodsley, 1756–62	0	2
James Dodsley, 1765–84	5	0
Andrew Millar & the Cadells, 1748–		
Andrew Millar, 1748–66	39	4
Andrew Millar & Thomas Cadell, Sr., 1766–68	5	0
Thomas Cadell, Sr., 1768–94		
Thomas Cadell, 1768–93	30	9
[William] Strahan and Cadell, 1769–84	32	0
[Andrew] Strahan and Cadell, 1786–94	20	0
Thomas Cadell, Jr., & William Davies, 1794–		
Cadell & Davies, 1794–1800	10	1
A. Strahan and Cadell & Davies, 1796–98	4	0
Thomas Becket & Peter de Hondt, 1760–78		
Becket & de Hondt, 1762–74	13	1
Thomas Becket, 1760, 1773, 1778	3	0
Edward & Charles Dilly, 1767–1800		
Edward & Charles Dilly, 1767–76	8	3
Edward Dilly, 1768	1	0
Charles Dilly, 1780–97	7	2
George Robinson & partners, 1767–		
Robinson & Roberts, 1767–76	2	1
George Robinson, 1773–87	9	0
G. G. J. & J. Robinson/the Robinsons, 1785–94	18	1
G. G. & J. Robinson, 1793, 1795–1800	8	2
Joseph Johnson, 1768–1800	15	1
William Strahan & Andrew Strahan, 1769–98		
William Strahan and [Thomas] Cadell, 1769–84	32	0
Andrew Strahan, 1786–98		
Andrew Strahan and [Thomas] Cadell, 1786–94	20	0
Andrew Strahan and Cadell & Davies, 1796–98	4	0
John Murray, 1771–94	29	4
Edinburgh		
Alexander Kincaid, his partners, and his successor,		
William Creech, 1747–		
Alexander Kincaid, 1747–48	2	1
Kincaid with Alexander Donaldson, 1751–57	8	0
Kincaid with John Bell, 1758–71	22	1

Table 5 (*continued*)

	"Printed For"	"Sold By"
Kincaid with William Creech, 1772–73	5	0
William Creech, 1774–1800	52	6
Gavin Hamilton, John Balfour, and successors, 1748–		
Hamilton & Balfour [& Neill], 1748–60	14	1
John Balfour, 1765–80	13	0
John & Elphinston Balfour, 1782	1	1
Elphinston Balfour, 1789–1800	4	1
Charles Elliot, 1775–89	15	0
John Bell/John Bell & John Bradfute, 1758–		
John Bell with Alexander Kincaid, 1758–71	22	1
John Bell, 1778–89	10	0
Bell & Bradfute, 1790–1800	12	2

Life Dates and Birthplaces
Robert Dodsley (1704–1764), Near Nottingham
Gavin Hamilton (1704–1767), Near Edinburgh
Andrew Millar (1705–1768), Port Glasgow
Alexander Kincaid (1710–1777), Falkirk
John Balfour (1715–1795), South Leith
William Strahan (1715–1785), Edinburgh
Thomas Becket (ca. 1722–ca. 1813), Unknown
James Dodsley (1724–1797), Near Nottingham
Alexander Donaldson (1727–1794), Edinburgh
Edward Dilly (1732–1779), Bedfordshire
John Bell (1735–1806), Berwickshire
George Robinson (1736–1801), Near Carlisle
John Murray (1737–1793), Edinburgh
Joseph Johnson (1738–1809), Near Liverpool
Charles Dilly (1739–1807), Bedfordshire
Thomas Cadell, Sr. (1742–1802), Bristol
William Creech (1745–1815), Near Edinburgh
Charles Elliot (1748–1790), Selkirk
Andrew Strahan (1750–1831), London
Elphinston Balfour (b. 1754), Edinburgh
John Bradfute (b. 1763), Lanarkshire
Thomas Cadell, Jr. (1773–1836), London
Peter de Hondt (Life dates unknown), The Netherlands
William Davies (d. 1819), Unknown

Note: Figures indicate the number of imprints listed in table 2 in which an individual or partnership is named, without taking into account publishing information from other sources. In several instances involving Hamilton & Balfour or Hamilton, Balfour, & Neill, imprints bearing the phrase "Printed By" have been counted as "Printed For" because of that firm's inconsistent use of these phrases.

Table 6. *Principal Publishers of Dublin First Editions of Scottish Enlightenment Books*

Bookseller or Firm	No. of Imprints in Table 2
1. Patrick Byrne (108 Grafton St.)	35
2. Chamberlaine–Rice (5 College Green)	31
3. James Williams (20 Dame St.)	28
4. Luke White (86 Dame St.)	28
5. John Exshaw (Sr. and Jr.) (98 Grafton St.)	26
6. Leathley–Hallhead–M'Kenzie (63 Dame St.)	25
7. Peter and William Wilson (6 Dame St.)	23
8. Thomas Walker (79 Dame St.)	21
9. Richard Moncrieffe (16 Capel St.)	20
10. William Sleater Jr. and Sr. (North Strand)	20
11. James Potts (74 Dame St.)	19
12. William and Anne Colles (17 New Buildings, Dame St.)	18
13. Caleb Jenkin (58 Dame St.)	17
14. James Moore (45 College Green)	17
15. William Jones	16
16. John Beatty (12 Capel St.)	15
17. Patrick Wogan (23 Old Bridge)	13
18. William and Henry Whitestone (91 Dame St.)	13
19. George Burnet (197 Abbey St.)	12
20. James Hoey, Jr.	12
21. John Jones (39 College Green)	11
22. Arthur Grueber (15 Dame St.) (also Grueber & M'Allister)	11
23. John Cash (14 Capel St.)	10
24. William Gilbert (26 S. Great George's St.) (also Gilbert & Hodges)	10
25. William Watson I and II (Capel St.)	10

Note: The addresses given are those of the firms in 1786. None is given for William Jones because he was not yet in business in 1786, nor for James Hoey, Jr., because he was deceased in that year. Three books in table 2 bearing the Dublin imprint "Company of Booksellers" (nos. 156, 182, and 192) have not been counted in this table, even though many of the firms above would have been among the publishers.

Table 7. *Printing Account of Thomas Cadell, Sr., in the Strahan Archive, 1793–1798*

	Author and Title	Quantity
1793		
January	Gillies, *History of Ancient Greece*, 3rd ed.	1,000
March	[C. F. Lindenau], *Extracts from Colonel Tempelhoffe's History of the Seven Years War*	500
	Tahsin al-Din, *The Loves of Camarúpa and Cámelatà*	500
April	Blair, *Lectures on Rhetoric*, 5th ed.	1,500
May	Henry, *History of Great Britain*, vol. 6 (4°)	750
	Richard Burn, *Justice of the Peace*, 17th ed.	5,000
June	Adam, *Roman Antiquities*	2,000
	Edward Morris, *False Colours, a Comedy*	2,500
	Moore, *View of Society in France*, 8th ed.	1,000
July	Gregory, *Father's Legacy*, 13th ed.	1,500
October	Ferguson, *Essay on Civil Society*, 6th ed.	1,000
December	Smith, *Wealth of Nations*, 7th ed.	2,500
	Hume, *History of England*	2,000
	Twining's Letter [Richard Twining, *Substance of a Speech Delivered at East India House?*]	2,390?
1794		
January	Mackenzie, *Mirror*, 9th ed.	1,000
	Mackenzie, *Lounger*, 6th ed.	1,000
	Mackenzie, *Man of Feeling*, 11th ed.	1,500
April	Watson, *History of Philip II*, 6th ed.	1,000
	Lewis Chambaud, *A Grammar of the French Tongue*, 11th ed.	8,000
May	Ferguson, *Astronomy Explained*, 9th ed.	2,000
August	Buchan, *Domestic Medicine*, 14th ed.	6,000
	Samuel Johnson, *The Rambler*, 13th ed.	1,000
September	Blair, *Sermons*, vol. 1, 19th ed.	2,000
	Blair, *Sermons*, vol. 2, 16th ed.	2,000
	Blair, *Sermons*, vol. 3, 8th ed.	2,250
	Blair, *Sermons*, vol. 4, 3rd ed.	3,000
October	Robertson, *India*, 2nd ed.	1,500
1795		
March	Nathanial Wraxall, *The History of France*, vols. 1–3	1,000
	Samuel Hearne, *A Journey from Prince of Wales's Fort in Hudson's Bay*	750
	Blair, *Sermons*, vol. 4, 4th ed.	3,000
April	Beattie, *Evidences of Christianity*, 4th ed.	1,000
	Smith, *Essays on Philosophical Subjects*	1,000
	Blackstone, *Commentaries on the Laws of England*, 12th ed.	5,000

(*continued*)

Table 7 (*continued*)

	Author and Title	Quantity
May	Henry, *History of Great Britain*, vols. 11 and 12 (8°)	1,000
	Charlotte Smith, *Elegiac Sonnets*, 7th ed.	1,000
	Moore, *View of Society in Italy*, 6th ed.	1,000
June	Mackenzie, *Man of the World*, 5th ed.	1,000
August	Blair, *Sermons*, vol. 3, 9th ed.	2,500
	Mackenzie, *Julia de Roubigné*, 5th ed.	1,000
December	*An Appendix to . . . Burn's Justice of the Peace*	1,500
1796		
January	*Ossian's Works [Poems of Ossian]*	1,250
	Blair, *Lectures on Rhetoric*, 6th ed.	1,500
	Robertson, *History of America*, 7th ed.	1,500
March	Edward Gibbon, *Miscellaneous Works*	2,500
June	Blair, *Sermons*, vol. 4, 5th ed.	2,500
	Robertson, *History of Charles V*	2,000
September	Smith, *Wealth of Nations*, 8th ed.	2,500
October	Blair, *Sermons*, vol. 1, 20th ed.	2,000
	Blair, *Sermons*, vol. 2, 17th ed.	2,000
December	Edward Gibbon, *Decline and Fall of the Roman Empire*, vols. 7–12 (8°)	2,000
1797		
January	Smith, *Theory of Moral Sentiments*, 8th ed.	1,000
	Lewis Chambaud, *Chambaud's Dictionary . . . Carefully Abridged*, pt. 2	8,000
	John Lemprière, *Bibliotheca Classica*, 3rd ed.	5,000
	Gregory, *Father's Legacy*	1,500
February	Buchan, *Domestic Medicine*, 15th ed.	6,000
March	Richard Burn, *Justice of the Peace*, 18th ed.	3,500
May	Edward Gibbon, *Decline and Fall of the Roman Empire*, vols. 1–6 (8°)	1,500
June	Moore, *Zeluco*, 4th ed.	1,000
August	Richard Burn, *Ecclesiastical Law*, 6th ed.	2,000
	Robertson, *History of America*, bks. 9 and 10 (8°)	1,500
	Robertson, *History of America*, bks. 9 and 10 (4°)	750
November	Robertson, *History of Scotland* (18°)	2,000
	Robertson, *History of Scotland*, "common"	1,000
1798		
February	Hume, *History of England*	2,000

Table 7 (*continued*)

	Author and Title	Quantity
May	Blair, *Sermons,* vol. 1, 21st ed.	2,000
	Blair, *Sermons,* vol. 2, 18th ed.	2,000
	Blair, *Sermons,* vol. 3, 10th ed.	2,250
	Blair, *Sermons,* vol. 4, 6th ed.	2,500
July	Buchan, *Domestic Medicine,* 16th ed.	6,000
August	Robertson, *History of Charles V* (18°)	2,000

Source: BL, Add. MSS 48817, fols. 18–20, 62, 79.

Bibliography

PRIMARY SOURCES

Manuscripts

Aitken, Robert. Ledgers. Historical Society of Pennsylvania, Philadelphia.

Autograph File. Houghton Library, Harvard University.

Bassler, Margaret A. "The Story of William Young." Typescript. Historical Society of Delaware, Wilmington, DE.

Beattie, James. Papers. MS 30. Aberdeen University Library.

Bell & Bradfute Ledgers. Edinburgh City Chambers.

Bell & Bradfute Papers. Acc. 10662 and Deps. 117, 193, and 317. National Library of Scotland.

Bell, John. Letterbooks. Bodleian Library, University of Oxford.

Boswell, James. Yale editions of the private papers of James Boswell. Yale University. Citations in this volume follow the referencing system in Pottle, Abbott, and Pottle, *Catalogue of the Papers of James Boswell at Yale University*.

Bruce, James. Papers. Microfilm copies, from the James Bruce Archive at the Yale Center for British Art. National Library of Scotland.

Buchan Papers. Baillie MSS 32225. Mitchell Library, Glasgow.

Cadell and Davies Correspondence. New York Public Library.

Cadell and Davies Correspondence and Documents. Beinecke Library, Yale University.

Cadell, Thomas. Papers in the Longman Archive (MS 1393) and other Cadell Papers (MS 2770). University of Reading Library, Reading, UK. See also *Archives of the House of Longman* under Published Work.

———. Papers. William R. Perkins Library, Duke University.

Carson, Marian S. Collection. Library of Congress.

Chamberlain Autograph Collection. Boston Public Library, Boston.

Constable, Archibald. Papers. National Library of Scotland.

Creech, William. Letterbooks in the Blair Oliphant of Ardblair Muniments. Consulted on microfilm, RH4 26/1–3. National Archives of Scotland.

———. Papers. Edinburgh Central Library.

Dreer Autograph Collection. Historical Society of Pennsylvania, Philadelphia.

Edinburgh Town Council Minutes. Edinburgh City Chambers.

Edinburgh University matriculation records. Edinburgh University Library.

Egerton Manuscripts. British Library, London.

Ferguson, James. Papers. New York Public Library.

Fettercairn Manuscripts. Acc. 4796. National Library of Scotland.

Foulis Papers. Baillie MSS 37886. Mitchell Library, Glasgow.

Fraser-Tytler of Aldourie Papers. NRAS 1073, from Aldourie Castle. Highland Council Archive, Inverness Library, Inverness.

Gordon Castle Muniments. National Archives of Scotland.

Graisberry, Daniel. Ledgers. Trinity College, Dublin.

Gratz Collection. Historical Society of Pennsylvania, Philadelphia.

Hall, David. Letterbook. Microfilm copies. Salem County Historical Society, Salem, NJ.

———. Papers. B/H 142.1–3. American Philosophical Society, Philadelphia.

Hyde, Donald and Mary. Collection. Houghton Library, Harvard University.

Johnson, Joseph. Letterbook, 1795–1810. Carl H. Pforzheimer Collection. New York Public Library.

Laing Manuscripts. Edinburgh University Library.

Lea and Febiger Papers. Historical Society of Pennsylvania, Philadelphia.

Literary and Historical Manuscripts. Pierpont Morgan Library, New York City.

Maconochie, Allan [Lord Meadowbank]. Meadowbank Papers. Microfilm copies. Edinburgh University Library.

McAllister Family Papers. Historical Society of Pennsylvania, Philadelphia.

"Memoir of W. Young by his Grandson W. Y. John McAllister." Microfilm copy; original in the Historical Society of Pennsylvania. American Antiquarian Society, Worcester, MA.

Minto Papers. National Library of Scotland.

Miscellaneous manuscripts from the Beinecke Library, Yale University; Bodleian Library, University of Oxford; British Library (Add. MSS); Edinburgh Central Library; Edinburgh University Library; Glasgow University Library; Historical Society of Pennsylvania, Library Company of Philadelphia (on loan); Houghton Library, Harvard University; National Archives of Scotland; National Institute of Medicine, Bethesda, MD; National Library of Scotland; Royal College of Physicians of Edinburgh.

"Miscellaneous Material relating to William Buchan." Royal College of Physicians of Edinburgh.

Murray, David. Papers. Glasgow University Library.

Murray, John. Archive (now in the National Library of Scotland). John Murray, Ltd., London.

Osborn Collection. Beinecke Library, Yale University.

Parish records of births and baptisms. Microfilm. Scottish Genealogy Society, Edinburgh.

Register of Printed Books. Stationers' Hall, London. See also *Records of the Worshipful Company of Stationers, 1554–1920*, under Published Work.

Robertson-Macdonald Papers. National Library of Scotland.

Royal Society of Edinburgh Manuscripts (including the David Hume Papers). National Library of Scotland.

Sloane Manuscripts. British Library, London.

Smellie, William. Papers. (Consulted before their removal from the library of the Society of Antiquaries of Scotland.) National Museum of Scotland, Edinburgh.

Stowe Manuscripts. British Library, London.

Strahan Archive. Add. MSS 48800–48918. British Library, London. See also *The Strahan Archive from the British Library* under Published Work.

Strahan, William. Journals. B/St 83. American Philosophical Society, Philadelphia.

Thomson of Banchory Papers. New College Library, Edinburgh.

Wodrow–Kenrick Correspondence. MS 24157. Dr. Williams's Library, London. See also *Wodrow–Kenrick Correspondence* under Published Work.

Young, William. Business Papers. Historical Society of Pennsylvania, Philadelphia.

———. Collection. Historical Society of Delaware, Wilmington, DE.

———. Papers. William L. Clements Library, University of Michigan.

Young-McAllister Papers. Historical Society of Pennsylvania, Philadelphia.

Published Work

This section excludes British, Irish, and American first editions as found in table 2.

Adam, Robert, and James Adam. *The Works in Architecture of Robert and James Adam.* Ed. Robert Oresko. London and New York, 1975.

Agnew, Jean, ed. *The Drennan-McTier Letters, 1776–1793.* 3 vols. Dublin, 1998.

[Aitken, Robert]. *R. Aitken, Printer, Book-Binder, and Bookseller, Opposite the Coffee-House, Front-Street, Philadelphia, 1779 Performs All Kinds of Printing-Work.* [Philadelphia, 1779].

———. *This Day Is Published, at Samuel Loudon's Book Store, Near the Coffee-House, New-York, a New Book, Printed and Sold by R. Aitken, Bookseller, Opposite the London Coffee-House, Front-Street, Philadelphia, on a New Type and Fine Paper, Essay on the Character, Manners and Genius of Women, in Different Ages.* [New York, 1774].

[Allen, Thomas]. *Thomas Allen's Sale Catalogue of Books, Consisting of a Very Extensive Collection of Valuable Books in Every Branch of Science and Polite Literature, Ancient and Modern, which Will Be Disposed of, Wholesale and Retail, on Reasonable Terms, at His Book and Stationary Store, No. 12, Queen-Street, New York.* New York, 1792.

Alves, Robert. *Sketches of a History of Literature: Containing Lives and Characters of the Most Eminent Writers in Different Languages, Ancient and Modern, and Critical Remarks on Their Works.* Edinburgh, 1794.

A[nderson], J[ames]. "Second Anecdote of Mr. Andrew Millar." *The Bee, or Literary Weekly Intelligencer* 3 (1 June 1791): 131–33. See also Authenticus.

Anderson, John. *A History of Edinburgh.* Edinburgh and London, 1856.

Anderson, John. *Institutes of Physics. Volume First.* Glasgow, 1777.

Archives of the House of Longman, 1794–1914. Microfilm. 73 reels. Cambridge, 1978. Originals at the University of Reading Library.

Arnot, Hugo. *The History of Edinburgh.* 2nd ed. Edinburgh, 1788.

Authenticus. "Anecdotes of Mr. Andrew Millar." *The Bee, or Literary Weekly Intelligencer* 3 (1 June 1791): 127–30. See also A[nderson], J[ames].

Bailey, N[athan]. *The New Etymological English Dictionary.* 5th ed. London, 1760.

Beattie, James. *The Correspondence of James Beattie.* 4 vols. Ed. Roger J. Robinson. Bristol, 2004.

———. *James Beattie's Day-Book, 1773–1798.* Ed. Ralph S. Walker. Aberdeen, 1948.

———. *James Beattie's London Diary, 1773.* Ed. Ralph S. Walker. Aberdeen, 1946.

Beccaria, Cesare. *An Essay on Crimes and Punishments.* Philadelphia, 1778.

Belknap, Jeremy. *Belknap Papers. Collections of the Massachusetts Historical Society,* 6th ser., 4 (1891).

Bell, John. *Travels from St. Petersburg in Russia, to Diverse Parts of Asia.* 2 vols. Dublin, 1764. With an advertisement for *Bell's Sale Catalogue of Books for 1763 and 1764.*

[Bell, John, and John Bradfute]. *A Catalogue of Books for the Year M,DCC,XCIV.* [Edinburgh, 1794].

Bell, Robert. *Catalogue of Books, to be Sold by Auction, by Robert Bell, Bookseller and Auctioneer* (for auction running 25 Mar.–8 Apr. 1768). [Philadelphia, 1768]. (Photocopy in the Library Company of Philadelphia)

———. *A Catalogue of Books, to be Sold by Auction by Robert Bell, Bookseller and Auctioneer* (for auction running 4–7 May 1768) [Philadelphia, 1768]. (Photocopy in the Library Company of Philadelphia)

[———], ed. *An Interesting Appendix to Sir William Blackstone's Commentaries on the Laws of England.* America [Philadelphia], 1773.

———. *Memorandum.* Philadelphia, 1774.

———. *Miscellanies for Sentimentalists.* Philadelphia, 1778.

———. *New and Old, Medical, Surgical, and Chemical Works, Lately Imported, and Now Selling at Bell's Book-Store, near St. Paul's Church in Third-Street, Philadelphia; with the Lowest Price Printed to Each Book.* [Philadelphia, 1784].

———. *Now in the Printing-Press, and Speedily Will Be Published by Subscription, in One Volume Octavo, Price One Dollar, Sewed in Blue Boards, although the English Edition Is Sold at Four Dollars. An Essay on the History of Civil Society. By Adam Ferguson, LL.D., Professor of Moral Philosophy, in the University of Edinburgh.* America [Philadelphia, 1771].

[———]. *Observations relative to the Manufactures of Paper and Printed Books in the Province of Pennsylvania.* [Philadelphia, 1773].

———. *Proposals, Addressed to Those Who Possess a Public Spirit. The Real Friends to the Progress of Literary Entertainment . . . Are Requested to Observe, that a Handsome*

American Edition of Hume's Celebrated History of England, Is Now in Contemplation to Be Published Periodically, by Subscription. [Philadelphia, 1771].

———. *Robert Bell's Sale Catalogue of a Collection of New and Old Books, in All the Arts and Sciences, and in Various Languages, Also, a Large Quantity of Entertaining Novels; with the Lowest Price Printed in Each Book; Now Selling, at the Book-Store of William Woodhouse, Bookseller, Stationer, and Bookbinder, in Front-Street, near Chestnut-Street, Philadelphia.* Philadelphia, 1773.

———. *To the Encouragers of Literature. The Third Volume of Blackstone's Commentaries Is Now Published.* [Philadelphia, 1772].

———. *To the Sons of Science in America, Robert Bell, Bookseller of Philadelphia, Notifieth, that in the Fall of This Present Year 1773, He Will Publish by Subscription, Ferguson's Essay on the History of Civil Society.* [Philadelphia, 1773].

[Bent, William]. *The London Catalogue of Books.* London, 1791.

Black, Adam. *Memoirs of Adam Black.* Ed. Alexander Nicolson. Edinburgh, 1885.

Blackburne, Francis. *Memoirs of Thomas Hollis.* 2 vols. London, 1780.

Blacklock, Thomas. *Poems by Mr. Thomas Blacklock. To which Is Prefixed, An Account of the Life, Character, and Writings, of the Author, by the Rev. Mr. Spence.* London, 1756.

———. *Poems by the Late Reverend Dr. Thomas Blacklock.* Edinburgh, 1793.

———. *Poems on Several Occasions.* Glasgow, 1746.

Blackstone, William, Sir. *Commentaries on the Laws of England.* 4 vols. America [Philadelphia], 1771–72.

Blair, Hugh. *Sermons.* 5 vols. London, 1818.

Boswell, James. *Boswell: The English Experiment, 1785–1789.* Ed. Irma S. Lustig and Frederick A. Pottle. New York, 1986.

———. *Boswell: The Great Biographer, 1789–1795.* Ed. Marlies K. Dansiger and Frank Brady. New York, 1989.

———. *Boswell: Laird of Auchinleck, 1778–1782.* Ed. Joseph W. Reed and Frederick A. Pottle. New York, 1977; reprint, Edinburgh, 1993.

———. *Boswell: The Ominous Years, 1774–1776.* Ed. Charles Ryskamp and Frederick A. Pottle. New York, 1963.

———. *Boswell for the Defence, 1769–1774.* Ed. William K. Wimsatt, Jr., and Frederick A. Pottle. New York, 1959.

———. *Boswell in Search of a Wife, 1766–1769.* Ed. Frank Brady and Frederick A. Pottle. New York, 1956.

———. *Boswell's Life of Johnson.* 6 vols. (including the *Journal of a Tour to the Hebrides with Samuel Johnson* in vol. 5). Ed. George Birkbeck Hill; revised by L. F. Powell. Oxford, 1934–64.

———. *Boswell's London Journal, 1762–1763.* Ed. Frederick A. Pottle. New York, 1950.

———. *The Correspondence and Other Papers of James Boswell relating to the Making of the "Life of Johnson."* Ed. Marshall Waingrow. 2nd ed. Edinburgh and New Haven, CT, 2001.

―――. *The Correspondence of James Boswell and William Johnson Temple, 1756–1795.* Vol. 1. Ed. Thomas Crawford. Edinburgh, 1997.

―――. *The Correspondence of James Boswell with Certain Members of The Club.* Ed. Charles N. Fifer. New York, 1976.

―――. *The General Correspondence of James Boswell, 1766–1769.* Ed. Richard C. Cole, with Peter S. Baker, Rachel McClellan, and James J. Caudle. Vol. 1, *1766–1767.* Edinburgh and New Haven, CT, 1993.

The British Coffee-House. 1764.

Brougham, Henry, Lord. *Lives of Men of Letters and Science Who Flourished in the Time of George III.* 2 vols. London, 1845.

Brown, John. *The Elements of Medicine of John Brown, M.D. Translated from the Latin, with Comments and Illustrations, by the Author. A New Edition, Revised and Corrected, with a Biographical Preface by Thomas Beddoes, M.D. and a Head of the Author.* 2 vols. London, 1795.

Brunhouse, David L., ed. *David Ramsay, 1749–1815: Selections from His Writings. Transactions of the American Philosophical Society,* n. s., vol. 55, pt. 4 (1965).

Buchan, William. *Domestic Medicine: or, A Treatise on the Prevention and Cure of Diseases by Regimen and Simple Medicines.* 13th ed. Philadelphia, 1793.

Buffon, Georges Louis Leclerc. *Buffon's Natural History, Abridged.* London, 1791; Dublin, 1791.

Burdy, Samuel. *The Life of the Rev. Philip Skelton.* Dublin, 1792.

Burgh, James. *The Art of Speaking.* Philadelphia, 1775.

―――. *Political Disquisitions; or, An Enquiry into Public Errors, Defects, and Abuses.* 3 vols. London, 1774–75; reprint, Philadelphia, 1775.

Burke, Edmund. *Reflections on the Revolution in France, and on the Proceedings in Certain Societies in London, Relative to the Event.* Philadelphia, 1792.

[Burney, Frances]. *Camilla: or, a Picture of Youth.* 5 vols. London, 1796.

―――. *The Journals and Letters of Fanny Burney (Madame D'Arblay).* 12 vols. Ed. Joyce Hemlow, with Patricia Boutilier and Althea Douglas. Oxford, 1972–84.

Burns, Robert. *The Letters of Robert Burns.* 2 vols. Ed. J. De Lancey Ferguson; revised by G. Ross Roy. Oxford, 1985.

Burton, J. E. [i.e., H.], ed. *Letters of Eminent Persons Addressed to David Hume.* Edinburgh and London, 1849.

Büsching, Anton Friedrich. *A New System of Geography.* Trans. Patrick Murdoch. London, 1762.

"Cadell (Thomas)." In *The New Biographical Dictionary,* 8:13–15. London, 1812–17.

[Cadell, Thomas], *Books Printed for and Sold by T. Cadell, opposite Catherine-Street in the Strand.* [London, 1767?].

[―――]. *A Select Catalogue of the Most Approved English Books.* London, 1768–.

[Cadell, Thomas, Jr., and William Davies]. *A Catalogue of Valuable Books, All the Latest and Best Editions, and Many of Them in Various Sizes, Printed (the Greater Part Exclusively) for T. Cadell and W. Davies.* London, 1816.

Cadogan, William. *A Dissertation on the Gout, and All Chronic Diseases, Jointly Consid-*

ered, as Proceeding from the Same Causes; What Those Causes Are; and a Rational and Natural Method of Cure Proposed. London, 1771.

[Callender, James Thomson]. *American Annual Register, or, Historical Memoirs of the United States, for the Year 1796.* Philadelphia, 1797.

———. *The Political Progress of Britain; or an Impartial Account of the Principal Abuses in the Government of This Country.* London, 1792; reprint, Philadelphia, 1795; reissued in Carey, *Select Pamphlets,* 1796.

[Campbell, Robert]. *Robert Campbell's Sale Catalogue of Books. To Be Sold on the Most Reasonable Terms, at No. 54, South Second-Street, Second Door, below the Corner of Chestnut-Street, on the West Side, Philadelphia.* [Philadelphia, 1791?].

Campbell, Thomas. *Dr. Campbell's Diary of a Visit to England in 1775.* Ed. James L. Clifford. Cambridge, 1947.

Carey, Mathew. *Autobiography.* New York, 1942.

———. *Mathew Carey, No. 158, Market-Street, Philadelphia, Has Imported from London, Dublin, and Glasgow, an Extensive Assortment of Books.* [Philadelphia, 1792].

———. *Miscellaneous Essays.* Vol. 1. Philadelphia, 1830; reprint, New York, n.d.

———, ed. *Select Pamphlets.* Philadelphia, 1796.

———. *Sir, Having, on Mature Deliberation, Resolved to Withdraw from the Company of Booksellers.* [Philadelphia, 1796]. Reproduced in Clarkin, *Mathew Carey,* 43.

———. *Vindicaiae Hibernicae: Or, Ireland Vindicated.* Philadelphia, 1819.

Carlyle, Alexander. *The Autobiography of Dr. Alexander Carlyle of Inveresk, 1722–1805.* Ed. J. H. Burton. New ed., 1910; reprint, Bristol, 1990.

A Catalogue of Books and Copyrights, including the Entire Stock of the Late William Creech, Esq. Which will be Offered, or Sold by Auction to A Company of Booksellers, at the Exchange Coffee-House, Edinburgh, on Monday, 17th July 1815. Edinburgh, 1815.

A Catalogue of Books, Published by the Different Members of the Philadelphia Company of Printers and Booksellers, and Now for Sale, at Wm. Spotswood's Book-store. Philadelphia, 1794.

A Catalogue of Books, which Will Begin to Be Sold by Auction, by the Sheriff's of the City of Dublin; Being the Bound Stock in Trade of Mr. Robt. Bell, Bookseller, at His Great Theatre in Caple-Street, on Wednesday the 2d of December 1767; Consisting of above Five Thousand Books in All Languages and Faculties; Also, the Interest of the Lease of that Large and Valuable Concern, which Mr. Bell, at a Very Considerable Expence, Has Fitted Up, and Subject to a Small Ground Rent. [Dublin, 1767].

A Catalogue of the Copies and Shares, of the late Mr Andrew Millar; which will be sold by Auction, to a Select Number of Booksellers of London and Westminster, at the Queen's-Arms Tavern, in St. Paul's Church-Yard, on Tuesday the 13th of June, 1769. [London, 1769]. Annotated copy, Murray Archive.

Chambers, John. *Proposals for Printing by Subscription, by John Chambers, No. 5 Abbey-Street, (A New Edition, Considerably Enlarged and Improved,) A System of Modern Geography . . . By William Guthrie, Esq.* London, n.d.; reprint, Dublin, n.d.

Chambers, Robert, and Thomas Thomson, eds. *A Biographical Dictionary of Eminent Scotsmen.* 2 vols. 1834; reprint, London, 1870.

Character of the Celebrated Dr Robertson, Author of the History of Scotland, and of the Emperor Charles the Fifth. Philadelphia, 1772. Also published in the *Pennsylvania Packet* for 10 Aug. 1772.

Chesterfield, Philip Dormer Stanhope, Earl of. *Principles of Politeness, and of Knowing the World.* Philadelphia, 1778. Also contained in Bell, *Miscellanies for Sentimentalists.*

————. *Principles of Politeness, and of Knowing the World.* Philadelphia, 1781.

Cockburn, Henry. *Memorials of His Time.* 1856; reprint, Edinburgh, 1988.

Collyer, Mary. *The Death of Abel. In Five Books. Attempted from the German of Mr. Gessner.* 8th ed. Dublin, 1767.

[Constable, Archibald]. *Catalogue of Books Printed for Archibald Constable & Co. Edinburgh.* Edinburgh, 1814.

Constable, Thomas. *Archibald Constable and His Literary Correspondents.* 3 vols. Edinburgh, 1873.

The Constitution, Proceedings, etc. of the Philadelphia Company of Printers & Booksellers. [Philadelphia], 1793 [i.e., 1794].

"Correspondence between William Strahan and David Hall, 1763–1777." *Pennsylvania Magazine of History and Biography* 10 (1886): 86–99, 217–32, 322–33, 461–73; 11 (1887): 98–111, 223–34, 346–57, 482–90; and 12 (1888): 116–22, 240–51.

Crawfurd, George, and William Semple. *The History of the Shire of Renfrew.* Paisley, 1782.

Creech, William. *Edinburgh Fugitive Pieces.* Edinburgh, 1815. Originally published anonymously in 1791.

[————]. *Letters, Addressed to Sir John Sinclair, Bart. Respecting the Mode of Living, Arts, Commerce, Literature, Manners, etc. of Edinburgh, in 1763, and since that Period.* Edinburgh, 1793.

[————]. *Letters containing a Comparative View of Edinburgh in the Years 1763 and 1783.* Edinburgh, 1783.

"Critical Remarks on Some of the Most Eminent Historians of England." *The Bee, or Literary Weekly Intelligencer* 3 (25 May 1791): 89–96.

Cumberland, Richard. *The Memoirs of Richard Cumberland.* 2 vols. 1807; reprint, New York, 2002.

Deanina [Denina], Carlo. *Extract from an Essay on the Progress of Learning among the Scots, Annexed to An Essay on the State of Learning in Italy.* N.p., 1763.

Denina, Carlo. *An Essay on the Revolutions of Literature.* Trans. John Murdoch. London, [1771].

Diderot, Denis. *The Encyclopedia: Selections.* Ed. and trans. Stephen J. Gendzier. New York, 1967.

[Donaldson, Alexander]. *Some Thoughts on the State of Literary Property Humbly Submitted to the Consideration of the Public.* London: printed for Alexander Donaldson. Dublin: reprinted for Robert Bell, [1767].

Du Ponceau, Peter Stephen. "The Autobiography of Peter Stephen Du Ponceau." Ed.

James L. Whitehead. *Pennsylvania Magazine of History and Biography* 63 (1939): 432–61.

Encyclopaedia Britannica; or, a Dictionary of Arts, Sciences, etc. 2nd ed. Edinburgh, 1778–82.

Encyclopaedia Britannica; or, a Dictionary of Arts, Sciences, and Miscellaneous Literature. 3rd ed. 18 vols. Edinburgh, 1788–97.

[*Encyclopaedia Britannica.*] *Supplement to the Third Edition of the Encyclopaedia Britannica.* 2 vols. Edinburgh, 1799–1801. Also 2nd ed. 2 vols. Edinburgh, 1803.

Erskine, David Stewart, eleventh Earl of Buchan. *The Anonymous and Fugitive Essays of the Earl of Buchan.* Edinburgh, 1812.

[Ewing, Thomas]. *Select Catalogue of Books. Printed for, and Sold by Thomas Ewing Bookseller in Capel-Street, Dublin.* [Dublin, 1774].

Ferguson, Adam. *The Correspondence of Adam Ferguson.* 2 vols. Ed. Vincenzo Merolle. London, 1995.

———. "Minutes of the Life and Character of Joseph Black, M.D." *Transactions of the Royal Society of Edinburgh* 5 (1805): 101–17.

Fielding, Henry. *The History of the Adventures of Joseph Andrews, and of His Friend Mr. Abraham Adams.* 3rd ed. 2 vols. London, 1743.

———. *Miscellanies.* 3 vols. London, 1743.

Fieser, James, ed. *Scottish Common Sense Philosophy: Sources and Origins.* 3 vols. Bristol, 2000.

[Fleming, Robert]. "An Account of the Life of the Late Mr William Creech." In Creech, *Edinburgh Fugitive Pieces,* xi–xli.

Forbes, Sir William. *An Account of the Life and Writings of James Beattie, LL.D.* 2 vols. 1806; reprint, Bristol, 1997.

Franklin, Benjamin. *The Papers of Benjamin Franklin.* 37 vols. Ed. Leonard W. Labaree et al. New Haven, CT, 1959–.

[Gaine, Hugh]. *Hugh Gaine's Catalogue of Books, Lately Imported from England, Ireland, and Scotland, and to Be Sold at His Book-Store and Printing-Office, at the Bible in Hanover-Square.* New York, 1792.

Gibbon, Edward. *Memoirs of My Life.* Ed. Georges A. Bonnard. London, 1966.

Goethe, Johann Wolfgang von. *The Sorrows and Sympathetic Attachments of Werter.* Philadelphia, 1784.

Goldsmith, Oliver. *An History of the Earth, and Animated Nature.* 8 vols. Dublin, 1776–77.

———. *An History of the Earth, and Animated Nature.* 4 vols. Philadelphia, 1795.

———. *The Traveller; or, A Prospect of Society, a Poem.* America [Philadelphia], 1768.

———. *The Vicar of Wakefield: A Tale.* 2 vols. Dublin, 1767.

———. *The Vicar of Wakefield: A Tale.* 4th ed. 2 vols. Dublin [i.e., Boston], 1767.

Graydon, Alexander. *Memoirs of His Own Time.* Ed. John Stockton Littell. Philadelphia, 1846.

Guthrie, William. *An Improved System of Modern Geography; or, A Geographical, Historical, and Commercial Grammar; Containing the Ancient and Present State of All the*

Empires, Kingdoms, States, and Republics in the Known World. . . . Originally Compiled by William Guthrie, Esq. A New Edition, Considerably Enlarged and Corrected, Inscribed, by Permission, to the Royal Irish Academy. Dublin, 1789. Marked "Chambers's Edition" at the top of the title page.

———. *A New Geographical, Historical, and Commercial Grammar.* Dublin, 1780, 1789 (10th ed.), 1794.

———. *A New Geographical, Historical, and Commercial Grammar; and Present State of the Several Kingdoms of the World.* 11th ed. London, 1788.

———. *A New System of Modern Geography: or, A Geographical Historical, and Commercial Grammar; and Present State of the Several Kingdoms of the World.* London, 1792.

———. *A New System of Modern Geography: or, A Geographical, Historical, and Commercial Grammar, and Present State of the Several Nations of the World.* 2 vols. Philadelphia, 1794–95.

[Hall, David]. *Imported in the Last Vessels from England, and to Be Sold by David Hall, at the New Printing-Office, in Market-street, Philadelphia, the Following Books.* [Philadelphia, ca. 1768].

Hallett, Robin, ed. *Records of the African Association.* Edinburgh and London, 1964.

[Hamilton, Elizabeth]. *Short Memoir of Gavin Hamilton, Publisher and Bookseller in Edinburgh, in the Eighteenth Century.* Aberdeen, 1840.

Hawkesworth, John. *An Account of the Voyages undertaken by Order of His Present Majesty for Making Discoveries in the Southern Hemisphere.* London, 1773.

Heron, Robert. "Memoir of the Life of the Late Robert Burns." *Monthly Magazine and British Review,* 1796. Reprinted in Lindsay, *Burns Encyclopedia,* 166–82.

———. *Observations Made in a Journey through the Western Counties of Scotland.* 2 vols. Perth, 1793.

History of the Speculative Society of Edinburgh. Edinburgh, 1845.

Home, Henry, Lord Kames. *Elements of Criticism.* 4th ed. 2 vols. Edinburgh, 1769.

Homer. *The Iliad of Homer. Translated from the Greek by Alexander Pope, Esq.* Philadelphia, 1795.

Hume, David. *Essays and Treatises on Several Subjects.* London, 1758.

———. *Essays and Treatises on Several Subjects.* 2 vols. London, 1768.

———. *Essays and Treatises on Several Subjects.* 2 vols. London, 1777.

———. *The History of England, from the Invasion of Julius Caesar to the Revolution in 1688.* 8 vols. Dublin, 1772.

———. *Letters of David Hume to William Strahan.* Ed. G. Birkbeck Hill. Oxford, 1888.

———. *The Letters of David Hume.* 2 vols. Ed. J. Y. T. Greig. Oxford, 1932.

———. *The Life of David Hume, Esq. Written by Himself.* London, 1777.

———. *A Treatise of Human Nature.* 3 vols. London, 1739–40.

Hume, David, and others. *The Life of David Hume, Esq; the Philosopher and Historian, Written by Himself. To which Are Added, The Travels of a Philosopher, containing Observations on the Manners and Arts of Various Nations, in Africa and Asia. From the*

French of M. Le Poivre, Late Envoy to the King of Cochin-China, and Now Intendant of the Isles of Bourbon and Mauritius. Philadelphia, 1778. Also contained in Bell, *Miscellanies for Sentimentalists.*

Jefferson, Thomas. *The Papers of Thomas Jefferson.* Ed. Julian P. Boyd et al. Princeton, 1950–.

Johnson, Samuel. *The History of Rasselas, Prince of Abissina: An Asiatic Tale.* America [Philadelphia], 1768.

Kenrick, Norah. *Chronicles of a Nonconformist Family.* Birmingham, 1932.

Kerr, Robert. *Memoirs of the Life, Writings, and Correspondence of William Smellie.* 2 vols. 1811; reprint, Bristol, 1996.

Knox, John. *A View of the British Empire, More Especially Scotland; with Some Proposals for the Improvement of that Country, the Extension of Its Fisheries, and the Relief of the People.* 2 vols. 3rd ed., London, 1785; 4th ed., London, 1789.

Lackington, James. *The Confessions of J. Lackington, Late Bookseller, at the Temple of the Muses, in a Series of Letters to a Friend.* London, 1804.

———. *Memoirs of the Forty-Five First Years of the Life of James Lackington.* 8th ed. London, 1794.

La Rochefoucauld, François, duc de. *Maxims and Moral Reflections.* Philadelphia, 1778. Also contained in Bell, *Miscellanies for Sentimentalists.*

Lambert, Sheila, ed. *House of Commons Sessional Papers of the Eighteenth Century.* Wilmington, DE, 1975.

Lee, John. *Memorial for the Bible Societies in Scotland.* Edinburgh, 1824.

Leechman, William. "The Preface, Giving Some Account of the Life, Writings, and Character of the Author." In Francis Hutcheson, *A System of Moral Philosophy*, 1: i–xlviii. Glasgow, 1755.

Leland, Thomas. *The History of Ireland from the Invasion of Henry II.* 3 vols. Dublin, 1773; London, 1773.

Lockhart, J. G. *Memoirs of Sir Walter Scott.* 5 vols. London, 1900.

———. *Peter's Letters to His Kinfolk.* 2 vols. 3rd ed. Edinburgh, 1819.

MacBride, David. *A Methodical Introduction to the Theory and Practice of Physic.* London, 1772.

———. *A Methodical Introduction to the Theory and Practice of the Art of Medicine.* 2 vols. Dublin, 1777.

MacCormick, Joseph. *State-Papers and Letters, Addressed to William Carstares.* London, 1774.

Mackenvie, William. *Annals and Statistics of the United Presbyterian Church.* Edinburgh, 1873.

Mackenzie, Henry. *Account of the Life and Writings of John Home.* 1822; reprint, Bristol, 1997.

———. *The Anecdotes and Egotisms of Henry Mackenzie, 1745–1831.* Ed. Harold William Thompson. 1927; reprint, Bristol, 1996.

———. *Letters to Elizabeth Rose of Kilravock: On Literature, Events and People, 1768–1815.* Ed. Horst W. Drescher. Edinburgh and London, 1967.

————. *Literature and Literati: The Literary Correspondence and Notebooks of Henry Mackenzie. Volume 1/Letters, 1766–1827.* Ed. Horst W. Drescher. Frankfurt, 1989.

Mackintosh, Sir James. *The Miscellaneous Works of Sir James Mackintosh.* 3 vols. London, 1854.

[Macky, John]. *A Journey through England.* London, 1714.

Macpherson, James. *The Rights of Great Britain Asserted against the Claims of America: Being an Answer to the Declaration of the General Congress.* Philadelphia, 1776.

Marmontel, Jean François. *The History of Belisarius, the Heroick and Humane Roman General.* America [Philadelphia], 1770.

M'Culloch, John. *A Concise History of the United States, from the Discovery of America till 1795.* 2nd ed. Philadelphia, 1795.

————. *Introduction to the History of America.* Philadelphia, 1787.

————. *Memoirs of the Late Rev. William Marshall.* Philadelphia, 1806.

McCulloch, William. "William McCulloch's Additions to Thomas's *History of Printing.*" Ed. C. S. B[righam]. *Proceedings of the American Antiquarian Society* 31 (1921): 89–247.

McKean, H. S. *Questions upon Adam's Roman Antiquities: For the Use of Students in Harvard College.* Cambridge, MA, 1834.

[McLewes, Jon]. *The Philadelphiad.* 2 vols. Philadelphia, 1784.

Millar, Robert. *The History of the Church under the Old Testament, from the Creation of the World.* Edinburgh, 1730.

————. *The History of the Propagation of Christianity, and the Overthrow of Paganism.* 2 vols. 3rd ed. London, 1731.

Mizuta, Hiroshi, ed. *The Edinburgh Reviews and the Scottish Intellectual Climate: Materials for the Study of the Scottish Enlightenment.* Nagoya, 1975.

Moore, John. "The Life of T. Smollett, M.D." In *The Works of Tobias Smollett, M.D.*, 1: xcvii–cxcvi. London, 1797.

More, Hannah. *Essays on Various Subjects, Principally Designed for Young Ladies.* Philadelphia, 1786.

A New and Correct Catalogue of All the English Books which Have Been Printed from the Year 1700, to the Present Time, with Their Prices. London, 1767.

New Statistical Account of Scotland. 15 vols. Edinburgh and London, 1845.

Nichols, John. *Illustrations of the Literary History of the Eighteenth Century, Consisting of Authentic Memoirs and Original Letters of Eminent Persons; and Intended as a Sequel to the Literary Anecdotes.* 8 vols. 1817–58; reprint, New York, 1966.

————. *Literary Anecdotes of the Eighteenth Century.* 9 vols. London, 1812–16.

O'Halloran, Sylvester. *A General History of Ireland, from the Earliest Accounts to the Close of the Twelfth Century.* 2 vols. London, 1778.

————. *An Introduction to the Study of the History and Antiquities of Ireland.* Dublin, 1772; reissued in London, 1772.

"On the History of Authors by Profession." *The Bee, or Literary Weekly Intelligencer* 1 (12 Jan. 1791): 62–65; 3 (11 May 1791): 13–15; 3 (18 May 1791): 52–54; 3 (25 May 1791): 87–89.

Paine, Thomas. *Common Sense; Addressed to the Inhabitants of America.* Philadelphia, 1776.

Park, Mungo. *Travels in the Interior Districts of Africa.* Ed. Kate Ferguson Marsters. Durham, NC, and London, 2000.

Payne, John [Robert Heron?]. *A New and Complete System of Universal Geography.* Montrose, 1796.

Pinkerton, John. *The Literary Correspondence of John Pinkerton, Esq.* 2 vols. Ed. Dawson Turner. London, 1830.

Playfair, John. "Account of Matthew Stewart, D.D." *Transactions of the Royal Society of Edinburgh* 1, pt. 1 (1788): 57–76.

———. "Biographical Account of the Late Dr. James Hutton F.R.S. Edin." *Transactions of the Royal Society of Edinburgh* 5 (1805): 39–99.

Pomfret, J. E. "Some Further Letters of William Strahan, Printer." *Pennsylvania Magazine of History and Biography* 60 (1936): 455–89.

Pope, Alexander, trans. *The Iliad of Homer.* 6 vols. London, 1715–20.

———, trans. *The Odyssey of Homer.* 5 vols. London, 1725–26.

———. *The Works of Mr. Alexander Pope.* London, 1717.

Pratt, S. J. *Supplement to the Life of David Hume, Esq.* London, 1777.

Ramsay, Allan. *The Tea-Table Miscellany: or, A Collection of Choice Songs, Scots and English.* 10th ed. 4 vols. London, 1740.

Ramsay, David. *The History of the American Revolution.* 2 vols. Philadelphia, 1789.

———. *The History of the Revolution of South-Carolina, from a British Province to an Independent State.* 2 vols. Trenton, NJ, 1785.

Ramsay, John. *Scotland and Scotsmen in the Eighteenth Century.* 2 vols. Ed. Alexander Allardyce. Edinburgh and London, 1888; reprint, Bristol, 1996.

Records of the Worshipful Company of Stationers, 1554–1920. Reels 6–9. Ed. Robin Myers. Microfilm. 115 reels. London, 1985. Originals at Stationers' Hall, London.

Rees, Thomas. *Reminiscences of Literary London from 1779 to 1853.* New York, 1896.

Reid, Thomas. *The Correspondence of Thomas Reid.* Ed. Paul B. Wood. Edinburgh, 2002.

———. *Philosophical Works.* 2 vols. Ed. Sir William Hamilton. 1895; reprint, Hildesheim, 1967.

Richardson, Samuel. *The Correspondence of Samuel Richardson.* 6 vols. Ed. Anna Laetitia Barbauld. London, 1804.

Rider, William. *An Historical and Critical Account of the Living Authors of Great-Britain.* London, 1762.

Roberts, William. *Memoirs of the Life and Correspondence of Mrs. Hannah More.* 2 vols. New York, 1835.

Robertson, William. *The Works of William Robertson.* 12 vols. Ed. Richard B. Sher and Jeffrey Smitten. Bristol, 1996.

Romans, Bernard. *A Concise Natural History of East and West Florida.* New York, 1776. Originally published in 1775.

Rudiman, Thomas. *The Rudiments of the Latin Tongue; or, A Plain and Easy Introduction to Latin Grammar.* Philadelphia, 1786.

Rush, Benjamin. *The Autobiography of Benjamin Rush.* Ed. George W. Corner. Princeton, 1948.

————. *An Eulogium in Honour of the Late Dr. William Cullen, Professor of the Practice of Physic in the University of Edinburgh; Delivered before the College of Physicians of Philadelphia, on the 9th of July, Agreeably to Their Vote of the 4th of May, 1790.* Philadelphia, 1790.

————. *The Letters of Benjamin Rush.* 2 vols. Ed. L. H. Butterfield. Philadelphia, 1951.

[Russell, William]. *The History of Modern Europe.* 5 vols. London, 1786.

Salmon, Thomas. *A New Geographical and Historical Grammar: Wherein the Geographical Part Is Truly Modern; and the Present State of the Several Kingdoms of the World Is So Interspersed as to Render the Study of Geography Both Entertaining and Instructive.* 11th ed. London, 1769.

Scott, Thomas. *The Holy Bible, containing the Old and New Testaments, with Original Notes, Practical Observations, and Copious Marginal References.* 5 vols. Philadelphia, 1804–9.

Scott, Sir Walter. *The Letters of Sir Walter Scott.* 12 vols. Ed. H. J. C. Grierson. London, 1932–37.

Sheridan, Thomas. *A General Dictionary of the English Language.* 3rd ed. Philadelphia, 1789.

Sibbald, J[ames]. *A New Catalogue of the Edinburgh Circulating Library: containing Twenty Thousand Volumes, English, French, and Italian . . . Including All the Books that Have Been Lately Published in Every Branch of Literature; Likewise Music and Prints.* Edinburgh, 1786.

Sinclair, Sir John. *The Correspondence of the Right Honourable Sir John Sinclair, Bart. With Reminiscences of the Most Distinguished Characters Who Have Appeared in Great Britain, and in Foreign Countries, during the Last Fifty Years.* 2 vols. London, 1831.

[Smellie, William]. *In the Press, and to be Published by William Creech, in Eight Volumes, 8vo, the Count de Buffon's Natural History; Translated into English, from the Paris Edition in Sixteen Volumes, Quarto, Illustrated with above Two Hundred and Forty Beautiful Copper-plates, and Embellished with an Elegant Portrait of the Author.* Edinburgh, 1779.

Smiles, Samuel, ed. *A Publisher and His Friends: Memoir and Correspondence of the Late John Murray, with an Account of the Origin and Progress of the House, 1768–1843.* 2 vols. London, 1891.

Smith, Adam. *The Correspondence of Adam Smith.* Ed. Ernest Campbell Mossner and Ian Simpson Ross. 2nd ed. Oxford, 1987.

————. *The Theory of Moral Sentiments.* Ed. D. D. Raphael and A. L. Macfie. 1976; reprint, Indianapolis, IN, 1982.

Smith, Elihu Hubbard. *The Diary of Elihu Hubbard Smith (1771–1798).* Ed. James E. Croinin. Philadelphia, 1973.

Smith, John. *Galic Antiquities.* Edinburgh, 1780.

Smith, Samuel Stanhope. *An Essay on the Causes of the Variety of Complexion and Figure in the Human Species. To Which Are Added Strictures on Lord Kaims's Discourse, on the Original Diversity of Mankind.* Philadelphia, 1787.

[Smollett, Tobias], ed. *A Compendium of Authentic and Entertaining Voyages, Digested in a Chronological Series.* 7 vols. London, 1756.

———. *Continuation of the Complete History of England.* 4 vols. London, 1762–65.

———. *The Expedition of Humphry Clinker.* Ed. O. M. Brack, Jr., and Thomas R. Preston. Athens, GA, and London, 1990.

———. *The History of England, from the Revolution to the Death of George the Second (Designed as a Continuation of Mr. Hume's History).* 5 vols. London, 1785.

———. *The Letters of Tobias Smollett.* Ed. Lewis M. Knapp. Oxford, 1970.

Smollett, Tobias, and others. *The History of England, from the Revolution to the End of the American War, and Peace of Versailles in 1783.* 8 vols. Edinburgh, 1791. Otherwise known as the Mudie edition; see also Society of Gentlemen.

[Society of Gentlemen]. *The History of the British Empire, from the Year 1765, to the End of 1783. Containing an Impartial History of the Origin, Progress, and Termination of the American Revolution. By a Society of Gentlemen.* 2 vols. Philadelphia, 1798. (Also published as vols. 5 and 6 of Robert Campbell's edition of Smollett and others, *The History of England,* and vols. 7 and 8 of the Mudie edition of Smollett's *History.*)

Somerville, Thomas. *My Own Life and Times, 1741–1814.* 1861; reprint, Bristol, 1996.

Sprague, William B. *Annals of the American Pulpit.* 9 vols. New York, 1869.

Stark, J. *Picture of Edinburgh: containing a Description of the City and Its Environs.* Edinburgh, 1819.

———. *Picture of Edinburgh; containing A History and Description of the City, with a Particular Account of Every Remarkable Object in, or Establishment Connected with, the Scottish Metropolis.* Edinburgh, 1806.

Sterne, Laurence. *A Sentimental Journey, through France and Italy.* North-America [Philadelphia], 1770.

Stevens, George Alexander. *Songs, Comic, Satyrical, and Sentimental.* Philadelphia, 1778.

Stewart, Dugald. "Account of the Life and Writings of Adam Smith, LL.D." (1794). Ed. I. S. Ross. In Adam Smith, *Essays on Philosophical Subjects,* ed. D. D. Raphael and A. S. Skinner, 269–351. Oxford, 1980.

———. "Dissertation: Exhibiting the Progress of Metaphysical, Ethical, and Political Philosophy, since the Revival of Letters in Europe." In *Collected Works of Dugald Stewart,* vol. 1. Edinburgh, 1854.

The Strahan Archive from the British Library. Microfilm. 23 reels. Woodbridge, CT, and Reading, UK, 1990. Originals at the British Library, London, Add. MSS 48800–48918.

[Strahan, William, and Thomas Cadell], *Books Printed for W. Strahan, and T. Cadell in the Strand.* [London, 1781]. Numerous versions were printed during the late 1770s and early 1780s.

Temple, William Johnston. *Diaries of William Johnston Temple, 1780–1796.* Ed. Lewis Bettany. Oxford, 1929.

Thomas, Isaiah. *The History of Printing in America.* Ed. Marcus A. McCorison. 2nd ed. New York, 1970.

[Thompson, William]. Thomas Newte, *Prospects and Observations; on a Tour in England and Scotland: Natural, Oeconomical, and Literary.* London, 1791.

Thomson, James. *James Thomson (1700–1748): Letters and Documents.* Ed. Alan Dugald McKillup. Lawrence, KA, 1958.

———. *The Seasons.* Philadelphia, 1777.

———. *The Works of James Thomson. With His Last Corrections and Improvements. To which Is Prefixed, An Account of His Life and Writings* [by Patrick Murdoch]. 2 vols. London, 1762.

Timperley, C. H. *Encyclopaedia of Literary and Typographical Anecdote.* 2 vols. 1839; reprint, New York and London, 1977.

[Topham, Edward]. *Letters from Edinburgh; Written in the Years 1774 and 1775.* 1776; reprint, Edinburgh, 1971.

Turnbull, George. *The Principles of Moral and Christian Philosophy.* 2 vols. London, 1740.

———. *A Treatise on Ancient Painting, containing Observations on the Rise, Progress, and Decline of that Art amongst the Greeks and Romans.* London, 1740.

Tytler, Alexander Fraser, Lord Woodhouselee. *Elements of General History, Ancient and Modern.* 2 vols. Edinburgh, 1801.

———. *Memoirs of the Life and Writings of the Honourable Henry Home of Kames.* 2 vols. Edinburgh, 1807.

An Universal History, from the Earliest Account of Time. 21 vols. London, 1747–54.

Voltaire. *Letters concerning the English Nation.* Ed. Nicholas Cronk. Oxford, 1999.

———. "M. De Voltaire to the Authors of the *Literary Gazette:* On the Elements of Criticism." *Edinburgh Advertiser,* 10–14 Dec. 1773.

———. *Miscellanies by M. de Voltaire.* Philadelphia, 1778.

Walpole, Horace. *The Works of Horatio Walpole, Earl of Oxford.* 5 vols. London, 1798.

———. *The Yale Edition of Horace Walpole's Correspondence.* 48 vols. Ed. W. S. Lewis. New Haven, CT, 1937–83.

Warburton, J., J. Whitlaw, and Robert Walsh. *History of the City of Dublin.* 2 vols. London, 1818.

[West, William]. *Fifty Years' Recollections of an Old Bookseller.* Cork, 1835.

———. "Letters to My Son at Rome." *Aldine Magazine of Biography, Bibliography, Criticism, and the Arts* 1 (1838): 1–4, 18–20, 33–37, 50–52, 66–71; (1839): 82–87, 99–117, 132–35, 156–57, 200–210, 248–254, 308–311.

"William Thomson." In *Public Characters of 1802–1803.* London, 1803.

Williams, Helen Maria. *Letters containing a Sketch of the Politics of France.* Philadelphia, 1796.

Willison, John. *A Treatise concerning the Sanctifying the Lord's Day.* 2nd ed. Edinburgh, 1722.

Wilson, William. *A Defence of the Reformation-Principles of the Church of Scotland. With a Continuation of the Same.* 1739; reprint, Glasgow, 1769.

Witherspoon, John. *The Dominion of Providence over the Passions of Men. A Sermon Preached at Princeton, on the 17th of May, 1776. Being the General Fast Appointed by the Congress through the United Colonies.* Philadelphia, 1776.

———. *Ecclesiastical Characteristics: or, the Arcana of Church Policy. Being an Humble Attempt to Open Up the Mystery of Moderation.* Glasgow, 1753.

Wodrow, Robert. *The Correspondence of the Rev. Robert Wodrow.* 3 vols. Ed. Thomas M'Crie. Edinburgh, 1843.

Wodrow–Kenrick Correspondence, c. 1750–1810. Microfilm. 1 reel. East Ardsley, Wakefield, UK, 1982. Originals in Dr. Williams's Library, London, MS 24157.

Woodfall, William. *An Impartial Sketch of the Debate in the House of Commons of Ireland, on a Motion Made on Friday, August 12, 1785, by the Rt. Hon. Thomas Orde.* Dublin, [1785].

Young, I. Gilbert. *Fragmentary Records of the Youngs, Comprising, in Addition to Much General Information Respecting Them, a Particular and Extended Account of the Posterity of Ninian Young.* Philadelphia, 1869.

Young, William S. "Yellow Fever in Philadelphia in 1793, and a Death-Bed Scene." *Evangelical Repository, and United Presbyterian Review* (April 1866): 615–25.

Zachs, William, ed. *Hugh Blair's Letters to His Publishers, 1777–1800.* Edinburgh, forthcoming.

SECONDARY SOURCES

Abbattista, Guido. "The Business of Paternoster Row: Towards a Publishing History of the *Universal History* (1736–65)." *Publishing History* 17 (1985): 5–50.

Adams, J. R. R. *The Printed Word and the Common Man: Popular Culture in Ulster, 1700–1900.* Belfast, 1987.

Adams, Thomas R., and Nicholas Barker. "A New Model for the Study of the Book." In Barker, *Potencie of Life,* 5–43.

Addison, W. Innes. *The Matriculation Albums of the University of Glasgow from 1728 to 1858.* Glasgow, 1913.

Ahlstrom, Sydney E. "The Scottish Philosophy and American Theology." *Church History* 24 (1955): 257–72.

"*AHR* Forum: How Revolutionary Was the Print Revolution?" *American Historical Review* 107 (2002): 84–128. See also Elizabeth L. Eisenstein as well as Adrian Johns.

Alden, John. "John Mein: Scourge of Patriots." *Transactions of the Colonial Society of Massachusetts* 34 (1945): 571–99.

———. "John Mein, Publisher." *Papers of the Bibliographical Society of America* 36 (1942): 199–214.

Aldridge, A. Owen, ed. *The Ibero-American Enlightenment.* Urbana, IL, 1971.

Allan, David. "Eighteenth-Century Private Subscription Libraries and Provincial

Urban Culture: The Amicable Society of Lancaster, 1769–c.1820." *Library History* 19 (2001): 57–76.

———. *Making British Culture: English Readers and the Scottish Enlightenment.* Forthcoming.

———. "Opposing Enlightenment: Revd Charles Peters' Reading of the Natural History of Religion." *Eighteenth-Century Studies* 38 (2005): 301–21.

———. "A Reader Writes: Negotiating *The Wealth of Nations* in an Eighteenth-Century English Commonplace Book." *Philological Quarterly* (2004): 207–33.

———. "The Scottish Enlightenment and the Readers of Late Georgian Lancaster: 'Light in the North.'" *Northern History* 36 (2000): 267–81.

———. "Some Methods and Problems in the History of Reading: Georgian England and the Scottish Enlightenment." *Journal of the Historical Society* 3 (2003): 91–124.

———. *Virtue, Leaning and the Scottish Enlightenment: Ideas of Scholarship in Early Modern History.* Edinburgh, 1993.

Alston, Robin. "Library History: The British Isles–to 1850." www.r-alston.co.uk/contents.htm.

Amory, Hugh. "'*De Facto* Copyright?' Fielding's *Works* in Partnership, 1769–1821." *Eighteenth-Century Studies* 17 (1984): 449–76.

———. "Hugh Blair." In *Sale Catalogues of Libraries of Eminent Persons*, ed. A. N. L. Munby, vol. 7, *Poets and Men of Letters*, 159–64. London, 1971–75.

Amory, Hugh, and David D. Hall, eds. *The Colonial Book in the Atlantic World.* Cambridge, 2000.

Anderson, John, ed. *Catalogue of Early Belfast Printed Books, 1694 to 1830.* Belfast, 1890.

———. *History of the Belfast Library and Society for Promoting Knowledge, Commonly Known as The Linen Hall Library.* Belfast, 1888.

Anderson, R. G. W., M. L. Caygill, A. G. MacGregor, and L. Syson, eds. *Enlightening the British: Knowledge, Discovery, and the Museum in the Eighteenth Century.* London, 2003.

Andrew, Edward G. *Patrons of Enlightenment.* Toronto, 2006.

Andrews, Corey. *Literary Nationalism in Eighteenth-Century Scottish Club Poetry.* Lewiston, NY, 2004.

Andrews, Stuart. *Unitarian Radicalism: Political Rhetoric, 1770–1814.* Basingstoke, UK, 2003.

Annals of The Club 1764–1915. London, 1914.

Armbruster, Carol, ed. *Publishing and Readership in Revolutionary France and America.* Westport, CT, and London, 1993.

Armitage, David. "Three Concepts of Atlantic History." In *The British Atlantic World, 1500–1800*, ed. David Armitage and Michael J. Braddick, 11–27. Basingstoke, UK, 2002.

Arner, Robert D. *Dobson's Encyclopaedia: The Publisher, Text, and Publication of America's First Britannica, 1789–1803.* Philadelphia, 1991.

————. "Thomas Dobson's American Edition of the *Encyclopaedia Britannica*." In *Notable Encyclopedias of the Late Eighteenth Century: Eleven Successors of the "Encyclopédie*," ed. Frank A. Kafker, 201–54. Oxford, 1994.

Austen-Leigh, Richard A. *The Story of a Printing House*. 2nd ed. London, 1912.

Axelrod, Alan. "Mathew Carey." In *American Writers of the Early Republic*, ed. Emory Elliott, 89–96. Detroit, 1985.

Baines, Paul. "Robert Heron." In *Eighteenth-Century British Literary Biographers*, ed. Steven Serafin, 161–69. Detroit, 1994.

Baker, Keith Michael, and Peter Hanns Reill, eds. *What's Left of Enlightenment: A Postmodern Question*. Stanford, 2001.

Barber, Giles. *Studies in the Booktrade of the European Enlightenment*. London, 1994.

Barker, Nicholas. *Form and Meaning in the History of the Book: Selected Essays*. London, 2003.

————, ed. *A Potencie of Life: Books in Society*. London, 1993.

Basker, James G. "Scotticisms and the Problem of Cultural Identity in Eighteenth-Century Britain." In Dwyer and Sher, *Sociability and Society in Eighteenth-Century Scotland*, 81–95.

————. *Tobias Smollett: Critic and Journalist*. Newark, DE, 1988.

Bassnett, Susan. *Translation Studies*. 3rd ed. London, 2002.

Bate, W. Jackson. *Samuel Johnson*. New York and London, 1975.

[Beath, Robert B.], ed. *An Historical Catalogue of the St. Andrew's Society of Philadelphia*. 2 vols. Philadelphia, 1907–13.

Beauchamp, Tom L. Introduction to *An Enquiry concerning Human Understanding: A Critical Edition* by David Hume, xi–civ. Oxford, 2000.

————. Introduction to *An Enquiry concerning the Principles of Morals: A Critical Edition* by David Hume, xi–lxxx. Oxford, 1998.

Becker, Carl. *The Heavenly City of the Eighteenth-Century Philosophers*. New Haven, CT, 2003. Originally published in 1931.

Belanger, Terry. "Booksellers' Sales of Copyright: Aspects of the London Book Trade 1718–1768." Ph.D. diss., Columbia University, 1970.

————. "Booksellers' Trade Sales, 1718–1768." *Library*, 5th ser., 30 (1975): 281–302.

————. "A Directory of the London Book Trade, 1766." *Publishing History* 1 (1977): 5–48.

————. "From Bookseller to Publisher: Changes in the London Book Trade, 1750–1850." In *Bookselling and Book Buying: Aspects of the Nineteenth-Century British and North American Book Trade*, ed. Richard G. Landon, 7–16. Chicago, 1978.

————. "Publishers and Writers in Eighteenth-Century England." In Rivers, *Books and Their Readers*, 5–26.

Benedict, Barbara. *Making the Modern Reader: Cultural Mediation in Early Modern Literary Anthologies*. Princeton, 1996.

————. "Readers, Writers, Reviewers, and the Professionalization of Literature." In *The Cambridge Companion to English Literature, 1740–1830*, ed. Thomas Keymer and Jon Mee, 3–23. Cambridge, 2004.

————. "'Service to the Public': William Creech and Sentiment for Sale." In Dwyer and Sher, *Sociability and Society in Eighteenth-Century Scotland*, 119–46.

Bennett, Stuart. *Trade Bookbinding in the British Isles, 1660–1800*. New Castle, DE, and London, 2004.

Benson, Charles. "Printers and Booksellers in Dublin 1800–1850." In Myers and Harris, *Spreading the Word*, 47–59.

Bentley, G. E., Jr. "Copyright Documents in the George Robinson Archive: William Godwin and Others 1713–1820." *Studies in Bibliography* 35 (1982): 67–110.

Berman, Eleanor Davidson. *Thomas Jefferson among the Arts*. New York, 1947.

Berry, Christopher J. *Social Theory of the Scottish Enlightenment*. Edinburgh, 1997.

Besterman, Theodore, ed. *The Publishing Firm of Cadell & Davies: Select Correspondence and Accounts 1793–1836*. Oxford, 1938.

Birn, Raymond. *Forging Rousseau: Print, Commerce and Cultural Manipulation in the Late Enlightenment*. Oxford, 2001.

Bishop, Edward L. "Book History." In Groden, Kreiswirth, and Szeman, *Johns Hopkins Guide*, 131–36.

Blagden, Cyprian. *The Stationers' Company: A History, 1403–1959*. Cambridge, MA, 1960.

Blanning, T. C. W. *The Culture of Power and the Power of Culture: Old Regime Europe, 1660–1789*. Oxford, 2002.

Bloom, Edward. *Samuel Johnson in Grub Street*. Providence, RI, 1957.

Bonnell, Thomas F. "Bookselling and Canon-Making: The Trade Rivalry over the English Poets, 1776–1783." In *Studies in Eighteenth-Century Culture*, ed. Leslie Ellen Brown and Patricia Craddock, 19:53–69. East Lansing, MI, 1989.

————. "John Bell's *Poets of Great Britain*: The 'Little Trifling Edition' Revisited." *Modern Philology* 85 (1987): 128–52.

Bonner, Stephen Eric. *Reclaiming the Enlightenment: Toward a Politics of Radical Engagement*. New York, 2004.

Botein, Stephen. "The Anglo-American Book Trade before 1776: Personnel and Strategies." In *Printing and Society in Early America*, ed. William L. Joyce, David D. Hall, Richard D. Brown, and John B. Hench, 48–82. Worcester, MA, 1983.

Box, M. A. *The Suasive Art of David Hume*. Princeton, 1990.

Brack, O. M., Jr. "Tobias Smollett Puffs His Histories." In Brack, *Writers, Books, and Trade*, 267–88.

————. "William Strahan: *Scottish* Printer and Publisher." *Arizona Quarterly* 31 (1975): 179–90.

————, ed. *Writers, Books, and Trade: An Eighteenth-Century Miscellany for William B. Todd*. New York, 1994.

Bracken, James K., and Joel Silver, eds. *The British Literary Book Trade, 1700–1820*. Detroit, 1995.

Brady, Frank. *James Boswell: The Later Years 1769–1795*. New York, 1984.

Brewer, John. "The Misfortunes of Lord Bute: A Case-Study in Eighteenth-Century Political Argument and Public Opinion." *Historical Journal* 16 (1973): 3–43.

————. *The Pleasures of the Imagination: English Culture in the Eighteenth Century*. New York, 1997.

British Book Trade Index (BBTI). www.bbti.bham.ac.uk.

Broadie, Alexander, ed. *The Cambridge Companion to the Scottish Enlightenment*. Cambridge, 2003.

Brock, C. Helen. "The Happiness of Riches." In Bynum and Porter, *William Hunter*, 35–54.

Brown, Iain Gordon. *Building for Books: The Architectural Evolution of the Advocates' Library, 1689–1925*. Aberdeen, 1989.

————. *Monumental Reputation: Robert Adam and the Emperor's Palace*. Edinburgh, 1992.

Brown, Michael. *Francis Hutcheson in Dublin, 1719–1730*. Dublin, 2002.

Brown, Stephen W. "Robert and Andrew Foulis." In Bracken and Silver, *British Literary Book Trade*, 135–42.

————. "William Creech, Kincaid and Creech, Creech and Smellie." In Bracken and Silver, *British Literary Book Trade*, 75–80.

————. "William Smellie and Natural History: Dissent and Dissemination." In Withers and Wood, *Science and Medicine*, 191–214.

————. "William Smellie and the Culture of the Edinburgh Book Trade, 1752–1795." In Wood, *Culture of the Book*, 61–88.

————. "William Smellie and the Printer's Role in the Eighteenth-Century Edinburgh Book Trade." In Isaac and McKay, *Human Face of the Book Trade*, 29–43.

Brown, Stephen W., and Warren McDougall, eds. *The Edinburgh History of the Book in Scotland*, vol. 2: *1707–1800*. Edinburgh, forthcoming.

Brown, Stewart J., ed. *William Robertson and the Expansion of Empire*. Cambridge, 1997.

Brunton, Deborah C. "The Transfer of Medical Education: Teaching at the Edinburgh and Philadelphia Medical Schools." In Sher and Smitten, *Scotland and America*, 242–74.

Bryson, Gladys. *Man and Society: The Scottish Inquiry of the Eighteenth Century*. 1945; reprint, New York, 1968.

Buchan, James. *Capital of the Mind: How Edinburgh Changed the World*. London, 2003. Published in North America as *Crowded with Genius: The Scottish Enlightenment; Edinburgh's Moment of the Mind*. New York, 2003.

Butterfield, L. H. "The American Interests of the Firm of E. and C. Dilly, with Their Letters to Benjamin Rush, 1770–1795." *Papers of the Bibliographical Society of America* 45 (1951): 283–332.

Bynum, W. F., and Roy Porter, eds. *William Hunter and the Eighteenth-Century Medical World*. Cambridge, 1985.

Cadell, Patrick, and Ann Matheson, eds. *For the Encouragement of Learning: Scotland's National Library, 1689–1989*. Edinburgh, 1989.

Carnie, R. H. "Scholar-Printers of the Scottish Enlightenment, 1740–1800." In Carter and Pittock, *Aberdeen and the Enlightenment*, 298–308.

Carnochan, W. B. "The 'Trade of Authorship' in Eighteenth-Century Britain." In Barker, *Potencie of Life*, 127–43.

Carrick, J. C. *William Creech: Robert Burns' Best Friend*. Dalkeith, 1903.

Carter II, Edward C. "The Political Activities of Mathew Carey, Nationalist, 1760–1814." Ph.D. diss., Bryn Mawr College, 1962.

Carter, Jennifer J., and John H. Pittock, eds. *Aberdeen and the Enlightenment*. Aberdeen, 1987.

Carter, Philip. *Men and the Emergence of Polite Society: Britain, 1660–1800*. Harlow, UK, 2001.

Cassirer, Ernst. *The Philosophy of the Enlightenment*. Trans. Fritz C. A. Koelln and James P. Pettegrove. Princeton, 1951. Originally published in German in 1932.

Chambers, Neil A. *Joseph Banks and the British Museum: The World of Collecting, 1770–1830*. London, 2006.

Chambers, Robert, ed. *The Life and Works of Robert Burns*. 4 vols. Revised by William Wallace. Edinburgh and London, 1896.

Chaplin, Joyce E. "Expansion and Exceptionalism in Early American History." *Journal of American History* 89 (2003): 1431–55.

Chard, Leslie F. "Bookseller to Publisher: Joseph Johnson and the English Book Trade, 1760–1810." *Library*, 5th ser., 32 (1977): 138–54.

Chartier, Roger. "The Man of Letters." In *Enlightenment Portraits*, ed. Michel Vovelle, 142–89. Trans. Lydia G. Cochrane. Chicago, 1997.

———. *The Order of Books: Readers, Authors, and Libraries in Europe between the Fourteenth and Eighteenth Centuries*. Trans. Lydia G. Cochrane. Stanford, 1994.

Christensen, Jerome. *Practicing Enlightenment: Hume and the Formation of a Literary Career*. Madison, WI, 1987.

Clark, J. C. D. *Samuel Johnson: Literature, Religion and English Cultural Politics from the Restoration to Romanticism*. Cambridge, 1994.

Clark, Peter. *British Clubs and Societies, 1580–1800: The Origins of an Associational World*. Oxford, 2000.

Clarkin, William. *Mathew Carey: A Bibliography of His Publications, 1785–1824*. New York and London, 1984.

Clayton, Timothy. *The English Print, 1688–1802*. New Haven, CT, and London, 1997.

Cloyd, E. L. *James Burnett Lord Monboddo*. Oxford, 1972.

Cochrane, J. A. *Dr. Johnson's Printer: The Life of William Strahan*. Cambridge, MA, 1964.

Cole, Richard Cargill. *Irish Booksellers and English Writers, 1740–1800*. London, 1986.

Colley, Linda. *Britons: Forging the Nation, 1707–1837*. New Haven, CT, and London, 1992.

Collins, A. S. *Authorship in the Days of Johnson: Being a Study of the Relation between Author, Patron, Publisher and Public, 1726–1780*. New York, 1929.

———. *The Profession of Letters: A Study of the Relation of Author to Patron, Publisher and Public, 1780–1832*. 1928; reprint, Clifton, NJ, 1973.

Connell, Philip. "Death and the Author: Westminster Abbey and the Meaning of the Literary Monument." *Eighteenth-Century Studies* 38 (2005): 557–85.

Conrad, Stephen A. *Citizenship and Common Sense: The Problem of Authority in the Social Background and Social Philosophy of the Wise Club of Aberdeen.* New York, 1987.

Court, Franklin E. *Institutionalizing English Literature: The Culture and Politics of Literary Study, 1750–1900.* Stanford, 1992.

Crawford, J. "Reading and Book Use in 18th-Century Scotland." *Bibliotheck* 19 (1994): 23–43.

Crawford, Robert, ed. *The Scottish Invention of English Literature.* Cambridge, 1998.

Curtin, Nancy J. *The United Irishmen: Popular Politics in Ulster and Dublin, 1791–1798.* Oxford, 1994.

Curwin, Henry. *A History of Booksellers, the Old and the New.* London, [1873].

Dane, Joseph A. *The Myth of Print Culture: Essays on Evidence, Textuality, and Bibliographical Method.* Toronto, Buffalo, and London, 2003.

Darlow, T. H., and H. F. Moule, eds. *Historical Catalogue of Printed Editions of the English Bible, 1525–1961.* Revised by A. S. Herbert. London, 1968.

Darnton, Robert. *The Business of Enlightenment: A Publishing History of the Encyclopédie, 1775–1800.* Cambridge, MA, and London, 1979.

———. "The Case for the Enlightenment: George Washington's False Teeth." In R. Darnton, *George Washington's False Teeth: An Unconventional Guide to the Eighteenth Century.* New York, 2003.

———. *The Forbidden Best-Sellers of Pre-Revolutionary France.* New York and London, 1996.

———. *The Great Cat Massacre and Other Episodes in French Cultural History.* New York, 1984.

———. *The Kiss of Lamourette: Reflections in Cultural History.* New York, 1990.

———. *The Literary Underground of the Old Regime.* Cambridge, MA, 1982.

———. "The Science of Piracy: A Crucial Ingredient in Eighteenth-Century Publishing." *Studies on Voltaire and the Eighteenth Century (SVEC)* 2003 (12): 3–29.

———. "The Social History of Ideas." In Darnton, *Kiss of Lamourette*, 219–52. Originally published in 1971.

———. "Sounding the Literary Market in Prerevolutionary France." *Eighteenth-Century Studies* 17 (1984): 477–92.

———. "Two Paths through the Social History of Ideas." In Mason, *Darnton Debate*, 251–94.

———. "What Is the History of Books?" In Darnton, *Kiss of Lamourette*, 107–35. New York, 1990.

Darnton, Robert, and Michel Schlup, eds. *Le rayonnement d'une maison d'édition dans l'Europe des Lumières: La Société typographique de Neuchâtel, 1769–1789.* Neuchâtel, 2005.

Davies, Ronald E. "Robert Millar: An Eighteenth-Century Scottish Latourette." *Evangelical Quarterly* 62 (1990): 143–56.

Davison, Peter, ed. *The Book Encompassed: Studies in Twentieth-Century Bibliography.* Cambridge, 1992.

Dawson, Deidre, and Pierre Morère, eds. *Scotland and France in the Enlightenment.* Lewisburg, PA, and London, 2004.

Dean, Dennis R. *James Hutton and the History of Geology.* Ithaca, NY, and London, 1992.

Deazley, Ronan. "The Myth of Copyright at Common Law." *Cambridge Law Journal* 62 (2003): 106–33.

———. *On the Origin of the Right to Copy: Charting the Movement of Copyright Law in Eighteenth-Century Britain (1695–1775).* Oxford, 2004.

De Jong, J. A. *As the Waters Cover the Sea: Millennial Expectations in the Rise of Anglo-American Missions, 1640–1810.* Kampen, 1970.

Devine, T. M. *Scotland's Empire and the Shaping of the Americas, 1600–1815.* Washington, DC, 2003. Published outside North America as *Scotland's Empire, 1600–1815.* London, 2003.

Dobson, Austin. "Fielding and Andrew Millar." *Library,* 3rd ser., 7 (1916): 177–90.

Donaldson, A. M. "Burns's Final Settlement with Creech: A Revealing Document." *Burns Chronicle* (1952): 38–41.

Donoghue, Frank. "Colonizing Readers: Review Criticism and the Formation of a Reading Public." In *The Consumption of Culture, 1600–1800: Image, Object, Text,* ed. Ann Bermingham and John Brewer, 54–74. London and New York, 1995.

———. *The Fame Machine: Book Reviewing and Eighteenth-Century Literary Careers.* Stanford, 1996.

Donovan, A. L. *Philosophical Chemistry in the Scottish Enlightenment: The Doctrines and Discoveries of William Cullen and Joseph Black.* Edinburgh, 1975.

Duffill, Mark. "Notes on a Collection of Letters Written by Mungo Park between 1790 and 1794, with Some Remarks concerning His Later Published Observations on the African Slave Trade." *Hawick Archaeological Society Transactions* (2001): 35–55.

Duncan, Douglas. *Thomas Ruddiman: A Study in Scottish Scholarship of the Early Eighteenth Century.* Edinburgh, 1965.

Durey, Michael. *Transatlantic Radicals and the American Republic.* Lawrence, KS, 1997.

———. *"With the Hammer of Truth": James Thomson Callender and America's Early National Heroes.* Charlottesville, VA, and London, 1990.

Dwyer, John. "The *Caledonian Mercury* and Scottish National Culture, 1763–1801." In *Politics and the Press in Hanoverian Britain,* ed. Karl Schweizer and Jeremy Black. *Journal of History and Politics* 7 (1989): 147–69.

———. *Virtuous Discourse: Sensibility and Community in Late Eighteenth-Century Scotland.* Edinburgh, 1987.

Dwyer, John, and Richard B. Sher, eds. *Sociability and Society in Eighteenth-Century Scotland.* Edinburgh, 1993. Also published as a special issue of *Eighteenth-Century Life* 15 (1991).

Eaves, T. C. Duncan, and Ben D. Kimpel. *Samuel Richardson: A Biography.* Oxford, 1971.

Egerer, J. W. *A Bibliography of Robert Burns.* Edinburgh, 1964.

Eisenstein, Elizabeth L. *Grub Street Abroad: Aspects of the French Cosmopolitan Press from the Age of Louis XIV to the French Revolution.* Oxford, 1992.

———. *Print Culture and Enlightenment Thought.* Chapel Hill, NC, 1986.

———. *The Printing Press as an Agent of Change.* 2 vols. Cambridge, 1979.

———. "An Unacknowledged Revolution Revisited." *American Historical Review* 107 (2002): 87–105.

Emerson, Roger L. "*Catologus Librorum A.C.D.A.:* The Library of Archibald Campbell, Third Duke of Argyll (1682–1761)." In Wood, *Culture of the Book,* 12–39.

———. "Lord Bute and the Scottish Universities, 1760–1792." In Schweizer, *Lord Bute,* 147–79.

———. "The Philosophical Society of Edinburgh, 1737–1747." *British Journal for the History of Science* 12 (1979): 154–91.

———. "The Philosophical Society of Edinburgh, 1748–1768." *British Journal for the History of Science* 14 (1981): 133–76.

———. "The Philosophical Society of Edinburgh, 1768–1783." *British Journal for the History of Science* 18 (1985): 255–303.

———. *Professors, Patronage and Politics: The Aberdeen Universities in the Eighteenth Century.* Aberdeen, 1992.

———. "The Scientific Interests of Archibald Campbell, 1st Earl of Ilay and 3rd Duke of Argyll (1682–1761)." *Annals of Science* 59 (2002): 21–56.

———. "Scottish Cultural Change, 1660–1710, and the Union of 1707." In *A Union for Empire: Political Thought and the Union of 1707,* ed. John Robertson, 121–44. Cambridge, 1995.

———. "The Scottish Enlightenment and the End of the Philosophical Society of Edinburgh." *British Journal for the History of Science* 21 (1988): 33–66.

———. "The Scottish Literati and America, 1680–1800." In Landsman, *Nation and Province,* 183–200.

———. "The Social Composition of Enlightened Scotland: The Select Society of Edinburgh, 1754–1764." *Studies on Voltaire and the Eighteenth Century* 114 (1973): 291–329.

———. *University Patronage and the Scottish Enlightenment.* Edinburgh, forthcoming.

Emerson, Roger L., and Paul Wood. "Science and Enlightenment in Glasgow, 1690–1802." In Withers and Wood, *Science and Medicine,* 79–142.

English Short-Title Catalogue (ESTC). Restricted on-line access through Research Libraries Group.

Essick, Robert N. *William Blake's Commercial Book Illustrations: A Catalogue and Study of the Plates Engraved by Blake after Designs by Other Artists.* Oxford, 1991.

Ewan, Joseph. "One Professor's Chief Joy: A Catalog of Books Belonging to Benjamin Smith Barton." In *Science and Society in Early America: Essays in Honor of Whitfield J. Bell, Jr.,* ed. Randolph Shipley Klein, 311–44. Philadelphia, 1986.

Ezell, Margaret J. M. *Social Authorship and the Advent of Print.* Baltimore and London, 1999.

Fabian, Bernhard. *The English Book in Eighteenth-Century Germany.* London, 1992.

———. "English Books and Their Eighteenth-Century German Readers." In Korshin, *Widening Circle,* 117–96.

Fagg, Jane B. "Biographical Introduction." In *The Correspondence of Adam Ferguson,* ed. Vincenzo Merolle, 1:xix–cxxxvi. London, 1995.

Fairfull-Smith, George. *The Foulis Press and the Foulis Academy: Glasgow's Eighteenth-Century School of Art and Design.* Glasgow, 2001.

Farren, Donald. "Subscription: A Study of the Eighteenth-Century American Book Trade." D.L.S. thesis, Columbia University, 1982.

Fawcett, Arthur. *The Cambuslang Revival: The Scottish Evangelical Revival of the Eighteenth Century.* London, 1971.

Feather, John. *Book Prospectuses before 1801 in the Gough Collection.* Oxford, 1980.

———. *Book Prospectuses before 1801 in the John Johnson Collection.* Oxford, 1976.

———. "The Commerce of Letters: The Study of the Eighteenth-Century Book Trade." *Eighteenth-Century Studies* 17 (1984): 404–24.

———. "The Country Trade in Books." In Myers and Harris, *Spreading the Word,* 165–83.

———. *A History of British Publishing.* London and New York, 1988.

———. "John Nourse and His Authors." *Studies in Bibliography* 34 (1981): 205–26.

———. "The Power of Print: Word and Image in Eighteenth-Century England." In *Culture and Society in Britain, 1660–1800,* ed. Jeremy Black, 51–68.

———. *The Provincial Book Trade in Eighteenth-Century England.* Cambridge, 1985.

———. *Publishing, Piracy and Politics: An Historical Study of Copyright in Britain.* London and New York, 1994.

Febvre, Lucien, and Henri-Jean Martin. *The Coming of the Book: The Impact of Printing, 1450–1800.* Trans. David Gerard. 1958; London and New York, 1990.

Festa, Lynn. "Personal Effects: Wigs and Possessive Individualism in the Long Eighteenth Century." *Eighteenth-Century Life* 29 (2005): 47–90.

Fieser, James. Introduction to *Essays and Treatises on Several Subjects,* by David Hume, 1: v–xviii. 2 vols. Facsimile of 1777 edition. Bristol, 2002.

Fish, Stanley. *Is There a Text in This Class? The Authority of Interpretive Communities.* Cambridge, MA, 1980.

Fisk, William Lyons. *The Scottish High Church Tradition in America: An Essay in Scotch-Irish Ethnoreligious History.* Washington, DC, 1995.

Fitzpatrick, Martin, Peter Jones, Crista Knellwolf, and Iain McCalman, eds. *The Enlightenment World.* London and New York, 2004.

Fleischacker, Samuel. "Adam Smith's Reception among the American Founders, 1776–1790." *William and Mary Quarterly,* 3rd ser., 59 (2002): 869–96.

———. "The Impact on America: Scottish Philosophy and the American Founding." In Broadie, *Cambridge Companion,* 316–37.

Fleming, Patricia Lockhart, Gilles Gallichan, and Yvan Lamonde, eds. *History of the Book in Canada*, vol. 1: *Beginnings to 1840*. Toronto, 2004.

Forbes, Duncan. *Hume's Philosophical Politics*. Cambridge, 1975.

Forbes, Margaret. *Beattie and His Friends*. 1904; reprint, Bristol, 1990.

Foster, John. "A Scottish Contributor to the Missionary Awakening: Robert Millar of Paisley." *International Review of Missions* 37 (1948): 138–45.

Foucault, Michel. "What Is an Author?" In *The Foucault Reader*, ed. Paul Rabinow, 101–20. London, 1986.

Fox, Adam. *Oral and Literate Culture in England, 1500–1700*. Oxford, 2000.

Foxon, David. *Pope and the Early Eighteenth-Century Book Trade*. Oxford, 1991.

Franklin, Benjamin, V, ed. *Boston Printers, Publishers, and Booksellers, 1640–1800*. Boston, 1980.

Fraser, Andrew G. *The Building of Old College: Adam, Playfair and the University of Edinburgh*. Edinburgh, 1989.

Free, William J. *The Columbian Magazine and American Literary Nationalism*. The Hague, 1968.

Fry, Michael. *"Bold, Independent, Unconquer'd and Free": How the Scots Made America Safe for Liberty, Democracy and Capitalism*. Ayr, 2003. Published in North America as *How the Scots Made America*. New York, 2005.

———. *The Scottish Empire*. Edinburgh, 2001.

Fulton, Henry L. "An Eighteenth-Century Best Seller." *Papers of the Bibliographical Society of America* 66 (1972): 428–33.

———. "John Moore, the Medical Profession and the Glasgow Enlightenment." In Hook and Sher, *Glasgow Enlightenment*, 176–89.

Furdell, Elizabeth Lane. *Publishing and Medicine in Early Modern England*. Rochester and Woodbridge, Suffolk, 2002.

Furet, François, Geneviève Bollème, and Daniel Roche, eds. *Livre et société dans la France du XVIII siècle*. 2 vols. Paris and The Hague, 1965–70.

Gaines, William H., Jr. "The Continental Congress Considers the Publication of a Bible, 1777." *Studies in Bibliography* 3 (1950): 274–81.

Gargett, Graham, and Geraldine Sheridan, eds. *Ireland and the French Enlightenment, 1700–1800*. Basingstoke, UK, and New York, 1999.

Garrard, Graeme. *Counter-Enlightenments: From the Eighteenth Century to the Present*. Abingdon, UK, and New York, 2006.

———. "The Enlightenment and Its Enemies." *American Behavioral Scientist* 49 (2006): 664–80.

Gascoigne, Bamber. *How to Identify Prints*. New York, 1986.

Gascoigne, John. *Joseph Banks and the English Enlightenment: Useful Knowledge and Polite Culture*. Cambridge, 1994.

Gaskell, Philip. *A Bibliography of the Foulis Press*. 2nd ed. Winchester, UK, 1986.

———. *A New Introduction to Bibliography*. 1972; reprint, Winchester, UK, and New Castle, DE, 1995.

Gaskill, Howard, ed. *The Reception of Ossian in Europe*. Bristol, 2004.

Gay, Peter. "Carl Becker's Heavenly City." In Gay, *Party of Humanity*, 188–210.

———. *The Enlightenment: An Interpretation*. 2 vols. New York, 1966–69.

———. *The Party of Humanity: Essays in the French Enlightenment*. New York, 1959.

———. "The Social History of Ideas: Ernst Cassirer and After." In *The Critical Spirit: Essays in Honor of Herbert Marcuse*, ed. Kurth H. Wolff and Barrington Moore, Jr., 106–20. Boston, 1967.

Genette, Gérard. *Paratexts: Thresholds of Interpretation*. Trans. Jane E. Lewin. Cambridge, 1997.

Gilhooly, J., comp. *A Directory of Edinburgh in 1752*. Edinburgh, 1988.

Gillespie, Raymond, and Andrew Hadfield, eds. *The Oxford History of the Irish Book*, vol. 3: *The Irish Book in English, 1550–1800*. Oxford, 2006.

Gimbel, Richard. *Thomas Paine: A Bibliographical Check List of Common Sense with an Account of Its Publication*. New Haven, CT, 1956; reprint, Port Washington, NY, and London, 1973.

Goldstein, Philip. "Reader-Response Theory and Criticism." In Groden, Kreiswirth, and Szeman, *Johns Hopkins Guide*, 793–97.

Golinski, Jan. *Science as Public Culture: Chemistry and Enlightenment in Britain, 1760–1820*. Cambridge, 1992.

Goodman, Dena. *The Republic of Letters: A Cultural History of the French Enlightenment*. Ithaca, NY, and London, 1994.

———. "Difference: An Enlightenment Concept." In Baker and Reill, *What's Left of Enlightenment*, 129–47.

Goodman, Dena, and Kathleen Wellman, eds. *The Enlightenment*. Boston, 2004.

Gordon, Daniel. *Citizens without Sovereignty: Equality and Sociability in French Thought, 1670–1789*. Princeton, 1994.

———. "On the Supposed Obsolescence of the French Enlightenment." In Gordon, *Postmodernism and the Enlightenment*, 201–21.

———. "Post-Structuralism and Post-Modernism." In Kors, *Encyclopedia of the Enlightenment*, 3:341–46.

———, ed. *Postmodernism and the Enlightenment: New Perspectives in Eighteenth-Century French Intellectual History*. New York and London, 2001.

Gough, Hugh. "Book Imports from Continental Europe in Late Eighteenth-Century Ireland: Luke White and the Société Typographique de Neuchâtel." *Long Room* 38 (1993): 35–48.

Graham, Henry Grey. *A Group of Scottish Women*. New York, 1908.

———. *Scottish Men of Letters in the Eighteenth Century*. London, 1908.

Grant, Ian R. "Note on Publicity for, Distribution and Management of, the *Statistical Account of Scotland*." In *The Statistical Account of Scotland, 1791–1799*, ed. Sir John Sinclair, 1:xlvii–lxxiii. Reprint. East Ardsley, UK, 1983.

Grant, James. *Cassell's Old and New Edinburgh*. 3 vols. London, n.d.

Gray, John. *Enlightenment's Wake: Politics and Culture at the Close of the Modern Age*. London, 1995.

Green, James N. "Benjamin Franklin as Publisher and Bookseller." In *Reappraising*

Benjamin Franklin: A Bicentennial Perspective, ed. J. A. Leo Lemay, 98–114. Newark, DE, 1993.

———. "English Books and Printing in the Age of Franklin." In Amory and Hall, *Colonial Book*, 248–98.

———. "From Printer to Publisher: Mathew Carey and the Origins of Nineteenth-Century Book Publishing." In *Getting the Books Out: Papers of the Chicago Conference on the Book in 19th-Century America*, ed. Michael Hackenberg, 26–44. Washington, DC, 1987.

———. *Mathew Carey: Publisher and Patriot.* Philadelphia, 1985.

———. "The Rise of Book Publishing in the United States, 1785–1840." In Gross and Kelley, *Extensive Republic*.

Griffin, Dustin. "Fictions of Eighteenth-Century Authorship." *Essays in Criticism* 43 (1993): 181–94.

———. *Literary Patronage in England, 1650–1800.* Cambridge, 1996.

Griffin, Robert J., ed. *The Faces of Anonymity: Anonymous and Pseudonymous Publication from the Sixteenth to the Twentieth Century.* London, 2003.

Griffiths, Antony. *Prints and Printmaking: An Introduction to the History and Techniques.* London, 1980.

Groden, Michael, Martin Kreiswirth, and Imre Szeman, eds. *The Johns Hopkins Guide to Literary Theory and Criticism.* 2nd ed. Baltimore and London, 2005.

Gross, Robert A., and Mary C. Kelley, eds. *An Extensive Republic: Books, Culture and Society in the New Nation, 1790–1840. A History of the Book in America.* Vol. 2. Chapel Hill, NC, forthcoming.

Guerrini, Anita. "'A Scotsman on the Make': The Career of Alexander Stuart." In Wood, *Scottish Enlightenment*, 157–76.

Gutjahr, Paul C. *An American Bible: A History of the Good Book in the United States, 1777–1880.* Stanford, 1999.

Haakonssen, Knud. *Natural Law and Moral Philosophy: From Grotius to the Scottish Enlightenment.* Cambridge, 1996.

Habermas, Jürgen. *The Structural Transformation of the Public Sphere.* Trans. Thomas Burger. Cambridge, MA, 1991.

Hall, Carol. "Andrew Millar." In Bracken and Silver, *British Literary Book Trade*, 184–90.

Hall, David D. *Cultures of Print: Essays in the History of the Book.* Amherst, MA, 1996.

Hancock, David. "Scots in the Slave Trade." In Landsman, *Nation and Province*, 60–93.

Harlan, Robert D. "David Hall's Bookshop and Its British Sources of Supply." In *Books in America's Past: Essays Honoring Rudolph H. Gjelsness*, ed. David Kaser, 2–23. Charlottesville, VA, 1966.

———. "Some Additional Figures of Distribution of Eighteenth-Century English Books." *Papers of the Bibliographical Society of America* 59 (1965): 160–70.

———. "William Strahan: Eighteenth Century London Printer and Publisher." Ph.D. diss., University of Michigan, 1960.

———. "William Strahan's American Book Trade, 1744–76." *Library Quarterly* 31 (1961): 235–44.

Harrison, Eliza Cope, ed. *Philadelphia Merchant: The Diary of Thomas P. Cope, 1800–1851.* South Bend, IN, 1978.

Hart, Edward L., ed. *Minor Lives: A Collection of Biographies by John Nichols.* Cambridge, MA, 1971.

Hauser, Arnold. *The Social History of Art.* 4 vols. New York, 1951.

Herman, Arthur. *How the Scots Invented the Modern World: The True Story of How Western Europe's Poorest Nation Created Our World and Everything in It.* New York, 2001. Published outside North America as *The Scottish Enlightenment: The Scots' Invention of the Modern World.* London, 2001.

Hernlund, Patricia. "Three Bankruptcies in the London Book Trade, 1746–61: Rivington, Knapton, and Osborn." In Brack, *Writers, Books, and Trade,* 77–122.

———. "William Strahan, Printer: His Career and Business Procedures." Ph.D. diss., University of Chicago, 1965.

———. "William Strahan's Ledgers: Standard Charges for Printing, 1738–1785." *Studies in Bibliography* 20 (1967): 89–111.

Hesse, Carla. "Books in Time." In *The Future of the Book,* ed. Geoffrey Nunberg, 21–33. Berkeley, CA, 1996.

———. *The Other Enlightenment: How French Women Became Modern.* Princeton, 2001.

———. "Print Culture in the Enlightenment." In Fitzpatrick et al., *Enlightenment World,* 366–80.

Himmelfarb, Gertrude. *The Roads to Modernity: The British, French, and American Enlightenments.* New York, 2004.

Hind, Arthur M. *A History of Engraving and Etching.* 3rd ed. New York, 1963.

Hodgson, Norma, and Cyprian Blagden. *The Notebook of Thomas Bennet and Henry Clements (1686–1719) with Some Aspects of Book Trade Practice.* Oxford, 1956.

Hollinger, David A. "The Enlightenment and the Genealogy of Cultural Conflict in the United States." In Baker and Reill, *What's Left of Enlightenment,* 7–18.

Hont, Istvan, and Michael Ignatieff, eds. *Wealth and Virtue: The Shaping of Political Economy in the Scottish Enlightenment.* Cambridge, 1983.

Hook, Andrew. *From Goosecreek to Gandercleugh: Studies in Scottish-American Literary and Cultural Relations.* East Linton, UK, 1999.

———. *Scotland and America: A Study of Cultural Relations, 1750–1835.* Glasgow, 1975.

Hook, Andrew, and Richard B. Sher, eds. *The Glasgow Enlightenment.* East Linton, UK, 1995.

Horkheimer, Max, and Theodor W. Adorno. *Dialectic of Enlightenment.* Trans. John Cumming. New York, 1988.

Howell, Wilbur Samuel. *Eighteenth-Century British Logic and Rhetoric.* Princeton, 1971.

Hudak, Leona M. *Early American Women Printers and Publishers, 1639–1820.* Metuchen, NJ, and London, 1978.

Hunter, Ian. *Rival Enlightenments: Civil and Metaphysical Philosophy in Early Modern Germany.* Cambridge, 2001.

Hutchison, Henry. "An Eighteenth-Century Insight into Religious and Moral Education." *British Journal of Educational Studies* 24 (1976): 233–41.

Hyland, Paul, with Olga Gomez and Francesca Greensides, eds. *The Enlightenment: A Sourcebook and Reader.* London and New York, 2003.

Isaac, Peter. "Charles Elliot and Spilsbury's Antiscorbutic Drops." In *The Reach of Print*, ed. Peter Isaac and Barry McKay, 157–74. Winchester, UK, and New Castle, DE, 1998.

———. "Charles Elliot and the English Provincial Book Trade." In Isaac and McKay, *Human Face of the Book Trade*, 97–116.

Isaac, Peter, and Barry McKay, eds. *The Human Face of the Book Trade: Print Culture and Its Creators.* Winchester, UK, and New Castle, DE, 1999.

Jacob, Margaret C. *Living the Enlightenment: Freemasonry and Politics in Eighteenth-Century Europe.* Oxford, 1991.

Jacobs, Edward H. *Accidental Migrations: An Archaeology of Gothic Discourse.* Lewisburg, PA, and London, 2000.

Jayne, Allen. *Jefferson's Declaration of Independence: Origins, Philosophy, and Theology.* Lexington, KY, 1998.

Johns, Adrian. "How to Acknowledge a Revolution." *American Historical Review* 107 (2002): 106–28.

———. *The Nature of the Book: Print and Knowledge in the Making.* Chicago, 1998.

Jones, Vivien, ed. *Women and Literature in Britain, 1700–1800.* Cambridge, 2000.

Jordanova, Ludmilla. *Defining Features: Scientific and Medical Portraits, 1660–2000.* London, 2000.

Justice, George L., and Nathan Tinker, eds. *Women's Writing and the Circulation of Ideas: Manuscript Publication in England, 1550–1800.* Cambridge, 2002.

Kafker, Frank A. "The Achievement of Andrew Bell and Colin Macfarquhar as the First Publishers of the *Encyclopaedia Britannica*." *British Journal for Eighteenth-Century Studies* 18 (1995): 139–52.

Karras, Alan L. *Sojourners in the Sun: Scottish Migrants in Jamaica and the Chesapeake, 1740–1800.* Ithaca, NY, and London, 1992.

Keen, Paul. *The Crisis of Literature in the 1790s: Print Culture and the Public Sphere.* Cambridge, 1999.

Kennedy, Máire. "The Domestic and International Trade of an Eighteenth-Century Dublin Bookseller: John Archer (1782–1810)." *Dublin Historical Record* 49 (1996): 94–105.

———. *French Books in Eighteenth-Century Ireland.* Oxford, 2001.

———. "Readership in French: The Irish Experience." In Gargett and Sheridan, *Ireland and the French Enlightenment*, 3–20.

Kennedy, Máire, and Geraldine Sheridan. "The Trade in French Books in Eighteenth-Century Ireland." In Gargett and Sheridan, *Ireland and the French Enlightenment*, 173–96.

Kent, Elizabeth E. *Goldsmith and His Booksellers*. Ithaca, NY, 1933.

Kernan, Alvin. *Printing Technology, Letters and Samuel Johnson*. Princeton, 1987.

Kinane, Vincent. "'Literary Food' for the American Market: Patrick Byrne's Exports to Mathew Carey." *Proceedings of the American Antiquarian Society* 104 (1994): 315–32.

Kinane, Vincent, and Charles Benson. "Some Late 18th- and Early 19th-Century Dublin Printers' Account Books: The Graisberry Ledgers." In *Six Centuries of the Provincial Book Trade in Britain*, ed. Peter Isaac, 139–50. Winchester, UK, 1990.

Klemme, Heiner, "'And Time Does Justice to All the World': Ein unveröffentlichter Brief von David Hume an William Strahan." *Journal of the History of Philosophy* 29 (1991): 657–64.

———, ed. *Reception of the Scottish Enlightenment in Germany: Six Significant Translations, 1755–1782*. 7 vols. Bristol, 2000.

Knapp, Lewis M., ed. *The Letters of Tobias Smollett*. Oxford, 1970.

———. "The Publication of Smollett's *Complete History* . . . and *Continuation*." *Library* 16 (1935): 295–308.

———. "Smollett's Works as Printed by William Strahan, with an Unpublished Letter of Smollett to Strahan." *Library* 13 (1932): 282–91.

———. *Tobias Smollett: Doctor of Men and Manners*. 1949; reprint, New York, 1963.

Knott, Sarah. "The Culture of Sensibility in the Era of the American Revolution." D.Phil. thesis, Oxford University, 1999.

Kors, Alan Charles, ed. *Encyclopedia of the Enlightenment*. 4 vols. Oxford, 2003.

Korshin, Paul J. "Types of Eighteenth-Century Literary Patronage." *Eighteenth-Century Studies* 7 (1974): 453–73.

———, ed. *The Widening Circle: Essays on the Circulation of Literature in Eighteenth-Century Europe*. Philadelphia, 1976.

Kropf, C. R. "The Accounts of Samuel Harrison Smith, Philadelphia Printer." *Papers of the Bibliographical Society of America* 74 (1980): 13–25.

Landsman, Ned C., ed. *Nation and Province in the First British Empire: Scotland and the Americas, 1600–1800*. Lewisburg, PA, and London, 2001.

Leerssen, Joep. *Mere Irish and Fíor-Ghael: Studies in the Idea of Irish Nationality, Its Development and Literary Expression prior to the Nineteenth Century*. 2nd ed. Cork, 1996.

Levere, T. H., and G. L'E. Turner, with Jan Golinski and Larry Stewart. *Discussing Chemistry and Steam: The Minutes of a Coffee House Philosophical Society, 1780–1787*. Oxford, 2002.

Lillywhite, Bryan. *London Coffee Houses*. London, 1963.

Lindsay, Maurice. *The Burns Encyclopedia*. 3rd ed. London, 1995.

Livingston, Donald W. "Hume, English Barbarism and American Independence." In Sher and Smitten, *Scotland and America*, 133–47.

Lockwood, Thomas. "Subscription-Hunters and Their Prey." *Studies in the Literary Imagination* 34 (2001): 121–35.

Lonsdale, Roger. "Thomas Gray, David Hume and John Home's *Douglas*." In *Re-*

constructing the Book: Literary Texts in Transmission, ed. Maureen Bell, Shirley Chew, Simon Eliot, Lynette Hunter, and James L. W. West III, 57–70. Aldershot, UK, 2001.

Lough, John. *Writer and Public in France: From the Middle Ages to the Present Day.* Oxford, 1978.

Love, Harold. *The Culture and Commerce of Texts: Scribal Publication in Seventeenth-Century England.* Oxford, 1993.

Loveland, Jeff. "Georges-Louis Leclerc de Buffon's *Histoire naturelle* in English, 1775–1815." *Archives of Natural History* 31 (2004): 214–35.

Lundberg, David, and Henry F. May. "The Enlightened Reader in America." *American Quarterly* 28 (1976): 262–71.

Lupton, Kenneth. *Mungo Park the African Traveler.* Oxford, 1979.

Lutes, Richard. "Andrew Strahan and the London Sharebook System, 1785–1825: A Study of the Strahan Printing and Publishing Records." Ph.D. diss., Wayne State University, 1979.

Mack, Maynard. *Alexander Pope: A Life.* London and New York, 1985.

Mackay, John. *A Biography of Robert Burns.* Edinburgh, 1992.

Mackenzie, Allan. *History of the Lodge Canongate Kilwinning No. 2 Compiled from the Records, 1677–1888.* Edinburgh, 1888.

Macleod, Jennifer. "Freemasonry and Music in Eighteenth-Century Edinburgh." In *Freemasonry on Both Sides of the Atlantic: Essays concerning the Craft in the British Isles, Europe, the United States, and Mexico,* ed. R. William Weisberger, Wallace McLeod, and S. Brent Morris, 123–52. New York, 2002.

Malherbe, Michel. "The Impact on Europe." In Broadie, *Cambridge Companion,* 298–315.

Mali, Joseph, and Robert Wokler, eds. *Isaiah Berlin's Counter-Enlightenment.* Philadelphia, 2003.

Mann, Alastair. *The Scottish Book Trade, 1500–1720: Print Commerce and Print Control in Early Modern Scotland.* East Linton, UK, 2000.

Manning, Susan. *Fragments of Union: Making Connections in Scottish and American Writing.* Basingstoke, UK, 2002.

Marshall, Rosalind K. *Virgins and Viragos: A History of Women in Scotland from 1080 to 1980.* Chicago, 1983.

Martz, Louis L. *The Later Career of Tobias Smollett.* New Haven, CT, 1942.

Maslen, K. I. D. "Slaves or Freemen? The Case of William Bowyer, Father and Son, Printers of London, 1699–1777." In Brack, *Writers, Books, and Trade,* 145–55.

———. "William Strahan at the Bowyer Press, 1736–8." *Library,* 5th ser., 25 (1970): 250–51.

Maslen, Keith, and John Lancaster, eds. *The Bowyer Ledgers: The Printing Accounts of William Bowyer, Father and Son.* London and New York, 1991.

Mason, Haydn T., ed. *The Darnton Debate: Books and Revolution in the Eighteenth Century.* Oxford, 1998.

Mathison, H. "'Gude Black Prent': How the Edinburgh Book Trade Dealt with Burns's *Poems*." *Bibliotheck* 20 (1995): 70–87.

Maxted, Ian. *The British Book Trades, 1710–1777: An Index of Masters and Apprentices.* Exeter, 1983.

———. *The London Book Trades, 1775–1800: A Preliminary Checklist of Members.* Old Woking, Surrey, 1977.

May, Henry F. *The Enlightenment in America.* Oxford, 1976.

Mayhew, Robert J. *Enlightenment Geography: The Political Languages of British Geography, 1650–1850.* Basingstoke, UK, and New York, 2000.

———. "William Guthrie's *Geographical Grammar*, the Scottish Enlightenment and the Politics of British Geography." *Scottish Geographical Journal* 115 (1999): 19–34.

Maza, Sarah. *Private Lives and Public Affairs: The Causes Célèbres of Prerevolutionary France.* Berkeley, CA, 1993.

McBride, Ian. "William Drennan and the Dissenting Tradition." In *The United Irishmen: Republicanism, Radicalism and Rebellion*, ed. David Dickson, Dáire Keogh, and Kevin Whelan, 49–61. Dublin, 1993.

McClelland, Aiken. "Amyas Griffith." *Irish Booklore* 2 (1972): 6–21.

McCosh, James. *The Scottish Philosophy, Biographical, Expository, Critical, from Hutcheson to Hamilton.* New York, 1875.

McCullough, Lawrence B. *John Gregory and the Invention of Professional Medical Ethics and the Profession of Medicine.* Dordrecht, 1998.

McCusker, John J. *How Much Is That in Real Money? A Historical Commodity Price Index for Use as Deflator of Money Values in the Economy of the United States.* 2nd ed. Worcester, MA, 2001.

———. *Money and Exchange in Europe and America, 1660–1775: A Handbook.* 2nd ed. Chapel Hill, NC, 1992.

McDougall, Warren. "A Catalogue of Hamilton, Balfour and Neill Publications, 1750–1762." In Myers and Harris, *Spreading the Word*, 187–232.

———. "Charles Elliot and the London Booksellers in the Early Years." In Isaac and McKay, *Human Face of the Book Trade*, 81–96.

———. "Charles Elliot's Book Adventure in Philadelphia, and the Trouble with Thomas Dobson." In *Light on the Book Trade: Essays in Honour of Peter Isaac*, ed. Barry McKay, John Hinks, and Maureen Bell, 197–212. London and New Castle, DE, 2004.

———. "Charles Elliot's Medical Publications and the International Book Trade." In Withers and Wood, *Science and Medicine*, 215–54.

———. "Copyright Litigation in the Court of Session, 1738–1749, and the Rise of the Scottish Book Trade." *Edinburgh Bibliographical Society Transactions* 5, pt. 5: 2–31.

———. "Gavin Hamilton, Bookseller in Edinburgh." *British Journal for Eighteenth-Century Studies* 1 (1978): 1–19.

———. "Gavin Hamilton, John Balfour and Patrick Neill: A Study of Publishing in Edinburgh in the Eighteenth Century." Ph.D. diss., University of Edinburgh, 1974.

———. "Hamilton, Balfour, and Neill's *Edinburgh Chronicle*." *Scottish Book Collector* 2 (June–July 1991): 24–28.

———. "Scottish Books for America in the Mid 18th Century." In Myers and Harris, *Spreading the Word*, 21–46.

———. "Smugglers, Reprinters, and Hot Pursuers: The Irish-Scottish Book Trade, and Copyright Prosecutions in the Late Eighteenth Century." In *The Stationers' Company and the Book Trade, 1550–1990*, ed. Robin Myers and Michael Harris, 151–83. Winchester, UK, and New Castle, DE, 1997.

McDowell, Paula. *The Women of Grub Street: Press, Politics, and Gender in the London Marketplace, 1678–1730*. Oxford, 1998.

McDowell, R. B. "The Personnel of the Dublin Society of United Irishmen, 1791–4." *Irish Historical Studies* 2 (1941): 12–53.

McElroy, David D. *Scotland's Age of Improvement: A Survey of Eighteenth-Century Literary Clubs and Societies*. [Pullman, WA], 1969.

McGuirk, Carol. *Robert Burns and the Sentimental Era*. Athens, GA, 1985.

McKendrick, Neil, John Brewer, and J. H. Plumb. *The Birth of a Consumer Society: The Commercialization of Eighteenth-Century England*. Bloomington, IN, 1982.

McKenzie, D. F. *Making Meaning: "Printers of the Mind" and Other Essays*. Ed. Peter D. McDonald and Michael F. Suarez. Amherst, MA, 2002.

———. *Stationers' Company Apprentices, 1701–1800*. Oxford, 1978.

McKitterick, David. *Print, Manuscript and the Search for Order, 1450–1830*. Cambridge, 2003.

McLaverty, James. "The Contract for Pope's Translation of Homer's *Iliad*: An Introduction and Transcription." *Library*, 6th ser., 15 (1993): 206–25.

———. *Pope, Print and Meaning*. Oxford, 2001.

McMahon, Darrin M. *Enemies of the Enlightenment: The French Counter-Enlightenment and the Making of Modernity*. Oxford, 2001.

———. "Happiness and *The Heavenly City of the Eighteenth-Century Philosophers:* Carl Becker Revisited." *American Behavioral Scientist* 49 (2006): 681–86.

McMillan, Dorothy, ed. *The Scotswoman at Home and Abroad: Non-Fiction Writing, 1700–1900*. Glasgow, 1999.

Melton, James Van Horn. *The Rise of the Public in Enlightenment Europe*. Cambridge, 2001.

Metzdorf, Robert F. "The First American 'Rasselas' and Its Imprint." *Papers of the Bibliographical Society of America* 47 (1953): 374–76.

Meyer, Donald H. *The Instructed Conscience: The Shaping of the American National Ethic*. Philadelphia, 1972.

Millburn, John R. *A Bibliography of James Ferguson, F.R.S. (1710–76)*. Aylesbury, UK, 1983.

———. *Wheelwright of the Heavens: The Life and Work of James Ferguson, FRS*. London, 1988.

Miller, C. William. *Benjamin Franklin's Philadelphia Printing, 1728–1766: A Descriptive Bibliography.* Philadelphia, 1974.

Miller, Thomas P. *The Formation of College English: Rhetoric and Belles Lettres in the British Cultural Provinces.* Pittsburgh, 1997.

Millgate, Jane. "Archibald Constable and the Problem of London: 'Quite the connection we have been looking for.'" *Library,* 6th ser., 18 (1996): 110–23.

Mishoff, Willard O. "Business in Philadelphia during the British Occupation, 1777–78." *Pennsylvania Magazine of History and Biography* 61 (1937): 165–81.

Mitchison, Rosalind. *Agricultural Sir John: The Life of Sir John Sinclair of Ulbster, 1754–1835.* London, 1962.

Mizuta, Hiroshi, ed. *Adam Smith's Library: A Catalogue.* Oxford, 2000.

M'Lean, Hugh A. "Robert Urie, Printer in Glasgow." *Proceedings of the Glasgow Bibliographical Society* (1913–14): 88–108.

Moonie, Martin. "Print Culture and the Scottish Enlightenment, 1748–86." D. Phil. thesis, Somerville College, Oxford University, 1999.

Moore, James. "The Two Systems of Francis Hutcheson: On the Origins of the Scottish Enlightenment." In Stewart, *Philosophy of the Scottish Enlightenment,* 37–59.

Moran, Mary Catherine. "From Rudeness to Refinement: Gender, Genre and Scottish Enlightenment Discourse." Ph.D. diss., Johns Hopkins University, 1999.

Mossner, Ernest Campbell. *The Life of David Hume.* 2nd ed. Oxford, 1980.

Mossner, Ernest C., and Harry Ransom. "Hume and the 'Conspiracy of the Booksellers': The Publication and Early Fortunes of the *History of England.*" *Studies in English* 29 (1950): 162–82.

Muir, James. *John Anderson: Pioneer of Technical Education and the College He Founded.* Glasgow, 1950.

Mumby, Frank Arthur. *Publishing and Bookselling: A History from the Earliest Times to the Present Day.* 4th ed. London, 1956.

Munck, Thomas. *The Enlightenment: A Comparative Social History, 1721–1794.* London, 2000.

Muthu, Sankar. *Enlightenment against Empire.* Princeton, 2003.

———. "Enlightenment Anti-Imperialism." *Social Research* 66 (1999): 959–1007.

Myers, Robin, and Michael Harris, eds. *Spreading the Word: The Distribution Networks of Print, 1550–1850.* Winchester, UK, and New Castle, DE, 1998.

Namier, Sir Lewis, and John Brooke, eds. *The House of Commons, 1754–1790.* 3 vols. London, 1964.

Nangle, Benjamin Christie. *The Monthly Review First Series, 1749–1789: Indexes of Contributors and Articles.* Oxford, 1934.

Neeley, Kathryn A. *Mary Somerville: Science, Illumination, and the Female Mind.* Cambridge, 2001.

Nichol, Donald W. *Pope's Literary Legacy: The Book-Trade Correspondence of William Warburton and John Knapton with Other Letters and Documents, 1744–1780.* Oxford, 1992.

Nichols, R. H., and F. A. Wray. *The History of the Foundling Hospital.* London, 1935.

Nobbs, Douglas. "The Political Ideas of William Cleghorn, Hume's Academic Rival." *Journal of the History of Ideas* 26 (1965): 575–86.

Nolan, J. Bennett. *Printer Strahan's Book Account: A Colonial Controversy.* Reading, PA, 1939.

Noll, Mark A. *Princeton and the Republic, 1768–1822: The Search for Christian Enlightenment in the Era of Samuel Stanhope Smith.* Princeton, 1989.

O'Brien, Karen. *Narratives of Enlightenment: Cosmopolitan History from Voltaire to Gibbon.* Cambridge, 1997.

Ó Ciosáin, Niall. *Print and Popular Culture in Ireland, 1750–1850.* Basingstoke, UK, and New York, 1997.

O'Halloran, Clare. *Golden Ages and Barbarous Nations: Antiquarian Debate and Cultural Politics in Ireland, c. 1750–1800.* Cork, 2004.

Okie, Laird. "William Guthrie, Enlightenment Historian." *Historian* 51 (1989): 221–38.

O'Leary, Patrick. *Sir James Mackintosh: The Whig Cicero.* Aberdeen, 1989.

Oliver, Vere Langford. *The History of the Island of Antigua.* 3 vols. London, 1896.

Ormond, Richard, and Malcolm Rogers, eds. *Dictionary of British Portraiture.* Vol. 2, *Later Georgians and Early Victorians.* Comp. Elaine Kilmurray. London, 1979.

Outram, Dorinda. *The Enlightenment.* 2nd ed. Cambridge, 2005.

Oz-Salzberger, Fania. *Translating the Enlightenment: Scottish Civic Discourse in Eighteenth-Century Germany.* Oxford, 1995.

Parks, Stephen. "Justice to William Creech." *Papers of the Bibliographical Society of America* 60 (1966): 453–64.

Paul, Sir James Balfour. *The Scots Peerage, Founded on Wood's Edition of Sir Robert Douglas's Peerage of Scotland.* 9 vols. Edinburgh, 1904–14.

Phillips, Hugh. *Mid-Georgian London: A Topographical and Social Survey of Central and Western London about 1750.* London, 1964.

Phillips, James W. *Printing and Bookselling in Dublin, 1670–1800: A Bibliographical Enquiry.* Dublin, 1998.

Phillipson, N. T. "Culture and Society in the 18th Century Province: The Case of Edinburgh and the Scottish Enlightenment." In *The University in Society,* vol. 2: *Europe, Scotland, and the United States from the 16th to the 20th Century,* ed. Lawrence Stone, 407–48. Princeton, 1974.

———. *The Scottish Whigs and the Reform of the Court of Session, 1785–1830.* Edinburgh, 1990.

Philp, Mark. *Godwin's Political Justice.* London, 1986.

Piper, David. *The Image of the Poet: British Poets and Their Portraits.* Oxford, 1982.

Plant, Marjorie. *The English Book Trade: An Economic History of the Making and Sale of Books.* 3rd ed. London, 1974.

Plomer, H. R., et al. *Dictionaries of the Printers and Booksellers Who Were at Work in England, Scotland and Ireland, 1557–1775.* London, 1977.

Pocock, J. G. A. *Barbarism and Religion.* 3 vols. Cambridge, 1999–2003.

Pointon, Marcia. *Hanging the Head: Portraiture and Social Formation in Eighteenth-Century England.* New Haven, CT, and London, 1993.

Pollard, Graham. "The English Market for Printed Books: *The Sandars Lectures, 1959.*" *Publishing History* 4 (1978): 7–48.

Pollard, M. *A Dictionary of Members of the Dublin Book Trade, 1550–1800.* London, 2000.

———. *Dublin's Trade in Books, 1550–1800.* Oxford, 1989.

———. "John Chambers, Printer and United Irishman." *Irish Book* 3 (1964): 1–22.

Pooley, Julian. "The Papers of the Nichols Family and Business: New Discoveries and the Work of the Nichols Archive Project." *Library,* 7th ser., 2 (2001): 10–52.

Popkin, Jeremy D. "Publishing." In Kors, *Encyclopedia of the Enlightenment,* 372–78.

Porter, Dorothy, and Roy Porter. *Patient's Progress: Doctors and Doctoring in Eighteenth-Century England.* Stanford, 1989.

Porter, Roy. *Enlightenment: Britain and the Creation of the Modern World.* London, 2000. Published in North America as *The Creation of the Modern World: The Untold Story of the British Enlightenment.* New York, 2000.

———. "William Hunter: A Surgeon and a Gentleman." In Bynum and Porter, *William Hunter,* 7–34.

Porter, Roy, and Mikuláš Teich, eds. *The Enlightenment in National Context.* Cambridge, 1981.

Pottle, Frederick A. *James Boswell: The Earlier Years, 1740–1769.* New York, 1966.

Pottle, Marion S., Claude Colleer Abbott, and Frederick A. Pottle. *Catalogue of the Papers of James Boswell at Yale University.* 3 vols. Edinburgh and New Haven, CT, 1993.

Powell, J. H. *Bring Out Your Dead: The Great Plague of Yellow Fever in Philadelphia in 1793.* Philadelphia, 1993.

Prescott, Sarah. *Women, Authorship and Literary Culture, 1690–1740.* Basingstoke, UK, and New York, 2003.

Price, Leah. "Introduction: Reading Matter." *PMLA* 121 (2006): 9–16.

Rankin, Ian. *Fleshmarket Alley.* New York, 2005. Originally published in the United Kingdom in 2004 as *Fleshmarket Close.*

Rashid, Salim. *The Myth of Adam Smith.* Cheltenham, UK, and Northampton, MA, 1998.

Rauser, Amelia. "Hair, Authenticity, and the Self-Made Macaroni." *Eighteenth-Century Studies* 38 (2004): 101–17.

Raven, James. "The Anonymous Novel in Britain and Ireland, 1750–1830." In Griffin, *Faces of Anonymity,* 141–66.

———. "The Book Trades." In Rivers, *Books and Their Readers: New Essays,* 1–34.

———. "Commodification and Value: Interactions in Book Traffic to North America, c. 1750–1820." In *Access Boundaries: The Book in Culture and Commerce,* ed. Bill Bell, Philip Bennett, and Jonquil Bevan, 73–90. Winchester, UK, and New Castle, DE, 2000.

————. "The Export of Books to Colonial North America." *Publishing History* 42 (1997): 21–49.

————. "From Promotion to Proscription: Arrangements for Reading and Eighteenth-Century Libraries." In Raven, Small, and Tadmor, *Practice and Representation of Reading in England*, 175–201.

————. "The Importation of Books in the Eighteenth Century." In Amory and Hall, *Colonial Book*, 183–98.

————. "Introduction: The Practice and Representation of Reading in England." In Raven, Small, and Tadmor, *Practice and Representation of Reading in England*, 1–21.

————. "Location, Size, and Succession: The Bookshops of Paternoster Row before 1800." In *The London Book Trade: Topographies of Print in the Metropolis from the Sixteenth Century*, ed. Robin Myers, Michael Harris, and Giles Mandelbrote, 89–113. New Castle, DE, and London, 2003.

————. *London Booksellers and American Customers: Transatlantic Literary Community and the Charleston Library Society, 1748–1811.* Columbia, SC, 2002.

————. "Memorializing a London Bookscape: The Mapping and Reading of Paternoster Row and St. Paul's Churchyard, 1695–1814." In *Order and Connexion: Studies in Bibliography and Book History*, ed. R. C. Alston, 177–200. Woodbridge, Suffolk, and Rochester, NY, 1997.

————. "New Reading Histories, Print Culture and the Identification of Change: The Case of Eighteenth-Century England." *Social History* 23 (1998): 268–87.

————. "Publishing and Bookselling, 1660–1780." In *The Cambridge History of English Literature, 1660–1780*, ed. John Richetti, 13–36. Cambridge, 2005.

Raven, James, Helen Small, and Naomi Tadmor, eds. *The Practice and Representation of Reading in England.* Cambridge, 1996.

Reid-Maroney, Nina. *Philadelphia's Enlightenment, 1740–1800: Kingdom of Christ, Empire of Reason.* Westport, CT, and London, 2001.

Remer, Rosalind. *Printers and Men of Capital: Philadelphia Book Publishers in the New Republic.* Philadelphia, 1996.

————. "A Scottish Printer in Late Eighteenth-Century Philadelphia: Robert Simpson's Journey from Apprentice to Entrepreneur." *Pennsylvania Magazine of History and Biography* 121 (1997): 3–25.

Rendekop, Benjamin W. "Reid's Influence in Britain, Germany, France, and America." In *The Cambridge Companion to Thomas Reid*, ed. Terence Cuneo and René Woudenberg, 313–39. Cambridge, 2004.

Renwick, John. "The Reception of William Robertson's Historical Writings in Eighteenth-Century France." In S. J. Brown, *William Robertson*, 145–63.

Richardson, Lynn N. *A History of Early American Magazines, 1741–1789.* New York, 1931.

Rivers, Isabel, ed. *Books and Their Readers in Eighteenth-Century England.* London and New York, 1982.

———, ed. *Books and Their Readers in Eighteenth-Century England: New Essays.* London and New York, 2001.

Roberts, William. *Memoirs of the Life and Correspondence of Mrs. Hannah More.* 2 vols. New York, 1835.

Robertson, John. *The Case for the Enlightenment: Scotland and Naples, 1680–1760.* Cambridge, 2005.

———. "The Case for the Enlightenment: A Comparative Approach." In Mali and Wokler, *Isaiah Berlin's Counter-Enlightenment,* 73–90.

———. "The Scottish Contribution to the Enlightenment." In Wood, *Scottish Enlightenment,* 37–62.

Robinson, Roger J. Introduction to *Elements of Moral Science,* by James Beattie, 1: v–xxxvi. 2 vols. Reprint. London, 1996.

———. Introduction to *An Essay on the Nature and Immutability of Truth,* by James Beattie, v–xli. Reprint. London, 1996.

———. Introduction to *Essays: On Poetry and Music,* by James Beattie, v–xxviii. Reprint. London, 1996.

Roche, Daniel. *Le siècle des lumières en province: Academies et académiciens provinciaux, 1680–1789.* 2 vols. Paris and The Hague, 1978.

Rogers, Pat. *Grub Street: Studies in a Subculture.* London, 1972.

Roman, Cynthia Ellen. "Pictures for Private Purses: Robert Bowyer's Historic Gallery and Illustrated Edition of David Hume's *History of England.*" Ph.D. diss., Brown University, 1997.

Roper, Derek. *Reviewing before the Edinburgh, 1788–1802.* Newark, DE, 1978.

Rose, Mark. *Authors and Owners: The Invention of Copyright.* Cambridge, MA, and London, 1993.

Rosenau, Pauline Marie. *Post-Modernism and the Social Sciences: Insights, Inroads, and Intrusions.* Princeton, 1992.

Ross, Ian Simpson. *The Life of Adam Smith.* Oxford, 1995.

———. *Lord Kames and the Scotland of His Day.* Oxford, 1972.

Ross, John D. *The Story of the Kilmarnock Burns.* Stirling, 1933; reprint, New York, 1973.

Ross, Trevor. "Copyright and the Invention of Tradition." *Eighteenth-Century Studies* 26 (1992): 1–27.

Rubin, Joan Shelley. "What Is the History of the History of Books?" *Journal of American History* 90 (2003): 555–76.

Sakamoto, Tatsuya, and Hideo Tanaka, eds. *The Rise of Political Economy in the Scottish Enlightenment.* London, 2003.

Sale, William M., Jr. *Samuel Richardson: Master Printer.* Ithaca, NY, 1950.

———. "Sir Charles Grandison and the Dublin Pirates." *Yale University Library Gazette* 7 (1933): 80–86.

Salih, Sara. "*Camilla* in the Marketplace: Moral Marketing and Feminist Editing in 1796 and 1802." In *Authorship, Commerce and the Public: Scenes of Writing, 1750–*

1850, ed. E. J. Clery, Caroline Franklin, and Peter Garside, 120–35. Basingstoke, UK, 2002.

Sambrook, James. Introduction to *The Seasons*, by James Thomson, ed. James Sambrook. Oxford, 1981.

———. *James Thomson, 1700–1748: A Life*. Oxford, 1991.

———. "'A Just Balance between Patronage and the Press': The Case of James Thomson." *Studies in the Literary Imagination* 34 (2001): 137–53.

Sanderson, Margaret H. B. *Robert Adam and Scotland: Portrait of an Architect*. Edinburgh, 1992.

Saunders, David. *Authorship and Copyright*. London, 1994.

Schellenberg, Betty A. *The Professionalization of Women Writers in Eighteenth-Century Britain*. Cambridge, 2005.

Schmidt, James. "What Enlightenment Was, What It Still Might Be, and Why Kant May Have Been Right after All." *American Behavioral Scientist* 49 (2006): 647–63.

———, ed. *What Is Enlightenment? Eighteenth-Century Answers and Twentieth-Century Questions*. Berkeley, CA, 1996.

Schmidt, Wolf Gerhard, ed. *"Homer des Nordens" und "Mutter der Romantik": James Macpherson's Ossian und seine Rezeption in der deutschsprachigen Literatur*. 4 vols. Vol. 4 co-edited by Howard Gaskill. Berlin and New York, 2003–4.

Schmitz, Robert Morrell. *Hugh Blair*. New York, 1948.

Schweizer, Karl W., ed. *Lord Bute: Essays in Re-interpretation*. Leicester, 1988.

Scott, Hew, ed. *Fasti Ecclesiae Scoticanae: The Succession of Ministers in the Church of Scotland*. New ed. 7 vols. Edinburgh, 1915–28.

Scott, William Robert. *Francis Hutcheson: His Life, Teaching, and Position in the History of Philosophy*. 1900; reprint, New York, 1966.

Scott, Mary Jane W. *James Thomson, Anglo-Scot*. Athens, GA, and London, 1988.

Scottish Book Trade Index (SBTI). www.nls.uk/catalogues/resources/sbti/index .html.

Scouller, James Brown. *A Manual of the United Presbyterian Church of North America, 1751–1887*. Pittsburgh, 1887.

Sefton, Henry R. "The Early Development of Moderatism in the Church of Scotland." Ph.D. diss., Glasgow University, 1962.

Selwyn, Pamela E. *Everyday Life in the German Book Trade: Friedrich Nicolai as Bookseller and Publisher in the Age of Enlightenment*. University Park, PA, 2000.

Sher, Richard B. "The Book in the Scottish Enlightenment." In Wood, *Culture of the Book*, 40–60.

———. "Boswell on Robertson and the Moderates: New Evidence." *Age of Johnson* 11 (2000): 205–15.

———. "*Charles V* and the Book Trade: An Episode in Enlightenment Print Culture." In S. J. Brown, *William Robertson*, 164–95.

———. *Church and University in the Scottish Enlightenment: The Moderate Literati of Edinburgh*. Princeton and Edinburgh, 1985.

———. "Commerce, Religion and the Enlightenment in Eighteenth-Century Glasgow." In *Glasgow*, vol. 1: *Beginnings to 1830*, ed. T. M. Devine and Gordon Jackson, 312–59. Manchester and New York, 1995.

———. "Corporatism and Consensus in the Late Eighteenth-Century Book Trade: The Edinburgh Booksellers Society in Comparative Perspective." *Book History* 1 (1998): 32–93.

———. "Early Editions of Adam Smith's Books in Britain and Ireland, 1759–1804." In *A Critical Bibliography of Adam Smith*, ed. Keith Tribe, 13–26. London, 2002.

———. "'The Favourite of the Favourite': John Home, Bute and the Politics of Patriotic Poetry." In Schweizer, *Lord Bute*, 83–98.

———. "Introduction: Scottish-American Cultural Studies, Past and Present." In Sher and Smitten, *Scotland and America*, 1–27.

———. "Moderates, Managers and Popular Politics in Mid-Eighteenth-Century Edinburgh: The Drysdale 'Bustle' of the 1760s." In *New Perspectives on the Politics and Culture of Early Modern Scotland*, ed. John Dwyer, Roger Mason, and Alexander Murdoch, 179–209. Edinburgh, 1982.

———. "New Light on the Publication and Reception of the *Wealth of Nations*." *Adam Smith Review* 1 (2004): 3–29.

———. "Professors of Virtue: The Social History of the Edinburgh Moral Philosophy Chair in the Eighteenth Century." In Stewart, *Philosophy of the Scottish Enlightenment*, 87–126.

———. "Science and Medicine in the Scottish Enlightenment: The Lessons of Book History." In Wood, *Scottish Enlightenment*, 99–156.

———. "Scotland Transformed: The Eighteenth Century." In *Scotland: A History*, ed. Jenny Wormald, 177–208. Oxford, 2005.

———. "'Something That Put Me in Mind of My Father': Boswell and Lord Kames." In *Boswell: Citizen of the World, Man of Letters*, ed. Irma Lustig, 64–86. Lexington, KY, 1995.

———. "William Buchan's *Domestic Medicine*: Laying Book History Open." In Isaac and McKay, *Human Face of the Book Trade*, 45–64.

———. "Witherspoon's *Dominion of Providence* and the Scottish Jeremiad Tradition." In Sher and Smitten, *Scotland and America*, 46–64.

Sher, Richard B., with Hugh Amory. "From Scotland to the Strand: The Genesis of Andrew Millar's Bookselling Career." In *The Moving Market: Continuity and Change in the Book Trade*, ed. Peter Isaac and Barry McKay, 51–70. New Castle, DE, 2001.

Sher, Richard B., and Andrew Hook. "Introduction: Glasgow and the Enlightenment." In Hook and Sher, *Glasgow Enlightenment*, 1–17.

Sher, Richard B., and Alexander Murdoch. "Patronage and Party in the Church of Scotland, 1750–1800." In *Church, Politics and Society: Scotland, 1408–1929*, ed. Norman Macdougall, 197–220. Edinburgh, 1983.

Sher, Richard B., and Jeffrey R. Smitten, eds. *Scotland and America in the Age of the Enlightenment*. Princeton and Edinburgh, 1990.

Sherman, Brad, and Alain Strowel, eds. *Of Authors and Origins: Essays on Copyright Law.* Oxford, 1994.

Short, John Rennie. *Representing the Republic: Mapping the United States, 1600–1900.* London, 2001.

Silver, Rollo G. "The Costs of Mathew Carey's Printing Equipment." *Studies in Bibliography* 19 (1966): 103–22.

———. *Typefounding in America, 1787–1825.* Charlottesville, VA, 1965.

Sinton, James. "Robert Heron and His Writings." *Publications of the Edinburgh Bibliographical Society* 15 (1935): 17–33.

Sitwell, O. F. G. *Four Centuries of Special Geography: An Annotated Guide to Books That Purport to Describe All the Countries in the World Published in English before 1888.* Vancouver, 1993.

Skinner, Basil. *Burns: Authentic Likenesses.* 2nd ed. Alloway, 1990.

Sloan, Douglas. *The Scottish Enlightenment and the American College Ideal.* New York, 1971.

Sloan, Kim, with Andrew Burnett, eds. *Enlightenment: Discovering the World in the Eighteenth Century.* London and Washington, DC, 2003.

Smart, Alastair. *Allan Ramsay: A Complete Catalogue of His Paintings.* Ed. John Ingamells. New Haven, CT, and London, 1999.

———. *Allan Ramsay: Painter, Essayist and Man of the Enlightenment.* New Haven, CT, and London, 1992.

Smith, Janet Adam. "Some Eighteenth-Century Ideas of Scotland." In *Scotland in the Age of Improvement: Essays in Scottish History in the Eighteenth Century,* ed. N. T. Phillipson and Rosalind Mitchison, 107–24. Edinburgh, 1970.

Smith, Merrit Roe, and Leo Marx, eds. *Does Technology Drive History? The Dilemma of Technological Determinism.* Cambridge, MA, and London, 1994.

Smith, Norah. "The Literary Career and Achievement of Robert Wallace." Ph.D. diss., University of Edinburgh, 1973.

Smith, Preserved. *The Enlightenment, 1687–1776.* New York, 1962. Originally published in 1934 as volume 2 of Smith, *A History of Modern Culture.*

Smitten, Jeffrey. "Robertson's Letters and the Life of Writing." In S. J. Brown, *William Robertson,* 36–54.

Snyder, Franklin Bliss. *The Life of Robert Burns.* New York, 1932.

Solomon, Harry M. *The Rise of Robert Dodsley: Creating the New Age of Print.* Carbondale and Edwardsville, IL, 1996.

Spawn, Willman. "Extra-Gilt Bindings of Robert Aitken, 1787–88." *Proceedings of the American Antiquarian Society* 93 (1983): 415–17.

Spawn, Willman, and Carol Spawn. "The Aitken Shop: Identification of an Eighteenth-Century Bindery and Its Tools." *Papers of the Bibliographical Society of America* 57 (1963): 422–37.

Spencer, Mark G. *Hume and Eighteenth-Century America.* Rochester, NY, 2005.

———, ed. *Hume's Reception in Early America.* 2 vols. Bristol, 2002.

St. Clair, William. "The Political Economy of Reading." John Coffin Memorial Lecture in the History of the Book. University of London, 2005. www.sas.ac.uk/ies/ Publications/johncoffin/stclair.pdf (as updated on 5 Sept. 2005).

———. *The Reading Nation in the Romantic Period.* Cambridge, 2004.

Steintrager, James A. *Cruel Delight: Enlightenment Culture and the Inhuman.* Bloomington, IN, 2004.

Stewart, M. A. "Hume's Intellectual Development, 1711–1752." In *Impressions of Hume,* ed. M. Frasca-Spada and P. J. E. Kail, 11–58. Oxford, 2005.

———, ed. *Studies in the Philosophy of the Scottish Enlightenment.* Oxford, 1990.

Stockdale, Eric. *'Tis Treason, My Good Man! Four Revolutionary Presidents and a Piccadilly Bookshop.* New Castle, DE, and London, 2005.

Sturrock, John. *The Language of Autobiography: Studies in the First Person Singular.* Cambridge, 1993.

Suarez, Michael F. "The Business of Literature: The Book Trade in England from Milton to Blake." In *A Companion to Literature from Milton to Blake,* ed. David Womersley, 131–47. Oxford, 2000.

———. "The Production and Consumption of the Eighteenth-Century Poetic Miscellany." In Rivers, *Books and Their Readers: New Essays,* 217–51.

Suarez, Michael F., and Michael Turner, eds. *The Cambridge History of the Book in Britain,* vol. 5: *1695–1830.* Cambridge, forthcoming.

Suderman, Jeffrey M. *Orthodoxy and Enlightenment: George Campbell in the Eighteenth Century.* Montreal and Kingston, 2001.

Sullivan, Alvin, ed. *British Literary Magazines: The Augustan Age and the Age of Johnson, 1698–1788.* Westport, CT, and London, 1983.

Tanselle, G. Thomas. "The Concept of Format." *Studies in Bibliography* 53 (2000): 67–116.

———. *Literature and Artifacts.* Charlottesville, VA, 1998.

Taylor, Richard C. "'The Evils I was born to bear': Two Letters from Charlotte Smith to Thomas Cadell." *Modern Philology* 91 (1994): 312–18.

Teichgraeber III, Richard F. "Adam Smith and Tradition: The *Wealth of Nations* before Malthus." In *Economy, Polity, and Society: British Intellectual History, 1750–1950,* ed. Stefan Collini, Richard Whatmore, and Brian Young, 85–104. Cambridge, 2000.

———. "'Less Abused Than I Had Reason to Expect': The Reception of *The Wealth of Nations* in Britain, 1776–90." *Historical Journal* 30 (1987): 337–66.

Thaddeus, Janice Farrar. "Elizabeth Hamilton's Domestic Politics." In *Studies in Eighteenth-Century Culture,* ed. Carla H. Hay and Syndy M. Conger, 23:265–84. East Lansing, MI, 1994.

———. *Frances Burney: A Literary Life.* Basingstoke, UK, and New York, 2000.

Thompson, Harold William. *A Scottish Man of Feeling: Some Account of Henry Mackenzie, Esq. of Edinburgh and of the Golden Age of Burns and Scott.* London and New York, 1931.

Thomson, H. F. "The Scottish Enlightenment and Political Economy." In *Pre-Classical Economic Thought: From the Greeks to the Scottish Enlightenment,* ed. S. T. Lowry, 221–55. Boston, 1987.

Thorne, R. G. *The House of Commons, 1790–1820.* 5 vols. London, 1986.

Tierney, James E. "Advertisements for Books in London Newspapers, 1760–1785." In *Studies in Eighteenth-Century Culture,* ed. Timothy Erwin and Ourida Mostefai, 30:153–64. Baltimore and London, 2001.

————, ed. *The Correspondence of Robert Dodsley, 1733–1764.* Cambridge, 1988.

————. "Dublin–London Publishing Relations in the 18th Century: The Case of George Faulkner." In *The Book Trade and Its Customers, 1450–1900: Historical Essays for Robin Myers,* ed. Arnold Hunt, Giles Mandelbrote, and Alison Shell, 133–39. Winchester, UK, and New Castle, DE, 1997.

Todd, Janet, ed. *Dictionary of British and American Women Writers, 1660–1800.* Totowa, NJ, 1987.

Todd, William B. "David Hume: A Preliminary Bibliography." In *Hume and the Enlightenment: Essays Presented to Ernest Campbell Mossner,* ed. William B. Todd, 189–205. 1974; reprint, Bristol, 1990.

Tompson, Richard S. "Scottish Judges and the Birth of British Copyright." *Juridical Review* (1992): 18–42.

Tucoo-Chala, Suzanne. *Charles-Joseph Panckoucke et la librairie francaise, 1736–1798.* Pau and Paris, 1977.

————. "Panckoucke, Charles Joseph." In Kors, *Encyclopedia of the Enlightenment,* 3:234–36.

Turner, Cheryl. *Living by the Pen: Women Writers in the Eighteenth Century.* London, 1992.

Turner, Katherine. *British Travel Writers in Europe, 1750–1800: Authorship, Gender, and National Identity.* Aldershot, UK, 2001.

Turnovsky, Geoffrey. "The Enlightenment Literary Market: Rousseau, Authorship, and the Book Trade." *Eighteenth-Century Studies* 36 (2003): 387–410.

Tyson, Gerald P. *Joseph Johnson: A Liberal Publisher.* Iowa City, IA, 1979.

Uglow, Jenny. *The Lunar Men: The Friends Who Made the Future.* London, 2002.

Ulman, H. Lewis, ed. *The Minutes of the Aberdeen Philosophical Society, 1758–1775.* Aberdeen, 1990.

Van Holthoon, Frederic L. "Hume and the 1763 Edition of His *History of England:* His Frame of Mind as a Revisionist." *Hume Studies* 23 (1997): 133–52.

Venturi, Franco. "The European Enlightenment." In *Italy and the Enlightenment: Studies in a Cosmopolitan Century,* by F. Venturi, ed. Stuart Woolf, trans. Susan Corsi, 1–32. New York, 1972. Originally published in Italian in 1960.

Wall, Thomas. *The Sign of Doctor Hay's Head: Being Some Account of the Hazards and Fortunes of Catholic Printers and Publishers in Dublin from the Later Penal Times to the Present Day.* Dublin, 1958.

Walsh, Marcus. "The Superfoetation of Literature: Attitudes to the Printed Book in the Eighteenth Century." *British Journal for Eighteenth-Century Studies* 15 (1992): 151–61.

Walters, Gwyn. "The Booksellers in 1759 and 1774: The Battle for Literary Property." *Library* 29 (1974): 287–311.

Ward, Robert E., ed. *Prince of Dublin Printers: The Letters of George Faulkner.* Lexington, KY, 1972.

Warner, Michael. *The Letters of the Republic: Publication and the Public Sphere in Eighteenth-Century America.* Cambridge, MA, and London, 1990.

Weindorf, Richard. *Sir Joshua Reynolds: The Painter in Society.* Cambridge, MA, 1996.

Wiles, Roy McKeen. "The Relish for Reading in Provincial England Two Centuries Ago." In Korshin, *Widening Circle*, 85–115.

Williams, Howard. "An Enlightenment Critique of the *Dialectic of Enlightenment*." In Fitzpatrick et al., *Enlightenment World*, 635–47.

Wilson, David A. *United Irishmen, United States: Immigrant Radicals in the Early Republic.* Ithaca, NY, and London, 1998.

Wilson, Douglas L. "Thomas Jefferson's Library and the Skipwith List." *Harvard Library Bulletin* 3 (1992–93): 56–72.

Wilson, Susan. "Postmodernism and the Enlightenment." In Fitzpatrick et al., *Enlightenment World*, 648–59.

Winans, Robert B. *A Descriptive Checklist of Book Catalogues Separately Printed in America, 1693–1800.* Worcester, MA, 1981.

Wind, Edgar. *Hume and the Heroic Portrait: Studies in Eighteenth-Century Imagery.* Ed. Jaynie Anderson. Oxford, 1986.

Withers, Charles W. J. *Geography, Science and National Identity: Scotland since 1520.* Cambridge, 2001.

Withers, Charles W. J., and Paul Wood, eds. *Science and Medicine in the Scottish Enlightenment.* East Linton, UK, 2002.

Withrington, Donald J. "What Was Distinctive about the Scottish Enlightenment?" In Carter and Pittock, *Aberdeen and the Enlightenment*, 9–19.

Wolf II, Edwin. *The Book Culture of a Colonial American City: Philadelphia Books, Bookmen, and Booksellers.* Oxford, 1988.

Woloch, Isser. *Eighteenth-Century Europe: Tradition and Progress, 1715–1789.* New York, 1982.

Wood, Paul B. "Aberdeen and Europe in the Enlightenment." In *The Universities of Aberdeen and Europe: The First Three Centuries*, ed. Paul Dukes, 119–42. Aberdeen, 1995.

———. *The Aberdeen Enlightenment: The Arts Curriculum in the Eighteenth Century.* Aberdeen, 1993.

———, ed. *The Culture of the Book in the Scottish Enlightenment.* Toronto, 2000.

———. Introduction to *An Essay on the Causes of Complexion and Figure in the Human Species*, by Samuel Stanhope Smith, v–xxv. Edinburgh, 1788; reprint, Bristol, 1995.

———. "Jolly Jack Phosphorous in the Venice of the North; or, Who Was John Anderson?" In Hook and Sher, *Glasgow Enlightenment*, 111–32.

———, ed. *The Scottish Enlightenment: Essays in Reinterpretation.* Rochester, NY, and Woodbridge, Suffolk, 2000.

Woodmansee, Martha. "The Genius and the Copyright: Economic and Legal Conditions of the Emergence of the 'Author.'" *Eighteenth-Century Studies* 17 (1984): 425–48.

Woodmansee, Martha, and Peter Jaszi, eds. *The Construction of Authorship: Textual Appropriation in Law and Literature*. Durham, NC, and London, 1994.

Wright, Johnson Kent. "The Pre-Postmodernism of Carl Becker." In Gordon, *Postmodernism and the Enlightenment*, 161–77.

Yeo, Richard. *Encyclopaedic Visions: Scientific Dictionaries and Enlightenment Culture*. Cambridge, 2001.

Zachs, William. *The First John Murray and the Late Eighteenth-Century London Book Trade*. Oxford, 1998.

———. "Gilbert Stuart." *Book Collector* 37 (1988): 522–46.

———. "John Murray and the Dublin Book Trade, 1770–93; with Special Reference to the 'Mysterious' Society of Dublin Booksellers." *Long Room* 40 (1995): 26–33.

———. *Without Regard to Good Manners: A Biography of Gilbert Stuart, 1743–1786*. Edinburgh, 1992.

Index

Page numbers in italics refer to figures and tables. Subentries for published works follow other subentries under each author's name.

Aberdeen: enlightened culture of, 116: Enlightenment publishing in, 268; Johnson and Boswell in, 144; Thomson's *Tour* on, 145

Aberdeen, University of. *See* King's College, Aberdeen; Marischal College, AberdeenAberdeen Philosophical Society, 107–8, 116

abridgments, 89, *357*, *358*

academic degrees: awarded to Grub Street Scots, 128; awarded to literati, 103–4; on title pages, 156–62

Account of Corsica (Boswell), 268–69

Account of Sir Isaac Newton's Philosophical Discoveries (C. Maclaurin), 212, 225, 285

Account of the Life and Writings of James Beattie (Forbes), 438

Account of the Life, Writings, and Inventions of John Napier (Earl of Buchan and Walter Minto), 211, 268

Adam, Alexander: Creech and, 406, 419–20; Creech cites, 76, 419–20; Kincaid and, 406, 419; publishing plans of, 237; rector of Edinburgh High School, 104, 419; *Roman Antiquities*, 92, 237–38, 243, 349, 604; *Summary of Geography and History*, 238, 604

Adam, James. *See* Adam, Robert

Adam, Robert: British Coffee House redesigned by, 130–31; in Edinburgh and London, 118–19; Millar's home designed by, 294; in Oyster Club, 109; *Spalatro* and his career, 225–26; Thomson monument designed by, 281–82; *Ruins of the Palace of the Emperor Diocletian at Spalatro*, 135, 225–26; *Works in Architecture of Robert and James Adam*, 131, *130*

Adams, William, 47, 84

Addison, Joseph, 72, 268

Addresses to Young Men (J. Fordyce), 371

Adorno, Theodor W., 12–13

advertisements: author function and, 150, *364*; Bell's "To the American World," *520–21*; cost, 362–63; in *Dublin Chronicle*, 487–88, 493, 496–

advertisements (*continued*)
97; in *Dublin Evening Post*, 451, 455,
472n50, 485; in *Dublin Gazette*, 473;
in *Dublin Magazine*, 460; in *Dublin
Mercury*, 456, 473; in *Edinburgh Evening Courant*, 253, 362, 395n157, 423,
424; in *Freeman's Journal* (Dublin),
482, 484; in *Freeman's Journal* (Philadelphia), 552–53; in *Gazette of the
United States*, 592; in *Hibernian Journal*, 451, 455, 458; in *London Chronicle*, 363, 364; in *Magee's Weekly Packet*,
451; in *Pennsylvania Journal*, 553; in
Pennsylvania Mercury, 560; in *Pennsylvania Packet*, 534; in *Public Gazetteer*,
482; in *Universal Asylum*, 565–67, 568.
See also publicity
Advocates' Library, 112
African Association, 186
Agis (J. Home), 88, 205
Aiken, John, 381
Aiken, Robert, 230
Aikman, William, 535
Aitken, Jane, 539
Aitken, Robert: American Revolution
and, 537–38; antiburghers and, 534,
570–71, 592; Bell and, 528–30, *529*,
535–37; binding, 539; on Johnson's
offensiveness, 537; logo of, 532, *533*;
in Paisley, 532, 534; *Pennsylvania
Magazine* and, 535–37; portrait, *533*;
religious publishing, 532, 534–35;
as Scottish Enlightenment reprinter,
38, 534–39; in St. Andrew's Society,
537–38, 549; Witherspoon and, 534;
Young and, 550, 552
Aitken, Mrs. Robert (Janet Skeoch),
532
Aldridge, A. Owen, 14
D'Alembert, Jean Le Rond, 98
Alexander, William, 121, 156
Alfred (J. Home), 457, 476
Aliamet, François, 167, 169
Alison, Archibald: Blair's *Sermons* re-
viewed by, 138; Woodhouselee biog-

raphy by, 140; *Essays on Taste*, 91, 142,
394–95
Alison, Mrs. Archibald (Dorothea
Gregory), 132
Allan, David (artist), 113–14, *113*
Allan, David (historian), 30–31
Allardice, Samuel, 560, 585, 587
Allen, Ethan, 531
Allen, Thomas, 39, 505, 555, 558, 561,
586
Alonzo (J. Home), 450
Alonzo and Ormisinda. See *Alonzo*
Alston, Charles, 76, 97–98, 105; *Lectures
on the Materia Medica*, 105
Alves, Robert, 34, 76–77; *Sketches of a
History of Literature*, 76–77
Amelia (Fielding), 288
America: availability of books in, 504–
6, 514–15; in Carey's edition of Guth-
rie's *Geography*, 576; growing book
market in, 439, 531–32, 535
American Annual Register, 589–90
American Behavioral Scientist (special is-
sue on end of Enlightenment), 11
American Copyright Act of 1790, 561
American Geography (Morse), 559
American Monthly Review, 590–91
American Museum, 544
American Philosophical Society, 538,
565
American Revolution: Aitken and, 537–
38; Balfour and, 337n24; Bell and,
528, 530–31; M'Culloch and, 548;
Ramsay and, 539; seceders and, 550
American Society of United Irishmen,
545
Amory, Hugh, 275
Amsterdam, 9, 407
*Anatomical Description of the Human
Gravid Uterus* (W. Hunter), 135
Anatomy of the Human Bones (Monro), 98
Ancient Scotish Poems (Pinkerton),
125n68
Anderson, James (antiquarian): his li-
brary sold by Millar, 279–80; *Collec-*

tions Relating to the History of Mary Queen of Scots, 279–80

Anderson, James (political economist): Callender cites, 577n100; in Carey's edition of Guthrie's *Geography*, 581, 582; defends Andrew Millar against Authenticus, 292–93; on false London imprints, 438; in prime generation, 98; *The Bee*, 139, 202–3; *Essays Relating to Agriculture and Rural Affairs*, 141–42, 390, 395; *Recreations in Agriculture, Natural-History, Arts, and Miscellaneous Literature*, 157n132

Anderson, John, 547; *Institutes of Physics*, 105, 269

Anderson, Mrs. (Helen Douglas), 129, 131

Anderson, Robert, 231

Anderson, Walter, 77; *History of France*, 250, 332, 350, 537

Anderson, William, 356, 448, 466

Anderston Club, 109

Andrews, Loring, 586

Anecdotes of the Russian Empire (Richardson): anonymity and, 154; patronage and, 206; Scotticisms and, 361

Anglo-Scottish relations. *See* Scottish-English relations

Annals of Scotland (Hailes), 254, 383, 420

anonymous publication: age and genre and, 149–50; author function and, 94, 149–50, 155; Foucault on, 149–50; institutional affiliations and, 161–62; *Mirror* no. 2 and, 150–51; Reid on, 152–53; mitigated anonymity and, 151–53; modesty and anxiety and, 149, 151–54; rare in nonfiction books, 154–55; Richardson and, 153–54; subterfuge and, 148–49, 154; temporary anonymity and, 152–53; true anonymity and, 148–51

antiburghers (Associate Synod or General Associate Synod in Scotland): Aitken and, 532; Bryce and, 534; Scottish ties in America, 551; Young

and, 547, 550–51. *See also* Associate Presbyterian Church (Philadelphia); Scots Presbyterian Church or Scots Church

anti-Enlightenment thought. *See* counter-Enlightenment

Antient Metaphysics (Monboddo): elitist attitude of author, 210; Hume's skepticism and, 146–47; print run, 86n80

Appeal to Common Sense in Behalf of Religion (Oswald): anonymity and, 148; Bell on, 324; Cadell buys into, 324; Hume's skepticism and, 146

appendix. *See* tables

Arbuthnot, Robert, 255

Archer, John, 389, 450, 452n14, 493

Argyll, 3rd Duke of, and Earl of Ilay (Archibald Campbell), 204

Aristotle's Ethics and Politics (trans. Gillies), 78, 240

Armour, Jean, 233

Armstrong, Dr. John, 283–84

Arner, Robert, 558, 560

Arnot, Hugo, 423–24

Art of Drawing in Perspective (J. Ferguson), 335, 336

Art of Speaking (Burgh), 513, 535

Associated Booksellers, 354

Associate Presbyterian Church (Philadelphia), 592. *See also* antiburghers; Scots Presbyterian Church or Scots Church

Associate Reformed Church (America), 550, 551n35. *See also* burghers; Covenanters

Associate Synod (later General Associate Synod) (Scotland). *See* antiburghers

Astronomy Explained (J. Ferguson): best seller, 92; commercial subscription book, 228; honorary copyright and, 354; self-published by subscription, 217; used in *Encyclopaedia Britannica*, 135

Atlantic studies, 24

Auld, William, 307

Aurelius, Marcus, *Meditations* (trans. Hutcheson and Moor), 133

Austen, Jane, 386

Authenticus. See *Bee, The*

author construction, 58, 75. *See also* author function

author function: anonymity and, 94, 149–50, 155; author identification and, 159–60, 455, 579; definition and critique of, 58; ordering print culture and, 7, 58, 94; publisher function and, 265–67. *See also* author construction; Foucault; publisher function

author identification: in America, 572, 579; verbal, 156–62, *158*, 572; visual, 163–92

author-publisher relations: authors' motives and expectations and, 209, 219, 249, 256–57, 260; Beattie and Creech, 417–19; Beattie on, 212–14; *The Bee* on, 202–3; Burns and Creech, 181, 234–35, 419; Creech and his authors, 417–22; Creech on profits, 347; Dublin as scapegoat, 447; Grub Street and, 122–28; Hume on, 201; Hume and Millar, 289–90; importance of, 7, 266–67; Mackenzie on, 213; mutual support, 220–24, 282–83, 292–94, 359–61, 417–19; mutual suspicions, 212–14, 240, 244–45, 250–52; 288–90; 345–52; patronage of authors, 195–203, 260; publishers' tactics and, 348–50; Robertson on, 201; Smellie and *Encyclopaedia Britannica* and, 216; transitional period for, 5. *See also* authors, Scottish Enlightenment; copy money; publication, terms of; publishers (in Britain)

authors, Scottish Enlightenment: in Aberdeen, 116, 146; academic degrees, 103–4; academic employment, 104; anonymity in books of, 148–54; author identification, 156–62, *158*; in clubs and societies, 106–10; copy money, 35–36, 257–60, 344–50; dis-

agreements and differences among, 146–47; Dublin reprints and, 458–59; in Edinburgh, 110–16; education of, 101–4; emulation of Robertson, 249–50, 346; fifty cited by Smollett, Creech, and Alves, 74–77, 92, 98–99, 117–18, 451, 454; family ties among, 132, 140–41; generations, 97–99; geographical backgrounds, 100–101; in Glasgow, 116–17; list of: 77, *613–18;* in London, 117–31, 284; patronage and, 35, 203–9; political divisions among, 147; professional character of, 104–5; return to Scotland of, 119–21; rising expectations and disappointments of, 219, 249, 260, 344–50; social status, 99–100; in St. Andrews, 117; subjects and genres of their books, 84–85, *700;* towns preferred by, 114–15; women among, 101–3. *See also* author-publisher relations; copy money; literati, Scottish; publication, terms of

Bailey, Nathan, 407

Baillie, Joanna: education of, 101; encouraged by Dugald Stewart, 102n9; father of, 100; in London, 102; in table 1, 77; in younger generation, 99

Baillie, Matthew: Hunter's *Anatomical Description of the Human Gravid Uterus* completed by, 135; medical practice, 121; published by Joseph Johnson, 381

Baillie, Mrs. James (Dorothea Hunter), 132

Baine, John I, 560

Baine, John II, 560

Baine & Co., 558, 560

Baldwin, Henry, 200, 221–24

Baldwin, Robert, 476

Baldwin, Richard, 169, 461

Balfour, Alexander, 552n39

Balfour, Elphingston (or Elphinston), 273, 307, 310, 343

Balfour, James, of Pilrig: brother of bookseller John, 310; opposition to Hume's skepticism, 146; in table 1, 77; *Delineation of Morality*, 310; *Philosophical Dissertations*, 310; *Philosophical Essays*, 310

Balfour, John, I: accused of selling pirated edition, 321, 356; against American Revolution, 337n24; on book trade, 357; civic and political activities, 310–11; death, 604; at Edinburgh University, 295; family connections, 309–10; intimacy with Strahan, 304, 336–37; partnership with Smellie, 307, 334; as a publisher of Scottish Enlightenment books, 36, 273, 307–11, 702–3; rivalry with Creech, 37, 340–43, 415; Robertson's histories and, 310, 321–22; violates honorary copyright, 355; wealth of, 358. *See also* Strahan (William) and Cadell; *names of individual authors whose works he published*

Balfour, John, II, 307

Balfour, Mrs. Elphingston (Margaret Bruce), 310

Ballantyne, James, 435–36

Banks, Sir Joseph, 120

Barclay, James, 402

Barnard, Thomas (Bishop of Killaloe), 458

Bath, 118, 199, 267, 270, 330–31

Baxter, Andrew, 98, 280

Beattie, James: Alves cites, 76; American editions of his books, 556; American readers and, 503; on authors and publishers, 212–14, 223, 235; Campbell and, 136, 238; in Carey's edition of Guthrie's *Geography*, 581, 582; contributes to *Edinburgh Magazine and Review*, 128n78; copy money and pension, 226–27, 254–55, 418; Creech and, 226–27, 255, 417–19; declines Church of England offers, 120; Dilly brothers and, 226–27, 255,

380, 417–18; disowns his early poetry, 53n13; in Dublin press, 455–56; Hume and, 53, 69n48, 89; on Kincaid, 417; on London–Edinburgh copublication, 317; popularity of, 30; in prime generation, 98; on puffing books, 138; on quarto histories, 249; Scotticisms and, 52; Strahan and, 304; *Dissertations, Moral and Critical*, 254, 340; *Elements of Moral Science*, 105, 254, 418, 574n95; *Essay on the Nature and Immutability of Truth*, 92, 138, 146, 226–27, 249, 250–51, 317–18, 380, 563; *Essays*, 105, 226–27, 418; *Evidences of the Christian Religion*, 254; *The Minstrel*, 87n81, 92, 152, 380, 417, 419, 531; *Scoticisms*, 416

Beatty, John, 472

Beavan, Arthur H., 601–2

Beccaria, Cesare, 530; *Essay on Crimes and Punishments*, 530

Becker, Carl, 12–13; *Heavenly City of the Eighteenth-Century Philosophers*, 12–13

Becket, Andrew, 374

Becket, Thomas, 254, 374

Becket & de Hondt (Thomas Becket and Peter de Hondt), 272, 702–3

Beddoes, Thomas, 187–88

Bee, The (James Anderson): Authenticus on Andrew Millar, 290–92; on authors, publishers, and the public, 202–3; on authors writing for wages, 257; biographies of Scottish authors in, 139; "On the Death of William Cullen, M.D." by Mungo Park, 139; response to Authenticus, 292–94; on subscription publishing, 224–25

Beechey, Sir William, 377

Beeswing Club, 129n81

Belfast, 449–50

Bell, Andrew, 216, 496

Bell, Benjamin: portraits, 183–84, *184*; subscriber to Burns's *Poems*, 136, *137*; *System of Surgery*, 91, 142, 157, 183–

Bell, Benjamin (*continued*)
84, 390, 563; *Treatise on Gonorrhoea Virulenta and Lues Venerea*, 454n19
Bell, John (author), 513
Bell, John (Edinburgh bookseller): accuses Balfour of piracy, 321; apprenticeship and early career, 316; Bell & Bradfute formed by, 388, 394; bookshop in Parliament Square, 112–13, *112;* career after leaving Kincaid, 387–88, 412, 428–29; character of, 324–25; in conflict over Ferguson's *Essay*, 37, 318–26; conflict with Cadell over Ferguson's *Essay*, 37, 318–26, 414; Constable and, 428–29, 435; as Creech's employer, 407; death, 604; George Robinson and, 325, 387, 389–98; Kames's *Loose Hints* and, 348; Murray and Stuart and, 325, 388, 420; leaves Kincaid partnership, 410; as publisher of Scottish Enlightenment books, 37, 272, 420, 702–3; radicalism, 396–98; Samuel Campbell and, 546; wealth of, 358. *See also* Bell & Bradfute; Creech, William; Kincaid & Bell
Bell, Malcome, 512
Bell, Mrs. Robert (Anne James), 513
Bell, Robert: advertising, 520–21; Aitken and, 528–30, 529, 535–37; American Revolution and, 528, 530–31; as auctioneer, 512n18, 516, 531; bankruptcy, 514; birth and background, 511–13; circulating library, 517; death, 531; Dublin career, 472–76, 513–14; as importer of books, 517–18; on Ireland, 520, 522; Kames's *Sketches* abridged by, 528–30, 529, 535; on literary property, 475–76; patriotic publishing, 519–24; Philadelphia bookshop, 516; Philadelphia career, 515–31; printing press purchased by Carey, 544; proposals for Hume and Ferguson editions, 523–26, 582; religion and, 512–13, 516–17, 593; Scottish

Enlightenment reprinting and, 38, 518–31; *Bell's Sale Catalogue of Books for 1763 and 1764*, 513; *Interesting Appendix to Sir William Blackstone's Commentaries on the Laws of England*, 593; *Miscellanies for Sentimentalists*, 531; *New and Old, Medical, Surgical, and Chemical Works, Lately Imported*, 517; *Now in the Printing Press, and Speedily Will Be Published by Subscription*, 524–25; *Robert Bell's Sale Catalogue of a Collection of New and Old Books*, 517; *To the Sons of Science in America*, 525
Bell & Bradfute. *See* Bell, John; Bradfute, John
Bell's Sale Catalogue of Books for 1763 and 1764 (R. Bell), 513
Benedict, Barbara, 404
Benger, Elizabeth, 101
Berkeley, Bishop George, 489
Berlin, 103
Berwick-upon-Tweed, 512
best sellers, 92–93
Bethune, John: *Highlander*, 100; *Essays and Dissertations on Various Subjects*, 146, 229
Beugo, John, *166*, 181, *182*, 190n169
bibles: Aitken and, 535; Carey and, 592; Kincaid patent, 312; Strahan patent, 312
binding, 83–84, 539
Birch, Thomas, 283–84
Black, Joseph: as author and teacher, 22; birth, 101; Creech cites, 76; Ferguson's biography of, 141; in Oyster Club, 109; in prime generation, 98; Smith's *Essays on Philosophical Subjects* co-edited by, 135; subscriber to Burns's *Poems*, 136, *137; Experiments upon Magnesia Alba*, 133
Blacklock, Thomas: Alves cites, 76; Beattie and, 138; Burns patron and subscriber, 136, *137*, 231; contributes to Donaldson's *Collection*, 314; contributes to *Edinburgh Magazine and*

Review, 128n78; contributes to *Encyclopaedia Britannica*, 494; *Lusiad* reviewed by, 73; Mackenzie's biography of, 140; prologue to *Sir Henry Gaylove* by, 102n9; *Poems on Several Occasions*, 224–25

Blackstone, Sir William: among Cadell's "four B's," 292; Creech cites, 446; his publishers, 327, 378; *Commentaries on the Laws of England*, 518, 521–23

Blackwell, Thomas: *Enquiry into the Life and Writings of Homer*, 98; *Letters concerning Mythology*, 89; *Memoirs of the Court of Augustus*, 133, 228

Blackwood, 602

Blair, Hugh: American readers and, 503; on book formats, 82; Burns patron and subscriber, 136, *137*; among Cadell's "four B's," 292; copy money and pension, 245–47; Creech cites, 446; Dublin reprinting of works by, 454; on engraving, 176; Heron and, 126; portraits of, *166*, 173, 176–79, *178*, *179*; Logan's *Sermons* edited by, 135; Macpherson's Ossian patronized by, 136; in Oyster Club, 109; patronizes authors, 135–36, 247; popularity of, 30; publication terms, 245–47; review in original *Edinburgh Review*, 64, 136; Robertson and, 136; Rose and, 368; on sensibility and humanity, 32–34; in Sibbald's circulating library, 113–14, *113*; Smollett cites, 74–75; teaching of, 403; Watson's *Philip III* and, 352; wealth of, 247; *Critical Dissertation on the Poems of Ossian*, 78, 90, 92, 152, 562; *Lectures on Rhetoric and Belles Lettres*, 92, 105, 176–79, 246–47, 340, 368, 459, 463, 538–39; *Sermons*, 32–34, 79, 82, 92, 138, 173, 176–77, 245–47, 339, 351–52, 359, 362, 368, 416, 451, 465, 561–62, 599

Blair, John, 283–84

Blake, William, 187–90, *188*

Blanning, T. C. W., 3

Blyth, Robert, 131

book history: international and interactive, 8–9; literary bias in, 10; nature of, 4–5, 11; rigorous historical method in, 29; subject matter of, 9–11

booksellers. *See* Dublin book trade; Philadelphia book trade; publishers (in Britain)

bookshops (Dublin), 468, *704*

bookshops (Edinburgh): Luckenbooths (M'Euen/Kincaid/Kincaid & Bell/ Creech), 110, *111*, 150–51, 198, 312, 317, 410, 412, 421–22, 439–40; Parliament Square (Elliot/Bell & Bradfute), 112–13, *112*, 386, 388

bookshops (London): Fleet Street (Murray), 382; Paternoster Row (Robinson), 388–89; Poultry (Dillys), 380; St. Paul's Churchyard (Johnson), 380; Strand (Donaldson), 314; Strand (Elliot & Kay), 387; Strand (M'Euen/ Millar/Cadell), 279–80

bookshops (Philadelphia): corner of Chestnut and Second Streets (Young), 553; Front Street (Aitken), 532; Market Street (Aitken), 532n62, (Carey), 545; Second Street (Campbell), 554; Second Street (Dobson), 546; Third Street (Bell), 516

Books Printed for W. Strahan, and T. Cadell in the Strand (Strahan [William] and Cadell), 56–58, *57*, 369–71

Bordeaux, 101

Boston, 509–10, 572, 574n90, 586

Boswell, Alexander, Lord Auchinleck, 122

Boswell, James: in The Club, 120; on Creech's shop, 422; Donaldson and, 198, 314; Dublin edition of *Tour* and, 458; education, 101; folio format considered by, 82; freemason, 108; on history writing among Scottish clergy, 250; on honorary copyright, 26; on Irish books in Scotland, 465; Johnson and Boswell on book profits, 256;

Boswell, James (*continued*)
London and, 118, 122, 405; on patronage for Johnson's *Dictionary*, 195–96;
publishing *Life of Johnson*, 220–24;
on Smith's letter on Hume, 59; social
background of, 100; on Strahan, 304;
in younger generation, 99; *Account of
Corsica*, 200, 269; *Journal of a Tour to
the Hebrides with Samuel Johnson*, 59,
144–45, 197, 200, 201, 220, 455, 458;
Life of Samuel Johnson, 82, 87, 195–96,
200, 220–24, 243, 363, 380, 449
Bowyer, Robert, 584
Bowyer, William, the younger, 297, 334
Bradford, Andrew, 514
Bradford, William, 514
Bradfute, John, 325, 388, 435
Bradley, Hulton, 473
Brewer, John: on authors and book-
sellers, 7, 39–40; on English fear of
Scots, 70; on publishing revolution, 2
British Coffee House (London): Adam
brothers redesign of, 130–31, *130*;
center of Scottish culture in London,
128–29; target for Scots baiters, 129–
30. *See also* London
British Museum (London), 22, 118–19
British Poets, The (Balfour-Creech edi-
tion), 355
Brook, Edward, 445
Brown, Iain Gordon, 226
Brown, John (English author), 289
Brown, John (Scottish physician): in
Carey's edition of Guthrie's *Geography*, *581*, 582; Cullen and, 121, 187;
freemason, 108; moves to London,
121; portraits, 187–90, *188*; *189*; *Elements of Medicine*, 187–90, 560
Brown, William, 295
Brown & Alfred, 124
Bruce, James: biography in *Encyclopaedia Britannica*, 494; in Carey's edition
of Guthrie's *Geography*, 582; death,
243; education, 101; freemason, 108;
returns to Stirlingshire estate, 120;

Robinson and, 242–43, 396; in Sib-
bald's circulating library, 113–14, *113*;
*An Interesting Narrative, of the Travels
of James Bruce, Esq.* (abridgment of
Travels), 89; *Travels to Discover the
Source of the Nile*, 89, 92, 141, 242–43,
395–96, 450, 495
Bruce, John, 403, 419; *First Principles of
Philosophy*, 85, 419
Bryce, John: Aitken and, 533–34; evangelical reprinter in Glasgow, 269;
Young and, 547–48
Brydone, Patrick, Walpole on, 71; *Tour
through Sicily and Malta*, 92, 253, 346,
454, 476, 536
Buccleuch (or Buccleugh), Duchess of,
137
Buccleuch (or Buccleugh), third Duke of
(Henry Scott), *137*, 207n25
Buchan, 11th Earl of (David Stewart
[or Steuart] Erskine): background,
99; on Creech, 433; freemason, 108;
life of Steuart in *The Bee* by, 139; patriotic ideals of, 210–11; subscriber
to Burns's *Poems*, 136, *137*; *Account
of the Life, Writings, and Inventions of
John Napier* (with Walter Minto), 211,
268; *Essays on the Lives and Writings of
Fletcher of Saltoun and the Poet Thomson*, 145, 211
Buchan, Countess of, *137*
Buchan, William: among Cadell's "four
B's," 292; copy money, 219–20, 256;
freemason, 108; moves to London,
121–22; plans for *Preventive Medicine*,
349; in prime generation, 98; in table
1, 77; *Domestic Medicine*, 30, 87n80,
92–93, 135, 142, 219, 228, 243, 256,
273, 329, 340–41, *341*, 343, 349, 354,
371, 413, 415, 454, 456, 531, 534–35,
571–73
Buchanan, George, 64–67
Buchanan's Head: Aitken's Paisley shop,
532; M'Euen's London shop, 279;
Millar and, 280

Buffon, Georges-Louis Leclerc de. *See* Smellie, William

Buley (or Bulley), Mary. *See* Creech, Mrs. William

Burgh, James: *The Art of Speaking*, 513, 535; *Political Disquisitions*, 527–30, 535

burghers, 550. *See also* Associate Reformed Church

Burke, Edmund: authorizes Dublin edition, 459n30; in The Club, 120; Ireland and, 500; *Reflections on the French Revolution*, 254, 397, 572

Burn, Richard: among Cadell's "four B's," 292; Millar's generosity to, 292; Millar wills money to, 282–83, 293; *Justice of the Peace, and Parish Officer*, 292

Burnett (or Burnet), Elizabeth (or Eliza): Burns's "Fair B[urnett]," 114; in Sibbald's circulating library, 113–14, *113*; subscriber to Burns's *Poems*, 136, *137*

Burnett, James, Lord Monboddo: on booksellers' profits, 346–47; in Dublin press, 456; elitist attitude toward book trade, 210; freemason, 108; frontispiece portrait of, 191n171; mocked by Walpole, 72; prefers Home's *Douglas* to Shakespeare, 69; in prime generation, 98; in Sibbald's circulating library, 113–14, *113*; title of, 99; visits London annually, 118n37; *Antient Metaphysics*, 86n80, 146, 210; *Origin and Progress of Language*, 191n171, 210n32, 338, 536

Burney, Charles, 196

Burney, Frances (Fanny), Mme. d'Arblay, 227–28, 376

Burns, Gilbert, 230

Burns, Robert: Creech and, 181, 234–35, 419, 421–22, 433; in Crochallan Fencibles, 109; in Dublin press, 455, 456; first American edition of, 556; freemason, 108; Heron's biography of, 127, 141; occupations of, 105, 114;

portraits of, *166*, 181–82, *182*; in Sibbald's circulating library, 113–14, *113*; in table 1, 77; in younger generation, 99; *Poems, Chiefly in the Scottish Dialect*, 108, 113–14, 136, 180–82, 230–35, 268, 273, 413, 450

Burton, Robert, 479

Büsching, Anton Friedrich, 156n130

Bute, 3rd Earl of (John Stuart): attacked by English, 69–71, 148; as patron, 204–5, 208; subscribes to Thomson's *Works*, 281

Byrne, Patrick: Company of Booksellers and, 479; *Dublin Chronicle* and, 469; emigration to America, 498; George Robinson and, 389, 452n14; Henry's *History*, 460, 495; prominent Roman Catholic, 470; radicalism and imprisonment, 498

Byron, George Gordon, Lord, 386

Cadell, Mrs. William (Mary), 330

Cadell, Thomas (of Bristol), 330

Cadell, Thomas, I: account in the Strahan ledgers, 600–601, 705–7; birth and background, 330; civic and political activities, 333; conflict with Bell over Ferguson's *Essay*, 37, 318–26, 414; on copy money and literature, 446; Creech and, 415; on Dublin book trade, 445–46, 468, 479, 481; early catalogues, 368–69; Elliot and, 336; enlightened motives, 360–61; fame, 430; Fordyce's ode to, 213–14; the "four B's" that kept him rich, 292; Hannah More consults, 5; intimacy with Strahans, 328–30; on Irish reprinting, 445–46; joins with Baldwin to publish Smollett's *History of England* as a continuation of Hume, 169–71; on literary property, 354, 445–46; marriage and family, 333; master of Stationers' Company, 333; as Millar's protégé, 287, 330–31, 334; Monboddo and, 210; Moore

Cadell, Thomas, I (*continued*)
and, 244–45; portraits of, *328, 377*;
publishes Denina, 74; retirement and
death, 378, 604; Russell and Hume's
History, 124; Scottishness of, 330;
wealth of, 359. *See also* Cadell &
Davies; Creech, William; Strahan,
William; Strahan (William) and
Cadell

Cadell, Thomas, II, 415, 602.*See also*
Cadell & Davies

Cadell, William, 330

Cadell & Davies: Boswell's *Life of Johnson* and, 223; Constable and, 602–5;
Creech and, 415, 428, 602–4; difficulties encountered by, 39, 599–604,
606; Moore's *Edward* and, 245; *Prize
Essays of Highland Society*, 212; publication catalogues, 379; as publishers
of Scottish Enlightenment books, 37,
272, 378–79, 396, 599–600, 702–3;
successors to Cadell I, 378; *The Following Valuable Books Are Printed for
T. Cadell, Jun. and W. Davies (Successors to Mr. Cadell) in the Strand, 1796*
(and subsequent years), 379. *See also*
Cadell, Thomas, I; Cadell, Thomas,
II; Strahan, Andrew; Strahan (Andrew) and Cadell; *names of individual
authors whose works they published*

Cadière, Catherine, 291

Cadogan, William, 534; "Dissertation
on the Gout," 534

Caldwall (or Caldwell), James: Blair,
portraits engraved by, *166, 173,
176–79, 178, 179*; Brown, portraits
engraved by, 188–90, *189*; criticized
for delaying publications, 176, 190;
Henry, portraits engraved by, 173,
177; Leechman, portraits engraved
by, 190, *193*; prices for line engravings, 167, 190*Caledonia* (Chalmers),
606

Caledonian Hunt, 231, 234

Caledonian Mercury, 74

Callender, James Thomson: buys copy of
Rights of Man from Bell, 397; contributions to Carey's edition of Guthrie's
Geography, 577–78; emigration to
America, 577–78; on immigrant publishers, 589–90; Scottish sources of,
577n100; *Political Progress of Britain*,
577–78. *See also* Carey, Mathew

Cambridge, 103, 145

Camilla (Burney), 227–28, 228n84

Camões, Luís de, 72

Campbell, George: Beattie and, 136,
238; Blair and, 136; in Carey's edition
of Guthrie's *Geography*, 582; on frus-
trations of authorship, 240; in prime
generation, 98; *Dissertation on Miracles*, 91, 286, 317, 560; *Four Gospels*,
86, 238–40; *Lectures on Ecclesiastical
History*, 105, 381; *Philosophy of Rhetoric*, 90, 137–38, 339

Campbell, Robert: Creech and, 554;
death of, 589; Dobson's *Encyclopaedia* and, 558; embellished editions
of Hume's and Smollett's *History of
England*, 582–89, *583*; emigration to
America, 541–42, 554; family ties,
554; meteoric rise, 554–55; prominence, 38–39; as Scottish Enlightenment reprinter, 555, 561–62, 582–89;
supplement to his *History of England*
by "A Society of Gentleman," 587–88

Campbell, Samuel, I, 546, 554

Campbell, Samuel, II: Dobson's *Encyclopaedia* and, 558; emigration to America, 546, 554; in New York, 555; as
a Scottish Enlightenment reprinter,
39, 561–62; staked by John Bell, 546;
subscriber to Campbell's edition of
Hume and Smollett, 586

Campbell, Thomas, 70

Carey, James, 545

Carey, Mathew: in *American Annual
Register*, 590; in American Society
of United Irishmen, 545; Anglopho-
bia of, 543, 575–78; assists Dobson

after fire, 592; book importing, 515; co-founds *Columbian Magazine*, 544; co-founds *Pennsylvania Evening Herald*, 544; in Dublin, 542–44; edition of Guthrie's *Geography*, 487, 573–82; emigration to America, 541–42, 544; founds *American Museum*, 544; in France, 543; in Hibernian Society, 545; Irish nationalism, 573–77; location, 545; Philadelphia Company of Printers and Booksellers and, 555, 571–73, 592; Robinson and, 576; Roman Catholicism and, 543–44, 592; as a Scottish Enlightenment reprinter, 38–39, 562, 571–82; subscribes to antiburgher church fund, 592; *Mathew Carey, No. 158, Market-Street, Has Imported from London, Dublin, and Glasgow, an Extensive Assortment of Books*, 515; "Urgent Necessity of an Immediate Repeal of the Whole Penal Code against the Roman Catholics," 543

Carey, William, 545

Carey's American Atlas, 576

Carlyle, Alexander, 74–75, 163, 284

Cash, John, 472, 479

Cassirer, Ernst, 12n31

Catalogue of Books Printed for Archibald Constable & Co., 438

Catalogue of the Royal and Noble Authors of England (Walpole), 71

Cathcart, Lord, 154, 206

censorship, 3–4, 148–49

Chalmers, George, 306; *Caledonia*, 606; *Life of Thomas Ruddiman*, 306

Chambaud, Louis, 336

Chamberlaine, Dillon: in Company of Booksellers, 479; founds key Dublin firm, 470–71; in price war of 1767, 472–75; subscribes to Steuart's *Inquiry*, 483

Chamberlaine, Hannah, 471

Chamberlaine & Rice, 471

Chamberlaine–Rice, 470–71, 704

Chambers, John: Carey and, 545, 573–76; emigration to America, 498; his edition of Guthrie's *Geography*, 486–93, 545; patriotic publishing, 488, 492; radicalism and imprisonment, 491–92, 498; rivalry with Exshaw, 492; ties to George Robinson, 398, 452n14

Chapman, William, 322

Chapman and Duncan, 269

Chapter Coffee House (London), 26, 357, 382

Characteristics of the Present Political State of Great Britain (R. Wallace): author's copy money from, 332n15; Dublin edition, 453–54; publication, 287; Strahan and, 332

Charlotte Square (Edinburgh), 119

Chartier, Roger: on literary patronage, 203; on pictorial representation of authors, 163; on space between text and object, 607; on tension between reading and publishing, 31

Chesterfield, 4th Earl of (Philip Stanhope), 195–96; *Principles of Politeness*, 530–31, 538

Chesterfield, 5th Earl of (Philip Stanhope), 207n25

Cheyne, George, 98

Christensen, Jerome, 47–48

Christie, Thomas, 247

Church of Scotland, 142

Cleghorn, Mrs. William (Jean Hamilton), 310

Cleghorn, William, 310

Clephane, John, 52

Clérisseau, Charles-Louis, 226

Clinical Experiments, Histories and Dissections (F. Home), 423

Club, The (Literary) (London), 120

clubs and societies: in Edinburgh: 62, 106–10, 115; in London: 119–20, 129. *See also names of specific clubs and societies*

Cockburn, Alison, 102

Cockburn, Henry, Lord Cockburn: on
    Creech, 434; on Creech's shop, 422,
    439; on the Edinburgh literati, 99
Cole, Richard Cargill, 444, 500
Collection of Original Poems (Donald-
    son), 314
*Collections Relating to the History of Mary
    Queen of Scotland* (James Anderson),
    sold by M'Euen and reissued by Mil-
    lar, 279–80
College of New Jersey (Princeton), 532
Colles, Anne, 470
Colles, William: Company of Booksell-
    ers and, 476; death, 470; London ties,
    451
Colley, Linda, 70
Collins, Benjamin, 362
Collyer, Joseph, the younger, 169–71,
    170, 171
Columbian Magazine, 544. See also
    *Universal Asylum, and Columbian
    Magazine*
Coming of the Book (*L'Apparition du Livre*)
    (Fevre and Martin), 9
Commentaries of Caesar (trans. W. Dun-
    can), 78, 215
Commentaries on the Laws of England
    (Blackstone), 518, 521–23
Common Sense (Paine), 528
common sense philosophy, 565–67
communications circuit, 30
Company of Bookbinders (Dublin), 477
Company of Booksellers (Dublin):
    Buffon's *Natural History* and, 496–97;
    corporate imprints of, 476, 477; de-
    cline and demise, 499; Ferguson's *Ro-
    man Republic* and, 462–63; history of,
    473–82, 510; identification of mem-
    bers, 478–79
Comparative View of Man (John Greg-
    ory), 92–93
*Compendium of Authentic and Entertain-
    ing Voyages* (Smollett), 215n44
Complete History of England (Smol-
    lett): best seller, 92; mass-marketed,

    229–30; Smollett's copy money from,
    215–16; used to construct Smollett's
    History of England (continuation of
    Hume), 169, 582–83
Complete History of the English Peerage
    (Guthrie), published in parts or num-
    bers, 229
*Concise Natural History of East and West-
    Florida* (Romans), 537
congers, 271
Constable, Archibald: background and
    career, 434–36, 605; bankruptcy, 436;
    as a bookseller and publisher, 430–31,
    438; Cadell & Davies and, 602–5; on
    Charles Elliot, 386, 434; on Creech,
    37–38; on decline of Cadell & Davies,
    601; on John Bell, 325, 428–29; like-
    ness of, 435–36, *437*; myth of, 438;
    purchases Creech's best copyrights,
    604–5; rise of, 39; Stark on, 431; un-
    dermines Creech, 602–3; *Catalogue of
    Books Printed for Archibald Constable
    & Co.*, 438
Constable & Co. *See* Constable,
    Archibald
*Continuation of the Complete History of
    England* (Smollett): best seller, 92;
    frontispiece portrait, 167; on Hume
    and Robertson, 170, 172; used to con-
    struct Smollett's *History of England*
    (continuation of Hume), 169, 582–83
Cook, Captain James, 347
Cook, Thomas, 182–83, *183*
Cooke, Charles, 584
*Cooke's Pocket Edition of Select British
    Poets*, 85
copy money: aristocratic disdain for,
    209–11; authors' emulation of Robert-
    son, 249–50, 346; book formats and,
    82–83, 249, 418; Cadell's testimony
    on, 327; charitable uses of, 211–12,
    424–27; French envy of, 261; as a mo-
    tive for writing books, 209, 256–59;
    Murray offers service instead of, 383;
    patronage and, 204, 208–9; publish-

ers boasting about, 327, 344–45; publishers' resentment of authors' demands, 345–50; publishers' tactics for countering rising demands of authors, 348–50; Scottish Enlightenment authors set new standard for, 261, 344–45. *See also* author-publisher relations; authors, Scottish Enlightenment; copy money paid to individual authors; profit motive; publication, terms of

copy money paid to individual authors: Alexander Adam, 237–38; Beattie, 226–27, 254–55, 418; Blair, 245–47; Boswell, 223–24; Bruce (James), 242–43; Brydone, 253; Buchan, 219–20, 256; Burney, 228n84; Burns, 231, 234; Cullen, 241–42, 253; Duncan (William), 215; Ferguson (Adam), 252–54, 600; Ferguson (James), 217; Gerard, 254; Gibbon, 259n161; Gillies, 240, 384; Hailes, 254; Hawkesworth, 347; Henry, 218–19; Hume, 241, 308; Kames, 253; Leland, 501n90; MacCormick, 351; Mackenzie, 254; Mackintosh, 254; Macpherson (John), 254; Mickle, 226; Millar, 254; Moore, 244–45; Park, 217; Reid, 393; Robertson, 201, 214, 259–60, 282; Smellie, 216, 228–29; Smith, 236–37; Smollett, 215–16; Somerville, 250–52; Steuart, 236; Stewart (Dugald), 253; Stuart (Gilbert), 254; Wallace, 332n15; Watson, 240, 349–50. *See also* copy money

copyright. *See* literary property

Copyright Act of 1709–10. *See* Statute of Anne

counter-Enlightenment, 11–13, 81

Court of Session, 99

Covenanters, 550

Covent Garden (London), 118

Cowper, William, 381

Cranstoun, George, 401–2

Cranstoun, Lord, 401–2

Creech, Mrs. William (Mary Buley, William's mother), 401–2

Creech, Rev. William (William's father), 401–2

Creech, William: Adam (Alexander) and, 419–20; ambiguous situation of, 404; Andrew Strahan and, 375–76, 379; Arnot's *History of Edinburgh* and, 423–24; Beattie and, 226–27, 255, 417–19; birth and education, 401–4, 407; bookshop in Luckenbooths, 110, *111*, 150–51, 198, 312, *317*, 410, 412, 421–22, 439–40; Bruce (John) and, 403, 419; Burns and, 181, 234–35, 419, 421–22, 433; Cadell & Davies and, 415, 428, 602–4; complains about review of *Mirror*, 367; Constable and, 428–30, 602–5; Continental tours, 407, 410; on copy money, 344–45, 359; database of Scottish authors and, 34, 75–77; decline and death of, 39, 604; *Edinburgh Magazine and Review* published by, 73; on engraving of Blair's portrait, 176; enlightened motives of, 418–19, 423–28, 434; freemasonry and, 108, 181, 420–21; Kames and, 359, 420; as Kincaid's employee, 403, 406–10; as Kincaid's partner and successor, 326, 337–39, 410–12, *411*; on literary property, 414–15; in London, 233, 404–8, 410, 412; Mackenzie and, 211–12, 420, *421*; Monro's *Nervous System* and, 424; Murray and Stuart and, 414, 420; order of names in imprints by, 415–16, 423, 429; patronage of authors by, 198, 417–22, 440; portraits of, 428, *429*, 436; reputation of, 37, 428–40; Richardson and, 153–54; rivalry with Balfour, 37, 340–43, 415; on Rousseau, 403; in Royal Society of Edinburgh, 404; Rush and, 553–54; Scott on, 435; as a Scottish Enlightenment publisher, 37, 272, 337–61 passim, 375–76, 378–79, 413–28, 440, 702–3;

Creech, William (*continued*)
as silent partner in publications, 273;
on slave trade, 433; Smellie and, 420,
433; Society of Antiquaries of Scotland and, 343, 404; Speculative Society cofounder, 403; *Statistical Account* and, 424–27, 433, 440; Strahan and Cadell and, 337–61 passim, 408–18 passim, *411*, 422–24; violates honorary copyright with Balfour, 355;
wealth of, 358; Woodhouselee and, 403, 419; *Edinburgh Fugitive Pieces*, 420, *421*; 428; *Letters Containing a Comparative View of Edinburgh in the Years 1763 and 1783* (revised as *Letters Addressed to Sir John Sinclair*), 75–76, 271, 344–45, 419–20, 424, 425. *See also* Cadell, Thomas, I; Kincaid, Alexander; Strahan, William; Strahan (Andrew) and Cadell; Strahan (William) and Cadell; *names of individual authors whose works he published*

Critical Dissertations on the Ancient Caledonians (John Macpherson), 135, 254

Critical Dissertation on the Poems of Ossian (Blair): extracts in *Universal Asylum*, 562; included in table 2, 78; popularity of, 90, 92; temporary anonymity of, 152

Critical Review: as guide to books, 4; Pinkerton and, 126, 138; on popularity of Blair's *Sermons*, 33; Scottish connections with, 365–66; Smollett and, 123; used in Dublin, 451; Walpole cites note in, 71

Crochallan Fencibles, 109

Cross, The (Edinburgh), 110, *110*

Crukshank, Joseph, 556, 561, 573

Cullen, William: acts against Brown and Buchan, 121; as author and teacher, 22, 121; in *The Bee*, 139; in Carey's edition of Guthrie's *Geography*, *581*, 582; Denina praises, 68; in Dublin press, 456; Elliot and, 241–42; meets with Strahan in Edinburgh,

304; Murray and, 241–42; named in Gregory's *Observations*, 151–52; in Oyster Club, 109; in prime generation, 98; Rush and, 527, 541; Stark praises, 430, 605; *First Lines of the Practice of Physic*, 92, 241–42, 243, 384, 386, 485, 527n54; *Institutions of Medicine*, 556; *Lectures on the Materia Medica*, 105, 253, 454n19, 465, 526–27, 536; *Treatise of the Materia Medica*, 157, *158*, 386–87, 508–9, 554, 561

Dalkeith Academy, 402–3, 419

Dalrymple, Sir David, Lord Hailes: Creech cites, 76; education, 101; freemason, 108; praises A. Ferguson, 525; in prime generation, 98; on proper format for history books, 86; titles of, 99; *Annals of Scotland*, 254, 383, 420; *Disquisitions concerning the Antiquities of the Christian Church*, 269

Dalrymple, Sir John: Creech cites, 76; title of, 99; *Essay towards a General History of Feudal Property*, 141, 287; *Memoirs of Great Britain and Ireland*, 249, 339, 369–71, 536

Darnton, Robert: on book history and Enlightenment, 4, 8; on communications circuit, 30; on definition of the Enlightenment, 14–15; on "low-life of literature," 128; on postmodern critique of the Enlightenment, 13n36; on production and reception, 32; on profit motive of publishers, 294, 360; on Société typographique de Neuchâtel, 4n11; on women authors in France, 102n7

Darwin, Erasmus, 381

Davidson, Archibald, 247–48

Davies, Thomas, 198

Davies, William, 602

Death of Abel, 473

Decline and Fall of Roman Empire (Gibbon): anti-religion theme in, 253; author's copy money from, 259n161;

commercial success of, 252; Dublin edition, 464, 471; Hume's backhanded compliment of, 69; print run, 252n142; publishing dominance of Strahan and Cadell and, 357–58

dedications: mitigated anonymity and, 151, 153–54; Scottish Enlightenment books and, 141–44; in Young's editions of Reid and Stewart, 567, *569*

Defence of the Reformation-Principles of the Church of Scotland (Wilson), 534

Defoe, Daniel, 314

de Hondt, Peter, 254

Delineation of Morality (Balfour), 310

Dell, Henry, 288

Dempster, George, 315

Denina, Carlo: on Augustan age in England, 68; Scottish literature praised by, 34, 68, 94; Scottish response to, 73–74, 94

Dialectic of Enlightenment (Horkheimer and Adorno), 12

Dialogues concerning Natural Religion (Hume), 56n22

Dickinson, John, 519, 527

Dickinson, T., 186–87, *186*

Dickson, Adam: *Husbandry of the Ancients*, 228; *Treatise of Agriculture*, 324

Dictionary of National Biography (*DNB*), 265–66

Dictionary of the English Language (Johnson): author paid by the job for, 216; Boswell on writing of, 195–96; definition of "publisher," xv; exchange with Millar after completion of, 289

Diderot, Denis, 98

Didot the younger, 543

diffusion of knowledge, 1–2, 14–15, 564, 608

Dilly, Charles: bid for second volume of Blair's *Sermons*, 246; copublisher of Guthrie's *Geography*, *134*; on copy money, 348; death, 604; generosity toward Boswell, 200; Gerard's *Sermons* published by, 256–57; Pinkerton's *History of Scotland* and, 138, 348–49; shields Boswell from stigma of self-publication, 200. *See also* Dilly brothers

Dilly, Edward, 213, 418. *See also* Dilly brothers

Dilly brothers (Edward and Charles): authors entertained by, 199; Beattie and, 226–27, 255, 380, 417–18; Boswell patronized by, 200; as Scottish Enlightenment publishers, 37, 272, 380, 702–3. *See also* Dilly, Charles; Dilly, Edward

Disquisitions concerning the Antiquities of the Christian Church (Hailes), 269

Dissenters, 131, 380–81, 389, 399, 598

Dissertation on Miracles (Campbell): Dobson's Philadelphia edition, 560; good seller, 91; publication, 286, 317

"Dissertation on the Gout" (Cadogan), 534

Dissertation on the Numbers of Mankind in Antient and Modern Times (R. Wallace), 287

Dissertations, Moral and Critical (Beattie), 254, 340, 418

Dissertations on Different Subjects in Natural Philosophy (Hutton), 210, 242

Dissertations on Subjects relating to the Genius and Evidence of Christianity (Gerard), 286, 317

Dobson, Mrs. Thomas (Jean Paton), 546

Dobson, Thomas: in *American Annual Register*, 590; birth and background, 545; Carey and, 574n90; Charles Elliot and, 387, 545–46; early career in Philadelphia, 546, 553; emigration to America, 541–42, 545–46; *Encyclopaedia*, 556–61, *557*, 585; Philadelphia Company of Printers and Booksellers and, 555, 571–73, 592; on the profit motive in publishing, 591–92; religion and, 592; as a Scottish Enlightenment reprinter, 38–39, 556–61; subscriber to Campbell's edition of

Dobson, Thomas (*continued*)
Hume and Smollett, 586; Young and, 551–53, 592

Dodsley, James, 534. *See also* Dodsley brothers

Dodsley, Robert: commissions William Duncan to write *Commentaries of Caesar*, 215; coowner of *London Chronicle*, 363; literary bias in favor of, 10; praised by Johnson, 196; *Preceptor*, 90. *See also* Dodsley brothers

Dodsley brothers (Robert and James): fame of, 430; as Scottish Enlightenment publishers, 272, 702–3; Spence's edition of Blacklock's *Poems*, 224. *See also* Dodsley, James; Dodsley, Robert

Doig, David, 494

Domestic Medicine (Buchan): American editions, 531, 534–35, 571–73; author identification, 572; author's copy money from, 220; dedication of, 142; Dublin editions, 454; in Dublin press, 456; edited by Smellie, 135; later editions, 329, 340–41, *341*, 343, 354, 413, 415, 534; an octavo best seller, 92–93; *Preventive Medicine* and, 349; print runs, 87n80, 219–20; self-published by subscription, 219–20, 228, 243

Dominion of Providence over the Passions of Men (Witherspoon), 534

Donaldson, Alexander: career, 313–16; Edinburgh shop, 198, 314; freemason, 108; Kincaid's partner, 311–14; London shop, 314–15; multidimensionality of, 315; not the leader of the Edinburgh book trade, 315–16; subscriber to Thomson's *Works*, 282; supported by Bell and Murray, 382; wealth of, 315; *Collection of Original Poems*, 314; *Some Thoughts on the State of Literary Property*, 475–76

Donaldson, James, 314–15

Donaldson, John (artist): drawing of Brown by, 187; drawing of Hume by, 168; engravings from drawing of

Brown by, 187–90, *188, 189*; engravings from drawing of Hume by, *48*, 49, 164, 168–71, *170*

Donaldson, John (bookseller), 314

Donoghue, Frank, 366n86

Don Quixote (trans. Smollett), 488

Douglas, James, 121

Douglas, John, Bishop of Salisbury: brother of Helen Anderson, 129, 131; brother-in-law of Pinkerton, 125; mediates publication of Scottish Enlightenment books, 83, 239; in Millar's circle of literary counselors, 283–84

Douglas, Sylvester (later Lord Glenbervie), 212, 223, 235, 254

Douglas, Tragedy of (J. Home): in Belfast, 449; best seller, 92; Company of Booksellers and, 476; forces Home to resign his parish, 205; Hume's controversy with Garrick over, 289; Monboddo rates it over Shakespeare, 69; published by Hamilton & Balfour, 308; supported by Hume and Scottish literati, 62, 66, 142–43

Dow, Alexander, 101; *History of Hindostan*, 87n81

downsizing books: in Britain, 27–28, 84, 93; in Dublin, 459–63; in Philadelphia, 509, 535, 560. *See also* formats of books

Draper, George, 498

Drennan, William, 491–92

Drury Lane (London), 118

Dryden, John, 268, 314

Dublin: as a center of print culture, 468–69; in Guthrie's *Geography*, 489;

Dublin book trade: bankruptcies and, 498; collaboration in Dublin, 468, 478, 481; collaboration with British publishers, 383, 452–53; collapse of, 498–502; communication with Britain, 451–52; compared with Edinburgh, 444; extension of British copyright to, 499; geography of, 468; fathers and sons in, 470; guild,

469–70; leading firms in, 468–72, 479, *704;* literary property in, 451, 473–78; location of, 468; organization of, 469–81; paper duty and, 467, 499; parasitical nature of, 469, 501; patriotic publishing in, 484, 486, 488, 492–95; political crisis of the 1790s and, 498–99; price war of 1767, 472–76; profits, 468; quality publishing, 479–97; religious divisions in, 470; Roman Catholics in, 470; Scottish backgrounds or surnames of publishers, 449; as subscribers to Dublin editions, 483–84, 486n65; use of literary counselors by publishers, 453; widows in, 470–72. *See also* bookshops (Dublin); Company of Booksellers (Dublin); Guild of St. Luke the Evangelist (Dublin); Irish editions in America; Irish editions in Britain; reprinting books (in Dublin); *names of individual booksellers and publishers in Dublin*

Dublin Chronicle, 456, 469, 487–88, 493, 496–97

Dublin Evening Post, 451, 455, 472n50, 485, 498

Dublin Gazette, 473

Dublin Journal, 469

Dublin Magazine, 460

Dublin Mercury, 456, 469, 473

Dublin's Trade in Books, 461, 464

Duff, William, 156; *Sermons on Several Occasions*, 229, 268

Dunbar, James, 371; *Essays on the History of Mankind*, 371

Duncan, Andrew: biography of Monro I by, 139; contributes to *Encyclopaedia Britannica*, 494; Creech cites, 76; freemason, 108; frontispiece portrait of, 191n171; in younger generation, 99; *Elements of Therapeutics*, 363, *363;* *Medical and Philosophical Commentaries*, 142, 162, 363, *364; Medical Cases*, 157, 191n171, 212

Duncan, Robert, 537–39

Duncan, Thomas, 537

Duncan, William: returns to Scotland, 120; *Commentaries of Caesar*, 215; *Elements of Logic*, 89–90, 92, 135, 508

Dundas, Henry, Viscount Melville, 402, 424

Dunlop, Mrs. (Frances Anna Wallace), 234

Du Ponceau, Peter Stephen, 516

Durham, Thomas, 373

Eadie, John, 548n25

Ecclesiastical Characteristics (Witherspoon), 81

Edgar, James, 252n143

Edgeworth, Maria, 381

Edinburgh: "Athens of Britain" (Sheridan), 67, 115; book trade in, 306–18; centrality of, 115–16; compared with London, 118–20; engravers in, 168, 176; "hot-bed of genius" (Smollett), 74–75, 115; intellectual culture of, 106–14; Johnson and Boswell in, 144–45; "modern Athens" (Knox), 115–16

Edinburgh, University of: Creech studies at, 403, 419; education of Scottish authors at, 103; in *Encyclopaedia Britannica*, 494; in Guthrie's *Geography*, 579; Heron's *Observations* on, 145–46; need for new buildings, 301, 456; significance of Ferguson's *Essay* for, 161; Stuart gets LL.D. from, 128; Thomson's *Tour* on, 145

Edinburgh Advertiser, 315

Edinburgh Booksellers' Society, 325, 355–56, 432, 478

Edinburgh Chamber of Commerce, 403, 433

Edinburgh Chronicle, 307

Edinburgh Evening Courant, 67, 253, 312, 362, 410

Edinburgh Fugitive Pieces (Creech), 420, 421, 428

Edinburgh Magazine (Sibbald's), 114, 231

Edinburgh Magazine and Review: Edinburgh literati and, 128; Gilbert Stuart and, 128; Murray and Creech and, 73, 366, 420

Edinburgh Musical Society, 421

Edinburgh Philosophical Society. *See* Philosophical Society of Edinburgh

Edinburgh Review (1755–56): preface defines goals of, 64–67; on printing, 65–66, 306; published by Hamilton & Balfour, 308; reprinted by Mackintosh, 135–36; review of Hutcheson's *System of Moral Philosophy* in, 64; Scottish literary identity and, 34, 64–67

Edinburgh Review (est. 1802), 39, 431–32, 436, 438

Edinburgh Society for the Encouragement of Arts, Sciences, Manufactures, and Agriculture in Scotland, 62, 107, 311

Edinburgh Trained Bands, 311, 403

Edridge, Henry, 186

Edward (Moore): author's copy money from, 245, 254, 398; authorship of, 150; publication, 398

Edwards, Miss, 102n9

Eisenstein, Elizabeth, 6

Eldridge, Charles Lucas, 333

Elements of Agriculture and Vegetation (G. Fordyce), 381

Elements of Criticism (Kames): copyright, 333; dedication, 141; Denina neglects, 74; publication, 286; strong seller, 91; Voltaire on, 67–68

Elements of Euclid (Simson): best seller, 92; included in table 2, 78; printed by the Foulis brothers, 268–69

Elements of General History, Ancient and Modern (Woodhouselee), 419, 604

Elements of Geometry (Playfair/Euclid), 78

Elements of Logic (W. Duncan): American edition, 508; duodecimo best seller, 92; popularity of, 89–90; used in *Encyclopaedia Britannica*, 135

Elements of Medicine (Brown): Dobson's Philadelphia edition, 560; frontispiece portrait in 1795 edition, 187–90, *188*

Elements of Moral Philosophy (D. Fordyce), 89–90, 92, 135

Elements of Moral Science (Beattie): author's copy money from, 254, 418; Carey's Philadelphia edition, 574n95; from university lectures, 105

Elements of the Philosophy of History, Part First (Logan): based on lectures, 106; Carey's edition of Guthrie's *Geography* praises, *581*, 582; Young's Philadelphia edition, 567

Elements of the Philosophy of the Human Mind (D. Stewart): author's copy money from, 253; dedication to Reid, 144; good seller, 91; later volumes, 606

Elements of the Practice of Midwifery (A. Hamilton), 447

Elements of the Practice of Physic (G. Fordyce), 381

Elements of the Science of Ethics (John Bruce), 419

Elements of Therapeutics (A. Duncan), 363, *364*

Elliot, Anne. *See* Murray, Mrs. John, II (Anne Elliot)

Elliot, Charles: bookshop of, 112–13, 386–87; Cadell and, 336; career, 386–87; copy money paid to authors, 386; copyright to Smellie's *Philosophy of Natural History* purchased by, 229; Creech and, 429; Dobson and, 387, 546–47; *Encyclopaedia Britannica* and, 556; expands to London, 387; Irish books and, 356, 452, 465–66; publishes Smiths' *Galic Antiquities*, 352; as Scottish Enlightenment publisher, 272, 386–87, *702–3*; shortcomings, 387; stroke and death, 387, 604;

wealth of, 358, 387. *See also* Dobson, Thomas; *names of individual authors whose works he published*

Elliot, Gilbert, of Minto, 43, 61, 66, 205

Elmsley, Peter, 336

Emerson, Roger, 204n20, 504

Encyclopaedia, The. See Dobson, Thomas; *Encyclopaedia Britannica*

Encyclopaedia Britannica (Smellie, editor of first edition): in Belfast, 449; Bell (Andrew) and, 496; compiled largely from Scottish Enlightenment books, 135; Dobson's edition, 556–61, *557*, 585; included in table 2, 78–79; Moore's Dublin edition, 493–95; Murray's piracy suit against, 135n89; popularity of, 88–90, 92–93; print run, 87n80; published in parts or numbers, 230; publishers get rich from, 216; Scottish biographies in third edition, 494, 559, 591; Smellie receives £200 for, 216; "a Society of Gentlemen in Scotland" ostensible authors of, 162; *Supplement to the Third Edition* (Edinburgh), 234; *Supplement to the Third Edition* (Dublin), 494; *Supplement to the Third Edition* (Philadelphia), 558–60

Encyclopédie, 80

English Review, 366

engraving: Blair on, 176; compared with original portraits, 164–65; copper plates compared with steel, 167; high cost of, 167; importance for defining visual images of authors, 165; line engraving, 165, *166*; in Philadelphia, 585; problem for Dublin reprinters, 495–96; stipple, 165, *166*. *See also* frontispiece portraits of authors

"Enlightened Reader in America" (Lundberg and May), 503

Enlightenment, American, 39, 589–95

Enlightenment, British, 19–21

Enlightenment, English, 22, 119–20

Enlightenment, French, 14–15, 149, 261

Enlightenment, nature of, 11–17, 33

Enlightenment, Scottish: Atlantic dissemination, 38; Augustan England contrasted with, 60–61; authors' opportunities for success, 260–61; Blair on values of, 32–34; book history of, 79–80; Continental dissemination of, 23; cosmopolitan ideal of, 142–47; database of authors from, 77–81; decline of, 39, 597–98; defined, 19–20, 79–81; deprecation of, 19–21; English Enlightenment contrasted with, 22; exaggerations about significance of, 18–19; London–Edinburgh axis and, 285–87; national identity and, 34, 61–73, 147; opposition to, 81; origin of term, 79; preceded by formative period, 79, 98; reading and reception of, 30–31; Smollett on, 75; tone of, 105; urban character, 114–31

Enquiry concerning Political Justice (Godwin), 397

Enquiry concerning the Principles of Morals (Hume), 45

Enquiry into the Elementary Principles of Beauty (W. Thomson), 381

Enquiry into the Life and Writings of Homer (Blackwell), 98

Enquiry [Philosophical Essays] concerning Human Understanding (Hume), 45, 151, 287

Epigoniad, The (Wilkie), 43, 66, 152, 308

Episcopalianism, Scottish, 116

epitexts. *See* paratexts; publicity

Erskine, Andrew, 314

Erskine, David Stewart [or Steuart]. *See* Buchan, 11th Earl of Erskine, Henry, 396

Erskine, John, 434

Essay on Crimes and Punishments (Beccaria), 530

Essay on Genius (Gerard), 254, 339

Essay on Man (Pope), *335, 336*

Essay on Taste (Gerard), 285, 297

Essay on the Causes of the Variety of Complexion and Figure in the Human Species (S. Smith), 538

Essay on the Character, Manners, and Genius of Women in Different Ages (Thomas; trans. Russell), 535

Essay on the Contents and Virtues of Dunse-Spaw (F. Home), 313

Essay on the Health of Seamen (Lind), 285

Essay on the History of Civil Society (A. Ferguson): author's copy money from, 254; Balfour accused of smuggling Irish edition of, 321, 356, 464; Bell's planned edition, *521, 523–26*; Cadell's first major publication, 324, 331; conflict between Cadell and Bell over, 37, 318–26, 414; Dublin edition, 463; first three editions of, *319;* good seller, 91; publication, 286; significance of, for Edinburgh University, 161

Essay on the Nature and Immutability of Truth (Beattie): author fixes review of, 138; author requests copublication, 317; author's copy money from, 254; best seller, 92; excerpt in *Universal Asylum,* 563; impolite language in, 146; publication, 318, 380; in quarto edition of *Essays,* 226–27

Essay on the Principles of Translation (Woodhouselee), 153

Essay on the Right of Property in Land (W. Ogilvie), 152–53

Essays (Beattie): quarto edition of, 226–27, 418; university lectures, drawn from, 105

Essays and Dissertations on Various Subjects (Bethune), 146, 229

Essays and Observations, Physical and Literary, 152

Essays and Treatises on Several Subjects (Hume): autobiographical advertisement in, 53; best seller, 92; Boswell resents quarto copy, 47; Dublin editions, 457, 462, 482–83; fashioning and refashioning of, 45–50; frontispiece portrait of Hume in, *48,* 168; neglected by Hume scholars, 55; not mentioned in "My Own Life," 54–55; publication, 285, 323; quarto, 81–82; Scottish literary identity and, 34; in Smith's library, 138; title page, *49;* variety of formats and prices, *51,* 56–58

Essays, Moral and Political (Hume): 1741–42 volumes, 312; authorship of, 151; 1748 edition, 285, *286,* 297

Essays on Philosophical Subjects (A. Smith): charitable purposes, 212; commercial failure of, 600; edited by Black and Hutton, 135

Essays on Shakespeare's Dramatic Characters (Richardson), 89

Essays on Taste (Alison), 91, 142

Essays on the Active Powers of Man (Reid), 394, 565–67, *568*

Essays on the History of Mankind (Dunbar), 371

Essays on the Intellectual Powers of Man (Reid): author's copy money from, 393; dedication, 143; Dublin edition, 463–64; publication, 391–94; Rush on, 565; Young's Philadelphia edition, 565–67, *568*

Essays on the Lives and Writings of Fletcher of Saltoun and the Poet Thomson (Earl of Buchan), 145, 211

Essays on the Principles of Morality and Natural Religion (Kames): authorship of, 149, 153; in Belfast, 449; publication, 313

Essays on the Trade, Commerce, Manufactures, and Fisheries of Scotland (Loch), 160, 228n85

Essays Relating to Agriculture and Rural Affairs (James Anderson): advertisement praises John Gregory, 141–42; imprint contains "the Robinsons,"

390; publication, 395; second edition dedicated to Cullen, 141

Essays upon British Antiquities (Kames), 312–13

Essays upon Several Subjects in Law (Kames), 153, 312

Essay towards a General History of Feudal Property (J. Dalrymple), 141, 287

ESTC (English Short-Title Catalogue), 156, 416, 443, 499, 510, 531

Eulogium in Honour of the Late Dr. William Cullen (Rush), 561, 563

Eurydice (Mallet), 280

Evidences of the Christian Religion (Beattie), 254

Ewing, Thomas: in Dublin price war, 473; expanded edition of Home's *Experiments on Bleaching*, 457; purchases rights to Millar's *Origin of Ranks*, 383, 453; quarto edition of *Charles V*, 482; subscribes to Steuart's *Inquiry*, 483

Experiments on Bleaching (F. Home), 457

Experiments upon Magnesia Alba (Black), 133

Exshaw, John, I: in Dublin price war, 473–74; *Exshaw's Magazine* and, 469; Guthrie's *Geography* and, 487; succeeded by son, 470

Exshaw, John, II: *Exshaw's Magazine* and, 469; George Robinson and, 389, 452n14; Guthrie's *Geography* and, 487–93; succeeds father, 470

Exshaw's Magazine, 455–56, 469

Faculty of Advocates, 106

Fairbairn, James, 604

Fairbairn, John, 428

Farquhar, John, 371; *Sermons*, 371

Fatal Discovery (J. Home), 148

Father's Legacy to His Daughters (John Gregory): Aitken's Philadelphia edition, 538; best seller, 92–93; honorary copyright and, 354; publication of, 339; on women's learning, 103

Faulkner, George: cheated by Rivington, 453; *Dublin Journal* and, 469; in Dublin price war, 473–54; uncle of Thomas Todd, 500

Faulkner, Thomas Todd, 469, 500

Febvre, Lucien, 9

Ferdinand Count Fathom (Smollett), 92–93, 453

Ferguson, Adam: Advocates' Library keeper, 112; American readers and, 503; biography of Black by, 141; a Highlander, 100; on London, 406n11; meets Strahan in Edinburgh, 304; negotiations for his *Roman Republic*, 252–53, 345–46, 348, 356; in Oyster Club, 109; praised by J. Dalrymple, 525; in prime generation, 98; promotes patronage for John Home, 205–6; resented by Strahan for condescending attitude, 350; in Sibbald's circulating library, 113–14, *113*; Smollett cites, 74–75; as tutor, 207n25; wants octavo edition of his *Essay* for class use, 320–21; *Essay on the History of Civil Society*, 37, 91, 161, 254, 286, 318–26, *319*, 331, 356, 369, 371, 414, 463, 464, *521*, 523–26 ; *History of the Progress and Termination of the Roman Republic*, 90, 159, 252–53, 340, 346, 348, 350, 356, 462; *Institutes of Moral Philosophy*, 85, 105; *Principles of Moral and Political Science*, 105, 600

Ferguson, James: in Carey's edition of Guthrie's *Geography*, 582; Denina praises, 68; patronized by Millar, Cadell, and Strahan, 199, 217; portrait painting by, 168; portraits of, 182–83, *183*; praised in *Universal Asylum*, 566; in table 1, 77; unschooled, 101; *Art of Drawing in Perspective*, 335, *336*; *Astronomy Explained*, 92, 135, 217, 228, 273, 354; *Lectures on Select Subjects*, 92, 105–6, 135, 287; *Select Mechanical Exercises*, 182–83, *335*, *336*; *Tables and*

Ferguson, James (*continued*)
Tracts, relative to Several Arts and Sciences, 368n94
Fergusson, Robert, 77, 191n171; *Poems*, 92, 191n171
Fielding, Henry, 280, 282–83; *Amelia*, 288; *Joseph Andrews*, 297; *Miscellanies*, 297; *Tom Jones*, 282, 473–74
Fingal ("trans." James Macpherson): best seller, 92; Denina neglects, 74; Dublin edition, 459–60, 454n19; format of, 86; as Scottish national epic, 66
Finn's Leinster Journal, 484
First Lines of the Practice of Physic (Cullen): American edition, 527n54; best seller, 92; Dublin edition, 485; Elliot purchases, 386; Murray loses, 384; publication, 241–42; registered at Stationers' Hall, 243
First Principles of Philosophy (John Bruce), 85, 419
Fish, Stanley, 31
Fisher, George, 519
Flaxman, John, 180
Fleeming (or Fleming), John, 475, 511
Fleming, Robert (Creech's factor): anonymous life of Creech by, 296, 428; on bond among Barclay's Scholars, 402–3; on Creech and Strahan, 408; on Creech in London, 404; on Kincaid, Millar, and Strahan as apprentices of "James Macewen," 296
Fleming, Robert (printer), 312
Fletcher, Andrew, Lord Milton, 205
Flin, Lawrence, 453, 513
Folingsby, George, 470, 493
Forbes, Duncan, 283
Forbes, John, 283
Forbes, Sir William, 255, 438; *Account of the Life and Writings of James Beattie*, 438
Fordyce, David: *Elements of Moral Philosophy*, 89–90, 92, 135; *Theodorus*, 133, 141

Fordyce, George: in The Club, 120; settles in London, 121; *Elements of Agriculture and Vegetation*, 381; *Elements of the Practice of Physic*, 381
Fordyce, James: intimately acquainted with Strahan's daughter, 198–99; portrait of, 180, *180*; praises brother David in *Theodorus*, 141; praises Cadell in poem, 213–14; in table 1, 77; *Addresses to Young Men*, 371; *Poems*, 180, 213–14; *Sermons to Young Women*, 92, 152, 198–99, 371, 471, 473, 475, 511
Fordyce, (Sir) William, 371
formats of books: American editions and, 509; book sales and, 84; compared, *51*, 46–47, 81–84, 488; copy money and, 82–83, 249, 418; Dublin editions and, 459–61; engraving and, 173, 176; folios ambitious, commercially impractical, and rare, 81–82, 85, 215, 225–26, 424; Hume's works and, 46–48, 56–58; prices and, 82–83, 526–27; reading and, 27–28; regarding Ferguson's *Essay*, 318–26; small books, 85; subjects and genres and, 85–86, 249, *700. See also* downsizing books
Foucault, Michel: on anonymity, 149–50; on author function, 7, 58, 77, 94, 159–60; on print culture, 3; "What Is an Author?" 58. *See also* author function
Foulis, Andrew (brother of Robert). *See* Foulis brothers
Foulis, Robert. *See* Foulis brothers
Foulis brothers (Robert and Andrew Foulis): arts academy, 117; *Edinburgh Review* alludes to, 66; fame of, 486; printing and publishing by, 63, 268–69
Foundling Hospital (London), 333, 378
Four Dissertations (Hume), 46, 142–43
Four Gospels (trans. Campbell): author resents high price and commercial failure of, 239–40; format of, 86; in-

cluded in table 2, 78; terms of publication, 238

Fragments of Ancient Poetry (James Macpherson), 308

Franklin, Benjamin: Carey and, 543; entertained by Strahan, 304; frontispiece portrait in Campbell's *History of England*, 587; as Philadelphia printer, 514; subscriber to Dobson's *Encyclopaedia*, 558

Freeman's Journal (Dublin), 482, 483, 543

Freeman's Journal (Philadelphia), 552–53

freemasonry: Burns and, 181; Creech and, 420–21; Scottish authors and, 108

French Revolution, 251–52, 254, 396, 567, 576, 578

Friends, The (Guthrie), 150

frontispiece portraits of authors: accessories for, 163, 182–85, 191; B. Bell, 183–84, *184;* Blair, 173, 176–79, *178, 179;* Brown, 187–90, *188;* Burns, 180–82, *182;* Henry, 173, *177;* Hume, *48*, 168–69, *170, 583, 585;* J. Ferguson, 182–83, *183;* J. Fordyce, 180, *180;* Johnson, 223; Leechman, 190, 192–93, *193,* 248–49; Macpherson, 172–73, *176;* not shown, 190n171; Park, 185–87, *186;* Pinkerton, 184–85, *185;* Pope, 59–60; Robertson, 172, *175;* Smollett, 167, 169, *171,* 587; staged nature of, 164, 191–92; vanity and, 168. *See also* engraving

Gaine, Hugh, 515; *Hugh Gaine's Catalogue of Books,* 515

Galic Antiquities (J. Smith), 352

Galloway, Robert, 551

Gardiner, William Nelson, 184–85, *185*

Garrard, Graeme, 11, 16

Garrick, David, 148, 205, 289, 304, 406

Gay, Peter, 3, 12, 98, 147

Geddes, Andrew, 435–36, *437*

General History of Scotland (Guthrie), 190n171, 389

generations of Scottish Enlightenment authors, 98–99

Genette, Gérard, 58–59, 371–72. *See also* paratexts

Geneva, 9

genres. *See* subjects and genres of Scottish books

Gentleman Farmer (Kames): advertising for, 362–63, *364;* dedication, 142; publication, 420; registered at Stationers' Hall, 243; Strahan on publication, 83, 345, 359

George III (king), 281

Gerard, Alexander: on importance of copy money for, 256–57; in prime generation, 98; on Strahan and Warburton, 350; *Dissertations on Subjects relating to the Genius and Evidence of Christianity,* 286, 317; *Essay on Genius,* 254, 339; *Essay on Taste,* 285, 297; *Sermons,* 256

Gibbon, Edward: in The Club, 120; Creech cites, 446; in Dublin press, 456; emulates Hume and Robertson, 259; his publishers, 327, 378; *Decline and Fall of the Roman Empire,* 69, 259, 358, 370, 464, 471

Gilbert, William: London ties, 451; master of William M'Kenzie, 471; radicalism and imprisonment of, 498

Gillies, John: career, 367–68; frontispiece portrait of, 191n171; Pinkerton's *History* to be reviewed by, 138; as tutor, 206–7; in younger generation, 99; *Aristotle's Ethics and Politics,* 240; *History of Ancient Greece,* 141, 191n171, 367–68, 449; *Orations of Lysias and Isocrates,* 367, 384; *View of the Reign of Frederick II of Prussia,* 207, 460

Girard, Jean-Baptiste (Father), 291

Glasgow: enlightened culture of, 116–17: Enlightenment publishing in, 268–69; Johnson and Boswell visit, 144

Glasgow, University of: eminent professors in, 116–17; Hutcheson at, 62–63, 133; lecture outlines by faculty at, 269; Thomson receives LL.D. from, 128; Thomson's *Tour* on, 145; William Hunter's gift to, 121; William Young attends, 547

Glasgow Literary Society, 107–8, 116–17

Gleig, George, 494

Glencairn, 14th Earl of (James Cunningham): Creech and, 402–3, 410; freemason, 181n159; patron of Burns, 231

Glorying in the Cross of Christ (J. Maclaurin), 553

Godwin, William, 397; *Enquiry concerning Political Justice*, 397

Goethe, Johann Wolfgang von, 531; *Sorrows and Sympathetic Attachments of Werter*, 531

Goldsmith, Oliver: in The Club, 120; in Guthrie's *Geography*, 489; Ireland and, 500; on the public as patrons, 197; *History of the Earth*, 485–86, 573; *The Traveller*, 518; *Vicar of Wakefield*, 473–75

Golinski, Jan, 22

good sellers, 91

Graisberry, Daniel, 461–63, 478

Graisberry ledgers, 461–63, 478–79, 480, 487

Grant, James, 77

Grant, Sir Archibald, of Monymusk, 277n21

Gray, John, 13

Gray, Thomas, 268

Graydon, Alexander, 129n82

Green, Ashbel, 539

Green, James, 540, 573

Green, Margaret (Bell's daughter), 516

Greenfield, William, 422

Gregory, George, 584

Gregory, James: arranges publication of father's *Works* and *Father's Legacy*, 141, 339; Creech and, 403, 421–22; freemason, 108; Reid and, 143–44, 391, 567, *569*; in younger generation, 99; *Philosophical and Literary Essays*, 144

Gregory, John: freemason, 108; frontispiece portrait of, 190n169; in prime generation, 98; returns to Scotland, 120; Stark praises, 430, 605; with Strahan in Edinburgh, 304; Tytler's biography of, 141; *Comparative View of Man*, 92–93; *Father's Legacy to His Daughters*, 92–93, 103, 339, 371, 538; *Lectures [Observations] on the Duties and Qualifications [Offices] of a Physician*, 105, 142, 151, 526–27; *Works*, 141, 190n169

Grierson, Boulter, 321, 449, 464, 487

Griffin, Dustin, 203–4, 208

Griffin, Robert, 155n128

Griffiths, Ralph, 366–67

Groningen, 103

Grub Street (Edinburgh), 126n71

Grub Street (London): anonymity and, 149; attitudes toward Scotland, 145–46; author identification and, 160; copy money and, 215–16; Scottish authors in, 35, 122–28; younger authors in, 99

Grueber (or Grubere), Arthur, 496, 498

Grueber & M'Allister, 493

Guild of St. Luke the Evangelist (Dublin), 469–70, 476, 478, 492, 513

Guthrie, William: background, 100; frontispiece portrait, 190n171; as a Grub Street author, 122; ostensible author of Guthrie's *Geography*, 155–56; *Complete History of the English Peerage*, 229; *The Friends*, 150; *General History of Scotland*, 190n171, 389; *The Mother*, 150; *New Geographical, Historical, and Commercial Grammar* (Guthrie's *Geography*), 1, 92–93, 133, 155–56, 273, 487–93, 508, 573–82, *580*, *581*, 597, 608

Guthrie's *Geography.* See Knox, John; *New Geographical, Historical, and Commercial Grammar* (Guthrie)

Habermas, Jürgen, 2, 196–97
Hague, The, 407
Hailes, Lord. *See* Dalrymple, Sir David, Lord Hailes
Hall, David: "Fellow-prentice" of William Strahan, 295–96; Philadelphia importer and bookseller, 514–15; Strahan's letters to, 298, 301, 305, 333–34, 373; *Imported in the Last Vessels from England,* 515
Hall, John, 172, *175*
Hallhead, Sarah, 471
Hallhead, William, 451–52, 471
Halpen (or Halpin), Patrick, 168, 485
Hamilton, Alexander: *Elements of the Practice of Midwifery,* 447; *Outlines of the Theory and Practice of Midwifery,* 142, 560
Hamilton, Archibald, 365–66, 373
Hamilton, Balfour, and Neil. *See* Hamilton & Balfour
Hamilton, Duke of, 122, 207n25
Hamilton, Elizabeth: birth, 100; contributes to *Lounger,* 102n9; education, 101; as educator of young women, 104; encouraged by Dugald Stewart, 102n9; in London and Edinburgh, 101–2; in younger generation, 99; *Memoirs of Modern Philosophers,* 152, 267
Hamilton, Gavin (bookseller): civic and political activities, 310–11; death, 307; family connections, 309–10; as a founding publisher, 36, 274, 598; with Hamilton & Balfour, 307–11; intimacy with William Strahan, 308; matriculates at Edinburgh University, 295; outbid for Robertson's *History of Scotland,* 282; publishes first volume of Hume's *History,* 308–9
Hamilton, Gavin (friend of Burns), 230

Hamilton, James, 276
Hamilton, Mrs. Gavin (Helen Balfour), 309
Hamilton, Mrs. James (Elizabeth Millar), 276
Hamilton, William: Edinburgh divinity professor, 280–81, 303, 310; praised by Strahan, 303; subscriber to Millar's *History of Propagation of Christianity,* 276
Hamilton & Balfour (including Hamilton, Balfour, & Neill): American trade, 515; dissolution, 308; family connections of, 309–10; history of, 36, 307–11; publications of, 308, 310, 458; as Scottish Enlightenment publishers, 273, 309–9, 702–3; subscribers to Thomson's *Works,* 282; vertical integration of, 308. *See also the names of individual authors whose works they published*
Hancock, John, 528
Harding, Silvester, 184
Hardwicke, 2nd Earl of (Philip Yorke), 367
Hart, Thomas, 297
Hauser, Arnold, 196
Hawkesworth, John, 289, 347
Hay, George, 542
Hay, James, 450
Heath, James, 223
Heavenly City of the Eighteenth-Century Philosophers (Becker), 12–13
Henry, Robert: attacked by Gilbert Stuart, 128, 366; portraits, 173, *177*; in prime generation, 98; *History of Great Britain,* 79, 91, 133, 173, 218–19, 243, 257, 460, 495, 536, 599–601
Herman, Arthur, 18–19, 567
Heron, Robert: affiliation with Morisons of Perth, 268; biography of Burns by, 127, 141, 234; contributes to *Encyclopaedia Britannica,* 494; as a Grub Street author, 126–27, 215; in table 1, 77; *New General History of Scotland,*

Heron, Robert (*continued*)
126, 141; *Observations Made in a Jour-
ney through the Western Counties of
Scotland*, 145–46
Hesse, Carla, 3
Hibernian Journal, 451, 455
Hibernian Magazine, 455–56, 469
Hibernian Society (Philadelphia), 545
Highland Society of Scotland, 107
High Street (Edinburgh), 110–11, *111*
Hill, Peter, 434
Himmelfarb, Gertrude, 19–20
Historical Disquisition on India (W. Rob-
ertson): author identification in, 159;
author's copy money from, 214; in
Belfast, 449; best seller, 92; E. Bal-
four and, 310; excerpts in *Universal
Asylum*, 565; format, 82; print run,
87n80; Young's Philadelphia edition,
565
*Historical Dissertation concerning the
Antiquity of the English Constitution*
(Stuart), 322–23
Historical Law-Tracts (Kames), 285,
366n84
Historical View of the English Government
(Millar), 383, 385, 454n19
History and Adventures of an Atom (Smollett), 389
History of America (Russell), 229
History of America (W. Robertson):
author's copy money from, 214; best
seller, 92; Company of Booksell-
ers and, 478–79, *481*, 482; Dublin
editions, 464–65, 482; frontispiece
portrait in Dublin edition, 478, *481;*
print run, 87n80; in Strahan printing
ledger, *335, 336*
History of America, bks. 9 and 10 (W.
Robertson), 87n80
History of Ancient Europe (Russell), 124
History of Ancient Greece (Gillies): in Belfast, 449; dedication, 141; success of,
367–68
History of Belisarius (Marmontel), 518

History of Charles V (W. Robertson): advertised, *57;* author's copy money for,
201, 260–61; Bell's Philadelphia edition, 511, 518–22, 524, 526, 536; best
seller, 92; dedication, 141; Dublin editions, 454, 465, 482; frontispiece portrait, 172, *175;* plans for, 321–22; print
run, 87n80; sale of shares to London
trade, 354; significance for Strahan
and Cadell, 332
History of Edinburgh (Arnot), 423–24
History of England (Hume): advertising,
57, *521;* in Belfast, 449; Bell's planned
Philadelphia edition, *521*, 523–24,
526; best seller, 92; Campbell's Philadelphia edition, 508, 582–89; Carey
criticizes treatment of Ireland in,
576; Company of Booksellers and,
476, 483; continuation of, 69; Dublin editions, 458, 466, 476, 482–85,
583–84; excerpts from, 363, 537; failure of first volume, 308–9; fashioning and refashioning of, 50; frontispiece portraits, 168–69, *170*, 485, *583*,
585; Gibbon inspired by, 259; given
preferential treatment in table 2, 79;
Life of David Hume in, 56, 141, 168;
Macpherson's *History* and, 172; Millar publishes after first volume, 287;
Millar's deception about, 290; in "My
Own Life," 54–55; print runs, 87;
registered at Stationers' Hall, 243;
review in *American Monthly Review,*
590–91; Smollett's *History of England*
and, 169, 582–89; in Strahan printing
ledger, *335, 336*; on "Trouble and Perplexity" of negotiating each edition
separately, 244; unauthorized British
reprints, 354, 584; variety of formats
and prices of, 56–58; Walpole distorts
and critiques footnote in, 71–72
History of England (Smollett) (continuation of Hume): in Belfast, 449; Campbell's Philadelphia edition, 582–89;
created by Cadell and Baldwin as a

continuation of Hume's *History*, 169, 582–83; frontispiece portrait, 169, *171;* praises Hume and Robertson, 170, 172; unauthorized British reprints, 584; White's Dublin edition, 461, 483. See also *Complete History of England* (Smollett); *Continuation of the Complete History of England* (Smollett)

History of France (W. Anderson): excerpt in *Pennsylvania Magazine,* 537; reviewed by Gilbert Stuart, 250; Strahan a silent publisher of, 332; Strahan upset about prejudiced recommendations for, 350

History of Great Britain (Henry): author's copy money from, 218–19; Dublin edition, 460, 495; frontispiece portrait, 173, *177;* good seller, 91; Laing completes, 135, 599–601; in *Pennsylvania Magazine,* 536; registered at Stationers' Hall, 243; in Smith's library, 138; Strahan on Henry's motives, 257; treated as a single book in table 2, 79

History of Great Britain (Hume). See *History of England* (Hume)

History of Great Britain (James Macpherson): advertising, 57, 363, *364;* frontispiece portrait in second edition, 172–73, *176*

History of Great Britain during the Reign of Queen Anne (Somerville): author identification in, 157; author's copy money from, 251, 600; dedication, 141; publication, 251–52

History of Hindostan (Dow), 87n81

History of Ireland (Leland), 501n90

History of Mary Queen of Scots (T. Robertson): dedication, 141; publication and reception, 395–96

History of Modern Europe (Russell): anonymity and, 153; in Dublin press, 456; on Hume's skepticism, 146–47; struggle to complete, 124

History of Philip II (Watson): author sells rights to one edition of, 240, 349–50;

in Dublin, 451; pirated Dublin edition, 465; publication, 339; registered at Stationers' Hall, 243; Strahan annoyed by author's demands, 346; in Strahan printing ledger, *335, 336*

History of Philip III (Watson): completed by William Thomson, 135, 390; co-published by Robinson, 390; Hallhead edition, 471; Strahan declines, 352

History of Political Transactions and of Parties, from the Restoration to the Death of King William (Somerville), 250–51

History of Scotland (Laing), 601, 603

History of Scotland (Pinkerton): frontispiece portrait, 184–85, *185;* reviews of, 138; terms of publication, 348–49

History of Scotland (W. Robertson): advertised, *57;* author's copy money from, 214, 260; in Belfast, 449; best seller, 92; Creech told to purchase, 407; Dublin edition, 485; false dating of, 89; Hume's *History* delayed to accommodate, 283–84; Millar outbids Hamilton for, 282, 287; pirated Dublin edition, 465; plans for Philadelphia edition, 523n47; sale of shares to London trade, 354; Scottish cultural revival and, 43

History of the American Revolution (Ramsay), 539

History of the Church under the Old Testament (R. Millar), 277n20

History of the Earth, and Animated Nature (Goldsmith), 485–86, 573

History of the Progress and Termination of the Roman Republic (A. Ferguson): author identification in, 159; commercial failure of, 252–53; Dublin printing charges for, 462–63; late bloomer, 90; print run, 252; publication and reception, 252–53, 340, 345–46, 348, 356; safety clause, 252–53

History of the Propagation of Christianity (R. Millar): publication, 275–76, 279,

History of the Propagation of Christianity (R. Millar) *(continued)* 297; reprinted by Andrew Millar, 277n20, 280; on significance of printing, 276

History of the Public Revenue of the British Empire (Sinclair), 191n171

History of the Reformation in Scotland (Stuart), 191n171

History of the Revolution of South-Carolina (Ramsay), 539

History of the Sufferings of the Church of Scotland (Wodrow), 279–80

Hoadly, Benjamin, Bishop of Winchester, 71

Hodge, Robert, 561

Hoey, James, I, 473

Hoey, James, II: *Dublin Mercury* and, 469; in Dublin price war, 473; location of, 468; prominent Roman Catholic, 470

Hoey, Jane, 468

Hoey, Peter, 479

Hollis, Thomas, 289

Home, Francis: in prime generation, 98; *Clinical Experiments, Histories and Dissections*, 423; *Essay on the Contents and Virtues of Dunse-Spaw*, 313; *Experiments on Bleaching*, 457; *Medical Facts and Experiments*, 285

Home, Henry, Lord Kames: active before 1746, 80; American readers and, 503; anonymity and, 151, 153; biography of in *Encyclopaedia Britannica*, 494; in Carey's edition of Guthrie's *Geography*, 582; Creech and, 359, 420; in Dublin press, 455; fears piracy of *Sketches*, 84; in formative generation, 98; meets with Strahan in Edinburgh, 304; mocked by Walpole, 72; patronage of younger authors by, 133; praised by Reid, 143; Stark praises, 430, 605; title of, 99; Voltaire on, 67; Woodhouselee's biography of, 140; wrote books on many subjects, 85;

Elements of Criticism, 91, 141, 286, 333, 407, 515; *Essays on the Principles of Morality and Natural Religion*, 149, 153, 313, 449; *Essays upon Several Subjects concerning British Antiquities*, 153, 312–13; *Essays upon Several Subjects in Law*, 312; *Gentleman Farmer*, 83, 142, 240, 243, 345, 362–63, 420; *Historical Law-Tracts*, 285, 366n84; *Principles of Equity*, 286, 318; *Introduction to the Art of Thinking*, 324; *Loose Hints upon Education*, 348, 384; *Six Sketches on the History of Man*, 530, 535; *Sketches of the History of Man*, 82–84, 91, 253, 338–39, 341–42, 371, 416, 420, 449, 476, 477, 526–30, 536, 538

Home, John (David Hume's brother), 55–56

Home, John (playwright): Alves cites, 76; contributes to Donaldson's *Collection*, 314; Denina praises, 68; on literati, 61–62; mocked by Walpole, 72; patronage of, 205–6, 208; *Agis*, 87n80, 88; *Alfred*, 457, 476; *Alonzo*, 450; *Douglas*, 62, 66, 92, 142, 205, 289, 308, 450, 476; *Fatal Discovery*, 148; *Siege of Aquileia*, 87n80, 88, 468; *Works*, 139

Homer: *Iliad*, 59–60, 572; *Odyssey*, 59–60

honorary copyright: in Edinburgh, 355, 444; importance after 1774, 26, 30; in London: 353–54, 584; popularity ratings and, 90. *See also* literary property; piracy

Hood, Thomas, 354

Hook, Andrew, 504, 572

Hopetoun, Earl of, 207

Horkheimer, Max, 12–13

House of Commons (Ireland), 577

Hugh Gaine's Catalogue of Books (Gaine), 515

Hume, David: active before 1746, 80; on advantages of printing for authors, 50–51; Advocates' Library keeper,

112; American readers and, 503; anxiety of, 54–55; on author-publisher relations, 201; on authors' motives for writing books, 257; biography of in *Encyclopaedia Britannica*, 494; Boswell and, 59; Carey's edition of Guthrie's *Geography* praises, *581, 582*; change of name, 52; comparison with Turnbull, 44; copy money from *History*, 241, 308; cosmopolitan ideal of, 142–43; Creech, cites, 446; deceived by Millar about editions of *History*, 290; Denina praises, 68; disdain for London and English culture, 69, 118–19; on Dublin edition of *History*, 458; in Dublin press, 455–56; Edinburgh moral philosophy chair denied to, 310; Gibbon and, 69; Henry's *History* evaluated by, 215, 257; idealized in "Story of La Roche" in *Mirror*, 139–40; on literary property, 25–26; on the literary public, 201; Millar and, 282–85, 289–90; mitigated anonymity and, 151; mocked by Walpole, 72; moves to Edinburgh, 114, 119; on Paris, 119; patronizes Blacklock, 224; philosophical opponents of, 53, 146; philosophical persona reshaped by *Essays and Treatises*, 45–52; Pope and, 60–61; popularity of, 30, 92; portraits, *48*, 164, 167–68, *170;* in prime generation, 98; on prominence of Strahan and Cadell, 357–58; Scotticisms and, 52–53, 299; on Scottish cultural revival, 43–44, 259; Smollett cites, 74–75; Stark praises, 430, 605; Strahan and, 47, 55–56, 69n48, 89, 218, 304, 346; terms of publication negotiated by, 244; *Universal Asylum* deletes sentence on, 563; wealth of, 240–41; *Dialogues concerning Natural Religion*, 56n22; *Enquiry concerning Principles of Morals*, 45; *Essays and Treatises on Several Subjects*, 34, 45–50, *49, 51*, 54, 92, 138, 168, 285, 323, 369–71, 457, 462,

482–83, 515; *Enquiry [Philosophical Essays] concerning Human understanding*, 45, 151, 287; *Essays, Moral and Political*, 45, 151, 285, *286*, 297, 312; *Four Dissertations*, 46, 142; *History of England*, 46, 69, 87, 92, 168, 172, 241, 243–44, 257, 259, 287, 308–9, *335*, *336*, 354, 363, 369–70, 458, 466, 476, 482–85, 508, 515, *521*, 523–24, 526, 537, 576, 582–89, *583*, 590–91; *Life of David Hume, Esq.* (incorporating "My Own Life"), 55–56, 482, 530–31; "My Own Life," *53*–56, 329, 591; *Political Discourses*, 313; *Three Essays, Moral and Political*, 45, 285; *Treatise of Human Nature*, 44, 53, 60, 148, 240–41

Hume–Smollett *History of England*. See *History of England* (Hume); *History of England* (Smollett) (continuation of Hume)

Humphreys, James, 523n47

Humphry Clinker (Smollett): advertising, 362, 456; best seller, 92; calls Edinburgh "a hot-bed of genius," 74–75; Dublin editions, 454, 466n41, 471, 476

Hunter, John: disagreements, 147; painted by Reynolds, 184n165; in prime generation, 98; published by Joseph Johnson, 381; settles in London, 121; *Observations on Certain Parts of the Animal Oeconomy*, 217; *Treatise on the Venereal Disease*, 217

Hunter, Mrs. John (Anne Home), 132

Hunter, William: in Carey's edition of Guthrie's *Geography*, 582; disagreements, 147; mocked by Walpole, 71; painted by Ramsay, 184n165; published by Joseph Johnson, 381; settles in London, 121; *Anatomical Description of the Human Gravid Uterus*, 135; *Medical Commentaries*, 147; *Two Introductory Lectures*, 106

Husbandry of the Ancients (Dickson), 229

Hutcheson, Francis: birth, 100; career, 62; death, 79; Denina praises, 68; in Dublin press, 455; Foulis brothers and, 268; Guthrie's *Geography* cites, 579–80; patronage of younger authors, 133; published anonymously, 149; Scottish literary identity and, 34, 63–64; subscriber to Robert Millar's *History of the Propagation of Christianity*, 276; in table 1, 77, 80; *Inquiry into the Original of Our Ideas of Beauty and Virtue*, 98; *Short Introduction to Moral Philosophy*, 85, 269, 556; *System of Moral Philosophy*, 62–64, 79, 225, 269

Hutton, James: aristocratic approach to publishing, 210; in Dublin press, 456; in Oyster Club, 109; Playfair's biography of, 139; in prime generation, 98; Smith's *Essays on Philosophical Subjects* co-edited by, 135; in table 1, 77; *Dissertations on Different Subjects in Natural Philosophy*, 210, 242

Ilay, Earl of. *See* Argyll, 3rd Duke of
Iliad (Homer), 59–60, 572
Illustrations of the Huttonian Theory of the Earth (Playfair), 139
Imported in the Last Vessels from England (Hall), 515
importing books (America): compared with reprinting, 506–7; delinquent payments for, 507, 546, 554, 572n81; in late eighteenth century, 514–15
imprints: Company of Booksellers (Dublin) and, 476–79, 477, 481; false date, 89; false place, 416–17, 438, 474–75, 511n16, 518, 527; order of publishers' names in, 415–16, 423, 429; place of printing, 267–70; publishers' names in, 273, 601; spurious editions, 89; statistics on, 270, 443, 509–10. *See also* printing
Indians, The (Richardson), 154
Ingham, Charles, 483

Inquiry into the Causes of the Infidelity and Scepticism of the Times (J. Ogilvie), 146
Inquiry into the Human Mind (Reid): 21st-century value of copy money, 258; Beattie on copublication of, 317; Company of Booksellers and, 476; publication, 286, 323; Rose reviews, 392; Strahan and Cadell purchase Millar's share of, 333; strong seller, 92
Inquiry into the Original of Our Ideas of Beauty and Virtue (Hutcheson), 98
Inquiry into the Principles of Political Oeconomy (Steuart): author's copy money from, 236; commercial failure of, 236, 483; Dublin edition, 483–84; publication, 236, 283, 287, 332; used in *Encyclopaedia Britannica*, 135
Institutes of Moral Philosophy (A. Ferguson), 85, 105
Institutes of Natural History (J. Walker), 105
Institutes of Physics (John Anderson), 105, 269
Institutions of Medicine (Cullen), 556
Interesting Appendix to Sir William Blackstone's Commentaries on the Laws of England (R. Bell), 593
Interesting Narrative, of the Travels of James Bruce, Esq., An (James Bruce) (abridgment of *Travels to Discover the Source of the Nile*), 89
Introduction to the Art of Thinking (Kames), 324
Introduction to the History of America (M'Culloch), 591
Introduction to the Study of the History and Antiquities of Ireland (O'Halloran), 501n90
Ireland: after 1800, 439; in Carey's edition of Guthrie's *Geography*, 575–77; in Chambers's edition of Guthrie's *Geography*, 488–93
Irish editions in America, 356, 447–47, 463, 467, 484, 487

Irish editions in Britain: Anderson and, 356; Boswell on, 465; controversy over extent of, 463–67; Elliot and, 356; Ferguson's *Essay*, 321, 356, 464; London booksellers on, 445–46, 447; prosecutions relating to, 356, 448; Strahan on, 355–56. *See also* piracy

Irish Volunteers, 455, 490–92, 577

Jackson, William, 546

Jackson and Dunn's Bookstore, 539, 541, 546

Jacob, Margaret, 108n18

Jardine, George, 547

Jefferson, Thomas, 504–5, 527, 558

Jenkinson, Charles. *See* Liverpool, 1st Earl of

Jervas, Charles, 59–60

John Bull (England), 206, 305

John Wilson & Co., 552

Johns, Adrian, 6, 8–9

Johnson, A., 543

Johnson, Joseph: death, 604; on Dobson's *Encyclopaedia*, 561; entertains and patronizes authors, 199; friend of George Robinson, 389; negotiates for Leechman's sermons, 247–48; print runs, 87n82; as Scottish Enlightenment publisher, 37, 272, 380–81, *702–3*

Johnson, Samuel: on Blair's sermons, 245, 351; on booksellers and patrons, 195–98; Boswell and, 47; in The Club, 120; Creech cites, 446; on Donaldson, 315; in Dublin press, 456; literary bias in favor of, 10; definition of "publisher," xv; equates patronage with the "multitude" in, 197; Irish preferred to Scots by, 70; Millar and, 196, 282; paid by the job, 216; on pecuniary motives for writing, 257; pension of, 207–8; Scots and Scotland ridiculed by, 70–72, 94; among Strahan and Cadell's authors, 327; on Strahan and Warburton, 350; *Dictio-

nary of the English Language*, 195–96, 216, 289; *Journey to the Western Islands of Scotland*, 536–37; *Lives of the Poets*, 216; *Rasselas*, 518. *See also* Boswell, James

Johnston, William, 320–21, 323, 362, 389, 453, 466n41

Johnstone, William Borthwick, 113, *113*

Jones, John: Company of Booksellers and, 479; George Robinson and, 389, 452n14; Henry's *History* and, 460, 495; subscriber to Moore's *Britannica*, 493

Jones, William: bankruptcy of, 498; Company of Booksellers and, 479; George Robinson and, 389, 452n14; location of, 468; subscriber to Moore's *Britannica*, 493; succeeds White, 472

Joseph Andrews (Fielding), 297

Journal during a Residence in France (Moore), 398, 575n95

Journal of a Tour to the Hebrides with Samuel Johnson (Boswell): Charles Dilly and, 200, 220–24; Dublin edition, 458; in *Hibernian Magazine*, 455; print runs, 220n58; promotes Scottish authors, 144–45; Smith's letter on Hume in, 59

Journey to the Western Islands of Scotland (Johnson), 536–37

Julia de Roubigné (Mackenzie): advertising, 363, *364;* American edition, 509; author's copy money from, 254; authorship of, 148; Company of Booksellers and, 476; Dublin edition, 455; linked to earlier novels by the author, 150; publication, 339; in Strahan printing ledger, *335, 336*

Justice of the Peace, and Parish Officer (Burn), 292

Kames, Lord. *See* Home, Henry, Lord Kames

Kant, Immanuel, 13, 16–17

Kay, Thomas, 387

Keen, Paul, 597
Keimer, Samuel, 514
Kello, Marion, 512
Kelly, Hugh, 500
Kennedy, Máire, 444
Kenrick, Samuel: on Andrew Millar by, 282–84; on Leechman's *Sermons*, 190, 247–49; on Strahan's service to Millar, 297
Kernan, Alvin, 6, 197, 298
Kerr, Lord Charles, 404
Kerr, Miss (Creech's fiancé), 412
Kerr, Robert, 110
Kidd, William, 479
Kilmarnock, 230–31, 546
Kilmaurs, Lord. *See* Glencairn, 14th Earl of
Kincaid, Alexander, I: American trade, 515; apprentice and successor of M'Euen, 311–12; Beattie and, 417; Bell and, 316–18; bookshop in Luckenbooths, 110, *111*, 312, 410; career, 272, 311–18, *702–3*; civic and political activities, 311; Creech and, 326, 337–39, 403–12, *411*; decline and death, 318n145, 412, 423; Donaldson and, 312–16; early publications of, 312; a founding publisher, 36, 274, 598; freemason, 108; intimacy with William Strahan, 296, 304, 311, 336–38; marries Caroline Kerr, 312; purchases copyright of Blair's *Sermons*, 245; saintly character of, 311. *See also* Creech, William; Kincaid & Bell; Kincaid & Donaldson: *names of individual authors whose works he published*
Kincaid, Alexander, II, 404, 412
Kincaid, Mrs. Alexander (Caroline Kerr or Ker), 403–4
Kincaid, Peggy, 406
Kincaid & Bell: bookshop in the Luckenbooths, *111*, *317*, 439; collaborative publishing with Millar, 285–87, 316–18; conflict with Millar & Cadell over Ferguson's *Essay*, 37, 318–26; cultural

and political circumstances, 316, *317*; Dilly and, 255; dissolution of, 407–10; subscribers to Thomson's *Works*, 282. *See also* Bell, John; Cadell, Thomas; Creech, William; Kincaid, Alexander
Kincaid & Creech. *See* Creech, William; Kincaid, Alexander; Kincaid & Bell
Kincaid & Donaldson: dissolution of, 314, 316; establishment of, 312–13; Hume's *Essays and Treatises* and, 45–52, *48*, *49*, *51*, 285; publications of, 285, 313–14. *See also* Donaldson, Alexander; Kincaid, Alexander
King's College, Aberdeen, 116
Knapton, John, 332
Knockroon, 221–22
Knox, John: "philanthropist" in *DNB*, 266; publisher and principal compiler of Guthrie's *Geography*, 134, 155–56, 575, 578; returns to Scotland, 120; *View of the British Empire*, 115, 144, 155. *See also* Guthrie, William; *New Geographical, Historical, and Commercial Grammar* (Guthrie)
Korshin, Paul, 234, 235n105

Lackington, George, 354
Lackington, James, 354, 555
Lafayette, Marquis de, 544
La Harpe, Jean-François de, 261
Laing, Malcolm: completes Henry's *History*, 135, 218, 601; Stark on, 605; *History of Scotland*, 601, 603
language in Scotland: attempts at "improving," 62, 107; *Edinburgh Review* on, 65–66; Hume on, 43, 52–53; Scottish accents in London, 128–29. *See also* Scotticisms
La Rochefoucauld, François, duc de, 530–31; *Maxims and Moral Reflections*, 530–31
Lawless, Robin, 331
Lawson, Alexander, 560, 585
Leathley (or Leathly), Ann, 471, 473
Leathley (or Leathly), Joseph, 471

Leathley–Hallhead–M'Kenzie, 471–72, 704

Lectures on Ecclesiastical History (Campbell), 105, 381

Lectures on Materia Medica (Cullen), 465

Lectures on Rhetoric and Belles Lettres (Blair): Aitken's edition, 537–38; author's copy money from, 246–47; best seller, 92; Creech's concerns about, 359; Dublin edition, 459, 463; frontispiece portraits, 173, 176–79, *178*, *179*; publication, 340; Rose's review, 368; university lectures and, 105

Lectures on Select Subjects (J. Ferguson): best seller, 92; guide to public lectures, 105–6; publication, 287; used in *Encyclopaedia Britannica*, 135

Lectures on the Duties and Qualifications of a Physician (John Gregory): Bell's plans for Philadelphia edition, 526–27; dedication, 142; mitigated anonymity and, 151–52; from university lectures, 105

Lectures on the Materia Medica (Alston), 105

Lectures on the Materia Medica (Cullen): Bell's Philadelphia edition, 526–27, 536; Dublin edition, 454n19; from university lectures, 105

Ledwich, Edward, 501n90

Leechman, Mrs. William (Bridget Balfour), 132, 310

Leechman, William: Hutcheson's protégé and biographer, 63, 133, 139; James Wodrow and, 190, 247–49; portraits, 190, *192–93*; student of William Hamilton, 310; ties with English Dissenters, 131; *Sermons*, 190, 247–49

Leiden, 103

Leland, Thomas, 501n90

Le Poivre, Pierre, 530

Letters concerning Mythology (Blackwell), 89

Letters concerning the English Nation (Voltaire), 405–6

Letters Containing a Comparative View of Edinburgh in the Years 1763 and 1783 (revised as *Letters Addressed to Sir John Sinclair*) (Creech), 75–76, 271, 344–45

Letters containing a Sketch of the Politics of France (Williams), 572

Letters on Toleration (Locke), 289

libraries: Adam Smith's library, 138–39; Advocates Library, 112; circulating libraries, *111*, 113–14, *113*, 312, 421, 517, 532; Library Company of Philadelphia, 535, 538, 543; Linen Hall Library, 449–50; reading revolution and, 2–3, 28

Library Company of Philadelphia, 535, 538, 543

Life of David Hume, Esq. Written by Himself, 55–56. *See also* "My Own Life"

Life of David Hume, Esq; the Philosopher and Historian, Written by Himself (Hume and Le Poivre), 530–31

Life of Samuel Johnson (Boswell): advertising, 363; author's copy money from, 223–24; in Belfast, 449; best seller, 92; Dilly brothers and, 380; format of, 82; print run, 87, 221; publication, 220–24; registered at Stationers' Hall, 243

Life of Thomas Ruddiman, 306

Lind, James: *Essay on the Health of Seamen*, 285; *Treatise of the Scurvy*, 313; *Two Papers on Fevers and Infection*, 108

Linen Hall Library (Belfast), 449–50

Lintot, Bernard, 59–60, 430

Literary and Characteristical Lives (Smellie), 140

literary property: authors' copy money and, 258; Creech's dilemma on, 414–15; Donaldson and, 313–16; in Dublin, 451, 473–78; importance of, 25–27; Millar's protection of, 288–89; Murray on, 382; restricted by House

literary property (*continued*)
of Lords in 1774, 28; revised editions extend, 349; St. Clair on, 27–30; Strahan syndicate on, 352–56. *See also* honorary copyright; Statute of Anne (Copyright Act of 1709–10)

literati, Scottish: in clubs and societies, 106–10; corporate identity of, 61–62; dedications among, 141–44; disagreements and differences among, 146–47; family connections among, 132; left-leaning literati, 147n117; mutual support for publications, 133–38; patronage among, 132–33; puffing among, 137–38, 41; sociability of, 106. *See also* authors, Scottish Enlightenment; Enlightenment, Scottish

Liverpool, 1st Earl of (Charles Jenkinson), 446

Lives of the Poets (Johnson), 216

Lizars, W. & D., 428, 429

Lloyd, T. A., 584

Loch, David: background, 101; *Essays on the Trade, Commerce, Manufactures, and Fisheries of Scotland*, 160, 228n85

Locke, John, 71–72, 289, 314; *Letters on Toleration*, 289

Lockhart, J. G.: on Creech and Constable, 431–32, 435–36; *Peter's Letters to His Kinfolk*, 431–32, 435, 439–40

Lockwood, Thomas, 235n105

Logan, John: as a Grub Street author, 123; patronized by Strahan, 303; tutor of Sinclair, 101, 140n107; *Elements of the Philosophy of History, Part First*, 106; *Sermons*, 135, 395

Logan, John, of Laight, 230

London: attracts Scottish literati, 121–22; British Coffee House, 128–31; Chapter Coffee House, 73, 357, 382; compared with Edinburgh, 118–20; integration problems for Scots in, 128–30; medical training in, 103; Scottish authors and, 117–31; Scottish physicians and, 121–22. *See also* book-

shops (London); Grub Street (London); *names of individual members of the book trade and of individual institutions and sites*

London Chronicle: advertising, 363, 364; excerpts in, 363, 365; Johnson on Scottish invasion of London, 70; Strahan and Cadell and, 372; Strahan's concerns about John Bull's perception of Scottish bias, 305

London–Edinburgh publishing axis: Beattie on, 317; beginnings, 285, 286, 598; delicacy of, 325–26; disintegration, 604; dominated by Millar–Strahan–Cadell syndicate, 274, 598–99; economic advantages of, 271; external evidence of, 273–74; failure of first volume of Hume's *History* boosts, 309; framework of, 267–75; imprint evidence of, 270; personal relationships and, 336; tradition of copublishing within London and, 271; transportation and communication and, 271, 274; summary of, 36. *See also* publishers (in Britain); *names of individual publishers and firms*

London Magazine, 519

London Review, 392

Longman, Thomas: entertains men of letters, 199; friend and executor of Andrew Millar, 284; Hutcheson's *System of Moral Philosophy* copublished by, 63; testifies before parliamentary committee, 445

Loose Hints upon Education (Kames), 348, 384

Lothian, 3rd Marquess of (William Kerr), 402, 404

Lothian, Marchioness, I (Margaret Nicholson, first wife of the third marquess), 402

Lothian, Marchioness, II (Jean Janet Kerr, second wife of the third marquess), 404

Loudon, Samuel, 535

Lounger, The (Mackenzie et al.): American edition, 561; charitable purposes of, 211; Elizabeth Hamilton's first publication in, 102n9; excerpted in *London Chronicle*, 365; good seller, 91; Mirror Club and, 109; obituary of William Strahan in, 295, 303; in table 2, 79;

Luckenbooths, The (Edinburgh), 110, *111*, 439

Lundberg, David, 503, 505–6

Lusiad, The (trans. Mickle): author's copy money from, 226; Dublin edition, 450; format of, 86; included in table 2, 78; Oxford imprint of, 267–68; review in *Edinburgh Magazine and Review*, 72–73

Lutes, Richard, 377–78, 600–601

Lynch, Elizabeth, 483

Lyttelton, 1st Baron (George Lyttelton or Lyttleton), 446

Macaulay, Catharine, 173n155

MacBride, David, 459; *Methodical Introduction to the Theory and Practice of Physic*, 459n30

MacCormick, Joseph, 83n74, 351

Macfarquhar, Colin, 216

Mack, Maynard, 60

Mackenzie, Henry: biography of Blacklock by, 140; biography of John Home by, 139; chooses Edinburgh career over London, 120; Creech and, 211–12, 420, *421*, 421–22; Dublin reprinting of works by, 454; freemason, 108; as intermediary with publishers for Burns, 232–33; as intermediary with publishers for Highland Society and Smith's heir 212; as intermediary with publishers for Hutton, 210; as intermediary with publishers for "the poor," 211; in Mirror Club, 109, 211; in Oyster Club, 109; Scottish authors patronized by, 136; in Sibbald's circulating library, 113–14, *113*; Strahan

visits, 304; in younger generation, 99; *Julia de Roubigné*, 148, 150, 254, *335*, 336, 363, *364*, 371, 455, 476, 509; *Lounger*, 91, 211, 273, 295, 303, 365, 561; *Man of Feeling*, 148, 150, 213, 254, 336, 371, 531; *Man of the World*, 148, 150, 254, 371, 531; *Mirror*, 79, 92–93, 139–40, 150–51, 211, 301, 339, 365, 367, 371, 416; *Prince of Tunis*, 476; *Prize Essays and Transactions of the Highland Society of Scotland*, 212

Mackintosh, Sir James: educated in law and medicine, 104; law professor, 104; reprints first *Edinburgh Review*, 135–36; title of, 100; *Vindiciae Gallicae*, 254, 397

Maclaurin, Colin: brother John, 553; death, 79; Denina praises, 68; Guthrie's *Geography* cites, 579; patronage of younger authors by, 133; in table 1, 77, 80; *Account of Sir Isaac Newton's Philosophical Discoveries*, 212, 225, 285, 297; *Treatise on Fluxions*, 98

Maclaurin, John, 553; *Glorying in the Cross of Christ*, 553

Maconochie, Allan, Lord Meadowbank, 403, 410

Macpherson, James: Callender cites, 577n100; in Dublin press, 455; edits John Macpherson's *Critical Dissertations*, 135; patronage and, 208; portraits, 172–73, *176*; in prime generation, 98; *Fingal*, 66, 86, 460, 454n19; *Fragments of Ancient Poetry*, 308; *History of Great Britain*, 57, 172–73, 363, *364*, 369; *Rights of Great Britain Asserted against the Claims of America*, 528; *Temora*, 66, 86, 460, 471

Macpherson, John, *Critical Dissertations on the Ancient Caledonians*, 135, 254

Macpherson, Sir John, 254

Madison, James, 293

Magee, James, 450

Magee, John, 449

Magee, William, 493

Magee's Weekly Packet, 451

Main, Molly, 552n40

Main, Patrick, 552n40, 552n42

Main, Robert, 449, 453, 474

Mallet, David: cited by Jefferson, 504; Denina praises, 68; early poetry published by M'Euen, 278; first play (*Eurydice*) published by Millar, 280; in Millar's circle of literary counselors, 283–84; Scotticisms and, 52

M'Allister, Randal, 496, 498

Malone, Edmund: Boswell's *Life of Johnson* and, 220–22; on impracticality of folio format, 82; Ireland and, 500

Mammuth (W. Thomson), 150

Man in the Moon (W. Thomson), 150

Mann, Alastair F., 306

Manners & Miller, 603–4

Mannheim, Karl, 21

Man of Feeling (Mackenzie): author's copy money from, 254; authorship of, 148, 150; author's relations with publishers, 213; Bell's Philadelphia edition, 531; best seller, 92–93; in Strahan's printing ledger, 335, 336

Man of the World (Mackenzie): author's copy money from, 254; authorship of, 148, 150; Bell's Philadelphia edition, 531

Marischal College, Aberdeen, 44, 116

Marishall, Jean (or Jane Marshall), 102n9

Marlborough, Duke of, 72

Marmion (Scott), 435

Marmontel, Jean-François, 518; *History of Belisarius*, 518

Marshall, Jane. *See* Marishall, Jean

Marshall, William, 550–51, 574n90, 592

Marsters, Kate Ferguson, 186

Martin, David: "painting away" in Edinburgh, 173; portraits of Robert Henry and Blair, 173; unflattering engraving of Rousseau, 164

Martin, Henri-Jean, 9

Martin & Wotherspoon, 124

Mason, William, 71–72

Mather, Cotton, 278

Mathew Carey, No. 158, Market-Street, Has Imported from London, Dublin, and Glasgow, an Extensive Assortment of Books (Carey), 515

Mathie, Peter, 295

Maxims and Moral Reflections (La Rochefoucauld), 530–31

May, Henry F., 14, 503, 505–6, 594

Mayhew, Robert, 156, 488–89

McCosh, James, 44

M'Culloch, John (bookseller in Glasgow), 546–47

M'Culloch, John (bookseller in Philadelphia): on American print culture, 591; subscriber to Campbell's edition of Hume and Smollett, 586; yellow fever and, 570; Young and, 548–53, 592; *Introduction to the History of America*, 591; *Memoirs of the Late Rev. William Marshall*, 550n33

M'Culloch (or McCulloch), William, 512, 516–17, 532

McDonnel (formerly McDaniel), Thomas, 542–43

McDougall, Warren: on Charles Elliot, 386, 452; on the first volume of Hume's *History*, 309; on Hamilton & Balfour, 307, 309, 311; on Scottish reprinting, 313; on smuggling Dublin editions into Scotland, 452, 464, 466

McLaverty, James, 60

McLaws, Agnes (first wife of William Young), 547–48, 570

McLaws, John, 551–52

McLaws, Mrs. John (Elizabeth M'Culloch), 547n22

McLaws, William, 551

McLewes, Jon, 516; *The Philadelphiad*, 516

McWhinnie, David, 230

Medical and Philosophical Commentaries
(A. Duncan): advertising, 363, *364;*
attributed to "a Society of Physicians
in Edinburgh," 161–62; dedication,
142; in table 2, 79

Medical Cases (A. Duncan): author identification in, 157; charitable purposes
of, 212; frontispiece portrait, 191n171;
life of Monro I in second edition, 139

Medical Commentaries (W. Hunter), 147

Medical Facts and Experiments (F.
Home), 285

Meditations (Marcus Aurelius; trans.
Hutcheson and Moor), 133

Mein, John, 475, 511

Melton, James Van Horn, 2, 235n105

Memoirs of Great Britain and Ireland
(J. Dalrymple): Beattie critical of, 249;
excerpt in *Pennsylvania Magazine,*
536; publication, 339

Memoirs of Modern Philosophers (E.
Hamilton), 267, 152

Memoirs of the Court of Augustus (Blackwell), 133, 228

*Memoirs of the Late Rev. William Mar-
shall* (M'Culloch), 550n33

*Memoirs of the Life and Writings of the
Hon. Henry Home of Kames* (Woodhouselee), 140, 419

M'Euen (or McEuen), James: auction catalogues of, 278; bookshop at
Buchanan's Head, Strand, London,
279; bookshop in Luckenbooths, 110,
111, 312, *317,* 439; in Edinburgh, 306;
founds *Edinburgh Evening Courant,*
278, 312; in London, 36; master of
Andrew Millar, 278–80; master of
Kincaid, 311–12; master of William
Strahan, 296; publications of, 278;
shops in London, Edinburgh, and
Glasgow, 279; stock in London shop,
279

Mickle, William Julius: change of name,
72–73, 125; fear of English reviewers, 72–73, 94; frontispiece portrait

of, 191n171; as a Grub Street author,
124–25; *The Lusiad,* 72–73, 86, 226,
267–68, 450; *Poems, and a Tragedy,* 191n171, 228n85; *Voltaire in the
Shades,* 146

Millan, John, 281

Millar, Andrew: Andrew Strahan's
godfather, 374; *The Bee* on, 290–94;
birth and education of, 275–78; book
catalogues by, 279–80; copyrights
sold posthumously to the trade, 333;
delays Tudor volumes of Hume's *History,* 283–84; early career, 280–82; on
Edinburgh, 301; fame of, 430, 486;
Fielding and Johnson and, 280; as
a founding publisher, 36, 274, 598;
"habitually drunk," 288; Hume and,
45–52, 48, 49, 51, 167–68, 285, 289–
90, 309; James Ferguson and, 199,
217; James Thomson and, 280–84,
289; Kincaid and, 285, 289; literary
counselors of, 278, 283–84; mentor of Cadell and Strahan, 287, 334;
M'Euen and, 278–80; migration of
Scots to London and, 284–85; need
for balanced view of, 294; outbids
other publishers for desirable works,
282; parents of, 277, 300; partiality
for Scottish authors, 284–85; presents
and legacies given to authors, 282–
83, 293–94; as a publisher of Scottish
Enlightenment books, 36–37, 63, 88,
272, 282, 285–87, 334, *702–3;* raised
price of literature, 196, 282; retirement and death, 330–31; ridiculous
at Harrogate, 287–88; ruthlessness,
288–90; Stationers' Company and,
305; unfavorable characteristics of,
287–91; ungracious remark to Johnson, 289; wealth of, 283, 292, 294.
See also Cadell, Thomas, I; Kincaid &
Bell; Kincaid & Donaldson; Millar,
Robert, I; Millar & Cadell; Strahan,
William; *names of individual authors
whose works he published*

Millar, Archibald, 277

Millar, Henry, 276, 277n21, 302

Millar, John (minister), 276

Millar, John (professor): freemason, 108; in prime generation, 98; progressive politics of, 397; *Historical View of the English Government*, 383, 385, 454n19; *Observations concerning the Distinction of Ranks in Society*, 91, 254, 383–84, 453

Millar, John, II (son of the professor), 132, 397n164

Millar, Mrs. Andrew (Jane Johnston), 277n21, 287, 291

Millar, Mrs. John (Robina Cullen), 132

Millar, Robert (father of Andrew): background and education of, 275; as ecclesiastical historian, 275–76; visited by William Strahan, 302; *History of the Church under the Old Testament*, 276; *History of the Propagation of Christianity*, 275–76, 279, 280, 297; *Whole Works*, 277

Millar, William (painter), 190, *192*

Millar, William, of Walkinshaw (brother of Andrew), 277, 302

Millar & Cadell, 37, 318–26

Miller, Robert, 603

Milliken, John, 483, 493

Milton, John, 72, 268, 289, 313–14, 562; *Paradise Lost*, 562; *Paradise Regained*, 562

Milton, Lord. *See* Fletcher, Andrew

Minstrel, The (Beattie): Bell's Philadelphia edition, 531; best seller, 92; Creech's poem on, 419; Dilly brothers and, 380; marketing of, 417; print run, 87n81; temporary anonymity and, 152

Minto, Walter, 268; *Account of the Life, Writings, and Inventions of John Napier*, 211, 268

Mirror, The (Mackenzie et al.): anonymity of, 150–51; charitable purposes of, 211; a duodecimo best seller, 92–93; excerpted in *London Chronicle*, 365;

Hume idealized in "Story of La Roche," 139–40; Mirror Club and, 109, 211; order of names in imprint, 416; publication, 339; reviewed in *Monthly*, 367; Strahan's anonymous letter on Edinburgh in, 301; in table 2, 79

Mirror Club, 109

Miscellanies (Fielding), 297

Miscellanies by M. de Voltaire, 530

Miscellanies for Sentimentalists, 531

Miscellanies, in Prose and Verse (Edwards), 102n9

Mitchell, Sir Andrew, 283–84

Mizuta, Hiroshi, 139

M'Kenzie (or McKenzie), William, 471–72

M'Lehose, Agnes Craig, 132, 233

Moderate Party (Church of Scotland), 142, 316, 351, 565

modest sellers, 90–91

Monboddo, Lord. *See* Burnett, James, Lord Monboddo

Moncrieff, William, I, 548

Moncrieffe, Richard: copy money for Leland's *History of Ireland*, 501n90; printing in Graisberry ledgers, 461–63; Williams and, 461, 472, 483

Moncur, John, 295

Monkwell Street meeting house (London), 131

Monro, Alexander, I: born outside Scotland, 101; Donald Monro's biography of, 140–41; Duncan's biography of, 139; in formative generation, 80, 98; Guthrie's *Geography* cites, 579; patronage of younger authors by, 133; taught William Hamilton, 121; *Anatomy of the Human Bones*, 98; *Works*, 140–41, 390

Monro, Alexander, II: his father's *Works* published by, 140; freemason, 108; Joseph Johnson and, 381; named in Gregory's *Observations*, 151–52; in prime generation, 98; *Observations on the Structure and Functions of the Nervous System, 51*, 81–82, 424; *Structure and Physiology of Fishes,* 449

Monro, Donald, 140–41

Montagu, Elizabeth, 69, 226–27

Montesquieu, Charles-Louis de Secondat, 98

Monthly Review: as guide to new books, 4; review of Campbell in, 239–40; review of Pinkerton in, 138; Scottish connections to, 365–66, 372; used in Dublin, 451

Moor, James (author), 133

Moore, James (Dublin bookseller): Company of Booksellers and, 479; Dublin reprint of *Encyclopaedia Britannica,* 493–95, 558; George Robinson and, 389, 452n14; Henry's *History,* 460, 495; patriotic publishing by, 493–95; a prominent Roman Catholic, 470; radicalism of, 498; retirement and death, 499

Moore, John: biography of Smollett by, 141; Burns and, 230–34; dealings with publishers, 244–45; Dublin reprinting of works by, 454; moves to London, 122; in prime generation, 98; on self-publication, 245; as tutor, 122, 207n25; *Edward,* 150, 245, 254, 398; *Journal during a Residence in France,* 398, 575n95; *Mordaunt,* 150; *View of Society and Manners in France, Switzerland, and Germany,* 92, 152, 244, 363, 365, 367, 451, 454, 466, 478, 509, 531; *View of Society and Manners in Italy,* 87n80, 91, 478–79, 509, 531; *View of the Causes and Progress of the French Revolution,* 398; *Zeluco,* 150, 244–45, 254, 561

Moore, Peter, 389, 493

Mordaunt (Moore), 150

More, Hannah, 5, 69

Morellet, Abbé André, 201

Morison, Robert, & Son (also Morison & Son), 268, 465

Morse, Jedidiah, 559, 576; *American Geography,* 559

Mosman, John, 295

Mother, The (Guthrie), 150

Mrs. William M'Kenzie. *See* Hallhead, Sarah

Mudie, George, 584, 587

Muir, Robert, 230

Munck, Thomas, 3

Murdoch, John, 74

Murdoch, Patrick: edits Maclaurin's book on Newton, 285; Millar praised in his biography of James Thomson, 281; Millar's literary counselor and chief literary associate, 283–85; Millar's will leaves money to, 282–83; translates Büsching's *Neue Erdbeschreibung* for Millar, 156n130

Murphy, Arthur, 70, 500

Murray, John, I: accuses Creech and Balfour of hypocrisy on literary property, 355, 382, 414–15; advertising costs, 362–63; on authors' fame and book sales, 94; change of name, 382; Creech and, 416, 420, 428; death, 604; Gilbert Stuart and, 123, 135n89, 366–67, 384–85; Irish trade and, 383, 453, 476; John Bell and, 325, 388; on literary property, 355, 382; magazines owned by, 366; Millar's *Distinction of Ranks* and, 383, 453; rivalry with Strahan and Cadell, 383–85; as Scottish Enlightenment publisher, 37, 273, 381–86, 702–3; spurious editions by, 89; wealth of, 385; William McLaws and, 551; William Richardson and, 206; William Thomson and *English Review* and, 124. *See also the names of individual authors whose works he published*

Murray, John, II, 385–86, 435, 603

Murray, Mrs. John, II (Anne Elliot), 386, 435

Muthu, Sankar, 14

"My Own Life" (Hume): fails to acknowledge *Essays and Treatises*, 54–55; Philadelphia reprint of, 591; publication of, 55–56; on reception of Hume's works, 45–46; 53–54; Strahan shares with Cadell, 329. See also *Life of David Hume, Esq. Written by Himself*

Nasmyth, Alexander, 113–14, *113*, 181, *182*
Natural History, General and Particular (Buffon; trans. Smellie): in Belfast, 449; failure of Dublin edition, 495–7; included in table 2, 78; publication, 339, 420, 423
Nature of the Book (Johns), 8
Neill, Patrick, 307
Neilston, 277n21
Neuchâtel, 9
Newall, John, 547n19
New and Old, Medical, Surgical, and Chemical Works, Lately Imported (R. Bell), 517
New Geographical and Historical Grammar (Salmon), 575
New Geographical, Historical, and Commercial Grammar (Guthrie): Carey's Philadelphia edition, 508, 573–82, *580–81*, 590; Chambers's Dublin edition, 487–93; Dilly and Robinson's editions, *134*, 490; Exshaw's Dublin editions, 487–92; Guthrie the ostensible author, 155–56; on Irish Catholics, 489–93; James Ferguson's astronomical introduction, 133, *134*; Knox the publisher and compiler, 155–56, 489; an octavo best seller, 92–93, *134*; preface to, 1–2, 597, 608; on Scottish and English universities, 579; on the Scottish Enlightenment, 579, *581*, 582, 591; supposed borrowings from Büsching's *Neue Erdbeschreibung*, 156n130*New System of Modern*

Geography. See *New Geographical, Historical, and Commercial Grammar* (Guthrie)
New General History of Scotland (Heron), 126, 141
Newte, Thomas (pseudonym). *See* Thomson, William
New York, 509–10. *See also* Campbell, Samuel, II
Nichols, John, 29, 221, 275, 283
Nisbet, Charles, 546, 570
Noon, John, 240–41
Nourse, John, 485
Now in the Printing Press, and Speedily Will Be Published by Subscription (R. Bell), 524–25

Observations concerning the Distinction of Ranks in Society (Millar): author's copy money from, 254; Cadell rejects, 384; Dublin edition, 383, 453; good seller, 91; Murray and, 383
Observations Made in a Journey through the Western Counties of Scotland (Heron), 145–46
Observations on Certain Parts of the Animal Oeconomy (J. Hunter), 217
Observations on the Diseases of the Army (Pringle), 91
Observations on the Dropsy (Whytt), 157
Observations on the Duties and Offices of a Physician (John Gregory). See *Lectures on the Duties and Qualifications of a Physician*
Observations on the Structure and Functions of the Nervous System (Monro II), *51*, 81–82, 424
O'Conor, Charles, 501n90
"Ode to Independence" (Smollett), 537
Odyssey (Homer), 59–60
Ogilvie, John: Alves cites, 76; *Inquiry into the Causes of the Infidelity and Scepticism of the Times*, 146; *Philosophical and Critical Observations on the*

Nature, Character, and Various Species of Composition, 452; *Providence,* 511; *Rona,* 384

Ogilvie, William, *Essay on the Right of Property in Land,* 152–53

O'Halloran, Clare, 500

O'Halloran, Sylvester, *Introduction to the Study of the History and Antiquities of Ireland,* 501n90

"old canon," 30, 606

"On the Death of William Cullen, M.D." (Park), 139

Orations of Lysias and Isocrates (Gillies), 367, 384

Origin and Progress of Language (Monboddo), 191n171, 338, 536

Orme, Robert, 76, 101

Orphan Hospital (Edinburgh), 211

Ossian: Aitken on offensiveness of Johnson's attacks on, 537; *Fragments* starts craze, 308; mocked by Walpole, 71–72; poems in *Universal Asylum,* 562. *See also* Macpherson, James

Oswald, James: in formative generation, 98; student of William Hamilton, 310; *Appeal to Common Sense in Behalf of Religion,* 146, 148, 324

Outlines of Moral Philosophy (D. Stewart), 105

Outlines of Natural Philosophy (Playfair), 606

Outlines of the Theory and Practice of Midwifery (A. Hamilton), 142, 560

Outram, Dorinda, 14

Owen, William, 377

Oxford, 47, 103, 145, 267, 270

Oxford Dictionary of National Biography (*ODNB*), 266

Oyster Club, 109–10

Paine, Thomas, 397, 528, 578; *Common Sense,* 528; *Pennsylvania Magazine,* 535; *Rights of Man,* 397, 578

Paisley, 276–77, 532, 534–35

Pall Mall (London), 118, 294

Panckoucke, Charles-Joseph, 196, 242–43, 310

paper, 50, 307–8, 467, 499

Paradise Lost (Milton), 562

Paradise Regained (Milton), 562

paratexts, 58–59, 371, 591. *See also* Genette, Gérard

Paris: as capital of the Enlightenment, 15; Creech sent to, 407; medical training in, 103

Park, Mungo: copy money received by, 217; "On the Death of William Cullen, M.D." (*The Bee*), 139; portraits, 185–87; *Travels in the Interior Districts of Africa,* 92, 185–87, 217

Parliament Square (or Close) (Edinburgh), 111–12, *112*

Parsons, John, 584

part or number books, 84, 229–30

patronage of authors: aristocratic, 203–9; in Augustan England, 60; *The Bee* on, 202–3; by booksellers or publishers, 195–203; democratizing of, 234; by funding risky projects, 197–8; Goldsmith on, 197; from government, 207–8; importance of all forms of, 260–61; Johnson and, 207–8; patronage of literature may differ from, 203; Pinkerton on, 198; by providing bridge to the public, 201–3; by providing copy money, 212–61; by providing hospitality and services, 198–200; Samuel Johnson and, 195–98; tutoring and, 101, 122, 206–7, 406

Pattison, Alexander, 232, 234

Pearson, Walter, 296

Pennsylvania Evening Herald, 544

Pennsylvania Journal, 553

Pennsylvania Magazine; or American Monthly Museum (Aitken), 535–37

Pennsylvania Mercury, 560

Pennsylvania Packet, 534

Percy, Thomas, 120, 219

Peregrine Pickle (Smollett), 92–93, 454
peritext. *See* paratexts
Perth, 268
Pery, Edmund Sexton, 486
Peter's Letters to His Kinfolk (Lockhart),
    431–32, 435, 439–40
Philadelphia book trade: Aitken and,
    534–39; Bell and, 515–31; collab-
    orative publishing, 571–73; mutual
    support, 592; Philadelphia Company
    of Printers and Booksellers, 555,
    571–73, 592; reprinting of Scottish
    Enlightenment by, 39–40, 556; rise
    of, 509–10, 514–15. *See also* book-
    shops (Philadelphia); importing
    books (America); reprinting books (in
    America); *names of individual publish-
    ers in Philadelphia*
Philadelphia Company of Printers and
    Booksellers, 555, 571–73, 592
Philadelphiad, The [McLewes], 516
Philadelphia Medical School, 527
Phillips, James W., 444, 476; *Printing
    and Bookselling in Dublin*, 444
philosophes, 62
*Philosophical Analysis and Illustration of
    Some of Shakespeare's Remarkable Char-
    acters* (Richardson): anonymity and,
    153–54; in *Pennsylvania Magazine*,
    536; printed by the Foulis brothers,
    268–69; Spotswood's Philadelphia
    edition, 556
*Philosophical and Critical Observations
    on the Nature, Character, and Various
    Species of Composition* (J. Ogilvie),
    452
Philosophical and Literary Essays (James
    Gregory), 144
Philosophical Essays (Balfour), 310
*Philosophical Essays concerning Human
    Understanding* (Hume). See *Enquiry
    concerning Human Understanding*
Philosophical Dissertations (Balfour), 310
Philosophical Society of Edinburgh,
    106–8, 121, 449

Philosophy of Natural History (Smellie):
    author's copy money for, 386; a late
    bloomer, 90–91; Robert Campbell's
    Philadelphia edition, 562; subscrip-
    tion and copyright, 228–29;
Philosophy of Rhetoric (Campbell): a late
    bloomer, 90; publication, 339; review-
    ing of, contemplated, 137–38
Picture of Edinburgh (Stark), 430–31,
    435, 438–39, 605–6
Pinkerton, John: British booksellers as
    "the sole patrons of literature," 198;
    on Creech, 433; as a Grub Street
    author, 125–26; portraits, 184–85,
    185; Scottish poetry compilations
    of, 125n68; *Antient Scotish Poems*,
    125n68; *History of Scotland*, 184–85,
    348–49; *Scottish Poems, Reprinted from
    Scarce Editions*, 125n68; *Scotish Tragic
    Ballads*, 125n68; *Treasury of Wit*
    (pseudonym H. Bennet), 126
piracy: downsizing and, 84; within
    Dublin, 473; honorary copyright and,
    353–55; smuggling Dublin editions
    into Britain, 355–56, 445–48, 463–
    67. *See also* honorary copyright; Irish
    editions in Britain; Statute of Anne
    (Copyright Act of 1709–10)
Pitt, William, Lord Chatham, 205
Playfair, John: biographer of Matthew
    Stewart and James Hutton, 139; in
    Oyster Club, 109; praised by Stark,
    605; in younger generation, 99; *Illus-
    trations of the Huttonian Theory of the
    Earth*, 139; *Outlines of Natural Philoso-
    phy*, 606
PMLA (special issue on book history
    and literature), 10
Pocock, J. G. A., 14
Poems (Fergusson), 92–93, 191n171
Poems (J. Fordyce), 180, *180*, 213–14
Poems, and a Tragedy (Mickle), 191n171,
    228n85
Poems, Chiefly in the Scottish Dialect
    (Burns): in Belfast, 449; freemasonry

and, 108; frontispiece portrait in Edinburgh (second) edition, 180–82, *182*; Kilmarnock (first) edition of, 114, 230–31, 268; sale of copyright, 232–33, 413; subscribers to Edinburgh edition, 136, *137*, 232; takes Edinburgh by storm, 113

Poems, Chiefly Rural (Richardson), 154, 536

Poems of Ossian (James Macpherson), 354. *See also* Macpherson, James; Ossian

Poems on Several Occasions (Blacklock), 224–25, 231–32

Pointon, Marcia, 163

Poker Club, 109

Political Discourses (Hume), 45, 313

Political Disquisitions (Burgh), 527–30

Political Progress of Britain (Callender), 577–78

Pollard, Mary, 444, 461, 464, 467, 497; *Dublin's Trade in Books*, 461, 464

poor sellers, 90–91

Pope, Alexander: Donaldson editions, 314; Foulis editions of, 268; image of, in books, 59–60; *Essay on Man*, 336; *Iliad* (trans.), 59–60, 572

popularity of books, 88–94, *701*

Popular Party (Church of Scotland), 535

Porter, Roy: on the British (English) and Scottish Enlightenment, 19–21; on "lively England and languishing Scotland," 118–19; on print culture, 2; on publishers as "cultural middlemen," 197

portraits. *See* engraving; frontispiece portraits of authors; *names of individual artists and subjects*

postmodernism, 12–14, 31, 34

Potts, James: in Company of Booksellers, 479; *Hibernian Magazine* and, 469; in price war of 1767, 472–75; subscriber to Steuart's *Inquiry*, 483

Preceptor, The (Dodsley), 90

presentation copies, 60, 139, 426

Present State of All Nations (Smollett), 389

Preston, William, 601

Price, Leah, 10

Price, Samuel, 479

prices, 27–30, 82–84

Priestley, Joseph, 22, 381, 592

Prince of Tunis (Mackenzie), 476

Principles of Equity (Kames), 286, 318

Principles of Moral and Christian Philosophy (Turnbull), 44, 297

Principles of Moral and Political Science (A. Ferguson), 105, 600

Principles of Politeness (Chesterfield), 530–31, 538

Pringle, Sir John: books dedicated to, 142; in Carey's edition of Guthrie's *Geography*, 582; entertained by Strahan, 304; on London, 118; in Millar's circle of literary counselors, 283–84; title of, 100; *Observations on the Diseases of the Army*, 91

printing: *The Bee* on, 202; in Dublin, 460–63; in Edinburgh, 65–66, 306, 355, 427, 431, 438–39; Foulis brothers, 63, 268–69; history and, 6; Hume on, 50–51; in Philadelphia, 586; preference of Scottish authors for Edinburgh printing, 317, 416; Robert Millar on, 276; Strahan firm and, 297–98, 334–36, *335*, 361, 377–78. *See also* imprints; print runs

Printing and Bookselling in Dublin (Phillips), 444

print runs, 86–87, 245, 417, 589. *See also* printing; *individual book titles*

Prior, Matthew, 72

Prize Essays and Transactions of the Highland Society of Scotland (Mackenzie), 212

profit motive: importance of, 250, 256–57, 290–92, 349; limitations of, 7, 256–57, 292–94, 329–30, 359–61, 418–19, 434, 591–92. *See also* author-publisher relations; copy money

Providence: An Allegorical Poem (J. Ogilvie), 511

public: authors' perceptions of, 159–60, 201–3; meanings of, 201; publishers and, 7

public dispensary (Edinburgh), 212, 396

Public Gazatteer, 482

publication, terms of: aristocratic ideal of, 209–12; complex and variety of, 214–15, 255–56; conditional bargains, 214, 252; copyright sold in advance of publication, 214, 244–55, 347–48; payment by the sheet or the job, 215–16; profit-sharing, 235–40, 347–48; rights to single edition sold, 240–44, 349–50; safety or saving clauses, 252–53, 348–49; self-publication, 216–24; subscription, 224–35. *See also* author-publisher relations; copy money; subscription publishing

publicity: advertising, 361–63, 455, 469; biographical articles, 371n96; 455–56, 494, 519; catalogues, 56–57, 57, 368–71, 554; epitexts, 371–72; excerpts, 74, 363, 365, 456, 536–37, 562–63, 591; reviews, 73, 137–38, 239–40, 365–68, 385n131, 456, 590; specimens, 507, 524–25, 528. *See also* advertisements

publisher-author relations. *See* author-publisher relations

publisher function, 7–8, 210, 265–67, 370. *See also* author function; Foucault

publishers (in America). *See* Philadelphia book trade

publishers (in Britain): ambiguous social status of, 210; attitudes toward authors, 344–52; *The Bee* on, 202–3, 290–93; complaints about financial conditions, 352; complaints and actions about literary property, 352–56; complex motives of, 294, 359–61; concentration in London and Edinburgh, 267–71; as first cause of great

literature, 446; London publishers visit Edinburgh, 355; as midwives, 213; as outsiders, 380; presents given to popular authors by, 246, 254, 282, 293–94; role of, 6–7; scholarly bias against, 265–66; significance of second wave of, 398–400; tricks by, 89; twelve principal firms, 271–74, 702–3; use of literary counselors by, 213, 215, 278, 283–84; wealth of, 358–59. *See also* author-publisher relations; London–Edinburgh publishing axis; *names of individual publishers in Edinburgh and London*

publishers (in Ireland). *See* Dublin book trade

publishing: complexity of, 6–7; Johnson's definition of, xv; reading and, 31–34

Pulteney, William, 253

Quarme, Mr., 402, 406

Raeburn, Sir Henry, 183–84, 428, 436

Ramsay, Allan (painter, son of the poet), 164, 168, 184n165

Ramsay, Allan (poet): circulating library of, *111*, 312, 421; close connection with M'Euen, 279; *Tea-Table Miscellany*, 279–80, 297

Ramsay, David: Aitken and, 539–40; *History of the American Revolution*, 539, 563; *History of the Revolution of South-Carolina*, 539

Randolph, Edmund, 574n90

Ranelagh (London), 118, 406

Rankin, Ian, 18–19

Rasselas (Johnson), 518

Raven, James, 31

Ravenet, Simon François, *48, 49*, 168

Raynal, Guillaume, 343

Read, James, 295

reading: empirical research on, 30–31; Jefferson on, 504–5; literary property and, 27–30; in post-Union Dublin,

499; publishing and, 31–34; Smith (Elihu Hubbard) on, 505

Reading Nation in the Romantic Period (St. Clair), 27–30

Recreations in Agriculture, Natural-History, Arts, and Miscellaneous Literature (James Anderson), 79, 157n132

Reflections on the French Revolution (Burke), 254, 572

Reformed Presbyterian Church in America. *See* Covenanters

Reich, Philip Erasmus, 242–43

Reid, John, 307

Reid, Thomas: American readers and, 503; on anonymity, 152–53; in Carey's edition of Guthrie's *Geography*, 582, *581*; contrasts people of Aberdeen and Glasgow, 116; dedication to Stewart and Gregory, 143, 567, *569*, 591; Dugald Stewart's biography of, 139; on cosmopolitan ideal, 143; in prime generation, 98; William Young and, 547; *Essays on the Active Powers of Man*, 394, 565–67; *Essays on the Intellectual Powers of Man*, 143, 391–94, 463–64, 565–67; *Inquiry into the Human Mind*, 92, 258, 286, 317, 323, 391–92, 476

Reid-Maroney, Nina, 504, 563n70

Remer, Rosalind, 555

Renfrewshire, 276–77

Rennell, James, 186

reprinting books (in America): after 1800, 593–94; as appropriation, 506; compared with importing, 506–7; compared with Irish reprinting, 507–10; Enlightenment and, 589–95; geographical issues, 509–10; pace of, 508–9; reducing costs, 509; Rush on profitability of, 554; scale of, 508; subscription publishing and, 507, 510; three reasons for, 506. *See also names of individual publishers in America*

reprinting books (in Dublin): attempts to outdo British editions, 484–86,

488, 495; best sellers, 453–54; compared with American reprinting, 507–10; importance for Scottish Enlightenment, 502; London booksellers on, 447; markets, 463–67; pace of, 457–58, 460–61; preference for British bestsellers, 450–51; printing costs, 461–63; reducing costs, 459–61. *See also names of individual publishers in Dublin*

reviewing books. *See* publicity

Revolution of 1688–89, 65

Reynolds, Sir Joshua: charges for painting, 167; founds The Club, 120; portraits by John Hunter, 184n165; portraits by Macpherson, 172–73; portraits by Robertson, 172, *174*, 478: portraits by Smollett, 167, *171*; portraits by Strahan, 428

Rice, Henry, 572

Rice, John: American connections, 572; career, 471; George Robinson and, 389, 452n14; his edition of Bruce's *Travels*, 495

Rice, Mrs. John (Maria Chamberlaine), 471

Rice, Patrick, 572

Richardson, Samuel, 299–300

Richardson, William: Alves cites, 76; anxiety about Scotticisms, 361; contributes to *Edinburgh Magazine and Review*, 128n78; patronage and, 206–7; William Young matriculates with, 547; *Anecdotes of the Russian Empire*, 154, 206, 361; *Essays on Shakespeare's Dramatic Characters*, 89; *The Indians*, 154; *Philosophical Analysis and Illustration of Some of Shakespeare's Remarkable Characters*, 153–54, 206, 269, 536, 556; *Poems, Chiefly Rural*, 154, 536

Riddell, Maria, 432

Rider, William, 68

Rights of Great Britain Asserted against the Claims of America (James Macpherson), 528

Rights of Man (Paine), 397

Rivington, James: in America, 515; Smollett's *Complete History* and, 215–16, 453; subscriber to Campbell's edition of Hume and Smollett, 586

Rivington, John, 389

Robert Bell's Sale Catalogue of a Collection of New and Old Books (R. Bell), 517

Roberts, John, 389–90

Robertson, John, 15

Robertson, Thomas, *History of Mary Queen of Scots*, 141, 395–96

Robertson, William: annual pipe of wine from Millar, 294; attacked by Gilbert Stuart, 128, 366; on author-publisher relations, 201; biography of in *Encyclopaedia Britannica*, 494; Blair and, 136, 368; cited by Smollett, 74–75, 170, 172; Carey's edition of Guthrie's *Geography* praises, 581, 582; copy money received by, 201, 214, 259–60, 282; Creech cites, 446; *Critical Review* and, 365–66; Denina praises, 68; on dignity of quarto format, 82; Dublin reprints of his works, 454; in Dublin press, 455–56; Dugald Stewart's biography of, 139; edits Robert Adam's *Spalatro*, 135; emulated by other authors, 218, 249–50, 259–60; among founders of original *Edinburgh Review*, 64, 136; on the literary public, 201; in Oyster Club, 109; patronage and, 208; patronizes younger authors, 135–36, 250; popularity of, 30; portraits, 172, *174*, *175*; practice of withdrawing to write, 97; in prime generation, 98; resists move to London, 120; Stark praises, 430, 605; Strahan's irritation at him concerning Blair's *Sermons*, 351–52; *Historical Disquisition on India*, 82, 87n80, 92, 159, 214, 449, 565; *History of America*, 87n80, 92, 214, *335, 336*, 464–65, 465, 478–79, 482; *History of America*, bks. *9 and 10*, 87n80; *His-*tory of Charles V, 87n80, 92, 141, 172, 201, 214, 243, 260–61, 321–22, 332, 354, 369, 454, 465, 482, 511, 518–22, 524, 526, 536; *History of Scotland*, 43, 87n80, 89, 92, 214, 260, 282, 283–84, 287, 294, 354, 369, 407, 449, 465, 485, 515, 523n47, 601

Robin Hood Club, 406

Robinson, G.G.J. & J. (and variations). *See* Robinson, G.G.J. & J. (and variations) and Bell & Bradfute; Robinson, George, I

Robinson, G.G.J. & J. (and variations) and Bell & Bradfute: Alison's *Principles of Taste* and, 394–95; limited success of, 396; other Scottish Enlightenment publications by, 395, *702–3;* Reid's *Essays* and, 391–95; second edition of Ferguson's *Roman Republic*, 253

Robinson, George, I: birth and background, 389; career and character, 388–98; Carey and, 576; *Critical Review* and, 366; death, 604; expansion of business in mid-1780s, 390; Guthrie's *Geography* from late 1770s, *134;* Irish trade and, 389, 445, 452; John Bell and, 325, 387, 389–98; men of letters entertained by, 199; offers to buy the copyright to Boswell's *Life of Johnson*, 220–22; Mackintosh and, 254; radicalism, 396–98; on the Rice brothers, 572n81; as Scottish Enlightenment publisher, 37, 272–73, 389–96, *702–3;* wealth of, 358–59; William Russell and, 124; wishes he and Bell could visit Ireland together, 397–98

Robinson, George, II, 388, 390

Robinson, John, 390

Robison, John, 494

Roderick Random (Smollett), 92–93, 454, 574n95

Roman Antiquities (Adam): Constable and, 604; a duodecimo best seller, 92;

publishing arrangements for, 237–38, 349; registered at Stationers' Hall, 243

Roman Catholics in Ireland, 489–93, 576–77

Romans, Bernard, 537; *Concise Natural History of East and West-Florida*, 537

Rona (J. Ogilvie), 384

Rose, Samuel, 391

Rose, William: in Millar's circle of literary counselors, 283–84; as Reid's publication agent, 391–93; reviews Blair in *Monthly Review*, 368

Rosenau, Pauline Marie, 31, 34

Ross, James, 337n24

Rotterdam, 407

Rouet, William, 283–84

Rousseau, J.-J.: Creech on, 403; generation of, 98; Glasgow editions of his writings, 269; portraits, 164

Rowe, Nicholas, 282

Rowlandson, Thomas, 187

Royal College of Physicians of Edinburgh, 106, 161

Royal College of Surgeons of Edinburgh, 106, 161

Royal Exchange (London), 405–6

Royal Infirmary (Edinburgh), 311

Royal Irish Academy (Dublin), 487, 501n90

Royal Society of Edinburgh, 106–7, 139–40, 156–57, 161–62, 456; *Transactions of the Royal Society of Edinburgh*, 449

Royal Society of London, 106–7, 119, 142, 156–57, 162, 182

Ruddiman, Thomas, 306

Ruins of the Palace of the Emperor Diocletian at Spalatro (R. Adam), 135, 225–26

Rush, Benjamin: on Andrew Millar's generosity, 293–94; on Bell and Paine, 528; Creech and, 553–54; Cullen and, 527, 541; Marshall and, 550; on Philadelphia book culture, 539,

541, 553; on Reid and common sense philosophy, 565; subscriber to Burgh, 528; subscriber to Guthrie's *Geography*, 574n90; in *Universal Asylum*, 563, 565–66; Young and, 550, 570; *Eulogium in Honour of the Late Dr. William Cullen*, 561, 563; "Thoughts on Common Sense," 565–66

Russell, James, 132, 403

Russell, Lord, 72

Russell, William: apprenticed to book trade in Edinburgh, 101; as a Grub Street author, 124; receives LL.D., 128; Thomas's *Essay on Women* (trans. and expanded), 535; *History of America*, 229; *History of Ancient Europe*, 124; *History of Modern Europe*, 124, 146, 153, 456

Salmon, Thomas, *New Geographical and Historical Grammar*, 575

Sandby, William, 382

Sands, William, 386

Saunders, Henry, 473, 483

Scot, Robert, 560, 585

Scoticisms (Beattie), 416

Scotish Tragic Ballads (Pinkerton), 125n68

Scots Magazine, 140, 74

Scots Presbyterian Church or Scots Church (Philadelphia), 534, 551. *See also* antiburghers; Associate Presbyterian Church

Scott, George, 283–84

Scott, Mrs. Peter (Anna Millar), 276

Scott, Peter, 276

Scott, Sir Walter: age of, 39; Constable and, 431–32, 436, 438; on Creech, 435; on death of Robert Heron, 127; on Millar's handling of Fielding's *Amelia*, 288; Murray II publishes, 386; praised by Stark, 605; in Sibbald's circulating library, 113–14, *113*; *Marmion*, 435; *Waverley*, 438

Scott, Thomas, 570

Scott, William Robert, 79
Scotticisms, 52–53, 299, 361. *See also*
language in Scotland
Scottish Book Trade Index (SBTI),
466
Scottish–English relations: English resentment and animosity, 69–72, 94,
129–30, 148; integration problems
among Scots in London, 128–30;
Scottish boasting, 43, 69, 73–74,
94–95, 365
Scottish Enlightenment. *See* Enlightenment, Scottish
Scottish national identity, 34, 147
*Scottish Poems, Reprinted from Scarce
Editions* (Pinkerton), 125n68
Seasons, The (J. Thomson): Bell's Dublin
editions, 513–14; Bell's Philadelphia
edition, 530; Millar protects literary
property of, 288–89; one of Millar's
most popular titles, 281
seceders. *See* antiburghers; burghers
Select Mechanical Exercises (J. Ferguson):
frontispiece portrait, 182–83, *183*; in
Strahan printing ledger, *335, 336*
Select Society (Edinburgh), 62, 107.
See also Edinburgh Society for the
Encouragement of Arts, Sciences,
Manufactures, and Agriculture in
Scotland; Society for Promoting the
Reading and Speaking of the English
Language in Scotland
Sentimental Journey (Sterne), 518
Sermons (Blair): advertising, 362, 451;
Alison and, 138; American editions,
470, 561–62; author fixes reviews
of, 138; author's copy money from,
245–46; extraordinary popularity,
33–34, 92, 247; format, 82; frontispiece portrait planned, 173, 176–77;
imprints, 416–17; Johnson's reading
of, 351; pirated Dublin edition, 465;
publication of, 339, 416–17; Rose's review, 368; on sensibility and humanity, 32–34; Strahan's irritation over,

351–52; table 2 categorizes as a single
book, 79
Sermons (Farquhar), 371
Sermons (Gerard), 256–57
Sermons (Leechman), 190, *193*, 247–49
Sermons (Logan), 135, 395
Sermons on Practical Subjects (R.
Walker), 535
Sermons on Several Occasions (Duff), 229,
268
Sermons to Young Women (J. Fordyce):
American edition, 511; best seller,
92; in Dublin price war, 473, 475;
Leathey edition, 471; Rachel Strahan
and, 198–99; temporary anonymity
and, 152
Seymour, Joseph H., 585
Shakespeare: Monboddo prefers *Doug-
las* to, 69; monument in Westmin-
ster Abbey, 282; in *North Briton*, 71;
Works, 313
Sheridan, Mrs. Frances, 282
Sheridan, Thomas, 67, 94, 500
Sherwin, John Keyse, 173, *176*
*Short Introduction to Moral Philoso-
phy* (Hutcheson): American edition,
556; duodecimo for classroom use,
85; printed by the Foulis brothers,
268–69
Sibbald, James, 113–14, *113*, 231
Sibbald's circulating library in Parliament Square, Edinburgh, 113–14,
113
Sidney, Algernon, 71–72
Siege of Aquileia (J. Home), 87n80, 88,
468
Simson, John, 132
Simson, Robert: Denina praises, 68;
Guthrie's *Geography* cites, 579; Stewart praises, 139; *Elements of Euclid*,
92, 269
Sinclair, Sir John: Callender cites,
577n100; in Carey's edition of Guthrie's *Geography*, 582; correspondence
of, 140; Creech and, 425–27, 433;

Creech cites, 76; education, 101; freemason, 108; frontispiece portrait of, 191n171; in London and Edinburgh, 120; title of, 100; in younger generation, 99; *History of the Public Revenue of the British Empire*, 191n171; *Statistical Account of Scotland*, 133, 211, 424–27, 430, 440

Sir Harry Gaylove (Marishall), 102n9

Sir Launcelot Greaves (Smollett), 92–93, 150

Six Sketches on the History of Man (Kames), 530, 535

Skelton, Philip, 257

Sketches of a History of Literature (Alves), 76–77

Sketches of the History of Man (Kames): author's copy money from, 82–83, 253; in Belfast, 449; Bell and Aitken's abridged Philadelphia edition, 526–30, *529;* challenged by Samuel Stanhope Smith, 538; Company of Booksellers and, 476, 477; excerpts in *Pennsylvania Magazine*, 536; format of, 84; order of names in imprint, 416; popularity of, 91; publication, 339, 420; Strahan fails to get Balfour added as copublisher, 341–42

Skipwith, Robert, 504

Sleater, William, I, 470, 483

Sleater, William, II, 469–70

Sloan, Douglas, 504

Sloane, Hans, 283–84

Smellie, Alexander, 140

Smellie, William (physician): Guthrie's *Geography* cites, 579; settles in London, 121; *Treatise on the Theory and Practice of Midwifery*, 92, 133, 135, 273

Smellie, William (printer): affinity to Grub Street writers, 126; apprenticed, 101; Buchan's *Domestic Medicine* edited by, 135; Creech and, 420, 433; Creech cites, 76; in Crochallan Fencibles, 109; on Edinburgh intellectual culture, 109–10; *Edinburgh Magazine*

and Review co-edited by, 128n78; on engraving in Dublin, 496; on expansion of Edinburgh printing, 306; fee for editing *Encyclopaedia Britannica*, 216; freemason, 108; partnership with Balfour, 307, 337; resists move to London, 120; Strahan and, 337; in younger generation, 99; translation of Buffon, *Natural History, General and Particular*, 339, 371, 420, 423, 449; *Encyclopaedia Britannica*, 92, 135, 216; *Literary and Characteristical Lives*, 140; *Philosophy of Natural History*, 90, 228–29, 386, 562

Smith, Abigail, 505

Smith, Adam: American readers and, 503; author identification of, 162; in *The Bee*, 139; biographical letter on Hume, 55–56, 59, 141, 591; in Carey's edition of Guthrie's *Geography*, *581*, *582;* in The Club, 120; Dugald Stewart's biography of, 139; in Dublin press, 455; among founders of original *Edinburgh Review*, 64; library of, 138–39; meets Strahan in Edinburgh, 304; mocked by Walpole, 72; nephew and heir of, 212; in Oyster Club, 109; popularity of, 30; in prime generation, 98; Smollett cites, 74–75; Stark praises, 430, 605; as tutor, 207n25; *Essays on Philosophical Subjects*, 135, 212, 348, 600; *Theory of Moral Sentiments*, 92, 105, 162, 285, 317, 333, 369–71, 457–58, 460, 515, 562–63, 601; *Wealth of Nations*, 92, 105, 162, 236–37, 240, 243, *335*, 336, 340, 358, 370–71, 413, 456, 457–59, 463–64, 471–72, 508–9, 560, 579, 601

Smith, Elihu Hubbard, 505

Smith, James, 230

Smith, John (Dublin bookseller), 449, 458

Smith, John (Scottish clergyman), 352

Smith, Preserved, 12

Smith, Samuel Harrison, 586

Smith, Samuel Stanhope, 538; *Essay on the Causes of the Variety of Complexion and Figure in the Human Species*, 538

Smith, W. & W., 473

Smith, William, 474, 483

Smollett, Tobias: Alexander Carlyle and, 74–75, 163; Alves cites, 76; author identification of, 160; biography of, by Moore, 141; in Carey's edition of Guthrie's *Geography*, 582; *Critical Review* and, 365–66; database of Scottish authors and, 34, 77; Denina praises, 68; disdain for England, 123; in Dublin press, 455; Dublin reprints of his works, 454; Edinburgh literati lauded by, 74–75; English resentment toward Scots noted by, 69; as a Grub Street author, 122–23, 127, 215, 257; Moore and, 69; in *Pennsylvania Magazine*, 537; popularity of, 30, 92–93; portraits, 167, 169, *171*; praises Millar for commemorative edition of Thomson's *Works*, 281–82; in prime generation, 98; *Compendium of Authentic and Entertaining Voyages*, 215n44; *Complete History of England*, 92, 169, 215–16, 229–30, 453; *Continuation of the Complete History of England*, 92, 169, 170n151, 273; *Don Quixote*, 488; *Ferdinand Count Fathom*, 92, 453; *History and Adventures of an Atom*, 389; *History of England* (continuation of Hume), 169–71, 461, 582–89; *Humphry Clinker*, 74–75, 92, 144, 362, 454, 456, 466n41, 471, 476; "Ode to Independence," 537; *Peregrine Pickle*, 92, 371, 454; *Roderick Random*, 92, 454, 574n95; *Sir Launcelot Greaves*, 92, 150; *Travels through France and Italy*, 471

Social History of Art and Literature (Hauser), 196

Société typographique de Neuchâtel, 4n11

Society for Promoting the Reading and Speaking of the English Language in Scotland (Edinburgh), 62, 107

Society for the Benefit of the Sons of the Clergy (Edinburgh), 211, 403, 425–27

Society in Scotland for Propagating Christian Knowledge (Edinburgh), 311

Society of Antiquaries of Scotland (Edinburgh), 106, 343, 456

Society of United Irishmen. *See* United Irishmen

Somerville, Mary, 102n9, 132

Somerville, Thomas: chaplaincy and pension, 252; emulates Robertson, 250–51, 304; encouraged by Strahan to try London, 304; encourages niece Mary, 102n9; freemason, 311; frustrating literary career, 250–52, 256, 348; in London, 131, 199; "pecuniary embarrassments" his motivation, 250, 256; resentment toward publishers, 251–52; transports Donaldson's money, 315; *History of Great Britain during the Reign of Queen Anne*, 141, 157, 251–52, 600; *History of Political Transactions and of Parties, from the Restoration to the Death of King William*, 250–51

Some Thoughts on the State of Literary Property (Donaldson), 475–76

Songs, Comic, Satyrical, and Sentimental (Stevens), 530

Sophonisba, Tragedy of (J. Thomson), 281

Sorrows and Sympathetic Attachments of Werter (Goethe), 531

Spectator, The, 33, 313

Speculative Society, 403, 419

Spence, Joseph, 224

Spencer, Mark G., 503, 586

Spotswood, William: in Boston, 572, 574n90, 586; Carey and, 542, 544, 562, 574n90; in Dublin, 486n65, 542; edition of Richardson's *Philosophical Analysis*, 556; in Philadelphia, 544,

556, 562, 571; Philadelphia Company of Printers and Booksellers and, 571–72; sells *Columbian Magazine* to Young, 562; subscriber to Campbell's edition of Hume and Smollett, 586
Spring (J. Thomson), 281
St. Andrews, 117, 144
St. Andrews, University of, 104, 128
St. Andrew's Society (Philadelphia), 538, 545, 549–50
Stark, John, 434–36; *Picture of Edinburgh*, 430–31, 435, 438–39, 606–6
State-Papers and Letters, Addressed to William Carstares (MacCormick), 83n74, 350–51
Stationers' Company (London): Cadell and, 333; imitated by Dublin Company of Booksellers, 476; importance of its Stationers' Hall, 243; Millar and, 278, 305; Strahan and, 299, 305
Stationers' Hall (London): books registered to Millar at, 281, 332, 334; Boswell's *Life of Johnson* registered at, 223; Burns's *Poems* registered to Creech and Cadell at, 233; portraits of A. Strahan and Cadell in, 377; registration of Scottish Enlightenment books at, 243–44
Statistical Account of Scotland (Sinclair): Creech and, 424–27, 433, 440; Heron helps to compile, 133; publication, 424–27, 433, 440; Sinclair's charitable intentions for, 211, 424–27
Statute of Anne (Copyright Act of 1709–10): Creech and, 355; defined, 4; Donaldson and, 313–14; Dublin trade ignores, 444; London copyright owners fear Irish violations of, 445–46; modern copyright law and, 25; prosecutions of violators of, 356; Strahan and Cadell wish to protect owners of copyrights not protected by, 353. *See also* honorary copyright; literary property; piracy
St. Clair, William, 6, 27–30, 606

Steele, Sir Richard, 489
Sterne, Laurence, 446, 518; *Sentimental Journey*, 518
Steuart, Sir James: in *The Bee*, 139; in Carey's edition of Guthrie's *Geography*, 581, 582; *Inquiry into the Principles of Political Oeconomy*, 135, 236, 283, 287, 332, 371, 483–84, 515
Stevens, George Alexander, 530; *Songs, Comic, Satyrical, and Sentimental*, 530
Stewart, Dugald: biographies of Smith, Robertson, and Reid by, 139; in Carey's edition of Guthrie's *Geography*, 581, 582; Creech and, 420–22; Creech cites, 76; in Dublin press, 456; on emergence of Scottish Enlightenment, 79; encourages women authors, 102n9; on Hutcheson's *System of Moral Philosophy*, 64; in Oyster Club, 109; praised by Stark, 605; Reid and, 143–44, 567, *569;* in younger generation, 99; *Elements of the Philosophy of the Human Mind*, 91, 144, 253, 567, 582, 606; *Outlines of Moral Philosophy*, 105
Stewart, James H., 562
Stewart, Matthew: freemason, 108; Playfair's biography of, 139; *Tracts, Physical and Mathematical* (and *Supplement* to), 139, 286
Stewart, Peter, 549, 553, 556
Stewart, Thomas, 449
St. Giles Church (Edinburgh), 110, *111, 112,* 403
St. James Chronicle, 67
Stockdale, John, 253
Stockton, Richard, 574n90
Strachey, Mrs., 406
Strahan, Andrew: on author identification, 159–60; birth and training, 373–75; Cadell & Davies and, 378–79, 599–602; character and portrait, 377–78, *377;* continues publishing partnership with Cadell and Creech, 374–76, 379, 599; declining inter-

Strahan, Andrew (*continued*)
est in publishing, 601; entertains
authors with Cadell, 199; success
of, 39; wealth of, 378. *See also* Cadell, Thomas, I; Strahan, William;
Strahan (Andrew) and Cadell Strahan
(Andrew) and Cadell: Adam's *Roman
Antiquities* and, 237–38, *239;* Bruce's
First Principles, 419; Burns's *Poems*
and, 232–33; Cadell's post-retirement
printing account in the Strahan ledgers, 599–600, *705–7;* Creech and,
375–76, 378–79; Ferguson's *Principles*
and, 253, 600; Henry's *History* and,
218–19; House of Strahan and Cadell
continued by, 375–76, 396; Hutton's
Dissertations and, 210; Leechman's
Sermons and, 248–49; new warehouse,
378; publication catalogues, 379;
publishing collaborations, 378–79;
Somerville's histories and, 250–52;
*The Following Valuable Books Are
Printed for A. Strahan and T. Cadell,
in the Strand, 1788* (and subsequent
years), 379. *See also* Cadell, Thomas,
I; Cadell & Davies; Strahan, Andrew;
Strahan, William; Strahan (William)
and Cadell; *names of individual authors
whose works they published*
Strahan, George (bookseller in Cornhill, London), 296–97
Strahan, George (son of William), 299,
373–74
Strahan, Mrs. William (Margaret
Elphingston), 297–98, 375
Strahan, Rachel, 198–99
Strahan, William: Adam's *Spalatro*
and, 226; advertising and, 362–63;
authors' demands for copy money
provoke, 345–50; background and
education, 294–95; change of name,
52, 299; chief printer of Millar's
Scottish Enlightenment books, 297,
331; Creech as correspondent and
disciple, 337–61 passim, 408–16, *411,*

423; death, 372, 390; declares end of
public interest in Gaelic poetry, 352;
Dublin trade and, 453; enlightened
motives of, 360–61; fame of, 430;
family of, 297–98, 373–75; a founding
publisher, 36, 274, 598; Hume and,
47, 55–56, 69n48, 89, 218, 304, 346;
intimacy with Balfour and Kincaid,
296, 304, 311, 336–38; Irish reprinting and, 355–56, 447–48, 465; on
John Bell, 412; Johnson and, 208; as
judge of manuscripts, 339; *London
Chronicle* and, 363; love of London,
305; member of Parliament, 299–300;
M'Euen's apprentice, 295–96; Millar's protégé, 287, 331, 334; *Monthly
Review* and, 366–68; obituary of,
in *The Lounger,* 295, 303; patronage of Scottish authors by, 196, 198,
303; perpetual copyright defended
by, 299; portraits, *328, 428;* possibly
in Millar's circle of literary counselors, 283n41; praised by Beattie and
Mackenzie, 213; printing charges
compared to Graisberry's, 461–63;
printing facility of, 298; publication
of Hume's "My Own Life,", 55–56;
on publishing for reasons other than
profit, 359; on publishing profits,
329–30; publishing strategy, 329,
336–38; pushes Kincaid to replace
Bell with Creech, 409–12, *411;* rejects
Gerard's *Sermons,* 256; Robertson
and, 89, 303, 336–37; on Robertson
and Blair's shortcomings as literary
counselors, 350–52; on Scotland and
England, 305–6; Scotticisms and,
52, 299, 361; self-consciousness as a
printer-publisher, 333–34; as silent
partner in publications, 273, 331–32;
in Stationers' Company, 299, 305; visits to Scotland, 300–305, 336; wealth
of, 359. *See also* Cadell, Thomas, I;
Creech, William; Strahan (William)
and Cadell

Strahan, William (Billy, son of William), 373–74

Strahan (William) and Cadell: acquisition of Millar copyrights by, 333; "Agreement" between, 329–30, 332; association with Balfour, 336–37, 340–44; association with Kincaid & Creech and, 337–40; Campbell's *Four Gospels* and, 238–40; catalogues of their books, 56–58, *57,* 329, 369–71; Creech and, 337–61 passim, 408–18 passim, *411,* 422–24; disciples of Millar, 330; division of labor between, 327, 361; Ferguson (James) and, 217; frontispiece portraits of authors and, 172–80, 182–83; intimacy of, 327–28, Mackenzie and, 211; outbid for Reid's *Essays,* 391–93; printing ledger of, 334–36, *335;* publicity, 361–72; rivalry with Murray, 383–85; scheme for a coalition with Balfour and Creech, 340–45, *341;* as Scottish Enlightenment publishers, 37, *57,* 82–83, 210–55 passim, 327–61 passim, *335, 341,* 372, 398, *702–3;* silent collaborations, 329; *Books Printed for W. Strahan, and T. Cadell,* 56–58, *57,* 329, 369–71. *See also* Balfour, John; Cadell, Thomas, I; Creech, William; Strahan, Andrew; Strahan, William; Strahan (Andrew) and Cadell; *names of individual authors whose works they published*

Strand (London), The. *See* bookshops (London)

strong sellers, 91–92

Structure and Physiology of Fishes (Monro II), 449

Stuart, Gilbert: in Carey's edition of Guthrie's *Geography,* 582; Creech and, 420; in Crochallan Fencibles, 109; in Dublin press, 455; *Edinburgh Magazine and Review* and, 128; frontispiece portrait, 191n171; as a Grub Street author, 123; on history writing by Scottish clergy, 249–50; Murray and, 123, 135n89, 366–67, 384–85; receives LL.D., 128; resentment toward Robertson and Edinburgh literati, 123, 384–85; in younger generation, 99; *Historical Dissertation concerning the Antiquity of the English Constitution,* 322–23; *History of the Reformation in Scotland,* 191n171; *Observations concerning Public Law,* 385n131; *A View of Society in Europe,* 89, 385n131, 455

Stuart, John. *See* Bute, 3rd Earl of

Suard, J.-B.-A., 201

Suarez, Michael F., 232n99, 265

subjects and genres of Scottish books: anonymity and, 149–50; best sellers and, 93; copy money and, 258; formats and, 85, *700;* individual authors and, 85; wide range of, 84–85, 94

subscription publishing: American characteristics of, 507, 510; associations with avarice, 227–28; in Augustan England, 60; of Blacklock's *Poems,* 224–25; of books by Scottish women, 102n9; of Buchan's *Domestic Medicine,* 219; of Buffon's *Natural History* (Dublin), 496; of Burney's *Camilla,* 227–28; of Burns's *Poems* (Edinburgh ed.), 136, *137,* 231–35; of Burns's *Poems* (Kilmarnock ed.), 230–31; for charitable purposes, 212; commercial, 228; of Cullen's *First Lines* and *Lectures* (Philadelphia), 526–27; difficulty of determining, 229; of Dobson's *Encyclopaedia,* 555–56; in Dublin, 450, 483–87, 493–96; *Encyclopaedia Britannica* (Dublin), 493; of of Goldsmith's *History of the Earth* (Dublin), 485–86; Guthrie's *Geography* (Dublin), 486–87, (Philadelphia), 574; of Hume's *History* (Dublin), 484–85; of Hume's *History* (Philadelphia), 583–89; of Hutcheson's *System of Moral Philosophy,* 63; hybrid modes of, 229–30, 232; less significant than usually thought,

subscription publishing (*continued*)
235; part or number books, 84, 229–
30; proposals for Robert Bell's editions (Philadelphia), *521*, 523–30, *529*;
of Robert Millar's books, 276–77;
of Robertson's *Charles V* (Philadelphia), 518–22; of Robertson's *Historical Disquisition* (Philadelphia), 565;
of Smollett's *History* (Philadelphia),
583–89; of Steuart's *Inquiry* (Dublin),
483–84; subscription lists, 102n9,
225, 228, 483–84, 493, 522, 527–28,
558, 574n90, 585–87; of Thomson's
Works, 281–82; traditional, 225–28;
variety and complexity of, 234–35.
See also publication, terms of
Summary of Geography and History
(Adam), 238, 604
Swift, Jonathan, 313–14, 489
System of Moral Philosophy (Hutcheson):
Leechman's life of Hutcheson in, 63,
139; printing and publication, 63,
225, 269; Scottish literary identity
and, 34, 62–64, 79
System of Surgery (B. Bell): author identification in, 157; dedication, 142;
excerpt in *Universal Asylum*, 563; frontispiece portrait, 183–84, *184*; publication, 390; strong seller, 91

tables (in appendix): table 1, 77, *613–18*;
table 2, 78–81, 448; *620–699*; table 3,
84–86; *700*; table 4, 90–93, *701*; table 5, 272–74, *702–3*; table 6, 468–72,
704; table 7, 599–600, *705–7*
*Tables and Tracts, relative to Several Arts
and Sciences* (J. Ferguson), 368n94
Talbot, Christopher, 544
Taylor, Robert, 512n18
Taylor, Samuel, 512
Tea-Table Miscellany (Ramsay), 279–80,
297
Temora ("trans." James Macpherson):
best seller, 92; Dublin edition, 460,

471; format, 86; as Scottish national
epic, 66
Temple, William Johnson, 119
Theodorus (D. Fordyce), 133, 141
Theory of Moral Sentiments (A. Smith):
Beattie on copublication of, 317; best
seller, 92; publication, 285; Dublin
edition, 457–58, 460; excerpts in *Universal Asylum*, 562–63; imprint, 601;
Strahan and Cadell purchase Millar's
share of copyright, 333; university
lectures, based on, 105
Thomas, Antoine Léonard, 535; *Essay
on the Character, Manners, and Genius
of Women in Different Ages* (trans. Russell), 535
Thomas, Isaiah, 512, 518, 537, 558, 586
Thomson, James: cited by Jefferson,
504; connected with Andrew Millar
and Anglo-Scots, 280–84; Denina
praises, 68; Donaldson editions, 314;
early poetry published by M'Euen,
278; monument in Westminster Abbey, 281–82; *The Seasons*, 281, 513–14,
530; *Spring*, 281; *Tragedy of Sophonisba*, 281; *Works*, 281–82
Thomson, William: as a Grub Street author, 123–24; patronized by Blair and
Robertson, 135, 367; receives LL.D.,
128; *Enquiry into the Elementary Principles of Beauty*, 381; *Mammuth*, 150;
Man in the Moon, 150; *Tour in England
and Scotland* [second edition by "Captain Newte"], 145
"Thoughts on Common Sense" (Rush),
565
Three Essays: Moral and Political (Hume),
285
Tierney, James E., 362
Tom Jones (Fielding), 282, 473–74
Tonson, Jacob, 486
Topham, Edward, 358
To the Sons of Science in America (R.
Bell), 525

Tour in England and Scotland (W. Thomson), 145

Tourneisen, J. J., 23n64

Tour through Sicily and Malta (Brydone): author's copy money from, 253, 346; best seller, 92; Company of Booksellers and, 476; Dublin best seller, 454; excerpts in *Pennsylvania Magazine*, 536

Town and Country Magazine, or, Irish Miscellany, 456

Townshend, John, 182–83

Tracts, Physical and Mathematical (and *Supplement* to) (M. Stewart), 139, 286

Transactions of the Royal Society of Edinburgh, 449

Traveller, The (Goldsmith), 518

Travels in the Interior Districts of Africa (Park): author's copy money from, 217; best seller, 92; Bruce's *Travels* compared with, 185–86; frontispiece portrait, 185–87, *186*; self-published, 217

Travels from St. Petersburg (J. Bell), 513

Travels of a Philosopher (Le Poivre), 530

Travels through France and Italy (Smollett), 471

Travels to Discover the Source of the Nile (James Bruce): in Belfast, 450; dedication, 141; Dublin edition, 495; Park's *Travels* compared with, 185–86; popularity of abridgments of, 89, 92; publication arrangements, 242–43

Treasury of Wit (Pinkerton; pseudonym H. Bennet), 126

Treatise concerning the Sanctifying of the Lord's Day (Willison), 279

Treatise of Agriculture (Dickson), 324

Treatise of Human Nature (Hume): anonymity not maintained, 148; commercial failure of, 44; copy sent to Pope, 60; disowned by Hume, 53; Hume's "hasty bargain" to publish, 240–41; Millar involved with, 280

Treatise of the Materia Medica (Cullen): American edition, 509, 554, 561; author's copy money from, 253, 386; author identification in, 157, *158;* bypassing London trade, 387; nearly simultaneous reprinting of, 508

Treatise of the Scurvy (Lind), 313

Treatise on Ancient Painting (Turnbull), 44

Treatise on Fluxions (C. Maclaurin), 98

Treatise on Gonorrhoea Virulenta and Lues Venerea (B. Bell), 454n19

"Treatise on Taste" (R. Wallace), 347–48

Treatise on the Theory and Practice of Midwifery (Smellie), 92, 133, 135

Treatise on the Venereal Disease (J. Hunter), 217

Trinity College Dublin, 468, 488–89

Trotter, Thomas, 180, *180*

Tunbridge Wells, 248, 330–31

Turnbull, George: active before 1746, 98; contrasted with Hume, 44–45; studies divinity under William Hamilton, 280–81; *Principles of Moral and Christian Philosophy*, 44, 297; *Treatise on Ancient Painting*, 44

Turner, Cheryl, 227

Two Introductory Lectures (W. Hunter), 106

Two Papers on Fevers and Infection (Lind), 108

Tytler, Alexander Fraser, Lord Woodhouselee: on anonymity, 153; biography of John Gregory by, 141; biography of Kames by, 140; Creech and, 403, 419, 421–22; Creech cites, 76; in Dublin edition of Boswell's *Tour*, 458; title of, 99; *Elements of General History, Ancient and Modern*, 419, 604; *Essay on the Principles of Translation*, 153; *Memoirs of the Life and Writings of the Hon. Henry Home of Kames*, 140, 419

Tytler, William, 145

Ulster, 100–101, 449–50

Union of 1603, 43

Union of 1707, 43, 65

Union of 1800–1801 (Great Britain and Ireland), 467, 471, 499

United Company of Booksellers (Dublin). *See* Company of Booksellers (Dublin)

United Irishmen, 398, 491, 498, 545, 577

United Presbyterian Church, 551n35

Universal Asylum, and Columbian Magazine: deletes sentence on Hume, 563; excerpts from Scottish Enlightenment books in, 562–63; Rush on Cullen and Brown in, 563; on stages of American print culture, 563–65; Young and, 562–68, *568*, 608. See also *Columbian Magazine*

Universal History, 297

universities: author identification and, 161; authors employed at, 104; books derived from lectures at, 105–6; cosmopolitan ideal and, 143; education of authors at, 103–4; English and Scottish compared, 579. *See also* Edinburgh, University of; Glasgow, University of; King's College, Aberdeen; Marischal College, Aberdeen; St. Andrews, University of

"Urgent Necessity of an Immediate Repeal of the Whole Penal Code against the Roman Catholics" (Carey), 543

Urie, Robert, 269

Utrecht, 103

Vallance, James, 483

Vallance, John, 560

Vauxhall (London), 118, 406

Venturi, Franco, 20–22

Vernor, Thomas, 354

Vernor & Hood, 354

Vertue, George, 59–60

Vicar of Wakefield (Goldsmith), 473–75

View of Society and Manners in France, Switzerland, and Germany (Moore): author compensated for each new edition, 244; Bell's American edition, 509, 531; best seller, 92; Company of Booksellers and, 478; Dublin advertisement for, 451; Dublin best seller, 454; excerpted in *London Chronicle*, 363, 365; pirated Dublin edition of, 466; reviewed by Gillies in *Monthly*, 367; temporary anonymity and, 152

View of Society and Manners in Italy (Moore): Bell's Philadelphia edition, 509, 531; Company of Booksellers and, 478–79; print run, 87n80; strong seller, 92

View of Society in Europe (Stuart), 89, 455

View of the British Empire (Knox), 115, 144, 155–56

View of the Causes and Progress of the French Revolution (Moore), 398

View of the Reign of Frederick II (Gillies), 206–7, 460

Vindiciae Gallicae (Mackintosh), 254, 397

Voltaire, François Marie Arouet de: anonymity of works by, 149; focal point of postmodernist scorn, 13; generation of, 98; Glasgow editions, 269; impressed by copy money paid to Robertson, 261; men of letters defined by, 80–81; Scottish literary criticism acknowledged by, 67–68; *Letters concerning the English Nation*, 405–6; *Miscellanies by M. de Voltaire*, 530

Voltaire in the Shades (Mickle), 146

Volunteer's Journal, 543–44

Waddington, Mrs., 228n84

Walker, John, *Institutes of Natural Philosophy*, 105

Walker, Joseph Cooper, 458

Walker, Robert, 535; *Sermons on Practical Subjects*, 535

Walker, Thomas, 469, 498

Walker, W. & J., 183–84, *184*

Wallace, George: author identification of, 156; biography of father Robert by, 140; Strahan and, 303, 347–48

Wallace, Robert: connected with Millar and Strahan, 280, 302–3; in formative generation, 98; published anonymously, 149; Smollett cites, 74–75; son George's biographical sketch of, 140; student of William Hamilton, 280, 310; *Characteristics of the Present Political State of Great Britain*, 287, 332, 453–54; *Dissertation on the Numbers of Mankind in Antient and Modern Times*, 287; "Treatise on Taste," 347–48

Waller, Thomas, 504

Wallis, John, 476

Walnut Street Church (Philadelphia). *See* Associate Presbyterian Church (Philadelphia)

Walpole, Horace: growing antipathy toward Scotland and Scottish authors, 71–72, 94; on Millar's generosity to Fielding, 282; on Strahan and Cadell, 330, 359n66; *Catalogue of the Royal and Noble Authors of England* (Walpole), 71

Warburton, William, 350

Ware, Sir James, 475

Warren, Hugh, 450, 493

Washington, George, 527, 545, 558, 574n90

Watson, James, 296

Watson, Robert: *History of Philip II*, 240, 243, 335, 336, 339, 346, 349–50, 451, 465; *History of Philip III*, 135, 352, 390, 471

Watson, Samuel, 473, 482, 483

Watson, William, I: in Dublin price war, 473; edition of MacBride's *Methodical Introduction*, 459n30; quarto edition of *Charles V*, 482; succeeded by son William, 470

Watson, William, II, 470

Watt, Adam, 295

Waverley (Scott), 438

Wealth of Nations (A. Smith): American editions, 508–9, 560; based on Smith's university lectures, 105; best seller, 92; Creech a silent partner in, 340, 413; Dublin editions, 457–59, 463–64, 471–72; in Dublin press, 456; imprint, 601; marks publishing dominance of Strahan and Cadell, 357–58; registered at Stationers' Hall, 243; on Scottish and English universities, 579; in Strahan printing ledger, 335, 336; terms of publication, 236–37

Wedderburn, Alexander, Lord Loughborough: among Barclay's Scholars, 402; among founders of original *Edinburgh Review*, 64; arranges Johnson's pension, 207

Weems, Mason Locke, 555

Wells, Robert, 484

West, William, 388

Westminster Abbey (London), 281–82

"What Is an Author?" (Foucault), 58

White, Luke: Boswell's *Tour* and, 458; Buffon's *Natural History* and, 496; career, 472; George Robinson and, 389, 452n14; Hume's *History* and, 483; London ties, 452; lottery tickets and medicines sold by, 481–82; Reid's *Intellectual Powers* and, 464; retirement, 499; as Scottish Enlightenment reprinter, 458, 472; Smollett's *History of England*, 461, 483; smuggling and, 464, 466

Whitestone, Henry, 470

Whitestone, William, 470

Whole Works of the Reverend Robert Millar, 277

Whytt, Mrs. Robert (Louisa Balfour), 132, 310

Whytt, Robert: Alves cites, 76; Guthrie's *Geography* cites, 579; in prime

Whytt, Robert (*continued*)
generation, 98; *Observations on the Dropsy*, 157
Wight, William, 269
Wilkes, John, 69–71
Wilkie, William: Alves cites, 76; Denina praises, 68; Smollett cites, 74–75; *Epigoniad*, 43, 66, 152, 308
Williams, Helen Maria, 572; *Letters containing a Sketch of the Politics of France*, 572
Williams, James: ambition of, 486; apprentices of, 472; in Company of Booksellers, 479; competition with Strahan and Cadell, 461–62, 484–86; death, 499; editions of Hume's works, 450, 457, 482–85; goals, 485–86; Guthrie's *Geography*'s and, 487; Kames's *Sketches* and, 528, 530; London ties, 451; lottery tickets and medicines sold by, 481–82; Moncrieffe and, 461, 472, 483; in price war of 1767, 472–75; printing in Graisberry ledgers, 461–62; as Scottish Enlightenment reprinter, 472, 482–86; subscription editions, 483–84
Williams, Mrs. James (Dorothea), 472
Willison, John, 278–79; *Treatise concerning the Sanctifying of the Lord's Day*, 279
Wilson, Alexander, 374, 552
Wilson, Andrew, 374
Wilson, James, 528, 574n90
Wilson, John, 230–31
Wilson, Peter, 470, 473, 483
Wilson, William, 451, 455, 470, 483
Wilson, William (Scottish clergyman), 534; *Defence of the Reformation-Principles of the Church of Scotland*, 534
Wind, Edgar, 191
Wise Club. *See* Aberdeen Philosophical Society
Wishart, George, 295, 302
Wishart, William, I, 295, 302

Wishart, William, II: connected with Millar and Strahan, 280; disciple of William Hamilton, 280; principal of the University of Edinburgh, 295
Witherspoon, John: Aitken and, 532, 534, 538; in America, 567; critic of Scottish Enlightenment, 81; *Pennsylvania Magazine* and, 535; Walker and, 535; *Dominion of Providence over the Passions of Men*, 534; *Ecclesiastical Characteristics*, 81
Wodrow, James: correspondence with Samuel Kenrick of, 190, 247; edits and publishes Leechman's *Sermons*, 190, 247–49; frontispiece portrait of Leechman arranged by, 190, 248–49
Wodrow, Robert, 278–80
Wogan, Patrick: Carey and, 542–43; location of, 468; prominent Roman Catholic, 470, 542; as Scottish Enlightenment reprinter, 542, 704
Wollstonecraft, Mary, 381
Woloch, Isser, 3
women: among authors in Scotland, England, and France, 101–3; in circulating libraries, 114; in Dublin book trade, 470–72; freemasonry and, 108n18; *Julia de Roubigné* intended for, 455; Woodhouse, William, 512, 527–28
Woodhouselee, Lord. *See* Tytler, Alexander Fraser, Lord Woodhouselee
Woodward, William, 553, 570
Works (Pope), 59–60
Works (Thomson), 281–82, 287
Works in Architecture of Robert and James Adam (R. Adam), *130*, 131
Works of Alexander Monro, 140, 389
Works of John Gregory, 141
Works of John Home, 139
Works of Ossian. *See* Macpherson, James; Ossian
Works of Shakespear, 313
Writers to the Signet, 106

yellow fever in Philadelphia, 559, 568–70

Young, Edward, 314

Young, George, 547

Young, Mrs., I (Agnes Wallace, William's mother), 546

Young, Mrs., II (Elizabeth Wallace, William's stepmother), 546

Young, Mrs. William (Agnes McLaws), 547–48, 570

Young, Stewart, & M'Culloch, 553

Young, William: Aitken and, 550, 552; in *American Annual Register*, 590; antiburghers and, 547, 550–51, 565, 570–71, 592; birth, education, and apprenticeship, 546–48; on diffusion of knowledge, 564, 593, 608; Dobson and, 551–53, 592; Dobson's *Encyclopaedia* and, 558; early career in Philadelphia, 551–54; emigration to America, 541–42, 549–53; lures Baines to Philadelphia, 560; Marshall and, 550–51; paper-maker in Rockland, DE, 553, 570; Philadelphia Company of Printers and Booksellers and, 555, 571–73, 592; portrait, 570, *571;* in Scotland, 546–49; as a Scottish Enlightenment reprinter, 38–39, 561–71; on stages of American print culture, 563–65; yellow fever and, 568, 570; *Universal Asylum, and Columbian Magazine* and, 562–68, *568*, 608

Zachs, William, 78, 383

Zeluco (Moore): American edition, 561; author's copy money from, 245, 254; authorship of, 150; author suspects Cadell of cheating him, 244–45